ISBN 978-1-332-52530-0
PIBN 10056724

Forgotten Books is a registered trademark of FB &c Ltd.
Copyright © 2015 FB &c Ltd.
FB &c Ltd, Dalton House, 60 Windsor Avenue, London, SW19 2RR.
Company number 08720141. Registered in England and Wales.

For support please visit www.forgottenbooks.com

1 MONTH OF
FREE
READING

at

www.ForgottenBooks.com

By purchasing this book you are eligible for one month membership to ForgottenBooks.com, giving you unlimited access to our entire collection of over 700,000 titles via our web site and mobile apps.

To claim your free month visit: www.forgottenbooks.com/free56724

Similar Books Are Available from
www.forgottenbooks.com

BAEDEKER'S GUIDE BOOKS.

Published at net prices

Great Britain. *England, Wales, and Scotland.* With 28 Maps, 65 Plans, and a Panorama. Seventh edition. 1910. . . . . 10 marks
London and its Environs. With 10 Maps and 19 Plans. Sixteenth edition. 1911 . . . . 6 marks
Greece, the *Greek Islands,* and an Excursion to *Crete.* With 16 Maps, 30 Plans, and a Panorama of Athens. Fourth edition. 1909. 8 marks
Holland, see *Belgium and Holland.*
India, in German:
·Indien, Ceylon, Vorderindien, Birma, die malayische Halbinsel, Siam, Java. Mit 22 Karten, 33 Plänen und 8 Grundrissen. 1914. 20 marks
Italy: *l. Northern Italy,* including Leghorn, Florence, Ravenna, and Routes through France, Switzerland, and Austria. With 36 Maps, 45 Plans, and a Panorama. Fourteenth edition. 1913 . . . 8 marks
II. Central Italy and Rome. With 19 Maps, 55 Plans and Views, and the Arms of the Popes since 1417. Fifteenth edition. 1909. 7 marks 50 pf.
III. Southern Italy and Sicily, with Excursions to Malta, Sardinia, Tunis, and Corfu. With 30 Maps and 34 Plans. Sixteenth edition. 1912 . . . . 6 marks
Italy from the Alps to Naples. With 25 Maps and 52 Plans and Sketches. Second edition. 1909 . . . . 8 marks
The Mediterranean. Seaports and Sea Routes, including Madeira, the Canary Islands, the Coast of Morocco, Algeria, and Tunisia. With 38 Maps and 49 Plans. 1911 . . . . 12 marks
Norway, Sweden, and Denmark, with Excursions to *Iceland* and *Spitzbergen.* With 62 Maps, 42 Plans and 3 Panoramas. Tenth edition. 1912 . . . . 8 marks
Palestine and Syria, including the principal routes through *Mesopotamia* and *Babylonia.* With 21 Maps, 56 Plans, and a Panorama of Jerusalem. Fifth edition. 1912 . . . . 14 marks
Portugal, see *Spain and Portugal.*
Riviera, see *Southern France.*
Russia, with Teheran, Port Arthur, and Peking. With 40 Maps and 78 Plans. 1914 . . . . 18 marks
Manual of the Russian Language with Vocabulary and List of Phrases. 1914 . . . . 1 mark 50 pf.
Scotland, see *Great Britain.*
Spain and Portugal, with Excursions to *Tangier* and the *Balearic Islands.* With 20 Maps and 59 Plans. Fourth edition. 1913. 15 marks
Switzerland and the adjacent portions of Italy, Savoy, and Tyrol. With 77 Maps, 21 Plans, and 14 Panoramas. Twenty-fifth edition. 1913 . . . . 8 marks
Tyrol, see *The Eastern Alps.*
The United States, with Excursions to *Mexico, Cuba, Porto Rico,* and *Alaska.* With 33 Maps and 48 Plans. Fourth edition. 1909. 15 marks

Published at net prices

RUSSIA

Money Table

English			Russian		American	
£	s.	d.	rb.	cop.	Doll.	Cts.
	2	$1\frac{1}{4}$	1	—	—	$51\frac{1}{4}$
	4	$2\frac{3}{4}$	2	—	1	$2\frac{1}{2}$
	6	4	3	—	1	$53\frac{3}{4}$
	8	$5\frac{1}{4}$	4	—	2	5
	10	$6\frac{3}{4}$	5	—	2	$56\frac{1}{4}$
—	12	8	6	—	3	$7\frac{1}{2}$
	14	$9\frac{1}{2}$	7	—	3	$58\frac{1}{4}$
	16	$10\frac{3}{4}$	8	—	4	10
	19	—	9	—	4	$61\frac{1}{4}$
1	1	$1\frac{1}{2}$	10	—	5	$12\frac{1}{2}$
1	3	$1\frac{3}{4}$	11		5	$63\frac{3}{4}$
1	5	$4\frac{1}{4}$	12		6	15
1	7	$5\frac{1}{2}$	13		6	$66\frac{1}{4}$
1	9	7	14		7	$16\frac{1}{2}$
1	11	$8\frac{1}{4}$	15	—	7	$67\frac{3}{4}$
1	13	$9\frac{1}{2}$	16	—	8	20
1	15	11	17	—	8	$71\frac{1}{4}$
1	18	—	18	—	9	$22\frac{1}{2}$
2		$1\frac{1}{4}$	19	—	9	$73\frac{3}{4}$
2	2	$2\frac{3}{4}$	20	—	10	25
2	12	$9\frac{1}{2}$	25	—	12	$81\frac{1}{4}$
5	5	7	50	—	25	$62\frac{1}{2}$
10	11	$2\frac{1}{4}$	100	—	51	25
£	**s.**	**d.**	**rb.**	**cop.**	**Doll.**	**Cts.**
—	1	—	—	47.9	—	$24\frac{1}{4}$
	5	—	2	39.5	1	$21\frac{1}{4}$
	10	—	4	79	2	$42\frac{1}{2}$
1		—	9	58	4	85
5		—	47	90	24	25
10			95	80	48	50
20			191	60	97	—

Distances

Versts	Miles
10	6.63
20	13.26
30	19.89
40	26.52
50	33.15
60	39.78
70	46.41
80	53.04
90	59.67
100	66.29
250	165.72
500	331.43
750	497.15
1000	662.87
1500	994.30
Miles	**Versts**
10	15.09
20	30.17
30	45.26
40	60.34
50	75.43
60	90.51
70	105.60
80	120.69
90	135.77
100	150.86
250	377.14
500	754.28
750	1131.42
1000	1508.57
1500	2262.85

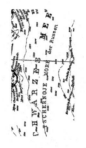

RUSSIA

WITH

TEHERAN, PORT ARTHUR, AND PEKING

HANDBOOK FOR TRAVELLERS

BY

KARL BAEDEKER

WITH 40 MAPS AND 78 PLANS

LEIPZIG: KARL BAEDEKER, PUBLISHER
LONDON: T. FISHER UNWIN, 1 ADELPHI TERRACE, W.C.
NEW YORK: CHARLES SCRIBNER'S SONS, 597 FIFTH AVE.
1914

'Go, little book, God send thee good passage,
And specially let this be thy prayere
Unto them all that thee will read or hear,
Where thou art wrong, after their help to call,
Thee to correct in any part or all.'

PREFACE.

The Handbook for Russia†, now issued in English for the first time, is intended to supply the traveller with such information as will render him as nearly as possible independent of hotel-keepers, commissionnaires, and guides, and thus enable him the more thoroughly to enjoy and appreciate the objects of interest he meets with on his tour.

The Handbook is based mainly upon the personal observation of the Editor and his Associates, who have repeatedly explored the country with a view to procuring the latest possible information. As, however, absolute accuracy is unobtainable, and changes are constantly taking place, the Editor will highly appreciate any suggestions with which travellers may favour him. Hotel-bills, with annotations showing the traveller's opinion of his treatment and accommodation, are particularly useful.

The MAPS and PLANS, on which special care has been bestowed, will often render material service to the traveller, and enable him at a glance to ascertain his bearings and select the best routes.

DISTANCES are generally given in versts (1 V. = 0.663 M.). HEIGHTS are given in English feet (1 Engl. ft. = 0.3048 mètre = 0.1429 sazhen), and the POPULATIONS in accordance with the latest data obtainable.

HOTELS. Besides the first-class hotels, the Editor names others of a less pretending kind. The asterisks indicate hotels which the Editor believes to be well-managed, reasonable, and adapted to

---

† The contents have been divided into eight sections, each of which may be separately removed from the volume by cutting the gauze backing visible on opening the book at the beginning and end of the portion to be detached. These sections are — (1) General Government of Warsaw (Poland), pp. 1-30; (2) Western Russia (Baltic Provinces), pp. 31-84; (3) St. Petersburg and Environs, pp. 85-196; (4) Grand Duchy of Finland, pp. 197-246; (5) Central and Northern Russia, pp. 247-370; (6) Southern Russia, pp. 371-436; (7) The Caucasus, pp. 437-496; (8) Teheran, Railways in Asiatic Russia, Port Arthur, Peking, pp. 497-568.

modern requirements. The more modest houses are sometimes described as 'good', 'fair', or 'very fair'. The hotel and other charges are stated either from the personal experience of the Editor and his staff or from that of his numerous correspondents, and will enable the traveller to form an estimate of his expenditure.

To hotel-keepers, tradesmen, and others the Editor begs to intimate that a character for fair dealing towards travellers is the sole passport to his commendation, and that no advertisements of any kind are admitted to his Handbooks. Persons calling themselves agents for Baedeker's Handbooks are impostors.

For the transliteration of Russian names, comp. p. xiii and the *Manual of the Russian Language* (published separately; 1s. 6d.).

Abbreviations.

R. = room, route.	yd. = English yard.
B. = breakfast.	ft. = „ foot.
déj. = déjeuner, luncheon.	N. = North, etc.
D. = dinner.	S. = South, etc.
S. = supper.	E. = East, etc.
pens. = pension.	W. = West, etc.
rfmts. = refreshments.	incl. = including.
omn. = omnibus.	comp. = compare.
carr. = carriage.	Pl. = plan.
r. = right.	ca. = circa, about.
l. = left.	inhab. = inhabitants.
hr. = hour.	adm. = admission.
min. = minute.	rb. = ruble, rouble.
O.S. = Old Style (Russian Calendar).	cop. = copeck.
M. = English mile.	ℳ = German mark.
S.M. = sea-mile, knot.	pf. = „ pfennig.
V. = verst.	m. = Finnish mark.
Kil. = kilomètre.	p. — „ penni.
m. = mètre.	$ = (Mexican silver) dollar
kg. = kilogramme	c. = cent.

The letter *d* with a date, after the name of a person, indicates the year of his death. The number of feet given after the name of a place shows its height above sea-level. The number of versts, miles, or kilomètres placed before the stations on railway and carriage routes indicates their distances from the starting-point of the route.

In the case of HOTEL NAMES ending in -*aya* the word *Gostínitza* (hotel) is understood, in the case of STREET NAMES ending in the same way the word *Úlitza* (street) is understood.

ASTERISKS denote objects of special interest or imply commendation.

CONTENTS.

Introduction.

I. General Government of Warsaw (Poland).

II. Western Russia (Baltic Provinces).

III. St. Petersburg and Environs.

IV. Grand Duchy of Finland.

V. Central and Northern Russia.

Maps.

Plans.

INTRODUCTION.

I. PRACTICAL INFORMATION.

1. Travelling Expenses. Language. Money. Equipment.

EXPENSES. The cost of travelling in Russia is considerably higher than in Central Europe. The railway fares, regulated by the zone tariff, are comparatively moderate, in spite of the long distances to be traversed, but the ordinary traveller will none the less find it difficult to keep his average expenses for hotels (6-10 rb.) cab-hire, commissionnaires, etc., down to less than 12-15 rb. per day. Travellers who know the country and language, and a party of two or three travelling together may do a little better than this.

LANGUAGE. Even the slightest acquaintance with the language is a considerable help, and all who visit the country should at least learn the Russian alphabet, in order to be able to read street-names, etc. The *Manual of the Russian Language* (price 1*s.* 6*d.*), issued by the publishers of this Handbook, will be found of service in teaching the rudiments of the language. It contains useful vocabularies, common phrases, and the grammatical rules necessary for the construction of simple sentences.—In the upper classes French is almost universally understood; the middle classes are more familiar with German. Outside the capital, Moscow, and the seaports, English is little spoken. In the Baltic Provinces and in the larger towns of Finland, German is generally understood.—For a list of *Polish* words, see p. 2; for *Finnish*, see p. 203; for *Persian*, see p. 498; and for *Chinese,* see p. 549.

The system of TRANSLITERATION employed in our text as given below follows mainly that of the Royal Geographical Society, but diverges from it in a few points intended to make the pronunciation easier for the traveller.

А, а	a	И, и	i	Р, р	r	Щ, щ	shtch
Б, б	b	й	i or mute	С, с	s	ъ	mute
В, в	v	I, i	i	Т, т	t	ы	ui, i
Г, г	g, h	К, к	k	У, у	u	ь	mute
Д, д	d	Л, л	l	Ф, ф	f	Ѣ, ѣ	ye
Е, е	e, ye	М, м	m	Х, х	kh	Э, э	e
ё	o, yo	Н, н	n	Ц, ц	tz	Ю, ю	yu
Ж, ж	zh	О, о	o	Ч, ч	tch	Я, я	ya
З, з	z	П, п	p	Ш, ш	sh	Ѳ, ѳ	f

Most of the maps and plans follow the R.G.S. system, differing from the text in such points as ch for ч and shch for щ. Some of them, however, are transliterated according to other systems. Thus the general maps of Russia, the maps of the Caucasus and Volga, and the plan of Novgorod follow the German usage (в = w, ж = sh, з = s, с = ss, x = ch, ц = z, ч = tsch, ш = sch, щ = schtsch, ы = y, ъ = je, ю = ju, я = ja), while the maps of the Crimea and of the Environs of Warsaw are French (ж = j, y = ou, ш = ch, щ = ehtch, ъ = ie, ю = iu, я = ia).

Money. The Russian monetary unit is the *Ruble* or *Rouble* (Рубль), divided into 100 *Copecks* (Копейка). The gold coins are pieces of 5, $7^1/_2$, 10, and 15 rb. The pieces of 15 and $7^1/_2$ rb., known as imperials and half-imperials, are scarce. The old imperials and half-imperials still occasionally met with have the same value as the current coins of these names, though nominally worth only 10 and 5 rb. Half-imperials may easily be mistaken for pieces of 10 rb. The silver coins include pieces of 1 rb. and of 5, 10, 15, 20, 25. and 50 cop. Silver coins with a hole in them should be refused. In copper there are coins of $^1/_4$, $^1/_2$, 1, 2, 3, and 5 cop. The paper-money (the so-called credit-notes) consists of notes of 1. 3. 5, 10, 25, 50, 100, and 500 rb. The notes of 5, 10, and 25 rb. issued in 1887, and those of 100 rb. issued in 1866 are no longer legal tender. The ruble is worth about 2s. 1d. and the copeck about $^1/_4$d. The ordinary rate of exchange is $1l. = 9$ rb. 58 cop., 100 rb. $= 10l.$ 11s. 2d. ($\$ 1 = 2$ rb.). Comp. Table at p. ii.— *Finnish Currency*, see p. 201.

English banknotes and sovereigns may be changed without loss in Moscow, Odessa, Riga, St. Petersburg, and Warsaw. *Circular Notes* or *Letters of Credit*, obtainable at the principal English and American banks, are the most convenient form in which to carry large sums; and their value if lost or stolen is recoverable. The *Travellers' Cheques* issued by the American Express Companies and by the American Bankers Association may also be recommended. It is not advisable to carry on one's person larger sums than are necessary for current expenses. A supply of Russian money should be obtained in London or Berlin, so as to avoid trouble at the frontier or on arrival at one's destination. Russian banks are all closed on the numerous holidays (comp. p. lxi). — The traveller should always be provided with small change (10, 15, and 20 cop. pieces) as the habit of *Tipping* is very widely spread in Russia.

Clothing should not be too light, for even in summer the nights are often chilly, and changes of temperature are frequent and extreme. Woollen underwear is recommended. The traveller should be provided with a pillow or an air-cushion, linen sheets (useful on long railway journeys and in provincial hotels), towels, a coverlet or rug, a small india-rubber bath, and some insect-powder. Visitors to S. Russia should have a light summer suit; the Russians themselves often wear suits of linen.— For winter-journeys warm furs and well-lined rubber-boots (best obtained in Russia) are indispensable. In spring a spell of warm weather is often succeeded by a sudden frost; it is therefore safer not to discard winter clothing until summer has actually arrived. — *Unboiled Water* should be avoided. Tea is a good substitute.

In making Purchases in Russia the traveller should not rely quite so implicitly on the bona fides of the shopkeeper as he does at home. It is quite customary, especially in the less fashionable shops, to accept 10-20 per cent less than the price originally demanded. In the Caucasus a third of the price is often abated in this way. The best furs are dearer than in England. Footgear of all sorts is good.

2. Plan of Tour. Routes from England to Russia.

Those who visit Russia for the first time will naturally be anxious to gain a general impression of the country, for which the geographical and historical sketch at p. xxxiii will form a useful preparation. The Western Provinces (the former kingdom of Poland), the Baltic Provinces, and Finland have all preserved their national idiosyncrasies. The land in its general features resembles the great North German plain, and the architecture of the towns is also of a predominantly W. European character. Russia proper begins at the line drawn from St. Petersburg viâ Smolensk and Kiev to Bessarabia. Both country and people are so uniform that the long railway journeys are of themselves enough to give a superficial acquaintance with them. Those who have visited the chief places of one or two provinces will discover little that is new by further exploration. Moscow, however, the heart of the Russian empire, is of extraordinary interest.

The busy industrial city of *Warsaw*, once the capital of Poland, and still its intellectual centre, impresses the visitor as an essentially Western European town, to which a Russian tinge is given by the numerous Russian officials and officers. More than one-third of its inhabitants are Jews. *Willanów*, near Warsaw, deserves a visit on account of its association with John Sobieski. — *Vilna*, the former capital of Lithuania, is charmingly situated, and contains many quaint old buildings. — *Riga*, the most important town in the Baltic Provinces, is a seaport and a busy manufacturing town, still substantially German. It has, however, little except its churches to remind us of its mediæval importance. *Narva*, however, and *Reval*, the ancient walls of which are still in great part extant, are both more mediæval in appearance. The valley of the Aa near *Kremon* is very attractive (Livonian Switzerland). — *Pskov (Pleskau)* possesses an interesting Kremlin.

St. Petersburg, on the banks of the wide *Nevá*. the capital of the empire since 1712, combines the character of a great modern centre of trade and industry with that of a political city swarming with officials. Its museums are the most important in Russia, and the Hermitage is one of the finest art-collections in the world, especially in the spheres of painting and the minor productions of the Greek genius. The season is in winter; the imperial theatres are closed at the beginning of May (O.S.; comp. p. xxxii). The spring parade of the Guards generally takes place at the end of April. The early summer (middle of May to middle of June, O.S.) is to be recommended for a visit to St. Petersburg; during this part of the year the environs of the city *(Peterhof, Pavlovsk, Tzarskoye Selo)* can be seen with their magnificent grounds in the glorious illumination of the 'white' summer nights. On June

21st the sun does not set at St. Petersburg till 9.22 p.m., and it rises at 2.43 the next morning.

FINLAND, the 'Land of a Thousand Lakes', is geographically as well as ethnographically allied to Sweden rather than to Russia. Travellers, however pressed for time, should not fail to visit *Viborg*, with the beautiful park of 'Monrepos', the *Imatra Falls*, and the *Mankala Rapids*. *Helsingfors* is the modern, *Åbo* the ancient capital. Finland is seen at its best from the middle of June to the end of August. Comp. p. 203.

The railway from St. Petersburg to Moscow forms an almost absolutely straight line. At Tchudovo a branch-line diverges for sleepy *Novgorod*, 'the Great', once the capital of a powerful commercial republic. *Tver* is the starting-point for a trip down the *Volga*, the chief artery of traffic in E. Russia. On the journey from Warsaw or Riga to Moscow we touch at the ancient walled city of *Smolensk*.

Moscow, the 'white-walled, golden-crowned holy city', for centuries the capital of the empire, shares with Kiev the most interesting associations with the real growth and history of the Russian race. Moscow is the most important trading and manufacturing town in the Russian Empire. In the middle of the town rises the Kremlin, the storehouse of Moscow's past memories. The Tretyakov Gallery contains a collection of pictures as important as the Alexander III. Museum in St. Petersburg for the study of the Russian school of painting. The season, as in St. Petersburg, is in winter. In summer the surroundings will be found very beautiful, and excursions may be made with advantage to places of interest like *Tzaritzuino* and the *Troitzko-Sergiyevskaya Lavra*, to which pilgrims from all parts of Russia resort.

To the E. of Moscow lies *Rostov-Yaroslavski*, with a Kremlin dating from the 17th century. On the *Volga* are *Yaroslavl*, with churches of great architectural interest, the picturesque *Nizhni-Novgorod*, which should be visited at the time of its world-famed yearly fair (comp. p. 344), and *Kazan*, the population of which includes many Tartars. — A *Trip on the Volga* from Nizhni-Novgorod to (2 days) *Samara* viâ Kazan may be recommended. It is hardly worth while to continue the voyage to (3 days) *Astrakhan*, although its mixed population and harbour traffic are interesting.

From Samara a railway journey of three days towards the W. brings us to *Kiev*, in Little Russia, the 'Mother of all Russian towns', beautifully situated on the *Dnieper*, with its renowned Lavra, the most famous convent in Russia. The churches, from the architectural point of view, are inferior to those of Moscow.

Odessa, the most important of Russian commercial ports on the *Black Sea*, is a modern town, and offers little of interest to the tourist.

The *Crimea* is described in R. 58, the *Caucasus* at p. 437.
For the Crimea and the Caucasus early summer and the autumn
are the best seasons, and for the Caucasian mountains, July to
October.—For the *Transcaspian Provinces, Teheran,* the *Trans-
Siberian Railway,* and *Peking,* comp. RR. 75, 74, 77, and 80.

For a TOUR OF 8-9 WEEKS the following time-table is recommended.
The use of express trains is everywhere presupposed.

	Days
From London viâ Berlin to *Warsaw* (R. 1)	2
Warsaw (R. 4) and *Willanów* (p. 24)	1¹/₂
From Warsaw to *Vilna* (R. 9)	¹/₂
Vilna (p. 36)	¹/₂
From Vilna viâ *Pskov* (half-a-day) to *St. Petersburg* (R. 8)	1-1¹/₂
St. Petersburg and environs (RR. 15-21)	7
From St. Petersburg to *Viborg* and the *Imatra,* and back to	
St. Petersburg (RR. 22 & 23)	2-3
From St. Petersburg viâ *Novgorod* and *Tver* to *Moscow* (RR. 36 & 37)	3
Moscow (R. 38)	5
From Moscow to the *Troitzko-Sergiyevskaya Lavra* (R. 40)	1
From Moscow to *Nizhni-Novgorod* (R. 43)	¹/₂-1
Nizhni-Novgorod (R. 44)	1
From Nizhni-Novgorod by steamboat down the Volga viâ *Kazan*	
to *Samara* (R. 45)	2-3
From Samara by rail viâ *Tula* and *Kursk* to *Kiev* (RR. 48 & 46)	3
Kiev (R. 54)	1
From Kiev to *Odessa* (RR. 55 b & 56)	1
From Odessa to *Sebastopol* by steamboat (R. 58 a)	1
The *Crimea* (R. 58 b-e; comp. p. 404)	6
From *Yalta* (Crimea) to *Batum* (RR. 58 e & 62)	3-5
The *Caucasus* (comp. p. 446)	10
From *Pyatigorsk* (Caucasus) viâ *Rostov-on-the-Don* to *Birzula*	2-3
From Birzula to London viâ *Lemberg* and *Vienna*	3-4
	57-64 Days

Three to four weeks suffice for a visit to *St. Petersburg, Moscow,*
and *Warsaw.* At Vilna we may deviate from the direct route to St.
Petersburg and travel viâ *Riga, Reval,* and *Narva,* an extension in-
volving 3 additional days.—*Finland* (comp. p. 203) may be visited from
St. Petersburg.—Those who are able to divide their visit into two parts
are advised to confine their first tour to N. Russia, and return from Kiev
viâ Warsaw or Lemberg. The second tour could begin at Kiev, and embrace S. Russia. From *Odessa* we may go by steamer to Constantinople
(comp. *Baedeker's Mediterranean*).

Routes from England to Russia.

RAILWAYS. The quickest route from London to St. Petersburg
is that followed by the *Nord Express,* starting from Charing
Cross station. This train runs daily as far as Berlin (viâ *Ostend,*
Brussels, Cologne and Hanover), and twice a week (daily service
projected) goes on to St. Petersburg (carriages changed at the frontier-station of Wirballen), taking just under two days for the whole
journey (1745 M.; fare 14*l.* 1*s.* 8*d.*; ticket from Sleeping Car Co.).
Other routes (change at Wirballen in all cases) lead viâ *Ostend,*
Brussels, Cologne, Magdeburg, and Berlin (1739 M., in 2¹/₂ days
from Charing Cross; fares 10*l.* 7*s.* 6*d.*, 6*l.* 17*s.* 7*d.*); viâ *Flushing,*
Wesel, Dortmund, Hanover, and Berlin (1683 M., in 2-2¹/₂ days

from Victoria; fares 9*l*. 12*s*. 4*d*., 6*l*. 6*s*. 11*d*.); viâ *Calais*, Lille, Brussels, Cologne, Hanover, and Berlin (1766 M., in 2¹/₂ days from Charing Cross; fares 10*l*. 19*s*. 2*d*., 7*l*. 5*s*. 7*d*.); and viâ *Hook of Holland*, Rotterdam, Utrecht, Hanover, and Berlin (1647 M., in 2¹/₂ days from Liverpool Street; fares 9*l*. 12*s*. 4*d*., 6*l*. 6*s*. 11*d*.).

On Tues. (Mon. from London) the *Nord Express* (p. xvii) connects at Berlin with a train to Warsaw (carriages changed) and Moscow, which is reached from London in 2¹/₂ days (1937 M.; through-fare 14*l*. 6*s*. 3*d*.). Other trains to Moscow (change at Warsaw), taking 2¹/₂-3 days, travel viâ Ostend, Boulogne, Flushing, or Hook of Holland. The fares by these trains are somewhat lower.

STEAMERS. To *St. Petersburg* direct from *London* by the *St. Petersburg Express Line* viâ the Kiel Canal, once weekly in 4 days (fares 7*l*. 10*s*., 5*l*., including meals); direct from *Hull* by the Wilson Line once weekly in 4¹/₂-5 days (fare 7*l*. 10*s*.).

To *Riga* from *London* by the *St. Petersburg Express Line* viâ the Kiel Canal, once weekly in 4 days (fares 6*l*. 15*s*., 5*l*., incl. meals); during the winter, if Riga is closed by ice, the service is maintained between London and *Windau* (same fares). From *Hull* by the Wilson Line once weekly in 4 days (6*l*. 15*s*.).

To *Libau* from *London* by *Det Forenede Dampskibs-Selskab* once weekly (fare 5*l*. 15*s*); from *Hull* by the *Wilson Line* once weekly (fares 5*l*. 15*s*., 2*l*. 5*s*.).

Libau is also reached from *New York* viâ Rotterdam (1¹/₂ day's stay) by the *Russian America Line* once fortnightly in 17 days (fare $ 70-120 or $ 50).

To *Odessa* from London by the *Westcott and Laurance Line* about every 3 weeks in 28 days, viâ Malta, Alexandria, Piræus, Salonica, and Constantinople (fares 15*l*. 15*s*., including food).

For steamers to ports in *Finland*, see p. 201.

3. Passport and Customs Regulations.

A PASSPORT (Пáспортъ) is *indispensable* for all foreigners visiting Russia. It must be furnished with the visa of a Russian consul in the traveller's own country (fee 2¹/₄ rb. = 4*s*. 9*d*.) before the frontier is crossed. The visa is good for six months, and allows the frontier to be crossed more than once. The Russian Consulate General in London issues a circular for the information of visitors to Russia.

Passports may be obtained in England direct from the *Foreign Office*, Whitehall (fee 2*s*.), or through any of the usual tourist-agents (fee 3*s*. 6*d*. to 5*s*.). In the United States applications for passports should be made to the *Bureau of Citizenship*, State Department, Washington, D.C.

The passport is demanded at the frontier, but the manner of procedure varies. Usually the passports are collected by gendarmes (p. xxi) before the passengers leave the train; sometimes the baggage examination (p. xix) does not take place until the passports are returned. At some frontier-stations the passports are collected as passengers enter the baggage room, and the baggage examination begins at once. When the baggage is passed, the passengers receive their passports back or ask for them from the gendarmes. At other stations passports are not returned till the travellers have taken their seats in the Russian train. If a passport is not in order, its unhappy owner has to recross the frontier, the train by which he came waiting for this purpose.

Passengers going to Russia by sea give their passports to the shipping agent, and get them back on landing.

For TURKESTAN, comp. p. 506.

The passport is valid for six months. It must be shown to the police in each place where the traveller stays, this duty being generally undertaken by the hotel-keeper. It is often of use in securing admission to galleries and museums, so that it is advisable to carry it on one's person. — Visitors who stay longer than six months deposit their passports at the Government Passport Office and receive a Russian permit of residence (Видъ на жйтельство), good for one year throughout the empire (fee 60 cop. or more).

On leaving Russia, the traveller has to report his intentions to the *Police Authorities* (stamp 75, office fee 30-40 cop.), handing in his passport and a certificate from the police officials of the district in which he has been living to the effect that nothing stands in the way of his departure. As the preparation of this application takes several hours at least, it is advisable to procure the necessary form as soon as possible at the last town in which the traveller resides. The passport is returned, provided with a permission to cross the frontier unimpeded within the next fortnight or more (according to the distance from the frontier). This function also is usually left to the landlord. — Strangers holding a permit of residence (see above) have on leaving Russia to procure a special travel-permit ($5^1/_2$ rb.), which is given up at the frontier-station.

At the Russian frontier-stations passports are examined and returned to passengers in their carriages after the second bell.

Travellers holding direct through-tickets to China or Japan need no permit to leave the country, even when they break their journey in Russian territory.

Customs. Whether at the railway frontier-station or at a seaport the customs examination of passengers' luggage is generally thorough. The examination takes place in the presence of the passenger, who should give his luggage-ticket to a porter (p. xx) and observe where his boxes are placed. Passengers are strongly advised not to send their luggage in advance. Unprinted paper only should be used for packing, to avoid any cause of suspicion.

The only things that pass DUTY FREE are *Used Objects* indispensable for the journey, such as clothing (not in quantities exceeding the usual needs of a traveller), cushions, bed-linen, and the like (all in very small quantities); one set of fur garments, such as coats, muffs, or caps; gold and silver objects not exceeding 3 lbs. in weight; 1 dozen pairs of new gloves; 100 cigars; one opened packet of tobacco or snuff; and needful provisions. — Photographic cameras and appliances, even if not new, are subject to duty, which is recoverable on leaving the country, provided the traveller has taken the precaution to get a receipt for the duty paid at the frontier-station (comp. also p. xxviii). Small cameras, however, are usually admitted free of duty.

b*

For the introduction of firearms a special permit is necessary, for which application must be made some months beforehand to the ambassador at St. Petersburg. This permit is valid for six months, and the traveller may be required to deposit the amount of duty leviable, which refunded only after considerable delay. After the expiration of six months full duty must be paid. — Books in large quantities are submitted to a censor. Travellers should avoid works of a political, social, or historical nature; bound books are subject to duty. — Luggage booked through to Eastern Asia. China, or Japan is not examined in Russia.

For all dutiable articles present in larger quantities the duty is charged according to a tariff, generally levied by weight. Travellers found in possession of dutiable articles which they have not declared have to pay (in addition to the duty) a fine of two-thirds of the amount levied. Prohibited goods, such as gunpowder and playing cards, are confiscated. When the total levy is less than $4^1/_2$ rb., no charge is made. Passengers are particularly warned against offering gratuities; the porters who assist at the customs examination receive 10 cop. for each large piece of luggage.

The *Russian Duty* on cigars is 7 rb. 20 cop. per lb. (Russian); on cognac ca. $1^1/_2$ rb. for an ordinary quart bottle ($^3/_4$ litre); on firearms (including gun-cases, etc.; see above) 43 rb. 20 cop. per pud (36 lbs.), on bicycles 30 rb. each.

The *German Duty* on jam, marmalade, and preserved fruits is 60 pf. per kg. ($2^1/_5$ lbs.), on chocolate 80 pf. per kg., on tea 1 ℳ per kg., on cigarettes 10 ℳ per kg., on tobacco 7 ℳ per kg.

LETTERS OF INTRODUCTION to officials will be found most useful, especially when one is travelling off the great railway routes.

4. Railways and Other Means of Communication.

For the railways in *Finland*, see p. 202.

Railways (Желѣзныя дороги). The sale of tickets begins $1/_2$-1 hr. before the departure of the train. The traveller should reach the station in good time, and leave the purchase of his ticket (Билётъ), the registration of his luggage, and the securing of his seat to one of the numerous *Porters* (Nosilshtchik; fee 30-50 cop.), who are thoroughly trustworthy. The porter's number should of course be noted. A bell is rung 3 times before the departure of the train: the first time (pervi zvonók) $1/_4$ hr. before, and the second (vtorói zvonók) 5 min. before, while the train leaves immediately after the third (treti zvonók). — The speed of the *Ordinary Trains* (Пассажірскіе or Почтóвые поѣздá) is very low, not exceeding 20-25 M. per hr., besides which they make long halts at the stations. The *Express Trains* (Курьéрскіе or Скóрые поѣздá) attain a speed of 35-40 M. per hr. The trains are frequently late. On many lines there are only two trains daily in each direction. The gauge (5 ft. $1/_2$ in.) is wider than the standard of Europe (4 ft. $8^1/_2$ in.). Most of the railways belong to the State. — The stations (Вокзáлъ) are usually at some distance from the centre of the towns. At Kiev, Moscow, Nizhni-Novgorod, St. Petersburg, Warsaw, and other large towns, tickets may be purchased and luggage registered in the town-offices of the State Railway (Городскія станціи; small commission charged). In many cases no one is allowed to enter the platform without a railway ticket or a platform ticket (Перрóнный билéтъ; 10 cop.).

The chief railway and steamer guide is the Официáльный указáтель желѣзнодорóжныхъ пароходныхъ и другихъ пассажирскихъ сообщéній (price 85 cop.), appearing twice yearly (April & Oct.) and obtainable at all railway stations. The local trains are dealt with in a separate section and are not shown in the tables referring to international or long-distance trains. The 'Kursbuch für Russland', published in Riga by N. Kymmel (80 cop.), is sufficient for the more important routes, and gives the names of stations in both Russian and German. St. Petersburg time is given throughout, except in regard to the steamers, which are scheduled according to local time. — St. Petersburg time is 61 min. in advance of Central European, and 2 hrs. 1 min. in advance of Greenwich time; comp. the table at p. xxxii. The station clocks keep St. Petersburg time, and occasionally local time as well.

Order at railway stations is maintained by *Gendarmes* (Жандáрмъ). Complaints may be registered in the Complaint Book (Жáлобная книга), kept at every station for this purpose. — There are three kinds of employés on the trains: the *Head Guard* (Óберъкондýкторъ), who comes to examine the tickets; the *Guard* (Кондýкторъ), who assigns the seats; and the *Provodnik* (Проводникъ) or attendant, who gives out the bedding, makes the beds, locks the compartments at the stopping-places, and makes himself generally useful. This last, like the negro porter in Pullman cars, expects a fee for his services. The head-guard and guards are dressed in a uniform consisting of a black blouse with belt, wide trousers tucked into the boots, and a round fur cap; the head-guard may be recognized by his silver and red braid and shoulder straps.

The *Carriages* (Вагóнъ; 1st cl. blue, 2nd cl. yellow, 3rd cl. green) are corridor coaches, with doors at each end; they are divided into compartments and are provided with lavatories (Убóрная). The Russian takes as much hand-luggage (Ручнóй багáжъ) into the carriage as he possibly can. The traveller should provide himself with pillows, towels, and soap (comp. p. xiv). All the trains have carriages for non-smokers (для некурящихъ) and for ladies (для дамъ). In winter double windows are universal. The carriages are steam-heated or are provided with stoves. — First-class carriages have compartments for two or four persons, with a lockable corridor-door, and broad upholstered seats without arm-rests; at night the back-cushion is hoisted up by the provodnik to form an upper berth. — Second-class carriages on the long-distance trains are fitted up in much the same style as the first-class, but are often overcrowded; there are also compartments for travellers without seat-tickets (p. xxiii), as on the ordinary trains. Passengers who wish to transfer from second to first class, buy a third-class ticket, which costs exactly the difference between the first and the second class fares. — Third-class carriages have a central corridor and wooden seats.

FARES are reckoned according to a *Zone Tariff*. Finland has its own tariff, and reckons by Finnish marks (see p. 202). Zone tariff of the Chinese Eastern Railway, see p. 532.

For *Ordinary Trains* the Russian zone tariff starts at the minimum of 6 V., and then rises with each verst up to 300 V. After 300 V. it rises with each 25 V. to 500 V., then with each 30 V. to 710 V., etc. For details, consult the following table, which gives the principal fares:—

Engl. Miles		1st class	2nd class	3rd class	Excess Luggage, per 10 lbs.
		rb. cop.	rb. cop.	rb. cop.	rb. cop.
1-4	1-6 V.	—.23	—.14	—.09	—.00.35
17	25 V.	—.95	—.57	—.38	—.01.44
33	50 V.	1.88	1.13	—.75	—.02.88
49	75 V.	2.83	1.70	1.13	—.04.32
66	100 V.	3.75	2.25	1.50	—.05.75
133	200 V.	7.00	4.20	2.80	—.11.50
199	300 V.	9.50	5.70	3.80	—.17.25
215	301-325 V.	10.15	6.10	4.05	—.17.25
232	326-350 V.	10.75	6.45	4.30	—.18.75
249	351-375 V.	11.40	6.85	4.55	—.20.25
265	376-400 V.	12.00	7.20	4.80	—.21.75
	From 401V. to 500V. add for *each 25V.*	—.50	—.30	—.20	—
331	500 V.	14.00	8.40	5.60	—.27.75
	From 501V. to 710V. add for *each 30V.*	—.50	—.30	—.20	—
471	710 V.	17.50	10.50	7.00	—.38.25
	From 711V. to 990V. add for *each 35V.*	—.50	—.30	—.20	—
656	990 V.	21.50	12.90	8.60	—.50.25
	From 991V. to 1510V. add for *each 40V.*	—.50	—.30	—.20	—
1001	1510 V.	28.00	16.80	11.20	—.69.75
	From 1511V. to 2860V. add for *each 45V.*	—.50	—.30	—.20	—
1896	2860 V.	43.00	25.80	17.20	1.14.75
	From 2861V. to 3010V. add for *each 50V.*	—.50	—.30	—.20	—
1995	3010 V.	44.50	26.70	17.80	1.19.25
	From 3011V. upwards add for *each 70V.*	1.00	—.60	—.40	—
2691	4060 V.	59.50	35.70	23.80	1.41.75
3314	5040 V.	73.50	44.10	29.40	1.62.75
3990	6020 V.	87.50	52.50	35.00	1.83.75
4640	7000 V.	101.50	60.90	40.60	2.04.75
5336	8050 V.	116.50	69.90	46.60	2.27.25
5985	9030 V.	130.50	78.30	52.20	2.48.25

Every ticket costing over 2 rb. is subject to a tax of 10 cop. for the benefit of the Red Cross Society.

Tickets are available as follows: 1-200 V. 1 day, 201-500 V. 2 days, 501-800 V. 3 days, 801-1100 V. 4 days, 1101-1500 V. 5 days, 1501-1900 V. 6 days, 1901-2300 V. 7 days; each additional 400 V. increases the validity of the ticket by 1 day.

The fares in the text of this Handbook refer to first and second class, except where otherwise stated. Third-class fares can be ascertained by deducting the second from the first.

In 1912 a system of *Circular Tour Tickets* (Круговые билёты), available for both express and ordinary trains, was introduced. These are valid for 3 months, and allow 1 pud of luggage free. Reserved seats (p. xxiii) are extra.

LUGGAGE. The allowance of free luggage is 1 pud (36 lbs.).
Each additional 10 lbs. (Russian) is charged for according to the
distance (comp. the table at p. xxii). In breaking the journey the
traveller is entitled to obtain access to his luggage on production of
a voucher, which has to be produced on again booking or registering
his baggage. Luggage may be deposited in the Left Luggage Office
(Ка́мера для хране́нія ручно́й кла́ди) for three days (fee 5 со́р.
daily for each article).

For EXPRESS TRAINS it is necessary to take not only *Supplementary Tickets* (Припла́та за ско́рость) but also *Reserved Seat
Tickets* (Плацка́рта). Early application is advisable (town-offices,
see p. xxi). As the number of seats is limited, the traveller cannot
count on securing one at an intermediate station. — Seat-tickets
must be procured at the booking-office and not from the train-
conductor. The charges are reckoned according to a zone-tariff:
1st and 2nd class up to 650 V., $1^1/_2$ rb.; from 651 to 2250 V.,
$1^1/_2$ rb. + 30 cop. per 200 V.; from 2251 V. to 4250 V., 3 rb.
90 cop. + 20 cop. per 200 V.; from 4251 V. onwards, 6 rb. 10 cop.
Third-class seat-tickets cost half the above charges. Trans-Siberian
Railway, see R. 77. When one passenger wishes to reserve a double
compartment for himself, he has to take four seat-tickets. At the
time of taking their tickets passengers must state whether they
prefer a smoking, a non-smoking, or a ladies' compartment, and
whether they prefer a lower (ни́жнее ме́сто; *odd* numbers, except
on the Baltic Railway) or an upper berth (ве́рхнее ме́сто; p. xxi).
Bedding is obtained from the provodník for 1 rb.; the passenger
is entitled to occupy his berth from 9 p.m. to 9 a.m. (local time).

SLEEPING CARS (Спа́льный ваго́нъ) of the International Sleeping
Car Co. run from St. Petersburg to Wirballen (Berlin). to Vienna (viâ
Warsaw), and to Moscow & Sebastopol; from Moscow to Nizhni-Novgorod,
to Warsaw, and to Siberia, and so on. By purchasing two supplementary
tickets a passenger can secure the exclusive use of a first-class compartment; advance booking is necessary ($^3/_4$-1 rb. for each ticket). —
RESTAURANT CARS (Ваго́нъ-рестора́нъ) are run on a few trains (B. 35 cop.,
déj. $1^1/_4$, D. $1^1/_2$ rb.), with sections for smokers and non-smokers.

On some lines the conductor collects the tickets in the evening,
giving a receipt in exchange, and returns them the following morning.

Passengers who desire to BREAK THE JOURNEY (отме́тка объ
остано́вкѣ) at an intermediate station must on quitting the train
present their tickets to the stationmaster (Нача́льникъ ста́нціи)
to be stamped, and on resuming the journey must present them at
the booking-office (Ка́сса) at least 10 min. before the departure of
the train to be again stamped.

On most railways the RAILWAY RESTAURANTS (Буфе́тъ) at the
chief stations may be safely recommended. The food is good and
inexpensive; the prices, which are fixed by the Railway Management, are usually to be found on the dishes. Tea is procurable at

any hour of the day or night (10 cop.). — Those who leave their compartment during a stoppage at any station should ask the conductor or the provodnik to lock it, or at least get a nosilshtchik (porter) to look after their belongings (fee 20-30 cop.).

The *Railway Book Stalls* of the larger stations generally offer a small assortment of English, French, and German books (not cheap), but foreign newspapers are seldom met with.

Posting (Почта). There are no diligences or stage-coaches in Russia, but travellers by road can obtain carriages and horses at a regular tariff at the various posting-stations. The horses are always good, but the carriages leave much to be desired. In winter sleighs (kibitka) with hoods are provided.

The *Teléga* (Телѣга) or mail cart, is a four-wheeled conveyance without springs and somewhat resembling a rude edition of the American buckboard. As a rule no seats are provided except for the driver, the passengers sitting on their trunks or on the hay or straw with which the bottom of the cart is littered. As the roads are bad, travelling is very rough and often painful. The so-called *Mail Teléga* (Перекладная телѣга) is somewhat better. Where procurable, as it is in most towns, the *Tarantass* is to be preferred. It is somewhat like a hooded victoria, the body swung by leathers on the wooden frame, or furnished with springs. The *Tarataíka* (Таратайка) is generally a two-wheeled vehicle, and is especially common in Finland.

The *Posting Tariff* (Progón, Прогонная плата) amounts to 3-7$^1/_2$ cop. per verst and horse; to this must be added the government tax (Государственный сборъ), amounting generally to 20 cop. per stage, and sometimes toll or road-money (Шоссейный сборъ). From two to six horses are used according to the state of the road and the character of the weather. The carriage is seldom paid for separately. Horses, driver, and vehicle are changed at every station, unless the traveller has hired the vehicle or horses for the whole journey (на долгихъ). The driver (Ямщикъ) expects a tip of 20-30 cop., and the ostler receives 5-10 cop. for helping to change horses.

Carriages. The straggling nature of Russian towns necessitates a frequent use of cabs. These are fast and comparatively cheap; берегись (beregís), the warning of the driver, means 'look out!' The usual *Droshkies* or *Izvóshtchik* (Извощикъ, *i.e.* 'cabby') are one-horse vehicles with the well-known Russian harness (p. xxv). They have barely room for two persons and often lack a cover.

The *Fare* for a drive of $^1/_4$ hr. is about 20-30 cop. either day or night, and if the driver has driven fast he expects a tip of 5-10 cop. Even in the towns possessing a fixed tariff a bargain should always be made beforehand. Pleasure drives (Катаніе по городу) do not usually come under the tariff. The drives mentioned in the tariff are not reckoned by time. Disputes should be referred to the nearest policeman (gorodovói) or to the police station. The driver often does not know•how to read; he does not always know his way about the town and sometimes raises difficulties about giving change. — Comp. the *Manual of the Russian Language*.

The *Karéta* is a four-seated vehicle with two horses, found only in the larger towns. The *Tróika* (Тройка), drawn by three horses, is a fairly comfortable conveyance, but its tariff is high. The middle horse runs between the shafts under a wooden arch or hoop (dugá); the two side-horses are loosely harnessed, and are 'checked up' so that their heads are turned outwards; they canter or gallop, while the middle horse never breaks from a sharp trot. Karétas and tróikas (unlike the one-horse cabs) occupy fixed stands. The driver is called Yamshtchik. — In S. Russia, the Caucasus, and Transcaspia the characteristic vehicle is the *Phaeton*, a two-horse four-wheeled carriage with a cover. — *Motor Cabs* and *Taximeter Cabs* exist in a few towns only.

The little one-horse *Sleighs* (Cáни) in the towns are wider and more comfortable than the cabs. When they are going fast, passengers must be on their guard against being thrown out.

The 'LINE' DROSHKIES or LINEIKAS (Линéйка) correspond to the old-fashioned 'knife-board' omnibuses. The passengers sit back to back, with their feet on a running footboard.

Commissionnaires or **Guides** (called *Factors* in Poland) are to be found at the larger hotels; they are paid 4-5 rb. a day (half-day 2-3 rb.).

Messengers (Посы́льный, Носи́льщикъ) receive 20-40 cop. for an errand; they belong to a guild (Artel, Артéль), which is responsible for all its members, and they are therefore thoroughly trustworthy.

5. Motoring. Cycling.

Motoring. The great national highroads connecting St. Petersburg, Moscow, Warsaw, and Kiev are admirably adapted for motoring and are kept in good condition. Petrol stations, established by Nobel of Baku, occur on these highways at intervals of 200 Kil. (124 M.). Lists of these stations and good motoring maps (printed in German) may be obtained from the Baltic Automobile Club, Nikolai-Str. 23, Riga. The highroad from Tiflis to Vladikavkaz (Caucasus; Georgian or Gruzinian Military Road; see p. 473) is good and passes through magnificent scenery. The roads maintained by the provincial authorities are of a very different character, and the traveller is advised not to try any of them until he has made enquiries at a local motor club. The roads in Finland and the Baltic Provinces, however, are often very fair. The best months for motoring in Russia are May, June, and August. The duty on a motor-car entering Russia varies from ca. 15l. to ca. 23l. (according to size), which is refunded if the car leaves the country within 12 months. Members of the Royal Automobile Club, of the English Automobile Association, and of the American Automobile Club, however, may deposit the amount of the duty with their clubs, in exchange for a document ('triptyque'), which exempts them from any customs formalities. The new International Customs Pass ('Carnet de Passages en Douanes'), also obtainable from the above-named clubs, serves the same purpose as the 'triptyque' but is available for nearly every European country (Germany and Finland excepted). There are no speed regulations

applying to the whole country, but the experienced motorist will
find no difficulty on this head if he adheres to the rules usual in other
European lands. In St. Petersburg the chauffeur should report himself at the Police Station, Nevski 91 (8 p.m.). The rule of the road is
to pass to the right and overtake on the left. The chauffeur must stop
when horses are shy. Imperial Russian Automobile Club, see p. 93.

The best route for a motor-car entering Russia from Germany is viâ
Tilsit. Tauroggen, and Riga to St. Petersburg. A Russian soldier accom-
panies the car from the Russian frontier-station (Plekishki) to Tauroggen,
where the customs formalities are observed. Motorists bound for Moscow
leave the St. Petersburg road at Feofilova-Pústuin (between Pskov and
Luga) and follow the highroad viâ Novgorod.

Cycling. On entering Russia cyclists deposit the duty (30 rb.
or 3l. 3s. 4d.; motor-cycles 20 rb. or 2l. 2s. 3d.) at the frontier
custom house. The deposit is returned at any custom house if the
cyclist leaves the country within six months. Seals are attached to
the machine in such a way as not to interfere with the rider's movements; and these seals must be kept intact until application is made
for the return of the duty. Members of the Cyclists' Touring Club
receive the privileges of the Touring Club of Russia without payment. Comp. the 'Road Book for N. and Central Europe' published by
the C. T. C. (280 Euston Road, London, N.W.). Maps, comp. p. lxiv.

6. Hotels. Furnished Rooms. Restaurants.

The large **Hotels** (Гостиница, Отéль) in St. Petersburg, Moscow, Warsaw, Riga, Odessa, and Kiev are little inferior to those
of Western Europe. The usual charges are: R. from 2¹/₂ or 3, B. ³/₄,
déj. 1-1¹/₂, D. 1¹/₂-2¹/₂ rb. The managers and porters all speak
German and French, and many of them English. The hotels in
provincial towns, especially the older ones, satisfy as a rule only
the most moderate demands, and they often leave much to be desired
in point of cleanliness. In spite of these failings they frequently
have high-sounding names, such as Grand-Hôtel, etc. The traveller
is thrown back upon Russian, as no other language is understood.
He should at once ask the charge for his room in case there is no
card of rates shown on the wall. The washing arrangements are
generally unsatisfactory, usually consisting of a tiny wash-basin
communicating with a small tank, from which the water trickles
in a feeble stream. Bed-linen and towels are often charged for
separately. Every candle used appears in the bill (10-15 cop.).
There is no charge for attendance; but it is customary, when the
bill is fairly high, to give about 10 per cent in tips; in respect of
a bill of 3-10 rb. the waiter, chambermaid, and porter receive at
least 25 cop. each. When the traveller pays his reckoning he
should not forget to reclaim his passport (comp. p. xix). Most of
the hotels have restaurants attached, but there is no compulsion
to take meals in them. Meals are usually paid for at the time.

Breakfast is often taken in one's own room; the tea is usually better than the coffee. Foreign newspapers are very scarce, even in the best hotels. — No notice should be taken if the izvóshtchik declares there is no room in the hotel he has been told to drive to.

Furnished Rooms (Меблирóванныя кóмнаты) or *Numbers* (Номерá) are not recommended unless the traveller means to make a prolonged stay in one place and finds hotel life too expensive. Previous enquiry should be made in each case. A bedroom costs 20-30 rb. per month, exclusive of bed linen and gratuities. The front door is closed at 10 or 11 p.m., after which hour the porter (dvornik) receives a tip (на чай) of 10 cop. for opening it.

Restaurants (Ресторáнъ) are opened at 11 a.m. (on Sun. usually at noon), and remain open until 2 or 3 a.m.; in the large towns déjeuner is served from 12 to 2, and dinner from 5 to 8 p.m. Beer-saloons, tea-rooms (Трактúръ), and eating-houses or cookshops (Кухмúстерская) are frequented by the lower classes only. — *Cafés* exist in a few towns only.

The *Restaurants of the First Class* are lavishly decorated and sumptuously furnished. In them the foreigner makes the acquaintance of the Russian cuisine at its best. Moscow is perhaps better than the capital in this particular, as in St. Petersburg the influence of French and German cuisine is very noticeable. Déjeuner costs $1-1^1/_2$, dinner $1^1/_2$-$2^1/_2$ rb.; meals à la carte are considerably dearer. A striking characteristic is the enormous number of waiters (often Tartars). They answer to the call of *Tchelovyék* (man). Tips range high (10 per cent of the bill, with a minimum of 30 cop.). Overcoats, overshoes (goloshes), and hats are left in the vestibule, and a gratuity of at least 10 cop. is given to the attendant, who does not as a rule give a check for articles left in his charge. There is no compulsion to take wine; good beer and the refreshing kvass (rye-beer) may be had almost anywhere. — In *Restaurants of the Second Class* it is possible to have a good midday meal for 50-75 copecks. — The *Delicatessen Shops* (Гастронóмій) found in a few of the larger towns generally have a restaurant attached, which may be recommended for déjeuner (closed on Sun. and holidays). — Foreign wines are dear; the native Bessarabian, Crimean, and Caucasian vintages (from the imperial domains, Удѣльное вѣдомство, and elsewhere) are good and cheap (from 1 rb. per flask).

A peculiarity of the Russian cuisine is the so-called *Zakúska* (Закуска; hors-d'œuvre, snack, relish), resembling the Finnish Smörgåsbord (comp. p. 202). In the larger restaurants there is always a sideboard or even a separate room for the zakúska, which consists of caviare, different kinds of fish, patties (Пирожкú), pickled cucumbers and mushrooms, and so forth, along with vodka or other spirits. The visitor regales himself on these dainties in order to get an appetite for dinner, though sometimes the zakúska takes the place of luncheon. The zakúska is always charged for extra, and it is not included in the meals à prix fixe. It is also an institution in private houses. — For the names of the commonest dishes, see the *Manual of the Russian Language*.

7. Consulates. Public Safety. Police. Photography.

In the event of any difficulty, and particularly in the case of differences with the Russian officials, the traveller should at once communicate with the nearest *Consul* of his own nation or of some friendly power.

Public safety is maintained in Russia in pretty much the same way as in the rest of Europe. Weapons may not be carried without a police-licence (comp. also p. xix). The *Police (Gorodovói)*, at least in the larger towns, are helpful and obliging.

The taking of photographs near fortresses is naturally forbidden; and even in less important places the guardians of the law are apt to be over-vigilant. In order to escape molestation the photographer should join the Russian Photographic Society (Русское Фотографическое общество). Its headquarters are in Moscow (Kuznétzki Most, Dzhamgárov Arcade; entrance fee 2 rb., annual subscription 6 rb.). Imperial châteaux and the like may not be photographed without the permission of the majordomo.

8. Post and Telegraph Offices.

Post Offices. The addresses of letters should be written in Russian or legible Roman characters. Important letters should be registered. Letters containing money must be declared, or they are liable to be confiscated. In the country-districts addressees have to collect their own letters from the nearest post office or railway station. The post offices (Почтámтъ) are generally open on weekdays from 8 a.m. to 2 p.m. (Sun. 8-10 a.m.). — *Postage Stamps* (see p. xxix) are best purchased at the post offices; if they are obtained at shops, hotels, or restaurants, a commission has to be paid.

The post offices are closed throughout the country on Jan. 1st, March 25th, Easter Day, Dec. 6th, and Christmas Day. Letters are, however, delivered on these days.

Postal Rates. *Letters* (Письмó), inland, 7 cop. per lot (0.45 oz. av.); foreign, 10 cop. per 15 grammes (1¹/₆ lot). — *Post Cards* (Открытое письмó), inland 3, foreign 4 cop. — *Registration Fee*, in addition to the postage, inland 7, foreign 10 cop. — *Postal Wrappers* containing printed matter (Бандерóльныя отправлéнiя), inland, 2 cop. per 4 lots or fraction thereof (maximum 4 Russian lbs.); foreign, 2 cop. per 50 grammes (3.9 lots) or fraction thereof (minimum charge 10 cop.; maximum weight (2 kg. or 4 lbs. 28 lots). — *Parcel Post*, inland, under 2 lbs. 25-65 cop. (according to distance), 2-7 lbs. 45 cop. to 1¹/₄ rb., over 7 lbs. and under 12 lbs. 65 cop. to 1 rb. 85 cop.; to England 1 rb. 20 cop. per 5 kg. (11 lbs.), to France 90 cop., to Germany 70 cop. — *Inland Money Orders and Telegraphic Money Orders* are issued up to 5000 rb. (poundage 15 cop. to 12¹/₂ rb.). — *Foreign Money Orders* are issued to or from England (up to 30*l*.), the United States ($100), France (800 fr.), Belgium (800 fr.), Germany (650 ℳ), Austria-Hungary (762 *K*), and Switzerland (800 fr.); poundage 10 cop. per 10 rb., for the United States 20 cop. per 20 rb.

Registered letters must be marked заказнóе (registered). If a letter is meant to lie at a post office till called for (up to 6 months), it must be marked до востребованiя (poste restante). Parcels containing books must bear the words съ книгами (books). — In the larger towns money sent through the post and parcels containing valuables (in St. Petersburg up to 500 rb.) are delivered at the addressee's residence. In other places the addressee receives an *Advice Note* (Повѣстка) telling him that the parcel has arrived at the post office. If the addressee is not known at the office, a certificate of identity from the local police or from the hotel proprietor must be shown also. — *Postage Stamps* (Почтóвыя мáрки) are issued for 1, 2, 3, 4, 5, 7, 10, 14, 20 cop., and upwards.

For postal arrangements in Finland, comp. pp. 202, 203.

Telegraph Offices. In the large towns messages are accepted in almost all languages, but at rail. stations and the smaller offices, Russian messages only are accepted.

Telegraph Rates. *Inland Telegrams.* Each word 5 cop. (to Manchuria 12 cop.), besides an initial payment of 15 cop.; words of more than 15 letters count as two. Telegrams marked срóчная (urgent), at treble rates, take precedence of other messages. — *Telegrams within the Town Limits* cost 1 cop. a word, plus the initial rate of 15 cop. — *Foreign Telegrams.* To Great Britain 18 cop. per word; United States from 73 cop. upwards; Australia 97 cop.; Germany and Austria-Hungary 11 cop.; Sweden 12 cop.; France 13 cop.; Belgium, Holland, and Denmark 14 cop.; Norway 15 cop.; Switzerland 16 cop.; Italy 17 cop.; Spain 20 cop.; Rumania 8 cop.; Turkey in Europe 25 cop.; Persia 24 cop.; China 75 cop.; Japan 1 rb. 31 cop.

9. Theatres. Concerts. Amusements. Sport.

The Imperial **Theatres** in St. Petersburg and Moscow receive a considerable subvention from the State. The larger houses are closed in summer, and all theatres are closed on the eves of the chief church festivals, and also for several weeks in Lent. The price of a reserved seat usually varies between 2 rb. and 5 rb., but is often considerably higher for benefit performances.

The peculiar talent of the Russians is seen at its best in Comedy and Comic Opera. Operas are presented with great magnificence, and the excellence of the Russian Ballet has been amply demonstrated both in other parts of Europe and in America. The stranger will be chiefly interested in the Russian National Dances (see p. xxx). — A visit should also be paid to the so-called *People's Houses* or *Palaces* (Нарóдный домъ), institutions subsidized by Government for theatrical and musical performances, and so on.

Concerts are given daily in summer in the parks and pleasure resorts near the larger towns by military and other bands, but during winter orchestral music is found in a few towns only. Those who do not shrink from an expensive supper and somewhat Bohemian society should make a point of hearing one of the Russian or Gipsy Choirs. The very characteristic performances of these choirs are generally given in the fashionable restaurants on the outskirts of the large towns, which on winter evenings are much frequented by the jeunesse dorée in their three-horse sleighs.

The Russians are great lovers of *Music.* Social entertainments without singing are almost unheard of. The workman also lightens his labour and the soldier his long marches with characteristic songs. The concertina or accordion is very common, but the old *Balaláika*, a kind of three-stringed zither, has lately become again very popular.

The Russian **National Dances** (generally round or country dances; Khorovódi, Хороводы) have a markedly dramatic stamp.

Among these national dances are the *Golubétz (i.e.* pigeon dance), representing the falling out and reconciliation of two lovers; the *Trepák;* the *Kamarinskaya;* the *Kazatchók* or Cossack Dance. Polish dances, such as the *Mazurka* (Мазурка) and the *Cracovienne (Krakoviák),* are also very popular.—A feature of all Russian dances is the so-called *'prisvádku* or peculiar method of bending the knee.

Among the Russian **National Amusements** are swinging, tobogganing, the so-called gulyáni (from гулять, to take a walk), and racing, especially trotting-races in summer and sleigh-races in winter. Most of these are best seen in the Maslenitza (Масленица) or *'Butter Week' (i.e.* the week before Lent). In spite of the name the *Gulyáni* (Гулянье) are really drives (Катанье), not walks, as the Russians have no taste for pedestrian exercise. Gulyáni, corresponding to the corso of West Europe, are held in the large towns on the chief holidays; ordinary cabs are not allowed to take part in the more fashionable displays. The gulyáni arranged from time to time in the various pleasure-gardens are a kind of fair. The *Toboggan Slides* or *Montagnes Russes* (Горы) resemble those familiar to every American, Canadian, or winter visitor to Switzerland.

Sport. All who wish to shoot must take out a shooting-licence (3 rb.; good for a year). In European Russia, except a few provinces in the N., shooting rights belong to the owner of the ground. The state-forests are let out on lease. The shooting of the aurochs or bison is forbidden under a penalty of 500 rb. The same rule applies to the elk-cow, the hind, and the doe.

The *Elk*, which is by no means rare in N. Russia and Siberia, is hunted with hounds or decoys.—The *Bear* is hunted in winter with beaters. There are men who earn a livelihood by locating the bear's den and offering the bear to a hunter at so much per pud. The Siberian natives hunt the bear with small dogs and dispatch him with a kind of lance (Рогатка). —The *Wolf* is hunted with beaters, generally after he has gorged himself with a carcase provided as bait at a suitable place. A more exciting sport is coursing him with wolf-hounds, a method in vogue in Central Russia and on the steppes. The Kirghizes hunt the wolf on horseback and kill him with knouts.—The *Tiger* still exists in the Lenkoran Territory, around the shores of the Caspian, in Turkestan, and on the Chinese bank of the Amur.—*Foxes* are coursed with greyhounds.—*Lynxes, Roes, Wild Boars, Grey* and *White Hares,* and *Badgers* are hunted in the same way as in other countries, as are also *Capercailzies, Black Game, Ptarmigans, Wood Grouse,* and *Partridges.* In N. Russia large quantities of these birds are shot during the winter months for exportation in a frozen condition.—In the steppes *Bustards* are chased with greyhounds.—Small fur-bearing animals are caught in traps or shot with small-calibre guns; great care is taken to hit only the head, so as not to spoil the pelt; the native Siberians especially show great skill in doing this.—Waterfowl-shooting has no peculiarly Russian characteristics. In the N.E., where wild duck and similar birds are very numerous, they are caught in nets. --In the Baltic Sea the *Seal* is hunted with harpoons or short guns, or is clubbed to death as on the White Sea.

Close Season (O.S.):—Bull Elk, Jan. 1st to Aug 15th.—Stag, March 1st to July 15th.—Roebuck, Nov. 15th to May 31st.--Capercailzie Cock and Blackcock, May 15th to July 15th.—Capercailzie Hen and Gray Hen,

Wood Grouse, and Ptarmigan, March 1st to Aug. 31st. — Woodcock, June 1st to July 15th. — Wild Duck, March 1st to June 29th. — Partridge, Dec. 1st to Aug. 15th. — Pheasant and Hare, Feb. 1st to Aug. 31st.

10. Tobacco.

The smoking of cigarettes is common among all classes of society and both sexes; the Russian smokes even at meals, between the courses. The Old Believers (p. lviii) do not smoke. Cigarettes (Папиро́сы, papirósi) cost 15-50 cop. per 25 in the tobacco shops. Russians generally roll their own cigarettes. Imported cigars are dear, owing to the prohibitive duty, but 100 may be taken in duty free. Smoking is forbidden near certain buildings, *e.g.* the Custom Houses (куре́ніе табака́ воспреща́ется, no smoking allowed). In government offices this injunction applies to the public only.

The *Cigarette Tobacco* comes from Bessarabia, the Crimea, and the Caucasus. Crimean tobacco is easily mistaken for genuine Turkish.

11. Baths.

St. Petersburg, Moscow, and the larger provincial towns generally possess two kinds of baths; the ordinary bath-houses (Ба́ни) containing one large room for all sorts and conditions of bathers (Простонаро́дье), and the more pretentious establishments, which have, in addition to the common rooms (О́бщія; 20-50 cop.), private suites or 'numbers', as they are called (Номера́; from 1 rb.). At the entrance a bánshtchik or (for ladies) a bánshtchitza (bath-attendant; fee 25-50 cop.) may be hired. The *Numbers* generally consist of three rooms: the dressing-room, an anteroom with a bath, and the vapour ('Turkish') bath proper, containing several rows of wooden couches in amphitheatrical form, opposite which is a large stone stove radiating great heat. Saturday is the most popular day. — Compare the *Manual of the Russian Language.*

12. Weights and Measures. The Calendar.
Weights (Вѣсъ).

1 *Bérkovetz* = 10 pud = 163.80 kg. = 361.12 lbs. = 3.22 cwt.

1 *Pud* = 40 pounds (Russian) = 16.38 kg. = 36.11 lbs. (62 pud = 1 ton).

1 *Pound* (Russian) = 32 lot = 96 zolotnik = 410 gr. = 14.44 oz. av.

1 *Lot* = 3 zolotnik = 12.80 gr. = 0.45 oz. av.

1 *Zolotník* = 96 doli = 4.26 gr. = 0.15 oz. av.

Measures of Length (Лине́йныя мѣры). Comp. p. ii.

1 *Verst* (Верста́) = 500 sazhen = 1.067 km. = 0.663 M. (7 V = ca. 1 geogr. M.).

1 *Sazhen* (Са́жень; fathom) = 3 arshin = 48 vershók = 2.134 mètres = 7 Engl. ft. (1 ft. = 0.305 m. = 0.143 sazhen).

1 *Arshín* = 16 vershók = 712 millimètres = 28 inches.

1 *Vershók* = 44.45 mm. = 1³/₄ inch.

Square Measure (Поземе́льныя ме́ры).

1 *Desyatina* = 2400 sq. sazhen = 1.0925 hectare = 2.7 acres.
1 *Square Verst* = 104.17 desyatina = 1.138 sq. km. = 281 acres.

Measures of Capacity (Ме́ры ёмкости).

1 *Botchka* (cask or barrel) = 40 vedró = 4.92 hectolitres (108.28 gallons).
1 *Vedró* = 10 krushka = 12.299 litres.
1 *Tchetvert* = 8 tchetverik = 64 garnetz = 2.099 hectolitres = 184.797 gallons.
1 *Tchetverik* = 8 garnetz = 26.238 litres = 23.099 gallons.
1 *Cubic Sazhen* = 9.71 cub. m. = 343 cubic ft.

THE CALENDAR.

In all parts of Russia except Finland the Julian Calendar established by Julius Cæsar in 46 B.C., and adopted by the Council of Nicæa in 325 A.D., still remains in force. This reckoning is 13 days behind the rest of Europe, which long ago adopted the Gregorian Calendar; thus Jan. 1st in Russia is really Jan. 14th. When the dates in the text are given according to the Russian Calendar the letters O.S. ('Old Style') are appended.

13. Table of Local Time.

Twelve o'clock midday in St. Petersburg is in:

Åbo . . .	11.28 a.m.	Moscow .	12.29 p.m.	Taiga .	3.44 p.m.
Archangel .	12.33 p.m.	Nizhni-Nov-		Tambov .	12.45 ,,
Astrakhan .	1.11 ,,	gorod . .	12.56 ,,	Tashkent .	2.36 ,,
Baku . . .	1.18 ,,	Odessa .	12.12 ,,	Tchelya-	
Erivan .	12.57 ,,	Omsk .	2.52 ,,	binsk .	2.04 ,,
Grodno . .	11.35 a.m.	Orel . .	12.23 ,,	Tiflis . .	12.58 ,,
Helsingfors	11.39 ,,	Orenburg .	1.39 ,,	Tobolsk .	2.32 ,,
Irkutsk .	4.56 p.m.	Peking .	5.48 ,,	Tomsk .	4.39 ,,
Kazan .	1.15 ,,	Penza .	12.50 ,,	Tula .	12.29 ,,
Kertch .	12.25 ,,	Perm .	1.44 ,,	Tver .	12.23 ,,
Kharbin . .	6.25 ,,	Petroza-		Tzaritzuin .	12.57 ,,
Kharkov .	12.24 ,,	vodsk .	12.16 ,,	Ufa . . .	1.43 ,,
Kherson .	12.09 ,,	Poltava .	12.17 ,,	Viborg . .	11.54 a.m.
Kiev . .	12.01 ,,	Pskov .	11.52 a.m.	Vilna .	11.40 ,,
Kishinev .	11.44 a.m.	*Reval .	11.37 ,,	Vitebsk .	12.00 noon
Kostroma .	12.43 p.m.	*Riga .	11.35 ,,	Vladimir .	12.40 p.m.
Kovno .	11.34 a.m.	Rostov-on-		Vladivostok	6.46 ,,
Krivosh-		the-Don .	12.38 p.m.	Vologda .	12.38 ,,
tchekovo .	3.30 p.m.	Ryazan . .	12.38 ,,	Voronezh .	12.36 ,,
Krasno-		Samara . .	1.19 ,,	Warsaw .	11.23 a.m
yarsk	4.10 ,,	Saratov .	1.03 ,,	Wirballen .	11.30 ,,
Kursk	12.24 ,,	Sebastopol .	12.13 ,,	Yaroslavl .	12.38 p.m.
Kutaïs	12.50 ,,	Simbirsk .	1.12 ,,	Yekaterin-	
*Libau	11.23 a.m.	Smolensk .	12.07 ,,	burg . .	2.01 ,,
Minsk	11.49 ,,	Sryetensk .	5.49 ,,	Yekaterin-	
*Mitau	11.34 ,,	Taganrog .	12.35 ,,	oslav . .	12.19 ,,

* In the Baltic Provinces St. Petersburg time was introduced in 1899.

II. GEOGRAPHICAL AND ETHNOGRAPHICAL SKETCH OF EUROPEAN RUSSIA

by

Professor Alfred Philippson.

a. The Land.

The E. half of Europe consists of an enormous plain, which is sharply distinguished from the smaller and more articulated W. part of the continent by its uniformity and unbroken continuity. It is bounded on the S.W. by the Carpathians, on the S. by the mountains of the Caucasus and the Crimea, and on the E. by the Urals. Its edge is touched by four seas, one of which, the Caspian Sea, to the S.E., is really a large inland lake, while the three others (the Arctic Ocean, the Baltic, and the Black Sea) are all so much separated from the ocean as to be practically lakes. This great plain connects with Central Asia by the so-called Caspian Depression, or gap between the Caspian and Ural mountains, and with Sweden through the narrower and lower part of Finland ('Finnish Bridge', p. xxxvii). On the W. it merges into the great North German plain, and on the S.W. into the plain of the Danube. This territory corresponds approximately to European Russia, which (without the Caucasus) has an area of 2,075,700 sq. M. and contains 131,200,000 inhabitants.†
The political and natural boundaries do not always coincide; in Poland, for instance, the political boundary lies beyond the natural frontier, while in the Carpathians it falls short of it. In the S.W. it just touches it at the mouth of the Danube; while on the S. it includes the mountains of the Crimea. In the S. part of the Urals the European boundary encroaches upon what is naturally Asiatic Russia, while, on the contrary, the N. part of the Caucasus is left to Asia. European Russia, with the exception of the group of Arctic islands known as Nova Zembla (Novaya Zemlya), reaches from 70° N. lat. (*i.e.* from a point within the Arctic Circle) down to 44° N. lat. (the same latitude as Florence). This huge territory forms, with regard to the other lands of Europe, as clearly defined a natural as a political whole. Russia's position as a world-power is hampered by the fact that it nowhere reaches the open sea; the scanty coast-line that it does possess is not of much use to it, since, if we except Lapland on the N. and the Crimea on the S., it is completely ice-bound in winter. Its E. frontier towards Asia is very much longer than its W. frontier towards the rest of Europe. Russia

---

† The total area of the Russian Empire, including its Asiatic possessions, is 8,600,000 sq. M., and its population (1909) 162,400,000. Europe has a total area of 3,800,000 sq. M., and a population of 443,500,000.

is thus a thoroughly continental country. Its natural outlets on the W. are the Baltic Sea and the Bosphorus. Its Baltic gateway has already been utilized; whether equal success will attend its endeavours in the S.W. remains to be seen. One advantage of its position is that all its European neighbours (Norwegians, Swedes, Germans, Austrians, and Rumanians) are on the same side, while its rear is protected by its huge Asiatic possessions. The enormous extent of the country, combined with its scanty population (63.7 per sq. M.), renders it practically invulnerable to military attack, as was illustrated by the campaign of Napoleon in 1812 and the Crimean War of 1854-55.

GEOLOGY. The Russian plateau may be described as consisting of one gigantic and homogeneous mass which has remained rigid since the earliest days of the earth's history, and so has escaped the folding from which the rest of Europe has suffered. The greater part of Scandinavia also belongs to this region. We thus find that only the Archæan or primæval rocks (gneiss, granite, crystalline slate) in this vast territory are found in a *folded* or tilted position, while all the sedimentary formations from the earliest to the latest remain in a *flat* or horizontal position. In the surrounding mountain-ranges and in the rest of Europe these formations have all been folded by lateral pressure. This is the main geological peculiarity of the land under consideration.

Two subordinate divisions may also be noticed:—

(1). The so-called *Baltic* or *Scandinavian Shield,* in which the folded Archæan rocks form the surface, since the overlying sedimentary rocks have nearly all been carried away. This includes Sweden and the so-called 'Finnish Bridge', the S. boundary being formed by the Gulf of Finland, Lake Ládoga, Lake Onéga, and the White Sea.

(2). The *Russian Tableland,* consisting of flat layers of sedimentary rocks of various ages, including early Palæozoic in the W., Carboniferous in the middle, Permian in the N.E., and Cretaceous and Tertiary in the S. Within this may be mentioned the following special zones: — the *Timan,* a branch of the Ural mountains, running N.W. to the Tcheskaya Bay of the White Sea, and consisting of folded sedimentary rocks; the *South Russian Granite Floor,* leading N.W. from the Sea of Azov to Volhynia; and the *Donetz Coal District,* adjoining the granite. These are exceptions to the general flat structure of the Russian tableland. *Breaks* or faults, however, occur in the tableland, so that different formations have often been brought to the same level through vertical disturbance. All these earth movements have, however, long ceased; there are no volcanoes, and earthquakes are very rare. In spite of this, the geological map of Russia is still a fairly variegated one, since, as we have said, the most heterogeneous formations are represented in the outcropping strata, albeit without much vertical expression. As a rule, however, each formation occupies an extensive area, and there is by no means so much variety as in the folded regions of W. Europe.

It follows then that the level character of the surface is conditioned by the horizontal stratification of its rocks, but is not altogether caused by it. The truth is rather that during a comparatively recent geological era destructive external forces wore down the territory to an almost level surface or *Peneplain,* which renders almost indistinguishable such various formations as those of the primæval mountains of the Baltic Shield, the Granite Floor, and the Timan Hills. The whole of this peneplain was elevated at a later epoch, so that it now forms a *Plateau,* the variation in level of which, occurring in gentle undulations and shallow valleys, is very insignificant compared with its vast area. In the greater part of Russia this plateau stands between 650 ft. and 1000 ft. above sea-level. Towards the sea it gradually diminishes in height, but it generally ends in a low marginal or littoral scarp, and absolutely flat coast-districts are rare. Hills attaining a height of 1300 ft. occur at a few points only in Russia.

RIVER SYSTEM. The position of the plateau at a height of a few hundred feet above the sea causes it to be split up by various rivers into *Valleys.* Absolute plains are thus for the most part found only on the watersheds and in the broader parts of the river-valleys. The Russian plateau is thus by no means a monotonous expanse, but a more or less undulating district, which at certain points, as, *e.g.,* on the banks of the Volga and in the Volga ravine above Samara, actually assumes mountainous features. Here and there the walls of the valleys attain a height of 1000 ft. and become quite picturesque. The upper parts of the river valleys are often narrow and winding, while farther down the great rivers have carved out large shallow *Basins.* It is a characteristic and well-known feature of the great rivers of S. Russia, such as the Volga, the Don, and the Dnieper, that they always incline to the right (W.) side of these basins, with the result that their right bank is always a 'mountain bank' and their left a wide plain or 'meadow bank'. — In S.W. Russia the lower as well as the higher river-valleys are apt to be narrow.

The rivers thus provide an orographical dissection of the Russian plateau which is quite independent of the geological constitution. For the better understanding of this fact it is necessary to bear in mind that, though the Russian rivers flow slowly (only a few, such as the Dnieper and the Narova, having rapids), they are very copious on account of the vast size of their drainage-basins, and carry down enormous quantities of water, especially during the spring-floods and the break-up of the winter ice and snow. In summer, on the

c*

other hand, it is true that they often dwindle away to shallow streams at the bottom of their broad channels, and in consequence of the increasing deforestation have often become so silted-up that navigation is seriously impeded. The Volga is an especial sufferer; all the same it and the Dnieper are really imposing streams even in summer. Of quite a different nature is the short but impetuous Nevá, which is kept uniform by the waters of Lake Ládoga.

The Petchora, Mezen, and Dvina flow into the Arctic Ocean, the Nevá, W. Dvina, and Niemen into the Baltic. The S. rivers are much larger. The Volga, the largest river in Europe, describes a gigantic arc open on the S.W., and then (at Tzaritzuin) bends sharply to the S.E. and enters the Caspian Sea. The Don and the Dnieper also describe huge 'bows' before they flow into the Black Sea. The Bug, Dniester, and Pruth flow in a straight S.E. direction. A glance at the map will show how many of the Russian rivers radiate from the comparatively unimportant Altai Hills in N.W. Russia. This fact, combined with the relative insignificance of the watersheds, has facilitated the union of the rivers by means of *Canals* into one vast network of inland navigation. This has proved an immense economic advantage for Russia, although it is subject to interruption in winter, when most of the rivers are frozen.

The parts of the Russian plateau lying between the broad river basins are generally known as '*Heights of Land*' or '*Land Ridges*'. These are, as may be gathered from what has already been said, not isolated elevations but broad flat tablelands. Many of these ridges radiate from the Valdai Hills, the hydrographic centre of the country. The main ridges are:—

(1). The *North Russian Ridge,* leading to the Urals, from which diverges the subsidiary *Timan Ridge,* extending between the broad plains of Arctic Russia to the White Sea.

(2). The *West Russian Ridge,* leading to the Prussian frontier, with one side sloping towards the Baltic Sea.

(3). The *Central Russian Plateau,* sloping towards the S., and connecting with the *South Russian Ridge* (the Granite Floor), from which the S. Russian tableland descends to the Black Sea. Between the W., Central, and S. Ridges lies the basin of the Dnieper, which extends on the W. through the marshy district of the Polyezye (the Pripet Swamp) to the Vistula. The basin of the Vistula itself, *i.e.* Poland, naturally belongs rather to the N. German plain than to Russia. Its physical configuration resembles that of N. Germany, which it is beyond our province to describe.

On the other side, starting from the neighbourhood of Moscow, in the middle of the central Russian plateau, the real heart of Russia, is a land ridge running E. between the basins of the Don and the upper course of the Volga. This ultimately expands into the *Volga Plateau,* which terminates on the 'mountain-bank' of that river.

Towards the S. it is continued by the Yergeni Hills. Beyond the Volga the *Ural Plateau* slopes up to the Urals. On the S. the Ural plateau is bounded by an elevated semicircular border formed by the Obshtchi-Suirt and the Yergeni Hills. This forms the step by which the Russian tableland descends to the *Caspian Depression,* which is in part below sea-level. This also forms practically the frontier between the cultivated land and the nomadic steppes, and thus is by many authorities considered as the real boundary between Europe and Asia.

The latest superficial deposits are of the utmost importance for the Russian empire, since they form the soil of the land, and so condition not only its scenic features but also its productive capacity. They are independent of the geological structure of the underlying strata. From this point of view we may distinguish their characters in the following regions: —

(1). The *Finnish Bridge,* including the peninsula of Kola, is part of the centre of the great N. European *Glacier Area* of the Ice Age. The process of glaciation has here worked mainly as a destructive agent, so that the predominant feature of the landscape consists of barren rocks of the primæval crystalline group polished by glaciers with kames or eskers of glacial detritus. Long trough-like valleys have been cut between gently rounded ridges, and they are often filled by long, narrow, and much ramified lakes. The rivers form numerous rapids and waterfalls. Lakes and waterfalls, rocks and woods thus combine to cause the unique charm of Finnish scenery, which resembles that of N. Sweden. This 'Finnish Lake Plateau' is traversed and bounded by large terminal moraines.

(2). *North-East Russia,* the basin of the Petchora and the Dvina, is covered with the clay and sand deposits of the Arctic Ocean, which flooded these lowlands at the end of the Ice Age.

(3). The rest of *North Russia,* down to a line drawn through Lemberg, Tula, Nizhni-Novgorod, and Perm, is occupied by the *Deposits of the North Glacial Area,* consisting of lateral and terminal moraines and sand. The continuation of the Baltic plateau running from E. Prussia across the Valdai Hills to Lake Onéga is specially distinguished by morainal hills and lakes. The glacial deposits gradually disintegrate into a light sandy soil known as 'podzol', the fertility of which varies but is seldom more than moderate.

(4). To the S. of this comes the region of the *Loess,* a yellowish steppe soil, transported by the wind during the so-called interglacial periods of the Ice Age. From the above-mentioned boundary down to the neighbourhood of the Black Sea it forms a continuous covering, the superficial black colour of which is due to the so-called *Black Earth* (Tchernozyóm), a humus of quite extraordinary fertility. To the E. of the Volga, and on the coast of the Black Sea,

this loess envelope is more or less intermittent; the underlying
strata come to the surface, while the percentage of humus and
consequent fertility of the soil decrease.

(5). *The Caspian Depression* consists for the most part of
unfertile sandy and salt-earth steppes, deposits of the Caspian Sea
in its earlier and more extensive form.

The **Climate** of Russia is quite continental, *i. e.* the variation
between summer and winter temperatures is very great. Thus at
Moscow the mean January temperature is 54° lower than that of
July, as compared with a range of 34° in Central Germany; the
July temperature corresponds to that of Paris, the January to that
of Haparanda. Owing to the enormous extent of Russia from N.
to S., the temperatures in different parts of the empire are naturally
very different. The cold and length of winter decrease as we go
from N.E. to S.W.; summer heat increases from N.N.W. to S.S.E.
The greatest extremes of temperature consequently occur in the S.E.
The following table gives a summary of the mean temperatures
according to the Fahrenheit scale. The coldest month is January,
except in Uleåborg and Helsingfors, where February is colder.
The warmest month throughout the whole empire is July:—

Town	Latitude	Coldest Month	Warmest Month	Variation	Mean Minimum	Mean Maximum
Uleåborg	65°1′	12.6	60.4	47.8	−17.4	78.3
Archangel	60°33′	7.3	60.4	53.1	−32.1	84.6
Helsingfors	60°10′	19.6	61.9	42.3	− 9.0	77.4
St. Petersburg	59°56′	15.3	63.9	48.6	−19.3	84.7
Riga	56°57′	22.8	64.2	41.4	—	—
Moscow	55°46′	12.2	66.0	53.8	−22.9	88.5
Kazan	55°47′	7.2	67.5	60.3	−26.3	88.0
Warsaw	52°13′	25.9	65.8	39.9	− 6.3	89.6
Kiev	50°26′	20.8	66.6	45.8	− 9.8	89.8
Orenburg	51°46′	3.4	70.9	67.5	−27.8	96.1
Odessa	46°29′	25.3	72.7	47.4	—	—
Astrakhan	46°21′	19.0	77.9	58.9	−15.0	97.3

The winters in the S. are thus very severe, except on the S.
coast of the Crimea; Odessa *(e.g.)* is colder than East Prussia and
Poland. Sudden variations of temperature are very frequent. The
snow lies for months, except in S. Russia, where the traces of its
violent snowstorms soon disappear. Winter in Poland, the Baltic
Provinces, and S.W. Russia is comparatively mild; it is coldest in
N.E. Russia and to the E. of the Volga. In the higher latitudes
the summers are generally cool, with one or two exceptionally hot
days. The summer climate of the Russian and Finnish coasts of

the Baltic Sea resembles that of the German Baltic coast, having much fog and a heavy rainfall; spring is late and autumn very short. In Central Russia the summer climate corresponds to that of Central Germany, while on the Volga and in S. Russia, especially near Astrakhan, very high temperatures are reached. The heat, however, is generally dry and neither oppressive nor sultry. The traveller must always be on his guard against sudden falls of temperature, especially in the evenings.

The ANNUAL RAINFALL in N. and Central Russia is moderate (20-24 in.), but quite sufficient for the vegetation, as it is spread over the whole year. As we go S. it decreases rapidly (8-12 in.), and in the extreme S. it is very low indeed in late summer, autumn, and winter, so that the period of vegetation is too short to allow of the growth of trees. Thus we find the *Forests* of N. Russia counterbalanced by the *Steppes* of S. Russia, a contrast which makes itself felt in every department of economic and national life. The boundary between the two territories coincides roughly with that of the glacial deposits (p. xxxvii), and may be considered as a line drawn from Lemberg through Kiev, Kazan, and Ufa to Orenburg. The extreme N. consists of a treeless wilderness known as the *Tundra*.

The **Forest District** begins at the Arctic Circle with the *Coniferous Belt,* including firs, pines, and birches, and extending almost uninterruptedly to St. Petersburg and to the upper course of the Volga (Kazan). In Russia scarcely any attention is given to arboriculture, so that the forests often present a very primæval appearance. The scanty population (1.3 to 36 per sq. M.) is clustered round the navigable rivers, and supports itself by timber-cutting, hunting, and fishing. Even in the somewhat warmer Finland (density of population, 21 per sq. M.) agriculture and cattle-rearing are relatively unimportant. Central and W. Russia form the region of the *Mixed Forests,* including both deciduous trees and evergreens; beeches, however, occur only in Poland and Podolia. The agricultural districts, which alternate with the forest in larger and smaller areas, are mainly confined to the cultivation of rye and oats, and produce little more than is necessary for the comparatively dense population (52-145 per sq. M., exclusive of Moscow). The products of the Baltic Provinces are more varied, and the returns higher, partly on account of a more rational system of agriculture, partly on account of their more favourable situation (density of population 60-80 per sq. M., exclusive of St. Petersburg). The fertile Poland supports a dense agricultural and industrial population (238 per sq. M.).

The **Steppes** (p. xxxvii) in the provinces of Bessarabia, Podolia, Kiev, Poltava, Kharkov, Kursk, Voronezh, Tambov, and Penza are almost wholly under tillage, and the population varies in density between 119 and 228 per sq. M. The excellent soil of the Black Earth, moistened by a moderate rainfall, produces all kinds of grain, and also sugar beets. The huge Russian exports of wheat and other grain are due entirely to the yield of these provinces, which include numerous small and moderate-sized towns, besides a large rural population. Near and beyond the middle course of the Volga (density 54-124 per sq. M.) and towards the Black Sea agriculture gives place more and more to cattle-rearing. Large portions of the steppes are still untilled, but the wandering nomads are increasingly hampered by the progress of Russian colonization. Genuine nomadic life, however, is still found in the desert salt-steppe of the Caspian Depression, where oases are non-existent except in the vicinity of the Volga. In spring the Pontic Steppe is a grassy carpet gay with flowers, which withers away completely in autumn, when the only growth of the soil consists of thistles and dun-coloured shrubs such as wormwood. — Wine is grown in Bessarabia, in the Crimea, and on the Lower Don.

The great Russian plateau is thus moulded on simple general lines, and lacks the manifold variety of W. Europe; still it can show considerable diversity in scenery, climate, vegetation, and culture, though this occurs rather in gradual transitions than in sharp contrasts. The traveller, if he is on the alert, will notice these differences even from the windows of the railway carriage. The greatest contrast is between the N. and the S., and after a night's journey the traveller will often awaken to a scene strikingly different from that of the evening before. In the forest-district the train often runs for hours at a time through lonely woods, consisting of a wild chaos of all kinds of trees and shrubs, and showing no trace of human activity except the numerous felled and rotting tree-trunks. Between these gloomy forests occur tracts of arable land and straggling villages of small blockhouses, dominated by the shining dome of a church. The fields are enlivened with the red shirts and petticoats of the men and women workers. Now and again the more numerous domes and larger houses of a town may be descried in the distance. The railway stations are usually crowded with a motley throng, full of interest to the stranger as displaying all the different racial types and every class of society. Every variety of uniform is to be seen. Outside the stations stand the curious country carts and little droshkies. In many districts we find gently rounded hills, winding valleys, and verdant meadows; at other times we traverse endless plains. Other features of the landscape include large rivers with quaint boats and rafts, and extensive swamps dotted with alders. — In the Black Earth region the characteristic feature is the wide expanse of huge and treeless tilled fields, with large though infrequent settlements; but even here we may suddenly come across a narrow valley with steep wooded sides, or meet with picturesque rocks. In the Steppes proper, to the S. and E., we traverse an undulating district with numerous furrows and vast uncultivated stretches of rocky soil, green in spring and grey in autumn. The only signs of life in this sparsely populated district are the whitewashed mud-huts and the half-wild cattle.

b. **The People.**

Alongside of the physical diversities of the country range those of its inhabitants. The various peoples have gradually become united to form one nation, but are still far from being welded into one race. They still show wide discrepancies in type, customs, and dress. The phlegmatic forest-dwellers in the N. have always differed in many respects from the more emotional inhabitants of the Steppe district in the S. In the beginning of the historical period we find an ethnographical distinction between the *Aryans* in the S.W. and the *Finns* in the N.E., the latter being a branch of the Mongolian race.

The Slavs are of Aryan descent. Their original home was on the Upper Dnieper and the Upper Dvina, whence they gradually spread over the whole country, branching into several different peoples. The most important Slav people is the—

Russians (Русскіе), who number about 78,000,000†, and so account for 75 per cent of the population of European Russia. All of these are members of the Greek Catholic Church or of its sects. They are divided into three stocks: the *Great Russians* (the standard-bearers proper of the Russian feeling of nationality), the *White Russians,* and the *Little Russians.* The first two of these are closely connected as regards language.

The White Russians (Бѣлоруссы) occupy what were probably the original homes of the Slavs in White Russia (provinces of Minsk, Mohilev, Vilna, Vitebsk, and Grodno). They number about 6,000,000, and probably derive their name from the light colour of their clothing. They are the poorest and the least advanced of the three stocks. Their villages are small, and solitary farms are frequent. A disease of the hair known as *Plica Polonica* (Колтунъ) is very common among them.

The Great Russians (Великоруссы), of whom there are 52,000,000 in European Russia, migrated in early times from their original homes towards the E., driving the Finnish peoples before them. They have, however, to some extent mingled with the Finnish race, which probably accounts for the broad faces, flat noses, and other Mongolian features found frequently among them. They now occupy not only 'Great Russia' (*i.e.* N. and Central Russia, with the N.E. part of the Black Earth region), but also E. and S.E. Russia,

---

† The figures for the individual peoples are taken from the census of 1897.

the former territory of the Tartar Khans. Their speech, customs, and character are spread over the whole empire. Physically they are blond, blue-eyed, and vigorous, with broad shoulders and bull necks, often somewhat clumsy and with a strong tendency to obesity. Their character has been influenced not only by a long history of subjugation to feudal despotism, but also by the gloomy forests, the unresponsive soil, and the rigorous climate, and especially by the enforced inactivity of the long winters. In disposition they are melancholy and reserved, clinging obstinately to their traditions, and full of self-sacrificing devotion to Tzar, Church, and feudal superior. They are easily disciplined, and so make excellent soldiers, but have little power of independent thinking or of initiation. The normal Great Russian is thus the mainstay of political and economic inertia and reaction. Even the educated Russian gives comparatively little response to the actual demands of life; he is more or less the victim of fancy and temperament, which sometimes lead him to a despondent slackness, sometimes to emotional outbursts. Here we have the explanation of the want of organization, the disorder, and the waste of time which strike the western visitor to Russia. This pessimistic outlook finds expression in the word that is forever on Russian lips — ничего (nitchevó), 'it doesn't matter'; the Russian derives his faults as well as his virtues from his 'wide nature' (широкая натура). The important and fascinating literature of Russia reflects this dreamy and melancholy outlook on life, which is seen also in the national songs and music.

The **Towns** of Great Russia generally cover a great deal of ground, and are all laid out on the same pattern. The centre is occupied by a spacious square, from which radiate broad and badly paved streets crossing each other at right angles. In the central part of the town the houses are built of stone and painted white, yellow, or pink. The public buildings seldom possess any architectural interest. In the suburbs the houses are of wood and stand at considerable distances from one another. The only effective architectural features are the large churches, which generally stand in open spaces at the intersection of the streets. Their gilded, silvered, or brightly coloured cupolas are very conspicuous. The commerce of the place, especially its retail trade, is often concentrated in Oriental fashion in bazaars or 'factories' (гостиные дворы). Each shopkeeper has his abacus (счёты) and samovar or tea-machine (самовáръ). A large proportion of the population wear uniforms, including not only soldiers but civil servants, students, schoolboys, and so on.

The **Villages** (Селó, village with church; Дерéвня, village without church) generally consist of one long straggling and unpaved street. In N. Russia the miserable houses (избы) are composed of logs placed horizontally one above the other, the interstices being filled with tow (пакля) and moss. The interior consists of a single room. The brick stove (печь) is used for heating, cooking, and baking, and also as a couch and bed. Every house in town and country has its ikon (образъ), with a perpetually burning lamp (лампáда), before which every Russian crosses himself on entering the room. The court is surrounded by an open shed, adjoined by the stables, barns, and threshing-floor. Every village possesses a simple kind of vapour bath, which is much frequented, especially on Saturdays (comp. p. xxxi).

The regular dress of the Great Russian peasant consists of a coloured shirt *(Rubáshka)* generally of red cotton *(Kumátch),* which is worn outside the trousers and not tucked in. Broad leathern boots *(Sapogi),* reaching to the knees, or puttees *(Onútchi),* fastened to sandal-like bast shoes *(Lapti),* cover the ends of the coloured and baggy trousers *(Portki).* In winter felt boots *(Válenki)* are common. The long-skirted coat *(Kaftán),* with a low collar, is held together by a belt or coloured sash. In summer the upper garment is the *Armyák,* made of coarse cloth with a broad collar, in winter the sheepskin *Tulúp* or the fur *Shuba.* The head is covered by the low *Shapka,* made of felt or fur, or by the peaked *Kartúz.* The ordinary Russian lets his beard grow, and allows only the hair of his head to be cut. — The chief garment of the women is the *Sarafán,* a skirt and bodice with shoulder-straps, all in one piece, or the *Panyóva,* a linen skirt. Above these is a short *Kaftán.* Round the head they wear a gaudy handkerchief, which is often replaced on holidays by a sort of tiara *(Kokóshnik)* adorned with imitation pearls.

The Little Russians (Малороссы; 20,000,000) are settled in the Black Earth district (*i.e.* in Little Russia proper), and in the Ukraine, which includes the provinces of Kiev, Poltava, Kharkov, and Tchernigov. They are also found in Volhynia and Podolia, whence, under the name of Ruthenians, they spread into Galicia and N.E. Hungary. In recent times they have also colonized Bessarabia, Kherson, and Taurida, in which provinces they now form a majority of the inhabitants. They are slender and dark, and they have the emotional southern temperament; their poetry and music are of a high order, as is evidenced by their popular songs and proverbs. Their dialect is very different from those of the Great and White Russians. The settlements of the Steppes are still more straggling than those of the forest region; owing to the lack of timber the houses are generally built of mud or clay.

The *Cossacks* are not a distinct stock, but are descended from the refugees and outlaws who occupied the frontier districts between the settled and the nomadic tribes. These were afterwards organized as a frontier militia and as light cavalry. The only Cossacks now in European Russia are those in the lower valley of the Don and in the Urals (Orenburg Cossacks).

A unique position is held by the **Poles,** a Slav race occupying the Russian part of the old kingdom of Poland. They are also to be found sporadically throughout W. Russia, which was formerly under their sway. Their total number is about 8,000,000. Their history and their mode of life as well as their religion (they are Roman Catholics) all bring them into much closer connection with W. Europe than with Russia. The Polish language is a member of the W. Slav family, employing Roman characters (comp. p. 2). The Poles are of the middle height, with slender but muscular bodies and light hair. The contrast between the lower classes and the noblesse is very striking, the latter being physically and in character refined to an almost excessive pitch of elegance. Polish women are renowned for their grace and beauty.

To the Slavs also belong, broadly speaking, the *Letts* (1,400,000), who occupy Courland and S. Livonia, and the *Lithuanians* (1,200,000), who form the bulk of the population in Russian Lithuania. The former are Lutherans, the latter Roman Catholics.

The **Non-Slavonic Aryans** in European Russia number 3,500,000. The most numerous are the *Germans* (2,000,000), who are the country gentlemen and citizens of the Baltic provinces in virtue of their descent from the former masters of the country. There are also agricultural settlements of Germans on the Upper and Lower Volga, in S.W. Russia, and in the Caucasus and the Crimea, many of them established in the reign of Catherine II. German manufacturers, merchants, and artisans are found in all the large towns. German influence on Russia has always been considerable. In Finland the *Swedes* were the pioneers of civilization. They now number about 370,000, and are especially numerous in the coast-towns. *Rumanians* (1,100,000) form the bulk of the population in Bessarabia. *Bulgarians* and *Greeks* are also more or less numerous in S. Russia.

The **Jews** (5,100,000) migrated in the middle ages from Germany to Poland, and speak a German dialect intermingled with Hebrew expressions. Many of them, however, now speak the language of the country. They are not allowed to live either in Great Russia or in E. Russia. Strictly limited in their privileges, and subject to numerous economic restrictions as well as to the caprice of the Russian officials, they subsist for the most part in a state of physical and moral degradation. As a result, they migrate in large numbers to other countries.

The **Mongolian Race** is represented in Russia by 9,000,000 souls, belonging partly to the *Ural* and partly to the *Turkish* group. The former are found in the N., N.E., and N.W., the latter in the S. and S.E. In the province of Astrakhan there are also 170,000 nomadic *Kalmucks*, who are of pure Mongol blood and profess the religion of Lamaism.

In the **Ural Group** (5,400,000) the *Samoyedes* or reindeer-possessing nomads of the Tundra (p. xxxix) are an insignificant item. The great bulk of the group consists of the *Finnish Peoples,* who were the aboriginal inhabitants of the whole of N. and N.E. Russia, but were split into two groups (E. and W.) by the Russian advance.

The **East Finns** include the *Ugrians* and the *Permiaks,* who along with the *Syryenians* and the *Votyaks* (650,000 in all) occupy the river districts of the Petchora, Dvina, and Kama, and also the *Volga Finns* (1,860,000) on the Middle Volga, a remnant of a people that flourished in the Middle Ages (Tcheremisses, Mordvins, Tchuvashes). They are all agriculturists, and occupy colonies interspersed among the Russians. They have, however, mingled freely with their Russian neighbours, and thus present no distinct Mongolian type. They belong to the Greek Catholic Church.

The WEST FINNS comprise two main stocks. The *Finns* proper, including the Karelians (2,800,000), live in Finland and the adjoining parts of Russia. They are also strongly mixed with Aryan blood, and are consequently fair-haired, blue-eyed, strong, and of medium stature. Civilized by the Swedes (comp. p. 198) and converted to Protestantism, they have considerable achievements to show in science, art, and literature. Their patriotism is very keen and they cling obstinately to their own language (comp p. 199). The *Esthonians* (about 900,000) are also Protestants, and inhabit Esthonia and the N. of Livonia. — With these may be mentioned about 3000 *Lapps*, who live in the extreme N. of Finland and in Kola as reindeerowning nomads and fishermen. They are small in stature and of a strong Mongoloid type. A few *Tchudes* and *Livonians* also belong to this group.

The **Turkish Group**, all of whom are Mohammedans, is predominantly represented by the TATARS or TARTARS, descendants of those tribes of the Turkish family who migrated from Central Asia along with the Mongolians and once dominated the whole of E. and S. Russia. They have now, however, almost lost their Mongolian features. Geographically, they are divided into agricultural *Crim Tartars*, whose number (200,000) is constantly decreasing through emigration to Turkey, and *Kazan Tartars* (1,700,000), who are known in the province of the Volga not only as agriculturists but also as shrewd merchants and pedlars. They are also met with throughout Russia as waiters and porters. The Kazan Tartars are of the middle height and light-yellow in colour, with an oval face, narrow and oblique black eyes, and scanty beards.

Their COSTUME consists of a long sleeveless coat surmounted by a kind of kaftán *(Khalát)*. The head is shaved and covered with a skull cap *(Yermólka)*, over which the ordinary man wears a white felt hat or a grey or black fur cap *(Burnik)*. The well-to-do classes wear a finer fur cap, broader at the top than at the bottom. Their feet are shod with bright-coloured morocco-leather boots without soles and slippers *(Bashmák)* or leathern overshoes. — Their Mosques *(Metchét)* are large and simple prayer halls, dominated by a minaret.

The BASHKIRS (1,400,000), in the provinces of Ufa and Orenburg, are a Finno-Turkish mixed race, speaking the Turkish language and having Mongoloid features. The *Mountain Bashkirs*, a tall and strong race, with dark hair, had their own military organization ('Bashkir Army') down to 1874, and are now in a transition-state between the nomadic and the settled life. The *Steppe Bashkirs*, the result of intermixture with the Meshtcheryaks, are still all nomads, but live in houses during the winter. They subsist mainly on Kumiss (p. 358).

The KIRGHIZES are a Turkish nomadic race, extending from

Central Asia to the Lower Volga. In the province of Astrakhan, where they live side by side with the Kalmucks (p. xliv), they number 250,000.

Alongside the present official division into governments (p. lvi) there still subsists a vivid recollection of the great **Historical Districts** which played their rôles in the past. In the census of 1909 the population and area of these latter were as follows: —

	Area in sq. M.	Population	Density, per sq. M.
Great Russia, N. division (govts. of Archangel, Olonetz, Vologda, and Novgorod) .	577,905	4,089,000	7.0
Great Russia, S. division .	303,112	34,621,000	114.2
Baltic Provinces	53,638	5,456,000	101.5
W. Russia	161,235	19,763,000	122.2
Little Russia	80,212	14,059,000	174.8
S. Russia	156,104	13,995,000	83.6
E. Russia	526,715	24,522,000	46.6
Poland	49,017	11,672,000	237.8
Finland	144,252	3,059,000	21.2
Total:	2,052,190	131,236,000	63.7

Religion (p. lvii). About 87,000,000 of the total population belong to the Greek Catholic Church; 2,000,000 are Raskolniks or Old Believers. The Roman Catholic Church has 11,400,000 adherents. Besides these there are 6,500,000 Protestants, 5,100,000 Jews, and 3,600,000 Mohammedans. There are about 300,000 Pagans.

III. SKETCH OF THE POLITICAL, ECONOMIC, AND SOCIAL HISTORY OF RUSSIA.

The formation of states in the great E. European plain radiated from two main centres. In the N. the Swedish Northmen, the *Variags (Varags)* or *Varangians* (foreigners) of the Russian annals, founded the oldest kingdom about the 9th century of our era. The name *Ros* or *Rus*, applied to them by the Finns (probably because they came from the Swedish coast-district of Roslagen), is supposed to be the origin of the present name of the people. At a somewhat later date flourished the commercial republics of *Novgorod* and *Pskov (Pleskau)*. In the S., *Kiev* was under the influence of Byzantium, to which the Russians owed the introduction of Christianity (10th cent.), the Greek alphabet, their ecclesiastical art, and other important elements in their civilization. To these must be added certain Mohammedan races, such as the E. Finnish *Bulgars* on the Volga, and the *Khazars* and other constantly varying occupiers of the Steppes farther to the S. All these states were overthrown in the 13th century by the aggressions of the *Mongols*. Out of the Mongolian empire emerged the Mohammedan khanates of the *Tartars*. On the W. side of the plain we find the *Teutonic Order* in possession of the Baltic Provinces, the *Swedes* ruling over Finland, and *Lithuania* and *Poland* stretching over the whole of W. and Little Russia. The *Principalities of Great Russia* were subject to the Tartars, until the *Grand-Princes of Moscow* shook off the yoke at the end of the 15th century. This may be taken as the beginning of the conscious expression of the GREAT RUSSIAN POWER. The other Russian principalities and republics were next overthrown, and then (1552-54) the khanates on the Volga. This opened the way to Siberia, and the Pacific Ocean was reached as early as the middle of the 17th century. On the W. side of the plateau Little Russia was wrested from Poland in 1667, while in the following century the Baltic Provinces were conquered from Sweden, which had already driven out the Teutonic Order. The foundation of *St. Petersburg* on the Baltic Sea inaugurated a new phase in the development of the empire. In the three partitions of Poland between 1772 and 1795 the whole of that country as far as the Niemen was absorbed, while the rest of what is now Russian Poland was added by the Vienna Congress of 1815. Finland had already been ceded by Sweden in 1809. In the meantime there was no break in the progress towards the S.; in 1774 the Turkish sovereignty over the Tartars was overthrown, and the Russians established themselves on the Black Sea and at the foot of the Caucasus. During the 19th century Bessarabia, to the S.W., and the Asiatic side of the Caucasus and part of Armenia were added, Siberia much extended, and Turkestan conquered.

The following short **Chronological Outline** will supplement the above general remarks: —

1. Old Russia. Period of the Local Principalities.

862. Invasion of the Norsemen, led by the Variags **Rurik, Sineus,** and **Truvor,** in answer to the invitation of the Slav republic of Novgorod, worded, according to the Chronicles, as follows: 'Our land is great and fruitful, but there is no order in it; come and reign and rule over us.' On the death of his kinsmen, Rurik became sole ruler.

879-912. **Olég,** regent during the minority of Rurik's son Igor, conquered the duchy of Kiev in 882.

912-945. **Igor.** Treaty made with the Byzantine Emperor, 945. — Christianity established at Kiev.

945-957. **Olga (St.),** widow of Igor and regent for her son Svyatoslàv, accepted the Christian faith at Kiev in 957.

957-972. *Svyatoslàv I. Ígorevitch.*—Division of the territory
among Svyatoslàv's sons.—Civil war.

980-1015. **Vladímir I. (St.;** the Apostle). Greek Church established as the state religion (988). Vladímir married
the Greek Princess Anna, sister of Theophano, wife of
Emperor Otho II. Succession disputed on Vladímir's
death.

1019-1054. **Yaroslàv I.,** *the Wise,* married a daughter of Olaf,
King of Sweden. Of his daughters, the eldest married
Harold, King of Norway; another Henry I. of France;
a third, Andreas I. of Hungary. Many towns founded.
The first Russian Code (Ру́сская пра́вда) issued.—
On his death, the kingdom was divided, and civil and
foreign wars ensued.

1113-1125. **Vladímir II. Monomákh.** Defeated the Polovtsi.
His wife was Gyda or Gytha, daughter of Harold II. of
England.

1125-1132. *Mstislàv I.,* Grand-Prince of Kiev. — Innumerable
divisions and endless wars. — Great Novgorod became
an independent republic.

2. Period of the Mongol Supremacy.

1224. First invasion of the Tartars under Genghis or Jenghiz
Khan. Defeat of the Russians on the Kalka.

1237-1242. Second Tartar invasion under *Baty-Khan.*—The king-
doms of the Bolgars, Polovtsi, etc., destroyed.

1238-1246. *Yaroslàv II. Vsévolodovitch,* Grand-Prince of Vladimir. The whole of Russia under Tartar suzerainty.

1252-1263. **Alexander Nevski,** Grand-Prince of Vladimir, the
Russian national hero and saint.—His son Daniel, as
Prince of Moscow, founded the line of Moscow princes
of the Rurik dynasty. — Alexander's victory over the
Swedes on the Nevá (whence his surname), 1240. Defeat
of the Teutonic Order on the ice of Lake Peipus (1242).

1328-1340. *Ivan I. Danílovitch Kalitá,* Grand-Prince of Moscow,
Vladimir, and Novgorod.—The Metropolitan removes
his seat from Vladimir to Moscow.

1363-1389. *Demetrius of the Don (Dmitri Donskói);* defeated the
Tartars on Kulikóvo Field on Sept. 8th, 1380.

1425-1462. *Vasíli II. Vasílyevitch.*

1462-1505. **Ivan** *(Ioánn)* **III. Vasilyevitch,** Grand-Prince of
Moscow, and the real founder of the Russian Empire.

Marriage with Sophia Palæologos, 1472. Perm reduced to subjection, 1472. Novgorod overthrown, 1478. Rout of the Golden Horde, 1478. Overthrow of the tribes on the Ob and the Irtuish, 1483-99. Kazan conquered and held for a short time, 1487. Karelia captured, 1496. Unsuccessful campaign against the Livonian Order, 1501-1503.

3. Period of Muscovite Unification.

FORMATION OF THE RUSSIAN EMPIRE.

1505 1533. *Vasíli III. Ivánovitch* united most of the independent principalities with Moscow.

1533-1584. **Iván** *(Ioánn)* **IV. Grozni** (the Terrible) ruled at first under the influence of Shúiski, Glinski, and the Boyars; then under that of the monk *Sylvester* and *Alexis Adáshev.* — Title of Tzar of all the Russias assumed, 1547. Conquest of Kazan (1552) and Astrakhan (1557). — The English begin to trade with Muscovy viâ Archangel, 1582. — Beginning of the conquest of Siberia by the Stróganovs, Yermák, and other bold Cossack chieftains. — Russian Law Code (Sudébnik) formulated; printing introduced at Moscow.

1584-1598. *Feódor* or *Theodore I. Ivánovitch,* the last sovereign of the line of Rurik. Peasants deprived of right of free migration. Patriarchate established. — After the murder of all the blood-relatives of Theodore and also of his step-brother *Dmitri* or Demetrius (d. 1591), Borís Godunóv, the brother of Theodore's wife, became sole ruler.

INTERREGNUM. PERIOD OF THE FALSE DEMETRIUS.

1598-1605. **Borís Feódorovitch Godunóv.** Appearance of the First and Second False Demetrius, both of whom were supported by the Poles. The *First False Demetrius* (1605-1606) was murdered on May 17th, 1606. — The *Second False Demetrius* appeared after the boyar *Vasíli Shúiski* (1606-10) had been elected Tzar.

1610-1613. **Interregnum.** *Kosmá Minin* and *Prince Pozhárski;* the Poles driven from Russia.

RISE OF THE ROMÁNOV DYNASTY.

1613-1645. **Mikhaíl Feódorovitch Románov,** kinsman of Theodore I., elected Tzar and founder of the present dynasty. Peace of Stolbovo, 1617 (cession of Ingermanland to Sweden); Armistice of Deulino, 1618; Peace of Polyanovka, 1634 (territory ceded to Poland; claims to Livonia, Courland, and Esthonia renounced).

1645-1676. **Alexis I., Mikháilovitch.** — Introduction of the new code ('Ulozhéniye') 1649. — Treaty of Andrúsovo (occupation of Smolensk and the Ukraine, suzerainty etablished over Kiev and the Cossacks), 1667. — Schism in the Russian Church due to innovations by Nikon (see p. lviii).

1676-1682. **Feódor (Theodore), Alexéyevitch.** Abolition of the system of preferment by 'hereditary rank' (Myéstnitchestvo). — On the death of Theodore, *Grand-Duchess Sophia Alexéyevna* (1682-1689) became regent on behalf of her half-brothers, the Tzars Iván and Peter (b. 1672).

4. The St. Petersburg Period.

1689-1725. **Peter I., the Great,** immured Sophia Alexéyevna in a convent and became, with the free consent of his brother Iván (d. 1696), sole ruler of the empire. Far-reaching innovations; introduction of W. European customs and culture. — Northern War (1700-1721), carried on, in alliance with Frederick IV. of Denmark and Augustus II. of Poland, against Charles XII. of Sweden. Victory of Poltava, 1709; loss of Azov, 1711. By the treaty of Nystad (1721) Russia gained Livonia and Esthonia. — Foundation of St. Petersburg, 1703. — War with Persia; Russian dominion extended to the S. shore of the Caspian Sea. — Peter's son *Alexis (Alexéi)* died in 1718. — Assumption of the imperial title, 1721.

1725-1727. **Catherine I.,** widow of Peter I., ruled under the influence of Prince Menshikov. Foundation of the Academy of Sciences, 1725.

1727-1730. **Peter II., Alexéyevitch,** grandson of Peter the Great, removed the court to Moscow and ruled during his minority under the influence of the Dolgorúki.

1730-1740. **Anna Ivánovna,** daughter of Iván, half-brother of Peter the Great, took part (at the instigation of her favourites Biron and Field-Marshal Münnich) in the War of the Polish Succession (1733-38), and regained Azov in a war waged against Turkey (1735-1739).

1740-1741. *Iván VI.,* great-grandson of Iván, half-brother of Peter the Great, succeeded as an infant to the throne, which he occupied for a short time under the regency of his mother, Anna (Elizabeth) Leopóldovna. He was deposed in 1741 (d. at Schlüsselburg in 1764).

1741-1761. **Elizabeth Petróvna,** daughter of Peter the Great. In 1742 Elizabeth's nephew, Karl *Peter* Ulrich of Holstein-Gottorp was created heir-apparent. War with Sweden (1741-43), resulting in the Peace of Åbo, by which Russia acquired Finland as far as the Kymmene-Elf. — Alliance with Austria against France and Spain, 1746; alliance with Austria and France against Prussia (Seven Years War), 1756. — Foundation of Moscow University (1755) and of the St. Petersburg Academy of Arts (1757).

HOUSE OF ROMÁNOV-HOLSTEIN-GOTTORP.

1761-1762. **Peter III.** died six months after his accession.

1762-1796. **Catherine II.,** widow of Peter III. Russia becomes a Great Power. — Russian territory greatly extended by the three Partitions of Poland. — First Turkish War (cession of parts of the Crimea and the Caucasus; protectorate of the Danubian Principalities), 1768-74. — Rebellion of the Cossack Pugatchóv put down, 1773-75. — Conquest of the Crimea, 1783. — Second Turkish War, ending in the Peace of Jassy, by which Russia acquired the whole district up to the Dniester, 1787-92. — Unsuccessful war with Sweden, 1788-90. — Annexation of Courland, 1795.

1796-1801. **Paul I., Petróvitch,** son of Catherine, entangled Russia in a war with France (1798).

1801-1825. **Alexander I., Pávlovitch,** son of Paul I. — War with France terminated by the Treaty of Tilsit (June 25th, 1807); that with Austria by the Peace of Vienna (1809); that with Sweden by the Peace of Fredrikshamn (Sept. 5th, 1809); that with Turkey by the Peace of Bucharest (May 16th, 1812). — Napoleon's invasion of Russia; annihilation of the Grande Armée, 1812. — Treaty of Paris (April 21st, 1815).

1825-1855. **Nicholas I., Pávlovitch,** third son of Paul I. — War with Turkey and Persia, 1828. — Publication of the final and complete form of the Russian Code of Laws, 1830. — Opening of the Nikolai (Nicholas) or Nikolá-yevski Railway from St. Petersburg to Moscow, 1851. — Crimean War (1853-1856).

1855-1881. **Alexander II., Nikoláyevitch.** — Treaty of Paris, 1856. — Conquest of the Caucasus. — Liberation of the serfs, 1861. — Introduction of the new Judicial Procedure, 1866. — New Municipal Law, 1870. — Institution of compulsory military service, 1874. — Russo-

Turkish war (1877-78), ended by the Treaty of San Stefano and the Berlin Congress.

1881-1894. **Alexander III., Alexándrovitch.** Conquests in Central Asia. — Beginning of the Trans-Siberian Railway.

1894 et seq. **Nicholas II., Alexándrovitch.** Completion of the Trans-Siberian Railway, 1903. — Russo-Japanese war (1904-5), ending in the defeat of the Russians. Peace of Portsmouth (U.S.A.), 1905. — Opening of the first parliament (Imperial Duma), 1906.

Russian Civilization. Like the Russian state itself, Russian civilization is the result of a combination of very diverse elements. In the development of the Slav the Greek Christian culture of Byzantium came into contact with the Mohammedanism adopted by the races from the steppes of Asia. Nor must we forget the influence of W. Europe, which first made itself felt through the Variags and later, and to a greater extent, through the Germans on the Baltic and the Poles in W. Russia. The interior of the country, however, remained so isolated that the inhabitants of W. Europe had scarcely any idea of it even at the time of the great transoceanic discoveries. It was the growth of the Muscovite state towards the middle of the 16th century that aroused the attention of other countries. The first detailed information was revealed in 1549 in a book by Baron Sigismund von Herberstein, whom Charles V. had entrusted with an embassy to the Great or High Prince. About the same time English mariners under Sir Hugh Willoughby penetrated the White Sea viâ the N. Cape, and established the Russia Company, of which the most famous members were Sir Anthony Jenkinson and Sir Jerome Horsey (p. lxii). From this time forward Archangel became a seaport of some importance. Towards the end of the 17th century began the 'Europeanization' of Russia through its relations with France and Germany. The most zealous promoter of the new spirit was Peter the Great. It was, however, only the upper classes that received a veneer of W. European culture; the masses still held fast to their primitive Slavonic, Byzantine, and Asiatic predilections. Hence arose that cleavage of interests between Russia proper and the sophisticated W. parts of the empire which is typified in the contrast between the two great cities, the Old Russian Moscow in the heart of the country and the upstart St. Petersburg on the coast.

The PEASANTS lost their liberty as early as the Middle Ages to the *Boyars* or territorial nobility, who at first held seignorial rights over the land and later on became absolute owners of it. The military services of these nobles during the enormous expansion of the empire were rewarded by constant extensions of their manorial rights, until at last in 1592 the peasants were reduced to a condition of absolute serfdom. The ancient communal system of the

Mir (comp. p. lvii) was further developed about the same time in Great Russia. The Muzhiks or peasants form corporations which hold the land in common and are responsible for the payment of dues to the state and the landlord. The ground is distributed afresh every 12, 15, or 20 years, with the result that, as no one has any permanent interest in its improvement, no trouble is taken over it and the laws of scientific agriculture are disregarded. As there is not enough land for the increasing population, the younger peasants seek temporary employment in the towns as domestic servants or factory hands, without thereby losing their right to a share in the soil. The emigration to Siberia also is not inconsiderable. In 1861 serfdom was abolished; but its demoralizing effects have by no means disappeared, since practically nothing is done for the elevation of the peasant. It must, however, be noted that the percentage of recruits who can neither read nor write has sunk from 79.1 in 1876 to 51.1 in 1900. The dues payable by the peasants to the ground-landlords as compensation for their emancipation were so oppressive that in 1905 all arrears were remitted. In 1906 and 1910 the compulsory character of the Mir was likewise modified.

The Russian Nobles are very different from those of W. Europe. The political rights of the owners of property were at an early stage limited in favour of an absolute monarchy, and were totally abolished by Peter the Great. The privileges of the comparatively few ancient noble families now left are limited to precedence in holding offices at court and in the Imperial Guards. The mainstay of the supremacy of the government and the police is the so-called *Tchin* or *Official Noblesse*. This is constantly recruited from all classes of the population, as everyone who attains the rank of Privy Councillor or Colonel thereby acquires hereditary nobility. The personal or life nobility, attainable by officials of a lower class, is of no importance. The hereditary nobility form special corporations in the provinces, which exercise considerable influence on the administration (comp. p. lvi).

The Citizen or Middle Class is still little developed. There are only 33 cities in the vast empire with populations exceeding 100,000. The chief of these are St. Petersburg, with 2,075,000 inhabitants; Moscow, with 1,617,000; Warsaw, with 872,000; Odessa, with 630,000; Kiev, with 590,000; Riga, with 530,000; and Lodz, with 450,000. Citizens are usually divided into burgesses (or upper class citizens), shopkeepers, and artisans, the first class consisting of members of the learned professions, the leading artists, wholesale merchants, manufacturers, and so on. Among the shopkeepers and artisans are many Germans (especially in St. Petersburg). Poles and Jews are also strongly represented. An Artisan Class began to come into existence in 1861, on the abolition of serfdom (comp. above). It consists mainly of peasants employed in manufactures, and has not yet attained a high standard of productiveness. Both burghers and artisans are, however, growing rapidly not only in numbers, but in intellectual development as well.

The total population of Russia, apart from the Jews and the Nomads in the East and North, is divided into four classes: nobles and officials, clergy, citizens or townspeople, and peasants, the last including the labourers. The really sharp distinction, however, is that between the great mass of the people on the one side and the hereditary and official nobility and the burgess class on the other. Even in the upper ranks of society the consequences of the sudden transition from the Old Russian civilization to that of W. Europe are easily discernible. Alongside of admirable achievements in all spheres of intellectual activity, we find also a great deal of merely outward imitation of western forms, with a tendency to rest content with a veneer of western culture and a stock of western catchwords. Side by side with the unquenchable desire for scientific knowledge, which shuns no sacrifice and is constantly drawing new elements from the lower classes, there is only too often a total inability to put into practice and make an effectual use of what has been learned. Fancy and emotion are much more widely developed in the soul of the Russian than true energy and joy in creation. The upper classes are noted for their luxury and extravagance and for their reckless gambling, their better side showing itself in their unlimited hospitality. The lower classes live in unspeakable poverty and destitution. Beggars are very troublesome, especially in the vicinity of churches.

Economic Conditions. Russia's situation as well as its natural features and its history make it a land of RAW PRODUCTS, though in the last 50 years manufacturing industry has developed fast. Fully 80 per cent of the population live by *Agriculture.* Yet only 26.2 per cent of the total area is under tillage and 15.9 per cent occupied by gardens, meadows, and pasturage. Forests cover 38.8 per cent; 19.1 per cent is wholly barren. Moreover, in the greater part of the empire, agriculture has to struggle against the poverty of the soil and the rigour of the climate. A failure in crops is regularly followed by famine, especially in the unproductive provinces on the Volga. A striking contrast to this, however, is afforded by the fertility of the Black Earth district (p. xxxvii), which exports its surplus grain by way of the harbours of the Black Sea, and is one of the most important sources of the world's corn-markets. Flax also is extensively cultivated, especially in the provinces of Pskov, Vyatka, Smolensk, Livonia, and Yaroslavl. —The *Furs* obtained in the hyperborean parts of the empire are very valuable, but their yield is steadily decreasing.

MANUFACTURING INDUSTRY is still much less important than agriculture. It is true that the Government has done much to elevate it in recent times, but there is a great lack both of native capital and of competent workmen (comp. pp. liii, liv). The entrepreneurs and managers of factories are largely foreigners. The products are limited to articles of common use for distribution in Russia and the interior of Central Asia. In *Poland* the manufacture of cotton and other textiles is the predominant industry; it flourishes chiefly to the W. of the Vistula, near the coal-fields of Upper Silesia and Poland (Lodz, p. 5). The important *Industrial District of Central Russia* centres in Moscow and extends on the S. to the coal-fields of Kaluga and Tula (p. 360), on the N. to Tver und Yaroslavl (pp. 267, 330), and on the E. to Ivanovo and Vladimir (pp. 338, 337). The chief manufactures here are textile and metal wares, but the domestic industries of the forest-zone still persist to a certain extent. The huge expansion of the iron industry of *South Russia*, where iron and coal are found together on the Donetz (p. 429), has already materially decreased the imports from foreign countries and has even led to a small export trade. Its production is now more than twice as great as that of the old and familiar iron industry of the *Ural*, which has to depend on lignite for fuel. The manufactures of *St. Petersburg, Riga*, and other towns on the Baltic are very varied, and include cotton, metal wares, machinery, and chemicals. In *Finland* there are wood-pulp, paper, and allied industries, which depend on that country's wealth in timber and water-power. The only industries of the *Steppes* (p. xxxix) centre round such quasi-agricultural institutions as flour-mills and sugar-factories.

The FOREIGN TRADE of Russia is still small compared with the extent of the country. The commercial coasting fleet is insignificant. The Russians are not a maritime nation, and their captains and pilots often come from Finland and the Baltic. On the other hand, owing to the number and size of the rivers, the inland navigation is of considerable importance. The most important exports are corn and flour, timber, flax, eggs, sugar, and butter, the last coming chiefly from Siberia and rapidly becoming of great importance. The imports include raw cotton, machinery, tea, wool, metal wares, and coal. Germany now heads the list both in exports and imports, with Great Britain in the second place.

The RAILWAY SYSTEM of European Russia is nearly as large as that of Germany so far as its mileage is concerned (35,447 M. being open for traffic in Jan. 1st, 1912), but the proportion of mileage to area (1 M. for every 53 sq. M. of territory) is less than for any other country except Norway (United Kingdom 1 M. per 5.3 sq. M.; Germany 1 M. per 5.8 sq. M.; United States 1 M. per 15.7 sq. M.). The difference of gauge (p. xx) is a serious hindrance to through traffic with W. Europe. — The HIGH ROADS are almost universally in bad repair (comp. p. xxv).

IV. GOVERNMENT AND ADMINISTRATION.

LEGISLATURE. Since 1905 the Russian Empire (Россійская Имперія or Россія) has been a constitutional monarchy with an autocratic sovereign (Императоръ, Государь, or Царь) at its head. The legislative power is exercised by the Tzar, the *Imperial Council* or First Chamber (Государственный Совѣтъ), and the *Imperial Duma* or Second Chamber (Государственная Дума). The First Chamber consists of 98 members nominated by the Tzar and of 98 additional members elected for a period of nine years; the Second Chamber consists of 442 members elected for five years.

EXECUTIVE. The executive power is vested in the Tzar and is delegated to: (1). The *Council of Ministers* (Совѣтъ Министровъ), consisting of the eleven ministers and of three other high officials enjoying similar privileges. This forms the Supreme Council of the Tzar in all matters of administration that are beyond the competence of individual ministers. — (2). The *Ruling Senate* (Правительствующій Сенатъ), divided into various departments. Its functions include the publication and registration of laws, and it constitutes the final Court of Appeal in both civil and criminal cases. — (3). The *Holy Synod*, see p. lviii.

LOCAL GOVERNMENT. The Russian Empire is divided into *Governments* (Губерніи) or provinces, and *Territories* (Области), *i.e.* Asiatic provinces under military rule. Sometimes several governments are united to form a *General Government* (Генералъ-губернаторство) or (as in the case of the Caucasus) a *Viceroyalty*. European Russia, exclusive of Finland, contains 59 governments and 1 territory. St. Petersburg, Odessa, Sebastopol, and certain other cities, are each under a City Governor (Градоначальникъ). Each government is divided into *Districts* (Уѣзды), *Towns*, and *Rural Cantons* (Волости). — For Finland, comp. p. 199.

ZEMSTVA. In European Russia the provincial executive is assisted by the *Zemstva* (Земство, pl. Земства) or provincial assemblies, representing the nobles on the one side and the rest of the electors on the other. Representatives of the peasants are elected by the 'volost' or cantonal assemblies, and must be approved by the Governor. These provincial assemblies, in which the nobles are the predominant factor, represent the economic interests of the province; the public health and to a certain extent the educational system also fall within their sphere. — There are both District and Provincial Zemstva (Уѣздныя и губернскія земскія собранія). The *District Zemstvo* consists of a representative assembly and of an executive board known as the Uprava (Управа), nominated by the assembly and formed of three members elected for three years. The *Syezd*, a committee of provincial officials, is specially concerned with the affairs of the peasants. — The *Provincial Zemstvo* consists of the provincial representative assembly, the members of which are elected by the district assemblies for three years, and is presided over by the president of the provincial nobility (Предво- дитель дворянства). The business of the province is carried on by the Provincial Board (Губернская Земская Управа), consist- ing of a chairman and six members chosen by the provincial assembly. Both District and Provincial Zemstva meet twice a year. The Governor has the right to veto any action of the Zemstvo which in his opinion oversteps its province. — Finland has its own diet or assembly.

Municipal Dumas. Municipal administration in the Russian provinces is regulated by the *New Municipal Ordinance* of June 16th, 1870. The *Municipal* or *Town Council* (Городская Дума) consists of members elected by the citizens, and it in turn appoints a *Town Board* or *Board of Aldermen* (Городская Управа). Council and Board are both under the presidency of the *Mayor* (Городской Голова).

Peasant Assemblies. The Russian peasants are divided into self-governing communities. Their rights have, however, been seriously curtailed since 1889, when a new class of officials named *Rural Supervisors* or *Land Captains* (Земскіе Начальники) was introduced. Communal ownership of the land (Mir) still prevails in Great, South, and Eastern Russia, while individual ownership is the rule in Western Russia (comp. p. liii). There are two kinds of communities, the *Village Community* (Сельское Общество), which regulates its affairs in the Communal Assembly (Сельскій Сходъ or Міръ; Громада in Little Russia) under the presidency of the Starost (Староста), and the *Cantonal* or *Volost Assembly*, consist- ing of several village communities grouped together. The executive authorities of the Volost are the Volost Assembly (each group of 10 farms sends a deputy), the Starshiná (Старшина) or Elder of the Volost, the Volost Council, and the Volost Court.

V. THE RUSSIAN CHURCH.

Christianity was late in coming into Russia. It was not till the year 988, in the reign of *Vladímir I.*, that Greek monks from Byzantium introduced the Orthodox or Greek Catholic faith (Пра- вославный) into Kiev. Vladimir converted his people to Christi- anity by baptizing them by hundreds at a time in the Dnieper. The Russian historian Kostomárov remarks: 'the introduction and propagation of the new faith was unattended by any great disturbances, since the ancient Russian Slavonic paganism, consisting in nature-worship, possessed no definite priesthood'. In the time of the Mongols, who suffered the Russians to keep their hereditary princes and did not interfere with their religion, the Grand-Prince Iván Kalitá migrated in 1328 from Vladimir to Moscow, which thus became the political and religious centre of the Russian race. The power of the Muscovite Patriarch developed side by side with the increasing influence of the Tzar. But long before the State grew strong enough to throw off the yoke of the Mongols the Church had ceased to recognize the supremacy of Byzantium, and had separated itself from the trend of Occidental Christianity. The attempts of the Popes to bring about a reconciliation with the Roman Catholic Church met with no success. In 1591 the Oriental patriarchs recognized the Metropolitan of Moscow as the fifth patriarch. About the middle of the 17th century, in the reign of Alexis Mikháilovitch, *Nikon*, Patriarch of Moscow (p. 295), placed himself at the head of a movement to revise the ceremonies and liturgy of the Russian Church. A council held at Moscow in 1667 approved this liturgical reform, and resolved to introduce it into the church after its confirmation at Jerusalem in 1672. This led to a schism. Those who left the mother-church on account of the new liturgy call themselves to this day *Raskólniks* (Separatists) and *Starovyéri* (*i.e.* Old Believers). At a later date the schism became still more acute. Peter the Great made the church closely dependent on the state, by appointing no successor to the patriarchate after it became vacant in 1700, and by substituting in 1721, in the form of the 'Holy Synod', a collegiate body of practically government officials for the supreme personal rule of the church. The *Holy Synod* (Святѣйшій Синóдъ) consists of the highest dignitaries of the Russian church, summoned by the Tzar. Its president is the Metropolitan of St. Petersburg. The Tzar is represented by the Procurator General, a layman, who introduces the subjects to be discussed, and without whose consent no resolution is valid. Catherine II. seized the church property in 1764, giving fixed salaries in return. — According to the census of 1897 the empire contains over 87,000,000 members of the Greek Catholic church (69.54 per cent of the total population), and over 2,000,000 Old Believers.

Ever since the Oxford movement there has been a question of a possible union between the Anglican and the Eastern Orthodox Churches. Though the obstacles seem to be insurmountable, especially in view of the Anglican retention of the *Filioque* clause in the Creed, the two churches have nevertheless much in common, such as their denial of the universal supremacy of the Pope. Efforts to find a *modus vivendi* have not been wanting on either side; and there have been interchanges of courtesies between high dignitaries with a view to promote 'the brotherly feeling between the two churches'.

Russia is divided into 66 EPARCHIES or dioceses, each of which is under an Archbishop (Arkhiepískop) or a Bishop (Epískop). Three of these eparchies (St. Pétersburg, Moscow, and Kiev) are ruled by Metropolitans or ecclesiastics of the highest rank. In each eparchy there is a Consistory, of which the bishop is president. — The general *Clergy*, strictly separated from the laity by tradition and assent, though not by law, are divided into two entirely distinct classes, the *Black Clergy* or *Monks* (Чёрное духовéнство), representing the Greek tradition, and the *White Clergy* or *Secular Priests* (Бѣлое духовéнство), representing the national element. In spite of their name, the White Clergy wear robes of a brown or blue colour. The higher officers of the church are pledged to celibacy, and are chosen exclusively from the Black Clergy. They include the Arkhicréi (metropolitans, archbishops, and bishops), the Archimandrites (abbots), and the Igumens (priors). The Secular Clergy consist of the Protoicréi or Protopopes (ranking next to the igumens), the Ieréi or Popes (Священникъ; known popularly as Бáтюшка or Little Father), and the Protodeacons, invested with deacon's orders only. The secular priest must be married; if his wife dies he may not marry again, but he may enter a monastery if he does not want to lead a secular life. The rivalry and enmity between the monks and the secular clergy is a noteworthy peculiarity of the Russian church. The Black Clergy are the ruling order, and maintain the management of the church almost entirely in their own hands, since they have a monopoly of the highest offices, and supervise and manage the theological training-colleges (seminaries, academies). They keep a jealous eye on their privileges. — Dissenting *Sects* are numerous, and the importance they have attained proves how strong religious feeling is in Russia. — The relations between the clergy and the laymen are very different from those obtaining elsewhere. The function of the parish priest is not so much the cure of souls as the regular performance of the ceremonial duties of his office. He is more honoured in his status than in his person.

CHURCH BUILDINGS AND SERVICES. Most of the Russian churches are rectangular in form, with five domes, the largest of which is in the middle. Each of these domes is gilded, silvered, or painted some bright colour, and surmounted by a Greek cross. The main entrance is on the W. side, and in front of it there generally rises a detached bell-tower or campanile (Колокóльня) without a clock. The bells are fixed (not swung), only the tongues being movable. There is usually a well-harmonized chime of several bells. The interior has no seats, organ, or sculptures. At the E. end is the raised choir for the priests and the singers. The choir is separated from the inner sanctuary (Алтáрь) by the Ikonostás, a screen with sacred pictures (Икóны or Образá). In front of the sacred pictures, which are enclosed in costly frames, burn perpetual lamps (in the wealthier churches only) and numerous wax candles placed by the devout. The ikonostás has three doors, of which the central one, known as the 'holy door' (Цáрскія вратá), may be used by the priests only. In the sanctuary, opposite the sacred door, stands the altar (Престóлъ), on which lie a New Testament and the Host. Women are not allowed to enter the sanctuary, and men must lay aside hat and umbrella before doing so. It is forbidden to pass in front of the altar. The language of the church services is Slavonic,

but the sermon. when one is given, is in Russian. The singing is of
very high quality, especially at the chief festivals in the larger churches.
The music consists mainly of three-part tunes, striking in their stern
simplicity, and generally sung by men and boys without accompaniment.
The words 'Góspodi pomílui' (Lord have mercy upon us) are used very
frequently. The congregation does not usually join in the singing.

The most important festivals are Easter (the chief festival of the
Greek Catholic church), the Jordan Festival or Blessing of the Waters
(Jan. 6th, O.S.), and the birthdays and saints' days of the Tzar and
Tzaritza (Tzarina). On Good Friday the churches are draped in black,
while a curtain with a representation of the Entombment (Плащаница)
is exhibited on a catafalque. Shortly before midnight on Easter Eve, the
priests, followed by the people, proceed round the outside of the church,
bearing pictures of saints and church banners. At midnight precisely all
the bells are rung, the lights are turned on full, and the procession enters
the church. The priests then greet the congregation with the words 'Christ
is risen' (Христосъ воскрéсе), and the people answer 'He is risen indeed' (Во йстину воскрéсе), and kiss one another.

The *Dress* of the priests consists of the Stikharion or alb (a long
garment with sleeves), the Orarion or stole, the Over-sleeves, the Girdle,
a sleeveless outer garment known as Phelonion or Riza, with an opening
for the head, and the Kamilavkion (Gk. χαμιλαυκιον) or cylindrical hat. —
The bishop wears the Sakkos instead of the Phelonion and a mitre instead of the Kamilavkion; he also carries a pastoral staff.

Every foreigner will be struck by the frequency with which
the people cross themselves, by their obeisances or prostrations
before every open church door, and by the kissing of the floor and
the relics (Мóщи) inside the churches. The pious Russian also
salutes the ikon on entering a room. Though the Russian attaches
great importance to the observance of all these rites and customs,
he welcomes strangers to his churches, and places no difficulties in
their way in examining the churches and their contents even during
divine service.

The following are some of the most frequent NAMES OF CHURCHES
(Цéрковь or Храмъ, church; Собóръ, cathedral): —

Цéрковь Благовѣщенія Пресвятóй Богорóдицы, Благовѣщенская
цéрковь, Church of the Annunciation.
Богоявлéнская цéрковь, Church of the Epiphany.
Цéрковь Вознесéнія Госпóдня, Вознесéнская цéрковь, Church of
the Ascension.
Воскресéнская цéрковь, Church of the Resurrection.
Знáменская цéрковь, Church of the Apparition of the Virgin.
Цéрковь Іоáнна Предтéчи, Church of John the Baptist.
Крестовоздвѝженская цéрковь, Church of the Elevation of the Cross.
Покрóвская цéрковь, Church of the Protection and Intercession of
the Virgin.
Цéрковь Преображéнія Госпóдня, Преображéнская цéрковь,
Church of the Transfiguration.
  „   Рождествá Пресвятóй Богорóдицы, Church of the Nati-
vity of the Virgin.
  „   Святóй Трóицы, Church of the Holy Trinity.
  „   Успéнія Пресвятóй Богорóдицы or Бóжіей Мáтери,
Успéнская цéрковь, Church of the Assumption.

Next to the Greek Church the **Roman Catholic Church**
has more adherents than any other (11,420,000). Most of the
Roman Catholics live in Poland and the adjoining governments.

The **Protestant Church** has 3,743,000 adherents (not counting Finland), most of whom are Lutherans. It is most strongly represented in Finland, the Baltic Provinces, Poland, Lithuania, and the German colonies in South Russia.

For the *Armenian Church*, comp. p. 441.

The **Jews** (p. xliv) include *Talmudists* (in Poland) and *Karaïtes* (in Taurida).

Russia contains about 14,000,000 *Mohammedans*, most of whom are found in the S. and E. Provinces. Many persons of the Finnish stock are *Pagans*, especially in the Volga and Kama districts.

Russia in Asia has, of course, many Buddhists and adherents of other Oriental faiths.

List of the Russian Ecclesiastical and National Festivals.

Old Style		Old Style	
Jan. 1st	New Year's Day.	Aug. 30th	St. Alexander Nevski.
„ 6th	Epiphany and Jordan Festival.	Sept. 8th	Nativity of the Virgin.
Feb. 2nd	Purification of the Virgin.	„ 14th	Elevation of the Cross.
		„ 26th	St. John the Evangelist.
Mar. 25th	Annunciation.		
Apr. 23rd	Saint's day of the Tzarina. St. George.	Oct. 1st	Protection and Intercession of the Virgin
May 6th	Birthday of the Tzar.	5th	Saint's day of the Tzarévitch.
9th	Festival of the Transference of the Relics of St. Nicholas the Wonder-Worker.	„ 21st	Accession of Tzar Nicholas II.
„ 14th	Coronation.	„ 22nd	Festival of the Wonder-Working Ikon of the Kazan Virgin.
„ 25th	Birthday of the Tzarina.		
June 29th	SS. Peter & Paul.	Nov. 14th	Birthday of the Dowager Empress.
July 22nd	Saint's day of the Dowager Empress.	„ 21st	Presentation of the Virgin.
„ 30th	Birthday of the Tzarévitch Alexis Nikoláyevitch.	Dec. 6th	Festival of St. Nicholas the Wonder-Worker and saint's day of the Tzar.
Aug. 6th	Transfiguration.		
„ 15th	Assumption.	„ 25th, 26th, 27th	Christmas.
„ 29th	Beheading of John the Baptist.		

In addition to these may be mentioned the Friday and Saturday of 'Butter Week' (*i.e.* the week before Lent), the Thursday, Friday, and Saturday of Holy Week, the Sunday, Monday, and Tuesday of Easter Week, Ascension Day, Whitsunday, and Whit Monday.

BIBLIOGRAPHY.

The following is a brief list of English books on Russia, mainly of recent date. Except where otherwise indicated. the place of publication is London. - -For books on *Finland*, see p. 204; the *Crimea*, see p. 403; the *Caucasus*, see p. 446; *Persia*, see p. 498; *Turkestan*, see p. 509; *Siberia* and *Manchuria*, see p. 525.

NOTE. The Russian names in this bibliography do not follow any particular system of transliteration, but are spelt, in order to facilitate reference, as they appear on the title-pages of the books.

GENERAL INFORMATION.

Baring, Maurice, The Russian People (1911; 15s.).
Wallace, Sir D. M., Russia (new edition, 1912; 12s. 6d.).
These are perhaps the two best English works giving a general description of the social and political institutions of Russia. The former has the merit of being written more recently, but the latter is somewhat fuller, and has been brought up to date in the last edition.
Williams, Harold W., Russia of the Russians (1914; 6s.), another admirable work.
Alexinsky, G., Modern Russia (Engl. trans. by Bernard Miall; 1913; 15s.). This book is a well-informed work on Russia by a native, intended, in his own words, 'to be a small encyclopedia of Russian life in all its manifestations.' It is written in a somewhat severely critical spirit.
Graham, Stephen, Undiscovered Russia (1912; 12s. 6d.); Changing Russia (1913; 7s. 6d.); With the Russian Pilgrims to Jerusalem (1913; 7s. 6d.). These are three charming books written from a somewhat romantic and idealistic standpoint by a man who has had most unusual opportunities for studying Russian peasant life.
Leroy-Beaulieu, A., L'Empire des Tsars (3 vols., 1882-88; Engl. trans., 1893-96).
Legras, J., Au Pays Russe (Paris, 1895; 3 fr. 50 c.).
Palmer, F. H. E., Russian Life in Town and Country (1901; 3s. 6d.).
Rappoport, A. S., Home Life in Russia (1913; 10s. 6d.).
Reynolds, Rothay, My Russian Year (1913; 10s. 6d.), a very readable work.
Meakin, Annette M. B., Russia: Travels and Studies (London, 1906; Philadelphia, 1907; 16s.).
Steveni, W. B. Things seen in Russia (1912; 2s.), a convenient little manual.
Baring, M., What I saw in Russia (1913; 1s.); The Mainsprings of Russia (1914).
Hare, A. J. C., Studies in Russia (1885; 10s. 6d.).
Norman, Sir Henry, All the Russias (1902; 18s.).
Drage, Geoffrey, Russian Affairs (1904; 21s.).
Dobson (G.), Grove (H. M.), and *Stewart (H.),* Russia (with coloured illustrations by *F. de Haenen;* 1913; 20s.).
Jarintzoff, Mme. N., Russia, the Country of Extremes (1914; 16s.).
Winter, N. O., The Russian Empire of To-day and Yesterday (1914; 10s. 6d.).
'Stepniak', The Russian Peasantry (new ed., 1905; 3s. 6d.).
Kovalevsky, M. M., Modern Customs and Ancient Laws of Russia (1891; 7s. 6d.); Russian Political Institutions (Chicago; 1902).
Urusov, Prince, Memoirs of a Russian Governor, an interesting personal record, of which an English translation appeared in 1898 (6s.).
Swinton, Andrew, Travels into Norway, Denmark, and Russia (1792).
Horsey, Sir Jerome, Travels (ca. 1588).
Fletcher, Giles, Russe Commonwealth (1590).
These two books were republished by the Hakluyt Society in 1856 in one volume, entitled Russia at the close of the Sixteenth Century.

The article on Russia in the 11th edition of the *Encyclopaedia Britannica* (1911) is an exhaustive account of the country. It is written by Walter Alison Phillips (government and administration), John Thomas Bealby (geography and statistics), Prince Kropotkin (geography and statistics), Sir D. M. Wallace (recent history), Ellis Hovell Minns (language), and W. R. Morfill (literature). See also the *Russian Year Book* (annual; edited by Dr. H. P. Kennard; 10s. 6d.); the Official Report on the Industries and Trade of Russia prepared for the Glasgow Exhibition (1901); the Russian section (by *D. Aitoff*) of the International Geography edited by *H. R. Mill* (1907); and the *Russian Review*, published quarterly by the Board of Russian Studies, Liverpool University.

Among other English books on Russia, some of which are now a little out of date, are those by *Albert J. Beveridge, John Foster Fraser, Wirt Gerrare, R. Martin, Wm. English Walling, Edmund Noble, Isabel F. Hapgood*, and *Edna Dean Proctor*.

The traveller will find his tour much more interesting if he has some acquaintance with the novels and romances of Turgenyev (Turgeniev), Dostoyevski (Dostoievski), Gorki, and Tolstoi. Most of them are to be had in English translations, of which those by Mrs. Garnett may be specially commended.

History.

Rambaud, Alfred N., History of Russia (from the French; 3 vols.; 1895-1900).

Munro, H. H., Rise of the Russian Empire (Boston; 1900).

Ralston, W. R. S., Early Russian History (1874; 4s. 6d.).

Skrine, F. H., The Expansion of Russia, 1815-1900 (Cambridge; 1903).

Bain, R. Nisbet, The Pupils of Peter the Great (1897; 15s.); The Daughter of Peter the Great (1899; 15s.); The First Romanovs, 1613-1725 (1905; 12s. 6d.); Peter III. (1902; 10s. 6d.); Slavonic Europe (1908; 5s. 6d.).

Kelly, W. K., History of Russia (1888; 7s.).

Kluchevsky, V. O., History of Russia (Engl. trans. by C. J. Hogarth; 3 vols. at 7s. 6d. each; 1911-13).

Waliszewski, K., Paul the First of Russia (1913; 15s.).

Rappoport, A. S., Russian History (1905; 1s.), a brief but convenient manual; The Curse of the Romanovs (1907; 16s.).

Vogüé, Vicomte E. M. de, A Czarevitch of the 18th Century and Other Studies in Russian History (Engl. trans. by C. Mary Anderson; 1913; 7s. 6d.).

Morfill, W. R., Russia ('Story of the Nations' Series; 3rd edit., 1897); History of Russia (1902; 7s. 6d.).

Parmele, Mary Platt, A Short History of Russia (New York; 1899; $1).

Dole, Nathan Haskell, Young Folk's History of Russia (Boston; 1881).

Steuart, A. Francis, Scottish Influences in Russian History (Glasgow; 1913; 4s. 6d.).

John Milton's Brief History of Moscovia (1682) may be glanced at for the sake of its illustrious author, but it has no historical value.

Mavor, Prof. James, An Economic History of Russia (2 vols., 1914; 31s. 6d.).

The Russian revolutionary movement may be studied in the works of *'Stepniak', Kropotkin, Arnaud, Von der Brüggen* (Engl. trans.), *Nevinson, Miliukov* (Engl. edit., 1905; French edit., 1907), *Bernard Pares, G. Perris*, and others.

Comp. the chapters on Russia in the *Cambridge Modern History* (1902-10) by Bernard Pares, R. N. Bain, J. Holland Rose, G. Drage, and other writers.

Art.

Holme, Charles, Peasant Art in Russia (special autumn number of the *Studio*, with 550 illustrations; 1912; 7s. 6d.).

Atkinson, J. B., An Art Tour to Northern Capitals of Europe (with a long account of the Hermitage Picture Gallery; 1873; 12s.).

Viollet-le-Duc, L'Art Russe (Paris, 1877; 25 fr.).

Maskell, Alfred, Russian Art and Art Objects in Russia (1875; out of print).

Antiquities of the Russian Empire (Moscow, 1849-53; 5 vols.; 500 plates with English text).

LITERATURE.

Wiener, Leo, Anthology of Russian Literature (New York, 1903; 12s. 6d.).

Brückner, A., Literary History of Russia (Engl. trans. by E. H. Minns; 1908; 12s. 6d.).

Volkonski, Prince Sergius, Pictures of Russian History and Russian Literature (1898).

Waliszewski, K., History of Russian Literature (1900; 6s.).

Morfill, W. R., Slavonic Literature (1883; 2s. 6d.).

Kropotkin, Prince P. A., Ideals and Realities in Russian Literature (1905; 7s. 6d.).

Voynich, E. L., Humour of Russia (New York; 1895; $ 1.25).

Ralston, W. R. S., Russian Folk Tales (1873; 12s.).

Ossip-Lourié, La Psychologie des Romanciers Russes (Paris; 1905; 7½ fr.).

Dole, N. H., The Great Masters of Russian Literature in the 19th Century (translations; Boston; 1886 et seq.).

Vogüé, Vicomte de, The Russian Novel (trans. from the French by Col. Sawyer; 1913; 7s. 6d.).

Garnett, Edw., Three Great Russian Novelists (1914).

Phelps, W. L., Essays on Russian Novelists (New York; 1911).

Merezhkovsky, Tolstoi as man and artist, with an essay on Dostoyevski (Engl. trans., 1901).

Patouillet, J., Ostrovsky et son Théâtre de Mœurs Russes (Paris; 1912).

Baring, Maurice, Landmarks in Russian Literature (1910; 6s.).

Among the best-known Russian histories of literature are those of *A. Pypin, A. Skabichévski*, and *Ovsianiko-Kulikovsky*.

MAPS.

RUSSIAN. The Russian General Staff has issued a *Military Topographical Map* of European Russia on a scale of 1 : 126,000 (3 versts = 1 English inch); price 50 cop. Between 500 and 600 sheets of this have appeared, but there are none as yet for E. and N. Russia. — *New Special Map* of European Russia, on a scale of 1 : 420,000 (10 versts = 1 English inch). The 177 sheets are issued in two forms, at 50 or 75 cop. per sheet. — The *Marcks Atlas* contains Russia in 16 sheets (1 : 2,000,000). For maps of the Caucasus, comp. p. 447.

GERMAN. *Karte des europäischen Russland*, in 6 sheets (1 : 3,700,000; from **Stieler's** Handatlas; 7 ℳ.). The *Topographische Spezialkarte von Mitteleuropa* (Reymann; 1 : 200,000) and the *Übersichtskarte von Mitteleuropa* (1 : 300,000), both published in Berlin, include W. Russia; the *Generalkarte von Mitteleuropa* (1 : 200,000), published in Vienna, includes S.W. **Russia**.

ENGLISH. Stanford's *London Atlas Map of Russia and Poland*, in 1 sheet (1 : 5,702,400; 3s.); W. & A. K. Johnston's *Royal Atlas Map of Russia* (1 : 3,270,000; 3s., on cloth and in case 4s. 6d.).

I. GENERAL GOVERNMENT OF WARSAW (POLAND).

Warsaw time, which prevails throughout the General Government of Warsaw, is 37 min. behind that of St. Petersburg and 24 min. ahead of that of Central Europe. — Polish names are given with Polish letters and spelling, except a few (like Warsaw) which have become familiar in their English dress; rules for pronunciation, see p. 2.

Chronological Outline of Polish History. — In the 9th cent. the Slav colonies along the Vistula gradually fell under the dominion of the Poles, whose leader, according to tradition, was *Piast*, the founder of the dynasty of that name.

962-992. MIECZYSLAW I., the fourth successor of Piast. Introduction of Christianity, 966.

992-1025. BOLESLAUS I. CHROBRY (the Bold), founder of the Polish Kingdom.

1102-1139. BOLESLAUS III. KRZYWOUSTY ('Wry Mouth'). At his death he divides the kingdom among his four sons.

1241. Mongol invasion. Battle of Liegnitz.

1306-1333. WLADISLAUS I. LOKIETEK (the Short) builds up the dominion; Cracow becomes the royal residence (1320-1610) and henceforth the Polish kings are crowned there.

1333-1370. CASIMIR III. (the Great).

1386-1434. WLADISLAUS II. JAGIELLO, Grand-Prince of Lithuania; marries Jadwiga, daughter of Louis of Hungary (d. 1382).

The LITHUANIANS, the northern neighbours of the Poles, were the last to abandon paganism. *Ryngold* (1176-1240) was the first Lithuanian Grand-Prince. In 1320 *Gedymin* (1315-40) conquered Volhynia, Vitebsk, and Tchernigov. The campaigns of *Olgierd* (1345-77) extended as far as Moscow. His son *Jagiello*, who introduced Christianity into Lithuania, became King of Poland.

1410. Victory over the Teutonic Order at Tannenberg.

1506-1548. SIGISMUND I., fourth son of Casimir IV.

1548-1572. SIGISMUND II. — 1569. Union of Poland and Lithuania.

1575-1586. STEPHEN BATHORY. Successful campaigns against Russia; treaty of Zapolye, 1582. Counter-Reformation.

1587-1632. SIGISMUND III., son of John III. of Sweden and of Catherine, sister of Sigismund II.

1674-1696. JOHN III. SOBIESKI. — 1683. Defeat of the Turks at Vienna.

1697-1733. AUGUSTUS II. (the Strong), Elector of Saxony. Northern War.

1733-1763. AUGUSTUS III. (Brühl, chief minister and favourite).

1763-1795. STANISLAUS II. PONIATOWSKI (d. 1798).

    1772. First Partition. — Insurrection, 1792.

    1793. Second Partition. — Insurrection, 1794.

    1795. Third Partition. Poland loses its independence.

    1815. Union of the Grand-Duchy of Warsaw with Russia.

1831 1863. Rebellions. — 1866. Poland (grand-duchy of Warsaw) reduced to the condition of a Russian province.

The **Polish Language** surpasses all the other Slav tongues in richness, flexibility, and conciseness. — Of the consonants *c* is pronounced as ts, *c* before i and *ć* = tsy, *cz* = tsh (like the Italian c in città), *dż* = j (dsh), *h* or *ch* are guttural aspirates resembling the Spanish j, *j* = y, *l* = ll, *ń* = ny, *rz* or *ż* = z (as in azure; like the French j in jour), *ś* = sy, *sz* = sh, *w* = v, *ź* = zy. The vowels have the Italian value (ah, eh, ee, oh, oo); *q* is pronounced as the French on, *ę* like the French ain, while an accent over the o *(ó)* lengthens the vowel. In Polish the accent is upon the penultimate. Among the most important words for tourists are: *hotel, gospoda*, hotel; *restauracya*, restaurant; *pokój*, room; *łóżko*, bed; *świeca*, candle; *ogień*, fire; *jadalnia*, dining-room; *widelec*, fork; *nóż*, knife; *szklanka*, glass; *flaszka*, bottle; *woda*, water; *wino*, wine; *piwo*, beer; *kawa*, coffee; *herbata*, tea; *mleko*, milk; *chleb*, bread; *masło*, butter; *mięso*, meat; *jaja*, eggs; *ser*, cheese. — *Kolej żelazna*, railway; *foksal, dworzec kolei*, railway station; *konduktor*, guard; *pakunek*, luggage; *tragarz*, porter; *wejście*, entrance; *wyjście*, exit. — *Miasto*, town; *wieś*, village; *ulica*, street; *plac*, square; *dom*, house; *palac*, palace; *kościół*, church; *klasztor*, convent; *poczta*, post office; *telegraf*, telegraph office; *teatr*, theatre; *kawiarnia*, café; *cukiernia*, confectioner's. — *Powóz*, carriage; *koń*, horse; *przewodnik*, guide (please guide me to the Hotel X, proszę zaprowadzić mnie do hotelu X). — *Droga*, way; *most*, bridge; *ogród*, garden; *drzewo*, tree; *las*, wood; *łąka*, meadow; *góra*, mountain; *dolina*, valley; *potok*, brook; *rzeka*, river; *jezioro*, lake. — *Rano*, morning; *dzień*, day; *południe*, midday; *wieczór*, evening; *noc*, night; *poniedzialek*, Monday; *wtorek*, Tuesday; *środa*, Wednesday; *czwartek*, Thursday; *piątek*, Friday; *sobota*, Saturday; *niedziela*, Sunday. — *Pan*, Mr.; *pani*, Mrs.; *mężczyzna*, man; *dziecko*, child. — *Angelski*, English; *amerikanski*, American; *niemiecki*, German; *ruski*, Russian; *polski*, Polish; *austryacki*, Austrian. — *Wielki*, large; *maly*, small; *wysoko*, high; *nisko*, low; *blisko*, near; *daleko*, far; *wcześnie*, early; *późno*, late; *powolny* (adv. *powoli*), slow; *prędki* (adv. *prędko*) fast; *dobrze*, good; *źle*, bad; *za drogo*, too dear; *u dolu*, below; *u góry*, above; *na lewo*, to the left; *na prawo*, to the right; *pól*, half; *caly*, whole. — *Czerwony*, red; *niebieski*, blue; *bialy*, white; *czarny*, black; *zielony*, green. *Święty*, holy; *zabroniony*, forbidden; *jest*, is; *ma*, has; *dziękuję*, I thank you; *proszę*, please. — *Jeden*, one; *dwa*, two; *trzy*, three; *cztery*, four; *pięć*, five; *sześć*, six; *siedm*, seven; *ośm*, eight; *dziewięć*, nine; *dziesięć*, ten; *jedenaście*, eleven; *dwanaście*, twelve; *piętnaście*, fifteen; *dwadzieścia*, twenty; *trzydzieści*, thirty; *czterdzieści*, forty; *pięćdziesiąt*, fifty; *sto*, hundred; *tysiąc*, thousand.

1. From Berlin viâ Alexandrovo to Warsaw (*St. Petersburg, Moscow*).

392 M., viâ Bromberg (or Frankfort) and Alexandrovo. Express train in 11¹/₂ hrs.; fares 52 ℳ 80, 34 ℳ 70 pf. ('train de luxe' in 10¹/₄ hrs.; fare 74 ℳ 60 pf.). Sleeping-car 10 ℳ 55, 8 ℳ 44 pf. Besides the sleeping-car, there is one through-car (1st & 2nd class) attached to the night-express to Warsaw; in other cases there is a change of carriages at Alexandrovo. — FROM BERLIN (Stadtbahn stations) TO ALEXANDROVO, 251 M. (405 Kil.), express train in 6¹/₂ hrs. (fares 33 ℳ 30, 21 ℳ 45, 13 ℳ 80 pf.; sleeping-car 8 ℳ, 6 ℳ 50 pf.).—FROM ALEXANDROVO TO WARSAW, 140 M. (211 V.), express train in 4 hrs. (fares 9 rb. 3 cop., 6 rb. 12 cop.; reserved seat 1¹/₂ rb., see p. xxiii); ordinary train in 6 hrs. (fares 7 rb. 28, 4 rb. 37 cop.). — Baggage is examined at Alexandrovo (in the reverse direction at Thorn). Money is exchanged to the best advantage in Berlin, but Russian money may also be obtained in Warsaw or at the money-changer's stall in Alexandrovo. For Warsaw time, see p. 1.—*Passports*, see p. xviii.—Pronunciation of Polish words, see p. 2.

The route from Berlin to Warsaw viâ Kalisz and Lodz (comp. R. 2) takes longer. Alternative routes to Kalisz are viâ Sagan (carriages changed) and Ostrowo (express train in 13¹/₂ hrs.; fares 54 ℳ 35, 35 ℳ 60 pf., reserved seat 1¹/₂ rb. extra) and viâ Bentschen and Ostrowo (15 hrs.; sleeping-car 8 ℳ, 6 ℳ 50 pf.).

From Berlin to (240 M.) *Thorn* (Thorner Hof), see *Baedeker's Northern Germany.* — The train then passes (248 M.) *Ottlotschin,* the last Prussian station, and crosses the Russian frontier, which is here formed by the *Tąszyna*, a tributary of the Vistula.

252 M. **Alexandróvo**, Александрóво, Polish *Aleksandrów* (*Railway Restaurant,* fair, D. 75 cop.), where a halt of about 1¹/₄ hr. is made. Passports and luggage are examined here (pp. xviii, xix; for greater details, comp. p. 34).

FROM ALEXANDROVO TO CIECHOCINEK, 7 V. (5 M.), branch-railway in ¹/₄ hr. — Ciechocinek, Цѣхоцинскъ (120 ft.; *Railway Restaurant; Hôtel Müller,* at the station, R. from 1¹/₄ rb., D. 75 cop.; cab from the rail. station to the town 30, from the steamer-pier 70 cop.; visitors' tax, after 3 free days, 5 rb.), a watering-place with salt-springs and salt-works, situated 1¹/₂ M. from the left bank of the Vistula. In the Kur-Park is the Kursaal, with reading-room and café-restaurant. Steamer to Warsaw, see pp. 27, 26.

Between Alexandrovo and Warsaw the train traverses the plains of the present Government of Warsaw, the ancient Kujavia and Masovia. The country is dotted with miserable-looking villages and is largely populated by Jews. As far as Włocławek the river Vistula is visible at intervals, on the left.

14 V. (9 M., *i.e.* from Alexandrovo) *Nieszawa*, Нешáва (p. 27). The little town of that name, 2²/₃ M. to the N. of the station, contains 5000 inhab., a Roman Catholic church of the 14th cent., and a Protestant church in the Gothic style (1890).

35 V. (23 M.) **Włocławek**, Влоцлáвскъ. — *Railway Restaurant.* — HOTELS. *Three Crowns (Pod Tremyá Koróuami,* Подъ Тремя Корóнами), Stary Rynek 9, R. 1-3 rb., D. (12-3 p.m.) 50 cop., omn. 20 cop.; *Mazowiecki.* — CAB from the railway station or the steamboat-landing to the town 30-50, per hr. 75 cop.

1*

Włocławek, a busy industrial town of 37,400 inhab., the capital of a district in the Government of Warsaw, is situated on the left bank of the *Vistula*. It is one of the oldest towns in Poland, having been founded at the end of the 11th cent., and destroyed in 1329 and 1431 by the Teutonic Knights. From the railway station we keep to the right, turning to the left after a few paces and following the Żelazna, which leads to (12 min.) the cathedral, passing the Town Hall (l.), crossing the Brzeska, and then passing the Lutheran Church (l.) and the Post Office (l.). The handsome *Cathedral*, with its two towers, built in the Gothic style in 1365, contains hatchments and the monuments of several bishops. A little to the N., on the Vistula, is the *Episcopal Palace*, dating from the 17th century. — Steamer to Warsaw, see pp. 27, 26.

About 8½ M. to the W. of Włocławek, in a plain surrounded by swamps, lies **Brześć**, Russ. *Brest-Kuyávski* (Брестъ-Куявскій), a place of 3500 inhab., formerly the capital of Kujavia. It is surrounded by its old walls, ramparts, and moats, and contains an interesting Roman Catholic church of 1240.

87 V. *Kutno* (Rail. Restaurant), a town on the *Ochnia*, with 15,200 inhab.; 104 V. *Pniewo*, Пнево. Before reaching Łowicz we cross the *Bzura*.

129 V. **Łowicz** (*Łowicz Wiedeński*, Ловичъ Вѣнскій; *Warszawski Hotel*), a district-town in the Government of Warsaw, with 14,500 inbah., lies on the right bank of the Bzura. It contains a handsome abbey-church, several other churches, an old château in a fine park, and cavalry-barracks.

From Łowicz to *Kalisz*, see pp. 6, 5. The station (Łowicz Kaliski) is connected with the station of Łowicz Wiedeński by a branch-line, 2 V. long.

About 3 M. to the S.E. of Łowicz is **Arcadia**, a magnificent château belonging to Prince Radziwill, containing rich collections of art. It stands in a large park.

Near (139 V.) *Nieborów* (Неборовъ) is an old château of the Radziwill family, with valuable pictures, a library, fine gardens, and a large orangery.

149 V. (99 M.) **Skierniewice**, Скерневйцы (405 ft.; *Railway Restaurant*, fair), a district-town of 11,500 inbah., which was formerly the residence of the Archbishop of Gnesen, Prince Primate of Poland. To the S. of the station is an imperial château, in a fine park. — To *Vienna*, see pp. 8-6.

The train crosses the *Rawka*, a tributary of the Bzura, and then runs due N.E. to Warsaw. — 171 V. *Żyrardów* (Жирардóвъ; pop. 32,000), with a large woollen and linen factory (Żyrardów) founded by a Frenchman named Gérard. In the vicinity are several important sugar-refineries.

183 V. *Grodzisk* (Гродзискъ), with a fine park. About 23 M. to the N. (carr. there and back 3½ rb.) lies *Żelazowa-Wola* (p. 26), the birthplace of Chopin (1810-49), to whom an obelisk with a medallion-portrait was erected in 1894. — 186 V. *Milanówek*, with many

villas. Beyond (196 V.) *Pruszków* we traverse woods, passing numerous country-houses.

211 V. (140 M.) *Warsaw* (Vienna Station; p. 9). — Thence to *St. Petersburg,* see R. 9.

2. From Breslau to Kalisz and Warsaw (St. Petersburg, Moscow).

250 M. Express train in 10¹/₂ hrs. (fares 35 ℳ 15, 23 ℳ 10 pf.; reserved seat 1¹/₂ rb. extra, see p. xxiii). Through-carriages from Kalisz to St. Petersburg, Moscow, Kiev, and Baku. Baggage is examined at Kalisz, in the reverse direction at Skalmierzyce or Ostrowo. Warsaw time, see p. 1. — *Passports,* see p. xviii. — Pronunciation of Polish words, see p. 2.

The route from Breslau to Warsaw viâ Sosnowice and Ząbkowice (comp. R. 3) takes longer: express train in 12¹/₂ hrs. (fares 42 ℳ 10, 28 ℳ 15 pf.; reserved seat 1¹/₂ rb. extra). Baggage is examined at Sosnowice, in the reverse direction at Kattowitz. — There are no express trains on the (Breslau) Oppeln-Herby-Częstochowa section.

From Breslau to (78 M.) *Ostrowo,* see *Baedeker's Northern Germany.* — Beyond (89 M.) *Skalmierzyce,* the last station in Prussia, the train crosses the Russian frontier.

93 M. **Kalisz,** Ка́лишъ, Ger. *Kalisch (Rail. Restaurant; Stadt Wien),* the capital of the government of that name, lies on the *Prosna,* and contains 52,500 inhabitants. Above the high-altar of the Roman Catholic Church of St. Nicholas is a Descent from the Cross by Rubens. Lutheran church.

The railway crosses the Prosna and proceeds to the E. — Beyond (50 V. from Kalisz) *Sieradz* (Сѣрадзъ), with 8500 inbab., it crosses the *Warthe* (Pol. *Warta*). — 92 V. *Pabianice,* a factory-town with 39,000 inhabitants. An electric tramway runs hence to Lodz.

105 V. (69¹/₂ M.) **Lodz,** Polish *Łódź,* Лодзь. — The RAILWAY STATION (restaurant) for *Warsaw* and *Kalisz* lies on the W. side of the town, that for *Koluszki* on the E. — HOTELS. *Grand-Hôtel,* Piotrkowska 72, at the corner of the Krótka, with a café-restaurant, R. 1¹/₂-7, B. ¹/₂, déj. (12-3 p.m.) 1¹/₄, D. (6-11 p.m.) 2 rb.; *Savoy Hotel,* Krótka, new; *Manteuffel,* Zachodnia 45, with concert-garden and variety theatre, R. 1¹/₄-5 rb., B. 40 cop., déj. (12-3 p.m.) ³/₄, D. (from 6 p.m.) 1¹/₂ rb.; *Victoria,* Piotrkowska 67, R. from 1 rb., D. 75 cop.; *Imperial,* Piotrkowska; *Hôtel de Pologne,* Piotrkowska 3.

RESTAURANTS in the hotels; also *A. Stempkowski,* Passage Maier, D. à la carte.

CAB from the Warsaw & Kalisz station to the town 50, with two horses 60 cop. (to the suburbs 10 cop. more in each case), to the station 40 or 50 cop. (from the suburbs 10 cop. more in each case); from the Koluszki station to the town 30 or 40 cop. (to the suburbs 20 cop. more in each case), to the station 25 or 30 cop. (from the suburbs 20 cop. more in each case); drive in the town 20 or 25 cop., to the suburbs 40 or 50 cop. At night (10-6) 10 cop. more in all cases; luggage over 1 pud, 10 cop. Cabs with rubber tyres demand 5 cop. more.

ELECTRIC TRAMWAYS traverse the main streets and the environs.

POST & TELEGRAPH OFFICE, corner of the Widzewska and Przejazd.

Thalia Theatre (German), Dzielna, open in winter only; *Helenenhof,* a pleasure-resort to the N.E. of the Old Town.

Lodz (700 ft.), a long straggling place on the sandy hills border-ing the *Lodka* and the *Jasien*, contains ca. 450,000 inhab. (220,000 Poles. 121,000 Germans, 100,000 Jews; pop. 190 in 1793, 60,000 in 1860). It is the central point of the textile industry of Poland, its annual products reaching a value of ca. 150,000,000 rubles. The Carl Scheibler Factory alone employs about 7500 workmen. The main street, named the Piotrkowska, intersects the town from S. to N.

From Lodz a branch-line runs to (25 V.) *Koluszki* (p. 8).

From (115 V.) *Zgierz* (Згержъ), an industrial town with 23,200 inhab., an electric tramway runs to Lodz. 161 V. *Łowicz* (Kalisz Station; p. 4).

236 V. (157 M.) *Warsaw*, see p. 9. The express train halts at the Kovel Station and then goes on to the Brest Station. The ordinary train stops at the Kalisz Station.

3. From Vienna to Warsaw *(St. Petersburg, Moscow).*

FROM VIENNA (North Railway Station) TO WARSAW, 433 M., express train in 16 hrs.; fares 84 *K* 10, 52 *K*, 31 *K* 20 *h*; sleeping-carriage (through to Warsaw) 20 and 16 *K*. In winter a 'train de luxe' runs from Nice viâ Vienna and Warsaw to St. Petersburg; fare from Vienna (North Railway Station) to Warsaw 112 fr. 40, to St. Petersburg 208 fr. 85 c. From Vienna express train to (244 M.) *Granitza* in 8½ hrs. (fares 47 *K* 50, 29 *K*, 18 *K* 50 *h*; sleeping-carriage 12 *K* 50 *h*, 11 *K*). From Granitza express train to (288 V.; 191 M.) *Warsaw* in 6 hrs. (fares 11 rb. 45, 7 rb. 77 cop.; reserved seat, see p. xxiii, 1½ rb.); ordinary train in 8 hrs. (fares 9 rb. 20, 5 rb. 52 cop.). — FROM VIENNA TO ST. PETERSBURG (through-carriages from Granitza viâ Ivangorod and Warsaw; comp. below and pp. 7, 27), 1141 M., express train in 37½ hrs. (fares 157 *K* 90, 99 *K* 30 *h*).

The customs examination for travellers entering Russia takes place at Granitza, for those leaving Russia at Szczakowa. Warsaw time, see p. 1. — *Passports*, see p. xviii. — Pronunciation of Polish words, see p. 2.

From Vienna to (242 M.) *Szczakowa*, see *Baedeker's Austria*. — We then cross the Russian frontier and reach (244 M.) **Granitza**, Гранйца, Polish *Granica (Railway Restaurant)*. A delay of fully one hour takes place here. Passports and luggage are examined (process similar to that at Wirballen, p. 34).

FROM GRANITZA TO IVANGOROD (Moscow), 279 V. (185 M.), railway in 6¾-9 hrs. — 6 V. *Strzemieszyce* (p. 7). — 29 V. *Olkusz*, with an old collegiate church and zinc mines. A pleasant excursion may be made hence to (21 V.; carr. 2-3 rb.) the village of *Oyców*, at the entrance of the so-called **Polish Switzerland**, a name given to the narrow rocky valley, about 10 M. in length, of the trout-stream *Prądnik*. At the widest part of the valley are the hotels *Pod Łokietkiem* and *Pod Kaźmierzem*, as well as numerous villas and summer boarding-houses. — Beyond (64 V.) *Miechów* (Мѣховъ), to the left, rise the finely wooded *Łysa Góra*, the last foot-hills of the Carpathians on the N. On the highest summit is a quaint-looking monastery. — 87 V. *Sędziszew*, Сендзишёвъ (Rail. Restaurant). — 146 V. **Kielce**, Кѣльцы (875 ft.; *Railway Restaurant*; *Hôtel Bristol*; carr. & pair from the station to the town 25, with luggage 35, at night 35 and 45 cop.), an industrial town and capital of a province, with 32,100 inhab., picturesquely situated on the *Sielnica.* In the old episcopal palace, now occupied by the provincial authorities, are portraits of the bishops from 1293 onwards. There is a Lutheran church. A pleasant walk may be taken to the suppressed Bernardine convent of (2 V.) *Karczowka,* which commands an attractive view. A branch-line runs to (110 V.) Częstochowa (see below). — 188 V. *Skarzysko* (Rail. Restaurant; p. 8). — 226 V. **Radom** (570 ft.; *Railway Restaurant; Hôtel Europejski,* Sobórnaya Square 3, R. 1¹/₄-3 rb., D. 60, omn. 25 cop.; *Hôtel de Rome* or *Rzymski,* Lubelska 13, R. ³/₄-2, D. ³/₄ rb., omn. 25 cop.; cab from or to the station 45 cop.) is the capital of a government, with 49,200 inhab., tanneries, and a Lutheran church. — We cross the *Vistula* just short of (279 V.) *Ivángorod* (see p. 27).

The Warsaw Railway leads through the busy manufacturing province of Piotrków (cotton and woollen mills, etc.), at first intersecting the great plateau of Upper Silesia and Poland, with an average height of 650-1000 ft. above the sea. Between Ząbkowice and Częstochowa we cross the watershed of the Vistula, Oder, and Warthe. Below the surface is a prolongation of the great coal-beds of Upper Silesia; and iron and zinc ores also occur. Beyond Częstochowa the plateau subsides; to the N. of Novo-Radomsk begins the fertile plain of Poland.

6 V. (from Granitza) *Strzemieszyce,* Стржемешйцы (p. 6).

13 V. **Ząbkowice,** Зомбковйцы *(Railway Restaurant),* the junction for the line from Kattowitz and Sosnowice.

30 V. *Zawiercie* and (43 V.) *Myszków,* both factory-towns. We cross the Warthe. As we approach Częstochowa, we see on the left the lofty tower of the Pauline monastery (see below).

72 V. (48 M.) **Częstochowa,** Ченстохóвъ. — *Rail. Restaurant,* fair, D. 1 rb. — HOTELS. *Angielski,* opposite the station, R. 1¹/₂-4, D. (1-4 p.m.) ¹/₂-1 rb.; *Victoria,* clean. — CAB (two horses) from the station to the town 35, to the convent 50 cop.; from the town to the convent 25 cop.

Częstochowa (800 ft.), capital of a district of the government of Piotrków, is an industrial town with 72,600 inhab., situated on the left bank of the Warthe. It is a celebrated place of pilgrimage.

On the *Jasna Góra,* 1¹/₂ M. to the W. of the railway station, stands the famous **Pauline Monastery,** surrounded by a pentagonal wall with bastions. [On leaving the station we turn to the left; in 3 min. more we cross the railway bridge to the left, and follow the Ulica Panny Maryi, a well-shaded avenue.] To the E. of the monastery, at the end of the Ulica Panny Maryi, is a bronze statue of Emp. Alexander II., erected in 1889. The entrance (Brama Lubomirskich; 1723) is on the S. side.

The Pauline Monastery, founded by King Wladislaus Jagiello, was once so wealthy that it is said to have owned or held in pledge one-fifteenth of all the landed estates in Poland. It was attacked and plundered by the Hussites in 1430; the fortifications, begun in 1500, were repeatedly strengthened at later dates. In 1655 the monastery was bravely defended by Prior Kordecki (p. 8) against the Swedes, and in 1705 the monks again successfully resisted the attack of an army of 10,000 Swedes. In 1772 it had to surrender, after an obstinate resistance, to the Russian troops, and it was again taken by the Prussians in 1793. The fortifications were dismantled in 1813.

The spacious *Church,* rebuilt after a fire of 1690, has a tower, 302 ft. in height. The battle-paintings on the ceiling are by the Swedish painter, P. Dankwart (1695). In a chapel on the N.E. side, above the altar, hangs the celebrated and wonder-working picture known as the 'Black Madonna' (Regina Regni Poloniæ). This consists of a painting of the Virgin and Child on cypress-wood, much darkened by age and adorned with costly jewels. The picture, which has been in Częstochowa since 1382, is shown unveiled twice daily during the chief services. The treasury, adjoining the sacristy, contains many valuable and interesting objects. The chief festival of the church is that of the Nativity of the Virgin (Sept. 8th). — On the ramparts, to the right of the entrance to the church, stands a bronze statue of Prior Kordecki (p. 7), erected in 1861. The ramparts afford an extensive view of the surrounding country.

From Częstochowa a branch-line runs W. to (16 V.) *Herby* (Гербы), on the Prussian frontier, which is connected by railway with *Vossowska* (Oppeln, Breslau). — Another line runs E. from Częstochowa to (110 V.) *Kielce* (P. 6).

Beyond Częstochowa the railway is accompanied on the left by the foot-hills of the mountainous district, and on the right by the marshes of the Warthe. The train returns to the right bank of the Warthe just before reaching (110 V.) *Novo-Rádomsk* ('New Radomsk'), a district-town of 19,700 inhabitants.

152 V. (101 M.) **Piotrków,** Петроковъ, German *Petrikau.* —
Railway Restaurant. — HOTELS. *Litewski,* Marinskaya Square 8; *Polski,* opposite the station, R. from 1 rb. 10 cop., B. 40, D. (12-4 p.m.) 50 cop. — CAB from the station to the town 30, with two horses 40 cop.; per drive within the town 15 and 20 cop.

Piotrków (685 ft.), capital of the government of that name, is a town of 41,200 inhab., situated on the small river *Strawa.* It contains four old convents and the ruins of a royal palace, now incorporated in a Russian regimental chapel ($^3/_4$ M. to the E. of the station). Lutheran church. — Piotrków is one of the oldest towns in Poland. In the 15-16th cent., under the Jagiellos, the Diets were held and the Kings were elected here; at a later date it was the seat of the supreme court for the provinces of Great Poland.

189 V. (125 M.) **Koluszki,** Колюшки *(Railway Restaurant).*

FROM KOLUSZKI TO OSTROWIEC, 152 V. (101 M.), railway in $6^3/_4$ hrs. — 26 V. *Tomaszów* (Томашевъ), an industrial town of 27,500 inhab. in the government of Piotrków. Near it is the imperial hunting-lodge of *Spala,* surrounded by beautiful woods. — 73 V. *Końskie,* with 10,000 inhab.; 108 V. *Skarzysko,* see p. 7. — 152 V. *Ostrowiec* (Островецъ), a town of 13,500 inhab. in the government of Radom.

Another railway runs from Koluszki to (25 V.) *Lodz* (p. 5).

226 V. (150 M.) **Skierniewice** (p. 4), the junction of the Alexandrovo and Warsaw Railway. From Skierniewice to —

288 V. (191 M.) *Warsaw,* see p. 4. Thence to *St. Petersburg,* see R. 9. .

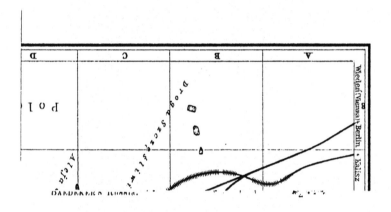

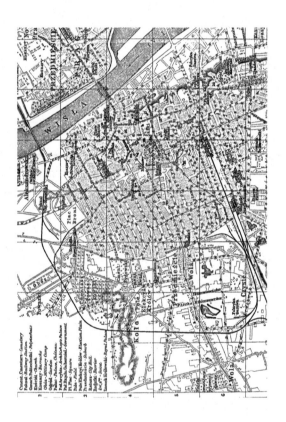

4. Warsaw and Environs.

The NAMES OF STREETS on our two plans of the city are given in Polish; at the street-corners they are given both in Polish and in Russian. It should be noticed that the adjective follows the noun in Polish street-names (thus, Ulica Petersburska).

Arrival. The larger hotels send carriages to meet the trains. *Cabs* and *Tramways*, see p. 10. — **Departure.** Tickets of the state-railways may be purchased at an advance of 10-20 cop., and baggage may be registered at an extra charge of not less than 50 cop. at Dluga, No. 30 (Pl. E, 4; *I*) and Moniuszki, No. 2 (Pl. F, 5; *II*); open 9-4, on Sun. & holidays 9-12. The office of the International Sleeping Car Co. is in the Hôtel Bristol (see below; open 8.30 to 4.30, on Sun. & holidays 10-12).

Railway Stations. Warsaw has five railway stations. On the *Left Bank of the Vistula:* 1. VIENNA STATION (Вѣнскій вокзалъ; Foksal Warszawsko-Wiedeński; Pl. E, F, 6, *I*), for Cracow, Vienna, Thorn, Berlin, and Sosnowice. A policeman, posted at the exit, hands the traveller a metal ticket with the number of a cab. 2. KOVEL STATION (Ковельскій вокзалъ; Foksal War.-Kowelski; Pl. D 2, *I*), to the S.W. of the citadel, for Mlawa (Marienburg), Lublin, Kovel (Kiev), and Moscow (three express trains daily; the other Moscow trains start from the Brest station). 3. KALISZ STATION (Кáлишскій вокзалъ; Foksal War.-Kaliski; Pl. D 6, *I*), near the Vienna Station, for Lodz and Kalisz (express trains from the Brest and Kovel stations). — On the *Right Bank of the Vistula*, in Praga: 4. ST. PETERSBURG STATION (Петербýргскій вокзалъ; Foksal War.-St-Petersburski; Pl. H, 2, 3, *I*), for Vilna, Dünaburg, and St. Petersburg. 5. BREST STATION (Брéстскій вокзалъ; Foksal War.-Brzeski; Pl. H, I, 3, *I*), for Brest-Litovsk, Moscow (see above), Kiev, Odessa, and Granitza (Vienna). — The various stations are connected by a junction-line.

Hotels. *HÔTEL BRISTOL (Pl. a, F 4; *I*), Krakowskie Przedmieście 44, first-class, R. from 3, B. ³/₄, déj. (12-3 p.m.) 1¹/₂, D. (5-8 p.m.) 2, omn. 1 rb.; *HÔTEL DE L'EUROPE (Europejski; Pl. b, F 4, *I*), Krakowskie Przedmieście 13, R. from 1¹/₂ rb., B. 50 cop., D. (2-8 p.m.) 1¹/₂ rb., omn. 50 cop.; *GRAND-HÔTEL BRÜHL (Brühlowski; Pl. c, E 4, *I*), Ulica hrabiego Kotzebue 12, R. 1¹/₂-3³/₄ rb., B. 50 cop., déj. (11-1) ³/₄, D. (1-7 p.m.) 1¹/₄ rb.; POLONIA PALACE HOTEL, Aleja Jerozolimska 53, new, opposite the Vienna Station (Pl. E F, 6; *I*), R. 2-15, B. ³/₄, déj. (12-3 p.m.) 1¹/₂-2, D. (6-8 p.m.) 2-2¹/₂, omn 1¹/₂ rb.; HÔTEL DE ROME (Rzymski; Pl. e, F 4, *I*), Nowosenatorska 1, frequented by country gentlemen, R. from 1¹/₂ rb., B. 40 cop., déj. (12-3 p.m.) 1 D. (3-6 p.m.) 1¹/₄ rh., omn. 50 cop.; SAVOY (Pl. i, F 5; *I*), Nowy Swiat 58 R. from 1¹/₄ rb., B. 50 cop., D. (1-7) 1-1¹/₄ rb., omn. 50 cop.; VICTORIA (Pl. d, F 5; *I*), Jasna 26, commercial, R. 1-3 rb., B. 40 cop., déj. (12-2 p.m.) ³/₄ D. (1-6 p.m.) 1, S. (from 9 p.m.) ³/₄ rb.; HÔTEL DE FRANCE (Francuski; Pl. f, E 5, *I*), Zielony Plac 11; HÔTEL D'ANGLETERRE (Angielski; Pl. g, F 4, *I*), Wierzbowa 6. — Second-class: HÔTEL DE PARIS (Paryski; Pl. h, E 4, *I*), Bielańska 9, R. from 1¹/₄ rb., B. 35 cop., D. (1-6 p.m.) ¹/₂-1¹/₂ rb.; HÔTEL ROYAL (Pl. o, F 5; *I*), Chmielna 31, R. from 1 rb., D. (1-6 p.m.) 60-75 cop.; POLSKI (Pl. k, E 4; *I*), Dluga 29; NIEMIECKI (Pl. l, E 4; *I*), Dluga 31; KRAKOWSKI (Pl. m, E 4; *I*), Bielańska 7.

Pension Wielhorska, Jasna 4 (Pl. F, 5, *II*), R. 1-4, board 1¹/₄-1¹/₂ rb. The *Home of the Protestant Association for Young Women* ('Jungfrauenverein'), Widok 20 (Pl. F, 5, 6; *I*), and the *Home Français,* Warecka 15 (Pl. F, 5; *II*), are intended for women-teachers and girls travelling alone.

Restaurants. **Hôtel Bristol,* **Hôt. Brühl* (Munich or Pilsen beer on draught), **Hôtel de l'Europe, Polonia Palace Hotel, Hôt. de Rome,* see above; *Versailles,* Aleja Ujazdowska (Pl. G, 6, 7; *I*); *Hôtel d'Angleterre* (see above); *Café-Restaurant Ostrowski,* Marszalkowska, corner of the Zlota (Pl. E, F, 5, 6; *I*), D. (1-5 p.m.) 75 cop.; *Wróbel,* Mazowiecka 14 (Pl. F, 5; *II*), D. 50 cop., well spoken of. · WINE. *Lijewski,* Krakowskie

Przedmieście 8 (Pl. F, 4; *I*); *Eremitage*, at the corner of the Widok and Marszałkowska (Pl. F, 5, 6; *I*), near the Vienna Station, plat du jour, 40 cop.; *Fukier*, on the W. side of the Plac Stare Miasto (No. 27; Pl. F 3, *I*), an old establishment which has occupied its present unpretending quarters since 1590. — CAFÉS-RESTAURANTS. *Empire*, Krakowskie Przedmieście 7, opposite the University (Pl. F, 4; *II*); *Cristal*, Aleja Jerozolimska 60 (Pl. F, G, 5, 6; *I*), near the Vienna Station; *Varsovie*, Nowy Świat 5 (Pl. F, 5, 6; *I*), near the Aleja Jerozolimska. — BARS (moderate prices; quite respectable). *Bar à la Hawełka*, Nowy Świat 59 (Pl. F, 5; *II*) and Marszałkowska 129 (Pl. E, 5; *II*); *Bar Artystyczny*, Sienna 2 (Pl. D, E, 6; *I*); *Bar Centralny*, Nowy Świat 21 (Pl. F, 5; *II*); *Bar Express*, Aleja Jerozolimska 80 (Pl. F, G, 5; *I*).

Cafés and Confectioners (Cukiernie; glass of coffee 15, tea 10-15, chocolate 20 cop.; also cold viands and beer). *Lardelli*, Nowy Świat 27 (Pl. F, 5, 6, *I*; near the Aleja Jerozolimska), Marszałkowska 87 (Pl. E, F, 5-7. *I*; to the S. of the Vienna Station), and Boduina 5, a side-street of the Szpitalna (Pl. F, 5; *I*); *Hôtel Bristol* (p. 9), a large café; *Hôt. de l'Europe* (p. 9); *Café de Saxe*, in the Saxon Garden (p. 15); *Semadeni*, in the Grand Theatre (p. 19); *Udziałowa*, cor. of Nowy Świat and Aleja Jerozolimska (Pl. F, 5; *I*), with dairy restaurant; *Bott*, Krakowskie Przedmieście 37, at the corner of the Trębacka (Pl. F, 4; *II*). Warsaw PASTRY is good. Good milk can be obtained in the larger *Dairy Restaurants* (Mleczarnia).

Theatres. *Grand Theatre* (Teatr Wielki; Pl. E, F, 4, *II*), in the Plac Teatralny, for operas and ballets; box 6³/₄-14 rb., parquet from 1 rb. 40 to 4 rb. 75 cop.; closed in summer. *Teatr Rozmaitości*, in the W. wing of the Grand Theatre, for Polish dramas; box from 10 rb. 40 to 15 rb. 10 cop., parquet from 1 rb. 35 to 3 rb. 35 cop.; performances usually begin at 8 p.m.; closed in summer. *Teatr Polski*, Oboźna (Karasie; Pl. F, 4, 5, *II*), for comedies and dramas. *Mały Teatr*, Moniuszki 5, in the building of the Philharmonic Society (p. 16), for modern plays. — Second-class: *Teatr Nowoczesny*, Boduina 4 (a side-street of the Szpitalna; Pl. F, 5, *I*), for short dramas, comedies, and operettas (performances at 8 and 10 p.m.); *New Theatre* (Teatr Nowy), Królewska (Pl. E, F, 5; *II*), in summer only; *Novelty Theatre* (Teatr Nowości; Pl. E 4, *II*), operettas and comedies, in winter only.

Polish Summer Theatre, in the Saxon Garden (p. 15), parquet from 1 rb. 50 to 3 rb. 35 cop. — VARIETY, THEATRES. *Aquarium*, Chmielna 9 (Pl. D-F, 6, 5; *I*); *Renaissance*, Nowy Świat 43 (Pl. F, 5; *I*). — CABARET. *Oaza*, Wierzbowa 9 (Pl. E, F. 4; *II*). — *Circus* (Pl. F, 5; *II*), Ordynacka, in winter only.

Pleasure Resorts. *Vallée Suisse* (Dolina Szwajcarska; Pl. F, G, 7, *I*), Ulica Szopena 5, not far from the Aleja Ujazdowska, with roller skating-rink, and good music on summer-evenings (30 cop.), symphony concerts on Wed. & Sat. (50 cop.); *Dynasy*, Oboźna (Pl. F, 4, 5; *I*), light music (25 cop.); *Bagatela*, in the Bagatela (Pl. G, 8; *I*), operettas in summer; *Marcellin*, *Sielanka*, both beyond the Rogatki Belwederskie (Pl. G, 8; *I*). — In winter the Philharmonic Orchestra gives concerts almost every day in the hall of the *Philharmonic Society* (p. 16).

Cabs (*Dorożki*, Извóщики). Per drive within the barriers (Rogatki) 20, at night (12-7 a.m.) 35, with two horses 35 and 50 cop.; per hr. 55, 70, 80, 95 cop., every additional hr. 35, 50, 55, 70 cop. From the railway stations (except the Vienna Station) to the town 55, 75, 90 cop., 1 rb. 15 cop.; to the stations in Praga, from the Vienna Station to the town, or from the town to Praga, the citadel, Łazienki, Czerniakowska, or Solec 30, 45, 50, 70 cop. — Baggage 10 and 15 cop. per pud. — The ordinary one-horse cabs drive slowly, but the two-horse cabs, equipped with good horses, drive very fast. The drivers of the two-horse cabs with rubber tyres expect a gratuity of 20-50 cop. — *Motor Cabs* charge 20 cop. per Kil. (ca. 30 cop. per mile).

Electric Tramways (fare per section, 1st class 7, 2nd class 5 cop.). The chief intersecting points are the Krakowskie Przedmieście (Statue of Mickiewicz; Pl. 23, F 4, *I*), for Nos. 0, 1, 3, 5, 7, 9, 17, 18, 22; Aleja Ujazdowska (Pl. G, 6, 7; *I*), Nos. 0, 1, 9, 14, 21; Vienna Station (Pl. E, 6; *I*), Nos. 0, 3, 8, 14, 16, 17, 18; St. Petersburg Station (Pl. H, 2, 3; *I*), Nos. 5, 18;

Brest Station (Pl. H, I, 3; *I*), Nos. 4, 22; Willanów Station (p. 11), Nos. 1,
3, 9,.14, 18, 21.— O (circular line). From the *Plac Zbawiciela*, viâ the
Marszałkowska, Złota, Karmelicka, Nalewki, Miodowa, Krakowskie Przedmieście, and Aleja Ujazdowska to the *Plac Zbawiciela*; 7¹/₄ M., in 62 min.
—1. *Mokotów* (Pl. F, 8; *I*) to *Cmentarz Powązkowski* (Pl. B, C, 3; *I*); 4³/₄ M.;
37 min.—3. *Mokotów* (Pl. F, 8; *I*) to *Plac Krasińskich* (Pl. E, 3, 4; *I*); 3 M.;
25 min.—4. From the corner of the *Dzika* and the *Gęsia* (Pl. D, 3, 4; *I*)
to *Foksal Warszawa Brzeski* (Pl. H, I, 3; *I*); 3 M.; 26 min.—5. From
Wola (Pl. A, 6; *I*) to *Praga* (Pl. H, 2; *I*); 4¹/₄ M.; 36 min.—7. *Towarowa*
(Pl. D, 6; *I*) to *Cmentarz Powązkowski* (Pl. B, C, 3; *I*); 4 M.; 35 min.—
8. *Foksal Kowelski* (Pl. D, 2; *I*) to *Rogatki Jerozolimskie* (Pl. D, 6; *I*);
4 M.; 33 min.—9. *Wola* (Pl. A, 6; *I*) to *Mokotów* (Pl. F, 8; *I*); 4³/₄ M.;
36 min.—14. *Plac Muranowski* (Pl. D, E, 3; *I*) to *Mokotów* (Pl. F, 8; *I*);
4 M.; 34 min.—16. *Wola* (Pl. A, 6; *I*) to *Plac Zbawiciela*; 3 M.; 25 min.
—17. *Foksal Kowelski* (Pl. D, 2; *I*) to *Plac Zbawiciela*; 3³/₄ M.; 36 min.—
18. *Mokotów* (Pl. F, 8; *I*) to *Praga* (Pl. H, 2; *I*); 4²/₃ M.; 37 min.—
21. *Plac Muranowski* (Pl. D, E, 3; *I*) to *Mokotów* (Pl. F, 8; *I*); 4²/₃ M.;
38 min.—22. *Towarowa* (Pl. D, 6; *I*) to *Foksal Brzeski* (Pl. H, I, 3; *I*);
4 M.; 33 min.

Light Railways. From the Rogatki Mokotowskie (Pl. F, 8; *I*) viâ
(7 V.) *Willanów* (p. 24) to (23 V.) *Piaseczno;* also to (15 V.) *Piaseczno*
direct and thence to (31 V.) *Góra Kalváriya* (p. 29). From the Most
Aleksandrowski (Alexander Bridge; Pl. F, G, 3, *I*) to the N. to (17 V.)
Jablonna (p. 25), and to the E. to (5 V.) *Wawer* (p. 25).

Steamboats. Small passenger-steamboats (50 cop.; restaurant on
board), starting from the Alexander Bridge (Pl. F, G, 3; *I*), ply up and
down the Vistula in summer (May-Oct.), in the afternoon and evening.

District Messengers (recognizable by their red cap). Per message
in the inner city 10 cop., longer distances 20 cop. and upwards.

Baths. *Central Baths* (Łaźnia Centralna), Krakowskie Przedmieście 16
(Pl. F, 4; *I*). — *River Baths* in summer near the Most Aleksandrowski
(Alexander Bridge; Pl. F, G, 3, *I*; 10 cop.). — PUBLIC LAVATORIES (5 cop.)
in the Plac Teatralny (Pl. E, F, 4; *II*), the Saxon Garden (p. 15), etc.

Booksellers. *Gebethner & Wolff*, *E. Wende & Co.*, Krakowskie
Przedmieście 15 & 9 (Pl. F, 4; *I*); *F. Hösick*, Senatorska 22 (Pl. E, F, 4; *I*).

Banks. *Imperial Bank* (Bank Państwa; Pl. E 4, *II*), Bielańska 10,
open 10-3; *Commercial Bank*, Włodzimierska 27; *Discount Bank,* Ulica
hrabiego Kotzebue 8.

Consulates. British Consul, *H. M. Grove*, Służewska 3 (10-2). American Consul, *T. E. Heenan*, Aleja Ujazdowska 18 (10-3). — Branch of the
RUSSO-BRITISH CHAMBER OF COMMERCE (p. 93).

Physicians (English-speaking). *Dr. Horodyński*, Nowogrodzka 34;
Dr. Raum (surgeon), Bracka 5; *Dr. Solman*, Jerozolimska 63; *Dr. Zabo-
rowski* (for ladies), Jerozolimska 58. — PROTESTANT HOSPITAL (Szpital
Ewangelicki; Pl. D, E, 4, *I*), Karmelicka 10.

Post Office (Pl. 21, F 5; *I*), Plac Warecki 8. The department for
parcels and money-order business is to the left (open 8 a.m. to 2 p.m.;
entrance at the corner of the Warecki Square and the Ulica Święto Krzyzka)
The department for ordinary, registered, and poste restante letters is to
the right (8 a.m. to 8 p.m.; entrance from the Warecki Square). Letter
within the town 3 cop. — **Telegraph Office** (Pl. 24, E, F, 4; *I*), Ulica
hrabiego Kotzebue 3.

Police Station and *Passport Bureau* in the City Hall (Ratusz;
Pl. E, F, 4, *I*). The official *Register of Addresses* is also kept here and
may be consulted daily (9-3 & 5-8, Sun. and holidays 9-12).

Churches. *English Church Service* (11 a.m.) at Hortensja 3; chaplain, Rev. H. C. Zimmermann. — *Lutheran Church* (p. 15). — *German Reformed Church* (p. 20). — The *Roman Catholic Churches* are open all day.

Collections, etc.
Art Union (p. 15). Daily 10-7; adm. 30 cop. The Chojnowski Collection
is open daily 10-3; adm. 30 cop.

Belvedere (p. 18), open in winter only, daily, except Sat., 10-3. Adm.
by tickets given out gratis at the Palace Office (p. 12).

Łazienki (p. 17), open daily, except Sat., 10-6, holidays 1-6, in winter
10-3 or 1-3: adm. by tickets which may be obtained gratis at the Palace
Office (p. 12) or from the majordomo at Łazienki.

Museum of Industry and Commerce (p. 14), open daily, except Mon.,
10-3; adm. 20 cop., Sun. 5 cop.

Palace, Royal (p. 13), open daily, except Sat., 10-6, holidays 1-6 (in
winter 10-3 or 1-3); adm. by tickets obtained gratis at the Palace Office
(Дворцовое управленіе; open week-days 9-3), to the left of the S. main
entrance of the Palace (second floor).

Picture Gallery (P. 19), open free, Tues., Thurs., & Sun. 11-3.

University Library (p. 16), open on week-days 10-4; during the vacation
on Mon., Wed., & Frid. 11-2.

Willanów, Palace of (P. 24), open on week-days 2-6.

Principal Attractions (1 day). Royal Palace (p. 13); street scenes
in the Krakowskie Przedmieście, the Marszałkowska, and the Nowy Świat;
Saxon Garden (p. 15); view from the lantern of the Lutheran Church
(p. 15); Aleja Ujazdowska (p. 17), especially towards evening; Imperial
Château of Łazienki (p. 17); Cathedral of St. John (p. 21); Old Town (p. 21);
Alexander Bridge (p. 22).—Those who have a little more time should not
omit a visit to Willanów (p. 24).

Warsaw (*Warszawa*, Варшáва; Ger. *Warschau*, Fr. *Varsovie;* 320 ft.), the capital of the General Government of Warsaw
or Poland and an important railway centre, lies on the left bank of
the *Vistula*, on the elevated edge (120-130 ft.) of a valley, descending abruptly to the river, here $1/4$-$1/3$ M. in width, and gradually
merging on the W. in a wide and undulating plain. The city contains 872,500 inhab., including 15,000 Protestants, 300,000 Jews,
and a strong garrison. It is the intellectual centre of Poland, and
its appearance is far more like that of West Europe than of Russia.
Warsaw is the seat of the Governor-General of Warsaw, of a Civil
Governor, of Archbishops of the Greek and Roman Catholic churches,
of the Commandant of the military district of Warsaw, and of those
of the 15th, 19th, and 23rd Army Corps, and of a Russian university
and a Russian technical college. The city, which is divided into
twelve police precincts (including Praga), consists of the *Old Town*
(Стáрое Мѣ́сто, *Stare Miasto*), of the *New Town* (Нóвое Мѣ́сто,
Nowe Miasto), to the N., and of *Wola, Mokotów*, and other suburbs.
On the right bank of the Vistula lies *Praga*. The river is crossed by
three bridges. The streets teem with activity; the great shopping
district lies in the Marszałkowska and the Krakowskie Przedmieście.
Whole quarters of the town (p. 19) are occupied by Jews, whose
inattention to personal cleanliness has become proverbial. Warsaw
is a flourishing industrial centre (machinery, wooden wares, leather,
and tobacco) and carries on a considerable trade.

The HISTORY of Warsaw makes a great part of the history of Poland
(comp. p. 1). It is said to have been founded in the 12th cent., and from
the beginning of the 14th cent. till 1526 it was the residence of the Dukes
of Masovia, on whose extinction it fell to Poland. King Sigismund II.
Augustus fixed his residence here in 1550, and Sigismund III. made it
the capital of Poland. After the extinction of the Jagiello family in
1572, all the kings of Poland were elected on the field of Wola. The

WARSZAWA II (WARSAW)

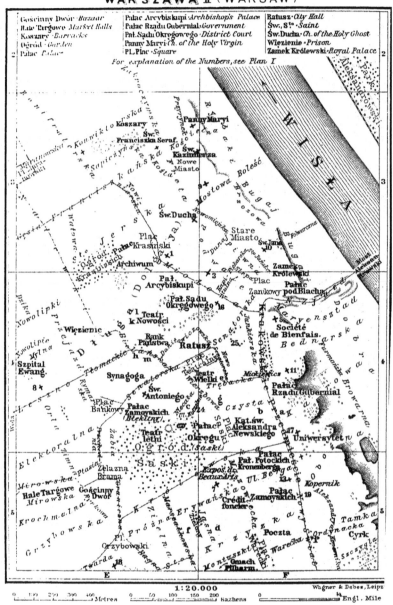

1:20,000

Wagner & Debes, Leipz

three days' battle of Warsaw was fought on July 28-30th, 1656 (see p. 24).
— Both Augustus II. and Augustus III. took great pride in the beautification of their capital. On May 24th, 1702, during the great war of the
Northern Powers, Warsaw was captured by Charles XII. After the death
of Augustus III. (Oct. 5th, 1763) Warsaw was for a time the scene of
constant disorder, until the Russians under Prince Repnin took possession
of the city (1764) and (with the co-operation of the Prussians) forced the
electors to choose the colourless Stanislaus Poniatowski as their king.
The quiet thus secured was of short duration. Fresh disorder in 1794
ended in the storming of Praga (P. 23) by Suvorov on Nov. 5th, and
led to the third partition of Poland. Poniatowski (p. 2) abdicated; Warsaw fell to the share of Prussia and became capital of the province of
South Prussia. — On Nov. 28th, 1806, the French, under Davout and Murat,
entered Warsaw. By the Peace of Tilsit (July 7th, 1807) South Prussia
was separated from Prussia, and Warsaw was made the capital of the Saxon
Grand-Duchy of Warsaw. — The Congress of Vienna (1814) transferred the
grand-duchy to Russia, which raised Warsaw to the rank of capital of the
kingdom of Poland. The great Polish Revolution of 1830 began with an
uprising in Warsaw, and ended on Sept. 7th, 1831, with the storming of
the city by the Russians under Paskévitch. Warsaw was also the focus of
the risings against Russian rule in 1861-64. Since the restoration of quiet
the growth of Warsaw's prosperity has been continuous.

a. **Palace Square. Lazienki. The Southern Quarters.**

In the centre of traffic, between the Old Town and the S.E.
suburbs which have supplanted it in importance, lies the Palace
Square (Зáмковая плóщадь, Plac Zamkowy; Pl. F 4, *II*), adorned with a *Monument to King Sigismund III. (Vasa)*, erected in
1644 by his son, Wladislaus IV. On a monolithic column of light
Cracow marble, 36 ft. high, stands a bronze statue of the king,
$8^1/_2$ ft. in height, holding a sword in his right hand and a cross in
his left. The Tritons at the foot of the column were modelled by
Kiss (1854). The total height of the monument is 66 ft.

On the E. side of the square, near the Vistula, stands the **Royal
Palace** (Королéвскій Зáмокъ, *Zamek Królewski;* Pl. F, 3, 4, *II;*
adm., see p. 12), founded by the Masovian dukes, rebuilt and fitted
up as a royal residence by Sigismund III. and Wladislaus IV., and
greatly embellished by John Sobieski and Stanislaus Poniatowski.

The E. part of the palace, with the former apartments of the Polish
kings, is now occupied by the Governor-General of Poland; the W.
part, surmounted by a tower, is used by military officials. Among the
most notable apartments are the Throne Room, the rooms formerly used
by the Senate and Chamber of Deputies, and the Marble Ball Room, with
its ceiling-painting by Bacciarelli. Most of the older works of art and
objects of value were removed to St. Petersburg and Moscow in 1831,
but the palace still contains several portraits of Polish kings, views of
Warsaw by Canaletto, scenes of Polish history by Bacciarelli, etc.

On the S. the Royal Palace is adjoined by the small *Palais pod
Blachą* (Домъ подъ бляхой; Pl. F 4, *II*), which lies on a somewhat lower level. This palace once belonged to Count Lubomirski,
but was purchased by King Stanislaus Augustus and presented by
him to his nephew Joseph Poniatowski.

By following the *Zjazd* (Съѣздъ; Pl. F 4, *II*), the wide street which descends from the Palace Square to the Alexander Bridge (p. 22). we obtain a good view of the water-front of the palace, with its terraced gardens. Below the terrace lie some of the stables of the sótnyas (squadrons) of *Circassians* and *Cossacks* forming the Governor-General's body-guard.

The KRAKOWSKIE PRZEDMIEŚCIE ('Cracow Suburb'; Краковское предмѣстье; Pl. F 4, *II*), one of the liveliest streets in Warsaw, with large palaces and imposing churches, leads from the Palace Square towards the S. Immediately to the left, opposite the prolongation of the Miodowa, is the **Church of St. Anne** (*Kościół św. Anny;* Pl. 5, F 4, *II*), founded in 1454 and formerly connected with a Bernardine convent. The remains of the original building include part of the cloisters on the S. side and the sacristy (fine intarsia). The aisleless interior was painted in 1749; the façade dates from 1788.

No. 66, adjoining the church, is the *Museum of Industry & Commerce* (Muzeum przemysłu i handlu; adm., see p. 12). The collection of industrial art and the Polish ethnographical collection, both on the second floor (the latter to the left of the entrance), merit notice. To the left, farther on, at the corner of the Bednarska, is the *House of the Charitable Society* (Warszawskie Towarzystwo Dobroczynności; Pl. F 4, *II*), bearing the inscription 'Res sacra miser'. Louis XVIII. spent part of his exile here. In front of the house is a small *Statue of the Virgin* (1683).

Farther on in the Cracow Suburb is the *Monument to Adam Mickiewicz* (1798-1855; Pl. F 4, *II*), by Cyprian Godebski (1898). On a podium of dark-grey granite rises a column of light-red granite, forming the pedestal for a bronze statue of the poet, 13 ft. in height. The total height of the monument, which is enclosed by a handsome railing, is $47^1/_2$ ft.

To the left is the *Church of St. Joseph* (Pl. 11, F 4; *II*), founded in 1643 as a Carmelite church. The façade dates from 1782. No. 46 is the *Palais Rządu Gubernialnego,* formerly the Palais Radziwill, now the seat of the *Provincial Government* (Зданіе Министерства Внутреннихъ Дѣлъ). In front of the palace is a *Bronze Statue of Prince Paskévitch* (p. 13), by Pimenov (1870).

Farther on, to the right, is the PLAC SASKI ('Saxon Square'; Саксонская площадь; Pl. F 4, *II*), in which rises the Greek Catholic **Cathedral of St. Alexander Nevski** (Соборъ св. князя Александра Невскаго), built in the Byzantine style in 1894-1912 from the plans of Benois. It has five gilded domes and a detached belfry, 240 ft. high. — To the W. of the cathedral stands the former **Saxon Palace** (Зданіе Управленія Варшавскаго военнаго округа, *Palac Okręgu Wojennego;* Pl. E, F, 4, *II*), once the residence of the Polish kings, torn down in 1842, and supplanted by two unsightly masses of building connected by a colonnade. Since

1869 it has been the headquarters of the Warsaw Military District.
— To the N. of the Saxon Palace is the former *Brühl Palace,* built
by Count Brühl (d. 1763), the favourite of Augustus III., and now the
Telegraph Office (Pl. 24, E, F, 4, *II;* p. 11).

Behind the Saxon Palace, and reached by the Colonnades, lies the
Saxon Garden (Саксо́нскій садъ, Ogród Saski; Pl. E, 4, 5, *II*),
a public park of 17 acres in extent, laid out by Augustus the Strong
and containing fine old trees (open in summer from 6 a.m. to 11 p.m.,
in winter 8 a.m. to 9 p.m.; café, see p. 10). In the N.W. part of
the garden is a *Summer Theatre* (Лѣтній теа́тръ, Teatr letni;
p. 10). On a mound near the Niecała gate, opposite the pond, is a
round temple containing the reservoir of the old aqueduct.

The W. gate of the park leads to the Market Place (Желѣзная
бра́ма, Żelazna Brama; Pl. E 5, *II*), with a *Bazaar* (Гости́ный
дворъ, Góscinny Dwór) and large market-halls (Hale targowe). —
The S. side of the garden abuts on the Królewska, where stands the
Exchange, with its portico of six columns.

To the S. of the Saxon Garden is the **Lutheran Church**
(Евангели́ческо-Аугсбу́ргскій храмъ, *Kościół Ewangielicki;*
Pl. 7, F 5, *II*), a large and conspicuous rotunda, begun in the time
of King John Sobieski and completed in 1799 (sacristan in the passage at Królewska 19, in the first house to the right, Quarter 10).
The lofty dome is surmounted by a lantern of considerable architec-
tónic interest, which affords, perhaps, the best *View of Warsaw
and its environs (185 steps).

From the lantern we see the Palace Square to the N., and to the
right of it the Zjazd leading to the Alexander Bridge. The main lines of
thoroughfare are clearly defined. Two of these run N. and S. and nearly
parallel: the one leading from the Old Town across the Palace Square to
the Krakowskie Przedmieście, Nowy Świat, and Aleja Ujazdowska, the
other running from the Nalewki viâ Przejazd, Żabia, and Graniczna to
Królewska and Marszałkowska. The third great artery of traffic runs
W., viâ Elektoralna and Chłodna. The winding course of the Vistula can
be traced for a long distance.

In the Erywańska, to the S. of the church, is the office of the
Crédit Foncier (Pl. F, 5; *II*), by Marconi (1856). The Erywańska
leads W. to the Plac Zielony ('Green Square'; Pl. E, F, 5, *II*). Here
rises the *Monument* commemorating the loyal Polish generals who
fell on Nov. 29th, 1830. The monument, which was originally erected
in the Saxon Square by Tzar Nicholas I. in 1841, was transferred
to its present site in 1898. It consists of a truncated steel obelisk
on an octagonal marble base, surrounded by eight lions couchant.

No. 17, Królewska, to the N. of the Lutheran Church, is the build-
ing of the **Art Union** (Зда́ніе о́бщества поощре́нія худо́жествъ,
Dom Towarzystwa Sztuk Pięknych; Pl. F 5, *II*), erected in 1898-
1900 from the plans of *St. Szyller* (adm., see p. 11; entr. in the
Mazowiecka). On the groundfloor, to the left, is the Chojnowski
Collection, comprising prehistoric objects, Greek, Roman, Sarmatian,

and Gothic antiquities found in Russia, Polish and Russian weapons, and modern pictures. The first floor contains rooms used for picture exhibitions and also the Bloch Collection of 1000 original drawings by old and modern masters. — At the corner of the Królewska and Mazowiecka is the *Palais Kronenberg*, by Hitzig (1869).

We now return through the Królewska to the KRAKOWSKIE PRZEDMIEŚCIE. Here, facing the Królewska, is the *Wizytek Church* or *Church of St. Joseph* (Pl. 17, F 4; *II*), a rococo building of 1760.

Close by, but standing a little back from the street, is the *University Library*, built in 1894 and containing ca. 576,000 vols. and 1384 MSS. (adm., see p. 12). Behind the library is the **University** (Pl. F, 4; *II*), which was founded in 1816, suppressed in 1832, reopened as a high school in 1861, and again made a university in 1869, with Russian as the language of instruction. There are about 2400 students. At No. 26, Krakowskie Przedmieście, is the entrance to the extensive *Zoological Museum* (open in winter on Thurs. & Sun., 12-3).

Nearly opposite the university is the **Church of the Holy Cross** (Костёлъ Святáго Крестá, *Kościół Św. Krzyża;* Pl. 13, F 5, *II*), one of the largest churches in Warsaw, built by Giovanni Bellotto in 1682-96. The towers were added from the plans of A. Fontanna in 1726-56. The upper church contains a monument to Fr. Chopin (see p. 4; by the first pillar, to the left of the entrance), with a marble bust by Marconi. The heart of the great musician is buried in the lower church, whither it was brought from Père Lachaise at Paris. The iron-work of the pulpit (upper church) is noteworthy.

At the end of the Krakowskie Przedmieście, in the fork between the Aleksandrya and Nowy Świat, lies the *First High School* (Pl. 19, F 5; *II*), with a tasteful Greek Catholic chapel. In front of it is a seated bronze figure of *Copernicus* (b. at Thorn in 1473, d. at Frauenburg in 1543), by Thorvaldsen, unveiled in 1830. — To the right of the gymnasium, in the Nowy Świat, stands the old *Zamoyski Palace* (Pl. F, 5; *II*), now used by the military authorities. The *Russian Club* occupies one of the rear buildings. — Near this point is the Warecki Square (Pl. F, 5; *II*), with the *Post Office* (p. 11). At No. 8, Moniuszki Street, is the large building of the *Philharmonic Society* (Gmach Filharmonji; Pl. F 5, *II*), erected from Kozłowski's plans in 1899-1901.

We return through the Święto Krzyzka to the NOWY ŚWIAT ('New World'; Нóвый Свѣтъ; Pl. F, 5, 6, *I*), forming the S. continuation of the Krakowskie Przedmieście. To the left diverges the Ordynacka, with the former *Palais Ordynacki*, begun in 1597 and used since 1859 as a Conservatorium of Music. The Nowy Świat now intersects the Aleja Jerozolimska (p. 21), the left branch of which leads over a viaduct, 765 yds. long, to the *New Vistula Bridge*, 550 yds. in length, built in 1904-14. Farther to the S. the Nowy Świat reaches the ALEXANDER SQUARE (Площадь Святаго Александра, Plac Św. Aleksandra; Pl. F 6, *I*), with the **Church of St. Alexander** (Pl. 4), built in 1826 and enlarged in 1891. The last station of the long-vanished chapels, 28 in number, of the Aleja Ujazdowska, stood in front of this church. Two of its three crosses still remain (restored in 1910), and between them is a statue of St. John Nepomuc. Farther to the E., on the left side of the Książęca, is the *Hospital of St. Lazarus* (Szpital Św. Łazarza; Pl. F, G, 5, *I*). To the S., on the Wiejska, lies the *Frascati Park* (Ogród Frascati; Pl. G 6, *I*), belonging to Count Branicki and inaccessible to strangers.

Three streets (Mokotowska, Aleja Ujazdowska, Wiejska) run from the Alexander Square towards the S. We follow that in the middle, the ALEJA UJAZDOWSKA (Уяздовская аллея; Pl. F, G, 6, 7, *I*), an avenue of stately lime-trees. The avenue is particularly lively towards evening. To the E. are the *Ujazdowski Park*, laid out in 1895, where a monument to Chopin (see p. 4) by W. Szymanowski is to be erected, and the *Church of the Archangel Michael*, belonging to the Lithuanian Regiment of Guards; behind the latter is the *Military Hospital* (Szpital Ujazdowski; Pl. G 7, *I*), formerly a royal summer-palace. Farther to the S. is the *Botanic Garden* (Ogród Botaniczny; Pl. G 7, *I*), containing the *Observatory*.

The small imperial château of **Łazienki (i.e.* 'Baths'; Лазенковскій дворецъ, Łazienki Królewskie; Pl. G, H, 8, *I)* makes a most attractive impression, especially when viewed from the artificial water, and its light colouring contrasts very effectively with the verdure of the park (adm., see p. 12; entr. in the Agrikola Górna). It was built in the Italian style for King Stanislaus Poniatowski in 1767-88 and was acquired by Emp. Alexander I. in 1817. The so-called Solomon Room has a ceiling painted by Bacciarelli with scenes from the life of Solomon; portraits of Stanislaus Poniatowski and his suite are introduced in the picture of Solomon's Sacrifice. The bathroom is adorned with reliefs. On the walls of the 'Green Cabinet' hang the portraits of numerous beauties of Warsaw in the reign of Stanislaus. Other rooms contain portraits of Polish kings and celebrities and pictures of momentous events in the history of Poland. To the W., connected with the château by a bridge, is the *Alexander Nevski Chapel*, built in 1876. The beautiful **Park contains several small villas; a Chinese palace; a *Rotunda*, with marble busts of Polish kings; and a *Natural Theatre*, the auditorium of which has been constructed in the form of a stone amphitheatre, while the stage, framed by Corinthian columns and shrubbery, lies on an island in the lake. Opposite the château, to the N., on the bridge of the Agrikola Dolna, is an *Equestrian Statue of John Sobieski* (Pl. 22, G 7; *I*), in sandstone, erected in 1788.

To the W. of the Łazienki Park is the château of **Belvedere** (Pl. G, 8; *I*), the beautiful garden of which, laid out in the English style, extends to the *Belvedere Barrier* (Бельведéрская застáва, Rogatki Belwederskie). The château (adm., see p. 12; entr. from the Aleja Ujazdowska), now the summer-residence of the Governor General, was rebuilt in 1822 and occupied by Grand-Duke Constantine Pávlovitch (d. 1831). The rooms used by the Grand-Duke and his wife, Princess Łowicz, are still in very much the same condition as during their life-time. In the upper floor are pictures illustrating the uniforms of old Polish regiments.

From the Belvedere the Bagatela leads to the W. to the *Mokotów Barrier* (Мокотóвская застáва, Rogatki Mokotowskie; Pl. F 8, *I*). To the right stretches the extensive *Mokotów Military Exercise Ground*, where horse-races are held in Oct. and June. To Willanów, see p. 23.

From the Mokotów Barrier we return to the N.W. through the Marszałkowska (Pl. E, F, 5-7, *I; p.* 21) to the Święto Krzyzka (Pl. E, F, 5, *II;* 1¹⁄₃ M.), turn here to the left, and follow the Bagno to the Plac Grzybowski (Pl. E, 5; *II*). On the S. side of this square stands the large *Church of All Saints* (Pl. 18, E 5; *II*), completed in 1893. Thence we return along the Królewska to the Krakowskie Przedmieście (p. 14).

b. Theatre Square. The Western Quarters.

From the Palace Square (p. 13) the Senatorska and its prolongations, the Elektoralna and Chłodna, lead to the S.W. to the Wola Barrier. To the left, in the Senatorska (Pl. E, F, 4, *II;* No. 15), stands the former *Palace of the Prince Primate,* now the headquarters of the Artillery (Pl. 25, F 4; *II*).

Nearly opposite the Palace, to the right, diverges the Miodowa (Медóвая; Pl. E, F, 4, *II*), on the left side of which is the **Church of the Transfiguration** (Pl. 16, F 4; *II*), erected by John Sobieski in 1693 in gratitude for his victory over the Turks before Vienna. In the Chapel of St. Peter (to the right of the high-altar) are a sarcophagus of grey marble, containing Sobieski's heart, and a marble urn, with a bronze crown, holding the heart of King Stanislaus Augustus Poniatowski. The urn is inscribed: 'Morte quis fortior? Gloria et amor.'   Adjacent is the *Palais Pac* (No. 11), built in 1823 and now occupied by the District Court (Окружнóй суд, Pałac Sądu Okręgowego; Pl. E 4, *II*). Opposite is the Greek Catholic *Church of the Assumption* (Pl. 3). Next, No. 13, comes the *Palace of the Archbishop of Warsaw* (Pałac Arcybiskupi; Pl. E 4, *II*), containing the Roman Catholic, Lutheran, and Reformed Consistories.

The Miodowa ends at the Plac Krasiński (Красńнская плóщадь; Pl. E 3, *II*). To the right, at the corner of the Miodowa and the

Długa, is the Greek Catholic **Cathedral of the Trinity** (Соборъ
Святóй Трóицы, *Cerkiew Katedralna Św. Trójcy;* Pl. 1, E 3,
II), rebuilt in 1837 in the Renaissance style, with five gilded domes
and an elaborate ikonostás. Prior to 1832 it belonged to the Piarists.
— On the W. side of the Plac Krasiński are the *Judicial Archives*
and the handsome **Krasiński Palace** (Pl. E, 3; *II*), built in the
Italian Renaissance style in 1692. Bequeathed by Count Krasiński
to Poland, the palace was used during the 18th cent. as the meeting-
place of the Chamber of Deputies. It was burned down in 1782, but
was rebuilt and has been used since 1876 as the seat of the Supreme
Court of the District of the Vistula.(Судéбная палáта, Pałac Izby
Sądowej). — Behind the palace lies the *Krasiński Garden* (Кра-
сíнскiй садъ, Ogród Krasińskich), open to the public and frequented almost exclusively by Jews. To the W. of the garden lies
the Jewish quarter of Warsaw.

We now return through the Miodowa to the Senatorska, which
soon expands into the PLAC TEATRALNY ('Theatre Square'; Теат-
ра́льная плóщадь; Pl. E, F, 4, *II*), with its flower-beds. On its
N. side stands the **City Hall** (Ра́туша, *Ratusz*), originally built
in 1725, destroyed by fire in 1863, and rebuilt in 1870. The chief
feature of the interior is the Alexander Hall, two stories in height.
The tower is 190 ft. high. — On the S. side of the square is the
Grand Theatre (Большóй теáтръ, *Teatr Wielki;* Pl. E, F, 4, *II;*
p. 10), dating from 1833, with colonnades on the groundfloor. The
ballet is at its best in such national dances as the mazurka and
cracovienne.

The **Municipal Picture Gallery** (Музéй изя́щныхъ
искýсствъ, *Muzeum sztuk pięknych*), lying to the W. of the Grand
Theatre (entr., Wierzbowa 11), contains 350 paintings by masters of
the older schools. Among its treasures are pictures by Jordaens
(No. 42), Dürer (72), Rembrandt (173), Stokade (191), Zurbaran
(308), and Clouet (330). Adm., see p. 12; catalogue 10 cop.

From the entrance we traverse Room V, and then turn to the left into Room I, which lies at the end of the building. On the end-wall:
1. *Flemish School* (beginning of the 16th cent.), Winged altar-piece, with
the Pietà, the donors, and their patron saints; 8. *Barend van Orley* (Jan
Gossaert?), Madonna; 7. *Mostaert* (Ambr. Benson?), Sibylla Persica;
2. *School of Bruges* (early 16th cent.), Triptych, with the Immaculate
Conception and the donors; 22, 23, 28, 29. *B. Spranger*, Spain, Austria,
Rome, and France. — Room II (second half of Room I): NETHERLANDS
SCHOOL. 42. *Jordaens*, Holy Family; 46. *Jan Brueghel*, Robbers in a
wood; *Snyders*, 56. Fruit, 58. Song-birds. -- Room III: GERMAN SCHOOL.
60. *Flüger*, Venus and Vulcan; 62. *L. Cranach the Elder*, Wooing; 63.
Hans Baldung Grien, Deposition in the Tomb; 66. *Holbein the Younger (?)*,
Portrait; 67. *Schäufelin*, Mocking of Christ; 68. *H. S. Beham* (not Grüne-
wald), Portrait; 72. *Dürer*, Portrait of a young man; 75. *A. Kauffmann*,
Feast of Venus. — Room IV: DUTCH SCHOOL. To the left of the entrance,
107. *Sir A. More* (Mierevelt?), Portrait of a woman. To the right of
the entrance, 113. *N. Maes*, Rembrandt's brother; 136, 137. *G. Dou*,
Portraits, the flowers and fruit by *Seghers;* 141. *Schalcken*, Old woman

with a candle; *Rembrandt*, 173. The artist's sister, 175. Portrait of himself; 174. *B. van der Helst*, Portrait of A. van den Hulst; 178. *G. van den Eeckhout*, Jacob's Dream; 183. *W. Cl. Heda*, Still-life; 184. *Ph. Wouverman*, Starting for the chase; 186. *Lievens*, Jacob blessing the sons of Joseph; 170. *F. Bol.* Judgment of Paris. — Room V: DUTCH SCHOOL. — Room VI. To the left. 195. *Florentine School*, John the Baptist and St. Francis; 196. *A. Previtali (?)*, Deposition in the Tomb. To the right of the entrance, 191. *Helt Stokade*, The artist and his family; 204. *Tintoretto*, Baptism of Christ; 223. *Pinturicchio (?)*, Madonna. — Room VII: 239. Holy Family with the Lamb, a replica of *Raphael's* picture in the Prado Gallery at Madrid. — Room VIII: 292. *French School of the 18th cent.*, Venus, Mars, and Mercury; 297, 298. *Callot*, Genre-scenes; 300. *N. Poussin*, Last Supper; 308. *Zurbaran*, Capuchin monk. — Room IX: 318. *Pedro de Moya (?)*, Cheesemonger; 330. *Clouet*, Finding of Moses, with portraits of Diana of Poitiers, Catherine de Medici, and the sons of Henry II. of France. Also drawings. — Rooms X and XI (to the left of R. VI) contain 18th cent. portraits and modern Polish pictures.

To the N.W. of the Plac Teatralny (Theatre Square) is the large new building of the *Imperial Bank* (Bank Państwa; Pl. E 4, *II*).

To the S.W. of the Theatre Square, in the Senatorska, is the *Church of St. Anthony* (Kościół Św. Antoniego; Pl. E 4, *II*), built in 1679. In front of it is a *Statue of the Virgin*.

A little to the S.W. of St. Anthony's is the PLAC BANKOWY ('Bank Square'; Pl. E 4, *II*), with the *Palace of Count Zamoyski* or the *Blue Palace*, built in a few weeks by King Augustus II. for his daughter, the Countess Orzelska. It is now the property of the rich family of Zamoyski, a familiar name in Polish history, and contains valuable art-collections and an extensive library. Opposite is the *Merchants' Resource* or *Club* (Resursa Kupiecka), with a *Statue of St. John Nepomuc* (1831) in front of it.

To the N. of the Bank Sq., in the Rymarska, rises the columned façade of the building of the *Financial Administration* (Зда́ніе казённой пала́ты). In the Tłomackie is a large *Synagogue* (Pl. E, 4; *II*), built by Marconi in the German Renaissance style (1877). — A little to the N. is the *Prison* (Więzienie; Pl. E 4, *II*), the scene of the bloodiest fighting at the outbreak of the Revolution on Nov. 29th, 1830.

We retrace our steps and turn into the LESZNO STREET (Лѣшно у́лица; Pl. E 4, *II*). Here, to the right, stands the *Reformed Church* (Pl. 8, E 4; *II*), a Gothic building with a lofty open-work tower (1882), and a little farther on is the *Church of the Nativity of the Virgin* (Костёлъ Рождества́ Пресвяты́я Богоро́дицы; Pl. 14, D 4, *I*), erected in 1683-1731, and containing a high-altar-piece (Crown of Thorns) ascribed to Correggio (?).

We now follow the Solna (Pl. D, 4, 5; *I*) to the ELEKTORALNA (Электора́льная; Pl. D, E, 4, 5, *I*), in a small square at the end of which is the *Church of St. Charles Borromeo* (Pl. 12, D 5; *I*), with two graceful towers (1849).

The Chłodna, a continuation of the Elektoralna, leads W. to the

Wola Barrier (Вóльская застáва, Rogatki Wolskie; Pl. C, D, 5, *I*),
beyond which lie the suburbs of *Wola* (p. 23) and *Czyste.*

From the Wola Barrier the Towarowa leads to the S.E. to the
Jerusalem Barrier (Іерусалúмская застáва, Rogatki Jerozo-
limskie; Pl. D 6, *I*), at the W. end of the *Aleja Jerozolimska*
(Іерус. Аллéя; Pl. D-G, 6, 5, *I*), which crosses the Nowy Świat
(p. 17) and descends to the new bridge over the Vistula. — To the
S.E. of the Jerusalem Barrier, in the Koszykowa, is the *Filtration
Station* of the City Water Works (Stacya Filtrów; Pl. D, E, 7, *I*)
constructed in 1884-87. Adjacent are the extensive buildings (1901)
of the *Hospital of the Infant Jesus* (Больнúца Младéнца Іисýса,
Szpital Dzieciątka Jezus; Pl. E 6, *I*), with the university clinics.
— In the Nowogrodzka is the *Pomological Garden* (Ogród Pomo-
logiczny; Pl. E 6, *I*). To the E. is the Romanesque *Church of SS.
Peter & Paul* (Pl. 15, E 6, *I;* 1886). Adjacent is the *Church of St.
Barbara.* To the S. stands the *Polytechnic School* (Gmach Poli-
techniki; Pl. E, F, 7, *I;* 600 students), built in 1901.

At the *Vienna Railway Station* (Foksal War.-Wiedeński; Pl.
E, F, 6, *I*) we bend to the N. into the Marszałkowska (Маршал-
кóвская), one of the chief shopping-streets, and then either proceed
in a straight direction to the Saxon Garden (p. 15), or follow the
Królewska to the right to the Krakowskie Przedmieście (p. 14).

c. Old Town. The Northern Quarters.

To the N. of the Palace Square (p. 13) lies the somewhat un-
savoury **Old Town** (Стáрое Мѣ́сто, *Stare Miasto;* Pl. F 3, *II*),
with its narrow, crooked streets. In the ŚwiĘto Jańska (Свя́то
Янскáя), to the right, stands the —

Cathedral of St. John (Каѳедрáльный костёлъ свя́таго
Іоáнна, *Kościół katedralny Świętego Jana;* Pl. 10, F 3, *II*), connected with the Palace by a covered gallery. It is a Gothic edifice,
with nave and aisles of equal height, founded by the Masovian dukes
about the middle of the 13th cent. and embellished by John III. Sobieski and others.

Interior. By the first pier to the left is a mosaic portrait of *Prince
Primate Michael Poniatowski* (brother of King Stanislaus Augustus). At
the high-altar is a Madonna with John the Baptist and St. Stanislaus, by
Palma Giovane. There are many monuments of eminent Poles. In the S.
aisle is Thorvaldsen's monument of *Count Stanislaus Malachowski* (1736-
1809), Marshal of the Diet, the chief author of the constitution of May 3rd,
1791; it is inscribed 'Przyjacielowi ludu' ('to the Friend of the People').
Adjacent is the tomb of *Bishop Albertrandi* (d. 1808), a man of great
learning. The stalls are in the rococo style. Most of the numerous hatchments are of the 17th century.

A little to the N.W. of the Cathedral of St. John we cross the
Plac Stare Miasto ('Old Town Square'; Pl. F 3, *II*), formerly the
market-place. It contains many quaint old buildings, bearing the

coats-of-arms of former owners, mottoes, images of saints, and reliefs. One of the most noteworthy of these is the house at the N.W. corner of the Dunaj. Here also is the office of the Society for the Protection of Historical Monuments. Continuing our walk towards the N.W., we next reach the FRETA (Pl. E, 3; *II*), where the so-called **New Town** *(Nowe Miasto)* begins. At the corner of the Długa (Дóлгая), which diverges to the left, is the *Church of the Holy Ghost* (Kościół Św. Ducha; Pl. E 3, *II*), also known as the *Pauline Church*, founded in the 13th cent., rebuilt in 1717, and restored in 1819. Opposite stands the Dominican church of *St. Hyacinth* (Kościół Św. Jacka; Pl. 9, F 3, *II*), dating from 1638. In the chapel to the left of the entrance are some elaborate marble sculptures. Farther on, to the right, is the New Town Square, with the *Sacramental Church of St. Casimir* (Kościół Św. Kazimierza; Pl. E, F, 3, *II*) and the convent connected with it, both erected in 1683-88 by Marya Kazimiera, wife of John Sobieski. — To the N. is the *Church of the Virgin* (Kościół Panny Maryi; Pl. E, F, 3, *II*), a Gothic edifice of 1419, the exterior of which was altered to the Romanesque style in 1883.

We now follow the Zakroczymska (Закрочймская; Pl. E, 2, 3, *II*), passing the *Franciscan Church* (Kościół Św. Franciszka Serafickiego; 1737), at the corner of the Franciszkańska, and the *Sapieha* and *Sierakowski Barracks* (Koszary), built at the expense of the families of these names. We then pass between the forts of *Alexéi* and *Vladimir*, cross the railway, and reach the **Alexander Citadel** (Александровская цитадéль, *Cytadela Aleksandrowska;* Pl. E 2, *I*), situated on the Vistula, at the N. end of Warsaw. It was built in 1832-35, at the cost of the city, as a punishment for the revolution of 1830. In the interior (adm. only by permission of the Commandant) are barracks, a prison for political offenders, and the Alexander Nevski Church. An obelisk of bronze, 50 ft. in height, was erected in honour of Alexander I. in 1835. — Just below the Citadel the Vistula, here $1/4$ M. wide, is crossed by a *Railway Bridge*, constructed in 1876. On the right bank is *Fort Śliwicki*, a tête-de-pont; the left bank is very steep.

d. Praga.

Again starting from the Palace Square (p. 13), we follow the Zjazd (p. 13) towards the E. and reach the **Alexander Bridge** *(Most Aleksandrowski;* Pl. F, G, 3, *I)*, an iron girder-bridge supported on five piers rising from the river. It is 560 yds. long and was constructed by Kierbedź in 1865. Smoking on the bridge is forbidden.

The bridge affords a pretty view of Warsaw. To the N. we see the Citadel, commanding the Vistula, the railway-bridge, and the buildings of the Old and New Towns, extending down to the brink of the river.

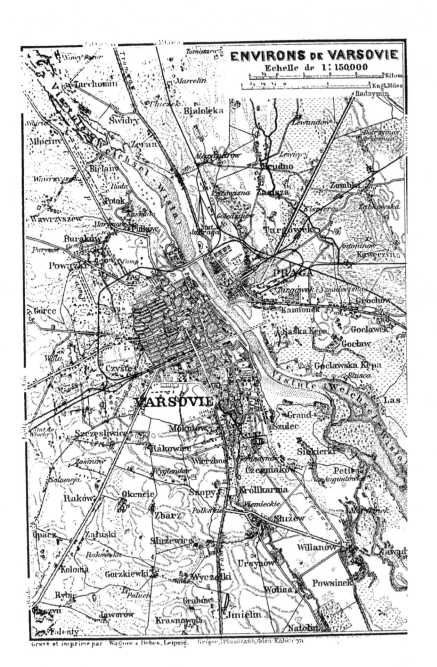

ENVIRONS DE VARSOVIE

Echelle de 1 : 150,000

In front of us, on the hill, lies the Royal Palace, forming a charming group with its terraced garden and the church of St. Anne. Above the bridge are the streets skirting the Vistula and the promenades and gardens surrounding the imperial château of Łazienki.

The bridge leads to the once fortified suburb of **Praga,** on the right bank of the Vistula.

After the second partition of Poland Praga was defended by ca. 23,000 soldiers and 5000 civilians, but was captured by *Suvorov*, at the head of 25,000 Russians, on Nov. 5th, 1794, after a struggle lasting 12 hours. Two days later Warsaw also fell. Suvorov informed the Empress of his victory in the three words 'Hurrah, Praga, Suvorov', and she replied, as laconically, 'Bravo, Field-Marshal, Catherine.'

In the Alexandrowska, to the right, is the Gothic *Church of SS. Florian & Michael* (Kościól Św. Florjana; Pl. G 3, *I*), erected in 1901; to the left is the small Greek Catholic *Church of Mary Magdalen* (Pl. 2), with five gilded domes (1869). The *Alexander Park* (Park Aleksandrowski; Pl. F, G, 2, 3, *I*), stretching along the Vistula, is frequented mainly by the lower classes.

e. Environs of Warsaw.

Carriages (with two horses), see p. 10; fare 4-5 rb. per half-day, 8-10 rb. per day (bargaining advisable).

The Młociny Road, on the LEFT BANK OF THE VISTULA, leads to the N.W. from the *Marymont Barrier* (Rogatki Marymonckie; Pl. C, D, 1, *I*) to (¹/₄ hr.) *Marymont* (Маримóнтъ), with a château and park, once a summer-resort of Marya Kazimiera, wife of John Sobieski, but now fallen wholly into decay.

About 2 M. to the N. of Marymont, beyond *Potok* and *Ruda*, is the *Forest of Bielany*. On a height here stands the imposing palace of **Bielany** (Бѣля́ны), with a suppressed convent and a small but interesting Camaldulensian church. To the W. of Bielany is a military summer-camp.

About 3 M. to the S. of Marymont lies the great **Election Plain** *(Pole Elekcyi Królów;* Pl. B 4, *I*), where, during the 16-18th cent., the Kings of Poland were elected, often amid scenes of storm and bloodshed. The famous, not to say notorious Polish *Diets* were also held here.

To the W. of the Wola Barrier (Rogatki Wolskie; Pl. C, D, 5, *I*) is (1¹/₂ M.) the village of **Wola** (Вóля). The *Russian Cemetery* (Wolski cmentarz prawosławny; Pl. A, 5, 6, *I*) occupies the site of the earthworks thrown up in Sept., 1831. Close to the Wolska is the *Church of the Vladimir Madonna,* the interior of which is adorned with military emblems, even the chandeliers being formed of gun-barrels.

From the Mokotów Barrier a light railway (see p. 11) runs to the S. to (7 V., in 35 min.) *Willanów* (return third-class fare 45 cop.; carr there & back 3-5 rb.) viâ (3¹/₂ V.) *Czerniaków,* with a beautiful little pilgrimage-church, built by Prince Stanislaus Lubomirski in 1691.

Willanów (*i.e.* Villa Nuova; Вилянóвъ) belongs to Count Branicki. From the station we proceed in a straight direction to (3 min.) the handsome domed church, built in 1857-72. Opposite is the *Želechowski Restaurant.*

The *Palace, 4 min. farther on, built in the Italian villa style, on a terraced height, lies at the entrance of the beautiful park, which contains a lake formed by an old arm of the Vistula, the river itself being fully 2 V. distant. The central structure and the two towers were erected by John III. Sobieski in 1678-94, from the plan of *J. Belotti;* the wings were added by later occupants.

The interior (adm., see p. 12) is handsomely fitted up in the style of the period of its erection. — GROUND FLOOR. From the *Ante-Chamber* of the main building we enter the *Velvet Room (II),* containing a magnificent chest which belonged to Sobieski. Adjacent is the room in which Sobieski died (June 17th, 1696), converted into a *Chapel* by the Countess Alexandra Potocka. In the *Amaranth Room (V)* are a fine card-table and three paintings by Fr. Silvestre. A cabinet here contains the swords of Stephen Bathory, Sigismund III., and Grand-Marshal Felix Potocki; in a second cabinet is a reliquary of John Casimir. The *Japanese Room (VI)* contains a chess-board that belonged to Sobieski. The walls of the *Cabinet of the King (VII)* are adorned with painted decorations. *Room VIII* has furniture in the style of Louis XIV. It contains a cabinet with a clay statuette of Moses, by Michael Angelo (?), and another with Limoges enamels, dishes of the 15th cent., and works by B. Palissy. *Room IX* (bedroom), with portraits of Sobieski, his son Constantine, and his daughter Theresa, contains a writing-table inlaid with ebony, presented by Pope Innocent XI. to Sobieski after his relief of Vienna (1683). In the *Room of the Mirrors (XI)* is a bust of Queen Marya Kazimiera, the wife of Sobieski. The *Dressing Room (XII)* has a fine painted ceiling, two pictures by Silvestre, and tasteful furniture. Among the portraits are Sobieski on horseback; Queen Marya Kazimiera; Marya Anna and Marya Clementina, granddaughters of Sobieski, the latter the wife of James Stuart, the Elder Pretender; Sobieski in the bosom of his family; Francis Bacon; Bishop Denhof. The remaining rooms contain a collection of Etruscan antiquities and paintings by Raphael Mengs, Jordaens, Guido Reni, Paolo Veronese, and others.

On the FIRST FLOOR are the so-called *Chinese Rooms.*

The *Library* contains numerous beautiful prayer-books, one of which belonged to Queen Bona Sforza.

About ²/₃ M. to the N.E. of Willanów lies *Morysinek,* another château of Count Branicki's, with a large deer-park.

By following a road leading to the S. from Willanów and then an avenue diverging from it to the right, we reach *Natolin,* a charming villa with a beautiful garden, also belonging to Count Branicki. It lies 6 M. from Warsaw and 2¹/₂ M. from the Vistula, on an eminence rising abruptly from the riverine plain.

On the RIGHT BANK OF THE VISTULA lie the battlefields of Bialolęka, Grochów, and Wawer. To the N., between Praga and (3¹/₂ M.) **Bialolęka,** lies the battlefield on which took place the great *Battle of Warsaw* (July 28-30th, 1656), in which the allied Swedish and Brandenburg troops, under Charles X. Gustavus and the Great Elector, routed the Polish army of 60,000 men and so gained possession of Warsaw. — To the E. of Praga are the battlefields of **Grochów** (Гро́ховъ) and **Wawer** (Ваве́ръ; light railway, see p. 11). About ³/₄ M. beyond the Moscow Barrier (Rogatki Moskiewskie; Pl. K 4, *I*) and 220 yds. to the left of the road rises a *Monument*, erected in 1846 by Tzar Nicholas I. on the spot where, during the battle of Grochów (1831), the Prince Albert Cuirassiers made their decisive charge. About ¹/₄ M. farther on, also to the left, is an *Obelisk* erected in the reign of Alexander I. Farther on extends the wide plain in which Joseph Poniatowski defeated the Austrians on April 25th, 1809, and where some of the closing scenes of the Polish drama of 1831 were also enacted.

From Warsaw to *Alexandrovo* (Berlin), see R. 1; to *Kalisz* (Breslau), see R. 2; to *Granitza* (Vienna), see R. 3; to *Mława* (Marienburg), see R. 5; to *Kovel* (Kiev, Odessa), see R. 6; to *Vilna* and *St. Petersburg*, see R. 9; to *Brest* and *Moscow*, see R. 32; to *Kiev* and *Odessa*, see R. 52.

5. From Warsaw to Mława *(Marienburg)* and Ciechocinek.

RAILWAY from Warsaw (Kovel Station) to (116 V.; 77 M.) *Mława* in 4 hrs.; from Mława to (93 M.) *Marienburg* in 4 hrs. This forms the most direct line between Warsaw and Danzig (Elbing, Königsberg). The Russian custom-house is at Mława, the German at Illowo.

The STEAMBOAT VOYAGE on the Vistula from Warsaw to (174 V.; 115 M.) *Ciechocinek* (15 hrs.; fare 3 rb. 60 cop.; no provisions supplied on board) cannot be recommended. The time-table varies according to the state of the water, so that careful inquiries should be made beforehand.

a. Railway from Warsaw to Mława.

Warsaw, see p. 9. The train crosses the *Vistula* by the railway-bridge mentioned at p. 22 and turns towards the N., traversing parts of the battlefields of 1656, 1794, and 1831. The line runs at no great distance from the right bank of the river, but the stream itself is seldom visible.

17 V. *Jabłonna,* Яблóнна (also reached by light railway, p. 11), a favourite resort of the Warsovians, with a fine old park and an interesting château, belonging to the Potocki family. — We now enter a wooded region. At (31 V.) *Nowy-Dwór* the train crosses a girder-bridge over the *Narew*, near its junction with the Vistula.

35 V. **Novo-Geórgiyevsk** (Ново-Гео́ргіевскъ; pop. 10,500) lies 2 M. to the S. of the fortress of that name (365 ft. above the sea, 100 ft. above the Vistula), constructed by Napoleon I. in 1807. Down to 1831 it was known as *Modlin*.

50 V. *Nasielsk,* Насѣ́льскъ.

About 26 V. (17 M.) to the N.E. of Nasielsk, and connected with it by diligence, lies **Pułtusk,** or Пулту́скъ (260 ft.; *Inn*, Jewish, in the market-place), a town of 18,600 inhab., on the right bank of the *Narew*. It contains several churches (one Lutheran) and convents, and is dominated by a large château on a hill, formerly occupied by the Bishops of Płock. In 1703 Charles XII. here defeated and captured a Saxon army under Steinau; and the French were here victorious over the Russians on Dec. 26th, 1806.

116 V. (77 M.) **Mława,** Млáва *(Railway Restaurant;* pop. 18,600), the Russian frontier-station. — Hence to *Marienburg,* see *Baedeker's Northern Germany.*

b. Steamer down the Vistula from Warsaw to Ciechocinek.

The **Vistula** (German *Weichsel,* Polish *Wisła,* Russian Вíсла) rises amid the Jablunka Mts., in Austrian Silesia, and is formed by the union of three streams, the White (Biala), the Little (Malinka), and the Black (Czarna) Vistula. Its total length is 715 M., of which 342 M. are in the Russian Empire. The stream enters Russia below Sandomierz and flows across the country in a wide curve, opening towards the W. As far as Pulawy the banks are steep and wooded. Farther on the banks become more level, and the river attains a width of $^1/_3$-$^2/_3$ M. Beyond Novo-Georgiyevsk the right bank again increases in height. As there are no artificial limitations of the channel within Russia, the flat banks are flooded at high water, which generally occurs thrice a year. The chief flood takes place at the beginning of March; those in summer, the so-called Janówka and Jakobówka (about the time of the festivals of St. John and St. James, June 24th and July 25th) are less serious. Navigation is considerably impeded at midsummer by sandbanks and shoal water.

Warsaw, see p. 9. The boats start at the Alexander Bridge (Pl. F, G, 3 ; *I*). The steamer passes under the railway-bridge and steams past the Citadel (p. 22), Bielany (p. 23), and Mlociny. — 15 V. *Jablonna* (railway, see p. 25).

31 V. *Noro-Geórgiyevsk,* see p. 25. The dark-green water of the Narew contrasts sharply with the yellow water of the Vistula.

34 V. *Zakroczym,* Закрóшимъ, a small town with 6900 inhab. on the right bank of the Vistula. The prettily situated Capuchin Monastery was converted into barracks in 1893.

55 V. *Czerwińsk* was the point where the Polish army under Wladislaus Jagiello crossed the Vistula in 1410 on its campaign against the Teutonic Order. The two handsome rubble towers of the former conventual church are conspicuous far and wide.

64 V. *Wyszogród,* Вышегрóдъ, a town with 4600 inhab. and a brisk trade, lies on the right bank of the Vistula, opposite the mouth of the *Bzura.* In the middle of the town rises a hill, formerly crowned by the castle of the Dukes of Masovia. The Protestant church formerly belonged to a Franciscan convent built in the 12th or 13th century. About $1^1/_2$ M. below Wyszogród is an old entrenchment known as the 'Okrągla Géra' ('round hill'). — To the S., 11 M. from Wyszogród, lies Żelazowa-Wola (p. 4).

101 V. (67 M.) **Płock,** Плоцкъ (290 ft.; *Polski,* R. $1^1/_4$-3, D. from $^1/_2$ rb.; *Warszawski;* cab to the town 60 cop.), one of the oldest towns in Poland, was formerly the seat of a bishop and the residence of the Dukes of Masovia and Poland, and is now the capital of a government. Pop. 31,000, mostly Jews. Plock is prettily situated on the right bank of the Vistula, here 200 ft. in height, and is divided into an Old Town and a New Town, the latter laid out

at the beginning of the 19th century. Among its numerous churches is the Romanesque *Cathedral* (early 12th cent.; restored in 1903), lying high above the river and containing the tombs of the Dukes of Poland and of Kings Wladislaus Hermann (1081-1102) and Boleslaus Krzywousty ('Wry Mouth'; 1102-39). It commands an attractive view. A little to the E. is the *Protestant Church*, built in the 17th cent., and formerly belonging to a Dominican monastery.

129 V. *Dobrżyń*, Добржинь (155 ft.), a small town on the right bank of the Vistula, with the ruins of an old castle which formed a frequent object of dispute between the Poles and the Teutonic Order. It was in the possession of the latter from 1233 to 1410. — Near *Skempe*, 17 M. to the N. of Dobrżyń, is a wonder-working image, to which numerous pilgrimages are made.

143 V. *Wloclawek*, see p. 3. — 158 V. *Bobrowniki*, a village on the right bank, with the ruins of an old castle, perched on a hill projecting into the river. — 164 V. *Nieszawa*, the Russian customs-station for the river-traffic (comp. p. 3).

174 V. (115 M.) *Ciechocinek*, see p. 3.

6. From Warsaw to Ivangorod and Kovel
(Kiev, Odessa).

315 V. (209 M.), Railway in 10 hrs. The ordinary trains start from the Kovel Station (p. 9), the Warsaw, Ivangorod, and Granitza express from the Brest Station (p. 9).

Warsaw, see p. 9. The railway crosses the *Vistula* and traverses the plain on its right bank, passing extensive forests, intermingled with cornfields.

26 V. *Otwock*, frequented by the Warsovians in summer. From (51 V.) *Pilawa* a branch-railway runs to (25 V.) Novo-Minsk (p. 248).

97 V. (64 M.) **Ivángorod**, Ивангородъ, Polish *Iwangród* (375 ft.; *Railway Restaurant*). The fortress, which lies 2 M. to the S., at the confluence of the *Wieprz* with the Vistula (here about 220 yds. wide), forms along with Novo-Georgiyevsk (p. 25) and Brest-Litovsk (p. 249) the important Polish Trilateral. — To Granitza, see pp. 7, 6; to Luków (Moscow), see p. 249; steamer, see p. 30.

Beyond (101 V.) *Fort Ivángorod* (Ивангородъ-Крѣпость) we cross the *Wieprz*.

119 V. (79 M.) **Novo-Alexandríya**, Ново-Александрія, Pol. **Puławy**. About 2 M. to the W. of the rail. station, on the right bank of the Vistula (cab 30, with two horses 50 cop.), lies the little town of *Novo-Alexandríya* (Hôtel-Restaurant Bristol). To reach it we turn to the right at the station and again after a few yards; after 8 min. we follow the highroad to the left (*not* crossing

the railway) direct to (35 min.) the Bristol Hotel. The Instytowka, 5 min. beyond the hotel, leads to the left to (5 min.) the former château of Prince Czartoryski, now occupied by an Institute of Forestry and Agriculture. In the shady park is the Temple of the Sibyls, built in imitation of the temple at Tivoli. — Steamer, see p. 30. — About 10 V. (7 M.) to the S.W. (cab there & back 1¹/₂ rb.) is Kazimierz (p. 30).

Beyond Pulawy the train turns to the S.E., and skirts the N. margin of the hill-district of Kazimierz (to the right). — About 3 M. from the station of (143 V.) *Nalęczów* (Налéнчовъ; cab 1¹/₂-2 rb.) lies the prettily situated watering-place of that name (710 ft.), with a hydropathic institute (pens. from 4, visitors' tax 8 rb.), a Kurhaus, and chalybeate and mud baths (65 cop. to 1 rb. 20 cop.).

164 V. (109 M.) **Lublin,** Люблинъ. — *Railway Restaurant.*
HOTELS. *Polski,* Kapucyńska, opposite the theatre, with restaurant, R. 1¹/₄-3, D. (1-4 p.m.) ³/₄ rb.; *Victoria,* Krakowskie Przedmieście; *Yevropéiskaya,* Krakowskie Przedmieście 29, R. from 85 cop. — CAFÉ in the Industrial Bank (p. 29). — CAB from the station to the town 45, per hr. 60 cop. — POST & TELEGRAPH OFFICE, Krakowskie Przedmieście.

Lublin (630 ft.), an important city with 65,800 inhab., stands on an eminence rising from the *Bystrzyca* and is surrounded by hills, lakes, and swamps. It is the capital of a province, the seat of a Roman Catholic bishop, and the headquarters of the 14th Army Corps. The old town, still retaining its ancient gates, rises above the lower-lying modern quarters.

Lublin was founded in the 10th century. Under the Jagiello dynasty the whole trade of Podolia, Volhynia, and Red Russia passed through the hands of its merchants, its markets were renowned far and wide, and its population increased to 70,000 souls. It became the seat of the Polish Royal Tribunal, and several diets were held within its walls, the most important being the Diet of 1569 in the reign of Sigismund Augustus, which lasted a whole year and completed the union of Poland and Lithuania. Even in the 18th cent. Lublin was one of the most important towns of Poland.

From the railway station, which lies to the S. of the town, we bear to the right, cross the Bystrzyca, and follow the Zamojska. At (25 min.) the N. end of this street, to the right, stands the *Roman Catholic Cathedral* (16th cent.). We then pass to the left through the *Trinity Gate* (fine view from its lofty belfry) and proceed direct to the market-place, in the middle of which is the *Palace of the Royal Tribunal* (14th cent.), now occupied by the Court of Arbitration. Or we may turn to the right beyond the Trinity Gate, follow the Jezuicka, turn to the left (3 min.), and reach the *Dominican Church,* with the Firlej Chapel, built by Casimir the Great. From the N.E. corner of the market-place the Grodzka descends to the E. to (5 min.) the *Old Castle* (r.), now a prison, with the Trinity Chapel built by Jagiello. — To the W. of the market-place is the *Cracow Gate,* through which and past the (r.) *Town Hall* and *Church of the*

Holy Ghost we reach the Krakowskie Przedmieście, the chief street of the town. Here stand an *Obelisk* (1825; r.), commemorating the union of Poland and Lithuania; the *Greek Catholic Cathedral* (r.); the *Post Office* (l.); the *Industrial Bank* (l.; 1900); and (standing back from the street) the *Lutheran Church* (r.; 1784). Behind the obelisk is the *Residence of the Governor*. At the end of the Krakowskie Przedmieście, ³/₄ M. from the market-place, are the pretty *Municipal Gardens*, with an unpretending café (military band on Thurs. & Sun.). — We now return along the Krakowskie Przedmieście to the Hotel Victoria and turn to the right (along the Kapucyńska) to visit the *Church of the Virgin* (Wizytkowski Church), built by Jagiello in 1426 to commemorate the victory of Tannenberg. The church has a N.W. tower and a crow-stepped gable. Opposite, to the N., is the *Theatre*, and a little to the E. is the *Bernardine Church*, containing the marble tomb of Oczko, the physician (16th cent.; at the end of the S. aisle). The Bernardyńska and the Zamojska lead hence to the S. back to the railway station.

A branch-railway runs to the N. from Lublin to (104 V.) *Łuków* (p. 249).

Beyond Lublin the train crosses the *Wieprż*.

231 V. (153 M.) **Kholm,** Холмъ, Polish **Chełm** (610 ft.; *Rail. Restaurant; Victoria Hotel,* R. ¹/₂-3 rb.; carr. & pair from the rail. station to the town 35, with rubber tyres 50 cop.), a provincial capital with 23,100 inhab. and the seat of a Greek Catholic bishop, lies in a fertile grain-growing district on the *Ucherka,* a feeder of the Bug. The festival of the Kholm Virgin is celebrated in the conspicuous cathedral on Sept. 8th (O.S.). Close by is a small museum of ecclesiastical antiquities. — About 5¹/₄ M. to the S.E. of the town is the German colony of *Kamień,* with a Lutheran church in the Gothic style (1885). — From Kholm to Brest-Litovsk, see p. 249.

Beyond (251 V.) *Dorochusk* (Дорогускъ) we cross the *Bug*.

On the Bug, 10 M. to the S. of Dorochusk, lies the small town of **Dubienka** (Дубенка), where Kościuszko, the 'Hero of Dubienka', offered a gallant but unavailing resistance to the overwhelming Russian forces on July 17th, 1792.

315 V. (209 M.) *Kovel,* Ковель, the junction of the railway from Brest-Litovsk to Kiev and Odessa (see p. 374).

7. The Vistula from Warsaw to Sandomierz.

210 V. (189 M.). Steamer-fares 2¹/₂, 1¹/₂ rb. — Comp. p. 25.

Warsaw, see p. 9. The steamer passes under the new Vistula bridge (p. 17).

34 V. (22¹/₂ M.) *Góra Kalváriya,* Гора Кальварія, a village

with a large convent, picturesquely situated $1^1/_8$ M. from the pier, on a hill rising steeply from the left bank of the Vistula. Light railway to Warsaw, see p. 11.

At *Mniszew* the Vistula receives the *Pilica* on the right.

75 V. *Maciejowice*, a village on the right bank, with a château belonging to Count Zamoyski. On Oct. 10th, 1794, Kościuszko was here defeated and taken prisoner by the Russians.

106 V. (70 M.) *Ivángorod*, see p. 27; the fortress is about 5 V. from the landing. On the left bank, $3^1/_4$ M. from the river, lies *Sieciechów*, one of the oldest Benedictine abbeys in Poland. — The steamer passes under the bridge of the Radom railway.

Near *Gniewoszew* (Гнѣвошóвъ), $6^1/_2$ M. to the S. of Ivangorod, the hills on each side begin to approach the river, and beyond Novo-Alexandriya the Vistula flows through a valley enclosed by the N. spurs of the Sandomierz Mts. on the W. and the S. Poland Hills on the E.

126 V. *Novo-Alexandriya*, Polish *Puławy*, see p. 27.

132 V. *Parchatka*, on the right bank.

138 V. *Kazimierz*, Казмержъ, an ancient town in the province of Lublin, pleasantly situated near the right bank of the Vistula and on the steep sides of a small lateral valley. It contains 4700 inhab., mostly Jews. The Gothic parish church was built by Casimir the Great (1333-70), the founder of the town. Outside the town is a ruined castle, also built by Casimir. — Opposite Kazimierz, on the left bank of the Vistula, lies *Janowiec*, with the ruins of an old castle of the Firlej family on a steep hill to the N.

194 V. *Zawichost*, Зáвихостъ, a small town on the left bank is the station of the Russian custom-house.

210 V. (139 M.) **Sandomierz** *(Sandomir)*, Сандóмиръ *(Polski Hotel)*, a small town of 7300 inhab. and the seat of a Roman Catholic bishop, is situated on a lofty bluff on the left bank of the Vistula, above the mouth of the navigable *San*. It was founded in 1236 and possesses an old cathedral and a castle built by Casimir the Great. In 1570 Sandomierz was the scene of a General Synod of the Protestants of Poland, which produced the Act of Union known as the Consensus Sandomiriensis.

Opposite Sandomierz, on the right bank of the Vistula, lies the Austrian village of *Nadbrzezie*, connected by railway with (121 M.) *Cracow*.

II. WESTERN RUSSIA (BALTIC PROVINCES).†

St. Petersburg time, which was adopted by the Baltic Provinces in 1899, is 61 min. in advance of that of Central Europe.

The **Baltic Provinces** of Courland, Livonia, and Esthonia are bounded on the W. by the *Baltic Sea,* and on the E. by the *West Russian Ridge,* which runs as a continuation of the Baltic Hills from the middle course of the Niemen to the Valdai Hills. The greater part of the provinces consists of a lowland district, but towards the coast they are intersected by several outliers of the great Russian plateau, which is interrupted by various broad openings. The most important river is the *Dwina* or *Dvina* (German *Düna;* Russian Западная Двина́, *i.e.* Western Dvina; Lettish *Dáugáwa*), which flows into the Gulf of Riga, but is navigable in its short lower course only. In the S. the inhabitants are Letts, in

---

† The lettering of the maps and plans in this section (except in the town-plans of Vilna, Pskov, and Narva) is given in German, that being the predominant tongue in the Baltic Provinces.

the N. Esthonians; in the towns, however, and among the landed
proprietors, clergy, and the like, are many Germans, while there
are also Russians, Poles, and Swedes. The chief occupations are
grain-growing and cattle-raising. Courland and Livonia possess
extensive forests of pine, fir, and birch. Of late an active industrial life has sprung up in Riga, Libau, and Reval. Railways
furnish the ports with a wide 'hinterland'.

COURLAND, the southernmost of the Baltic Provinces, 10,237
sq. M. in area, consists of a plateau, 625 ft. high, jutting out into
the Gulf of Riga between the *Niemen* and the wide depression of
the *Dvina*. — LIVONIA, 18,154 sq. M. in area, stretches N. from
the Dvina, across the *Aa-Plateau* (Livonian Switzerland) and the
East Livonian Heights, to a depression through which runs the
Embach, a river connecting *Lake Wirzjärw* with *Lake Peipus*.
The *Great Munamägi* (1063 ft.), one of the East Livonian Heights,
is the highest summit in the Baltic Provinces. The inhabitants of
Livonia are (as in Courland) Letts, with some Esthonians in the N.
part of it. — ESTHONIA, the northernmost of the Baltic Provinces,
7817 sq. M. in area, consists of a tableland of Silurian limestone,
which descends abruptly to the coast in the so-called 'Glint' (p. 81)
and is overlain in the S. by Devonian sandstone and dolomite strata.
The islands of *Dagö* and *Oesel*, in the Baltic Sea, form a prolongation of this tableland.

The LETTS, who (like the Esthonians) belong to the Lutheran church,
live in separate farms (mahja) which are often grouped together in pairs,
but seldom in greater numbers. Their wooden dwelling-houses, barns
(rihja), corn-lofts (klehts), and bath-houses (pirts) still retain their ancient appearance. Few traces of the old national dress have been retained, though sandals of leather, tied round the ankle with strips of
flax, are still often seen, while shoes of bast also occur. — The ESTHONIANS
belong to the Mongolian race. Their speech is poor in the expression of
abstract ideas, but their folk-lore is exceptionally rich. The dwelling-
house of the Esthonians, with wooden cross-bars on the top of the thatched
roof (wares-pun), consists of three parts — the living-room, the corn-loft
(serving in winter as a kitchen and often also as living-room), and the
threshing-floor, used in winter as stables. Round the dwelling-house lie
the barns (ait), the cow-stable (laut), the summer-kitchen (koda), and the
bathroom (saun). The farmyard (õue) and the fields are surrounded by
lattice fences. In the less advanced regions (on the islands and among
the Esthonians in the government of Pskov or Pleskau) the picturesque
national costume is still retained, but it is giving way rapidly to newer
fashions, especially among the men.

Chronological Outline of the History of the Baltic Provinces.

In the middle of the 12th cent. the Germans established themselves on the banks of the lower Dvina.

1188. Foundation of the bishopric of Üxküll in Livonia; introduction of Christianity by *Bishop Meinhard*, an
Augustine monk from Segeberg in Holstein.

1201. Foundation of Riga and (1202) of the Order of the Sword by *Bishop Albert.*—1207. Division of Livonia between Bishop Albert and the first Master of the Order, *Venno.*

1219. *Waldemar II.* of Denmark takes Lindanissa (Reval) from the Esthonians.

1237. Union of the Order of the Sword with the Teutonic Order.

1245. Appointment of an archbishop for Livonia and Prussia; in 1251 Riga is chosen as his see.

1330. *Eberhard von Munheim,* Master of the Order, conquers Riga. Predominance of the Order.

1346. Esthonia sold to the Teutonic Order by Denmark.

1422. Samogitia (belonging partly to Livonia, partly to Prussia) is lost to the Order; Livonia and Prussia are thereby isolated from each other.

1452. Agreement between the Archbishop and the Order at Kirchholm, by which the government of Riga is divided between them.

1494-1535. Under the rule of *Master Walter von Plettenberg* the Teutonic Order reaches the zenith of its power.

1522. Introduction of the Reformation into Livonia and Riga.

1558-1561. Invasion of *Ivan IV.,* 'the Terrible'. Loss of the territories of the Order. *Master Gotthard Kettler* becomes hereditary Duke of Courland and Semgallen; Livonia is annexed to Poland, Esthonia to Sweden, and Ösel to Denmark.

1562. Grant by Sigismund Augustus of privileges whereby Livonia is guaranteed civil and religious freedom and right to use the German tongue.

1600. Beginning of the Polish-Russo-Swedish war, ended by the Peace of Stolbovo in 1617.

1621. Conquest of Riga by *Gustavus II. Adolphus* of Sweden; Livonia, with the exception of the Polish districts, falls under his sway.

1656. *Tzar Alexis Mikháilovitch* devastates Livonia and lays siege to Riga (without success).

1700-1721. The Northern War; the *Peace of Nystad* (1721) assigns Livonia and Esthonia to Russia. *Peter the Great* confirms the privileges granted by Sigismund Augustus.

1795. Courland annexed to Russia.

1819. Abolition of serfdom in Livonia.

1881-1894. Introduction under *Alexander III.* of the Russian language and judicial system.

8. From Berlin to St. Petersburg.

1017 M. Express train in 26 hrs.; fares 115 ℳ, 73 ℳ 15 pf. (exclusive of the charge for reserved seat, see below). The North or Nord
Express (see p. xvii) takes 25¹/₂ hrs. (fare 187 ℳ 90 pf.). — FROM BERLIN
(Stadtbahn stations) TO WIRBALLEN VIÂ DIRSCHAU AND KÖNIGSBERG, 462 M.,
express train in 10¹/₂ hrs. (fares 62 ℳ·80, 37 ℳ 70 pf.; sleeping berth
12 or 10 ℳ; tickets for the latter may be obtained of the conductor,
but it is safer to order them in advance). Another express runs viâ
Posen, Thorn, and Insterburg. — FROM WIRBALLEN TO ST. PETERSBURG,
837 V. (555 M.), express train in 15 hrs. (fares 24 rb. 20, 16 rb. 40 cop.;
seat-ticket, p. xxiii, 1 rb. 80 cop.; sleeping-car 6 rb. 70 cop., 5 rb.); ordinary
train in 28 hrs. (fares 19 rb. 50, 11 rb. 70 cop.). — FROM WIRBALLEN TO
VILNA, 179 V. (119 M.), express train in 3 hrs. (fares 8 rb. 3, 5 rb. 44 cop.;
seat-ticket 1¹/₂ rb.), ordinary train in 5¹/₂ hrs. (fares 6 rb. 48, 3 rb. 89 cop.).
— FROM VILNA TO ST. PETERSBURG, 658 V. (436 M.), express train in
11¹/₂ hrs. (fares 19 rb. 5, 12 rb. 25 cop.; seat-ticket 1 rb. 80 cop.; sleeper
5 rb. 25, 3 rb. 95 cop.), ordinary train in 19¹/₂ hrs. (fares 17 rb., 10 rb. 20 cop.).
  Passports, see p. xviii. — *Russian Money* (p. xiv) may be obtained at
the money-changers' stalls at Eydtkuhnen or Wirballen, but it is better
to procure it at Berlin before starting.
  To ST. PETERSBURG BY STEAMER (fares incl. meals): from *Stettin*
(70 ℳ) once weekly in 65 hrs.; from *Lübeck* (60 ℳ) twice weekly in
80 hrs.; from *Stockholm* (36 kr.) four times weekly in 42 hrs. Comp.
pp. xviii, 201.

From Berlin to (462 M.) *Eydtkuhnen*, see *Baedeker's Northern
Germany*. — **Eydtkuhnen** *(Welter's Hotel*, R. from 2¹/₄ ℳ; *Hôtel
de Russie)*, a village with 5500 inbab., on the frontier-stream *Lepone*,
is the last Prussian station. The train halts here for ¹/₄ hr. (in the
reverse direction 1 hr.).

1 V. (from Eydtkuhnen) **Wirballen** (Вержболóво; *Railway
Restaurant*, with bedrooms, fair) is the first Russian station. Passports and baggage are examined here (see pp. xviii, xix), causing a halt
of 1 hr. — When the customs revision is finished, the traveller should
engage a porter (p. xx) to take care of the small articles and bring
them afterwards to the train; he should give him his seat-number.

As far as Kovno the railway lies through Polish territory, traversing the province of *Suwalki*, which is included in the General
Government of Warsaw. The N. part of the province is inhabited
by Lithuanians, the S. by Poles, intermixed with whom, especially
in the towns, are numerous Russians, Germans, and Jews. The
district to the N. and S. of the Niemen is intersected by ranges
of small hills and dotted with small lakes. It forms a continuation
of the terminal moraine ridge of E. Prussia, which is crossed
obliquely by the railway in its course through Lithuania.

16 V. *Wilkowyszki*. The small town of this name, 1¹/₃ M. to the
S. of the station, was the headquarters of Napoleon on June 22nd,
1812, before he crossed the Niemen, and here he dated his procla-
mation announcing the beginning of a 'Second Polish War'.
  At the beginning of the campaign the 'Grande Armée' consisted of
684,000 men. The total number of French troops that eventually crossed

the Russian frontier was 612,000, including 300,000 French, 190,000 Germans, 90,000 Poles and Lithuanians, and 32,000 Italians, Spaniards, and Portuguese, with 1242 field-pieces and 130 siege-guns. In December, 1812, only 110,000 were left. — The entire military force of Russia amounted to 480,000 men, of whom 428,000 actually came into touch with the French. The total loss of the Russians amounted to 200,000 men.

Beyond (28 V.) *Pilwiszki* and (63 V.) *Mavrútzi* we reach the *Niemen* (Нѣманъ), which the train crosses by an iron tubular bridge, $^1/_4$ M. long.

83 V. (55 M.) **Kovno**, Ковна. — The *Railway Station* (restaurant) lies to the E. of the town. — Hotels. *Métropole* (R. $^1/_2$-3 rb.), *Lewinsohn*, *Versailles* (R. from 75 cop.), all three in the Nikoláyevski Prospékt. — Restaurant in the small *Municipal Garden*, Nikoláyevski Prospékt. — Cab from the station to the old town 50, to the new town 40 cop. — Tramway from the station through the town to the market-place (3 V.; fares 10,6 cop.). — Steamers, starting at the bridge-of-boats, ply viâ Georgenburg (25 cop.) to Tilsit (an attractive trip).

Kovno (110 ft.), the capital of a government of the same name, is prettily situated on a tongué of land between the *Viliyá* (Вилія) and the Niemen, the banks of which are here about 200 ft. in height. The town, which contains 88,000 inhab. (one-half of whom are Jews), consists of the old town and the new town, the latter stretching up the river. It is strongly defended by advanced works.

Kovno, supposed to have been founded in the 13th cent. (?), was in the 14th cent. a great bone of contention between Lithuania and the Teutonic Order. It passed, together with Lithuania, into the hands of Poland under Wladislaus Jagiello, and in the 15-16th cent. it became the centre of the export-trade from Poland and Lithuania to Russia. An English Trading Factory was also established here. In 1655 Kovno was plundered and burned down by a Russian army under Tzar Alexis. At the Third Partition of Poland in 1795 it was finally annexed to the Russian empire. On June 23rd, 1812, the French army reached the left bank of the Niemen, opposite Kovno; and a hill near the village of (3 V.) *Ponyémon* (p. 36) is still known as *Napoleon's Hill*.

From the rail. station we follow the Mikháilovski Prospékt, turning after 10 min. to the left into the Pestchánaya. In 4 min. more we take the Kíyevskaya to the right and reach (6 min.) the Greek Catholic *Cathedral of SS. Peter and Paul*, completed in 1895. Turning to the left at this point, we reach the Nikoláyevski Prospékt, the chief thoroughfare of the town. At (18 min.) the W. end of the Prospékt we turn to the left and enter the Old Town through the Peterbúrgskaya, a little to the E. of which stands the old *Chapel of St. Gertrude*. We then follow the Vílenskaya, in which (r.; 12 min.) is the Gothic *Church of SS. Peter and Paul*, the largest Roman Catholic church in Lithuania, built of brick in the 15th century. Close by is the Market Place, with a pyramidal *Monument* in cast-iron, erected in 1843 in commemoration of the discomfiture of the French in 1812. On the W. side is the *Town Hall*, a building of the 16th cent. (rebuilt in 1638), with a tower. A little to the W. of the market-place is the *Church of St. George* (1471). To the S. is a bridge-of-boats across the Niemen. To the E. of the bridge is the *Lutheran Church*, built in 1686 in the early-Gothic style. — The industrial suburb of *Shantzi* is adjoined by large barracks. Opposite lies *Ponyémon* (p. 35), best reached by the railway-bridge.

About 21 M. to the S. of Kovno (motor-omnibus 1 rb. 90 cop.) lies **Birshtáni** (Бирштаны; *Stáraya, Nóvaya,* and *Málaya Gostinitza,* R. 15-35 rb. a month), with saline springs, pleasantly situated on the right bank of the Niemen (season from May 20th to Aug. 20th, O.S.). Visitors' tax 5 rb.

Beyond Kovno the train threads a long tunnel and skirts the Niemen (right) for a short distance.

117 V. (78 M.) **Koshedári** (Кошедары; *Railway Restaurant*), the junction of the line viâ Muravyevo (Libau, p. 49) to Riga (R. 10 b).

163 V. (128 M.) **Landvaróvo** *(Railway Restaurant)*, the junction of the St. Petersburg & Warsaw Railway (p. 46).

We now approach the valley of the *Viliyá*, penetrate the *Ponári Hills* by a tunnel, and reach (179 V. or 119 M.) *Vilna.*

[Those who leave their compartment during the long wait here should hire a porter to guard their belongings (comp. p. xx).]

Vilna, Вильна, Polish *Wilno.* — *Railway Restaurant*, D. 1 rb., fair.

HOTELS. *Geórgiyevskaya* (Pl. a; A, 2), Geórgiyevski Prospékt 20, with restaurant, fair, R. 1-10 rb., B. 40 cop., D. (2-6 p.m.) 1¼ rb., omn. 60 cop.; *Palace Hotel* (Pl. d; B, 4), Bolshaya 9, new; *Grand-Hôtel* (Pl. e; B, 5), Ostrovorótnaya 5, with restaurant; *Bristol* (Pl. f; A, 2), Geórgiyevski Prospékt 22; *Yevrópa* (Pl. b; A, B, 4), Blagovyéshtchenskaya 1, with restaurant, R. 1-8 rb., B. 45 cop., D. (2-5 p.m.) ³/₄-1 rb., omn. 60 cop., well spoken of; *Continent* (Pl. c; B, 4), Nyemétzkaya 37, opposite the theatre, with restaurant, R. from 1 rb., B. 45 cop., D. (1-6 p.m.) ¹/₂-1 rb. — *Restaurant Narushevitch*, Bolshaya 86 (1st floor), a little to the E. of the theatre (Pl. B, 4). — PLEASURE RESORTS. *Bernadinski Garden* (Pl. D, 3), with military music in summer; *Botanical Gardens* (Pl. C, 2), with vaudeville stage. — POST & TELEGRAPH OFFICE (Pl. B, C, 3), Bolshaya.

CAB from the rail. station to the town 35, with two horses 50 cop. (at night, 12-7, 40 & 60 cop.); per drive in the town, 20 cop.; per hour 50 cop., with two horses 1 rb., each additional hour 45 and 90 cop.

TRAMWAYS (fare 5 cop.) from the railway station (Pl. A, B, 6) through the town to the Zelyóni Bridge (Зелёный мостъ; Pl. A, 1); from the Pretchístenski Cathedral (Pl. C, 4), along the Geórgiyevski Prospékt to the Nikoláyevski Bridge (beyond Pl. A, 1); from the Stanislaus Cathedral (Pl. B, 2) to the suburb of Antokól (beyond Pl. D, 1).

CHIEF ATTRACTIONS (3 hrs.). Ostra Brama Chapel (p. 37); Cathedral of St. Stanislaus (p. 38); Castle Hill (p. 38).

Vilna (525 ft.), the capital of the General Government of the same name and formerly the capital of Lithuania, is pleasantly situated, with its suburbs *(Antokól, Zaryétchye, Pogulyánka,* and *Lukíshki),* on a group of sand and clay hills (820 ft.) rising at the confluence of the *Viléika* and the Viliyá. It is now an important railway and commercial centre, with a trade in timber and ca.

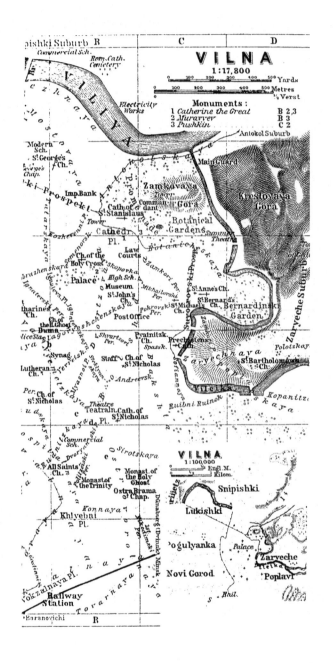

192,700 Jewish, Lithuanian, and Polish inhabitants. It contains
the headquarters of the 3rd Army Čorps and is the seat of a Greek
Catholic archbishop and of a Roman Catholic bishop. The streets
in the older parts are narrow and badly paved, but contain many
quaint old churches.

The history of Vilna stretches back to the earliest times, when it
was a great centre of Pagan worship. A sacred fire was kept constantly
burning at the foot of the hill upon which Gedymín, Grand-Prince of
Lithuania, built his castle. In 1323 Vilna was raised to the dignity of a
town and was made the capital of Lithuania. The Grand-Prince Wladislaus
Jagiello, who became King of Poland in 1386, introduced Christianity in
1387 and erected a cathedral (St. Stanislaus) on the site of the heathen
temple. Vilna is afterwards often mentioned in the history of the
struggles of the Poles with the Teutonic Order, the Tartars, and the
Russian Grand-Prince. During the 17-18th cent. Vilna was frequently
pillaged by the Swedes, Russians, and Cossacks, and lost much of its
former importance. In 1794 it offered a gallant resistance to the Russian
army, but was captured on Aug. 12th after a severe bombardment. At
the opening of the war of 1812 Napoleon fixed upon the line of the
Niemen as his base of operations and made Vilna (at the point of intersection of the roads from Königsberg and Warsaw to St. Petersburg
and Moscow) the strategic centre of the French lines. On his retreat
from Russia he again visited Vilna, which he finally left in disguise on
the night of Nov. 24th (Dec. 6th), 1812.

From the railway station (Pl. A, B, 6), which lies at the S. end of
the city, we follow the Vokzálnaya to the right (E.) and turn to the
left into (6 min.) the Ostrovorótnaya (Pl. B, 5, 6). Here stands the
Óstruiya Voróta (Polish, Ostra Brama), a town-gate of the 16th century. Above this gate, on the N. side (entrance), is the **Ostra Brama
Chapel** (Pl. B, C, 5), containing a large wonder-working image of the
Virgin, which is highly revered by Greek and Latin Catholics alike.
The street is always filled with kneeling worshippers; but the image
is not visible except during divine service, when the chapel windows
are opened. Beyond the gate, to the right, is the R. C. *Church of
St. Theresa*, with a marble façade, founded in 1626. Farther on,
also to the right, is the Greek Catholic *Monastery of the Holy Ghost*
(Свято-Ду́ховскій монастьірь), founded in 1597, opposite which
is the *Monastery of the Trinity* (Свято-Тро́ицкій монастьірь),
dating from the end of the 15th cent. and belonging to the same
confession. — The Ostrovorótnaya ends at the THEATRE SQUARE (Pl.
B, 4), with the *Theatre*, originally the town hall, rebuilt by Gutze-
vitch in 1783, and converted to its present uses in 1845. Opposite
rises the imposing *Cathedral of St. Nicholas*, erected in 1596-1604
and in the hands of the Greek Catholics since 1832. — At the S.W.
corner of the Theatre Square begins the Nycmétzkaya or 'German
Street', now exclusively occupied by Jews but containing the
Lutheran Church (Pl. A, 4), built in 1555.

The main thoroughfare of the city, named the Bolshaya, runs
to the N. from the Theatre Square. To the right stands the *Church
of St. Nicholas* (Pl. B, C, 4), founded at the beginning of the 16th

century. Farther on, in the midst of a small square, is the *Pyát-nitzkaya Church* (Pl. B, 4), built in 1345 and last restored in 1865. — From this point we proceed to the E. through the Spásskaya to the *Pretchistenski Cathedral* (Pl. C, 4), which, after a career full of vicissitudes, was rebuilt in 1867. — Farther on in the Bolshaya, to the left, is the R. C. *Church of St. John* (Pl. B, 3), begun by Jagiello in 1388, completed in 1426, restored in 1571 and 1826.

Beyond St. John's the Mikháilovski Pereúlok leads to the right from the Bolshaya to the handsome *Church of St. Anne* (Pl. C, 3), a Gothic brick structure of the close of the 14th century. Adjacent is the *Church of SS. Bernard and Francis,* founded in 1469 by King Casimir.

The Bolshaya ends at the CATHEDRAL SQUARE (Pl. B, 2, 3), in which is a bronze *Statue of Empress Catherine II.* (Pl. 1), by Antokólski (1903). — On the N. side of the square stands the R.C. **Cathedral of St. Stanislaus,** a building in the form of a Greek temple, founded in 1387 on the site of a sanctuary of Perkunas, a pagan god of light. The lower part of the tall belfry is said to date from the 14th century. Six massive Doric columns form the portico. In the pediment is a group of the Sacrifice of Noah; above it are statues of SS. Helena (with the cross), Stanislaus, and Casimir. The whole church was restored in 1801.

INTERIOR. A baroque marble chapel to the right of the high-altar contains the silver coffin of St. Casimir and eight silver statues of Polish kings and queens. On the E. wall (l.) is the tomb of Grand-Prince Witowt (d. 1430); under the epitaph is a picture of the Virgin, presented to him by the Greek emperor Manuel Palæologus in 1386. The vault to the right of the tomb is the oldest part of the church. There are also numerous monuments of scions of distinguished Polish and Lithuanian families.

On the **Castle Hill** (Зáмковая горá; Pl. C, 2; adm. 3 cop.), which rises 165 ft. above the Viliyá and is most easily ascended from the Botanic Gardens (7 min. to the tower), are the fragmentary remains of a castle built by Gedymín (p. 37). The tower (rfmts.) commands a view of the city and its surroundings.

In the Geórgiyevski Prospékt, leading to the N.W. from the Cathedral Square, are the *Imperial Bank,* the *District Court* (1898), and the *Girls' High School.*

The Dvortzóvaya leads to the S. from the Cathedral Square to the palace and the buildings of the former university. The PALACE (Pl. B, 3), occupied by the archbishops in the 16-18th cent., is now the residence of the Governor-General. Here also is the *Muravyév Museum,* with reminiscences of Count M. Muravyév, who was Governor of Vilna in 1863-65 and suppressed the Polish revolt (entrance through the office of the Governor-General, Dvortzóvaya 6, first floor). In front of it is a bronze statue, by Gryaznov (1898), of *Count Muravyév* (Pl. 2). — Opposite the palace, to the E., is the former UNIVERSITY (Dvortzóvaya 5), established as an academy by Stephen Bathory in 1578, made a university by Alexander I. in 1803, and suppressed in 1832. On the groundfloor, to the left, is the *Public Library* (open on week-days 12 - 8; closed ·in July, but accessible to strangers), which contains 220,000 vols. and 10,000 MSS. (most important exhibited in show-cases). To the right is the Zoological Department; on the first floor is the *Antiquar̃ian Museum* (Музéй дрéвностей; Pl. B, 3; open on Sun., 12 - 3, except in July, to strangers at other times also); it contains numerous objects of the stone, bronze, and iron ages, coins, weapons, portraits,· and other paintings.

In the suburb of Antokól (beyond Pl. D, 1; tramway, see p. 36) are the *Church of SS. Peter & Paul,* prettily situated on a slope, and completed in 1684, and the *Military Hospital,* built in 1691 as the château of the Princes Sapieha.

About 5 M. to the N. of Vilna (pleasant steamer trip; 35 cop.) is the manor of *Verki,* picturesquely situated on the high right bank of the Viliyá, with a garden in the English style. On the bank of the river is a restaurant.

From Vilna to Rovno, 480 V. (318 M.), express train in 10¹/₂ hrs. The railway traverses the provinces of Vilna, Minsk, and Volhynia, and its S. part intersects the Polyesye (p. 249) from N. to S. — 49 V. *Binyakóni* (Rail. Restaurant); 89 V. *Lida* (Rail. Restaurant; p. 249), a district-town with 14,800 inhabitants. Beyond (113 V.) *Nyemán* we cross the *Niemen.* 138 V. *Novogrudok* (Rail. Restaurant). — 188 V. (125 M.) **Baránovitchi** (Барановичи; *Rail. Restaurant*), the junction of the railway from Warsaw to Moscow (p. 250) and of a branch-line to Bialystok (see p. 45).— 297 V. *Luninétz* (Rail. Restaurant), the junction of the railway from Brest-Litovsk to Bryansk (p. 249). We cross the *Pripet.* — 397 ·V. *Sarni* (Rail. Restaurant), the junction of the Kovel and Kiev railway (p. 374). — 435 V. *Mokvin* (Rail. Restaurant). — 480 V. (318 M.) *Rovno,* see p. 374.

From Vilna to Romni, 711 V. (471 M.), railway in 20 hrs. — At (9 V.) *Novo - Viléisk* (p. 40) this line diverges to the S.E. from the St. Petersburg line. — 79 V. *Zalyésye* (Залѣсье; Rail. Restaurant); 101 V. *Molodétchno* (p. 249); 173 V. *Minsk* (p. 250); 273 V. *Ósipovitchi* (Rail. Restaurant). — 313 V. (208 M.) **Bobrúísk** or Бобруйскъ *(Rail. Restaurant; Berézina.* R. from 1 rb., D. from 60 cop.; *Syévernaya),* a town in the province of Minsk, lies 2¹/₂ V. (cab 30 cop.) from the railway, in the midst of the forests of the *Polyésye* (p. 249) and on the commanding right bank of the *Berézina,* here 330 ft. in width. About half of the 40,800 inhab. are Jews. Down to 1897 Bobruisk was strongly fortified. — We cross the Berézina. 374 V. *Zhlobin* (Жлобинъ; Railway Restaurant); hence to Vitebsk, see pp. 258, 257. The train crosses the *Dnieper.* — 454 V. (301 M.) **Homel** (Гомель; *Rail. Restaurant; Continent,* Zámkovaya, R. from 75, D. from 60 cop.; *Syévernaya,* Rumyántzevskaya 30; cab to the town 20, with two horses 30, per drive 15 or 25, per hr. 30 or 45, in spring and autumn 5-15 cop. more) is a town in the government of Mohilév, with 97,900 inhab. and a considerable trade. It lies on the lofty right bank of the *Sozh,* a tributary of the Dnieper. On the terrace of Prince Paskévitch's château (on the Sozh; 25 min. from the station viâ the Zámkovaya) is an equestrian statue of Joseph Poniatowski, cast in bronze from Thorvaldsen's model and originally destined for Warsaw. The monument of Chancellor N. P. Rumyántzev (d. 1826), in the adjacent Cathedral of SS. Peter & Paul, is by Canova. Railway to Brest-Litowsk and to Bryansk, see p 249; steamer to Kiev (p. 378). — 549 V. *Snóvskaya* (Rail. Restaurant). We cross the *Desná.* 638 V. *Bakhmatch* (Бахмачъ; Rail. Restaurant), see p. 376. — 711 V. (471 M.) *Romni,* see p. 391.

. From Vilna to *Warsaw,* see R. 9.

CONTINUATION OF THE RAILWAY TO ST. PETERSBURG. The first
station beyond Vilna is (187 V.) **Novo-Viléisk** (Ново-Вилейскъ ;
Railway Restaurant), the junction of the line from (Libau) Vilna
to Romni (see p. 39). — From (251 V.) *Novo-Svyentzyáni* (Railway Restaurant) a light railway runs to the N.W. to (136 V.)
Ponevyezh (p. 48).

334 V. *Kalkuhnen* (Калку́ны; Rail. Restaurant), the junction
of the line to (187 V.) Radzivilishki (p. 48). — The train now crosses
the *Dvina* (p. 31) by an iron bridge and enters the station of
Dünaburg.

340 V. (225 M.) **Dünaburg**, Russian *Dvinsk*, Двинскъ. — RAIL-
WAY STATIONS. *St. Petersburg Station* (fair restaurant), 1¹/₃ M. from the
town, for St. Petersburg, Vilna, Wirballen, and Warsaw; *Riga Station*
(restaurant), for Riga (R. 10 a) and Moscow (R. 33 a). The two stations are
connected by a junction line 2 M. long. — HOTELS. *Central*, Alexándro-
Névskaya, R. from 60 cop. to 2¹/₂ rb., B. 50, D. (1-5 p.m.) 50-75 cop.;
Grand-Hôtel (Большая гостиница), Ofitzérskaya, R. 2-5 rb., B. 50 cop.;
Kapp, at the Riga Station, R. 1-2 rb., B. 50 cop., D. (12-4 p.m.) ¹/₂-1¹/₄ rb.
— CABS. From the St. Petersburg Station to the town, first-class 50, second-
class 40 cop.; from the Riga Station 20 or 15 cop.; at night 50 per cent
more; per hr. 50 cop.

Dünaburg (330 ft.), built by Stephen Bathory in 1582 and
officially named *Dvinsk* since 1893, is a fortified depôt and capital
of a district in the government of Vitebsk (Polish Lithuania). It
lies on the right bank of the Dvina (German, Düna), carries on a
brisk trade in flax, grain, and timber, and is an important railway
centre. Pop. 110,900. — About 1¹/₄ M. from the St. Petersburg Station
and 3 M. from the Riga Station lies the Greek Catholic *Garrison
Church*, a two-towered structure of the middle of the 18th cent.,
formerly belonging to the Jesuits. The barrel-vaulting of the nave
is borne by piers, each of which is articulated by four slender
columns. The choir-ending is rectangular. The Lutheran Church
was built in 1892.

On the Warsaw highroad, 9 M. to the S.W. (carr. 2 rb.), lies *Meddum*,
a climatic resort on a small lake. — Amid pine-woods on the Dvina, 5 M.
to the W. of Dünaburg (steamboat in ¹/₂ hr.; fare 15 cop.), lies the open-
air resort of *Pogulyanka*, with a hydropathic institute.

Beyond Dünaburg the railway traverses the government of
Vitebsk, the scenery of which offers little variety. 401 V. *Antonópol*
(Rail. Restaurant); 419 V. *Ryézhitza* (Rail. Restaurant; to Moscow,
see R. 33 b), with the picturesque ruins of the castle of *Rositten*
(right); 460 V. *Kórsovka* (Rail. Restaurant). From (491 V.) *Puita-
lovo* (Rail. Restaurant) a branch-line runs viâ *Marienhausen*, with
a ruined castle of the Archbishops of Riga, to (63 V.) *Sita*. — On
passing the boundary of the government of Pskov, we enter Great
Russia proper. We cross the *Velíkaya*. — 531 V. *Ostrov* (Rail.
Restaurant), a town of 7300 inhab., carrying on a brisk trade in flax,
great quantities of which are grown in the government of Pskov.

About 52 V. (35 M.) to the S.E. of Ostrov, and reached viâ (30 V.) *Novgoródki*, lies the village of *Tabalenétz*, with the Svyatogórski Convent, where Pushkin lies buried (comp. p. 115).

580 V. (384 M.) **Pskov,** Псковъ, Ger. *Pleskau* (Plan, see p. 42). —*Railway Restaurant*, good. — Hotels. *London* (Pl. b; B, 2), Sérgiyev-skaya, R. 1-3, D. ³/₄ rb., very fair; *St. Petersburg* (Pl. a; B, 2), Sérgiyev-skaya, R. 1-2 rb., B. 50, D. (1-6 p.m.) 75 cop. — Restaurant at the *Kutúzov Garden* (Pl. 20; B, C, 2, 3). — *Military Band* thrice weekly in the Muni-cipal Garden (Pl. C, 3). — Electric Tramway from the rail. station through the town (6 cop.). — Cab from the railway station to the town 30, per drive 15, per hr. 50 cop.

Pskov, an ancient town with 36,000 inhab. and an important trade in flax, the capital of a government of the same name, and the seat of a Greek Catholic archbishop, is situated on both sides of the *Velíkaya* (German *Muddau*) and the *Psková*. Pskov is divided into four parts: the Kremlin (see below), with the adjoining forti-fications by Dóvmont; the town proper, built in the 14-15th cent. between the Velíkaya and the Psková; the Zápskovye, or quarter on the right bank of the Psková, reached by an arched iron bridge (1898; fine view of the cathedral); and the Závelitchye, or quarter on the left bank of the Velíkaya, connected with the town by two bridges. All of these quarters, except the last, are surrounded by partly preserved walls and towers. — The town contains a Lutheran church (Pl. 12; B, 3), a Roman Catholic church (Pl. 10; B; 3), and 45 Greek Catholic churches.

Pskov, which is said to have been founded in 965, was united with Novgorod to form a bishopric in 992. A republic like Novgorod (comp. p. 262), Pskov rose in the middle ages to be the emporium of a con-siderable trade with Germany and other countries, and it became a member of the Hanseatic League. The German factory lay on the left bank of the Velíkaya, and the German merchants were debarred from crossing the bridge-of-boats which connected it with the town. During the Mongolian invasions of Russia the town asserted its independence and it also beat off the attacks of the Teutonic Order, under the leadership of the cou-rageous Lithuanian Prince Dóvmont (p. 43). Walter von Plettenberg, Grand Master of the Teutonic Order, failed in his attempt to capture Pskov in 1502, but won a victory over the Russians at the lake of Smólina on his way back to Livonia (Sept. 13th, 1502). In 1510 Grand-Prince Vasili III. Ivánovitch at last succeeded in destroying the independence of the city and incorporated the republic with the principality of Moscow. In 1570 Tzar Iván the Terrible advanced against Pskov, whose inhabitants he suspected of treason, but he allowed himself to be turned from his plan of destroying the city by the representations of the monk Nicholas Salos, who feigned madness to effect his end.

The *Kremlin* (Кремль; Pl. B, 1, 2), situated in the angle be-tween the Velíkaya and the Psková, is surrounded by a limestone wall, dating from 1266. It commands a good view of the town and of the valleys of the two rivers. — In the middle of the Kremlin rises the conspicuous —

*Cathedral of the Holy Trinity (Pl. 6; B, 1), founded about 1138 but dating in its present form from 1691-99. It is 196 ft. long, 124 ft. wide, and 256 ft. high (to the top of the cross). There are

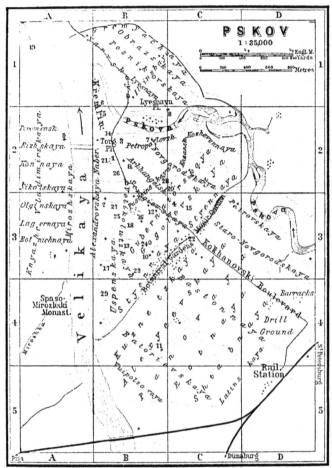

PLAN OF PSKOV. No. 1 (B, 2), Alexander II. Monument; 2 (B, 3), Arch-bishop's Palace; 3 (B, 2), Bazaar; 4 (C, 3), Cadet Academy. — *Cathedrals:* 5 (B, 2), Annunciation; 6 (B, 1), Holy Trinity; 7 (B, 2), SS. Peter & Paul. - *·Churches:* 8 (C, 2), Apparition of the Virgin; 9 (A, 2), Assumption; 10 (B, 3), Roman Catholic; 11 (B, 4), St. Alexis; 12 (B, 3), St. James (Lutheran). — 13 (B, 3), Club of the Noblesse; 14 (B, 2), Consistory; 15 (C, 3), Girls' High School; 16 (B, 3), Governor's House; 17 (B, 3), High School; 18 (B, 3), Imperial Bank; 19 (A, 1), John the Baptist Convent; 20 (C, 2, 3), Kutúzov Garden; 21 (B, 2), Law Courts; 22 (C, 3), Modern School; 23 (B, 3), Novo-Voznesénski Convent; 24 (B, 3), Pogankin House; 25 (B, 3), Police Sta-tion; 26 (B, 2), Post & Telegraph Office; 27 (B, 3), Seminary; 28 (B, C, 2), Theatre; 29 (B, 4), Training College.

five domes. The entrance is preceded by a wide vaulted flight of
steps, thirty-three in number.

The lofty vaulting of the central space is borne by four massive
piers. To the left of the ikonostas is the *Tomb of St. Gabriel (Vsévolod)*,
the first Prince of Pskov (d. 1138); the tomb is of silver and dates from
1834. Vsévolod's sword is also shown, bearing the inscription 'honorem
meum nemino *(sic)* dabo'. — On the pier to the right of the ikonostás is
the *Crucifix of St. Olga* (reconstructed in 1623). The oak *Tomb of Prince
Dóvmont* (d. 1299), who was afterwards canonized, is in a chapel to the
right of the ikonostas. Above hangs Dóvmont's sword, with which the
princes were girt at their coronation in the cathedral. — To the right of
Dóvmont's tomb is that of *St. Nicholas Salos* (Николай Юродивый;
p. 41). — The *Sacristy* contains some ecclesiastical antiquities, old town-
seals, and coins of Pskov. — The vaults below the church contain the tombs
of Princes of Pskov.

The *Pogánkin House* (Поганкины палаты; Pl. 24, B 3), built
about the middle of the 17th cent. and restored in 1902, contains a
small museum of antiquities (open free daily, except Mon., 10-3;
entrance from courtyard). A little to the N. of the Archiepiscopal
Palace (Pl. 2) is a *Museum of Ecclesiastical Antiquities* (Музей
церковнаго историко-археологическаго комитета, open free
daily 11-1, Sun. 12-1). In front of the *Law Courts* (Pl. 21; B, 2)
is a bronze statue of Alexander II., by Opekúshin (1886). — The
Cathedral of the Transfiguration, belonging to the *Spaso-Mirozhski
Convent* (Pl. A, 4), is adorned with frescoes of the 12-13th cent.,
restored in 1900.

About 7 V. (5 M.) to the S. of Pskov lies *Tchereókha* (Kurhaus, with
restaurant), a pleasant group of villas, reached by ascending the Velíkaya
by steam-launch for 35 min. and then taking the tramway (7 min.; through-
fare 20 cop.). — The village of *Vúibutino (Libutino)*, on the Velíkaya,
12 V. (8 M.) to the S. of Pskov, is said to have been the birthplace of
St. Olga (d. 969; comp. p. xlviii), wife of Igor, Prince of Kiev.

From Pskov to *Bologóye*, see p. 266; to *Walk*, see p. 80. — Steamboats to *Dorpat*, see p. 69 (pier at the bridge-of-boats; Pl. A, B, 2).

644 V. *Strugi-Byélaya* (Rail. Restaurant); 708 V. *Luga* (Rail.
Restaurant), a town of 11,600 inhab., in the government of St. Petersburg. 757 V. *Divenskaya*, 773 V. *Siverskaya*, both with railway
restaurants. — Shortly before entering the station of Gatchina, at the
S.E. end of the town, we intersect the Baltic Railway, which has a
station on the W. side of the town.

794 V. (526 M.) *Gátchina* (Rail. Restaurant), see p. 186. To
Taps (Riga, Reval), see pp. 83-80. A branch-line also runs to (46 V.)
Tosno (p. 262). — 816 V. *Alexándrovskaya*. The train now describes a wide curve; to the left, in the distance, is a range of hills,
skirting the Gulf of Finland from this point to St. Petersburg. On
one of its summits lies the observatory of Pulkovo (p. 189).

837 V. (555 M.) *St. Petersburg* (p. 88; Warsaw Station).

9. From Warsaw to St. Petersburg viâ Vilna.

1046 V. (693 M.). Express train in 18¹/₂ hrs.; fares 27 rb. 90, 18 rb. 90 cop. (reserved seat 2 rb. 10 cop., comp. p. xxiii; sleeping-car 8 rb. 35, 6 rb. 30 cop.). [In winter this route is also traversed by the Nice and St. Petersburg Express; comp. p. 6.] Ordinary train in 31 hrs.; fares ²² 1h. 50, 13 rb. 50 cop. — From Warsaw to Vilna, 388 V. (257 M.), express train in 7 hrs. (fares 14 rb. 90, 10 rb. 10 cop.; seat-ticket 1¹/₂ rb.); ordinary train in 11 hrs. (fares 12 rb., 7 rb. 20 cop.).

Warsaw, see p. 9. The train runs N.E. through the ancient duchy of *Masovia*, which embraced the three modern governments of Warsaw, Kholm, and Lomza, and traverses extensive forests. — From (32 V.) *Tłuszcz* (Тлущъ; Rail. Restaurant) branch-railways run N.E. to (70 V.) Ostrołęka (see below) and S. to (33 V.) Novo-Minsk (p. 248). —51 V. *Łochów* (Rail. Restaurant). — Just short of (79 V.) *Małkinia* (Rail. Restaurant) we cross the *Bug*.

From Małkinia to Ostrołęka, 52 V. (35 M.), railway in 2 hrs. — Ostrołęka (Остроленка), a town with 16,000 inbah., on the left bank of the *Narew*, which is here spanned by a bridge. The French defeated the Russians here in 1807, and the Russians gained a victory over the Poles on almost the same field in 1831.

Another line runs from Małkinia to (63 V.) *Siedlce* (p. 248).

141 V. (93 M.) *Łapy* (Rail. Restaurant).

From Łapy to Ostrołęka, 83 V. (55 M.), railway in ca. 4 hrs. 49 V. *Tchervónni-Bor*. About 14 V. (9 M.) to the N. lies *Łomża* (Лómжа; Pólskaya Hotel), the fortified capital of a government of the same name, situated on the left bank of the Narew and containing 27,800 inhabitants. 83 V. (55 M.) *Ostrołęka*, see above.

The railway now crosses the *Narew* and passes under the line from Brest-Litovsk to Grajewo (see p. 45).

162 V. (107 M.) **Białystok**, Бѣлостóкъ. — The Railway Station (*Restaurant*) lies to the N.W. of the town. — Hotels. *Nyemétzkaya*, Bazárnaya, with restaurant, R. 1-4 rb.; *Grand-Hôtel*, Nikoláyevskaya, with café, R. 1-4 rb. — *Restaurant Eremitage*, Nyemétzkaya. — Izvóshtchik from the station to the town 40-50, per drive 15-20 cop. — Tramway from the station to the town, 5 cop.

Białystok (440 ft.), the capital of a district in the government of Grodno and headquarters of the 6th Army Corps, lies on the river *Biała* and is strongly garrisoned. Of its 86,200 inhab. about three-fourths are Jews. The town is the centre of an important woollen-manufacturing district. We turn to the right at the rail. station, then cross the railway-bridge (r.), and proceed through the Novo-Shosséinaya, Lípovaya, Túikotzkaya, Bazárnaya, and Nyemétzkaya, to (¹/₂ hr.) the Town Park, passing on the right the Tzar Nicholas Institute for Girls, in a converted château, formerly belonging to the Counts Branicki. A little to the E., in the Alexándrovskaya, is the new Lutheran Church, the tower of which commands a view of the town and of the well-wooded and hilly surroundings.

FROM BIAŁYSTOK TO BREST-LITOVSK, 126 V. (84 M.), railway in 4 hrs.
5 V. *Starosielce*, where the afternoon train to Brest-Litovsk is separated
from that to Grajewo (see below). — From (45 V.) *Bielsk* (9400 inhab.) a
branch-railway runs viâ (28 V.) *Gáinovka* (p. 249) to (49 V.) the village
of *Byelovyézh* (Pol. *Bialowieża*), with a prettily situated shooting-lodge of
the Tzar, built by Count Rochefort in 1893. The **Byelovyézh Forest**
(Бѣловѣжская пу́ща), 396 sq. M. in area and attaining a height of 645 ft.,
is a bleak hilly district in the government of Grodno, overgrown with firs
and pines. The aurochs or bison (Bison bonasus L.; зубръ) occurs here as
in the Caucasus (comp. p. 440). There are believed to be about 600 head,
which may not be shot or hunted without the permission of the Tzar. —
78 V. *Tcherémkha* (p. 249). — 126 V. (84 M.) *Brest-Litóvsk*, see p. 249.

FROM BIAŁYSTOK TO GRAJEWO, 78 V. (52 M.), railway in 3¹/₂ hrs. —
5 V. *Starosielce*, see above; 54 V. *Osowiec* (Оссовецъ), a strong fortress.
— 78 V. *Grajewo*, the Russian frontier and customs station. The German
frontier station is *Prostken*, whence a railway runs to (121 M,) *Königsberg*.

FROM BIAŁYSTOK TO BARANOVITCHI, 201 V. (133 M.), railway in 8 hrs.
The line runs to the E., through the government of Grodno. — 87 V. *Bagrationovskaya* (Rail. Restaurant; p. 249). At (90 V.) *Volkovúisk* (Polish
Wolkowysk; Rail. Restaurant), a district-capital with 15,600 inhab., Jagiello assumed the Polish crown in 1386. — 154 V. *Slonim-Albértin* (Rail.
Restaurant), a district-town of 21,400 inhab., on the *Shtchará*. — 201 V.
(133 M.) *Baránovitchi*, see p. 39.

201 V. *Sokólka* (Rail. Restaurant); 216 V. *Kúznitza*. We cross
the *Niemen* by a lofty viaduct and reach —

241 V. (160 M.) **Grodno**, Гродна. — *Rail. Restaurant.* — HOTELS.
Métropole, Bánkovaya, R. ¹/₂-2 rb., with restaurant; *Yevropéiskaya*,
Slavyánskaya (hôtel garni; R. ³/₄-4 rb.), both in thè Sobórnaya. — IZVÓSH-
TCHIK from the railway station to the town 30, per drive 15, per hr. 40 cop.

Grodno (385 ft.), the chief town of the government of that
name and headquarters of the 2nd Army Corps, with 66,500 inhab.
(two-thirds Jews), is situated on the right bank of the Niemen, at
the point where that river begins to penetrate a barrier of hills
and forms a valley enclosed by sides 100 ft. in height.

Grodno, first heard of in 1120, was almost totally destroyed by the
Mongolians in 1241 and by the Teutonic Knights in 1284 and 1391. Stephen Bathory, King of Poland, made Grodno his residence and died here
in 1586; his grave, however, is in the palace church of Cracow. At the
Grodno Diet of 1793 the Second Partition of Poland was signed, and at
that of 1795 (Sept. 25th) the abdication of King Stanislaus Poniatowski
was accepted. — The town was occupied by the French on June 18th,
1812, and King Jerome fixed his headquarters here.

From the railway station, which lies on the N.E. side of the
town, we at first proceed in a straight direction and then (2 min.)
bend to the left into the Úlitza Grafa Muravyéva. This leads to
(13 min.) the *District Court* (Окру́жный судъ), passing the *House
of the Governor* on the right and the *General Post Office* on the
left. We turn (l.) into the Sobórnaya and follow this street to the
(7 min.) Parade Ground, in which, immediately to the right, is the
Cathedral of St. Sophia. We then proceed (r.) through the Zám
kovaya to the (5 min.) *Old Palace*, a 15th cent. building, now used
as the Officers' Club, its garden affording a view of the valley of the
Niemen. On the E. side of the Parade Ground stands the *Parish*

Church, erected in the baroque style in 1610. About $^1/_4$ M. to the
S., reached by the Myeshtchánskaya, is the *Bernardine Church*,
erected in 1595, and containing some good contemporary stone-
carvings of the Stations of the Cross.

FROM GRODNO TO SUWALKI, 98 V. (65 M.), railway in 4 hrs. — 69 V
Augustów (Августовъ; Rail. Restaurant), a district-capital in the government of Suwalki, with 15,200 inhab., contains some factories and dye
works, and is the scene of important cattle and horse fairs. The horses,
the so-called 'Lithuanians' ('Litauer'), are small but wiry. — 98V. **Suwalki**,
Сувалки (*Rail. Restaurant; Yevropéiskaya*, R. $^3/_4$-$3^1/_2$ rb., D. 60, omn.
30 cop.; cab to the town, 60 cop.), the capital of the government of that
name, contains 33,000 inhab. and a Lutheran church. Hence to Orani,
see below. About 17 V. to the S.W. of Suwalki (carriage 8 rb.) lies *Raczki*
(Рачки), a market-town which formerly belonged to the Pac family. The
church is elaborately decorated with sculpture; the Gothic town hall has
a tall and slender tower. About $^3/_4$ M. from Raczki is the handsome
château of *Rospuda*, which also belonged to the Pacs. In 1815 General
Louis Pac settled a number of Scottish colonists at Rospuda, and with
their help made that estate famous for its admirable cultivation. About
9 V. to the E. of Suwalki, in a beautiful situation, is the former Camaldulensian convent of *Wigry*.

A branch-line runs from Grodno to (55 V.) *Mosti* (see p. 249).

270 V. (179 M.) *Druskyentki* (Rail. Restaurant).

A highroad (motor-omnibus 1 rb.) runs hence to the N.W. to. (17 V.
or 11 M.) *Druskyentki* (635 ft.; Kurórtnaya, Yevropéiskaya, R. $^1/_2$-$3^1/_2$ rb.),
a watering-place on the right bank of the Niemen, with cold saline springs
containing iodine and bromine. The season lasts from May 1st to Sept. 10th,
O.S. (visitors' tax 6 rb.).

The train enters the government of Vilna. — 315 V. *Oráni* (Rail.
Restaurant). A branch-railway runs hence to (133 V. or 88 M.)
Suwalki (see above), passing (9 V.) *Artilleriskaya*, with artillery
ranges and a summer-camp for sappers and infantry. — 371V. *Landvaróvo* (p. 36). Beyond a tunnel we reach —

388 V. (257 M.) *Vilna* (p. 36). Thence to (1046 V. or 693 M.)
St. Petersburg, see pp. 40-43.

10. From Berlin to Riga. Libau.

Instead of the railway routes described below, travellers may use the
STEAMERS plying once weekly from *Stettin* to (45 hrs.) *Riga* (fares 36 *M*,
25 *M*; meals extra). The steamer 'Regina' takes 38 hrs. only (fares 55 *M*,
35 *M*, incl. meals). — Another steamer plies once a week from *Lübeck* to
Riga, viâ Warnemünde, in 50 hrs. (fares 55 *M*, 40 *M*, with meals).

a. Viâ Vilna and Dünaburg.

823 M. Railway (express train as far as Wirballen or Dünaburg) in
$26^1/_2$ hrs. (fares 100 *M* 75 pf., 62 *M* 80 pf.). Sleeping-car from Berlin to
Eydtkuhnen 12 or 10 *M*. As far as Dünaburg use may also be made of the
North (Nord) Express (p. 34). *Passport*, see p. xviii. — FROM WIRBALLEN
TO RIGA, 544 V. (361 M.), express train in $14^1/_2$ hrs. (fares 17 rb. 60 cop.,
11 rb. 60 cop.; reserved seat $1^1/_2$ rb., see p. xxiii); ordinary train in $19^1/_2$ hrs.
(fares 15 rb., 9 rb.).

From Berlin to (462 M.) *Eydtkuhnen* and thence viâ *Wirballen* to (340 V. or 225 M.) *Dünaburg,* see R. 8. In Dünaburg we are transferred by the junction-line to (3 V.) the Riga Station.

Beyond Dünaburg the line skirts the right bank of the *Dviná* (p. 31), traversing the wooded districts of Polish Livonia. On the left bank of the river lies Courland, this part of it being named *Semgallen.*

423 V. (280 M.) **Kreuzburg** (300 ft.; *Rail. Restaurant*), with an old palace, formerly belonging to the Roman Catholic Archbishops of Riga and now to the Von Korff family. — Opposite, on the left bank of the Dvina, lies (4 V.) the Courland town of *Jakobsstadt,* with 5900 inhabitants.

From Kreuzburg to Tuckum, 181 V. (120 M.), railway in 5¹/₂ hrs. — We cross the *Dvina* by a bridge 245 yds. in length. 17 V. *Selburg,* with the scanty remains of a lodge of the Teutonic Order on the steep bank of the Dvina; 58 V. *Tauerkaln,* amid extensive woods; 99 V. *Gross-Eckau,* with the estate of Count von der Pahlen. Near (129 V.) *Mitau* (p. 51) we cross the *Semgaller Aa.* — 181 V. *Tuckum II.,* see p. 64.

From Kreuzburg to (744 V. or 493 M.) *Moscow,* see R. 33 b.

The train crosses the *Ewst* and enters the government of Livland (Livonia). — 439 V. (291 M.) **Stockmannshof** (255 ft.; *Railway Restaurant; Plawingkrug,* on the Dvina, ¹/₄ M. from the station, R. ³/₄-1 rb., unpretending), a small place with the château of Count Medem. It is famous for its orange liqueur ('Pomeranzenlikör'). On the steep rocky bank of the Dvina is the ruined castle of *Loxten.*

A pleasant trip down the Dvina may be made from Stockmannshof to (25 V.) Kokenhusen (6-8 hrs., including stops; boat with two rowers 5-6 rb.). On the Courland bank (left) rises the moss-clad rock of *Stabburags* ('Rock of Tears'). The following stretch, as far as *Grütershof,* is accompanied by picturesque limestone cliffs. On the left is the ruined castle of Altona (p. 48). We land at the ruin of *Kokenhusen.*

About 22 M. to the N.E. of Stockmannshof lies the manor of *Tootzen,* the birthplace of the Austrian Field Marshal von Laudon (1717-90).

From Stockmannshof to Walk, 197 V. (131 M.), light railway in 12 hrs. — 123 V. *Marienburg* (Rail. Restaurant), with the relics, on an island in a lake (625 ft.), of a lodge of the Teutonic Order, built in 1342. The future Empress Catherine I. (1679-1727) was brought up in the parsonage here as the foster-daughter of Pastor Glück. — 197 V. *Walk II.* (p. 71).

456 V. (302 M.) **Kokenhusen** (285 ft.; *Inn,* opposite the railway station, unpretending, R. 70 cop.; in summer local train service to Riga). The ruins of the *Castle of Kokenhusen* are picturesquely situated on the Dvina, 1³/₄ M. by road from the railway. On quitting the station we first turn to the left and then (2 min.) to the right, into an avenue of poplars. At (¹/₄ hr.) the end of this avenue we turn to the left, and at (5 min.) the unpretending Moscow Inn we descend to the right to the bank of the Dvina, which we then skirt (to the right) to (¹/₄ hr.) the mouth of the *Perse* and the ruin. [By keeping to the right at the end of the poplar avenue, we reach the new château of Kokenhusen, belonging to Herr von Löwenstern.]

About ¹/₂ M. to the N. of the ruin, high up on the left bank of the Perse, is an arbour affording a view of the ruin and the wooded valley of the Perse. The castle of Kokenhusen, built by Bishop Albert in 1209 and occupied by the Archbishops of Riga from 1397 to 1566, was blown up by the Saxon and Polish troops in 1701, during the Northern War. — On the left bank of the Dvina, 2 M. above Kokenhusen, is the ruined castle of *Altona*, erected by the Teutonic Order.

The train crosses the *Perse.* — 476 V. *Römershof* (260 ft.; Rail. Restaurant).

About 3 M. to the E. of Römershof lies *Ascheraden*, the property of the Barons von Schoultz, with the ruins of a lodge of the Teutonic Order, built after 1211. — On the left bank of the Dvina, 2¹/₂ M. to the S. of Römershof, is *Friedrichsstadt*, a Courland town with 6500 inhabitants.

496 V. *Ringmundshof* (150 ft.). On the Dvina, 1¹/₃ M. from the railway station, on the left, is the manor of *Lennewarden* (Von Wulf family), with the ruins of a castle of the Archbishops of Riga. — Short of (512 V.) *Oger* (90 ft.; several pensions), a summer-resort of the people of Riga, we cross the river *Oger*.

519 V. *Üxküll* (110 ft.). About 1³/₄ M. to the S. is the Church of Üxküll, the oldest in Livonia, a double-naved building of 1186, altered in 1881 and provided with a tower. — About 15 V. to the S. of Üxküll (carr. & pair 3 rb., omn. 70 cop.) are the small sulphur baths of *Baldohn*, with a Kurhaus (restaurant).

Near (525 V.) *Kurtenhof* lies a summer-camp. An earthwork near the Lutheran Church of St. George, 1¹/₂ M. to the S., marks the scene of a defeat of Charles IX. of Sweden by the Poles (Sept. 17th, 1605). On the Dvina are the ruins of the castle of *Kirchholm*.

544 V. (363 M.) *Riga* (Orel Station; p. 53).

b. Viâ Koshedari and Mitau.

763 M. Railway (express train as far as Eydtkuhnen or Koshedari; sleeping-car 12 or 10 ℳ) in 24 hrs. (fares 94 ℳ 15, 57 ℳ 50 pf.). *Passport*, see p. xviii. — From Wirballen to Riga, 457 V. (303 M.), railway in 12 hrs. (fares 13 rb. 50, 8 rb. 10 cop.; sleeping-car 3 rb. 60, 2 rb. 70 cop.); to *Mitau*, 413 V. (274 M.), in 16 hrs. (fares 12 rb. 50, 7 rb. 50 cop.); to *Libau*, 412 V. (273 M.), in 15¹/₂ hrs. (fares 12 rb. 50, 7 rb. 50 cop.; sleeping-car 3 rb. 30, 2 rb. 50 cop.). Seat-ticket 1¹/₂ rb.

From Berlin to (462 M.) *Eydtkuhnen* and thence viâ *Wirballen* to (117 V. or 78 M.) *Koshedári*, see pp. 34-36. Our line now diverges to the N. from that to Vilna (R. 8). Near (143 V.) *Yánov* we cross the Viliyá. — 172 V. *Keidáni* lies on the right bank of the *Nevyazha*, which formed the E. boundary of the dominions of the Teutonic Order from 1384 to 1422. Beyond Keidani the wooded region (the old Samogitia) becomes hillier. — From (233 V.) *Radzivilishki* (Rail. Restaurant) a branch-line runs viâ (51 V.) *Pónevyezh* (Rail. Restaurant; p. 40) to (187 V. or 124 M.) Kalkuhnen (p. 40). — 251 V. *Schaulen*

(Шáвли; Rail. Restaurant), a district-capital in the government of Kovno, with 22,700 inhab., many of whom are Jews.

324 V. (215 M.) **Muravyévo**, Муравьево, or *Mozheiki* (245 ft. · *Railway Restaurant*).

FROM MURAVYEVO TO LIBAU, 86 V. (57 M.), railway in $2^1/_2$ hrs. — Just short-of (8 V.) *Venta* the train crosses the *Windau*, and beyond (19 V.) *Lusha* we enter the government of Courland. — 86 V. *Libau* (Railway Restaurant; tramway, see below).

Libau, Либáва, Lettish *Léepaja.* — HOTELS. *Hotel de Rome* (Pl. a; B, 3), Neuer Markt 1, R. from $1^1/_3$ rb., B. 60 cop., D. (1-4 p.m.) $1^1/_4$ rb., good; *Hôt. St. Petersburg* (Pl. b; B, 3), Grosse-Str. 15, with garden, R. from 1, B. $^1/_2$, D. (1-6 p.m.) 1 rb., well spoken of; *Hôt. Impérial* (Pl. c; B, 3), Neumarkt 11, with concert-garden. — RESTAURANTS at the hotels also in the *Kurhaus* (p. 50). — *Café Bonitz*, Korn-Str. 42 (Pl. B, 2, 3), with garden. — *Cettinje* (Pl. D, 2), a pleasure-resort on an island in the Lake of Libau (small boat from the Stadt-Brücke 5 cop.).

CABS. Per drive inside one of the four zones 15, with two horses 20 cop.; to the Main Railway Station 30, 40 cop.; from the Main Railway Station to the town 40, 60 cop.; each article of luggage 5 cop.; per $^1/_2$ hr. 30, 40, each $^1/_4$ hr. additional 15, 20 cop.

ELECTRIC TRAMWAYS. From the Main Railway Station (Pl. C, 1) to the Neumarkt (Pl. B, 3) and to the Kurhaus (Pl. A, 2), 20 minutes. From the Kurhaus to the Naval Harbour (beyond Pl. B, 1), $^1/_2$ hr

POST & TELEGRAPH OFFICE (Pl. 10; B, 2), Helenen-Str.

CONSULATES. British, Vice-Consul, *C. J. Hill*, Stender-Str. 14; United States Consular Agent, *Alfred Seligmann*, Nordost-Hafen-Quai. — LLOYD' AGENTS, *Helmsing & Grimm*, Grosse-Str. 13.

ENGLISH CHURCH and BRITISH SEAMEN'S INSTITUTE, Helenen-Str. 2 (Pl. B, 3); services at 8.30, 11, & 7; chaplain, *Rev. F. Hamilton Banks*.

Numerals on the Plan of the Town. No. 1 (Pl. B, 3), District Court; 2 (C, 2), Exchange; 3 (B, 3), Church of St. Anne; 4 (C, 3), Greek Catholic Church; 5 (B, 3), Roman Catholic Church; 6 (B, 3), Trinity Church; 7 (B, 3), High School for Girls; 8 (B, C, 3), House of Peter the Great; 9 (B, 3), Police Station; 10 (B, 2), Post & Telegraph Office; 11 (C, 3), Modern School; 12 (B, 3), Town Hall; 13 (B, 3), Synagogue; 14 (C, 3), Theatre.

Libau, being the N. terminus of the Romni & Libau Railway, which opens up a wide 'Hinterland', is the chief port and commercial town of Courland, containing 90,000 inhab.; it lies at the point where the Lake of Libau (17 sq. M. in area) discharges into the Baltic Sea through a channel dug in 1703. The chief exports are timber, grain, and eggs; the chief imports are coal and herrings. The harbour is open all the year round. — To the N. of the town is the fortified 'Naval Harbour of Emperor Alexander III.' (no admission), with the Greek Catholic Marine Cathedral, consecrated in 1903.

Libau, originally a fishing-village but long known for its excellent harbour, was burned down by the Lithuanians in 1418 and given in pawn to Duke Albert of Prussia in 1560. In 1609 it reverted to Courland, and in 1625 it received its municipal charter from Duke Frederick (Kettler). On Sept. 13th, 1701, it was taken by Charles XII., who fortified it at the expense of the citizens. In 1812 it was occupied by the Prussian allies of Napoleon, under Macdonald.

From the *Main Railway Station* (Pl. C, 1) the Bahnhof-Str. leads to the S. to the (25 min.) Stadt-Brücke, or bridge over the Commercial Harbour (Pl. B, C, 2). On the other side of the bridge, to the left, is the Säger-Platz, with the *Exchange* (Pl. 2). From the bridge the Grosse-Str. leads to the S.W. to the (10 min.) Neuer Markt, passing the Lutheran *Church of the Trinity* (Pl. 6; 1758; fine organ) and the *Town Hall* (Pl. 12). To the S.E. of the Neuer Markt, at Herren-Str. 24, is the house (Pl. 8), which Peter the Great occupied in 1697.

Libau has a good sandy beach and well laid out pleasure-grounds, and is frequented to some small extent for sea-bathing (June-Sept.). The Korn-Strasse, running to the N.W. from the Neuer Markt, and then the Kurhaus-Prospékt (left) bring us to (20 min.) the *Kurhaus* (Pl. A, 2; R. $1^{1}/_{4}$-4, B. $^{1}/_{2}$, D. 1 rb.; concert daily in summer). A little to the S. are the Municipal Baths (Kurbad), the Nikolaibad (warm bath 60 cop.), and the bathing-places for ladies and gentlemen (bath 15 cop.).

STEAMERS to *Riga*, see p. 54; to *Reval* and *St. Petersburg* fortnightly (first-class fare 8 rb.); to *Stettin* fortnightly (18 rb., including meals); to *Lübeck* weekly (19 rb., incl. meals); to *Copenhagen* once a week (18 rb.); also to *London, Hull, New York* (comp. p. xviii), etc.

FROM LIBAU TO HASENPOTH, 46 V. (31 M.), light railway in $2^{1}/_{2}$ hrs. (station by the bridge, Pl. C 2).—11 V. *Grobin*, on the *Alandbach*, with 1500 inhab. and the remains of a lodge of the Teutonic Order. Beyond (21 V.) *Legen* we skirt the W. bank of the *Lake of Durben* (3 sq. M.).— About 6 V. to the N.W. of (40 V.) *Marienhof* is the manor of *Zierau*, near which are the so-called *Servants of Kinte (Kintegesinde)*, a series of pagan Standing Stones, consisting of blocks 10-13 ft. long and 3-6 ft. broad, enclosing an area 300 yds. in length by 170 yds. in breadth. Other stones of equal size stand in a circle hard by, under the shade of venerable oaks. This is believed to have been a pagan place of sacrifice or assembly. The erection of the stones is popularly ascribed to Kinte, a man of gigantic strength. — 46 V. **Hasenpoth** (*Railway Restaurant; Baltischer Hof*, R. from 70 cop.), a town of 3800 inhab., picturesquely situated on the *Tebber*. On the left bank is a ruined castle of the Teutonic Knights, while on the right bank lay the bishop's castle. Parts of the church-walls date from the 15th century.

About 37 V. (25 M.) to the N.E. of Hasenpoth by road (diligence) lies **Goldingen** (*Vereinshaus*, R. from $^{3}/_{4}$ rb.), a town on the left bank of the *Windau*, with 10,500 inhab. and the scanty remains of a lodge of the Teutonic Order. St. Catharine's Church dates from 1672. — The old manor of *Edwahlen*, 14 V. (9 M.) to the W. of Goldingen, which was formerly the property of the Bishops of Pilten, has belonged since the 16th cent. to the Barons von Behr. The château stands in a large and fine park. The church contains old armour and coats-of-arms.

CONTINUATION OF RAILWAY FROM MURAVYEVO TO RIGA. Near (343 V. or 227 M.) *Ringen* the train enters the government of Courland. 361 V. *Autz* (310 ft.). — 392 V. *Friedrichshof*.

About 9 V. (6 M.) to the N.W. of Friedrichshof (diligence thrice daily, fare 30 cop.) lies **Doblen**, a small town with 2000 inhab., picturesquely situated on the *Behrse*. It is commanded by the well-preserved ruin of a *Castle* of the time of the Teutonic Knights, which stands on the top of a hill descending precipitously to the river. The castle is surrounded by a strong and high wall, measuring nearly ¹/₂ M. in circumference. At the N. end of the castle-square lie the ruins of the castle of Duke Gotthard Kettler, including the chapel. On the E. side are the remains of a palace -of the ducal period (16th cent.). The commandery of the Teutonic Order has been destroyed.

399 V. *Pfalzgrafen.*

413 V. (274 M.) **Mitau,** Митáва (Plan, see p. 49).—The RAILWAY STATION (Pl. C, 4; restaurant) lies in the S. part of the town. — HOTELS. *Linde* (Pl. a; C, 2), Schloss-Str. 7, with restaurant, R. from 1, B. ¹/₂, D. (1-5 p.m.) ¹/₂-1¹/₄ rb.; *Courland* (Pl. b; C, 2), Markt, R. from 75, B. 25, D. (1-5 p.m.) from 60 cop.; *Imperial* (Pl. c; C, 3), Palais-Str. 39.—RESTAURANTS (D. from 1 to 4 p.m.). *Gewerbeverein* (Pl. 2; C, 3), Palais-Str. 37, with garden; *Purring* (late *Torchiani;* also confectioner), Grosse-Str. 6 (Pl. A, B, 2); *Sanssouci* (Pl. S; C, 1), in the Palace Gardens, concerts in summer daily at 8 p.m., except on Sat. & Sunday. — CONFECTIONER. *Leutzinger,* See-Str. 1 (Pl. B, C, 1).—CAB from or to the railway station 20, with two horses 30 cop., per drive in the town 15 or 20 cop., from the station to the Palace 30 or 40 cop., per ¹/₂ hr. 30 or 40, per hr. 40 or 60 cop. — STEAMBOAT (comp. Pl. D, 1) to Dubbeln (p. 64) in 3¹/₂ hrs. (fare 45 cop.).

Mitau (Lettish *Jélgawa;* 25 ft.), the capital and intellectual centre of the government of Courland and the seat of a General Superintendent of the Lutheran Church, lies in a flat and fertile district on the left bank of the navigable *Semgaller Aa.* Its 40,000 inhabitants include Germans (9500), Jews (6500), Letts, Russians, and Poles.

The castle of Mitau was founded in 1265 by the Grand-Master Konrad von Mandern and was made a commandery of the Teutonic Order. The town, which was not founded till 1561, became the residence of the Dukes of Courland. Gustavus Adolphus of Sweden took Mitau in 1621 and again in 1625. The Duchy of Courland reached the height of its prosperity under Duke James of the family of Kettler (1642-82). In his time Courland had colonies on the Gambia (Africa) and owned the W. Indian island of Tobago. In 1658 Mitau was captured by the Swedes under Count Douglas, but they relinquished it in 1660. The Russians made themselves masters of the town in 1706 and destroyed the old castle of the Teutonic Order. In 1795 Courland was permanently incorporated with the Russian empire. In 1812 Mitau was occupied by the French and their Prussian allies under Macdonald.

The most prominent building in Mitau is the **Palace** (*Schloss;* Pl. C, D, 1), an extensive edifice in the early rococo style, situated outside the town upon an island formed by the Aa and the Drixe (about 1¹/₂ M. from the railway station). It was begun in 1738 by Duke John Ernest Biron, on the site of the old castle of the Teutonic Order (see above), and was finished in 1772. The architect was Count Rastrelli (p. 112). The palace was occupied in 1798-1801 and 1804-7 by Louis XVIII. of France, who here found a temporary asylum during his exile. It now serves as the residence of the Governor of Courland. The entrance is in the Schloss-Str; the castellan's rooms are in the E. wing, entrance on the S. side (Pl. *K;* fee 30 cop). Visitors are shown the rooms reserved for the emperor and also the Ducal Burial Vault (Pl. *G*), containing 25 coffins.

4*

The COURLAND PROVINCIAL MUSEUM (Pl. C, 1) is housed in a building in the Museums-Platz (No. 1), erected by Neumann in 1898. It was founded by J. F. von Recke in 1818 and is closely connected with the Courland *Society of Arts and Letters,* founded three years earlier by the author Schlippenbach. It is open on Sun., 12-2 (adm. 20 cop.), and at other times on application to the janitor (next house to the left; adm. 40 cop.). Director, H. Diederichs.

GROUND FLOOR. To the right is the library (20,000 vols.). To the left are the collections of natural history. — FIRST FLOOR. To the right is the room of the Society of Arts & Letters, on the end-wall (r.) of which is a contemporary portrait of the Livonian patriot, Joh. Reinhold Patkul (d. 1707). Room I (r.) contains prehistoric antiquities, armour, and views of old castles of Courland. In Room II are documents, coins, and portraits, the last including those of the Duchess Dorothea of Courland (d. 1821) and Duchess Dorothea of Dino (d. 1862), by Gérard (on the exit-wall). Room III (second section): Portrait of Elisa von der Recke (d. 1833), by A. Graff. Room IV: Modern pictures and a torso of Eros, after Praxiteles (found in Italy)

The *Church of the Trinity* (Pl. C, 2) contains stained-glass windows with scenes from the history of Courland. — At No. 6, Palais-Str., one of the oldest houses in the town, is the *Katharinenstift* (Pl. C, 2), a home for indigent gentlewomen, founded by Katharina von Bismarck in 1775. — In the Grosse-Str., the principal business-street of the town, is the *Church of St. Anne* (Pl. A, B, 2), built in 1573. — The *Government High School* (Pl. 3; C, 2), built in the baroque style in 1775, contains a library of 50,000 vols., established by Duke Peter. — In the Roman Catholic Graveyard (entr. from the Kalwensche Chaussée) is the neglected sepulchral chapel of *Abbé Edgeworth* (d. 1807; Pl. *E,* C 4), the father confessor of Louis XVI., who accompanied the king to the scaffold.

Among the pleasure-resorts near Mitau are (1½ V.) *Sorgenfrei* and (4 V.) *Langerwald.* The former is reached by a footpath leading to the left from the bridge over the Aa; the latter, with a restaurant and wooded park, lies to the right of the highroad to Riga and is visited by a Sun. steamer in summer.

From Mitau a highroad leads to the S. to (44 V. or 29 M.) **Bauske** *(Hotel Petersburg),* a Courland town with 7500 inhab., picturesquely situated on a height at the confluence of the Memel and the Muhs, which unite to form the Kurische Aa. It contains the imposing remains of a lodge of the Teutonic Order.

Railway from Mitau to *Kreuzburg* and to *Tuckum,* see p. 47.

Just beyond Mitau the train crosses the *Semgaller Aa* and the *Eckau,* and near (432 V.) *Olai,* where the delta of the Dvina begins, we enter the government of Livonia. 451 V. *Thorensberg* (p. 63). — The train now crosses the Dvina by the bridge mentioned at p. 60 and enters the Tuckum Station or the Orel Station at

457 V. (303 M.) *Riga* (see R. 11).

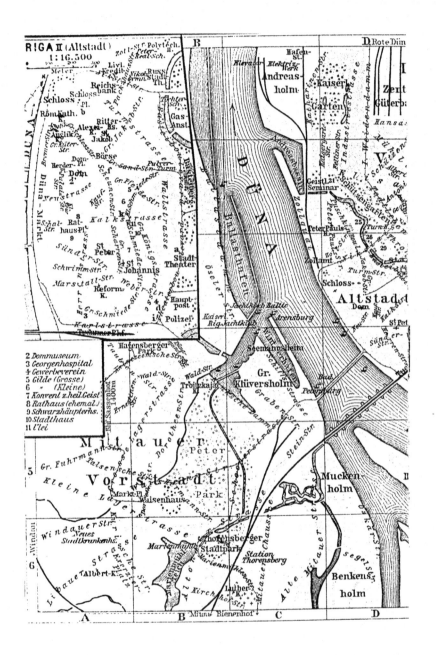

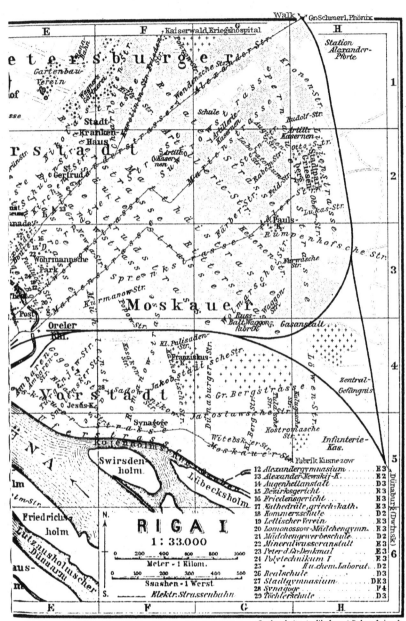

RIGA I

1 : 33.000

12 Alexandergymnasium E3
13 Alexander-Newskij-K. E2
14 Augenheilanstalt D3
15 Bezirksgericht D3
16 Friedensgericht E3
17 Kathedrale, griech.-kath. . . . E3
18 Kommerzschule D2
19 Lettischer Verein E3
20 Lomonossow-Mädchengymn. . . E3
21 Mädchengewerbeschule D2
22 Mineralwasseranstalt E3
23 Peter d. Gr.-Denkmal E3
24 Polytechnikum I E3
25   " d. chem. Laborat. . . D2
26 Realschule D3
27 Stadtgymnasium DK3
28 Synagoge F4
29 Töchterschule D3

Geograph. Anst. v. Wagner & Debes, Leipzig.

11. Riga and Environs.

In the plan-references in the text, the main plan of the city is indicated by *I*, the plan of the inner (or old) town by *II*.

Arrival. The main railway station is the OREL or DVINSK STATION ('Riga I'; Pl. E 4, *I*; *Restaurant*), in the Moscow suburb, for *Dünaburg* (Moscow, Warsaw, Wirballen), *Mühlgraben*, *Pskov* (St. Petersburg), and *Dorpat* (Reval, St. Petersburg). The TUCKUM STATION ('Riga II'; Pl. D, E, 4, *I*), for *Mitau* (Libau, Wirballen), *Tuckum* (Riga Coast), *Windau*, and *Bolderaa*, is to be demolished in 1914. Cabs and tramways, see below and p. 54.—Agency of the International Sleeping Car Co., Kauf-Str. 4; open on week-days 9.30-4, holidays 10-12.—*Steamers* from foreign ports lie to in the customs harbour ('Zollquai'; Pl. C, 2, 3, *I*).

Hotels. HÔTEL DE ROME (Pl. a; *II*), Theatre Boulevard 5, with restaurants on the groundfloor and in the basement, R. 2-8 rb., B. 60 cop., D. (1-6 p.m.) 1½ rb., omn. 50 cop.; ST. PETERSBURG (Pl. b; *II*), Schloss-Platz 4, in a quiet situation, R. from 1½ rb., B. 60 cop., D. (1-5 p.m.) 1-1½ rb.; IMPÉRIAL (Pl. c, E 3; *I*), Alexander Boulevard 3, R. from 1¼ rb., B. 50 cop., D. (2-7 p.m.) 1¼ rb.; BELLEVUE (Pl. g, E 3; *I*), Thronfolger Boulevard 33, near the Orel Station; MÉTROPOLE (Pl. d; *II*), Theatre Boulevard 12, with restaurant on the groundfloor; FRANKFURT-AM-MAIN (Pl. e, E 2; *I*), Alexander-Str. 25, with garden, R. from 1½, D. (2-6 p.m.) 1¼ rb.; CENTRAL HOTEL (Pl. f; *II*), Scheunen-Str. 25; VICTORIA (Pl. h, E 2; *I*), Alexander-Str. 7, with concert-garden; HÔTEL DE COMMERCE (Pl. i; *II*), Theatre Boulevard 13, with Russian fare; STADT LONDON (Pl. k; *II*), Kalk-Str. 21, commercial.—CHRISTIAN HOSPICE, Nikolai-Str. (Pl. C, 2, 3; *I*).

Pensions. *Eckardt*, Andreas-Str. 1 (Pl. D, 2; *I*), pens. 2½-4 rb.; *Von Goetschel*, Paulucci-Str. (Pl. E, 3; *I*), R. 1¾-4, board 1 rb. 90 cop.; *Keussler*, Thronfolger Boulevard 3 (Pl. D, E, 3; *I*), pens. 2 rb. 65 cop. to 3 rb. 15 cop.; *Hasen*, Alexander-Str. 2 (Pl. E, F, 2; *I*).

Restaurants. *Hôt. de Rome, Métropole, Impérial, Frankfurt-am-Main* (D. 1-1½ rb.), see above; *A. Kröpsch*, Scheunen-Str. 30, opposite the Exchange ('Börse'; Pl. *II*); *Johannis-Keller*, in the house of the Small Guild (p. 59; garden), D. 65 cop.; *Kloster-Keller*, in the house of the Great Guild (p. 59); *Roland*, Kauf-Str. 22 (Pl. D, 3; *I*), opposite the former city hall, D. from 60 cop. to 1 rb.; restaurant in the *Wöhrmann Park*, see p. 60.—WINE ROOM. *Otto Schwarz*, Bastei Boulevard 2 (Pl. D, 3; *I*); hot dishes served; closed in summer at 8.30 p.m.—*Automatic Restaurant*, Scheunen-Str. 19.

Cafés and **Confectioners.** *Börsen-Café*, Grosse Sand-Str. 11 (Pl. *II*); *Reiner*, Ständer-Str. 4 (Pl. D, 4; *I*) and Kalk-Str. 6 (Pl. D, 3; *I*); *Basteiberg Pavilion* (p. 56), open in summer only.

Cabs (here called 'Fuhrleute'; each driver must show the tariff in German and Russian). The town is divided into eight 'rayons' or districts, the most important of which for the stranger is the first, including the whole of the inner town, and the St. Petersburg suburb as far as the Elizabeth-Str. and Turgényev-Str.

	One horse.	Two horses.
1. BY DISTANCE.		
Drive within one rayon	15 cop.	30 cop.
Extra payment for each additional rayon	5 „	10 „
2. BY TIME.		
Within rayons, per ½ hr.	30 „	60 „
Each additional ½ hr.	25 „	40 „
Beyond rayons, per ¼ hr.	30 „	60 „
Each additional ¼ hr.	20 „	30 „

The above tariff covers 1-2 pers.; each additional person pays ⅓ more. An extra fee of 10 or 15 cop. is paid for drives from the Orel Station.

Each piece of *Luggage* 5 cop. *At Night* (12-7) double fare is charged. The passenger pays *Bridge Toll* in both directions.

Electric Tramways (6 cop.). 1. From the *Bank of the Dvina* (pontoon bridge; Pl. D 4, *I*) round the *Inner City*, either viâ the Tuckum Station (Pl. D, E, 4; *I*) or viâ the Castle (Pl. D, 3; *I*), to (3¹/₄ M.; 28 min.) the *Phoenix Factory* (beyond Pl. H, 1; *I*). Name-boards red. — 2. Round the *Inner City* as in No. 1, going on viâ the cemeteries (beyond Pl. F, 1; *I*) to (3¹/₄ M.; 28 min.) the *Military Hospital Station.* Name-boards green. 2 b. From the *Military Hospital* to the (2 M.; 13 min.) *Kaiserwald.* Name-boards white and green. — 3. From the *Bank of the Dvina* (railway bridge; Pl. D 4, *I*) viâ the Orel Station (Pl. E, 4; *I*) to (2 M.; 19 min.) the *Pernauer-Strasse* (Griesenberg Park; Pl. H 2, *I*). Name-boards white. -- 4. From the *Exchange (Börse; Pl. II)* to (2 M.; 17 min.) the corner of the *Marien-Strasse* and the *Revaler-Strasse* (Pl. G, 2; *I*). Name-boards green and white. — 5. From the *Bank of the Dvina* (railway bridge; Pl. D 4, *I*) to (3 M.; 25 min.) the *Kuznetzóv Factory* (beyond Pl. H, 5; *I*). Name-boards yellow. — 6. Round the *Inner City* as in No. 1, going on to (3²/₃ M.; 25 min.) the *Red Dvina* (beyond Pl. D, 1; *I*). Name-boards blue. — 7. From the *Bank of the Dvina* (Pl. D 4, *I*) over the pontoon-bridge to (4¹/₂ M.; ¹/₂ hr.) the *Bienenhof* or to the *Children's Hospital* (beyond Pl. C, 6; *I*). Name-boards white and red. — 8. From the *Bank of the Dvina* (Pl. D 4, *I*) over the pontoon-bridge to the (3¹/₂ M.; 28 min.) *Regimentshof* viâ the Schlocksche-Str. (beyond Pl. A, 4; *I*). Name-boards green and red. — 9. From the *Phoenix Factory* (comp. No. 1) to (2 M.; 11 min.) *Gross-Schmerl.* Name-boards blue and red.

Post Office (Pl. E, 3, 4; *I*), at the corner of the Suvorov-Str. and the Theatre Boulevard, open on week-days 8 a.m. to 2 p.m. and 4-9 p.m., Sun. 8-10 a.m. Letter within the town 3 cop. — **Police Station** (Pl. *II*), in the Theatre Boulevard. — *Passport Bureau* (10-3) for foreign passports, in the Castle ('Schloss'; Pl. D 3, *I*).

Theatres. *City Theatre (Stadttheater;* Pl. *II*), German, performances from Aug. 20th to May 20th (O. S.), 1st parquet 1 rb. 85 cop. to 2¹/₂ rb. — *Hagensberg Summer Theatre,* in the Hagensberg Park (Pl. A, B, 4; *I*), German. — *Russian Theatre (Russisches Stadttheater;* Pl. *II*), Nikolai-Str. — *Lettish Theatres,* Pushkin Boulevard (Pl. D, 2, 3; *I*), etc. — *Circus,* Paulucci-Str. 4 (Pl. E, 3; *I*).

Pleasure Resorts. *Wöhrmann Park* (Pl. E 3, *I; p.* 60), military band in summer daily, except Sat., 5-11 p.m., no charge; on winter-evenings, concerts in the winter-garden 20 cop. — *Imperial Garden (Kaiserlicher Garten;* Pl. D 1, *I; p.* 61), concerts and variety performances in summer, skating and tobogganing in winter. — *Arcadia,* near the station of Thorensberg (Pl. C, 6; *I*). — *Casino,* Alexander-Str. 80 (Pl. E, F, 2; *I*).

Baths. *Dr. S. Kroeger's Medical Baths,* Kirchen-Str. 18 (Pl. E, 2; *I*), with small swimming-bath, etc. — *River Baths* in the Rosenbach Bathing Establishment (Pl. C, D, 4; *I*), at the pontoon-bridge.

Consulates. Great Britain, *V. H. C. Bosanquet,* Paulucci-Str. 21. U. S. A., *W. F. Doty,* Albert-Str. 11. — Lloyd's Agents, *Helmsing & Grimm,* Grosse Schloss-Str. 21.

English Church *(St. Saviour's;* Pl. *II*), on the Dvina, near the Roman Catholic Church; services at 11 a.m. and (in winter) 6 p.m. — English Club, see p. 58.

Steamboats. To (7 min.) *Hagensberg,* every 6 min., fare 5 cop.; to *Ilgezeem,* every ¹/₂ hr., 10 cop.; to *Bolderaa* (p. 62; 1 hr.), hourly, 15 cop.; to *Mühlgraben* (p. 62), every ¹/₂ hr., 15 cop.; to *Mühlgraben* and the *Stint-See,* thrice daily, 25 cop.; to *Dubbeln,* twice daily, 30 cop. — To *Libau* viâ *Windau,* once a week, in 20 hrs., fare 7 rb. (to Windau, in 12-13 hrs., fare 6 rb.). — To *Pernau,* twice a week, in 8-9 hrs., fares 5 & 3 rb. — To *St. Petersburg* viâ *Arensburg* and *Reval,* see p. 84. — To *Stettin* or *Lübeck,* see p. 46. — To *Stockholm,* in 24 hrs., fares 17 & 13 rb. — To *Copenhagen,* in 48 hrs., fare 19 rb. — To *London,* in 4 days, fares 65 & 48 rb., including meals (comp. p. xviii). — To *Hull,* in 4 days, fare 65 rb., including meals (comp. p. xviii).

Principal Attractions (one day). Cathedral (p. 57), Dom-Museum (p. 58), St. James's Church (p. 59), Ritterhaus (P. 59), Castle (p. 58), Hall of the Blackheads (p. 56), St. Peter's Church (p. 59), Great and Small Guilds (p. 59), Art Museum (p. 60), Imperial Garden (p. 61). — Pleasant excursions may be made to various beach-resorts and to the Livonian Switzerland.

Riga (20 ft.), Púra, Lettish *Rihga,* the capital of the government of Livonia, is situated in a sandy plain on both sides of the *Dvina* (p. 31), here ¹/₂ M. wide, about 9 M. above its mouth in the Gulf of Riga. Riga is, after St. Petersburg, the most important Russian commercial and industrial town on the Baltic Sea, and it is the headquarters of the 20th Army Corps and the residence of the Greek Catholic Archbishop of Riga and Mitau, as well as the seat of the National Consistory of the Lutheran Church. The population is estimated at 530,000. The Germans, Letts, and Esthonians belong almost without exception to the Lutheran church (²/₃ of the total population). The town consists of the *Inner Town* or *Old Town,* the *St. Petersburg Suburb* (with handsome modern dwellings) to the N., the *Moscow Suburb* to the E., and the *Mitau Suburb* to the W., on the left bank of the Dvina. Riga, with its many towers and domes, makes a pleasing impression, especially when approached by sea. The inner town, which is surrounded by a ring of boulevards (p. 56), is the quarter of the trading and official classes. Its chief streets are the Kalk-Str., Kauf-Str., and Scheunen-Str.; the Alexander-Str. is the main street of the St. Petersburg Suburb. The exports consist of wheat, skins and hides, timber, eggs, oilcake, linseed, flax, and hemp; the chief imports are herrings, coal, and machinery. The value of the over-sea exports in 1912 was 225,628,000 rb., of the imports 155,000,000 rb.

HISTORY (comp. also p. 32). About the middle of the 12th cent., some German merchants penetrated, viâ Wisby, to the mouth of the Dvina, and formed settlements here. In 1201 *Bishop Albert* (d. 1229) built the town · of Riga on the Rege, an .affluent of the Dvina, and colonized it with German settlers; next year he founded the *Order of the Brethren of the Sword,* which became united with the Teutonic Order of Prussia in 1237. Riga soon acquired great privileges and possessions, and at the end of the 13th cent. adopted the Hamburg Code. In 1282 it joined the *Hanseatic League.* The bishops (after 1255 archbishops), citizens, and knights were almost constantly at variance with each other, the two former parties generally uniting against the third, which, however, maintained the upper hand. In 1522 Riga embraced the tenets of the *Reformation,* and in 1541 it joined the League of Schmalkalden. In 1561 Livonia was ceded to Poland, and Riga also became Polish in 1582. In the wars between Sweden and Poland, Riga was captured by Gustavus Adolphus on Sept. 15th, 1621, after a protracted siege, and from that time on it remained in the hands of Sweden. In the wars between Sweden and Russia, the town was unsuccessfully besieged by the Tzar Alexis Mikháilovitch in 1656. In the Northern War the city resisted the Russians under General Sheremétycv for eight months, but was finally compelled to open its gates on July 4th, 1710. By the *Peace of Nystad* (1721) Livonia and Riga were incorporated with the Russian empire. Herder lived in Riga as a teacher and preacher from 1764 to 1769, and Hardenberg here wrote his memoir on the reorganization of the Prussian state in 1807. The French bombarded Riga in 1812, setting fire to the wooden houses of the suburbs, and the English under Admiral Sir Charles Napier blockaded it in 1854. In 1857 the fortifications were demolished, in 1877 the old constitution was abrogated, and in 1889 Riga was organized on the model of the Russian towns.

In the square in front of the Orel Railway Station (Pl. E, 4; *I*) stands a *Chapel*, erected to commemorate the escape of the imperial family at Borki (p. 400). From this point a series of **Boulevards*, flanked on both sides by handsome houses, runs towards the N. These follow the course of the old ramparts, which have been transformed into an attractive park traversed by the city canal. On the E. side of the boulevards lie the *Lomonósov High School for Girls* (Pl. 20, E 3; *I*), the *Alexander High School* (Pl. 12, E 3; *I*), the *Polytechnic* (Pl. 24, E 3, *I*; 2000 students), built in 1869 from Hilbig's designs, and the *City High School* (Pl. 27, D, E, 3; *I*).— On the W. side are the *Chief Police Office*, the *Post* and *Telegraph Office* (Pl. E, 3; *I*), and the *City Theatre* (Pl. E 3, *I*; p. 54), built by Bohnstedt in 1863 and restored after a fire in 1887. Farther on is the so-called *Powder Tower* (Pulverturm; Pl. *II*), which dates from 1650 and is the only wholly preserved tower of the former fortifications. In 1892 it was provided with a pointed roof, and taken possession of by the 'Rubonia', a student society (visitors admitted to see the interior). Adjacent is a monumental fountain with the figure of a Knight of the Teutonic Order, by Neumann (1898). The castle-like structure a little to the N. is the *Gas Works* (Pl. *II*), now used as offices only.— The *Basteiberg* (Pl. *II;* café, see p. 53) affords a view over the ring of boulevards.

In front of the old town, at the S. end of the Alexander Boulevard, is a bronze equestrian *Statue of Peter the Great* (Pl. 23, E 3; *I*), by Schmidt-Cassel (1910). On the left side of the busy Kalk-Str., which leads hence into the old town, is the Russian club *Ulei* (No. 30; Pl. 11, *II*). Opposite, at Grosse König-Str. 4, is the house of the German *Mussen-Gesellschaft*, where the theatrical performances took place until 1863; Richard Wagner was conductor of the orchestra here in 1837-39.— The Kalk-Str. runs into the Rathaus-Platz, in the middle of which is a fountain with a figure of Roland, in sandstone, by Neumann and Volz (1897). On the N.W. side of the square is the former **City Hall** *(Rathaus;* Pl. 8, *II)*, built in 1750-65 by Von Öttinger, which now contains the *Office of the City Orphanages*, the *Municipal Discount Bank*, and the *City Library*, with 100,000 vols., incunabula from the former Riga convents, letters of Luther and Herder, etc. (week-days 1-4; from June 12th to Aug. 12th, O. S., on Wed. and Sat. only).—Opposite the City Hall, to the S., stands the—

*Hall of the Blackheads *(Schwarzhäupterhaus;* Pl. 9, *II)*, one of the oldest buildings in the city, built in 1330. The Gothic gable was reconstructed in the Renaissance style in 1620, and in

1889 it was adorned with figures of Neptune, Unity, Peace, and Mercury, above which are the arms of Riga, Hamburg, Lübeck, and Bremen. At the entrance on the side next the square are two 'Beischlagsteine' (slabs from a 'stoop') of 1522, with reliefs of the Virgin Mary and St. Maurice. Among the objects of interest in the interior are the Golden Book, with autographs of royal and other eminent visitors, some silver plate (table-ware and loving-cups of the 16-17th centuries), weapons, and portraits of Swedish and Russian rulers (admission on application on the groundfloor of Grosse Waage-Str. No. 1).

The *Blackheads*, a society of unmarried citizens of the better class, are first mentioned in 1413. Originally they formed merely a kind of club of the unmarried merchants from other towns living in Riga, but they soon acquired a very considerable influence in the town. The so-called 'Blackheads' in the small Livonian towns and in the castles of the Teutonic knights, were, on the contrary, military companies in the service of the Order, which were of a later origin than the Blackheads of Riga and disappeared with the abolition of the Order in 1561. — The Blackheads chose St. George as their chief patron-saint, and associated with him St. Maurice, who is always represented as a Moor. One of their chief festivals takes place upon the first Saturday after Shrove Tuesday, when the 'Fastnachtsdrunken', or Carnival drinking-bout, is still observed in the ancient fashion.

Proceeding to the N.W. from the Rathaus-Platz through the Kleine Neu-Str. and the Palais-Str., we reach the Herder-Platz, in which there is a bronze *Bust of Herder* (p. 55), by Schaller (1864). On the S. side of the adjacent Dom-Platz stands the *Cathedral or Church of the Virgin *(*Dom;* Pl. D 3, *I;* sacristan in the adjoining Domkirchenhaus), a brick building in the late Romanesque style with a square tower. The cathedral was begun in 1211, and in the second half of the 15th cent. it was converted into a basilica; it was restored after a fire in 1547 and again in 1883-1910.

The S. aisle contains stalls belonging to the Blackheads (17th cent.) and six modern stained-glass windows, with scenes from the life of Christ. On the N. wall of the chancel is the monument of Bishop Meinhard (d. 1196; p. 32). The choir-stalls date from the 14th century. In the floor of the N. transept is the tombstone of William of Brandenburg (d. 1563), the last Archbishop of Riga. The pulpit was made in 1641. The Ecke Chapel (N. side, the third to the left of the main entrance) has two stained-glass windows, the one representing Grand-Master Walter von Plettenberg confirming the religious freedom of the city in 1525, and the other the reception of Gustavus Adolphus of Sweden by the town council in 1621 at the entrance of the cathedral. The windows in the bridal chapel (adjacent, to the left) represent Engelbrecht von Tiesenhausen and the foundation of the cathedral. — The *Organ*, which was built in 1884 and is contained in an organ-case made by Jacob Raab in 1601, has 125 stops (frequent recitals). — The *Cloisters*, with their Romanesque columns and Gothic arcades, and the Tonsorium were reconstructed in 1893 (admission-ticket 15 cop.). The cloister-garth, adjoining the S. wall of the church, contains an embossed copper statue of Bishop Albert (p. 55), by K. Bernewitz (1897), and (on the E. side) a font from the church of Üxküll (p. 48).

In the old cathedral convent, remodelled in 1889, is the so-called

Dom Museum (Pl. 2, *II;* entrance in the Palais-Str.), containing the *Municipal Archives* (open on week-days, 10-3), the museum of the Historical Society (see below), and the *Collections of the Natural History Society* (open on Sun. 12-2; admission 15 cop.; guide, 1911, 20 cop.).

The *Museum of the Historical Society*, which occupies the first and second floors, is open on Sun., 12-3 p.m. (adm. 20 cop.), and at other times on application to the castellan, next door, Palais-Str. 2 (30 cop.). Illustrated catalogue (1911) 50 cop.

FIRST FLOOR. Room I. (Session Room). Pictures of the 17th century. — Room II. Locksmith's work, musical instruments, town-banners of Riga of the 17-18th cent.; chemist's shop of Riga in the 18th century. — Room III. Objects found in graves from the flint period to the later iron period; ecclesiastical robes; so-called goblet of Emperor Otho (10th cent.; window-case 38). — Room IV. Riga corporation room of the middle of the 18th century. — Room V. Suite of furniture of the second half of the 18th cent.; ceramic ware; objects in glass and silver. — Rooms VI-VIII. Arms and armour. — Room IX (entered from Room V.). Furniture, miniatures, coins, dies for medals.

SECOND FLOOR (reached from R. II). Room X. Portraits of eminent ecclesiastics, generals, scholars, and artists of Livonia; costumes and embroidery. — Room XI. Portraits, views of Riga (including a large and unique copper-plate of 1612), plans, and albums. — Room XII. Portraits of representatives of the Livonian noblesse. — In the cloisters of the cathedral (p. 57) are some Riga cannon of the 16-17th cent. and some architectural fragments.

Near the cathedral, at the corner of the Jakob-Str., is the **Exchange** *(Börse;* Pl. *II),* built in the Venetian Renaissance style from the plans of H. von Bosse in 1852-55 (business-hours 10.30-12). In the Grosse Schloss-Str., which leads to the Schloss-Platz, is the *English Institution* (with a Sailors' Home and the English Club; entrance in the Anglikanische-Str.), behind which is the *English Church* (Pl. *II),* a tasteful Gothic structure, built in 1859 from the designs of J. D. Felsko. At the end of the Grosse Schloss-Str. is the *Roman Catholic Church* (Pl. *II),* consecrated in 1785. — The SCHLOSS-PLATZ contains a granite *Column of Victory,* 26 ft. in height and surmounted by a bronze figure of Victory erected in 1818 in memory of the momentous years 1812-1814. On the W. side of the square stands the —

Castle *(Schloss;* Pl. D 3, *I),* formerly the commandery of the Teutonic Order and now occupied by the Governor of Livonia. It was erected in 1330, rebuilt in 1491-1515, and again altered in 1682 and 1783.

From the Schloss-Platz we enter the court of the old outer castle by the so-called 'Schwedentor' ('Swedish Gate'). To the right are the rooms occupied by the Governor. To the left is the main gate of the old castle, outside which, to the right, are a statue of the Virgin Mary, patron saint of the Order, and another of the Grand-Master Walter von Plettenberg (p. 67). Both the figures date from 1515. The gateway, with its two star-vaults, leads to the court of the old inner castle, on the opposite side of which is another vaulted archway leading to the Roman Catholic Church (see above). — Within the castle are still preserved the old chapel of the Order and the refectory, but both have been remodelled to serve as office-rooms.

From the Schloss-Platz we proceed to the E. to the Grosse Jakob-Str., in which stands the so-called **Ritterhaus** (Pl. *II;* open on week-days, 10-3), rebuilt in 1864-66 in the style of the Florentine Renaissance and extended in 1908. On the main façade, which is turned towards the Kloster-Str., is a statue of Walter von Plettenberg, after Schwanthaler. The Hall of the Knights, in which the Diet of Livonia meets, contains the armorial bearings of the noble families of Livonia. The *Library* (open on week-days, 1-3 p.m.; librarian, K. von Löwis) contains the original MS., engrossed with Indian ink on parchment, of the Rhymed Chronicle of Livonia (14th cent.). — Opposite is the *Church of St. James* (St. Jakobs-kirche; Pl. *II*), a brick structure in the Transition style of the beginning of the 13th cent., practically rebuilt in the 15th century. The sacristy contains portraits of former general superintendents.

Passing the Exchange (p. 58) and following the Scheunen-Str. and the Grosse Pferde-Str., we reach the house of the ***Great** or **Virgin's Guild** (Pl. 5; *II*), the guild of the merchants, probably dating from the second half of the 13th cent., but rebuilt from plans by Beyne in 1853-59 (caretaker in the house).

The great hall on the groundfloor has a vaulted ceiling, supported by six slender pillars, and is adorned with a modern painted frieze of municipal coats-of-arms. On one side is the seat of the 'Dockmann' or president, so called from the 'Docke' (*i.e.* doll), an image of the Virgin Mary, dating from the beginning of the 16th cent., which is placed behind the seat at meetings of the guild. Above the door leading to the Bridal Chamber are the remains of a gilded wood-carving (from an altar), representing the Death of the Virgin (end of the 15th cent.). The beautiful sandstone chimney-piece of the Bridal Chamber dates from 1633.

Opposite is the *Small* or *St. John's Guild* (Pl. 6; *II*), the guild-hall of the artisans, built by J. D. Felsko in the Gothic style in 1866. The Hall of the Elders contains stained-glass windows representing the presidents of the guild in mediæval costume (1888).

From the Guilds we proceed to the S.E. through the Scheunen-Str. and the Scharren-Str. to the **Church of St. Peter** (Pl. *II;* sacristan, Petri-Friedhof 7), the choir of which was erected in 1409 after the model of the Church of St. Mary in Rostock, while the nave was added in 1456-66. The three portals in the baroque style date from 1692. The interior contains interesting hatchments of the 17-18th cent., a marble pulpit of 1793, and an altar-piece by Steinle (Descent of the Holy Ghost). In the ambulatory (r.) is a seven branched brazen candelabrum of 1596. The *Tower* (404 ft.), topped by a spire with three galleries, dates in its present form from 1746. The first gallery commands a splendid view of the town and sea.

A little to the E. is the ancient *Church of St. John* (Pl. *II*), formerly belonging to the Dominicans, with a fine W. gable. Adjacent are the remains of the cloisters of the Dominican Convent, which was the episcopal residence down to 1234. Close by are a hospice called *Ecke's Convent*, built in 1596 and renewed in 1770,

and another hospice known as the *Convent of the Holy Ghost* (Pl. 7; *11*), incorporating the remains of the St. George's Church of the Brethren of the Sword, dating from 1202 and thus the oldest building in Riga.

From St. Peter's the Sünder-Str. leads S.W. to the *Dvina,* across which three bridges lead to the Mitau Suburb (p. 62). One of these is a *Pontoon Bridge,* 575 yds. long, another an iron *Girder Bridge* (Pl. D, 4; *I*), $^1/_2$ M. long, supported by eight granite piers, and the third a new *Railway Bridge,* adjoining the Girder Bridge.

The busiest scenes on the quays of the Dvina are witnessed near the *Market Place* (Pl. *II*), beside the *Customs Harbour* ('Zollquai'; Pl. C, 2, 3, *I*), and at the *Ambaren,* or warehouses, above the rail way-bridge. At the Ambaren may be seen the so-called *Strusen,* i.e. large flat barges, which descend the Dvina loaded with country-products during the high-water of spring and after discharging their cargoes are taken to pieces and sold for fire-wood. — On June 22nd (O.S.) the so-called 'Krautabend', a floral fête with illuminations and fire-works, is held on and near the Dvina.

To the E. of the circle of boulevards (p. 56) lies the attractive **Wöhrmann Park** (Pl. E 3, *I;* music, see p. 54), presented to the town in 1817 and containing a *Mineral Water Establishment* (Pl. 22), and a fair *Restaurant* (p. 53).

In the Paulucci-Str. (No. 13) is the *House of the Lettish Society* (Pl. 19, E 3; *I*), containing an ethnographical collection, with interesting figures in local costumes (open on Sun. and Wed., 11-2; adm., 20 cop; new museum proposed for the Pushkin Boulevard).

To the N. of the Wöhrmann Park are the *District Court* (Pl. 15, E 3; *I*) and the *Court of the Justices of the Peace* (Pl. 16; *I*). Opposite, in the Esplanade (Pl. D, E, 2, 3; *I*), which is partly adorned with pleasure-grounds, is the *Greek Catholic Cathedral* (Pl. 17; *I*), erected in 1877-84 from the plans of Pflug. To the N.E. of it stands a monument, to *Field-Marshal Barclay de Tolly* (1761-1818), by W. Wandschneider (1913). On the N.W. side of the Esplanade, to the left, stands the *Commercial School* (Pl. 18; *I*), built by Bockslaff in 1905 in the Gothic style. To the right is the—

Municipal Museum of Art *(Kunstmuseum;* Pl. E 2, *I),* a building in the S. German baroque style, erected by Neumann in 1905. It contains 500 pictures and is open from March 1st to Sept. 30th on week-days (except Mon.) 11-4 (adm. 30 cop.), on Sun. 11.30 to 4 (20 cop.); in winter it closes at 3 p.m. Visitors are not admitted between June 15th and July 15th (O.S.). Catalogue 30 cop., with illustrations 1 rb. Director, Dr. W. Neumann.

Ground Floor. On the left are Sculptures, mostly casts. — On the right is the collection of Engravings.

Upper Floor. On the left are the rooms of the Riga Art Union. On the same side is also the Brederlo Gallery. Room I. *J. A. Ingres,*

Raphael and the Fornarina; 89. *Sir E. Landseer*, Resting; 102. *B. Manfredi*, Musical entertainment; 188. *H. Vernet*, Flight of the Kabyles from Constantine; 198. *Sir D. Wilkie*, Illicit still in Ireland. — Room II. 17. *Jan de Bray*, Christ appearing to the Virgin; 36. *A. van Dyck*, Prince William of Orange as a child; 40. *A. Elsheimer*, Landscape; 86. *Chr. van der Laenen*, Prodigal Son; 97. *Lübeck Master of 1520*, Domestic altar (triptych); 115. *Josse de Momper*, River-scene. — Room III: 4. *L. Bakhuisen*, Rough sea; 35. *J. Droochsloot*, Village-festival; 67. *M. d'Hondecoeter*, Cock-fight; 96. *J. van Loo*, Portrait of a scholar; 98. *G. Lundens*, Boors playing cards; 127. *E. van der Neer*, At the cradle; 140. *E. van den Poel*, Farm. — Room IV: 19. *Q. Brekelenkam*, Visiting the sick; 54. *Harmen Hals*, Pancake-baker; 69. *L. de Jongh*, Family-scene; 114. *P. Molyn the Elder*, River-scene; 141. *J. Porcellis*, Rough sea; 159. *S. van Ruysdael*, River-scene; 176. *M. Sweerts*, Shepherds in a cave; 196. *J. Wynants*; Scene on the dunes. — Room V: (lit from above): 1, 2. *A. Achenbach*, Landscapes; 22. *H. Bürkel*, Italian rural life; 46. *K. D. Friedrich*, Sea-beach by moonlight; 49. *F. Gauermann*, Stag-hunt; 82. *A. Koch*, Italian landscape; 84. *Franz Krüger*, Groom; 90. *K. F. Lessing*, Scene in the Eifel; 151. *L. Richter*, Tiber at Acqua Acetosa.

On the right is the MUNICIPAL GALLERY. Cabinet I: *K. Spitzweg*, 199. Old Commandant, 200. Hermit; *F. Sonderland*, 196. On the way to school, 197. The two malefactors. — Cab. II: 11. *A. Beyeren*, Fish; 59. *Wybrandt de Geest*, Portrait of a gentleman; 147. *J. Mancadam*, Ruins. — Cab. III: 73. *Harmen Hals*, Cobbler's workshop; 81. *H. Herschop*, Portrait of the physician, Seyger van Rechteren; 137. *J. M. de Jonge*, Cavalry skirmish. — Cab. IV: 39 a. *L. Dill*, Fishermen at Chioggia; also, paintings by modern Baltic artists. — Of the three rooms lit from above, the first contains pictures by Baltic and Russian artists (*G. von Bochmann, E. Dücker, E. von Gebhardt, A. Spring, K. von Winkler, N. Kasátkin, J. Aivazóvski*, and *N. Bogolyúbov*); the second pictures by *H. Makart* (9), *F. von Lenbach, A. Feuerbach* (Pietà, Study), *W.* and *H. von Kaulbach, K. Rottmann*, and others; the third works by Flemish masters of the 17th cent. and by Italian and French masters.

To the N.W. of the Esplanade lies the pleasant *Schützen-Garten* (Pl. D, 2; *I*), to which strangers may obtain entrance on introduction by a member of the Schützenverein. Farther to the N. is the **Imperial Garden (Kaiserlicher Garten;* Pl. D 1, *I; Restaurant;* comp. p. 54), laid out in the time of Peter the Great and containing some fine old lime-trees. — We now return to the centre of the town by the Peter-Paul-Str., passing the Greek Catholic *Cathedral of SS. Peter and Paul* (Pl. C, D, 2; *I*), built in 1786 within the citadel, which has since been demolished. Farther to the S. are the building of the *Livländischer Kredit-Verein* (Pl. *II*), completed in the Renaissance style from Koch's designs in 1890, and the *Russian Theatre* (Russisches Stadttheater; Pl. *II*), by Reinberg (1901).

The ST. PETERSBURG SUBURB, to the N.E. of the old town, contains the *Municipal Hospital* (Stadt-Krankenhaus; Pl. E, F, 1, 2; *I*) and the *Church of St. Gertrude* (Pl. E, 2; *I*), completed in the Gothic style from J. D. Felsko's designs in 1867. Not far off, in the Nikolai-Str., are the extensive *Wagner Nursery Gardens* (Pl. E, F, 1, *I;* open to the public on week-days till 7 p.m.).

. In the Petersburger Chaussée, prolonging the Alexander-Str. (Pl. G, 1; *I*) towards the N.E., are several large factories. — On the S. bank of the Stintsee (p. 65) is the *Kaiserwald* (restaurant at the terminus of the tramway mentioned at p. 54), with a group of villas, a recreation-ground (30 cop.), and a zoological garden.

In the Moscow SUBURB, which is inhabited by the poorer classes, may be mentioned the *Church of St. Paul* (Pl. G, 2, 3; *I*), built in 1887 from the designs of Hilbig; the Greek Catholic *Church of the Annunciation*, dating from 1814-18; the wooden *Church of Jesus* (Pl. E 4, *I;* Lutheran); the *Synagogue* (Pl. F, 5; *I*); and the Roman Catholic *Church of St. Francis* (Pl. F, 4; *I*), built in 1889-92 in the Gothic style. To the left of the last is the grave of *Konradin Kreutzer* (d. 1849), the composer.

The MITAU SUBURB, reached by one of the bridges mentioned at p. 60, contains the *Seamen's Home* (Pl. C, 4; *I*), built by Scheel in 1884. For the Hagensberg Summer Theatre, see p. 54. — In Thorensberg (p. 63) are the large and new *Peter Park,* the *Luther Church* (Pl. C, 6; *I*), built by Koch in 1891, and (farther to the W.) the Roman Catholic *Church of St. Albert* (Pl. A, 6; *I*), built from plans by Bockslaff in 1903. Hagensberg contains the *Church of St. Martin,* near which, on the bank of the Dvina, is a promenade known as the Philosopher's Walk, so named after J. G. Hamann, who lived in Riga in 1755 and 1759.

FROM RIGA TO HAFENDAMM, 18 V. (12 M.), railway in $^3/_4$ hr. (steamer to Bolderaa, see p. 54).—From Riga to (6 V.) *Sassenhof,* see p. 63. Beyond (15 V.) *Bolderaa* the train crosses the *Courland Aa* (*Kurische, Buller,* or *Bolder Aa*), which here joins the Dvina, and reaches (17 V.) *Dünamünde,* officially named *Ust-Dvinsk,* a fortified town on the left bank of the Dvina, at the point where it flows into the Gulf of Riga. Dünamünde owes its origin to a Cistercian convent founded on the right bank by Bishop Albert I. in 1205. This was purchased by the Brethren of the Sword in 1305 and turned into one of their lodges. The fortifications on the left bank were constructed in the 17th century. — 18 V. *Hafendamm,* with a winter-harbour. Visitors who wish to ascend the lighthouse must obtain permission from the commandant of the fortress.

FROM RIGA TO MÜHLGRABEN, 10 V. (7 M.), railway in $^1/_2$ hr., starting from the Orel Station. The train passes the *Military Hospital* (left) and the *Alexandershöhe,* on which are two lunatic asylums. — *Mühlgraben* has a winter-harbour, important shipbuilding-yards, and several large manufactories. Steamboat to Riga, see p. 54.

The excursion to the **Island of Runö** (100 V. or 66 M. to the N. of Riga) offers little to the ordinary tourist, but is interesting to ethnographers. There is no regular communication with the island, but a sail-boat, which may be hired for 2-3 days for about 10 rb., crosses the intervening strait in 12 hrs. Excursion-steamers also sometimes ply to Runö in June. The traveller should take his own provisions, including coffee, tea, and sugar, and may apply for accommodation to the pastor (Pastor och Kyrkeherre på Runö). — From Riga to (17 V.) *Dünamünde,* see p. 72. Beyond this we traverse the Gulf of Riga. — The island of *Runö* is $3^1/_2$ M. in length, $2^1/_2$ M. across at its widest part, and at its highest point 100 ft. above sea-level. It is inhabited by 300 Swedes of pure blood. The E. portion is covered with coniferous trees; on the W. coast are large erratic blocks. The village lies in the middle of the island. The wooden church of Mary Magdalen, built in 1641, is situated on a hill to the E. of the village. From the platform of the iron light-house (177 steps) a wide view is obtained. The inhabitants are engaged in fishing and sealing, but do not allow strangers to share in either of these.

From Riga to *Berlin* (Mitau, Libau), see R. 10; to *Reval,* see R. 12; to *St. Petersburg,* see R. 14; to *Moscow,* see R. 33.

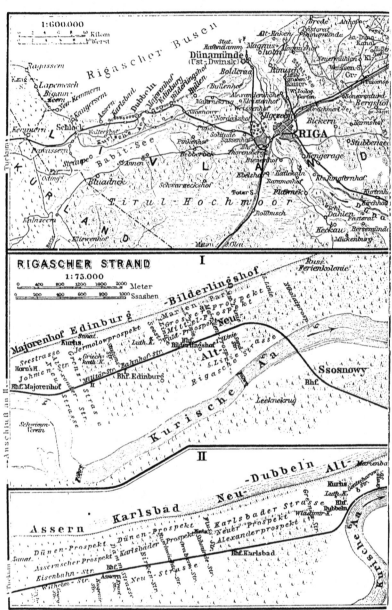

From Riga to Windau.   The Riga Coast.

RAILWAY from Riga to Windau, 165 V. (109 M.) in 5¹/₂ hrs.; the trains start from the Tuckum Station (p. 53). Reduced fares to Bilderlingshof 50 or 30 cop., to Majorenhof (1 hr.) or to Dubbeln 65 or 40 cop., to Kemmern 1 rb. 15 cop. or 70 cop. — STEAMER to Majorenhof and Dubbeln, or to Windau, see p. 54.

Riga, see p. 53. After leaving the Tuckum Station, the train crosses the *Dvina* by the bridge mentioned at p. 60. — 2 V. *Thorensberg* (p. 52).; 6 V. *Sassenhof* (p. 62). Near (9 V.) *Solitude* is a racecourse. Beyond (16 V.) *Sosnóvi* we cross the *Courland Aa* (p. 62), an arm of which runs into the Gulf of Riga a little farther to the E.

We now reach the first of a series of bathing-resorts, situated on a peninsula between the Courland Aa and the *Gulf of Riga,* and surrounded by pine-woods. These resorts stretch from Bilderlingshof to Assern, a distance of 8 M., and are annually frequented in June, July, and Aug., by 80,000 visitors. There are numerous summer-villas (datchas), and the sandy beach is good. The cabtariff, visitors' tax, and hours for bathing are in each case the same as those at Majorenhof (see below).

19 V. *Bilderlingshof* (Railway Restaurant; Hotel Bilderlingshof, Pl. a, at the corner of the Grosser Prospékt and Marien-Prospékt, with concert-garden, R. 1-3 rb., D. from 60 cop., pens. 60-90 rb. monthly; Pension Tannenheim, corner of the Grosser Prospékt and 10th Linie) is the first of the resorts, and is especially visited by the citizens of Riga. On the dunes is the Marien-Park.

20 V. *Edinburg,* with two stations (Kurhaus, with a sea-pavilion, D. 60 cop. to 1 rb.; Pension Klapper, Yermólov Prospékt 46; Pens. Kevitch, Yermólov Prospékt 39, pens. from 3¹/₂ rb.), is the most fashionable of the resorts, with handsome villas in the Yermólov or Jermólow Prospékt. Next door to the Kurhaus is the Sanatorium of Dr. Maximovitch.

22 V. **Majorenhof.** — *Rail. Restaurant.* — HORN'S HOTEL (burnt down in 1913), Jobmen-Str. 11, 4 min. from the station, with concert-garden and sea-pavilion, R. from 1¹/₂, B. ¹/₂, D. (1-5 p.m.) ³/₄-1¹/₂ rb., pens. 25-35 rb. weekly. Admission to the concert-garden 50 cop., for the season 6 rh. — PENSIONS. *Radecki,* See-Str. 63, pens. 4-6 rh.; *Mischke,* See-Str. 61. — CABS. Each resort forms a cab-district, except Assern, which is divided into two. Per drive 15 cop., with two horses 25 cop.; from one district to the next 25 or 35 cop., through two districts into a third 35 or 45 cop., per hour 50 or 65 cop. — STEAMBOAT WHARF, near the Rail. Station. — BATHING HOURS: men till 10 a.m. & 1-3 p.m., women 10-1 & 3 to 5.30 p.m. Bath 10 cop. — VISITORS' TAX 1 rb.

Majorenhof is the most crowded and popular of the resorts on the Riga coast. Those who wish quieter quarters should select the See-Str. in preference to the lively Jobmen-Str. Among the visitors are many Russians. Boating may be had on the Aa, but caution must be observed with sailing-boats.

24 V. **Dubbeln.** — *Railway Restaurant.* — HOTELS. *Kurhaus*, opposite the rail. station, with concert-garden, R. 2-5 rb., D. (1-6 p.m.) 85 cop., pens. from 4 rb.; *Brückmann* (Pl. b), Gontcharov-Str. 3. — *Marienbad Hydropathic*, on the beach.

Dubbeln, the oldest of the Riga bathing resorts, is (like Majorenhof) very noisy; among the visitors are many Jews. The Kurhaus is the centre of activity.

26 V. *Karlsbad* (Kurhaus) and (29 V.) *Assern*, the westernmost of the larger Riga beach-resorts, are both simpler and quieter than the others. Strawberries are grown in the neighbourhood.

33 V. *Schlock*, a small town with 4500 inhab., has a large celluloid factory. The railway enters the government of Courland.

42 V. **Kemmern** (*Rail. Restaurant; Annenhof*, Tuckumer-Str.; *Kurhaus*, Direktor-Allée; cab from the rail. station to the village 25 cop.) is a spa with six cold sulphur-springs, mud-baths, and a pleasant Kur-Park. It is visited annually by over 6000 persons. The season lasts from May 15th to August 25th (O.S.). Visitors' tax 3 rb. A sulphur bath costs 80 cop. to 1 rb. 30 cop., a mud bath 1 rb. to 1 rb. 10 cop. — About $4^1/_2$ M. to the N.E. is the sea-bathing place of *Neu-Kemmern*, to which an electric tramway runs from the railway station.

61 V. **Tuckum** (*Railway Restaurant; Riga*, in the market-place), a district-town with 12,000 inhab. and the remains of a castle of the Teutonic Order, founded ca. 1300. About $4^1/_2$ M. to the N.E. (carr. & pair in $^3/_4$ hr.; return fare, incl. 1 hr.'s stay, 3 rb.) rises the *Hüningsberg* (365 ft.), the view from which has been partly spoiled by the growth of the trees. — From (63 V.) *Tuckum Vtoрói* (i.e. *Tuckum II.*) a railway runs to Mitau and Kreuzburg (see p. 47). — 86 V. *Zehren*.

About 4 M. to the S. of Zehren lies *Kandau* (Jägermann, R. 1, D. $^3/_4$-1 rb.), a village in the so-called 'Courland Switzerland', with 2400 inhab. and the tower of a castle of the Teutonic Order erected ca. 1250.

104 V. *Stenden* (Railway Restaurant), with a fine park.

About 8 M. to the N. lies *Talsen* (St. Petersburg, R. 1-2 rb.), a prettily situated village with 5000 inhab. and a public park affording a fine view. — The prettily situated village of *Zabeln*, 8 M. to the S. of Stenden, contains 1800 inhab., most of whom are Jews.

Beyond (122 V.) *Spahren*, to the left, lies *Lake Usmaiten* (16 sq. M. in area), with four islands, one of which, named the *Moritzholm*, is noted for its luxuriant vegetation and is maintained as a natural park.

165 V. **Windau**, Виндава. — *Railway Restaurant.* — HOTELS. *Hôtel de Rome*, R. $^3/_4$-5 rb., B. 30 cop.; D. (1-5 p.m.) 1 rb., omn. 50 cop.; *Hôtel Royal.* — CAB, with one horse, from the railway station to (10 min.) the town 50, in the reverse direction 30 cop.; per drive 10, per hr. 40 cop. —

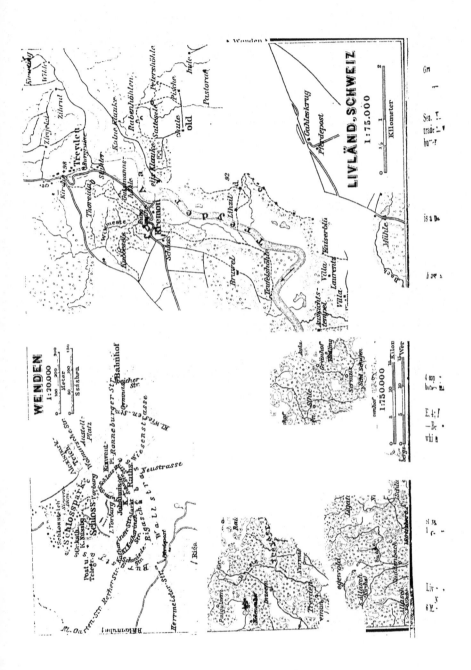

British Vice-Consul, *E. H. Ruffmann.*—Lloyd's Agents, *Helmsing & Grimm,* Wasser-Str.—Steamer to Libau (6-7 hrs.) and Riga (see p. 54). Steamers also ply to London (p. xviii), *Copenhagen,* and other ports.

Windau, the capital of a district in Courland, with 25,000 inhab., lies on the left bank of the *Windau,* at its mouth in the Baltic Sea. The harbour is open all the year round. Windau has a large trade in wood and grain and is the chief shipping port for Siberian butter (see p. 524). The railway station and the grain elevator lie on the right bank, and are reached by a bridge-of-boats (railway bridge in course of construction). The *Castle,* an unpretentious building erected in 1290, was once the seat of a lodge of the Teutonic Order; the well-preserved chapel is now used by the Greek Catholics. There is a good bathing-beach; at the edge of the wood is a pavilion with a restaurant.

About 50 V. (33 M.) to the N.E. of Windau lies *Dondangen,* the largest estate in Courland, surrounded by extensive forests in which the elk is still hunted. To the N. of this point Courland tapers off to a long narrow tongue reaching out into the sea. About 3¹/₂ M. to the N., at the extremity of this peninsula, which is named *Domesnäs,* there is a lighthouse, situated on an artificial island.

12. From Riga to Reval.

a. By Railway viâ Walk and Dorpat.

414 V. (274 M.). Railway in 13 hrs. (fares 12 rb. 50, 7 rb. 50 cop., reserved seat 1¹/₂ rb.). In summer there are local trains to Wenden.

For land-journeys it is advisable to order horses in advance (horse 4 cop. per verst, calèche 50 cop.). The railway stations at which post horses may be procured are indicated below.

Riga, see p. 53. The train starts from the Orel Station (Pl. E, 4; *I*), and makes its first stop at (6 V.) *Alexander-Pforte* (25 ft.). —Beyond (10 V.) *Jägel* we reach a bridge across the river *Jägel,* which connects the *Jägelsee* (right) with the *Stintsee* (left; p. 61). To the left is the Aa and Dvina Canal, completed in 1903. Herder (comp. p. 55) used to spend his summers on Lake Jägel. — 39 V. *Hintzenberg* (175 ft.; posting-station). The line now ascends.

50 V. (33 M.) **Segewold.** —*Rail. Restaurant,* well spoken of.— Hotels. *Hotel Segewold* (Pl. a), R. from 75, D. 70 cop.; *Central Hotel* (Pl. b), R. from 60, D. (1-3 p.m.) 65 cop., pens. 40-70 rb. monthly.— Pensions. *Schwenn* (Pl. c); *Nachtigal* (Pl. d); *Weisses Haus* (Pl. e), pens. 1³/₄-2¹/₂ rb. — Cab from the rail. station to the château of Segewold 25 cop., to Kremon or Treyden 75 cop., per hour 50 cop. — Segewold is a posting station.

Segewold (330 ft.), the property of Prince Krapotkin, is visited as a summer-resort and is the best starting-point for exploring the Livonian Switzerland (p. 66). It is also frequented for winter sports.

Nurmis, the estate of Count Dunten-Dalwigk, with a fine park, lies 6 M. to the N.E. of Segewold; 5 M. to the S.E. of Nurmis is *Ligat* (p. 67).

Between Kronenberg on the W. and Segewold and Treyden
on the E. the *Livonian Aa* flows in a winding course through a
valley, the geological formation of which consists mainly of red
sandstone. Since the beginning of the 19th cent., this valley, with
its prettily wooded slopes (rising to a height of 265 ft.), its three
ruined castles, and its two large caverns, has been known as the
Livonian Switzerland (Livländische Schweiz). A hurried
visit may be made to it in 4 hrs. — From the railway station of
Segewold (p. 65) we proceed in a straight direction, passing the
Segewold Hotel (Pl. a) on the right. After 9 min. we keep on in
the same direction, avoiding the road to the left, and in 5 min.
more we pass the Central Hotel (Pl. b) on the left. In 3 min. more
we reach a fork, where we either descend the road to the left to
the Aa ferry (see below) or go on in a straight direction to (4 min.)
the ruin of Segewold, passing the new château of Prince Krapotkin
on the left. The castle of *Segewold*, of which imposing remains
are preserved, was built of rubble by the Teutonic Order in 1208,
and was destroyed at the beginning of the 17th cent., during the
wars between Sweden and Poland. A pavilion to the left of the
entrance commands a fine view of the valley of the Aa, with the
château of Kremon on the opposite bank.

We now return to the fork mentioned above, and descend to
the right to the ($^1/_4$ hr.) ferry across the Aa (fare 1 cop.). On
reaching the opposite bank we keep to the right; after 3 min. we
may either ascend, by the curving road to the left, to ($^1/_4$ hr.) the
Schweizerhaus Inn at *Kremon* (Pl. f; R. 75 cop., D. 65 cop. to 1 rb.,
pens. $1^1/_2$-2 rb.), or we may turn to the right for (12 min.) the
Gutmanns-Höhle (see below). A little to the E. of the Schweizerhaus
are the scanty remains of a castle erected by the canons of Riga.
Between the Schweizerhaus and the new château of Princess Lieven
is a pavilion affording a view of Segewold.

If time allows, we may descend by the 325 steps beginning at the
pavilion, and proceed to (1 hr.) the *Teufels-Höhle*, a cavern situated on
the Aa.

Near the ruin of Kremon, at the *Bellevue* (just before reaching
which we have an open view of the valley of the Aa), we descend
a series of 380 steps. At the bottom we turn to the right, cross
the brook, ascend a little, and then proceed along the side of the
hill to the (25 min.) *Gutmanns-Höhle*, a large sandstone cavern
containing a spring, and with its walls covered with roughly carved
inscriptions.

From the cave we go on in the same direction (N.E.) along the
slope, and after 5 min. turn to the left into the road, from which,
after 6 min. more, a steep footpath ascends to the right to the ruin
of Treyden. The road continues to ascend to (9 min.) a fork, the
left branch of which leads to (5 min.) the Schweizerhaus Hotel

(Pl. g; R. 60-75, D. 50-60 cop., pens. 1$^1/_2$ rb.), while the right leads to (5 min.) the ruined castle of *Treyden* (1214), formerly belonging to the Archbishops of Riga but now the property of Baron Staël von Holstein. The chief feature of the ruins is a round brick tower, 90 ft. high. The garden affords a good view of the Aa valley. From this point we regain the railway station of Segewold in 1$^1/_2$ hr.

Beyond (61 V.) *Ligat* (395 ft.) we cross the stream of that name. About 6 V. to the N. (shadeless road) lies the prettily-situated paper-mill of *Ligat.* — About 5 V. to the N.E. of (70 V.) *Ramozki* (385 ft.), in the smiling valley of the *Ammat*, lies the manor of *Karlsruhe.* — To the left lies *Arrasch* (485 ft.), the highest point of the line, situated on a small lake, on the S. bank of which are the scanty remains of a ruined castle.

88 V. (58 M.) **Wenden**, Венденъ (Plan, see p. 65). — *Railway Restaurant.* — Hotels. *Baltischer Hof* (Pl. a), Rigasche-Str. 21, $^1/_3$ M. from the station, with garden, R. 1-1$^3/_4$ rb., D. 65 cop.; *Central Hotel* (Pl. b), Rigasche-Str. 17, R. $^3/_4$-1$^1/_2$ rb.; *Schloss Wenden* (Pl. c), near the castle, R. $^3/_4$-1$^1/_2$ rb., D. (1-4 p.m.) 75 cop. — Cab from the station to the town 20, per hr. 40 cop. — Post & Telegraph Office, Burg-Str. 19.

Wenden (Lettish *Zehsis;* 355 ft.), capital of a district, with 6800 inhabitants, is pleasantly situated 2 M. to the E. of the *Aa.*

The castle of Wenden was built by Volkquin (1209-36), second Grand Master of the Brethren of the Sword, and from 1237 on it was occupied by Masters of the Teutonic Order. It was considerably enlarged by Walter von Plettenberg (1494-1535), the most celebrated and fortunate of all the Masters who resided here. In 1577 the garrison blew themselves up in the castle in order to avoid falling into the hands of Iván the Terrible. At a later date the castle became the residence of Bishop Patricius Nidecki, who had been appointed by King Stephen Bathory of Poland in 1583. Since a destructive fire in 1748 the castle has been little more than a ruin.

From the railway station we proceed, in a straight direction, along the Ronneburger-Str. and the Rigasche-Str. After 6 min. we either proceed to the right, through the Schloss-Str., to the castle, or in a straight direction to (3 min.) the market-place. A few paces to the right of the latter is the *Church of St. John*, built in 1283-87 and last restored in 1900 (sexton, to the W., at Schmiede-Str. 1). In the vestibule, to the left, are some remains of the tombstone of Walter von Plettenberg; in the choir, to the right, are those of Grand-Masters Brüggeney and Freitag. At the end of the S. aisle is a bronze bust of Walter von Plettenberg, a replica of that by Schwanthaler in the Walhalla, near Ratisbon. At the end of the N. aisle, in the wall, is the monument of Bishop Patricius Nidecki (d. 1587; see above), with an effigy of the deceased.

A little to the N. of the Church of St. John (viâ the Turm-Str.), in the middle of a park belonging to the estate of Count Sievers, lie the well-preserved ruins of the old *Castle of the Teutonic Order*, built in 1210 (adm. 20 cop.). The most interesting feature is the late-Gothic reticulated vaulting of the Grand-Master's room in the W. tower. The top of the tower commands an extensive view of the town, and of the hilly country round it.

Birkenruhe (³/₄ M. to the W. of Wenden), a well-known school for boys, commands a fine view of Wenden and the ruined castle. — About 2 M. to the S.W. of Wenden is the wooded park of *Meiershof.* — *Ronneburg*, with the extensive ruins of an archiepiscopal château, lies 14 M. to the E. of Wenden. — About 40 M. to the S.E. of Wenden rises the *Gaisingkalns* (1030 ft.), the second-highest hill in the Baltic Provinces.

The railway crosses the *Valley of the Raune*, by a viaduct 80 ft. in height. — 114 V. (76 M.) **Wolmar** (165 ft.; *Rail. Restaurant; Riga*, R. ³/₄-1 rb.; cab to the town 40 cop.; posting-station), a town of 5800 inhab., with the scanty ruins of a castle of the Teutonic Order, founded in the 13th cent. and destroyed by the Russians in 1702.

To the N.E. the town is adjoined by *Wolmarshof*, the property of the Von Löwenstern family, the extensive woods of which teem with game. In the château are souvenirs of Queen Louise of Prussia. — About 13 V. (9 M.) to the W. of Wolmar is the *Blauberg* (425 ft.), said to be an old pagan sacrificial station. — To the S.W. of Wolmar is the finely situated church of *Papendorf* (12 V.).

Light railways run from Wolmar to *Haynasch*, on the Gulf of Riga, and to *Smilten*, with the remains of a castle of the Archbishops of Riga.

Just short of (133 V.) *Stackeln* (posting-station) the train crosses the Aa. It then traverses the extensive *Forest of Luhde*.

158 V. (105 M.) **Walk** (240 ft.; *Railway Restaurant; Baltischer Hof*, R. 1¹/₂-3, B. ¹/₂, D. 1 rb.; cab to the town 25 cop.), a pleasant little town with 20,500 inhabitants.

From Walk to *Pskov* and *St. Petersburg*, see R. 14a. — Light railways to *Pernau* and *Reval*, see R. 12b; to *Stockmannshof*, see p. 47.

The train now leaves the Lettish part of Livonia for the Esthonian, and crosses the Embach just before reaching (171 V.) *Sagnitz.* — 192 V. *Bockenhof* (410 ft.; posting-station); near *Odenpäh*, 10 M. to the E., is the beautiful *Heiliger See*, a little to the S. of which is the *Kleiner Munamägi* (800 ft.). — 212 V. *Elwa* (posting-station), a summer-resort on the Lake of Uddern.

236 V. (156 M.) **Dorpat**, officially styled *Yuryev*, Юрьевъ.

Rail. Restaurant. — HOTELS. *London* (Pl. a; B, 4), Promenaden-Str. 2, R. 1¹/₂-2 rb., B. 35 cop., D. (1-3 p.m.) ¹/₂-1 rb., no public dining room; *St. Petersburg* (Pl. b; C, 4), Neumarkt-Str. 22, 3 min. from the steamboat-landing, R. ³/₄-3 rb., B. 35, D. (12-4 p.m.) 50-75 cop.; *Bellevue* (Pl. c; C, 3), Rathaus-Str. 2; *Commerz Hotel* (Pl. d; B, 4), Rigasche-Str. 39.

RESTAURANTS. *Poirier*, Grosser Markt 2 (Pl. B, 3), at the corner of the Johannis-Str., D. (1-5 p.m.) 45 cop.; *Luchsinger*, Johannis-Str. 20 (Pl. B, 3), confectioner and wine-room. — The *Handwerkerverein* (Pl. A, B, 4), Teich-Str. 58, where all strata of society meet, has a large garden (concerts) and a German summer-theatre.

POST & TELEGRAPH OFFICE (Pl. 4; B, 3), Ritter-Str. — RIVER BATHS at the *Schwimmanstalt* (Pl. C, 3).

CAB per drive 10, with two horses 20, per hr. 50 cop. or 1 rb.; from the station 30 or 50, to the station 20 or 35 cop.

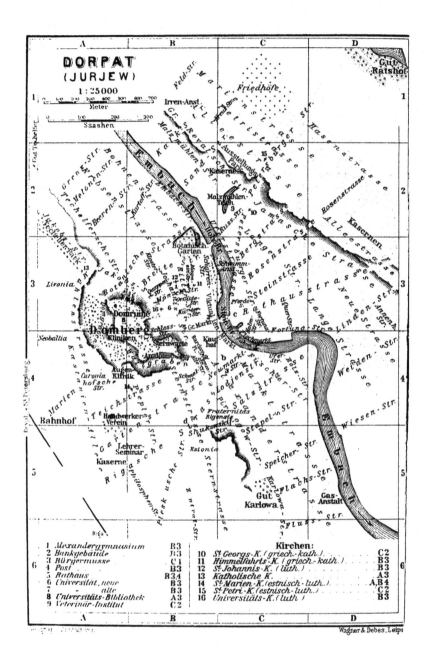

DORPAT
(JURJEW)

1 : 25000

Meter

Ssashen

Kirchen:

1	Alexandergymnasium	B 3
2	Bankgebäude	B 3
3	Bürgermusse	C 1
4	Post	B 3
5	Rathaus	B 3.4
6	Universität, neue	B 3
7	„ alte	B 3
8	Universitäts-Bibliothek	A 3
9	Veterinär-Institut	C 2

10	St. Georgs-K. (griech.-kath.)	C 2
11	Himmelfahrts-K. (griech.-kath.)	B 3
12	St. Johannis-K. (luth.)	B 3
13	Katholische K.	A 3
14	St. Marien-K. (estnisch-luth.)	A, B 4
15	St. Petri-K. (estnisch-luth.)	C 2
16	Universitäts-K. (luth.)	B 3

STEAMBOAT (landing-place at the end of the Neumarkt-Str.; Pl. C, 4) to *Pskov* (p. 41), thrice weekly in 9-10 hrs. (fare 4 rb.).

Dorpat (195 ft.), the capital of a district in the government of Livonia and the seat of a university, is situated on the navigable *Embach* and contains 50,000 inhabitants. The Embach, of which the right bank, with the Domberg, is about 115-130 ft. higher than the left bank, is crossed here by two bridges, one of stone (Steinbrücke; Pl. C, 3) built by Catherine II. in 1783 and having two gates in the middle of it, and the other one, farther up, of wood (Holzbrücke; Pl. B, C, 2, 3). — A much-frequented agricultural show is held at Dorpat yearly in the last days of August (O. S.).

The Russian Grand-Prince Yuri is said to have established a fortress called Yuryev on the site of the present Dorpat, once a sanctuary of the Esthonians. Later we find here an Esthonian castle called 'Castrum Tarbatum', which came into the hands of the Germans in 1224 and was made the seat of a bishop. The town, of which we find no mention before the middle of the 13th cent., was already a member of the Hanseatic League in the 14th cent., and attained considerable prosperity through its trade with Pskov and Novgorod. It accepted the doctrines of the Reformation in 1525. In 1558 Dorpat passed to Russia and in 1582 to Poland, while in 1625 it was captured by the Swedes after an obstinate resistance, during which the town was partly burned down. Peter the Great besieged it in 1704 and compelled its gallant defender Skytte to surrender on July 13th. In 1708 the town became once more a prey to the flames. The Peace of Nystad (1721) allotted it to Russia. — The university was founded by Gustavus Adolphus of Sweden in 1632, was suppressed in 1710 during the Northern War, and was reopened by Alexander I. in 1802, with German as the language of instruction. The number of students amounts to about 2680. With the exception of those in the Lutheran theological faculty, the lectures have all been delivered in Russian since 1895.

From the railway station (Pl. A, 4) we first follow the Marienhofsche-Str. in a straight direction, then descend to the left to the Wallgraben, bear to the left, and ascend to the (12 min.) —

DOMBERG (Pl. A, B, 3), which formerly bore the old pagan and then the episcopal fortress and is now laid out with shady grounds. On the N. side lie the picturesque **Ruins of the Cathedral** (Domruine; Pl. A, B, 3). The cathedral, an early-Gothic brick building dedicated to SS. Peter and Paul, with two towers, was burned down on June 23rd, 1624, owing to the careless use of the fire of St. John. It is worth while ascending the N. tower for the sake of the view. The choir has been rebuilt and is occupied by the *University Library* (Pl. 8), containing 247,000 vols. and 202,000 graduation theses (open on week-days 11-3, in vacation 12-2). Among the chief contents of the library are the collection of books made by Klinger (d. 1831), a friend of Goethe's youth, drawings by Goethe, and portraits of Goethe (1808), Wieland, and Herder by Von Kügelgen. — A little to the N. is the seated bronze figure of the naturalist *Karl Ernst von Baer* (1792-1876), by Opekúshin (1886). To the S., in front of the Surgical Clinic (Pl. A, B, 3, 4), is a monument (1913) with a bust of Ernst von Bergmann (1836-1907), the surgeon of Emp. Frederick III. — On the S.E. side of the Domberg stands the

Observatory (Sternwarte; Pl. B, 4; 225 ft.), the name of which is widely known through the achievements of F. G. W. von Struve (1820-39), J. H. von Mädler (1840-65), and other eminent directors.

From the Domberg the Schloss-Str. leads to the E. to the GROSSER MARKT (Pl. B, 3), in which stands the *Town Hall* (Pl. 5), containing the municipal archives. From the Grosser Markt the Ritter-Str., the chief street of the town, runs towards the N., and at the corner is the *Old University* (Pl. 7; B, 3), containing the important collections of the *Esthonian Society of Scholars* (adm. on application to the keeper).

A little to the S. of the Grosser Markt is the Barclay-Platz (Pl. B, 4), adorned with a bronze bust of *Field-Marshal Barclay de Tolly* (p. 60), by Demuth-Malinovski (1849).

To the N. of the Markt, in the Johannis-Str., are the *Buildings of the University* (Pl. 6; B, 3). Between the two wings which it sends out towards the Domberg is the spireless *University Church* (Pl. 16; Lutheran). In the university is the *Art Museum*, containing terracottas, plaster casts, and a few original sculptures (adm. on application to the attendant).

Farther to the N. is the Lutheran *Church of St. John* (Pl. 12; B. 3), dating from the beginning of the 13th century. The W. tower, 200 ft. in height, is adorned with terracotta busts and figures of saints. — On part of the former ramparts lies the *Botanic Garden* (Pl. B, 3) of the university.

On the W. side of the town lies the *Techelfer Park* (Pl. A, 2, 3).

From the wooden bridge over the Embach the Russische-Str. and its continuation the Petersburger-Str. lead past the (left) *Veterinary Institute* (Pl. 9, C 2; 350 students) and the *Show Grounds* (Ausstellungs-Park; Pl. C, 2; view of the town) to (20 min.) the **Ratshof** (Pl. D, 1), the château of the Von Liphart family, containing one of the most important collections of pictures in the Baltic Provinces (visitors sometimes admitted on personal application).

B. Boccaccino, Madonna and Child; *A. Bronzino*, Portrait of the Grand-Duchess Christina of Tuscany; *Piero di Cosimo*, Mary and Joseph returning to Nazareth after finding Jesus in the Temple; *A. van Dyck*, Karl Malery, the engraver, and Jacob Hagboldt; *Jan van Eyck*, Portrait of a man (small); *Garofalo*, Madonna with SS. Rochus and Sebastian; *Frans Hals*, Portrait of a man; *B. van der Helst*, Two portraits; *D. Puligo*, Holy Family; *S. van Ruysdael*, River-scene; *Jan Steen*, Portrait of a man; *D. Teniers the Elder*, Adoration of the Magi (1609); *Terburg*, Young scholar; *Tintoretto*, Venetian nobleman (1547). — Among the sculptures may be mentioned: *Donatello*, St. Jerome; *Michael Angelo (?)*, Marble relief with Apollo and Marsyas (16 in. high & 12 in. wide); *Luca della Robbia*, Children's heads.

On the left bank of the Embach (11 V. or 7½ M. up the river) lie the ruins of the Cistercian abbey of *Falkenau.* — A steamboat plies 5 times daily (1 hr.) down the Embach to the summer-resorts of *Haselau* (right), *Kabbina* (left), and *Kawershof* (right; 25 cop.), the last containing the remains of the episcopal fortress of Oldentorn.

Beyond Dorpat the train crosses the *Embach*. About 12 V. (8 M.) to the E. of (281 V.) *Laisholm* lie the ruins of *Lais*, a castle

of the Teutonic Order. Just short of (299 V.) *Wäggewa,* we enter
the government of Esthonia. — 341 V. **Taps** (305 ft.; *Railway Restaurant*). Hence to *St. Petersburg,* see R. 14 b. — 401 V. *Laakt.*
— As we approach (414 V. or 274 M.) *Reval* (p. 74), we have the
Oberer See to our left, while on the right we enjoy a fine view of the
town, the S. and W. sides of which the train skirts.

b. By Railway viâ Walk and Moiseküll.

405 V. (268 M.). State Railway from Riga to (158 V.) *Walk* in 3½-5 hrs.
(fares 5 rb. 93 cop., 3 rb. 56 cop.; reserved seat 1½ rb.). Light railway
from Walk to (247 V.) *Reval* in 14 hrs. (fares 8 rb. 5 cop., 4 rb. 75 cop.;
no first class; sleeping-berth 1½ rb. extra).

From Riga to (158 V. or 105 M.) *Walk,* see pp. 65-68. — 164 V.
Walk Vtoróï (i.e. *Walk II.*), station for the light railway to (197 V.)
Stockmannshof (p. 47). — 174 V. *Ermes* (Rail. Restaurant), with the
picturesque ruins of a castle. About 1³/₄ M. to the S. of (205 V.)
Rujen (Rail. Restaurant; posting-station) are the remains of another
castle. The train now leaves the Lettish and enters the Esthonian
Livonia. — 225 V. (149 M.) *Moiseküll* (Railway Restaurant).

From Moiseküll to Pernau, 50 V. (33 M.), narrow-gauge railway in
2½ hrs. — **Pernau,** Пéрновъ, Esthonian *Pärnu (Rail. Restaurant; Hôtel
du Nord,* near the harbour, R. from 60, B. 50 cop. to 1 rb. 50 cop. to 1 rb.
20 cop.; *Hotel Bristol,* near the rail. station; restaurants at the *Kurhaus*
or *Strand-Salon* and at the *Park-Salon,* open in summer only; cab from
the station to the town 50 cop.; British vice-consul, *J. Dicks;* Lloyd's
Agent, *W. A. Schmidt*), a flourishing town with 25,000 inhab., situated
on the Gulf of Pernau and at the mouth of the river of that name, was
founded about the middle of the 13th century. Of its former fortifications,
the Reval Gate and parts of the circumvallation still remain. The church
of St. Nicholas dates from 1529. There is a sandy beach, and the sea-
bathing is good. To the S. of the town is the large wood-pulp factory
of *Waldhof.* Steamer to Riga, see p. 54. — About 25 V. to the N.E. of
Pernau lies *Torgel,* with a well-known stud.

267 V. (177 M.) **Fellin,** Esthonian *Willandilin (Rail. Restaurant; Park Hotel,* R. 1 rb. 15 cop. to 1 rb. 65 cop., B. 35, D. 60-
75 cop.), with 7700 inhab., is situated on the high N.W. bank of the
small lake of Fellin (150 ft.). The station lies about 1 M. to the
S.W. of the town (cab 35 cop.). On the castle-hill are pleasure-
grounds and the noteworthy remains of the large lodge of the Teutonic Order. The Museum of the Fellin Literary Society contains
many valuable objects found amid the ruins of the castle and in
prehistoric graves, and also industrial products from the 18th cent.
onwards (adm. free on Sun., 12-2). The horses of Fellin are renowned.

Beyond (296 V.) *Wechma* the railway enters Esthonia. — 316 V.
Allenküll (Rail. Restaurant).

A branch-line runs from Allenküll to the N. to (13 V.) *Weissenstein*
(Klub-Hotel, R. 1 rb.), a small town with 3000 inhabitants. Of the castle
of the Teutonic Order, which was built here in 1266, the keep (100 ft.
high) is still extant (wide view from the top). In the Revalsche-Str. is
a museum of provincial antiquities (open on Sun., 12-2; adm., 20 cop.).

311 V. *Lelle* (posting-station); 357 V. *Hermet* (Rail. Restaurant; posting-station). — 405 V. (268 M.) *Reval* (Town Station); 409 V (271 M.) *Reval* (Harbour Station; p. 74).

c. By Sea viâ Arensburg.

Steamboat twice weekly to *Arensburg* in 8½ hrs. (fares 5 and 3 rb.); to *Hapsal* in 17-18 hrs. (fares 6 and 4 rb.); to *Reval* in 25-26 hrs. (fares 6 and 4 rb.). Stoppages are not reckoned in the above times. Dinner, 1¼ rb. (first class) or 1 rb. (second class). In spring and autumn most of the steamers leave Arensburg untouched.

Riga, see p. 53. The steamer at first descends the Dvina for 1 hr., passing on the left the *Meadow of Spilwe*, where Charles XII. of Sweden defeated the Saxon and Polish army in 1701. Of the fortress of *Dünamünde* (p. 62) nothing is visible from the steamer but a few ramparts and walls. To the right is the former mouth of the Dvina, with the so-called 'Schanze', a remnant of the castle of Dünamünde. The steamer now enters the *Gulf of Riga*, the coasts of which gradually disappear as we advance. In about 4 hrs. more the *Island of Runö* (p. 62) is seen to the right. Another 3½ hrs. bring us to *Romasaar*, the landing-place for *Arensburg* on Oesel (160 V. or 106 M. from Riga; carr. from the pier to the town, 3 V., 1 rb. 20 cop.).

Arensburg. — Hotels. *Meissner*, R. from 80 cop. to 3 rb., B. 40 cop., D. (1-4 p.m.) ½-1, pens. 40-70 rb. per month; *Hotel Osilia*. Pensions of *Baroness Stackelberg* (2½ rb. daily) and *Frau E. Michelsen* (60-75 rb. monthly). — Lloyd's Agent, *Carl Bergmann.*

Arensburg, the capital and only town of the large island of Oesel, is situated on the S. coast of the island and on the Gulf of Riga, and contains 5000 inhabitants. It has a Lutheran and a Greek Catholic church and a gymnasium (high school). To the S.W. of the town is the well-preserved *Bishop's Castle*, a building of the 14th cent., with two towers, a handsome chapel, cloisters, and rooms for the knights; the cellar is also interesting. In the outer court of the castle is a well-arranged *Museum*, with objects found in graves of the bronze period and the middle ages. The costumes worn by the inhabitants on market-days are interesting. — The town is frequented annually by 3500 visitors, who here enjoy sea-bathing and salt mud-baths (three establishments). The season lasts from May 20th to Aug. 20th. There is a Kurhaus (restaurant) in the town park.

The **Island of Oesel**, Esth. *Kure-Saare* (i.e. Island of the Courlanders) or *Saare-Ma* (i.e. Insular Land), is about 1010 sq. M. in extent and contains 65,000 inhab., mostly Esthonians. Like Gothland, it consists of a limestone plateau covered with a diluvial stratum which at places is very thin. Along with Moon, Runö, and other islands, it forms the Oesel district of the province of Livonia. The small horses of Oesel are known for their mettle and endurance. — In the 13th cent. the island of Oesel (Osilia, with the strong town of Valdia) was occupied by Waldemar,

King of the Danes, but the castle which he erected was soon destroyed by the Esthonians. Soon after the conquest of the island by the Brethren of the Sword in 1227, the Esthonians embraced Christianity and were placed under the sway of a bishop. Johann von Münchhausen, the last bishop, sold the island in 1559 to Denmark, in whose hands it remained till its surrender to Sweden in 1645. In 1721 Oesel (with the rest of Livonia) was incorporated with Russia. — Excursions (diligence per verst and horse 4 cop., calèche 50 cop.). The church of *Carmel*, 12 V. to the N. of Arensburg (carr. there & back in 3-4 hrs., 2-3 rb.), contains a fine wooden carving of the Coronation of the Virgin, dating from the 15th century. About 17 V. to the N.E. of Arensburg is *Lake Sall*, a crater-like basin, with a high margin, formed by a volcanic upheaval and now filled with water. A visit may also be paid to the so-called 'Pank' at *Mustel*, a perpendicular cliff on the N.W. coast, 24 M. from Arensburg. Some fine sculptures in Esthonian marble may be seen in the church of *Karris*, 22 M. to the N.E. of Arensburg. Hill-fortresses and lofty ring-walls of pagan date are met with in several parts of the island.

After quitting Arensburg, the steamer at first pursues an easterly course, and after a voyage of 4$^{1}/_{2}$ hrs. anchors off *Kuiwast*, on the island of *Moon*. It thence proceeds to the N. through the *Great* or *Werder Sound*, passing on the right the lighthouse of Werder and the rocky island of *Schildau*, and in 3 hrs. reaches Hapsal.

Hapsal, Гапсаль, Esthonian *Haapsalolin (Hotel St. Petersburg*, in the market-place, R. from 50, B. 30 cop., D. $^{1}/_{2}$-1 rb.; cab from the harbour to the town or per hr. 40 cop., from the station to the town 25 cop.; Lloyd's Agent, Julius Blauberg), the capital of the district of *Wiek* in Esthonia, is situated upon a bay and contains 3300 inhabitants. It was founded in 1279 and contains the picturesque ruins of an episcopal palace, with which the Lutheran church has been incorporated (good view from tower). It is frequented for sea-bathing and mud-baths. — Railway (station in the S.W. part of the town) to *Reval*, see p. 79.

The steamer leaves Hapsal in the same direction in which it approached it, but on reaching the island of *Worms* (34 sq. M. in area) steers to the N. After 1$^{1}/_{2}$ hr. it calls at the island of *Harry*, the station for the large island of *Dagö* (350 sq. M. in area). — On the voyage between Dagö and (6$^{1}/_{2}$ hrs.) Reval, we see to the left the small island of *Odinsholm* (2 hrs. from Harry), with a light-house and the so-called tumulus of Odin. To the right, 1$^{3}/_{4}$ hr. farther on, is the lighthouse of *Packerort* (p. 79), 1 hr. beyond which we see the light of *Surop* on the mainland to the right, and that of the island of *Nargen* to the left.

On entering the Gulf of Reval we enjoy a fine view of *Reval* (p. 74), with the Domberg; to the left are the Laaksberg (p. 78) and the ruined Convent of St. Bridget (p. 79).

13. Reval.

The *Main Railway Station* (Pl. A, 3; restaurant), for Dorpat (Riga), St. Petersburg, Baltic Port, and Hapsal, lies to the W. of the lower town; the *Fellin Station* (Pl. D, 2) lies to the E. — The *Harbour* (Pl. C, D, 1, 2), 1 M. from the Main Railway Station, is on the N. side of the town.

Hotels (prices of rooms raised and sometimes doubled during the fairs held March 1st-12th, June 22nd-25th, and Sept. 1st-12th, O. S.). St. Petersburg (Pl. a; A, 3), corner of Dunker-Str. and Rader-Str., R. 1-5 rb., B. 50 cop., D. (2-6 p.m.) 60 cop. to 1 rb., good restaurant; Goldener Löwe (Pl. c; A, B, 4), Schmiede-Str. 40; Hôtel du Nord (Pl. b; A, 3), Rader-Str. 3; Royal (Pl. d; A, 3), Süstern-Str. 8; Hôtel de Russie (Pl. e; B, 3), Schmiede-Str. 21, R. 1-3, B. 1/2, D. (2-6 p.m.) 1/2-1 rb. — *Evangelical Hospice*, Falkensteg 4 (Pl. A, 4), R. 3/4-11/4 rb.

Restaurants at the hotels. Summer restaurants at the *Strandpforte* (Pl. A, B, 2; concerts) and the *Schmiedepforte* (Pl. A, 4; variety entertainments). — *Stude* (confectioner), Lang-Str. (Pl. B, 2, 3). — For Katharinental, see p. 78.

Post and Telegraph Office (Pl. B, 3), Russ-Str. 9.

Police Station (Pl. B, 3), Russ-Str. 23. — *Passport Bureau*, in the Palace (Schloss; Pl. A, 4; 11-3).

Theatre (Pl. B, 4), German performances from Sept. to April.

Cab per drive within the town 10, with two horses 15 cop.; from the main station into the town 15 or 20, to the suburbs 25 or 35 cop.; from the main station to the Fellin Station 60 or 80 cop.; from the harbour to the town or suburbs 30 or 50 cop.; per 1/4 hr. 20 or 25, per 1/2 hr. 30 or 40, per hr. 50 or 60, each addit. hr. 40 or 50 cop. At night (10-6) 50 per cent more. Drives to the Dom (see below) 5 or 10 cop. more. Small articles of luggage free, trunk 10 cop. — To *Katharinental* 30, with two horses 45 cop.; to *Ziegelskoppel* 60 or 70 cop.

Tramways from the Alter Markt (Pl. B, 3) to Katharinental, in 12 min., every 5 min., 5 cop.; from the Russischer Markt (Pl. B, C, 3) through the Grosse Dörptsche-Str. (Pl. C, D, 3, 4) and the Pernausche-Str. (beyond Pl. B, 4).

Baths. *Krauspsche Seebadeanstalt* (Pl. 15; B, 2), Hafen-Str.; *Stempel* (Pl. 16; B, 3), Neugasse. Also sea-bathing at Katharinental (p. 78).

Steamboats to *St. Petersburg*, see p. 84; to *Riga*, see p. 72; to *Helsingfors*, in 4 hrs. (fare 6 or 5 rb.); to *Stettin*, in 42 hrs. (fare 56 or 40 ℳ, meals 6 ℳ per day), and to *Lübeck* (fare 56 or 40 ℳ). — *Rowing Boats* may be hired at the Kauffahrtei-Brücke in the harbour.

Consulates. British Vice-Consul, *W. Girard*. United States Consular Agent, *Rustan Radau*. — Lloyd's Agent, *C. R. Cattley*, Hafen-Str.

Principal Attractions (1 day). Forenoon: Grosser Markt (p. 75), Church of St. Nicholas (p. 77), Domberg (p. 76), Lang-Strasse (p. 77), Strandpforte (p. 78). — Afternoon: Strand Promenade (p. 79), and then (best by cab) Katharinental, Kosch, and ruins of the Convent of St. Bridget (p. 79).

Reval (45 ft.) or Ревель, Esth. *Tallinna* or *Tannilin* (i.e. 'Town of the Danes'), the capital of the government of Esthonia, contains 131,000 inhab. and is picturesquely situated on a bay of the Gulf of Finland. The town, which is more mediæval in appearance than any other in the Baltic Provinces, is divided into three parts, the Upper Town or 'Dom', the Lower Town, and the Suburbs. The *Dom* lies on the Domberg, at a height of 140 ft. above the sea; the *Lower Town*, or town proper, the seat of the merchants and municipal authorities, extends from the Domberg to the sea, and is surrounded

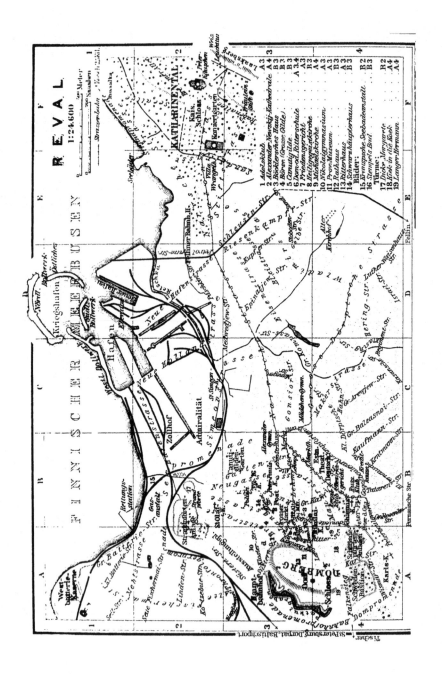

REVAL.

1:24.600

1 Adelsklub .... A 3
2 Alexander-Newski-Kathedrale ... A 4
3 Bröckers Haus .... B 3
4 Börse (Grosse Gilde) .... B 3
5 Canutgilde .... A 3,4
6 Domkl. Ritterschule .... A 3
7 Friedensgericht .... A 3
8 Heiligengeistkirche .... A 3
9 Michaeliskirche .... B 3
10 Nikolaigymnasium .... A 3
11 Prov.-Museum .... A 3
12 Rathaus .... B 3
13 Ritterhaus .... A 3
14 Schwarzhäupterhaus .... B 3
    Bilder:
15 Kunstgewbe. Seebadeanstalt ... B 2
16 Stempels Bad .... B 3
    Türme:
17 Dicke Margarete .... B 2
18 Kiek in die Kök .... A 4
19 Langer Hermann .... A 4

by promenades, the old bastions, and the tower-strengthened wall, dating from the 14th cent. and still well preserved in parts. The extensive *Suburbs*, beyond the town proper and extending along the shores of the bay, are the headquarters of a flourishing industrial activity. The chief articles of commerce are cotton (imported to the amount of 97,000,000 lbs. in 1910), coal, grain, flax, bristles, and hides. A special branch of industry is the capture and pickling of a small silvery fish resembling the sardine *(Killoströmlingen,* Кйлька; clupea latulus), large quantities of which are exported in all directions.—The construction of a naval harbour was begun in 1912.

The Esthonian fortress of *Lindanissa* (p. 76) was captured and destroyed in 1219 by Waldemar II., King of Denmark, and a new one was built in its place. During the contest, says the legend, a red banner with a white cross on it fell from heaven, and this was forthwith adopted as the national standard ('Danebrog') of the Danes. In 1228 a town began to grow up under the walls of the castle; this became the seat of a bishop and in 1248 it was invested by the Danish king with the same legal and civic rights as were enjoyed by Lübeck. In 1284 it joined the Hanseatic League. From its very foundation Reval was divided into two parts: the *Dom,* under the sway of the royal and (later) knightly officials, and the *Town Proper,* ruled by the municipal authorities. In 1346 Esthonia, and with it Reval, was purchased from the Danes by the Teutonic Order. In 1524 the town became Protestant. Having placed itself under Swedish protection in 1561, it was bombarded in 1569 by a fleet of 30 Lübeck and Danish war-ships, while it was unsuccessfully besieged by the Russians for 4¹/₂ months in 1570-71 and for seven weeks in 1577. As a result of the Northern War Esthonia and Reval passed into the hands of Russia. Peter the Great did much for the prosperity of the town, and expanded its harbour for the use of his navy. In 1790 an attack by the Swedish fleet was beaten off. In 1809 the harbour was blockaded by the British, and in 1854-55, during the Crimean War, it was again blockaded by the combined British and French fleet.

From the Main Railway Station (Pl. A, 3) the Süstern-Strasse leads slightly to the left. To the right rises the Domberg (see p. 76), while to the left stand the buildings used at the Agricultural Show held here in June. From the end of the Süstern-Strasse the 'Langer Domberg' (Pl. A, 3, 4) leads to the right, through an old gateway, to the Domberg (see p. 76), while the Fuhrmann-Strasse leads straight on to the GROSSER MARKT (Pl. B, 3), situated in the heart of the inner town.

On the S. side of the Grosser Markt stands the **City Hall** (Pl. 12), a plain Gothic building of the 14th cent., with a slender tower added about 1635. It is the only extant mediæval city hall in the Baltic Provinces. The former 'Lauben' or arcades have been converted into shops.

The groundfloor contains a collection of *Archives* (open on week-days, 10-2), of especial interest in connection with the history of the Hanseatic League. On the same floor is the *Chancellery* (shown on application to the attendant), with four pieces of Flemish tapestry (1547) and some old silver ware. On the first floor, to the left of the staircase, is the room of the *Town Council,* containing old carved furniture (15-16th cent.). The beautiful carved frieze, with hunting-scenes, was presented in 1697 by Charles XI. of Sweden. Above it are eight oil-paintings of Biblical incidents by Hans Aken (1667), chiefly after engravings by Rubens and Rembrandt.

The Grosser Markt is adjoined on the E. by the ALTER MARKT, where we may notice the *Böckler House* (No. 8; Pl. 3, B 3). Its gable is adorned with reliefs of the 16th cent., representing the Evangelists (sides), the Trinity (middle), and the Saviour (at the top). From this point the busy Lehm-Strasse leads to the E. (to Katharinental, see p. 78), and the Russ-Strasse (Pl. B, 3) to the N. On the right side of the latter are the Roman Catholic *Church of SS. Peter & Paul*, built in 1845 in the refectory of an old Dominican convent and having two-storied cloisters, and also the Greek Catholic *Church of St. Nicholas,* dating from before 1422.

Proceeding to the S. from the Grosser Markt (p. 75) through the Goldschmiede-Strasse and then to the right viâ the Nikolai-Strasse (Pl. A, B, 3) and the 'Kurzer Domberg' (stone steps, ending at a gateway), we reach the *DOMBERG* or CASTLE HILL (Pl. A, 3, 4), on which lies the upper town. The Esthonians believed the hill to be the burial-place of the demigod Kalev, the father of the legendary hero Kalevi-poeg (*i.e.* 'son of Kalev'). Their old fortress on this site was named Lindanissa after Linda, the wife of Kalev.

In the middle of the Schloss-Platz rises the *Alexander Nevski Cathedral* (Pl. 2), with its five gilded domes, built by Preobrazhénski in 1894-1900. — On the W. side of the square stands the *Palace,* now the residence of the governor, originally dating from the 13th cent. but rebuilt in 1772. A splendid view of land and sea is obtained from the S. tower, the so-called 'Long Herman' (150 ft. · Pl. 19), the key of which is kept in the right corner of the first court (15 cop.; ascent not recommended to ladies). — From the Schloss Platz the Douglas-Strasse leads N. to the —

Cathedral *(Domkirche),* originally dating from the 13th cent., burned down in 1433, 1553, and 1684, but rebuilt on each occasion.

The INTERIOR (sacristan in the 'Kirchenhaus', opposite the S. side of the church) contains a fine altar-piece (Crucifixion) by *Ed. von Gebhardt.* To the right, by the S. wall of the choir, is the monument of the Swedish general Pontus de la Gardie (d. 1585) and his wife (d. 1583), a natural daughter of John III. of Sweden, with effigies, by *Passer* (1589). Count Matthew von Thurn (d. 1640), a prominent figure in the Thirty Years' War, was also buried in the choir. Outside the choir-screen, to the right, in the floor, are the tombstones of the Swedish marshal Karl Horn (d. 1601) and his wife (d. 1611). On the N. wall of the church, near the organ, is the marble monument of the Russian admiral Sir Samuel Greig (1735-1788), a native of Scotland. Adjacent, to the left, rests Admiral Krusenstern (p. 172). Numerous hatchments hang on the walls.

Opposite the choir of the cathedral lies the *Ritterhaus* (Pl. 13), the meeting-place of the Esthonian chamber of nobles. The large hall is decorated with the coats-of-arms of the Esthonian noblesse, and other rooms contain their archives. — To the E., opposite the Ritterhaus, is the *Provincial Museum* (Pl. 11), with prehistoric, ethnographic, natural history, and other collections (open on Wed., Sat., and Sun., 12-3, adm. 25 cop.; at other times through the castellan, fee 50 cop.).—To the N. (left) of the Ritterhaus is the *Borough Court* (Pl. 7), behind which (passage on the right) is a stone parapet affording a fine view of town and sea. Below is the Patkul Promenade.

We now descend again from the Schloss-Platz by the 'Kurzer Domberg' and turn to the right into the Ritter-Strasse. In this street rises the—

*Church of St. Nicholas (Nikolai-Kirche; Pl. A, 3, 4), a building of limestone, known to have been in existence in 1316. On the W. side rises a huge tower, erected in 1681-95. The sacristan is to be found in the small house to the right of the tower (door at the back of the house).

INTERIOR. By the W. wall are the carved *Stalls of the Blackheads (1556; p. 78). Behind is a beautifully carved screen, representing angels with instruments of torture (18th cent.). By the third pillar in the S. aisle is the oaken pulpit of 1624; by the fourth pillar is a seven-branched brazen candlestick, 16$^1/_2$ ft. high, with a small figure of the Madonna on its middle arm (1519). Numerous hatchments.—On the W. wall of the Chapel of St. Anthony (entrance in the W. wall, to the left) are the remains of a *Dance of Death*, forming a reduced reproduction of that in the church of the Virgin at Lübeck, with rhymed verses in Low German (16th cent.). The same chapel contains a large winged altar-piece by a Netherlandish painter of the school of Gerard David (retouched in 1654). On the N wall of the same chapel is a carved altar, 10 ft. in height, with double wings painted by *Hermann Rode* of Lübeck (scenes from the lives of SS. Victor and Nicholas) and also a beautifully carved reredos, with pictures by *Bernt Notke* (1483).

We next follow the Rader-Strasse, or N. prolongation of the Ritter-Str., and turn to the right into the LANG-STRASSE (Pl. B, 2, 3), the busiest street in Reval. Here, to the right, at the end of the Heiligegeist-Strasse, is the *Church of the Holy Ghost* (Pl. 8), a small building with two naves of equal height, known to have existed as the chapel of the municipal poorhouse in 1316. The slender spire dates from the 17th century. It contains stalls with mediæval carvings representing the story of Virgil. — No. 17, opposite the church, is the so-called *Grosse Gilde* (Pl. 4), now used as the Exchange as well (business-hour 12-12.30), a Gothic gabled structure of 1410, with two door-knockers of 1430. The vaulting of the great hall rests on three pillars. — No. 20, farther on, to the right, is the *Canutigilde* (Pl. 5), built in 1864, with bronze statues of Luther (r.) and St. Canute (l.) on its façade.

The **Schwarzhäupterhaus** (Pl. 14; No. 26), or *Hall of the Blackheads*, has a Renaissance façade adorned with a blackamoor's head and several reliefs. It has been in the possession of the society since 1531. The portal dates from 1597, while the 'Beischlagsteine' (p. 57) immured to the right and left of it are 22 years older. The interior contains archives. In the upper floor is a Flemish winged altar-piece from the church (Katharinen-Kirche) of the old Dominican convent (end of 15th cent.). The building also contains the rooms of the Blackhead Society, with portraits of Swedish and Russian rulers, valuable silver-plate, weapons, and other antiquities.

The *Society of Blackheads* (comp. p. 57) was founded in the 14th cent. by the foreign merchants. They formed a military organization, had their own peculiar ceremonies and usages, and often fought under their own banner, inscribed 'aut vincendum aut moriendum', against the numerous foes of the wealthy town of Reval.

At the N. end of the Lang-Str. rises the Gothic *Olai-Kirche* (Pl. B, 2; sacristan opposite the S. entrance), one of the largest and finest churches in the Baltic Provinces. It is consecrated to St. Olaus or Olaf, King of Norway, who introduced Christianity into his dominions at the beginning of the 11th century. The church, which is heard of as early as 1267, has been struck by lightning nine times. After the last fire, in 1820, twenty years were allowed to elapse before it was restored. The *Tower*, 456 ft. in height, is the loftiest in Russia, and its gallery commands an extensive panorama. On the S. side of the choir is the *Bremer Chapel*. On its exterior, on the side next the Lang-Str., is the fine monument of Hans Paulsen, at whose cost the chapel was built in 1513.

To the N. of the Olai-Kirche is the *Strandpforte,* with an old tower known as the 'Dicke Margarete' or 'Rosenkranz' (Pl. 17). To the left is a small park (restaurant, see p. 74). — In the S. suburb, reached viâ the Schmiedepforte, with the tower called 'Kiek in die Kœk' (Pl. 18, A 4; restaurant, see p. 74), are the *Church of St. John* (Johannis-Kirche; Pl. B, 4), with a handsome tower (1867), a bronze *Statue of Peter the Great* (by Bernstamm; 1910), and the Esthonian *Dom-Karls-Kirche* (Pl. A, 4), with two towers (1870). — To the S. of the *Lehmpforte* (Pl. B, 3), two towers of which are still extant, are the *Esthonian Bank*, by Saarinen, and the *Esthonian* and the *German Theatres* (Pl. B, 4), the former by Lindgren & Lönn (1913), the latter by Bubuir and Vasilyev (1910). — A pleasant walk (1 hr.) may be taken round the promenades encircling the inner town, which afford a good view of the towers of the city-wall.

ENVIRONS OF REVAL. — From the Alter Markt (p. 76; cabs and tramway, see p. 74) the Lehm-Strasse (Pl. B, 3) and its prolongation the Narvsche-Strasse lead to (1¹/₂ M.) *Katharinental* (Pl. F, 2; *Restaurant*, with concert-garden), an imperial château, surrounded by a fine park. Peter the Great, who was a frequent visitor to Reval, erected the *Château* in 1719 (architect, Michetti) and presented it to his wife, Catherine. A little to the E. is the so-called *Peterhäuschen*, the modest little house which Peter first occupied here and now containing various reminiscences of him (shown by an attendant; 20 cop.). About 200 yds. farther to the E., on the *Laaksberg*, is the *White Lighthouse* (view best in the forenoon). On the

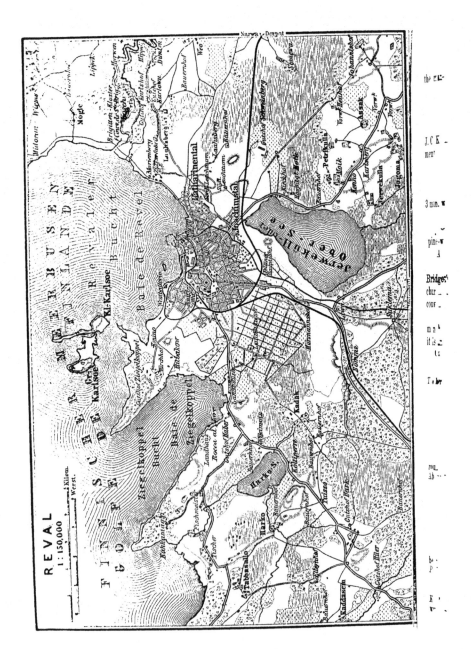

REVAL

1 : 150,000

adjacent STRAND PROMENADE (view; sea-baths) is the *Rusalka Monument* (Pl. F, 1), erected in 1902 to commemorate the loss of the man-of-war of that name in 1893. The bronze angel on the lofty granite pedestal is by Adamsohn.

About $2^1/_2$ M. to the N.E. of Katharinental (cab in 25 min., fare 65 cop.; omn. 20 cop.) lies **Kosch,** situated in a charming little wooded valley, watered by the *Brigittenbach* (tickets obtained from J. C. Koch, Lang-Str. 68, Reval). Starting from the Rusalka Monument (see above), we proceed to the N.E. along the esplanade, then follow the seashore, passing the *Chateau of Marienberg* on the right (1 M.), with a fine retrospective view of the town. After 9 min. more we turn to the left (not to the right or inland); after 3 min. we come to a fork in the road near a country-house on the left, the left branch leading downhill to ($1/_2$ hr.) St. Bridget's Nunnery (see below), and the other branch running straight through the pine-woods to (1 M.) Kosch.

About 1 M. to the W. of Kosch, on the right bank of the stream (ferry), not far from the sea, lie the picturesque *Ruins of St. Bridget's Nunnery (Brigittenruine)*, including the walls of the church, the lofty W. gable, and some of the window-tracery. The convent, which was erected in 1407-36, was destroyed by the Russians in 1577. The space in front of the church was the common burial-ground of the district. Among the houses surrounding it is an unpretending *Restaurant*.

On the coast, about $3^3/_4$ M. to the W. of Reval, is the villa of *Rocca al Mare*, with a park and some old tombstones (tickets at the office of Thomas Clayhills & Son, Brokusberg, Reval). The fishing-village of *Tischer* lies $4^1/_2$ M. farther to the W. (omn. from Reval, 50 cop.).

FROM REVAL TO BALTIC PORT, 45 V. (30 M.), railway in 2 hrs. — 9 V. (6 M.) *Nömme*, a summer-resort. — 26 V. (17 M.) *Kegel* (posting-station; carriages and horses should be ordered by telephone from Reval). About 2 M. to the N., near the old double-naved church, is a bronze statue of Martin Luther, by Baron Klodt (1862). About 13 V. ($8^1/_2$ M.) to the N.W. (carr. & pair there & back 2 rb. 38 cop., with fee of 50 cop.), at the point where the *Kegel* enters the Gulf of Finland, is Prince Volkonski's *Château of Fall*, built by Stakenschneider in the English Gothic style and surrounded by a large and well-kept park, containing a waterfall (16 ft. high). About $7^1/_2$ M. to the N. of Kegel and 5 M. to the S.E. of Fall is Baron von Stackelberg's château of *Fähna*, containing a collection of pictures (carr. & pair from Kegel viâ Fähna to Fall and back to Kegel 2 rb. 86 cop., with fee of 50 cop.). A highroad leads S.W. from Kegel, past the marble quarry of *Wasalem*, to (21 V.; 14 M.) the fine ruins of the monastery of *Padis*, built by the Cistercians in 1310. Railway from Kegel to *Hapsal*, see below. — 45 V. (30 M.) **Baltic Port** or Балтійскій Портъ *(Railway Restaurant: Hotel Guida;* Lloyd's Agent, *(G. F. Hinrichsen),* a small town on the W. coast of Esthonia, with 1200 inhab. and an ice-free harbour. A walk may be taken to the N. along the rocky coast to (3 M.) the lighthouse of *Packerort*, where the Glint (see p. 81) ends (extensive view from the gallery). The park of *Leetz* is $2^3/_4$ M. to the E. of Baltic Port.

FROM REVAL TO HAPSAL, 98 V. (65 M.), railway in 3 hrs. — To (26 V.) *Kegel*, see above. — 49 V. *Riesenberg*, the estate of Baron von Stackelberg, with a fine park; 78 V. *Pallifer*, the manor of Herr von Lueder. - 98 V. *Hapsal*, see p. 73.

FROM REVAL TO ST. PETERSBURG, 347 V. (229 M.), railway (no express trains) in 10¹/₂ hrs. (fares 10 rb. 75, 6 rb. 45 cop.; reserved seat 1¹/₂ rb.; sleeping-car 2 rb. 75, 2 rb. 10 cop.). To (73 V. or 48 M.) *Taps*, see p. 71; thence to (274 V.) *St. Petersburg*, see R. 14 b. — To St. Petersburg by sea, see R. 11 c.

From Reval to *Riga*, see R. 12.

14. From Riga to St. Petersburg.

a. By Railway viâ Pskov.

519 V. (364 M.). Express train in 11 hrs. (fares 17 rb. 20, 11 rb. 20 cop.; reserved seat 1¹/₂ rb. extra; sleeping car 4 rb. 40, 3 rb. 30 cop.).

From Riga to (158 V.) *Walk*, see pp. 65-68. — 186 V. *Antzen* (posting-station). About 25 V. (17 M.) to the N. lies Odenpäh (p. 68). — 205 V. *Sommerpahlen*. Farther on we have a view to the right of the Grosser Munamägi and the Welamägi (see below). — 214 V. (142 M.) **Werro** (275 ft.; *Rail. Restaurant; Hotel Alexander*, Katharinen-Str. 4; cab from the rail. station to the town 40 cop.). The town, which contains 5000 inhab., lies on *Lake Tammula* (2¹/₃ sq. M. in area), on the N. margin of the E. Livonian Hills, which reach a height of 1065 ft. in the *Grosser Munamägi*, 9¹/₂ M. to the S. (carr. & pair there and back 6 rb.) and of 1010 ft. in the *Welamägi*, 7¹/₂ M. to the S. — Beyond (231 V.) *Neuhausen* we enter the government of Pskov. The village of Neuhausen, with a picturesque ruined castle, lies 12 V. (8 M.) to the S. of the railway. — Farther on we descend somewhat rapidly to (249 V.) *Petchóri*, Печоры (Rail. Restaurant). About 2 M. to the S.W. of the station is a cave-monastery occupied by Greek Catholic monks. — A little short of Pskov we cross the *Velikaya*.

292 V. (194 M.) **Pskov** *(Pleskau)*, see p. 41. Thence to (549 V. or 364 M.) *St. Petersburg* (Warsaw Station), see p. 43.

b. By Railway viâ Dorpat.

615 V. (408 M.). Railway (no express trains) in 21 hrs. (fares 16 rb., 9 rb. 60 cop.; reserved seat 1¹/₂ rb.).

From Riga to (341 V. or 226 M.) *Taps*, see pp. 65-71. — 367 V. *Wesenberg*, Esth. *Rákwerelin* (235 ft.; Rail. Restaurant; Hôtel du Nord; cab to the town 25 cop.), the capital of a district, on the *Söli*, with 5900 inhab. and the considerable remains of a castle of the Teutonic Order.

A private railway runs from Wesenberg to the N.E. to (18¹/₂ V.) *Kunda*, with cement-works, a fine park, and a harbour. Hard by, on a promontory jutting out into the sea, are the ruins of the *Tolsburg* or *Fredeburg*, a castle of the Teutonic Order, built in 1471 (fine view).

427 V. (283 M.) *Jewe* (Rail. Restaurant).

From Jewe we may proceed by diligence viâ *Kuckers* and *Türpsal* to (44 V.) *Ontika*, in order to visit the rocky coast of the Glint. From Ontika the island of *Hogland* (p. 216) is visible on the N. horizon, 65 V.

(43 M.) distant. — The *Glint* is the precipitous N. scarp of the great Esthonian plateau, stretching along the Gulf of Finland from Narva to Packerort (p. 79). The cliffs, which reach a height of 185 ft., are clothed with luxuriant vegetation. Their upper strata consist of limestone, containing numerous fossils, while below are layers of clay and sandstone.

466 V. (309 M.) **Narva,** Нарва (Plan, see p. 82). — *Rail. Restaurant.* — HOTEL ST. PETERSBURG (Pl. a), Vuishgorodskáya, R. 1¹/₂ - 6 rb., B. 40 cop., D. (2-6 p.m.) ₁ rb. — CAB (stands in front of the hotel and in the market-place) from the rail. station to the town 25, per hr. 50 cop.; fares at night (11-8) 35 & 60 cop. — STEAMBOATS 6 times daily to Hungerburg in 1 hr. (fare 30 cop.) and twice weekly to St. Petersburg in 6-7 hrs. (fare 3 or 2 rb.). — BRITISH VICE-CONSUL, *George Cottam*, Krähnholm Factory. — LLOYD'S AGENT, *F. N. Dieckhoff.* — Those whose time is limited will find 2-3 hrs. enough, especially with the aid of a cab, to visit the town and the waterfalls.

Narva (70 ft.), formerly an Esthonian fortress and now a town in the government of St. Petersburg, contains 50,000 inhab. and lies picturesquely on the left bank of the *Naróva,* which issues from Lake Peipus and flows into the Gulf of Finland, 8 M. below the town. The town has several Lutheran and Greek churches and a harbour. Its inhabitants are engaged in fishing (lampreys and salmon), manufacturing (p. 83), and the export of timber.

Narva, founded in the 13th cent. under Danish supremacy and inhabited almost exclusively by Germans, carried on a brisk trade with the interior of Russia. In 1347 it came into the hands of the Teutonic Order, and later it had much to suffer as a frontier-town in the wars of the Order and of those (after 1581) between the Swedes and Russians (Novgorod). In 1558 Narva was captured by Ivan the Terrible, and it was again besieged by the Russians in 1590 and 1700. In the last case, however, it was relieved by Charles XII. of Sweden, who gained a brilliant victory over the Russians in spite of the fact that they outnumbered his army three to one (comp. p. 84). In 1704 the town was taken by Peter the Great after a gallant resistance under Horn, and from that time on it has continued in Russian possession.

The inner town has been compressed into a very narrow space by the unusually strong and high fortifications, which rise over the precipitous bank of the Naróva (here 165 yds. in width). The *Castle of the Teutonic Order* is now used as an arsenal and barracks. The lofty square tower on the S.E. side, known as 'Long Herman', dates from the middle of the 16th cent. and affords a wide view of the town and its environs (keeper at the foot of the tower). — Opposite, on the high rocks on the right bank of the river (bridge from the site of the old water-gate), lie the imposing walls and towers of the dismantled *Fortress of Ivángorod* (or John's Town), built by the Russians in 1492 when the left bank was still German.

From the station we turn to the left and in 3 min. reach a fork. By turning to the left and crossing the tracks, we reach (¹/₄ hr.) the large buildings of the Krähnholm cotton-mill and the waterfalls (p. 83). By keeping to the right we reach (8 min.) the Baltiskaya, which we follow to the right (leaving the Petróvskaya Sq. to the left), descend a little, and then (4 min.) ascend to the left through the Vuishgorodskáya, passing the Cathedral of the Transfiguration (see

BAEDEKER'S Russia.

p. 83) and in 5 min. reaching the market-place of the inner town.
On the W. side of the market-place, which is embellished with an
obelisk erected in honour of Peter the Great in 1872, rises the *Town
Hall* (Pl. 2), built in 1671 and containing a few curiosities. On its

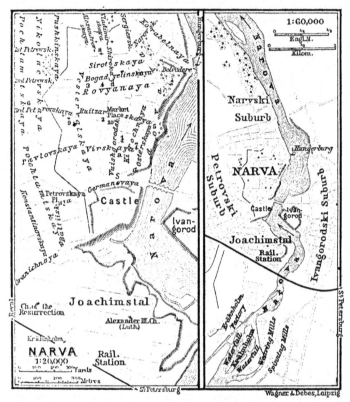

1. Cathedral of the Transfiguration. — 2. Duma (Town Hall). — 3. Girls'
High School. — 4. High School. — 5. Peter the Great's House. — 6. Post
Office. — 7. St. John's Church. — 8. St. Michael's Church. — 9. St. Peter's
Church. — 10. Theatre.

S. side is the *Theatre* (Pl. 10), built in 1698 as the Exchange. At
the E. end of the Rúitzarskaya, to the right, at the corner of the
Österskaya, stands the so-called *House of Peter the Great* (Pl. 5),
recognizable by the four columns in front. It now contains the Muni-

cipal Museum (furniture, books, pictures) and various objects which belonged to the Tzar (keeper in the Österskaya; fee 15 cop.; Russian catalogue 20 cop.). The Rúitzarskaya ends at the *Promenades* laid out above the river, which afford a good idea of the picturesque situation of the town (we turn to the right). On the right bank is Ivangorod, on the left are the Castle and the new Lutheran church (in the background). A still more extensive view, especially down the river, is obtained from the pavilion above the steamboat-wharf.— About 300 yds. to the S. of the market-place is the Greek Catholic *Cathedral of the Transfiguration* (Преображенскій соборъ; Pl. 1), a Gothic building with a circular W. tower and a dome, built before 1502. The interior of the church, which was formerly used both for Roman Catholic and Lutheran services, is interesting. A little to the E. is the Prot. *Church of St. John* (1636-48; Pl. 7).

About 1 V. above the town (cab from the station in 6 min., 20 cop., comp. p. 81; from the market-place in $^1/_4$ hr., 30 cop.) the Naróva forms two broad **Waterfalls,** 26-33 ft. high, the waters of which unite again below the island of *Krähnholm*. The river rushing over layers of hard limestone here falls upon soft clay, the gradual washing-away of which has formed the falls. Below the falls the channel of the river is deep and enclosed by precipitous banks, but above the falls the banks are more level. The beauty of the falls is much impaired by the mills erected to utilize the water-power. On the left bank, on this side of the bridge leading to the island, is a bronze statue of Baron Knoop, the founder of the Krähnholm Mills, by Tchizhóv (1899). The bridge commands a good view, to the right, of the W. fall. The view of the E. fall is finer, but special permission from the management of the mills is required for the island.

The *Hermannsberg,* 2 M. to the W. of Narva (cab there & back, in $^3/_4$ hr., 1 rb.), commands a good survey of the battlefield of 1700. — On the sea lie the bathing-resorts of *Hungerburg* (Kurhaus; Lloyd's Agent, A. A. Peters; steamer, see p. 81), which is prettily situated and has a good sandy beach, *Schmetzke,* and *Merreküll* (Kurhaus). The last, which is 15 V. (10 M.) from Narva (carr. 2-2$^1/_2$ rb.), is within $^1/_2$ hr.'s drive of Hungerburg (cab 1 rb., with two horses 1$^1/_2$ rb.).

The train now crosses the *Naróva* by an iron bridge (good view of Narva and Ivangorod to the left and of the waterfalls to the right) and enters the government of St. Petersburg. A little short of (488 V.) *Jamburg* (Swedish, *Jama*) we cross the *Luga*. 536 V. *Volósovo* (Rail. Restaurant). — 573 V. *Gátchina* (Baltic Station; Rail. Restaurant), and thence to —

615 V. (408 M.) *St. Petersburg* (Baltic Station), see R. 17.

c. By Sea viâ Reval.

Steamer in 43-45 hrs., exclusive of stops (fares 9 & 6 rb.); from Reval to St. Petersburg in 18 hrs. (fares 5 & 4 rb.).

From Riga to *Reval*, see R. 12 c. — On leaving Reval the steamer at first proceeds to the N. across the Gulf of Finland, but it strikes a N.E. course at the island of *Wulf* (1 hr. from Reval) and steers to the E. when off the island of *Kokskär* (pron. Kokshare), 1 hr. farther on. — The naval battle of Hogland (p. 216) took place off the island of *Ekholm*, 3½ hrs. from Reval. To the right, 5¾ hrs. from Reval, rises the lighthouse of *Stenskär*.
8 hrs. To the left are seen the picturesque granite and porphyry cliffs of the island of *Hogland* (p. 216); to the right are the flat islands of *Great* and *Little Tütters*. — 10½ hrs. To the right, the island of *Lavensaari*. — 12 hrs. *Seskär*, with a lighthouse.
14 hrs. The steamer steers into the narrowing E. end of the Gulf of Finland. The coast on each side becomes more distinct.
16 hrs. *Cronstadt* (p. 184). We enter the *Sea Canal* (p. 129). Farther on we pass *Oranienbaum* (p. 182) and *Peterhof* (p. 179) on the right. St. Petersburg gradually comes into sight ahead, dominated by the conspicuous gilded dome of St. Isaac's Cathedral (p. 109). — 18 hrs. The steamer reaches its berth at St. Petersburg, in the Vasili Ostrov, below the Nikoláyevski (Nicholas) Bridge (p. 111).

III. ST. PETERSBURG AND ENVIRONS.

INDEX TO THE PLAN OF ST. PETERSBURG.

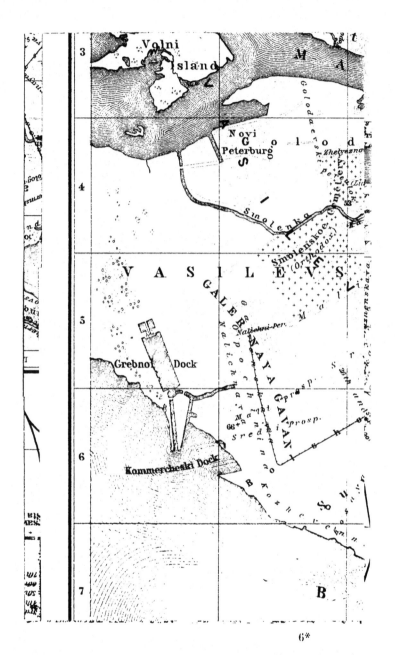

St PETERSBURG I

15. St. Petersburg.

PLANS OF THE CITY. In the following pages the large general plan of the city (p. 87) is referred to as Pl. *I*, the plan of the central part of the city (p. 103) as Pl. *II*.

I. Arrival. Departure. Railway Stations.

ARRIVAL. Conveyances from the principal hotels meet the trains at *Stations 1-5* (see below). Most of the commissionnaires from the hotels speak French and German, and some of them speak English. Cabs, see p. 90. — The landing-stage for *Steamers* from foreign ports is on the Gutúyevski Island (Pl. B, 7, 8; *I*); those from Russian and Finnish ports are berthed at the Nikoláyevskaya Náberezhnaya (Pl. C, D, 5, 6; *I*).

DEPARTURE. Tickets for the State Railways, with the exception of the Finnish Railway, may also be obtained (for an extra fee of 10-40 cop.) at the city booking-office (Городская станція казённыхъ желѣзныхъ дорóгъ), Bolshaya Konyúshennaya 29 (Pl. F, 5; *II*), which is open on week-days 10-4 and on holidays 10-1. Luggage may also be booked here for a fee of 7 cop. per pud (minimum 50 cop.). For Tourist Agencies, see p. 96.

Railway Stations. St. Petersburg has seven railway stations:

1. *Warsaw Station* (Варшáвскій вокзáлъ; Pl. E 8, *I*), at the S. end of the Izmáilovski Prospékt, for Pskov, Dünaburg, Vilna, Warsaw (Berlin, Vienna; RR. 8, 9), Riga (R. 14 a), and Gatchina (pp. 43, 186). — Tramways Nos. 3, 8, 9 (p. 91).

2. *Baltic Station* (Балтíйскій вокзáлъ; Pl. E 8, *I*), on the S. bank of the Obvódni Canal, for Reval, Baltic Port, Dorpat (or Yuryev), and Riga (R. 14 b), and also for Peterhof and Oranienbaum (R. 16), and for Krasnoye Selo, Gatchina (R. 17), and Tosno (p. 43). — Tramways Nos. 3, 8, 9 (p. 91).

3. *Nicholas Station* (Николáевскій or Москóвскій вокзáлъ; Pl. H 6, *I*), in the Známenskaya Square, for Tver and Moscow (R. 37), Novgorod (R. 36), Ruibinsk (p. 267), and Vologda (Archangel) and Tchelyabinsk (Siberia; R. 35). Tramways Nos. 5, 7, 11, 13, 14, 19 (pp. 91, 92).

4. *Finland Station* (Финляндскій вокзáлъ; Pl. H 3, *I*), on the Viborg side, near the Alexándrovski Bridge, for Finland. — Tramways Nos. 1, 8, 9, 10, 19 (pp. 91, 92).

5. *Tzárskoye Seló Station* (Царскосéльскій вокзáлъ; Pl. F 7, *I*), in the Zágorodni Prospékt, for Tzarskoye Selo, Pavlovsk (R. 18), and Vitebsk (R. 34). — Tramways No. 9, 15, 16 (pp. 91, 92).

6. *Sestroryétzk Station* (Сестрорѣцкій вокзáлъ; Pl. D 1, *I*), in Nóvaya Derévnya, for Ozerki, Lakhta, and Kurort Sestroryetzk (R. 20). — Tramways Nos. 2, 3, 15 (pp. 91, 92).

7. *Irinovka Station* (Ирúновскій вокзáлъ; Pl. K 4, *I*), for Sheremetyevka (Schlüsselburg, comp. R. 19). — Tramways Nos. 13 & 14 (p. 92) and steamer from the Smolni Convent (Pl. I, K, 4; *I*) to Okhta (2 cop.).

II. Hotels. Restaurants. Cafés. Confectioners.

Hotels. *ASTORIA (Pl. c, E 6; *II*), at the corner of the Morskáya and Voznesénski Prospékt, R. with bath from 4, B. 1, déj. (12-3) 1¹/₄, D. (6-9) 2¹/₄ & 3, omn. 1¹/₂ rb.; *Hót. DE L'EUROPE (Европéйская гостúница; Pl. a, F 5, *II*), at the corner of the Nevski and the Mikháilovskaya, R. from 3 (with bath from 7¹/₂), B. 1, déj. (12-3) 1¹/₄, D. (6-9) 3, omn. 1¹/₂ rb. — *GRAND-Hótel (Pl. e, E 5; *II*), Ulitza Gógolya 18, R. from 2 rb., B. 60, déj. (11-3) 60 cop., D. (4-8) 1¹/₂, pens. from 5, omn. ³/₄-1¹/₂ rb.; *Hót. D'ANGLETERRE (Áнглія; Pl. d, E 5, *II*), Voznesénski Prospékt 10, opposite St. Isaac's Cathedral, R. from 2, B. ³/₄, déj. (12-3) ³/₄, D. (5-8) 1¹/₂, pens. from 5, omn. 1-1¹/₂ rb.; *Hót. DE FRANCE (Фрáнція; Pl. b, F 5, *II*), Morskáya 6, R. from 2³/₄ rb.,

B. $^3/_4$, déj. (11-3) 1, D. (4-8.30) $1^1/_2$, pens. from 7, omn. 1 rb.; *Hôt. Regina (Pl. o, F 5; *II*), Móika 61, R. from 2 rb., B. 60, déj. (11-3) 75 cop., D. (4-9) $1^1/_4$-2, pens. from 6, omn. $^3/_4$ rb.; Grand-Hôtel du Nord (Сѣверная гостй- ница; Pl. g, H 6, *II*), Nevski 118, opposite the Nicholas Station, R. from 2 rb., B. 60 cop., déj. (11-3) 1, D. (3-8) $1^1/_4$-2 rb.; Hôtel de Paris (Парйжъ, Pl. f, E 5, *II*), Ulitza Gógolya 23, R. from $1^1/_2$, déj. (11-3) $^3/_4$, D. (3-8) $^3/_4$-$1^1/_2$ rb.; Hôt. Dagmar (Pl. h, G 5; *II*), Sadóvaya 9, R. from 2 rb., B. 50, déj. (11-2) 75-90 cop., D. (4-8) 1-$1^1/_4$, omn. 1 rb.; Rossíya (Pl. i, E, F, 6; *II*), Móika 60, hôtel garni, R. $1^1/_4$-8 rb.; Victoria .(Pl. k, E, F, 6; *II*), Kazánskaya 29, R. from $1^3/_4$ rb., B. 40, déj. 60 cop., D. 1 rb.; Hermitage (Pl. p, H 6; *II*), Nevski 116, R. from 1 rb. 10, B. 35, déj. 60-75 cop., D. 60 cop. to 1 rb.; Old Riga (Стáрая Рйга; Pl. m, E 6, *II*), Novi Pereúlok 8, modest, R. from 1 rb., déj. 35 cop., D. $^1/_2$-1 rb.—Hotels in the Russian style: Moskvá (Pl. l, G 6; *II*), Nevski 49; Balábinskaya (Pl. n, H 6; *II*), Nevski 87.

Pensions. *Pens. Ritterholm,* Nevski 11, R. from 2, B. $^3/_4$, déj. (12-2) 1, D. (4-7) 1-2 rb.; *Pens. Sperk,* Mikháilovskaya 2 (Pl. F, 5; *II*), pens. from $6^1/_2$ (in winter $8^1/_4$) to 12 rb.; *Hospice of the Evangelical Society* (Госпйцъ Евангелйческаго Óбщества), Vasili Ostrov, Tenth Line, No. 15 (Pl. C, D, 4, 5; *I*), R. $1^1/_4$-5, D. (12-3) $^3/_4$, pens. $2^3/_4$-6 rb. — Furnished Rooms (Меблирóванныя кóмнаты) are numerous in the Nevski (e.g. *St. Petersburg,* No. 54) and the Morskáya (30-100 rb. a month).

Restaurants (comp. p. xxvii). Most of the large restaurants are in the hands of French or German proprietors or of Waiters' Unions, and entirely lack those national peculiarities which characterize the Moscow 'traktirs'. Wine is dear, but beer is usually to be had. Many of the restaurants have an orchestra. — Restaurants at the *Astoria,* *Europe,* *Grand,* *France,* *Angleterre,* and *Paris Hotels* (see p. 88). Other first- class restaurants are the following. In the City: *Restaurant de Paris* (late *Cubat*), Morskáya 16 (corner of Kirpítchni Pereúlok; Pl. F 5, *II*), déj. (1-3) $1^1/_4$, D. (6-9) $2^1/_2$ and 3 rb.; *A l'Ours* ('Медвѣдь'), Bolsháya Konyúshennaya 27, near the Nevski (Pl. F, 5; *II*), with large dining- room (closed from May 1st to Sept. 1st; much frequented in winter after the theatre), déj. (12-3) $1^1/_4$, D. (6-9) $2^1/_2$ rb.; *Donon,* Móika 24, near the Pyévtcheski Bridge (Pl. F 5, *II;* entrance by the porte cochère), with a small garden, déj. (12-3) $1^1/_2$, D. (5-8) $2^1/_2$ rb.; *Contant,* Móika 58, by the Krasni Bridge (Pl. F, 6; *II*), with garden, déj. (12-3) $1^1/_4$, D. (6-9) $2^1/_2$ rb.; *Old Donon,* Blagovyéshtchenskaya 2, near the Nikoláyevski Bridge (Pl. D, 5, 6; *II*), D. (3-7) $2^1/_2$ rb., frequented by the demi-monde at night after the theatre; *Pivato Frères,* Morskáya 36, near the Mariinskaya Square (Pl. E, 6; *II*), déj. (12-3) 1, D. (5-9) 2 rb. — Outside the City: *Datcha Ernest* (Pl. E, 2; *I*), Kámenno-Ostróvski Prospékt 60, D. (6-9) 3 rb.; *Cubat Frères* (formerly Bellevue; Pl. D 1, *I*), Kámenni Ostrov 24, near the Bol- shaya Nevka, D. from May 1st to Aug. 1st (5-8) 3 rb., at other times à la carte.

Less pretentious: *Vienna* (Вѣна), Ulitza Gógolya 13 (Pl. E, F, 5; *II*), déj. (11-3) $^3/_4$, D. (3-8) $^3/_4$-1 rb.; *Leinner,* Nevski 18, near the Politzéiski Bridge (Pl. F, 5; *II*), déj. (12-3) $^1/_2$-$^3/_4$, D. (3-8) 1 rb., with view of the Nevski, much frequented by Germans; *Restaurant Français Albert,* in the same building, déj. (11-3) $^3/_4$, D. (3-8) 1-$1^1/_2$ rb.; *Dominique,* Nevski 24, opposite the Kazan Cathedral (Pl. F, 5; *II*), a favourite luncheon-resort, with billiard-room, déj. (12-3) 40-75 cop., D. (3-8) $^3/_4$-1 rb. — *Métropole,* Sadóvaya 14, at the corner of the Nevski (Pl. F, G, 5; *II*), D. (3-8) $^3/_4$- 1 rb.; *Bernhard,* Vasili Ostrov, at the corner of the Nikoláyevskaya Náberezhnaya and Eighth Line (Pl. D, 5; *I*), déj. (12-3) $^3/_4$, D. (3-8) 1 rb.; *Brockmann,* Yekaterininski Canal 45, near the Kámenni Bridge (Pl. F, 6; *II*); *Quisisana,* Nevski 46, opposite the Gostíni Dvor (Pl. F, 5, 6; *II*), déj. (12-3) $^3/_4$, D. (3-8) $^3/_4$-1 rb. — *Cave la Grave,* Bolshaya Konyúshen- naya 14 (Pl. F, 5; *II*), near the Nevski, a small bar, with good cooking and Russian wines, moderate charges; *Makáyev,* Nevski 23, bar with Russian cooking and wines of the Caucasus. — There are also restaurants near the landing-stages of the Nevá steamers at the Alexander and Summer Gardens.

RUSSIAN DINING ROOMS. *Solovyóv* (late *Palkin*), Nevski 47, at the corner of the Vladimirski Prospékt (Pl. G, 6; *II*), déj. (12-2.30) 1, D. (2.30-8) 1¹/₄-2 ıb.; *Malo-Yaroslávetz*, Morskáya 8, next to the Hôt. de France, déj. (12-3) ³/₄, D. (3-8) 1, S. (10-2.30) 1¹/₄ rb.; *Kuznetzóv*, Nevski 29, near the Duma (Pl. F, 5; *II*), a 'Delikatessen' shop with a small restaurant on the first floor, déj. 80 cop., D. (from 5) 1¹/₂ rb.; *Grand-Hôtel du Nord* (p. 89).

Cafés and **Confectioners.** *Reiter*, Nevski 50, at the corner of the Sadóvaya (Pl. F, G, 5; *II*); *Tzvyetkóv* (late *Andréyev*), Nevski 6, near the Admiraltéiski Prospékt (Pl. E, 5; *II*); *Dominique*, see p. 89; *Café Central*, Nevski 44; *Polish Café*, Mikháilovskaya 2 (Pl. F, 5; *II*), also frequented by ladies for luncheon (50 cop.). — PIES AND PASTRY (Пирожки́) at *Filippov's*, at the corner of the Nevski (No. 45) and the Tróitzkaya (Pl. G, 6; *II*).

III. Carriages. Tramways. Steamers.

Carriages (comp. xxiv and the *Manual of the Russian Language*). St. Petersburg contains about 23,000 public vehicles of various kinds.

The IZVÓSHTCHIKS, or one-horse cabs, hold two persons and are fitted with folding hood and rubber tyres.

Tariff	¹/₄ hr.	20 min.	25 min.	¹/₂ hr.
By Day	20 cop.	25 cop.	30 cop.	35 cop.
At Night (12-7) . .	30 „	35 „	40 „	50 „

Tariff	35 min.	40 min.	³/₄ hr.	1 hr.
By Day	40 cop.	45 cop.	50 cop.	60 cop.
At Night (12-7) . .	55 „	60 „	70 „	90 „

This tariff is for the district enclosed by the Vólkovskoye (Pl. H, 8, 9; *I*) and Mitrofániyevskoye (Pl. E, 9; *I*) Cemeteries on the S., the Smolénskoye Cemetery (Pl. B, 4, 5; *I*) and Petrovski Ostrov (Pl. C, D, 3; *I*) on the W., and Aptékarski Ostrov (Pl. D-F, 2; *I*) and the Roman Catholic Cemetery (Pl. H, 2, 3; *I*) on the N.

From railway stations, landing-stages, theatres, and places of entertainment 15 cop. extra. One person is entitled to 3 puds of luggage free, two persons to 1 pud. The drivers are bound by the tariff and must drive at the rate of at least 10 versts (6²/₃ M.) per hour. For all drives of any length it is, however, better to make a bargain beforehand, paying 40-45 cop. for ¹/₂ hr., 60 cop. for ³/₄ hr.; drive to the Admiralty Quarter from the Warsaw and Baltic Railway Stations 80, from the Nicholas Station 60 cop., from the Finland Station ³/₄-1 rb.

Travellers with much luggage who do not wish to use the hotel omnibus should engage a four-seated carriage (Каре́та; 1¹/₂ rb. from the Warsaw or Baltic Station to the Admiraltéiski Prospékt).

TAXIMETER CABS (scarce) for the first verst 20, for every following verst 10 cop. From railway stations, etc., 15 cop. extra.

The LIKHATCHI (Лихачи), superior one-horse cabs with pneumatic tyres, are not bound by the tariff and usually charge 1 rb. for a short drive.

The ordinary charge for a TWO-HORSE CARRIAGE, taken from the rank, is 1-1¹/₂ rb. per drive on the hither side of the Nevá, and 1¹/₂-2 rb. beyond the Nevá; to the Islands 2-3 rb.; for 4-6 hrs., 3-5 rb.; for the whole day 10-15 rb.; for the night 6-8 rb., with a gratuity of 1 rb. on all the longer drives. *Stands* (Изво́щичьи би́ржи): Isaákiyevskaya Square (Pl. E, 5; *II*); Sini Bridge (Pl. E, 6; *II*); between the Kazan Cathedral (Pl. F, 5; *II*) and the Yekaterininski Canal, etc.

TRÓIKAS (p. xxiv), used in winter only (chief stand behind the Kazan Cathedral; Pl. F 5, *II*), are expensive, the price ranging from 8 to 20 rb. according to distance, besides a gratuity of 1-2 rb. to the driver.

MOTOR CABS (Та́ксо-мото́ры; Росси́йское Та́ксомото́рное Акцио-не́рное Общество, abbreviated to P.T.A.O.; headquarters at Bolshaya

Konyúshennaya 17): 1-2 persons per verst 20, at night (12 to 7 a.m.) 30; 3-4 pers. 30 or 40; waiting 5 cop. for 2½ minutes. — Motor Cars may be hired outside the Gostíni Dvor (Pl. F, 5, 6; *II*). They are subject to no fixed tariff.

The **Electric Tramways** run from 8 a.m. to midnight and even later on holidays in summer. Services 4, 5, 7, 11, 13, & 14 touch the Nevski Prospékt, 4, 5, & 7 the Admiraltéiski Prospékt, and 2, 4, 7, 10, & 12 Mikháilovskaya Square. Fare for one section 5 cop. — In winter an electric tramway runs over the frozen surface of the Nevá from the Winter Palace to the Múitninskaya Náberezhnaya (Pl. E, 4; *I*), fare 3 cop.

1. *Finland Station* (Pl. H, 3; *I*) to *Narva Triumphal Arch* (Pl. C, 9; *I*), viâ Sampsóniyevski Bridge (Pl. G, 3; *I*), Tróitzki Bridge (Pl. F, 4; *I*), Suvórovskaya Square (Pl. F, 4; *I*), Sadóvaya (Pl. D-G, 5-7; *I*), Syennáya Square (Pl. F, 6; *I*), Kalinkinski Bridge (Pl. D, 7; *I*), and Peterhófski Prospékt (Pl. D, 7, 8; *I*). Fare 15 cop.; 4 sections; blue and yellow lights.

2. *Mikháilovskaya Square* (Pl. F, 5; *I*) to *Nóvaya Derévnya* (for Sestroryétzk Railway Station; Pl. D 1, *I*), viâ Mársovo Pole (Pl. F, 4, 5; *I*), Suvórovskaya Square (Pl. F, 4; *I*), Tróitzki Bridge (Pl F, 4; *I*), Kámenno-Ostróvski Prospékt (Pl. E, F, 2-4; *I*), and Stróganovski Bridge (Pl. E, 1; *I*). Fare 10 cop.; 2 sections; blue and red lights.

3. *Nóvaya Derévnya* (for Sestroryétzk Railway Station; Pl. D 1, *I*) to *Baltic Station* (Pl. E, 8; *I*), same route as Service 2 to Mársovo Pole, then viâ the Sadóvaya (Pl. F, G, 5, 6; *I*), Syennáya Square (Pl. F, 6; *I*), Zabalkánski Prospékt (Pl. F, 6, 7; *I*), First Rota (Pl. E, F, 7; *I*), and Izmáilovski Prospékt (Pl. E, 7, 8; *I*). Fare 15 cop.; 4 sections; green and red lights.

4. *Lafonskaya Square* (Pl. I, 4; *I*) to *Smolénskoye Cemetery* (Pl. B, C, 4, 5; *I*) viâ Suvórovski Prospékt (Pl. H, I, 4, 5; *I*), Eighth Rozhdéstvenskaya (Pl. H, I, 5; *I*), Basséinaya (Pl. G, H, 5; *I*), Inzhenérnaya (Pl. F, G, 5; *I*), Mikháilovskaya Sq. (Pl. F, 5; *I*), Mikháilovskaya (Pl. F, 5; *I*), Nevski (Pl. E, F, 5; *I*), Admiraltéiski Prospékt (Pl. E, 5; *II*), Kónno-Gvardéiski Bulvár (Pl. D, E, 5, 6; *I*), Nikoláyevski Bridge (Pl. D, 5; *I*), Eighth Line (Pl. C, D, 4, 5; *I*), Bolshói Prospékt (Pl. C, D, 5; *I*), Sixteenth Line (Pl. C, 4, 5; *I*), and Mali Prospékt (Pl. B-D, 4, 5; *I*). Fare 15 cop.; 4 sections; yellow lights.

5. *Známenskaya Square* (Pl. H, 6; *I*) to *Galérnaya Gávan* (Nalítchni Pereúlok; Pl. B 5, *I*), viâ Nevski, Admiraltéiski Prospékt, thence as in Service 4, as far as Bolshói Prospékt, the whole length of which it then traverses. Fare 10 cop.; 3 sections; red lights.

7. *Mikháilovskaya Square* (Pl. F, 5; *I*) to *Známenskaya Square* (Pl. H, 6; *I*), viâ Sadóvaya, Tróitzki Bridge (Pl. F, 4; *I*), Krónverkski Prospékt (Pl. E, F, 3, 4; *I*), Vedénskaya (Pl. E, 3; *I*), Bolshói Prospékt (Pl. D, E, 3, 4; *I*), Tutchkóv Bridge (Pl. D, 4; *I*), Kadétskaya Líniya (Pl. D, 4, 5; *I*), Nikoláyevski Bridge (Pl. D, 5; *I*), Kónno-Gvardéiski Bulvár (Pl. D, E, 5, 6; *I*), Admiraltéiski Prospékt (Pl. E, 5; *II*), and Nevski. Fare 15 cop.; 5 sections; green lights.

8. *Finland Station* (Pl. H, 3; *I*) to *Tutchkóv Bridge* and *Baltic Station* (Pl. E, 8; *I*), viâ Sampsóniyevski Bridge (Pl. G, 3; *I*), Arkhiyeréiskaya (Pl. F, 2, 3; *I*), Bolshói Prospékt (Pl. D, E, 3, 4; *I*), Tutchkóv Bridge (Pl. D, 4; *I*), Nikoláyevski Bridge (Pl. D, 5; *I*), Úlitza Glinki (Pl. E, 6; *I*), and Izmáilovski Prospékt (Pl. E, 7, 8; *I*). Fare 15 cop.; 4 sections; green and yellow lights.

9. *Finland Station* (Pl. H, 3; *I*) to *Baltic Station* (Pl. E, 8; *I*), viâ Alexándrovski Bridge (Pl. G, 4; *I*), Litéini Prospékt (Pl. G, 4, 5; *I*), Zágorodni Prospékt (Pl. F, G, 6, 7; *I*), First Rota (Pl. E, F, 7; *I*), and Izmáilovski Prospékt (Pl. E, 7, 8; *I*). Fare 10 cop.; 3 sections; white lights.

10. *Mikháilovskaya Square* (Pl. F, 5; *I*) to *Wylie Clinical Hospital* (Pl. 95, G 3; *I*), viâ Inzhenérnaya (Pl. F, G, 5; *I*), Litéini Prospékt (Pl G, 4, 5; *I*), Alexándrovski Bridge (Pl. G, 4; *I*), Finski Pereúlok (Pl. G, H, 3; *I*), and Bótkinskaya (Pl. G, 3; *I*). Fare 5 cop.; red and yellow lights.

11. *Známenskaya Square* (Pl. H, 6; *I*) to the *Putílov Railway* (beyond Pl. F, 9; *I*), viâ Nevski, Sadóvaya (Pl. F, 6; *I*), Syennáya Square (Pl.

F, 6; *I*), Zabalkánski Prospékt (Pl. F, 6-9; *I*), and Moscow Triumphal Arch (Pl. F, 9; *I*). Fare 10 cop.; 3 sections; red and blue lights.

12. *Mikháilovskaya Square* (Pl. F, 5; *I*) to *Vedénskaya* (Pl. E, 3; *I*), viâ Sadóvaya, Tróitzki Bridge (Pl. G, 4; *I*), and Krónverkski Prospékt (Pl. E, F, 3, 4; *I*). — Fare 5 cop.; yellow and green lights.

13. *Palmenbákhskaya* (Pl. I, K, 4; *I*) to *Pokróvskaya Square* (Pl. D, 7; *I*), viâ Suvórovski Prospékt (Pl. H, I, 4-6; *I*), Nevski, and Sadóvaya (Pl. D-G, 5-7; *I*). — Fare 10 cop.; 3 sections; white and red lights.

14. *Palmenbákhskaya* (Pl. I, K, 4; *I*) to *Narva Triumphal Arch* (Pl. C, 9; *I*), viâ Suvórovski Prospékt (Pl. H, I, 4, 5; *I*), Second Rozhdéstvenskaya (Pl. H, 6; *I*), Známenskaya Square (Pl. H, 6; *I*), Nevski, Sadóvaya (Pl. D-G, 5-7; *I*), and so on as in Service 1. Fare 15 cop.; 4 sections; yellow and red lights.

15. *District Court* (Pl. G, 4; *II*) to *Nóvaya Derévnya* (for Sestroryetzk Railway Station (Pl. D, E, 1; *I*), viâ Litéini Prospékt (Pl. G, 4, 5; *I*) and Zágorodni Prospékt (Pl. F, G, 6, 7; *I*) to the Zabalkánski Prospékt, thence as in Service 3. Fare 20 cop.; 6 sections; blue lights.

16. *Putilov Railway* (beyond Pl. F, 9; *I*) to *Bolshaya Bolotnaya* (Pl. I, 5; *I*), viâ Moscow Triumphal Arch (Pl. F, 9; *I*), Zabalkánski Prospékt (Pl. F, 7-9; *I*), Zágorodni Prospékt (Pl. F, G, 6, 7; *I*), and Basséinaya (Pl. G, H, 5; *I*). Fare 10 cop. 3 sections; white and green lights.

17. *Smolni Prospékt* (Pl. I, K, 4; *I*) to *Corner of Sredni Prospékt and Twenty-fifth Line* (Pl. C, 5; *I*), to the Nikoláyevski Bridge (Pl. D, 5; *I*) as in Service 4, thence viâ First Line (Pl. D, 5; *I*), Bolshói Prospékt (Pl. D, 5; *I*), and Eighth Line (Pl. D, 5; *I*). Fare 15 cop.; 4 sections; white and yellow lights.

18. *Tverskáya* (Pl. I, 4; *I*) to *Mikháilovskaya Square* (Pl. F, 5; *I*), viâ Shpalérnaya (Pl. H, I, 4; *I*), Voskresénski Prospékt (Pl. H, 4; *I*), and Litéini Prospékt (Pl. G, 4, 5; *I*). Fare 5 cop.; white and blue lights.

19 (?). *Nicholas Station* (Pl. H, 6; *I*) to *Finland Station* (Pl. H, 3; *I*), viâ Známenskaya (Pl. H, 5; *I*) and Litéini Prospékt (Pl. G, 4, 5; *I*), in course of construction.

Horse Tramways. The chief lines run from *Universitétskaya Náberezhnaya* (Pl. D, E, 5; *I*) to *Krestóvski Island* (Pl. C, 2; *I*), and from *Suvórovski Prospékt* to *Alexander Nevski Monastery.*

Steam Tramways. 1. From the *Lígovskaya* (near Známenskaya Square; Pl. H 6, *II*) to the S.E. viâ the Nevski (Alexander Nevski Monastery, see p. 130) and Schlüsselburg Prospékt (6²/₃ M.; Imperial Porcelain and Glass Factory, see p. 192) to the village of *Murzinka* (8 M.); every 12 min., 20 and 12 cop. (To the Alexander Nevski Monastery in 9 min.; 5 and 3 cop.) — 2. From the *Wylie Hospital* (Pl. 95, G 3; *I*) to the (4 M.) *Forestry Institute*, every 11 min., in 34 min., fare 6 and 4 cop.; thence to the *Polytechnic* 3 and 2 cop.

Steamboats. a. FERRIES (Перевóзы; 2 cop., at night 3 cop.). Perevóznaya (Pl. C, D, 6; *I*) to Mining Institute (Pl. 105, C 6; *I*); Senate House (Pl. E, 5; *II*) to Rumyántzev Square (Pl. D 5, *II*; temporarily suspended); Dvortzóvi Bridge (Pl. E, 5; *I*) to Múitninskaya Náberezhnaya (Pl. E 4, *I*; Zoological Gardens); Frantzúzskaya Náberezhnaya (Alexándrovski Bridge; Pl. G 4, *I*) to House of Peter the Great (Pl. 146, F 4; *I*). — b. LONGER TRIPS. From Lyetni Sad (Summer Garden; Pl. F, G, 4, *I*) down the Bolshaya Nevka to Krestóvski Ostrov (Pl. C, 2; *I*), every ¹/₄ hr., 10 cop.; from the Eleventh Line on Vasili Ostrov (Pl. D, 5; *I*) to Lyetni Sad (Pl. F, G, 4; *I*) and Irínovka Railway Station (Pl. K, 4; *I*); from the Wylie Hospital (Pl. 95, G 3; *I*) to Lyetni Sad (Pl. F, G, 4; *I*), Fontánka, and Kalínkinski Bridge (Pl. D, 7; *I*); from the Eleventh Line on Vasili Ostrov (Pl. D, 5; *I*) to Lyetni Sad (Pl. F, G, 4; *I*) and Seló Smolénskoye (beyond Pl. K, 8; *I*), every ¹/₄ hr.; from the Twelfth Line on Vasili Ostrov (Pl. D, 5; *I*) to the Harbour and Morskói Canal (Pl. A, 8, 9; *I*).

The time of departure of the steamers to *Cronstadt* (p. 184) and *Schlüsselburg* (p. 191) is often changed; particulars will be found in the (Russian) Police Gazette.

IV. Post and Telegraph Offices. Commissionnaires.

Post Office. The *General Post Office* (Главный почтамтъ; Pl. E 6, *II;* p. 111), Potchtámtskaya, near St. Isaac's Cathedral, is open on week-days 9-7 (for money orders and letters or parcels containing valuables, 9-4 only), on Sun. and festivals (comp. p. xxviii) 9-11 a.m. The various offices for public business are in the large covered court entered from the Potchtámskaya. Window No. 8 (to the right) is for foreign money orders, No. 16 for foreign registered letters, Nos. 18 & 19 for the payment of money orders, No. 26 for the delivery of parcels from abroad, and Nos. 28 & 29 for the despatch of foreign parcels. Window No. 43, in the middle of the court, is for *poste restante* letters, No. 44 for the delivery of registered letters, and Nos. 45 & 61 for the sale of postage stamps. Money orders and parcels not exceeding 500 rb. in value are delivered at the addressee's residence (10 or 20 cop.). — Branch-offices are open on week-days from 8 to 2, on Sun. and holidays from 8 to 10. — City letters cost 3 cop.

Telegraph Office. The *General Telegraph Office* (Главная телеграфная станція; Pl. E 6, *II;* p. 111), Potchtámtskaya 15, is always open. So also is the telegraph office at the Warsaw Station. The branch-offices are open from 9 a.m. to 9 or 11 p.m. Telegrams within the city 15 cop. plus 1 cop. per word. Letters may be registered at the General Telegraph Office between 8 p.m. and 8 a.m.

Commissionnaires (Посыльные). The *1st St. Petersburg Commissionnaires* wear orange caps, the *2nd* red, the *3rd* blue, and so on. The charge for an ordinary message or parcel is 20 cop., for long distances 40 cop.; at night double those rates.

V. Embassies. Clubs. Police. Churches.

Embassies and Consulates. GREAT BRITAIN: Ambassador, *Sir George William Buchanan, G.C.V.O., K.C.M.G., C.B.,* Dvortzóvaya Náberezhnaya 4 (Pl. E, F, 4, 5, *II;* 11-3); Consul, *Arthur W. Woodhouse,* Konno-Gvardéiski Bulvár 13 (Pl. E, 5, 6, *II;* 10-3); Vice-Consul, *C. H. Mackie.* — UNITED STATES OF AMERICA: Ambassador *(vacat)*, Furshtátskaya 34 (Pl. G, H, 4, *II;* 11-3); Consul, *Dr. J. E. Conner,* Nevski 1 (Pl. F 5, *II;* 10-12 & 1-3); Vice-Consul, *H. Vesey.*

LLOYD'S AGENT, *Chas. R. Cattley,* Konno-Gvardéiski Bulvár (Pl. E, 5, 6; *II*). — RUSSO-BRITISH CHAMBER OF COMMERCE, Gorokhováya 4 (12-4).

Clubs and Societies. — *New English Club* (Новый Англійскій клубъ), Morskáya 36 (Pl. E, 6; *II*), for Englishmen and Americans. — *Imperial Yacht Club* (Морской Яхтъ клубъ; Pl. E 5, *II*), Morskáya 31 (for the high aristocracy and diplomatic corps). — *English Club* (Англійское собраніе; Pl. F 4, *II*), Dvortzóvaya Náberezhnaya 16 (for the nobility, high officials, etc.). — *New Club* (Новый клубъ), Dvortzóvaya Náberezhnaya 14, similar to the preceding. — *Army & Navy Club* (Офицерское собраніе армiи и флота; Pl. G, 4, 5, *II*), Litéini Prospékt 20. — *Club of the Noblesse* (Благородное собраніе; Pl. F 5, *II*), Nevski 15, cor. of the Morskáya. — *Commercial Club* (Коммерческое собраніе), Angliskaya Náberezhnaya 18 (Pl. D, E, 5, 6, *II;* rich merchants). — *Literary and Artistic Society* (Литературно-артистическій кружокъ), Dvortzóvaya Náberezhnaya 12 (Pl. E, F, 4, 5; *II*); the Society is lessee of the Little Theatre (p. 94). — *Imperial River Yacht Club* (Рѣчной Яхтъ клубъ; Pl. B 1, *I*), Krestóvski Island. — *Imperial Automobile Club* (Императорское Россійское Автомобильное Общество), Dvortzóvaya Náberezhnaya 10 (Pl. E-G, 4, 5; *II*).

Count V. P. Súbov's Institute of Art and History (Институтъ исторіи искусствъ), Isaákiyevskaya Square 5 (Pl. E, 5; *II*). — *Institut Français de St. Pétersbourg,* Gorókhovaya 13 (Pl. E, F, 5, 6; *II*).

Police. *City Governor,* or *Prefect of Police* (Градоначальникъ; Pl. E 5, *II*), Gorókhovaya 2. For passports, certificates of residence, etc., see p. xviii. — *Address Bureau* (Pl. 4, E 7; *I*), Sadóvaya 58 (week-days 9-6; holidays 10-3).

Churches. *St. Mary & All Saints* (Pl. 43, D 6; *I*), Angliskaya Náberezhnaya 56; chaplain, Rev. Bousfield S. Lombard, M. A.; services at 8.15, 10.30, & 6.30. *Mission Church*, in the Schlüsselburg Quarter; services in summer on 2nd & 4th Sundays, at 8.30, 11, & 6.—*British and American Congregational Chapel* (Pl. 42, E 6; *II*), Novo-Isaákiyevskaya 16; minister, Rev. W. Orr; services at 11 & 6.—*Methodist Episcopal Church*, Tenth Line 37, Vasili Ostrov (Pl. D, 4, 5; *I*).—*French Protestant Church* (Pl. F. 5; *II*), Bolshaya Konyúshennaya 25.—There are also several *German Protestant Churches*.

Roman Catholic Churches. *Cathedral of the Assumption*, First Rota of the Izmáilovski Regiment 11 (Pl. E, F, 7; *I*).—*Church of St. Boniface* (German; Pl. 54, E 3, *I*), Gesleróvski Pereúlok 11, new building at Tzerkóvnaya 9 (Pl. D, E, 4; *I*).—*Salvator Chapel* (German), Ninth Line 60, Vasili Ostrov (Pl. D, 5; *I*).—*Church of St. Catharine* (Pl. F, 5; *II*), Nevski 34.— *Church of St. Stanislaus*, Málaya Masterskáya 9 (Pl. D, 6, 7; *I*).

Y. M. C. A., Nadézhdinskaya 35 (Pl. G, H, 5, 6; *II*).—*Girls' Friendly Society*, Galérnaya 57 (Pl. D, E, 5, 6; *II*).—*Princess Alice Home for Governesses*, Kuznetchni Pereúlok 18 (Pl. G, H, 6; *II*).

VI. Theatres. Pleasure Gardens. Places of Entertainment.

Theatres. The season lasts from the end of Aug. to the beginning of May (O. S.). Tickets may be procured in advance four days before the performances. There is a Central Theatre Agency at Nevski 23 (booking-fee 10 per cent of price of ticket).

Imperial Marie Theatre (Маріинскій театръ; Pl. 180, E 6, *I*; p. 123), for Russian opera and ballet (both very good; ballet every Sun. and also often on Wed.). The building seats 2000 persons. Performances begin at 8 p.m. Most of the seats are let to subscribers.—Prices (booking in advance). First tier boxes for ballet 24 rb. 90 and for opera 22 rb. 70; baignoire 22 rb. 70 and 18 rb. 85 or 20 rb. 50 and 17 rb. 20; bel-étage 24 rb. 90 and 27 rb. 10 or 22 rb. 70 and 24 rb. 90; second tier 17 rb. 75 or 16 rb. 10; third tier from 10 rb. 60 to 12 rb. 80 or 9 rb. 50 to 11 rb. 70; fourth tier 9 rb. 50 or 8 rb. 40; parquet from 3 rb. 40 to 11 rb. 10 or 3 rb. 40 to 8 rb. 90; third balcony 2 rb. 85 cop. Much higher prices rule at benefit performances.

Imperial Alexandra Theatre (Александрийскій театръ; G 6, *II*; p. 106), for Russian drama and comedy.—Tickets (in advance). First tier and bel-étage boxes 11 rb. 60 and 13 rb. 80; second tier 9 rb. 40 and 10 rb. 50; third tier 7 rb. 20 and 9 rb. 40; fourth tier 5 rb. 80 and 7 rb. 20; parquet from 2 rb. 30 to 4 rb. 50; balcony 1 rb. 50 cop.

Imperial Michael Theatre (Михайловскій театръ; F 5, *II*; p. 119), for French and Russian drama and comedy, and Russian opera.—Prices in advance. First tier and bel-étage boxes 18 rb. 20 to 22 rb. 60; second tier 11 rb. 60 to 13 rb. 80; third tier 7 rb. 20 to 9 rb. 40; fourth tier 5 rb. 80 to 7 rb. 20; parquet 2 rb. 30 to 6 rb. 70 cop.

Grand Opera in the theatre of the Conservatoire of Music (Театръ музыкáльной дрáмы; Pl. E 6, *II*) in winter; boxes 10-30 rb., parquet 1 rb. 40 cop. to 7 rb.—Performances are also sometimes given in winter in the Aquarium (p. 95).

Little Theatre (Мáлый театръ; Pl. F 6, *II*), in the Fontánka, leased by the Literary & Artistic Society (p. 93), for plays by modern Russian dramatists; boxes 8-18 rb., parquet 1-6 rb.

Palace Theatre (Pl. F, 5; *II*), Mikháilovskaya Square 13; Russian comic operas.—*Casino Theatre*, Kryukov Canal 12 (Pl. D, E, 6; *I*). *Russian Dramatic Theatre*, Admiraltéiskaya Náberezhnaya 4 (Pl. E, 5; *II*).—*Nevski Farce*, Nevski 56.—*Arcade Theatre*, in the Arcade (Passage; Pl. F, G, 5, *II*), entrance in the Italyánskaya, for Russian operettas.— *Opéra Comique*, Ofitzérskaya 39 (Pl. E, 6; *II*), at Luna Park.—*Théâtre Zon*, Kámenno-Ostróvski Prospékt 40 (Pl. E, F, 2, 3; *I*).—*Emperor*

Nicholas II.'s People's Theatre (Pl. E, F, 3, *I*; tickets booked in advance at the Central Theatre Agency, p. 94), opera and drama; seat for opera 1 rb. 55 to 3 rb. 40 cop., box $2^1/_2$ rb.

Music. In winter symphony concerts take place under the direction of Kusevitzki, Zilóti, Safónov, etc. Other good concerts are given by Count Sheremétyev's orchestra at the Assembly of Nobles (Pl. 17, F 5, *II;* seat 20 cop. to $1^1/_2$ rb.) and by the Imperial Court Orchestra.

Pleasure Gardens (the summer season lasts till the middle or end of Aug., O. S.). *Pávlovsk,* see p. 189. — *Zoological Gardens* (Pl. E 4, *I;* p. 175), on the Petersburg Side, with band, adm. 32 cop.; steam-ferry, see p. 92; tramway No. 7 (Krónverkski Prospékt), see p. 91. — *Arcadia* (Pl. D, E, 1; *I*), near the Sestroryetzk station, in Nóvaya Derévnya, opera in summer; tramways Nos. 2 & 3, see p. 91. — *Aquarium* (Pl. F, 3; *I*), Kámenno-Ostróvski Prospékt 10; tramways Nos. 2 & 3, see p. 91. — *Villa Rode* (Pl. E, 1; *I*), near the Stróganovski Bridge; tramways Nos. 2 & 3, see p. 91. — *Luna Park,* Ofitzérskaya 39 (Pl. E, 6; *II*).

Ciniselli Circus (Pl. G, 5; *II*), on the Fontánka; performances in winter only. Side-boxes (6 pers.) 15 rb. 60, barrière-boxes (4 pers.) 10 rb. 40, first tier boxes (4 pers.) 8 rb. 40; stalls 4 rb. 10 and 3 rb. 10; reserved seat 2 rb. 10 cop. — *Cirque Moderne,* corner of Kámenno-Ostróvski Prospékt and Krónverkski Prospékt (Pl. E, F, 3; *I*).

Sport. GOLF COURSE (nine holes) at Murino (p. 194). — ROWING. *Arrow Rowing Club,* at the Krestovski Ostrov. — LAWN TENNIS at the Pargolóvo, Krestovski, Tavritcheski, and Cadet Corps clubs. — SHOOTING CLUBS (the members of which enjoy the right of shooting over the club preserves): Krásnoye Seló, Pavlovsk, Málaya Víshera, Tcherentzovo, etc. — SKATING (Катóкъ) in the *Ice Palace* of the Aquarium (Pl. F 3, *I*; see above), adm. 1-7 p.m. 1 rb., 8.30 p.m. to 1 a.m. 2 rb. (restaurant, D. 3 rb.); also in the Yusúpov Garden (Pl. E, F, 6, 7, *I;* p. 123), on the Fontánka, near the Semyónovski Bridge (Pl. F, 6; *I*), etc.

Horse Races (Скáчки) are held from June 1st to Aug. 15th (O. S.) thrice weekly on the racecourse in the Kolomyágskoye Chaussée (p. 177). — TROTTING RACES (Бѣгá) take place in the Semyónovski Square (Pl. F, G, 7; *I*), in autumn and winter; entr. to the stands opposite the Nikolá-yevskaya.

Public Entertainments (Нарóдныя гулянья; good theatrical performances, etc.) are arranged by the Temperance Society (Горóдскóе попечительство о нарóдной трéзвости) every Sun. and holiday, in Emperor Nicholas II.'s People's Theatre (see above), the Petróvski Park (Pl. D, 3, 4; *I*), the Tauric or Tavritcheski Garden (Pl. H, 4; *I*), and Yekaterinhóf (Pl. C, 8; *I*).

VII. Baths. Physicians. Chemists.

Baths (Бáни; comp. p. xxxi). *Central Baths* (Pl. F, 6, 7; *I*), Kazátchi Pereúlok 11; *Tzelibyéyev* (Pl. G, 5; *II*), Basséinaya 14; *Vorónin* (Pl. E, 6; *II*), Móika 82, warm bath at these two 1 rb. — RIVER BATHS (very primitive), on the Admiraltéiskaya Náberezhnaya, near the Dvortzóvi Bridge (Pl. E, 5; *II*). Bath 5-10, sheet 10, towel 5 cop.

PUBLIC LAVATORIES (Клозéты). Alexander Garden, near the Senate (Pl. E, 5; *II*); in the Duma (Pl. F, 5; *II*), entrance in the Dúmskaya; near the Public Library (Pl. G, 5; *II*); Yekateríninskaya Square (Pl. I, 4; *I*); Lyetni Sad (Pl. F, G, 4; *II*); Známenskaya Square (Pl. H, 6; *II*).

Physicians (Врачй; English-speaking). *Dr. Webb,* at the Alexander Hospital (see below); *Dr. Baron Sternberg,* Angliski Prospékt; *Dr. Gersoni* (for diseases of women), Fifth Rozhdestvenskaya 4; *Dr. Butz* (surgeon), Second Line 19, Vasíli Ostrov.

ALEXANDER HOSPITAL (Pl. 78, C, D, 5; *I*), Fifteenth Line 4, Vasíli Ostrov, for men, founded by Germans and maintained by voluntary contiibutions (25-30 rb. per week; without private room 10 rb.). — PROTESTANT HOSPITAL (Pl. H, 5; *II*), Ligovskaya 4, for women (fees as above).

Chemists (Аптéки). *Friedländer*, Gorókhovaya 24 (portable medicine chests); *Dietz*, Nevski 66, near the Anítchkov Bridge; *Kressling*, Bolshaya Konyúshennaya 14; *Homeopathic Chemist*, Gorókhovaya 17, etc.

VIII. Tourist Agencies. Banks. Shops.

Tourist Agencies. *International Sleeping Car Company* (Междунарóдное Óбщество спáльныхъ вагóновъ), Nevski 22 (fee 2 per cent of price of tickets); open on week-days 9-5 (cash department closed at 4 p.m.), on Sun. and holidays 9.30-12. — *Nordisk Resebureau*, Bolshaya Konyúshennaya 29 (Pl. F, 5; *II*), mainly for travellers to Finland, Sweden, and Norway. — *R. Edgren* (bookseller), Bolshaya Konyúshennaya 8 (Pl. F, 5; *II*), is the agent for the Finland Tourist Society (p. 203).

Banks. *Imperial State Bank* (Госудáрственный банкъ; Pl. F 6, *I*), Sadóvaya 19, entrance at Yekateríninski Canal 30; *Azóv-Don Commercial Bank* (Азóвско-Донскóй коммéрческій банкъ), Morskáya 5; *Commercial Bank of Siberia* (Сибíрскій торгóвый банкъ), Nevski 44; *Crédit Lyonnais* (Ліóнскій кредíтъ), Nevski 48 (Arcade); *Russian Bank for Foreign Trade* (Рýсскій для внѣшней торгóвли банкъ), Morskáya 32; *Russian & English Bank* (Рýсско-Англíйскій банкъ), Nevski 28; *Russo-Asiatic Bank* (Рýсско-Азіáтскій банкъ), Nevski 62; *St. Petersburg Commercial Bank* (С. П. торгóвый банкъ; formerly G. Wawelberg), Nevski 7; *St. Petersburg Commercial Joint Stock Bank* (Чáстный коммéрческій банкъ), Nevski 1; *St. Petersburg Discount Bank* (С. П. Учéтный и Ссýдный банкъ), corner of the Nevski and Yekateríninski Canal; *St. Petersburg International Commercial Bank* (С. П. Международный коммéрческій банкъ), Nevski 58; *Volga-Kama Commercial Bank* (Вóлжско-Кáмскій коммéрческій банкъ), Nevski 38, cor. of the Mikháilovskaya. — *J. W. Junker & Co.*, Nevski 12; *E. M. Meyer & Co.*, Angliskaya Náberezhnaya 30. — Usual office-hours 10-4; State Bank 10-3.

Shops. — ANTIQUES. *L. Grisard*, Alexandrinskaya Square 5; *Sávostin*, Sadóvaya 13.

BOOKSELLERS. English, *Watkins*, Morskáya 36. French, Russian, and German, *Mellier & Co.* (A. Zinserling & Co.), Nevski 20, near the Politzeiski Bridge; *M. O. Wolff*, Nevski 13 and Gostíni Dvor 18. German, *Eggers & Co.*, Móika 42; *A. Isler*, Nevski 20; *Karl Ricker*, Nevski 14. Russian, *I. Glazunóv*, Nevski 27; *A. S. Suvórin* ('Nóvoye Vrémya'), Nevski 40. — Second-hand Booksellers, *W. I. Klotchkóv*, Litéini 55; *L. F. Mellin*, Litéini 51.

BOOTS. *Mechanical Shoe Factory*, Nevski 61 and Morskáya 26; *Weiss*, Nevski 66.

CIGARS. *Feik & Co.*, Nevski 20; *Laferme*, Nevski 26; *A. Schramm & Co.*, Morskáya 11; *Ten-Cate & Co.*, Nevski 18.

CONFECTIONERY (excellent). *Ballet*, Nevski 54; *Berrin*, Úlitza Gógolya 8; *Bormann*, Nevski 30 & 21; *Conradi*, Nevski 20 & 36; *Kotchkuróv*, Mikháilovskaya Square 4, corner of Italyánskaya; *Krafft*, Italyánskaya 10; *Rabon*, Nevski 30. — *Abrikósov*, Nevski 42 (good candied fruit; мармелáдъ). — Dried Fruit from Kiev, *Balábukha*, Vladimirski Prospékt 15.

DOMESTIC INDUSTRIES (including lace, fancy work, etc.) at Nevski 3 (Óбщество улучшéнія нарóднаго трудá), Morskáya 30 (Óбщество пóмощи ручнóму трудý въ С. Петербýргѣ), Litéini 28 (Кустáрный склáдъ), and Fontánka 21 (Склáдъ кустáрныхъ издѣлій графíни Шувáловой). Also *Frau Behrens*, Universitétskaya Náberezhnaya 17 (Academy of Arts; entr. from the Fourth Line), and *Vogt*, Gostíni Dvor, Perínnaya Line 1 h.

FURS. *Mertens*, Nevski 21.

GOLOSHES, Indiarubber Boots, and Overshoes. *Kirschten*, Admiraltéiski Prospékt 8; *Malm*, Morskáya 34; *Provodnik*, Morskáya 14.

Jewellers. Russian Goldsmith's and Silversmith's Work: *Gratchev* Nevski 19; *Y. E. Morózov*, Gostíni Dvor 85; *M. P. Ovtchínnikov*, Morskáya 35. — Goldsmith's Work and Jewellery: *K. I. Bock*, Morskáya 9; *K. E. Bolín*, Morskáya 10; *L. E. Burchard*, Nevski 34; *C. Fabergé*, Morskáya 24; *A. Tillander*, Morskáya 25. — Bronzes and Objects in malachite, lapis lazuli, and other Siberian stones: *A. K. Denísov-Urálski & Co.* Morskáya 27; *Wörffel*, Nevski 36.

Maps and Plans. Depot of the General Staff (Гла́вный штабъ), Nevski 4, and *A. Ilyin*, Yekateríninskaya 3.

Newsvendors in every street. St. Petersburger Zeitung, Herold (German), 5 cop.; Russian papers 7 cop.; foreign papers at *Wolff's*, Nevski 13 and at *Viollet's*, Málaya Konyúshennaya 16.

Photographs. *A la Palette de Raphaël* (Avanzo), Morskáya 9, near the Nevski; *Avanzo*, Nevski 5; *Daziaro*, Morskáya 11; *J. Fietta*, Morskáya 36; *Trenti*, Morskáya 21; *Velten*, Nevski 20. — Photographic Materials: *O. & K. Jochim*, Nevski 1; *Kodak*, Bolshaya Konyúshennaya 19; *J. Steffen*, Kazánskaya 5.

Porcelain. *Kornílov Bros.*, Nevski 66 (cups, etc., with paintings after Karázin); *Kuznetzóv*, Nevski 64.

Tea. *P. Botkin & Sons*, Nevski 38; *K. & S. Popóv Bros.*, Nevski 26.

IX. Museums, Collections, and other Sights.

Gentlemen are not allowed to wear their hats in museums and galleries. All collections are closed on the chief holidays.

Academy of Arts (p. 169), open free daily, except Mon., 10-4 (in winter 10-3). It is closed in July (O. S.), but foreigners are admitted on application. — For temporary *Exhibitions of Art*, see the daily papers.

Academy of Sciences, see p. 166. — *Library*, on Wed. in summer 11-3, in winter on Mon., Tues., Thurs., & Frid. 11-3; closed for a fortnight at Christmas and Easter.

Agricultural Museum (p. 126), open free daily, except Mon., 11-3; closed on holidays.

Anthropological & Ethnographical Museum of Peter the Great (p. 166), Sun. & Mon., 11-3, free; Wed. & Frid., 11-3, adm. 25 cop.; closed on Frid. from June 20th to Sept. 1st.

Artillery Museum (p. 174), Mon., Wed., & Frid., 11-3; entrance by ticket, procured free of charge at the Depot, corner of Málaya Dvoryánskaya and Konni Pereúlok (Pl. F, 3; *I*); closed on festivals.

Asiatic Museum (p. 167), daily, except Sat., Sun., and festivals, 11-3 (closed on Wed. in summer and for a fortnight at Christmas and Easter).

Botanical Gardens, Imperial (p. 176), open daily from 7 a.m. till dusk; *Hot Houses* in summer from 10 a.m. to 7 p.m. (Sun., and festivals till 3 p.m.), in winter till dusk; *Museum*, Tues., Thurs., & Sat., 1-3; *Library* and *Herbarium*, week-days 11-3.

Botkin Collection (p. 172), shown on application.

Carriages, Museum of Imperial (p. 117), open free on week-days (except Mon.) 11-3, Sun. 1-3.

Commissary-General, Museum of (p. 124), open free on Tues. & Frid., 10-3; closed on holidays and from July 10th to Aug. 15th (O. S.).

Education, Museum of (p. 126), open on week-days (in winter also on Sun.), 12-3.

Guard Mounting at the Winter Palace at midday.

Hermitage (P. 131), open daily, except Mon. and most of the high festivals, 11-4 (Oct. 1st to March 1st, 11-3).

Industrial Art Museum (P. 110), week-days in summer (except Mon.) 10-4, in winter daily 10-3; 30 cop.

Kustarni Museum (p. 126), open free on week-days (except Mon.) 11-3, Sun. 12-3.

Marine Museum (p. 108), open free on Tues., Thurs., & Frid., 11-4, Sun. 12-4; closed from May 15th to Aug. 15th (O. S.).

Michael Nikoláyevitch, Museum of Grand-Duke (p. 116), Thurs. & Sun.
11-2; tickets obtained free on the previous day in the office, Milliónnaya 19
(open 2-4 p.m.).

Mining Academy & Museum (p. 172), open free from June 1st to
Aug. 31st, on Tues., Wed., & Thurs., 10-3 (closed on festivals); from
Sept. 1st to May 31st, on Tues., Wed., Frid., & Sat. 10-3, Sun. and
festivals 12-3.

Ministry of Ways of Communication, Museum of the (p. 123), Tues.,
Thurs., & Sun. 10-3; 25 cop.

Old St. Petersburg, Museum of (p. 169), Mon. & Frid., 2-5; free.

Porcelain and Glass Factory, Imperial (p. 192), open free on week-
days in summer, 10-12 & 2-5 (Sat. 10-12 only); in winter on week-days
10-3 (Sat. 10-12).

Public Library, Imperial (p. 105). The *Reading Room* is open to the
public daily from 10 a.m. to 9 p.m. (Sun. & holidays 12-3); it is closed
during Passion Week, for three days at Easter, from July 1st to July 3rd,
and from Dec. 24th to Jan. 1st (O. S.). Those who wish to consult MSS.,
engravings, or the like, require a special permission from the Director. —
Inspection permitted on Tues. & Sun., except on the days on which the
Library is closed (see above), under the guidance of an official. Visitors
assemble in the entrance-hall at 1 p.m. The explanations by the guide
are usually given in Russian.

Russian Museum of Emperor Alexander III. (p. 119), open free daily
(except Mon.) 10-4, in winter 10-3.

Seménov Gallery (p. 171), adm. on application.

Stieglitz Museum of Industrial Art (p. 125), open free daily, 10-3.

Stróganov Gallery (p. 103), open every forenoon, except Sat., Sun.,
and holidays, on application at the 'Kontor' in the court (left).

Suvórov Museum (p. 127), open free daily, except Mon., 11-4.

Technical Society, Imperial (p. 126), open free on week-days (except
Mon.) 11-4, on Sun. & holidays 1-3; from June 15th till Sept. 1st (O.S.)
on Wed., 11-4, only.

Tolstói Museum (p. 169), daily, except Mon , 11-5; 20 cop.

University Library (p. 169), open from Aug. 20th to June 10th (O. S.)
on week-days, 10-3, and also on Mon., Wed., & Frid., 6-10 p.m. (during
the Christmas holidays on Wed. & Frid. only, 11-2); from June 11th to
Aug. 19th, Mon. & Thurs. 11-2.

Winter Palace (p. 112), open daily, 11-3, during the absence of the
imperial family. Visitors obtain cards of admission on presenting their
passports at the office of the Chief of the Palace Police (to the left of the
chief entrance, opposite the Alexander Column).

Zoological Museum (p. 167), daily, except Mon. & Thurs., 11-3; adm.
on Tues. 70 cop., Wed. and Frid. 25 cop., Sat. & Sun. free. It is closed
from June 15th to Aug. 1st, but foreigners are admitted, on application
at the office, Tamózhenni Pereúlok.

The *Greek Orthodox Churches* are generally closed at 6 p.m.

Chief Sights. At least a week is necessary to see the chief objects
of interest in St. Petersburg and its environs. As the distances are often
considerable, a liberal use of cabs will be found an economy of time.
It should be noted that most of the collections are closed on Mon., and
open only from 10 or 11 a.m. to 3 p.m. on other days.

DRIVE THROUGH THE TOWN (13½ M.; 3-4 hrs.). Fare for an izvóshtchik
(one with a good horse should be selected) 2½ rb., with two horses (preferable; stand at the Admiralty), 3½ rb. A motor-cab costs 5-8 rb. — From
the Admiralty (p. 107) we follow the Nevski (p. 103) to the Litéini Prospékt
(P. 124), follow this to the left to the Frantzúzskaya Náberezhnaya, cross
the Tróitzki Bridge (l.; T. Most, p. 173; view), follow the Kámenno-
Ostróvski Prospékt to Kámenni Óstrov (K. Island; p. 177), traverse this
island by its chief avenue, and cross the First Yelágin Bridge to Yelágin
Óstrov (p. 177); we then make the circuit of this island (to the right),
pass the 'Pointe', and cross the Second Yelágin Bridge to Krestóvski

Ostrov (p. 177) and then the Krestóvski Bridge to the St. Petersburg Side.
Here we follow the Bolshaya Zelénina to the Bolshói Prospékt and cross
the Tutchkóv Bridge to Vasíli Óstrov (p. 165). On Vasíli Óstrov we drive
through the First Line to the Nevá, skirt its bank to the right, cross the
Nicholas Bridge (p. 111; view), and follow the Angliskaya and Admiraltéiskaya Náberezhnaya, passing the Winter Palace Garden, to the Admiralty
Square.—An excursion by steamboat on the Nevá (p. '92) is interesting.

1st Day. Drive through the town (see p. 98).—Afternoon, *Alexander
Nevski Monastery* (p. 130).—Towards evening, steamboat excursion to
the Islands (p. 176; Botanic Gardens, Pointe).

2nd Day. *Hermitage* (p. 131).—Afternoon and evening, *Pavlovsk* (p. 189).

3rd Day. *Kazán Cathedral* (p. 104); *Carriage Museum* (p. 117); *Church
of the Resurrection* (p. 118); *Russian Museum of Emperor Alexander III.*
(p. 119).—Towards evening, *Sestroryétzk* (Kurort; p. 194).

4th Day. *St. Isaac's Cathedral*, with ascent of dome (p. 109); *Peter
the Great Monument* (p. 108); *Winter Palace* (p. 112); *Imperial Library*
(p. 105).—Afternoon, *Tzárskoye Seló* (p. 186).

5th Day. *Hermitage* (second visit); *Marine Museum* (p. 108); *Industrial
Art Museum* (p. 110).—Afternoon, *Cathedral of SS. Peter & Paul* (p. 173);
Peter the Great's House (p. 175).—Evening, *Zoological Garden* (p. 175).

6th Day. *Mineralogical Museum of the Mining Academy* (p. 172);
Zoological Museum (p. 167) or *Anthropological & Ethnographical Museum*
(p. 166); *Stieglitz Museum of Industrial Art* (p. 125).—Afternoon, *Smolni
Convent* (p. 127).—Evening, *Aquarium* (p. 95).

7th Day. *Peterhof* (p. 179).

Excursion to the *Imatra Waterfall*, see p. 207.

St. Petersburg, Санктъ-Петербу́ргъ (popularly known as
Пи́теръ), is named after its founder Peter the Great. It is the
second capital of the Russian Empire, the chief residence of the
Tzar, the seat of the highest government officials, the headquarters
of the Commander of the Guards and of the 1st and 18th Army
Corps, the most important commercial town on the Baltic, and one
of the principal manufacturing towns in Russia. Pop. (with the
suburbs) 2,075,000 (192,000 in 1784; 425,000 in 1825; 861,000 in
1881), including 11,200 Germans, 2400 Frenchmen, and 2100 Englishmen. It lies on a flat plain, at the mouth of the *Nevá* in the Gulf
of Finland, in 59° 57' N. lat. and 30° 20' E. long., and covers an area
of 35 sq. M. The Nevá, 42 M. long, flows out of Lake Ládoga
(p. 195), reaches the town at the Alexander Nevski Monastery, and
farther on takes a sharp turn to the W. and (now 650 yards in
breadth) divides into three branches: the *Great* or *Bolshaya Nevá,*
which is spanned by five bridges, and into which the four drainage
canals of the left bank (Móika, Catherine Canal, Fontánka, and
Obvódni Canal) open at both ends; the *Small* or *Málaya Nevá;*
and the *Great* or *Bolshaya Névka,* from which two arms diverge,
enclosing the 'Islands'. Floods are not uncommon, especially in
autumn during prolonged and violent S.W. winds. From the middle
of Nov. to the beginning of April (O.S.) the river is frozen.

St. Petersburg has on the whole the outward appearance of a
modern and western city; its national or Russian features are less
obvious. It is seen to greatest advantage from the Nevá. Except

for the imperial palaces and some of the public offices, the buildings in the chief thoroughfares are wholly modern and of large (sometimes of huge) proportions. They are, however, somewhat monotonous in style, and their only unusual characteristic is the bright colours with which they are painted. The rows of secular edifices are interrupted by numerous churches. Both private and public buildings usually stand on piles, necessitated by the swampy nature of the ground.

The main part of the city lies on the LEFT BANK OF THE NEVA and includes the following districts. 1. The *Admiralty Quarter* (Адмиралтейская часть; pp. 107, 112), between the Nevá and the Móika, forming with the two following quarters the most fashionable part of St. Petersburg. It contains the Senate House, Falconet's monument to Peter the Great, St. Isaac's Cathedral, the Admiralty (at the head of the main thoroughfare of the town, the Nevski Prospékt), the Winter Palace, and the Hermitage, one of the most important galleries in Europe. — 2. The *Kazán Quarter* (Казáнская часть; pp. 117, 122), between the Móika and the Yekateríninski or Catherine Canal, contains the Marie Palace, where the Imperial Council sits, and the Kazán Cathedral. — 3. The *Spásskaya Quarter* (Спáсская часть; pp. 117, 122), between the Catherine Canal and the Fontánka, contains the Government Offices, the Imperial Public Library, the collection of Russian paintings in Tzar Alexander III.'s Museum, and the new Cathedral of the Resurrection. — 4. *Kolómenskaya Quarter* (Колóменская часть; p. 124), to the W. of the three above. — 5. The *Narva Quarter* (Нáрвская часть; p. 128), to the S. of the Kolómenskaya Quarter, contains factories, the harbour, and the Baltic and Warsaw Railway Stations. — 6. *Moscow Quarter* (Москóвская часть; p. 128), between the Fontánka and Obvódni Canal. — 7. The *Litéinaya Quarter* (Литéйная часть; p. 124), to the N. of the Moscow Quarter, contains the most fashionable residential streets (Sérgiyevskaya, Furshtátskaya, and Mokhováya; also hospitals and barracks). — 8. The *Rozhdéstvenskaya Quarter* (Рождéственская часть; p. 124), to the E. of the Litéinaya Quarter, contains the Tauride Palace, in which the Imperial Duma or House of Representatives meets. — 9. The *Alexander Nevski Quarter* (Александро-Нéвская часть; p. 128), to the S. of the Rozhdéstvenskaya Quarter, contains the Nicholas Railway Station and the Alexander Nevski Monastery. The two last-mentioned quarters are chiefly inhabited by workmen. — On the RIGHT BANK OF THE NEVÁ are the following districts: 10. The *Vasílyevskaya Quarter* (Васúльевская часть; p.165), on the Vasili Óstrov (island of Vasili), contains the Mining Academy, the Academy of Arts, the University, the Academy of Sciences, and the Exchange. — 11. The *St. Petersburg Quarter* (Петербýргская часть; p. 173), between the Nevá and Bolshaya Nevka, is the oldest part of the

town, containing the Peter Paul Fortress and the house of Peter the
Great. The Islands (p. 176) adjoin this quarter on the N.—12. The
Viborg Quarter (Выборгская часть; p. 177), with its factories,
lies to the E. of the Petersburg Quarter.

The STREETS in St. Petersburg are wide (50-100 ft.) and straight,
but the paving is sometimes defective. Streets of the first class are
called *Prospékti*, or Perspectives. Among these are the Nevski and
Voznesénski Prospékts (radiating from the Admiralty), the Litéini
Prospékt, the Vladímirski Prospékt, and others. Streets of the
second rank are called *Ulitzi*, amongst which are the Gorókhovaya
(named after a Count Harrach; often mistakenly called Pea Street,
from горóхъ = pea), the Morskáya (Sea Street), the Gogol Street
(formerly Málaya Morskáya), the Milliónnaya, the Sadóvaya (Garden
Street), the Kazánskaya, the Konyúshennaya (Stable Street), and the
Ofitzérskaya. Streets of the third rank are called *Pereúlki* (lanes).
On Vasíli Óstrov every street consists of two *Lines,* the right side
of the street (reckoned from the Great Nevá) being denoted by
even numbers (Line II, IV, etc.), the left side by uneven.—The
business of St. Petersburg centres round the Nevski (between the
Admiralty and the Fontánka) and the neighbouring streets. Promena-
ders throng the Nevá Quays in spring, the Kámenno-Ostrovski Prospékt (p. 176) and the Islands in summer (especially towards evening),
and the Morskáya in winter (particularly from 2 to 4 p.m.).—The
town possesses about 80 open *Squares,* some of which can accom-
modate 60-100,000 persons.

The Streets of St. Petersburg are much less animated than those of
other European capitals, though they are a little less dull on Sun. and
holidays. The horses are generally good, especially those of the private
carriages; and the drivers, in their heavy wadded gowns, usually urge
them through the streets at great speed. The scarlet liveries of the royal
carriages are conspicuous. Nearly one-tenth of the male population of
St. Petersburg wear some kind of uniform, including not only the numerous
military officers, but civil officials, and even students, schoolboys, and
others. Characteristic street figures, which are, however, fast disappearing,
are the vendors of ices (morózhenoye) and kvass (a cooling drink brewed
from rye-bread or fruit), who carry their pails and glass jugs on their heads;
the itinerant cooks, with pirogís (pasties), various purées (especially 'kisél
malínovi' and 'kisél gorókhovi', raspberry-purée and purée of peas), and
pancakes (bliní); the raznóshtchiks (pedlars), especially near the Gostíni
Dvor; the vendors of old clothes (mostly Tartars; offering 'khaláti', *i.e.*
dressing-gowns) and linen (polotnó). Other street cries are: 'tzvyetí,
tzvyetótchki' (flowers); 'kartóffel' (potatoes); 'ókuni, yershi, sigi, loso-
sina, rúiba zhiváya' (perch, ruff, char, salmon, live fish); 'gribí molodúiye,
gribótchki' (mushrooms); 'apelsíni, limóni khoróshiye' (oranges, lemons);
'klubníka sadóvaya, klubníka' (strawberries); 'klyúkva podsnyézhnaya,
klyúkva' (cranberries); 'zemlyaníka spyélaya, zemlyaníka' (ripe wild strawberries).—At night numerous *Dvórniks* or yard-porters (from dvor = yard
or court), clad in polushúboks (short fur coats), sit by the house-doors.
They combine the functions of the French concierge, the American chore-
man, the English hall-porter, and a subordinate police-official. — The
Gorodovóis or policemen are clad in a black uniform with green facings,
the officers in grey.

The wet nurses, dressed in bright and rich national costume (blue, when their charges are boys, and pink for girls) are a conspicuous feature. They generally wear a white mantle richly ornamented with silver tassels; their becoming headgear (kokóshnik), is of the same colour, shaped like a diadem, and adorned with imitation pearls and silver.

The CLIMATE of St. Petersburg is raw, damp, and very unsettled; woollen underclothing is the best protection against chills. *Unboiled water should on no account be drunk.* — July is the warmest month (64° Fahr.) and January the coldest (15° Fahr.), the annual mean being 40° Fahr. Rain or snow falls on about 200 days in the year. Winter lasts for six months, and snow often falls as late as May. June, July, and (often) August are pleasant summer months, but sometimes the second half of August is raw and inclement. In September and the first half of October the weather is generally more settled. — In summer, owing to the long light nights, most people go late to bed (comp. p. xv); the more important shops do not open until 9 a.m.

HISTORY. Ingermanland, the land between Lake Peipus, the Naróva, and Lake Ládoga, which belonged at one time to Novgorod, then to Moscow, and in 1617 at the peace of Stolbovo was given to Sweden, was reconquered in 1702 by *Peter the Great,* who wished to erect, at the mouth of the Nevá, a new capital that could be reached more easily from W. Europe ('a window towards Europe', in Algarotti's phrase). On 16th (27th) May, 1703, was laid the foundation-stone of the Peter Paul Fortress, the citadel of the town. In 1704 the first houses on the N. bank of the Nevá were built. The work was carried on for many years by 40,000 men from all parts of the empire, whose numbers were frequently decimated by the poisonous exhalations of the swamps and the enormous strain of the work. The Tzar built his first small house in 1703, not far from the Tróitzki Church (p. 128); then, in 1711, the Summer Palace in the Summer Garden (p. 116). Later on he built a winter residence for himself (on the site of the present Hermitage), with its chief façade towards the Nevá. An attack on the town by the Swedes in 1708 failed, and the defeat of the Swedes at Poltava (1709) removed all danger threatening from that quarter. In 1712 St. Petersburg was made the imperial capital. In 1713 the celebrated architect and sculptor, Andreas Schlüter, was summoned to St. Petersburg, but he died in the following year. In order to confer on the town the dignity of a shrine of the national religion, Peter had the bones of Alexander Nevski brought to St. Petersburg in 1724, and over his tomb he built a church and monastery (Lavra). In 1725 the city contained 75,000 inhabitants. — Peter's death was followed by years of inactivity. Catherine I. (1725-27) and Peter II. (1727-30) preferred Moscow. Anna Ivánovna (1730-40) was the next ruler who took up her residence in St. Petersburg, and under her and her successor Elizabeth Petrovna (1741-61), the town grew rapidly. Anna built the Admiralty Tower, with its gilded spire, and also began the Winter Palace; Elizabeth erected the Anitchkov Palace. Most of the public buildings, including some of the finest, date from the reign of Catherine II. (1762-96); amongst others, the Academy of Arts, the Marble Palace, and the Tauride Palace (in which the Imperial Duma now assembles); the Winter Palace was finished and the equestrian statue of Peter the Great erected. Emperor Paul I. (1796-1801) fostered the spirit of building (Old Michael Palace, now the Engineering Academy; Kazan Cathedral). Alexander I. built the Exchange and the New Michael Palace (now the Alexander III. Museum) and began St. Isaac's Cathedral. Nicholas I. erected the Hermitage in its present form.

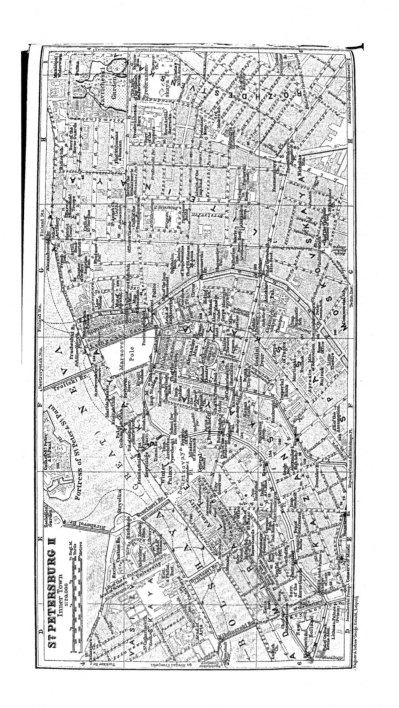

I. QUARTERS ON THE LEFT BANK OF THE NEVA.

a. Nevski Prospekt.

Stróganov Palace. Kazan Cathedral. Imperial Public Library.

The Nevski Prospékt, from the Admiraltéiski Prospékt to the Známen-skaya Square, is traversed by tramways Nos. 5 & 7, and portions of it also by Nos. 4, 11, 13, 14, & 17 (comp. pp. 91, 92).

The *Nevski Prospékt (Невскій проспектъ; Pl. E-I, 5, 6, *II*) is 115 ft. wide and $2^3/_4$ M. long, being the longest street in St. Petersburg. From the Admiralty (p. 107) it runs in a straight line as far as the Známenskaya Square (Pl. H, 6; *II*), where it trends slightly to the S. and runs through a poorer quarter to the Alexander Nevski Monastery (p. 130). As far as the part W. of the Anítch-kov Bridge is concerned, it is the busiest street in St. Petersburg.

Between the Admiralty and the *Politzéiski Bridge* the Nevski is flanked on both sides by business houses. On the right, at the corner of the Úlitza Gógolya, is the *St. Petersburg Commercial Bank* (p. 96), built by Peretyátkovitch (1912). Farther on the Nevski crosses the Morskáya (p. 110), No. 5 in which, to the left, is the *Azov & Don Commercial Bank* (p. 96), by Lidval (1909).

Immediately beyond the Politzéiski Bridge, on the right, Nevski 17, is the **Stróganov Palace** (Pl. F, 5; *II*), built in the baroque style by *Rastrelli* (p. 112) in 1754.

The palace contains an interesting **Art Gallery** (adm., see p. 98). Passing through some anterooms adorned with bronzes, views of Italy, and copies of the paintings in the loggie of the Vatican, we enter the Picture Gallery proper. The most notable works are the following: *Perugino*, Ma-donna, a good school-piece; *A. van Dyck*, Portrait of a man; *Rubens*, Helena Fourment; *A. Bronzino*, Madonna with angels; *Boltraffio*, St. Louis; *Rubens*, The artist and his son; *Tintoretto*, *Portrait of a general with a white beard, a masterpiece of the artist; *Tintoretto*, L. Garzoni, Governor of Ætolia; *Claude Lorrain*, *Heroic landscape; *Le Sueur*, St. Cecilia; *Filip-pino Lippi*, Annunciation; *Andrea Orvitani*, St. James the Great; *Petrus Cristus*, Madonna (1441); *Ortolano*, Gathering manna (after the engraving by Marc Antonio). The room also contains miniatures, works in glass and porcelain, prehistoric antiquities from E. Asia and Mexico, busts by *Houdon*, and other objects of interest. — Adjoining the picture-gallery is the library, containing the so-called *Apollo Stróganov*, a bronze statuette held by Furtwängler to be a modern forgery based on the Apollo Bel-vedere; the left hand, holding a skin, formerly taken for the ægis, does not belong to the statuette. The library also contains a Dancing Satyr and a silver statuette of Venus (both antique), a bust of Ludovico Gonzaga by *Donatello*, terracottas, Byzantine silver cups, works in ivory, and enamels.

To the left stands the *Dutch Church* (Цéрковь Голлáндская; Pl. F 5, *II*), completed in 1837 and inscribed 'Deo et Servatori sacrum'. — Farther on, beyond the Bolshaya Konyúshennaya (p. 117) and standing a little back from the street, is the Lutheran *Church of SS. Peter & Paul*, erected in 1832 by A. Bryullóv, and possessing two low towers. The altar-piece (Crucifixion) is by K. P. Bryullóv.

7*

Nearly opposite St. Peter's, in a large open space, rises the —
*Kazán Cathedral (Собóръ Казáнской Бóжіей Мáтери;
Pl. F 5, *II*), approached by a semicircular colonnade of 136 Corinthian columns, modelled on that of St. Peter's at Rome. The
church, erected in 1801-11 from the designs of Voroníkhin and at a
cost of 4 million rubles, is in the form of a cross 236 ft. long and
180 ft. wide. It is surmounted by a metal dome 65 ft. in diameter,
the drum of which is adorned with 16 pilasters. The total height
to the top of the cross is 260 ft. On the N. façade, turned towards
the Nevski, are niches containing colossal statues of SS. John the
Baptist (by Martos), Vladímir, Alexander Nevski (these two by
Pímenov), and Andrew (by Demut-Malinóvski). The bronze doors of
the main entrance are copies of the doors of the Baptistry in Florence. The church is closed at 6 p.m. in winter and 7 p.m. in summer.

INTERIOR. The dome is borne by four piers, from which radiate four
rows of Corinthian columns, leading to the high-altar and to the three
principal entrances of the church. The columns, 56 in number, are mono-
liths of Finland granite, 40 ft. in height; the bases and capitals are of
bronze. The *Ikonostás*, with its beautiful modern paintings, and the
balustrade in front of it are made of silver (about 3600 lbs. in weight),
presented, as the inscription on the balustrade records, by the Cossacks
of the Don after the war of 1812. On the left side of the ikonostás is
the *Wonder-Working Virgin of Kazan*, found in Kazan in 1579, removed
to Moscow in 1612, and transferred thence to St. Petersburg in 1710. On
the altar behind the ikonostás is the *Tabernacle*, presented by Count Stróganov, with columns of costly stone.
On the pillars and walls are 103 banners and eagles captured from
Napoleon, which give the church a military aspect. On the two pillars
of the bay to the right of the main entrance are the keys of 25 captured
towns (Hamburg, Leipzig, Dresden, Rheims, Breda, Utrecht, etc.) and
the baton of Marshall Davoût. — To the right of the entrance is the *Tomb
of Prince Kutúzov* (d. 1813), on the spot where he is said to have performed
his devotions before starting in 1812 to join the army at Smolensk.

The grounds in front of the cathedral contain the monuments of
Prince Kutúzov-Smolénski (l.) and *Prince Barclay de Tolly* (r.;
p. 60), from the designs of Orlóvski (1837). — To the W. of the cathedral is a square with handsome railings designed by Voroníkhin.

Beyond the *Kazánski Bridge* is the Roman Catholic **Church of
St. Catharine** (Pl. F, 5; *II*), built by De la Mothe in 1763, and
approached by a large archway. Inside, on the floor of the N.E.
arm of the transept, is a simple slab marking the grave of *Stanislaus Augustus Poniatowski* (d. 1798), King of Poland. The French
general *J. V. Moreau,* mortally wounded at the battle of Dresden
(1813), rests under the first window to the right of the entrance.

To the right is the **City Hall,** or *Duma* (Горóдская Дýма;
Pl. F 5, *II*), built in 1802 by Ferrari, with a pentagonal tower.

The **Gostíni Dvor,** or *Bazaar* (Гостиный Двóръ; Pl. F, 5,
6, *II*), bounded on the E. by the Sadóvaya and on the S. by the
Tchernuishóv Pereúlok, is an extensive building painted white and
enclosing several courts. It was erected in 1761-85 by Vallin de la

Mothe and completely rebuilt at the end of the 19th century. The arcades on the groundfloor and the first floor contain about 200 shops, which, however, are less elegant than the other shops of the Nevski.

To the left, opposite the Gostíni Dvor, and lying back a little from the street, is the *Armenian Church of St. Catharine* (Армянская Церковь Святой Екатерины; Pl. F 5, *II*), built in 1772 by Velten, at the cost of Lázarev (p. 115).

To the right (No. 37), between the Sadóvaya and the Alexandra Square, rises the —

Imperial Public Library (Императорская публичная библиотéка; Pl. G 5, *II*), the entrance to which is in the Alexandra Square (adm., see p. 98). The main façade is adorned with Ionic columns and statues of Greek philosophers. The building was begun in 1794 under the superintendence of Sokolóv. The corner building was finished in 1810; the wing in the Alexandra Sq. was added in 1828-30 by Rossi; and a further extension was completed in 1902. The library, which was opened in 1814, now contains 2,044,000 books, 21,900 maps, 102,120 engravings and photographs, and 124,140 MSS., autographs, and documents. Director, D. F. Kobéko.

GROUND FLOOR. ROOM 1 ('Cabinet of Faust') was fitted up in 1857 in imitation of a monastic library, and contains over 7000 *Incunabula.* — Room 2. *Specimens of Printing of the 16-17th cent.* (Elzevir). — Room 3. *Department of Languages.* Bibles, including a Gutenberg Bible (ca. 1450); Imitatio Christi in the Paris édition de luxe of 1855. In the Oriental Section is an Arabic Gospel, printed in 1708 for the Cossack 'hetman' Mazeppa. Greek and Latin Classics. — We then cross a hall to Room 4, containing *Modern Classics* and *Hebrew Literature* and *Hebraica.* — Room 5. *Bulgarian, Servian, & Ruthenian Literature;* also modern printing (since 1880) in Ecclesiastical Slavonic letters. — Room 6. *Slavonic* and *Oriental MSS. Ecclesiastical Slavonic* and *Old Russian Printed Books.* In the front of the first case on the right is the first Russian newspaper (Московскія Вѣдомости; 1703), and at the back is the first Russian Bible (1581); in the second case (r.) is the first book printed in Russia, the Acts of the Apostles (Дѣянія апóстольскія; Moscow, 1564); in the case to the left is the translation of the Bible by Dr. Fr. Skorina of Prague (1516-19). — Room of Alexander I., or Oval Room. *Ecclesiastical Slavonic Printed Books* down to 1880; *Hebrew MSS.*, including 47 rolls of the Pentateuch of the first millennium A.D.; marble bust of Tzar Alexander I. by Demut-Malinóvski; portraits of Russian writers.

MAIN HALL. Section I. On the left, by the windows: *Slavonic-Russian MSS.* of the 11-18th cent., including the Svyatosláv Collection (1076) and the Chronicle of Nestor (1377); *Servian, Bulgarian, and Glagolitic MSS.* from the 12th cent. onwards; *Greek MSS.*, including papyrus-leaves of the 2nd cent. A.D., epistles of St. Paul in Greek and Latin (7th cent.), a psalter of 862, a book of the Gospels of 835, and palimpsests. On the right, under the windows, autographs of composers; in the row of glass-cases, *Oriental MSS.*, including Eusebius's church-history in Syrian (462), the epistles of St. Paul in Arabic (892), a Gruzinian book of the Gospels (995), fragments of richly decorated Korans of the 9th and 10th cent., Persian and Turkish miniatures, and sumptuous bindings; *Latin MSS.*, from the 6th cent. onwards. *Bindings*, including a Greek book of the Gospels on purple parchment with letters of gold (9th cent.). In the centre of the hall: Koran of Caliph Osman in Cufic characters (9th cent.), captured at Samarkand; *Jagataic MSS.* In the glass cases between the columns: *MSS. on Parchment with Miniatures* (in Case 4

a prayer-book of Mary, Queen of Scots; in Case 6 a Gospel of Demetrius
Palæologus, adorned with Greek and Italian miniatures, and a portrait
of Emp. Manuel II. Palæologus). On the walls: Autographs of sovereigns
and famous men (arranged according to countries). In a case by the rear
wall, the Zographu Gospel in Glagolitic characters (from the monastery
of Zográphu on Mt. Athos; 11th cent.). — Section II. In the centre: on
the left, the celebrated Codex Sinaiticus, found by Professor Tischendorf
in the Sinai Monastery in 1859, and next to that of the Vatican the oldest
Greek text of the New Testament (4th cent.). To the right is the Sarmasakhli Gospel, written in Greek on purple parchment (6th cent.; purchased in Sarmasakhli near Kaisariyeh in 1896). Between these, farther
back, is the Ostrómir Gospel (1056), the oldest dated Russian MS. On the
right: *Autographs* of Russian sovereigns (Románov dynasty), writers, and
ecclesiastics. On the left: *Musical Scores* and autographs of Russian and
European celebrities. On the walls: Autographs of famous Russians,
including a passport in the name of the 'Emperor' Constantine Pávlovitch.

FIRST FLOOR. Circular Room: *Theology* above, *Russian Section* below.
— In the four rooms to the left the Russian Section is continued. — We
retrace our steps through the Circular Room, and turn to the right into
Room I, the lower part of which is devoted to *Art* and *Technology*, the
upper to *Theology*. On the right side, adjoining the entrance and exit, are
two cases containing the 7000 volumes of *Voltaire's Library*, bought by
Catherine II. In the centre of the room, on a low case, is a woodcut of
1576, representing the Embassy of Prince Súgorski to Emp. Rudolf II. —
Room II *(Peter Gallery)*, with portraits of Peter the Great and the
Rovinski Collection of over 30,000 foreign portraits (engravings). — Room 3.
Historical Section. Catherine II., a highly idealized painting by Levitzki;
in the second case to the right are two portraits of Empress Elizabeth,
one of which was suppressed in 1744; in the third case is a Cat of Tzar
Alexis Mikháilovitch, engraved by Kollar (1661). — *Korff Room*, with a
collection of all foreign works on Russia (over 150,000 vols., including
periodicals). — To the right in the Vestibule is Zvenigoródski's book on
cloisonné enamel. — *Larin Room.* Works on Russia and History.

The groundfloor of the EXTENSION mentioned at p. 105 is devoted to
the departments of *Natural History* and *Mathematics.* — The upper floors
are reached by a marble staircase. On the first floor are the department
of *Jurisprudence* and the handsome *Reading Room*, accommodating 500 persons. It is adorned with busts of Russian emperors and authors. — The
second floor is devoted to *Polygraphy* and *Philosophy*, while the third
floor contains the duplicates.

To the E. of the Library is the ALEXANDRA SQUARE (Алек-
сандрийская площадь), which is adorned with flower-beds and
contains the **Monument of Catherine II.** (Памятникъ Екате-
ринѣ II.; Pl. G 6, *II*), erected in 1873 from the designs of Mikéshin
and Opekúshin. A base of reddish granite supports a bell-shaped
pedestal bearing a figure of the Empress, 13 ft. in height, clad in an
ermine mantle, and holding the imperial sceptre in her right hand
and a wreath in her left. Round the pedestal are nine colossal bronze
figures of celebrated contemporaries of the Empress.

On the S. side of the square stands the **Alexandra Theatre**
(Александрийскій Театръ; Pl. G 6, *II*; see p. 94), built from
Rossi's designs in 1832 and named after the consort of the then
reigning Tzar, Nicholas I. The main façade consists of a loggia of
six Corinthian columns, and the pediment is surmounted by a
quadriga in bronze. — To the W. of the theatre is a private house
in an elaborate Russian style.

From the Alexandra Square the Teatrálnaya; passing the *Imperial Dramatic School* on the left, leads to the Tchernuishóvskaya Square on the Fontánka (Pl. F, G, 6; *II*). On the S.W. side of this square is the *Ministry of the Interior* (Министéрство внýтреннихъ дѣлъ), while to the W. is the *Ministry of Public Instruction* (М. нарóднаго просвѣщéнія), both designed by Rossi. In the middle of the square is a *Memorial Bust of the Poet Lomonósov* (1711-65; Pl. 131, G 6, *II*), erected in 1892.

Farther on in the Nevski, to the right, adjoining the Fontánka, is the **Anítchkov Palace** (Анíчковъ Дворéцъ; Pl. G 6, *II*; no admission), erected in 1741-47 by the Empress Elizabeth, from the designs of *Rastrelli,* for Count Razumóvski (d. 1771). It was resumed by the Crown in 1785, rebuilt by Sokolóv and again under Alexander II. in 1866, and is at present the winter-residence of the Dowager-Empress Marie Feódorovna.

On the E. side of the Palace the Fontánka is crossed by the **Anítchkov Bridge** (Анíчковъ мостъ; Pl. G, 5, 6, *II*), which is adorned with four colossal bronze groups of horse-tamers, cast at St. Petersburg in 1841 from the models of Baron Klodt. — Beyond the bridge, to the right, rises the *Palace of the Grand-Duchess Elizabeth Feódorovna,* an elaborate baroque structure formerly belonging to Prince Byelosélski-Byelozérski.

Beyond this point the Nevski offers nothing of interest. The Známenskaya Square (Pl. H 6, *II;* p. 129) contains a massive bronze *Equestrian Statue of Tzar Alexander III.* by Prince P. Trubetzkói, erected in 1909. On the S. side of the square is the *Nicholas Railway Station.* For the Alexander Nevski Monastery, see p. 130.

b. **Western Admiralty Quarter.**

Admiralty. Equestrian Statue of Peter the Great. St. Isaac's Cathedral.

The **Admiralty (Глáвное Адмиралтéйство; Pl. E 5 *II*), on the left bank of the Nevá, lies to the W. of the Dvortzóvaya Square (p. 112), to the N. of the Alexander Garden (p. 108), and to the E. of the Peter Square (p. 108). It was founded by Peter the Great in 1705, and re-erected in 1806-23 after the plans of A. Sakhárov (d. 1811). The extensive building consists of a central block, 458 yds. long, and two wings, turned towards the Nevá and each 196 yds. long. The space between the wings has been filled up since 1871 by other buildings (No. 4, the former Panáyev Theatre; No. 8, Palace of Grand-Duke Mikhaíl Mikháilovitch, now appropriated by the Ministry for Trade and Industry; Nos. 12-14, Land Bank of the Noblesse), so that the ends of the wings are the only part of the Admiralty visible from the river side. The entrance is in the centre of the façade towards the Alexander Garden; to the right and left are groups (by Th. Shtchedrín) of three female figures bearing the terrestrial globe. The attic contains a relief by A. I. Terebenev (Foundation of the Russian Navy), and at each of the four corners is a figure of a seated warrior, by Shtchedrín. Over the gateway rises the Admiralty Tower, 230 ft. high, ending in a tapering gilded spire, and surmounted by a weather-vane in the form of a crown and ship. The lower part of the tower is adorned with 28 pillars and 28 statues. The extensive inner rooms contain the Board of Admiralty, a library, and (on the first floor) the —

*Marine Museum (Морско́й музе́й; adm., see p. 97; entr. opposite the Alexander Garden, first door to the left of the main entry). Director, Capt. A. A. Попо́в.

Room I. Models of the churches on the Shipka Pass and at Borki; paintings (Arrival of William II. at Reval in 1892; French fleet at Cronstadt in 1897). — Rooms II & III. Model ships and 19th century uniforms. — Room IV. Models of Russian and captured foreign ships; uniforms and flags of the time of Catherine II. — *Peter the Great Room* (Залъ Петра́ Вели́каго), containing souvenirs of him: seat which he used at naval court martials; a wooden model made by him of a small battleship; his working overalls, etc. In the middle are models of an English warship, presented by King William III., and of a French galley, a gift of Louis XIV.; also other model ships and uniforms of Peter's day. In a cabinet near the entry is a naval uniform of Catherine II. — In the passage are models of more recent Russian warships. — As we retrace our steps along the passage the second room on the left is the *Hall of Heroes* (Залъ геро́евъ), containing portraits of officers and men who have distinguished themselves in naval battles; also souvenirs of the Chinese campaign of 1900 and the Japanese war of 1904-5. In the fourth room is the model of a merchant-vessel built at Archangel in 1697.

In front of the Admiralty, on the N., are two bronze *Statues of Peter the Great,* by Bernstamm (1909). In one he is represented as building a boat, in the other as saving drowning men.

To the S. of the Admiralty is the **Alexander Garden** (Алекса́ндровскій садъ; Pl. E 5, *II*), with a fountain, near the Горо́ховая, and several bronze busts. To the E. are the poets *Zhukóvski* (1783-1852) and *Le´rmontov* (1814-41), and the composer *Glinka* (1804-57); to the W., the poet *Gogol* (1809-52) and the Asiatic traveller *Przheva´lski* (1839-88).

To the W. of the Admiralty lies PETER SQUARE (Пло́щадь Петра́ I.), with flower-beds, and (near the Нева́) the famous *Equestrian Statue of Peter the Great (Па́мятникъ Петру́ I.; Pl. E 5, *II;* comp. p. 119). The Tzar, riding up a rocky slope, has his face turned to the Нева́, and points with his right hand towards the scene of his labours. The horse is balanced on its hind-legs and tail, while its hoofs trample on a writhing snake. The statue is 16^1/$_2$ ft. high. The sculptor *E. M. Falconet* (1716-91) made the model in 1769 and supervised the work of casting it (1775). The Tzar's head was modelled by *Marie Collot,* who later became Falconet's daughter-in-law. The enormous granite block which forms the pedestal is 46 ft. long, 19^1/$_2$ ft. wide, and 16^1/$_2$ ft. high. On one side it bears the proud inscription, Петру́ Пе́рвому Екатери́на Втора́я 1782; on the other side, 'Petro Primo Catharina Secunda MDCCLXXXII'. The monument was unveiled on Aug. 7th, 1782, and cost 425,000 rb.

The whole of the W. side of Peter Square, between the English
Quay (p. 111) and the Konno-Gvardéiski Bulvár (see below), is occu-
pied by the large **Senate House** (Правительствующій сенáтъ;
Pl. E 5, *II;* comp. p. lv), and the **Holy Synod** (Правитель-
ствующій святѣйшій синóдъ; Pl. E 5, *II;* comp. p. lviii) of the
Greek Catholic Church, both built in 1829-32 after plans by Rossi.
The two buildings are joined by a high archway, adorned with
sculptures, and spanning the Galérnaya ('Galley Street').

On the S. side of the wide KONNO-GVARDÉISKI BULVÁR (Horse
Guards Boulevard; Pl. E, 5, 6, *II*), which extends W. to the Blagovyéshtchenskaya (p. 111), lies the *Manège of the Horse Guards*
(Конногвардéйскій Манéжъ), or *Nicholas Riding School,* built
in 1804 by Quarenghi.

To the S.W. of the Alexander Garden (p. 108) lies ISAAC SQUARE
(Pl. E, 5; *II*), bounded on the E. side by the *War Office* (Воéнное
Министéрство), a large triangular building by Ricard de Mon-
ferrand. In the centre of the square stands —

*St. Isaac's Cathedral, or *Cathedral of St. Isaac of Dal-
matia.* (Собóръ Исаáкія Далмáтскаго; Pl. E5, *II*), the largest
church in St. Petersburg, built in 1819-58, in the place of an earlier
church, after plans by the French architect, *Ricard de Monferrand.*
The cost of the building amounted to more than 23,000,000 rb. — The
cathedral, built of granite and marble with a lavish disregard of
cost, is in the shape of a cross 364 ft. long and 315 ft. wide, and is
crowned by an enormous gilded dome, visible at a great distance. The
doors are approached by wide granite steps. The chief entrances, in
the longer (N. and S.) sides, form beautiful *Porticoes,* modelled on
that of the Pantheon in Rome, each with 16 monolith columns of
polished red Finnish granite, 54 ft. high and 7 ft. thick, with bronze
bases and capitals, arranged in three rows. In the shorter sides (E.
and W.) are smaller porticoes, with eight columns each. The columns
are surmounted by four pediments (those on the longer sides 112 ft.
long), adorned with large bronze reliefs: on the S., 'Adoration of the
Magi', by Vitali; on the E., 'St. Isaac foretelling his approaching
death to Emperor Valentinian', on the N., 'Resurrection of Christ',
these two by Lemaire; on the W., 'Meeting of St. Isaac with Emperor Theodosius', by Vitali. (The portrait-heads in the last relief
include one of Alexander I.) Above are statues of the Evangelists
and Apostles; the statues of angels at the corners of the roof are by
Vitali. — The gilded *Centre Dome,* 87 ft. in diameter, rests on a drum
surrounded by 24 hollow columns encased in granite, and each $42^1/_2$ ft.
high. The dome is crowned by a lantern $40^1/_2$ ft. high, with 8 pillars;
from the top rises a cross 19 ft. high. The inner height of the dome
from the floor is 269 ft. (St. Peter's in Rome 404 ft., St. Paul's in
London 225 ft.); the height of the whole building to the top of the
cross is $333^1/_2$ ft. Four smaller gilt domes surround the central dome.

Interior (closed at 6 p.m.). — Four colossal bronze doors, richly adorned with sculptures by Vitali and others, lead to the interior, which is dimly lighted by twelve windows in the dome and nine others on the sides. The walls are lined with beautiful polished marble of various kinds, and are adorned with about 200 paintings by Russian artists (now being replaced by mosaics). The *Ceiling Painting of the Central Dome* ('Virgin surrounded by Saints, Apostles, and Evangelists') was begun by Bryullóv and finished by Basin. Under the windows of the dome are bronze-gilt figures of angels.

On the *Ikonostás* (223 ft. long), which is of richly gilded marble, are 33 large mosaics of saints, arranged in three tiers. The beautiful 'holy' door in the centre, 23 ft. high and 13 ft. wide, was cast in bronze after a design by Vitali. On each side of it stand five semicircular columns, the two nearest being of lapis lazuli 16 ft. high and 5 ft. in diameter, while the rest are of malachite 29^1/$_2$ ft. high and 2^1/$_2$ ft. in diameter; the bases and capitals are richly gilded. [The columns are really hollow cylinders of iron, veneered with malachite and lapis lazuli.] Adjacent are two pilasters, also overlaid with malachite. — The tabernacle in the Holy of Holies is in the form of a model of the Cathedral, in silver-gilt. The stained-glass window with the Resurrection was made in Munich. In front of it is the marble Chair of the Metropolitan.

With the exception of the seven bronze chandeliers, all the ecclesiastical vessels are of gold and silver, their exquisite workmanship being worthy of their pecuniary value (the silver articles weigh over a ton). Special mention may be made of the 15 large silver chandeliers, of a beautiful Evangelarium (in the binding of which 44 lbs. of gold were used), and of a model of the Holy Sepulchre in silver and silver-gilt (in the S.W. corner of the church).

The Dome (562 steps up to the lantern) affords a fine *View over the city and the Nevá. It is reached from the S. side, to the right of the entrance to the church (1-5 persons 1 rb., each addit. pers. 20 cop.).

To the S. of the Cathedral, in the Marie Square, stands the **Monument of Emperor Nicholas I.** (Пáмятникъ Николáю I.; Pl. E 6, *II*), by *Baron Klodt*, 49 ft. high and erected in 1859. The Tzar, in the uniform of the Chevalier Guards, is represented on a prancing horse. The pedestal is adorned with bronze trophies, and four reliefs depicting events in the Tzar's life. At the corners are figures of Justice, Strength, Wisdom, and Faith (portraits of the Tzar's wife and daughters).

To the S. of the Nicholas monument, on the other side of the Sini (Blue) Bridge, at the corner of the Voznesénski Prospékt, stands the **Hall of the Imperial Council** (Pl. E, 6; *II*), formerly the *Marie Palace*, built in 1844 in the Italian style by Stakenschneider and presented by Nicholas I. to his eldest daughter Marie, Duchess of Leuchtenberg, and her husband. In the Council Chamber is a large painting by I. E. Ryépin (Session of the Council held in celebration of its centenary in 1901).

To the E. of the monument, at the corner of the Marie Square and the Morskáya, stands the *Ministry of Agriculture* (Pl. 11, E 6; *II*). No. 38 in the Morskáya is the *Industrial Art Museum of the Society for the Advancement of Art* (Худóжественно-промы́шленный музéй óбщества поощрéнія худóжествъ; Pl. E 6, *II;* curator, M. P. Botkin), a permanent exhibition of objects of applied art and paintings (adm., see p. 97). — No. 41 in the

Morskáya (to the W. of the Nicholas monument), at the N.W. corner of the Marie Square, is the *German Embassy* (Pl. E, 6; *II*), rebuilt in 1912 after the designs of Peter Behrens; on the roof stands a copper group, 16 ft. in height, by B. Encke. No. 43 is the *Italian Embassy;* farther on (l.) is the *German Reformed Church* (Реформатская Церковь; Pl. E 6, *II*), built in 1863-65.

To the N. of the church diverges the Potchtámtski Pereúlok, in which are (r.) the *Office of the Postmaster-General* (Главное Управленіе Почтъ и Телеграфовъ), and (l.; No. 3) the **General Post Office** (Главный Почтámtъ; Pl. E 6, *II;* p. 93). The *General Telegraph Office* (Pl. E 6, *II;* p. 93) is at Potchtámtskaya 15.— In the Novo-Isaákiyevskaya (No. 16) is the *British and American Chapel* (Pl. 42, E 6; *II*).

The Potchtámtski Pereúlok ends on the N. at the Konno-Gvardéiski Bulvár, in which are (r.) the Manège (p. 109) and (l.) the long *Stables* and *Barracks of the Horse Guards*. At the W. end of the boulevard, in an open space adjoining the Blagovyéshtchenskaya, is the *Church of the Annunciation* (Церковь Благовѣщенія Пресвятыя Богородицы; Pl. D, E, 6, *II*), built under Nicholas I. after plans by Thon. The edifice is in the shape of a Greek cross, with a gilded tower above the intersection and four gilded domes at the sides. To the N. of the church stands the *Institute of Grand-Duchess Xenia* (Ксéньинскій институтъ; Pl. D 6, *II*), a school for girls of the upper classes, built in 1862 by Stakenschneider as the *Palace of Grand-Duke Nicholas Nikoláyevitch* (d. 1891), and converted to its present use in 1895.

We follow the Blagovyéshtchenskaya to the ENGLISH QUAY (Ángliskaya Náberezhnaya), on the Nevá (Nicholas Bridge, see below). Turning to the left, we pass (No. 56) the *English Church* (Церковь Англійская; Pl. D 6, *II*), an unpretending building of 1815, originally designed by Quarenghi, with six columns in front and a statue of Christ above the pediment.— At the W. end of the Galérnaya is the **New Admiralty** (Новое Адмиралтейство; Pl. D 6, *I*), built under Nicholas I., with docks and wharves. There are always some men-of-war at anchor here. To the right of the entrance stands the *Church of Our Saviour on the Water* (Церковь во имя Спáса на водáхъ), erected from the plans of Peretyátkovitch & Smirnóv (1910) and commemorating the seamen killed in the Russo-Japanese War of 1904-5.

The **Nicholas Bridge** (Николáевскій мостъ; Pl. D 5, *I;* view), which leads from the English Quay to Vasíli Ostrov (p. 165) is a granite and iron structure resting on seven piers, and was built in 1842-50 by Kierbedź. At the N. end is an opening for ships (1.15-2.15 a.m. and 5.15-6.15 a.m.). At the farther end of the bridge is a small *Marble Chapel* erected in 1854 and dedicated to St. Nicholas, containing a mosaic portrait of the saint after an original in Bari.

c. Eastern Admiralty Quarter.

Winter Palace. Summer Garden.

To the E. of the Admiralty (p. 107) lies the Dvortzóvaya Square (Palace Square; Pl. E, F, 5, *II*), on the N. side of which stands the Winter Palace (see below), and on the S. and E. the large crescent-shaped buildings of the General Staff (p. 115). In the centre of the square rises the *Alexander Column (Алекса́ндровская Коло́нна), erected by Nicholas I. in 1834 to the memory of Alexander I. after a design by *Monferrand*. On a pedestal 26 ft. high, hewn out of a single piece of granite, stands a huge pillar, of polished red Finnish granite, the largest monolith of modern times, 98¹/₂ ft. high and 13 ft. in diameter; the bronze capital is 13 ft. high. On the ball at the top a bronze angel by Orlóvski, 13 ft. in height, holds a cross (20 ft. in length) in his left hand, while his right is lifted towards heaven, and his foot tramples on a snake. The height of the whole monument is 153¹/₂ ft. On the side facing the Winter Palace is the inscription: "Алекса́ндру Пе́рвому Благода́рная Росси́я" (Grateful Russia to Alexander I.).

The *Imperial Winter Palace (Зи́мній Дворе́цъ; Pl. E, F, 5, *II;* adm., see p. 98), the imperial winter residence, finished in 1764 from a design by *Rastrelli,* was partly burned down in 1837 and restored by the beginning of 1839. The building, which is 499 ft. long, 384 ft. wide, and 92 ft. high, is painted a brownish red and faces the Nevá on the N. and the Palace Square on the S. On the W. side of the palace is the garden, laid out by Nicholas II. and surrounded by a beautiful wrought-iron railing.

The State (private) entrances are in the Dvortzóvaya Náberezhnaya (Jordan Gateway) and in the Dvortzóvaya Square. The Jordan entrance on the Nevá Quay leads up to the Imperial State apartments by means of the *Grand* or *Ambassadorial Staircase* (P. 114), of which the steps are of Carrara marble. The entrance-hall is lined with stucco-work in the Renaissance style and ornamented with statues; below is a gallery adorned with marble groups (by Falconet, Pigalle, etc.) and busts.—The following description of the rooms is given in the order in which they are shown to visitors. Entr. from the Dvortzóvaya Náberezhnaya through the Councillors' Entrance (Сове́тскій подъѣздъ) in the Hermitage. The visit takes two hours.

We first enter the so-called *New Rooms* (Но́выя ко́мнаты) of the Old Hermitage of Empress Catherine II., used for the accommodation of royal visitors, and facing the Nevá.

The rooms retain their old decoration of beautiful furniture and fine inlaid doors. Room I: Mosaic furniture (old Florentine workmanship); four vases of pink agate. — Passing through the small adjoining Room II, we reach Room III, containing a Florentine cabinet in pietra dura and a table of malachite. — The two following rooms (IV and V) lead into the semicircular Room VI, with pictures by *Bassano* and *Maratta.*—Then through the Boudoir (VII), overlooking the courtyard, into the Bedroom (VIII), in blue silk; over the door is a painting (Turkish Ladies) by *J. B. Vanloo.* The ceiling of the Bathroom (IX) is also by *J. B. Vanloo* (Genii doing homage to Venus).—We return through the boudoir and an adjoining room (X) into the Large State Room (Жёлтый залъ; XI), with 8 pillars of black marble veined with white, resting on high bases of brown marble decorated with gilded bronze foliage. The two fire-places are flanked by columns of ribbon-jasper; the mantelpieces are of white marble ornamented with lapis lazuli; the ceiling-paintings are of the Venetian School. Cabinets of Florentine mosaic. Doors of buhl work.— Room XII contains paintings by *De Vos, Bloem,* and *D'Hondecoeter.*— Corner Room XIII (Свинцóвый залъ): *Snyders,* Still-life; Italian mosaic tables.

We return and enter the SMALL or FIRST HERMITAGE OF EMPRESS CATHERINE II.

Adjoining the *Pavilion,* which contains four fountains, a fine mythological mosaic, and two large portraits (Empress Marie Feódorovna, by Mme. Vigée-Lebrun, and Catherine II., by Lampi), is the *Winter Garden,* decorated with marble statues.

Then follows the *Románov Gallery,* with good portraits of members of the House of Románov, beginning with the Patriarch Philarét Nikititch, father of Tzar Michael.

Among the portraits the following are worthy of notice: Sophia Alexéyevna as Regent.—Peter the Great, by *K. de Moor, Nattier (?), Belli* (copy of the portrait by Kneller at Hampton Court), etc.—Catherine I. as Empress, by *Nattier.*—Elizabeth I., by *Tocqué.*—Catherine II., by *Eriksen* (on horseback, in the uniform of the Preobrazhénski Regiment), *P. Falconet the Younger* (1769), *Shebánov,* etc.—Paul I. with his first wife, Natalie of Hesse, and his second, Marie of Wurtemberg, by *Falconet, Roslin* (1777), *Borovikóvski,* etc.—Queen Anna Pávlovna with her husband, King William II. of the Netherlands, by *N. de Keyser.*—Sons and daughters of Emperor Nicholas I., by *Mme. Robertson.*

At the exit we notice the curious *Instructions* issued by Catherine II. in regard to the Hermitage, with which everyone had to comply. Every visitor 'has on entering to leave his title, hat, and sword outside', and so on.

We next enter the *St. George's Saloon* (Геóргіевская зáла), 154 ft. long and 65½ ft. wide, with white marble Corinthian pillars and six beautiful chandeliers; at the N. end stands the throne, behind which is a large imperial coat-of-arms embroidered in gold on red velvet. In this room the first Russian Parliament was opened on April 27th (May 10th), 1906. St. George's festival is celebrated here on Nov. 26th (Dec. 9th), and the Emperor receives here the congratulations of the diplomatic corps on New Year's Day.—The rococo *Palace Chapel* (Собóръ Спáса Нерукотвóрнаго óбраза) contains some valuable church-plate.

The following room is the *Armorial Saloon* (Гербóвая зáла), with gilt pillars; in the four corners are groups of ancient Russian warriors, holding military banners on which the coats-of-arms of the various Russian provinces are represented. By the side-wall, in nine sections, are exhibited the bowls in which salt and bread were presented to the Emperors.

We now come to the *Throne Room of Peter the Great* (Пе-тро́вская за́ла), the walls of which are hung with red velvet strewn with Russian eagles worked in gold. In a niche between two jasper pillars is a picture by Amigoni (Peter the Great led by Glory); in front is the imperial throne. The chandeliers, candelabra, and tables are of silver.

Next comes the *Field Marshals' Room* (Фельдма́ршалская за́ла), with portraits of famous Russian marshals, and other pictures.

The *East* or *Pompeian Gallery* (Восто́чная or Помпе́йнская галере́я), which is hung with battle-scenes from the Russo-Turkish War of 1877-78, leads hence into the *Avant Saloon,* which is decorated with the vessels in which the symbolic 'salt and bread' were presented to Catherine II. and her successors. To the right of this room is the Grand or Ambassadorial Staircase (p.112). To the left lies a second Winter Garden. — We turn to the right into the *Nicholas Saloon,* which is the largest in the palace, being 200 ft. long by 61 ft. broad. Here the court balls are held. It has 16 windows overlooking the Nevá, and is adorned by a portrait of Emperor Nicholas I. on horseback, by Krüger, and four large wall-trophies with vessels of gold. Adjoining is a Concert Hall. — Then follows the *Moorish Saloon* (Ара́пская ко́мната), which leads (l.) to the *Rotunda,* containing lifesize portraits of Emperor Nicholas I. by Bothmann, Alexander I. and Alexander II. by Angeli, and Empress Alexandra Feódorovna by Winterhalter.

The *Dark Corridor,* which opens out of the Rotunda, contains lifesize portraits of the Knights of the Order of St. Andrew. To the left is the Marine Room, with paintings of the battles of Grenham (1720) and Hangö (1714), by Bogolyúbov. — It was in Alexander II.'s Dining Room, which contains a few models of ships, that an explosion in 1880 nearly caused the death of the Tzar. — We pass from the Dark Corridor into the *Smaller Field Marshals' Room,* with portraits of Russian generals of Nicholas I.'s time. The cannon was presented by Emperor William I. to Alexander II.

Then follow three *Rooms of Alexander II.,* viz. his Library, his Study (with the iron bed on which he died), and a Reception Room. Beyond these are the rooms of Empress Marie Alexándrovna, wife of Alexander II. — We return through the Dark Corridor into the *Golden Saloon* (Золота́я за́ла), fitted up in Byzantine style, with a fine mosaic (view of the temples of Pæstum) over the fireplace. In a corner is a seated marble figure of Empress Alexandra Feódorovna, by Wichmann. — In the next room we find a few smaller pictures and a clock which requires to be wound up once a year only.

We now come to the beautiful *White Saloon* (dining-hall), with fine marble statues. — The next seven rooms are adorned with battle-scenes by Aivazóvski, Bogolyúbov, P. Hess, Kotzebue, Rechlin, Rosen,

Sauerweid, Sukhodólski, and Willewalde. — The *Hall of Columns,* which follows, leads into apartments for royal guests. — The *Gallery of 1812* contains several flags and half-length portraits of 250 princes and generals who distinguished themselves in 1812 and succeeding campaigns, painted by Dawe (and his assistants).

On the upper floor of the Winter Palace is the *Crown Jewel Room (Брилья́нтовая ко́мната); adm. obtained only from the Court Chamberlain at the request of the traveller's ambassador. The glass-case in the centre contains the *Imperial Regalia* (copies, see p. 163). Of these the *Sceptre* (Ски́петръ) is the most valuable (2,400,000 rb.); among the jewels with which it is set is the *Orlóv Diamond,* weighing 185 carats. This diamond originally came from India, where it was stolen by a sepoy, and afterwards fell into the hands of an Armenian merchant named Lázarev, from whom Count Orlóv bought it in Amsterdam, afterwards presenting it to Empress Catherine II. The price paid was 450,000 rb., besides which the merchant received an annuity of 2000 rb. and a title. — The exquisite *Imperial Crown,* of Byzantine form, was ordered by Empress Catherine II. from the court-jeweller Loubié, but was finished only in time for Paul I.'s coronation. It is valued at 1,100,000 rb. On the top is a cross of five magnificent diamonds, resting on a very large unpolished ruby and held by a gold ring containing 7 large diamonds. On each side of the ring is a half-circle of 38 big pearls, which give the crown the form of a mitre, symbolizing the supremacy of the Russian Emperor in the Church. The circle of the crown resting on the forehead is set with 28 brilliants. — The *Crown of the Empress* is also studded with the most valuable diamonds. — The *Orb* is surmounted by a large diamond cross resting on a magnificent sapphire. — Other cases contain *Sets of Jewellery, Diadems,* etc. The unset *Shah Diamond,* a present from a Persian prince to the Tzar, is elongated in form, weighs 86⁷/₁₆ carats, and is engraved with the names of Eastern potentates. Noteworthy also are an exquisite pale-red *Ruby,* an *Order of St. Andrew* set with five rose-diamonds and two Siberian beryls, the diamond chains of the Order of St. Andrew, etc.

Opposite the Winter Palace, on the S.E. side of the Dvortzóvaya Square (p. 112), stands the **Office of the General Staff** (Гла́вный Штабъ; Pl. F 5; *II*), the façade of which (three stories, with 768 windows), 570 yds. in length, is broken by a large archway, through which a passage leads to the Morskáya and the Nevski Prospékt. The archway is surmounted by a bronze group of Victory in a six-horse chariot, by Démut-Malinóvski and the elder Piménov. The building, which was erected in 1819-47 after plans by *Rossi,* contains considerable collections of books and maps, a printing-office, and a cartographical institute. — The *Ministry of Finance* and the *Ministry for Foreign Affairs* are in the same building.

Near by, on the other side of the Pyévtcheski Bridge (Pl. F, 5; *II*), is the *Court Singing School* (Придво́рная Пѣ́вческая Капе́лла), in which pupils are prepared for the imperial choir. — Not far off (Móika 12) stands the house in which *Pushkin* died on Jan. 29th, 1837 (marble memorial tablet; comp. pp. 41, 193).

Adjoining the Winter Palace on the E. rises the Hermitage (p. 131). Following the Dvortzóvaya Náberezhnaya towards the E., we cross the Winter Canal at its junction with the Nevá by means of the *Hermitage Bridge* (Эрмита́жный мостъ). To the right is the *Imperial Hermitage Theatre* (Pl. 178, F 5; *II*), built in 1785 by G. Quarenghi (p. 131), and used for court festivals. Behind the theatre, and facing the Milliónnaya, are the *Barracks of the 1st Battalion of the Preobrazhénski Regiment* (Казармы Преображéнскаго полкá; Pl. F 5, *II*).—Farther on (No. 26), with its façade towards the Nevá, stands the *Palace of Grand-Duchess Marie Pávlovna* (Pl. F, 5; *II*), widow of Grand-Duke Vladimir Alexándrovitch; it is an elegant building of 1870 in the Florentine style. No. 18 is the *Palace of Grand-Duke Nicholas Mikháilovitch* (Pl. F, 4, 5; *II*), built by Stakenschneider in 1863, and somewhat over-elaborate in its ornamentation. It contains the Museum of the Grand-Duke Mikhail Nikoláyevitch (d. 1909), with souvenirs of him (entr. to the left of the main door; adm., see p. 98). No. 14 is the New Club (p. 93), No. 16 the English Club (p. 93).—A little farther on stands the *Marble Palace* (Мрáморный Дворéцъ; Pl. F 4, *II*), built in 1768-85 of marble, granite, iron, and bronze from the plans of Rinaldi and presented by Catherine II. to Count Orlóv. It is occupied by Grand-Duke Constantine Constantínovitch.

To the E. of the Marble Palace lies the small SUVÓROV SQUARE (Pl. F, 4; *II*). In the middle rises the bronze *Suvórov Monument* (pp. 127, 130), by Kozlóvski, erected in 1801; the géneral is represented in Roman costume, wielding a sword in his right hand, while his left holds a shield over the Papal, Sardinian, and Neapolitan crowns.—Tróitzki Bridge (Pl. F, 4; *I*), see p. 173.

The MÁRSOVO POLE (Field of Mars; Pl. F, 4, 5, *II*) stretches to the S.E. of the Marble Palace as far as the Móika. The great military parades, usually held at the end of April (O.S.), took place here from 1818 till a few years ago, since when they have been held at Krasnoye Selo or Tzarskoye Selo. The mounts of each of the regiments of the household cavalry are all of one colour (Horse Guards black, Gatchina Hussars dapple-gray, Chevalier Guards chestnut, etc.).

To the E. of the Suvórov Square, in the Dvortzóvaya Náberezhnaya, are the *British Embassy* (No. 4; p. 93) and (farther on) the chief gate of the **Summer Garden** (Лѣтній садъ; Pl. F, G, 4, 5, *II*), in front of which is the principal landing-stage of the steamers plying to the Islands (p. 92). The Summer Garden was laid out by Leblond in 1712 in the Franco-Dutch style, and forms a long rectangle about 37 acres in area. On the side next the Nevá it is enclosed by a handsome iron palisade (by Velten, 1783). At the chief entrance stands a *Chapel* erected to commemorate the escape of Tzar Alexander II. from an assassin (April 4th, 1866). The park, with fine old trees, contains 75 marble sculptures (from Venice) of the early 18th cent., by V. Grupello, P. Baratta, G. Bonazza, etc.— A little to the left of the entrance on the Nevá side is the so-called *Small Palace of Peter I.* (Дворéцъ Петрá I.; Pl. G 4, *II*), an unpretentious two-storied building erected in 1711 as a 'Summer Palace'. The interior has been frequently restored. On the groundfloor are a clock, a chest of walnut-wood (stairway to the first floor), and other objects made by the Tzar himself; on the upper floor are a lifesize portrait of Peter, and numerous mediocre pictures (fee to the attendant, 20 cop.). — Farther on, to the left of the chief avenue, in the children's playground, is a seated bronze figure, by Klodt (1856), of *Iván Kruilóv* (Памятникъ Крылóву; 1768-1844), the La Fontaine of Russia. On the granite pedestal are four bronze reliefs with figures from his animal-stories. Hard by is a refreshment-kiosque. — On the S. side of the garden are a pond and a *Pórphyry Vase,* presented in 1839 by Charles XIV. John of Sweden.

If we leave the Summer Garden by the S. gate, turn to the left, and cross the Fontánka by the *Panteléimonski Bridge,* we reach the Stieglitz Museum of Industrial Art and the E. Quarters of the town (p. 125). Directly opposite the gate is the *Inzhenérni Bridge,* leading across the Móika to the Engineers' Palace (p. 118).

From the Field of Mars we return viâ the MILLIÓNNAYA (Pl. F, 4, 5; *II*) to the Dvortzóvaya Square (p. 112). In this street (l.), at the corner of the Tzarítzuinskaya, are the *Barracks of the Pávlovski Regiment,* while farther on are the **Hermitage** (r.; p. 131) and the *Office of the Imperial Archives* (l., opposite), built in 1883-7

d. Spasskaya and Kazanskaya Quarters to the N. of the Nevski.

Church of the Resurrection. Museum of Alexander III.

Michael Square (Mikháilovskaya Ploshtchad; Pl. F 5, *II*) is reached by tramways Nos. 2, 4, 7, 10, 12, 17, & 18.

From the Nevski (p. 103), to the E. of the Politzéiski Bridge, the BOLSHAYA KONYÚSHENNAYA (Pl. F, 5; *II*) runs towards the N. To the left is the *French Reformed Church,* founded in 1737 and rebuilt in 1862; it contains a chair which Peter the Great is said to have occupied at a christening on July 31st, 1724. To the right is the *Finnish Church of St. Mary,* built in 1801 by Velten (?). To the left, at the corner of the Volúinski Pereúlok, are the *Co-operative Stores of the Officers of the Guards,* which are open to the public. — At the end of the street is the —

Museum of Imperial Carriages (Придвóрно-конюшен-ный музéй; Pl. F 5, *II*), built in 1860 from the designs of Sadóvnikov. The entrance is at No. 2 Konyúshennaya Square (adm., see p. 97; illus. Russian catalogue 1 rb.; Director, N. A. Kavélin). The objects of interest on the upper floor include French and Russian tapestry (the latter made at the St. Petersburg factory, which existed from 1716 to 1857); a travelling-sleigh made by Peter the Great; the coronation-carriage of the empresses, presented by Frederick the Great to the Empress Elizabeth I.; several state-coaches with paintings by Watteau and Boucher; sleighs, saddles, and so forth. The shattered carriage occupied by the Emperor Alexander II. at the time of his assassination (p. 118) is also kept here (covered).

Opposite are the *Imperial Stables* (Зданіе придворныхъ конюшенъ; Pl. F 5, *II*).

To the E. of the Carriage Museum, beyond the Yekaterininski or Catherine Canal, extends the *Mikháilovski Garden,* which contains many fine old trees, and is open to the public in summer (entrance from the Sadóvaya and the Catherine Canal). — On the W. side of the garden, adjoining the Catherine Canal, stands the —

*Church of the Resurrection (Храмъ Воскресéнія Христóва; Pl. F 5, *II*) or Church of Expiation, erected between 1883 and 1907 by *A. Parland,* on the spot where Tzar Alexander II. was mortally wounded by the Nihilists on March 1st (O.S.), 1881. The church, which is built of granite, marble, and coloured bricks in the Russian style of the 17th cent., is 190 ft. long, 148 ft. wide, and 266 ft. high (to the top of the central dome). Of the nine domes the main dome is overlaid with mosaic, and the four side-domes and the two which surmount the entrances are adorned with brilliant enamel. The dome over the apse and that of the bell-tower (194 ft. high) are gilded. The best mosaic is a Crucifixion by Parland, under the large W. window. Inside, on the W., under the belfry, the exact spot of the assassination is marked by a canopy borne by four columns of jasper. The mosaics which cover walls, piers, and vaults have a total area of 176,400 sq. ft. (3600 sq. sazhens; St. Mark's, Venice, 45,790 sq. ft.). On the walls we have Scenes from the Life of Christ, from designs by Parland, Byeláyev (Deposition in the Tomb, on the W. side), Kharlámov (Last Supper, on the ceiling of the E. apse), Koshelév (Transfiguration, in the side-dome between the apse and central dome), and others. On the piers of the central dome are Apostles, Prophets, Martyrs, and Church Fathers.

To the E. of the Mikháilovski Garden lies the **Engineers' Palace**, or *Old Michael Palace* (Инженéрный Зáмокъ; Pl. G 5, *II;* adm. on application at the office), built in a mediæval style in the reign of Paul I. between 1797 and 1800, probably by Brenna from a design of Bazhénov, on the site of a summer-palace occupied by the Empress Elizabeth. Its total cost was 18,000,000 rubles. In 1822 the building was fitted up as an *Engineering Academy* (Николáевская инженéрная акадéмія). It forms a massive quadrangle enclosing a large octagonal court, on the W. side of which rises the tower of the palace-church. The main S. façade, looking over the great square, is relieved by groups of Ionic columns, while the pediment is adorned with reliefs of historical scenes and the imperial coat-of-arms. On the main frieze is an inscription, originally intended for St. Isaac's Cathedral: Дóму твоемý подобáетъ святыня Госпóдня въ долготý дней ('Holiness becometh thine house, O Lord, for ever'; Ps. xciii, 5). A magnificent marble staircase, beginning on the left side of the court, leads to the first floor, where the old Throne Room and the so-called Round Room still remain in their original form. The latter now contains the rich technical collection of the Academy.— Paul I. died in this palace on March 24th, 1801, and the room in which he died was converted into a chapel in the reign of Alexander II.

To the S. of the palace is an *Equestrian Statue of Peter the Great* (Pl. G 5, *II;* comp. p. 108), cast in the reign of Elizabeth from designs by Rastrelli the Elder, and set up under Paul I. The inscription on the marble pedestal runs 'To the Great-Grandfather by the Great-Grandson 1800' (Прáдѣлу Прáвнукъ 1800).

From this monument the Klenóvaya leads direct to the large *Michael Manège* or *Riding School* (Михáйловскій манéжъ; Pl. G 5, *II),* in front of which, to the S., is a bronze equestrian statue, 16 ft. high, of *Grand-Duke Nicholas Nikoláyevitch* (d. 1891), after a design by P. Canonica of Turin (1914). The reliefs on the pedestal, which is 23 ft. high, represent the battles of Plevna and the Shipka Pass. From the N. side of the Michael Manège we follow the Inzhenérnaya to the MICHAEL SQUARE (Михáйловская плó-щадь; Pl. F 5, *II),* which is laid out in pleasure-grounds. On the W. side of the square is the *Michael Theatre* (p. 94), erected by Rossi and Bryullóv in 1835.— On the N. side of the square stands the—

*Russian Museum of Emperor Alexander III., or *New Michael Palace* (Рýсскій Музéй Импéрáтора Алексáндра III.; Pl. F, G, 5, *II),* erected in 1819-25 in the Tuscan style, from designs by Rossi, for Grand-Duke Michael Pávlovitch, and converted into a Museum of Russian Art in 1895-98. The right wing is new and is destined for the new Ethnographical Museum. The collection of pictures rivals in importance the Tretyakóv Gallery at Moscow (P. 316) for the study of Russian painting.— Admission, see p. 98. Director, Grand-Duke George Mikháilovitch; Assistant Director, Count D. I. Tolstói. All the pictures and sculptures are labelled. Alterations in the arrangement are not infrequent. Russian catalogue 35 cop., with autotypes 80 cop.

GROUND FLOOR.—Room I, to the left of the entrance. Portraits of Russian Rulers and Grandees, mostly by unknown painters of the 18th century.— Room II. Portraits by *F. S. Rókotov* (1730-1810), *D. M. Levitzki* (1735-1822), and others.— Room III. To the right, 278. *I. M. Tankóv* (1756-99), Village-festival; 270. *P. I. Sokolóv* (1753-91), Mercury and Argus; 14. *F. Y. Alexéyev* (1753-1824), Kremlin of Moscow in 1810.— Room IV. Cartoons by *K. P. Bryullóv* (1799-1852).— Room V. Portraits by *V. L. Borovikóvski* (1757-1825): 3093 (on the right), Empress Catherine II.; 42. Khan Feth-Ali-Mustapha-Kuli; 2333. Mme. Neklyúdova; 43. D. P. Troshtchínski.— Room VI. Paintings by *A. O. Orlovski* (1777-1832); Italian landscapes by *S. F. Shtchedrín* (1791-1830); Allegories of the War of Liberation by *Count F. P. Tolstói* (1783-

8*

1873; wax reliefs); 1622. *O. A. Kiprenski* (1783-1836), Portrait of the artist. In the centre, *B. I. Orlovski* (1783-1838), 957. Satyr, 958. Paris (in marble).

Room VII. Main wall, 284. *V. A. Tropínin* (1776-1857) Guitar-player; *A. G. Venetziánov* (1780-1847), 90. Threshing-floor, 1620. Fortune-tellers, 97. Portrait of the artist. In the middle, 951. *K. M. Klímtchenko* (1817-1848), Girl with mirror (marble).

Room VIII. Drawings and Water-colours by artists of the 18-19th centuries. — Room IX. Cartoons by *F. A. Bruni* (1800-75).

Room X is devoted to sculpture. To the left of the entrance, 1002. *Edwards* (b. 1861), Glory to God in the highest; to the right, 1552. *L. A. Bernstamm* (b. 1859), Christ and the Woman taken in Adultery. On the main wall, 919. *V. A. Beklemíshev* (b. 1861), St. Barbara. On the exit wall, to the right, 918. *M. M. Antokólski* (1842-1902), Yermák, the conqueror of Siberia; to the left, 924. *P. A. Veliónski* (b. 1849), Russian bard with boy. — Room XI. Drawings and Water-colours by *Prince G. G. Gagárin* (1810-73). — Room XII. Drawings, Water-colours, and Engravings. — Room XIII. Watercolours and Drawings by *V. M. Vasnetzóv* (b. 1848). — Room XIV. To the right, 172. *I. B. Lampi* (1775-1837), Count P. V. Zavadóvski; portraits by *H. F. Voille* (1750-1812?). — Rooms XV & XVI. Watercolours and Drawings presented by Princess M. K. Ténisheva. — The next rooms, which are closed, contain pictures of saints.

Staircase. In the arcade at the top, 969. *K. B. Rastrelli* (d. 1744), Empress Anna Ivánovna (bronze).

Upper Floor. Room XXII. To the right, 36. *A. P. Bogolyúbov* (1824-96), Golítzuin Hospital; 2. *I. K. Aivazóvski* (1817-1900), Clouds. In the middle, 972. *P. A. Stavasser* (1816-50), Nymph (marble). — Room XXIII. To the right, 1619. *A. A. Ivánov* (1806-58), N. V. Gogol. Portraits by *P. V. Basin* (1793-1877), *Bruni*, and *K. P. Bryullóv*. — Room XXIV. To the left, 4. *I. K. Aivazóvski*, Odessa; *K. P. Bryullóv*, 2230. Count A. A. Perovski, 58. Last Days of Pompeii (1833; one of the artist's masterpieces); 50. *F. A. Bruni*, Brazen Serpent (1840).

Room XXV. To the right, 275. *V. I. Súrikov* (b. 1848), Yermák fighting with native Siberians; 243. *V. D. Polyénov* (b. 1844), Christ and the Woman taken in adultery. — 255. *I. E. Ryepin* (b. 1844), St. Nicholas the Wonder-worker. — 259. *I. E. Ryepin*, Cossacks preparing a letter to the Sultan of Turkey; 266. *H. I. Siemirádzki* (1843-1902), Phryne exhibiting her charms to the public; 188. *K. E. Makovski* (b. 1839), Kiss after the feast. — 260. *K. A. Savitzki* (b. 1845), Departure for the front. — In the middle, 914. *M. M. Antokolski*, Mephistopheles, in marble; 934. *F. F. Kamenski* (b. 1838), The first step (marble).

Room XXVI. To the right, 115. *N. N. Gay* (1831-94), Peter the Great examining the Tzarévitch Alexis at Peterhof; 1624.

I. N. Kramskói (1837-87), V. G. Peróv; 121. *N. D. Dmítriyev-Orenbúrgski* (1838-98), Drowned; 2883. *N. N. Gay,* N. A. Nekrásov; 1662. *N. A. Yaroshénko* (1846-98), Swing. — Room XXVII. Temporary exhibitions. — Room XXVIII. Works by *V. V. Vereshtchágin* (1842-1904). — Room XXIX. To the right, 35. *N. P. Bogdánov-Byelski* (b. 1868), Sunday School in the village; 3019. *I. I. Shishkin* (1831-98), Wintry landscape; 144. *A. D. Kivshénko* (1851-95), Sorting feathers. — Room XXX. Portraits by *I. E. Ryepin* (2244. Count Leo Tolstói; 1891). In the middle, 915. *M. M. Antokolski,* Tzar Iván the Terrible (bronze). — Room XXXI. To the right, 179. *A. D. Litóvtchenko* (1835-90), Tzar Iván the Terrible showing his treasures to the English ambassador; 298. *A. A. Kharlámov* (b. 1842), I. S. Turgényev (1875).

Room XXXII. To the right, 1883. *K. Y. Kruishítzki* (1858-1911), First snow; 231. *Orlovski,* Ai-Petri, in the Crimea; 130. *I. I. Yendo-*

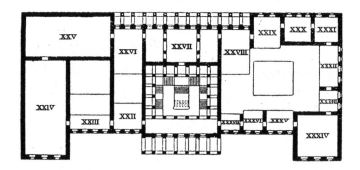

gúrov (1861-98), Beginning of Spring; 272. *R. G. Sudkovski* (1850-85), Gorge of Daryal, in the Caucasus; 220. *A. N. Novoskóltzev* (b. 1853), Last moments of the Metropolitan Philip. — Room XXXIII. To the right, 3139. *Marie Bashkírtzev* (1860-84), Landscape; 2183. *Y. E. Kratchkovski* (b. 1854), Spring in the Crimea. — Room XXXIV. Above the entrance, 3245. *N. M. Fokin* (1869-1908), Wintry landscape. To the left, 2009. *A. M. Vasnetzóv,* Old Moscow; 2018. *M. V. Nésterov* (b. 1862), St. Sergius; 2902. *B. M. Kustodiyev* (b. 1878), Child in a bath; 332. *A. Edelfelt* (1854-1905), Washerwomen. Studies by *I. I. Levítan* (1861-1900). — Room XXXV. To the right, 2968. *V. A. Syeróv* (1865-1911), Bathing; 3226. *K. A. Somov* (b. 1869), Portrait of his father. Room XXXVI. Water-colours. To the left of the entrance, 2229. *L. O. Pasternak* (b. 1862), Family of Count Leo Tolstói (1902). Room XXXVII. On the mantelpiece, 932. *V. P. Brodski* (1825-1904), Christ with two angels (marble).

In the ITALYÁNSKAYA, to the E. of the Michael Square, are the *Ministry of Justice* (Министе́рство юсти́ціи; Pl. G 5, *II*), on the right, and the *Alexander Cadet Corps* (Алекса́ндров-скій каде́тскій ко́рпусъ), on the left.—From the S. side of the Michael Square the MIKHÁILOVSKAYA leads to the Nevski Prospékt. On the W. side of this street stands the large Hôtel de l'Europe (p. 88), opposite which is the building of the *Assembly of the Nobles* (Дворя́нское собра́ніе; Pl. 17, F 5, *II*), containing a handsome concert-room.

c. Spasskaya and Kazanskaya Quarters to the S. of the Nevski. Kolomenskaya Quarter.

The Sadóvaya is traversed by Tramways Nos. 1, 3, 11, 13, & 14 (pp. 91, 92).—*Steamer* on the Fontánka, see p. 92.

To the S.W. of the Kazán Cathedral stands the large *Foundling Hospital* (Воспита́тельный Домъ; Pl. F 6, *II*), rebuilt at the end of the 18th cent. (office at Móika 54).

From the Gostíni Dvor (Pl. F, 5, 6, *II*; p. 104), adjoining the Nevski, we turn to the S.W. and enter the SADÓVAYA (Pl. D-G, 7-5; *I*). To the left, at the corner of the Tchornuishóv Pereúlok, is the building of the **Corps of Pages** (Па́жескій Его́ Импера́-торскаго Вели́чества Ко́рпусъ; Pl. F 6, *II*), built in 1756-58 by Rastrelli as the palace of Count Vorontzóv.

This building includes the *Roman Catholic Priory Church of the Maltese Order* of St. John of Jerusalem, and also a Chapel of John the Baptist, both built in 1799 by Quarenghi under the Tzar Paul I., Grand-Master of the Maltese Order. The present façade of the priory-church, which is turned towards the inner court, is articulated by four large pilasters and two smaller columns, and bears the inscription: 'Divo Joanni Baptistæ Paulus Imp. Hospit. Magister'. Two rows of yellow marble columns divide the church into a nave and aisles, each about 65 ft. in height. To the left of the high-altar is the gilded throne occupied by Paul at the meetings of the Order, and also the chapel in which Duke Maximilian of Leuchtenberg (d. 1852) is buried.—The *Chapel of the Baptist* was built by Paul in 1800, and handed over to the Corps of Pages in 1810. On its ceiling are 15 Maltese crosses.—The Corps of Pages educates 400 boys, whose fathers or grandfathers must have attained the rank of lieutenant-general.

Farther on, to the right, is the **Imperial Bank** (Госуда́р-ственный Банкъ; Pl. F 6, *II*), a large horseshoe-shaped building erected by Quarenghi in the reign of Alexander I. Opposite, to the left, are the *Marie* and *Apraxin Markets* (Мари́инскій ры́нокъ, Апра́ксинъ ры́нокъ). We next reach, beyond the Gorókhovaya, the *Parish Church of the Assumption* (Це́рковь Успе́нія Пресвятыя Богоро́дицы, popularly known as Спасъ; Pl. F 6, *II*), built in 1753-65 and enlarged in 1826. Most of the SYENNÁYA PLÓSHTCHAD ('Hay-market'; Pl. F 6, *II*) is occupied by four *Market Halls* of iron.

Following the Zabalkánski Prospékt (Pl. F, 6-9; *I*) to the left from
the Syennáya Square, we reach in 3 min. (No. 9, to the right) the **Institute
of the Engineers of Ways of Communication** (Институтъ Инженéровъ Путéй Сообщéнiя; Pl. 109, F 6, *I*), built in 1810 by Bétancourt (?).
From the Óbúkhovski Bridge, about 3 min. farther to the S., we obtain a
distant view of the Moscow Triumphal Arch (P. 128). For the Technological Institute, see p. 128.—To the N. of the Syennáya Square, at
Demídov Pereúlok 8 a, is the building of the *Imperial Geographical Society* (Pl. E, F, 6; *II*), which was founded in 1847.

In the Sadóvaya (No. 50) stands the *Museum of the Ministry of
Ways of Communication* or *Museum of Tzar Nicholas I.* (Музéй
вѣдомства путéй сообщéнiя úмени импéратора Николáя I.;
Pl. 137, E, F, 6, *I*), which was completed in 1902 (adm., see p. 98;
Russian catalogue 1 rb). On the first floor are models of bridges,
railway rolling-stock, locomotives, ships (including the paddle-
steamer made by Kulibin of Nizhni-Novgorod in 1804), locks, and
the like; also relics of Tzar Nicholas I. In a pavilion in the garden
is an imperial saloon-carriage constructed in 1847. — Adjoining
the Museum is the **Yusúpov Garden** (Юсуповъ садъ; Pl.
E, F, 6, 7, *I*), frequented chiefly by the lower classes in summer,
and by skaters in winter.— On the S.W. side of the garden, at
No. 117 Fontánka, is the *Ministry of Ways of Communication*
(Министéрство путéй сообщéнiя; Pl. 184, E 7, *I*), built by Quarenghi as the Yusúpov Palace.

At the corner of the Sadóvaya and Voznesénski Prospékt is the
New Alexander Market (Нóвый Алексáндровскiй рынокъ;
Pl. 119, E 7, *I*), a kind of rag-fair. — To the N., in the Voznesénski
Prospékt, is the *Church of the Ascension* (Pl. 40, E 6; *I*), built in
1772 by Rinaldi and altered at the beginning of the 19th century.

From the Sadóvaya (farther on) the Novo-Nikólski Bridge leads
to the right across the Catherine Canal to the Nicholas Square
(Никóльская плóщадь; Pl. E, 6, 7, *I*). Here, surrounded by attractive gardens, is the so-called 'Sailors' Church', or *Cathedral of St.
Nicholas* (Морскóй Николáевскiй Богоявлéнскiй Собóръ), built
in 1758 by S. I. Tchevakinski, a pupil of Rastrelli, and surmounted by
five gilded domes. A good view is obtained from the detached belfry.

Following the Glinka Street to the N. from the Cathedral, we
reach the Theatre Square (Театрáльная плóщадь; Pl. E 6, *II*),
in the middle of which stands the **Conservatorium** (Pl. E, 6; *II*).
This building, formerly called the 'Grand Theatre', was rebuilt in
1891-96 from the plans of V. Nikolá. On the first floor are the
Glinka and *Rubinstein Museums*, open in winter on Sun., 12-2.
The grand hall was reconverted into a theatre in 1912; the foyer
contains statues of the composers Tchaikovski (d. 1893), by Bekle
mishev, and Rubinstein (d. 1894), by Bernstamm (1902). — The im
perial **Marie Theatre** (Марíинскiй Теáтръ; Pl. 180, E 6, *I*,
p. 94), built in 1860, stands opposite. In front of this, on the S.,
is a *Statue of Glinka* (d. 1857; Pl. 129, E 6, *I*), by Bach (1906).

At No. 94 Móika, on the S. bank, is the **Palace of Princess Yusúpov,** which contains an extensive collection of paintings (adm. on application).

Rembrandt, *Portraits of a man and woman (companion-pictures), *Portrait of a youth; *G. van den Eeckhout,* Jacob and Rachel hearing the false report of the death of Joseph; *P. de Hooch,* Woman with cradle; *D. Teniers,* *Piper, *Girl with a drum, and four other pictures; *J. van Ostade,* Several genre-scenes; *J. Molenaer,* Concert; *J. van Ruysdael,* Moonlit landscape; *J. van der Does,* Landscape with sheep; *J. D. de Heem,* Fruit; *Demarné,* Scenes of popular and fashionable life. There are five tine specimens of *Ph. Wouverman. Claude Lorrain* is represented by three pictures, *Boucher* and *Greuze* by several.

From the Theatre Square the Ofitzérskaya and the Voznesénski Prospékt lead to the E. back to the Marie Square (p. 110). To the W. of the Theatre Square lies the unattractive Kolómenskaya Quarter.

Kolómenskaya Quarter.

At the corner of the Ofitzérskaya (Pl. D, E, 6; *I*), on the Kryukov Canal, beyond the Theatre Sq., rises the so-called *Lithuanian Palace* (Pl. D, 6; *II*) or *Prison* (Городская тюрьмá), which was built under Catherine II., but received its present form under Nicholas I. Farther to the W. in the Ofitzérskaya are the *Synagogue* (Pl. 176, D 6; *I*), erected in the Moorish style, and the Esthonian *Church of St. John* (Pl. 57, D 6; *I*).—New Admiralty, see p. 111.

Other noteworthy points in the Kolómenskaya Quarter are the *Commissariat Office* (Pl. 70, D, E, 6, 7; *I*), Yekaterinhóf Prospékt 51, which contains a collection of uniforms and accoutrements (adm., see p. 97); the *Church of the Resurrection* (Цéрковь Воскресéнія Христóва; Pl. 52, D 7, *I*); and the Roman Catholic *Church of St. Stanislaus,* at the corner of the Torgóvaya and the Málaya Masterskáya. To the S. of the Catherine Canal is the *Church of the Intercession of the Virgin* (Цéрковь Покрóва Богорóдицы; Pl. 45, D 7, *I*).

f. Liteinaya and Rozhdestvenskaya Quarters.

Stieglitz Museum. Imperial Duma. Smolni Convent.

The Litéini Prospékt is traversed by tramways Nos. 9, 10, 15, & 18 (PP. 91, 92).—Nos. 4, 5, 11, 13, 14, 17, 18, & 19 will also be found useful by the visitor to this quarter.

By crossing the Anítchkov Bridge (p. 107) in the Nevski, and taking the first cross-street to the left, we reach the Litéini Prospékt (Литéйный проспéктъ; Pl. G, 4, 5, *II*), the main street of the Litéinaya Quarter.

Near the beginning of the street is a large group of charitable institutions and gardens, occupying the whole space between the Fontánka and the Známenskaya. No. 53 is the *St. Catharine Institute for Girls* (Училище Óрдена святóй Екатерины; main entrance at Fontánka 36), built in 1804 by Quarenghi. Opposite this is the *Marie Hospital* (Маріинская больница), a huge building with two wings by Quarenghi (1803); in front is a bronze monument to *Prince Peter of Oldenburg* (d. 1881), by Schrœder (1889). At Nadézhdinskaya No. 12 is the *Alexandra Hospital* for women

(Александрінская женская больница), and at Známenskaya
No. 8 is the *Pávlovski Institute for Girls.*

Fontánka No. 34 is the *Palace of Count S. D. Sheremétyev* (Pl. G, 5;
II), built in the reign of the Empress Elizabeth, and containing a collection of weapons, which may be visited upon previous application. The
collection embraces about 1400 objects, including many rifles, muskets,
and pistols (illustrated description by E. von Lenz, *2l.*). Here also is the
Museum of the Society for the Study of Ancient Manuscripts (Музей
общества любителей древней письменности; adm.free).— In the Simeó-
novskaya, to the left of the Litéini Prospékt, is the *Church of SS. Simeon
and Anna* (Церковь Симеóна Богопріймца и Анны Пророчицы; Pl.
G 5, *II*), a domed structure erected in 1732-42 by M. G. Zemtzov.

Proceeding N. along the Litéini Prospékt, we pass the *Office of the
Administration of the Imperial Domains* (Главное управлéніе
удéловъ; No. 37), and in another 4 min. come to the Panteléimonskaya, which leads to the **Cathedral of the Transfiguration**
(Спáсо-Преображéнскій Собóръ; Pl. G 5, *II*), one of the most
important churches in St. Petersburg, built in 1742-54, burned down
in 1825, and restored in 1829 from the designs of Stasov.

The court of the church is surrounded by a railing, each of the
uprights of which is composed of the barrels of three Turkish and three
French cannon. Inside the enclosure are twelve Turkish guns, with their
carriages. — The INTERIOR of the church contains numerous Turkish and
Persian standards, horse-tail banners, and keys of fortresses. The altar-
cross dates from the time of Alexis Mikháilovitch, father of Peter the
Great. By the wall, to the left of the ikonostás, is a silver chalice presented to Count Ostermann-Tolstói by the Bohemians, and bearing the
names of the Russian staff-officers killed at Kulm. To the left of the
high-altar are the uniforms of Alexander I. and Nicholas I.; to the right
are the last uniform of Alexander II. and the sword which he wore at
the time of his assassination. Adjacent are the uniform of Alexander III.
and other relics of the same kind.

We now retrace our steps and follow the Panteléimonskaya, on
the right side of which, beyond the Litéini Prospékt, is the *Church
of St. Pantaleon the Martyr* (Церковь Святáго Пантелеймóна;
Pl. 61, G 5, *II*), built of wood by Peter the Great in 1722, and rebuilt
in stone in 1764. — Summer Garden, see p. 116.

A little to the N. of the church, at Solyanói Perculok 95, is the
Stieglitz Drawing School, built in 1881. Adjacent is the **Stieglitz
Museum of Industrial Art** (Pl. G, 5; *II*), built in the Renaissance style from plans by Mesmacher (1896). The collections are
extensive but include comparatively few Russian products (adm.,
see p. 98; Director, E. I. Gruzhévski).

GROUND FLOOR. To the right is the *Antiquarian Room*, with Egyptian,
Greek, and Roman antiquities, and clay vessels found by Schliemann in
Hissarlik. — The corridors contain textile fabrics of the 4-6th cent., and
Byzantine and Roman antiquities. — In the right wing are Oriental carpets,
objects of copper, and so forth. — The left wing contains wood-carvings,
carpets, furniture, and Russian antiquities.

FIRST FLOOR. In the middle is the *Venetian Room*, containing a
large jasper vase, five large paintings by J. B. Tiepolo, MSS., and miniatures (15-16th cent.). The *Lecture Hall* is hung with Flemish tapestry
representing the Four Seasons (16th cent.). To the right is the *Furnese
Room*, with Limoges enamels. — Right Wing. The so-called *Loggie of*

Raphael, round the light-well, contain Delft and other porcelain, an ebony cabinet (French, 16th cent.), and Gobelins tapestry representing the Elements, after drawings by Claude Audran. *Room of Henry II.*, with Hispano-Moresque and Urbino majolica, and Persian porcelain (15-17th cent.). *Room of Louis XIII.*, with majolica from Pesaro, Deruto, Faenza, and Castelli, and works by Bernard Palissy. *Room of Louis XIV.*, with Gobelins tapestry, Chinese, Meissen, and Sèvres porcelain, and fine French furniture of the 17-18th centuries. — Left Wing. Venetian, Bohemian, Spanish, and German glass. The *Flemish Room* contains pottery.

Adjoining the museum on the N., at Fontánka 10, is the huge building of the former SALT WAREHOUSE (Соляно́й городо́къ). This now contains the *Museum of Education* (entrance, Panteléimonskaya 2; adm., see p. 97; Director, Major-General S. A. Makshéyev), the *Museum of the Imperial Technical Society* (adm., see p. 98; Director, I. Popóv), the *Kustarni Museum* or Museum of Home Industries (entr., Solyanói Pereúlok 9; adm., see p. 97; Director, Y. P. Dyágilev), and the extensive *Imperial Museum of Agriculture* (Се́льско-хозя́йственный музе́й; entr., Rúinotchnaya 1; adm., see p. 97; Director, V. D. Bátyushkov). — Farther to the N., Fontánka 6, is the *Law School* (Учи́лище Правове́дѣнія; Pl. G 4, *II*), established in 1835 by Prince Peter of Oldenburg, and open only to the sons of the noblesse (330 pupils).

We now return through the Sérgiyevskaya to the Litéini Prospékt. To the right, at the corner, is the *Cathedral of St. Sergius* (Pl. G, 4; *II*), built in 1800 by Demirtzov. Opposite, with its main façade turned towards the Litéini Prospékt, is the building of the *Artillery Headquarters*, erected in 1808. In front of it are 20 old cannon. To the right, at the corner of the Litéini Prospékt and the Zakháryevskaya, is the *District Court* (Окружно́й Судъ), a large detached quadrangle of three stories, erected by Bazhénov in 1770 as an arsenal, with a handsome portal facing the Litéini Prospékt. — A little to the S., in the Furshtátskaya (Pl. G, H, 4; *II*), is the *United States Embassy* (No. 34; p. 93).

Between the Furshtátskaya and the Kirotchnaya is the Lutheran *Church of St. Anne* (Pl. G, 4; *II*), built in 1779 by Velten, and surmounted by a dome. Adjacent, to the W., is the large *Army and Navy Club* (Pl. G, 5; *II*), completed in 1898.

From the District Court we proceed to the E. along the Shpalérnaya. On the right (No. 45) is the building of the **Imperial Duma** (Госуда́рственная Ду́ма; Pl. I 4, *II*). This was once the *Tauride Palace*, built by Starov in 1783, by order of Catherine II., and, presented after the conquest of the Crimea, to Potyómkin (Potemkin), the 'Hero of Tauris'. After his death in 1791, the palace was resumed by the Crown. Since 1906 it has been used by the imperial Duma, which held its first sitting in the palace on April 27th (May 10th) of that year. The interior may be visited on presentation of passport. From the entrance-hall we pass into the Round Room (Кру́глій залъ), where there is a bust of Alexander II. Beyond this are the Catherine Room, the old ball-room, now used as a Salle des Pas Perdus, and the Hall of Session (444 seats), formerly a winter garden. — To the S. of the Duma lies the *Tauric Garden* (Tavrítcheski Sad); the S. part of it is open to the public (entrances in the Potyómkinskaya and Kírotchnaya).

To the S. of the Tauric Garden, at Kírotchnaya 41 d, is the **Suvórov Museum** (Сувóровскій музéй; Pl. I 5, *II;* adm., see p. 98), built from the plans of Von Hohen in 1904. The exterior is adorned with two mosaic pictures, that on the right representing Suvórov's departure for the Italian campaign, and that on the left his crossing of the Alps. Inside are five rooms containing relics of Field-Marshal Prince A. V. Suvórov (1720-1800) and his time. Farther to the S. is the *Suvórov Church,* transferred hither in 1900 from the village of Kontchánskoye, where the Field-Marshal often attended the services. To the S. of the church is a bronze bust of Suvórov on a lofty granite pedestal. The *Nicholas Military Academy* (Николáевская Воéнная Акадéмія; Pl. H, I, 5, *II*), at Suvórovski Prospékt 32, was built from the plans of Von Hohen in 1901.

To the N. of the Duma are the *Municipal Water Works* (Pl. I, 4; *II*). Farther to the E. in the Shpalérnaya are the *Araktchéyev Barracks* (Pl. 18, I 4; *I*) and the extensive buildings of the Smolni Convent.

The **Smolni Convent** (Смóльный монастырь; Pl. I, K, 4, *I*) was begun in 1748 as a nunnery for orphan girls by the Empress Elizabeth on the site of a palace of Peter the Great. In 1764 Catherine II. added a school for girls. The Empress Marie, consort of Paul I., further enlarged the institute in 1797. Connected with the convent is a Home for Widow Ladies.

The convent is separated from the Catherine Square by a tasteful railing. The five domes of its main church, the *CATHEDRAL OF THE RESURRECTION (Собóръ Воскресéнія Христóва всѣхъ учéбныхъ заведéній; Pl. 34, K 4, *I*), built in 1744-57 by Rastrelli, are visible from all points of the town.

The INTERIOR, which was completed in 1835 by Stasov, is severely simple, but very effective. The prevailing colours are white and gold; the floor, however, is of gray marble, and the steps leading to the three altars are of yellow Ural marble. The altars are enclosed by crystal balustrades. The pictures are all modern. The most conspicuous, both in size (20 ft. high) and quality, is the Resurrection by E. Jacobs over the high-altar (1834). The Apparition of the Virgin by Venetziánov also deserves mention. All the ecclesiastical vessels are of massive silver, including a tabernacle in the form of the Ark of the Covenant, borne by 56 jasper columns.

Those who wish to return from the Smolni Convent to the Nevski may use either the tramway (4, 13, or 14) or the steamboat.

To the S. of the convent is the *Peter the Great Bridge* (Pl. K, 5; *I*), completed in 1911. It is 1065 ft. long and 75 ft. wide.

g. Moscow, Narva, and Alexander Nevski Quarters.

Izmáilov Cathedral. Alexander Nevski Monastery.

Tramways (pp. 91, 92) in the Moscow Quarter, Nos. 9, 11, 15, 16; in the Narva Quarter, Nos. 3, 8, 9, 11, 16; in the Alexander Nevski Quarter. Steam Tramway No. 1 (p. 92). — *Steamers* ply on the Fontánka (see p. 92).

The second cross-street on the right in the Nevski beyond the Anitchkov Bridge (p. 107) is the VLADÍMIR PROSPÉKT (Pl. G, 6; *II*), which leads to the *Church of the Vladímir Mother of God* (Pl. G, 6; *II*), a white building with five gilded domes and a handsome bell-tower, constructed in 1761-85 by Rastrelli (?).

Farther on we follow the ZÁGORODNI PROSPÉKT to the S.W., passing (on the right) the *Empress Marie Alexándrovna's School for Girls* (Pl. 167, G 6; *I*). To the left lies the *Semyónovski Square* (Семёновскiй плацъ; Pl. F, G, 7, *I*), with a *Trotting Track* (p. 95), and the *Station of the Tzarskoye Selo Railway* (Pl. F, 7; *I*).

Proceeding to the W. from the Tzarskoye Selo station we reach the Obúkhov City Hospital (Городскáя Обýховская больнúца; Pl. 87, F 7, *I*), founded by Catherine II. in 1780, and adorned with a bronze bust of the empress on the side next the Fontánka. Farther to the W., in the Zabalkánski Prospékt, is the *Constantine Artillery School* (Pl. 153; F, 7).

At the corner of the Zágorodni Prospékt and the Zabalkánski Prospékt, to the right, is the *Technological Institute* (Техно-логúческiй Инститýтъ; Pl. F 7, *I*), founded in 1828.

Turning to the left into the ZABALKÁNSKI PROSPÉKT (tramway 11), we notice on the right the building of the *Civil Engineers* (Инститýтъ гражданскихъ инженéровъ; Pl. 100, F 7, *I*), while a little farther on, on the same side, is that of the *Imperial Agricultural Society* (Импе-ráторское Вóльное Экономúческое Óбщество; Pl. 10, F 7, *I*). Beyond the Novo-Moskóvski Bridge crossing the Obvódni Canal, to the right, are the *Cattle Yards* (Скотопригóнный Дворъ; Pl. E, F, 8, *I*), the main entrance of which is adorned with two colossal bronze oxen by Demut-Malinóvski (adm. upon application at the office; best time about 10 a.m.). To the left is the large *Novo-Dyevítchi Nunnery* (Pl. F, 9; *I*), built by Yefímov in 1845-61. — Beyond the Tzarskosélski Bridge, about 2 M. from the Obúkhov Hospital, is the Moscow Triumphal Arch (Москóвскiя Трiумфáльныя ворóта; Pl. F 9, *I*), erected from Stasov's plans in 1833-38. Twelve cast-iron Doric columns, each 4½ ft. in diameter and 75 ft. in height, support a cornice adorned with trophies and twelve genii in relief by Orlóvski. The inscriptions commemorate the campaigns of 1826-31 in Persia, Turkey, and Poland. The gate has five separate openings.

From the W. end of the Zágorodni Prospékt the Pérvaya Rota leads to the W., passing on the right the Roman Catholic *Cathedral of the Assumption*, and ending at the TRÓITZKAYA SQUARE. Here stands the white **Izmáilov Cathedral**, also known as the *Tróitzki* or *Trinity Cathedral* (Трóицкiй Собóръ; Pl. 33, E 7, *I*), erected in 1827-35, from the designs of Stasov, by the Empress Marie, widow of Paul I. Its five domes, painted blue and sprinkled with stars, are visible far and wide; that in the centre is 260 ft. high. The cathedral occupies the site of a wooden chapel in which, according to tradition, Peter the Great was married on a November night in 1707 to Catherine, the future empress.

The INTERIOR of the church is lighted solely from the domes. The ikonostás is adorned with costly pictures of saints; the high-altar of the Holy Trinity is marked by fine workmanship and elaborate gilding. The visitor should also notice the tabernacle, which is ornamented with crystal, and the bronze lustre in the centre, containing 300 candles. On the walls to the right and left of the high-altar are marble tablets bearing the names of officers of the Izmáilov Guards, who had fallen in battle prior to the consecration of the church.

In the square to the E. of the cathedral rises the **Monument of Fame** (Памятникъ славы), 89 ft. high, erected in 1886 from the designs of *Grimm*. A base of Finnish granite supports a cast-iron Corinthian column, the flutes of which contain five rows of captured cannon. At the top is a bronze Victory. At the base are four huge bronze tablets recounting the chief events in the war of 1877-78 and naming the regiments of Guards which took part in it. Ten captured guns form a semicircle round the monument.

To the S. of the Tróitzkaya Square is the NICHOLAS CAVALRY SCHOOL (Pl. E, 8; *I*), in which is the *Lérmontov Museum*, with autographs and other reminiscences of the poet; the garden is to contain a bronze figure of Lérmontov, by Mikéshin. Beyond the Obvódni Canal are the *Warsaw Railway Station* (Pl. E, 8; *I*) and the *Baltic Railway Station* (Pl. E, 8; *I*).

The WEST PART OF THE NARVA QUARTER offers little of interest. No. 144 in the Fontánka is the *Government Printing Office* (Экспедиція заготовленія государственныхъ бумагъ; Pl. 147, D 7, *I*), in which banknotes and public documents are produced. It employs 3700 workmen and may be visited by permission of the director.—In the Narva Square stands the **Narva Triumphal Arch** (Нáрвскія Тріумфáльныя ворóта; Pl. C, D, 9, *I*), built of granite in 1814 by Quarenghi to commemorate the victories of the Russian Guard in 1812-14 and altered in 1834 by Stasov. To the right and left of the archway are two warriors in old Russian dress, holding garlands; on the platform is a Victory in a chariot with six horses, by Baron Klodt; on each side of the attic are four genii with wreaths of laurel.—To the W. of this point lies the *Yekaterinhóf* (Екатерингóфъ; Pl. C 8, *I*), a wooden palace built under Peter the Great in 1703, and named in honour of his wife. The neglected garden contains a popular theatre.—In the Estlyánskaya (Pl. C, 7, 8; *I*), to the N. of the Yeka-terinhof, is the *Kalinkin Brewery* (Wm. Miller & Co.), the largest in Russia. On the *Gutúyev Island* (Pl. A-C, 8, 9; *I*) are the DOCKS and the *Chief Custom House* (Pl. C 8, *I*; comp. p. 166). The *Sea Canal* (Морскóй канáлъ), 17 M. long and 26 ft. deep, leads hence (at a distance of 2¹/₂-3 M. from the S. coast) to the roads of Cronstadt. It was constructed in 1875-88 at an outlay of 10 million rubles. On the mole of Gutúyev Island is a granite obelisk 43 ft. high, bearing inscriptions relating to this canal.

To the E. of the Vladimir Prospékt (p. 128) the Púshkinskaya runs S. from the Nevski Prospékt. It contains a *Bronze Statue of Pushkin* (1799-1837; Pl. H 6, *II*), by Opekúshin.

To the N. of the Známenskaya Square (p. 107) are the *Greek Church of St. Demetrius* (Грéческая цéрковь Святáго Димитрія; Pl. H 5, *II*), an edifice in the Byzantine style by Kuzmin (1865), and the imposing *Pro-testant Women's Hospital* (Pl. H, 5; *II*), with its towers and pinnacles. To the S.E. of the Známenskaya Square, at the corner of the Poltávskaya and Mirgorodskáya (Pl. H, 6; *I*), is the *Romanov Church*, built in the ancient Rostov style from the designs of S. S. Kritchinski in 1914; it commemorates the tercentenary of the Romanov dynasty.

From the Ligovskaya, just to the N. of the Známenskaya Square, a steam-tramway (No. 1) runs S.E. along the Nevski to the —

Alexander Nevski Monastery (Алекса́ндро - Не́вская Тро́ицкая Ла́вра; Pl. I 7, *I*), the seat of the Metropolitan of St. Petersburg and the third in importance of the so-called *Lavras*†. It is of great extent, including twelve churches and several chapels, all enclosed by walls and moats. According to tradition, the monastery stands upon the spot where the Grand-Prince Alexander (1218-53) won a great victory over the Swedes and the Knights of the Teutonic Order on July 15th, 1241 (hence the name Nevski, *i.e.* 'of the Nevá'). Peter the Great, in order to lend his new capital the prestige of a national sanctuary, built a church here (1713), brought the relics of St. Alexander Nevski all the way from Vladimir (1724), and endowed it with large estates and revenues, which now bring in an annual income of more than 500,000 rubles.

The first church of the monastery is the *Cathedral of the Trinity* (Свя́то-Тро́ицкій Собо́ръ), begun by Peter in 1724 and remodelled in 1776-90, when the dome (after plans by Starov) and the two rectangular towers were added.

In the interior, to the right of the marble ikonostás, is a *Reliquary*, containing the bones of St. Alexander Nevski and adorned with reliefs from the life of the saint. Over this is a canopy, borne by slender silver columns and supporting a cushion with the imperial regalia. The silver wall behind is elaborately adorned with sculptures. In 1752 the Empress Elizabeth devoted the first year's produce of the Koluiván silver-mines, amounting to 90 puds (3250 lbs.), towards the cost of this work. In front of the catafalque stands a reading-desk with a reliquary and a candelabrum, all made of silver and presented by Alexander I. in 1806. Among the paintings are an Annunciation by Raphael Mengs (behind the ikonostás) and a few copies of Rubens, Van Dyck, and others. The treasury (seldom shown) contains a large number of valuable objects.

Immediately to the left of the bridge is the *Church of the Annunciation* (Це́рковь Благове́щенія Пресвяты́я Богоро́дицы), the crypt of which contains the tombs of several members of the imperial house and other eminent Russian families. In the choir, in front of the third window to the left of the ikonostás, is the tomb of Field-Marshal Suvórov (d. 1800), a marble slab bearing the simple inscription selected by himself 'Здѣсь лежи́тъ Суво́ровъ' ('Here lies Suvórov'). — In the S.W. tower of the Lavra is a *Collection of Ecclesiastical Antiquities* (Дре́влехрани́лище; Pl. Dr.), shown on Tues. and Thurs., 2-4.30, and on Sun. and holidays, 2-5.30.

The churchyards of the convent contain the graves of numerous members of the Russian aristocracy, poets, and other celebrities. These

---

† Lavra is the name for those convents of the first class which are also seats of Metropolitans and contain theological academies. There are four lavras in Russia: that of Kiev (p. 380), the Tróitzkaya Convent of St. Sergius (p. 325), the Alexander Nevski Monastery, and the Potcháyevskaya Convent (p. 375). St. Saba in Jerusalem and the Monasteries on Mt. Athos and Mt. Sinai also claim the rank of Lavra.

burial-places are very expensive, but the monuments are often neglected and not always in the best taste. — The LAZARUS CHURCHYARD (Лáзаревское клáдбище; Pl. L.) lies on the left as we enter the precincts of the convent. Proceeding in a straight direction from the entrance, and then turning to the left at the chapel, we reach (on the right) in about 30 paces, at a point where the path forks, the grave of *Lomonósov* (1711-75), the founder of modern Russian literature. Following the plank path to the left for about 45 paces more, we see to the left the white marble slab on the grave of *Vizin* (1744-92), the writer of comedies. — The TÍKHVINSKOE CHURCHYARD (Тúхвинское клáдбище; Pl. T.) lies on the right of the entrance to the monastery. Immediately to the left of its entrance, on its main avenue, lies *Glinka* the composer (1804-57; comp. p. 123); farther on, also to the left, is the grave of *Kruilóv* (p. 117). The first path to the right of the entrance leads in a few paces to the tomb (left) of the historian *Karamzin* (1766-1826); opposite, on the right, is that of the author *Dostoyévski* (1821-81), behind which is that of the poet *Zhukovski* (1783-1852). The fourth path to the right, leading from the main avenue to the wall and then turning to the left, brings us to the tomb of the composer *Tchaikóvski* (1840-93; right). — The NICHOLAS CHURCHYARD (Никóльское клáдбище; Pl. N.; entr. behind the apse of the cathedral) contains the grave of the composer *Anton Rubinstein* (1829-94; comp. p. 123). To reach it we pass the mortuary chapel (left), go straight on, and turn to the right into the last walk but one.

Connected with the monastery are the *Imperial Theological Academy* (Императóрская Духóвная Акадéмія; Pl. 1, I 7, *I*), attended by 280 students, and an *Ecclesiastical Seminary* (Pl. 175).

About 1¼ M. to the S.W. of the Alexander Nevski Monastery is the *Vólkovo Cemetery* (Вóлковское клáдбище; Pl. H, 8, 9, *I*), containing the tomb of the novelist Ivśn Turgényev (1818-83).

h. Hermitage.

The **Hermitage** (Императóрскій Эрмитáжъ; Pl. F 5, *II*), Milliónnaya 35, is connected with the Winter Palace by the First Hermitage of Empress Catherine II. It forms a rectangle 170 yds. long and 124 yds. wide, with three courts, and contains the chief imperial art collections. The building, the interior of which is richly fitted up, has two chief façades, that on the N. being turned towards the Nevá, that on the S. towards the Milliónnaya. The latter has a portico of eight pillars, against which rest ten Atlantes of dark grey granite, 19¹/₂ ft. high. On either side of the portico are niches with zinc statues of famous artists, and on the side-façades are groups, representing Art fostered by the State and the Church.

In 1765 Catherine II. caused a two-storied building to be erected beside the Winter Palace by *Vallin de la Mothe*. This was at first called the 'Small Winter Palace', but its name was afterwards changed to FIRST HERMITAGE OF EMPRESS CATHERINE II., or the PAVILION HERMITAGE. It was connected by a still extant flying-bridge with the apartments occupied by the Empress, and contained three picture galleries. In 1775 *Velten*, the Director of the Imperial Academy, completed the enlargement of the so-called OLD HERMITAGE, and *Giacomo Quarenghi* of Bergamo added the Loggia Gallery (now the Raphael Gallery) in 1778-87. In 1840 Tzar Nicholas I. undertook a complete reconstruction and enlargement of the whole building; and the present pseudo-classical structure, from plans by *Leo von Klenze* (d. 1864), of Munich, and the court architect, *A. I. Stakenschneider* (d. 1865), was the result. It was completed in 1852.

ARRANGEMENT OF THE COLLECTIONS. *Ground Floor:* 1. Egyptian and Assyrian Antiquities; 2. Antique Sculptures; 3. Antiquities from Kertch; 4. Vases, Bronzes, Terracottas; 5. Drawings and Engravings; 6. Scythian and Siberian Antiquities; 7. Mediæval and Renaissance Collection. — *First Floor:* 1. Picture Gallery; 2. Collection of Coins; 3. Gems and Miniatures; 4. Gems and Ornaments; 5. Collection of Silver and Porcelain (in the First Hermitage of Catherine II.). The Old Hermitage, the Románov Gallery, the Marble Hall, and the Winter Garden can be entered only from the Winter Palace (comp. p. 112).

ADMISSION, see p. 97. — The ENTRANCE is in the Milliónnaya. — CATALOGUES on sale at the head of the staircase.

Director, *Count D. I. Tolstói.* — Chief Curator of Antiquities, *E. Pridik;* Curators, *O. Waldhauer, V. Goleníshtchev.* — Curators of the Picture Gallery, *E. von Liphart* (Chief Curator), *B. Veselovski, K. Iskerski, J. von Schmidt, Baron von Koskull.* — Chief Curator of the Collection of Coins, *A. von Markov;* Curator, *O. Retovski.* — Chief Curators of the Mediæval and Renaissance Collections, *E. von Lenz, I. Smirnóv.* — Chief Curator of Gems, Ornaments, Silver, and Porcelain, *Baron A. Völkersam.*

GROUND FLOOR.

The VESTIBULE is embellished with 16 columns of brown Finnish granite with marble capitals, two beautiful candelabra of manganite (орлецъ), and a vase of rare Finnish granite (grey with pink specks). A broad staircase faces the entrance and leads up to the first floor (p. 144). From the vestibule we turn to the left into —

ROOM 1. **Egyptian and Assyrian Antiquities.** The Egyptian Section consists mainly of the collections of Count Castiglione and of the Turkish ambassador Khalil-Bey. The Inventaire de la collection égyptienne (1891; 1 rb.) and the Description of the Assyrian Monuments (1897; in Russian; 25 cop.) are both by V. Goleníshtchev.

To the left of the entrance stands a sarcophagus of black granite which (according to the inscription) contained the mummy of *Ahmes* (Amasis; 31st Dyn.), the commander of the archers. By the first pillar to the left, No. 149, Granite statue of the lion-headed *Sekhmet*, of the time of Amenhotep III. (16th cent. B. C.). 729. Seated granite figure of *Amenemhȇt III.* (ca. 2300 B. C.), the builder of the Labyrinth; the projecting cheek-bones recall those of the so-called Hyksos statues. Pink granite sarcophagus of *Nana*, High Priest of Ptah in Memphis (20th Dyn.); behind, 769. Square wooden coffin of *Ata*, a woman of the 12th Dynasty. Farther on, 738. Kneeling statue of *Amenemnan*, a high official of the time of Ramses II. (14th cent. B. C.), with sacrificial table. 740. Granite group of a man sitting between his mother (l.) and his wife (r.). Sarcophagus of *Queen Nekht-Sebast-er-ro-u*, mother of Ahmes (see above); the names on her sarcophagus and on that of her son were partly effaced at the time of the Persian invasion. — Wall Cases 1-3, Figures of Egyptian gods; Case 4, Holy animals; Case 5, Small statuettes and household articles; Case 6, Vases and terracottas. In the lower portions of the cases are statuettes of the dead. — Below the windows, *Stelae* of limestone. To the right of the entrance, Painted wooden coffins and fragments of *Papyri*. Here also are glass-cases containing *Scarabs*, rings, and other small objects.

The *Assyrian Bas-Reliefs* (9th cent.) on the end-walls come from Nimrud and Khorsabad. To the left of the entrance, King Ashur-nasir-pal; behind him

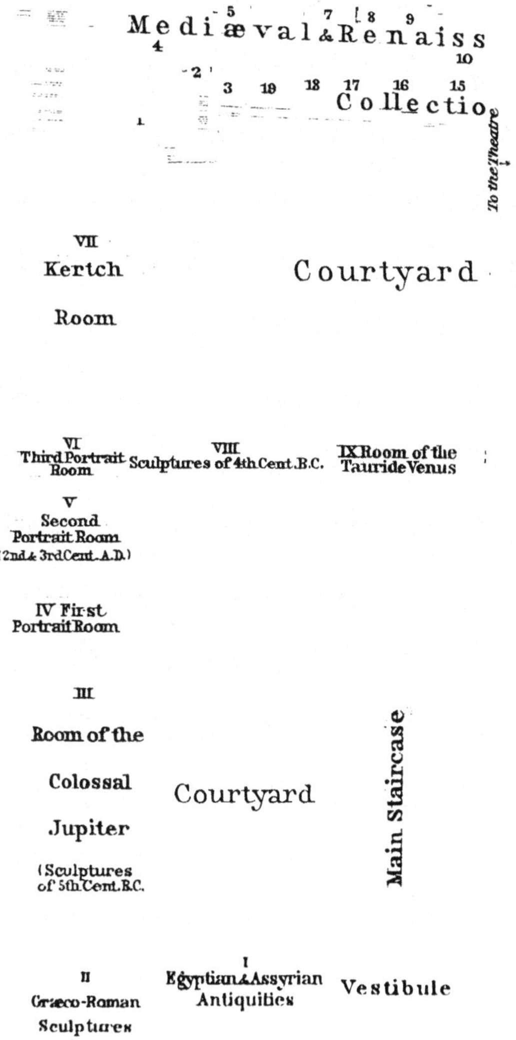

Mediæval & Renaiss Collectio

5 7 |8 9
4
-2 ' 10
3 19 18 17 16 15
1

To the Theatre

VII
Kertch
Room

Courtyard

VI
Third Portrait
Room
VIII
Sculptures of 4th Cent. B.C.
IX Room of the
Tauride Venus

V
Second
Portrait Room
(2nd & 3rd Cent. A.D.)

IV First
Portrait Room

III

Room of the

Colossal

Jupiter

(Sculptures
of 5th Cent. B.C.

Courtyard

Main Staircase

II
Græco-Roman
Sculptures

I
Egyptian & Assyrian
Antiquities

Vestibule

HERMITAGE (GROUN

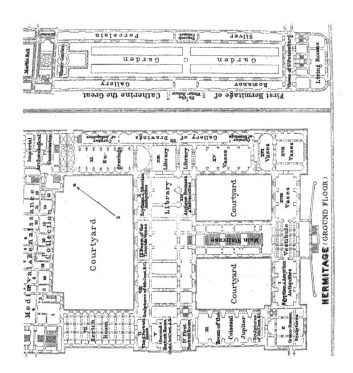

HERMITAGE (GROUND FLOOR)

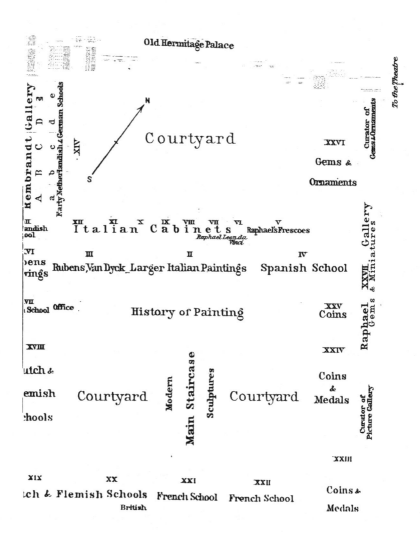

Old Hermitage Palace

Courtyard

N

S

XIV

XXVI

Gems &

Ornaments

Curator of Gems & Ornaments

To the Theatre

Rembrandt Gallery

A B C D E

a b c d e

F. arly Nether landish & German Schools

II.
andish
ool

XII   XI   X   IX   VIII   VII   VI
I t a l i a n   C a b i n e t s

V
Raphael's Frescoes

Gallery & Miniatures

Raphael Leon. da
Vinci

.VI
oens
vings

III   II

Rubens, Van Dyck – Larger Italian Paintings

IV

Spanish School

XXVII

VII
School   Office

History of Painting

XXV
Coins

Raphael   Gems

XVIII

XXIV

utch &
emish
chools

Courtyard

Modern
Sculptures

Main Staircase

Courtyard

Coins
&
Medals

Curator of Picture Gallery

XXIII

XIX   XX   XXI   XXII

ch & Flemish Schools   French School   French School

British

Coins &

Medals

HERMITAGE (FIRST FLOOR

a winged god. To the right, Assyrian warriors and priests from Khorsabad; between these, god with eagle's head (Nimrud). — On the exit-wall: Two bas-reliefs, representing winged gods (prototypes of the Cherubim and Seraphim), of grey alabaster blackened with fire; near them, Tomb-relief from Palmyra. On the left side-wall are four stone slabs with texts in cuneiform characters from the palace of Sargon II. at Khorsabad.

The next seven rooms contain the **Greek and Roman Sculptures.** This collection dates from the time of Peter the Great, who bought the Tauride Venus at Rome in 1718. Under Catherine II. were added the Shuválov and Lyde-Browne collections (the latter bought in 1787 for 23,000*l.*). Nicholas I. also made valuable additions (Demidov and Laval collections), and in 1861, under Alexander II., 78 pieces of sculpture were bought from the Campana Gallery in Rome. The most recent acquisitions came from the Galítzuin (p. 145) and Bludov collections. — The collection was renumbered in 1911; each work is labelled both in Russian and French. With the old illustrated catalogue (in Russian; 2 rb.), by G. von Kieseritzki, a list of the new numbers is supplied. New Russian catalogue by O. Waldhauer, without illustrations (1912), 80 cop.

II. ROOM OF HELLENISTIC AND ROMAN DECORATIVE SCULPTURES. — *Statues:* In the centre, 1. Aura (Goddess of the air) on a swan. To the left, in front of the middle window, 22. Statuette of a Satyr, a fine Roman work after a Hellenistic original. By the first pier, 15. Dancing Satyr. By the first column, 18. Herdsman. Between the columns, 21. Torso of a reclining hero, with a head belonging to a statue of Poseidon. By the second column, 23. Silenus. By the second pier, 26. Dancing Satyr, probably a companion-piece to No. 15. By the third window on the left, 7. Sleeping Silenus, from a fountain. — *Heads.* To the left, in front of the middle window, 72. Dionysus; in the window-niche to the right, *74. Zeus, with tragic expression; in front of the third window to the left, 76. Pan, from Pompeii(?), apparently an Alexandrine work.

III. FIFTH CENTURY ROOM, or ROOM OF THE COLOSSAL JUPITER. — *Statues.* To the right of the entrance, 94. Æsculapius (second half of 5th cent.); to the left, 95. Athena without the ægis (head from another statue; middle of 5th cent.). At the pier, 96. Statuette of Hercules; 97. Athlete resting, in the style of Polyclitus; 98. Athena Campana (middle of 5th cent; head modern); 100. Torso of a youth (beginning of 5th cent.); 101. Colossal statue of Jupiter (Roman); *102. Eros Soranzo, originally a victorious athlete (Pythagoras; 5th cent.); 103. Aphrodite, a variation of the statue by Alcamenes (end of 5th cent.); 104. Hermes, in the style of Polyclitus; 105. Early Hellenistic Dionysus. In the centre, 118. Suppliant Woman, a replica of the Barberini figure in Rome; to the left of the entrance, Caryatide. — *Heads.* In the centre, 141. Hermes, by Alcamenes the Elder; at the end of the same row, *143. Portrait (of the first half of the 5th cent.); at the beginning, 140. Head of the Westmacott Athlete (Polyclitus). — In the last niche, to the right, 377. Late-Roman sarcophagus, with figures of Hippolytus and Phædra. On the exit-wall, to the right, *352. Niobid Relief, a copy of a work of the 5th cent., of the school of Phidias; to the left, 333. Attic tombstone (5th cent.); near it, 371. Odysseus slaying the Suitors; *332. Tombstone of Philostrate (5th cent.); in front of the last, a head (Cyprus; 5th cent.), in limestone.

IV. FIRST PORTRAIT ROOM. At the window, 170. Socrates, 171. Demosthenes (in neither case does the body belong to the head); 182, 183. Scipio the Elder. To the right of the entrance, 133. Augustus as Jupiter. Mosaic Pavement, Hylas and the Nymphs.

V. Second Portrait Room (2nd and 3rd centuries A.D.). To the left, at the window, Princes of the Antonine period. To the right, Statues: 202. Augustus; ?201. Statue with restored head of Hadrian; 200. Marcus Aurelius. -- In the centre, large modern vase of green Ural porphyry.

VI. Third Portrait Room. By the window-wall, to the left, 245. Vespasian. 248. Titus; on the table in front, Children's heads of the time of Augustus. etc. To the right and left of the door to R. VIII, 249, 250. Heads of Dacians. On the wall adjoining R. VII, *List of Customs Dues of Palmyra* (137 A.D.), on a slab of marble, 21 ft. long and 5 ft. high, with Greek and Aramaic inscription. — Here we leave the Kertch Room (VII; see below) on the left and turn to the right into R. VIII.

VIII. Fourth Century Room. — *Statues* (beginning at the second niche). 271, 272. Figures of the Athena type, beginning of 4th cent. (Timotheus?); 275. Eros stretching his bow (Lysippus?); 276. Leda, by Timotheus(?); 279. Satyr pouring out wine, by Praxiteles; 278. Torso of the Leaning Satyr, by Praxiteles. To the left and right of the door to R. IX: Two statues of the same type. By the piers, 269. Dionysus; 274. Hercules (middle of 4th cent.); 277. Apollo. — *Heads.* In the middle niche, *299. Artemis, by Praxiteles; in the last niche on the right, *302. Sappho.

IX. Room of the Tauride Venus. — *Statues.* 314. Woman carrying water (from a fountain); *315. Tauride or Tauric Venus, a replica of the so-called Venus de Medici in Florence, and named after the Tauride Palace, in which it was first placed; 316. Apollo, of a Hellenistic type. — Cabinets 54, 55, 58-64, and 67-73, at the piers opposite the windows, contain *Ancient Glass*, one of the best collections of the kind in wealth of form and colour, chiefly found in S. Russia (1500 pieces). Of the so-called 'Phœnician' Thread Glass, in the Egyptian style, all three types (Alabastron, Amphoriskos, and Oinochoë) are exceedingly well represented, and the selection of coloured glass beads has hardly its equal anywhere. Especially noteworthy are the 15 vases of pink glass (Cab. 60, 4th row from bottom), the jugs, glasses, and dishes of blue glass (Cab. 61) and glass mosaic (Cab. 62), several glass bowls with handles all in one piece, the Murrina ware (Cab. 60, 4th row from bottom), a flat cup with a lid, bearing traces of a golden laurel wreath on a blue and red ground (Cab. 61, 3rd row), and the large plates in Cab. 61 (6th and 7th rows from bottom). — Cabinets 54 and 55 contain Pompeian and Syrian glass.

VII. **Kertch Room,** a large hall supported by 20 dark-grey granite columns, containing works of art and antiquities from the Cimmerian Bosphorus. This is the finest collection in the Hermitage; no other in the world possesses so many small specimens of Greek (especially Attic) work, many of them dating from the most flourishing period of art (5th and 4th cent. B.C.). The most valuable discoveries were made during excavations in the Crimea near Kertch, the ancient *Panticapaeum* (from 1831 onwards), and on the Asiatic side of the Straits of Kertch, on the peninsula of *Taman*, amid the ruins of *Phanagoria*, *Anapa*, etc. Other excavations were made among the ruins of the cities of Chersonesus and Olbia, and also at the mouth of the Don, on the site of ancient Tanaïs, and other places. The objects (amongst which are many of gold) are either of Greek origin, or are the work of Greek or native artists in the colonies. — The collection is to be re-arranged.

By the entrance-door are two large *Wooden Sarcophagi.* — We begin with the windows. Under each window is a glass-case, and in each window-niche are two tall cabinets, while opposite the windows are obelisks, glass-cases, tables, and columns.

I. Window. — *Case 9* (objects from the Kurgán or tumulus of Artyukhóv; 3rd cent.). Fine gold diadem, gold bangles, funeral wreaths, etc. Agate and granite necklaces; rings, earrings; bronze folding mirror with a representation of Scylla and traces of gilding; silver ladles; glass beads, knucklebones, etc.

Cab. 8. Terracotta masks and caricatures. — *Cab. 11.* Terracotta masks; below, Niobe and her children.

Column VII. Bronze-gilt hydria, containing ashes.

Obelisk. Silver articles. On the second glass-shelf, *575. Rhyton (drinking-horn) in the shape of a bull's head (murder of Polydorus, son of Priam, by Polymnestor, King of Thrace; Hecuba tearing out the eyes of Polymnestor). Above, 531. Cup with wild-boar hunt.

II. Window. — *Case 14* (Seven Brothers Tumuli, late 6th cent.; Ionian objects). Necklaces; rings. Deer, rams' heads, griffins, heads of Pallas (archaic), owls, and heads of river-gods, stamped in gold-leaf for sewing on garments; *Engraved vessels in silver-gilt.

Cab. 13. Terracottas; *575 B. Large silver drinking-horn ornamented with the head of a wild (bezoar) goat; gold rhyta (drinking-horns). — *Cab. 16.* Terracottas.

Column IX. Vase adorned with a relief representing the struggle between Poseidon and Pallas for the possession of Athens (4th cent.; a work inspired by the group on the pediment of the Parthenon).

Gilded Pyramid P. Rings, chains, and other gold jewellery especially from the Kurgán of Karagodeuakhsh.

III. Window. — *Case 19.* Various kinds of gold ornaments. Sword-handles studded with chalcedonies. Golden sword-hilt. Wooden articles, including a comb with an engraved but incomplete inscription (ἀδελφῆς δῶρον, a sister's gift). Paint-boxes, rouge-pots, etc.

Cab. 18. Terracottas. Children playing with cocks, dogs, and goats; children's toys. — *Cab. 21.* Objects taken from two graves at Elteghen (Nymphæum), 6-5th cent. B.C. On the lower shelves are silver objects, including a Kylix (No. 536), with a painting of Helios in his chariot.

Gilded Pyramid I. Gold ornaments: bracelets, brooches (for fastening robes at the shoulder), buckles, buttons, spiral bracelets, and earrings.

Column XI. Iron helmet, much oxydized, with silver ornaments.

IV. Window. — *Case 24.* *Gold ornaments for trimming dresses, in the form of heads of Medusa and Pallas, lotus-flowers, etc. Coins found with these objects prove that they belong to the time of Alexander the Great. Finely engraved ivory fragments. The objects in this case were found in three graves in the Great Bliznitza.

Cab. 23 and *26.* Terracotta figures.

Column XIII. *Vase, with coloured and gilt figures in relief (Persians hunting, figures of the legendary Arimaspians and their

9*

enemies the Griffins), the work of Xenophantes of Athens (a masterpiece of the 4th cent.).

Gilded Pyramid II. Necklaces; fine gold earrings.

V. Window. — *Case 28.* Gold articles (Kul-Oba Tumulus).
*Necklace with two Scythians on horseback. Two *Bracelets, each
with two sphinxes. Tablets with mounted Scythians, Pegasus, etc.
Scythian archers. *Fragments of ivory with fine engravings (Judg
ment of Paris, Pelops and Œnomaus, etc.).

Gilded Cabinet 27 (in the recess). Works in gold. *451. Vase
of electrum, decorated with figures of Scythians, one of whom is
binding up a comrade's foot, another extracting a tooth from his
companion, a third drawing a bow. Two beautiful silver-gilt vases,
with a frieze of animals and birds catching fish. Large dish ornamented with heads of Gorgons; the protuberance (omphalos) in the
centre served as a handle. Silver rhyton (drinking-horn). Gold
sword-sheath with a sea-horse and animal-figures. Greaves of gold
overlaid with iron.

Gilded Glass Cabinet 29 (opposite the last). *Large gold earrings with heads of Athene Parthenos (Pallas). Heads of Dionysus
(originally sewn on dresses). Mirror with gold handle. Recumbent
gold stag, with animal-figures in relief.

Wooden Stand XIX. *Bowl (Adorning of a bride).

Gilded Pyramid III. Gold ornaments. Gold and iron rings.
Section 5. *292 h. Chalcedony with gold ring (flying heron), a fine
work by Dexamenes of Chios (4th cent. B.C.). *294· Cornelian with
gold ring: two winged lions sejant, with crowned human heads. —
Sec. 6. *296· Chalcedony (Aphrodite) with gold chain, an excellent
work of the 4th cent.B.C. *295· Persian cornelian cylinder: below the
Ferver or tutelary genius we see the king wrestling with two winged
bulls with human heads. 328 a. Two large gold rings with heads
of Pallas (cut in stone). 299 a. Chalcedony on gold chain (head of
Medusa). — Sec. 7. Engraved gold rings. *246 b. Gold ring (Scythian
stringing his bow; by Athenades, 4th cent.). 245. Gold ring with
the inscription ψυχή ('dear soul'), others with χάρα ('greeting').

VI. Window. — *Case 32* (grave from the Great Bliznitza).
··Necklace, with goats and sheep, of finished workmanship. Two
gold diadems, representing coils of human hair. Gold plates: Goddess
of Victory, women on a griffin, panther, Mænads, Satyrs, etc. Textiles and boots from the Pávlovski Kurgán.

Cases 31 & 34. Earthenware figures.

Column XXII. *Amphora with gold ornaments (Birth of Bacchus,
Mission of Triptolemus).

Gilded Pyramid IV. Works in gold. Masks, lions, earrings
in the form of Cupids, heads of Kore (or Demeter), Sirens, heads of
lions, lynxes, etc.

VII. Window.— *Case 37.* Ornamentations of a wooden sarcophagus from Anapa (4th cent. B.C.), Nereids bringing arms to Achilles.

Cab. 36. Clay figures.— *Cab. 38* (partly covered). Beautiful earthenware vessels in the form of figures, coloured and gilded: *Sphinx; winged human figure with Krotala (rattles); *Venus rising from a shell; Atys. Below these, on the lowest shelf, *Vase with reliefs, from Kertch (Teucer with Tecmessa, his brother's wife Adonis, Aphrodite, Peitho) and a second similar vase from the same place (a copy of the vase at Column XIII).

Column XXVIII. Gold open-work helmet, of a rare dome-like shape. Two cups of ancient shape. Gold coin of Alexander the Great, found with the other objects.

Gilded Pyramid R. Rings and earrings. *Gold ornaments from Chersonesus (5-4th cent. B.C.).

VIII. Window. — *Case 42.* Bronze fish-hooks, scissors, strigils, keys, etc. Bronze folding-mirror with Dionysus and Ariadne.

Cab. 41. Bronze articles. Fine lion's head. Snake about to strike. Mirror, surgical instruments. Greaves.— *Cab. 44.* Bronze-gilt Phaleræ (horse-trappings); handle of a bronze amphora, with Medusa (6th cent.).

Obelisk. *Gold olive-branches and laurel wreaths. Golden head-dress in the form of a kalathos (Arimaspians fighting with Griffins).

IX. Window. — *Case 47* (grave from the Great Bliznitza). Fine necklace. Diadem in imitation of hair. Two bracelets, each adorned with two lionesses. Two pendants of a crown (Thetis with the arms of Achilles). — Female dancers, youthful heads of Hercules (for decorating costumes). Bronze lid of a mirror, with remnants of gilding (Aphrodite kissing Eros).

Cab. 46. Terracottas: caricatures.— *Cab. 49.* Terracottas, with representations of gods.

At the *End Wall,* opposite the entrance-door, stands a marble sarcophagus from Kertch (Achilles and the daughters of Lycomedes); the lid, with two recumbent figures, was found on the Taman Peninsula.— In front, limestone sarcophagus, found at Kertch, with paintings inside.

Between the columns on the left side of the room:

XXXIII. Amphora (Apollo Citharœdus). — *XXXI.* Bronze-gilt vase.— *XXIX.* Amphora.— *Tables XXIII-XXVI* (covered). Textiles.— *XX.* Panathenaic challenge-cup, decorated with races. — *Tables XIV-XVII* (covered). Interesting and very rare *Specimens of figured stuff with the inscription Ἰοκάστ, showing that the scenes refer to the myth of Œdipus.— *XVIII.* Bronze helmet with cheek-pieces.— *X.* Bronze greaves with heads of Medusa.— *VIII.* Amphora (Nessus and Dejaneira).

By the wall are gravestones from S. Russia. 93. Pedestal of a statue of Cybele, of the time of King Pairisades II. (284 B.C.). — *22 b. Statue, probably of an archon's wife, found in 1850 near Kertch, a beautiful work of the 1st cent. A.D. — *XXI. Sarcophagus of cypress-wood, with excellent figures of Apollo and Hera. — *127. Inscription in honour of Queen Dynamis, from the inhabitants of Agrippia (Phanagoria). — Two lions couchant with undeciphered inscriptions. — Ancient lion found in Kertch. Bronze couch and candelabra (one from the 6th cent. B.C.). — 83a. Grave formed of three limestone slabs, enclosing a cinerary urn of gilded bronze. — 22 a. Statue of an archon (magistrate), companion-figure to No. 22 b. (see above). — 88. Pedestal for two statues of Sanerges and Astara, of the time of King Pairisades I. — 27. Greek stele (tombstone).

From the Kertch Room we may enter the rooms containing the Mediæval and Renaissance Collection, a description of which will be found at the close of that of the other groundfloor collections (p. 141).

We return through the Sculpture Rooms to the Entrance Hall and enter four rooms on the right, which contain the valuable *Collection of Vases. Russian and German guide, by O. Waldhauer, 75 cop.

Room XVIII contains the earliest vases (down to the end of the 6th cent. B.C.). — To the right of the entrance, Shelves 2 & 3. Corinthian vases; Shelf 6. Oldest Attic vases; Shelf 7. Chalcidian vases; Shelf 8. Etruscan mixing-bowl (beginning of the 6th cent.); Shelves 9 & 10. Early black-figured Attic vases; Shelf 12 (on the right), Hydria, with Hercules and Triton (middle of 6th cent.); Shelf 14. Cratera (large mixing-bowl), with Hercules and Eurystheus; Shelf 15. Cups by the so-called 'Lesser Masters' (Attic); Shelf 19 (on the left), Achilles dragging the body of Hector round Troy; Shelf 23. Amphora (Sileni gathering grapes); Shelf 32 (in the middle), Hydria, with bridal procession of Zeus and Hera. — To the left, Shelves 51-62. Black-figured Etruscan vases; Shelf 41. Panathenaic amphora. — Down the middle of the room: at the two ends, Red Etruscan vases with stamped figures; in the centre, in two glass-cases, Vases from S. Russia (Case 1 from Olbia and district, and from the island of Berezán; Case 2 from Kertch and neighbourhood).

Room XVII. In the centre is the famous *Hydria (Ewer) of Cumae (4th cent. B.C.), 26 in. in height, found in 1853. The Eleusinian gods are represented in coloured relief, surrounded by Attic deities, who stood in close relationship to them. In the centre is a seated figure of Demeter (Ceres), conversing with her daughter Kore (Proserpine), who stands holding a torch, while between them is an altar on which the sacrificial flame is burning; to the left of Demeter are Dionysus, Triptolemus (in a car drawn by serpents), Hecate (?; upright, with torch), and Rhea (?; seated). The youth standing behind Kore, holding a pig, is supposed to be Eubuleus. Beyond him come Athena, Artemis (with two torches), and Aphrodite. — 349. Crater, with Orestes pursued by the Furies. 350. Apulian amphora, Triptolemus despatched by Demeter to disseminate a knowledge of agriculture. 355. Apollo and Marsyas. 406. Amphiaraus bidding farewell to his sons. 420. Orestes and Pylades received by Iphigeneia. 422. Priam begging for the dead body of Hector. 424. Hades, with the Danaïds and other figures. 523. Gigantomachia, Orestes in the Delphic Temple, Death of young Opheltes, the Seven before Thebes (the last two at the back). — Ancient floor from the Uvárov Basilica at Chersonesus (Sebastopol), a votive offering (according to an inscription near the pillar to the right of the entrance) of Malchus and his friends.

Room XVI. Vases from Lower Italy.

Room XV. To the left by the windows are red-figured Attic vases of the 5th cent., arranged in chronological order; to the right are vases from S. Italy. To the left, by the first window, is a psykter (cooling-vessel) with recumbent hetæræ by Euphronius. Cabs. 13 & 15. Attic vessels. Case 24. Drinking-horns in the shape of animals' heads. By the second window, to the left, pelike (small pot-like vase with two handles), with a man and three boys looking at a swallow, and inscriptions; to the right, below, dish with drinking and brawling scenes. Third niche, to the left, cratera, with Danaë and Perseus being confined in the chest; to the right below, in the middle, amphora with Hermes and Ganymede. By the last window, to the left, white attic lecythi; to the right, *Vases in the Phidian style. — In the middle of the room are cabinets with vases from S. Russia. Cab. 33. To the left, on the middle shelf (left & right), two vases with Paris and Helen; in the middle, high vase with a toilet-scene; to the left, pelike with Helen looking at the swan's egg; to the right, pelike with Dionysus on the panther. Below, in the middle, cratera with Apollo and Dionysus at Delphi. Cab. 30, in the middle, painted Hellenistic vases from Kertch (rare examples of black ware with coloured figures). Cab. 29. Hellenistic and Roman ware from Kertch, some of it with stamped reliefs.

The following room belongs to the *Archaeological Library* (Room XIII) and leads to the left into —

Room XIV. **Antique Bronzes, Silver Work, & Terracottas,** from the collections of Pizzati, Campana, Sabúrov, etc.

L. *Cab. 1.* Household articles, lamps, jewellery, etc. — *Cab. 2.* 96. Prochoos (ewer) of Pomponius Zoticus, found at Viterbo. Vases, household articles, etc. — *Cab. 3.* Smaller articles of jewellery, harness, and so on. — *Cab. 4.* *339. Silver rhyton in the form of a ram's head. *346. Silver rhyton with a horse's head. *347. Patera (sacrificial cup), Ajax carrying the dead body of Achilles. — *Cabs. 5, 12, & 19.* Earthenware lamps.

Cabs. 6 & 7. Bronze utensils, pots, and candelabra from Palestrina and Pompeii. — *Cab. 8.* *364. Etruscan silver-plated helmet, with inscription. Panoply of shields, breast-plates, and lances. — *Cab. 9.* Hatchets, locks, and hinges. — *Cab. 10.* Bronze animal-figures and utensils. — *Cab. 11.* *409. Mirror-cover, with female head, a fine piece of work. Gold jewellery from Italy, Greece, and Asia Minor.

Cabs. 13.-17. Small figures of gods and men; large shield, greaves, and lances; *423. Etruscan helmet, with three gold wreaths. — *Cab. 18.* Mirrors: *420. Eos with the dead body of Memnon. — *Cab. 20.* Small bronze figures. — On the cabinets are six bronze helmets.

In the centre of the room stands a *Glass Case*, with statuettes of gods, men, and animals. Above, to the left, *536 a. Bronze votive figure, inscribed Πολυκράτης ἀνέθηκε, a Greek work of the 6th cent. B.C., either representing the god to which it is dedicated (Apollo), or the typically idealized portrait of the donor. Below, *551. Satyr, found on the Don; *552. Large silver mirror; 553. Dionysus, with Christian inscriptions and monograms, found on the Don; Corinthian mirror with Aphrodite. — To the left and right of the glass-case, on stands: *373. Silver vase with gilding, with Centaurs (as handles), battle of Amazons, hunting-scenes, and Nereids (ca. 250 A.D.), found in Moldavia, on the bank of the Pruth; *431. Silver ewer, with Leda, Daphne, and Hylas, a fine work of the time of Augustus, found at the same place.

In the centre of the room, on stands: *123. Victor of chariot-race, lifesize bronze statue from Makri in Asia Minor; 388. Recumbent Etruscan with detachable necklace (from Perugia); 379 A. Cylindrical cist, with a Satyr and Mænads on the cover (from Palestrina); 437. Front part of a

Chimæra. Etruscan work. — On the end-wall is a case with *Silver Vessels from the province of Perm (Indian, Persian, and Sassanide). — Opposite the windows are three glass-cases containing terracotta lamps, arranged in chronological order.

Case 22. 338. Etruscan tripod, in the most archaic style, with the labours of Hercules. Above is a silver helmet, found in Moldavia. 547. Relief, Dionysus standing on a pedestal, adjoined by two Bacchantes. — *Cases 23 & 24.* Terracottas, masks, lecythi, rhyta. — *Cases 25 & 26.* Terracottas from Asia Minor. Votive relief from Ephesus (in 26). — *Cases 27-31.* *Tanagra figures. — *Cases 31-33.* Reliefs from Campana (below). — *Case 32.* Hermes and other terracottas from Corinth. — *Case 33.* Bœotian terracottas. — *Case 34.* Attic terracottas. — *Cases 35-37.* Terracottas from Italy. Earthenware figures, animals, sphinxes, toys, heads, etc.

We return through the Library (p. 139) and pass into —

Room XII. **Gallery of Drawings.** The nucleus of the collection, which comprises 12,000 specimens, was obtained from Count Brühl, though many other purchases have since been added. The French school is especially well represented, including 1067 drawings by Callot, and 132 portraits of great Frenchmen from Francis I. to Charles IX., by Dumoustier, and others.

Room XIII is adjoined on the N. by the large —

Room XI. **Collection of Engravings.** The collection contains over 200,000 specimens, French and English engravers of the 18th cent. being specially well represented. There are also numerous portraits of Russian princes and famous Europeans, maps, and costume-pieces. The beautiful cabinets in which the engravings are kept are adorned with porphyry and jasper vases. Many of the engravings are exhibited on tables and special stands. — From the semicircular hall at the entrance to Room XI. a door leads into —

Room X. **Scythian and Siberian Antiquities.** Relics found in the tumuli of Scythian kings in the province of Yekaterinosláv and the like.

We begin at the opposite end, to the left of the entrance to R. IX. *Cabinets 95-93.* Relics from Alexandropol. Cab. 95: 793. Gold pig; 794. Gold circlet, with two horses' heads; bronze and bone jewellery; bronze buttons for decorating carriages and horses, generally plated with either silver or gold. Cab. 93: 511. Bronze horse-trappings with bells; bronze carriage-fittings. Cab. 96: Broad iron sword, 39 inches long; bronze and bone arrow-heads. — *Cab. 92.* Gold ornaments. 432. Gold dagger-sheath; bronze sword.

Cab. 91-89. Shelves 1 & 2: *Objects from Kelermés (Caucasus), including a golden sword, a golden axe with animal-reliefs, a drinking-cup of gold, a golden emblem for a shield (representing a couched beast of prey), a mirror (of Ionian work), crowns, etc. Shelf 3: Treasure of Maikop, probably the most ancient in S. Russia, including golden bulls, four hollow poles (probably used for supporting the canopy of a funeral-car), figures of animals to be sewn on garments, and gold and silver vessels. Shelf 4: Objects from Bori (1st cent. A.D.). Shelf 5: Hellenistic and Roman silver dishes. — Cab. 89: Objects from Ilyinetz (bottom shelf). Cab. 91: Objects from ancient Tanaïs (first shelf).

Cab. 87-84. Relics found at Nicopolis. Cab. 87: 370. Large quiver and bow-case, with scenes from the life of Achilles; 375. Gold scabbard, with fight between Greeks and Barbarians. Cab. 86: 176. Large silver-gilt vessel, 177. Ladle, both of Greek workmanship. Cab. 85: 381, 382. Swords with gold hilts; small gold lamellæ, for ornamenting dresses.

In the centre is the famous ****Silver Vase of Nicopolis** (No. 175; dating from the time of Alexander the Great), representing in high relief the capture and taming of the wild horse of the steppes; the men are of the characteristic Slav type.

Cab. 83-81. Shelf 4: Objects from Kertch (4th cent. A.D.), silver dish with the portrait of Emperor Constantius II., etc. Shelves 5-7: Golden wreaths.

Cabinet 77. Treasure of a nomad prince found in 1863 in the Kurgán of Novo-Tcherkassk: 890, 891. Two gold crowns, the larger surmounted by stags of the steppes and adorned in front with a female portrait in chalcedony, a Hellenistic work of the 3rd cent. B.C.; 896, 895. Two gold vases, the handles formed of animals; small gold plates for trimming dresses. Above, relics found in a grave at Melitopol (Province of Taurida); horse-trappings. — *Cabinet 79:* Gold articles, found in Siberia in the time of Peter the Great, including gold necklaces made of thick plaques of massive gold, with figures of lions. Family group beneath a tree; horses, set with turquoises. The so-called *Melgunóv Treasure, found in 1763, includes a gold scabbard with a fantastic frieze of animals, a diadem, a plaque with an ape and two birds, and the silver-gilt feet of a throne. Below is the Treasure of Kazínskoye (province of Stavropol), consisting of collars, goblets, and other gold objects.

On each side of the door leading to Room XI (p. 140) are bronze vessels, lamps, etc. — *Case 74.* Gold Ornaments. — *Case 65.* Two gold death-masks, one from a grave near Kertch, the other from the neighbourhood of Olbia. *577. Silver dish of Rhescuporis, a king of the Bosphorus, with niello ornamentation; gold ornaments blackened by fire.

We return to the Kertch Room (VII, p. 134), and pass through it to the rooms of the —

*Mediæval and Renaissance Collection (Отдѣленіе среднихъ вѣковъ н эпохи возрожденія), containing arms and armour from the Arsenal at Tzarskoye Selo (p. 188), and the Bazilevski, Narúishkin, Saltuikóv, Tatíshtchev, and other Collections. — Catalogue of the Renaissance Section, Part I (Weapons), $2^1/_2$ rb.; Russian guide to the collection of weapons, 35 cop.

In the ANTEROOM (1) are armour, fire-arms, flags and ensigns of the Zaporozhian Cossacks and Streltzi. — The two following CORRIDORS (2 & 3) contain oriental fire-arms, saddles, and trappings.

ROOM 4. *Oriental Room.* Five cabinets along the main and side walls contain presents from the rulers of Kokand (Ferghana), Persia, Kashgar, Bokhara, and Khiva; in glass-cases between these are Indian, Persian, and Caucasian arms, richly jewelled and enamelled. By the side-wall are Turkish weapons, and (in the middle) a large silken standard which fell into the hands of the Polish king, John Sobieski, in 1683 at the relief of Vienna. At the entrance are Malay arms. In the middle row is a table-case (XXII) with examples of damascened blades. The middle glass-case contains valuables from the treasury of the Khan of Khiva.

ROOM 5. *Spanish Room.* Under the arcade is the so-called *Vase of Fortuni, a Hispano-Moorish work of the 11th century. By the window-wall are swords, cross-bows, and fire-arms of the 16-17th cent.; in the glass-cases are fretted dagger-blades.

ROOM 6. *Italian Room.* In the cabinet on the right are offensive and defensive arms of the 16-17th cent., including an embossed state helmet (*I. 362) representing the head of a fantastic monster, made by Pifanio Tacito for Guidobaldo II. (1514-74), Duke of Urbino; underneath is a helmet (I. 615) of Ercole Bentivoglio (1459-1507). Behind the cabinet, on the wall, are trophies of rapiers, long swords, and daggers (held in the left hand) used to parry sword-thrusts; underneath is a round shield with 'blade-breakers'. On the back-wall, two cabinets with arms of state, mostly Milan work, chased and damascened, and shields with embossed leather-work. Between the cabinets and above them are Italian textiles of the 15-16th cent., below are fronts of Florentine wedding-chests. In Cab. 4. by the side-wall. is a targe (wooden shield), with the figure of St. George, a Venetian trophy from the sea-fight of Chioggia (1380); hammered and damascened work. In the centre of the room are two state cannon, the larger cast by Mazzaroli ca. 1670. Between the windows are swords by the most famous masters of the 16-17th cent. (mostly from Milan).

7. First German Room. By the window, Baz. (*i.e.* Bazilévski Collection) 409. Helmet (with straps) of the 7-8th cent.; above, on the wall, Nuremberg shirt-of-mail of the 15th century. On the window-sill: a trumpet of a shape peculiar to Scandinavia (Lur; 10-11th cent.). By the side-wall. to the left, Plate-armour of the 15th cent.; below, gun-barrel, said to have been captured at the battle of Granson (1476). On the wall above are pavises (standing shields) and cavalry shields from Deggendorf Bavaria, 15th cent.; H. 137 & 139, bearing the arms of the Shoemakers' nd Bakers' Guilds). On the rear wall, below, engraved and gilded plate-armour by Nuremberg and Augsburg masters; above, large wooden pavises of the 15th cent. (H. 95, with the figure of King Wenceslaus and Czech inscription; Baz. 347, with figure of St. George and arms of the town of Enns, ca. 1437). In the middle of the room is a full suit of tournament-armour (16th cent.) from Lüneburg. Between the windows are suits of field-armour, with extra pieces for tournaments.

Room 8. Weapons of the Chase. On the side-walls are cross-bows of the 16-18th cent., with the gaffles for setting them; below, in a glass-case, is a series of bolts. In the cabinet and by the windows are fowling-pieces, mostly of German origin. In the three glass-cases are powder horns, wheel-locks, hunting-knives, spurs, and so on.

9. Second German Room. Armour of the period of the Landskuechts, including two-handed and other swords and halberds of the 16-17th centuries. In the middle is a suit of plate-armour for man and horse. By the doors are richly engraved and gilded pikes. Between the windows is a·stand with swords by the most celebrated masters of Solingen.

10. French Room. By the windows are weapons of state: *F. 145. Wheel-lock musket of Henri IV. (1595); B. 195. Short sword with flamboyant blade, and pistol-barrel with the arms of Avignon; F. 281. Fowling-piece of Louis XIII. (?). By the window are other hunting-weapons and various gun-barrels made at Versailles (Boutet). In the middle is a glass-case with fine Limoges enamel. On the back and side walls are richly carved coffers and cabinets, above which hangs tapestry.

Room 11. To the right is a cabinet containing ivory carvings, including a goblet of Emperor Otho III. (*Baz. 70), diptychs, and statuettes of the Madonna. By the rear wall are two cabinets with silver and silver-gilt ecclesiastical vessels, reliquaries, chalices, and monstrances; in the middle is a large antependium, with Flemish carving of the 16th cent. To the left is a cabinet with Rhenish and Limoges enamels (12-14th cent.), reliquaries, candelabra, jugs, book-covers, and crucifixes. In the middle of the room is a large glass-case with monstrances and processional crosses, including a large monstrance by Hans Ryssenbach of Reval (end of 15th cent.). Between the windows is a mosaic figure of an angel. On the chimney-piece are marble figures from the tomb of Philip the Bold at Dijon (Baz. 105, 106). In the glass-case by the window, to the left, are prayer-books with miniatures of the 14-15th centuries.

Room 12. *Majolica and Glass.* Opposite the entrance is a large *Majolica Altar-piece (16-17th cent.), ascribed to Giovanni della Robbia; adjacent, by the window, is a bust of John the Baptist, probably by Donatello. In the cabinets, fayence from Faenza, Deruta, Caffagiolo, Urbino, and Gubbio; the cabinet on the right contains specimens from the workshop of Bernard Palissy; in the little cabinet adjacent, by the door, is French majolica, including three very valuable specimens from Oiron (Henri II.). On the walls are four examples of tapestry of the end of the 15th century. In the central glass-case is Venetian glass. — Another row of cabinets stretches along the side next the court.

᠅Cab. 13. *Polish Silver Work and Weapons.* In the cabinet on the back-wall are weapons of state: B. 13. Hat and sword presented by Pope Innocent XI. to John Sobieski; Baz. 72. Sword of King Sigismund I., inlaid with mother-of-pearl; Baz. 334. Copy of the Polish coronation sword (the original of the 13th cent. is lost). By the front wall to the left is a gun-barrel of the period of Sigismund II. Augustus (1561). Under the window-ledge is an iron bar (Q. 72) said to have been bent by Augustus the Strong. — Cab. 14. *Russian Weapons of State* (15-18th cent.). To the right is a case with helmets and rapiers; in the centre, a helmet and a corslet covered with red velvet. On the door behind the case is part of a suit of armour made in Germany for the False Demetrius. On the back wall is a glass-case with weapons of the 16-17th cent.: A. 326. sabre-blade of 1642, presented by the Tzar Mikhaïl Feódorovitch; *A. 210. C. 313. sabres and daggers of the Boyar Demetrius Godunóv; below, I. 604, Corslet of Prince Vladímir Andréyevitch Stáritzki (1535-69). On the left side-wall are ornamented guns from the Tula factory; by the door to the left is a sabre from the Zlatoust factory. Between the windows are battle-axes of the Russian infantry of the 16-17th centuries. In the glass-case by the window are objects found in the Baltic Provinces, including a *Sword with a figure of Christ on the pommel. — Cab. 15. *Post-Mongolian Period.* The case on the right contains discoveries from the territory of the Golden Horde (13-14th cent.). On the back-wall are discoveries from Kuban (Caucasus), including glass vessels and textiles; to the left are objects from Siberia. In the large glass-case are discoveries from the Byelo-retchenskaya Stanitza, in the district of Kuban. — Cab. 16. *Pre-Mongolian Period.* By the door, swords of the 11-15th centuries. By the side-walls, relics from Caucasian burial-places. By the back-wall, relics from S., W., and E. Russia. Glass-case in the centre of the room, relics from Kiev, Ryazan, Vladímir, and Tchernigov, including a golden *Diadem, adorned with enamels (Christ, Apostles, and Angels). Between the windows is the so-called Stone of Tmutarakán, with an inscription stating that Prince Glyeb in the year 6576 (1068 A.D.) measured the distance over the ice-bound sea from Tmutarakan to Kertch and found it 10,004 fathoms. By the door to the left are amulets against fever, with figures of snakes.

Cab. 17. *Primitive Christian and Byzantine Antiquities.* The glass-cases by the windows contain crosses and images of saints; to the left are ornaments and images dating from the 6th cent. onwards, including two miniatures in mosaic, an *Enamel Portrait of St. Theodore, and a 5th cent. glass cup from Podgóritza in Montenegro. In the pyramidal case are carved-ivory caskets and pyxes (Byzantine work of the 5-11th cent.). To the left is a sarcophagus; above, a cabinet with primitive Christian bronzes and earthenware. By the back-wall, two cabinets with relics from Chersonesus (Sebastopol); next to these, a lamp in the form of a basilica, from Algiers (4th or 5th cent.). To the right, in the cabinet, Armenian *Reliquary of embossed silver (1293), with inscriptions and a portrait of the Armenian ruler, Hetum II. Above are remains of frescoes and other relics from Ani (Armenia). On the wall to the left are silken fabrics from Egypt. The Treasure of Poltava, found in 1912, is to be exhibited in this cabinet. — Cab. 18. *Coptic Antiquities.* Stone steles and wooden reliefs, bronze articles, and fabrics of the 3rd to 9th cent. (chiefly remains of winding-sheets, with fairly well preserved coloured patterns).

Cab. 19. *Moslem Antiquities.* In the middle is a large majolica vase, with equestrian figures, a Persian work of the 13-14th centuries. Between the windows is a magnificent wooden *Door from the Gur-Emir Mosque in Samarkand. Lock of a door found in Jerusalem. In the cabinet by the back-wall, relics from Samarkand and neighbourhood; damascened copper-work of the 14th and 15th centuries. In the side-pyramids are copper-work and three Arabian glass lamps. On the walls, coloured glazed tiles from Turkestan, Arabian fabrics from Egypt. The glass-cases by the windows contain ornaments.

First Floor.

The rooms on the first floor (p. 132) are reached by a fine *Marble Staircase*. The galleries at the sides are adorned with jasper and marble vases, and with several marble busts and statues, including (in the gallery to the left) a Nymph by *Dupré* (No. 1099).

The Entrance Room (I) adjoining the staircase is decorated after designs by Klenze. On the walls are 86 encaustic pictures representing the development of Greek and Roman painting, executed on bronze slabs by *Hiltensperger* at Munich in 1843. In the centre of the room are a bust of Catherine II., busts of Buffon (No. 259) and Voltaire (No. 213), by *Houdon*, and others of Falconet (No. 272) and Diderot (No. 270), by *Marie Collot*. To the left of the entrance, Cupid and Psyche, Dancer, Orpheus, Hebe, Paris, by *Canova;* Queen Louise, by *Rauch*. On the wall (behind the group of Amor and Psyche), Catherine II., marble medallion by *Marie Collot;* to the right and left, busts of Elizabeth (by *Guichard*) and Nicholas I. (by *Rauch*). To the right of the entrance, The Graces, by *Canova;* *Diana, by *Houdon;* Shepherd Boy, by *Thorvaldsen;* *Seated Figure of Voltaire, by *Houdon* (replica in the Théâtre Français at Paris); Amor, Pygmalion and Galatea, by *Falconet*. Tables, candelabra, and vases of malachite.

From the Entrance Room we pass into the —

**Picture Gallery †, housed in a series of magnificent rooms.

The Picture Gallery was founded by Peter the Great. In 1763 Catherine II. added the collection of the Prussian patriot *Joh. A. Gotzkówski*, consisting of pictures bought for Frederick II. (1755 et seq.), which the king was unable to accept owing to the war. In 1769 the Empress acquired the collection of *Count Brühl*, and in 1779 she bought (for 36,000*l.*) *Sir Robert Walpole's* collection at Houghton Hall, including a famous series of works by Van Dyck. She also purchased valuable paintings through Raphael Mengs and Reifenstein in Rome, Baron Grimm, Diderot, and Falconet in Paris, and other agents, besides ordering pictures from the most famous painters of her time. — In 1814 Alexander I. bought from the ex-Empress Josephine, a few days before her death, at Malmaison, 38 of her best pictures and 4 statues by Canova for the sum of 940,000 fr. Amongst these are 22 Flemish and Dutch canvases, including the Archers of Antwerp by D. Teniers the Younger (No. 672), the Farmhouse and the Huntsman's Life by Paul Potter (Nos. 1051, 1052), and the Four Periods of the Day by Claude Lorrain (Nos. 1428-1431), all of which were formerly at Cassel. In the same year, 67 pictures were purchased from the collection of Coesvelt, the banker, in Amsterdam, for 8700*l.* — In 1829 Nicholas I. bought 30 pictures from the collection of the Duchess

---

† Catalogues: Russian guide by Alex. Benois (1911; illus.) 2 rb.; short general catalogue, in Russian, 50 cop.; *Italian and Spanish Schools*, in French 60 cop. (illus. 1 rb. 40), in Russian 1 rb. 25 cop.; *Netherlandish and German Schools*, in Russian 85 cop.; *English and French Schools*, in French 25, in Russian 30 cop. (illus. 65 cop.).

of St. Leu (Queen Hortense), for 180,000 fr.; in 1831, 33 canvases from the collection of Don Manuel Godoy, the 'Principe de la Paz', for 567,935 fr.; in 1836, 7 pictures from the Coesvelt gallery (p. 144), including Raphael's Madonna Alba (No. 38), for the small sum of 9400*l*; and in 1850 the Barbarigo Gallery in Venice and several valuable paintings at the sale of the collection of the King of the Netherlands, including numerous masterpieces by Velazquez, Seb. del Piombo, and B. van der Helst. — Alexander II. added in 1880 the small Madonna Connestabile, an early work by Raphael (No. 1667). Alexander III. enriched the Hermitage gallery with 74 of the paintings purchased in 1886 from the Galitzuin Museum in Moscow for 800,000 rb., including a Triptych (No. 1666) by Perugino.

Among the acquisitions of the most recent period the following may be mentioned: Gir. Romanino, Madonna; Seb. Ricci, Rape of the Sabines; Perugino, St. Sebastian; Dom. Theotocopuli (El Greco), SS. Peter and Paul; Adrian Ysenbrant, St. Jerome; Hans von Kulmbach, Christ the Mediator. — In 1911 Counts Gregory and Paul Stróganov bequeathed to the gallery a Madonna by Filippino Lippi, a Pietà by Cima da Conegliano, and a landscape by Hobbema. In 1912 the Khitrovó Bequest, a collection of English portraits, was added.

The Hermitage Gallery incontestably ranks as one of the finest galleries in Europe, not on account of its size (though it contains nearly 2000 pictures) or the completeness of its representation of the great masters or even of the great schools (14th and 15th cent. art and German painting being scarcely represented at all), but because it includes so many masterpieces of the best period of the various schools of art. In Spanish works it is excelled only by the Museo del Prado in Madrid and the Louvre; the French school is better represented in the Louvre alone; as regards Flemish works it at least equals most of the chief European collections; while in Dutch paintings, especially in examples of Rembrandt, it ranks first of all.

Of the ITALIAN SCHOOL the earlier period is represented by only one good work, *viz.* the Adoration of the Magi, by *Sandro Botticelli.* — The most flourishing period of this school is better represented. Two works are ascribed to *Leonardo da Vinci.* The Holy Family by *Andrea del Sarto* is a striking as well as a picturesque creation of the master. Four pictures are attributed to *Raphael,* but though authorities are agreed as to the authenticity of three of these (the Madonna Alba, a good work of his early Roman period, the small Madonna Connestabile, and the St. George, two gems of his youth), there is some doubt as to the fourth (Holy Family with the beardless St. Joseph). By his rival, *Sebastian del Piombo,* the Hermitage possesses four original paintings, each of which in its own style is a chef d'œuvre of this rare master. A Judith, formerly ascribed to Moretto, is now recognized as a genuine work of *Giorgione. Titian* is represented almost solely by examples of his latest work, of which the Mary Magdalen is the most important. Notable among works by his contemporaries and successors in Venice are pictures by *Bonifazio, Bordone, Lotto,* and

Pordenone, the Nativity of the Virgin Mary by *Tintoretto,* and the Descent from the Cross by *Veronese.* — In harmony with the taste of the 18th and early 19th century, the Italian masters of the 17th cent., whether Academics or Naturalists, are represented almost without exception. Of the many pictures of this era a large proportion may be classed as choice and important works, particularly those by *Salvator Rosa.* The Italian schools close with some masterpieces of decorative colouring by *Tiepolo* and *Canaletto.*

The SPANISH SCHOOL is represented by some fine works by its chief exponents, Velazquez and Murillo. *Velazquez's* portrait of Philip IV. ranks as one of the most famous of the many portraits of that monarch. The 18 authentic pictures of *Murillo* reveal the master in all the various stages of his career, and often at his best. They include large canvases and decorative works, smaller paintings showing careful attention to detail, marvellous representations of mundane beauty under the spell of religious ecstasy, cheerful and homely renderings of Biblical subjects, and naïve scenes of Spanish popular life. The Assumption (No. 371), the Rest on the Flight into Egypt (No. 367), St. Peter in prison (No. 372), and Jacob's Ladder (No. 359) would rank as gems of the great painter's art even in Seville or Madrid.

The GERMAN SCHOOL, with the exception of some excellent pictures by Lucas Cranach, is, as has been already remarked, scarcely represented in the Hermitage. — The works of the EARLIEST NETHERLANDISH SCHOOL, though few in number, include some very characteristic examples, such as the Annunciation of *Jan van Eyck,* and the Healing of the Blind, the most important effort of *Lucas van Leyden.* The later phase in the development of Netherlandish art was affected more or less deleteriously by the influence of the Italian Renaissance and its misunderstood interpretation in the Low Countries. At the Hermitage, however, the period is represented by some of its happiest and most original efforts, including excellent portraits by *Sir A. More, Pourbus,* and others. The collection also boasts the best religious picture of the time, an Adoration of the Magi, by *L. Lombard,* which forms a worthy transition to the works of the great Flemish master, P. P. Rubens.

FLEMISH SCHOOL. Of *Rubens,* as of the other chief masters of this school, *Van Dyck, Teniers, Snyders,* and *Jordaens,* the Hermitage possesses a larger number of pictures than any other gallery in the world. Amongst the 50 pictures by Rubens there are not only many Biblical and mythological scenes of great and (in some cases) pre-eminent value, but also a number of such magnificent portraits (including that of his second wife) and sketches (notably those made for the entry of the Cardinal-Infante into Antwerp), that the Hermitage in this respect rivals the Munich Gallery. Two of the

CABINET XII. To the left, *307. *C. Maratta*, Pope Clement IX. On the screen, 1648. *Franc. Guardi*, Street-vista. — We return to Cab. VIII and thence proceed to Cab. VII.

CABINET VII. By the window, on a stand, **1667. *Raphael*, Madonna Connestabile, the smallest of the artist's Madonnas, from Perugia (about 1503), purchased by Alexander II. in 1880 for 310,000 fr.

'Mary, in a standing position, with only the upper part of the figure visible and with her mantle drawn over her head, holds the Infant Jesus, and has her glance directed slightly to the left. Her left hand supports the Child whilst her right holds an open prayer-book, at which Christ is devoutly gazing. A pleasing landscape, brightened by a river, and sloping up to a range of snow-covered mountains on the horizon, forms the background. The brightness and clearness of the colouring, which owes nothing to the effect of contrast, but is the result of the delicate fusion of the colours and the bold touch with which the tints are laid on, enable this work to rank as the worthy and promising commencement of a long and glorious series of representations of the Madonna.'

(*Springer*, Raphael and Michael Angelo.)

**39. *Raphael*, St. George, wearing the Order of the Garter; this picture was sent to Henry VII. of England in 1506 by Duke Guidobaldo of Urbino, on the occasion of his investiture with the Order. — To the right of the door of Cab. VIII, above, 58. *G. Romano*, Lady at her toilet (known as the Fornarina); *74. *Bern. Luini (Fr. Melzi?)*, So-called Colombina, a famous canvas once attributed to Leonardo da Vinci. — On the main wall, 24. *Andrea del Sarto*, Holy Family; 40. *Franc. Bacchiacca* (formerly ascribed to Raphael), Portrait of an old man, freely retouched; *38. *Raphael*, Madonna and Child with the youthful John the Baptist ('Madonna Alba'; from the beginning of the artist's Roman period); above, 20. *School of Fra Bartolomeo*, Madonna with the Holy Child and angels; 37. *Raphael*, Madonna and Child with St. Joseph (beardless); *14. *Cesare da Sesto*, Holy Family. — 1969. *Franc. Maineri*, Bearing of the Cross; above, 35. *G. Bugiardini*, Holy Family; 6. *Giorgione* (?), Madonna and Child; above, to the left, *15. *School of Leonardo da Vinci*, Portrait; 71. *Bern. Luini*, Madonna and Child. — In the middle, Dead boy on a dolphin, a marble group by *Pietro d'Ancona* (?), after a drawing by Raphael.

CABINET VI. By the window, on a stand, *13a. *Leonardo da Vinci (Ambrosio de Predis?)*, Madonna and Child ('Madonna Litta'), a work of the greatest charm; 1967. *Fra Filippo Lippi*, Madonna with the Holy Child and angels. — To the right, 4. *Cima da Conegliano*, Madonna and Child, with two saints; *1675. *Cima da Conegliano*, Annunciation (1495); above, 9. *Catena*, Holy Family. — *1666. *Perugino*, Triptych (in the centre, Crucifixion, with the Virgin and St. John; on the wings, St. Jerome and Mary Magdalen); above, 1. *School of Lor. di Credi*, Madonna and Child with angels; in the middle of the main wall, *1674. *Fra Angelico*, Virgin and Child with SS. Dominic and Thomas Aquinas (fresco from Flor-

master's rare landscapes are also of conspicuous beauty. — The collection of paintings by *Van Dyck*, 32 in number, is unrivalled even in the galleries of England. Among the Biblical scenes we find what is perhaps his best work, the Rest on the Flight into Egypt. The numerous portraits include a celebrated series of the Wharton family and another of the English royal family from the Walpole collection, but many authorities place even higher than these a series of portraits of his early period, including the Snyders family and Susanna Fourment and her daughter. *Jordaens* is also represented by paintings of every kind, including two admirable portraits. The 12 works by *Frans Snyders* seem to confirm Rubens's assertion that this master's forte was still-life, and not the representation of animated nature. A still larger number of his works are preserved at the imperial châteaux (Gatchina, etc.). Of the 38 pictures by *Teniers the Younger* it is only necessary to mention here his two unequalled masterpieces, the Feast of the Arquebusiers and the Guard-room.

The pictures of the DUTCH SCHOOL are even more numerous and important. Here again their value does not lie in the historical completeness of the collection (the early masters, excepting *Frans Hals*, being either missing or poorly represented) but in the number and value of works by the great masters, and especially by the greatest of them all, *Rembrandt*. Of the 42 pictures ascribed to him, 38 are certainly genuine; these (excepting his very rare landscapes) comprise works of every kind, of all sizes, and dating from almost every year of his artistic career. Among the works of the very first rank may be mentioned, Abraham entertaining the angels unawares, Joseph's coat of many colours, the Holy Family, the Return of the Prodigal Son, the Denial of St. Peter, the Descent from the Cross, and the so-called Danaë; while among the portraits, those known as Rembrandt's mother with her Bible, Sobieski, and several others of old men and women are specially worthy of study. — Of Rembrandt's pupils we miss scarcely one; but the portraits in the Hermitage by *Ferd. Bol*, *G. Flinck*, and others are far excelled by several works of *Bart. van der Helst*, especially by the charming Presentation of the Bride. Of the many works by the lesser masters of the early Dutch school we need only mention such gems as the Glass of lemonade, by *Terburg*, and the Breakfast, by *Metsu* (both formerly in Cassel). The numerous paintings by *J. Steen*, *A. van Ostade*, and *G. Dou*, however, include no such masterpieces. Of the 54 originals by *Ph. Wouverman* the large 'Course au Chat' and the Scene on the Dunes are of unusual beauty, as are two of the 13 pictures by *Jacob van Ruysdael*, the Sandy Path and the Mountain Tarn (No. 1147), the earliest and one of the latest of the master's works, both canvases of unusual size. Other landscape-painters, such as *A. van der Neer, A. Cuyp, Wynants,* and *J. van der Heyde* (9 pictures), are represented almost as fully. The Hermitage collection also includes 7 genuine pictures by *Paul Potter*, among them the finest of all his works, the Farmhouse, which, with two other excellent pictures by the artist, at one time had a place in the Cassel Gallery.

The FRENCH SCHOOL of the 17th cent. is brilliantly represented by its chief masters, *Nicolas Poussin* (18 works; amongst them the two landscapes with Polyphemus and Hercules) and *Claude Lorrain* (12 landscapes, including those known as the Four Periods of the Day). Among painters of the 18th cent., *Watteau, Boucher, Greuze,* and *Chardin* may be mentioned.

Leaving the Entrance Hall we first enter —

ROOM II. **Larger Italian Paintings.** This room, like the others, is adorned with huge vases of malachite and with candelabra of grey jasper. In the middle of the room, Bust of Tzar Nicholas I., the builder of the present museum, in Slav armour, by *N. Pimenov.* — By the entrance-wall, to the right, 92. *Bonifazio dei Pitati,* Holy Family; *73. *Bern. Luini,* St. Sebastian (said to be a portrait of Maximiliano Sforza); *Garofalo,* 61 (above), Bearing of the Cross, 59. Adoration of the Shepherds, 1848 (above), Wedding at Cana of Galilee. — On the right end-wall, 222. *Salvator Rosa,* Democritus and Protagoras; above, 239. *Guercino,* Assumption; 221. *Salv. Rosa,* Odysseus and Nausicaa. — Side-wall opposite the entrance, *318. *Ant. Canale (Canaletto),* Reception at Venice of Count Gergi, ambassador of Louis XV. of France; *317. *G. B. Tiepolo,* Banquet of Cleopatra; adjacent, 319. *Ant. Canale,* Marriage of the Doge with the Adriatic; above, 1942. *Seb. Ricci,* Rape of the Sabine Women; *216. *Caravaggio,* Crucifixion of St. Peter (a work which gave Rubens the idea of his painting in St. Peter's at Cologne); above, 291. *Giordano,* Descent from the Cross; *220. *Salv. Rosa,* Prodigal Son; above, 204. *Franc. Albani,* Rape of Europa. *224. *Salv. Rosa,* Portrait of a poet; above, 153. *Paolo Veronese,* Portrait; *191. *Guido Reni,* Virgin Mary at the sewing school, a charming study, with a naïve reproduction of contemporary (early 17th cent.) conditions; above, 313. *G. M. Crespi,* Holy Family; 240. *Guercino,* Martyrdom of St. Catharine. — Left end-wall, 89. *Dom. Capriolo (?),* Portrait of the artist; *100. *Titian,* Danaë; *121. *A. Schiavone,* Jupiter and Io, in a beautiful landscape by *Dom. Campagnola.* — Entrance-wall, 185. *G. Reni (Contarini?),* St. Francis adoring the Child Christ; *132. *Tintoretto,* Nativity of the Virgin, as rich and flower-like in colour as it is graceful in conception; *Titian,* 94. Ecce Homo, 1678. St. Sebastian (unfinished study); above, to the left, 101. *Titian,* Pope Paul III.; 219. *Bern. Strozzi,* Tobias healing his father; adjacent, **18. *Seb. del Piombo,*

Descent from the Cross (1516), a masterpiece of the
in composition and luminously clear in colouring, the
is represented at night; above, 241. *Guercino,* St.
desert. — A door opposite the main entrance leads fr
into the Italian Cabinets.

Italian Cabinets (V-XII). We first enter —

CABINET VIII. To the left, 124. *Aless. Allori (Bro*
trait; above, 115. *School of Parma* (16th cent.; *L*
Portrait. — 111. *Paris Bordone (?),* Lady with a c
Giorgione, Judith; *113. *Moretto,* Faith (painted ca.
the right, 125. *Aless. Allori,* Portrait. — *19. *Seb. d*
Cardinal Reginald Pole, Archbishop of Canterbury, adn
ceived; above, 109. *School of Bonifazio dei Pitati, A*
the Shepherds; 17. *Seb. del Piombo,* Bearing of the *(*
Seb. del Piombo (Titian?), Cardinal Ant. Pallavicini.
door leading to Cab. VII, 91. *School of Palma Vecchia*
and Child with saints.

CABINET IX. To the left, 154. *G. B. Moroni,* Portr
1916. *Romanino,* Madonna and Child; *98. *Titian, M*
dalen (the chief work by Titian in the Hermitage); above
Badile (teacher of Paolo Veronese), Portrait of a Venetia
*93. Replica of a lost original of *Giorgione,* Madonna a
— In the middle of the main wall, *145. *Paolo Veronese*
from the Cross, one of the most deeply felt works of th
marked by the finest colouring and by rare delicacy of chi
to the right, 138. *Paolo Veronese,* Finding of Moses;
the right, 1636. *Jac. Bassano,* Boy with his nurse. — Tit
Jesus Christ giving his blessing, *99. Toilet of Venus; abo
Padovanino (?), Portrait of a lady, probably Eleanor, D
Urbino; 96. *Titian,* Madonna and Child with Mary Magd

CABINET X. On the main wall, 1915. *Franc. Trevisan*
and Daphne; 201. *Lanfranco,* Annunciation; in the middle
Domenichino, St. John the Evangelist; 176. *Ann. Carac*
trait of the artist; adjacent, 202. *Franc. Albani,* Annun
1924. *Ann. Caracci,* Battle of the Lapithæ and the Cent
257. *Sassoferrato,* Madonna with a bird.

CABINET XI. Above the door of Cab. X: 189. *G. Ren*
of Europa. To the left, 236. *Dom. Feti,* Portrait of an actor;
225. *Salv. Rosa,* Bandit; 217. *Caravaggio,* Mandoline-pla
227. *Salv. Rosa,* Landscape with smugglers; below, to the
267. *Bart. Schidone,* Madonna and Child; adjacent, 232.
Feti, Tobias healing his father. — *C. Dolci,* 1639. St. Jo
Evangelist, 1640. Tobias and the angel; above (top row)
Ben. Luti, Holy Family; 252. *C. Dolci,* Mary Magdalen.
the door leading to Cab. XII: 237. *Lanfranco,* God the Fat

master's rare landscapes are also of conspicuous beauty. — The collection of paintings by *Van Dyck*, 32 in number, is unrivalled even in the galleries of England. Among the Biblical scenes we find what is perhaps his best work, the Rest on the Flight into Egypt. The numerous portraits include a celebrated series of the Wharton family and another of the English royal family from the Walpole collection, but many authorities place even higher than these a series of portraits of his early period, including the Snyders family and Susanna Fourment and her daughter. *Jordaens* is also represented by paintings of every kind, including two admirable portraits. The 12 works by *Frans Snyders* seem to confirm Rubens's assertion that this master's forte was still-life, and not the representation of animated nature. A still larger number of his works are preserved at the imperial châteaux (Gatchina, etc.). Of the 38 pictures by *Teniers the Younger* it is only necessary to mention here his two unequalled masterpieces, the Feast of the Arquebusiers and the Guard-room.

The pictures of the Dutch School are even more numerous and important. Here again their value does not lie in the historical completeness of the collection (the early masters, excepting *Frans Hals,* being either missing or poorly represented) but in the number and value of works by the great masters, and especially by the greatest of them all, *Rembrandt*. Of the 42 pictures ascribed to him, 38 are certainly genuine; these (excepting his very rare landscapes) comprise works of every kind, of all sizes, and dating from almost every year of his artistic career. Among the works of the very first rank may be mentioned, Abraham entertaining the angels unawares, Joseph's coat of many colours, the Holy Family, the Return of the Prodigal Son, the Denial of St. Peter, the Descent from the Cross, and the so-called Danaë; while among the portraits, those known as Rembrandt's mother with her Bible, Sobieski, and several others of old men and women are specially worthy of study. — Of Rembrandt's pupils we miss scarcely one; but the portraits in the Hermitage by *Ferd. Bol, G. Flinck,* and others are far excelled by several works of *Bart. van der Helst,* especially by the charming Presentation of the Bride. Of the many works by the lesser masters of the early Dutch school we need only mention such gems as the Glass of lemonade, by *Terburg,* and the Breakfast, by *Metsu* (both formerly in Cassel). The numerous paintings by *J. Steen, A. van Ostade,* and *G. Dou,* however, include no such masterpieces. Of the 54 originals by *Ph. Wouverman* the large 'Course au Chat' and the Scene on the Dunes are of unusual beauty, as are two of the 13 pictures by *Jacob van Ruysdael,* the Sandy Path and the Mountain Tarn (No. 1147), the earliest and one of the latest of the master's works, both canvases of unusual size. Other landscape-painters, such as *A. van der Neer*, *A. Cuyp*, *Wynants*, and *J. van der Heyde* (9 pictures), are represented almost as fully. The Hermitage collection also includes 7 genuine pictures by *Paul Potter*, among them the finest of all his works, the Farmhouse, which, with two other excellent pictures by the artist, at one time had a place in the Cassel Gallery.

The FRENCH SCHOOL of the 17th cent. is brilliantly represented by its chief masters, *Nicolas Poussin* (18 works; amongst them the two landscapes with Polyphemus and Hercules) and *Claude Lorrain* (12 landscapes, including those known as the Four Periods of the Day). Among painters of the 18th cent., *Watteau Boucher*, *Greuze*, and *Chardin* may be mentioned.

Leaving the Entrance Hall we first enter —

ROOM II. **Larger Italian Paintings.** This room, like the others, is adorned with huge vases of malachite and with candelabra of grey jasper. In the middle of the room, Bust of Tzar Nicholas I., the builder of the present museum, in Slav armour, by *N. Pimenov.* — By the entrance-wall, to the right, 92. *Bonifazio dei Pitati*, Holy Family; *73. *Bern. Luini*, St. Sebastian (said to be a portrait of Maximiliano Sforza); *Garofalo*, 61 (above), Bearing of the Cross, 59. Adoration of the Shepherds, 1848 (above), Wedding at Cana of Galilee. — On the right end-wall, 222. *Salvator Rosa*, Democritus and Protagoras; above, 239. *Guercino*, Assumption; 221. *Salv. Rosa*, Odysseus and Nausicaa. — Side-wall opposite the entrance, *318. *Ant. Canale (Canaletto)*, Reception at Venice of Count Gergi, ambassador of Louis XV. of France; *317. *G. B. Tiepolo*, Banquet of Cleopatra; adjacent, 319. *Ant. Canale*, Marriage of the Doge with the Adriatic; above, 1942. *Seb. Ricci*, Rape of the Sabine Women; *216. *Caravaggio*, Crucifixion of St. Peter (a work which gave Rubens the idea of his painting in St. Peter's at Cologne); above, 291. *Giordano*, Descent from the Cross; *220. *Salv. Rosa*, Prodigal Son; above, 204. *Franc. Albani*, Rape of Europa. *224. *Salv. Rosa*, Portrait of a poet; above, 153. *Paolo Veronese*, Portrait; *191. *Guido Reni*, Virgin Mary at the sewing school, a charming study, with a naïve reproduction of contemporary (early 17th cent.) conditions'; above, 313. *G. M. Crespi*, Holy Family; 240. *Guercino*, Martyrdom of St. Catharine. — Left end-wall, 89. *Dom. Capriolo (?)*, Portrait of the artist; *100. *Titian*, Danaë; *121. *A. Schiavone*, Jupiter and Io, in a beautiful landscape by *Dom. Campagnola.* — Entrance-wall, 185. *G. Reni (Contarini?)*, St. Francis adoring the Child Christ; *132. *Tintoretto*, Nativity of the Virgin, as rich and flower-like in colour as it is graceful in conception; *Titian*, 94. Ecce Homo, 1678. St. Sebastian (unfinished study); above, to the left, 101. *Titian*, Pope Paul III.; 219. *Bern. Strozzi*, Tobias healing his father; adjacent, **18. *Seb. del Piombo*,

Descent from the Cross (1516), a masterpiece of the artist, superb in composition and luminously clear in colouring, though the scene is represented at night; above, 241. *Guercino*, St. Jerome in the desert. — A door opposite the main entrance leads from this room into the Italian Cabinets.

Italian Cabinets (V-XII). We first enter —

Cabinet VIII. To the left, 124. *Aless. Allori (Bronzino)*, Portrait; above, 115. *School of Parma* (16th cent.; *Lor. Lotto?*), Portrait. — 111. *Paris Bordone (?)*, Lady with a child; *112. *Giorgione*, Judith; *113. *Moretto*, Faith (painted ca. 1530). — To the right, 125. *Aless. Allori*, Portrait. — *19. *Seb. del Piombo*, Cardinal Reginald Pole, Archbishop of Canterbury, admirably conceived; above, 109. *School of Bonifazio dei Pitati*, Adoration of the Shepherds; 17. *Seb. del Piombo*, Bearing of the Cross; 102. *Seb. del Piombo (Titian?)*, Cardinal Ant. Pallavicini. Above the door leading to Cab. VII, 91. *School of Palma Vecchio*, Madonna and Child with saints.

Cabinet IX. To the left, 154. *G. B. Moroni*, Portrait; above, 1916. *Romanino*, Madonna and Child; *98. *Titian*, Mary Magdalen (the chief work by Titian in the Hermitage); above, 152. *Ant. Badile* (teacher of Paolo Veronese), Portrait of a Venetian Senator; *93. Replica of a lost original of *Giorgione*, Madonna and Child. — In the middle of the main wall, *145. *Paolo Veronese*, Descent from the Cross, one of the most deeply felt works of the master, marked by the finest colouring and by rare delicacy of chiaroscuro; to the right, 138. *Paolo Veronese*, Finding of Moses; above, to the right, 1636. *Jac. Bassano*, Boy with his nurse. — *Titian*, *95. Jesus Christ giving his blessing, *99. Toilet of Venus; above, *105. *Padovanino (?)*, Portrait of a lady, probably Eleanor, Duchess of Urbino; 96. *Titian*, Madonna and Child with Mary Magdalen.

Cabinet X. On the main wall, 1915. *Franc. Trevisani*, Apollo and Daphne; 201. *Lanfranco*, Annunciation; in the middle, *1643. *Domenichino*, St. John the Evangelist; 176. *Ann. Caracci*, Portrait of the artist; adjacent, 202. *Franc. Albani*, Annunciation; 1924. *Ann. Caracci*, Battle of the Lapithæ and the Centaurs. — 257. *Sassoferrato*, Madonna with a bird.

Cabinet XI. Above the door of Cab. X: 189. *G. Reni*, Rape of Europa. To the left, 236. *Dom. Feti*, Portrait of an actor; above, 225. *Salv. Rosa*, Bandit; 217. *Caravaggio*, Mandoline-player. — 227. *Salv. Rosa*, Landscape with smugglers; below, to the right, 267. *Bart. Schidone*, Madonna and Child; adjacent, 232. *Dom. Feti*, Tobias healing his father. — *C. Dolci*, 1639. St. John the Evangelist, 1640. Tobias and the angel; above (top row), 288. *Ben. Luti*, Holy Family; 252. *C. Dolci*, Mary Magdalen. Above the door leading to Cab. XII: 237. *Lanfranco*, God the Father.

CABINET XII. To the left, *307· *C. Maratta*, Pope Clement IX. On the screen, 1648. *Franc. Guardi*, Street-vista. — We return to Cab. VIII and thence proceed to Cab. VII.

CABINET VII. By the window, on a stand, **1667. *Raphael*, Madonna Connestabile, the smallest of the artist's Madonnas, from Perugia (about 1503), purchased by Alexander II. in 1880 for 310,000 fr.

'Mary, in a standing position, with only the upper part of the figure visible and with her mantle drawn over her head, holds the Infant Jesus, and has her glance directed slightly to the left. Her left hand supports the Child whilst her right holds an open prayer-book, at which Christ is devoutly gazing. A pleasing landscape, brightened by a river, and sloping up to a range of snow-covered mountains on the horizon, forms the background. The brightness and clearness of the colouring, which owes nothing to the effect of contrast, but is the result of the delicate fusion of the colours and the bold touch with which the tints are laid on, enable this work to rank as the worthy and promising commencement of a long and glorious series of representations of the Madonna.'

(*Springer*, Raphael and Michael Angelo.)

**39. *Raphael*, St. George, wearing the Order of the Garter; this picture was sent to Henry VII. of England in 1506 by Duke Guidobaldo of Urbino, on the occasion of his investiture with the Order. — To the right of the door of Cab. VIII, above, 58. *G. Romano*, Lady at her toilet (known as the Fornarina); *74· *Bern. Luini (Fr. Melzi?)*, So-called Colombina, a famous canvas once attributed to Leonardo da Vinci. — On the main wall, 24. *Andrea del Sarto*, Holy Family; 40. *Franc. Bacchiacca* (formerly ascribed to Raphael), Portrait of an old man, freely retouched; *38· *Raphael*, Madonna and Child with the youthful John the Baptist ('Madonna Alba'; from the beginning of the artist's Roman period); above, 20. *School of Fra Bartolomeo*, Madonna with the Holy Child and angels; 37. *Raphael*, Madonna and Child with St. Joseph (beardless); *14· *Cesare da Sesto*, Holy Family. — 1969. *Franc. Maineri*, Bearing of the Cross; above, 35. *G. Bugiardini*, Holy Family; 6. *Giorgione* (?), Madonna and Child; above, to the left, *15· *School of Leonardo da Vinci*, Portrait; 71. *Bern. Luini*, Madonna and Child. — In the middle, Dead boy on a dolphin, a marble group by *Pietro d'Ancona* (?), after a drawing by Raphael.

CABINET VI. By the window, on a stand, *13 a. *Leonardo da Vinci (Ambrosio de Predis?)*, Madonna and Child ('Madonna Litta'), a work of the greatest charm; 1967. *Fra Filippo Lippi*, Madonna with the Holy Child and angels. — To the right, 4. *Cima da Conegliano*, Madonna and Child, with two saints; *1675· *Cima da Conegliano*, Annunciation (1495); above, 9. *Catena*, Holy Family. — *1666· *Perugino*, Triptych (in the centre, Crucifixion, with the Virgin and St. John; on the wings, St. Jerome and Mary Magdalen); above, 1. *School of Lor. di Credi*, Madonna and Child with angels; in the middle of the main wall, *1674· *Fra Angelico*, Virgin and Child with SS. Dominic and Thomas Aquinas (fresco from Florence); *3. *Sandro Botticelli,* Adoration of the Magi, a predella of rich and charming composition and colouring; *Leonardo da Vinci,* Madonna (purchased in 1914 from Mme. M. A. Benois for 15,500*l.*). Adjoining the door of Cab. V, 1938. *Perugino,* St. Sebastian; adjacent, 1965. *Cima da Conegliano,* Pietà; above, to the left, 25. *Dom. Puligo,* St. Barbara. — In the middle, *Michael Angelo,* Crouching youth, in marble (ca. 1513-16).

CABINET V. Frescoes by *Pupils of Raphael,* The Rape of Helen from the so-called Villa Raphael, the others from the former Villa Mills in Rome. Renaissance and later bronzes by *Giov. da Bologna,* etc. In the middle, equestrian statue of Louis XIV. by *Girardon* (model for the statue in the Place Vendôme in Paris which was destroyed in 1791). To the right is an old copy of the Boy extracting a thorn from his foot (original in the Capitol at Rome).

Room XXVI, adjoining (see p. 162), contains the collection of Gems and Ornaments.

From Cab. V we return through Cabs. VI-VIII to Room II, and pass through the door on the left into —

ROOM IV. **Spanish School.** To the left of the entrance, *Morales,* 401. Mater Dolorosa, 400. Madonna and Child; between these, 1962· *Dom. Theotocopuli (el Greco),* SS. Peter and Paul. — Left side-wall, *Murillo,* *369· Holy Family, a little gem distinguished by delicacy of composition, depth of feeling, and finished execution (ca. 1665); **371. Immaculate Conception, still better than the famous picture in the Louvre in its naïve charm of youth, its delicate chiaroscuro, and its perfect state of preservation (ca. 1675); to the left, 361. Annunciation; to the right, 374. Death of Peter Arbuez, the Inquisitor; *359· Jacob's Ladder, the angels seen through a golden haze, and depicted with great animation (ca. 1665); below, adjoining No. 371, 368. Rest on the Flight into Egypt; to the right, **367. Rest on the Flight into Egypt, with unusually beautiful figures bathed in deep glowing colour; above, to the right, 365. St. Joseph and the Child Christ; **373. Vision of St. Anthony (ca. 1675); adjoining the door of Room XXVI, 366. St. Joseph and the Child Christ; *377· Boy with dog, like No. 378, a naïve work of strong colouring and delicate tone (ca. 1655); above, to the right, 363. Adoration of the Shepherds; below, to the right, *378. Girl with flowers and fruit (ca. 1655). — End-wall, *Murillo,* *372· Angel delivering St. Peter from prison (ca. 1672); above, *362· Immaculate Conception ('Concepción Esquilache'; ca. 1665). — Right side wall, *354· *A. Cano,* Vision of a Dominican; *Velazquez,* *418· Pope Innocent X. (according to Justi a spirited replica of the head in the painting at the Palazzo Doria, Rome); adjacent, 1849. Luncheon; 419. Philip IV. of Spain (school-piece); adjacent, 349. *Zurbaran,* St. Lawrence; *421· *Velazquez,* Duke of Olivarez, minister of Philip IV.; below, 348. *Zurbaran,* Virgin as a child; above, to the right, *331. *Ribera*, St.Sebastian's martyrdom, a work of noble conception; below, 1850. *Ribera*, Ecce Homo. —415,416. *Pereda*, Still-life pieces; 333. *Ribera*, St. Jerome. —End-wall, 414. *Mayno*, Adoration of the Shepherds.

Entrance to the Raphael Gallery, see p. 162.

We return to the large Italian Room (II) and enter Room III.

Room III. **Netherlandish School.** To the left, 620. *A. van Dyck*, Sir Thomas Chaloner (?); **576. *Rubens*, Portrait of Helena Fourment, his second wife, as regards technical execution, one of the most perfect and carefully treated productions of his latest period (ca. 1632); 632. *A. van Dyck*, L. Maharkyzus, the physician; above, 653. *Jordaens*, Portrait, full of humour and life; above, 1315. *Fr. Snyders*, Large still-life piece. —Left side wall, *A. van Dyck*, 626. Inigo Jones, the architect, *609. Charles I. of England (see below); 646. *A. van Dyck (?)*, Study for a head of St. Peter; above, *603. *A. van Dyck*, Rest on the Flight into Egypt ('la Vierge aux perdrix'), one of the most brilliantly coloured of the master's religious paintings (ca. 1632); above, 1313. *Fr. Snyders*, Still-life; *574 (below No. 603). *Rubens*, Charles de Longueval, a large and spirited sketch; adjoining the door of Room I, 1784. *Rubens*, Madonna and Child; above, *610. *A. van Dyck*, Henrietta of England, companion-piece to No. 609, and, like it, remarkable for its air of aristocratic bearing (ca. 1638); 1316, *1320. *Fr. Snyders*, Large still-life pieces. Lower row, 622. *A. van Dyck*, Portrait of Jan van den Wouver (1632); 585, 584. *Rubens*, Franciscan monks; between these, *535. *Rubens*, Expulsion of Hagar, a finely coloured masterpiece (ca. 1616; smaller replica in Grosvenor House, London); 630. *A. van Dyck*, Lumagne, the Paris banker. Middle row, *A. van Dyck*, *607. Doubting Thomas (early work), 608. St. Sebastian; between these, *543. *Rubens*, Jesus in the house of Simon the Pharisee, the best of the artist's large Biblical compositions in the Hermitage (ca. 1615-20). —End wall, *538. *Rubens*, Virgin and Child (ca. 1615). *A. van Dyck*, **575. Portrait of Isabella Brant, first wife of Rubens (early work); **627. Family portraits, wrongly described as the painter Snyders and his family, the most finished work of his early period, when still under the influence of Rubens; *635. Susanna Fourment and her daughter Catherine (ca. 1620); above, 631. Portrait of the banker, E. Jabach, an early work still showing Italian influence in its brilliant colouring; adjacent, 624. Elderly lady. Below, 578. *Rubens*, Old lady in an armchair (early work). —Right side-wall, lower row, *Rubens*, 586. Head of an old man; *595. Rainbow; 582. Young man; 549. Venus and Adonis; 583. Young lady; *594. Landscape, with a waggon stuck in the mire (ca. 1635); *579. Maid of Honour to the Archduchess Isabella (ca. 1615); middle row, *550. Bacchus (ca. 1637-40). 634. *A. van*

Dyck (?), Two young English girls; top row, 1314. *Fr. Snyders,* Large still-life piece. Beyond the door of Cab. XII, lower row, *Rubens,* 591. Pastoral scene; *551. Bacchanalian scene; *593. Statue of Ceres crowned by putti (the garlands by *J. Brueghel the Elder*); *552. Perseus rescuing Andromeda (ca. 1615). 611. *Adr. Hannemann,* William III. of Orange. Middle row, 617. *A. van Dyck,* Sir Thomas Wharton (1639); 554. *Rubens,* Tigris and Abundantia (ca. 1610); *615. *A. van Dyck,* Henry Danvers, Earl of Danby.—End-wall, in the middle of the lower row, **616. *A. van Dyck,* Philip, Lord Wharton, a masterpiece (1632); to the left and right, 580, 581. *A. van Dyck,* Portraits; 618 (above No. 616), *A. van Dyck,* Elizabeth and Philadelphia Wharton; to the left and right, 559, 560. *Rubens,* Philip IV. of Spain (ca. 1628) and his wife Elizabeth; above, 1317. *Fr. Snyders,* Large still-life piece.

From Room III we pass into the first of a series of rooms lit by side-windows.

Room XVI. **Drawings by Rubens.** [All the works mentioned in this room are by Rubens, unless otherwise stated.] To the left of the entrance, *660. *Quellinus,* Holy Family, in a wreath of flowers by *D. Seghers;* below, to the right, 664. *Ph. de Champaigne,* Moses.—In the middle of the left wall, above, 647. *J. van den Hoecke,* SS. Paul and Barnabas at Lystra; below, to the right, 589. *Jordaens,* Heads of three children, a sketch; right at the end, 544. Last Supper, sketch for the picture in the Brera Gallery at Milan.—First window-stand, 569, 570. Sketches for the paintings ordered by Marie de Médicis for the Luxembourg, now in the Louvre (1621-25); between these, 573. Sketch for the ceiling-paintings at Whitehall (ca. 1629); above, 558. Sketch for statues of five German Emperors, executed for the triumphal arch at Antwerp (1635). On the back of the stand, 567, 568. Sketches like Nos. 569, 570 (see above); between these, *557. Sketch for the altarpiece of St. Ildefonso, now in Vienna (ca. 1630); upper row, *561, *566. Sketches for the triumphal arch for the entry of the Cardinal Infante Ferdinand into Antwerp (1635), affording a most brilliant proof of Rubens's extraordinary power of invention, skill in composition, and mastery of picturesque treatment; between these 572. Sketch like No. 573 (see above).—Second window-stand *562, *565. Sketches like No. 561; between these, 571. Sketch like No. 569 (see above); upper row, 590. Lion-hunt, a rough sketch for the famous Munich picture. On the back of the stand, *563, *564. Sketches like No. 561 (see above).—Right wall, 556. Study of a scene from Roman history; to the right of the door of R. XIII, above, 546. Descent from the Cross, the figure of Christ by the master himself, the rest the work of his pupils (ca. 1613); *650. *Jordaens,* Satyr and peasant; above, 1785. Caritas

Romana (ca. 1612).—Entrance-wall, 642. *C. de Vos,* The family constitutional; above, 536. Adoration of the Magi, a large work (ca. 1614); adjoining the door, 727. *G. Coques,* Portrait.—In the middle of the room is a large vase of 'orlétz' (manganite).

We now pass through the door on the right into —

Room XIII. **Netherlandish School.** In the middle of the entrance-wall, 1932. *A. van der Meulen,* Scene from Condé's campaigns. — To the right and left of the door leading to Room XII, above, 1377, 1376. *N. van Verendael,* Flora, Pomona. — To the right of the door leading to Room XV, 714. *D. Ryckaert III.,* Old woman with a cat; above, to the right, 1921. *Flemish School of the 17th cent.,* Studies of heads.

The door in the end-wall of R. XIII leads into Cab. XII.; we, however, pass through the door in the side-wall, and enter —

Room XV. **Rembrandt Gallery,** which is separated by partitions into 5 cabinets, and also contains 14 glass-cases with etchings by Rembrandt, bequeathed to the Hermitage by Senator D. A. Rovinski. [The pictures in Cabs. A-E mentioned below without the artist's name are all by Rembrandt.]

Cab. A. To the left, 801. Doubting Thomas (1634); 817. Saskia, the master's first wife, at her toilet (1654); *792. Abraham's sacrifice, lifesize figures (1635); above, to the right, 813. Portrait of an Oriental (ca. 1633).

**802. So-called Danaë (1636).

'Titian himself could not have depicted more truly or with greater charm the softness and delicacy of the warm and palpitating flesh, or the effect of light and shade on the skin. The cool green curtains, the gilt baroque frame of the gorgeous bedstead with its white linen, add to the glowing effect of the nude figure, on which the light is poured, and still further enhance the changing play of light and shade and the wonderful charm of the chiaroscuro.'   (*Bode,* Dutch Painting.)

Cab. B. **811. Portrait of a man (wrongly called John Sobieski), with exceptionally fine effects of light (1637); above, 828. Portrait of a young man (1634); *800. Descent from the Cross, a large masterpiece of his early period (1634); *808. Portrait of a scholar (wrongly called Coppenol, the writing-master; 1631); above, 1842. Young man. — In the lower row, 815. Old Jew; 814. Old warrior (ca. 1630); **796. Holy Family, an idyll of domestic happiness (1645); *798. Parable of the Labourers in the Vineyard, a small but vital composition (1637); *807. Old woman, so-called Mother of Rembrandt (1643). In the upper row, to the left, 824. Elderly man (1654); 822. Hannah teaching Samuel to read (ascription doubtful); *806. Half-length portrait of an old lady (ca. 1654).

Cab. C. *826. Girl with a broom ('La balayeuse'; 1651); 1777. David reconciled to Absalom (1642); above, **804. Old woman with a book (ca. 1658); *820. Portrait ('Rabbi'; 1645). — 809. Minerva (ca. 1650); 794. Potiphar's wife accusing Joseph (1655); above, 795. Fall of Haman (ca. 1650); *818. Old man (ca. 1654).

Cab. D. 825. Portrait of a young man; above, 821. Portrait (ca. 1661); *799. Peter denying Christ, a large and powerful composition (ca. 1656); 827. Elderly man. — *797. Return of the Prodigal Son, the largest Biblical canvas of Rembrandt's later years, abounding in sentiment (ca. 1668).

Cab. E. *829. Portrait of an old lady (ca. 1642); 819. Portrait of a young lady; above, *793 (?). Jacob's sons showing Joseph's blood-stained coat to their father. — *805. Portrait of an old woman (1654), masterly and broad in treatment; *791. Abraham entertaining the three angels (ca. 1636); 810. Old Jew (1654); above, *G. van Honthorst,* 750. Bon vivant, 751. Mandoline-player.

Main wall, beginning at Cab. E: 831. *J. van de Capelle,* River-scene; above, to the left, 854. *F. Bol,* Portrait of an old lady; 834. *F. Bol,* Half-length portrait of an officer; 856. *F. Bol,* Portrait of an old man (so-called Father of Rembrandt); above, to the right, 837. *S. Koninck,* Crœsus showing his treasures to Solon; above, 748. *G. van Honthorst,* Elector-Palatine Charles Louis; below, to the right, *F. Bol,* 853. Portrait of a young man, 848, 849. Portraits, 852. Philosopher; 844. *G. Flinck,* Portrait of a young officer; 1907. *School of Rembrandt,* Tobias taking leave of his parents before his journey with the angel; 867. *A. de Gelder,* Young officer, 1831. Portrait of the artist; 816. *J. Livens,* Portrait of an old man; *847. *F. Bol,* The scholar, the finest of this master's pictures in the Hermitage.

Two doors lead from the Rembrandt Gallery into the narrow parallel —

GALLERY XIV. **Early Netherlandish and German Schools,** arranged in five cabinets.

Cab. e. To the left, in the middle, 491. *Netherlandish School of the 16th cent.,* Adoration of the Shepherds. — On the opposite wall, *Jan Brueghel the Elder,* 518. Highroad, 515. Village-street; above, to the right, 1199. *P. Neeffs,* Interior of a Gothic church.

Cab. d. Opposite the windows, 1693. *P. Brueghel the Younger,* John the Baptist preaching; in the middle, 513. *Jan Brueghel the Elder,* Landscape (1607); 508. *A. Elsheimer,* Forest-scene; above, 1200, 1201, 1198. *P. Neeffs,* Gothic church-interiors.

Cab. c. 478, *479. *Chr. Amberger,* Portraits of a young man and his wife, finely characterized and brilliant in colouring; between these, 462. *L. Cranach the Elder,* Cardinal Albert of Mayence (1526). — *Sir Anthony More (Mor),* *480, *481. Sir Thomas Gresham, founder of the Royal Exchange in London, and his wife (ca. 1570); *482 (between 480 and 481), Portrait. *L. Cranach the Elder,* 459. Madonna under an apple-tree, 460. Madonna in a vine-arbour (early work); above, *485, 486. *Fr. Pourbus the Elder*, Portraits. — 466 .*Ambr. Holbein*, Portrait; 1913. *German School of the 17th cent.*, Emperor Rudolf II. — On the window-wall, 461. *L. Cranach the Elder*, Venus and Cupid, a good work of his early period (1509).

Cab. b. *487· *Fr. Pourbus the Younger*, Portraits. — 474. *Jan Gossaert*, surnamed *Mabuse*, Descent from the Cross; *468· *Lucas van Leyden*, Healing of the Blind Man, triptych (ca. 1531) the most important work of this rare painter; above, 1717, 1718. *Gortzius Geldorp*, Portraits of G. Hautappel and his wife. — 1867. *H. Bles*, Flight into Egypt; 475. *M. Coxie*, Annunciation.

Cab. a. To the right of the door leading to the Rembrandt Gallery, 445. *Roger van der Weyden*, St. Luke painting the Virgin (replica of the Munich picture); above, 476. *D. J. van Oostsaanen*, Guild of arquebusiers; to the left of the door, 444. *Jan van Eyck (?)*, Diptych with the Crucifixion and the Last Judgment; *443· *Jan* or *Hubert van Eyck*, Annunciation; 446. (above No. 444), *D. Bouts*, Annunciation; below, to the left, 1918. *A. Isenbrant*, St. Jerome in the desert; above, 458. *Gerard David*, Pietà, enclosed in a wreath of flowers; above, 477. *J. Cornelisz*, Guild of arque-busiers. — *Master of Flémalle*, 447. Trinity, 448. Madonna and Child; 449. *J. Provost*, Triumph of the Virgin.

We return through RR. XIII and XVI to —

Room XVII. German Masters of the 17th and 18th centuries. To the right, in the middle of the wall, 1303. *R. Mengs*, Portrait of the artist. Opposite, 1305. *Angelica Kauffmann*, Scene from Sterne's 'Sentimental Journey'; 1285, 1286. *B. Denner*, Portraits. — 1302. *R. Mengs*, Judgment of Paris. — To the left of the window, 1297. *R. Mengs*, Annunciation. — Adjoining is the long —

Room XVIII. Dutch and Flemish Schools. Each side of the gallery is divided into five cabinets.

Right Side. 1056. *P. Potter (?)*, Landscape; above, to the left, 782. *B. van der Helst*, Full-length portrait (1670); 788. *Th. de Keyser*, Portrait.

First short partition-wall, 1767. *Adr. van Ostade*, Brawl· above, 1702. *S. de Vlieger*, Sea-piece; 952. *Adr. van Ostade*, Beerhouse; above, *940· *Adr. Brouwer*, Flute-player. — 951. *Adr. van Ostade*, Village musician; 979. *Ph. Angel*, Kitchen; 902. *Jan Steen*, Tavern-scene.

First long partition-wall, 907. *G. Dou*, Rabbi; 1778. *P. Quast*, Doctor — *A. Cuyp*, *1104. Cows at pasture, *1105· Horses; be-tween these, 874. *Terburg*, Music-lesson; upper row, 740. *P. Miere-velt*, Portrait; 900. *Jan Steen*, Backgammon-players.

Second short partition-wall, *G. Dou*, 911. Soldier bathing, 905. Herring-seller, 912. Girl bathing.

Second long partition-wall, in the middle of the lower row,

**870. *Terburg,* The glass of lemonade, a masterpiece, in an excellent state of preservation; above, to the right, *1096. *J.B. Weenix,* Pastoral scene. — In the middle of the lower row, *771. *Fr. Hals the Elder,* Portrait; to the right, *1135. *A. van Everdingen,* Storm at the mouth of the Scheldt, a most effective composition; upper row, at the end, 1780. *R. de Vries,* Landscape.

Third short partition-wall, 1006. *Ph. Wouverman,* Highroad; 946. *Adr. van Ostade,* Peasant-family. — *Jan van der Heyde,* *1208. Haarlem Gate in Amsterdam, 1206. Street in Cologne; between these, *897. *Jan Steen,* Garden-party; upper row, *Adr. van Ostade,* 954. Peasant family, 948. Old woman; between these, 1122. *A. van der Neer,* Wintry landscape.

Third long partition-wall, 1788. *Jan Steen,* Tavern-scene; 1139. *J. van Ruysdael,* Landscape; *770. *Frans Hals the Elder,* Portrait; *1148. *J. van Ruysdael,* Scene near Groningen (very effective; 1647). — *998. *Ph. Wouverman,* Riding-school; above, 1776. *E. van der Poel,* Conflagration at night; *872. *Terburg,* Messenger; 1166. *A. Pynacker,* Italian landscape; 903. *G. Dou,* Doctor; *995. *Ph. Wouverman,* 'La Course au Chat', an exceptionally rich and picturesque masterpiece of his best period (ca. 1655).

Fourth short partition-wall, in the middle of the upper row 871. *Terburg,* Violin-player. — 937. *Adr. Brouwer,* Toper. •

Fourth long partition-wall, *J. van Ostade,* 964. Frozen lake, *963. Inn; between these, *880. *G. Metsu,* The breakfast, a masterpiece of great charm; *1032. *Wouverman,* Return from hawking; above, to the left, 1127. *Goyen,* Coast-scene; above, to the left, 1359. *A. Mignon,* Nosegay. — 1059. *G. Camphuysen,* Cattle; *896. *Jan Steen,* Doctor's visit; *1117. *A. van der Neer,* Village on an island in the Meuse, a famous work; *878. *G. Metsu,* Invalid · above, to the right, 781. *B. van der Helst (?),* Portrait.

Fifth short partition-wall, *G. Dou,* *913. Bible-reading, *909. Spinner; above, 1131, 1132. *J. van Goyen,* Landscapes. — 1162. *A. Pynacker,* Italian coast; *918. *F. van Mieris the Elder,* Small portrait of a lady (1665).

End wall, middle row, *1147. *J. van Ruysdael,* Norwegian landscape (the so-called Mountain Tarn), a masterpiece of his later period, distinguished by its superb composition and poetical feeling; 1107. *A. Cuyp,* Cattle; 1133. *A. van Everdingen,* Norwegian landscape; below, adjoining the door, 1106. *A. Cuyp,* Calm scene by moonlight. — In the middle, below, 1062. *A. van der Velde,* Cattle, a large canvas (1671); above, *1145. *J. van Ruysdael,* Norwegian waterfall, a large and elaborate composition; *1055. *P. Potter,* Watch-dog (1650), a masterly work (lifesize); 1138. *J. van Ruysdael,* Forest-brook.

Left Side of R. XVIII, beginning at the door to R. XIX.

First short partition-wall, *1052. *P. Potter,* The huntsman's life; different forms of hunting are delicately and often cleverly depicted in twelve small compositions, while two larger scenes in the centre represent the trial by the animals of the huntsman, and the execution of the sentence upon him. — *1051. *P. Potter,* Farmyard, the most important of all 'cattle-pieces', not only for its size but also for its exquisite morning light and the characteristic treatment of the various animals (1649).

First long partition-wall, *A. Cuyp,* 1102. The Meuse, 1103. Scene on the Scheldt; to the right, 1213. *Jan van der Heyde,* Fortified castle; above, to the left, 996. *Ph. Wouverman,* Riding-school. — 1128. *J. van Goyen,* Landscape; above, to the left, 877. *G. Metsu,* Prodigal Son.

Second short partition-wall, 1854. *J. van Goyen,* Landscape. — *G. Dou,* 904. Herring-seller, 906. Violin-player; between these, 1971. *Hobbema,* Wooded landscape; above, to the right, 1087. *K. du Jardin,* Landscape.

Second long partition-wall, below, to the left, 1130. *J. van Goyen,* River-scene; to the right, 898. *Jan Steen,* Merry toper· *1211. Jan van der Heyde,* View in Amsterdam. — 1137. *J. van Ruysdael,* Approaching thunderstorm; *772. *Fr. Hals the Elder,* Portrait; 1141. *J. van Ruysdael,* Path by a pond; above, *J. Vanloo,* 1252. Concert, 1253. Visit; 932. *A. Palamedesz,* Genre-scene.

Third short partition-wall, in the middle of the lower row, 861. *P. de Hooch,* Concert; above, to the left, 914. *G. Dou,* Portrait; 1186. *W. van de Velde the Younger,* Calm sea; 1248. *F. van Mieris the Younger,* Breakfast. — *860. *P. de Hooch,* Lady and cook, an excellent and sunny work of his middle period; 1057. *P. Potter,* Bull (ca. 1651); above, to the left, 910. *G. Dou,* Bather.

Third long partition-wall, 873. *Terburg,* Messenger; in the middle, 773. *Fr. Hals the Elder,* Portrait of an officer; *1017. *Ph. Wouverman,* Landscape; above, 975. *Benj. Cuyp,* Brawl; adjacent, 1204. *D. van Delen,* Entrance to a palace (1667). — 943. *P. de Hooch,* Bedroom; *901. *Jan Steen,* Peasant wedding; 1134. *A. van Everdingen,* Norwegian landscape; in the middle of the upper row, 761. *C. van Poelenburgh,* Diana and Callisto; above, to the right, 882. *C. Netscher,* Queen Mary II. of England (1683).

Fourth short partition-wall, 1111. *J. Wynants,* Landscape with sheep; *915. *F. Mieris the Elder,* Lap-dog; above, *Adr. Brouwer,* *938. Peasants in a tavern, 939. Peasants quarrelling. — 916. *F. van Mieris the Elder,* Oyster-breakfast, the earliest and yet perhaps the most finished work of the artist (1659).

Fourth long partition-wall, 1042. *Ph. Wouverman,* Landscape; *1053. *P. Potter,* Two huntsmen leaving a tavern, a masterpiece of colouring and distribution of light and shade (1650); *1136. *J. van Ruysdael,* Forest; *1054. *P. Potter,* Cattle (1651); below, to the right, 1040. *Ph. Wouverman,* Winter-scene; 1081 (above

No. 1136), *Cl. Berchem*, Italian landscape (1656). — *Jan van der Meer*, 1153. Landscape, *1154· Dutch village; between these, 742. *Jan van Ravesteyn (?)*, Portrait of a little girl; below, to the right, *881· *G. Metsu*, Family scene.

Fifth short partition-wall, *J. van Ostade*, 956. Touch, 957. Sight, 958. Taste; 1037 (above No. 956), *Ph. Wouverman*, Young bird-catchers; above, to the right, 990. *Adr. van der Werff*, Mary Magdalen in the desert; 879. *G. Metsu*, Concert. — *Adr. van Ostade*, *947· Itinerant musician, *949· Ballad-singer; between these, 955. *I. van Ostade*, Tavern-scene; above, *1142· *J. van Ruysdael*, Forest-path; to the right and left, *Adr. van Ostade*, 959. Peasant-scene, *950· Baker.

End-wall, in the middle, below, *1143· *J. van Ruysdael*, Sandy path, a large and early work, almost unrivalled in its faithful representation of a most insignificant fragment of the earth's surface (1646); above, 757. *C. van Poelenburgh*, Rest on the Flight into Egypt; to the left and right, 1861, 1862. *N. Elias*, Man and wife.

CORNER ROOM XIX. **Dutch and Flemish Schools** (continued). To the right of the entrance, 1218. *G. Houckgeest*, Monument of Admiral P. Hein in the Oude Kerk at Delft; 892. *J. Ochtervelt*, Breakfast; above the closed door, 1348. *J. Weenix*, Hunting trophies. To the left of the entrance, 999. *Ph. Wouverman*, Riding-school; in the middle, below, 1709. *D. Hals*, Merry company; above, in the third row, 1768. *J. Ochtervelt*, Buying fish; below, to the right, 1271. *J. Lingelbach*, Leghorn Harbour. — To the left of the door to Room XX, 1125. *A. van der Neer*, Dutch town by moonlight; above, to the left, 927. *Brekelenkam*, Hermit. To the right of the door to Room XX, 1124. *A. van der Neer*, River-scene. — First window-stand, 971. *Corn. Bega*, Peasant family; at the back, *Ph. Wouverman*, 1014. Travellers resting, 1002. Travellers; above, 1355. *J. D. de Heem*, Nosegay; 1704. *Ph. Wouverman*, Bathers. Second window-stand, 1730. *K. du Jardin*, Ford; at the back, 1003. *Ph. Wouverman*, Travellers. On the window-wall, *1116· Jan Wynants, Landscape. — To the right is the First Hermitage of the Empress Catherine II. (p. 131); to the left is —

ROOM XX. **Netherlandish and British Masters.** To the right of the entrance, **672. *David Teniers the Younger*, Guild festival in the square in front of the town hall of Antwerp (1643), the best and largest picture by the master in the Hermitage; above, *698· *D. Teniers the Younger*, Kitchen interior. — First window-stand, in the middle, above, *D. Teniers the Younger*, *677· Wedding-breakfast, *699· Monkeys in the kitchen; at the back, *673· *D. Teniers the Younger*, Guard-room (1642), remarkable for its brilliant and powerful colouring. — Second window-stand, *D. Teniers the Younger*, *674· Village-festival (1646), 688. Card-players. At the back, *Raeburn*, Mrs. Bethune; *Hoppner*, Thomas Sheridan, father of the dramatist; *Gainsborough*, Lady of quality (Duchess of Beaufort); above, 1914. *H. von Kulmbach*, Intercession of Christ and the Virgin for an abbot. — Exit-wall, *Romney*, Mrs. Hadley d'Oyly; *John Opie*, Frances Vinnicombe; *1872. *Lawrence*, Portrait of Count Vorontzóv; above, *Lawrence*, *Lady Raglan; 1392. *Reynolds*, Magnanimity of Scipio; *Kneller*, 1388. John Locke the philosopher, 1389. Grinling Gibbons the sculptor; *Reynolds*, 1390. Venus and Cupid, 1391 (above), Hercules throttling the snakes (painted to the order of Catherine II.). — Main wall, *778. *A. van den Tempel*, Family portrait (known, on Burger's authority, as the 'Potter Family'); 1312. *Fr. Snyders*, Large still-life piece; *1034. *Ph. Wouverman*, Stag-hunt; *779. *B. van der Helst*, Large family portrait (1652); *777. *B. van der Helst*, Presentation of the bride, showing a young couple greeting the parents of the bridegroom in a park, one of the artist's masterpieces; above, to the right, *1339. *M. d'Hondecoeter*, Water-fowl in a park, a similar picture to the 'Plume Flottante' in the Ryks Museum at Amsterdam. — This room also contains two vases of lapis lazuli.

The next two rooms contain works by —

French Masters of the 17th and 18th centuries. — Room XXI. On the entrance-wall, to the right, 1904. *L. Tocqué*, Portrait of the Dauphin Louis, father of Louis XVI.; to the right, **1413. *N. Poussin*, Italian river-scene with Hercules and Cacus (see below); 1487. *J. Clouet*, Duke of Alençon; above, *1438. *Claude Lorrain*, Italian forest-scene with Apollo and Marsyas; above, 1491. *Le Valentin*, Duet. On the entrance-wall, to the left, 1488. *School of Clouet*, Portrait of Mary, Queen of Scots, said to have been painted at the Castle of Fotheringay in 1586. — Main wall. To the left, above, 1875, 1876. *C. A. Vanloo*, Conversation-pieces; below, to the right, 1908. *J. M. Nattier*, Portrait of Louis XV. Above, 1421. *S. Bourdon*, Death of Dido; below, 1485. *C. A. Vanloo*, Portrait of the artist (1762); 1808. *J. B. Le Moyne*, The two knights on the island of Armida (from Tasso's 'Jerusalemme Liberata'). — End-wall, 1878. *L. M. Vanloo*, Concert. To the right of the door, **1414. *N. Poussin*, Italian mountain-scene with Polyphemus (1648); this painting and its companion-piece, No. 1413, are the almost unrivalled masterpieces of the artist, both in the delicacy of the colouring and in the majestic composition of the landscape. — First transverse wall (beginning at the entrance to Room XXII), 1809. *P. Mignard*, Portrait of a lady; above, 1458. *P. Mignard*, Duchess de la Vallière. Between the 1st and 2nd windows, 1554. *Cl. J. Vernet*, Death of Virginia. — Second transverse wall, at the back, 1537. *Largillière*, Preparations for a fête at the Hôtel de Ville in Paris.

Room XXII. On the entrance-wall, to the right, *Fr. Boucher*, *1797. Landscape; 1486. Rest on the Flight into Egypt (1757); above, to the right, 1798. Hermit. To the left of the entrance, *1435. *Claude Lorrain*, Seaport; above, 1546. *Cl. J. Vernet*, Near Sorrento; 1543. *Cl. J. Vernet*, Storm. — Main wall, **1428, **1429, 1430, 1431. *Claude Lorrain*, Periods of the Day (1672), Italian landscapes marked by the delicate treatment of the various light-effects, though Evening and Night have, unfortunately, become much darkened; between Nos. 1429 and 1430, *1400. *N. Poussin*, Triumph of Amphitrite, distinguished for its masterly treatment of the joy of motion and for the colour and beauty of its figures. Upper row, *J. de Troy*, 1498. Susannah at the bath, 1497. Lot and his daughters; between these, *1456. *P. Mignard*, Magnanimity of Alexander the Great. — End-wall, above, 1449. *E. Le Sueur*, Stoning of St. Stephen. To the right of the door, in the middle, *1520. *J. B. Greuze*, Death of the gouty patient, one of the master's chief works; above, 1480. *C. A. Vanloo*, Triumph of Galatea. — By the windows are two partition-walls and three stands. First stand (beginning at the entrance to R. XXIII), *1516. *J. H. Fragonard*, Country family; at the back, *M. Gérard*, 1805. Woman painting, 1804. Happy mother. First partition-wall, *J. S. Chardin*, 1514. Washerwoman, *1513. Saying grace; 1800. *J. B. Greuze*, Head of a girl; *1519. *J. B. Perronneau*, Portrait of a boy; *1517. *J. B. Greuze*, Head of a girl; at the back, 1874. *Ant. Watteau*, Camp; above, *N. Lancret*, 1509. Kitchen, 1510. The gallant servant. Second stand, *J. B. Pater* 1812. Breaking camp, 1811. Camp; above, 1515. *J. S. Chardin*, House of cards; at the back, 1845. *J. H. Fragonard*, Stolen kiss. Second partition-wall, *Ant. Watteau*, *1504. Burden of war; above, *1502. Bagpipe-player; *1503. Guitar-player; above, *1501. Conversation-piece; *1505. Camp; above, *1923. Female figure. Third stand, *N. Lancret*, *1508. Summer, *1507. Spring.

The three following rooms (XXIII-XXV) contain the large **Numismatic Collection** (more than 200,000 coins and medals).

The chief contents of the Coin Cabinet are the collections of the Academy of Sciences, and of Schroll, Reichel, Count Shuválov, Grant, Bartholomäi, Photiadi-Pasha, Lobánov, Velyaminov-Syornov, and Lishin. In 1899 the Kiev treasure trove of 16,000 pieces was added (including a gold medallion of Constantius II. and a medal of Constantine Ostrozhski). — Amongst the *Russian Coins* (12,000) are five gold coins of St. Vladimir; silver coins of Vladimir, Yaroslavl, and Svyatopolk; silver and gold bar-money (Grivni) from Kiev; silver bars from Novgorod and Tchernigov (11-15th cent.); coins of the Russian principalities (Удѣльные) from the middle of the 14th cent. (when the Russian coinage was instituted) onwards; bilingual Russo-Arabic and Russo-Tartar coins (14th & 15th cent.); coins of the Novgorod and Pskov Republics; a ducat of Ivan III., coined after the Hungarian pattern (unique); rare gold coins of the Tzars, presented as rewards, from the time of Ivan the Terrible to Peter the Great; imperial coins, valuable on account of the number of unique specimens, and proof coins. An octagonal glass-case contains laminated copper coins,

struck (as an experiment) under Catherine I. and Catherine II. in Yekaterinburg. The complete collection of Russian medals, remarkable for their
size rather than their beauty, includes some platinum medals from the
time of Nicholas I. and Alexander II.—Numerous sets of coins from Poland and the Baltic Provinces.—There are 25,000 Greek and 20,000 Roman
coins. The most noteworthy of the *Greek Coins* are those of the rulers
of the Bosphorus, of the Greek colonies in S. Russia, of the reign of
Alexander the Great, of Lysimachus (ca. 800 gold-pieces), and of Athens
(including the Beulé collection). The Byzantine series (3000) is also important.—Bactrian coins and coins of the Sassanides and Seleucides.—
Among the *Coins of Western Europe* may be mentioned the Anglo-Saxon
coins (incl. 1000 of the time of Ethelred II., found in Russia), the German
coins of the 10-12th cent., the Swedish copper money (including several
8-thaler pieces of the time of Charles XI., weighing 30 lbs.), and the Dutch
coins. There is also a fine collection of thalers of the 15-18th centuries.
—The rich collection of *Oriental Coins* (43,000) includes Chinese, Japanese,
and Corean coins; Persian and Tartar coins (representing more than 200
dynasties) are nowhere better represented.

The RAPHAEL GALLERY (XXVII), with copies of five of Raphael's
works in the loggie of the Vatican painted by the Tyrolese artist
Christopher Unterberger about 1786, contains the **Collection of
Gems and Miniatures**. It is entered from the Room of the
Spanish Masters (IV; see p. 151). The chief feature is the famous
collection of the Duke of Orleans, purchased by Catherine II. Intaglios and cameos are exhibited in pyramidal and flat glass-cases
(the intaglios accompanied by plaster casts), including (in the case
by the last window, to the right of the entrance) the *Gonzaga
Cameo*, or 'Camée de la Malmaison', with the busts of Ptolemy I.
and his wife and sister Arsinoë. Another large cameo adjoining it
represents the Emperor Trajan and the Tyche of Antioch.—We
now return to Room IV, and pass thence into—

ROOM XXVI, containing the *Collection of Gems and
Ornaments**. Like the Collection of Silver described at p. 164, it
is of great importance for the study of French goldsmith's work of
the 18th century.

We first enter a semicircular room separated from the main saloon
by four yellow marble columns. This room contains five coin-cabinets
(médailliers) of Catherine II., by Röntgen, with bronze decorations ascribed
to Gouthière. At the entrance, by the columns, are two dark bronze figures
of Egyptians, in gilded clothing, and holding dishes of yellow quartz
over their heads.

Scattered about the room are 26 cabinets (see p. 163), all exactly alike,
made to the order of Catherine II. Between them, in the middle row, are
some magnificent escritoires of Empress Catherine II. and Empress Marie
Feódorovna, wife of Paul I., with secret drawers and automatic devices,
three of them with musical boxes. Especially noteworthy is the escritoire
by Gambs (1815), in redwood, with inlays of dark American walnut and
bronze-gilt ornaments.—At the back of the room is a large chiming clock,
made by J. G. Strasser in 1793-1801. In front of the clock stands a large
*Glass-case, containing the most valuable pieces in the collection, including
some vases of Marie Antoinette by Gouthière; aigrettes of Potemkin and
Suvórov, set with brilliants; sprays set with precious stones, belonging
to the Empresses Anna and Elizabeth; table-clock; mirror, in a frame
set with brilliants and precious stones; vases, goblets, small articles of

jewellery (including examples by the Dinglingers); and silver-gilt caskets, richly ornamented with cameos, pearls, and precious stones, presented by King Sigismund I. to the Elector Joachim I. of Brandenburg, with the arms of both these rulers. In a small glass-case are Chinese and Indo-Persian objects in nephrite; in another, Persian goldsmith's work, mostly of the 16th century. In the middle of the room, between the escritoires, are two glass-cases, one containing snuff-boxes, the other polished stones from the Urals.

Cabinets (comp. p. 162). To the left and right of the entrance, Cabs 10 & 11. Fans, small articles of jewellery, and tortoise-shell of the 18th century. — Main wall. Cab. 2. Objects in crystal and rock-crystal, including a glass that belonged to Anne Boleyn (on a silver-gilt stand). Cab. 15. Bronze objects adorned with porcelain (18th cent.). Cab. 16. Objects belonging to Alexander I. and Napoleon I., including the gold travelling toilet-set of the latter. Cab. 4. Tula work in steel and silver; toilet-set of Catherine the Great. Cab. 14. Bibelots of the 17th cent. in stone, metal, tortoise-shell, and enamel. Cab. 12. Persian objects. Cabs. 19, 18, & 21. Objects in semi-precious stones, silver, and gold; filigree-work; toilet-set of the Empress Elizabeth. Cab 8. Clocks and watches of the 17-18th centuries. Cab. 1. Smaller *objets d'art* from the middle of the 19th cent. onwards, including a chess-set of Alexander III. and a gold casket presented with the Freedom of the City of London. — End-wall. Cab. 25. Objects in jasper, porphyry, and marble, adorned with bronze (18th cent.). Cabs 6 & 9. *Turkish saddle-cloth, and Turkish bridle, set with brilliants. Cab. 13 (between the last two), Swords and walking-sticks of the Tzars. — In the centre of the room are four cabinets. Cab. 7. *Watches and pendants of the 18th cent., a collection of unique value. Cab. 17. Gold toilet-set of Empress Anna Ivánovna, made at Augsburg. Cab. 23 contains the insignia of the Order of the Garter belonging to Nicholas I. and Alexander II. Cab. 20. All the Russian and many foreign Orders. — Window-wall, beginning at the end. Glass-cases II, I, 7, & 6: *Snuffboxes. Cabs. 3 & 24. Objects in ivory, walrus ivory, and malachite. Between the cabinets, in Glass-cases 4 & 3, Cameos and intaglios with Biblical scenes and portraits. Case 5. Chinese gold filigree work, chiefly head-ornaments. Cases 1 & 2. Souvenirs of the Empress Marie Feódorovna.

In this room are also seven obelisks ornamented with bronze. In the first two are bibelots of the 17th cent. (by the Dinglingers); in the next two, bibelots of the 18th cent. including some objects in bloodstone and gold; in the next two, objects in rock-crystal; and in the last, Persian gems and ornaments. — In the middle of the room, on a plinth of grey marble, is a miniature representation of the insignia of the crown (p. 115) in brilliants and gold, by Fabergé.

Especially noteworthy is the 18th cent. furniture scattered about the room; bureau or commode in redwood with bronze ornamentation; Louis XVI. bureau, with inlaid plaques, painted blue and white in the Wedgwood style; small coin cabinet of Catherine II. in redwood, probably by Gouthière; two tripod-tables in bronze and stone; two clocks by Röntgen, with musical boxes. On all the cabinets are vases in Siberian stone with bronze ornaments.

First Hermitage of Empress Catherine II., entered from Corner Room XIX (p. 159) across an archway.

I. Transverse Gallery, with views of St. Petersburg by *Gius. Valeriani* (reign of Empress Elizabeth), *B. Paterson* (time of Paul I. and Alexander I.), and *Alexéyev.*

II. Long Gallery, on the right, divided into three sections: the Silver Collection, the Peacock Cabinet, and the Porcelain Collection. [The Museum of Peter the Great is now in the Academy of Sciences, p. 166.]

A. Collection of Silver. Comp. p. 162.—CABINET I. Silver and gold salt-cellars. gold goblet presented to Field-Marshal Münnich after the Finnish campaign, gold tea-service by Köpping (St. Petersburg), etc.

CAB. II. *German and English Work.* *Silver-gilt goblet in the form of a two-headed eagle, made at Nuremberg (ca. 1590). Silver-gilt goblets and tankards, made at Nuremberg and Augsburg. Six tankards, 17th cent., made at Danzig.—To the left is a large dish; also tankards and pitchers of English workmanship made for Catherine I. Tankards and small bowls in gold, made at Augsburg. Dish with the arms of Riga.

CAB. III. Russian drinking-goblets, so-called 'kavshi' (ковши, ladles) and 'bratini' (братины, 'brother bowls', *i.e.* punch bowls). Collection of the Grand-Duke Alexis Alexándrovitch.

CAB. IV. Italian, French, & German filigree work.

CAB. V. Below are three epergnes, that to the left by Claude Ballin, that in the middle by Liebmann of St. Petersburg, that to the right (formerly belonging to Duke Biron of Courland) by Biller of Augsburg. There are also four soup-tureens of St. Petersburg workmanship. Above are two tureens from Turin, and a large silver bowl from Amsterdam.

CAB. VI. Large wine-fountain, made at Copenhagen (1795). On each side and above, smaller fountains from Augsburg and London (17th cent.).

CAB. VII. Silver-gilt toilet-service by Germain. Above, Parisian work of the 18th cent.

CAB. VIII. Collection of Grand-Duke Alexis Alexándrovitch: Silver-gilt pitchers from Nuremberg; goblet in the shape of an eagle's head; large tankard made at Riga in the 17th cent.; tea-service with niello, Siberian work. The objects on the upper shelf are of the 19th century.

CAB. IX. *Parisian Work.* *Six silver-gilt soup-tureens with supports, by Fr. Th. Germain (1758-9). *Silver dishes with lids, also by Germain Four silver-gilt soup-tureens with supports, by L. Lehendrick (1769-70). Silver-gilt candelabra, also by Lehendrick. Two silver-gilt soup-tureens with supports, by P. Charvel (1769-70). Silver soup-tureens and candelabra, by J. N. Rœtiers (1770). Silver wine-cooler and candlesticks by R. J. Auguste (1776-8).

Along the window-wall are large silver *Vases*, the first and fifth made at Augsburg, the others at London. Vase with the arms of Lord Scarsdale, by Paul de Lamerie (1726-27; London). Vase with the arms of the Duke of Kingston, the work of an unknown London master (1696-1720). Between the windows are four cabinets. The first (nearest the Peacock Cabinet) contains modern Sèvres figures and an epergne presented by the President of the French Republic to Tzar Nicholas II.; the next two cabinets contain the renowned Wedgwood 'Frog Service', made for Catherine II.; in the fourth cabinet, modern St. Petersburg porcelain.

B. In the middle is the **Peacock Cabinet,** so called from a bronze automatic toy, the work of a Prussian mechanic in London, bought by Potemkin and presented by him to the Empress Catherine II. When the works, concealed in an imitation mushroom, are wound up, the peacock turns round and spreads its tail, the cock by its side crows, and the owl rolls its eyes. By the window are cameos in porcelain, copied by Tassie for the Empress Catherine II.

C. Collection of Porcelain. By the MAIN WALL are eight cabinets containing *Dresden China* (Meissen). *Teapot in red stoneware, by Böttger, in a silver framework set with precious stones. Two *Coffee-services with Chinese scenes (ca. 1720), on silver stands, made by J. Engelbrecht and E. Adam of Augsburg. Clock with dial set with brilliants (1727). Writing-set of the Duchess of Courland (1731-37). Coffee and tea service of 1725-40. *Part of an epergne, with Neptune and Satyrs, one of the earliest examples of the work of Kendler. Birds (by Kendler), animals, and fruit. Two large vases, with flowers in relief and porcelain medallions, including a portrait of the Empress Elizabeth. Large vases with trophies of the chase and of war. Small figures of every kind. Dinner and coffee service of the Order of St. Andrew the Apostle (second half of the 18th cent.). Dinner-service with hunting scenes (second half of the 18th cent.). Large lilac vase, with the initials 'A. R.' (Augustus rex). Large blue vase, with Chinese scenes. — Then come three cabinets with *Sèvres Porcelain*. Green table service of 1756. Two pots with green and red covers. Blue *Service with the initials of Catherine II., ordered in 1778-79; it originally consisted of 744 pieces, and cost 300,000 livres; over 700 pieces are extant. To this set also belongs the allegorical group, the 'Parnassus of Russia', in biscuit china. — Next to these is a cabinet with *Chinese Porcelain*. — Then follow two cabinets with *Vienna Porcelain*. Large *Vessel in the shape of an elephant, surrounded by dancing peasants on a silver stand, one of the earliest productions of the Vienna factory, as are also a large number of dishes with the imperial Russian arms and small Chinese figures on the covers. Especially striking is the figure of a woman sitting by a shell, by L. von Lücke. — In the last cabinet is *Russian Porcelain*.

By the Window Wall, beginning at the door of the Director's office. Two cabinets with *Russian Porcelain* of the 19th century. — Glass-case with *Vienna Plates* of the beginning of the 19th cent., painted by Duffinger, Perger, Nigg, Herr, and others. — Six cabinets with *Berlin Porcelain*. *Dessert-service and epergne (1772; Catherine II., surrounded by the trophies of war and by captured Turks, receiving the homage of the different nations of Russia), a present from Frederick the Great to the Empress. Plates with views and plans of fortresses on the islands of the Mediterranean and of the Ægean Sea, presented to Tzar Paul as the 'Comte du Nord'. Epergne, figure in biscuit china between two vases with the signs of the zodiac and bronze ornaments, presented by Frederick William III. to Alexander I. — Between the cabinets with Berlin porcelain is a glass-case with *Sèvres Plates*. — Next come cabinets with *St. Petersburg Porcelain*. Table service with pink flowers and small figures of blackamoors, of the period of the Empress Elizabeth. Gilt tea-cups with gay garlands of flowers. Table service of the time of Catherine II. and Paul I. Four services of the Orders of St. Andrew, St. Alexander Nevski, St. Vladimir, and St. George, respectively, from the Gardner factory (second half of the 18th century). — Between the cabinets with St. Petersburg porcelain is a glass-case with snuff-boxes and small *objets d'art* from Berlin, Meissen, St. Petersburg, and other places.

II. QUARTERS ON THE RIGHT BANK OF THE NEVA.

i. Vasíli Óstrov.

Zoological Museum. Academy of Arts. Mining Academy.

The Vasíli Óstrov is reached by Tramway Lines 4, 5, 7, 8, & 17 (pp. 91, 92). — Steamers, see p. 92.

From the Peter Square (p. 108) the Vasíli Óstrov is at present reached by the *Dvortzóvi* or *Palace Bridge* (Pl. E, 5; *II*), a bridge-of-boats, but a new bridge is being constructed at the Dvortzó-vaya Square. At the E. extremity of Vasíli Óstrov is the so-called **Dutch Exchange** (Бйржа; Pl. E 5, *II*), an edifice in a pseudo-classical style, 272 ft. in length and 259 ft. in depth, built in 1804-11 from designs by the French architect Thomon. It is surrounded by a peristyle of 44 Doric columns; and over the façade is a group of Neptune and sea-monsters. The business-hours are from 11 to 12.30.

On the open space in front of the Exchange rise two *Rostral Columns,* 112 ft. in height, their pedestals adorned with two colossal statues and their shafts with the prows of ships. — The Birzhevói Bridge crosses to the Petersburg Side (p. 173).

The *View from the semicircular space between the columns, called the *Stryélka* (Pl. E, 4; *II*), is one of the most beautiful in St. Petersburg. To the left are the revetments of the Fortress of SS. Peter and Paul, topped by the gilded and needle-like spire of the Cathedral (p. 173); to the right are the quays of the Nevá with their palaces, over which gleam the golden pinnacle of the Admiralty (p. 107) and the huge dome of St. Isaac's. Immediately in front of the beholder is the imposing river, while the background is formed by the distant rows of houses in the N.E. quarters of the city.

Behind the Exchange is the semicircular Birzhevói Place, with its flower-beds. On the N. side is the *Chief Custom House* (comp. p. 129). On its S.E. side, on the Nevá Quay, lies the —

Imperial Academy of Sciences (Академія наукъ; Pl. E 5, *II*), built in 1784-87 by Quarenghi, and containing museums and a library. The plan for this Academy was formulated in 1724 by Peter the Great, with the aid of Christian von Wolff and Leibnitz, but it was not till after his death in 1725 that the plan was carried into effect by Catherine I. After a period of suspended animation, the Academy entered on a new lease of life in the reign of Catherine II. It now consists of three sections: Physics and Mathematics, Russian Language and Literature, History and Philology. The annual income of its endowment amounts to over one million rubles.

The Academy contains the following departments:

1. A *Library* of about 500,000 vols. and over 13,000 MSS. (in the building adjoining the Exchange; adm., see p. 97). A new building is being constructed in the Tutchkóva Náberezhnaya.

2. The **Anthropological & Ethnographical Museum of Tzar Peter the Great* (adm., see p. 97; Russian Catalogue, 1912, 50 cop.; Director, W. Radlov). Room I contains objects from N.W. America and N.E. Asia. Room II: Objects from Siberia and other parts of N.E. Asia. Staircase: Objects illustrative of Buddhism. Room III (upper floor): China, Japan, Corea, India. Room IV: Polynesia, Australia, Africa. Room V (third floor): Antiquities from Turfan in Eastern Turkestan; objects of the stone age (France, Switzerland, Sweden); results of excavations in S. Russia, Samarkand, Sarai, Perm, etc.; objects from Central and S. America.

3. *Department of Peter the Great,* containing reminiscences of that monarch. Room I: Writing-desk of the Tzar; by the window-wall, wax figure of Peter the Great, on a canopied throne; the glass-cases contain autographs of the Tzar, coins, and medals; in the centre, on a table, model of the house at Zaandam in which Peter lived; cabinet with ivory articles, carved by the Tzar. Room II: Tools of the Tzar. Room III: in the centre, carriage of the Tzar; telescopes; on the exit-wall, cabinet with glass cups. Room IV: Costumes of the Tzar, walking-sticks, etc.

4. The *Cabinet of Coins* (open to numismatists only; Director, C. Salemann), with Russian coins from the earliest times to the present day, including many rare specimens.

5. The *Botanical Museum* (open to botanists only; Director, I. P. Borodin) contains numerous plants from Siberia and elsewhere, collected by Steller, Gmelin, Pallas, and Przhevalski; also collections made by Counts Razumóvski, Uvárov, and Sivers.

6. The *Geological Museum of Peter the Great*, inferior in value to the collection of the Mining Academy (p. 172) but including some note-worthy meteorites and specimens from the Russian Silurian age.

7. The *Asiatic Museum* (open to Orientalists only; adm., see p. 97; Director, C. Salemann), containing Arabic, Persian, Turkish, and Hebrew MSS., coins, an extensive collection of Chinese and Tibetan woodcuts, and other objects of interest.

8. The *Zoological Museum* (see below)

The *Imperial Zoological Museum (Зоологи́ческій музе́й Импера́торской акаде́міи нау́къ; Pl. E 5, *II*), founded in 1728, consists of two departments, *viz.* the scientific collection (open to students only; entrance in the Tamózhenni Pereúlok) and the ex-hibition section, open to the public and occupying three large rooms. Adm., see p. 98; entrance at Universitétskaya Náberezh-naya 1. Russian catalogue (1912), 25 cop. The objects all bear labels in Russian and Latin. Animals found in Russia are denoted by red labels.—Director, N. V. Nasónov.

Adjoining the entrance, on the groundfloor, is a seated bronze figure of *K. E. von Baer* (Pl. B.), the naturalist, a replica of the monument at Dorpat (comp. p. 69). We ascend the steps to the right to —

Room I. To the left is a marble bust of *J. F. von Brandt* (Pl. Br.; d. 1879), the zoologist.—In the middle, between the pillars, are *Skeletons of Whales*, including one of the Balænoptera Sibbaldii, 102 ft. in length. Around the skeleton are stuffed *Sturgeons* (Delphinapterus leucas, Бѣлу́га), *Dolphins*, etc. By the steps leading to the gallery (Pl. G) is the rare skeleton of the *Sea Cow* (Rhytina Stelleri), which became extinct in the 18th cent.; a piece of its skin is shown in Glass-case 55 A, behind it.— Right side-wall: Cases 1-3, 5-10, 12-19, & 25-contain groups illustrating Mimicry, Protective Colouring, and so forth. Cases 4 (cuckoo) 11, 20, 21-24 (to the right of the last pillar), & 29-32 (behind the last pillar to the right), 36-39 (behind the last pillar to the left) contain groups, illus-trating Care for the young and Nest-building.—Cases 33, 34, & 40-42 (to the right and left of the approach to the gallery) contain *Sponges*.—Left side-wall (beginning at the steps to the gallery): Case 41 (in front of the end-wall) contains *Polyps;* Cases 46 & 48 contain *Corals*.—Gallery. To the left are *Insects* (Cases 730-778), *Butterflies* (780-802), *Crustacea* (830-875), *Spiders* (883-885), and so on.

Room II. Three cases at the entrance are devoted to a *Mammoth (Pl. M), dug out of the ice of the Berézovka in N.E. Siberia in 1901. The middle case contains its skeleton, that to the right a realistic reproduction of the monster in the position in which it was found, while that to the left contains its tongue, bits of its hide, and other fragments preserved in spirits. Adjacent to the left are *Molluscs* from the ice-age of N. Russia (Cases 72-77). In front of the windows are 25 desk-cases (14 to the right, 11 to the left) containing a collection of Mollusc Shells. The front half of the room, extending as far as the 5th pillar, contains *Molluscs* (pre-served in spirits), *Worms, Tortoises, Lizards, Crocodiles* (all these on the right), *Fish*, and *Snakes* (these on the left). The rear half of the room contains the COLLECTION OF BIRDS, including many realistically mounted groups. The example of the extinct *Cormorant* (Phalacrocorax perspicillatus; Case 566) from Behring Island and the bones of a *Moa* or *Dinornis* (Cases 579 & 580), a huge bird of New Zealand, which became extinct only in the 18th century, should also be noticed.

Room III. MAMMALIA, including several specimens of the diluvial epoch (mammoth, rhinoceros, etc.), some of which, found in the perennially frozen soil of N. Siberia, still retain fragments of their flesh, skin, and hair.

11*

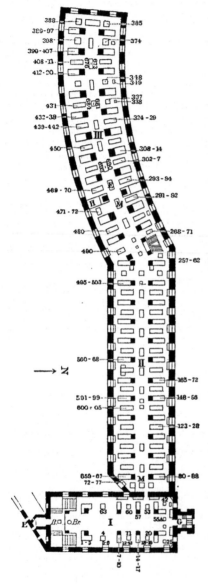

S. Side-wall: 480. Caucasian stag; 471, 472. Milk-teeth of a mammoth and a mastodon. To the right, in the central gangway, complete skeleton of a mammoth (Pl. M), with parts of the head and feet, and (on the floor) two colossal mammoth tusks. To the left, group of hippopotami and tapirs (Pl. H); above, antlers of the Irish elk (Cervus Megaceros or giganteus) and (farther on) of the maral (Cervus elaphus); 469, 470. Heads, horns, and feet of the diluvial rhinoceros; to the right, in the middle, Indian elephant, with skeleton (Pl. E); 690-693. Yaks; 450. Aurochs, from the Caucasus and Lithuania; 441. Elks; 438. Russian wildcats; 431. Musk oxen; in the middle, to the right, 683, 684. Camels; above Cases 412-420, Horns of the Bison priscus and other extinct varieties of cattle; 409, 410. Siberian tigers; in the middle, to the right, 677, 678. Wild horses; 402. Skeleton of a Tibetan bear (Ailoropus melanoleucus); 398. Fur seals (Otaria ursina) from the Behring Sea; 671, 672. Zebras; 395. Bears of Central Asia (Ursus lagomyiarius). — By the end-wall: 388. Caspian seals (Phoca caspica). — We now return along the N. side: 374. Caucasian leopards; 359. Kamtchatka ram; 360. Badger; 349. Steppe-foxes (Canis corsæ); 348. Arctic foxes; 338. Steppe-antelope (Saiga tatarica); 337. Mountain-goat; 326. Chamois; 310. Takin or mountain-antelope of Tibet (Budorcas taxicolor); 305. Chinese antelope (A. subgutturosa); 293, 294. Well-preserved skull of an Elasmotherium Fischeri; 291, 292. Feet and mane of mammoth, in perfect preservation; 283. Sea-lion; 268-271. Bears.

Continuing to follow the quay of the Great Nevá, we reach the **University** (Императорскій Университетъ; Pl. E 5, *II*), which was founded by Alexander I. in 1819. It possesses four faculties, *viz.* those of History and Philology, Physics and Mathematics, Jurisprudence, and Oriental Languages. The number of students is 7500. The lectures are given between Sept. 1st (O.S.) and Easter. The *University Library* (adm., see p. 98) contains upwards of 453,000 volumes.

At Kadétskaya Line, No. 21, is the *Museum of Old St. Petersburg* (Музей стараго Петербурга; adm., see p. 98), founded in 1907. This museum contains objects of artistic and historical interest relating to Old St. Petersburg. At First Line, No. 24, is the *Tolstói Museum,* containing reminiscences of Count Tolstói (adm., see p. 98).

Passing the long building of the *First Cadet Corps,* formerly the Palais Ménshikov, built in 1710 by Schädel, we arrive at the Rumyántzev Square (Румянцевскій Скверъ; Pl. D 5, *II*), containing the *Rumyántzev Obelisk* (Памятникъ Румянцеву), 89 ft. in height, erected in 1799 in honour of Count P. A. Rumyántzev-Zadunáiski (1725-96), who distinguished himself in the Turkish wars of 1768-74. The obelisk, designed by the architect Breno, was originally erected in the Mársovo Pole (p. 116), but was transferred to its present site in 1820.

Not far from the obelisk, on the bank of the Nevá, stands the —

Imperial Academy of Arts (Императорская Академія Художествъ; Pl. D 5, *II*), founded by Catherine II. in 1757, and guarded by two fine Egyptian *Sphinxes,* brought from Thebes in 1832. The building, which is one of the handsomest in the city, was erected in 1765-88 by *Kokórinov* from the plans of *Vallin de la Mothe,* and forms a square each side of which is 460 ft. long. The principal façade, looking towards the Nevá, is in two stories and is articulated by columns and pilasters. The central portico is adorned with statues of the Farnese Hercules and the Farnese Flora and is surmounted by a domed roof. — Adm. to the *Museum* of the Academy, see p. 97. The first floor is reserved for an annual exhibition of pictures, particulars of which will be found in the newspapers; adm. 32 cop.). Conservator, E. von Wiesel.

The MUSEUM OF ANCIENT AND RENAISSANCE SCULPTURES, arranged in Rooms 2-32 of the groundfloor, the rooms adjoining the main staircase, and Room 57 of the upper floor, contains few originals but has an extensive collection of plaster casts. — Room 57, on the first floor, known as the First Gallery of Antiques or Raphael Room, also contains copies of Raphael and other paintings. In the small Lecture Room (No. 58) are four magnificent pieces of tapestry after *Jouvenet* and a marble statue of Catherine II. by *Halberg.* The Assembly Room, with a large ceiling painting by *Shebúyev,* contains portraits of former presidents of the Academy and fine stained-glass windows by Svertchkóv. Room 66 (Second Gallery of Antiques, or Titian Room) contains copies of Venetian masters and a marble bust of Catherine II. by *Shubin.*

Russian Paintings and Sculptures. Rooms 40-54 and 77 on the main floor contain diploma-works by students of the academy. Room 43, to the left, 95. *Bryullóv*, The three angels appearing to Abraham. Room 44, to the right, 669. *Aivazóvski*, Sea-piece. Room 46, to the right, 184. *Orlovski*, Landscape. Room 47, on the exit-wall, 368. *Kivshénko*, Council of War in Fili, 1812. Room 48, to the left, 190. *Ryepin*, Daughter of Jairus. Room 49, to the left, *Kramskói*, Portrait of I. I. Shishkin, the landscape-painter. Room 50, to the left, *Brovar*, Autumn; on the side-wall, 1116. *Zhukovski*, Winter-scene. Room 51, to the right, 438. *Krui-zhítzki*, Village in Little Russia; to the left, 678. *Purvit*, The last of the snow; 620. *Polyénov*, Lagoon; 1005. *Nésterov*, Holy Russia. Room 52 to the left, 1072. *Pasternák*, Portrait of himself. Room 54, to the left, 1126. *Shélkovi*, Arrest of the Metropolitan Philip. — Sculptures: *Orlovski*, Paris; *Baron P. Klodt*, Horses; *Halberg*, Boy, Monument of Karamzin, Model of a colossal statue of Catherine II.; *Falconet* and *Ramazánov*, Milo of Crotona and the lion; *Demut-Malinovski*, Bust of Suvórov; *Tolstói*, Reliefs from the Odyssey; *Stavasser*, Nymphs.

Kúshelev Gallery (catalogue in Russian). Room 70. On the main wall, to the right, 160. *Gallait*, Last moments of Count Egmont; 196. *Daubigny*, Landscape; 332. *Troyon*, Peasants on the road to market; 360. *Ary Scheffer*, Faust; to the left, 187. *Paul Delaroche*, Cromwell at the bier of Charles I.; 333. *Troyon*, Sheep; 138. *Bouguereau*, Departure of Tobias. Cabinet I, to the left, *227. *L. Knaus*, Village-fire; to the right, 208. *Gérôme*, Duel after the masked ball. Cabinet II, to the left, 293. *L. Robert*, Neapolitan fisherfolk; 352. *Fourmois*, Landscape; to the right, 212. *F. Ziem*, Seashore; 127. *Rosa Bonheur*, Sheep at pasture. Cabinet III, to the left, 3. *Hoguet*, Angler; 211. *F. Ziem*, Venice; 353. *Hoguet*, Village in Normandy; to the right, *Courbet*, Dead horse in a wood; 271. *Fr. Millet*, Women carrying faggots. Cabinet IV, to the left, 357. *Chavet*, Duet; 159. *B. Vautier*, Manual training; *Meissonier*, 266. Soldier; *265. Smoker; to the right, 188, 190. *Diaz*, Scenes of child-life; 249. *Lehon*, On the shore. — Room 69. Cabinet I, to the left, 351. *Fromentin*, Caravan; 202. *Dupré*, Landscape; 111. *A. Achenbach*, Landscape. Cabinet II, 155. *Willems*, The answer; 146. *E. Verboeckhoven*, Sheep. Cabinet III, to the left, 317. *Stevens*, Unlucky organ-grinder; 223. *Ten-Kate*, Judicial examination; to the right, 256. *J. Lies*, Toper; 269. *Merle*, Children dancing; 24. *Greuze*, Girl at prayer. Cabinet IV, to the left, 219. *A. Calame*, Evening on the Lake of Lucerne; to the right, 368. *J. J. van der Eeckhout*, Soldier studying his map. Cabinet V, to the left, 53. *G. Netscher*, Children blowing soap-bubbles; to the right, *20. *Ph. Wouverman*, Halt at the tavern; *Terburg*, 74. Young lady, 73. Lovers; *50. *Metsu*, Woman sewing; 330. *Troyon*, Landscape; 36. *L. Cranach*, Christ Child; 37. *Jordaens*, Twelfth Night, one of the best representations of this favourite subject of the artist; 131. *Braekeleer*, Escaped bird. On the main wall, beginning at Cabinet IV 154. *Willems*, Imprisonment of Joan of Arc; 10. *J. B. Weenix*, Crossing the river; 22. *J. van Goyen*, River-scene; 9. *Boucher*, Apollo and Daphne; 203. *Dupré*, Cattle at pasture. — Next comes a room with the *Krausold Collection*, consisting of modern Russian and foreign paintings.

From Room 70 we enter a room on the left containing pictures by French Masters of the 18th century. Among these are 584. *Boucher*, Pygmalion; 585, 586. *J. Vernet*, Landscapes; 611. *N. Poussin*, Prodigal Son; 591, 592. *Greuze*, Portraits; 598-600. *Courtois*, Battle-scenes. Here also is a statue of Alexander the Great, by *J. Houdon* (No. 1119).

The Library (open daily 11-3 and also 7-10, except on Sat.; from May 15th to Sept. 15th on Tues. & Wed. only) contains a reading-room and includes a rich collection of engravings, photographs, and works on art.

Continuing to follow the Nevá Quay, we leave the Nicholas Bridge (P. 111) to the left. At the corner of the Seventh Line and the Bolshói Prospékt is the *Cathedral of St. Andrew* (Соборъ Апостола Андрея Первозваннаго; Pl. 36, D 5, *I*), built in 1764 by Ivánov.

At No. 39 Eighth Line is the *Semenov Gallery (pron. Sem-yónov; Pl. D 5, *I*), containing 600 paintings by 370 different masters and affording an excellent view of the historical development of the Flemish and Dutch Schools. The collection is to be incorporated with the Hermitage, to which it was bequeathed by its founder, P. P. Semenov, the explorer (d. 1914). Adm., see p. 98.

The group of the PREDECESSORS OF REMBRANDT is represented by works of *P. Lastman, J. van Schooten, Cl. Moyaert,* and *L. Bramer.* The chief masters belonging to the period previous to and during the separation of the Flemish and Dutch Schools are *K. van Mander, G. Coninxloo, C. Vinckboons, R. Savery,* and *Adr. van de Venne.* — Among the followers of the Italian Naturalistic School may be mentioned the rare *G. Smit* (Flora and Fortuna, 1636) and *G. Honthorst,* the latter represented by Esau selling his birthright, Old woman counting money, Prince of Orange as Cupid (1637), and Two young women (1649; the first two of these night-scenes, the last two daylight-scenes). — The earliest national development of the Dutch School of landscape-painting is represented by *Esaias van de Velde* (four works, dated 1621, 1623, 1626); *J. van Goyen* (four works, dated 1632, 1634, 1647, 1652); *S. van Ruysdael* (two); *P. Molyn* (four); and the rare masters *P. Nolpe, A.* and *J. van Croos* (1667), *Coelenbier* (1645), *J. Meerhout* (1633), and *H. de Meyer* (1657). The marine-painter *S. de Vlieger,* and *B. van Bassen, G. Hoeczgeest,* and *J. Vucht,* the painters of church-interiors, are also represented. — Among the painters of genre-scenes may be mentioned *Dirk Hals* (Concert, 1623; Artist in the tavern, 1626), *Frans Hals the Younger* (Still-life, 1640), *P. Palamedesz* (Battle, Sentinel), *A. Palamedesz, Peter Potter* (Landscape, 1637), *P. Quast, J. Verspronck* (1645), and *S.* and *J. de Bray.* — The portrait-painters represented include *W. de Geest, W. van der Vliet, M. Mierevelt, P. Moorelse,* and *Th. de Keyser.*

Though *Rembrandt* himself is represented only by a small study of a head, we find no less than 35 paintings by 26 masters of REMBRANDT'S SCHOOL. *G. Dou* (Sleeping lace-maker; Night-scene, similar to that in Dresden); *J. A. Backer; F. Bol* (Judas and Tamar); *G. Flinck* (Bathsheba receiving David's letter, 1657); *B. Fabritius; J. Victors* (Diogenes with his lantern); *J. Ovens* (Portrait of a lady, 1656); *Chr. Paudiss* (Old man); *N. Maes* (Portrait of Jan de Wit, Boy at a window); *J.* and *G. de Wet; J. van Loo;* and *H. van der Vliet.* — The genre-painters of the best period are represented by 40 paintings: *Jan Steen* (The artist's family); *G. Netscher* (Pomona and Vertumnus); *P. de Hooch* (Woman with the dropsy consulting a quack); *Q. Brekelenkam* (painting of 1669); *W. Mieris, J. Ochtervelt, Esaias Boursse,* and *G. Schalcken.* The painters of scenes of peasant-life include *Adr.* and *Is. van Ostade, C. Bega, J. Molenaer,* and *R. Brakenburgh.* — The collection includes three paintings by *B. van der Helst,* two of which, dated 1662 and 1649, are portraits of himself, the latter painted in the style of Rembrandt. *Abr. van den Tempel* (1670), *D. Santvoort, C. Janssen van Ceulen,* and *L. Bakhuysen* (Portrait of Rachel Ruysch, 1683) are also represented. — The 87 landscape-painters represented contribute 120 pictures. The most eminent names are *A. Everdingen, J. van Ruysdael* (two), the rare *Jacob Salomonsz Ruysdael, C. Decker, Van der Meer van Haarlem, G. Dubois, A. Verboom, Fr. Moucheron, F. Post* (1659), and *A. van der Neer.* — Among the animal-painters may be mentioned *Govert Camphuysen, Corn. Saftleven, Cl. Berghem,* and *K. du Jardin;* among the painters of battles and hunting-scenes, *Ph.* and *P. Wouverman, J. van Huchtenburgh,* and *A. Hondius;* and among marine-painters, *L. Bakhuysen, J. Beerstraten,* and *R. Zeeman* (1664). — The painters of still-life are represented by numerous works.

The FLEMISH SCHOOL is represented by 90 masters. Among those of the 16th cent. are *J. Gossaert (Mabuse;* Madonna), *Fr. Floris* (Compassion), *P. Brueghel* ('Two dancers, 1517), *H. Bol* (three paintings), *P. Bril, J. Brueghel* (Adoration of the Magi), *D. Alsloot,* and *H. van*

Balen (Venus, 1600). — *Rubens* is seen in the portrait of Cardinal-Infante Ferdinand. Among his pupils may be mentioned *J. Jordaens* (Holy Family), *A. Diepenbeck* (M. A. Capellus, Bishop of Antwerp), *E. Quellinus* (Virgin presenting a banner to St. Ildefonso, the wreath of flowers by *D. Seghers*), and *D. Teniers the Younger*. — Among the landscape-painters are *L. van Uden* (fine painting with figures by Teniers), *J. Wildens*, *J. van Arthois*, and *C. Huysmans*. *D. Seghers*, *A. Coosemans*, and *P. Verbrüggen* contribute pictures of fruit and flowers.

We now return to the Nevá Quay. In the Tenth Line, which here diverges to the right, is the *Patriotic Institute* (Pl. 106, D 5; *I*), a school for girls. To the right, between the Eleventh and Thirteenth Lines, is the *Nicholas Naval Academy* (Николáевская Морскáя Акадéмія; Pl. 6, D 5, *I*); in front of it, on the Nevá Quay, is a *Bronze Statue of Admiral Krusenstern*, the first Russian circumnavigator of the world (d. 1846; p. 76), erected in 1873. At the corner of the Fifteenth Line is the *Church of the Kiev Lavra* (Цéрковь Кíево-Печéрской Лáвры; Pl. 47, D, 5, 6, *I*), completed in 1898. At the corner of the Eighteenth Line is the house of the academician *M. P. Botkin* (d. 1914), containing a collection of terracottas, statues, Byzantine enamels, etc. (adm., see p. 97).

At the end of the quay is the *Institute of Mining Engineers* or **Mining Academy** (Гóрный Институтъ; Pl. 105, C 6, *I*), founded by Catherine II. in 1773. It is attended by 650 students, in training for posts in the Government Department of Mining. The huge edifice, covering an area of 14,350 sq. yds., was built by *Voronikhin* in 1806-11 and has a portico of 12 Doric columns on the side next the Nevá. In front of the portico are a Hercules by Piménov and the Rape of Proserpine by Démut-Malinóvski. The lecture-hall contains a bust of Tzar Paul I. by Shubin (d. 1805). — Adm. to the Museum, see p. 98; Director, N. P. Pokrovski. Russian catalogue, 60 cop. Visitors are conducted by an attendant (fee).

On the first floor is the *Museum of the Mining Academy, arranged according to the system of Groth of Munich. — Room I & II. Fossils and shells. — Room III. Elements, sulphides, oxides, haloid compounds, carbonate compounds. In the middle is a block of malachite weighing 94 puds (3394 lbs.), found in 1789 in the province of Perm, and valued at 26,000 rb. By the window-wall are two iron chests (closed) containing gold and platinum. By the exit-wall, to the left, is a block of copper 52 puds in weight. — Room IV. Minerals in natural crystals and in pseudomorphs. — Room V (with columns). Sulphuric acid compounds, aluminates, ferrides, and so on; phosphides; silicates (including some rare Siberian and Uralian topazes in Case 55); minerals of organic origin; meteorites. In the middle are beryls, including a sea-green transparent specimen 9½ in. long and 2546 grammes in weight. To the right of this is a block of meteoric iron from Augustinovka, found in 1890, and weighing 720 lbs. Farther on, to the left, is a wine-coloured topaz, 23 lbs. in weight. — Room VI contains vases, busts, swords, and other articles made of ores found in Russia; cut stones. — Room VII. Pearls and pearl-oysters. — We now return through Rooms VI and V and enter Room VIII, which, along with Room IX, to the left, contains the *Collection of Models* (mining implements, etc.). — No. X is the Lecture Room. — Rooms XI and XII are devoted to the palæontology of Russia, and include some beautiful variegated ammonites from the Volga district. — The cellar is laid out with full-size models of adits and shafts of mines.

The inner parts of the Vasili Óstrov offer no attractions to the stranger. *Novi Peterburg* (Pl. B, 4; *I*), on Golodai Island, is a growing residential quarter. — From the Mining Academy we may return to the Bolshói Prospékt and proceed thence to the Admiraltéiski Prospékt by tramway No. 4 or 5.

k. Fortress Island and St. Petersburg Quarter.

Cathedral of SS. Peter and Paul. Artillery Museum. House of Peter the Great.

Tramways 1, 2, 3, 7, 8, 12, & 15 (pp. 91, 92) serve this district. Steamer, see p. 92.

From the Suvórov Square (p. 116) the **Tróitzki Bridge** (Троицкій мостъ; Pl. F 4, *I;* *View) leads across the Nevá, which here attains its greatest width (645 yds.), to the Petersburg Side or Quarter. This iron bridge was constructed in 1897-1903 as a memorial of the silver wedding of the Tzar Alexander III. and the Tzarina Marie Feódorovna. It is supported by six piers and cost upwards of 5 million rubles. At the S. end is a draw for vessels.

We proceed from the N. end of the bridge to the Tróitzkaya Square (p. 175), traverse the Kronwerk Canal to the left, and so reach the Fortress Island; then, passing through the Gate of St. John, we enter the fortress by the E. or Peter Gate (1749).

The **Fortress of SS. Peter and Paul** (Петропа́вловская Крѣпость; Pl. E, F, 4, *I;* comp. p. 102) was built from the plans of Dom. Trezzini in 1703-40, the walls being faced with granite in the reign of Catherine II. It contains the State Prison, the Cathedral of SS. Peter and Paul, the Mint, and the old Arsenal with the Artillery Museum. The fortifications have now lost their importance. A cannon is fired here every day at noon (comp. p. 189).

The *Cathedral of SS. Peter and Paul (Петропа́вловскій Собо́ръ; Pl. F 4, *I*) is open all day long, but is best visited between 1 and 4 p.m. This cathedral, which is the burial-church of the Russian emperors, was founded at the same time as the fortress, but was rebuilt after a fire in 1753 and again altered under Nicholas I. It is a domed structure, 210 ft. in length and 98 ft. in breadth. The extremely slender gilded spire, which is one of the highest in Russia (394 ft.), is crowned by an angel bearing a cross 23 ft. in height. The clock in the spire, brought from Cologne in 1760, plays the hymn 'Kol Slaven' every hour and the national anthem at noon.

The INTERIOR is adorned with military trophies, flowers, and growing plants, and makes a very light and cheerful impression. The Russian emperors of the house of Románov since Peter the Great (with the exception of Peter II., see p. 285), their wives, and the imperial Grand-Dukes and Grand-Duchesses are all buried here in the *Imperial Vaults*. White marble sarcophagi, with gilded eagles at the corners, mark the sites of the graves of the Tzars. On the sarcophagus of Peter the Great is a large medal struck in 1903 to commemorate the bicentenary of St. Petersburg. On the adjacent wall is a naval flag taken in 1870 at the battle of Tchesmé. The tombs of Alexander II. and Alexander III. are adorned with numerous garlands of silver and gold. Fine ikonostás by Sarudni (1726). — Several works made by Peter the Great's own hand are shown here, including a carved ivory candelabrum (to the right of the ikonostás), 10 ft. in height and 6½ ft. in diameter.

To the N.E. of the cathedral, and connected with it by a passage beginning at the tomb of Tzar Nicholas I., is the *Grand-Ducal Mausoleum,* completed in 1906 from the designs of Grimm. Outside the cathedral, at its E. end, is a small graveyard, with the tombs of the commanders of the fortress, including that of the first commander, *General Roman Bruce* (1668-1720). A separate building (by M. G. Zemtzov) to the left of the cathedral contains a boat found by Peter the Great in 1691 at the village of Izmailovo (p. 320) and known as the 'Grandfather of the Russian Fleet' (Дѣдушка рýсскаго Флóта). — The *Imperial Mint* (Монéтный дворъ; no adm.), to the W. of the cathedral, was founded in 1716.

Leaving the fortress by the Peter Gate (p. 173) and turning to the left, we skirt the Kronwerk Canal until we reach the 'Kronwerk' itself. Here is the *Old Arsenal* (Крóнверкскій Арсенáлъ; Pl. E, F, 4, *I*), containing the interesting **Artillery Museum.** Adm., see p. 97; Director, Col. D. P. Strukov.

Ground Plan of the Cathedral of SS. Peter and Paul.

A. High Altar. B. Pulpit. C. Throne of the Tzar. D. Imperial Chamber. E. Entrance. — Imperial Tombs. 1. Peter the Great (d. 1725); 2. Catherine I. (d. 1727); 3. Elizabeth I. (d. 1761); 4. Anna Ivánovna (d. 1740); 5. Peter III. (d. 1762); 6. Catherine II. (d. 1796); 7. Paul I. (d. 1801) and 8. Marie Feódorovna (d. 1828; née Princess Sophia of Würtemberg); 9. Alexander I. (d. 1825) and 10. Elizabeth Alexéyevna (d. 1826; née Princess Louise of Baden); 11. Nicholas I. (d. 1855) and 12. Alexandra Feódorovna (d. 1860; née Princess Charlotte of Prussia); 13. Alexander II. (d. 1881) and 14. Marie Alexándrovna (d. 1880; née Princess of Hesse); 15. Alexander III. (d. 1894).

On the Ground Floor is an extensive collection of fire-arms of all kinds from the 15th cent. down to the present day; also old weapons, armour, standards, old and new engines of war, and figures of soldiers in the uniform of various periods, including Streltzi on foot and on horseback. To the left of the entrance is a standard-car of the time of the Empress Elizabeth. In a separate room to the right of the entrance are reminiscences of Russian rulers, including the felt hat, uniform, caftan, and spontoon of Peter the Great, the uniforms of several other Russian rulers, and a Streltzi banner of 1681, 11 ft. long and 10 ft. high. —

On the First Floor is the *Hall of Fame,* containing numerous captured banners, weapons, and other trophies, including many of Swedish, Prussian, Turkish, and Chinese origin. The Prussian banners, 120 in number, include a number belonging to the guilds of Berlin and carried off from the arsenal of that city on its capture in 1760 in the belief that they were military flags. The spoils of the battle of Kunersdorf include 20 regimental banners and the uniform and body-linen of Frederick the Great. Among the Turkish trophies is the gilded dome of the Mosque of Bender, captured in 1770. The Chinese guns and other trophies are part of the 'loot' of 1900. — This floor also contains weapons of the prehistoric period and two graves of warriors from the province of Kiev, dating from the 9-11th cent. (under glass).

To the W. of the Kronwerk, with its main entrance in the Krónverkski Prospékt, is the *Zoological Garden* (Зоологическій Садъ; Pl. E 4, *I;* p. 95; open from 10 a.m. onwards). Besides the collection of animals (feeding-hour in summer 5.30 p.m.),the garden also contains a summer-theatre, where concerts, etc., are given.

To the E. of the Zoological Garden, on the N. and E. sides of the Kronwerk, extends the *Alexander Park* (Александровскій Паркъ; Pl. E, F, 3, 4, *I*), a favourite resort of the lower classes. The park contains the so-called *People's Palace* or *House of Tzar Nicholas II.* (Народный домъ Императора Николая II.; Pl. E 3, *I;* comp. p. 95), completed in 1901, and containing a large theatre (4000 seats) added in 1911. A little farther on, to the E., is the *Ssteregúshtchi Monument* (Pl. 133, F 3 ; *I*), erected, from a design by Isenberg, to commemorate the heroic sinking of the torpedo-boat, Steregushtchi, off Port Arthur, on March 10th, 1904.

Near the E. entrance of the park, in the Tróitzkaya Sq., which was the chief square of the original St. Petersburg, is the *Cathedral of the Holy Trinity* (Соборъ Животворящей Троицы; Pl. 39, F 4, *I*), erected in 1710, rebuilt in 1756, and burned down in 1913. Peter the Great frequently attended service in the original church. A little to the N. is a large *Mosque* (Pl. F, 3; *I*), with fayence decoration and two minarets, built by Kretchinski (1912).

The **House of Peter the Great** (Домикъ Петра I.; Pl. 146, F 4, *I;* open daily 8-7, in winter 8-4) stands to the E. of the cathedral, in a garden on the Nevá Quay, surrounded by a green and gilt railing. Peter built this house, which was the first in the Petersburg Quarter, in 1703, and lived here while superintending the structure of his new capital. It is a one-story blockhouse about 62 ft. in length and 20 ft. in breadth, and contains only two rooms and a cabinet. [It is enclosed within a stone building erected by Chatherine II. in 1784 to protect it from the weather.] The bedroom on the left was converted by Nicholas I. into a Chapel of the Redeemer (Часовня Спасителя) and contains, in an elaborately ornamented frame, a wonder-working picture of the Redeemer, which Peter the Great always carried on his person. In the room on the right are a wooden chair with a leather cushion, a bench, and other articles made by Peter's own hands. At the back is a boat in which Peter saved the lives of some fishermen on Lake Ládoga in 1690. — The garden by the river contains a bronze bust of the Tzar.

To the N.E. of the Peter House, at Penykóvaya 8, are the *Ozone Waterworks* (Pl. 140, G 3 ; *I*), which were opened in 1910.

In the N. part of the Petersburg Side is the *Medical Institute for Women* (Жéнскій медицúнскій институтъ; Pl. 103, F 2, *I*). — To the W. are the *Second Cadet Corps* (Pl. 31, D 3; *I*) and the *Paul Military School* (Pl. 173, D 3; *I*). — At No. 21 Kámenno-Ostrovski Prospékt is the IMPERIAL ALEXANDER LYCEUM (Pl. 12, F 3; *I*), in which is the *Pushkin Museum,* containing relics of the poet, who was a pupil of the institute.

1. The Islands. Staraya Derevnya and Novaya Derevnya. Viborg Quarter.

There are about 100 islands in the delta of the Nevá, the most beautiful of which are Aptékarski, Kámenni, Yelágin, Krestovski, and Petrovski Ostrov, popularly known as 'the Islands'. In spring some of these are inundated, but by the beginning of summer all have assumed the appearance of verdant parks. The islands contain many 'datchas' or villas. — In the height of summer the islands are the scene of a fashionable corso, especially on the road leading to the Stryelka (p. 177).
· The Islands are served by *Tramway Lines* Nos. 2, 3, & 15 (pp. 91, 92). — *Steamers* (a pleasant trip), see p. 92. — *Restaurants,* see p. 89. — Those who have no time for more should at least visit the Kámenni and Yelágin Islands (comp. p. 98).

From the N. end of the Tróitzki Bridge (p. 173) the KÁMENNO-OSTROVSKI PROSPÉKT (tramways Nos. 2, 3, & 15) leads N. to (¹/₂ hr.) the **Apothecary Island** (Аптéкарскій Óстровъ; Pl. D-F, 2, *I*) on the S.E. side of which lie the Botanical Gardens.

The **Imperial Botanical Gardens** (Pl. F, 2; *I*), now known as the *Gardens of Peter the Great,* were laid out by Peter the Great in 1713 for the cultivation of medicinal herbs. Adm., see p. 97. The main entrance is in the Aptékarskaya Náberezhnaya, and there are other entrances in the Pesótchnaya and at the corner of the Kárpovka and Aptékarski Prospékt. Detailed information is given in the Иллюстрúрованный путеводúтель issued by the Director, with illustrations and plans (price 1 rb., abridged edition 20 cop.). Director, Prof. A. Fischer von Waldheim. — The gardens cover an area of about 50 acres, and since 1823 have been used for scientific purposes only. Besides a very extensive collection of plants (36,000 species and varieties, including 28,000 in the greenhouses), they also possess a *Library* of 38,400 vols., a *Herbarium* of 7387 vols., containing over two million plants, a *Botanical Museum* (with 48,000 specimens), a *Physiological Laboratory,* a *Phyto-pathological Station,* a *Seed-Testing Station,* and a *Horticultural School.*

To the N. is the *Church of the Transfiguration* (Цéрковь Преображéнія Госпóдня; Pl. 65, F 2, *I*), built in 1845 from the designs of Thon, and adorned with paintings by Bryullóv.

We now cross the Málaya Nevka by the Kámenno - Ostrovski Bridge (Pl. E, 1; *I*) and reach the **Kámenni Island** (Ка́менный Óстровъ; Pl. D, E, 1, *I*), the chief seat of the villas of the rich citizens of St. Petersburg. Beyond the bridge, to the right, is a three-storied *Palace* (Pl. 141, E 1; *I*), built by Bazhénov for the future Tzar Paul I. in 1766, and altered in the 19th century. To the N.W. of this point stands the *Church of the Birth of John the Baptist* (Це́рковь Рождества́ Iоа́нна Предте́чи; Pl. 41, E 1, *I*), dating from 1778. Opposite, to the left, is the *Naval Hospital of Paul I.* (Pl. 85, E 1, *I*). The *Imperial Summer Theatre* (Ка́менно-Острóвскiй Теáтръ; Pl. 179, D 1, *I*), by Shustov (1827), at the W. end of the island, has been closed.

The First Yelágin Bridge (Pl. C, D, 1; *I*) leads across the Sréd-nyaya Nevka to the **Yelágin Island** (Елáгинъ Óстровъ; Pl. B, C, 1, *I*). Alexander I. purchased this island from Count Orlóv in 1817 for 350,000 rb. and built the present *Yelágin Palace* (Елá-гинскiй Дворéцъ; Pl. 145, C 1, *I*) for his mother from plans by Rossi (1826). The English park in which the palace stands contains some fine old oaks. The other parks and parkways of the island are also well kept up. The so-called '*Stryelka*' or '*Pointe*', at the W. end of the island, commands a fine view of the Gulf of Finland.

From the Yelágin Island the Third Yelágin Bridge leads to the N. across the Bolshaya Nevka to **Stáraya Derévnya** and **Nóvaya De-révnya** (Pl. B-D, 1; *I*), containing villas of a less pretentious character. — About 1¹/₂ V. (1 M.) to the N. of Nóvaya Derévnya, adjoining the Kolo-myágskoye Chaussée, is the *Racecourse* (Скаковóй ипподрóмъ; p. 95), with a track 3 V. (2 M.) in length (station on the railway to Ozerki; p. 193).

From Yelágin Óstrov the Second Yelágin Bridge (Pl. C, 1, 2; *I*) leads to the S. over the Srédnyaya Nevka to the **Krestóvski Island** (Крестóвскiй Óстровъ; Pl. A-D, 2, *I*) containing the château and park of Prince Byelozérski. On the N. side is the boat-house of the *River Yacht Club* (Рѣчнóй Яхтъ-Клубъ; Pl. B 1, *I*). The W. end of the Bataréinaya Doróga affords a fine view of the Gulf of Finland.

The Bolshói Petrovski Bridge leads S. from the Krestovski Island to the **Petrovski Island** (Петрóвскiй Óстровъ; Pl. B-D, 3, 4, *I*), with its factories; it was a favourite resort of Peter the Great, who laid out the *Petrovski Park* here.

Those who wish to visit the unattractive Viborg District should use the tramway (No. 1, 8, 9, 10, 19, or steam-tramway No. 2; pp. 91, 92). To the E. of the *Sampsónyevski Bridge* (Pl. G, 3; *I*) is the *Wylie Clinical Hospi-tal* (Pl. 95, G 3; *I*), in front of which is a bronze statue of *S. P. Botkin* (d. 1889), the physician, by Beklemíshev (1909). A little farther to the E. is the *Military Medical Academy* (Вое́нно-Медици́нская Акаде́мiя; Pl. 4, G 3, *I*), established in 1798 by Paul I. In the court is a monument (Pl. 135; *I*) erected in 1859 to *Sir J. Wylie* (d. 1854), the famous British surgeon, who was once president of the Academy and bequeathed it two million rubles. The *Anatomical Museum*, founded in 1871 by Gruber (d. 1890), and the *Pirogóv Museum* are both interesting to professional visitors (adm. on application at the offices). To the S. of the Academy is the *Military Clinical Hospital* (Клини́ческий Вое́нный Гóспиталь; Pl. 83, G 3, *I*). To the E. of the Alexander Bridge is the *Michael Artillery Academy* (Михáйловская Артиллерíйская Акаде́мiя; Pl. 2, G 4, *I*). — In the N. part of the district is the *Church of Samson* (Церковь Св. Самсонія Странноприймца; Pl. 63, G 2, *I*), built in 1728-40. Opposite is a *Bronze Statue of Peter the Great.* — From the Michael Academy the Simbirskaya leads to the E., passing the *Finland Railway Station* (Pl. H, 3; *I*) and the *Prison* (Pl. H, 4; *I*), to the **New Arsenal** (Новый Арсеналъ; Pl. H, 3, 4, *I*), which includes a cannon-foundry, a cartridge-factory, and various other works.

16. From St. Petersburg to Peterhof and Oranienbaum. Cronstadt.

One of the pleasantest excursions from St. Petersburg is the day-trip to *Peterhof*, especially on a Sunday in June or July. The traveller should drive thither along the coast-road (p. 183) and return by railway. — *Stryelna*, the *Monastery of St. Sergius*, and *Cronstadt* offer few points of interest.

To the S. of St. Petersburg lies a range of hills, forming the N. margin of the Esthonian plateau and stretching from W. to E. viâ Krasnoye Selo to Tzarskoye Selo and Pavlovsk. One of its outlying spurs bears the observatory of Pulkovo (p. 189). Numerous brooks coming from the S. descend over this ridge to the Nevá, enlivening the scenery and contributing an important element to the beauty of the numerous landed estates and imperial parks. At Peterhof and Oranienbaum the hills approach close to the Gulf of Finland.

a. By Railway to Peterhof and Oranienbaum.

37 V. (25 M.). Railway in 1 hr. (fares 1 rb. 5, 65, 40 cop.); to *Sergiyevskaya Pustuin* in 28 min. (fares 50, 30, 20 cop.); to *Stryelna* in 35 min. (fares 60, 35, 25 cop.); to *New Peterhof* in 44 min. (fares 75, 45, 30 cop.); to *Old Peterhof* in 53 min. (fares 90, 55, 35 cop.).

The train starts from the Baltic Station (Pl. E 8, *I;* p. 88). After leaving the city-limits the railway leads through meadow and forest to (13 V.) *Lígovo* (to Krasnoye Selo, see p. 185) and then runs parallel with the coast-road, which lies a few versts to the N. (p. 183).

18 V. (12 M.) **Sérgiyevskaya Pústuin,** Сергіевская Пустынь. — *Railway Restaurant.* — *Izvóshtchik* to the Monastery 30, to the Stryelna Château 25 cop. — *Tramway* from the railway station, passing the monastery, to (2 M.) the E. entrance of the Stryelna Park.

From the railway station a mathematically straight road leads N. to (¹/₂ hr.) the *Monastery of St. Sergius* (Сéргіевская Пýстынь), a large quadrangular building founded in 1743, surrounded on three sides by avenues and ponds, and on the fourth by ramparts. In the inner court stand its four principal churches (excellent vocal music). Immediately opposite the main entrance of the convent is the Cathedral of the Holy Trinity, built by Rastrelli in 1760, and containing a miracle-working picture of St. Sergius (to the right of the ikonostás). Many eminent personages are buried in the churches and in the well-kept churchyard.

21 V. (14 M.) **Stryelna,** Стрѣльна, consisting of a group of datchas or villas. The grand-ducal *Château of Stryelna,* built in 1711 by Leblond and altered in the Gothic style by Rusko in 1804, lies high up on the seashore, about 1¹/₄ M. from the rail. station. We

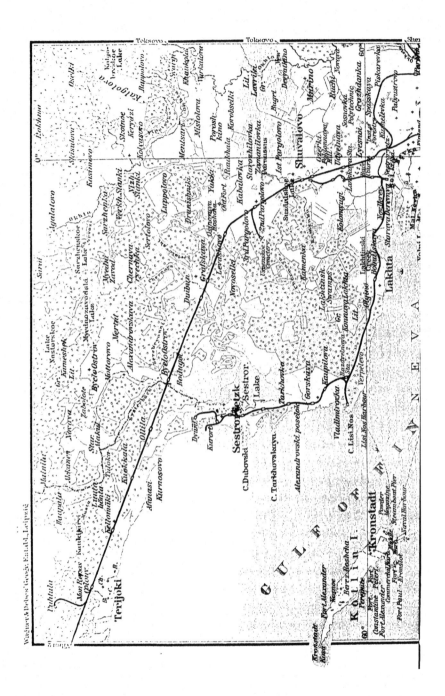

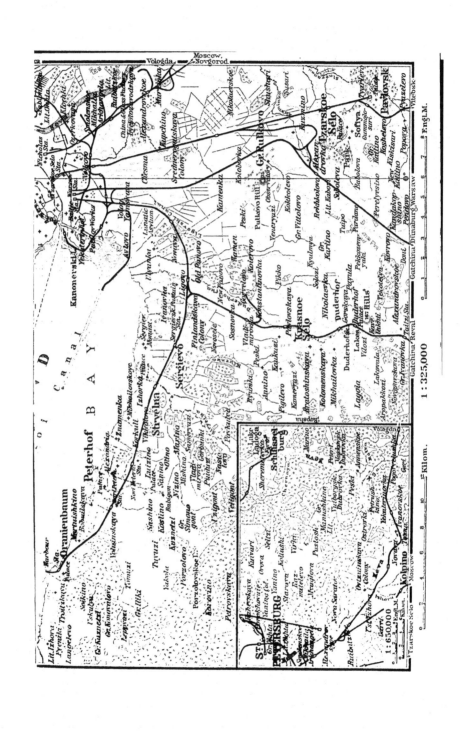

first turn to the right, then a few paces farther on to the left; after 9 min. we follow the main road to the right, then diverge to the left after 4 min., and immediately afterwards take a parkway to the right; in 4 min. more we pass a Russian church on the right and then proceed in a straight direction through the park to the (8 min.) château. The interior of the château is quite simple, but the charming grounds, laid out in the Dutch style with islands, canals, and a bath-house, are well worth seeing.

FROM THE CHÂTEAU OF STRYELNA TO SERGIYEVSKAYA PUSTUIN, a walk of 1 hr. From the château we follow the broad lower parkway to the E. to the (4 min.) park-gate, then turn to the right, and a few paces farther on to the left. After 3 min. we turn to the right again, and then (2 min.) follow the highroad to the left (tramway, see p. 178). In 18 min. we reach the Monastery of St. Sergius, which lies to the left. A straight path to the right leads hence to (¹/₂ hr.) the station of Sergiyevskaya Pustuin (p. 178).

27 V. (18 M.) **New Peterhof**, Но́вый Петерго́фъ. — *Railway Restaurant*, fair. — HOTEL SAMSON (Pl. a, D 2; German landlord), Peterbúrgskaya 44, also open in winter, with baths and garden, R. 1¹/₂-8, B. ³/₄, D. (2-8 p.m.) 1¹/₂ rb., well spoken of. — IZVÓSHTCHIK from the railway station into the town 30 cop.; from the rail. station to the harbour or to the lapidary works, or vice versâ, 40 cop. There is no tariff for pleasure-drives in the park, but the usual rate is 1 rb. per hr., or rather more on Sundays. The drive to Oranienbaum along the lower coast-road takes ³/₄-1 hr. (fare 1¹/₂ rb.). — Visitors are admitted to the Imperial Palace and other buildings in the park daily, 11-6, between May 15th and Sept. 15th (O.S.); tickets are obtained at the steward's office (Дворцо́вое упра-вле́ніе; Pl. D 2), Samsónyevskaya 3. — In summer the orchestra of the imperial court gives concerts in the lower park on Tues., Thurs., and Frid. 8-10 p.m., and a military band plays there daily 7-9 p.m.

COAST ROAD to St. Petersburg or to Oranienbaum (Cronstadt), see p. 183

New Peterhof, a town of 15,900 inhab., with numerous datchas belonging to St. Petersburgers, was founded by Peter the Great in 1711.

To the S. of the Imperial Palace, on the St. Petersburg road, is a *Bronze Statue of Francis I. of France* (Pl. 1; D, 2) by Dumont (1896), inscribed 'Le Commerce et l'Industrie du Havre à Sa Majesté Nicolas II'. A little farther to the N. is the *Neptune Fountain* (Pl. D, 2), executed in 1652-60 by Ritter and Schweigger, two Nuremberg masters, and acquired by Tzar Paul I. in 1797.

The ***Imperial Palace of Peterhof** (Большо́й Петер го́фскій Дворе́цъ; Pl. D, 2) was built by Peter the Great in 1720 from the plans of *Leblond*, and, though it was enlarged in 1746-51 by *Rastrelli* for Empress Elizabeth Petrovna, it has retained its original character of an imitation of Versailles. The main building is in three stories and is connected with the wings by galleries. Its red and white colouring harmonizes with the iron roof and the richly gilded domes. The *Terrace*, which is about 40 ft. in height, is formed by the natural slope of the ground towards Nevá Bay, and commands a distant view of the Finnish coast. When the fountains are playing (in June and July daily, 3-5 & 7-9 p.m., in Aug. & Sept., 4-6 p.m.), the spectacle here is very imposing. A huge cascade rushes down in two arms over six wide steps of coloured marble into a large basin, in the centre of which stands the *Samson Fountain*. This consists of a bronze-gilt figure of Samson, by Kozlovski, forcing open the jaws of a lion, from which a jet of water as thick as a man's arm shoots up to a height of 65 ft. The cascade is flanked with about 45 gilded statues, vases, and the like. The space between the palace and the beach, 330 yds. in width, is laid out as a park. The paths skirting the canal are enclosed by lofty pine-trees interspersed with 22 fountains (11 on each side).

Interior (adm., see p. 179; fee to the attendant who shows the rooms, 50 cop., for a party more in proportion). On the First Floor are the state rooms, the first of which is known as the *Portrait Room*, from the 328 por rai s of girls and young women from all parts of Russia, painted by Count C. Rotari during a journey of Catherine II. We then pass to the right into the *First Chinese Room*, the walls and furniture of which are lacquered in black and gilt. The *Reception Hall* contains four portraits (by Levitzki) of girls who received the first prize at the Institute of the Noblesse in the reign of Catherine II. In the *Divan Room* are portraits of the Empresses Elizabeth Petrovna and Catherine II. The *Boudoir of Empress Elizabeth Petrovna* contains a beautiful tortoise-shell and bronze-gilt cabinet (Italian work of the 16th cent.), and the adjoining *Cabinet* has a portrait of the Empress Elizabeth Petrovna by Rotari. The *Standard Room* is upholstered in yellow silk. On the left side of the *Cavalier Room*, in red silk, is a portrait of Peter the Great by Balerini, while to the right is a portrait of Peter the Great on the Gulf of Finland by Dobrovolski. The predominant feature in the decoration of the *Dining Room* is the monogram of Empress Elizabeth Petrovna. The *Blue Guest Chamber* contains an oil-painting by Saltzmann, representing the reception of the Emperor William II. at Cronstadt in 1888. We next reach the suite of eleven elaborately fitted-up *Rooms occupied by Queen Olga of Wurtemberg* (d. 1892), daughter of Emperor Nicholas I., and three *Rooms of Princes*. The *Cabinet of Nicholas I.*, in carved oak, contains a mosaic portrait of Peter the Great by Yunévitch (1855), a portrait of Nicholas I. by Bothmann after Krüger, a picture of a parade of the Horse Guards under Nicholas I. (by Sauerweid), and models of three ironclads. — We now return to the Portrait Room and proceed to the left into the *Second Chinese Room*, resembling the one above described. In the *White Room*, so called from its stucco decorations, are five beautiful chandeliers of rock-crystal. The *Room of the Maids of Honour* (Статсъ-дамская комната) is decorated in white and gilt. The *Room of Peter the Great* contains a piece of tapestry after Steuben, representing Peter the Great on Lake Ládoga (comp. below), and also four full-length portraits (by Buchholtz) of Peter the Great and the Empresses Catherine I., Anna, and Elizabeth. Opposite the tapestry are four scenes from the naval battle of Tchesmé (1770), by Erich. The *Saloon of the Guards* (Пикéтная комната) is decorated with twelve scenes from the battles of Tchesmé and Sinope, two of which are by Erich, while ten were painted by J. Ph. Hackert at Rome in 1772. The *Merchants' Room* (Купéческій залъ), which we next reach, is fitted up in the rococo style, and is the largest of all. In the *Anteroom of Peter the Great* are an oil-painting by Tanneur ('Storm') and the model of a group by Ustryálov (1864), representing Peter the Great saving the lives of some fishermen on Lake Ládoga (May 26th, 1690).

On the Ground Floor are the *Prussian Rooms*, so named because occupied from time to time by Prussian princes. They contain paintings by Lancret, Robert, Kügelgen, and others.

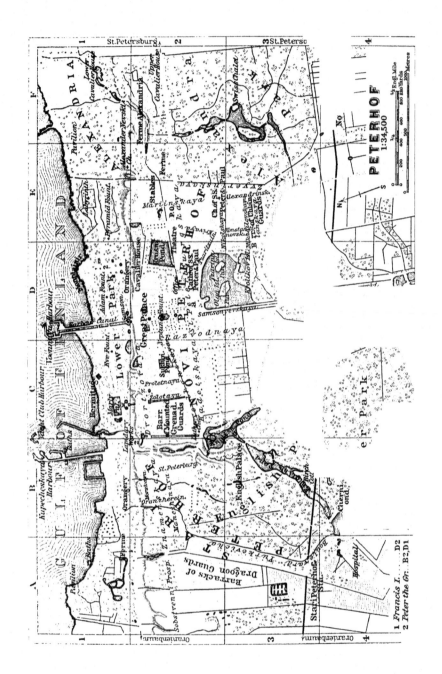

PETERHOF
1:34,500

At the E. corner of the palace is the *Church*, with its five gilt cupolas, built in 1751 by Rastrelli. Below the palace is a shell grotto (no admission). The palace is surrounded by the houses of various court-officials. Adjacent is the small *Winter Chapel*, built in 1832.

In the W. part of the Lower Park (Нйжнiй садъ) are the *Lapidary Works* (Гранйльная Фáбрика; Pl. B, C, 1, 2), established in the reign of Peter the Great. Adjacent is a bronze group by Bernstamm (Pl. 2, B 2; 1902), representing Peter the Great holding the little King Louis XV. of France in his arms. A little to the E., surrounded by water, stands *Marly* (Pl. C, 1; adm., see p. 179, or on application to the attendant), a small two-storied white house, built in 1714 by Peter the Great. In this, to the left, are a table made by the Tzar, and his bedroom, containing his bed and dressing-gown; to the right is the kitchen, with Delft tiles. Passing along the Marly Pond, we see on the right the *Marly Cascade* (Pl. M; C, 1), descending over 20 marble steps, some of which are gilded. To the N., on the shore, is the *Hermitage* (Pl. C, 1), built by Peter the Great. The dining-room, on the first floor, contains 113 paintings by Netherlandish masters. Part of the table is so constructed that it can be made to sink to the floor below.

Proceeding to the E. from the Marly Cascade along the broad avenue, and passing the *Lion Fountain* and the *Eve Fountain* (Pl. C, 1), we reach the *Harbour Canal* (to the right, the Palace, p. 179).

In the E. part of the park is the *Adam Fountain* (Pl. D, 1). To the N.E. of the Adam Fountain, on the beach, lies —

Monplaisir (Pl. D, 1; adm., see p. 179, or on application to the attendant), a villa built by Peter I. in the Dutch style and adorned with numerous paintings. Its terrace commands a fine view of the sea, with the dome of St. Isaac's on the E. horizon and Cronstadt on the W. The main building contains the bedroom of Peter the Great, with his bed and nightcap, and also a Dutch kitchen in which the Empress Elizabeth Petrovna sometimes prepared a meal for her guests with her own hands. The right wing is fitted up with baths. — To the S. is a *Bronze Statue of Peter the Great* (Pl. '); D, 1) by Antokolski, erected in 1883.

On the E. the Lower Park is adjoined by **Alexandria** (Pl. F, 1 2; no admission), including the so-called *Ferme*, a favourite resort of Alexander II. Hard by is the imperial *Villa of Alexandria*, originally built in the Gothic style by the Empress Alexandra Feódorovna, and now used as a summer-residence by Emperor Nicholas II.— Near Alexandria are the attractive little *Church of St. Alexander Nevski*, built in the Gothic style by Schinkel in 1832, the villa of *Renella*, a Tudor structure by Stavasser, and other buildings.

The *Stables* (Pl. E, 2) form an imposing pile of buildings in the Tudor style; the *Riding School* has a fine oaken ceiling.

Between the St. Petersburg Chaussée on the N. and the station of New Peterhof (p. 179) on the S. lies the ALEXANDRA PARK (Pl. E. F, 2, 3; entrances on the S. and N. sides), among the birch-trees of which lies a *Swiss Chalet* (Pl. F, 3).

To the W. of the palace, between the town of Peterhof and the station of Old Peterhof, is the ANGLISKI or ENGLISH PARK (Англійскій садъ; Pl. B, C, 2, 3), containing the *Palais Anglais* (by Quarenghi; 1789; with numerous paintings), the *Fasanerie*, and several large ponds.

To the S. of the railway stretches the large UPPER PARK, containing various imperial villas standing amid lakes, meadows, and woods. The most interesting of these is the château of **Babigon,** or *Belvedere* (beyond Pl. D, 4), situated on a view-commanding hill in a bare and somewhat marshy district, $2^2/_3$ M. from the station of New Peterhof. This château, which is of small size, was built in the classic style in the reign of Nicholas I. (1856) from the designs of Stakenschneider. The magnificent flight of steps ascending to the château is adorned with marble statues, and in the middle of it, in front of the portico, is a bronze group by Kiss (Scythian attacked by a panther), presented by Frederick William IV. to Nicholas I. A little to one side are two Horse Tamers by Baron Klodt (replicas of those at the Anitchkov Bridge, p. 107).

31 V. (21 M.) *Old Peterhof*, Старый Петергófъ (Railway Restaurant), $1^3/_4$ M. to the S.W. of the palace of Peterhof (p. 179).

37 V. (25 M.) **Oranienbaum.** — *Railway Restaurant.* — *Oranienbaum Garden & Theatre,* with military music on Sun. afternoons in summer, D. (2-7 p.m.) 1-$1^1/_2$ rb. — *Izvóshtchik* to $(^3/_4$-1 hr.) Peterhof, $1^1/_4$ rb. The cab should be dismissed here, as the Oranienbaum drivers are not always well acquainted with the Peterhof Park. — *Local Trains* run to Old Peterhof (tickets obtained from the conductors). — *Steamer* to Cronstadt, starting opposite the railway station, see p. 184.

Oranienbaum, a town of 8100 inhab., on the *Karasta* and the Gulf of Finland, was laid out by Ménshikov in 1714. Owing to the shallowness of the water, a long pier has had to be built far out into the Gulf. — From the railway station to the château, $^1/_4$ hr. On leaving the station, we proceed to the right along the Peterbúrgskaya Úlitza; after 4 min. we turn to the right into the Dvortzóvi Prospékt, which we quit in 3 min., opposite the fire-station, and enter the park of the château to the left. Here we at first keep to the left, but after 3 min. take the wide avenue on the right, which leads to (5 min.) the château. The *Château*, which contains nothing of special interest, is the property of Charles Michael, Duke of Mecklenburg-Strelitz. It was built in 1713-25 by the German architect G. Schädel and consists of a central structure with a dome-shaped roof surmounted by a crown, and of two long pavilions connected by galleries with the main building. Near the large terrace in front of the N. façade is a narrow canal leading to the sea. The *Park*, laid out in the Dutch style and consisting of an upper and a lower part, contains the so-called Chinese House, the House of Peter III., the remains of a fortress constructed by Peter III., the Hermitage of Catherine II. (Дámскій дómикъ), the 'Montagne Russe' (Катáльная горá) con-

structed by Rastrelli, and a Lutheran Church. The bead-work tapestry
in the Chinese House was made by the Empress Elizabeth Petrovna.
Drive to *Peterhof*, see below.

b. By the Coast Road to Peterhof and Oranienbaum.

33 V. (22 M.). Carr. & pair to Peterhof in 3 hrs., fare 8-10 rb. (on Sun.
10 rb. at least). From Peterhof to Oranienbaum it is better to take an
izvóshtchik (p. 182). Motor-cab for a day, 25-30 rb. — As far as Ligovo
few points of interest are passed; farther on the scenery is attractive, and
we enjoy a view of the Gulf of Finland to the right.

The ORANIENBAUM ELECTRIC RAILWAY, now under construction, will
run from the *Narva Triumphal Arch* (Pl. C, D, 9, *I;* tramways Nos. 1 & 14)
to (60 V. or 40 M.) *Krásnaya Gorka.* Chief stations: 13 V. Monastery of
St. Sergius; 16 V. Stryelna; 22 V. Alexandria; 24¹/₂ V. or 16¹/₂ M. Peterhof
(Square); 27 V. or 18 M. Peterhof (Kadetski Platz); 30 V. Stari Peterhof;
37 V. or 25 M. Oranienbaum; 45 V. Málaya Izhora.

The coast-road leaves the city by the Narva Triumphal Arch
(p. 129) and is at first flanked by houses and manufactories. 4¹/₂ V.
(3 M.) Village of *Ávtovo.* — 8 V. (5¹/₃ M.) *Lígovo.* To the left
diverges the road leading to (2 M.) the railway station of that name
(p. 178). — 11 V. (7 M.). To the left are the large buildings of a
lunatic asylum, popularly known in St. Petersburg as the 'House at
the 11th verst' (Домъ на одиннадцатой верстѣ). Also to the left
are the datchas of *Ivánovka.* — 15 V. (10 M.). To the right is the
Monastery of St. Sergius (p. 178). Opposite is a straight road
leading to (2 V.) the railway station.

16¹/₂ V. (11 M.). Village of *Stryelna.* The road forks here.
Our road, to the right, leads along the beach below the cliffs. The
main road runs in a straight direction along the top of the cliffs to
(9 V.) Peterhof. To the left is the chaussée leading to (11 V.) Krasnoye Selo (p. 185). — As we proceed we see the *Château of Stryelna*
(p. 178) to the right. On the left the coast-hills approach nearer
the sea. On both sides of the road are villas, palaces, and parks,
including *Mikháilovka* (the property of Grand-Duke Michael),
Kórkuli, Shuválovo, and *Známenskaya.* Before reaching *Alexandria* we quit the lower road.

26¹/₂ V. (18 M.). *Lapidary Works* of **Peterhof,** just on this
side of the palace (p. 181).

We now follow the lower road, which is lined on the left by
country-houses. To the right is the datcha of the Prince of Oldenburg. To the left (about 2¹/₂ M. from the palace at Peterhof) is the
imperial rococo villa known as *'My Property'* (Cóбственная Егó
Велúчества Дáча), built by Stakenschneider, in the reign of Nicholas I., for the future Tzar Alexander II. (adm. on application to the
steward at the Peterhof Palace, p. 179). A little farther on, to the
left, is *Sérgiyevskoye,* the datcha of the Duke of Leuchtenberg,
attractively situated on a hill in the midst of a beautiful park. We
now proceed through the village of *Martúishkino* and the town of
Oranienbaum to (33 V. or 22 M.) Oranienbaum rail. station (p. 182).

12*

c. **Cronstadt.**

Direct STEAMER from *St. Peteṛsburg* 4-5 times daily in 1½ hr. (fare 65 cop.); it starts from the Vasili Ostrov, just below the Nicholas Bridge (Pl. D, 5; *I*). — From *Oranienbaum* (p. 182) a steamer plies 11 times daily in ½ hr. (fare 15 cop.); its pier in Cronstadt is near that of the St. Petersburg boat. — From *Lisi Nos* (p. 194), steamer 7 times daily in ½ hr., fare 15 cop. (from Novaya Derevnya to Cronstadt, 1½ hr., fare 65 cop.).

The Nevá (p. 99) discharges itself into *Nevá Bay*, 19 M. long, which forms a part of the Gulf of Finland. The water is fresh and freezes in winter (Sea Canal, see p. 129). At the spot where Finland (N.) and Ingermanland (S.) approach nearest each other lies Cronstadt. The steamer lands at the St. Petersburg Gate, the E. extremity of the island, where a long pier projects into the sea.

Cronstadt, Кронштáдтъ. — HOTELS. *St. Petersburg, London*, both in the Nikoláyevski Prospékt. — *Restaurant* in summer on the steamboat-pier. — *British Vice-Consul & Lloyd's Agent*, A. Fishwick; *United States Commercial Agent*, Peter Wigius. — A general idea of Cronstadt may be obtained in a drive of 1 hr. (the fare should not exceed 60-80 cop.; previous understanding with the izvóshtchik desirable). From the pier we traverse the town to the Petrovski Garden, and then drive along the Nikoláyevski Prospékt and past the Naval Cathedral back to the pier.

Cronstadt, a fortified town with 65,000 inhab. and the station of the Baltic fleet, lies upon the island of *Kotlin*, which is 7¼ M. in length and 1¼ M. in width. Its batteries, built upon piles, and looking as if floating on the sea, command the entrance to Nevá Bay.

The original fortifications on the island were made in 1703. The present fortifications, which are deemed impregnable, were partly constructed by Tzar Nicholas I. and partly in 1856-71 from the plans of Count Todleben. In June, 1854, a combined British and French fleet under Admiral Sir Charles Napier appeared before Cronstadt, but made no attack on it.

The town is divided into the *Commercial Quarter* and the *Naval Quarter*. In the latter lie the *Admiralty* (constructed in 1785 in the reign of Catherine II), the *School of Naval Engineers*, a large *Naval Hospital* (seen to the right in approaching from St. Petersburg), and various barracks, arsenals, and shipbuilding-yards. In front of the engineering school is a bronze statue, by Laveretzki (1886), of P. K. Pákhtusov, who explored Nova Zembla in 1832-35. At the S.E. end of the island lies the *Naval Harbour* (Воéнная гáвань), adjoining which is the so-called *Middle Harbour* (Срéдняя гáвань), intended for the equipment of men-of-war. To the W. of the last is the *Commercial Harbour*. Permission to visit the harbours, the docks, and a man-of-war may be obtained on weekdays (10-12 & 3-4 or 3-5) from the Chief of Staff (Начáльникъ штáба пóрта), at the corner of the Knyázheskaya and the Makárovskaya. In front of the governor's residence lies the *Petrovski Garden* (rfmts.), commanding a view of the harbours; in the middle of it is a bronze statue of Peter the Great, by Baron Klodt (1841). A long *Mole* projects into the sea here, the end of which (also reached by boat across the harbour) commands a fine view of the harbour and forts. — The main street of the town is the Nikoláyevski Prospékt, running N. and S. On its E. side is the Greek Catholic *Cathedral of St. Andrew*, built in 1805-17 by Sakhárov. 'Father John of Cronstadt' (d. 1908) was one of the priests connected with this church. From the cathedral the Yekaterininskaya runs towards the E.; in the gardens on its S. side is a bronze statue of Admiral Bellingshausen (d. 1852), by Schröder (1870). About ¹/₄ M. from the Cathedral of St. Andrew a cross-street leads S. to the *Naval Cathedral*, built in 1903-13 by Kosyakov; in front of it rises a bronze statue of *Admiral Stephen Ósipovitch Makárov* (comp. p. 548), by Sherwood (1913). — Near the steamboat-pier are two *Lutheran Churches* and a *Roman Catholic Church*.

17. From St. Petersburg to Krasnoye Selo and Gatchina.

Railway to (24 V. or 16 M.) *Krasnoye Selo* in ³/₄ hr. (fares 70, 40, 25 cop.); to (43 V. or 29 M.) *Gatchina* in 1¹/₂ hr. (fares 1 rb. 25, 75, 50 cop.). — Gatchina may also be reached by the St. Petersburg and Warsaw Railway (p. 43; 42 V.) in 1 hr. (fares 1 rb. 20, 70, 45 cop.).

The excursion to Krasnoye Selo, where the Corps of Guards occupies a summer-camp in the months of June, July, and August (O.S), is mainly of interest to military men.

The trains start from the Baltic Station (Pl. E 8, *I;* p. 88). — Beyond (13 V.) *Lígovo* or Лигово (to Peterhof, see p. 178) we traverse the level and monotonous manœuvring-ground.

24 V. **Krásnoye Seló**, Красное Село (*Railway Restaurant*, with bedrooms; izvóshtchik to the dairy-farm and the château, in 1¹/₂-2 hrs., fare 1¹/₄-1¹/₂ rb.), pleasantly situated on the *Dúderhofka* and the three *Lakes of Duderhof*, is a large village, with numerous villas, grouped round the *Church of the Holy Trinity*, built by Anna Ivánovna in 1733. Near the theatre is a summer-restaurant.

To the S.E. of the village is the *Hill of Duderhof* (550 ft.), in the middle of the manœuvring-ground. From the small station of Duderhof (7 min. by railway from Krasnoye), we walk in 10 min. to the *Imperial Dairy Farm* (Ферма), situated at the foot of the hill. A further walk of 25 min. through the park brings us to a height bearing the so-called *Château* (Дворецъ), built in the style of a Swiss chalet. Like the farm and the grounds, this was a creation of the Empress Alexandra Feódorovna (1828). The balconies running round the château command a wide view. — At the N. base of the hill begins the extensive *Camp of the Guards*, which is reached most directly by crossing the railway close to the station (2 V.; izvóshtchik 20-30, per hr. 60 cop.).

From Krasnoye Selo a good road leads towards the W. to (10 V.) **Ropsha,** Ропша (izvóshtchik there and back, in 4 hrs., 2 rb.; the traveller must take his luncheon with him). The beautiful park here contains an imperial *Château*, in which Peter III. died in 1762; permission to visit it may be obtained from the steward at Krasnoye Selo. — The typical Finnish villages in the neighbourhood are interesting.

43 V. Gátchina, Гатчина (*Restaurants* at both railway stations, comp. p. 43; *Hôtel-Restaurant Veryóvkin,* Lutzévskaya; izvóshtchik from either station to the town 35, per hr. 50 cop.), a town with 18,200 inhab., pleasantly situated on both sides of the *White* and *Black Lakes* (Бѣлое и Чёрное Озеро) formed by the *Izhóra* (Ижора). The town, with its numerous villas and shady streets, is the private property of the imperial family. It has a Lutheran and a Roman Catholic church.

The PALACE OF GATCHINA (shown in the absence of the Empress Dowager on application to the steward), built by Rinaldi in 1766-81, lies on the W. side of the town, ¹/₄ M. from the Baltic Station, and at the foot of the Marienburg heights, and is surrounded by a beautiful park. It is a three-storied structure, built in a simple yet dignified style, and connected by colonnades with one-storied wings enclosing a large, rectangular court. In front of the palace is a statue of Tzar Paul I., by Baron Klodt. The interior contains 600 rooms, including three throne-rooms, a theatre, and numerous valuable pictures and sculptures. — The *Park* extends down to the pellucid lake, which contains several islands, united by bridges, and is fed by several rivulets. The *Priory*, said to be an imitation of that of the Knights of St. John at Malta, was erected by Paul I.

18. From St. Petersburg to Tzarskoye Selo and Pavlovsk.

Railway to (22 V. or 15 M.) *Tzárskoye Seló* in ¹/₂ hr. (fares 83, 50, 33 cop.); to (25 V. or 17 M.) *Pavlovsk* in 40 min. (fares 95, 57, 38 cop.). — The railway from St. Petersburg to Tzarskoye Selo, opened in 1837, is the oldest in Russia.

Soon after leaving the Tzarskoye Selo station in St. Petersburg (Pl. F 7, *I;* p. 88), we see the Novo-Dyevítchi Convent (p. 128) and the aerodrome of the Aviation Battalion, both on the right. Farther on the train runs to the S. through fields and pastures; in the background are the heights of Tzarskoye Selo.

22 V. **Tzárskoye Seló,** Царское Село. — *Railway Restaurant,* very fair. — HOTEL: *Sévernaya* (Pl. a; E, 2), Oranzheréinaya. — The imperial palaces in Tzarskoye Selo are shown from 10 a.m. till dusk by tickets obtainable in the *Palace Office* (Дворцовое управленіе; Pl. 11, D 2), at the corner of the Srédnyaya and Leóntyevskaya (entrance from the latter). The park is open to the public. — *Izvóshtchik* from the railway station to the palace 30, to Pavlovsk 80 cop. *Carriage* for a drive in the park, to which izvóshtchiks are not admitted, 1¹/₂ rb. per hr.

Tzárskoye Seló (*i.e.* Village of the Tzar), a town of 30,800 inhab., with broad and straight streets and numerous villas, makes a very pleasing impression. It contains two imperial palaces, several barracks and hospitals, and eight churches, including a Lutheran Church (Pl. E, 3) and a Roman Catholic Church (Pl. D, 1).

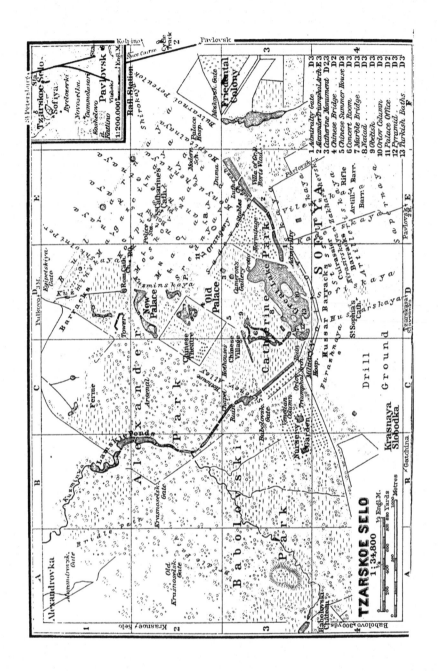

TZARSKOE SELO
1:34,800

Alexandrovka

Kransnoe Selo

St Petersburg
Tzárskoe Selo
Sofiya
Byelozerki
Yonrosetka
Samnoloster
Koshelevo
Fautino
Vitebsk
11:200,000°

Pavlovsk

Kolhino
Racе Course

Rail. Station

Frederal Colony

Mackov. Gate

Alexander Park

Babolovski Park

Babolovski Chateau

Babolovo 4300 yds.

R "Gatchina

Krasnaya Slobodka

Drill Ground

Catherine Park

Sofiya

Pavlovsk

1 Admiralty Gate D3
2 Alexander Triumphal Arch E3
3 Catherine Monument ... D2,3
4 Chinese Bridge D2
5 Chinese Summer House .. D3
6 Concert Room D3
7 Marble Bridge D3
8 Vauxhall D3
9 Obelisk D3
10 Orlov Column D3
11 Palace Office D2
12 Pyramid D3
13 Turkish Baths .... F

From the *Railway Station* (Pl. F, 1, 2) we first follow the Shiró-
kaya in a straight direction, and then turn to the right into the
Búlvarnaya, where we take the third street to the left, the Leóntyevskaya. In the last, to the left, stands the Greek Catholic *Cathedral
of St. Catharine* (Pl. E, 2), with five gilded domes, built in 1840
from plans by Thon. At the end of the street we turn to the right,
pass the Palace Church, and reach (ca. 35 min. from the railway
station) the Palace Square. — Here stands the —

Great Imperial Palace (Стáрый дворéцъ; Pl. D, 2; admission, see p. 186; attendant 50 cop., parties more in proportion).
This extensive building, re-erected in the rococo style in 1747-56,
from the designs of Rastrelli, is 326 yds. in length. The enclosure
of the spacious Palace Square, which is entered by three iron
gates, is completed by a semicircle of low buildings on the N.W.
The prevailing colours of the palace are light-green and white,
while its over-elaborate stucco ornamentation is bronzed. — Behind
the palace is a small statue of Catherine II. (Pl. 3), the model for
that mentioned at p. 106.

The *Palace Church* is richly decorated in gold and blue; opposite
the ikonostás is the gallery of the imperial family. The *Bedroom of
the Tzarina Marie Alexándrovna*, consort of Alexander II., has walls of
opalescent glass, pillars of violet glass, and a parquet-floor inlaid with
mother-of-pearl. Another room, once occupied by Catherine II., is adorned
with agate. The *Amber Room* (Янтáрная кóмната) is panelled in amber.
The *Silver Room* is resplendent with silver, the *Ball Room* (140 ft. in
length by 52 ft. in breadth) with mirrors and gold. The tables and chandeliers of the *Lapis Lazuli Room* (blue and gold) are adorned with lapis
lazuli. The decorations of the *Chinese Room* are black and gold. One
room is hung with pictures of the Netherlandish School. Among the
other noteworthy pictures may be mentioned the numerous sea-pieces by
Aivazovski, and two works by Willewalde (Submission of Shamyl, Coronation of Alexander II. at Moscow). There are also many paintings by
Bryullóv, the most interesting of which is the copy of the ceiling of St.
Isaac's Cathedral. — After leaving the state apartments, we are conducted
through the rooms of the *Empress Marie Feódorovna*, the *Emperor
Alexander I.*, and the *Empress Elizabeth*, etc. — On the groundfloor are
the rooms of Alexander II. — The open *Gallery* of the S. wing, built
by Cameron (p. 189), is 269 ft. long and adorned with bronze busts of
celebrated men of antiquity. A flight of stone steps, with tasteful iron
gates, descends from the gallery to the park. The front *Staircase*, in white
marble, ascending to the second story, is beautifully decorated and deserves
attention.

The N.W. gate of the Palace Square mentioned above leads into
the —

Park, which is laid out in the English style, is kept in excellent order, and contains numerous arbours, triumphal arches,
statues, grottoes, ruins, and picturesque bridges over the swan-
ponds. — Beyond the gate is the *Chinese Bridge* (Pl. 4), with a balustrade of imitation coral, on which sit four stone Chinamen with
parasols. A little to the S. of this is a vaulted *Suspension Bridge*
representing a cross, in the centre of which is a *Chinese Arbour* of
glazed red and yellow bricks (Pl. 5; D, 3). Farther to the S.W. is

the so-called *Chinese Village* (Pl. C, 3), built in 1782-6 from plans by Cameron. A little to the N. is a *Theatre* (Pl. C, 2). The more southerly of the two *Artificial Ruins* (Pl. C, 3) in the park, reproducing an ancient tower, commands a wide view of the extensive drill-ground. On the second floor of the other ruin stands a marble figure of Christ, by Dannecker (1824). Not far off are large *Orangeries* and *Greenhouses.*

Visitors should take the walk round the *Great Lake* (Pl. D, 3; 1 hr.). From the palace-church (p. 187) we proceed to the S.E. along the Sadóvaya, which leads along the canal. At the first bridge we diverge to the right, and skirt the outflow of the great pond. To the left we see the white *Hermitage* (Pl. E, 3), built by Rastrelli in 1752. On reaching the great pond, we turn to the left and begin our circuit of it on the E. side. The *Admiralty* (Pl. D, 3), where row-boats may be hired, contains three gilded barges of the time of Catherine II. Farther on, to the right, the *Orlóv Column* (Pl. 10), erected in 1778 in honour of the victorious Prince Orlóv Tchésmenski, rises from the lake. The yellow marble column, which rests on a base of granite, is crowned by an eagle and adorned with the prows of vessels. On a point projecting from the S. bank are the *Turkish Baths* (Pl. 13), built in 1852 in the Moorish style, with an elaborately decorated gilded dome. A *Granite Pyramid* (Pl. 12), rising from the shrubbery a little to the left, marks the burial-place of three of Catherine's pet dogs. We now cross a bridge of blue Siberian marble (Pl. 7), adorned with columns. On the W. bank is a large granite block bearing a *Bronze Naiad* (Pl. 8) by Sokolóv (1810), holding a broken pitcher out of which a stream of water flows.

Almost all the GATES of the park are of admirable workmanship. On the S. side is a large *Triumphal Archway* (Pl. C, 3) of marble, erected by Catherine II. to the memory of Prince Gregory Orlóv, who distinguished himself in 1771 by his pacification of Moscow during the plague. — On the E. side is another *Triumphal Arch* (Pl. 2; E, 3), erected by the Tzar Alexander I. in 1818 to the Russian Army and inscribed: Любéзнымъ мойм сослужи́вцамъ ('To my dear companions-in-arms'). — The so-called *Gate of Bábolovo* or *Bábolovski Gate* (Pl. C, 3) leads to the pretty grounds and small château of that name.

To the N. of the Great Palace, in what was once the Lyceum Garden, is a seated *Bronze Figure of Pushkin* (Pl. P. ; D, 2), by R. Bach (1900).

The ALEXANDER or NEW PALACE (Нóвый дворéцъ; Pl. D, 2), built by Catherine in 1796 from the plans of Quarenghi, is often occupied by the Tzar in spring. — In the Alexander Park are also the *Dairy Farm* (Фéрма, *Ferme;* Pl. C, 1), built in 1820, and the former *Arsenal* (Pl. C, 2), a red brick structure in the English Gothic style, with four towers. It now contains model-figures of Russian cavalry and examples of the work of the Imperial Porcelain and Glass Manufactory. The earlier collections have been removed to the Hermitage (p. 141).

PAVLOVSK

1:21,000

Near Tzarskoye Selo and Pavlovsk are several German settlements, including *Friedental* (Фридентáль; Pl. F, 3), established by Tzar Alexander I. in 1820. — To the S. of Tzarskoye Selo and its park is *Sofiya* (Софiя; Pl. D, E, 4), much frequented in summer by the wealthy inhabitants of St. Petersburg.

At the end of the park, beyond the Triumphal Arch of Alexander I. (Pl. 2; E, 3), begins a broad avenue which leads in an absolutely straight line, passing numerous country-houses, to (3 M.) Pavlovsk (see below; izvóshtchik, see p. 186). A little short of Pavlovsk, to the left, are the handsome iron gates of the grand-ducal park.

,FROM TZARSKOYE SELO RAILWAY STATION TO PULKOVO, 8 V. (5 M.), izvóshtchik there and back, with a stay of 1 hr., 2 rb. — **Púlkovo** is a village of about 2000 inhabitants. Close by, on a hill which commands a splendid view of St. Petersburg, is the imperial *Nicholas Observatory* (Обсерватóрiя; 253 ft. in height), built in 1839 at a cost of nearly 2,000,000 rb., and admirably fitted up (open on Wed. & Sat., 1-3 p.m.; in the evening only by special permission from Director O. Backlund). A cannon is fired every day at noon in the Fortress of SS. Peter & Paul (p. 173) by an electric current from the observatory. A flying visit to the observatory takes about 1 hr. Carr. & pair from St. Petersburg to Pulkovo and back, in 6-7 hrs, 8 rb.

A straight road leads from Pulkovo to (12 V or 8 M.) St. Petersburg (Moscow Triumphal Arch; p. 128). About 9 V. from Pulkovo on this road lies *Tchesmá* (Чесма), a château erected in 1773 by Catherine II. from the designs of Velten in commemoration of the victory won over the Turks at Tchesmé on July 5th & 6th, 1770. In 1836 the château was converted by Nicholas I. into a hospital for old soldiers.

From Tzarskoye Selo to *Vitebsk*, see R. 34.

CONTINUATION OF RAILWAY TO PAVLOVSK. Beyond Tzarskoye Selo the railway to Vitebsk diverges to the right.

25 V. **Pavlovsk,** ПАВЛОВСКЪ. — Near the station is the large railway restaurant of *Vauxhall* (Вокзáлъ; Pl. C, 2; D. 1¹/₄ & 2¹/₂ rb.); popular concerts with a good band every evening in summer (adm. free; reserved seats 10-50 cop.). — *Izvóshtchik* for the 1st hr. 60 cop., each following hr. 40 cop.; to Tzarskoye Selo 60 cop. It is, however, as well to make a bargain beforehand.

Pavlovsk, a town with 8400 inhab., was formerly a village presented by Catherine II. in 1777 to her son Paul and his wife Marie Feódorovna. It consists of two parts separated by the little river *Slavyánka* (Славянка). The attractive wooden houses surrounded by trees and gardens are mostly summer-quarters of the citizens of St. Petersburg.

The **Palace** (Pl. B, C, 2, 3), which has three stories and belongs to the Grand-Duke Constantine Constantínovitch, was built in 1782-84 from designs by the Scottish architect *Charles Cameron*, but received its present form after a fire in 1803. In the centre of the façade is a portico of eight Ionic columns surmounted by a large dome; at the sides are semicircular colonnades. In the middle of the Palace Square is a *Statue of Paul I.* (1872), a replica of that at Gatchina (p. 186). On a lawn behind the palace is a concave gallery adorned with marble statues and painted by Gonzague in such a way as to afford the perspective of a large and elaborate building. — Permission to visit the interior in the absence of the Grand-Duke may be obtained from the local authorities (Управленіе города). The original furniture and decorations in the Louis XVI. style are in an excellent state of preservation.

FIRST FLOOR. The *Cabinet of Paul I.* contains ivory carvings by the Empress Marie Feódorovna, Gobelin tapestry, with scenes from the fables of La Fontaine, and a portrait of the empress, by Lampi. Farther on are the *Gobelin Room* (Ковровая комната), the *Peace Room*, the *War Room*, the beautiful *Greek Room*, and the *Cabinet of the Empress Marie Feódorovna*. In the *State Bed Chamber* are a mirror with porcelain figures by Clodion and a toilet-set and tea-service in Sèvres china (two of the cups decorated with miniature portraits of Louis XVI. and Marie Antoinette). — The PICTURE GALLERY contains pictures by Rembrandt (Head of Christ), A. Cuyp, S. van Ruysdael, P. Veronese, Angelica Kauffmann, Van Mieris, Ribera, A. Caracci, Guido Reni, Mme. Vigée-Lebrun, and others. — Amongst the antiques of the ART COLLECTION may be mentioned: 1. Venus; 4. Eros; 7. Bacchus; 8, 9. Satyrs; 13. Polyhymnia; 15, 16. Boy and girl with bird; several Busts of Roman emperors; 42, 43. Tombstones; 89, 90-96. Statuettes in bronze. — The LIBRARY numbers about 21,000 vols., chiefly works of the 18th cent.; in the niches between the bookcases are marble statues of the Muses. The chief treasures of the collection are a New Testament in French, dating from 1559; the diary of J. G. Korb, secretary to the embassy sent by Leopold I. to Moscow in 1698-99 (Vienna; 1700); a collection of original physiognomic drawings by Lavater; and the Memoirs of Manstein (d. 1757). The collection of *Coins and Medals* is shown in five cases (1. Cameos; 2. Russian Coins; 3-5. Medals).

In the E. part of the park, ³/₄ M. from the Great Palace, lies the small *Constantine Palace* (Константиновскій дворецъ; Pl. D, 4), on the edge of a lake, in a small park of its own. The unpretending interior contains a few pictures by Russian artists (views of St. Petersburg and the Nevá).

The *Park of Pavlovsk constitutes one of the most successful achievements of landscape gardening on unpropitious soil. It offers a series of picturesque glimpses, hills and dales, lake-views, and foaming waterfalls, while Greek temples adorned with statues, attractive Swiss chalets, and moss-clad arbours peep in every direction from amongst fine trees of every variety.

To the S. of the palace is the *Trellised Arbour* (Трельяжъ; Pl. B, 3), affording a pleasant view. From it a flight of 70 steps adorned with marble vases descends to the lake, on the bank of which rises an *Obelisk* (Pl. B, 3), erected in commemoration of the foundation of Pavlovsk (1777). [About ¹/₃ M. to the S.W. is the fortress (p. 191).] Near the Sadóvaya is the *Temple of the Graces*, with marble statues by Trescorni. Near the stone bridge is a *Monument to the Grand-Duchess Helena Pávlovna* (Pl. B, 3), with a relief by Martos. To the N.W. is the *Temple of Apollo* (Pl. B, C, 2), with a double row of columns. The so-called *Family Grove* (Семейная роща; Pl. B, 2) is a small wood surrounded by water, with trees planted by members of the imperial family. The *Temple of Friendship* (Храмъ дружбы;

Pl. C, 2), a rotunda in the Doric style, contains a statue of Empress Catherine II. as Ceres.

A broad avenue runs E. from the palace. To the left, in a beautiful flower garden, is a *Marble Bust of Emp. William I.* of Germany, who visited Pavlovsk as Crown-Prince in 1817. To the right is an *Aviary* (Pl. C, 3). Bearing to the left at the end of the avenue, we reach the *Rondell* (Старая Сильвія; Pl. D, 3), from which radiate twelve different paths. In the centre of the rondell are figures of the Muses and a bronze replica of the Apollo Belvedere. A little to the N.W. is a small temple, with a pretty marble group by Martos, erected in memory of the Grand-Duchess Alexandra Pávlovna (d. 1801; Pl. D, 2). A semicircular temple to the S., inscribed 'To my Parents' (Родителямъ) was erected by Marie Feódorovna. On the left bank of the Slavyánka is the *Pil-Báshnya* (Pl. E, 2), a round tower with a thatched roof. Ascending along the bank of the stream from this point we reach (12 min.) the rectangular *Elizabeth Pavilion* (Елизаветинскій павильонъ; Pl. F, 2), a curious structure of 1799, the flat roof of which is reached by a broad flight of steps. We return through the *Nóvaya Sílviya* (Pl. E, F, 2, 3), on the right bank, to the *Monument of Paul I.* (Pl. E, 3), consisting of a temple, the façade of which is adorned by four columns of red granite. Inside is a granite pyramid with a marble medallion of Paul; below is a female figure, and on the base is a relief representing his mourning relatives. The sculptures are all by Martos. Over the entrance is the inscription: 'To the Husband and Benefactor' (Супругу благодѣтелю). To the S. stands the *Pavilion of Roses* (Розовый павильонъ; Pl. D, 3), the ceiling of which is decorated with garlands of artificial roses.

Pavlovsk also possesses a miniature *Fortress* (Pl. A, 2), with towers, bastions, and ordnance, situated about $^3/_4$ M. to the S.W. of the Great Palace, and surrounded on three sides by water. It occupies the site of a Swedish fortification destroyed by Peter the Great, and is seen to best advantage from the opposite bank of the river.

In the E. part of the park is the *Constantine Magnetic & Meteorological Observatory* (comp. Pl. D, E, 4), an admirably equipped institution, which is open to the public on Sat., 2-4 p.m. Director, V. Chr. Dubinski.

19. From St. Petersburg to Schlüsselburg.

Comp. Inset Map at p. 173.

STEAMBOAT from St. Petersburg to Schlüsselburg several times daily in 4 hrs. (fare 1 rb.), returning downstream in 3 hrs. It starts at the summer-garden (Pl. F, G, 4; I). There is a restaurant on board. An hour suffices for a visit to Schlüsselburg.

A LIGHT RAILWAY runs from Okhta (starting from the Irinovka Station, p. 88) twice daily to (39 V. or 26 M.) *Sheremétyevka*, in 2½ hrs. (2nd class fare, 1 rb.). Hence we go on to Schlüsselburg by steamer (10 cop.).

The STEAMBOAT TRIP up the Nevá to Schlüsselburg is by no means devoid of interest. At first we see factories, especially on the left bank (in the Schlüsselburg quarter is an English church), and settlements. After this the banks become wooded, and country-houses make their appearance. The whole effect is somewhat sombre. The broad stream is covered with huge rafts and with tugs hauling six or more boats in double row.

8 V. *Alexándrovskoye Seló,* on the left bank, with Thornton's Woollen Mill, the largest in Russia.

10 V. (7 M.) On the left bank is the interesting *Imperial Porcelain and Glass Manufactory* (Императорскій Фарфоровый и стеклянный заводы), the entrance to which is on the side next the Nevá. Admission, see p. 98. Steam-tramway, see p. 92. The porcelain factory was founded in 1744 under the Tzarina Elizabeth by K. Chr. Hunger of Meissen. The glass-works founded in 1772 became imperial property in 1792 and were united with the porcelain factory in 1890. The articles are not for sale. To the left of the entrance is the porcelain museum, to the right are the workshops, with specimens of glass ware.

On the left bank are the Obúkhov steel-works. — 15 V. On the right bank is the German colony of *Novo-Sarátov* (Ново-Саратовская Колонія). — On the left bank is *Ust-Izhóra;* farther on is a summer camp. — 32 V. *Ostrovki,* on the right bank, a château once belonging to Prince Potemkin, and situated in a wooded park. — Beyond *Dubróvka* (left bank) the steamer reaches Schlüsselburg. To the right are a huge cotton-mill and the town proper; in front, on an islet, is the small fortress; to the left lies *Sheremétyevka* (railway, see p. 191).

60 V. (40 M.) **Schlüsselburg,** Шлиссельбургъ, the chief town of a district in the province of St. Petersburg, with 7600 inhab., lies at the point where the Nevá issues from Lake Ládoga.

The Nevá and Lake Ládoga furnished the waterway by which the Vikings and, at a later period, the mariners of the Hanseatic Towns reached the Volkhov and Novgorod. In 1323 the inhabitants of Novgorod (P. 262), then at war with Sweden, established a fortress *(Orékhov)* upon the island lying opposite Schlüsselburg, and this long remained a bone of contention between Sweden and Russia. In 1617 the fortress became Swedish and its name was changed to *Nöteborg,* but in 1702 it was captured by Peter the Great after an assault of 35 hrs. and rechristened *Schlüsselburg.*

About 200 yds. to the right of the landing-stage are the *Locks of the Old Ládoga Canal* (p. 195). To the left of the landing-stage is the new canal, commanding a view of the island fortress, Lake Ládoga, and the red lighthouse of *Koshkin.* — The former *Fortress* (Крѣпость) is now used as a prison.

From Schlüsselburg to *Petrozavódsk* and to the *Kivátch,* see R. 21.

20. From St. Petersburg to Terijoki. Sestroryetzk. Toksovo.

FROM ST. PETERSBURG TO TERIJOKI, 49 Kil. or 30¹/₂ M., railway, starting from the Finland Station (Pl. H 3, *I;* p. 88), in 1¹/₂ hr. (fares 1 rb. 81,
1 rb. 9, 72 cop.). Fares to Lanskaya 20, 15, 10 cop.; to Udyelnaya 30, 20,
10; to Ozerki 40, 25, 15; to Shuvalovo 40, 25, 15; to Pargolovo 55, 35,
20; to Levashovo 60, 45, 25 cop. — Custom-house examination, see p. 204.

FROM NOVAYA DEREVNYA TO OZERKI, 7 V. (5 M.), railway, starting
from the Sestroryetzk Station (P. 88), in 20 min. (fares to Kolomyagi 18,
13, 8 cop.; to Ozerki 25, 15, 10 cop.).

FROM NOVAYA DEREVNYA TO SESTRORYETZK (station, see p. 88), 29 V.
(19 M.), railway in 1¹/₄ hr. Fares (tickets obtained from the conductor) to
Lakhta 30, 20, 15 cop.; to Sestroryetzk 80, 55, 40 cop. — To Cronstadt, see
p. 184.

FROM ST. PETERSBURG TO TERIJOKI (fares, see above). — 5 Kil.
Lanskáya, with a beautiful park. — 8 Kil. *Udyélnaya* (Удѣльная).
To the W. lies *Kolomyági* (see below), reached through the garden
and park of Udyelnaya by a walk of 20 minutes.

In Udyelnaya, near the Komendántskaya Datcha, stands a bust of
Pushkin, marking the spot where the poet fell mortally wounded in a
duel (Jan. 27th, 1837; comp. p. 115).

10 Kil. (6 M.) **Ozerkí,** situated on two lakes, with a large
pleasure-resort (concerts, etc.), much frequented in winter by sleigh-
ing-parties. There are also a number of summer-villas here.

FROM NOVAYA DEREVNYA TO OZERKI, 7 V. (fares, see above). *Nóvaya
Derévnya,* see p. 177. — 3 V. *Kolomyági* (Коломяги), a pleasantly situated
colony of datchas. To the left is the racecourse mentioned at p. 177. —
7 V. *Ozerki.*

11 Kil. **Shuválovo,** the family-seat of Count Shuválov, with a
beautiful park. Shuvalovo is also the summer-residence of numerous
St. Petersburg families, who have built themselves villas on the banks
of *Lake Suzdal* (steamboat 10 cop.). To reach the lake, we leave
the rail. station in a straight direction, after a few steps turn to the
left, and immediately after to the right.

16 Kil. **Párgolovo** is the common name of several villages on
the highroad to Viborg. On the lake to the E. of the road are the
datchas of several St. Petersburg families. The surrounding heights
command a fine view of St. Petersburg, especially *Mt. Parnassus,*
¹/₂ hr.'s walk to the S.E. of the rail. station.

19 Kil. *Levashóvo.* About 2 M. to the E. is the village of *Yukki,*
situated on a small lake with steep banks. The highest point of
the bank commands an extensive prospect in the direction of Finland. Close by is a fair restaurant.

The scenery now becomes somewhat monotonous, forests alternating with moors, and swamps. Beyond (32 Kil. or 20 M.) *Valkeasaari* or *Byelo-Ostrov* (customs examination for passengers from
Finland) the train crosses the *Snistera Ryeka* (Swedish, *Syster-
bäck*), a stream forming the frontier between Russia and Finland.

49 Kil. (30¹/₂ M.) **Térijoki** (comp. *Map*, p. 178). — *Railway Rest aurant*, pint of beer with roll and butter 1 m. — HOTELS. *Casino* (Map O), R. 1¹/₂-4 rb., déj. 75 cop., D. 1¹/₄ rb.; *Riviera* (Map R), R. 1¹/₂-10, déj. (12-2 p.m.) 1¹/₄, D. (6-8 p.m.) 1¹/₂, board 2¹/₂ rb.; *Bellevue* (Map B), R. from 1¹/₂, déj. ³/₄, D. 1¹/₄ rb.

Térijoki, a scattered village on the Gulf of Finland, with numerous villas, is the station for the custom-house examination of passengers from Russia (comp. p. 204). To reach the sea (1¹/₂ M. from the rail. station) we first turn to the left, then (3 min.) cross the railway to the left and pass the church (l.); after ¹/₄ hr. we keep to the right (avoiding the turn to the left), and in 4 min. turn to the left; in 2 min. we turn to the right and reach (4 min.) the Hôtel-Restaurant Casino.

About 5 M. from Terijoki is *Tchernaia Retchka* (Tchórnaya Ryetchka), a picturesque summer-resort, much visited by English residents of St. Petersburg.

From Terijoki to *Viborg*, see R. 22.

___

FROM NOVAYA DEREVNYA TO SESTRORYETZK (fares, see p. 193). *Novaya Derevnya*, see p. 177. — The railway leads through heath and swamp to (9 V.) *Lakhta*, a popular resort on the Gulf of Finland, with numerous datchas and a life-saving station. — Farther on we traverse wood. From (17 V.) *Razdyélnaya* a branch-line runs to (3 V.) *Lisi Nos*, whence a steamboat plies to Cronstadt (p. 184). To the left lies the Gulf of Finland. 21 V. *Górskayá*, a group of datchas; 26 V. *Sestroryétzk*, Сестрорѣцкъ, with an imperial small-arms factory, founded by Peter the Great. — 29 V. (19 M.) **Kurort Sestroryétzk**, a watering-place laid out in 1900 in the midst of the pine-woods on the shore of the gulf (Kurhaus, R. from 40, in winter from 35 rb. per month, board 2¹/₂ rb. per day, déj. 1, D. 2 rb.; visitors' tax 4-8 rb.). The place possesses a sanatorium, a beach-promenade (lighted by electricity in the evening), a covered promenade, and all the usual adjuncts of a bathing-resort. Near the Kurhaus, which contains a large concert-room, is a bronze statue of Peter the Great in the guise of a carpenter.

___

FROM ST. PETERSBURG TO TOKSOVO, 26 V. (17 M.), highroad. The School of Forestry and the Polytechnic are most easily reached by steam-tramway No. 2 (p. 92). — 6 V. The **Imperial Institute of Forestry** (Лѣсной Институтъ), founded in 1803, is attended by 560 students. Near it are numerous villas, a large and beautiful park, a mineral-water factory, and a summer-theatre. About 1 V. to the N. is the **Polytechnic** (Политехническій Институтъ), opened in 1902, and attended by 5200 students. — 12 V. *Múrino*, a pretty village on the *Okhta*. — 26 V. (17 M.) **Tóksovo**, a village in a small and picturesque lake-district known as the *St. Petersburg Switzerland*.

21. From St. Petersburg to Petrozavodsk.
The Kivatch.

STEAMER from St. Petersburg to *Petrozavodsk* thrice weekly, starting from the Voskresénskaya Náberezhnaya (Pl. H, 4; *I*) about 11 a.m. and taking 45 hrs. for the voyage (in the reverse direction 35 hrs.). Fare 9 or 6½ rb.; return-ticket for passengers coming back on the same steamer are issued at a reduction of 20 per cent. Meals cost about 3 rb. daily. This interesting but somewhat fatiguing excursion requires 5 days; the best months for it are June and July.

Steamboat voyage from St. Petersburg to *Schlüsselburg*, see R. 19. — Beyond Schlüsselburg, where it halts for ½ hr., the steamer enters Lake Ládoga, which it crosses toward the E. in ca. 8 hrs. Many lighthouses are seen during the transit.

Lake Ládoga (Ла́дожское О́зеро), formerly called by the Finns *Nevo*, lies about 16 ft. above sea-level and is, next to the Caspian Sea, the largest lake in Europe, being 124 M. long, 62 M. wide, and 7000 sq.M. in area. Its greatest depth is 730 ft., but it also contains many reefs and shoals, which, combined with the frequent tempests, make navigation somewhat dangerous. To avoid these perils, the *Ládoga Canal* was constructed in 1718-31, skirting the S. margin of the lake from Schlüsselburg to the mouth of the Volkhov. The new canal, constructed in 1861-1886, runs close to the lake, parallel with the old one. The banks of Lake Ládoga on the N. and W. are high and rocky, sometimes covered with woods but at other times entirely bare. The N. shore is penetrated by numerous bays flanked by steep and rugged cliffs. It finds an outlet into the Gulf of Finland by the Nevá. — During the most recent geological period, Lake Ládoga and Lake Onéga were for a time united with the Gulf of Finland, and formed a basin enclosing E. Finland.

About midnight the steamer reaches *Sermaks*, situated at the point where the *Svir*, a river 133 M. in length, enters the lake. We next ascend this river through a wooded region, passing many timber-rafts. This is perhaps the prettiest part of the whole journey, though in midsummer the voyage is at places obstructed by rapids. The stations are *Lodéinoye Pole* (4 a.m.); *Vázhini; Myátusovo*, and *Gag-Rutchéi.*—Towards 7 p.m. we reach *Voznesénye*, a busy place at the beginning of the Onéga Canal.

Lake Onéga (Оне́жское о́зеро; 125 ft.), the third largest lake in Europe, occupies the central part of the government of Olónetz, has an area of 3764 sq.M., and reaches a depth of 408 ft. The *Onéga Canal*, constructed in 1818-51 and 45 M. long, runs along the S. bank of the lake and connects the Svir with the Vúitegra, which together with the Shexná forms the *Marie Canal System*, enabling vessels to pass from the Volga (Ruibinsk) to St. Petersburg.

About 1 a.m. the steamer leaves Voznesenye and runs to the N. along the W. bank of Lake Onéga, hugging the coast. After steaming 6-8 hrs. it enters the picturesque Bay of Petrozavodsk, and soon after reaches the town itself.

Petrozavódsk (*Schmidt's Hotel*, Sobórnaya, R. from 75 cop., D. ½-1½ rb.; *Lagunóvitch*, Vladimirskaya Náberezhnaya, both unpretending), the capital of the government of Olónetz, contains

13.800 inhab. and was founded in 1703. At the E. end of the Sobór-naya, which ascends from the harbour to the town, is a bronze statue of Alexander II. by Schröder. Thence we proceed to the N.W. along the Mariinskaya to the Law Courts, in front of which is a bronze statue of Peter the Great, also by Schröder (1873). To the S. stands a Lutheran Church.

Those who drive to the Kivatch immediately after the arrival of the steamer can get back by midnight. [The trip by boat takes longer and is not recommended.] A pleasanter plan, however, especially in warm weather, is to start at 3 p.m. and spend the night at the Kivatch, In this case, however, the traveller should make himself sure in Petrozavodsk that he will not miss the return-voyage of the steamer. Carriages (return fare with 2 horses 12-16, tróika 18-20 rb.) may be best obtained with the help of the captain of the steamer. The traveller should take his provisions with him.

The road to the (67 V. or 45 M.) Kivatch passes several beautiful lakes. The posting-station of (47 V.) *Kontchézero* (simple refreshments) commands a fine view. — The ***Kivátch** (Кивачъ) is a waterfall 50 ft. in height and 60 ft. in width, formed by the *Suná*, a stream descending towards Lake Onéga. The water descends in four leaps and the river-banks are well wooded. The fall is seen to best advantage about sunrise, when rainbows are formed in the spray. The best point of view is the pavilion (nightquarters) at the head of the fall. There is another view-point on the right bank where, however, some caution is necessary in approaching the edge.

The Suna also forms the waterfalls of *Por-Poróg* and *Girvás* about 38 V. (25 M.) above the Kivatch (carr. & pair there & back 10 rb.).

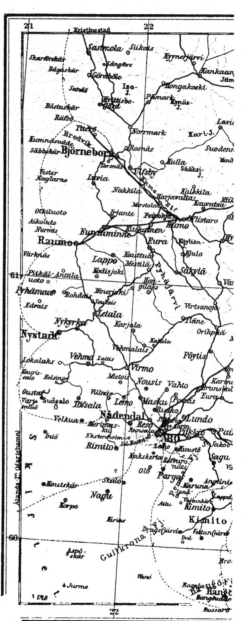

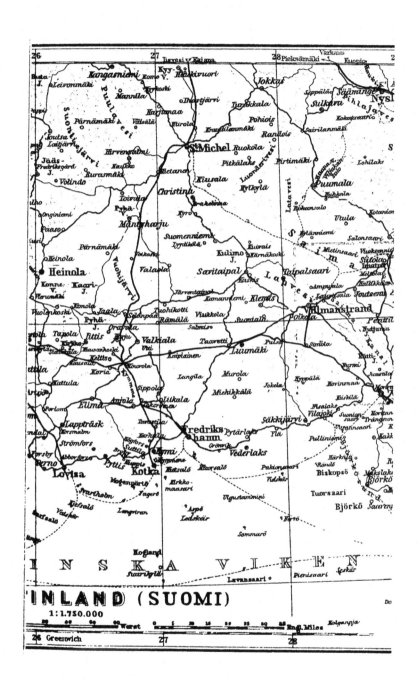

INLAND (SUOMI)

1:1.750.000

IV. THE GRAND DUCHY OF FINLAND.

In Finland Helsingfors time is kept. This is 22 min. behind St. Petersburg time, 39 min. ahead of Central European time, and 1 hr. 39 min. ahead of W. European time.

Finland (Finnish *Suomi*), the 'Land of a Thousand Lakes', is 145,686 sq.M. in area, and contains 3,200,000 inhab., nearly all of whom are Protestants (Lutherans). Geographically, Finland forms a transition from the mountainous district of Scandinavia to the great plain of Eastern Europe. Its geological formation is mainly accounted for by the long process of denudation of the superimposed sedimentary formations. The final appearance of its surface is due to the work of the glaciers of the Ice Age, which produced the long gentle ridges, the rounded hills, and the trough-like valleys. In the valleys the ice has hollowed out basins, which are now filled with the innumerable lakes of Finland, together covering 11 per cent of its total area. These lakes are often very irregular in form, and are dotted with hundreds of islands. The short but copious rivers connecting the lakes with each other and with the sea generally penetrate the intervening rocky barriers by means of rapids or waterfalls. The whole of the interior is occupied by the *Finnish Lake Plateau,* 250-1000 ft. in height, the scenery of which has a quiet and sombre beauty of its own, though seldom attaining to real grandeur. Its chief features are masses of dark granite, dense forests of both deciduous and coniferous trees (including, on the coast, many of quite recent growth), extensive morasses, clear and placid lakes, cheerful-looking little towns, churches with detached bell-towers, cottages painted a brownish-red, and meagre cornfields and pasture-lands. To all these the long light nights of summer lend a special magic. In the S. the lacustrine plateau is separated from the coast zone by the two great terminal moraines of the *Salpausselkä.* The S. and the W. coasts are fertile, and fringed by belts of low rocky islands, the *Skärgården* or *Skerries.* The N. part of Finland rises gradually to the higher plateau of Lapland.

The red granites of the S. coast at Hangö and between Kotka and Viborg are used for building purposes at St. Petersburg and elsewhere. Various kinds of marble, copper-ore, and iron-ore are also found. Finland has no coal, but has been able to develop a considerable industry through the use of its water-power. The chief articles of export include timber, paper, and butter.

Though Finland is not a wealthy country, there is much less poverty to be seen than in many other parts of Russia. The good roads, clean towns, and absence of uniforms are also characteristic. About 87.8 per cent of the population consists of **Finns** *(Suomalaiset).* These are divided into two main races: the *West Finns,* consisting of Finns proper or Suomalaiset and Tavastians or Hämäläiset, and the *East Finns* (Karelians, Karjalaiset). The *Lapps,* who occupied the district before the Finns, have been gradually driven more and more to the N.; they now number about 1300. On the sea-coast of Österbotten and Nyland and on the Aland Islands are numerous *Swedes* (Ruotsalaiset), forming 11.8 per cent of the population. They possessed the country down to 1809, and consequently the influence of their civilization is still strong. Swedish was the official language of the country down to 1863 and still holds equal rights with Finnish. The *Russians* (Venäläiset), about 8000 in number, live chiefly in the Län of Viborg. The *Germans* (Saksalaiset), now about 2000 in number, were formerly more numerous. The Finns are strongly built and of medium statue, and have somewhat angular brachycephalic skulls, with flat faces and prominent cheekbones. Their complexion is pale, often with a yellowish tinge, while their hair is fair, with a tendency to become brown with increasing age. These traits are much more marked in the Tavastian type than in the more slender and graceful Karelians. The Finns are honest, persevering, and industrious. Their educational system is admirably organized (only 1.48 per cent illiterate). Their dwellings, customs, dress, and mode of life have been strongly influenced by their intercourse with neighbouring races, but the national type is more obvious in the interior and the E. part of the country. The original Finnish 'Pirtti' is very similar to an American log-hut. It has, however, to a great extent given way to the 'Tupa', a more comfortable dwelling provided with proper windows and chimneys. As the coast is approached these cottages improve both in size and comfort. They generally stand alone, not in groups or villages, and in the wooded districts the boundaries of the different homesteads are often denoted by rail fences. The cottages of the S. coast and on the islands are very similar to the Swiss chalets. The Finns live very simply, chiefly on potatoes, fish, milk, and rye-bread. They are very fond of vapour-baths, tobacco, and coffee. — Many Finns emigrate to the United States and Canada, where they engage mainly in farming.

The FINNISH LANGUAGE (p. 203) is the most highly-developed member of the Baltic branch of the Finno-Ugrian root-language, and possesses many dialects, which may be divided into the two main groups of W. Finnish and E. Finnish. The Finnish literary language was established in the 16th century. The earlier literature consists mainly of religious works, but of late, owing mainly to the exertions of Lönnrot (1802-1884), the Finnish language has developed greatly and it is now capable of wide literary expression.

In 1835 Lönnrot edited the old Finnish epic of *Kalévala,* which deals with the contrast between the people of Kalevala (*i.e.* Finns) and the people of Pohjola (*i.e.* Lapps), and gives a graphic picture of the country and its inhabitants. Among the chief characters in the epic are Väinämöinen, an old magician and singer, the inventor of the harp Kántele; Ilmarinen, the smith, maker of the magical mill Sampo; Lemminkäinen, who glories in battle; the mischievous Kullervo; and the unhappy maiden Aino. It was the 'Kalevala', which Max Müller describes as the 'fifth national epic of the world', that suggested to Longfellow the metre of his 'Hiawatha'. An English translation by *W. F. Kirby* is published in 'Everyman's Library' (2 vols., 1*s.* each). There is another by *J. M. Crawford.* Comp. 'The Sampo: Hero Adventures from the Finnish Kalevala', by *James Baldwin* (illus.; New York, 1912).

ADMINISTRATION. Finland was conquered and christianized by Sweden in the 12th cent., but was gradually absorbed by Russia in conformity with the terms of the Treaties of Nystad (1721), Åbo (1743), and Fredrikshamn (1809). It is now a Grand-Duchy and forms part of the Russian Epmire with the right of self-government, which has, however, been considerably curtailed since 1899. It is divided into eight Governments (Län), over which the Tzar in his capacity as Grand-Duke exercises the supreme executive power. The Diet or House of Representatives has since 1906 consisted of one chamber of 200 members, elected for 3 years. Women vote and are eligible as members of the Diet, which formerly was composed of the four Estates of Nobles, Clergy, Burghers, and Peasants. At the head of the internal administration stands the Finnish Senate, presided over by a Governor-General appointed by the Tzar. Questions reserved for the personal decision of the Tzar reach him through the Secretary of State for Finland at St. Petersburg.

13*

Chronological Survey of the History of Finland.

1157. *Eric IX.* of Sweden (1150-60) landed on the coast of Finland, introduced Christianity (Bishop Henry of Upsala, an Englishman), and built Åbo. First hostile encounter between the Swedes and Russians (Novgorodians; 1164).

1249. *Birger Jarl,* of the Folkungar family, conquered Tavastland and founded Tavasteborg (Tavastehus).

1293. *Torkel Knutson,* the Swedish Viceroy, conquered Karelia and defended Finland against the Russians.

1495. Invasion of Finland by *Iván III.;* siege of Viborg. Truce with Russia, renewed by treaty, 1504. — Åbo plundered by the Danes, 1509.

1523-1560. *Gustavus Vasa.* 1548, New Testament first translated into Finnish, by Bishop Michael Agricola.

1572 & 1590. Invasions of Russians and devastation of Finland as far as Åbo.

1581. Finland becomes a Grand-Duchy.

1596-1597. Insurrection of the peasants ('Cudgel War').

1600-1611. *Charles IX.* founded Vasa, Uleåborg, etc.

1611-1617. Russo-Swedish war, under *Gustavus II. Adolphus* (1611-32). Karelia and Kexholm ceded to Sweden by the Treaty of Stolbovo (1617).

1632-1654. *Christina.* During her minority the able *Count Per Brahe* was Viceroy of Finland. University of Åbo founded in 1640. First complete printed Bible in the Finnish language (1642).

1654-1660. *Charles X. Gustavus.* Russo-Swedish war (1655-1661), ended in 1661 by the Treaty of Kardis in Livonia (ratification of the Treaty of Stolbovo).

1660-1697. *Charles XI.* Rapid development of Finland.

1697-1718. *Charles XII.* During the Northern War Finland suffered severely. The naval battle of Hangö-Udd placed Finland at the mercy of the Russians, who advanced as far as Åland.

1721. Treaty of Nystad, by which Sweden ceded the Baltic Provinces, Karelia, and Viborg to Russia.

1741. The 'War of the Hats'. By the Peace of Åbo (Aug. 7th, 1743) the Russian frontier was advanced to the river Kymmene.

1771-1792. *Gustavus III.* In 1788 an attack was made on Russia. Siege of Fredrikshamn and naval battle off Hogland. Conspiracy of Anjala. — Renewal of hostilities in 1789. Naval battle in the Svensksund. Peace of Värälä (1790) ratifying the frontier as defined in 1743.

1792-1809. *Gustavus IV. Adolphus* refused to recognize the Treaty of Tilsit. On Feb. 21st, 1808, the Russians crossed the frontier. In 1809 *Charles XIII.*, by the Peace of Frederikshamn, ceded Finland and the Aland Islands to Russia, the northern frontier being defined as the river Torneå.

1809. Diet of *Borgå*, at which *Alexander I.* undertook to recognize and maintain the constitutional and religious privileges enjoyed under Sweden. Grand-Duchy of Finland granted self-government under a Governor-General.

1812. Limits of the Grand-Duchy extended to include the territory ceded by the treaties of 1721 and 1743.

1863. First meeting of the Diet since 1809.

1899 et seq. Restriction of self-government under Nicholas II.

Foreigners visiting Finland require a **Passport** (p. xviii). The visa of a Russian consul is nominally unnecessary, but it is convenient to have it in order to prevent any difficulty in continuing the journey to Russia. The passport must be shown to the police authorities, whose endorsement (fee 1 m.) allows the traveller to remain in the country for 60 days. This may be done through the landlord of the hotel, who will also arrange for the passport to be *visé* when the traveller leaves the country. — Finland has its own customs-administration, and visitors are subjected to a *Customs Examination* on landing at any of the ports. Comp. also R. 22.

Money. Finland has its own coinage, the unit of which is the *Mark* (Markkaa), containing 100 *Penni* (Penniä) = 37^1/$_2$ cop. = 10d. = 20 cents (American) = 80 pf. = 1 franc. The Finnish mint issues gold coins of 10 and 20 marks, silver coins of ^{1}/$_4$, ^{1}/$_2$, 1, and 2 marks, and copper coins of 1, 5, and 10 penni. The legal paper-currency consists of the notes of the Finnish Bank at Helsingfors, which circulates notes of 5, 10, 20, 50, 100, 500, and 1000 marks. — Russian money is also legal tender throughout Finland (1 rb. = 2 m. 66^2/$_3$ p.), but it is more convenient, since all reckonings are made in marks and pennis, to change one's Russian money at the banks.

Steamers. From St. Petersburg to *Helsingfors* (and on viâ *Hangö* to *Stockholm*) 4 times weekly, in 20 hrs. (fares 18 & 15 m.); to *Viborg* twice weekly; to *Joensuu* and *Kuopio* once weekly. All these steamers start from the Vasili Ostrov, near the Tenth Line. — From Hull steamers of the Finland Steamship Co. (Helsingfors; John Good & Sons, Hull) ply weekly to *Åbo* (fares 5-6*l.*; 3*l.* to 3*l.* 15*s.*; return-fares 9-11*l.*, 5*l.* 10*s.* to 7*l.*), *Hangö* (in winter; fares as to Helsingfors), and *Helsingfors* (in summer; 4^1/$_2$-5 days; fares 6-7*l.*, 3*l.* 15*s.* to 4*l.* 5*s.*; return-fares 11*l.* to 12*l.* 10*s.*, 7*l.* to 7*l.* 15*s.*; through-fares to St. Petersburg, 1st class 6*l.* 5*s.* to 8*l.* 5*s.*, 2nd cl. 3*l.* 15*s.* to 5*l.*). — From Lübeck to *Helsingfors* viâ Reval once weekly (56 hrs.; fares 56 & 40 German marks, food extra); to *Åbo* viâ (58 hrs.) Hangö once weekly in 2^1/$_2$ days (fares 40 & 30 German marks; meals extra). — From Stettin to *Helsingfors* viâ Reval once weekly in two days (fares 56 & 40 German marks; food 6 $\mathcal{M}$ daily). — From Stockholm to *Helsingfors* 4 times weekly in 24 hrs. (fares 25^1/$_2$ & 20 kronor or crowns); to *Hangö* (with railway connection for St. Petersburg) in 15 hrs. (fares 23 & 19 kr.); to *Åbo* once daily in 14 hrs. (fares 23^1/$_4$ & 19 kr.; in winter 5^1/$_4$ & 4^1/$_2$ kr. extra; déj. 1^1/$_2$, D. 2^1/$_2$, S. 2^1/$_4$ kr.), connecting with the express train to Helsingfors and St. Petersburg (dining-car). — From Copenhagen to *Helsingfors* once weekly in 44 hrs. (fares 54 & 36 kr., including meals). — Details of all these routes may be found in the 'Turisten' (50 p.), appearing 6 times yearly (in Finnish and Swedish, with explanatory notes in English).

Railways. In Finland distances are reckoned by kilomètres. The trains run slowly, but the expresses from St. Petersburg to Helsingfors or Åbo reach a speed of ca. 40 M. an hour. First-class carriages are painted blue, second-class green, and third-class brown. Fares are reckoned according to a *Zone Tariff*. Thus the second-class fare for 10 Kil. (6 M.) is 55 p., for 50 Kil. (31 M.) 2 m. 70 p., for 100 Kil. (62½ M.) 5 m. 15 p., for 200 Kil. (125 M.) 9 m. 75 p., for 500 Kil. (310 M.) 20 m. 25 p., for 1000 Kil. (620 M.) 27 m. 45 p., for 1500 Kil. (930 M.) 31 m. 20 p. The third-class fares for these distances are 40 p., 1 m. 80 p., 3 m. 45 p., 6 m. 50 p., 13 m. 50 p., 18 m. 30 p., and 20 m. 80 p. First-class fares are equal to the second and third-class fares put together, but this class is little used. Tickets are available for 5 days, in addition to the day of issue. The journey may be broken once on showing the ticket to the stationmaster. There is no reduction of price for return-tickets. No charge is made for luggage under 55 lbs. (luggage-ticket 25 p.). — *Combination Tickets* (Kupongbiljetter) are issued by all railways for all three classes for distances not less than 800 km. (500 M.), and are valid for three months. These are also available on some of the steamer-routes. Tourist-tickets for shorter distances may be obtained from the tourist agency in Helsingfors (p. 222). — Porters receive 10 p. for each piece of luggage. At the smaller stations their place is taken by half-grown boys. The cloak-room charge is 10 p. per diem for each package. — *Railway Restaurants* are few and far between, and are open only at certain hours. The charge for breakfast is 1-1½, for dinner 2½-3 m. A bottle of beer costs 50 p., but cannot be bought alone, as the law of the country forbids the sale of spirituous liquor unless accompanied by food (minimum for food and beer 1 m.). A cup of coffee with a roll costs 50 p. Milk is a very common beverage.

Posting System. For excursions aside from the railway and steamboat routes, the traveller must have recourse to the Finnish posting-system (Finnish *kyyti;* Swedish *skjuts,* pron. shyss), which corresponds to that used in Sweden and Norway. The tariff for each of the small Finnish horses and for the very uncomfortable car is 14 p. per kilomètre in the country, or 18 p. per kil. from a town to the next station. Better carriages may be hired in the towns. — The Finnish *Private Posting Stations* (Finn. *kestikievari,* Swedish *gästgifveri*) are generally unpretentious, but coffee (tea not recommended), bread, butter, cheese, and fish can always be obtained at officially fixed prices (R. 1, D. 1½ m.). Every traveller must sign his name in the *Dagbok* (Finn. *päiväkirja*), which also contains the tariff.

Motor Cars and **Cycles** may be introduced on terms similar to those mentioned at p. xxv, but the duties are lower. The rule of the road is to keep to the right, passing to the right in meeting and to the left in overtaking other vehicles.

The **Hotels** in the larger towns are, as a rule, fairly comfortable, but those in the interior of the country are rather primitive. The traveller should see that his bedroom contains dark blinds or window-curtains on account of the light summer-nights. The best hotels in the smaller towns are often named Societetshus (Finn. Seurahuone); a temperance hotel is called Nykterhetsvärdshus in Swedish and Ráittiusrávintola in Finnish. The smörgåsbord, or course of *hors d'œuvre* with which a meal begins (cold meat, fish, cheese, etc.), is usually included in the regular charge, but may be ordered separately (1¼ - 2½ m.). Dinner (usually from 3 to 6 p.m.) costs 2-3½ m. Supper (sexa) corresponds more or less to the English late dinner and costs 2-5 m. 'Engelskt the' ('English tea') means tea with cold meat. 'Knäckebröd' is bread in thin, hard, round slices. Finnish beer (good) costs 40-50 p. a bottle. Wine is dear. The waiter or waitress generally receives a gratuity of 50 p. When the amount is higher than usual, 10 per cent. of the total bill is expected.

Good *Cigars* cost 20-50 p. each; *Cigarettes (Papyros)* 50-60 p. for 25.

Post and Telegraph Offices. There are Finnish postage-stamps for 2, 5, 10, 20, & 40 p., 1 m., & 10 m., but Russian stamps are also valid. The postage for a letter not exceeding 1 oz. in weight is 20 p. or 7 cop.

within Finland, 7 cop. to Russia, 10 cop. to foreign countries; foreign post-card, 4 cop. Money orders are issued up to 5000 m. for Finland and up to 500 m. for foreign countries.—*Telegrams* within Finland cost 50 p., plus 10 p. for each word; to Russia, 15 cop., plus 5 cop. for each word. Foreign telegrams cost from 21 p. per word upwards (to Great Britain 47 p., to the United States 1 m. 95 to 4 m. 65 p.).

Plan of Tour. The best time for travelling in Finland is from the middle of June to the end of August. The daily expenses, exclusive of railway, steamship, and other fares, should not exceed 15 marks.

Plan of Tour for 8-10 Days. 1st Day. Helsingfors.—2nd Day. Borgå, going by steamer and returning by train.—3rd Day. Train to Hangö, going on in the evening by train to Abo.—4th Day. Abo, proceeding in the afternoon by train to Helsingfors.—5th Day. Train to Lahti, steamer to Heinola.—6th Day. Trip down the Mankala Rapids. Train to Viborg.—7th Day. Viborg; going on in the afternoon viâ Villman-strand to the Imatra.—8th Day. The Imatra, returning viâ Rättijärvi to Viborg.—*Or:* 8th Day. Steamer to Nyslott.—9th Day. Punkaharju. —10th Day. Back to Viborg.

Plan of Tour for a Fortnight. 1st Day. Helsingfors.—2nd Day. Train to Borgå and back; night-train to the Imatra.—3rd Day. Imatra.—4th Day. Steamer to Nyslott.—5th Day. Punkaharju.—6th Day. Steamer to Kuopio.—7th Day. Train to Kajana.—8th Day. Kajana and environs. —9th and 10th Days. From Kajana down the Oulunjoki Rapids to Uleåborg, and thence by railway to Tammerfors.—11th Day. Tammerfors and Kanga-sala.—12th Day. Train to Abo.—13th Day. Abo and back to Helsingfors.

Information of every kind is willingly given to travellers by the representatives of the **Finland Tourist Society,** the headquarters of which are at Helsingfors (p. 222). Circular Tour Tickets and Hotel Coupons are issued by the *Finland Tourist Office* (p. 222). The 'Kartbok' of the society contains 49 maps (1 : 400,000) and costs 8 m.—The *Anglo-Finnish Society* of London (sec., *W. T. Good*), is intended to promote good relations between the two countries.

The **Shooting** in Finland is not very good, and it is altogether pro-hibited in forests belonging to the State. To the N. of Kajana black game, capercailzies, wood grouse, and wild ducks are fairly numerous. Shot-guns pay a duty of ca. 5 m. each. Especial permission (obtained through the visitor's Foreign Office) is necessary for the introduction of rifles.— **Fishing** (salmon and salmon-trout) is carried on mainly in the Uleå and in other rivers in the N. part of the country. Permission must be obtained from the riparian owners.

Language (comp. p. 199). A knowledge of Finnish and Swedish is not necessary for tourists who confine themselves to a visit to the larger towns, but will be found extremely useful in districts aside from the railway.—The *Accent* on Finnish words rests always on the first syllable. The single vowels are pronounced short and are lengthened by being doubled. Both letters of a diphthong are distinctly pronounced.—The *en (n)*, *et (t)*, and *ene (ne)* in such Swedish words as *gatan*, *källaren*, *torget*, *hotellet*, and *kongarne* represent the definite article.

Among the words most important for travellers are the following: Ho-tel, *hotelli;* posting station or inn, *kestikievari;* restaurant, *ravintola;* café, *kahvila;* bill of fare, *ruoka-lista;* room, *huone;* bed, *sänky;* candle, *kynttilä;* fire, *valkea;* dining room, *ruokasali;* fork, *kahveli;* knife, *veitsi;* spoon, *lu-sikka;* glass, *lasi;* bottle, *pullo;* water, *vesi;* wine, *viini;* beer, *olut;* coffee, *kahvi;* milk, *maito;* bread, *leipä;* meat, *liha;* fish, *kala;* egg, *muna;* cheese, *juusto;* butter, *voi;* salt, *suola.*—Railway, *rautatie;* station, *asema;* wayside station, *pysäkki;* luggage receiving office, *matkatavaran vasta-anotto;* luggage delivery office, *matkatavaran ulosanto;* entrance, *si-säänkäytävä;* exit, *uloskäytävä;* lavatory for men, *miehille* (Swedish, för Män), for women, *naisille* (Swedish, för Kvinnor).—Town, *kaupunki;* village, *kylä;* street, *katu;* road, *tie;* highroad, *maantie;* market-place, *tori;* house, *talo;* church, *kirkko;* preacher, *pappi;* school, *koulu;* teacher, *opettaja;* post office, *postikonttoori;* telegraph office, *sähkösanoma asema;*

posting-station, *majatalo.* — SHIP, *laiva;* boat, *vene, paatti;* steamer, *höy-ryläira;* harbour, *satama;* carriage, *vaunut;* car, *rattaat;* sledge, *reki;* horse, *hevonen;* riding-horse, *selkähevonen, ratsuhevonen;* reindeer, *poro;* driver, *ajuri;* guide, *opas;* guide me to the hotel x, *viekää minut x hotelliin;* to, *asti;* bridge, *silta;* garden, *puutarha;* tree, *puu;* wood, *metsä;* pasture, *niitty;* mountain, *vuori;* rock, *kallio;* valley, *laakso;* rain, *sade;* brook, *puro.* — MORNING, *aamu;* day, *päivä* (24 hrs. *vuorokausi*); noon, *puolipäivä;* evening, *ilta;* night, *yö.* — Mr., *herra;* Mrs., *rouva;* man, *mies;* child, *lapsi.* — English, *englantilainen;* American, *amerikka-lainen;* Finnish, *suomalainen;* Swedish, *ruotsalainen;* Russian, *venä-läinen.* — BIG, *suuri;* small, *pieni;* high, *korkea;* low, *matala;* half, *puoli;* whole, *koko;* near, *lähellä;* far, *kaukana;* early, *varhain;* late, *myöhään;* slowly, *hidas;* quickly, *nopea;* good, *hyvä;* bad, *huono;* what does it cost ? *mitä maksaa?;* too expensive, *liian kallis;* below, *alhaalla;* above, *yl-häällä;* left, *vasemmalle;* right, *oikealle;* is, *hän on;* has, *hänelläon;* I, *minä;* we, *me;* please, *pyydän;* thank you, *kiitän;* yes, please, *kiitoksia kyllä;* no, thank you, *ei kiitoksia;* goodbye, *hyvästi;* — ONE, *yksi;* two, *kaksi;* three, *kolme;* four, *neljä;* five, *viisi;* six, *kuusi;* seven, *seitsemän;* eight, *kahdeksan;* nine, *yhdeksän;* ten, *kymmenen;* eleven, *yksitoista;* twelve, *kaksitoista;* fifteen, *viisitoista;* twenty, *kaksikymmentä;* fifty, *viisi-kymmentä;* hundred, *sata;* thousand, *tuhat;* — SUNDAY, *sunnuntai;* Mon., *maanantai;* Tues., *tiistai;* Wed., *keskiviikko;* Thurs., *tuorstai;* Frid., *per-jantai;* Sat., *lauantai.*

In names of places it should be noted that *joki* means river; *järvi,* lake; *kangas,* sandy plain; *koski,* waterfall; *lahti,* gulf; *mäki,* hill; *niemi,* cape, promontory; *saari,* island; *salmi,* strait; *suo,* marsh; *vesi,* water.

Bibliography. Among recent English books on Finland the follow-ing may be mentioned: Finland To-Day, by *George Renwick* (1911); A Summer Tour in Finland, by *Paul Waineman* (1908); Through Finland to St. Petersburg, by *A. M. Scott* (1909); Finland, the Land of a Thousand Lakes, by *E. Young* (1912); Through Finland in Carts, by *Mrs. Alec Tweedie* (1897 ; 1s. ed., 1915); Finland and the Tsars, by *J. R. Fisher* (2nd ed., 1900); Finland as it is, by *Harry de Windt* (1901); A Peep at Finland, by *M. Pearson Thomson* (1911); Letters from Finland, by *Rosalind Travers* (1911); Finland and the Finns, by *Arthur Reade* (1914). — English and Finnish Dialogues and Vocabulary, by *Agnes Renfors* (price 2s.).

22. From St. Petersburg to Viborg.

129 Kil. (80 M.). RAILWAY in 2½-3½ hrs. (fares 11 m. 45, 6 m. 90, 4 m. 60 p., or 4 rb. 26, 2 rb. 56, 1 rb. 70 cop.). The trains start from the Finland Railway Station (p. 88), where there is a money-changer's office. — The luggage of passengers arriving in Finland is examined at Terijoki, that of passengers leaving the country at Valkeasaari (registered luggage in both cases at St. Petersburg).

From St. Petersburg to (49 Kil. or 30½ M.) *Terijoki,* see R. 20. — 59 Kil. *Raivola,* with beautiful larch-woods in the vicinity. About 11 M. to the W. of (75 Kil.) *Uusikirkko* lies *Halila,* an im-perial sanatorium for tubercular patients. 88 Kil. *Perkjärvi,* a favourite summer-resort of the citizens of St. Petersburg; 100 Kil. *Galitzina.* — 129 Kil. (80 M.) *Viborg* (Railway Restaurant).

Viborg.

HOTELS *Belvedere* (Pl. c; B, 5), Alexanders Perspektivet, R. 4-12, B. 1½, déj. 1½, D. (2-5 p.m.) 3 m.; *Hotel Andrea* (Pl. b; A, 4), Katarine-gatan, a commercial hotel, R. 6-11, déj. 2½, D. 3½, S. 2½ m.; *Societetshus* (Pl. a; B, 5), Rådhus-Torg, R. 3-12 m., B. 1 m. 20 p., déj. 1½, D. 3 m.: *Hotel Continental* (Pl. d; C, 5), R. 3-10, déj. 2½, D. 3 m., *Central Hotel*

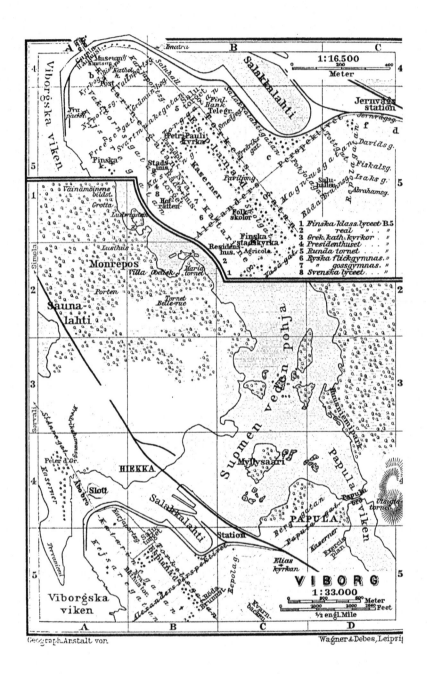

1:16.500

Meter

1	Finska klass.lyceet B.5
2	" real " .
3	Grek. kath. kyrkor "
4	Presidenthuset . . "
5	Runda tornet . . "
6	Ryska flickgymnas."
7	" gossgymnas. "
8	Svenska lyceet "

VIBORG

1:33.000

Meter
Feet
½ engl. Mile

Geograph.Anstalt von   Wagner & Debes, Leipzig

(Pl. f; C, 5), R. 2¹/₂-8, déj. 1¹/₂, D. 3 m., these two near the railway station.
—Hôtel Garni. *Karelia*, Repolagatan 4 (Pl. C, 5), well spoken of, R.
2¹/₂-12, B. 2 m.

Restaurants. *Esplanade Pavilion* (Pl. B, 5), on the Esplanade (music on summer evenings), déj. 2, D. (2.30 to 6 p.m.) 3¹/₂, S. 3 m.; *Aristo*, opposite the station. — *Café*, Katarinegatan 23, cor. of the Parad-Plats (Pl. B, 5).
— *Viborgs Kringlor*, a kind of twisted roll, are known throughout Finland.

Cabs. Drive within the so-called citadel 50 p., at night 1 m.; to the suburbs ¹/₂-1 m.; per hr. 2¹/₂ m. Drive from the railway station, 25 p. extra. — Electric Tramways from the rail. station through the town and to the Papula Bridge.

Post Office (Pl. A, 4), Katarinegatan. — Telegraph Office (Pl. B, 5), Torkelsgatan. — British Vice-Consul, *V. Frisk.* — Lloyd's Agent, *K. Lundberg.*

Banks (10 a.m. to 2 p.m.) *Finlands Bank*, Salu-Torg (Pl. B, 5); *Kansallispankki*, Torkelsgatan (Pl. B, 5); *Nordiska Aktiebanken för Handel och Industri*, Salu-Torg (Pl. B, 5).

Steamers. To *Helsingfors* twice weekly (fare 11¹/₂ m.); to *Joensuu* and *Kuopio*, thrice weekly; to (3¹/₄ hrs.) *Rättijärvi* by the Saima Canal (p. 209), once daily; to *Juustila* (p. 209), six times daily; to *Trångsund* (see below), six times daily. — Steam Launches ply to various points in the vicinity (5-10 p.).

Principal Attractions (5 hrs.). Visitors should drive from the railway station viâ the Salu-Torg to Monrepos (closed on Tues. and Frid.), returning on foot through the town, visiting the Museum en route, to the Papula Hill.

Viborg, Finn. *Viipuri*, the old capital of Karelia and now the chief town of a government, a pleasant-looking place entirely surrounded by water, lies at the head of the deeply-indented *Gulf of Viborg*, at the mouth of the *Saima Canal* (p. 209). It contains 35,000 inbab. and a strong garrison, and is the seat of the Greek Catholic Archbishop of Finland and of one of the three supreme courts of the grand-duchy. The inner harbour, where the steamboats land their passengers, is near the castle. The *Roads of Trångsund*, forming the outer harbour of Viborg, lie about 7 M. to the S. The town carries on a brisk trade, principally in boards and planks. — The fortifications of Viborg consist of advanced forts, chiefly on the E. side and on the Island of Trångsund (visitors not admitted).

In 1293 the Swedish viceroy *Torkel Knutson* built a castle here (P. 206), round which sprang up the town of Viborg. Civic rights were granted to it in 1403 by *King Eric XIII.*, and about 1477 it was surrounded by *Eric Axelsson Tott* with a wall. In 1495 Viborg withstood a three months' siege from a large Russian army, during which its gallant defender, *Knut Posse*, is said to have killed 16,000 Russians by an artfully contrived mine (Viborgska Smällen, *i.e.* 'Viborg Thunder'). Peter the Great made himself master of the place in 1710, after a hard struggle. By the Peace of Nystad (1721) the province of Viborg was adjudged to Russia. On June 6th, 1790, the Swedish fleet under *Gustavus III.* retired to the Gulf of Viborg, and while engaged in blockading the town was itself blockaded by the Russian fleet under Admirals Tchitchagóv and Kniso (later under the Prince of Nassau). On July 3rd, however, Gustavus managed to force his way through the Russian fleet to Svenborg ('Viborg Blockade Running'). In 1812 Viborg was again united with the grand-duchy of Finland.

From the *Railway Station* (Jernvägs Station; Pl. C, 5), completed in 1913 from the plans of E. Saarinen, we go straight along the Alexander Perspektive, with the Salakkalahti Harbour and the castle to the right (the latter in the background). After 8 min. we turn to the right into the ESPLANADE (Pl. B, 5; Restaurant, see p. 205), on the left side of which is a national school built by Sjöström and containing a concert-room. The Torkelsgata, running parallel with the Esplanade, is one of the main business thorough-fares of the town (Katarinegatan, see below). — On the N. the Esplanade ends at the Market Place (Salu-Torg), with the white *Round Tower* (Runda Tornet; Pl. 5, B 5), popularly known as 'Fat Catherine'. We now follow the Torggata, and then turn to the right into the Katarinegata (the chief artery of traffic in the old town), and so reach the OLD TOWN HALL MARKET (Gamla Rådhus-Torg; Pl. A, 4), with a bronze *Statue of Torkel Knutson* (p. 205) by Vall-gren. On the S.E. side of the square is the **Museum Viburgense** (open on week-days 11-1, on Sun. 12-3; fee 25 p.), on the first floor of which are pictures, pottery, and weapons; on the second floor are costumes and ornaments; on the third, ecclesiastical antiquities, farmhouse furniture, and implements for hunting and fishing.

Opposite the Museum is the Åbo Bridge (near the steamboat-quay), leading to a small granite island on which stands the ancient Gothic **Castle** (*Slott;* Pl. A, 4; 25 min. from the railway station). Built by Torkel Knutson (see above) in 1293, this castle formed the strong-hold of the Swedish power and of the Christian religion in Karelia, and was a constant bone of contention between Russia and Sweden. In the interior is the insignificant Museum of Peter the Great, con-taining portraits. An extensive *View is obtained from the top of the tower (165 ft. high); parties are formed each hour from 12 to 5 under the guidance of a gendarme (239 easy steps). To the N.W. of the castle, beyond the Åbo Bridge, are the gardens of Peter the Great; on the hill is a bronze *Statue of Peter,* by Bernstamm (1910; view of the castle and town).

We now recross the bridge and enter the Katarinegata (see above). This leads past the Parad-Plats, on the N. side of which stands the unpretending *Church of SS. Peter & Paul* (Pl. B, 5), used by Swedes and Germans. To the right of the Katarinegata lies the NEW TOWN HALL SQUARE (Nya Rådhus-Torg; Pl. B, 5), con-taining the Greek Catholic *Uspenski Cathedral* (Pl. 3). On the N.W. side of the square is the *Town Hall* (Stadshuset); to the W. are the *House of the President of the Supreme Court* (Presidenthuset; Pl. 4) and the *Supreme Court* (Hofrätten), the latter built in 1839 and containing portraits of former presidents. To the N.W. of the Nya Rådhus-Torg is the *Finnish Rural Parish Church* (Finska Kyrka; Pl. A, 5), formerly a Dominican convent (1481). — To the S.E. is the *Finnish Town Parochial Church* (Finska Stadskyrka: Pl. B, 5), in front of which is a monument to *Bishop M. Agricola,* by Wikström (1907; comp. p. 200).

About 1 M. to the N. of the Åbo Bridge, and reached by crossing

the railway after 12 min. and then following the broad avenue, lies
Monrepos (Pl. A, B, 2), the country-seat of Baron von Nikolay
and the finest point in the environs of Viborg. It is open to the
public daily (except Tues. & Frid.) from early in the morning till
dusk (fee 40 p.). A hasty walk through the park takes $1^1/_2$ hr. Cab
from the town $1^1/_2$ m. — A beautiful avenue leads direct from the
entrance to the *Villa,* which stands on a lawn surrounded by trees
and gardens. To the E. of the villa is an abrupt rock, affording a
striking view and crowned by an *Obelisk* erected by Paul von Nikolay to his brothers-in-law, the Ducs de Broglie, who fell at Auster-
litz and Kulm. To the E. of the obelisk is the *Marie Tower,* with
a bust of the Empress Marie (limited view from the roof). Proceeding to the W. along the bay, we reach an island (no admission) on
which is the *Ludwigsstein,* the family mausoleum, in the form of
a small Gothic castle. Farther on is a zinc cast of the marble statue
of *Väinämöinen* (comp. p. 199), by J. Takanen, the Finnish sculptor.

Following the Papulagata (Pl. C, D, 4, 5) from the railway
station and bearing to the right beyond the Papula bridge, we reach
($^1/_4$ hr.) the hill of **Papula,** with a park and a temperance restaurant, the view-tower (Utsigts-Tornet; Pl. D, 4) on which commands
a splendid view of the town and its environs.

About 5 M. to the N. of Viborg is the *Konkkala Sanatorium* (pens.
from 8 m.), rebuilt after a fire in 1913.

A steamboat-trip (p. 205) on the *Saima Canal* as far as Juustila
(p. 209) or Rättijärvi (p. 209) will be found very enjoyable.

From Viborg to the *Imatra,* see R. 23; to *Joensuu-Nurmes,* see R. 24;
to *Kajana-Uleåborg,* see R. 26; to *Helsingfors,* see R. 27.

23. From Viborg to the Imatra.

a. Vᴵᴀ Aɴᴛʀᴇᴀ. Railway to (72 Kil. or 45 M.) Imatra in $2^1/_4$ hrs. (fares
6 m. 25, 3 m. 75, 2 m. 50 p.; from St. Petersburg to Imatra 6 rb. 36, 3 rb. 82,
2 rb. 54 cop.). A visit to the Imatra by this (the shortest) route can be
accomplished in one day (there & back).

b. Vᴵᴀ Vɪʟʟᴍᴀɴsᴛʀᴀɴᴅ. Railway to (59 Kil. or 37 M.) Villmanstrand in
$1^3/_4$ hr. (fares 5 m. 15, 3 m. 10, 2 m. 10 p.). Thence we proceed by steamer
(twice daily) to ($2^3/_4$ hrs.; fare 3 m.) *Vuoksenniska,* and by railway thence
in $^1/_4$ hr. to (7 Kil.; fares 55, 40 p.) Imatra. Those who wish to use the
steamer starting from Villmanstrand about 7 a.m. must spend the previous
night in Villmanstrand.

c. Tʜʀᴏᴜɢʜ ᴛʜᴇ Sᴀɪᴍᴀ Cᴀɴᴀʟ. Steamer (starting from the quay of
the Salakkalahti Harbour; tickets sold on board) 5 times a week viâ
($3^1/_4$ hrs.) *Rättijärvi* (fare 2 m.) and (6 hrs.) *Lauritsala* to (1 hr.) *Villmanstrand* (10 hrs. from Viborg; fare 4 m.). Thence as in Route b.

d. Vᴵᴀ Rᴀᴛᴛɪᴊᴀʀᴠɪ. Steamer to Rättijärvi through the Saima Canal
as above. Thence by motor-car (fare 10 m.) to (36 Kil. or $22^1/_2$ M.) the Imatra
in $1^1/_4$ hr. Hand-luggage only is taken by this route.

Travellers in St. Petersburg who have no time to visit anything in
Finland except the Saima Canal and the Imatra Fall can make this excursion in two days. From June 1st to Sept. 15th circular tickets, including steamer and carriage, are issued for 15 rb. 12 cop. (1st class) and

10 rb. 88 cop. (2nd class). We take the morning train to Viborg, and go on thence by local steamer to Rättijärvi, where we take the motor-car to Imatra. Next day we return by train to St. Petersburg.

Owing to the crowds it is inadvisable to make this excursion on a Sunday or Russian holiday.

a. Viâ Antrea. On leaving *Viborg* (p. 204) the train runs to ward the N.E. through thick woods. Before reaching (40 Kil.) *Antrea* (Rail. Restaurant) we cross the Vuoksen by an iron girder bridge (view). Railway to Nurmes, see R. 24. — The line to Imatra follows the left bank of the Vuoksen (p. 210), which, however, is not visible. — 65 Kil. *Enso;* 72 Kil. (45 M.) *Imatra,* ³/₄ M. to the E. of the waterfall (p. 209; carr. 75 p.); 79 Kil. (49 M.) *Vuoksenniska,* where the Vuoksen issues from Lake Saima.

Some fishing may be obtained here. The 'English Club' of St. Petersburg has a fishing station on the island of *Vapra Saari.*

b. Viâ Villmanstrand. Railway to (40 Kil. or 25 M.) *Simola,* see p. 215. Here carriages are changed. The railway to (19 Kil. or 12 M.) *Villmanstrand* continues to run towards the N. The town lies to the E. of the railway station, but the trains run on to the harbour (tickets, 25 p. extra, obtained from the conductor).

Villmanstrand.—Hotels. *Patria* (Pl. c), Kauppakatu, R. 2¹/₂-3. déj. 2, D. 2¹/₂, S. 2 m.; *Societetshus* (Pl. a), R. from 4, déj. 2, D. 2¹/₂, S. 2 m.—There is a *Hydropathic* (Pl. d) on Lake Saima. The *Casino* has a restaurant (déj. 2, D. or S. 3¹/₂ m.).—Cab per drive 50 p., from the railway station to the town 75 p., from the steamer landing-stage 1 m.— Steamer on *Lake Saima,* to *Vuoksenniska* (see above); to *St. Michel* (p. 216) in 8-9 hrs. (fare 6 m.); to *Nyslott* and *Kuopio,* see R. 25.

Villmanstrand, Finn. *Lappeenranta,* a little town with 3000 inhab., is charmingly situated on the S. bank of the *Lappvesi* or S. arm of Lake Saima. About 10 min. to the N. of the railway station is a hill (195 ft. above Lake Saima; garrison church, Pl. 10) affording a view of the town and its environs. On a headland to the N. lies the old fortress, constructed in 1656 and now used partly as Barracks (Pl. 7) and partly as a Reformatory (Pl. 1). — About 2 M. to the W. of Villmanstrand, on a tongue of land stretching out into Lake Saima, is the new *Huhtiniemi Sanatorium.*

Lake Saima, often celebrated by native poets as the 'lake of a thousand isles', lies 255 ft. above sea-level and is 680 sq. M. in area. It may be described as a conglomeration of small lakes and bays united with each other by narrow straits and sounds. Its low S. bank is formed by the Salpausselkä (p. 198), which presents a barrier to its direct discharge on this side (Saima Canal, see p. 209). The name Saima in a restricted sense is given to the most southerly basin (37 M. long) of the group of lakes, the still, dark surface of which is covered with innumerable rocky islets. The Vuoksen (P. 210) flows hence to Lake Ládoga.

The steamer from Villmanstrand skirts the S. coast of Lake Saima and touches (¹/₄ hr.) at *Lauritsala* (Pension Urpain, déj. 1¹/₂, D. 2¹/₂, S. 1¹/₂, pens. 6 m.), in 2 hrs. more reaches *Jakosenranta* (Hôtel-Pension Rauha, with hydropathic, pens. from 18 m.; motor omnibus to and from Imatra, 4¹/₂ M., 2 m.), and thence proceeds to *Vuoksenniska.*

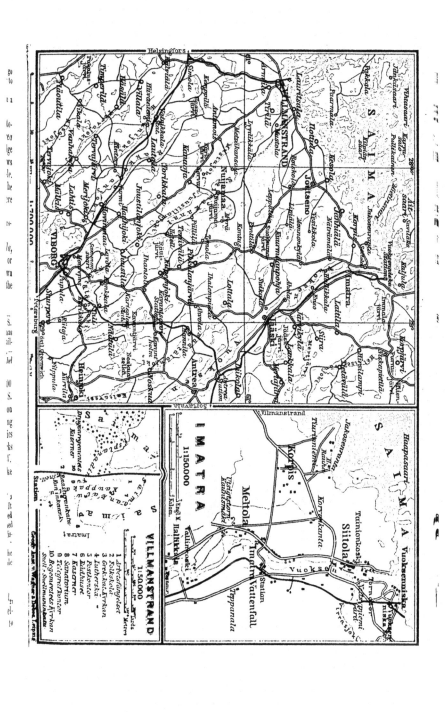

From this point we take the train (7 Kil. in $^1/_4$ hr.) to *Imatra* (see below). Walkers will also find it pleasant to follow the road (4$^1/_2$ M.), which is seldom at any great distance from the Vuoksen, and affords excellent views of its cascades and rapids. [The road leads to the right beyond the railway station, and after $^3/_4$ M. turns to the right.]

c. Viâ the Saima Canal. Soon after starting we enjoy a pleasant retrospect of Viborg. Farther on *Monrepos* (p. 207) lies to the left. In $^3/_4$ hr. we reach the *Lavola Lock*, where the Saima Canal begins.

The **Saima Canal**, 37 M. in length (20 M. of which are artificial waterway) and about 40 ft. wide, was constructed in 1845-56 and connects Lake Saima with the N. end of the Gulf of Viborg. The difference of level, amounting to about 250 ft., is surmounted by 28 locks, each 130 ft. long, 26 ft. broad, and 10 ft. deep. The banks are covered with coniferous and deciduous trees.

Soon after passing the first lock, the steamer enters the small and picturesque lake of *Juustilanjärvi*. At *Juustila* (Hotel Juustila, R. from 3, déj. 2$^1/_2$, D. 3$^1/_2$ m.), we ascend through three locks, a process taking $^1/_2$ hr. Passengers sometimes disembark before passing the locks, and walk to another steamer in waiting beyond. Four other locks are passed before we reach *Taipale*, where the canal is crossed by a drawbridge and the scenery increases in beauty. At the N.W. end of Lake Rättijärvi lies *Rättijärvi* (dépendance of the Grand-Hôtel Cascade, see below). Between *Mustola* and *Lauritsala* (p. 208) the canal has at various points been hewn out of the solid rock. From Lauritsala to the Imatra, see p. 208.

d. Viâ Rättijärvi. We follow the Saima Canal to *Rättijärvi* as above, and motor thence to (36 Kil. or 22$^1/_2$ M.) the waterfall. The road leads for the most part through woods, but here and there we pass some scantily tilled fields, or a dark and placid lake.

Imätra.—Hotels. *Grand-Hôtel Cascade* (Pl. a), close to the fall, on the right bank of the Vuoksen, open throughout the year, R. from 6, B. 1$^1/_2$, déj. 3, D. (5-7 p.m.) 4, omn. $^1/_2$ m.; *Turist-Hotel* (Pl. c), near the railway station, rebuilt after a fire in 1913.—*Pens. Vúoksela* (Pl. b), $^1/_3$ M. to the N. of the rail. station, R. from 3, déj. 2, D. 3, S. 2 m.—Cab from the rail. station to the Cascade Hotel or the Pension Vúoksela 50 p., to Jakosenranta 2$^1/_2$ m.

On leaving the railway station, we follow the road in a straight direction (shortcut by footpath bearing to the left); after 6 min. the road also bends to the left. In 5 min. more we cross an arched iron bridge (view), just beyond which, to the left (3 min.), is the imposing Grand-Hôtel Cascade (see above).—The ***Imätra Fall** of the Vuoksen is in reality a gigantic rapid, about 930 yds. in length and 65 ft. in width, with a gradual fall of 62 ft. It rushes with tremendous noise and impetuosity through the channel it has carved for itself in the granite rock (about 111,000 gallons of water pass per second). Both banks are wooded. A cursory visit to the fall takes 1$^1/_2$ hr.

The **Vuoksen** (Finn. *Vuoksi*), the only natural outlet of Lake Saima, issues from the Lappvesi or southernmost basin of the lake and flows towards the S.E., finally dividing into two arms and falling into Lake Ládoga. The great difference of level between Lake Saima and Lake Ládoga, amounting to upwards of 250 ft., and the comparatively short course of the river (about 95 M.), result in a large number of rapids and waterfalls. Behind the second important rapid, called the *Tainionkoski* or *Pikku-Imatra* (*Small Imatra;* cab from Imatra and back 4 m.), and from 110 to 220 yds. in breadth, lie several factories, which utilize the water-power of the river. About $2^1/_2$ M. to the S. of this begins the Imatra Fall.

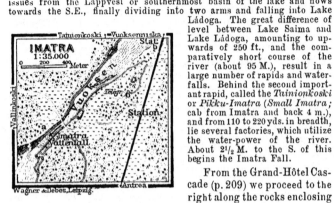

From the Grand-Hôtel Cascade (p. 209) we proceed to the right along the rocks enclosing the waterfall for a few paces and descend a flight of 58 steps (left) leading to the middle of the fall. Going on for $2^1/_2$ min. more we reach a cliff with a wooden platform close to the rapids. A general view of the fall from below is obtained from a point 3 min. farther down, at the end of the footpath, where the Imatra enters the large basin of the Mellonselkä.

A little above the Grand-Hôtel Cascade, we reach the bridge mentioned above, which affords a good bird's-eye view of the fall (to the right). This brings us to the LEFT BANK, where a flight of 46 steps descends to the right. Near the foot of this is a small pavilion. Following the path, we reach (3 min.) a rock protected by a hand-rail and affording a magnificent view of the foaming and rushing waters. A little lower down, the hand-rail guarding the path ends; here, by turning to the right, we can approach to the very brink of the fall (splendid view, but caution necessary). By bending sharply to the left (instead of descending in a straight direction) we reach (ca. 50 yds.) one of the so-called *Devil's Stones*, consisting, according to the legend, of the devil's broken butter-tub. These natural curiosities have been formed, like those in the Glacier Garden at Lucerne, by the continued action of small whirlpools and gravel in the beds of former rivers.

The curiously shaped IMATRA STONES, which are offered for sale in the neighbourhood as memorials of the visit, are found chiefly in the bay of *Miikinlahti*, on the left bank of the Vuoksen, about $^3/_4$ M. from Imatra, and in the brook *Lampsijoki*, below the Vallinkoski Falls (p. 211). They consist of chalk-marl, and are nodules formed in the glacial clays superimposed upon the granite. They frequently resemble spectacles, or prehistoric spindle-whorls.

A visit should also be made to the Vallinkoski, $2^1/_2$ M. to the S. of Imatra. Cab there & back $2^3/_4$ m., waiting 1 m. per hour.

Walkers turn to the left behind the Grand-Hôtel Cascade (p. 209), and follow the road (no views); after 17 min. we keep straight on, avoiding the path to the right; in 7 min. more we turn to the left at the finger-post pointing to Vallinkoski; 35 min. more brings us to the entrance-gate of the park by the *Vallinkoski Fall (close by is the *Restaurant Pavilion Vallinkoski;* déj. 2, D. 3 m.). From the entrance gate we follow the broad avenue, which forks halfway up the slope (3 min.). The right branch, which is at first level but begins to zigzag downwards opposite a country-house, leads to (3 min.) a pavilion, close to the Vallinkoski and affording a splendid view of the fall, between the arms of which rises the Vallinsaari cliff. [A fee of $1^1/_2$-2 m. is demanded for throwing a barrel into the water.]

24. From Viborg to Nurmes via Joensuu. Valamo.

473 Kil. (294 M.). Railway in $15^1/_2$ hrs.; fares 19 m. 60, 13 m. 5 p. (2nd and 3rd class only).

From Viborg to (40 Kil. or 25 M.) *Antrea,* see p. 208. Beyond Antrea the country is monotonous. — 93 Kil. *Hiitola.*

From Hiitola a road (posting-station near the rail. station; carr. 8 m.) leads S.E. to (38 Kil. or 24 M.) **Kexholm,** Finnish *Käkisalmi (Societets-hus,* R. $2^1/_4$-$4^1/_4$, D. $2^1/_4$ m.), a small town of 1800 inhab. situated at the N. mouth of the Vuoksen (p. 210), which is now silted up. The ruined castle contains a small historical museum. Steamers ply to Jaakkima, Valamo, Konevits, Schlüsselburg, St. Petersburg, etc.

About 19 M. to the S.E. of Kexholm (steamer in 2 hrs.; from Schlüsselburg in 6 hrs.) lies **Konevits,** Finn. *Kononsaari,* an island in Lake Ládoga, $4^1/_4$ sq.M. in area, belonging to the government of Viborg and containing a Greek Catholic *Monastery,* founded in 1393 by the monk Arsenius (d. 1444). The present conventual buildings date from the 19th century. Strangers are welcomed by the Igúmen or Abbot. The pagan *Sacrificial Stone* in the forest is now sheltered by a wooden chapel.

From (113 Kil.) *Elisenvaara* (Rail. Restaurant) a branch-line runs to Punkaharju and (82 Kil.) Nyslott (see p. 214). — 138 Kil. *Jaakkima* is the junction for ($1^1/_4$ M.) the port of *Lahdenpohja* on Lake Ládoga, whence a steamer runs thrice weekly to (3 hrs.) Valamo (p. 212; fare 5 m.).

178 Kil. (111 M.) **Sortavala.** — *Railway Restaurant.* — Hotels. *Societetshus,* Kyrkogatan, R. $3^1/_2$-6, déj. $1^1/_2$, D. 2 m.; *Nya Hotel.* — Cab from the station to the town 1 m., per drive 50 p. — Steamer twice a week viâ Valamo (p. 212) and Konevits (see above) to St. Petersburg (24 hrs.; fare 16 m.).

Sortavala, Russian Сердоболь, a small town dating from 1643, in the government of Viborg, is prettily situated at the N. end of Lake Ládoga. It contains 3200 inhab., a Lutheran and a Greek Catholic church, a Finnish normal seminary, and a historical and ethnographical museum (adjoining the town hall). On the W. side of the town lies the town park of Vakkosalmi.

Excursions may be made to (12¹/₂ M.; by boat) the island of *Kaar-nesaari*, with its interesting grotto, and to (9¹/₂ M. to the N.E.) *Kirjavalahti*, on a long arm of Lake Ládoga, and about 3 M. distant from the hill of *Pötsö-vaara*, which commands a magnificent view extending as far as Valamo.

From Sortavala to Valamo, steamer twice weekly in 2 hrs. (fare 3 m.). This forms an attractive excursion; the best plan is to leave Lahdenpohja (p. 211) on Thurs. for Valamo and to return on Sat. to Sorta-vala. — *Valamo, Валаамъ (6 hrs. by steamer from Kexholm and 22 hrs. from St. Petersburg), a wooded island (12 sq. M. in area) in the N. part of *Lake Ládoga* (p. 195), is surrounded by forty smaller islands. On the festival of SS. Peter and Paul (June 27-30th, O. S.) thousands of Russian pilgrims flock to Valamo. Free quarters may be found in the hospice adjoining the monastery, but the traveller should give a sum amounting to 1 rb. or 2 m. per day on his departure. Simple refreshments are provided, but the traveller should bring the bulk of his provender. Smoking, fishing, and shooting are forbidden on the island. — From the landing-place on the N. side a flight of 62 steps ascends to the *Greek Catholic Monastery*, which was founded in 992, suffered much during the Swedish and Russian wars, and was burned down in 1754. In its present imposing form it dates from the middle of the 19th century. In the *Church of the Transfiguration*, built in 1887-90, are the tombs of the monks Sergius and Herman, founders of the monastery. Extensive views are obtained from the square above the garden and from the belfry. In the older *Churchyard* (behind the convent) is the alleged tombstone of Magnus Erikson, King of Sweden, who, according to tradition, finished his life here as the monk Gregorius. More credible reports, however, state that he was drowned in 1374 near Bergen in Norway. The attractively situated churches of *All Saints* (1¹/₄ M.), *John the Baptist* (2¹/₂ M.), and the *Virgin Mary* (3³/₄ M.) may all be reached by boat. A boat-trip round Valamo and a visit to the *Holy Island*, 2¹/₂ M. to the E. of it, may be recommended (6-7 hrs.; rowing-boats at the landing-stage).

Beyond Sortavala the railway turns towards the N., traversing a dreary district of wood and marsh. — Just short of (240 Kil.) *Värtsilä* (Railway Restaurant), with large iron-works, we cross the boundary between the provinces of Viborg and Kuopio.

311 Kil. (193 M.) **Joensuu** (*Turist-Hotel*, R. 3-5, déj. 2, D. 3, S. 2 m.; *Seurahuone,* similar prices; cab from rail. station 50 p.), the chief town of Karelia (now the province of Kuopio), with 4700 inhab., is prettily situated on the W. bank of the *Pielisjoki* at its confluence with the *Pielisjärvi.* The town, founded in 1848, carries on a brisk trade in timber.

Steamers (8 m.) ply from Joensuu 4 times weekly through the *Pielisjoki*, the lower part of which was canalized in 1874-79, and the *Pielisjärvi* to *Koli* (see below) and (93 M.) *Nurmes* (see below). — Steamer to Nyslott, see p. 214.

We cross the Pielisjoki just beyond Joensuu, and the *Rukavesi* just short of (361 Kil.) *Uimaharju.* — 392 Kil. *Vuonislahti*, on the Pielisjärvi. On the W. bank of the Pielis (row-boat 5 m.) are *Koli* and *Mt. Kolivaara* (825 ft. above the Pielis), the summit of which (small hotel) affords a splendid view. — For the rest of the journey the Pielisjärvi is on the left.

473 Kil. (294 M.) *Nurmes* (accommodation at the posting-station and the Malmgren Pension), with 500 inhabitants.

From Nurmes we can make the journey by land to (80 Kil. or 50 M.) *Nothamo* (accommodation at the posting-station; comp. p. 217), and continue thence to Kajana (p. 217) by steamer in 5 hrs.

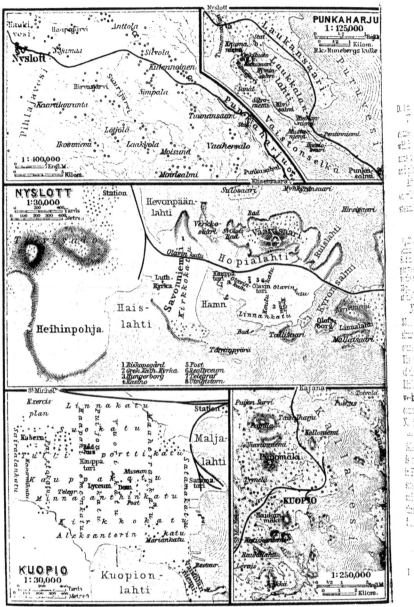

PUNKAHARJU
1:125,000

R.k. Runebergs kulle

NYSLOTT
1:30,000

1 Biskopsgård
2 Grek.Kath.Kyrka
3 Hangerborg
4 Kasino
5 Post
6 Reallyceum
7 Telegraf
8 Utrigtstorn

KUOPIO
1:30,000

1:250,000

Geogr. Anst. v. Wagner & Debes, Leipzig

25. From Villmanstrand to Nyslott and Kuopio. Punkaharju.

STEAMER to *Nyslott* daily in 8 hrs.; to *Kuopio* thrice weekly in 24-27 hrs. (from Nyslott to Kuopio once daily in 13 hrs.); to *Joensuu* thrice weekly in 22-24 hrs. Fare (varying with the steamers) to Nyslott 8, to Kuopio 14-19 m., to Joensuu 14 m. Restaurant on board (déj. 2, D. 3 m.).

Villmanstrand, see p. 208. The steamer pursues a winding course amid the numerous and beautifully wooded islands with which Lake Saima is dotted. The country becomes more monotonous and sombre as we proceed towards the N., thick woods of fir and pine stretching for miles along the narrow waterways.

After about 4 hrs. the steamer enters the *Sound of Puumala,* on which lie the church and village of that name. — Farther on we steam through the *Pihlajavesi,* and in 4 hrs. more reach —

140 Kil. (87 M.) **Nyslott.** — The steamer-wharf lies to the S. of the market-place (Kauppa Tori), the rail. station is to the W., outside the town, ³/₄ M. from the market-place. — HOTEL (advisable to telegraph for rooms in summer). *Turist-Hotel* (Pl. a), in the market-place, R. 3-8, déj. 2, D. 3, S. 2 m. — *St. Olofsbad Hydropathic,* R. 7-25 m. per week, treatment 15 m. per week, visitors' tax 3 m. per week. — *Casino Restaurant* (Pl. 4) attached to the St. Olofsbad. — CAB 50 p. per drive, from the rail. station to the town 75 p., per hr. 2 m. — *Operas* and *Concerts* are given by Mme. Aino Ackté at the beginning of July in the court of the Olofsborg

Nyslott ('New Castle'), Finn. *Savonlinna,* a small town with 3500 inhab. and the seat of a Lutheran bishop, is picturesquely situated, mainly on an island in the *Sound of Kyrönsalmi,* which connects the Pihlajavesi on the S. with the *Haukivesi* on the N. The island is united with the mainland by a bridge. To the S. of the Olavin Tori, on a hill, is the *Hungerborg* (Pl. 3), with the Lindforss Museum, containing collections of birds, etc. (open on week-days 1-2, on Sun. 12-2; adm. 50 p.). The tower (65 steps) commands a fine panorama, especially towards evening. To the N. of the town, on the peninsula of Vääräsaari, is *St. Olofsbad* (see above), with park and view-tower (Pl. 8). On a small rocky islet in the sound (bell for the attendant at the ferry; adm. 25 p.) is the **Olofsborg,* the finest and best-preserved mediæval castle in Finland, built by Erik Axelsson Tott in 1475. It was of considerable importance during the period of the Russo-Swedish wars and was restored in 1870, at the cost of the state. The castle has three strong round towers, one of which (the 'Church Tower') was formerly used as a state-prison.

FROM NYSLOTT TO PUNKAHARJU, a very pleasant afternoon's trip; we go by steamer in 2¼ hrs. (fare 2 m.), and return by railway from Punkasalmi (p. 214) in 1 hr. (34 Kil. or 21 M.; fares 1 m. 85, 1 m. 25 p.). — **Punkaharju,* 19 M. to the S.E. of Nyslott, is a steep and narrow ridge or esker, 4¹/₂ M. long and ca. 100 ft. high, intersecting an island between the *Puruvesi* on the N. and a bay of Lake Saima on the S. On the top, about $^1/_3$ M. from the steam-boat-pier, is the good but often overcrowded *Hotel Punkaharju* (Pl. a; R. from 2, déj. 2, D. $3^1/_2$, pens. 6-8 m.). To reach the ($^3/_4$ M.) rail. station from the hotel we first keep to the S. for one min. and then turn to the left, and to the left again after 11 min. more. About $^1/_2$ M. to the S. of the hotel, a little to the left of the main road, is the so-called *Runeberg Hill* (Runebergs Kulle, R. K. on the map), a fine point of view. The excellently kept road running S. to ($3^1/_2$ M.) *Punkasalmi* (see below) is best followed on foot; it leads up and down through woods, and offers charming glimpses of the somewhat sombre district and its lakes.

From Nyslott to Elisenvaara, 82 Kil. (51 M.), railway in $2^1/_2$ hrs. The railway crosses the Kyrönsalmi, affording a view of the Olofsborg (p. 213) to the right. Just before reaching (28 Kil. or $17^1/_2$ M.) *Punkaharju* (see above) we cross the *Tuunansalmi*. On a tongue of land, $^1/_4$ M. to the S. of the station, is the new *Hotel Finlandia* (Pl. b; rooms with baths). To reach the Hotel Punkaharju, we leave the station in a straight direction, turn to the right after a few paces, and then (after 12 min.) turn again to the right. By keeping to the left at the last fork, we reach (9 min.) the Runeberg Hill (see above). — Just before reaching (34 Kil. or 21 M.) *Punkasalmi* (to Punkaharju, see above) we cross the sound of that name, and just beyond (54 Kil.) *Särkisalmi* we cross the *Simpelejärvi*. 82 Kil. (51 M.) *Elisenvaara*, see p. 211.

From Nyslott to Joensuu (p. 212; 189 Kil. or 117 M.), steamer several times a week in 17 hrs., viâ the Haukivesi (see below), *Enonvesi*, and the beautiful *Oricirta* and *Pesolansalmi Sounds*. A railway from Nyslott to *Pieksämäki* (see p. 217) is to be opened in the summer of 1914.

The steamer from Nyslott to Kuopio viâ Taipale at first passes close to the Olofsborg (right, p. 213) and then traverses the *Haapavesi* and the *Haukivesi*. Just after reaching *Taipale* we pass through the two locks of the *Taipale Canal* (difference of level 23 ft.). About 1 M. to the N.W. of the canal (left) lies the manor of *Varkaus*, with iron-works, a paper-mill, and a saw-mill (railway to Pieksämäki, see p. 217). The steamer now enters the *Unnukkavesi*. To the left, on a finely wooded arm of the lake, is the thriving village of *Leppävirta*. About $^1/_2$ hr. farther on, to the right, is *Konnus*, with a lock between the Unnukkavesi and the *Kallavesi*, which latter we now follow towards the N. *Kuopio* (see below). — The steamboat from Nyslott to Kuopio viâ Heinävesi (19 hrs.; fare $6^1/_2$ m.; very fine scenery) turns to the N. in the Haukivesi (see above), passes through the *Orevi* and *Kerma Canals* (3 locks), and lies to for the night at *Heinävesi*. The next day it crosses *Lake Kerma*, and then passes through *Karvio Lock* and several rapids into the *Suvasvesi* and through the *Vehmersalmi Narrows* into the *Kallavesi*.

189 M. Kuopio. — Hotels. *Seurahuone* (Pl. a), Maaherrankatu, R. $2^1/_2$-$6^1/_2$, B. $1^1/_4$, déj. 2, D. (2·5 p.m.) 3, S. 2 m.; *Hot. Kuopio* (Pl. b), Kauppakatu, a temperance house, R. 2-5, déj. $1^1/_2$, D. 2, S. $1^1/_2$ m. — *Restaurant Peräniemi*, in the Väinölänniemi Park, déj. $1^1/_2$, D. 2, S. $1^1/_2$ m.,

open in summer only. — Cab from the rail. station to the town and vice versâ 75 p.; to the Puijomäki and back 4¹/₂ m.; per drive ¹/₂, per hr. 3 m.; ¹/₄ hr.'s waiting 25 p.

Kuopio, the capital of the province of that name, is a town of 16,300 inhab., founded in 1776 and picturesquely situated on a peninsula which divides the Kallavesi into two branches. It is overlooked on the N. by the Puijomäki. The stone *Cathedral* (Dom), on a small hill in the middle of the town, was completed in 1815 and contains an altar-piece by Söderhjelm. In the garden to the E. of the church is a bronze bust, by Takanen (1886), of the Finnish politician *J. V. Snellman* (d. 1881), formerly rector of the lyceum at Kuopio. In the *Museum* are ethnographical and biological collections from the district of Savolaks. To the S.E. is the public park of *Väinölänniemi* (Restaurant, see p. 214). Visitors are also shown the cottage of *Minna Canth* (d. 1897), the wife of a cobbler, who became one of the foremost dramatists in Finland.

A pleasant walk may be taken to (³/₄ hr.) the top of the **Puijomäki* (755 ft.; winter sports; cab, see above). From the Town Hall (Rådhus) we follow the Puijonkatu to the N., crossing the railway and keeping on in the same direction. After 9 min. we follow the road to the left (not ascending the steps). At (3 min.) a finger-post we keep straight on. In 5 min. more, we turn to the right at a finger-post, and climb a gentle hill to (25 min.) a stone view-tower (25 p.; 163 steps), affording a splendid view of the Kallavesi and Kuopio, especially towards evening. We now return to the road, from which after 2 min. a shorter footpath diverges to the right and leads through a wood, rejoining the road lower down. We turn to the right.

Environs. About 3 M. to the E. is the island of *Vaaiasalo,* affording a good view. — To the N.E. lie *Muuruvesi* (steamer), *Strömsdal* (hotel; iron works), and the *Pisavuori,* a hill (885 ft.) in Nilsiä, on the boundary between Savolaks and Karelia and known for its rock-crystals. — To the N.W. is the fine *Bay of Tuovilanlahti* (steamer in 4-5 hrs.).
From Kuopio to *Kajana,* see p. 217; to *Kouvola.* see pp. 217-215.

26. From Viborg to Kajana and Uleâborg.

From Viborg to *Kajana,* 562 Kil. (349 M.), railway in 14 hrs. (fares 22 m. 5, 14 m. 70 p.). Sleeping-car by the night-train as far as Kuopio. — For the excursion to Uleåborg (p 217) by the rapids hand-luggage only should be taken.

Viborg, see p. 204. Soon after leaving the town a view of the castle is obtained on the left. — 2 Kil. *Monrepos* (p. 207); 12 Kil. *Hovinmaa.* From (40 Kil. or 25 M.) Simola *(Rail. Restaurant)* a branch-line runs to (19 Kil.) Villmanstrand (see p. 208). — The line traverses a district of hills and lakes. 74 Kil. *Taavetti.*

121 Kil. (75 M.) **Kouvola** *(Rail. Restaurant; Hotel,* R. from 3, déj. 1¹/₂, D. 2¹/₂, S. 1¹/₂ m.), a village of 2500 inhab., is the junction of the line to Helsingfors (R. 27).

FROM KOUVOLA TO KOTKA, 51 Kil. (32 M.), railway in 2 hrs.—21 Kil.
Inkeroinen. with a large paper-mill. To the W., near *Anjala*, is the largest
fall of the Kymmene (p. 218). Anjala is known through the so-called 'Anjala
League', a conspiracy of the nobles against Gustavus III. of Sweden in
1788. Railway to Fredrikshamn, see below. — From (41 Kil.) *Kymi* a
branch-railway runs to (5 Kil.) the industrial village of *Karhula*. —Beyond
(46 Kil.) *Kyminlinna* we cross an arm of the Kymmene and reach (51 Kil.
or 32 M.) **Kotka** (*Societetshus*, near the wharf, R. 4-6, déj. 1½, D. 3, S. 1½ m.;
cab from the station to the town 1 m., per drive 50-75 p.; British vice-
consul, *A. Gullichsen;* Lloyd's Agent, *A. Lemke;* daily steamer to Fredrikshamn), a town of 11,000 inhab., founded in 1879 on an island in the Gulf
of Finland. It carries on a brisk trade in timber (incl. pit-props for the
collieries in the North of England) and contains many saw-mills. Good
views can be obtained from the tower of the fire station, near the harbour,
and from *Norska Bärget*, to the S.E. of the town. On the S. side of the
town is the *Catherine Lighthouse*, affording an extensive sea-view.

The *Svensksund*, which may be reached from Kotka by rowing-boat
in 1 hr., or by the just-mentioned Fredrikshamn steamer, is known for
the defeat of the Swedes on Aug. 24th, 1789, and for the brilliant victory
of Gustavus III. over the Russians on July 9th, 1790. — About 3½ M.
to the N. of Kotka lies *Langinkoski*, beautifully situated and formerly
a favourite summer-residence of the Tzar Alexander III. (carr. there and
back 3¾ m., waiting 1 m. per hr.). The house is a plain wooden building.

Visitors will generally find sailing-boats in Kotka ready for the
excursion to the island of **Hogland** (Finn. *Suursaari*), which lies about
25 M. to the S. and may be reached with a favourable wind in 3-5 hrs.
(provisions necessary). There is also a mail-boat twice weekly. This
rocky island, situated just about halfway between Finland and Esthonia,
is 7½ M. long from N. to S. and 1-2 M. broad. Its highest points are
the *Pohjaskorkia (i.e.* 'Hill of the North'; 350 ft.), which affords a fine
view, the *Haukkavuori* (480 ft.), and the *Lounatkorkia* (520 ft.), the
last at its S. end. The inhabitants, about 750 in number, live in two
villages on the E. coast, *Suurikylä*, the larger of the two, lying to the N.,
and *Kiiskinkylä*, the smaller, to the S. — Eckholm (p. 84), to the W. of
Hogland, was the scene, on July 17th, 1788, of an indecisive naval battle
between the Russians (under Sir Samuel Greig, see p. 76) and the Swedes.

FROM INKEROINEN TO FREDRIKSHAMN, 25 Kil. (15½ M.), railway in 1 hr.
—**Fredrikshamn**, Finn. *Hamina* (*Societetshus*, R. 2-5, déj. or S. 1½, D.
2½ m.; cab per drive 50 p., per hr. 2 m.; steamboat daily to Kotka; Lloyd's
Agent, *H. Ahlqvist*), a small seaport with 3400 inhab., lies upon a peninsula in the Gulf of Finland and was fortified down to 1836. The most
prominent building is the former *Finnish Cadet School*. It was at Fredrikshamn that the Peace of Sept. 17th, 1809, between Sweden and Russia,
was signed, by which the whole of Finland as far as the Torneå-Elf was
ceded to Russia.

The railway to Kajana diverges to the N. from the Helsingfors
line (R. 27) and runs along the boundary-line between the provinces
of Viborg and Nyland to (144 Kil.) *Seländpää.* Farther on it skirts
the large lake of *Vuohijärvi* (on the left).

234 Kil. (145 M.) **St. Michel.** — *Railway Restaurant.* — HOTELS.
Societetshus, opposite the rail. station, to the E. of the town, R. 3-6, déj.
1½, D. (2-4 p.m.) 2½, S. 1½ m. — CAB per hour 1½-2 m. — STEAMER to
Villmanstrand, see p. 208.

St. Michel, Finn. *Mikkeli*, capital of the province of that name,
is situated on one of the W. bays of Lake Saima. It has 4500 inhab.
and contains a lyceum. A good view is obtained from the water-
tower; hard by is the *Pavilion Naisvuori*, a temperance restaurant.

Beyond (248 Kil.) *Hiirola* the train runs through wood. —
305 Kil. *Pieksämäki*, at the S. end of the *Pieksänjärvi*, with an
old church. Railway to Nyslott, see p. 214; a branch runs E. to
(50 Kil.) Varkaus (p. 214). — Beyond (322 Kil.) *Haapakoski* we
cross the frontier of the province of Kuopio. — 343 Kil. (213 M.)
Suonnejoki (Rail. Restaurant).

From Suonnejoki a branch-line runs N. to (8 Kil.) *Iisvesi*, whence there
is a steamer to *Pielavesi*. — Suonnejoki is the starting-point of land-routes
leading to the S.W. through picturesque country to (19 Kil. or 12 M.)
Rautalampi, and thence viâ *Laukas* to (116 Kil. or 72 M.) Jyväskylä (p. 219).
Another route runs to the S.E. viâ *Sorsakoski* to (45 Kil. or 28 M.) Leppävirta (p. 214).

The train now runs towards the N.E. through a barren district.
A little beyond (383 Kil.) *Pitkälahti* the Kallavesi (see below) becomes visible, and just before Kuopio the Puijomäki (p. 215) is
seen on the left.

394 Kil. (245 M.) **Kuopio** *(Rail. Restaurant),* see p. 214. —
The railway now crosses the broad *Kallavesi* on a long causeway
(view). 408 Kil. *Toivola.* — 479 Kil. *Iisalmi* (Railway Restaurant,
D. $2^1/_2$ m.), a little town with 2200 inhabitants. About 3 M. to the
N. (carr. there and back 2-3 m.), by the bridge over the *Virta*, is
a monument commemorating the battle of Oct. 27th, 1808, between
the Russians and the Finns.

562 Kil. (349 M.) **Kajana**, Finn. *Kajaani* (*Turist-Hotel*, well
spoken of, R. $2^1/_2$, B. 1, déj. $1^1/_2$, D. $2^1/_2$, S. $1^1/_2$ m.; restaurant in
the posting-station), a town of 3000 inhab., lies on the *Kajaaninjoki*
(grayling and trout fishing), which forms two waterfalls within the
town. On an island between the waterfalls (view from the bridge)
are the ruins of the *Kajaneborg*, built in 1607-66, captured and
destroyed by the Russians in 1716. Johannes Messenius was a
prisoner in this castle from 1620 to 1635, and here wrote his history
of Finland. Elias Lönnrot (p. 199) lived in the Lönnrots Stuga, about
$^2/_3$ M. to the E. of Kajana, in the second quarter of the 19th century. A visit may be paid to the park of *Kyynäspää* and to the
Lycksalighetensö ('Isle of Blessedness'). The tower on the *Pölly-
vaara* (1 hr. to the N.) commands an extensive panorama.

Objects carved in stone, furs, fishing-tackle, etc., may be obtained
from H. Renfors, Manager of the Turist-Hotel, who also arranges for fishing privileges (he speaks English). The fishing season lasts from June 1st
to Sept. 15th, and the charge for each rod is 1 m. 50 p. per day. Trout,
grayling, perch, bream, roach, and pike may all be caught here.

About 25 M. to the S.E. of Kajana (steamer daily in 3 hrs; fare
1 m. 60 p.), on the bank of the *Nuasjärvi*, rises *Mt. Vuokatti* (985 ft.). It
is near the church of Sotkamo (p. 212), and about $4^1/_2$ M. from the steam-
boat-station of *Kärnälä*. A good view is obtained from both the towers.

From Kajana to Uleåborg by Water, 150 Kil. (93 M.), in $1^1/_2$
day (route open from the middle of June to Aug. 31st only). The
carriage-road is not recommended. — *Kajana*, see above. We take
the steamer (fare 5 m.; restaurant on board, déj. 2 m.), starting every
week-day at 7 a.m., for (5 hrs.) Vaala. The steamer steers N.W.

across the *Oulujärvi*, a lake 50 M. long, and divided into two parts
by the large island of *Manamansalo*. *Vaala* (Turist-Hotel, R. 3,
déj. $1^1/_2$, D. $2^1/_2$, S. $1^1/_2$ m.), at the beginning of the *Oulunjoki*, is
a harbour for tar-boats, and many salmon, sea-trout, and grayling
are caught here in July and August. Capt. Spolander, who speaks
English, attends to the wants of anglers. From Vaala we go in a
rowing-boat of the Finland Tourist Society through the **Oulunjoki
Rapids** (to Muhos 6 hrs., 10 m.). Immediately beyond Vaala are
the rapids of the *Niskakoski* (about 5 M. long). Beyond the *Ahmas-
koski* we are towed by motor-boat to *Merilä*, from which point we
again row to *Koskisaavi*. Thence a motor-boat takes us to *Pyhäkoski*, whence we descend (row-boat) the *Pyhäkoski* (with a fall of
195 ft. in 11 M.) and the large *Pälli* cataract to the village of
Muhos (bed and meals at the house beside the wharf). From Muhos
we go on either the same evening or the following morning by steamer
on the Oulunjoki to (2 hrs.; fare 2 m.) the Kurkela wharf at *Uleåborg* (p. 245), about 1 M. from the town (cab 75 p.).—A motor-
omnibus service between Uleåborg and Vaala is in view.

27. From Viborg to Helsingfors *(Hangö)*.
Mankala Rapids.

313 Kil. (194 M.). RAILWAY in 6-9 hrs. (fares 23 m. 90, 14 m. 35,
9 m. 55 p.). Passengers by the day-express pay a supplement of 6, 4, or 2 m.
respectively. The night-express, made up of sleeping-cars, conveys 1st
and 2nd class passengers only (supplement 2 m.; bed-ticket 12 or 6 m.)
Steamers from St. Petersburg to Helsingfors, see p. 201.

From Viborg to (121 Kil. or 75 M.) *Kouvola*, see p. 215.
The railway to Helsingfors keeps to the W., crosses the *Kymmene*
by a lofty iron bridge (view), and enters the province of Nyland.

The **Kymmene** (Finn. *Kymijoki*) is the outlet of the extensive
system of lakes and ponds which occupies a great part of the Finnish
uplands. It flows into the Gulf of Finland through five different branches
between Fredrikshamn and Lovisa. Its total length from Lake Ruotsalainen is 102 M., during which it makes a descent of 265 ft.

128 Kil. *Koria;* 152 Kil. *Sidikkala* (comp. p. 219). Just short
of (162 Kil.) *Uusikylä* we enter the government of Tavastehus.

183 Kil. (114 M.) **Lahti** (*Railway Restaurant*, small; *Hotel
Lahti*, R. $2^1/_2$-7, déj. $1^1/_4$, D. 2, S. $1^1/_4$ m.; *Societetshus*, same
charges), a town of 6000 inhab., with saw-mills and pulp-mills.
In the highest part of the town is the Town Hall, commanding an
extensive view over the Vesijärvi. Lahti is the starting-point for
the excursion to the Mankala Rapids (p. 219).

FROM LAHTI TO LOVISA, 82 Kil. (51 M.), railway in 4 hrs.—**Lovisa,**
Finn. *Loviisa* (*Societetshus*, facing the Kurhaus Park, R. from 3, déj. or
S. 2, D. 3 m.; *Pens. Central; Casino Restaurant*, to the S. of the town,
Kapellet Restaurant, in the park, both open in summer only; cab from
the rail. station to the town 75 p.; British vice-consul & Lloyd's agent,

A. Ljungqvist), a small town with 3200 inhab., is picturesquely situated on an arm of the sea and on the heights surrounding it. To the N. of the town lies a hydropathic establishment, in a pretty park. The inner harbour lies about 1 M. to the S.E. of the rail. station, and on an island 4¹/₂ M. from it are the ruins of the fortress of *Svartholm*, erected in 1755. — *Pernå*, 6 M. to the W., has a quaint old church.

From Lahti a branch-railway runs to the N. to *Vesijärvi* (see below), whence a STEAMER plies through the Anianpelto Canal (see below) and the narrow *Äijälä Sound* to (12 hrs., fare 8 m.) **Jyväskylä** (*Monopooli*, R. 2¹/₂-5, déj. or S. 2, D. 2¹/₂ m.), a town of 3800 inhab., picturesquely situated on the *Jyväsjärvi*, and containing a Finnish normal school and lyceum. Good views are obtained from the Pavilion (temperance restaurant) in the park by the sea, and from the belvedere of *Ihantola*, on the *Syrjänharju*. Railway to Haapamäki or Suolahti, see p. 242.

FROM LAHTI TO THE MANKALA RAPIDS VIÂ HEINOLA, a very attractive trip, practicable from June 4th to Aug. 31st. On the first day, we take the steamer to Heinola, and on the second day shoot the rapids and go on from Sidikkala by railway to Helsingfors or Viborg. Only small articles of luggage can be taken. Those whose time is limited can do it in one day by taking the night-steamer, which sails several times weekly from Vesijärvi to Heinola.

Lahti, see p. 218. A branch-railway runs N. to (4 Kil., in 8 min., 55 p.) the harbour of *Vesijärvi*. — We proceed by steamer, starting at the rail. station (to Heinola 5 hrs., fare 3 m.; restaurant on board), across *Lake Vesijärvi*, which is bordered by wooded hills. We then follow the winding *Anianpelto Canal*, through a lock at the end of which we enter the *Päijänne*. Our course then lies to the E. through the *Kalkis Canal*, with another lock, and across the *Ruotsalainen* and the *Jyränkö* to —

Heinola (Plan, see p. 220; *Societetshus*, Pl. a, temperance hotel, R. 2¹/₂-5, B. 1, déj. 2, D. 3, S. 2 m.; *Restaurant Casino*, Pl. 1; cab from the harbour to the town 75 p.), a pleasant little town with 1800 inhab. and a hydropathic. — Tickets for the excursion down the rapids (6 m.) are obtained from Mr. B. Rosenström, the representative of the Finland Tourist Society.

From Heinola the morning-steamer runs to the S.E. to (1-1¹/₄ hr.) *Vuolenkoski* (fare 2 m.), whence we walk (10 min.) to the starting-place of the motor-launch, which descends the *Kymmene* to (1 hr.) *Mankala* (Eskola Farm, déj. 1¹/₂, R. 1 m.). After a halt of an hour we go on by rowing-boat (best seats on the left) through the ***Mankala Rapids** of the Kymmene, which are framed in finer scenery than those of the Oulunjoki, and are quite as violent though much shorter (15-20 min.). The rowing-boat lands at *Perolahti*, whence another motor-launch takes us to (20 min.) the farm of *Hannula*. Thence we walk to *Sidikkala* railway 'halt' (p. 218) in 25-30 min. (conveyance 2 m.).

After passing the first two (and smaller) rapids above the Tolppakoski, we may disembark and walk along the top of the left bank (fine view of the Vähäkäyrä and the Isokäyrä; another path below) to (1¹/₄ M.) Pero-

lahti. During the time of high water (down to the beginning of July),
this is the only way in which this excursion can be made.

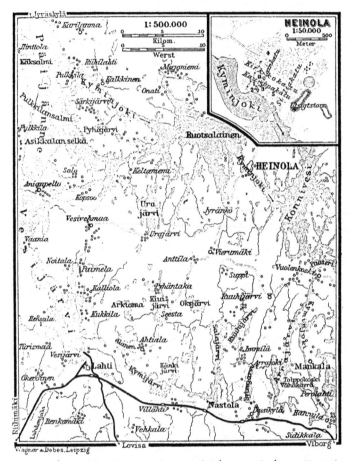

Explanation of the numerals on the plan of Heinola: 1. Casino, 2. Kursaal,
3. Post Office, 4. Normal School, 5. Telegraph Office.

242 Kil. (150 M.) **Riihimäki** *(Railway Restaurant,* déj. or
S. 1¹/₂, D. 2-2¹/₂ m.; *Inn),* a manufacturing place with 4000 inhab., is the junction for *Åbo* (R. 29 b) and *Tammerfors* (R. 31).

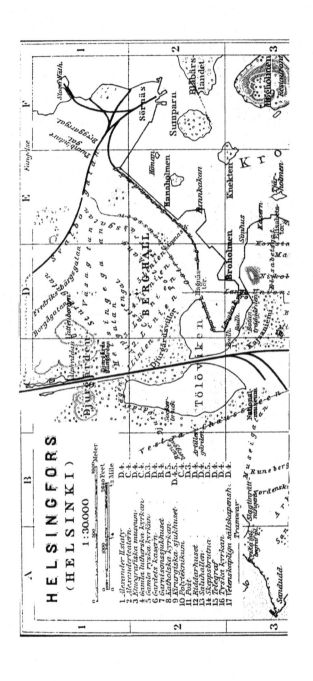

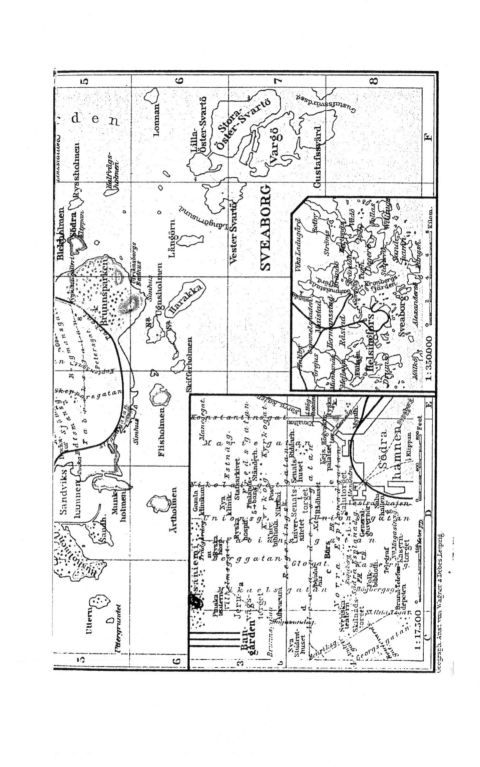

SVEABORG

1 : 350000

Geograph. Anst. von Wagner & Debes, Leipzig

1 : 17,300

The Helsingfors line turns to the S.—254 Kil. (158 M.) **Hyvinkää** (*Railway Restaurant; Hot. Hyvinge*, R. 2-3 m.).
FROM HYVINKÄÄ TO HANGÖ, 149 Kil. (93 M.), railway in 4 hrs. (fares 12 m. 50 p., 7 m. 50 p., 5 m.).—The district traversed is at first monotonous. —64 Kil. (40 M.) *Lohja.* The large village of this name (inn) lies'on°*Lake Lohja*, 2¹/₂ M. to the W. of the station, and contains an interesting church with mural paintings of the 16-17th centuries. Pleasant trips may be made on the lake and its banks; thus a steamer may be taken across the lake to *Härjänvatsa* and a conveyance thence to *Myllykylä* (6¹/₄ M. to the N.E.), which lies 2¹/₂ M. to the E. of the chapel of *Sammatti*, with the grave of E. Lönnrot (comp. p. 199).—84 Kil. *Svartå*, at the S. end of Lake Lohja. About 2¹/₂ M. to the N. of the railway station is the manor of Svartå, belonging to the Linder family.—99 Kil. (61¹/₂ M.) *Karis* (Rail. Restaurant). Hence to *Hangö*, see p. 231; to *Åbo*, see R. 29 a.

The scenery now becomes monotonous. From (284 Kil.) *Kerava* (Rail. Restaurant) a branch-line runs to (33 Kil.) Borgá (p. 229), affording a view of the cathedral to the left as we arrive. Beyond (302 Kil.) *Malm* we traverse the *Djurgård*, and cross the Gulf of Tölö by a long causeway.—313 Kil. (194 M.) *Helsingfors.*

28. Helsingfors and Environs.

ARRIVAL. At the *Bangård* or *Railway Station* (Pl. C, 3) cab-tickets are given out as at Warsaw (p. 9).— *Steamers* come to anchor in the Södrahamn (Pl D, E, 4).

Hotels (comp. plan of inner town). SOCIETETSHUS (Pl. b; C, 3), Brunnsgatan 12, a new building, opposite the rail. station, R. from 5 (with bath from 10), B. 1¹/₂, déj. (11-2) 2, D. (4-7) 3¹/₂, S. (8-12) 4 & 5 m.; HOT. KÄMP (Pl. c; D, 4), Norra Esplanadgatan 29, R. 5-7, B. 1¹/₄, déj. (10 a.m. to 2 p.m.) 1¹/₂-3, D. (3-6.30 p.m.) 3¹/₂-5, S. 3¹/₂ m., frequented by foreigners; FENNIA (Pl. a; D, 3), Mikaelsgatan 21, opposite the rail. station, R. 3-13, déj. 1¹/₂-2, D. 3¹/₂, S. 3¹/₂-5 m.; APOLLO (Pl. f; D, 4), Södra Esplanadgatan 10, R. 5-12, incl. bath, déj. 1¹/₂-2, D. 3-5 m.; KLEINEH (Pl. e; D, 4), Salu-Torget, R. 3-6, D. 3¹/₂ m.—Hotels Garnis. BRISTOL (Pl. g; D, 4), Unionsgatan 15, R. 4-8; PATRIA (Pl. d; C, D, 4), Alexandersgatan 17, R. 3-8.—*Kristillinen Matkailijakoti* ('Christian Hospice'; Pl. m, D 3), Berggatan 17, R. 2-7, déj. 1, D. 1¹/₂ m.--PENSIONS. *Central*, Alexandersgatan 46 (Pl. C, D, 4), in the Arcade, R. 3-8, déj. 1¹/₂, D. 1³/₄, pens. from 6 m.; *Touriste*, Boulevardsgatan 4 (Pl. C, 4), R. 3-7¹/₂, B. 1¹/₂ m.

Restaurants (open 9 a.m. till midnight). At the hotels; also *Kapellet* (Pl. i; D, 4), in the E. part of the Esplanade, D. 3¹/₂, 'sexa' 4 m.; *Operakällaren*, in the Swedish Theatre (Svenska Teatern; Pl. C, D, 4), déj. (10 a.m. to 2 p.m.) 1¹/₂ & 2¹/₂, D. (3-6.30 p.m.) 2¹/₂ & 3¹/₂, S. (8 p.m. to midnight) 3¹/₂ & 5 m., music at these two in summer; *Börs* (Pl. D, 4), Fabiansgatan 14, déj. 1¹/₂ & 2¹/₂, D. 3¹/₂, S. 3¹/₂ & 5 m.; *Catani*, Norra Esplanadgatan 31, next door to the Hotel Kämp, D. 3¹/₂ m., closed in summer; *Brunnshuset* (Pl. k; D, 5), in the Brunns-Park, D. 3¹/₂ m., in summer only; *Kajsaniemi* (Pl. l, C 3; p. 227); *Central*, Hagasundsgatan 4 (Pl. C, 3, 4), déj. 1¹/₂, D. 1¹/₂-2 m.; *Gradin*, Boulevardsgatan 2 (Pl. C, 4), new, for ladies; *Osmola* (students' co-operative temperance restaurant), Norra Esplanadgatan 21, in the court, first floor, déj. 1¹/₄, D. 1¹/₂, S. 1 m. (no tips; vegetarian dishes). *Automatic Restaurants:* Brunnsgatan 8 (Pl. C, 3), Boulevardsgatan 3 (Pl. C, 4), Unionsgatan 26 (Pl. D, 4), etc.—In the environs: *Klippan*, on the Södra Blekholm (Pl. E, 5), in summer only, with view of the town and the sea, D. 3¹/₂ m., band in the evening (steamer from the Salu-Torg every ¹/₄ hr., in 5 min.; fare 15 p.); *Alphyddan* (Pl. C, 1), in the Djurgård (p. 228) D. 3¹/₂ m; *Högholmen* (Pl. F, 3; p. 228), D. 2¹/₂ m.

Cafés and **Confectioners.** *Fazer*, Glogatan 3 (Pl. D, 4); *Löfström*, Alexandersgatan 40 (Pl. D, 4); *Brondin*, Södra Esplanadgatan 20 (Pl. D, 4); *Ekberg*,¨Alexandersgatan 52, first floor; *Brondin's Vienna Café*, City Arcade, Brunnsgatan 8 (Pl. C, 3).

Cabs per drive in the town, to the railway station, and in the Brunns-Park 75 p.; from the station to the town 1 m.; to the Djurgård 1¼ m.; per hr. 2, if no stops are made 3 m. Closed cabs 50 per cent more. Double fares at night (midnight to 7 a.m.). — *Motor Cabs*, for 1-3 persons, 600 mètres 70 p., each 200 mètres more 10 p.

Electric Tramways (15 p.). *Boulevardsgatan* (W. end; Pl. C, 4) to *Skatudden* (Pl. E, 4) and back, viâ Alexandersgatan (Pl. C, D, 4) and Salu-Torget (Pl. D, 4); name-board painted blue. — *Tölö* to *Hagnäs-Torget* (Pl. D, 2), viâ Vestra Chaussée (Pl. B, C, 2, 3), Salu-Torget (Pl. D, 4), Brunns-Park (Pl. D, 5), Henriksgatan (Pl. C, 3, 4), and Jernvägs-Torget (Pl. C, D, 3); colour yellow. — *Sörnäs* (Pl. F, 2) to *Skepparegatan* (Pl. C, 5) viâ Östra Chaussée (Pl. D, E, 2), Salu-Torget (Pl. D, 4), and Brunns-Park (Pl. D, 5); colour green. — *Hagnäs-Torget* (Pl. D, 2) to *Lappviksgatan* (Pl. B, C, 4) viâ Jernvägs-Torget (Pl. C, D, 3); colour red.

Theatres. *Swedish Theatre* (Svenska Teatern; Pl. C, D, 4), Esplanadgatan. — *Finnish Theatre* (Pl. C, D, 3), Jernvägs-Torget. — *Alexander Theatre* (Pl. 2; C, 4), Sandviks-Torget, Russian. — *Operetta Theatre*, in the Brunns-Park (Pl. D, 5), open in summer only. — *Apollo Theatre*, Esplanadgatan, for operettas, open in winter only.

Post Office (Pl. D, 3), Nikolaigatan 6 (probably to be transferred to the new railway station buildings; Pl. C, 3); open on week-days 10 a.m. to 7 p.m., Sun. 9-11 a.m. Letter within the town 10 p. or 4 cop. — **Telegraph Office** (Pl. D, 4), Norra Magasingatan 9 (open day and night).

Baths. *Ulrikasborgs Badhus*, in the Brunns-Park (in summer only); *Bad Central*, Arcade, Alexandersgatan 46 (Pl. D, 4); *Saima*, Högbergsgatan 2b (Pl. D, 4, 5). — SEA BATHS on the S. side of the town (Pl. 'Simhus', C 5).

Banks. *Finlands Bank* (Pl. D, 3), Kyrkogatan 15 (11 a.m. to 3 p.m.); *Föreningsbanken*, Alexandersgatan 36 (Pl. D, 4); *Nordiska Aktiebanken* (Pl. N. A.; D, 4), Unionsgatan 32. — Money may be changed at the *Finland Tourist Society* (see below; 10-2 & 4-6).

Shops. Books: *AkademiskaBokhandeln*, Alexandersgatan 7 (Pl. D, 4); *Waseniuska Bokhandeln*, Norra Esplanadgatan 25 (Pl. D, 4); *Helsingfors Bokhandeln*, Norra Esplanadgatan 19. — Photographs: *Nyblin*, Fabiansgatan 31 (Pl. D, 3, 4); *Atelier Apollo*, Alexandersgatan 13. — Photographic Materials: *Bögelund* (Kodak), Norra Esplanadgatan 25. — Native Handiwork: *Union of the Friends of Handicraft* (Finska Handarbetets Vänner), Unionsgatan 23, first floor (Pl. D, 4), near the Salu-Torg; *Pirtti*, Boulevardsgatan 2, first floor (Pl. C, 4); *Hemflit* ('Home Industry'), Unionsgatan 30, first floor; *Finlands Slöjdförening*, Alexandersgatan 15. — Angling requisites from *R. Renfors*, Mikaelsgatan 4 (Pl. D, 3, 4).

Finland Tourist Society, Norra Esplanadgatan 21 (Pl. D, 4; 10 a.m. to 3 p.m. on week-days). In the same building is the official *Finland Tourist Office*, open on week-days 10 a.m. to 6 p.m.

Consuls. British, *V. K. Kestell-Cornish*, Alexandersgatan 48 (Pl. C, D, 1; vice-consul, *S. W. Wancke*); American, *Viktor Ek*, Vestra Kajen 8 (Pl. D, 4). — LLOYD'S AGENTS, *Lars Krogius & Co.*, Södra Magasinsgatan 4.

Steamboat Offices. FINLAND STEAMSHIP CO. (Finska Angfartygs Aktie Bolaget; F. Å. A.), Södra Magasinsgatan 4 (Pl. F. D.; D, 4), for St. Petersburg, Åbo, Stockholm, Reval, Stettin, Copenhagen, Hamburg, London, and Hull; VICTOR EK, Vestra Kajen 16 (Pl. D, 4), for St. Petersburg, Viborg, Fredrikshamn, Kotka, Lovisa, Åbo, Björneborg, Stockholm, Reval, and Lübeck. — *Steamers* ply to Borgå (see p. 229); to St. Petersburg (4 times a week; fare 18 or 15 m., comp. p. 201); to Åbo (5 times a week; fare 10 or 8 m.); to Stockholm (4 times a week, in 26 hrs.; fare 36 or 28 m.).

Principal Attractions (one day). Esplanade (p. 224), Athenæum (p. 224), Senate Square (p. 225), National Museum (p. 228), Brunns-Park (p. 227). Afternoon: drive to Fölisön (p. 228); in the evening, Djurgården (p. 228) or Klippan (p. 221).

Helsingfórs, Finn. *Helsinki*, the capital of Finland, the seat of the Governor-General, of the Senate, of all the central offices for the government and administration of the grand-duchy, and of the Alexander University, and headquarters of the 22nd Russian Army Corps, is situated on a much-indented peninsula, which stretches towards the S.E. and divides a deep bay into two smaller bays. The main bay and the sea just outside it are dotted with numerous rocky islets, upon a group of which lies the naval fortress of Sveaborg (p. 229). Pop. 150,000 inhab., of whom half speak Swedish. The appearance of the town is entirely modern, in some respects suggesting America rather than Europe. Many granite buildings erected since 1900 show a praiseworthy attempt at originality of style. The Lutheran Emperor Nicholas Church, the Berghäll Church, and the Greek Catholic Church of the Assumption are especially conspicuous. —Helsingfors is at its busiest between Sept. and June.

The first town of Helsingfors was founded by *Gustavus I. Vasa* of Sweden in 1550, on the bank of the Wanda-A, where it flows into the Gulf of Finland, 3 M. from the present town. Its remains, called by the Finns Gammelstaden (*i.e.* old town), are still visible (see p. 229). The site, however, proved unfavourable for the commercial prosperity of the town, and in 1639, by the command of Queen Christina, it was removed to its present position on the Estnäs peninsula. Devastated by pestilence (1710), fire, and war (1713), the town was rebuilt and fortified in 1749. In 1808 Helsingfors was occupied by the Russians under General Bux-höwden, and by the Peace of Fredrikshamn (Sept. 17th, 1809) it was annexed to Russia. At that time it was still a small and unimportant place of 5000 inbah., but its size has rapidly increased since it was made the capital of Finland in 1812. In 1828 the University of Abo was transferred to Helsingfors. Comp. p. 229.

The busiest parts of Helsingfors are the vicinity of the HARBOUR, with its handsome granite quays, and the neighbouring SALU-TORG or MARKET PLACE (Pl. D, 4). The former is divided into the *Norra* and *Södra Hamnen* by the peninsula of Skatudden (see below). At the N.E. corner of the market-place rises the *Imperial Palace* (Kejserliga Palatset), an unpretending three-storied building, containing a handsome throne-room in which take place the opening and closing scenes of the Finnish Diet (p. 199). Not far off, on the S. quay, rises the *Alexandra Monument*, an obelisk erected in memory of the visit of the Empress Alexandra Feódorovna in 1833. Farther W. is an *Ornamental Fountain*, by Vallgren (1908). — To the S. is a market-hall (Saluhallen).

To the E. of the Salu-Torg is a bridge which crosses the canal connecting the two harbours. This leads to the quarter of SKA-TUDDEN (Pl. E, 4), with its modern apartment buildings. — On the N.W. side of Skatudden is the Greek Catholic **Cathedral of the Assumption** *(Ryska Kyrkan)*, completed in 1868 from the plans of Gornostáyev. This church stands high, and its white roofs and gilded domes are conspicuous far and near. It commands a good view of the town. To the S. of the cathedral is a chapel consecrated in 1913. Also to the S., below the cathedral, is the *Mint*

(Mynthuset). Farther to the E. is the *Custom House,* and at the extreme end of the peninsula are some marine barracks.

From the Salu-Torg the ESPLANADE (Esplanadgatan; Pl. D, 4), the finest street in the town, embellished with four rows of lime-trees, leads towards the W. Its N. side (Norra Esplanadgatan) forms, in conjunction with the parallel Alexandersgata, the chief business quarter of Helsingfors. At the beginning of the Norra Esplanadgata (No. 19) is the *Private Bank* (Pl. P. B.), erected in 1904 by Sonck & Jung (interior worth seeing). In the Södra Esplanadgata, at the corner of the Fabiansgata, is the *Residence of the GovernorGeneral,* opposite which is the *Kapellet Restaurant* (Pl. i; p. 221). In the middle of the Esplanade is a bronze statue of the poet *Runeberg* (p. 230), by his son Walter (1885). No. 12 Södra Esplanadgatan is the *Vasa Bank* (Pl. V. B.), by Gran, Hedman, & Vasastjerna (1899); No. 16 is the *Finnish Mortgage Bank* (Finlands Hypothek Förening; Pl. F. H.), by Lars Sonck (1909). At the W. end of the Esplanade is the **Swedish Theatre** (*Svenska Teatern;* Pl. C, D, 4), built by Chiewitz in 1858-60, burned down in 1863, and restored by Bénoit (Restaurant Operakällaren, see p. 221).

To the N.W. of the Swedish Theatre is the *Students' Club House,* built in 1870 by A. H. Dalström, with a large banqueting hall; adjoining, on the N., is the *New Student's Club House* (Pl. C, 4), erected by A. Lindgren in 1911. At the corner of the Mikaelsgata and the Alexandersgata is the office of the *Pohjola Fire Insurance Co.* (Pl. D, 4), by Gesellius, Lindgren, & Saarinen (1901).

To the N. lies the JERNVÄGS-TORG or Railway Square (Pl. C, D, 3), with the *Railway Station* (Bangården), now being built to the designs of Saarinen, the Athenæum (see below), and the *Finnish Theatre,* by Tarjanne (1902).

The **Athenæum** (Pl. C, D, 3) was built by *Höijer* in 1887, and its façade is elaborately decorated by *Sjöstrand* and *Vallgren.* Besides the collection of art (see below), it contains several schools for the cultivation of the fine and industrial arts, and also the *Museum of the Union for Industrial Art* (open 11-4, in winter 12-3; adm. 50 p., Sun. 10 p.).

The spacious HALL and STAIRCASE are adorned with sculptures, including (No. 768; to the right of the entrance) the Death of Kullervo by *C. Sjöstrand* (1828-1906).

The UPPER FLOOR contains the *Gallery of the Finnish Art Union, consisting mainly of works by native artists, and also a part of the Antell Collection (open 12-3; adm. 25 p., Sun. 10 p.). The collection is continually being added to, and consequently the pictures are frequently re-arranged. We therefore give a list of the more important works with the names of the artists in alphabetical order.—No. 2. H. Ahlman-Biese (b. 1867), View in winter from the Pyynikke; 34. A. von Becker (1831-1909), Card-players; 46. G. Berndtson (1858-95), Song of the bride; A. Edelfelt (1854-1905), 128. Duke Karl of Sweden at the bier of Count Clas Fleming, 132. Women in front of a church, 133. Christ and Mary Magdalen, 142. Mme. Ackté, the tiger, and Illustrations for Runeberg's 'Fänrik Stål' (a collection of ballads);

156. *R. W. Ekman* (1808-73), Scene from Runeberg's 'Elgskyttarna'; *M. Enckell* (b. 1870), 165. Concert, 630. Resurrection; 637. *A. W. Finch* (b. 1854), Storm; *A. Gallén* (b. 1865), 188. Ilmarinen's smithy (scene from the Finnish national epic of Kalevala; comp. p. 199), 189. Triptych from the Myth of Aino, 191. The Imatra in winter, 193. Lemminkäinen's mother resuscitating her son, 650. Kullervo; 216. *P. Halonen* (b. 1865), Clearing a path in the primæval forest; 228-236. *W. Holmberg* (1830-60), Landscapes; 255. *K. E. Jansson* (1846-74), Wooing in the Aland Islands; *E. Järnefelt* (b. 1863), 259. Clearing the forest, 265. Landscape; *A. Lauraeus* (1783-1823), 286. Portrait, 299. Monk in a wine-cellar; 308. *A. Liljelund* (1844-99), Buying costumes for the museum; 325. *B. Lindholm* (b. 1841), Storm in the Cattegat; *E. J. Löfgren* (1825-1884), 335. Portrait, 853. King Eric XIV. and Karin Månsdotter; 370. *H. Munsterhjelm* (1846-1905), November evening; 879. *J. Rissanen* (b. 1873), Fortune-teller; 470. *H. Schjerfbeck* (b. 1862), Convalescent; 890. *H. Simberg* (b. 1873), Portrait; 504. *V. Soldan-Brofeldt* (b. 1863), Heretics; 903. *V. Thomé* (b. 1871), Boys playing; 530. *A. Uotila* (1858-86), Vegetable market at Nice; 536. *T. Waenerberg* (b. 1846), Summer day on Hogland; *V. Westerholm* (b. 1860), 547. Landscape, Vallinkoski (no number); *F. von Wright* (1822-1906), Animal pictures. — Sculptures by *E. Halonen* (b. 1875), *F. A. Nylund* (b. 1879), *W. Runeberg* (b. 1838). *C. A. Sjöstrand* (1828-1906), *R. Stigell* (1852-1907), *J. Takanen* (1849-85), *V. Vallgren* (b. 1855), *E. Vikström* (b. 1864), *A. Rodin* (Nos. 723-726), and *J. T. Sergel* (1740-1814; No. 749. Faun). — Here also are some old Dutch and modern Belgian, French, and Swedish pictures.

To the E. of the Athenæum, at the corner of the Berggata and Regeringsgata, is the *House of the Old Finnish Party,* now also the meeting-place of the Diet (comp. p. 226). Still farther to the E. is the SENATE SQUARE (Senats-Torget; Pl. D, 4), bounded on the N. by the Emperor Nicholas Church, on the W. by the University, on the S. by the *Town Hall* (Rådhuset), and on the E. by the Senate House. In the middle of the square rises the bronze *Statue of Tzar Alexander II.* by W. Runeberg, erected in 1894 by the Finnish people.

The Lutheran **Emperor Nicholas Church** (Pl. D, 3), stands upon a huge mass of granite, which raises it about 30 ft. above the level of the square, and is approached by a broad flight of 45 granite steps. It was begun in 1830 in a pseudo-classical style, but, as the architect *Engel* died in 1840 with his work unfinished, the design was altered, and the building was completed in a different style in 1852. It has four porticoes, with six columns in each, and five domes. At the sides are two lofty and narrow wings. High up on the façade are statues of the Apostles, cast in zinc from the models of Schievelbein and Wredow (1850). The interior, which is supported by pillars, contains an altar-piece by Neff (Entombment) and a good organ. The tower (custodian in the E. pavilion on the terrace) affords the best view of the town and sea.

The **University** (*Alexanders Universitet;* Pl. D, 4), another palatial structure, was also built by *Engel* (1828-32). The staircase is adorned with a plaster frieze by Sjöstrand, the subject of which is taken from the 'Song of Väinämöinen' (between the ground-floor and the first floor). On the groundfloor, opposite the entrance, is the large Aula (reception room), decorated in 1905 et seq. with frescoes by *Edelfelt,* depicting the opening of the Åbo Academy in 1640. The Conference Room and the adjoining Chancellor's Office (first floor) contain portraits of Russian tzars and eminent natives of Finland, a marble bust of Queen Christina of Sweden, etc. — The University has 86 professors and 95 instructors; the total number of students is about 3530, including 830 women. They are divided into twelve 'nations' (Afdelningar) and are distinguished by a white cap with a black band and lyre, which is also worn by the female students. The lectures are delivered in Swedish and Finnish.

In the same building is the *Zoological Museum* (open on Sun. 1-3 p.m.). — Other institutions of the University are in separate buildings, including the Library (p. 227), the *Chemical Laboratory,* the *Mineralogical Museum* (W ed. & Sat. 12-1), and the *Collection of Plaster Casts* (Wed. 1-2, Sun. 2-4). — The Botanical Gardens (p. 227), the *Pathological and Anatomical Institute* (Nikolaigatan 10), the *Anatomical Museum* (Fabiansgatan 35), and the Observatory (Pl. D, 4; p. 227) also belong to the University.

The imposing **Senate House** (Pl. D, 4), 660 ft. long and 330 ft. deep, was built by *Engel* in 1822, and contains various government offices (adm. on application to the porter; fee). On the first floor is the handsome Senate Room. The antechamber contains portraits of governors-general of Finland.

Behind the senate-house (E.) lies the **Riddarhus** or *House of the Knights* (Pl. D, 4), erected by *Chiewitz* in the Renaissance style in 1858-61 (castellan in the vestibule, to the right of the stairs). The spacious hall on the first floor, embellished with the armorial bearings of the leading Finnish families, was the meeting-place of the Nobles before the introduction of the new constitution in 1906 (comp. p. 199). The adjoining apartments contain portraits of Presidents of the Finnish Diet and two paintings by Ekman (Opening of the Diet at Borgå by Alexander I. in 1809, Opening of the Diet at Helsingfors by Alexander II. in 1863).

To the S., opposite the University (Unionsgatan 32), is the *Nordiska Aktiebank* (Pl. N. A.; D, 4), built in 1904 by Gesellius, Lindgren, & Saarinen, and containing a noteworthy hall. Farther to the S.W., at Fabiansgatan 14, is the *Exchange* (Börs; Pl. D, 4), a granite building by Lars Sonck (1912).

To the left, in the NIKOLAIGATAN, which runs towards the N. from the Senate Square, is the *Finland Bank* (Pl. D, 3), built in 1883 by Bohnstedt. Opposite, to the right, is the former **House of the Estates** (*Ständerhuset;* Pl. D, 3), now used for committees of the Diet (comp. p. 199). The building was completed in 1891 from the plans of G. Nyström, and the pediment of the portico contains a bronze group by Vikström (1903), representing Alexander I. receiving the oath of fealty at the Diet of Borgå (1809). The building is to be enlarged by a new hall for the meetings of the Diet (comp. p. 225). — To the left, at the corner of the Fredsgata, is the *National Record Office* (Statsarkivet; Pl. D, 3), erected in the Renaissance style by G. Nyström in 1890 (open daily, 10-3).

Leaving Senate Square and following the Unionsgata towards
the N., we come (on the left, opposite St. Nicholas's) to the *University Library* (Pl. D, 3), erected by Engel in 1836-45 (open on week-
days 10-3 and 5-9, in the summer vacation in the morning only).
It contains about 250,000 vols., including (on the groundfloor) the
valuable collection of books and maps made by Baron A. E. von
Nordenskiöld, the distinguished Arctic voyager (b. in 1832 at Helsingfors; d. 1901). Among many other rare volumes it includes a
primer (A b c kiria) of 1542, probably the first book printed in
Finland (shown on request).— Farther on in the Unionsgata, on
the left, is the Russian *Military Hospital*. Nos. 35 and 37, on the
right, are the *New* and the *Old Clinical Institutes*. Opposite the
latter is the entrance to the *Kajsaniemi Park* (Pl. C, D, 3). A band
sometimes plays on summer evenings in the restaurant here (p. 221).

At No. 44, Unionsgatan is the entrance to the *Botanical Gardens* of the University (Botaniska Trädgården; Pl. D, 3), prettily
situated on the Tölö Bay and containing fine orangeries and green-
houses (open on Tues. and Frid. 11-1, Sun. 2-3).— Farther N., on
a small hill in the suburb of *Berghäll*, is an imposing church built
by Lars Sonck in 1912 (Pl. D, 2); the tower commands a fine view
(caretaker on the E. side).

We now return to the Salu-Torg (p. 223) in order to visit the
South Quarter of the Town. We ascend along the Unionsgata,
passing the *German Church* (Pl. 16; l.) and the *Swedish Normal
Lyceum* (r.). We then reach the *Observatory Hill*, which is laid out
with pleasure-grounds and affords a panorama of the town and sea.
On the top of the hill is the *Astronomical Observatory* (Pl. D, 4),
open on Thurs., 1-2 p.m. A little to the E., on the side next the sea,
is 'Shipwrecked' (Pl. 14), a bronze group by Robert Stigell (1898).
Descending the S. slope of the Observatory Hill, and passing the *Roman Catholic Church* (Pl. 8; 1859), we reach the entrance to the —

Brunns-Park (Pl. D, 5; restaurant, see p. 221), which contains
numerous villas and is rather a suburb than a park properly so-
called (electric tramways, see p. 222). In the S. part of the park
are the *Ulrikasborg Baths* (p. 222); farther to the W. are salt-
water baths. Above is an old battery commanding a view of Sveaborg and of the sea. In the E. part of the park, at Östra Brunns-
parken 17, is the unimportant *Picture Gallery of the Poet Cygnäus*
(d. 1881; Pl. D, E, 5; open daily 11-4; adm. 25, on Sun. 10 p.).

From the Brunns-Park we return through Högbergsgatan to the
Esplanade. On our way we pass on the left the *New Lutheran
Church* (Pl. C, 4, 5), a Gothic building by Melander (1893), with
two towers 245 ft. in height. Farther on, to the left, is a *Fire
Station* (Branddepoten), built by Höijer in 1892; its tower commands a wide view (open 2-3; fee 25 p.). On the right are the *Offices
of the Telephone Co.*, a granite building by Lars Sonck (1905).

15*

Mention may be made of the following buildings in the Kaserngata, which runs parallel to the Högbergsgata: the *Surgical Clinics* (Pl. 9); the *Scientific Societies' Building*, erected in 1899, at the corner of the Ulrikaborgsgata (No. 24; Pl. 17); the old *Finnish Guards Barracks* (Pl. 6), with a monument in the court to the soldiers who fell in the Russo-Turkish war of 1877-78; and the striking *Club House of the Nyland Students' Society* (No. 40), built by Hård af Segerstad in 1901.—To the E., at Södra Magasinsgatan 4, are the *Offices of the Finland Steamship Co.* (Pl. F. D.; D, 4), by H. Neovius (1904).

The WEST QUARTER OF THE TOWN is intersected by the wide and shady Boulevardsgata (Pl. C, 4). Between the Boulevardsgata and the Andreegata rises the *Old Lutheran Church* (Pl. 4), a wooden building by Engel (1826), surrounded by a garden. It contains an altar-piece by Ekman, representing Christ blessing little children. To the N., opposite the church, in the Andreegata, is a *Bronze Monument to Elias Lönnrot* (Pl. L.-St.; see p. 199), by E. Vik-ström (1902); Lönnrot is represented seated, listening to the song of Väinämöinen (p. 199). At the corner of the Andreegata and Georgs-gata (Pl. C, 4) are the offices of the *Suomi Life Insurance Co.*, by Lindgren (1911). To the S.W., in the Sandviks-Torg, is the *Technical High School* (Pl. 10), with 40 instructors and 470 students.

At Vestra Chaussée 6 is the **National Museum,** built by *E. Saarinen* in 1912, with a high tower (Pl. C, 3; not yet opened).

GROUND FLOOR. To the left of the entrance-hall (refreshment room on the right), in the S. part of the building, are the historical collections. Farther on, to the W., is the prehistoric and early historic section (from the stone age to the end of the 13th cent.). Adjoining, on the N., is the ethnographical section. — FIRST FLOOR. Baroque furniture; fayence; glass; room with mural paintings, from the manor of Jackarby in Nyland; Empire and modern furniture; costumes; embroidery; peasant gear. —BASEMENT. Ethnography of the Finno-Ugrian peoples in Russia proper.

About 12 min. to the N. of the National Museum, on the right, is the **Djurgård** (Pl. C, 1) or *Tölö Park* (cab, see p. 222; tram-way), an attractive park with a large greenhouse (Alphyddan Re-staurant, see p. 221), picturesquely situated on the Bay of Tölö. On a small hill are the municipal waterworks (Vattenborgen; view).

About 2 M. to the W. of the Djurgård is the island of *Fölisön*. To reach it we follow the Vestra Chaussée to the N., then turn to the left into the Mäjlansgata, a little beyond the Runebergsgata (Pl. B, 2), and finally skirt the shore. Or we may go by steamer (every hour, in 20 min., from the N. side of the inner Sandviks Harbour, Pl. B 5; fare 25 p.), or take a carriage (fare from the town 3 m.). The island of **Fölisön,** which is connected with the main-land by a bridge, boasts an interesting *Open Air Museum* (with an 18th cent. farm from Konginkangas in N. Tavastland), an admirably laid out public park, and a temperance restaurant (D. $1^1/_2$-$2^1/_2$ m.).

On the island of **Högholmen** (Pl. F, 3), to which a ferry plies from the Norra Hamn every $^1/_2$ hr. in 10 min. (fare 10 p.), is a small

Zoological Garden containing native and other animals (admission free) and a restaurant (p. 221). The highest part of the island (to the left of the landing-stage) commands a fine view of the town and the Archipelago.

Environs of Helsingfors.

An excursion among the numerous islands in the bay is pleasant and interesting, especially in the direction of Borgå. Steamers ply several times daily to various points, and one steamer, starting from the Norra Hamn at 11.30 a.m., makes a round trip of 2 hrs. Among the points chiefly frequented by the inhabitants of Helsingfors are the islands of *Knekten, Degerö* (the largest), *Vådö, Sumparn,* and *Villinge,* and also *Hertonäs* and *Botby* on the mainland. All these lie to the N.E. — The favourite points for excursions by land include *Gammelstaden* (p. 223), *Sörnäs* (with a harbour, brewery, and large prison), *Mäjlans,* and *Munksnäs.* The first two lie to the N.E., the other two, which are separated from one another by a narrow sound, lie to the N.W.

To the S. of Helsingfors (steamer hourly in 20 min.; fare 25 p.) lies **Sveaborg** (Pl. E, F, 6, 7), Finn. *Viapori,* a strong Russian naval fortress, occupying a chain of seven islands, and commanding the entrance to the Bay of Helsingfors. The fortress cannot be visited except by permission of the commandant; the gendarme who meets the traveller at the pier conducts him to the Greek Catholic church and to the grave of Ehrensvärd (in all 20 min.; gratuity $^{1}/_{2}$-1 m.).

After the Peace of Åbo in 1743, Sweden began (1749) to convert Sveaborg into a fortified harbour, after plans by Field-Marshal Count Ehrensvärd (see below). The most difficult part of the operation was the construction of the docks, and not the erection of the ramparts, which are 50 ft. in height. — In the spring of 1808 the fortress was blockaded by the Russians and soon fell into their hands, it is alleged through the treachery of its commandant Admiral Cronstedt. It was bombarded on Aug. 9-11th, 1855, by an Anglo-French squadron, with no other effect than the destruction of the buildings in the interior of the fortress, while a simultaneous attempt at landing on the islands of Drumsö and Sandhamn was also repulsed. The hostile fleet withdrew on Aug. 14th. Since then the works have been materially strengthened.

The steamer lands at the Stora-Öster-Svartö, which contains the Greek Catholic church and the commandant's residence. — On Vargö is the grave of *Field-Marshal Count Ehrensvärd,* with a monument designed by Gustavus III., modelled by Sergel, and erected in 1788. This consists of a granite rock, armour-plated in the style of a man-of-war and bearing a trophy of weapons, inscribed (in Swedish): 'Here lies Ehrensvärd, surrounded by his works, the Fortress of Sveaborg and the National Fleet'.

FROM HELSINGFORS TO BORGÅ. Steamer (restaurant on board) in 4 hrs. (fare 3 m., there & back 5 m.). The return-journey may also be made by railway viâ *Kerava* (p. 221) in $2^{1}/_{2}$ hrs. (62 Kil. or 39 M.; fares 3 m. 40, 2 m. 25 p.).

Borgå. — The steamboat wharf is on the left bank of the Borgå, to the W. of the Salu-Torg; the railway station is on the right bank of

the Borgåå, outside the town. — HOTELS. *Societetshus* (Pl. a), Salu-Torget,
R. 3¹/₂-5, déj. 1¹/₂, D. 2¹/₂, S. 1¹/₂ m.; *Phoenix*, R. from 3 m.; *Elim Hospice*,
R. 2¹/₂ m. – CAB from rail. station to town or vice versâ 75 p., per hr. 2¹/₄ m.
BRITISH CONSULAR AGENT, *Einar Paavola*, Krämar-Torg (Förenings-Bank).
LLOYD'S AGENT, *A. W. Karlsson*, Stadhusgatan 3.

Borgå (Finnish *Porvoo*), a small town of 5500 inhab., founded
as early as 1346(?), is situated at the point where the *Borgåå* enters
a bay of the Gulf of Finland, and lies picturesquely on and around
the heights enclosing the river and the fjord. To the N. is the
high-lying Old Town. To reach this from the steamboat, we proceed
to the N. through the Ågata to (9 min.) the Borgåå bridge, and
then ascend to the right; from the railway station we turn to the
left, cross the bridge, and ascend in a straight direction (9 min.).

BORGÅ

1:50.000

0   250   500
        Meter

1 *Eug. Schaumanns Graf*   8 *Runebergs graf*
2 *Finska Kyrkan*   9   *hem*
3 *Konsistorium*   10   *staty*
4 *Lyceum*   11 *Stadshuset*
5 *Museum*   12 *Telegrafkontor*
6 *Postkontoret*   S · *Salutorget*
7 *Realskola*

Wagner & Debes, Leipzig

[By ascending to the right
4 min. after leaving the rail.
station and before crossing the
railway, we reach (3 min.) the
Cemetery.] At the top of the
hill is the Gothic *Cathedral*
(1414), the white gable-front
of which, diversified with brick
ornamentation, faces the river.
There is no tower. The interior
(verger in the first house to the
left) is decorated in the rococo
style. Opposite the pulpit
(1764) is a bronze statue of
Tzar Alexander I., erected in
1909. It was here that the
Estates took the oath of fealty
to the Tzar on March 29th,
1809. A little to the N. is the

Consistorium (Pl. 3), formerly the Grammar School, in which
Alexander I. opened the Finnish Diet on March 27th, 1809, at the
same time confirming the privileges of the country, an incident commemorated in a picture by Thelning. From the cathedral we descend
to (3 min.) the *Museum*, in the Old Town Hall (Pl. 5), containing
weapons, uniforms, costumes, and so on (adm. 50 p.). About 5 min.
farther to the S. is a bronze *Statue of Runeberg* (Pl. 10), a reduced
replica of that in Helsingfors (p. 224), erected in 1885. About
3 min. farther on is the *House of J. L. Runeberg* (Pl. 9; key at the
back door), the poet, who taught at the Borgå Lyceum from 1837
to 1857 (d. 1877; comp. p. 244). The house is now national property. His grave is in the cemetery mentioned above (Pl. 8). Here,
too, is the grave of *Eugene Schauman* (d. 1904), the Finnish patriot.

FROM HELSINGFORS TO HANGÖ, 137 Kil. (85 M.), railway in 4 hrs.
(fares 11 m. 75, 7 m. 5, 4 m. 70 p.). — Beyond (3 Kil.) *Fredriks-*

berg the line diverges to the left from that to Riihimäki (p. 220). About 2¹/₂ M. to the N. of (52 Kil.) *Sjundeå* is the old church of that name. — 87 Kil. (54 M.) **Karis** *(Rail. Restaurant).* To *Hyvinkää,* see p. 221, to *Åbo,* see R. 29 a.

103 Kil. *Ekenäs* (Finnish *Tammisaari;* Continental Hotel, R. 3-4 m., with restaurant open in winter only, déj. 1¹/₂, D. 2¹/₂, S. 1¹/₂ m.; Knipan Restaurant, at the harbour, open in summer; cab from the rail. station to the town 75 p.) is a small town of 2800 inhab., situated on a peninsula. At the E. entrance to the town is the Slottsbacke ('Castle Hill') commanding a view of the sea. — In May, 1854, the British ships *Hecla* and *Arrogant* destroyed the batteries of Ekenäs and captured a large merchantman.

About 10 M. to the E. of Ekenäs (carr. there & back 8 m.) are the interesting remains of the old castle of *Raseborg* (Tourist Inn). The station of *Raseborg,* on the Helsingfors & Hangö railway, lies 3¹/₂ M. to the N. of this point. — From Ekenäs steamers ply 4 times weekly (fare 5 m.) to Helsingfors through the *Barösund.* On the small island of *Makilo,* in this sound (said to be named after a Scot called McEliot), is a simple memorial to English and French sailors buried here during the Crimean War. — A motor omnibus runs daily from Ekenäs to Bromarv (see below).

We cross the *Bay of Pojo.* — 119 Kil. *Lappvik.* From the N. side of the Bay of Lappvik we may row in 2 hrs. to the picturesque parish of *Bromarv* (Pension Wickström, plain), which may also be reached from Ekenäs (see above) or Hangö (see p. 232). Not far off lies *Rilaks,* a château in the Early English style, with a picture-gallery and park. On July 26th, 1714, Peter the Great defeated the Swedish fleet in the Bay of Rilaks, thus winning the first victory of his infant navy. — We pass through woods to —

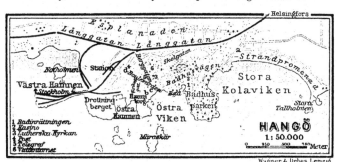

137 Kil. (85 M.) **Hangö.** — HOTELS: *Bellevue* (Pl. a), situated on the sea-front, to the E. of the town, and suitable for a long stay, open from June to Aug. only, R. 3-10, B. 1¹/₂, D. (3-5 p.m.) 3¹/₂, pens. from 7¹/₂ m.; *Grand-Hôtel* (Pl. c), Boulevard, on the sea-front, R. from 3, déj. 3, D. 3¹/₂, S. 2 m.; *Societetshus* (Pl. b), Torggatan, with a large glass veranda overlooking the sea, R. from 2, déj. 1¹/₂, D. 2¹/₂, S. 1¹/₂ m.; *Jernvägs-Hotel* (Pl. d), nearly opposite the rail. station, R. 2¹/₂-4, D. 2-4 m. — *Casino Restaurant* (Pl. 2), near the Baths, open in summer only, déj. 2, D. 3¹/₂,

S. 2½ m. — POST OFFICE (Pl. 4), Jernvägs-Torg; TELEGRAPH OFFICE (Pl. 5), Berggatan 3. — BRITISH VICE-CONSUL, *Uno Cairenius*, Boulevarden 11. — LLOYD'S AGENT, *K. Boström*, Bulevarden 17. — CAB per drive 50 p., from the rail. station or the harbour to the town 75 p. — *Season*, from June 10th to Sept. 1st. — *Visitors' Tax*, after three days of grace, 6 m. per week.

Hangö (Finnish *Hanko*) is a town of 7000 inhab., founded in 1878. Its harbour is open in winter, and it carries on a considerable export trade in butter. It is also a seaside and bathing resort. It lies on a sandy peninsula stretching for 19 M. into the sea, and forming the southernmost point of the Finnish mainland. Views are obtained from the *Drottningberg* and from the *Vattentorn* (Pl. 6; 160 steps), which is 102 ft. in height. The *Badhus Park*, with its pleasant drives and walks contains a well-defined 'pot-hole'. From the Bellevue Hotel the road runs E. along the seashore to the (1 M.) two *Tallholmen* (cafés).

Steamers to Bromarv (p. 231; five times a week), Stockholm, Hull, etc. (comp. p. 201; passport, see p. 201).

From Helsingfors to *Viborg* (St. Petersburg), see R. 27; to *Åbo*, see R. 29; to *Uleåborg* and *Tornea*, see R. 31.

29. From Helsingfors to Åbo.

a. VIÂ KARIS.

200 Kil. (124 M.). RAILWAY in 5-5½ hrs. (fares 16 m. 20, 9 m. 75, 6 m. 50 p.). — STEAMER preferable to the railway, see pp. 222, 237.

From Helsingfors to (87 Kil.) *Karis*, see pp. 230, 231. Beyond Karis the train turns towards the N.W. and passes through the only tunnel in Finland. From (97 Kil.) *Skuru* a branch-line runs to (4 Kil.) *Fiskars*, with a large iron-foundry, established in 1649. From the tower of the handsome church of (144 Kil.) *Salo* (Rail. Restaurant; Gästgifveri), a market-town in the parish of Uskela, we obtain a good view of the district. — 149 Kil. *Halikko*, with an old stone church. A little to the S. are the *Åminne* and *Viurila* estates. — 190 Kil. *Littoinen*, with a cloth-factory. — 200 Kil. (124 M.) *Åbo*, see p. 233; 203 Kil. *Åbo Harbour*

b. VIÂ RIIHIMÄKI.

275 Kil. (171 M.). RAILWAY in 8 hrs. (fares 21 m. 40, 12 m. 85, 8 m. 55 p.); from Helsingfors to (108 Kil. or 67 M.) *Tavastehus* in 3 hrs. (fares 9 m. 40, 5 m. 65, 3 m. 75 p.) — STEAMER, see above.

From Helsingfors to (71 Kil. or 44 M.) *Riihimäki*, see pp. 221, 220. The railway continues to the N. and enters the province of Tavastehus, the S. part of which is admirably cultivated.

108 Kil. (67 M.) **Tavastehús.** — The *Railway Station* lies to the E. of the town. — HOTELS. *Stads-Hotel*, on the N. side of the Main Square, R. 3-8, D. (2.30 to 6 p.m.) 3 m.; *Hôtel-Restaurant Teatern*, Itäinen Linnan Katu, a little to the N. of the Main Square, R. 3-7, D. 3 m. — CAB from the rail. station to the town 75 p., per hr. 2 m.; to Karlberg & back 3 m., to Aulango Tower & back 4½ m., waiting 1 m. per hr. — STEAM LAUNCH from the town to the Public Park several times a day.

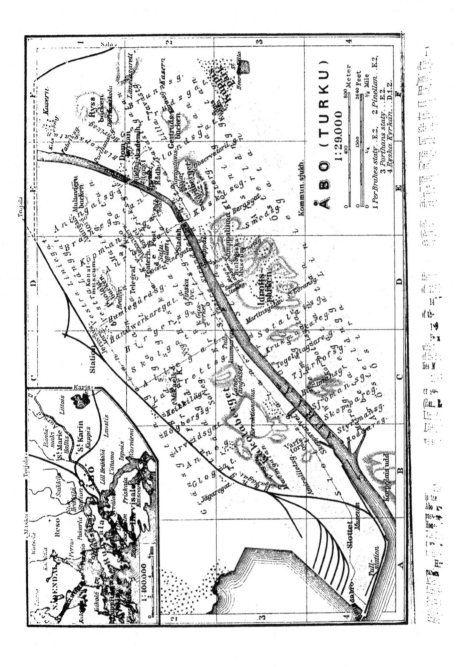

ÅBO (TURKU)
1:29,000

1 Per Brahes stdy. . E.2,   2 Pinellan. . E.2,
3 Porthans stdy. . E.2.
4 Ryska Kyrkan. . D.1.2.

Tavastehús, Finn. *Hämeenlinna,* a town with 6500 inbab. and
of little commercial importance, is pleasantly situated on the *Vanajavesi,* which is bounded on the S. by the wooded heights of the
Hattelma. To reach the (12 min.) Main Square (Finn. Iso-Tori) we
turn to the left on leaving the railway station, turn to the right in
4 min., and then cross the bridge over the Vanajavesi. On the E.
side of the square stands the *Lutheran Church,* built in 1798.
Leaving the square on the N. side by the Itäinen Linnan Katu, we
pass the *Finnish Lyceum* on the right, and in 10 min. reach the
Castle of Kronoborg, founded in 1249 and still in a good state of
preservation. It is now used as a penitentiary for women. About
$^3/_4$ M. to the N. is the *Public Park,* containing an artificial ruin
(view; temperance restaurant in summer).

On the E. bank of the Vanajavesi, 2 M. to the N. of the rail. station
(cab, see p. 232), is the manor-house of **Karlberg,** with large greenhouses
(shown on application). In the well-kept park is the *Aulango Tower*
(110 ft. high), from the top of which an extensive view is obtained; in a
cave below is a group of bears by Stigell.

Beyond Tavastehus we skirt the E. bank of the Vanajavesi and
then cross the river. The church of *Hattula,* $1^1/_2$ M. to the N.E.
of (116 Kil.) *Parola,* has interesting old mural paintings.

147 Kil. (91 M.) **Toijala** *(Railway Restaurant),* the junction
of the line to Tammerfors (p. 240).— We proceed towards the S.W.

189 Kil. *Humppila.*

From Humppila a branch-railway runs to (23 Kil.) *Forssa,* a village
with 7000 inhab. and a cotton-mill, in front of which is a colossal bust
of its founder by W. Runeberg (1887).— About $5^1/_2$ M. to the E. of Forssa
lies *Mustiala,* with an agricultural institute.

199 Kil. *Ypäjä.* The railway now traverses the Län of Åbo and
crosses the *Loimaanjoki* shortly before reaching (209 Kil.) *Loimaa*
(Rail. Restaurant). We are now in the most fertile region of the
Län of Åbo and indeed of all Finland.— 219 Kil. *Mellilä;* 257 Kil.
Lieto. Just before reaching (275 Kil. or 171 M.) *Åbo* (see below),
we see the cathedral to the left. 278 Kil. (173 M.) *Åbo Harbour.*

30. Åbo and Environs.

The STEAMER coming from Stockholm (comp. p. 201) lies to at the quay
in the outer harbour, where through passengers (not making any stay in
Abo) are transferred to the express train. Passports are scrutinized as the
passengers leave the steamer, and luggage is examined in the Custom
House (Pl. A, 4). Cab to the town $1^1/_2$ m.; cab-tickets are given out.—
The RAILWAY STATION (Pl. C, 1; refreshment room) lies to the N. of the
town; cab (tickets as at the harbour) to the town 75, vice versâ 50 p.,
to the Stockholm steamer $1^1/_4$ m.

Hotels. HAMBURGER BÖRS (Pl. c; E, 2), Köpmansgatan 6, with concert-
garden, R. from $2^1/_2$, déj. $1^1/_1$, D. 2 & 3, S. $1^1/_4$ m.; PHŒNIX (Pl. a; D, 1),
Alexanders-Torget, R. from $2^1/_2$, déj. $1^1/_2$, D. 3, S. $1^1/_2$ m., these two very
fair; STANDARD (Pl. d; D, 2), Kristinegatan 9, R. from $2^1/_2$, déj. $1^1/_4$, D.
$2^1/_2$ m ; JERNVÄGS-HOTEL (Pl. b; D, 1), near the rail. station, R. $2^1/_4$-8,
déj. $1^1/_4$, D. $2^1/_2$, S. $1^1/_4$ m.; SAIMA (Pl. c; D, 2). a temperance house,
Eriksgatan 15, R. $1^3/_4$-5, déj. 1, D. $1^3/_4$, S. 1 m.

Restaurants. *Hamburger Börs* (p. 233); *Samppalinna* (Pl. D, 2; concerts), prettily situated on the slope of a hill at the landing-place of the coasting-steamers; *Observatoricbacken* (open in summer only), on the Vårdberg (Pl. E, 2). — In the environs, *Lilla Bockholmen* (p. 237; steamer).

Cafés & Confectioners. *Lehtinen*, Nylandsgatan 2, at the corner of the Nikolai-Torg (Pl. E, 2); *City*, Köpmansgatan, opposite the Hamburger Börs (see p. 233).

Cabs. Per drive or to the Kuppis Park 50-75 p., to the Castle and to the Stockholm steamer 1 m., per hr. 1½ or (if no stops are made) 2½ m. At night (midnight to 6 a.m.) double fares. — MOTOR CABS. For 700 mètres 70, each 300 m. more 10 p.

Electric Tramway from the rail. station through the town to the Castle and the Harbour (fare 15 p.).

Steamers to the *Castle*, *Runsala* (40 p.), and *Lilla Bockholmen* (50 p.), several times a day; to *Hangö*, see p. 237; to *Helsingfors*, see p. 222; to *Stockholm*, see p. 201 (fares 32 and 26 m., winter supplement 8 and 7 m.); to *Salo* 4 times weekly; to *Nådendal* several times daily in 1¼ hr.; to *Nystad* daily; to *Björneborg* and *Vasa* twice weekly.

Post Office (Pl. D, E, 2), at the corner of Eriksgatan and Auragatan. **Telegraph Office** (Pl. D, 2), Puolalagatan.

Banks (10 a.m. to 3 p.m.). *Finlands Bank*, *Åbo Aktiebank*, both at the corner of Slottsgatan and Auragatan (Pl. D, E, 2); *Föreningsbanken*, Auragatan (Pl. D, E, 1, 2).

Consuls. British Vice-Consul, *W. J. B. Wilson*, Kaskisgränd 3; U. S. Commercial Agent, *Victor Forselius*, Slottsgatan 5. — LLOYD'S AGENT, *J. G. Wikeström*, Slottsgatan 35.

Baths. *Thermae*, Auragatan 14 (Pl. D, E, 1, 2), opposite the Phœnix Hotel; sea-bathing at Runsala and other points.

Principal Attractions (half-a-day). Cathedral, Vård-Berg, Biological Museum, and Castle.

Åbo (pron. Obo), Finn. *Turku*, situated at the mouth of the *Aura*, is the oldest and historically most interesting town in Finland, of which it was formerly the capital. It is also the seat of the Lutheran Archbishop of Finland and of the Governor of the Län, and it has contained one of the three Supreme Courts of Finland since 1623. It now has 50,000 inhab. and is the second largest town in the grand-duchy. Its chief imports consist of manufactured articles, colonial wares, grain, and salt, while the chief exports are oats, timber, and wooden wares.

The rise of Åbo dates from the time when the Swedes and Christianity entered the land together (1157). The town, which was at first of small importance and was repeatedly pillaged and burned, entered on a new era of prosperity in the 13th century. Bishop Magnus I. began the building of the cathedral, which was finished in 1300. In 1318, however, the town was burned by the Russians and the cathedral sacked. The real prosperity of Åbo begins with the Peace of Nöteborg in 1323. In 1509 it was captured by the Danes. At the time of the Reformation the Dominican monastery, founded in 1249, was suppressed and the bishopric became Protestant; in 1817 it was converted into an archbishopric. In 1630 Gustavus Adolphus founded a grammar-school, which was raised to the rank of a university by Queen Christina in 1640. The Peace of Åbo (Aug. 7th, 1743) put an end to the Russo-Swedish war, which had broken out in 1741 at the instigation of France. In 1808 the town and castle were occupied by the Russian General Buxhöwden, and in the following year, Åbo, like the rest of Finland, passed into Russian possession. In 1819 the seat of government was removed to Helsingfors, whither the university was also transferred after the destructive fire of 1827.

The chief seat of traffic is in the neighbourhood of the two *Bridges over the Aura*. Here, on the N. bank of the river, lies the *Town Hall* (Stadshuset; Pl. D, E, 2), containing a handsome banqueting-room. Adjacent is the ALEXANDERS-TORG (Pl. D, E, 2), in which are the *Theatre,* the *Post Office,* and the *Greek Catholic Church* (Pl. 4), the last containing paintings by the Finnish artist Godenhjelm. — A little to the W. of the post office is the *Market* (Saluhallen; Pl. D, 2).

To the N.W. of the Alexanders-Torg, upon a small hill (view), is the **Art Museum** *(Konst Museum),* by *G. Nyström* (Pl. D, 1; open daily, 12-2 p.m., adm. 25 p.; at other times 50 p.). In the entrance-hall and on the staircase are sculptures, including (up stairs) the marble busts of the founders of the Museum, E. and M. Dahlström. On the first floor are modern paintings, including 'The Defender of Sampo' by Gallén (comp. p. 199). — To the E. of the Alexanders-Torg, on the Aura, is the *Public Library* (Pl. E, 2), built in the style of the Riddarhus of Stockholm.

On the left bank of the Aura lies the NIKOLAI-TORG (Pl. E, 2), a square laid out with gardens. On the right side of this are the *Swedish Lyceum,* founded in 1630 as a grammar-school, the *Municipal Offices* (Rådhuset), and a seated bronze figure by Sjöstrand (1864) of *H. G. Porthan* (d. 1804; Pl. 3), the Finnish historian. To the left are the Cathedral, the Akademihus, and a bronze statue, by W. Runeberg (1888), of *Per Brahe* (Pl. 1), the able Governor-General of Finland from 1637 to 1654. On the pedestal is the inscription 'Jagh war med landett, och landett med mig wääl tillfreds' (I was satisfied with the country and the country with me).

The **Cathedral* (*Domkyrkan,* formerly *St. Henry's Cathedral;* Pl. E, 1, 2), a massive brick building of the late-Romanesque period (consecrated in 1300), with Gothic and Renaissance additions, stands in the middle of the former graveyard on the hill of Unikankari. It is 290 ft. long, 125 ft. wide, and 145 ft. high. The cathedral is open in summer 11-1 & 4-6; at other times on application to the sacristan Lampi, Lilla Tavastgatan 4 (Pl. F, 2).

Over the main W. entrance is the large *Organ,* the finest in Finland, possessing 5000 pipes and constructed in 1842 with a bequest left for the purpose by a patriotic baker called Anderson. — To the right of the main entrance is the chapel of the *Stålhandske* family, containing (right) the tomb of Torsten Stålhandske, with a recumbent figure in sandstone. — To the left of the entrance, on the N. side, is the Tavast Chapel, with the tombs of *Archbishop Magnus Tavast* (d. 1452), of *Field-Marshal Horn* and his wife (recumbent figures in low relief), and of *Colonel Cockburn* (d. at Abo in 1621), a Scottish officer who served under Charles XII. *General Wedderburn* and other Scots soldiers of fortune are also buried here. The stained-glass window by Vladimir Svertchkóv (d. 1888) represents Gustavus II. Adolphus at the bed of the dying Field-Marshal Horn. To the left of the choir is the *Kankas Chapel* or chapel of the families *Horn* and *Kurck* (comp. p. 239), the finest in the church.

In the middle of it is the granite sarcophagus (placed here in 1865) of the much-tried Karin or Catherine Månsdotter (d. 1612), the daughter of a common soldier, who became the consort of King Eric XIV. The central stained-glass window, by V. Svertchkóv, represents Catherine Månsdotter handing her crown to a page in Swedish dress and descending from the throne of Sweden, supported by a fair-haired page from Tavastland, who is emblematical of Finland. — To the right of the choir is the chapel of the *Tott* family, endowed in 1678 by Per Brahe. The marble figure of a knight in full armour is *Åke Tott* (d. 1640), a Swedish general in the Thirty Years' War; at his side is his wife Sigrid Bjelke. — In the vault below the choir lie Åke Tott, Sigrid Vasa (d. 1653), daughter of King Eric XIV. and Catherine Månsdotter (see above), and various other eminent personages. — The *Choir* contains an altar-piece by the Swedish painter Westin and is adorned with two frescoes by Ekman (d. 1873). The scene to the right shows Bishop Henry of Upsala (an Englishman; comp. p. 200) baptizing the Finns at the spring of Kuppis (p. 237); to the left Bishop Agricola, a pupil of Luther and Melanchthon, handing King Gustavus Vasa the New Testament that he has translated into the Finnish language.

The *Akademihus* (Pl. E, F, 2), built by Gustavus IV. Adolphus in 1802-15 for the old university, now contains the Residence of the Governor of the Län, the Supreme Court of Justice, the Government Archives, and other government offices. The former Aula, or Graduation Hall (keeper in the Swedish Lyceum, p. 235), is adorned with six alto-reliefs by the Finnish sculptor Cainberg (d. 1816), representing scenes from the history of the town and university.

At the foot of the **Vård-Berg** (Pl. E, 2), Stora Tavastgatan 28, is the building of the *Finland Economic Society,* established in 1797 for the promotion of agriculture, art, and industry. Farther up are attractive pleasure-grounds, containing a restaurant, the *School of Navigation,* with the observatory of the old university, and the reservoirs of the town water-works (hewn out of the rocks).

Farther to the W., reached from the Magasinsgata by following the Jungfrustig towards the S., is the *Biological Museum (Pl. D, 3; open in summer 10 a.m. to 8 p.m.; in winter 10-3; adm. 50 p.), founded by the consul A. Jacobsson, and affording (in ten lifelike groups) a good survey of the mammalia and birds of Finland. — A little to the W. is the *Recreation Ground* (Idrottsparken; Pl. D, 3).

Returning to the right bank of the Aura and following the SLOTTSGATA (Pl. B-E, 2-4) towards the W., we reach the *Castle of Åbo (*Slottet;* Pl. A, 4; tramway from Alexanders-Torget in 12 min.), an extensive and heavy-looking building, consisting of two parallel blocks connected at the ends by two low and massive square towers. Probably built about 1300, it was formerly the key of Finland and consequently a frequent object of contest. In the interior is the municipal **Historical Museum,** shown on week-days 10-7 (50 p.) and on Sun. 12-3 (25 p.) on application to the keeper, on the right side of the court, second floor (Swedish catalogue 50 p.). Its 51 rooms contain portraits, furniture, ornaments, articles in pewter, coins, and costumes, affording an admirable survey of the evolution of Finnish civilization. Visitors may also see the cell where Eric XIV. of Sweden was imprisoned by his brother John from 1569 to 1571.— The *Church of St. Michael* (Pl. C, 2) is an early work of L. Sonck.

ENVIRONS. From the Nikolai-Torg (p. 235) the Nylandsgata leads S.E. to the *Kuppis Park* (Pl. F, 3); at the S. end of the park is the *Spring of St. Henry,* in the waters of which the first Finnish Christians are said to have been baptized (comp. p. 236).

To the N.E. of the town, on the right bank of the Aura, lies ($1^1/_4$ M.) the well-preserved **Church of St. Mary,** a remarkable brick structure resembling the cathedral of Åbo. It is stated to have been built in 1161 at the bidding of Bishop Henry of Upsala and to have been the first Christian church in Finland. It was the cathedral of the country down to 1300.— On the other side of the river is *St. Karin,* another venerable church.

On the W. side of the town, near the castle, is a long bridge on piles (toll 10 p.) connecting it with the island of **Runsala** (*Ruissalo;* cab there & back $3^3/_4$ m.). This charming island, which is about $5^1/_2$ M. in length, was originally a royal domain and chasse and afterwards became the summer-residence of the governors of the Län of Åbo-Björneborg. In 1845 it was acquired by the town and parcelled out into lots for villas and gardens. It is famous for its rich flora and for its oak-woods — a rarity in Finland. In the centre of the island is a spring with an inscription in memory of the poet *Choräus* (d. 1806), who resided here for a time (Choräi Källa). In the prettiest part of the island is the restaurant of *Allmänna Promenaden.* Those who leave the steamer here may return by it in about 1 hr.

A trip may also be made either from Runsala or from the town to the harbour and pleasure-resort of *Lilla Bockholmen,* which lies between the islands of *Hirvensalo* (see below) and Runsala.

Excursions from Åbo.

a. To HANGÖ.

a. BY RAILWAY (163 Kil. or 101 M., in 5 hrs.; fares 13 m. 65, 8 m. 20, 5 m. 45 p.), see pp. 232, 231, 230.

b. BY STEAMER in 8-11 hrs. (fare 7 m.). The boats start at the Aura bridge. — On reaching the mouth of the Aura, the steamer turns to the S. and enters the sound between the mainland and the villa-studded island of *Hirvensalo.* Passing the promontory of *Lemo,* we steer first to the S. and then to the E., skirting the S. side of the island of **Kuustö.** On this island, somewhat inland, lie the ruins of the castle of *Kuustö,* which belonged to the bishops of Finland from the 13th cent. onward, and was razed to the ground on the introduction of Protestantism.

Some of the steamers pass through the sound of *Pargas*, on which lies the well-preserved château of *Quidja*, once belonging to the Fleming family and now to that of the Heurlins. These steamers rejoin the usual route at Sandö, in the Pemar Fjord (see below).

Beyond Kuustö the steamer threads another sound, passes the cape of *Röfvarnäs* on the right, and enters the spacious *Pemar Fjord*. We leave this fjord, between *Karuna* on the left and *Sandö* on the right, by a narrow strait separating the mainland from the island of *Kimito*, the largest of the coast-islands of Finland. It contains blast-furnaces and iron-works. To the right we see the manor of *Vestankärr*, and farther on *Lappdal* and the church of *Angelniemi*. The last is picturesquely situated at the end of the long promontory which forms the N.E. end of Kimito. We continue to the S., passing the island of *Vartsala* on the left. On the same side are the iron-works of *Kirjakkala* and *Mathildedal*, with the blast-furnaces of *Tykö* between them. Farther on we proceed through the pleasant *Strömma Canal* and past the island of *Finnby* to *Hangö* (p. 231).

b. The Åland Islands.

The local steamer from Åbo to Stockholm viâ the Åland Islands calls at Degerby (see below) and also at Mariehamn, but the daily mail-steamer does not touch at these ports. — The smaller steamers which ply 6 time a week to Mariehamn, calling at various intermediate stations, may also be used (fare 16 or 12 m.).

The steamer threads its way through the innumerable small islands opposite Åbo, the most important of which are *Nagu*, *Korpo*, and *Houtskär*, enters the *Skiftet Sound* (see below), and soon comes in sight of the **Åland Islands**. These islands are similar in appearance to those we have just seen, only they are more numerous and more scattered.

The ÅLAND ISLANDS (*Åländska Skärgården*, Finn. *Ahvenanmaa*), with a total area of 550 sq.M., are separated from Finland by the Skiftet Sound, 4-20 M. in width, and from Sweden by the Ålands Haf, which is about 25 M. broad. The inhabitants are of Swedish origin. Of the several hundred islands which the group contains, about 90 only are inhabited. The largest is the so-called *Åland Mainland (Fasta Åland)*, containing about half of the population. Åland formerly had a governor of its own, but now belongs to the province of Åbo-Björneborg.

About 8 hrs. after leaving Åbo the steamer reaches *Degerby*, a village on the island of Föglö. Thence to Mariehamn the voyage takes 2 hrs. more.

The smaller steamers hold more to the N. and pass through the sounds of *Lappvesi* and *Delet*, which run from N. to S. and contain numerous islands. In approaching Mariehamn they pass the fortifications of *Bomarsund*, destroyed in 1854, and the *Lemström Canal*, completed in 1882.

125 Kil. or 78 M. (from Åbo) **Mariehamn**, Finn. *Maarianhamina* (*Societetshus*, R. 3½-10, déj. 1½, D. 2½ m.; *Bad-Hotel*, open in summer only, similar charges; Lloyd's Agent, H. *Kors-*

ström; cab 50 p.), a pleasantly situated little town and bathing
resort with about 1400 inhabitants. — About 12^1/$_2$ M. to the N. of
Mariehamn lies *Kastelholm,* with the ruins of a castle, founded
in the 14th cent. and occupied down to 1634 by the governors of
Åland. This is one of the most picturesque points among the islands.
About 3 M. to the N.E. of Kastelholm lies the parish of *Sund,* containing a quaint old stone church, above the altar of which are some
ancient sculptures representing the Saviour, the Virgin Mary, and
the Apostles. In the parish of *Saltvik,* 3 M. to the N.W. of Sund,
are the hills of *Orrdalsklint* and *Asgårda Kasberg* (395 ft.), which
may be visited for their extensive views and picturesque cliffs of red
granite. — *Eckerö Storby,* the largest village in the Åland islands,
lies on the island of Eckerö, situated to the W. in the Ålands Haf.

c. From Åbo to Nystad viâ Nådendal.

High Road to (18 Kil. or 11 M.) Nådendal and (83 Kil. or 52 M.)
Nystad. — The sea-journey is, however, preferable. Steamer to Nådendal
and Nystad, see p. 234.

The steamer descends the Runsala Sound, between the islands
of Hirvensalo and Runsala, and enters the *Erstan*, a long fjord
running N. and S. It then turns to the N., leaving *Ekstenholm* on
the left, and enters the *Rauma Sound.* This continues to contract
as we approach Nådendal, before reaching which the steamer has
to pass through an aperture resembling a rocky gate.

20 Kil. (12^1/$_2$ M.) **Nådendal,** Finn. *Naantali* (*Suosio,* hôtel
garni, R. from 3 m.; restaurant in the *Brunnshus,* open in summer
only, D., 2-4 p.m., 3 m.), a small town with 900 inhab., sprang up
round the Bridgittine Nunnery, which was erected here in 1443 and
once enjoyed a great reputation. The ancient *Church,* situated on
the beach to the N. of the town, contains a few old monuments,
paintings, and sculptures. Nådendal is now much frequented as a
bathing-resort from June to Aug., and contains several bathhouses,
with mud and other baths (visitors' tax 12 m.). Visitors should
order their rooms well in advance.

About 15 M. to the N.E. of Nådendal, in the parish of Masku, lies
Kankas, the old domain of the family of *Horn,* the members of which
have played such important parts in the history of Sweden and Finland. The château, a quadrangular building of stone, was erected in the
14th century.

On quitting Nådendal, the steamer passes the sound and church
of *Merimasku* (steamb. stat.). The next part of our route leads to
the W., through an archipelago of innumerable small islands. Finally
we cross a stretch of open water and reach (6 hrs. from Åbo) —

103 Kil. (64 M.) **Nystad,** Finn. *Uusikaupunki* (*Hotel Valhalla,*
R. 2-4, déj. 1^1/$_2$, D. 3 m.; cab from the harbour to the town 1 m.),
a seaport and timber-trading town founded under Gustavus II.

Adolphus in 1617, and containing 4500 inhabitants. The old *Church* (1629) contains a small ethnographical collection. The harbour for the larger steamers is about $^2/_3$ M. to the W. of the town. The peace of Aug. 30th, 1721, which placed Russia in possession of Ingermanland, Esthonia, Livonia, and a part of Karelia, was concluded at Nystad. — About $4^1/_2$ M. to the S. lies *Sundholm*, a beautifully-situated old manor-house.

From Nystad travellers may visit the Finnish towns on the Gulf of Bothnia, by means of the steamers coming from Åbo (comp. p. 234). — *Raumo*, 4 hrs. by steamer from Nystad, see p. 242; *Björneborg*, 4 hrs by steamer from Raumo, see p. 241; *Kristinestad*, see p. 242; *Vasa (Nikolai stad)*, see p. 243.

31. From Helsingfors to Vasa-Nikolaistad, Uleåborg, and Torneå. Ounasvaara.

RAILWAY to (187 Kil. or 116 M.) *Tammerfors* in $5^1/_2$ hrs. (fares 15 m. 50, 9 m. 30, 6 m. 20 p.); to (493 Kil. or 306 M.) *Vasa-Nikolaistad* in 15 hrs. (fares 33 m. 55, 20 m. 15, 13 m. 45 p.); to (752 Kil. or 467 M.) *Uleåborg* in 23 hrs. (fares 42 m. 45, 25 m. 45 p., 17 m.); to (885 Kil. or 550 M.) *Torneå* in 27 hrs. (fares 44 m. 35, 26 m. 60, 17 m. 75 p.). — Sleeping-car to Seinäjoki.

From Helsingfors to (147 Kil. or 91 M.) *Toijala*, see pp. 232, 233. The train turns to the N., and at (166 Kil.) *Lempäälä* (church on the left) crosses a small isthmus between two lakes.

187 Kil. (116 M.) **Tammerfors.** — *Railway Restaurant*, very fair, déj. $1^1/_2$, D. $2^1/_2$ m. — HOTELS. *Central Hotel* (Pl. a; C, 2), Hämeenkatu 17, cor. of the market-place, R. from 5, B. $1^1/_4$-$1^3/_4$, déj. 2, D. 3, S. 2 m.; *Stads-Hotel* (Pl. b; C, 2), Kauppakatu 1, R. from 3, déj. $1^1/_2$, D. $2^1/_2$-3, S. 3 m.; *Emmaus* (Pl. c; D, 2), a so-called 'Christian Hospice', opposite the rail. station, temperance house, R. from $1^1/_2$, déj. 1, D. 2 m. — *Theatre Restaurant* (Pl. C, D, 2; p. 241), déj. $1^1/_2$, D. $2^1/_2$-3, S. $3^1/_2$ m.; *Café Engström.* Hämeenkatu 26, at the corner of Läntinenkatu (Pl. C, 2). — POST OFFICE (Pl. 3; C, 2), Hämeenkatu 22; TELEGRAPH OFFICE (Pl. 7; C, 2), Puuvilla-tehtaankatu 5. — CAB from the rail. station or steamer landing-stage to the town 75 p., per hr. 3 m.; waiting $1^1/_2$ m. per hr.; to the Pyynikki 1 m. -- STEAMERS ply on the Pyhäjärvi to Laukko, Vesilaks, Pirkkala, and Nokia; on the Näsijärvi to Ruovesi, Visuvesi. and Virdois. — BRITISH VICE-CONSUL, *E. Forsström.*

Tammerfors, Finn. *Tampere*, founded in 1779, the largest manufacturing town in the country, lies on both sides of the *Tammerkoski*, a torrent (with a fall of 60 feet in 1 M.) connecting the *Näsijärvi* on the N. with the *Pyhäjärvi* on the S. Pop. 46,500. The foundations of the industry were laid by two Scotsmen, Dr. Patterson and Mr. Finlayson, at the beginning of the 19th century. Several of the mill-managers hail from Lancashire or Yorkshire. — About $^1/_4$ M. to the N. of the rail. station is the *Johanneskyrka* (Pl. D, 2), a noteworthy granite structure by L. Sonck (1907). The somewhat jarring interior contains an altar-piece (Day of Resurrection) by Enckell, while round the front of the gallery runs a frieze (bv Simberg) of nude boys bearing a chain of roses and thorns

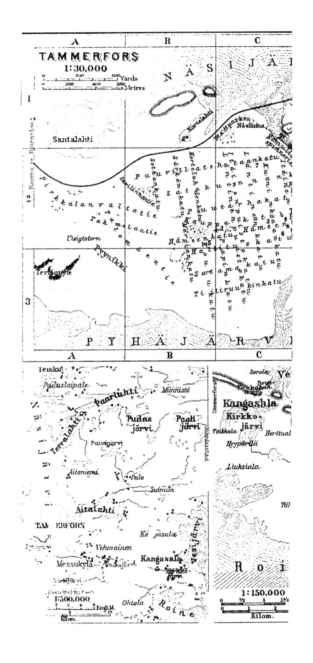

emblematical of the burden of life. In one of the aisles is a crude
piece of symbolism representing the Garden of Death. The Hämeenkatu, the main business thoroughfare, leads W. from the rail. station
to (5 min.) the lower bridge across the Tammerkoski. Both banks are
lined with factories making use of the water-power at their command:
on the right bank are the Frenckell paper works, the oldest in Finland (1805), and (farther to the N.) the cotton mill belonging to the
Nottbeck family. Opposite the latter, on the left bank, are the linen
spinning and weaving mills of the Tammerfors Linen & Iron Manufacturing Co. Beyond the bridge is the Market Place (Finn. Kaup-
patori), on the E. side of which is the *Theatre* (Pl. C, D, 2), with
a terrace overlooking the Tammerkoski (Restaurant, see p. 240).
About 12 min. to the N., on the Näsijärvi, is the *Town Park* (Stads
parken), with the imposing *Hämeen Museo Näsilinnassa* (Pl. C, 1),
containing au ethnological collection and other objects of interest
(open on week-days 10-7, on Sun. 10-2; adm. 50 p.).

About $^3/_4$ M. from the *Alexanderskyrka* (Pl. 1; B, C, 2) is the
view-tower (Utsigts-Torn) on the **Pyynikki** (Pl. A, 2, 3; cab, p. 240;
88 steps; adm. 10 p.), which commands an extensive panorama. To
reach it, we proceed from the church through the Hämeenkatu,
then cross the meadow and ascend through woods. Arriving at the
top of the ridge in 12 min., we turn to the right, and in 3 min. more
we reach the tower. Adjoining are the rocks known as *Thermopylae.*
To the S., on the Pyhäjärvi, is the Pyynikki Restaurant.

EXCURSIONS. A pleasant drive towards the W. (carr. 20-25 m.) may be
made viâ the lunatic asylum of *Pitkäniemi* and Pirkkala (steamer, see
p. 240) to *Nokia* (see below).—Another attractive route leads to the N.W.
viâ *Hämeenkyrö* to the (45 Kil. or 28 M.) *Falls of Kyröskoski* (82 ft.; view-
tower).—Another drive may be taken to Kangasala (p. 242; carr. or motor
car 20-25 m.).—The steamer on the **Näsijärvi** passes the picturesque
parish of *Ylöjärvi* on the left, and the chapel of *Teisko* on the right,
and reaches (2¹/₂ hrs.) *Kuru.* It then proceeds through the *Murole Canal,*
a little to the right of which is the Murole waterfall, and enters *Lake
Ruovesi.* [About 4 M. to the W. of the village of Ruovesi is the *Kovero-
järvi.*] Farther on we may either proceed to the E. through a picturesque
district to *Vilppula,* 1 M. from the station of that name on the Vasa railway (p. 242), or to the N.W. viâ *Visuvesi* to *Virdois,* with the interesting
Toriseva Lakes.

FROM TAMMERFORS TO BJÖRNEBORG, 136 Kil. (85 M.), railway in 4¹/₂ hrs.
(fares 7 m. 5, 4 m. 70 p.). In starting we have a picturesque view of the
town to the left and of the Näsijärvi to the right (see above).—17 Kil.
Nokia (see above), on the river of that name, with a paper mill. Beyond
(26 Kil.) *Siuro* we skirt the *Kulovesi* and then the *Rantavesi,* and beyond
(59 Kil.) *Tyrvää* we traverse an agricultural district. 86 Kil. *Kyttälä.*
Farther on we cross the Kumo-Elf three times, obtaining a good view from
the last bridge. 97 Kil. (60 M.) *Peipohja* (Rail. Restaurant); to Raumo,
see p. 242.—136 Kil. (85 M.) **Björneborg,** Finn. *Pori* (*Hotel Strömlund,*
Nikolaigatan 15; *Otava,* Nikolaigatan 5, R. 2¹/₂-6, déj. 1¹/₄, D. 3 m.; *Restaurant Teaterkällaren,* Rådhus-Torg; cab from the rail. station to the town
75, per drive 50 p.; British Consul, *C. G. Sundell;* Lloyd's Agents, *O. Heine
& Co.*), situated on the S. bank of the *Kumo-Elf,* 4¹/₂ M. from its mouth in
the Gulf of Bothnia, is a town of 16,600 inhab., carrying on a brisk trade in
timber. It received municipal privileges in 1558 and was rebuilt after the

conflagration of 1852. Its port *Mäntyluoto* lies 12¹/₂ M. to the N.W. (branch railway). From the rail. station we follow the Vestra Esplanade in a straight direction, and after 5 min. turn to the left into the Norra Esplanade, which is intersected by the Konstantinsgata and Nikolaigata. In 5 min. more we reach the *Town Hall*, situated on a height above the Kumo-Elf, and commanding a view of the town. About 5 min. to the E., also on the river, is the *Church*, erected by Chiewitz in the Gothic style in 1863, and containing an altar-piece by Ekman. At the corner of the Konstantinsgata and Vladimirsgata is the *Satakunta Museum*. There are many factories in the neighbourhood, and large quantities of salmon are caught in the Kumo.

FROM PEIPOHJA TO RAUMO, 47 Kil. (29 M.), railway in 2 hrs. — *Peipohja*, see p. 241. — Near (20 Kil.) *Panelia* are some prehistoric tumuli. — **Raumo**, Finn. *Rauma* (*Societetshus*, R. 1¹/₂-4¹/₂, déj. 1¹/₂, D. 2¹/₂ m.; cab from the harbour into the town 1 m., from the rail. station 75 p.; steamer to Nystad in 4 hrs.), a quaint old commercial town on the coast, contains 6000 inhab. and received its municipal charter in 1442. Bobbin-lace is made here. The Town Hall contains a museum. The church of Vuonjoki, with its mural paintings, belonged to a Franciscan monastery which was suppressed by Gustavus I. Vasa. — *Kauttua*, situated 30 M. to the E. in the parish of Eura, at the point where the *Eurajoki* emerges from the Pyhäjärvi, was the birthplace of Fredrika Bremer (d. 1866), the well-known novelist. It has a fine park.

Beyond Tammerfors the train runs in a N.E. direction to (200 Kil. or 124 M.) *Kangasala* (posting station).

About 3¹/₂ M. to the S.E. (omn. 50 p.) is the village of **Kangasala** (*Turist-Hotel*), where a good view is obtained from the tower on the *Kirkkoharju (Church Hill)*. To the S., on the N. bank of Lake Roine, we see *Liuksiala*, once the residence of Karin Månsdotter (p. 236). From the Church Hill we keep to the S.E. along the *Kangasala-Ås*, a high narrow ridge between *Längelmävesi* (N.) and *Lake Roine* (S.), and in 50 min. reach the *Keisarinharju (Emperor's Hill)*, the tower on which commands another fine view. The finest and most extensive view of all is, however, afforded by the tower on the *Vehoniemenharju* (to the right of the path), which lies farther to the S., beyond the Kaivanto Canal (simple tourist inn). Comp. Inset Map, p. 241.

229 Kil. *Orihvesi* (Rail. Restaurant). The scenery now becomes dreary. Before reaching (249 Kil.) *Korkeakoski* the train crosses the *Yrösjoki* by a long bridge, and farther on, between (260 Kil.) *Lyly* and (276 Kil.) *Vilppula* (p. 241), we cross the broad Straits of Keuruu. Near (287 Kil.) *Kolho* the train ascends rapidly and then crosses an arm of Lake Keuruunselkä. — 301 Kil. (187 M.) *Haapamäki* (Rail. Restaurant).

From Haapamäki a branch-line runs viâ *Jyväskylä* (p. 219) to (120 Kil. or 75 M.) *Suolahti*, whence the steamer may be taken to *Viitasaari* (Turist-Hotel), a good centre for trout-fishers.

334 Kil. *Myllymäki* (Rail. Restaurant). The railway now runs to the N.W., traversing much wood. 342 Kil. *Inha*, situated on a long and narrow lake surrounded by pine-woods.

419 Kil. (260 M.) **Seinäjoki** (*Railway Restaurant; Hotel* at the station, R. 2-3 m.), the junction of the railway to *Uleåborg* and *Torneå* (p. 244).

From SEINÄJOKI TO KRISTINESTAD, 112 Kil. (70 M.), railway in 3-4 hrs., traversing the fertile S. portion of Österbotten. — 88 Kil. (55 M.) *Perälä*, whence a branch-line runs to (15¹/₂ M.) *Kaskö*, a small seaport (1000 inhab.). — 112 Kil. (70 M.) **Kristinestad** or *Christinestad*, Finn. *Kristiinankau-*

punki (*Hotel Berg;* British vice-consul, *William Hagen*), a seaport upon a peninsula in the parish of Lappfjärd, contains 3300 inhab., and was founded in 1649 by Count Per Brahe. The railway station lies on the E. side of the bay, a bridge across which leads to the town. The hill of *Kvarnbacken*, near the harbour, commands a good view (restaurant). Steamers ply frequently, especially on Sat. and Sun., to the pleasure-garden and restaurant on the island of *Högholmen.* Steamers also ply to Åbo and other ports (comp. p. 240).

We cross the *Kyrönjoki* by a long bridge and enter the more cheerful district of East Bothnia, the fields and meadows of which are only here and there interrupted by marshes — 448 Kil. *Orismala* and (460 Kil.) *Tervajoki.* Both lie in the parish of Storkyrö, which is celebrated for its fields of grain. The parish church, built in 1304 and containing some interesting old mural paintings, lies 5 M. to the N.W. of Orismala. — Near (469 Kil.) *Laihia* are numerous Hunnish graves.

478 Kil. *Toby.* The train now passes *Gamla-Vasa* (see below).

493 Kil. (306 M.) **Vasa** or **Nikolaistad.** — The *Railway Station* lies to the E. of the town. — HOTELS. *Ernst,* Kyrko-Esplanade 16, R. 3-8, déj. 2, D. 3, S. 2 m.; *Central Hotel,* Hofrätts-Esplanade, not far from the rail. station, similar prices. — RESTAURANTS. *Pavilion* (closed in winter), near the Supreme Court and the steamboat-pier, with music frequently in the evenings; *Esplanade Café,* Hofrätts-Esplanade 12; *Sandviks Villa,* to the S. of the town 75 p., per drive 50 p., per hr. 1¹/₂-2 m. — POST OFFICE, at the rail. station. — TELEGRAPH OFFICE, Skolhusgatan 38. — STEAMER to the Finnish coast-towns (see p. 240), also to the Swedish coast-towns. — BRITISH VICE-CONSUL, *Karl Kurten.* — LLOYD'S AGENT, *Arvid Näsman,* Sandogatan 2. — Needlework, etc., may be purchased at the Slöjdbutik, Handels-Esplanade 20.

Vasa, officially styled *Nikolaistad,* Finn. *Nikolain-Kaupunki,* picturesquely situated on the peninsula of *Klemetsö,* is the seat of the Governor of the Län and of one of the three Supreme Courts of Finland, and also the chief commercial town of Österbotten (East Bothnia). Pop. 22,000. The town, which was founded in 1606, received its municipal charter, with the right to bear the name and arms of the Vasas, five years later. The original town (Gamla-Vasa, see above) was burned down in 1852 and was rebuilt on its present site (3 M. farther to the N.W.) under the name of Nikolaistad in 1862. — From the railway station we follow the Hofrätts-Esplanade to the Nikolai-Torg, containing the Lutheran *Church of the Trinity,* built in the Gothic style by Setterberg in 1863, and the *Town Hall,* built by Isæus. To the S. of this square is the *Greek Catholic Church,* commanding a view of the sea. To the W. of it, on the sea, is the *Supreme Court,* a large building surrounded by a park. Close by, to the N., Sandö-gatan 1, is a *Historical Museum* (adm. 25 p.).

A little to the N. lies the island of *Brändö,* connected with the town by a bridge, and containing docks, factories, and warehouses. To the W. of the town are the islands of *Sandö,* with a public park, and *Vasklot,* with a harbour and numerous villas, both also connected with the town by bridges. — *Korsholm,* a little to the S. of Old Vasa, formerly a royal domain and farm with a fortified château, is now an agricultural school. — The 'Great Quarken', forming the channel between Finland and Sweden, is here only about 30 M. wide, and in winter is generally frozen hard enough for traffic across it. Thus, on March 17th, 1809, the Russians under Barclay de Tolly marched from here to Umeå over the ice.

The RAILWAY FROM SEINÄJOKI TO TORNEÅ at first runs to the N. across the level plains of Österbotten (E. Bothnia). Farther on it bends somewhat to the E. and ascends gradually to the wooded region. Between Seinäjoki and Uleåborg we cross 121 bridges. Beyond (424 Kil. or 263 M. from Helsingfors) *Nurmo* we twice cross the *Lappoå* (Finn. *Lapuanjoki*). 442 Kil. *Lapua*, a large village with a monument commemorating the battle between the Russians and Finns on July 8th, 1808. 456 Kil. *Kauhava* (230 ft.; Rail. Restaurant) is known for its manufacture of curious knives (on sale at the railway station). 474 Kil. *Härmä*. The train descends along the Lapuanjoki to (497 Kil.) *Jeppo* (Finn. *Jepua*), and bends slightly to the N.E. —510 Kil. (317 M.) *Kovjoki*.

About 5¹/₂ M. to the W. of Kovjoki (branch-line), and 2¹/₂ M. from the mouth of the Lapuanjoki in the Gulf of Bothnia, on two rapids formed by that river (view from the bridge), lies **Nykarleby,** Finnish *Uusikar-lepyy (Stads-Hotel*, R. 2¹/₂-3¹/₂, déj. 1¹/₂, D. 2¹/₂ m.), a small town with 1250 inhab. and a normal school. *Zakris Topelius* (1818-98), a popular Finnish poet, was born here. —About 3 M. to the S. lies *Jutas*, the scene of a Swedish victory over the Russians on Sept. 13th, 1808. It contains a handsome monument erected in 1885, with a medallion-portrait of Colonel von Döbeln, leader of the Swedes. The decisive battle of the campaign, however, in which the Russians were victorious, took place on Sept. 14th, 1808, at *Oravais*, 21 M. to the S., on the road to Vasa.

The railway now once more approaches the coast. —519 Kil. (322 M.) *Bennäs*.

From Bennäs a branch-railway runs to (8 Kil. or 5 M.) **Jakobstad,** Finn. *Pietarsaari (Stads-Hotel*, R. 3¹/₂-6 m.; cab from rail. station to the town 75 p., from the harbour 1¹/₂ m.), an industrial and commercial town with 6700 inhabitants. Its port, with which it is connected by railway, lies 2 M. from the town, on the island of *Alholm* (Alheda Temperance Rest-aurant). A good view is obtained from the tower of the town-hall, which lies ¹/₄ M. to the W. of the rail. station. — Jakobstad was the birthplace of J. L. Runeberg (1804-77), and 2¹/₂ M. to the N.E. of the town (cab 1¹/₄ m.) and 1 M. to the E. of Alholm, is *Runeberg's Stuga*, a favourite resort of the poet in his youth. — About ²/₃ M. to the S. (cab 75 p.) is the parish church of *Pedersö*, built of granite blocks about 1250.

Farther on we cross several littoral streams. — 526 Kil. *Kållby*.

552 Kil. (343 M.) **Gamla-Karleby,** Finn. *Kokkola (Societets-hus,* opposite the rail. station, R. 2¹/₂-5 m.; Brit. vice-consul, *Carl J. Forsén),* a trading-town with 4100 inhab., founded in 1620. The port *Yxpila* lies 3 M. to the W. of the town (railway 6 times daily, fare 25 p.; carr. 2 m.).

In June, 1854, a small detachment of English sailors and marines landed here to compel the burgomaster to surrender the public funds in his hands, but fell into an ambuscade and lost their leader. A flotilla of small boats afterwards endeavoured to avenge this check, but were beaten off by the fire of the soldiery from Vasa, with the loss of a gun and 29 seamen. One of the boats was also captured, and is still exhibited here. The pretty *Cemetery* contains a monument to the memory of three English seamen who fell on this occasion.

The railway now turns to the E. and crosses the *Perhonjoki*. At (592 Kil.) *Kannus,* where a halt of 20 min. is made for dinner, we cross the *Lestijoki.* At (614 Kil.) *Sievi* we cross the *Sievijoki,* and at (631 Kil.) *Ylivieska* we cross the *Kalajoki.* At (643 Kil.) *Kangas,* the train turns to the N., and just short of (659 Kil.) *Oulainen* it crosses the *Pyhäjoki.* — 699 Kil. (434 M.) *Lappi* (Rail. Restaurant).

From Lappi a branch-railway runs to (28 Kil. or 17¹/₂ M.) **Brahestad,** Finn. *Raahe* (*Lagerstam*, R. 2-5 m.; cab from the rail. station to the town 50 p.; bathing-house on the beach), a clean-looking town of 3600 inhab. in the parish of Salo, founded by Count Per Brahe in 1649. It possesses a good harbour and carries on considerable trade and manufactures. About ¹/₃ M. to the N.W. of the rail. station is a square, with a bronze statue of Per Brahe, a replica of that in Åbo (p. 235). A little to the N. is a wooden church dating from 1651. — *Salo,* 3 M. to the S. of Brahestad, has a quaint church of 1622, with mural paintings and images of saints.

Near (706 Kil.) *Ruukki* we cross the *Siikajoki.* At (729 Kil.) *Liminka* the train reaches the coast, which it skirts to (742 Kil.) *Kempele.*

754 Kil. (468 M.) **Uleåborg.** — The *Railway Station* lies to the E. of the town. — HOTELS. *Societetshus,* R. 3¹/₂-6, déj. 2, D. 3, S. 2 m.; *Nya Hotel,* at the station, R. 1¹/₂-3, déj. 1¹/₄, D. 1¹/₂ m., a temperance house; *Turist-Hotel,* at the station, similar prices. — RESTAURANT. *Raatti,* on the island of that name. — CAB from the rail. station or the Kurkela bridge to the town 75, per drive 50 p., per hr. 2¹/₂ m. — BRITISH VICE-CONSUL, *J. R. Weckman.* — LLOYD'S AGENT, *Viktor Höckert.* — STEAM LAUNCHES to Raatti 10 p., to Toppila (see below) 20 p.

Uleåborg, Finn. *Oulu,* a prosperous commercial and industrial town (leather) with 21,000 inhab., founded in 1605, lies on the left bank of the *Oulunjoki,* at the point where it flows into the Gulf of Bothnia. From the rail. station we follow the Stationsgata for 7 min., and then proceed to the right through the Kyrkogata to the Franzén Esplanade, in which is a bronze bust (by Stenberg) of *F. M. Franzén,* the poet, who was a native of Uleåborg (1772-1847). On the N. side of the Esplanade is the house of the governor of the province; on the E. side is the church, near which is the grave of Messenius (p. 217). About ¹/₂ M. to the N., in the *Merikoski,* are the *Frihetsholmarne* or Islands of Freedom. A little to the N.W. of the Esplanade is a bridge leading to the island of *Raatti.* The curious funnel-shaped wooden structures (so-called Pata) here projecting into the river are for catching salmon, and are generally cleared about 5 p.m.

A branch-line runs to the N.W. to (4 Kil.) *Toppila,* the port of Uleåborg, containing a large tar-depot (50-60,000 barrels annually).

FROM ULEÅBORG TO THE RAPIDS OF THE OULUNJOKI. We first take the steamer to *Muhos* (p. 218), then go on by land to (8 M.) *Merilä* (p. 218), whence we descend the rapids in a small boat (comp. p. 218). A motor service to *Vaala* is in view.

The railway to Torneå (53 bridges) crosses the Oulunjoki just beyond Uleåborg, and then runs to the N. at a short distance from the E. coast of the Gulf of Bothnia.—859 Kil. (534 M.) *Kemi* (Rail. Restaurant; Anna Kiemelä's Inn), a small town with 2000 inhabitants.

From Kemi a branch-line (114 Kil. or 71 M., in 4¹/₂ hrs.) runs to the N.E. up the right bank of the *Kemijoki*, which is often visible from the train, to *Rovaniemi* (inn), a small town at the confluence of the *Ounasjoki*, descending from the N., with the Kemijoki. Opposite, on the left bank of the Kemijoki (short boat-trip, then ¹/₂ hr.'s walk), rises the hill of **Ounasvaara** (710 ft.), from which the midnight sun may be seen between June 18th and June 28th.

The train to Torneå crosses the Kemijoki (see above).

885 Kil. (550 M.) **Torneå,** Finn. *Tornio (Societetshus).* From the rail. station, which lies on the left bank of the wide and rapid *Torniojoki*, a steam-ferry plies to the little town (1700 inhab.), situated on the right bank. It is the northernmost town in Finland, and lies on the Swedish frontier. The wooden church built in 1684 is still in its original condition, and contains some ceiling paintings. Many salmon are caught in the Torniojoki.—To the S. is a bridge leading across a shallow arm of the river to the Swedish town of *Haparanda* (Stads-Hotel, very fair). For details, see *Baedeker's Norway and Sweden.*

About 54 M. (87 Kil.) to the N. of Torneå, on the Finnish side of the boundary, at the confluence of the *Tengeli* with the Torniojoki, rises the hill of **Avasaxa** (730 ft.), which is visited annually on June 22-25th by crowds of tourists for the view of the midnight sun (the Ounasvaara, see above, is more accessible). The top, on which stands a shelter-hut, is reached by a climb of ³/₄ hr. Numerous names of visitors have been carved in the rock here. The trip to Avasaxa and back takes three days by carriage (30 m., with two horses 50 m.); there is also a motor service. Nightquarters are provided at the farms of *Hannukka* and *Juuso,* but the traveller should bring his own provisions.

V. CENTRAL AND NORTHERN RUSSIA.

32. From Warsaw to Moscow viâ Brest and Smolensk.

1224 V. (811 M.). Express train, with through-carriages, in 24$^1/_2$ hrs. Fares 30 rb. 40, 20 rb. 60 cop.; reserved seat (p. xxiii) 2 rb. 40 cop.; sleeping-car 9 rb. 80, 7 rb. 35 cop. Train de luxe once weekly in 24 hrs. (fare 44 rb. 10 cop.). Ordinary train in 37 hrs.; fares 24 rb. 50, 14 rb. 70 cop. Most of the trains start from the Brest Station, but some of the expresses start from the Kovel Station. The line between Brest and Moscow was christened the *Alexander Railway* in 1912, in memory of the events of 1812.

From Wirballen viâ Vilna (carriages changed), Novo-Vileisk, and Minsk (junction-line between the two stations; change) to (1067 V. or 707 M.) Moscow in 25$^1/_4$ hrs. (fares 22 rb. 50, 13 rb. 50 cop.; extra charge for express train and reserved seat); the through-carriages from Wirballen to Moscow take no less than 36 hrs.

Warsaw, see p. 9. The train runs towards the E. and at first traverses the battlefield of Grochów (p. 25). — 35 V. *Novo-Minsk*, a town of 7000 inhab. on the *Srebrna*, which must not be confounded with the capital of the government of Minsk (p. 250). Branch-railways run to (25 V.) Pilawa (p. 27) and to (33 V.) Tłuszcz (p. 44).

84 V. (56 M.) **Siedlce**, Сѣдлецъ, or *Syedletz* (*Rail. Restaurant; Victoria*, R. 1-2 rb., D. 70 cop.; cab from the station to the town 25 cop.), a town of 34,000 inhab., contains a large château, formerly belonging to Prince Oginski, and an interesting old building, which once served as town hall. — A branch-railway runs hence to (63 V.; 2$^1/_2$ hrs.) Małkinia (p. 44).

FROM SIEDLCE TO POLOTZK, 594 V. (394 M.), railway in 18 hrs. —
Beyond (41 V.) *Plydterowo* we cross the *Bug.* 85 V. *Tcherémkha,* the
junction for the railway from Białystok to Brest-Litovsk (p. 45); 113 V.
Gáinovka (p. 45). Beyond (131 V.) *Nárevka* we cross the stream of that
name.—Just short of (185 V.) *Bagrationovskaya* (Rail. Restaurant; p. 45)
we cross the *Rossa,* and before reaching (219 V.) *Mosti* (Rail. Restaurant)
we cross the *Niemen.* From Mosti a branch-line runs to (55 V.) Grodno
(p. 45).—288 V. *Lida* (Rail. Restaurant; p. 39). Beyond (353 V.) *Voigyani*
(Rail. Restaurant) we skirt the *Berézina* at places. 407 V. *Molo'détchno*
(Rail. Restaurant; p. 39). We now cross the *Viliyá.* 488 V. *Parafíanovo*
(Rail. Restaurant). After passing (526 V.) *Podsvílye* the train traverses
a hilly and wooded region, dotted with numerous lakes.—As we approach
(594 V. or 394 M.) *Pólotzk* (p. 255) we cross the *Dviná.*

110 V. (73 M.) *Łukόw* (Rail. Restaurant), a town with 10,500
inhab., whence a branch-line runs S.W. to (57 V.; 2 hrs.) Ivangorod
(p. 27) and another to the S. to (104 V.; 4 hrs.) Lublin (p. 28).

159 V. *Biała,* Бѣла, a district town with 22,000 inhab. situated
on the *Krzna* or *Trzna.*—The train now skirts the fortifications
of Brest, and crosses the *Bug* by an iron lattice bridge.

199V. (132 M.) **Brest-Litόvsk** (Брестъ-Литовскъ), Pol. *Brześć
Litewski* (445 ft.; *Rail. Restaurant,* very fair; *Victoria, Bristol,
Yevrόpa,* R. 1¹/₂-5 rb.; cab from station to town 30 cop.), a town of
57,000 inhab. (half of them Jews) in the government of Grodno, is
the seat of a Greek Catholic bishop and the headquarters of the 19th
Army Corps. It consists of the new town, laid out in 1833 on the
right bank of the *Muchawiec,* which here flows into the Bug, and
of the strong fortress on the right bank of the Bug, 1¹/₄ M. distant.

FROM BREST-LITOVSK TO KHOLM, 107 V. (71 M.), railway in 4 hrs. —
61 V. *Włodawa,* a district town with 11,700 inhab. on the upper Bug; 100 V.
Ruda, with glass-works.—107 V. *Kholm,* see p. 29.

FROM BREST-LITOVSK TO BRYANSK, 757 V. (502 M.), railway in 26 hrs.
The railway traverses, from W. to E., the *Polyésye* (Полѣсье, i.e. 'forest land'), a large triangular district (33,600 sq. M. in extent) consisting
of forests, marshes, lakes, and meadows, between Brest-Litovsk, Mohilev,
and Kiev; drainage operations were begun in 1875.—At (24 V.) *Zhábinka*
(p. 250) our line diverges to the right from that to Minsk, and follows
the left bank of the Pripet. 46 V. *Kóbrin* (Rail. Restaurant), a district
town with 11,300 inhab. on the Dnieper & Bug Canal.—159 V. *Pinsk* (Rail.
Restaurant; Bassévitch, Bolshaya Kiyevskaya, R. 60 cop. to 2¹/₂ rb.; cab from
the station to the town 40 cop.), the chief town of a district in the government of Minsk, with 37,000 inhab. (incl. many Jews), situated on the *Pina.*
It contains large factories for making Russian leather. A steamer plies
hence viâ the prettily situated town of Mozuir (see below) to (2 days) Kiev
(p. 377).—214 V. *Luninétz* (Rail. Restaurant), see p. 39; 283 V. *Zhitkovitchi*
(Rail. Restaurant). About 12 V. (8 M.) to the S. of the station of (380 V.)
Mózuir (Rail. Restaurant) is the above-mentioned town of 10,700 inhab.
(izvόshtchik in summer 1¹/₂ rb.). 416 V. *Vasilevitchi* (Rail. Restaurant).
Beyond (456 V.) *Ryétchitza* (Rail. Restaurant) we cross the Dnieper, and
beyond (497 V.) *Homel* (p. 39) we cross the Sozh.--From (564 V.) *Novo-
zuibkóv* (Rail. Restaurant), a district-town in the government of Tchernigov, with 21,500 inhab., a branch-railway runs to (113 V.) *Nόvgorod-Syeversk*
(Rail. Restaurant), an old town of the government of Tchernigov, with
12,700 inhab., situated on the *Desná.*—628 V. *Unétcha,* 679 V. *Potchép,*
both with rail. restaurants.—757 V. (502 M.) *Bryansk,* see p. 376.

From Brest-Litovsk to *Odessa,* see R. 52; to *Białystok,* see p. 45.

16*

The train runs through the wooded and monotonous governments of Grodno (occupied by White Russians; p. xli), Minsk, and Smolensk. —224 V. *Zhábinką* (Жабинка); to Bryansk, see p. 249. 292 V. *Pogodino* (Rail. Restaurant); 389 V. *Baránovitchi*, the junction of the railways to Białystok (p. 45), and to Vilna and Rovno (p. 39).

520 V. (345 M.) **Minsk.** — There are two *Railway Stations* (both with restaurants), the Brest Station to the S.W. of the town, the Romni Station to the S. — Hotels. *Grand-Hôtel Garni*, Sakháryevskaya, at the corner of the Bogodyélnaya; *Paris*, Sakháryevskaya, adjoining the Lutheran Church, with a good restaurant; *Novo-Moskóvskaya*, Sakháryevskaya 86, R. 1-5¹/₂, D. (2-5 p.m.) 1 rb., with a restaurant frequented by Germans; *Odessa*, opposite the Grand-Hôtel. — Cab from the railway stations to the town 50 or 40 cop. — Tramway from the railway stations through the town 6 cop. — Post & Telegraph Office, Gubernátorskaya.

Minsk, the capital of the government of the same name, is situated on both sides of the *Svislotch,* a tributary of the Berézina, and is the seat of a Greek Catholic bishop and the headquarters of the 4th Army Corps. It contains 105,000 inhab., one-half of whom are Jews, and carries on an important trade, holding a yearly fair in March. The lines of streets leading from the railway stations (tramway, see above) unite at the corner of the Sakháryevskaya and the Kolómenskaya. To reach this point from the Brest Station we first take a few steps to the right, then proceed to the left through the Moskóvskaya, and, beyond the Libau & Romni Railway, turn to the right into the Sakháryevskaya (25 min.). From the Romni Station we turn to the left, then follow the Peterbúrgskaya to the right, and finally turn to the left and follow the Kolómenskaya to the Sakháryevskaya (10 min.). Proceeding along the Sakháryevskaya to the right, we reach (10 min.) the Gubernátorskaya, one of the chief business-streets. Here we proceed either in a straight direction, passing the *Lutheran Church,* to the *Alexander Square* (r.), or we may turn to the left along the Gubernátorskaya and reach the (4 min.) Sobórnaya Sq., on the right side of which are the *District Courts* and the *Greek Catholic Cathedral of SS. Peter & Paul,* founded in the 16th cent. and rebuilt in 1857, while to the left are the *House of the Governor* and the *Roman Catholic Cathedral.* About 5 min. to the E. of the Alexander Square is the *Governor's Garden,* where a band plays on summer evenings.

From Minsk to *Vilna* or to *Romni*, see p. 39.

597 V. (396 M.) **Borísov** *(Rail. Restaurant).* The town of the same name *(Kommértcheskaya Hotel),* the chief town of a district, lies 2 M. to the N. of the station (cab 50 cop.), on the left bank of the *Berézina* (p. 251) and contains 19,400 inhab. (half of them Jews). — About 8 M. to the N.W. of Borisov (carr. in 1¹/₂ hr.; fare, there & back, 3-4 rb.), lies the village of *Studyónka* (see p. 251) on a slope rising from the left bank of the Berézina. The spot where the French crossed the river in 1812 is now marked by two simple monuments. Comp. the Inset Map, p. 251.

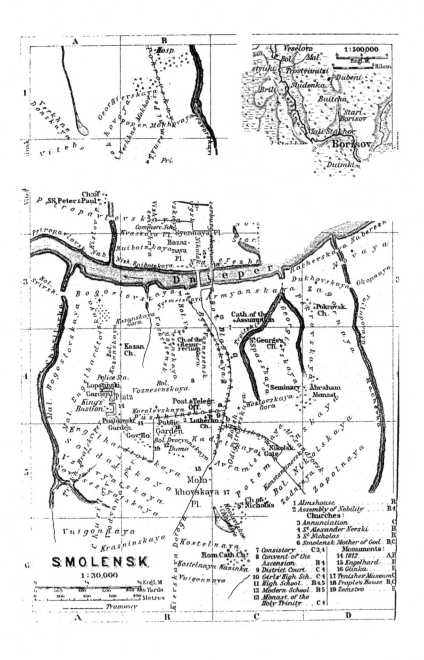

Hosp.

A   B

1:500,000
Engl. M
Kilom.

Veselovo
Bol.   Mal.
struki
Trostyanitsi
Dubeni
Brili   Studenka
Buitcha
Start.
Borisov
Mali Stakhor
Borisov
Duimki

Verkhne Donskaya
viteb.
Georgievskaya
Pop. Mokhora
Verkhne Mokhora
Tyurenkaya
Pri.

SMOLENSK

1:30,000

0   ¼   ½ Engl.M
250   500   750   800 850 Yards
200   400   600   800   Metres
Tramway

Ch. of
SS. Peter & Paul
Petropavlovskaya
Petropavlorsk. Nab.
Commerc. Sch.
Kvaskova Ul.   Syennaya Pl.
Ruibatzkaya   Bazar-
naya
Nizh. Ruibatskaya   Pl.

D n **i** e p e r

Kacherskaya Naberezh.
Naberezh.
Naberezhnaya Naberezh
Star.

Bol. Srtrsk.
Bogoslovskaya
Kuzanskaya Gora
Bol. Kazanskaya
Kazan. Ch.
Mal. Bogoslovskaya
Engelhardtovskaya
Police Sta.
Lopatinski Garden
King's Bastion
Pushkinski Garden
Gov. Ho.
Bol. Voznesenskaya
Kralevskaya
Push
Public
Garden
Bol. Dvoryanskaya
Duma
Engelhard
Solovskaya
Vsgratskaya
Resestrovskaya
Podvalnaya
Vuigonnaya
Krasninskaya
Kierskaya Doroga

Dremetskaya
Armyanskaya
Blagov
Ch. of the Resurrection
Nosovskaya
Post & Teleg. Off.
Kaduetskaya
Avramie
Konstantinovsk
Potem
Molo-
khovskaya
Pl.
Rom. Cath. Ch.
Kostelnaya
Kostelnaya Kazinka
Vuigonnaya

Cath. of the Assumption
St. George's Ch.
Spasskaya
Georgievskaya
Seminary   Abraham Monast.
Khovlovskaya Gora
Nikolsk. Gate
Bol. Nikolskaya
Zadnaya
Ch. of
St. Nicholas

Dukhovskaya   Okonnaya
Zago
Pokrovsk. Ch.
Zaprosslovskaya
Zaprosslovskaya
Kach
Zaprosslovskaya
Zapolnaya

1 Almshouse . . . . . . B
2 Assembly of Nobility . . . B4
    Churches:
3 Annunciation C
4 St. Alexander Nevski . . B
5 St. Nicholas . . . . . B
6 Smolensk Mother of God . BC
7 Consistory . . . C3,4   **Monuments:**
8 Convent of the   14 1812 . . . . . AB
    Ascension . . B4   15 Engelhard . . . B
9 District Court. . . C4   16 Glinka . . . . . B
10 Girls' High Sch. . C4   17 Tenishev Museum C
11 High School . . B4,5   18 People's House B,C
12 Modern School . B5   19 Zemstvo . . . . B
13 Monast. of the
    Holy Trinity . . C4

Beyond Borisov the course of the railway corresponds pretty closely with the line of retreat followed by the French Grande Armée in 1812. A certain historical interest is thus imparted to our journey, which offers few scenic attractions. Just beyond Borisov we cross the **Berézina** by a long bridge. This river, which is nowhere more than about 100 ft. wide, winds sluggishly and circuitously through a tract of marshy pastures, $1/_4$-$1/_2$ M. in width.

On the evening of Nov. 13th (Nov. 25th), 1812, the day before the famous passage of the Berézina by the French, the main body of Napoleon's crippled army was either at Borisov or on the way to it. In all Napoleon had 31,000 men under arms, with 250 guns, besides 35,000 disorganized and unarmed stragglers. — On Nov. 14th, when the French began to cross the Berézina, it had overflowed its banks and was full of large masses of ice. The right bank of the Berézina was guarded by a Russian corps of 31,500 men under Tchitchagóv, but Napoleon managed to deceive this general as to his intended place of crossing, and succeeded after incredible exertions in constructing two wooden bridges at *Studyónka* (Студенка). On Nov. 15th Napoleon crossed the river with the Old Guard. On Nov. 16th the French on the left bank, under Victor, were attacked by Wittgenstein at the head of 30,000 men, while a simultaneous attack was delivered by Tchitchagóv against Oudinot and Ney on the right bank. The French, however, succeeded in maintaining their positions. In the night of Nov. 16-17th Marshal Victor, who had covered the passage of the main body, also crossed to the right bank of the Berézina. All semblance of order was now lost, and the rumour that Kutúzov's army was approaching intensified the fear and confusion. A general *sauve qui peut* took place, and thousands of unhappy soldiers were drowned in the river. The total French loss amounted to 30,000 men. — Of the army of 108,000 men with which Napoleon had left Moscow nothing now remained but 36,000 demoralized fugitives, making their way as best they could to Vilna.

720 V. (477 M.) *Orsha* (Rail. Restaurant). The town of this name, which is first mentioned in 1067, is the capital of a district and is prettily situated on both banks of the *Dnieper*, 2 M. to the S. of the rail. station (cab 60 cop.). Pop. 21,000, mostly Jews. Branch-railways run N. to Vitebsk (p. 257) and S. to Mohilev (Zhlobin, pp. 257, 258). — 769 V. *Krásnoye* (Rail. Restaurant). At the little town of *Krásnoye*, 13 M. to the S. of (790 V.) *Gúsino*, the corps of Ney and Davout were almost annihilated in the battles of Nov. 3rd and 6th (O.S.), during the retreat of the French army.

832 V. (552 M.) **Smolénsk, Смоленскъ.** — *Rail. Restaurant*, very fair. — HOTELS. *Grand-Hôtel* (Pl. b; C, 4, 5), Bolshaya Blagovyéshtchenskaya, R. $3/_4$-3 rb.; *Yevropéiskaya* (Pl. a; C, 4), Púshkinskaya 2, with pleasure-garden and variety-theatre, R. $3/_4$-3 rb., B. 50, D. (1-5 p.m.) 50-70 cop. Rooms ($1^1/_2$-2 rb.; D. 1 rb.) may also be obtained in the *Club of the Noblesse* (Благородное собрáніе; Pl. c, B, C, 4), Púshkinskaya (well spoken of). — CAB (with two horses) from the railway stations to the town 50, from the town to the station 40, per drive 20, per hr. 40 cop. Sleighs (in winter) 30, 25, 15, 30 cop. — ELECTRIC TRAMWAYS run from the stations through the town. — POST & TELEGRAPH OFFICE (Pl. B, 4), in the Potchtamtskaya.

Smolénsk (590 ft.), the capital of the government of the same name and the headquarters of the 13th Army Corps, contains 71,000 inhab. and is prettily situated on both banks of the Dnieper. The main and older part of the town is enclosed by a wall and lies amid trees on the left bank, which slopes abruptly to the *Rátchevka*, the *Tchurílovka*, and the Dnieper. The St. Petersburg Suburb, containing the two railway stations, lies upon the right side of the river.

Smolensk, the 'Key and the Gate of Russia', was, according to the ancient chronicler Nestor, the capital of the Slavonic *Krivitchi* (Krevos or Krevs). Towards the end of the 9th cent. *Olég* (p. xlvii) descended the Dnieper to Kiev, conquering on his way Smolensk, Tchernigov, and the other Slavonic towns on that river. Down to 1054 the province of Smolensk formed part of the principality of Kiev, and afterwards it frequently changed masters. Among the numerous sieges it underwent was an attack by Muscovites and Tartars in 1340. In 1408 the town surrendered, after a siege of 7 weeks, to the Lithuanians. It attained its greatest prosperity in the 16th cent., when it is said to have contained 200,000 inhabitants. In 1514 it was captured by the Muscovites under Grand-Prince Vasili III., and in 1611 by the Poles, who ceded it to Russia in 1667. — At the beginning of Aug., 1812, the two Russian Armies of the West, under Bagration and Barclay de Tolly, joined their forces at Smolensk, to which Gneisenau had already advanced 'the real line of defence'. On Aug. 4th (16th) the French advanced against the town, which was defended by Dokhtúrov. During the two days' battle (Aug. 5th and 6th) for the possession of Smolensk, the greater part of the town was burned to the ground. On the retreat of the Grande Armée Napoleon entered the town on Oct. 28th (Nov. 9th) and spent four days here in a vain attempt to reorganize his demoralized forces.

From the railway stations (Pl. A, 2) we proceed to the S.E., cross the (25 min.) Dnieper bridge, and enter the old town. This is surrounded by the remains of a crenelated brick and stone wall fully 3 M. long, 30-50 ft. high, and 10-20 ft. thick, dating from the time of Boris Godunóv (1596-1602). It was originally strengthened with 38 square and other towers, but only 16 of these are extant.

On a hill to the S. of the bridge lies the *Cathedral of the Assumption* (Успéнскій соборъ; Pl. C, 3), a huge building with five domes, dominating the whole city. It was founded at the beginning of the 12th cent., destroyed by the Poles in 1611, after their capture of the town, and restored in 1772. In the interior is an ikonostás of gilded lime-wood, 33 ft. high. On the pillar in front of it, to the left, is a winding-sheet embroidered with the Entombment, dating from 1561 (Плащанйца), and on that to the right is a wonder-working picture of the Virgin, said to have been painted by St. Luke. This was brought to Tchernigov about the middle of the 11th cent. by the Greek Princess Anna and was transferred to Smolensk in 1103. — In the Bolshaya Blagovyésbtchenskaya, the main street of the town, stands the *District Court* (Окрýжной судъ; Pl. 9, C 4), from which the Púshkinskaya leads towards the W. On the left side of this latter street is the *Lutheran Church* (Pl. B, 4). In the Public Garden is a bronze statue of *M. I. Glinka* (Pl. 16; B, C, 5), the composer of the opera 'A Life for the Tzar' (b. in the province of Smolensk in 1804, d. in 1857). The monument, designed by Bock, was unveiled in 1885. In the Dvoryánskaya, a little to the S., is the *Duma* (Pl. B, 5), on the third floor of which is a small

Archæological Museum (open free on Wed. & Sun., 12-3). The fire-watcher's tower in the same building affords an admirable view (186 steps). The W. prolongation of the Púshkinskaya leads to the so-called *King's Bastion* (Королéвская Крѣпость; Pl. A, 4), the citadel built by Sigismund III. of Poland in 1611. To the E. of the citadel is the *Monument of 1812* (Pl. 14), a cast-iron pyramid erected in 1841 to commemorate the battles around Smolensk.—On the N. side of the Molokhovskaya Square (Pl. B, 5) are a memorial to *Lieut. Col. von Engelhard* (Pl. 15), who was shot here by the French in 1812, and (a little to the W.) the *New Monument of 1812*, by Schutzmann (1913). On the E. side of the square is the *Historical and Ethnological Museum of Princess M. K. Tenisheva* (Pl. 17), containing collections of archæology, ethnology, and local art, Old Russian silverware, pictures of saints, old prints & engravings, and musical instruments (including 'balaláikas' with modern paintings). The museum is open on Thurs. & Sun., 10-3 (adm. 15 cop.); it is closed from June to Sept., but strangers may obtain admission by applying to the Conservator Bartchevski, who lives in the building. The churches of *SS. Peter & Paul* (Pl. A, 2; the W. part rebuilt), and of the *Archangel Michael* (also called *Svirskaya;* beyond Pl. A, 3), are two quaint-looking buildings of the 12th century. In the latter church is the tomb of its founder, Prince David Rosti-slavitch (d. 1197).

FROM SMOLENSK TO OREL, 361 V. (239 M.), railway in 10 hrs. The railway runs through a wooded region viâ (56 V.) *Potchinók* (Rail. Restaurant) to (111 V.) *Róslavl* (650 ft.; Rail. Restaurant), a district-town in the government of Smolensk, situated on the *Oster* (pron. Ostyór) and containing 27,500 inhabitants.—Beyond (147 V.) *Syéshtchinskaya* the train enters the government of Orel. Interminable undulating plains lie on both sides of the track. Large areas are planted with rye, buckwheat, and flax. The villages lie closer together than in the governments more to the W. The houses are well built, clean, and larger; their façades are often adorned with quaint and attractive wood-carvings.—We next pass through the Bryansk Forest. 183 V. *Zhúkovka* (Rail. Restaurant); 236 V. *Bryansk* (525 ft.; Rail. Restaurant), see p. 376; 277 V. *Karátchev* (Rail. Restaurant), a district-town with 20,700 inhab., mentioned as early as 1146; 303 V. *Khotuinétz* (825 ft.), the highest point on the line from Riga to Orel.—361 V. (239 M.) *Orél*, see p. 361.

FROM SMOLENSK TO SUKHINITCHI, 220 V. (145 M.), railway in 8 hrs.—76 V. *Yélnya;* 133 V. *Spas-Demenskóye.*—220 V. *Sukhinitchi* (p. 376).

From Smolensk to *Riga*, see R. 33a.

891 V. *Yártzevo* (Rail. Restaurant).— Beyond (928 V.) *Doro-gobúzh* (Rail. Restaurant) we cross the Dnieper. The town of that name (pop. 7600) lies 14 M. to the S. of the Dnieper.

997 V. (661 M.) **Vyazma** or Вязьма (*Rail. Restaurant; Centrálnaya*, R. 1-2½ rb.; izvóshtchik from the station to the town 40-45 cop.), the chief town of a district in the government of Smolensk, lies on the *Vyazma*. Pop. 29,600. The Vyázemskiye Pry-ániki (a kind of gingerbread) made here enjoy a great reputation.

From Vyazma to Tula, 279 V. (185 M.), railway in 8 hrs. The railway runs towards the S.E. — 155 V. **Kalúga** (475 ft.; *Rail. Restaurant; Riga*, Kutúzovskaya 161, R. $^3/_4$-2, D. 1 rb., omn. 30 cop.; *Kulon*, Nikitskaya, good cuisine at both), the capital of the government of the same name and the seat of the Bishop of Kaluga and Bórovsk, lies on the left bank of the *Oká*, which is here about 220 yds. wide, and on the *Yátchenka*, which here joins the larger river. Pop. 55,000. The town lies about 2 M. to the S.W. of the railway station (izvóshtchik to the town in summer 50-60, in winter 40-50 cop.). There is a good bathing-establishment on the Oká. In 1611 the second False Demetrius was shot by the Tartar prince Urúsov while hunting near Kaluga. The house in which the False Demetrius lived with Marina Mniszek (Дворéцъ Марйны Мнйшекъ) is still well preserved, and now contains a historical museum (open daily, 11-3; adm., 10 cop.). The town park on the Oká contains a restaurant and music pavilion and commands a fine and extensive view. There is a Lutheran church. A branch-railway runs from Kaluga to (17 V.) Tikhonova-Pustuin (p. 376). — Between (220 V.) *Aléxin* (Rail. Restaurant) and (228 V.) *Ryúrikovo* the train crosses the Oká. — 279 V. (185 M.) *Tula*, see p. 360.

From Vyazma to *Likhoslávl*, see p. 267.

1056 V. *Gzhatsk* (Гжатскъ; Rail. Restaurant), a town of 9700 inbab. and capital of a district in the government of Smolensk. — 1095 V. *Uvárovka*. About 16$^1/_2$ M. to the N. (cab 4-5 rb., there & back) lies the village of *Poryétchye*, containing the château of Count Uvárov with its rich collections of art and archæology.

1111 V. (736 M.) *Borodinó*. At the rail. station is the Borodino Museum, with portraits, maps, etc. (key with the station-master).

The undulating plain that stretches N. from the station to the (2$^1/_2$ M.) village of Borodino was, on Aug. 26th (Sept. 7th), 1812, the scene of the **Battle of Borodinó**, which the French call the 'Bataille de la Moskova', though that river lies 4$^1/_2$ M. to the E. of the village. The Russian army under Kutúzov, consisting of 104,000 men, with 637 guns, took up its position here in a final effort to save Moscow from Napoleon, who had over 124,000 men with 587 guns, under his command. The points against which the French directed their chief attack were the three Bagration Redoubts near Semenovskoye and the Rayev Redoubt ('Grande Redoute'), all of which were assaulted with great spirit but no less valiantly defended. At the end of the day the French were in possession of the hard-won field, though they allowed the Russians to retire unpursued. It was the most sanguinary battle that Napoleon ever fought, as the French casualties amounted to 28,000 and those of the Russians to 44,000. — At the railway station carriages may be procured for a drive round the battlefield, taking 4-5 hrs. (3-3$^1/_2$ rb.). Borodino is best visited from Moscow (provisions should be taken). To the N.W. of the station is the village of *Semenovskoye*, where ($^1/_2$ hr. from the station) the road divides. To the left we reach in 8 min. the *Nunnery of Spáso-Borodínski*, founded in 1833 on the site of the Bagration Redoubts, whence another $^1/_2$ hr. brings us to the *Shevardinski Redoubt* (Шевардинскiй редутъ), a little to the W., with a French monument erected in 1913. The road straight on from Semenovskoye leads in $^1/_4$ hr. to the site of the *Rayev Redoubt* (Батарея Раевскаго), with a monument erected by the Russians in 1839; thence we proceed N. to the ($^1/_4$ hr.) village of *Borodinó*, on the *Kalótcha* brook, with an imperial château. The church-tower affords a view of the battlefield.

1121 V. *Mozháisk* (Можайскъ; Rail. Restaurant), the chief town of a district, with 5500 inhab., is dominated by the Cathedral of St. Nicholas, built in the time of Iván the Terrible.

1165 V. *Kubínka* (Rail. Restaurant). — 1183 V. *Golítzuino* (Rail. Restaurant).

About 18 V. (12 M.) to the N.W. of Golitzuino (seat in a linéika 75 cop., carr. & pair 2¹/₂-3 rb.), on the high left bank of the Moskvá, lies the *Monastery of St. Sabas* (Сáввинскiй монасты́рь), founded at the end of the 14th century. The enclosing wall, with its six towers, was built in 1654. The Cathedral of the Virgin (Собóръ Пресвятóй Богорóдицы) contains the relics of St. Sabas, in a silver coffin of 1680. The silvered canopy dates from 1840.

Beyond (1212 V.) *Kúntzevo* (p. 322) we cross the Moskvá. In the distance appear the numerous domes and towers of Moscow. — 1224 V. (811 M.) *Moscow* (Alexander or Brest Station), see p. 269.

33. From Riga to Moscow.

a. Viâ Smolensk.

970 V. (643 M.). Railway in 22 hrs., with change into express at Smolensk (fares 21 rb. 50, 12 rb. 90 cop.; seat-ticket 2 rb. 10 cop.). The through-carriages from Riga to Moscow by this route take 33¹/₂ hrs.

From Riga to (204 V.) *Dünaburg (Dvinsk)*, see R. 10a.

221 V. *Iozefóvo* (510 ft.); 244 V. *Kreslávka* (Rail. Restaurant). —294 V. *Drissa* (380 ft.; Rail. Restaurant). The town of this name, the capital of a district in the government of Vitebsk, lies 2¹/₂ M. to the W., at the confluence of the *Drissa* and the Dviná, and contains 5600 inhabitants.

355 V. (235 M.) **Pólotzk**, Полоцкъ. — *Rail. Restaurant*, very fair. —Hotels (prices raised in Aug.). *Grand-Hôtel; Hôt. Frankfurt*, Spásskaya, with garden, R. from 75, D. (1 p.m.) from 40 cop.—Izvóshtchik from the station to the town 30, at night 40 cop., per hr. 80 cop. & 1 rb.

Pólotzk (425 ft.), the capital of a district in the government of Vitebsk, is prettily situated upon a ridge between the *Dviná* and the *Polotá* (N.). Pop. 31,000, including many Jews. High above the Dviná rises the old Kremlin, enclosing the conspicuous Greek Catholic Cathedral of St. Sophia, a large building in the rococo style. In the square opposite the Greek Catholic Cathedral of St. Nicholas and the Cadet School, both of which were built under Stephen Bathory, rises a monument to the memory of the Russians who fell at Polotzk in 1812. On the bank of the Dviná there is a small Lutheran Church, and there is also a Roman Catholic Church. — About 1¹/₄ M. to the N. is the Spásski Monastery, or Monastery of Our Saviour, which played a rôle in the contests of 1812.

From Polotzk to Bologoye, 434 V. (288 M.), railway in 13 hrs. The line runs to the N.E. —93 V. *Nevel* (Rail. Restaurant), see p. 257; 143 V. *Velíkiye Luki* (Rail. Restaurant), see p. 256; 212 V. *Toropétz* (Rail. Restaurant), a district-town with 8700 inhab., on the Toropá. Before reaching (311 V.) *Sígovo* we cross the Volga. — 328 V. *Ostáshkov* (Rail. Restaurant), a district-town in the government of Tver, with 10,800 inhab., lies on *Lake Seliger*, and manufactures leather and iron. — 434 V. (288 M.) *Bologóye*, see p. 266.

From Polotzk to *Siedlce*, see p. 249.

As we leave Polotzk behind us and approach Vitebsk the district becomes hilly. The gentle undulations of the ground are partly covered with masses of granite, but the formations near Vitebsk are of limestone.—410 V. *Sirotino* (Rail. Restaurant).

448 V. (297 M.) **Vitebsk** *(Rail. Restaurant)*, see p. 257.

The undulating region between the Dviná and the Dnieper (ca. 650 ft. above the sea-level), forming the great 'Gate of the Nations' towards the W., is for the most part flat and marshy. — 516 V. *Rudnya* (Rail. Restaurant).

578 V. (383 M.) **Smolénsk** (590 ft.; *Rail. Restaurant)*, see p. 251. — Hence to (970 V. or 643 M.) *Moscow*, see pp. 253-255.

b. Viâ Kreuzburg and Rzhev.

865 V. (573 M.). Express train in 22¹/₂ hrs. (fares 20 rb., 12 rb.; reserved seat 2 rb. 10 cop.; sleeping-car 6 rb. 90, 5 rb. 20 cop.); ordinary train in 31¹/₂ hrs.

From Riga to (121 V.) *Kreuzburg*, see pp. 48, 47. — 210 V. *Ryézhitza* (Rail. Restaurant), see p. 40; local trains run to the station on the St. Petersburg line. — 233 V. *Lyútzin* or *Ludsen* (Rail. Restaurant), a town with 6900 inhab. and the ruins of a castle of the Teutonic Order; 287 V. *Sebézh* (Rail. Restaurant), with 7600 inhabitants.

391 V. (259 M.) *Novo-Sokólniki* (Rail. Restaurant). To St. Petersburg or Vitebsk, see p. 257. — We now cross the *Lovat* and reach (418 V.) *Velíkiye Lukí* (Rail. Restaurant), a town with 10,200 inhab.; to Polotzk or Bologoye, see p. 255. — 486 V. *Toropá* (Rail. Restaurant). Beyond (511 V.) *Západnaya Dviná* (Rail. Restaurant) we cross the *Dviná.* — 644 V. (427 M.) **Rzhev,** Ржевъ (pron. Rzhov; *Railway Station* with restaurant, on the right bank of the Volga; *Centrálnaya;* izvóshtchik from the stations to the town 40-50 cop.), a district-town in the government of Tver, with 23,600 inhab., is situated on the *Volga.* A branch-railway (station on the left bank of the Volga) runs hence to Vyazma and to Likhoslavl (see p. 267).

748 V. *Volokolámsk* (Rail. Restaurant), a town of 5100 inhab. in the government of Moscow. — 809 V. *Novo-Ierusalímskaya* (Rail. Restaurant).

About ²/₃ M. from the railway station is the **Monastery of the New Jerusalem,** founded by the Patriarch Nikon (d. 1681; comp. p. 295) in 1656 and resembling a fortress with its lofty walls. The large *Church of the Resurrection*, 220 ft. in height, was built by Nikon on the model of the Church of the Holy Sepulchre at Jerusalem. His grave is in the Chapel of John the Baptist, under the so-called 'Golgotha' (comp. p. 283).

865 V. (573 M.) *Moscow* (Windau Station), see p. 269.

34. From St. Petersburg to Vitebsk *(Kiev)*.

533 V. (353 M.). Express train in 14 hrs. (fares 15 rb., 9 rb.; seat-ticket 1½ rb.; sleeping-car 4 rb. 25, 3 rb. 20 cop.). Ordinary train in 14-17 hrs.

From St. Petersburg to (22 V.) *Tzárskoye Seló*, see p. 186. —
25 V. *Pavlovsk Vtorói* (comp. p. 189). — 56 V. *Vúiritza* (Rail
Restaurant); 121 V. *Oredézh* (Rail. Restaurant); 193 V. *Soltzi* (Rail.
Restaurant); 230 V. *Dno* (Rail. Restaurant), junction for Bologoye
and Pskov (pp. 266, 267); 319 V. *Súshtchevo* (Rail. Restaurant). —
395 V. *Novo-Sokólniki* (Rail. Restaurant). To Riga or Moscow,
see p. 256. — 437 V. *Nevel* (Rail. Restaurant), a district-town in
the government of Vitebsk, with 17,000 inhabitants. To Polotzk
or Bologoye, see p. 255. — 499 V. *Gorodok* (Rail. Restaurant).

533 V. (353 M.) **Vítebsk**, Витебскъ. — *Railway Restaurant*, very
fair. — HOTELS. *Hôtel Brosi*, Smolénskaya 1, near Sobórnaya Sq., R. 1-3½,
D. (1-6 p.m.) ½-1¼ rb.; *Bristol*, Zámkovaya. — *Albert* (Confectioner), adjoining the Hôt. Brosi, with a terrace. — IZVÓSHTCHIK from the railway
station to the town 40, per hr. 60 cop. — ELECTRIC TRAMWAY from the
railway station across Sobórnaya Sq. and through the town 5 cop. — POST
& TELEGRAPH OFFICE, Smolénskaya.

Vítebsk (470 ft.), the capital of the government of the same name,
prettily situated on the *Dviná*, contains over 103,900 inhab., including numerous Jews. Down to the 12th cent. the town belonged
sometimes to Smolensk, sometimes to Polotzk, but thereafter it
formed a small independent principality. In the 14th cent. it was
united with Lithuania, but its position on the frontier long made
it a bone of contention between Poland and Russia. It finally fell
to the latter at the First Partition of Poland (1772). On July 16th
(28th), 1812, Napoleon entered Vitebsk at the head of his Guards. —
The railway station lies on the right bank of the Dvina, the town
proper on the left bank. From the railway station we proceed a
few yards to the right, then turn to the left and follow the Vokzál-
naya, to the left of which, in the Petróvskaya, is a Lutheran church.
After 10 min. we cross the Dviná and enter the Zámkovaya, the
chief business thoroughfare, leading to (10 min.) Sobórnaya Square,
in which is the *Cathedral of St. Nicholas*, erected by the Jesuits
in 1664. Proceeding hence to the N., we cross the Vitba Bridge,
bear slightly to the left at the Roman Catholic *Church of St. Anthony*
(1731), and ascend the Suvórovskaya. We turn to the left into the
Uspénskaya, which leads to the (7 min.) high left bank of the
Dviná, on which stands the *Cathedral of the Assumption* (1777).
The terrace in front of this church overlooks the town and the
Dviná valley. A little to the N. is the *Residence of the Governor*.

FROM VITEBSK TO ZHLOBIN (Kiev), 265 V. (176 M.), railway in 7½ hrs.
— 78 V. *Orsha* (p. 251). — 146 V. (97 M.), **Mohilév**, Могилевъ (pron. Mohilyóv; *Rail. Restaurant; Bristol*, Dvoryánskaya 20, with restaurant, R.
1-4 rb.; *Frántziya*, Shklovskaya 18; izvóshtchik from the railway station
to the town, 1 M. to the S.E., 50, per hr. 50 cop.; steamer to Kiev, see p. 378),
the capital of the government of that name and the seat of a Greek

Catholic bishop, lies in a picturesque and hilly district on the left bank of the Dnieper. Pop. 54,000, including many Jews. The chief objects of interest are the Public Park, with view and restaurant; the tower of the Duma, which dates from the 16th cent.; the Bratstvo Church, erected in 1620; and the Roman Catholic Cathedral, containing fine old pictures. There are also a small Provincial Museum and a Lutheran church. Pleasant excursions may be made to *Piepenberg* (Буйничи; 5 M. to the S.), with a convent; to (1 M.) *Karabánovka;* to (2 M.) *Petchérsk,* the summer residence of the Greek Catholic bishop, with a fine park; and to (3¹/₄ M. to the N.) *Poluikóvitchi,* a pilgrim-resort on the Dnieper.—265 V. (176 M.), *Zhlobin* (p. 39). From Zhlobin to *Bakhmatch,* see p. 39; thence to *Kiev,* see p. 376. From Vitebsk to *Riga* or to *Moscou,* see R. 33a.

35. From St. Petersburg
to Tchelyabinsk *(Siberia)* viâ Vyatka.

2191 V. (1452 M.). Two ordinary trains daily, taking 3 days for the journey (fares 36 rb., 21 rb. 60 cop.; seat-ticket 3 rb. 90 cop.). The express from St. Petersburg to Irkutsk (p. 523) follows this route (twice weekly; 2¹/₄ days to Tchelyabinsk; 78 rb. 5, 50 rb. 95 cop.), but from the summer of 1914 onwards it will run viâ Yekaterinburg, Tyumen, and Omsk (see p. 261).

St. Petersburg (Nicholas Station), see p. 88. At *Obúkhovo* our line diverges to the left from the Moscow railway, traversing forests and marshes. 24 V. *Sapérnaya,* with a military camp; 86 V. *Voibokala* (130 ft.; Rail. Restaurant). 114 V. *Zvanka* (Rail. Restaurant); branch-line to (12 V.) *Gostinopólye,* a harbour on the Volkhov. We cross the *Volkhov.* — 137 V. *Skit,* with a convent.

187 V. **Tikhvin** (145 ft.; *Rail. Restaurant*), a district-town with 13,500 inhab. in the government of Novgorod. In the Cathedral of the Assumption is the wonder-working picture of the Tikhvin Virgin. — 239 V. *Tchudzi* (965 ft.), the highest point of the line between St. Petersburg and Vologda; 257 V. *Yefimovskaya* (Rail. Restaurant); 329 V. *Babáyevo* (Rail. Restaurant); 444 V. *Tcherepóvetz* (390 ft.; Rail. Restaurant), a district-town in the government of Novgorod (pop. 9400), on the *Shexná,* a tributary of the Volga, forming part of the Marie Canal System (p. 195). Before reaching (480 V.) *Shexná* we cross the river.

560 V. (371 M.) **Vólogda.** — *Rail. Restaurant.* — HOTELS. *Eremitage,* Alexándrovskaya Sq.; *Zolotói Yakor,* Moskóvskaya. — Izvósнтснiк from the station to the town 35, per drive 20, per hr. 40, in winter 30 cop.

Vólogda (395 ft.; pop. 38,700), founded in 1147, is the capital of the government of that name and lies on both sides of the Vólogda. The Cathedral of St. Sophia, 1¹/₂ M. to the N. of the railway station, was built ca. 1570 under Iván the Terrible, on the model of the Uspénski Cathedral at Moscow. A little to the W. is a Collection of Ecclesiastical Antiquities (Церковное древлехранилище). At the S.E. end of the Moskóvskaya, 1¹/₂ M. from the cathedral, is a house once occupied by Peter the Great (small museum). Lace making is an industry of this district.

Railway to *Yaroslavl* or *Archangel,* see R. 42. — Interesting steamer-trip before August (in 3¹/₂ days; fare 12 rb., without meals) down the

Vologda, the Súkhona, and the Syévernaya Dviná to (1162 V. or 770 M.) *Archangel* (p. 334), viâ (493 V.) *Ústyug Veliki* (with 18,700 inhab. and linen-factories) and (563 V.) *Kotlas* (see below).

Just before reaching (682 V.) *Bui* (Rail. Restaurant) we cross the *Kostromá*. The country becomes more populous and more hilly. —730 V. *Galitch* (Rail. Restaurant), a small town on the S.E. bank of Lake Gálitchskoye; 795 V. *Nikóla Polóma* (Rail. Restaurant). Beyond (871 V.) *Mantúrovo* we cross the *Unzhá*, and short of (916 V.) *Sharya* (Rail. Restaurant) we cross the *Vetlúga*. 1027 V. *Svyetcha* (Rail. Restaurant). Just beyond (1075 V.) *Kotélnitch* (Rail. Restaurant) the train crosses the *Vyatka* by a bridge 700 yds. long.

1156 V. (766 M.) **Vyatka**, Вятка (440 ft.; *Rail. Restaurant; Yevropéiskaya*, corner of Spásskaya and Nikoláyevskaya; *Restaurant Peterburg*, corner of Preobrazhénskaya and Nikoláyevskaya; izvóshtchik from the railway station to the town 40 cop.), founded in 1174, is the capital of the government of the same name and lies on the river Vyatka. Pop. 44,100. At the corner of the Moskóvskaya and Kazánskaya is a museum of domestic industries.

From Vyatka a railway runs to (359 V. or 238 M.) *Kotlas* (Rail. Restaurant) on the high left bank of the Syévernaya Dviná. From Kotlas steamers ply to Archangel and Vologda (see above).—From Vyatka a steamer runs once daily to (2½ days) Kazan (p. 352; fare 12 rb. 60 cop.).

We now traverse pine-woods. 1255 V. *Zuyevka* (Rail. Restaurant); 1351 V. *Glazov* (Rail. Restaurant), with 4500 inbab.; 1492 V. *Voznesénskaya* (Rail. Restaurant). Shortly before reaching Perm we cross the Kama by a bridge 970 yds. long. We have a good view of the town to the left.

1605 V. (1064 M.) **Perm**, Пермь.—*Rail. Restaurant.* — Hotel. *Klúbnuiye Nomerá*, Voznesénskaya. Rooms may also be obtained at the Club of the Noblesse (Благородное собрánie), with very fair restaurant.—Izvóshtchik from the railway station to the town 80, from the landing-stage to the town at least 30 cop.

Perm (300 ft.), capital of the government of the same name, prettily situated on the high left bank of the *Kama*, with 61,600 inbah., has 19 churches, including one Lutheran and one Roman Catholic. In the Zemstvo building is a collection of products of domestic manufacture. The Town Park is well kept.

From Perm to Yekaterinburg viâ Biser, 469 V. (311 M.), ordinary train in 28½ hrs. This line intersects part of the Central Urals (p. 369). — 4 V. *Motovilikha*, with a large government gun-foundry. Beyond (44 V.) *Suilva* (325 ft.; Rail. Restaurant) we cross the river of that name. 104 V. *Kálino* (Rail. Restaurant). Just before reaching (119 V.) the prettily situated *Tchusovskáya* (405 ft.; Rail. Restaurant) we cross the *Tchusováya.*—Beyond (211 V.) *Biser* (1510 ft.; Rail. Restaurant), in a marshy district, the railway reaches its highest point (1545 ft.). About 7 V. beyond (248 V.) *Yevropéiskaya* (1245 ft.) are two iron posts marking the geographical frontier between Europe and Asia. Farther on we pass several large foundries. To the left, near (291 V.) *Goroblagodátskaya* (760 ft.; Rail. Restaurant), with its government iron-works, rises the isolated double-peak of *Blagodát* (1155 ft.), with extensive layers of magnetic iron-ore containing 52-58 per cent of iron. On the S. peak stands a chapel. From Goroblagodátskaya a branch-line runs to (182 V.) *Nadézhdinski Zavód,* with a large rolling-mill. — 335 V. *Nizhni Tagíl* (780 ft.; Rail. Restaurant; pop. 45,000), with the offices of the Demídov Foundries; 382 V. *Nevyansk* (Rail. Restaurant). At (409 V.) *Verkh-Neivínsk* (875 ft.; Rail. Restaurant) the first gold in the Urals was found. — 469 V. (311 M.) *Yekaterinbúrg* (see below). Steamer from Perm to *Kazán*, see pp. 355, 354.

1699 V. *Kungúr* (Rail. Restaurant), a town with 19,600 inbab on the Suilva. In the neighbourhood there is an ice-cave (Ледяная пещера); 1764 V. *Kordón* (Rail. Restaurant); 1824 V. *Shalya* (Rail. Restaurant); 1889 V. *Koúrovka* (Rail. Restaurant).

1961 V. (1300 M.) **Yekaterinbúrg**, Екатеринбургъ. — *Railway Restaurant.* — HOTELS. *Palais Royal*, Glavni Prospékt; *Ameri-kánskaya*, Pokróvski Prospékt, with café, R. 1-4 rb.; *Atamánov*, Glavni Prospékt, hôtel garni, R. 1¹/₄-3¹/₂ rb. — Good cuisine at the *Club* (Обще-ственное собрание), Voznesénski Prospékt, with concert every evening in summer (except Sat.) in the garden.
Izvóshtcnik (fares vary according to the condition of the cab) from the rail. station to the town or vice versâ 35-50 (at night 50-70) cop.; per drive 20-40, per hr. 40-80 cop. — GENERAL POST OFFICE, Glavni Prospékt.
BRITISH VICE-CONSUL, *T. H. Preston.* — BRITISH AND FOREIGN BIBLE SOCIETY, Uspénskaya (chief depot for Siberia).
PRECIOUS STONES OF THE URALS. *Nurov*, opposite the Amerikánskaya Hotel (also statuettes from the Kazli iron-foundry); *Lipin*, Voznesénski Prospékt 23. The stones offered by the street-vendors, especially the emeralds, are mostly spurious.

Yekaterinbúrg (870 ft.), a district-town in the government of Perm, founded in 1721, was named after Empress Catherine I. and lies on both sides of the *Isét*. It is the most important place in the Urals. Pop. 75,000. From the chief railway station, situated to the N. of the town (there is another to the E. of the town), the Arsényevski Prospékt runs S. to the Voznesénski Prospékt, on the left side of which, a little back from the street, is the *Church of the Ascension* (wide view from the tower). Farther on, also on the left, are the *Club* (see above) and (at the intersection with the Glavni Prospékt) the *General Post Office* (1¹/₂ M. from the station). A little to the E. of the post office are the *Lutheran Church* and the *Town Theatre*. To the S.E. of this point is (25 min.) the *Magneto-Meteorological Observatory* (Магнитно-метеорологическая обсерватория; open 10-4, extensive view from the tower). In the Glavni Prospékt, to the W. of the General Post Office, is the *Cathedral of St. Catharine;* to the right is the *District Court*, on a pond formed by damming the Isét. We then follow the Isét Embankment (Плотина), with the imperial *Lapidary Works* (Имп. гранильная Фабрика) to the left, and bronze busts of Peter the Great and Catherine I. on the right. To the left, at the W. end of the Embankment, is the *Natural History Museum* of the Ural Society of Naturalists (Музей Уральскаго общества любителей естест-вознания; open daily 10-4, in winter 10-3; adm. 20 cop.). Farther on in the Glavni Prospékt, to the left, are the *School of Mines* (Уральское горное училище), the *Chief Department of Mines* (Уральское горное управление), and the *Bazaar*. To the right

(10 min. from the theatre) stands the *Cathedral*, in front of which is a bronze statue of Alexander II., by Popóv (1906).

From Yekaterinburg to Omsk viâ Tyumen, 841 V. (557 M.), railway in 32 hrs. — 53 V. *Bazhénovo* (785 ft.; Rail. Restaurant). On the Bolshói Reft, 23 M. to the N., are emerald mines. — 94 V. *Bogdanóvitch* (550 ft.; Rail. Restaurant). 134 V. *Kamuishlóv* (325 ft.; Rail. Restaurant; Nomerá Dembovski), a district-town with 9900 inhabitants. About 74 M. to the N. (diligence) lies *Irbít* (Sibirskoye Podvórye, R. from 1 rb.), a district-town in the government of Perm, with 8600 inhabitants. The turnover in furs at the annual fair (Feb.), founded in 1643, amounted in 1912 to 8,000,000 rb. — 201 V. *Poklévskaya* (255 ft.; Rail. Restaurant). — 304 V. (202 M.) **Tyumén,** Тюмень (280 ft.; *Rail. Restaurant;* furnished rooms at F. P. Loshkomoyev's, cor. of Sadóvaya and Známenskaya; cab to the town 50 cop.), a district-town in the government of Tobolsk, prettily situated on the lofty banks of the *Turá.* Pop. 50,000. The Modern School, on the Tzárskaya, contains a Natural History Museum (open in winter on Sun., 12-3). Before the opening of the Trans-Siberian Railway all the exiles used to pass through Tyumen, which thus witnessed, between 1823 and 1898, a melancholy procession of 908,266 persons, consisting of the prisoners and their families. Steamers run viâ (412 V.) Tobolsk (p. 527) to (1555 V.) Omsk (p. 526) or (2219 V.) Tomsk (p. 529). — Beyond (374 V.) *Yalutorovsk,* we cross the *Toból.* 440 V. *Vagai,* 576 V. *Ishim,* 701 V. *Nazuivayevskaya,* all three with rail. restaurants. — At (836 V.) *Kulomzino* the line joins the Trans-Siberian Railway. — 841 V. (557 M.) *Omsk,* see p. 526.

We now reach the S. part of the Urals (p. 369). The marble quarried at (2001 V.) *Mrámorskaya* (1260 ft.) is cut and polished at the Mrámorski Zavód. Specimens are on sale at the station. — 2030 V. *Poldnévaya* (1205 ft.), in a wooded district, has chrysolite mines. The train ascends to a height of 1480 ft. and then descends to (2059 V.) *Ufaléi* (1280 ft.; Rail. Restaurant). Near (2107 V.) *Kuishtuím* (830 ft.; Rail. Restaurant), which is prettily situated, are iron-works. 2140 V. *Argayásh* (840 ft.). We cross the *Miáss.*

2191 V. (1452 M.) *Tchelyábinsk* (760 ft.; Rail. Restaurant) see p. 370.

Trans-Siberian Railway, see R. 77.

36. From St. Petersburg to Staraya Russa (Pskov) viâ Novgorod.

268 V. (178 M.). Railway in 10 hrs. (fares 9 rb. 70, 5 rb. 22 cop.), to Novgorod in 6¼ hrs. The trains start from the Nicholas Station; carriages are changed at Tchudovo. — A pleasanter route than the railway from Tchudovo to Novgorod is the Steamboat Trip up the Volkhov from Volkhovo (p. 266) to Novgorod (4½ hrs.; 1¾ rb.). When taking tickets at St. Petersburg or Moscow, passengers must state whether they wish to use the railway from Tchudovo or the steamer from Volkhovo.

St. Petersburg, see p. 88. As soon as the immediate environs of St. Petersburg are left behind us, the scenery becomes dreary and desolate. — At *Slavyánka* we cross the *Slavyánka,* a marshy river which, along with its tributaries, waters the parks of Pavlovsk (p. 190) and Tzarskoye Selo (p. 187).

24 V. *Kolpino,* a town of 20,200 inbah., situated on both banks of the *Izhóra,* and containing an iron-foundry belonging to the

Admiralty. From (50 V.) *Tosno* a branch-railway runs to (46 V.)
Gatchina (p. 186). 78 V. *Lyubán* (Rail. Restaurant). — About
10 M. to the N. of (111 V.) **Tchúdovo**, Чудово (215 ft.; *Railway Restaurant*), lies the château of *Grúzino*, formerly the property of Count A. A. Araktchéyev (d. 1834), containing a collection
of Russian antiquities.

From Tchudovo to *Moscow*, see R. 37.

Our line now diverges to the S.W. from the Nicholas Railway.
135 V. *Spásskaya Polist* (Rail. Restaurant); 160 V. *Podberézye*
(Rail. Restaurant).

180 V. (120 M.) **Nóvgorod**, Новгородъ. — The Railway Station *(Restaurant)* lies to the W. of the town. — Hotel. *Solovyév* (Pl. a;
E, 2), Moskóvskaya, R. $^1/_2$-$3^1/_2$ rb. (bed-linen 25 cop.), B. 50 cop., D.
(1-6 p.m.) 60 cop. to 1 rb. — Restaurants in the *Summer Garden* (Pl. D, 3),
D. $^1/_2$ rb., with frequent concerts, and at the *Club of the Noblesse*, also
in the Summer Garden. — Izvóshtchik from the railway station to the
town 30, from the steamboat-pier to the town 15 or 20, per hr. 40 cop. —
Post & Telegraph Office (Pl. 35), Známenskaya. — Steamboats (comp.
Pl. D, E, 2) ply from Novgorod to ($3^3/_4$ hrs.) Volkhovo (p. 266) and across
Lake Ilmen to (4 hrs.) Staraya Russa (p. 265; fare, there & back, 2 rb.).

Nóvgorod (165 ft.), formerly called Novgorod the Great, now the
unimportant capital of the government of Novgorod, is the seat of
a Greek Catholic archbishop and contains 27,100 inhabitants. The
town lies on both sides of the *Volkhov*, which is crossed by a bridge
and is divided into the *Sophia Side* (Софійская сторона́) and the
Commercial Side (Торго́вая сторона́).

Novgorod (*i.e.* 'New Town') was founded by Scandinavian Vikings
in the earliest days of the Christian era. In 862 the Varangians or Varags
(Normans) under *Rurik* (P. xlvii) invaded the district and took possession of
the left bank, where the Kremlin now stands. In 882 *Olég* transferred the
seat of his government to Kiev, and Novgorod was administered by a
Viceroy (Namyástnik). *Yarosláv I.* (1019-1054) endowed the town with great
privileges. During the 11-12th cent. Novgorod grew greatly in power,
while at the same time its bond of union with Kiev became slacker and
slacker, until finally a kind of republican commonwealth, known as the
Volkhov Republic, was formed. The power of the frequently-changing
viceroy was faced by that of the Vyetche (Вече), or popular assembly,
and that of the Posádnik, or mayor elected by the citizens. The Novgorodian proverb, 'Koli khud knyaz, tak v gryaz' ('If the prince is bad, into
the mud with him'), was habitually acted on (see *Wallace's* 'Russia').
During their campaigns of conquest, which extended as far as the Baltic
Sea, the Novgorodians entered into relations with Wisby, which was then
the focus of the Baltic trade. They long possessed a factory there, while
at the beginning of the 12th cent. a German settlement ('Deutscher Hof')
was established at Novgorod. In its struggles with the Mongols Novgorod
was victorious, but it fostered, from motives of policy, a good understanding with the Khan of the Golden Horde. — The Novgorodians also extended their powers to the Volga and towards the N. From this period
date the saying 'Who can resist God and Novgorod the Great?' (Кто
про́тивъ Бо́га и Вели́каго Но́вгорода?) and the name 'Lord Novgorod
the Great' (Господи́нъ Вели́кій Но́вгородъ). The propinquity of the
Russian princes, however, prevented the Novgorodians from perpetuating
their empire. In 1471 their armies were defeated near Lake Ilmen (June
and July) by the Russian and Tartar hordes of *Iván III.*, Grand-Prince of
Moscow, and Novgorod was compelled to acknowledge his supremacy.
The brave Marfa Borétzkaya, who wanted to put the town under Polish

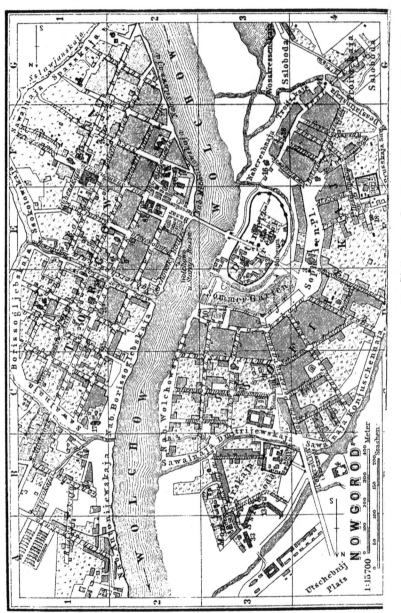

protection, ended her life as a prisoner at Nizhni-Novgorod. Six years later new dissensions arose, and in Jan., 1478, the town was captured and its citizens paid homage to Iván. *Iván the Terrible* destroyed the last relics of the former prosperity of Novgorod in 1570, when he, is said to have butchered 60,000 of its citizens. The foundation of St. Petersburg and numerous conflagrations completed the ruin of the once flourishing free city.

From the *Railway Station* (beyond Pl. D, 4), which lies to the W. of the town, the Legóshtchaya leads through the Sophia Side to ($^1/_4$ hr.) the —

Kremlin (Pl. E, 3), the brick walls of which, with their nine round and square towers, date from 1303 and 1490 (with restorations in 1698 and 1862). The popular assemblies referred to above were held in the great square of the Kremlin. In the middle of this square stands a *Millennial Monument* (Пáмятникъ Тысячелѣтію Россíи; Pl. 2), erected in 1862, from the design of Mikéshin, to commemorate the thousandth anniversary of the political existence of Russia. On a circular pediment, with relief-portraits of several eminent Russians, rests a large imperial orb, bearing a kneeling figure of Russia and the Guardian Angel of the Empire, leaning against the cross. The globe is encircled with bronze statues representing various periods of Russian history; the six chief figures counting from the S. are Rurik, Demetrius Donskói (*i.e.* of the Don), Iván III., Peter the Great, Mikhail Feódorovitch, and St. Vladimir.

The legendary account of the foundation of the Russian empire is thus related by the oldest chronicler, as quoted in the 'Russia' of Sir D. M. Wallace (new edit., 1912; p. 171). "At that time, as the southern Slavonians paid tribute to the Kozars, so the Novgorodian Slavonians suffered from the attacks of the Variags. For some time the Variags exacted tribute from the Novgorodian Slavonians and the neigh-

Key to the Numbers on the Plan of Novgorod.

1. Club of the Noblesse	E 4		19. Nativity of the Virgin	D 1
2. Millennial Monument	E 3		20. St. George	E 2
3. Monument of Liberation (from the French dominion, 1812)	D, E, 4		21. St. Joan Predtetcha	E 2
			22. St. Lazarus	B 3
			22a. Lutheran	D 1
4. Prison	B 4		23. Cathedral of St. Nicholas	F 2
5. District Court	E 3		24. SS. Peter and Paul	D 1
7. Gostini Dvor and Duma	E 2		25. St. Procopius	F 2
8. Governor's House	E 2		26. Cathedral of St. Sophia	E 3
9. Government High School	E 2		27. Známenski Cathedral	F 1
9a. Girls' High School	E 2		28. Troitzkaya	F 3
10. 1st Military Hospital	D 3			
11. 2nd Military Hospital	C 3		CONVENTS.	
12. District Hospital	C 3		29. St. Anthony	A 1
13. Barracks of the Sappers	B 3		30. Desyatinni	E 4
14. Barracks of the 22nd Artillery Brigade	C 3		31. Holy Ghost	B 3
16. House of Catherine the Great	F 3		32. Consistory	E 3
			33. Riding School	A 3
			34. Police Station	D 1
CHURCHES.			35. Post & Telegraph Office	F 1
			37. Archbishop's Palace	D 3
17. SS. Borís and Glyeb	C 1		40. Yaroslav Tower	F 2
18. St. Michael the Archangel	E 4		41. White Tower	G 4

bouring Finns; then the conquered tribes, by uniting their forces, drove out the foreigners. But among the Slavonians arose strong internal dissensions; the clans rose against each other. Then, for the creation of order and safety, they resolved to call in princes from a foreign land. In the year 862 Slavonic legates went away beyond the sea to the Variag tribe called Rus, and said, 'Our land is great and fruitful, but there is no order in it; come and reign and rule over us'. Three brothers accepted this invitation, and appeared with their armed followers. The eldest of these, Rurik, settled in Novgorod; the second, Sineus, at Byelo-Ozero; and the third, Truvor, in Isborsk. From them our land is called Rus. After two years the brothers of Rurik died. He alone began to reign over the Novgorod district, and confided to his men the administration of the principal towns."

On the N. side of the square is the **Cathedral of St. Sophia** (Софійскій Соборъ; Pl. 26), built by Greek architects in 1045-1052 and provided with six domes. It is an important monument of Russian architecture of the time of Yarosláv I. During a complete restoration of the cathedral in 1893-1900, the frescoes in the interior (with the exception of those under the central dome) were repainted, the exterior of the main dome was gilded, and the remaining domes were covered with zinc. — In the main W. entrance is the celebrated *Korsún* or *Plotzk Door*, which appears to have been made by Master Riquinus of Magdeburg, in the first half of the 12th cent., to the order of Bishop Alexander of Plotzk (Blucich), and was afterwards purchased by Russian merchants for Novgorod. The door, which is about 12 ft. high, consists of oak overlaid with 48 plates of bronze. Of these, 3 represent scenes from the Old Testament, and 23 scenes from the New Testament, while the remaining 22 are of allegorical or mythological subjects. The inscriptions are partly in Latin and partly in Slavonic, but the latter were probably not added until the beginning of the 15th century.

INTERIOR (fee to the sacristan 20-30 cop.). The massive piers supporting the domes are adorned from top to bottom with modern frescoes of saints. The head of Christ in the main dome, surrounded by two rows of angels and prophets, dates from the middle of the 11th century. The *Ikonostás* (16th cent.) is richly adorned with gold and silver. Among the paintings are many of early-Byzantine workmanship. The restored mosaic ornamentations behind the high-altar are said to be Byzantine work of the time of Yarosláv I. In front of the ikonostás are the *Thrones of the Tzar and the Metropolitan*, both of wood, painted and gilded (16th cent.). To the right of the ikonostás, at the entrance to the Chapel of the Nativity, is the *Sigtuna Door*, which the Novgorodians are said to have carried off from the Swedish town of Sigtuna in a foray of 1188. It is, however, properly speaking, merely a bronze sheathing for the oaken door and is of later date than the Korsun Door. — Among the monuments of princes and archbishops may be mentioned the silver sarcophagus of John of Novgorod (d. 1186; N. side). — By the staircase leading to the galleries are ancient figures and inscriptions scratched in the limestone and now protected by glass. — In the space adjoining the high-altar, various so-called 'Golosniki', or large earthenware vases for improving the acoustics, are built into the walls. Similar acoustic vases may also be seen in other Novgorod churches. — The *Treasury* contains many interesting antiquities.

To the N. of the Cathedral of St. Sophia is an interesting house of 1436, containing the so-called *Granovítaya Paláta*, a room in which the archbishops received the homage of the people after their election. — In the Court of St. Sophia (Дворъ св. Софіи or Дворъ Владычній) rises the *Yevfimiyevski Tower*, 155 ft. high and erected in 1436. It affords a good view of the city. — The *Museum*, on the S.W. side of the Kremlin, is open on week-days, 10 - 4 (in Nov. & Dec. 10.30-3), and on Sun. 12 - 3; adm. 25, on Sun. 15 cop. — On the N. side of the Kremlin lies the shady *Summer Garden* (Лѣтній садъ; Pl. D, 3), containing a restaurant (p. 262).

To the E. of the Kremlin is the iron *Volkhov Bridge* (Pl. E, 3; view, to the right, of the Monastery of St. George, see below), leading to the COMMERCIAL SIDE (p. 262). Immediately to the S. of the bridge once lay the so-called *Slavonian Konétz*, the focus of the commercial and political life of the city. The extensive Bazaar Square (Pl. E, 2) used to be bounded on the E. and S. sides by the stalls of the *German* and *Pskov Factories*. Here, at present, on the right, stands a large block of buildings in which are the *Gostíni Dvor* (Bazaar; Pl. 7) and a school-house incorporating the remains of the *Yaroslàv* or *Vyetche Tower* (Ярослава башня; Pl. 40). — In the Znàmenskaya is the *Znàmenski Cathedral* (Pl. 27; F, 1), adorned within and without with frescoes. On the ikonostàs, to the left, is a wonder-working image of the Virgin, which is said 'to have shed tears whenever Novgorod was molested'. — In the Moskóvskaya is the *Lutheran Church* (Pl. 22 a). To the N., on the bank of the Volkhov, lies the *Monastery of St. Anthony* (Pl. 29; A, 1), founded in 1106.

About 2 M. to the S. of Novgorod (there & back by rowing-boat in 4 hrs.), on the right bank of the Volkhov, is the village of *Ryurikovo Gorodishtche*. On a hill ³/₄ M. to the E. of it lies the small *Spaso-Nereditzkaya Church*, built in 1198 by Yaroslàv Vsévolodovitch and restored in 1904, containing interesting 13th cent. frescoes. — To the W., opposite Ryurikovo Gorodishtche, prettily situated on the left bank, is the *Monastery of St. George* (Юрьевъ монастырь), founded by Yaroslàv I. in 1030. The chief church was restored in 1902 and the 12th cent. frescoes of Nicholas Safónov of Suzdal were refreshed. — In the village of *Volotovo*, 2 M. to the E. of Novgorod, near the Moscow highroad, is the old Convent Church of the Assumption, built in 1353, with interesting contemporary frescoes.

Beyond (224 V.) *Shimsk* (Rail. Restaurant) the railway crosses the *Shelón*, and turns towards the S.E.

268 V. (178 M.) **Stàraya Russa**, Старая Русса. — *Railway Restaurant.* — HOTELS. *Kursaal*, adjoining the Salt Springs (p. 266), R. 1³/₄-5, déj. (11-2) ¹/₂, D. (3-7) ³/₄-1 rb.; *Eremitage*, in the market-place, R. 1¹/₂ rb. — Izvóshtchik to the town 40, per drive 20, per hr. 40 cop. — STEAMER to Novgorod (fare 1 rb. 40 cop.), see p. 262. — BATHING ESTABLISHMENTS, open from May 20th to Aug. 20th (O.S.). Salt baths 55 cop., peat baths 1 rb. 40 cop., pine-cone baths 75 cop. — Visitors' tax 5 rb.

Stàraya Russa (240 ft.), a district-town in the government of Novgorod, with salt and peat baths, lies on the slope of the Valdài Hills, at the point where the *Porùsya* and the *Pereruìlitza* enter the *Polist*. Pop. 20,000. The *Bathing Establishment* (Курóртъ),

17*

with well-kept grounds, lies on the E. side of the town. To reach it we leave the railway station in a straight direction, and then follow the Peterbúrgskaya to the left; beyond the bridge across the Polist we bear to the left through the Alexándrovskaya (street to the right leading to the Market Place), turn to the right (12 min.), and follow the Ilyínskaya to the (¹/₄ hr.) main entrance of the Baths. Going straight on and then turning to the right through the Arcade, we reach the Muravyév Saline Springs (52° Fahr.), to the W. of which is the Kursaal (p. 265). A little to the S. are some other baths, the Directorial Spring (54° Fahr.; contained in a chapel), and the Great Salt Lake.

From Staraya Russa to *Pskov* (Pleskau), or *Bologoye*, see below.

37. From St. Petersburg to Moscow.

610 V. (404 M.). *Nicholas Railway*, running in an almost mathematically straight line. Express train in 10-11 hrs. (fares 19 rb. 85, 13 rb. 45 cop.; reserved seat 1¹/₂ rb.; sleeping-car 4 rb. 90, 3 rb. 65 cop.). Ordinary train in 15 hrs. (fares 16 rb., 9 rb. 60 cop.). Travellers by the express trains should order their tickets in advance.—This journey may be advantageously performed at night, as little of interest is passed on the way.—For the railway or steamboat journey to Novgorod, compare the remarks at the beginning of R. 36.

From St. Petersburg to (111 V.) *Tchúdovo*, see p. 261.—Immediately beyond (118 V.) *Vólkhovo* the train crosses a lattice bridge, 325 yds. in length, spanning the *Volkhov*. Steamer (landing-place just below the railway station) to *Novgorod*, see p. 262.

152 V. *Málaya Víshera* (Rail. Restaurant). The train crosses the *Msta*, and then a ravine about 200 ft. in depth. The scenery becomes a little more varied as we approach the *Valdái Hills* (Валдайскія горы), which come into sight beyond (202 V.) *Torbinó*. These hills, though forming an important watershed and ethnographical barrier, separating Baltic Russia from the Volga districts, are of unimposing appearance, consisting of a series of low wooded ridges (highest point 1055 ft.). Farther on we pass numerous Kurgans (tumuli).

234 V. *Okúlovka* (Rail. Restaurant). — 252 V. *Úglovka* (Rail. Restaurant).

A branch-line runs hence in 1 hr. to (19 M.) *Borovitchi* (295 ft.; Rail. Restaurant), the capital of a district, situated on both banks of the Msta, and containing 13,900 inhabitants. Coal is mined in the neighbourhood.

300 V. (199 M.) **Bologóye** *(Rail. Restaurant).*

FROM BOLOGOYE TO PSKOV, 334 V. (221 M.), railway in 10¹/₂ hrs. — 48 V. **Valdái** *(Rail. Restaurant)*, a place with 5000 inhab., surrounded by mountains, and situated on the S. bank of the picturesque *Lake Valdái*, which is 16 sq. M. in area. The lake contains three wooded islands, on one of which is the *Iverski Convent*, built by the Patriarch Nikon in 1653, and now a frequented place of pilgrimage (3 V.; boat there & back 50 cop.). — Farther on we cross the *Pola* and the *Lovat*. 162 V. *Stáraya Russa* (p. 265). From (241 V.) *Dno* (Rail. Restaurant) branch-lines run to St. Petersburg and Vitebsk (see p. 257). A little short of (266 V.) *Porkhov* (Rail. Restaurant), a town of 6800 inhab. with old battlemented walls and towers, we cross the *Shelón.* — 334 V. (221 M.) *Pskov (Pleskau),* see p. 41.

FROM BOLOGOYE TO RUIBINSK, 280 V. (186 M.), railway in 7-8¹/₂ hrs. The most important stations, all (except Volga) with restaurants, are (57 V.) *Udómlya,* (106 V.) *Maxátikha,* (154 V.) *Byezhetzk,* (181 V.) *Sónkovo,* (208 V.) *Rodiónovo,* and (254 V.) *Volga* (P. 349). — 280 V. (186 M.) *Ruibinsk,* see p. 349.

From Bologoye to *Połotzk,* see p. 256.

342 V. *Vuishni-Volotchók* (Rail. Restaurant), the chief town of a district in the government of Tver, contains 17,600 inhab. and is situated on the *Tvéretzki* and *Tzninski Canals.* The canal system of Vuishni-Volotchok (538 M. in length) was constructed in 1703-1709, to connect the Nevá with the Volga, but it is no longer in use.

373 V. *Spirovo* (Rail. Restaurant). — 414 V. (274 M.) *Likhoslávl* (Rail. Restaurant).

FROM LIKHOVSLAVL TO VYAZMA, 244 V. (162 M.), railway in 7 hrs. — 32 V. *Torzhók* (Rail. Restaurant), an old and pleasant-looking town of 13,700 inhab., situated on the *Tvertzá.* Its chief industry is the making of fine gold embroideries on velvet and leather. — 88 V. *Stáritza* (Rail. Restaurant). Beyond (128 V.) *Rzhev* (see p. 256) we cross the *Volga.* 174 V. *Suitchévka* (Rail. Restaurant). — 244 V. (162 M.) *Vyazma,* see p. 253.

As we approach Tver, the forests give place more and more to meadows. The train crosses the *Tvertzá* and immediately afterwards the *Volga.*

453 V. (301 M.) **Tver, Тверь.** — The RAILWAY STATION (fair restaurant) lies W. of the town. — HOTELS (both in the Tryokhsvyatskáya). *Centrálnaya,* R. 1-3 rb., with good restaurant on the first floor; *London,* R. 1-3 rb., bed-linen 40 cop., D. (2-7 p.m.) 1-2 rb. — IZVÓSHTCHIK from the station to the town or to the steamboat-pier 40-50, per drive 25, per hr. 60 cop. — ELECTRIC TRAMWAY from the station to the town and along the Milliónnaya, 5-10 cop. — POST & TELEGRAPH OFFICE, Post Office Square.

Tver (415 ft.), the capital of the government of the same name, situated on the right bank of the Volga, at its confluence with the *Tvertzá* and the *Tmaká,* contains 62,600 inhab., and is the see of a Greek Catholic archbishopric. The largest of its considerable factories is the Morózov Cotton Mill.

Tver was founded in 1181 by the *Grand-Prince Vsévolod* of Vladimir. The chief part of the town then lay on the left bank of the Volga. It was not until 1240 that Grand-Prince Yarosláv Vsévolodovitch built the fortress on the right bank. At that time Tver was the residence of a prince of its own, dependent upon the principality of Suzdal. After the reign of Mikhaïl Borísovitch Tver fell, in 1490, into the hands of the Muscovite State. In 1569 Iván IV. passed through Tver on his campaign against Novgorod and delivered its inhabitants up to the brutality of his soldiers.

From the railway station the Tryokhsvyatskáya (electric tramway, see above) leads, in a straight direction, to the (40 min.) so-called OCTAGONAL SQUARE (Осьмиугóльная плóщадь), also known as the *Catherine Square.* This is surrounded by the *Law Courts,* the *Government Offices,* and other public buildings. A little way beyond this square, in the same direction, we reach the lofty bank of the Volga, along which runs a promenade planted with trees. Below (5 min.) is the landing-place of the Samolet steamers.

To the E. and W. of the Octagonal Square, parallel with the Volga, runs the MILLIÓNNAYA, the chief street of the city. The E. part of it leads to the right to the Post Office Square (post office, see p. 267). A little to the E. of this is the *Lutheran Church*. In following the Milliónnaya to the W. (left) from the Octagonal Square, we have on our left the *Gostíni Dvor* or *Bazaar*, and on our right the *Public Garden* (summer restaurant), which extends on the N. to the Volga. Farther on, to the left, is the *High School*. To the right, opposite (8 min. from the Octagonal Square), is the rectangular *Cathedral of the Transfiguration*, built in 1689. Five domes rise from its flat roof. In the interior, in a sarcophagus under a canopy between the two S. piers, are the remains of St. Mikhaíl Yaroslávitch, a Grand-Prince of Tver, who was murdered by the Tartars in 1318. To the N., behind the church, is the *Imperial Palace*, the left wing of which contains an interesting Museum (open on Sun. & Thurs. 12-2 p.m.; castellan in charge), with prehistoric, ecclesiastical, industrial art, and other collections. A little farther to the N. is an iron suspension-bridge, leading to the left bank of the Volga.

The Milliónnaya ends at the Tmaká. Hence we cross the bridge and proceed in a straight direction for about ¹/₂ M., then turn to the left and reach the *Tróitzi Church* (Церковь живоначáльной трóицы), with its seven domes, built in 1564. The so-called 'Little Church', in the interior, to the right of the ikonostás, contains a door adorned with decorations in lead (14th cent.). On the upper floor are the so-called Secret Chambers (Палáтки; inaccessible), with scarcely noticeable slits in the wall instead of windows. These were used by the clergy and citizens to conceal their treasure from hostile invaders.

On the left bank of the Volga, at the confluence of the Tvertzá, is the *Otrótch Monastery* (Отрóчь успéнскій мужскóй монастырь), founded in 1265. Here is shown the cell (now a chapel) of *Philip*, the former Metropolitan of Moscow, who was deposed by Iván the Terrible in 1568, and was strangled at Tver in the following year. — About 2¹/₂ M. to the S.W. of Tver, on the Tmaká, is the *Zhóltikov Monastery* (Жéлтиковъ успéнскій мужскóй монастырь), built by St. Arsenius in 1394. The Tzarévitch Alexis, son of Peter the Great, was once confined in a room above the fortified gateway.

From Tver a steamer of the Samolet Co. runs daily to (2 days) *Ruibinsk* (fares 8 rb. 5, 6 rb. 45 cop.; comp. R. 45).

After crossing the bridge over the *Shosha*, the train enters the fertile and industrious government of Moscow.

526 V. *Klin* (Rail. Restaurant), a town on the *Sestrá*, with 7000 inhab., was the ancestral home of the Románov family. The Tchaikóvski house was occupied by the composer, P. I. Tchaikóvski from 1885 till his death in 1893.

606 V. *Petróvsko-Razumóvskoye* (p. 323). — 610 V. (404 M.) *Moscow* (Nicholas or Kursk Station), see p. 269.

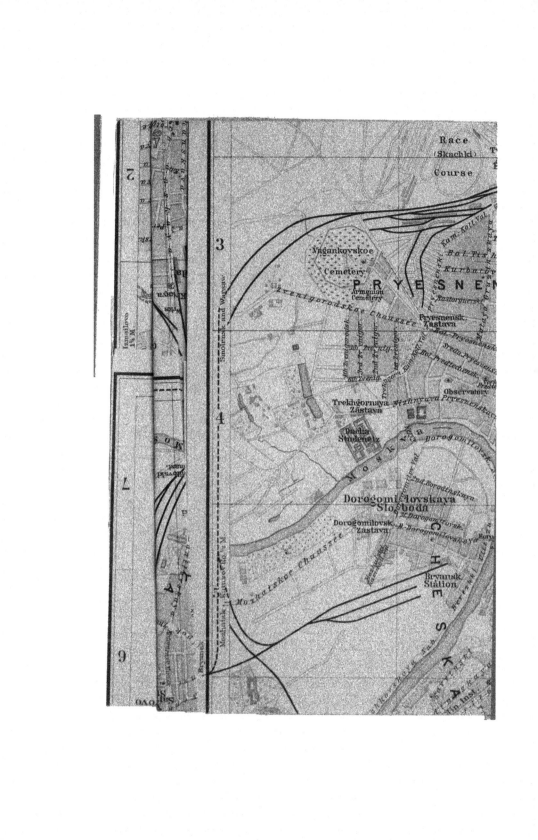

38. Moscow.

Moscow time is 29 min. in advance of that of St. Petersburg.
PLANS OF THE CITY. The principal plan (opposite) is referred to in the text as Pl. *I*, the plan of the inner city (p. 296) as Pl. *II*.

I. Arrival. Departure. Railway Stations.

ARRIVAL. *Izvóshtchik* from the railway stations to the inner city in summer 60-80, in winter 50-60 cop.; the cabs nearest the station-exits charge the most. *Motor Omnibuses* from the larger hotels (preferable) meet most of the trains.—DEPARTURE. Tickets should be bought in advance (comp. p. xxiii) at the *City Office of the State Railways* (Городская станція казённыхъ желѣзныхъ дорóгъ), in the Hôtel Métropole Buildings (Pl. c, D 4; *II*), Teatrálni Proyézd (open on week-days 9.30 to 5, Sun. & holidays 10-1); at the office of the *International Sleeping Car Co.*, at the same address (open week-days 9-5, Sun. & holidays 9.30 to 12); and at the tourist-agency of *E. Garbell*, Kuznetzki Most 13 (Pl. D, 4; *II*).

Railway Stations. Moscow has nine railway stations:

1. NICHOLAS or ST. PETERSBURG STATION (Николáевскій вокзáлъ; Pl. E, 2, 3, *I*), on the N.E. side of the town, for some of the St. Petersburg trains (R. 37). D. in the restaurant (12-8 p.m.) 1 rb.—Tramways Nos. 4, 6, 8, 10, 29, 30, & 34.

Key to the Numbers on the General Plan of Moscow.

1. Administration of Studs	C 4	24. Commercial School . .	C 5
2. Alexander & Marie School		25. Commissariat, New . .	E 5
for Girls	C 5	26. Commissariat, Old . .	E 5
		27. Deaf and Dumb Institute	C 7
ALMSHOUSES.		28. Duma (City Hall) . . .	D 4
		29. Fire Brigade	C 5
3. Artisans' . .	D 3	30. Governor-General's Resi-	
4. Catherine . .	G 1	dence	C D, 4
5. Kurakin . .	E 3	31. High School, 1st . . .	C 5
6. Merchants'	B 7	32. High School, 2nd. . . .	F 3
7. Nabilkov . .	E 2	33. High School, 6th. . .	D 5
8. Preobrazhenski	H 1	34. Historical Museum . .	D 4
9. Protestant . . .	G 3	35. Iberian Chapel	D 4
10. Archæological Society	D 5	36. Industrial Art Museum . D, 3, 4	
11. Archives of the Ministry		37. Industrial Art School	C 2
of Justice	B 6	38. Ivan Veliki . . .	D 4
		39. Krasniya Gate . .	E 3
BARRACKS.		40. Military Stores . .	C 5
12. Alexander	D 7	41. Nicholas Lyceum .	C 5
13. Cavalry	C 6	42. Orphanage	D 7
14. Khamovnitcheski	B, C, 6	43. Pirogov Monument	B, 5, 6
15. Spanski	E 3	44. Pokrovski Community,	
		Hospital of . . .	G 2
CATHEDRALS.		45. Pokrovski Monastery . .	F 5
		46. Polytechnic Museum . .	D 4
16. Kazan	D 4	47. Preobrazhenski Hospital	G 1
17. St. Basil Blazhenni	D 4	48. Protestant Hospital	E 4
18. Uspenski	D 4	49. Romanov House	D 4
		50. Shanyavski People's Uni-	
19. Catherine Institute for		versity	C, 2, 3
Girls	D 2	51. Sheremetyev Hospital . D, E, 3	
20. Church of St. Michael .	F 3	52. Surveying School . . .	F 3
21. Church of St. Nikita the		53. Widows' Home	B 4
Martyr	F 3	54. Zatchatiyevski Convent .	C 5
22. City Governor's Office .	C 4		
23. Commercial Institute . .	D 6		

2. Yaroslavl Station (Яросла́вскій вокза́лъ; Pl. E 2, *I*), near the Nicholas Station, for Yaróslavl, Kostroma (R. 41), and Archangel (R. 42). Tramways 4, 6, 8, 10, 29, 30, & 34.

3. Kazan and Ryazan Station (Каза́нскій вокза́лъ; Pl. E 3, *I*), opposite the Nicholas Station on the S., for Kazan, Ryazan, Orenburg-Tashkent, Kozlov-Saratov, Voronezh-Rostov (Baku), etc. — Tramways 4, 6, 8, 10, 29, 30, & 34.

4. Kursk and Nizhni-Novgorod Station (Ку́рско-Нижегоро́дскій вокза́лъ; Pl. F 4, *I*), not far from the Sadóvaya, for most of the St. Petersburg trains and for Tula (Ryazhsk, Siberia), Orel, Kursk, Kiev, Kharkov-Rostov (Baku), Odessa, Sebastopol, Vladimir, and Nizhni-Novgorod. — Tramways 1, 31, & Б.

5. Alexander or Brest Station (Алекса́ндровскій вокза́лъ; Pl. B 3, *I*), on the W. side of the town, outside the Arch of Triumph, for Smolensk (Riga), Brest, Warsaw, etc. — Tramways 1, 6, 8, 13, 16, & 36.

6. Bryansk Station (Бря́нскій вокза́лъ; Pl. B 5, *I*), in the Dorogomilovskaya suburb, for Bryansk (Kiev) and Kaluga. — Tramways 4 & 31.

7. Windau Station (Винда́вскій нокза́лъ; Pl. D 1, *I*), near the Krestóvskaya Zastáva, for Ryezhitza (Wirballen), Riga, and Windau. Tramways 17 & 19.

8. Savelovo Station (Саве́ловскій вокза́лъ; Pl. C 1, *I*), near the Butúirskaya Zastáva, for Savelovo (p. 348). — Tramways 18, 27, & 29.

9. Saratov Station (Сара́товскій вокза́лъ; Pl. E 6, *I*), in the S. side of the town, for Kozlov-Saratov (R. 60). — Tramways 19, 25, & 30.

II. Hotels. Restaurants.

Hotels. *Hôtel National (Націона́льная гости́ница; Pl. g, D 4; *II*), at the corner of the Tverskáya and the Mokhováya, R. from 3 rb. (with bath from 8 rb.), B. ³/₄, déj. (11-3) 1¹/₂, D. (3-8 p.m.) 2¹/₄, omn. 1 rb.; Hôtel Métropole (Pl. c, D 4; *II*), in the Theatre Square, a large house, R. 3-10, B. ³/₄, déj. (12-3 p.m.) 1¹/₄, D. (6-9 p.m.) 1¹/₂-3, omn. 1 rb.; Slavyánski Bazaar (Pl. a, D 4; *II*), Nikólskaya 9, R. from 2 rb., B. 65 cop., déj. (11-2) 1 rb. 20 cop., D. (3-7.30 p.m.) 1¹/₂ & 2¹/₂, omn. 1 rb., all three of the first class. — Hôtel Dresden (Pl. b, D 4; *II*), Tverskáya, opposite the Governor-General's House, R. from 1¹/₂ rb., B. 65 cop., déj. (12-2 p.m.) 1, D. (2-7 p.m.) 1¹/₂, omn. ³/₄ rb.; Alpine Rose (Альпі́йская Ро́за; Pl. l, D 4; *II*), Sofíka 4, R. from 2 rb., B. 60, déj. (11-3) 80 cop., D. (3-8 p.m.) 1 & 2, omn. 1 rb.; Savoy Hotel, adjacent, cor. of Rozhdéstvenka, similar charges (several rooms with baths); Hôtel Billo (Pl. d, D, 3, 4; *II*), Bolshaya Lubyánka 9, R. from 1¹/₂, B. ³/₄, omn. 1 rb., patronized by Germans; Hôtel Berlin (Pl. e, D 4; *II*), Rozhdéstvenka, commercial and German, R. 2-10 rb., B. 60 cop., déj. (11 to 2.30) ³/₄, D. (2.30 to 8 p.m.) 1-1³/₄, omn. ³/₄ rb.; Rossíya (Pl. f, D 3; *II*), at the corner of the Petróvka and the Petróvskiya Líniya; Yevrópa (Pl. h, D 4; *II*), Neglínni Proyézd; Grand-Hôtel de Paris (Pl. i, D 4; *II*), Tverskáya. — The following are run on Russian lines: Bolshaya Moskóvskaya Gostínitza (Pl. n, D 4; *II*), first-class, in the Voskresénskaya Square, R. 2-15 rb., B. ¹/₂, déj. (12-3 p.m.) 1¹/₄, D. (3-9 p.m.) 1¹/₂ & 2¹/₂ rb.; Frántziya (Pl. m, D 4; *II*), Tverskáya, Filíppov House; Loskútnaya Gostínitza (Pl. k, D 4; *II*), Tverskáya, R. from 1, D. (2-7 p.m.) 1¹/₄ rb.

Pensions. *Hollberg*, Lubyánski Proyézd 3 (Pl. D, 4; *I*), Stakhéyev House, pens. 3-4 rb.; *Takke*, Trubnikóvski Pereúlok 30 (Pl. C, 4; *I*), pens. 4-6 rb. (less in summer). — *Home of the Society for Protestant Girls* (Убе́жище евангели́ческаго попечи́тельства о де́вицахъ), Nóvaya Basmánnaya (Pl. E, F, 3; *I*), for governesses. — Furnished Rooms (Меблиро́ванныя ко́мнаты; R. 15-25 per month, with board 40-70 rb.).

Restaurants (open from noon). *Hermitage (Pl. D, 3; *II*), Trúbnaya Square, with concert-garden, déj. (12-2) 1¹/₄, D. (2-8.30) 1¹/₂ & 2¹/₂ rb.; *Hôtel National (see above); *Hôtel Métropole (see above); *Slavyánski Bazaar (see above); *Bolshaya Moskóvskaya Gostínitza (see above); *Praga, Arbátskaya Square, cor. of Arbát (Pl. C, 4; *II*), déj. 60 cop. & 1 rb., D. (2.30-9 p.m.) 1¼ & 2½ rb.; Tyestov, Theatre Sq. (Pl. D, 4; *II*), cor. of Voskresénskaya Sq.; New Peterhof, Mokhováya, near the Vozdvízhenka (Pl. D, 4; *II*), with garden, déj. (12-4 p.m.) 1, D. (4-7 p.m.) 1 rb.—Hôtel Billo (p. 270), beer; Hôtel Berlin (p. 270); in the Upper Rows (p. 299), D. (4-8 p.m.) 1¼ rb., very fair; Trekhgorni, Petrovka, Dom Gratcheva; Hôtel Yevrópa (p. 270), D. (4-8) 65 cop.; K. I. Kirpikóv, Kuznétzki Most (Pl. D, 4; *II*), in the Tretyakóv Building, frequented for luncheon.— *Outside the Town.* *Yar (D. 2½ rb.), Mauritania (in summer only), Stryelna (in winter only), all three in the Petróvski Park (p. 323) and much frequented in the evening (not cheap).

Cafés. Hôt. Métropole (p. 270); Filíppov, at the corner of the Tverskáya and the Gliníshtchevski Pereúlok (Pl. C, D, 3, 4; *II*), also cold dinners.— **Confectioners.** Cadet, Einem, both in the Petróvka; Siou, Kuznétzki Most, Dzhamgárov Arcade.

III. Carriages. Electric Tramways. Steamers.

Carriages (comp. p. xxiv). There is no definite tariff; the fares from the railway stations are given at p. 269.—Izvóshtchik (two seats, with movable top), short drive 20-30, longer drive 40-80 cop., at night rather more; within the town for the whole day (not recommended) 2½-3, outside the town 3-4 rb.—Likhatchí (p. 90) are found only in front of the best restaurants; short drive at least 1-2 rb. These vehicles are very popular for drives to the places of amusement outside the town (fare 5-10 rb., if engaged in the evening and kept all night 10-20 rb.).—Motor Cabs for 1-3 pers., first verst 40, each additional verst 30 cop.—Calèches (with two or four seats; stands on the Lubyánka Square and elsewhere): 60 cop. to 1 rb. per hr., 4-5 rb. per day.—Tróikas, suitable for excursions; fare 10-25 rb. according to time and distance.—Landaus (fare per half-day 5-8, per day 8-10, if outside the town 9-12 rb.) may be hired of *Yetch-kin*, Neglínni Proyézd (Pl. D, 3, 4; *II*).—Gratuity for the better class of carriages 30 cop. to 1 rb. On holidays, for 'corso' drives, and so forth, the charges for all kinds of carriages are often doubled.

Electric Tramways run from 6 or 7 a.m. till 10.30 p.m. or midnight. Fare according to zone (Станция) 5-10 cop.; transfer-tickets are also issued. The cars are entered by the back, and quitted by the front platform. The numbers of the lines are frequently changed, as the system has not yet been completed. The plan-references in the following list refer to Plan *I*.

1. *Alexander (Brest) Railway Station* (Pl. B, 3) to *Kursk Railway Station* (Pl. E, F, 4) viâ Petróvski Boulevard (Pl. D, 3) & Myasnítzkaya (Pl. D, E, 3, 4).—3. *Preobrazhénskaya Zastáva* (Pl. H, 1) to *Danílovski Ruinok (Serpukhovskáya Zastáva;* Pl. D, 7) viâ Pokróvskaya (Pl. F, G, 2, 3), Lubyánskaya Square (Pl. D, 4), & Kámenni Bridge (Pl. D, 5).—4. *Preobrazhénskaya Zastáva* (Pl. H, 1) to *Dorogomílovskaya Zastáva* (Pl. A, 5) viâ Kalantchévskaya Square (Pl. E, 3), Myasnítzkaya (Pl. D, E, 3, 4), & Arbát (Pl. C, 4).—5. *Preobrazhénskaya Zastáva* (Pl. H, 1) to *Smolénski Ruinok* (Pl. B, C, 5) viâ Pokróvskaya (Pl. F, G, 2, 3) & Sadóvaya.—6. *Petróvski Park* (Pl. B, 2) to *Sokólnitcheskaya Zastáva* (Pl. F, 1, 2) viâ Bolshaya Dmítrovka (Pl. D, 3, 4), & Myasnítzkaya (Pl. D, E, 3, 4).—7. *Kalúzhskaya Zastáva* (Pl. B, C, 7) to the *Sparrow Hills* (Pl. A, 7).—8. *Alexander (Brest) Railway Station* (Pl. B, 3) to *Kalantchévskaya Square* (Pl. E, 3) viâ Súkharevskaya Square (Pl. D, E, 3).

10. *Kalúzhskaya Square* (Pl. D, 6) to *Preobrazhénskaya Zastáva* (Pl. H, 1) viâ Polyánka (Pl. D, 5, 6), Sofíka (Pl. D, 4), & Súkharevskaya Square (Pl. D, E, 3).—11. *Máryina Roshtcha* (Kamer Kollézhski Val; Pl. D, 1) to *Kalúzhskaya Square* (Pl. D, 6) viâ Catherine Park (Pl. D, 2), Neglínni Proyézd (Pl. D, 3, 4), & Krásnaya Square (Pl. D, 4).—13. *Petróvski Park* (Pl. B, 2) to *Serpukhovskáya Square* (Pl. D, 6) viâ Arbátskaya Square (Pl. C, 4) & Polyánka (Pl. D, 5, 6).—15. *Tzarítzuinskaya Square* (Pl. B, 6)

to *Tagánskaya Square* (Pl. E, 5) viâ Trúbnaya Square (Pl. D, 3) & Lubyán-skaya Square (Pl. D, 4). — 16. *Spásskaya Zastáva* (Pl. F, 6) to *Alexander (Brest) Railway Station* (Pl. B, 3) viâ Tagánskaya Square (Pl. E, 5), Lubyán-skaya Square (Pl. D, 4), & Bolshaya Nikítskaya (Pl. C, 4). — 17. *Novodye-vítchi Convent* (Pl. A, 6) to *Windau Railway Station* (Pl. D, 1) viâ Arbát (Pl. C, 4, 5), Sofíka (Pl. D, 4), & Sryétenka (Pl. D, 3). — 18. *Butúirskaya* (Pl. B, 1) to *Kalúzhskaya Zastáva* (Pl. B, C, 7) viâ Bolshaya Dmítrovka (Pl. D, 3, 4) & Volkhónka (Pl. C, 5). — 19. *Windau Railway Station* (Pl. D, 1) to *Sarátov Railway Station* (Pl. E, 6) viâ Lubyánskaya Square (Pl. D, 4).
    20. *Sokólnitcheskaya Zastáva* (Pl. F, 2) to *Bogoródskoye* (beyond Pl. F, G, 1). — 21. *Pokróvskaya Zastáva* (Pl. F, 5) to *Pokróvskaya Zastáva* (Pl. F, 5) viâ Lubyánskaya Square (Pl. D, 4), Krásniya Gate (Pl. E, 3) & Nyemétzkaya (Pl. F, 3). — 22. *Pryésnenskaya Zastáva* (Pl. B, 3) to *Seménov-skaya Zastáva* (Pl. H, 2) viâ Bolshaya Nikítskaya (Pl. C, 4) & Myasnítzkaya (Pl. D, E, 3, 4). — 23. *Pokróvskaya Zastáva* (Pl. F, 5) to *Novodyevítchi Convent* (Pl. A, 6) viâ Lubyánskaya Square (Pl. D, 4) & Volkhónka (Pl. C, 5). — 24. *Tzaritzuinskaya* (Pl. B, 5, 6) to *Hospitálnaya Square* (Pl. G, 3) viâ Mokhováya (Pl. C, D, 4) & Lubyánskaya Square (Pl. D, 4). — 25. *Pryésnen-skaya Zastáva* (Pl. B, 3) to *Sarátov Railway Station* (Pl. E, 6) viâ Bolshaya Dmítrovka (Pl. D, 3, 4) & Krásnaya Square (Pl. D, 4). — 26. *Yelókhovskaya Square* (Pl. F, 3) to *Yekaterininskaya Square* (Pl. D, 2) viâ Marosséika (Pl. D, E, 4) & Sofíka (Pl. D, 4). — 27. *Butúirskaya* (Pl. C, 1) to *Rogózh-skaya Zastáva* (Pl. F, 5) viâ Bolshaya Dmítrovka (Pl. D, 3, 4). — 28. *Spás-skaya Zastáva* (Pl. F, 6) to *Simónovskaya Zastáva* (Pl. E, F, 7). — 29. *Petróvski Park* (Máslovka Vérkhnyaya; Pl. A, B, 1) to *Sokólnitcheskaya Zastáva* (Pl. F, 1, 2) viâ Butúirskaya Zastáva (Pl. C, 1), Málaya Dmítrovka (Pl. C, 3), Pokróvka (Pl. E, 4), & Kalantchévskaya Square (Pl. E, 3).
    30. *Spásskaya Zastáva* (Pl. F, 6) to *Kozhevnítcheskaya* (Pl. E, 6) viâ Dvortzóvi Bridge (Pl. F, G, 4), Kalantchévskaya Square (Pl. E, 3), & Krás-naya Square (Pl. D, 4). — 31. *Kursk Station* (Pl. E, F, 4) to *Dorogomílov-skaya Zastáva* (Pl. A, 5) viâ Pokróvka (Pl. E, 4) & Arbat (Pl. C, 4). — 32. *Rogózhskaya Zastáva* (Pl. F, 5) to *Máryina Roshtcha* (Kamer Kollézhski Val; Pl. D, 1) viâ Solyánka (Pl. E, 4), Sryétenka (Pl. D, 3), & Bozhedóm-skaya (Pl. D, 2). — 33. *Lubyánskaya Square* (Pl. D, 4) to *Serpukhovskaya Square* (Pl. D, 6) viâ Varvárskaya Square (Pl. D, E, 4) & Tchugúnni Bridge (Pl. D, 5). — 34. *Kalantchévskaya Square* (Pl. E, 3) to *Tzaritzuinskaya* (Pl. B, 5, 6) viâ Myasnítzkaya (Pl. D, E, 3, 4), Mokhováya (Pl. C, D, 4), & Pret-chistenka (Pl. C, 5). — 36. *Alexander (Brest) Railway Station* (Pl. B, 3) to *Danílovskaya Suburb* (Pl. D, 7) viâ Bozhedómskaya (Pl. D, 2), Sryétenka (Pl. D, 3), & Krásnaya Square (Pl. D, 4).
    A. *Circular Line* viâ the Boulevards. — B. *Circular Line* viâ the Sadó-vaya (p. 277). — B. *Circular Line* viâ the Kamer-Kollézhski Val (under construction).

Steam Tramway (to be electrified); from the *Butúirskaya Zastáva* (Pl. C, 1; *I*) to *Petróvsko-Razumóvskoye* (p. 323), every ¹/₂ hr.; fare 10 cop.

Steamers. From *Bolótnaya Square* (Pl. D 5, *I;* Tramways No. 3, 10, 13, & 18) to *Sparrow Hills* (Pl. A, 7; *I*), ¹/₂ hr., 10 cop. (holidays 15 cop.); from *Sparrow Hills* to *Borodinski Bridge* (Pl. B, 5; *I*), 10 or 15 cop.; from *Moskvoryétzki Bridge* (Pl. D, 4; *I*) to *Símonov Monastery* (Pl. E, F, 7; *I*), 5 or 10 cop.

IV. Post & Telegraph Offices. Consulates. Police Stations. Commissionnaires.

Post Office. The *General Post Office* (ПОЧТА́МТЪ; Pl. E 3, *II*), at the corner of the Myásnitzkaya and the Tchístoprúdni Boulevard (p. 311), is open on week-days 9-4 (for receiving and issuing registered letters, till 9 p.m.), on Sun. and holidays 9-11 a.m. There are branch-offices in the Exchange (Pl. D, 4; *II*), in the Upper Rows (Pl. D, 4; *II*), in the Hotel Métropole Buildings (Pl. c, D 4; *II*), and at numerous other points. They are open on week-days from 8 a.m. to 2 p.m. (registered letters also 5-7 p.m.), on Sun. and holidays 8-10 a.m. (comp. p. xxviii). An ordinary letter within the limits of the city delivery costs 3 cop.

Telegraph Office. The *General Telegraph Office* (Pl. E 3, *II;* p. 311), open day and night, is in the Myásnitzkaya, adjoining the General Post Office. Telegrams within the city cost 15 cop. plus 1 cop. per word.

Consulates. GREAT BRITAIN: Consul-General, *C. T. R. Clive-Bayley*, Bolshaya Moltchanovka 21bis (Pl. C 4, *II;* 10-2); Vice-Consul, *R. H. Bruce Lockhart.* — UNITED STATES OF AMERICA: Consul-General, *J. H. Snod grass*, Arkhángelski Pereúlok 9 (Pl. E, 3, 4, *II;* 10-1 & 2-4); Deputy Consul, *A. W. Smith.* — LLOYD'S AGENT, *John Foulis-Munro*, Bolshaya Orduinka

Police. *Chief of Police* or *City Governor* (Градоначáльникъ; Pl C 4, *II*), Tverskói Boulevard. — *Address Office* (Áдресный стóлъ), Známenski Pereúlok 3 (Pl. D, 3; *II*), open on week-days 9-4, Sun. and holidays 9-1. Fee for looking up each address 3 cop.

Commissionnaires (Posúilnuiye), distinguished by red caps and collars: message within the Kremlin and Kitái Gorod 10, in the Byeli-Gorod 20, in the Zemlyanói Gorod 30 cop.

V. Theatres. Concerts. Clubs.

Theatres (closed in summer). The performances generally begin at 7.30 or 8 p.m. and last till midnight. It is best to buy tickets at the box-office, open after 10 a.m.; in the evening the dealers exact high prices.

Great Imperial Theatre (Pl. D, 4; *II*), in the Theatre Square (p. 309). Operas and ballets. Prices of seats at the opera: box in 1st tier 15 rb.; 'bel étage' (dress-circle) 15 rb.; box in 2nd tier 9½; 3rd tier 7, 4th tier 5 rb.; lettered boxes in 3rd tier 10, in 4th tier 6 rb.; stalls 1 rb. 80 cop. to 6 rb.; third balcony 1 rb. 50 cop., fourth balcony 1 rb. 10 cop.

Little Imperial Theatre (Pl. D 4, *II;* p. 309), opposite the Great Theatre. Dramas. — Prices: lettered boxes 14, boxes and bel étage 12, stalls 2-5, amphitheatre 2½ rb.; first balcony 1 rb. 80 cop.; second balcony 1 rb. 10 cop. to 1½ rb.

New Imperial Theatre (Nezlobin Theatre; Pl. D 4, *II*), in the Theatre Square, for plays. Prices: bel étage 10 rb.; stalls 1 rb. 80 cop. to 5 rb.; first balcony 1½ rb.

Moscow Art Theatre (Худóжественный теáтръ; Pl. D 4, *II*), Kamergérski Pereúlok, stalls 2-5 rb.; for drama; noted for its admirable *ensemble* and its artistic stage-equipments; all seats taken by subscribers.

Korsh Theatre, Petróvka, cor. of Bogoslóvski Pereúlok (Pl. D, 3; *II*), for Russian plays, also used for German performances; *Solodóvnikov Theatre (Zimin Theatre)*, Bolsháya Dmitrovka (Pl. D, 3, 4; *II*), for opera; *Nikitski Theatre*, Kulashni Pereúlok, near the Nikitskiya Gate (Pl. C, 4; *II*), for operettas; *Independent Theatre*, at the Hermitage (see below; in winter only), for opera, drama, and comic opera.

VARIETY THEATRES. *Hermitage* (not to be confounded with the restaurant mentioned at p. 270), Karétni Ryad 3 (Pl. D, 3; *I*), for vaudeville, operettas, and variety performances (in summer only); *Aquarium*, Sadóvaya, near the Tverskáya (Pl. C, 3; *I*), in summer only. — *Zon's Theatre* (formerly *Bouffes*), Triumfálnaya Square (Pl. C, 3; *II*), in winter only. — CABARET. *The Bat* (Letútchaya Muish), Milyutinski Pereúlok 16 (Pl. C, 3, 4; *II*), with performances at 11 p.m. (adm. 5-10 rb.).

Truzzi Circus (Pl. D, 3; *II*), in the Tzvyetnói Boulevard. Prices: box 10½ rb.; seat 1 rb. 10, 2 rb. 10, or 3 rb. 10 cop. — *Nikitin Circus*, Triumfálnaya Sadóvaya (Pl. C, 3; *I*).

Concerts. The *Symphony Concerts* founded by Nicholas Rubinstein (d. 1881) take place in the large concert-hall of the Conservatorium (Pl. C, 4; *II*), Bolshaya Nikitskaya; the concerts of the *Philharmonic Society* in the hall of the Club of the Nobless (Pl. D, 4; *II*). — *Military Concerts* (in summer) on the Boulevards, in Sokólniki Park (p. 312), and in the Zoological Gardens (p. 307).

Clubs. English: *British Club*, at the Hôtel National (p. 270; subscription 35, entrance-fee 10 rb.); *British Sports Club* (subscription 10 rb.). — Russian: *English Club* (Англійскій Клубъ; Pl. C 3, II), Tverskáya, fashionable (strangers may be introduced by a member); *Club of the Noblesse* (Дворянскій Клубъ or Благорóдное Собрáніе; Pl. D 4, II), Bolshaya Dmítrovka (good balls, concerts, and fêtes); *Merchants' Club* (Купéческое Собрáніе), Málaya Dmítrovka 6 (Pl. C, 3; II).

VI. Churches. Physicians. Chemists. Baths. Shops. Banks.

Churches. ENGLISH CHURCH (*St. Andrew's;* Pl. C 4, II), Bolshói Tchernuishóvski Pereúlok, service on Sun. at 11 a.m., in winter also at 7 p.m. Chaplain, *Rev. F. W. North.* Lending Library, Bryusovski Pereúlok. — GERMAN PROTESTANT SERVICES at the *Church of SS. Peter & Paul* (p. 312; 10 a.m.), at *St. Michael's Church* (p. 313; 10.30 a.m.), and at the *Reformed Church* (Pl. E 4, II; 11 a.m.), Mali Tryokhsvyatítelski Pereúlok. — ROMAN CATHOLIC SERVICES at the *Church of SS. Peter & Paul* (p. 310) and the *Church of St. Louis* (p. 310).

Physicians. *Dr. L. Levin,* Mamonovski Pereúlok; *Dr. J. Goldendach; Dr. R. Hirschfeld; Dr. O. Schmidt; Dr. J. Taube; Dr. Wellberg* — AMERICAN DENTIST. F. *Lambie,* Kamergérski Pereúlok 2. — PROTESTANT HOSPITAL (Pl. 48, E 4; I), Vorontzóvo Pole 14. *Private Hospital of Dr. von Schiemann* (German), Yáuzski Boulevard (Pl. E, 4; II).

Chemists. *V. K. Ferrein,* Nikólskaya; *Sack,* Myasnítzkaya; *Wagner* (homœopathic), Marosseika.

Baths (Бáни). *Sandunóvskiya Baths* (Pl. D, 3; II), Neglínni Proyézd, bath ¹/₂ - 5 rb.; *Central* (Pl. D, 4; II), Teatrálni Proyézd, bath 1 - 10 rb. Both have good public baths (60 cop.) and are open from 6 a.m. to 11 p.m. Fee to attendant 20-50 cop.

Shops. The best shops are in the Kuznétzki Most (P. 309), in the neighbouring streets, such as the Lubyánka, Sofíka, Petróvka, and Tverskáya, in the Solodóvnikov, Golovtéyev, Petróvski, Lubyánski, Dzhamgárov, Póstnikov, and Alexander Arcades, and in the Upper Rows (p. 299) — BOOKSELLERS. German, *M. O. Wolff,* Kuznétzki Most; *J. Deubner,* Fur kásovski Pereúlok. French, *Tastevin,* Kuznétzki Most. Russian, *Karbasnikov,* Mokhováya; *A. S. Suvórin,* Neglínni Proyézd; *A. Ilin,* Petróvski Line (maps). — BOOTS. *M. Pironet,* Bolshaya Dmítrovka; *St. Petersburg Shoe Factory,* Upper Rows. — CIGARS. *Bernhardt, Reinhard,* both in the Kuznétzki Most. — DOMESTIC INDUSTRIES, *Museum of Domestic Industries* (p. 302); *Soyuz,* Neglínni Proyézd (Pl. D, 3, 4; II), Petróvski Arcade. — FURS. *P. Sorokoúmovski & Sons,* Ilyinka; *M. L. Byelkin,* Kuznétzki Most. — GENERAL MERCHANTS (dry goods). *Muir & Merrilees,* Petróvka, with a refreshment-room. — JEWELLERY AND ORNAMENTS (Russian workmanship). *M. P. Ovtchínnikov,* Kuznétzki Most. — ORIENTAL FABRICS of all kinds (wool, silk, etc.) in the Golovtéyev Arcade (company of a Russian friend desirable). — PHOTOGRAPHS. *Daziáro, Avanzo,* both in the Kuznétzki Most. Photographic Materials, *Kodak,* Petróvka. — PRESERVED FRUITS. *Abrikósov,* Solodóvnikov Arcade; *Cadet,* Petróvka, corner of Kuznétzki Pereúlok; *Einem,* Petróvka, Rudakóv Building. — RUBBER OVERSHOES. *Meyer & Co.,* Kamergérski Pereúlok. — RUSSIAN ANTIQUITIES may often be picked up cheaply in the *Sunday Market* in the Súkharev Square (Pl. D, E, 3; I) and in the adjoining streets. — TEA. *P. Botkin's Sons, K. & S. Popov, Caravan Co.* (Wogau and Co.).

Banks. *Imperial State Bank* (Pl. D, 3, 4; II), Neglínni Proyézd, open 10-3; *Russo-Asiatic Bank,* Ilyinka; *Commercial Bank of Siberia,* Ilyinka; *Union Bank,* Kuznétzki Most; *Crédit Lyonnais,* Kuznétzki Most; *J. W. Junker & Co.,* Kuznétzki Most; *G. Volkov & Sons,* Petróvka.

VII. Principal Attractions. Distribution of Time.

Botkin's Picture Gallery (p. 313), admission on application to the owner.
Domestic Industries, Museum of (p. 302), week-days 10-6, free.

Fine Arts, Museum of (p. 304), week-days, except Mon., 11-3, Sun. & holidays 12-3; free.

Historical Museum (p. 297), Sun., Tues., & Thurs., 11-3, free; from June 15th to Aug. 15th (O. S.) strangers are admitted on application.

Industrial Art Museum (p. 310), in summer, on week-days 11-3 (closed on Sun. and holidays); in winter 10-4, Sun. and holidays 10-3; free.

Kremlin. — *Cathedrals* and *Churches,* generally open 8-4. — *Court of Justice* (p. 296), week-days, 11-3. — *Great Palace* (p. 286), daily, except Sun. and festivals, 10-2; tickets obtained free (on exhibition of passport) 10-1, at the office of the Superintendent of Police in the Kremlin. — *Memorial Museum of the War of 1812* (p. 294), daily, 10-4, free. — *Oruzhéinaya Paláta* (P. 289), Mon., Wed., & Frid., except holidays, 10-2. Adm. as for the Great Palace (see above). — *Synodal Library* (p. 295), week-days 10-3; closed from May 15th to July 1st (O. S.). — *Synodal Treasury* (p. 282), week-days 10-1, on application at the Synod Building in the Kremlin; free.

Municipal Administration, Museum of (p. 311), daily 10-12 and 1-4, free.

Panorama (Battle of Borodinó; p. 313), daily, except Mon., 10-10; adm. 65, in the evening 75, on Sun. 32 cop.

Polytechnic Museum (p. 312), daily (except Mon. & Tues.) 11-3; on Wed. & Sat. 15 cop., at other times free.

Románov House (p. 300), Tues., Thurs., & Sat., 10-2, free; at other times, gratuity.

Rumyántzov Museum (p. 302), daily (except Mon. & holidays) 11-3, 20 cop. (Sun. free). Reading-room, open on week-days 10-8 (June 1st to Aug. 15th, 11-4).

Synodal Printing Office (p. 301), week-days except Sat., 10-3 in summer, 10-4 in winter, free.

Tolstoi Museum (p. 306), daily (except Mon.) 11-5, 30 cop.

Tretyakóv Gallery (p. 316), March 1st to Oct. 1st (O. S.), except Mon., daily 10-4, other months 10-3. Closed on Jan. 1st, Thurs., Frid. and Sat. of Holy Week, Easter Day, and Dec. 24th and 25th. The attendant takes care of overcoats and umbrellas, free of charge.

University. — *Botanical Gardens* (p. 311), on Wed. and Sun. 9-7 (Aug. 15th to May 15th 9-4), the Orangeries on Wed. and Sun. 2-4, free; strangers are admitted at any time by the Director. — *Library* (p. 302), week-days 10-3; in the summer vacation on Tues., Wed., and Thurs. only, 11-3. — *Zoological Museum* (p. 302), Sept. 1st to April 30th on Sun. 10-3, free.

Zoological Gardens (p. 307), daily 10-8 (in winter, 10-4); 35 cop.

Distribution of Time. In order to obtain a general impression of Moscow, it is advisable to begin our visit by the following circular drive of 1 hr.: from the Krásnaya Square (Pl. D 4, I; p. 296), viâ Nikólskaya (Pl. D 4, I; p. 300), Lubyánskaya Square (Pl. D 4, I; p. 310), and Neglínni Proyézd (Pl. D, 3, 4, I; p. 310); then to the left, viâ the *Boulevards,* to the Church of the Redeemer (Pl. C 5, I; p. 304), and thence along the S. wall of the Kremlin and back to Krásnaya Square.

1st Day. Kremlin (p. 278; Cathedrals and ascent of the Iván Velíki). — Petrovski Park (p. 323).

2nd Day. Kremlin (p. 278; Convents and Great Palace), Krásnaya Square (p. 296), Románov House (p. 300), Industrial Art Museum (p. 310). — Neskútchni Park (p. 320); Sparrow Hills (p. 320); Convent of the Maidens (p. 307).

3rd Day. Kremlin (P. 278; Oruzhéinaya Paláta and Synodal Treasury), Historical Museum (p. 297), Polytechnic Museum (p. 312), Súkharev Tower (p. 311). — Sokólniki Park (p. 312).

4th Day. Tretyakóv Gallery (p. 316). — Kuskovo and Kosino (p. 321).

5th Day. Rumyántzov Museum (p. 302), Church of the Redeemer (p. 304). — Excursion to Tzaritzuino (p. 322).

Those who have sufficient time may also make excursions to the *Troitzko-Sergiyevskaya Lavra (R. 40), to Ostankino (p. 324), to Arkhangelskoye (p. 324), and to New Jerusalem (p. 256).

Moscow (Москва, Moskvá; Ger. *Moskau*, Fr. *Moscou*), the sacred city of the Russians, the city with the 'white walls' (Бѣло-каменная), affectionately known as 'Little Mother Moscow' (Má-tyushka Moskvá), is situated at a height of 525-815 ft. above the sea, in 55° 45′ N. lat. and 37° 37′ E. long., and lies in a fertile undulating plain on seven hills rising in terraces from the banks of the *Moskvá* and its affluent the *Yáuza* (Яуза). It occupies an area of 27¹/₂ sq. M., the main part of it, including the Kremlin, being on the N. bank of the Moskvá, which is spanned by seven bridges. Moscow is the ancient capital of the empire and was the place where the Tzars held their court down to the time of Peter the Great. It is now the seat of the Metropolitan of Moscow and Kolomna, of the oldest Russian university, and of the Commandant of the Moscow Military District (incl. five Army Corps). It is also the chief railway centre as well as the chief commercial and industrial town of Russia, among the staples of its trade and produce being tea, cloth, and machinery. The population, including many Raskól-niks (p. lviii), increased from 602,000 in 1871 to 1,617,000 in 1912. The city contains about 450 churches, 25 convents, and 800 bene-volent institutions. The mean annual temperature is 40° Fahr.

Moscow is divided into 17 Districts *(T'chasti).* On the left bank of the Moskvá: I. *Gorodskáya,* II. *Tverskáya,* III. *Myasnítzkaya,* VI. *Pre-tchistenskaya,* VII. *Arbátskaya,* VIII. *Sryétenskaya,* IX. *Yáuzskaya,* X. *Basmánnaya,* XI. *Rogózhskaya,* XIII. *Khamovnítcheskaya,* XIV. *Présnen-skaya,* XV. *Sushtchévskaya,* XVI. *Myeshtchánskaya,* XVII. *Lefórtov-skaya Tchast.* — On the right bank of the Moskvá: IV. *Pyátnitzkaya,* V. *Yakimánskaya,* XII. *Serpukhóvskaya T'chast.* — These divisions form three police-districts, subdivided into 43 precincts.

According to an old historical distribution, which, however, is falling more and more into desuetude, Moscow, which has developed in concentric circles round its centre the Kremlin, is divided into five main parts, separated from each other by walls or boulevards. 1. The *Kremlin* (p. 278), the oldest part of the city. — 2. *Kitái-Gorod* (*i.e.* 'fortified city', Tartar Kitái = fortress; p. 296), the crowded and irregularly-built centre of business, with the Exchange, the Trading Rows, and so forth. The Kremlin and Kitái-Gorod are now combined to form the *Gorodskáya Tchast* (*i.e.* the 'City Quarter'). This inner city, generally known simply as *Gorod* ('City'), is surrounded by a whitewashed wall (built in 1534), about 1¹/₂ M. in length and relieved by numerous towers (chiefly of a bright green colour), turrets, and decorations. — 3. In a semicircle round the inner city stretches the *Byeli Gorod,* or *'White City',* the most elegant quarter of Moscow, with wide streets radiating from the Kremlin, numerous palaces and public buildings, and the most attractive shops. The 'White City' now embraces the Tverskáya Tchast (II) and the Myasnítzkaya Tchast (III) and is enclosed by a wide girdle of handsome *Boulevards,* 4¹/₂ M. in length. — 4. The White City' is adjoined by the *Zemlyanói Gorod,* or *'Earth City',*

so named after the earthen ramparts thrown up by Tzar Mikhail
Feódorovitch, the site of which is now occupied by the boulevard-
like *Garden Street (Sadóvaya),* 11 M. long. Zemlyanói-Gorod includes the 4-9th of the above-mentioned districts. — 5. The outermost zone is formed by the *Suburbs,* which occupy three-fourths
of the total area of Moscow and are surrounded by the Kamer-Kol-
lézhski ramparts, erected in 1742 but now fallen to decay. Of the
14 former Zastávas or barriers, the names alone remain. The suburbs embrace Districts X-XVII and contain many manufactories
(particularly on the banks of the Yáuza), several barracks, and the
railway stations. They are mainly occupied by the poorer classes.

If ever a city expressed the character and peculiarities of its
inhabitants, that city is Moscow, the 'heart of Russia', in which the
Russian 'wide nature' (широкая натура; p. xlii) is abundantly
obvious. The characteristic life and tendencies of the people are
seen in much, greater purity here than in St. Petersburg and are
much less influenced by W. Europe, though even Moscow is rapidly
becoming modernized of late years.

The TRAFFIC in the ill-paved streets is extraordinarily animated.
What is here known as the 'German' dress is predominant; but side
by side with· it we see the bearded muzhik in his bast slippers,
patched caftan, and gray armyák or sheepskin; the Russian pope in
his long brown robe, with his black hat and long hair and beard;
the merchant in his old-Russian fur cap, and his wife˜adorned with
strings of genuine pearls; Circassians, Tartars, and Bokhariots, all
in their national dress; Greeks in red fezes; Persians with high
conical caps of black sheepskin; and other types too numerous to
mention. The various costumes of the lower classes are best seen
at the POPULAR FESTIVALS and in the MARKETS. Of the latter the
most interesting is the *Okhótni Ryad* ('Hunter's Line'), or market
for vegetables, eggs, poultry, and game, held in the square of that
name (Pl. D 4, *II;* p. 308), near the Imperial Theatres. The Sunday market in the Súkharev Square, mentioned at p. 274, is also
notable. The most important market for fruit and flowers is held
in the *Bolótnaya Square* (Pl. D 5, *I;* p. 315); the chief flower-
market is held in the *Tzvyetnói Boulevard* (Pl. D 3, *I;* p. 309);
the horse-market takes place in the *Kónnaya Square* (Pl. D 6, *I;*
p. 319); while birds and dogs are bought and sold on Sun. in the
Trúbnaya Square (Pl. D 3, *II;* p. 309).

History. Moscow is mentioned by the chroniclers for the first time
in 1147, when Prince Yuri Dolgorúki of Suzdal invited Prince Svyatosláv
Olgovitch of Tchernigov to visit him here. It long remained a place of
no importance. In 1325 the *Metropolitan Peter* (d. 1326) transferred his
residence hither from Vladimir-on-the-Klyazma. This example was
followed in 1328 by *Grand-Prince Iván Danilovitch Kalitá* (1328-40),
who was recognized in 1333 by the Grand-Khan as chief ruler of Russia.
He surrounded the town with a palisade, and gave the name of Kremlin
to the castle. Under Demetrius Donskói (1363-89) the town was unsuccessfully besieged (1363) by the Grand-Prince Olgierd of Lithuania,

and in 1382 it was laid in ashes by the Khan Tokhtamysh. During the succeeding period it was frequently sacked by Mongolian hordes, and did not attain any great degree of prosperity until the reign of *Iván III. Vasilyevitch* (1462-1505), who made Moscow the centre of the now united kingdom, and beautified it by numerous buildings, erected by Italian architects. In 1520, during the reign of *Vasíli Ivánovitch* (1505-33), the town is said to have contained 45,000 dwelling-houses. Under I*ván the Terrible* (1533-84) the vigorous development of the city was interrupted by conflagrations (in 1547, etc.) and by hostile invasion, as in 1571, when it was captured by Devlet-Girei, Khan of the Crim-Tartars. In 1553 Iván concluded a commercial treaty with Queen Elizabeth of England, after the landing of Sir Richard Chancellor on the shore of the White Sea (comp. p. 335). In 1591 the Tartars, under Kara *G*irei, attacked Moscow for the last time. In 1612 the Poles, who had supported the claim of the False Demetrius to the throne of the Tzars, were expelled, and on Feb. 21st (March 4th), 1613, *Mikhail Feódorovitch Románov* (pp. xlix, 300), though under seventeen years of age, was chosen Tzar by the National Assembly. In 1711 the capital of the empire was, indeed, removed to the newly built St. Petersburg, but the immediate successors of Peter the *G*reat continued to favour the Kremlin rather than the still undeveloped town on the Nevá. In 1748 Moscow was raised to the dignity of an eparchy (see p. lviii), and in 1755 its university was founded.— The fate of Moscow in 1812 is universally known. On Sept. 2nd (14th) the *G*overnor, Count Rostoptchin, with the great majority of the population, left the city, and Napoleon entered it on the same day. On the following day began the conflagration, which was not subdued until Sept. 6th (18th), when three-fourths of all the houses in the city lay in ashes. On Oct. 11th (23rd) the French were compelled by famine to evacuate the city, but the order given to blow up the Kremlin, which so far had escaped comparatively uninjured, was carried out only in part. Of the 100,000 men who had entered Moscow with the Emperor Napoleon, 28,000 had either succumbed to famine or had been taken prisoners by the Russians. In 1813 began the rebuilding of the town, which quickly retrieved its former prosperity, while it was regarded with even greater veneration than before, on account of the aureola thrown around it by its stupendous fate. Comp. 'Moscow', by *Henry M. Grove* (1912), and 'The Story of Moscow', by *Wirt Gerrare* (1900).

a. The Kremlin.

In the centre of the city, on a hill rising 130 ft. above the Moskvá and dominating the whole of Moscow, rises the **Kremlin, in which all the reminiscences of Moscow's past are united. For the Russian the Kremlin is a holy spot. It is in the Kremlin that the power of the Tzars first receives the sanction of the church, when the bells of Iván Veliki announce to all Russia that the Tzar has ascended the throne of his ancestors. 'There is nothing above Moscow', says the proverb, 'except the Kremlin, and nothing above the Kremlin except Heaven'. — The best general views of the Kremlin are obtained from the Moskvoryétzki Bridge (p. 315) and from the Sofiskaya Náberezhnaya; Pl. D 5, *I*).

The ancient and fortress-like *Kremlin* (Кремль, formerly also called *Dyetinetz;* Pl. D 4, II) forms an irregular triangle, occupying an entire quarter of the city, and consists of a great conglomeration of ecclesiastical, palatial, and official buildings, enclosed by a battlemented brick wall 1¹/₄ M. in circumference and 65 ft. high, erected under Iván III. and

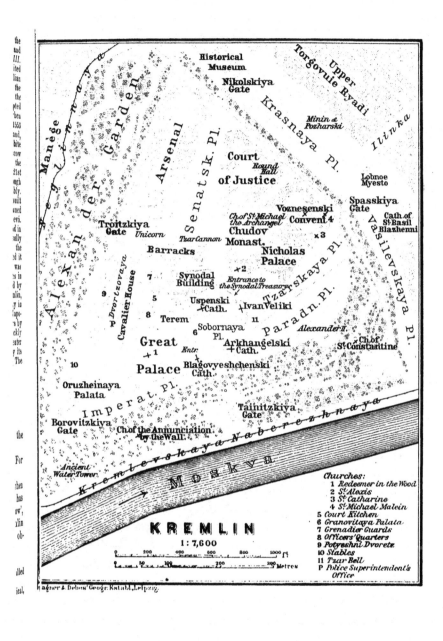

the
and
III.
ited
lian
the
the
pted
ben
1553
and,
bite
now
the
21st
ngh
bly.
built
uned
evi.
d in
ally
the
ed it
was
es in
d by
nlin,
y in
apos-
s by
ckly
nter
y its
The

the

For

rhen
has
ow',
nlin
ob-

lled

ical,

Manège

Historical Museum

Nikolskiya Gate

Upper Torgovuie Ryadi

Ilinka

Krasnaya Pl.

Neglinnaya

Alexander Garden

Arsenal

Senatsk. Pl.

Minin & Pozharski

Court of Justice

Round Hall

Lobnoe Myesto

Spasskiya Gate

Troitzkiya Gate

Unicorn

Ch. of St. Michael the Archangel

Voznesenski Convent 4

Cath. of St. Basil Blazhenni

Tzar Cannon

Chudov Monast.

×3

Barracks

Nicholas Palace

Dvortzovaya Cavalier House

7

×2

Synodal Building

Entrance to the Synodal Treasury

9

5

Uspenski Cath.

Ivan Veliki

Tzarskaya Pl.

Paradn. Pl.

Vasilevskaya Pl.

P

8

Terem

11

6

Sobornaya Pl.

Alexander II.

Great

+1

Entr.

Arkhangelski Cath.

Ch. of St. Constantine

10

Palace

Blagovyeshchenski Cath.

Oruzheinaya Palata

Imperat. Pl.

Tainitzkiya Gate

Borovitzkiya Gate

Ch. of the Annunciation by the Wall.

Ancient Water Tower

Kremlevskaya Naberezhnaya

Moskva

KREMLIN
1 : 7,600

0   200   400   600   800   1000 ft

0   50   100   150   200   250 Metres

Churches:
1 *Redeemer in the Wood*
2 *St. Alexis*
3 *St. Catharine*
4 *St. Michael Malein*
5 *Court Kitchen*
6 *Granovitaya Palata*
7 *Grenadier Guards*
8 *Officers' Quarters*
9 *Potyeshni Dvoretz*
10 *Stables*
11 *Tzar Bell*
P *Police Superintendent's Office*

Wagner & Debes' Geogr. Estabt., Leipzig.

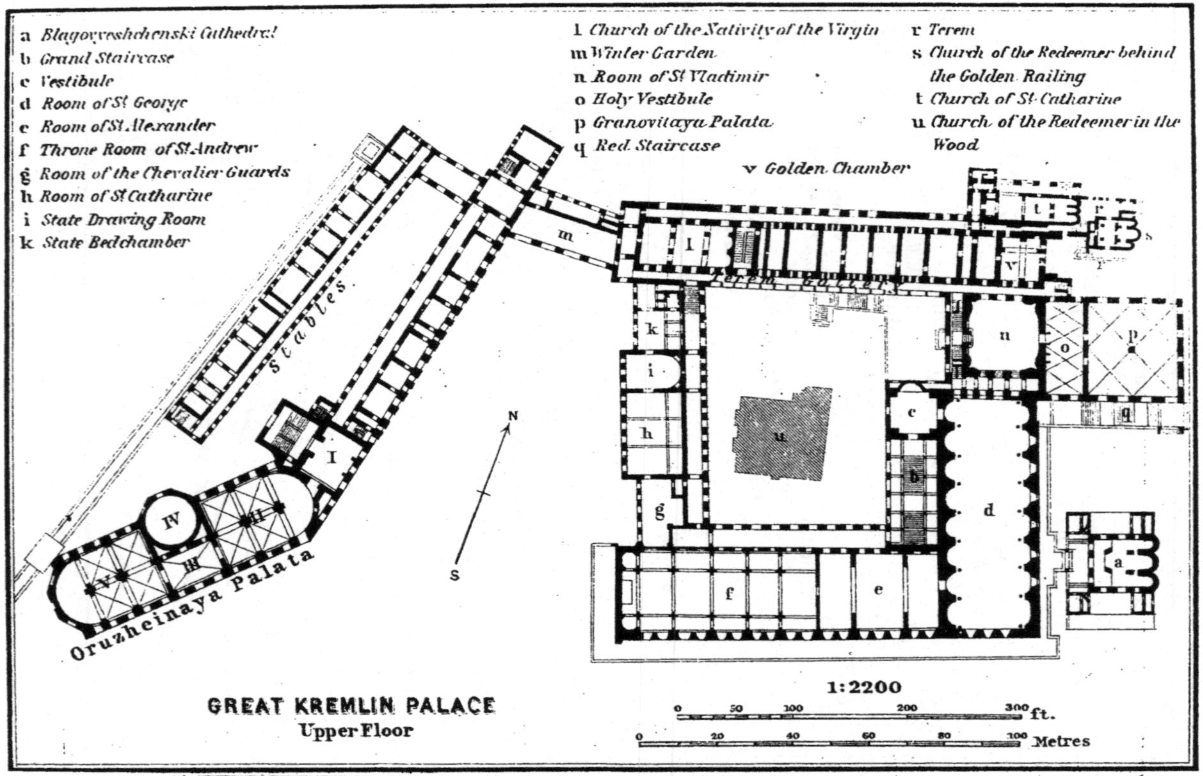

GREAT KREMLIN PALACE
Upper Floor

1:2200

a Blagovyeshchenski Cathedral
b Grand Staircase
c Vestibule
d Room of St George
e Room of St Alexander
f Throne Room of St Andrew
g Room of the Chevalier Guards
h Room of St Catharine
i State Drawing Room
k State Bedchamber

l Church of the Nativity of the Virgin
m Winter Garden
n Room of St Vladimir
o Holy Vestibule
p Granovitaya Palata
q Red Staircase
v Golden Chamber

r Terem
s Church of the Redeemer behind the Golden Railing
t Church of St Catharine
u Church of the Redeemer in the Wood

Oruzheinaya Palata

Stables

strengthened with nineteen towers. The characteristic Russian blend of
imperial and ecclesiastical power is nowhere more strongly expressed
than here, where the Palace of the Tzar stands surrounded by numerous
churches. — The Kremlin is entered by five GATES, almost all of which
are noteworthy, whether historically or on account of the style of their
architecture. On the E. is the *Spásskiya Gate* (see below); on the N.E.
is the *Nikólskiya Gate* (p. 296); on the W. is the *Tróitzkiya Gate* (p. 294);
on the S.W. is the *Borovitzkiya Gate* (p. 294); and on the S. is the *Tainitzkiya Gate*, the last used only by pedestrians.

From the Krásnaya Plóshtchad or Red Square (p. 296) we enter
the Kremlin by the **Spásskiya Gate** or **Gate of the Redeemer**
(Спáсскія ворóта), a tower-gateway 205 ft. in height, surmounted
by the Russian eagle. The lower part of the tower was built by
Pietro Antonio (p. 296) of Milan in 1491; the belfry was added by
the English architect Galloway in 1626; the present clock dates
from 1737. Outside the gate, on the right and left, are two small
chapels; above the entrance is the *Picture of the Saviour* placed
here by Tzar Alexis Mikháilovitch, in 1647, and regarded as the
Palladium of the Kremlin. The decree of Alexis that no man should
pass through this gateway with his hat on is still strictly enforced.

Passing through the gate, we find ourselves in a large open space
known as the SQUARE OF THE TZARS (Цáрская плóщадь, Tzárskaya
Plóshtchad). — To the right is the —

Voznesénski Nunnery, or *Convent of the Assumption*
(Вознесéнскій дѣвúчій монастырь), erected in 1389 by Eudoxia,
the wife of Grand-Prince Demetrius IV. Donskói, who retired to the
convent after the death of her husband, and died there in 1407. The
Church of St. Catharine (Pl. 3), the façade of which is painted
blue and is turned toward the Square of the Tzars, was built in
1817, in a mixed Gothic style. In the middle of the convent rise
the five gilded domes of the *Voznesénski Cathedral,* which was
built in 1519, and was last restored in 1721. It contains the relics
of 38 Grand-Princesses and Tzarinas, the series ending with Natalia
Alexéyevna (d. 1728), sister of Peter II. The tombs are mostly by
the W. wall. The Riznitza, or Sacristy, contains ancient palls and
numerous valuables. On the E. side of the convent is the *Church
of St. Michael Maléin* (Pl. 4), dating from 1634 and consisting of
two stories. To the left of the entrance to the upper church is a
painted relief of St. George and the Dragon (the arms of Moscow).

The Convent of the Assumption is adjoined by the **Nicholas**
or **Little Palace** (Николáевскій дворéцъ, Мáлый кремлéвскій
дворéцъ), which was erected from the plans of Kazakóv, in the
reign of Catherine II., for the Metropolitan Plato, purchased in 1817
for the Grand-Duke Nicholas, afterwards Tzar, and restored in 1872.
Alexander II. was born in this palace in 1818. The interior is very
simply fitted up. In Nicholas I.'s bedroom is his camp-bed. The
dining-room contains a painting by Belotto, representing the election
of Stanislaus Poniatowski on the plain of Wola in 1764. The larger

reception room is adorned with two large pictures by Aivazóvski, the Burning of Moscow (left) and the Church of the Redeemer (right). The palace is not shown except by special permission of the Superintendent of Police (p. 294).

Opposite the Nicholas Palace, on the side next the Moskvá, rises the large **Monument of Alexander II.**, unveiled in 1898. The bronze statue of the Tzar by *Opekúshin* is 21 ft. in height, and stands upon a pedestal of red granite, under a kind of canopy (118 ft. in height), which is supported by 16 bronze columns, in groups of four. The roof is covered with plates of copper-gilt and enamel, and is crowned with a Russian eagle. On three sides the monument is surrounded by an arcade, with two corner-pavilions. The ceiling of this arcade is adorned with the portraits of 33 Russian rulers, from St. Vladimir to Nicholas I., in Venetian mosaic.

At right angles to the Nicholas Palace stands the red **Tchudov Monastery** (Чу́довъ мужско́й монасты́рь), or *Convent of the Miraculous Apparitions of the Archangel Michael*. It was founded in 1358 by the Metropolitan Alexis, to whom the ground was presented by the Tartar Khan, Dzhani-Beg, whose wife he had healed of a severe illness. Later it was frequently destroyed by fire and as often rebuilt (last in 1771). It was made the Katedrálni Monastúir of the eparchy of Moscow, *i.e.* the seat of the Metropolitan of Moscow, and it is still known as the *Residential Convent of the Metropolitan*, although this dignitary no longer occupies it.

It was to the Tchudov Monastery that the Tzar Vasíli Shuiski retired after his abdication on July 17th, 1610. The False Demetrius (Brother Gregory) lived here before he entered upon his career as Pretender. In Dec., 1667, there met here the last Council in which the Greek Church took part through the personal presence of its leading officials, and at this Council the Patriarch Nikon (p. 295) was condemned to the loss of his position. The children of Iván IV., and Tzars Alexis, Peter I., and Alexander II., were all baptized in the Tchudov Convent.

To the right of the entrance to the Monastery is a curious image made of paper; seen from the front, it represents the Holy Ghost, from the left, Christ, from the right, God the Father. In the *Church of St. Alexis* (Pl. 2), in a niche in the wall, to the left of the ikonostás, is a silver sarcophagus placed here in 1686, and containing the wonder-working body of St. Alexis (d. 1378). *The Church of the Archangel Michael*, built in 1503 and several times restored, contains some interesting mural paintings. In the lower church is a chapel erected in 1912 to the memory of the Patriarch Hermogenes, starved to death in the Tchudov Monastery during the Polish invasion of 1612, and canonized in 1913. The *Riznitza* or *Sacristy* contains a copy of the Gospels written by St. Alexis, in a costly binding. In the *Churchyard* are the graves of many Metropolitans, Bishops, and Russian Princes, and also that of Edigér, the last Khan of Kazan.

On the W. side of the Square of the Tzars, on a granite pedestal, in front of the Iván Veliki (p. 281), stands the so-called **'Tzar Bell'** (Царь-ко́локолъ; Pl. 11). This is the largest bell in the world, measuring 26 ft. in height (including the ball and cross on the top) and 66 ft. in circumference. It weighs 200 tons, and is 22 inches thick at the bottom and $10^1/_2$ inches thick at the top. The exterior is adorned with inscriptions and reliefs. To the right of the fracture is the Tzar Alexis Mikháilovitch, with SS. Peter & John the Baptist above him; to the left is the Empress Anna Ivánovna, with the Saviour, the Virgin, and St. Anna above her. The piece broken out of the bell lies at the foot of the pedestal.

The bell, as the inscription records, was cast by Matórin of Moscow in 1735, at the command of the Tzarina Anna. On completion it was left in the factory and was there exposed to a fire (1737) which broke off a piece of it. It then lay imbedded in the ground for a century, before the architect Monferrand succeeded in raising it and bringing it to its present position in 1836.

The huge bell-tower of *Iván Veliki* (Колоко́льня Ива́на Вели́каго, or *John the Great*), begun under Feódor Ivánovitch, completed by Boris Godunóv in 1600, and last restored in 1813, rises in five stories to a height of 320 ft. (including the cross). The four lower stories are octagonal, the fifth one is round. The tower is surmounted by a gilded dome, 33 ft. in diameter, crowned by a gilded cross. This cross occupies the place of the original one, which was torn down by the French in 1812 (much to the detriment of the upper part of the tower), in the belief that it was made of gold. — On the groundfloor and in the adjacent building (entrance from the W. side) are two churches, one dedicated to St. John, (Russian, Iván), the other to St. Nicholas of Gostúnsk, the patron saint of betrothed lovers. In the latter church, to the left of the altar and behind the ikonostás, is a large Book of the Gospels, with reliefs upon its binding (1689). — Visitors should not omit the Ascent of the Iván Veliki, for which a bright day should be chosen. It is customary to place 20 cop. in the collection-box at the foot of the tower, and the guide (unnecessary) expects 50 cop. In ascending the 236 easy steps we pass 33 bells of various sizes. The largest of these is the so-called Bell of the Assumption (or Festival Bell; 65 tons in weight), in the second gallery, to the right.

The *View* from the top is especially beautiful by evening light. From this point Joseph II. viewed Moscow in 1780, Napoleon and his Marshals in 1812. We not only overlook the whole of the city and its suburbs, but also its environs for a distance of about 20 M., while we see the long windings of the Moskvá, which intersects the landscape like a shining, silver ribbon. At our feet lies the Kremlin, surrounded by the wall separating it from the city. Within these walls are the cathedrals, with their gilded domes; to the S.W. are the huge Imperial Palace, the Church of the Redeemer, and (more distant) the Convent of the Maidens and the Sparrow Hills; to the N. are the gleaming white Court of Justice, the Historical Museum, the Great Theatre, and the Súkharev Tower; to the E. are the Trading Rows, the Cathedral of St.

Basil, the Monument of Alexander II., and the Foundling Hospital. On all sides the Kremlin is surrounded by an ocean of houses, with number-less gaily-coloured church-domes, gradually losing themselves in the hilly and wooded environs, until all is merged in the blue horizon.

On the second floor of the Iván Veliki (entr. on the N. side, out-side the railing) is the rich **Synodal Treasury** (Синодáльная Рúзница; adm., see p. 275). Catalogue (1907) 30 cop.

From the vestibule a narrow passage leads into a room containing ecclesiastical vestments (mostly of Oriental silk), richly adorned with pearls and precious stones. We may then either enter the large room opposite the entrance (see below), or turn to the left into a room divided into three parts. At the end of the latter to the left are the palls *(Pokróv)* of three Tzars. To the left of the entrance, in the glass-cases in front of the 2nd, 3rd, & 4th windows, are the *Omophoria* (scap-ulars) of the Patriarchs Nikon, Job, and Adrian. In a cabinet oppo-site the 5th window is the *Sakkos* (episcopal cope) of the Metropolitan Photius, embroidered at Constantinople in the first quarter of the 15th cent., and bearing the Creed in Greek. By the 6th window is a case con-taining a copy of the Gospels belonging to Tzarina Marfa Matvéyevna, the wife of Tzar Feódor Alexéyevitch, with enamel and precious stones. Above is a copper pitcher *(Alaváster)*, inlaid with mother-of-pearl (Persian; 17th cent.), in which the sacred anointing oil (p. 295) is said to have been brought from Constantinople to Kiev in 988. The middle case contains (below) two mitres and two crowns belonging to the Patriarch Nikon; also some *Pórutchi*, or short oversleeves.—At the end of this room we turn to the right into a corner-room, containing several cases with epis-copal copes, all adorned with pearls and embroidery.—We now retrace our steps and turn to the left into the main room, in the middle of which is a glass case containing crosses and *Panagía (i.e.* pictures of the Virgin and of saints, borne by the archbishops upon their breast). In the four corners and by the rear wall are glass-cases with ecclesiastical vessels of silver and gold, chiefly German work of the 17th cent., but including some very fine English specimens.

An iron railing separates the Square of the Tzars (p. 279) from the CATHEDRAL SQUARE (Собóрная плóщадь, Sobórnaya Plóshtchad), which adjoins it on the S.W. This latter is bounded by the Uspenski Cathedral (see below) on the N., the Granovítaya Paláta (p. 288) and the Great Kremlin Palace (p. 286) on the W., and the Cathedral of the Annunciation (p. 285) and the Archangel Cathedral (p. 285) on the S.

The *Cathedral of the Assumption or Uspénski Ca-thedral (Успéнскій собóръ), the church in which the Tzars are crowned, and formerly the burial-place of the Patriarchs, was built by *Fioraventi* of Bologna in 1475-79, on the site of an earlier church, and on the model of the Cathedral of St. Demetrius of Vladimir (p. 337). Though repeatedly devastated (1493, 1547, 1682, 1812) by plunderers or fire, the church was always restored in its original form. It stands almost in the centre of the Kremlin, and forms a rectangle 82 ft. wide and 125 ft. long. In the middle rises a massive dome, 138 ft. in height, while at the four corners are smaller domes. The walls and pillars are adorned with pictures of saints.

We enter the INTERIOR by the main entrance on the W. side. On the walls to the right and left of the entrance are frescoes representing the Last Judgment. On the wall to the left (N.) are episodes from the life of the Virgin, while to the right (S.) are the seven Councils of the Greek

Church. The piers immediately in front of us are adorned with a series of pictures upon a gold ground, forming a garish mixture of angels, saints, monks, and fighting knights. Farther up, the walls and columns are adorned with gilding, reaching to the very top of the dome. In the central dome is a colossal figure of the Deity, while in the smaller domes are the Virgin, the Lord of Sabaoth, Immanuel, and the Saviour. Between the piers, in the nave, is the place where the Tzar is crowned. Nine *Patriarchs* (p. 295) rest here; Nikon, the 10th, is buried in the Convent of the New Jerusalem (Church of the Resurrection; p. 256). In the corner, to the left of the entrance, lies the *Metropolitan Jonas* (Pl. 5); to the right are the sarcophagi of *SS. Photius* and *Cyprian* (Pl. 6), and of the *Patriarch Hermogenes* (1606-1612; Pl. 11; p. 280). Between these is a rectangular chapel-like receptacle of copper-gilt, 23 ft. in height, adorned with open-work and surmounted by a pointed roof. This contains several relics, the shroud of Christ and the robe of the Virgin sent to the Tzar Mikhail Feódorovitch in 1625 by Shah Abbas of Persia, and also a nail of the True Cross, presented by the Georgian Tzar Artchil in 1686. In the right aisle, in front of the ikonostás, is a large throne of black walnut, which is said to date from the time of Iván the Terrible (1552). In front of the piers are the stone *Throne of the Patriarch* to the right, and the *Throne of the Tzarinas* to the left.

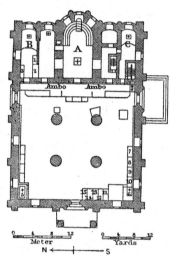

CHAPELS: A. Assumption; B. St. Peter and St. Paul; C. St. Demetrius Solunski. — RELICS: 1. St. Theognostus; 2. Metropolitan Peter; 3. Gregory the Theologian; 4. St. Philip; 5. Metropolitan Jonas; 6. St. Photius and St. Cyprian. — TOMBS OF PATRIARCHS: 7. Joseph (d. 1652); 8. Job (d. 1607); 9. Joasaph I. (d. 1641); 10. Philaret (d. 1633); 11. Hermogenes (d. 1612); 12. Joasaph II. (d. 1672); 13. Pitirim (d. 1673); 14. Joachim (d. 1690); 15. Adrian (d. 1700).

The *Ikonostás*, partly renewed in 1882, consists of a lofty vermilion wall of artistic perforated work, with five rows of saints, one above another, and lavishly adorned with precious stones. In the choir takes place the anointing of the Tzar. To the left of the holy door, in a costly frame, is the famous *Vladimir Picture of the Virgin*, said to have been painted by St. Luke. This picture was brought, about the middle of the 5th cent., from Jerusalem to Constantinople; in the beginning of the 12th cent. it came to Kiev, and in 1158 to Vladimir. In 1395, on the invasion of Timur the Tartar, it was brought to the Kremlin at Moscow, in order to protect the city (p. 310). To the right is a *Picture of the Redeemer*, said to have been painted by the Greek Emperor Manuel in 1143, and preserved down to 1476 in the Church of St. Sophia at Novgorod. — The net weight of the gold of the ikonostás, and of the altar-vessels and other sacred objects, is said to amount to 330 puds (11,900 lbs.). The French carried off the whole of this treasure with them, but their spoil was taken from them by the Cossacks, who in commemoration of this rescue, presented the church with a silver *Chandelier* with 46 branches, which weighs 880 lbs. and now hangs from the dome.

Behind the ikonostás is the *Sanctuary*. Behind the altar, upon a marble table, is a relief of *Mt. Sinai*, made of pure 'ducat-gold', and presented by Potemkin in 1788. In the making of this relief, 21 lbs. of gold and 22 lbs. of silver were used. On the top of the mountain stands a golden figure of Moses, with the Tables of the Law. In the mountain is a cavern containing a small golden pyx, used for keeping the Host. Below lie state documents. In the background is a niche in the wall, containing the throne of the Metropolitan of Moscow, on each side of which are mural paintings of Patriarchs and Fathers of the Church. In the side-chapel to the left (entr. from 'choir; Pl. B.) are the *Altar of SS. Peter & Paul*, the sarcophagi of the *Metropolitans Peter* (first Metropolitan of Moscow, d. 1326; Pl. 2) and *Theognostus* (d. 1353; Pl. 1), and a shrine containing relics. In the right side-chapel (that of St. Demetrius Solunski, the Martyr; Pl. C), Prince Yuri Glinski, a distant cousin of Iván the Terrible, was assassinated in 1547.—In front of the choir, to the right, is the silver reliquary of the *Metropolitan Philip* (p. 268; Pl. 4).—From the chapel of St. Demetrius Solunski a narrow flight of steps leads to the *Chapel of the Virgin*, where the election of the Patriarch used to take place, and to the *Sacristy* (Ри́зница).

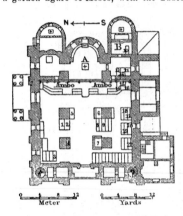

Ground-plan of the Archangel Cathedral.

CHAPELS: A. Archangel Michael; B. John the Baptist. — TOMBS: 1. Iván Alexéyevitch (d. 1696); 2. Féodor Alexéyevitch (d. 1682); 3. Vasíli Shuiski (d. 1613); 4. Tzarévitch Peter of Kazan; 5. Emperor Peter II. (d. 1727); 6. Tzarévitch Demetrius (d. 1591); 7. Prince Mikhail of Tchernigov and Boyar Feódor; 8. Alexis Mikháilovitch (d. 1676); 9. Mikhail Féodorovitch; 10. Mikhail Skopin-Shuiski (d. 1610); 11. Iván the Terrible (d. 1584); 12. Iván Ivánovitch (d. 1582), son of the preceding; 13. Feódor Ivánovitch (d. 1598); 14. Vasíli Ivánovitch (d. 1534); 15. Iván III. Vasílyevitch (d. 1505); 16. Vasíli Vasílyevitch (d. 1462); 17. Iván Danílovitch, Kalitá (d. 1340); 18. Simeón Ivánovitch, the Proud (d. 1353); 19. Demetrius Donskói (d. 1389); 20. Iván Ivánovitch (d. 1359); 21. Vasíli Dmítriyevitch (d. 1425).

Passing the *Palace Guard House*, we reach the foot of the so-called **Red Staircase** (Кра́сное крыльцо́; marked q on plan at p. 279), also called the Lion Staircase, on account of the lions on its landings. This staircase leads from the 'Sacred Floor' to the Cathedral Square, but is kept closed.

The staircase was originally covered by a pointed and painted wooden roof, for which Prince Vasíli Golítzuin substituted one of copper gilt in 1685. Since the fire of 1696 it has, however, been roofless. It was here that Iván the Terrible received Vasíli Shibánov, the messenger of Prince Kurbski, who had taken refuge among the Poles, thrusting the iron point of his staff through his foot and then listening to his message while leaning on the staff. Here, too, the False Demetrius received petitioners, and here (in 1682) the Strelitzi massacred the Boyar Matvéyev, three members of the Naruishkin family, and 69 opponents of the Tzarina Sophia. — The Tzars still descend the Red Staircase when on their way to the coronation in the Cathedral of the Assumption.

Opposite the Uspenski Cathedral, on the S. side of the Cathedral Square, lies the **Archangel Cathedral** (Архáнгельскій собóръ), or *Cathedral of the Archangel Michael,* the burial church of the Tzars of the House of Rurik and of the Románovs before Peter the Great (p. 173); also of Peter's feeble-minded brother Iván, and of Peter II. It was erected in 1505-8 by the architect *Alevisio Novi* of Milan, on the site of an older church, and was last restored in 1895.

The *Mural Paintings,* executed by Yermoláyev in 1680-81 under Feódor Alexéyevitch (restored in 1743 and 1772), represent the Last Judgment, and lifesize figures of the Tzars. By the walls, at the feet of the figures, are the plain *Sarcophagi* of the Tzars, 47 in number. Alexander, once Tzar of Kazan (d. 1566), and Peter, the Tzarévitch of Kazan (d. 1509), also rest here. In front of the small Chapel of John the Baptist is the sarcophagus of Iván the Terrible (Pl. 11). Adjoining are the coffins of his sons, Iván and Feódor Ivánovitch. In various small recesses are the Coffins of the Saints (Мóщи); the most revered are those of *St. Mikhail Vsévolodovitch* (Pl. 7) and *Demetrius Uglitzki* (Pl. 6). St. Mikhail was Prince of Tchernigov, at the time of the Mongolian supremacy. In 1246, when he went to do homage to the horde of Baty-Khan, he refused to pass through the sacred fire and was murdered in consequence. A similar fate befell his companion, Boyar Feódor. The body was brought back to Moscow, and Mikhail was declared a saint. The silver coffin was presented by Catherine II. in 1774. Demetrius, the last scion of the Rurik family, was assassinated at Uglitch (p. 348). On the pier above his sarcophagus are a portrait of him in low relief, made of fine gold, and also some articles of his attire. Adjacent is a candelabrum of silver.

To the W. of the Archangel Cathedral, rises the **Blagovyéshtchenski Cathedral** (Благовѣщенскій собóръ), or the *Cathedral of the Annunciation,* the church in which the Tzars are christened and wedded. It was founded by Vasíli Dmitriyevitch in 1397, rebuilt in 1482-9 by Pskov masters, and frequently restored, last in 1884-95. It possesses nine domes, each of which is surmounted by a golden cross, and a gilded roof.

Through the gate of the Cathedral Square we enter a corridor, with frescoes of 1508 (restored in 1890), which surrounds the inner church on three sides. Two doors lead from it into the church itself. The doors are covered with panels of chased bronze; the door-posts and lintels are adorned with precious stones and gold ornaments on a blue ground. The floor of the church consists of coloured jasper, presented to the Tzar Alexis by the Shah of Persia. The frescoes on the walls and domes are very curious. They represent patriarchs, prophets, apostles, martyrs, and Greek philosophers (these conceived of as the heralds of the coming Messiah) in conjunction with monsters of all kinds. These are but dimly illuminated by the feeble light finding its way through the central dome. The *Ikonostás* was almost entirely destroyed by the French in 1812, in their search for gold, but was afterwards restored. Adjoining the holy door, which is of massive silver, are the highly revered pictures of (right) the *Saviour,* of the 14th cent., and the *Annunciation* (from Greece), in a costly frame. To the left is the picture of the *Virgin of the Don,* which Demetrius Donskói had fastened to his black banner during the battle on the plain of Kulikóvo in 1380. The same holy banner was borne by Boris Godunóv in his battle with the Tartars under the walls of Moscow in 1591. On the back is the Assumption of the Virgin; the frame is of solid gold and still shows some scars made in 1812 by the French, who mistook it for copper-gilt. The side-door is adorned with reliefs. In front of the ikonostás, to the right, is the throne of Tzar Feódor Alexéyevitch, and in the wall behind is a niche in which Iván the Terrible often attended divine service.

We now enter the —

*Great Kremlin Palace (Большо́й кремлёвскій дворе́цъ) by a door in the main façade, which is turned towards the Moskvá. This handsome edifice, 395 ft. long and 92 ft. in height (exclusive of the dome), was erected from the designs of *Thon* in 1838-49, at a cost of 12,000,000 rb. The main building consists of two stories, the upper of which has two rows of windows. On the N. side lies the Belvedere Palace (p. 288), and on the E. side the Granovítaya Paláta (p. 288), while in the W. wing is the Oruzhéinaya Paláta (p. 289). Adm., see p. 275; entr. on the E. side (Pl. Entr.). The visit takes $^3/_4$ hr. The attendant expects a fee of 1 rb. (for a party 20-30 cop. each). See Plan, p. 279.

The palace stands upon the same spot on which the old wooden and stone palaces of the Tzars stood previous to 1737. Of these older buildings, only the Granovítaya Paláta and the Terem are now extant. In 1753 Empress Elizabeth erected the so-called Winter Palace (Кремлёвскій зи́мній дворе́цъ), a stone building designed by Count Rastrelli. Napoleon I. occupied this palace in 1812, and it was burned down the same year. Catherine II. intended to build a huge palace in the Kremlin from the designs of Bazhénov, but work on it was little more than begun.

To the left of the handsome vestibule, which is borne by four monolithic columns of granite, are the private rooms of the Tzar, which are not shown without the special permission of the Chief of Police. The magnificent granite *Staircase* (Пара́дная лѣ́стница; Pl. b), consisting of 58 steps, arranged in five flights, leads hence to the upper floor. To the right is a large picture of the battle on the plain of Kulikóvo, by the French painter Yvon (1850). At the top of the staircase are two huge crystal vases.

The small *Antechamber* (Pl. c) contains a painting by Ryepin, representing peasants doing homage to Alexander III. To the right is the *St. George Room* (Pl. d), the largest in the Kremlin (200 ft. long, 70 ft. wide, and 60 ft. high), which is furnished and decorated in white and gold. The ceiling is supported by 18 pilasters, in front of which are placed twisted columns. On the capitals are Victories, with shields bearing lists of the conquests of Russia, and the arms of conquered provinces. On the walls are marble tablets, inscribed in golden letters, with the names and dates of Russian regiments which have distinguished themselves in the field, and also the names of all officers who have been decorated with the Order of St. George, the highest Russian order for military bravery. At the end of the room is a group in silver, representing the Cossack leaders, Yermák (p. 522) and Platov (d. 1818), presented in 1870 by the Cossacks of the Don. Adjacent are two gilded bronze chests, containing the statutes and the names of the Knights of St. George. The six candelabra contain 3200 electric lights.

The *St. Alexander Room* (Pl. e), richly adorned in pink and gold, is 100 ft. long, 70 ft. wide, and 70 ft. high to the vaulting of the dome. It is named in honour of the Order of St. Alexander Nevski, instituted by Catherine I. in 1725. Opposite the two rows of windows (14 in all) are enormous mirrors, reflecting the view of the city seen from the windows. The room also contains six paintings of scenes from the life of St. Alexander Nevski, by Prof. Müller. On festivals the room is illuminated by 3500 electric lights. The floor, like that of the St. George Room, is skilfully put together from upwards of 20 varieties of wood.

The *Throne Room of St. Andrew* (Pl. f; 160 ft. long, 70 ft. wide, 60 ft. high), named after the Order of St. Andrew, instituted by Peter the Great in 1698, is decorated in light-blue and gold, and is supported by ten massive pillars. Opposite the entrance is the Imperial Throne with its three seats, constructed in 1896 for the coronation of Nicholas II. On the walls and pillars are the arms of the Imperial Family. — The three rooms last described are all used at the coronation of the Tzar.

The adjoining *Room of the Chevalier Guards* (Pl. g) contains a painting by Svertchkóv (Alexis Mikháilovitch reviewing troops). — The *St. Catharine Room* (Pl. h), called after the order of St. Catharine (1714), is decorated in white and red, and contains two pillars, partly covered with malachite.

The next series of rooms, known as the 'Inner Chambers', are sumptuously fitted up, and may be visited (in the absence of the Tzar) by permission of the Chief of Police. From the *Dressing Room*, adjoining the *State Bedroom* (Pl. k), the long *Terem Gallery* (inside wall old) leads to the Golden Chamber (see p. 288).

The Dressing Room is adjoined by the *Church of the Nativity of the Virgin* (Pl. l), the former domestic chapel of the Tzarinas, containing a silver-gilt ikonostás. It was originally founded in 1393, but was rebuilt by Alevisio in 1514. A staircase on the left leads through the *Winter Garden* (Pl. m), by which the Dvortzóvaya is bridged, to the APARTMENTS OF THE HEIR APPARENT, situated in the wing of the palace. The *Reception Room* is also known as the Silver Room on account of its seven silver tables, its silver mirror frames, and its silver chandeliers (all of good Augsburg work, from the beginning of the 18th cent.). The room also contains four pieces of tapestry with scenes from Don Quixote (1756). By the middle window is a model of the monument erected at Novgorod in 1862 (p. 263). In the *Bedroom* is a table with fine intarsia work. Beyond the *Dressing Room* we reach the *Sitting Rooms*, containing copies of pictures in the Dresden Gallery, executed by Seydelmann (d. 1829) in sepia, and a large work by Svertchkóv (Iván the Terrible in the Red Square). Farther on is the *Picture Gallery*, which contains six large pictures by Bacciarelli of scenes from Polish history (formerly in the Royal Palace at Warsaw), and a number of other pictures, some brought from the Hermitage at St. Petersburg, others from Warsaw.

The *Golden Chamber* (Золотáя or Цари́цына палáта ; Pl. v), dating from the end of the 16th cent., was the audience-room of the Tzarina. The paintings, on a gold ground, restored under Nicholas I., represent the Finding of the True Cross by St. Helena, scenes from the life of St. Olga, and other similar subjects. The octagonal *St. Vladímir Room* (Pl. n) is named after the Order of St. Vladímir, founded by Catherine II. in 1782.

From the Vladímir Room a door on the left leads to the *Sacred Vestibule* (Svyatúiya Seni ; Pl. o), from one side of which we reach the Red Staircase (p. 284), and from the other, the Granovítaya Palátá.

The **Granovítaya Palátá** (Грановѝтая палáта ; Pl. p), or *Hall of the Facets* (so-called from the form of the stone on the façade towards the Cathedral Square), was built in 1473-91 by the Italian architects *Marco Ruffo* and *Pietro Antonio,* and was last restored in 1882. It consists of a single low-vaulted chamber, supported in the middle by a rectangular pier. The iron ribs of the vaulting are covered with gilt, and on the vaulting appear mottoes in Slavonic characters.

In earlier days this room was the audience-chamber of the Tzars. It now serves as a banqueting-room, in which, after the coronation, the Tzar, clad in the Imperial robes and insignia, dines in state with the foreign princes. The central pier is surrounded by stands on which silver plate from the Imperial Treasury is exhibited on the coronation day. In 1882 the walls were covered with frescoes, reproducing those of the time of Tzar Feódor Ivánovitch, and symbolically representing, by means of scenes from the Old Testament, the wisdom and virtues of the Grand-Princes and Tzars. The chandeliers, of a dark bronze colour, are designed on ancient models. Around the sides of the room are benches covered with gaudily embroidered silk. Under a heavy canopy, copied from a design in the Uspenski Cathedral, is a throne of wood, with coats-of-arms embroidered on the back. The floor is entirely covered by a glorified rag-carpet, composed of bright-coloured pieces of cloth. Above the quaint-looking entrance are the arms of Iván III. High up on the same wall, to the left, is the golden frame of the window of the *Tainik* (i.e. hiding-place), from which the Tzarinas used to witness the festivities. This Tainik is a room hung with modern tapestry, to which the visitors are conducted after viewing the Terem (see below).

The ***Belvedere Palace** or *Terem* (Тéремный дворéцъ ; Pl. r), built in 1636 by Mikhaíl Feódorovitch for his sons and occupied by the Tzars Feódor and Alexis, consists of five floors, arranged in pyramidal form (the three lower not shown). This palace, the exterior of which produces a curious and barbaric effect, contains a series of small and low rooms, fitted up in mediæval style. [Terem means a garret, balcony, or belvedere, and also the women's apartment in the upper floor.]

FOURTH FLOOR. I. *Dining Room,* containing furniture of the Tzar Alexis Mikháilovitch, father of Peter the Great. The ceiling-paintings represent the Saviour, the Evangelists, Constantine the Great and his mother Helena, St. Vladímir, and St. Olga. — II. *Reception Room.* In the middle are two bronze coffers containing documents, including the electoral ukaze of Tzar Mikhaíl Feódorovitch Románov. — III. *Throne Room* of the Tzar Alexis. In the corner by the window is a chair belonging to that monarch. — IV. *Bedroom.* On the bed of Alexis lies a coverlet worked by his daughters. — V. Small *Oratory* of Tzar Alexis Mikháilovitch.

From the Hall of the Terem we overlook the small *Church of the Redeemer behind the Golden Railing* (Спáса за золотóй рѣшóткой; Pl. s), named after the so-called 'golden railing', which really consists of copper (cast in 1670). The chapel was founded in 1635.

The Kremlin Palace also includes the *Spas na Ború Church*, or *Church of the Redeemer in the Wood* (Pl. u), built in the 13th cent., when the hill on which the Kremlin now stands was covered with thick forest. In 1330 Iván Danilovitch Kalitá pulled down the original wooden church and erected in its place a church of stone, which received its present form in 1527 and was last restored in 1857-63.

A wing of the Kremlin Palace, entered from the W. side of the Imperátorskaya Square, contains the ***Treasury** or **Oruzhéinaya Paláta** (i.e. *Armoury*). — Adm., see p. 275; illustrated catalogue, 40 cop. (1911). Directors, V. K. Trutóvski and J. V. Arsényev.

The earlier so-called Treasury (Большáя Казнá) contained objects of gold and silver, and numerous other valuables. It included the *Oruzhéinaya Paláta* proper, the courts in which the weapons were forged, the *Royal Mews* (Коню́шенный прикáзъ), in which the imperial equipages and harness were kept, and the *Sapásnoi Dvor*, or Storehouse, a large three-storied building opposite the palace. In the reign of Tzar Alexis Mikháilovitch (1645-76) the Moscow Armoury (Брóнный москóвскій прикáзъ) existed as a separate institution, quite apart from the Treasury. Peter the Great removed all the chief objects in the collections to St. Petersburg, and established a Museum of Costumes and Armour, which was transferred by Alexander I. to the present Barracks (p. 294) in 1806. The present Oruzhéinaya Paláta was built by Nicholas I. in 1849-51 and became the final home of the Treasury.

In the VESTIBULE, to the left below, is a tocsin or alarm bell, recast in 1714. To the right are two iron tablets with inscriptions relating to the execution of Streltzi under Peter the Great (copies prepared by order of Catherine II., in 1771, of inscriptions placed in 1699 in the Red Square, where the execution took place). — To the left is the entrance to the rooms of the lower floor (p. 293). We, however, keep straight on and ascend the staircase to the —

Upper Floor. — On the STAIRCASE are arms, armour, and Russian tapestry of 1738 (Expulsion of Hagar). To the left of the entrance to Room I. are several suits of boy's armour worn by the Tzarévitch Alexis Mikháilovitch (1634).

I. ARMOUR ROOM (Брóнная зáла) Armour of Boyars of the 16-17th centuries. On the walls are weapons belonging to Knights of the Livonian Order of the Brethren of the Sword, and armour. Cuirasses and helmets of Grand-Princes and Tzars. To the left of the entrance, 9. Helmet of Tzar Feódor Ivánovitch, presented by Sigismund III. of Poland (Italian, end of 16th cent.); 10. Boy's helmet of Tzarévitch Iván, son of Iván the Terrible (Russian work, 1557);

11. Helmet said to be that of Grand-Prince Yaroslàv Vsévolodovitch (13th cent.). Towards the exit, on the left, are the helmet of Prince Mstislàvski (No. 41; Persian work of the 16th cent.) and a helmet of Byzantine work of the 13th cent. (No. 24).

II. WEAPON ROOM (Оружейная зала). Weapons of various styles, places, and dates, including some interesting muskets of the 18th century. — To the left of the entrance are muskets made at Tula in the 18th century. — The first case to the left and several cases in front of the windows contain Russian arquebuses. — In the case at the first window are Asiatic swords and daggers. — By the second window are Polish and Russian sabres, including (below; 5699) the sword of Stanislaus Augustus, King of Poland. — By the third window is the shield of Prince Mstislàvski (5067), above which are the sabres of Prince Pozhàrski (left, 5923) and Minin (right, 5924). In the glass-case behind are the arms of Tzars Alexis Mikhàilovitch and Iván Alexéyevitch. — By the fourth window are the arms of Peter the Great, while the glass-case behind contains those of the Tzars Alexis Mikhàilovitch, Peter II., the Tzarinas Elizabeth and Anna, and Alexander I. — On the first and second pillars (counting from the entrance) are remains of banners of the Streltzi (17th cent.); in Glass-case 78 are two shields and a mace of Tzar Alexis Mikhàilovitch. Adjacent, to the left, in Case 77, the banner of Prince Pozhàrski (p. 298); in Case 76 is his saddle. — Glass-case 75, near the exit, contains costly saddles and other objects. To the right is the large enamel quiver of Tzar Mikhaíl Feódorovitch (Moscow work), and to the left is another large quiver, which belonged to Tzar Alexis Mikhàilovitch (Greek work; 1656). — On the exit-wall, to the right, is an equestrian portrait of Empress Catherine II., by Erikson (1762).

To the right of the entrance are Russian arquebuses, Italian pistols, battle-axes, and maces. By the second window are Turkish arms and Russian pistols (17th cent.) By the third window are German, Dutch, and English pistols (17th cent.). By the fourth and fifth windows are Turkish arms, and Russian and other maces. At the fifth window hangs a Russian imperial banner of 1741.

III. TROPHY ROOM (Трофейная зала). To the left of the entrance are weapons from the battle of Poltava (1709), and the sedan chair of Charles XII. of Sweden. — To the right of the entrance are Hungarian banners of 1849. — On the wall with the door leading to Room V are Polish banners, those to the left given by Napoleon I., those to the right by Alexander I. and Nicholas I. To the right and left of the entrance to Room IV are the coronation banners of Alexander II. and Alexander III. — In the middle is the coronation banner of Nicholas II., with the sword and shield of the Emperor. The glass-case below contains trinkets that be-

longed to Peter the Great, a golden chain of Tzar Mikhaíl Feódorovitch, and the insignia of the earliest Russian Orders. In the glass-
case by the second window are watches and valuables belonging to
Mikhaíl Feódorovitch, Peter the Great, and his successors; medallion-portrait of Frederick the Great. — Against and opposite the
window-wall are 15 thrones. — The room also contains portraits of
Russian rulers and their contemporaries of the 18th century.
On the right, this room is adjoined by the circular —

IV. Room of the Crowns (Коронная зала). To the right and
left of the entrance, which is closed by an iron grating, are the
walking-sticks of Peter the Great and other Tzars. To the left is
the crown of Grand-Prince Vladímir Monamákh (12th cent., altered
in the 16th cent.). Adjacent is the Kazan Crown, prepared by order
of Iván IV. in 1553 for Edigér, last Tzar of Kazan, who assumed
the name of Simon on his baptism. — Behind, in Glass-case 5, are
clothes of the Tzar Alexis Mikháilovitch. — On a separate stand is
the crown of the Tzar Mikhaíl Feódorovitch (1627), now that of
Astrakhan. — By the wall behind is an ivory throne (altered in the
16th cent.), which was brought to Moscow in 1472 by Sophia,
daughter of Thomas Palæologus and wife of Iván III. — Adjacent,
on the right, is the throne of the Tzar Mikhaíl Feódorovitch. —
Crown of Iván Alexéyevitch (1682). Behind, in Glass-case 10, are
the coronation robes of the Empresses Catherine I., Elizabeth, and
Catherine II., and of the Tzars Peter the Great, Peter II., and
Paul I. — Throne of Tzar Alexis, with 876 diamonds and 1223 other
precious stones (1659). — To the right is the Siberian Crown,
studded with gems and dating from 1684. This is known as the
'Altabásnaya', because it is made of gold lace.

By the window, to the left, Imperial Orb of the Tzar Mikhaíl
Feódorovitch, first half of the 17th cent.; to the right, the Imperial
Orb of Tzar Alexis Mikháilovitch, the work of the Greek Yuryev
(Georgios) of Constantinople (1662). The glass-case contains the
sceptres of various Tzars; the barmi or collar of Alexis Mikháilo-
vitch, adorned with gold and enamel medallions (1665); valuable
necklaces and pendants; and sacred pictures from the barmi of
Vladímir Monomákh.

Crown of Peter the Great. Throne of the Tzar Borís Godunóv,
covered with thin plates of gold and studded with 2200 precious
stones and pearls (presented by Abbas, Shah of Persia, in 1604).
Farther on is another crown of Peter the Great. Behind, in Glass-
case 18, are the coronation robes of Alexander I. and Nicholas I. —
Double Throne of the Tzars Iván and Peter the Great, in silver-
gilt (1682). — In front is the crown of the Empress Anna Ivánovna
(Императорская корона), encrusted with numerous diamonds and
a large ruby. — Crown of Georgia. Behind, in Case 23, the coronation
robes of Alexander II. and his wife. By the entrance is the Maltese

crown of Paul I.—In the middle of the room are the canopy and
robes used at the last coronation (1894).

We now return through Room III. to the—

V. Silver Room (Серéбряная зáла), containing upwards of
1000 pieces of gold and silver plate.

The Silver Room contains the largest collection extant of works by
German goldsmiths. Most of the pieces were made in the workshops of
Nuremberg, Augsburg, and Danzig; during the Thirty Years' War they
were taken as booty to Sweden, whence they found their way to Russia
as presents to the Tzars. The collection also contains numerous specimens
of Dutch, Danish, and English workmanship. The oldest pieces date from
the second half of the 16th century. Most of the Russian works are utensils in actual use. There is also a large number of flat dishes and salt
cellars used at the presentation of bread and salt to the Tzars on their
journeys.

Cabinet 1 (opposite the first window on the left). Russian silver-ware of the 17th century.—*Cab.* 2 (to the left of the entrance),
Russian silver-ware and enamel of the 18th century.—*Cab. 3*
(between the 1st and 2nd windows on the left). Russian enamel
and niello work down to the beginning of the 18th century. 9707.
Writing materials of Tzar Mikhaíl Feódorovitch; plate of Tzar
Alexis Mikháilovitch; 542. Tankard given by the Patriarch Nikon to
Alexis Mikháilovitch.—*Cab. 4* (between the 3rd and 4th windows
to the left). Gifts received by the Tzars Nicholas I., Alexander II.,
and Nicholas II.—*Cab. 5* (at the 2nd window to the left). London
silver-ware of the 16-17th centuries. 1922, 1923. Two lifesize
panthers presented by Queen Elizabeth to Tzar Borís Godunóv.
—*Cab. 6* (at the 3rd window to the left). Hamburg silver-ware of
the 16-17th centuries. 1904-1906. Three large fumigators representing Danish palaces.—*Cab.* 7 (at the 4th window to the left). Silver-ware from Copenhagen, Stockholm, Bremen, and Hamburg.

In the circular recess at the end of the room. *Glass Case 8.*
9624. Silver table, English work (1724).—*Glass Case 9.* Russian
silver-ware from the 12th cent. down to 1613; 2106. Large goblet
of Prince Vladímir Davídovitch of Tchernigov (d. 1151); 1810.
Goblet of Prince Simeon Ivánovitch, uncle of Iván the Terrible;
1936. Cock belonging to Iván III. (1492); 1598. Beaker presented
by the Hospodar of Moldavia to Iván the Terrible, and now used
by the Tzar in proposing toasts at the coronation banquet; 527.
Goblet of Tzar Vasili Ivánovitch Shuiski; 526. Goblet of Tzar Borís
Godunóv.—*Pedestal 10.* Marble statue of Napoleon I. as a Roman
Emperor, by Chaudet.—We now retrace our steps towards the
entrance-wall.

Pillar Cabinet 11. Foreign works in crystal and stone. 2551.
Pitcher inlaid with mother-of-pearl.—*Pillar Cabinet 12.* Silver-
ware from Riga, amber-ware from Königsberg.—*Cab. 13* (in the
middle of the room). Nuremberg silver-ware of the 16-17th cen-

turies. 1930. Large silver-gilt eagle by Christopher Jamnitzer representing the coat-of-arms of Oesel, and presented by the district of Oesel to Christian IV. of Denmark in 1595 (purchased at Archangel in 1628); 2252. Small beaker by Wenzel Jamnitzer, curiously covered with silver plates of Russian work; 1056. Double goblet by Hans Pätzold (1578); 1071. Large goblet in the form of a bunch of grapes; 1057. Double goblet by Hans Pätzold. — *Pillar Cabinet 14.* Works in mother-of-pearl, cocoa-nut, and shell. — *Pillar Cabinet 15.* Caucasian and Russian silver-ware and ivory work of the 14-18th centuries. — *Cab. 16* (to the right of the entrance). Silver-ware from Danzig, Königsberg, Cracow, Bremen, and Halle (16-17th cent.); 4059 a. Relief, showing the Polish army, under John Casimir, giving thanks to God for a victory over the Cossacks in 1651. — We now retrace our steps towards the semicircle.

‑ *Pillar Cabinet 17.* Arabic, Chinese, and Japanese work down to the 18th century. — *Pillar Cabinet 18.* Ivory work; ostrich eggs. — *Pillar Cabinet 19.* Foreign glass. — *Pillar Cabinet 20.* Russian glass. Below, 2586. Small wine-glass of Peter the Great, probably the first made in Russia.

In the semicircle, at the end of the room. *Glass Case 21.* Foreign work in silver filigree, crystal, and so on (16-18th centuries). — *Glass Case 22.* Silver table made in Paris. — We now return towards the entrance-wall.

Cabinets 23-25. Augsburg silver-ware. Cab. 24 contains a large oval dish with the representation of the liberation of Vienna from the Turks, presented in 1684 by the Emperor Leopold I. (No. 1193). — *Cab. 26.* Dutch silver-ware.

Window-wall. *Cab. 27, Case 28, & Cab. 30.* Russian dishes for bread and salt, presented at the coronation of Nicholas II. — *Glass Case 31.* Addresses at the coronation of Nicholas II.

Entrance-wall. *Cab. 32.* Foreign silver-ware of the 16-17th centuries. — *Glass Case 33.* Knives, forks, and spoons of the 17th century. — *Cab. 34.* Foreign silver-ware of the 16-17th centuries. — *Cab. 35.* Silver-ware from Lübeck, Rostock, Leipzig, and Brunswick.

The glass-cases by the windows contain Russian coins and medals.

We now return through RR. III-I and descend the staircase to the right to the Lower Floor.

Lower Floor. I. MODEL ROOM (Модéльная зáла). By the entrance, to the left, is a huge porcelain vase. To the right is a large service of Sèvres porcelain, made in 1806, with scenes from the Egyptian Expedition of Napoleon. — Opposite, to the left, is an ivory eagle on a rock of ironwood presented by the Mikado of Japan to Nicholas II. Adjacent is a silk Japanese screen, embroidered with waves. — Table 21. Model of an old palace of the Tzars at Kolomna, near Moscow, razed to the ground in 1767. — Thrones of the Khan of Khiva (captured in 1873) and of Prince Abbas Mirza of Persia (captured in 1827). — By the right window-wall are the bed of Peter the Great, the travelling-bed of Alexander I., and two camp-beds of Napoleon I., captured at the Berézina.

II. PORTRAIT ROOM (Портрéтная зáла). In the middle is a terrestrial globe presented to the Empress Elizabeth by the Academy of Sciences in 1746. — To the left of this globe is a marble group of Jagiello and Jadwiga, by Soznóvski. — The cases contain valuable harness. On and by the walls are portraits and busts of Polish kings and celebrated men such as Copernicus, Zamoyski, and Potemkin.

III. DOMESTIC ROOM (Бытовáя зáла), with wearing apparel and other objects. — We now return to Room II, and enter the

IV. CARRIAGE ROOM (Карéтная зáла), which contains old equipages. To the left is a carriage of the Boyar Nikita Ivánovitch Románov, lined inside and outside with red velvet. To the right is an English carriage sent to Tzar Mikhaïl Feódorovitch in 1625, the inside lined with velvet and the outside adorned with carved and gilded scenes of war and the chase. — In the middle is the state chariot of the Empress Elizabeth, 30 ft. in length, presented by Count K. Razumóvski in 1754. — In the semicircle is a state chariot of the Empress Anna, made at St. Petersburg in 1739. — At the end of the right side-wall is the closed sleigh in which Elizabeth drove to her coronation at Moscow in 1742; it is fitted up as a small room, upholstered in green cloth, with a table and divans, two doors, and fourteen windows. Other gilded carriages, with beautiful paintings, made at Vienna, Berlin, and other places. — The glass-cabinets contain valuable harness.

To the S. of the Oruzhéinaya Paláta is the *Borovítzkiya Gate,* a structure 62 ft. in height, erected under Iván III., the upper part restored at the end of the 17th century. It was through this gate that Napoleon I. entered the Kremlin in 1812.

Through the Imperátorskaya Square a passage, under the arcade supporting the imperial winter-garden (p. 287), leads to the Dvortzóvaya, the only street in the Kremlin. To the right (1st door; Pl. P.), is the *Office of the Police Superintendent of the Kremlin,* where the tickets admitting to the Kremlin Palace are obtained. Farther on, to the left, is the **Potyéshni Dvorétz** (Pl. 9; see below), a green-painted building with a balcony supported by four buttresses, and interesting ornamentation on the windows and doors. It now contains the *Memorial Museum of the War of 1812* (adm., see p. 275).

The *Potyéshni Dvorétz,* or 'Pleasure Palace', the old home of the Miloslávski, came into the possession of the Románovs through the marriage of Tzar Alexis Mikháïlovitch with Marie Ilitchna Miloslávskaya in 1648. The first court theatre of Russia was opened here in the reign of Alexis, under the superintendence of the Boyar Artamon Matvéyev. Here Peter the Great is said to have been brought up by Zotov.

At the end of the Dvortzóvaya, to the left, is the *Tróitzkiya Gate,* with the *Imperial Archives.* We turn to the right and reach the large SENATE SQUARE (Сенáтская плóщадь), bounded on the S. by the Kremlin Barracks, on the W. by the Arsenal, on the E. by the Court of Justice (p. 296). On the N. side of the square is a cross, marking the spot where Grand-Duke Sergius Alexándrovitch was murdered on Feb. 4th, 1905.

The imposing *Kremlin Barracks* (Кремлéвскія казáрмы) are said to occupy part of the site of the old wooden palace of Tzar

Boris Godunóv. In front of the main façade are 20 old-fashioned cannon, among which may be especially noticed the two huge ones at the corners, that to the left being known as the Tzar Cannon, that to the right as the Unicorn. The somewhat over-ornamented *Tzar Cannon* (Царь-Пушка), cast by Tchokhov in 1586, in the reign of Feódor I. Ivánovitch, and supported on a carriage cast by Baird at St. Petersburg, is 17¹/₂ ft. long and 2400 puds (38¹/₂ tons) in weight. Its bore is ca. 40 inches, and the ball weighs nearly 2 tons. The *Unicorn* (Единорогъ), cast by Osipov in 1670, in the reign of Alexis Mikháilovitch, is a 60-pounder, weighing 779 puds (12¹/₂ tons).

Beyond the Kremlin Barracks, to the S., lies the **Synodal Building,** completed in 1655 and originally the *Residence of the Patriarch* (Синодáльный домъ). It contains the Church of the Twelve Apostles, the private chapel of the Metropolitan Philip, and the library of the Patriarchs.

The Metropolitan of Moscow, the first prelate of Russia, was solemnly invested with the style of 'His Holiness' in the middle of the 16th cent., and in 1589 the pious Tzar Feódor I. Ivánovitch, with the acquiescence of all the bishops of the Greek Church, granted him the title of Patriarch. On Jan. 23rd of the same year, Job (1589-1607), the first patriarch, was solemnly installed. The *Patriarchate* maintained itself until 1700, when it was superseded by the Holy Synod (p. lviii). Of the ten patriarchs who ruled during this period, the most important was *Nikon*, who was consecrated on July 25th, 1652, after the death of Joseph. For many years he enjoyed the highest confidence of the Tzar Alexis Mikháilovitch as his spiritual adviser and friend, as leader both of the Church and of the State. The nobles, however, at last succeeded in overthrowing his power. In 1666 Alexis summoned a solemn council to his palace in the Kremlin, and Nikon was formally deposed. Adrian (1690-1700) was the last patriarch. From 1700 to 1742 the Muscovite Eparchy remained under the immediate superintendence of the Synod, *i.e.* without a chief pastor. In the latter year the Empress Elizabeth confirmed the resolution of the Synod creating the archbishopric of Moscow.

On the second floor of the building is the *Church of the Twelve Apostles* (Цéрковь двѣнáдцати апóстоловъ), built in 1656 and containing a picture of the Apostles Peter and Paul, dating from the 12th or 13th century. On Maundy Thursday the holy chrism is prepared in silver kettles in the adjacent *Muirovárnaya Paláta.* — The *Church of the Apostle Philip* was formerly the domestic chapel of the patriarchs. Adjacent is the unpretending dwelling of the patriarchs. — The *Library of the Patriarchs,* now the *Synodal Library* (librarian, N. Popóv; adm., see p. 275), contains 500 Greek MSS. of the 9-12th cent. (Russian catalogue 5 rb., 1894) and 1800 Slavonic MSS. of the 11-14th centuries.

Opposite the Barracks, on the N., rises the huge *Arsenal* (Арсенáлъ; no admission), built in 1701-36, blown up by the French in 1812, and rebuilt by Nicholas I. In front are 875 cannon captured in 1812, including 366 French guns, 189 Austrian, 123 Prussian, and 70 Italian.

The **Court of Justice,** or former *Senate House* (Здáніе су-
дéбныхъ установлéній; adm., see p. 275), facing the Arsenal on
the E., erected by Kazakóv in 1771-85, in the reign of Catherine II.,
was restored after 1812 and in 1866. It is surmounted by a flat
dome, bearing a square pillar with a crown. On each of the four
sides of this pillar is inscribed the word 'Закóнъ' (law) in golden
letters. In the E. part of the building lies the handsome Round
Hall (Крýглая зáла), containing reliefs representing the deeds
of Empress Catherine II. Here, too, are portraits of the Empress
Catherine, under a canopy, and of the Tzars from Alexander I. to
Nicholas II. In a niche is a marble statue of Alexander II.

We leave the Kremlin by the *Nikólskiya Gate* (Никóльскія
ворóта; Pl. D 4, *II*), which leads to the Red Square. The tower was
erected by Pietro Antonio (p. 279) in 1491, and was rebuilt by
Rossi in the reign of Nicholas I., after the model of the tower of
the Church of the Virgin at Stargard in Pomerania. The gate takes
its name from the mosaic picture of St. Nicholas of Mozhaisk, the
patron-saint of the afflicted, which hangs above the archway. An
inscription on the gate, placed there by Alexander I., records that
when the gate was blown up by the French, no harm came to either
the portrait of the saint or to the lamp hanging in front of it, although the upper part of the tower was considerably damaged.

b. Inner City (Kitái-Gorod).

Chapel of the Iberian Virgin. Red Square. House of the Boyar Románov.

To the N., between the Kremlin (p. 278) and the Inner City, lies
the Krásnaya or Red Square (Крáсная плóщадь; Pl. D 4, *II*),
900 yds. long and 175 yds. broad, bounded on the W. by the battlemented wall of the Kremlin, on the E. by the Trading Rows (p. 299),
on the N. by the Historical Museum (p. 297) and the Kazan Cathedral (p. 300), and on the S. by the Cathedral of St. Basil (p. 299).

The main entrance to the Inner City on the W. side is formed
by the *Iberian* or *Voskresénskiya Gate* (Воскресéнскія ворóта;
Pl. D 4, *II*), which stands opposite the end of the Tverskáya. The
gate has two openings, over each of which is a pointed tower. Between the two openings, on the side towards the Krásnaya Square,
is the —

Chapel of the Iberian Virgin (*Íverskaya Tchasóvnya,*
Часóвня Йверской бóжіей мáтери; Pl. D 4, *II*), built in 1669,
and one of the most highly revered in Russia. Each time that the
Tzar comes to Moscow he visits this chapel before entering the
Kremlin. The chapel is generally crowded, even at night, and the
traveller should be on his guard against pickpockets.

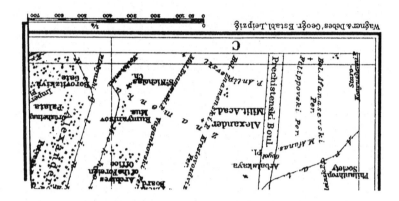

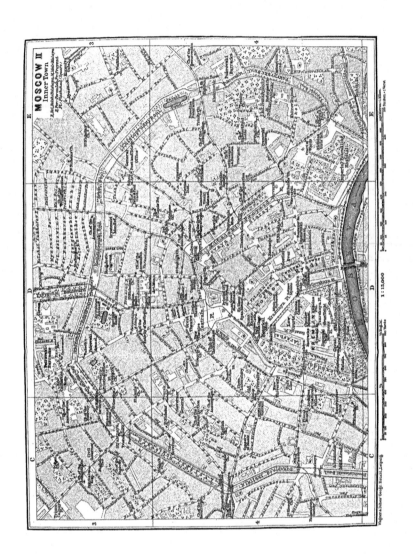

MOSCOW II
Inner Town

1:15,000

The INTERIOR (open till 7 p.m.) consists of one very small chamber. In the sanctuary is the picture of the wonder-working (Tchudotvórni) Iberian Virgin, the most celebrated picture of the kind in Moscow. It is an accurate copy, solemnly made in 1648, with an accompaniment of fasting and prayer, of the miracle-working picture of the Virgin (Vratárnitza) of the Iberian Monastery on Mt. Athos, which is said to date from the 8th century. It was presented to the Tzar Alexis Mikháilovitch by the Archimandrite Pakhomios and the brothers of the monastery. The scar on the right cheek of the Virgin was made by a Tartar. The head is enveloped in a net of pearls; one shoulder and the forehead are studded with large jewels; above is a diamond crown. In one corner of the picture is a shield bearing a Greek inscription. — Orthodox Russians are allowed, for a pecuniary consideration, to secure the presence of this sacred picture at sick-beds or at their family festivals. On these occasions the picture is placed upon a carriage, drawn by six horses and attended by two priests and several bare-headed attendants, and is carried from room to room of the house it visits. On the way it is greeted by everyone with the greatest reverence. During its absence it is replaced in the chapel by a copy.

On the N.E. the Iberian Gate is adjoined by the *Duma* (City Hall; Pl. D 4, *II*), a brick structure erected in 1892 from the plans of Tchitchagóv, facing toward the Voskresénskaya Square. — To the S.W. of the Iberian Gate, with its chief façade towards the Red Square, stands the —

Historical Museum (Импера́торскій Россі́йскій Истори́ческій музе́й; Pl. D 4, *II*), a massive building in the Russian style of the 16th cent., erected by *Sherwood* in 1875-83, at a cost of upwards of 2,000,000 rb. It contains collections relating to the history of Russian art and civilization. — Adm., see p. 275. Russian guide (1914). Director, Prince N. S. Shtcherbátov; chief conservator, A. V. Oréshnikov; librarian, A. I. Stankévitch.

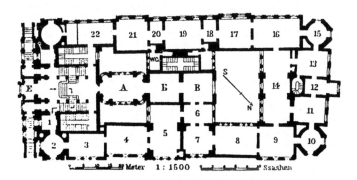

A flight of steps with bronze lions leads to the UPPER HALL. The ceiling-painting here, by Tóropov, represents the genealogical tree of the Russian reigning family; below are SS. Vladímir, Olga, Borís, and Glyeb; above, arranged in 10 rows, are 68 princes and tzars, ending with Alexander III. The decorations on the walls are in the style of the ornaments on the throne of the Tzars in St. Sophia's at Novgorod.—To the right of the vestibule is Room 1, containing objects of the *Stone Age* from Asiatic Russia. —Room 2. *Stone Age* in European Russia. Weapons and implements of stone and clay; bones of the mammoth. The frieze, by *Vaznetzóv*, represents scenes from the Stone Age.—Room 3. *Bronze Age*. Heads of lances and arrows; vessels and ornaments, including a few of gold and silver (in the glass-cases); objects connected with worship; objects found in the Caucasus.—Room 4. *Iron Age* (N. & Central Russia). The glass-cases contain models of Kurgáns or tumuli (chiefly fire-graves) and objects found in them. Those by the side-wall are from the Dnieper, those in the middle from Central Russia. Of especial interest are the objects found in the governments of Smolensk, Vladimir, Ryazan, Tambov (Finnish tribes), and Moscow. By the exit-wall are so-called Babi (*i.e.* roughly executed stone statues). The mural paintings by *Siemirádzki* represent the burning of the corpse of a rich Russian merchant in Bulgari (10th cent.), the burning of the bodies of fallen Russians, and the slaughter of prisoners of war outside Silistria (war of Svyatosláv with the Greek Emperor John Tzimisces, 10th cent.).—Room 5. *Iron Age* (S. & E. Russia). To the left is the collection made by *Prof. Samokvásov*. Babi (see above).— Room 6. *Scythia*. The glass-cases contain objects from the Caucasus, the Crimea, and other places. In the middle is a model of the tumulus of Kul-Oba.—Room B (to the left). Works of Christian art from the Caucasus and Crimea. Statues and limestone crosses from the Caucasus.— Room Б. *Greek Colonies in S. Russia*. Terracottas, bronzes, gold ornaments, vessels, etc. Over the door is a painting by Aivazóvski, representing the Gulf of Kertch with the Tzarski Kurgán.—Room A contains chiefly casts of works of Christian art down to the 6th century. The mural paintings are copies of those in the Roman Catacombs. The mosaics are after those in Ravenna and Constantinople.—We now return through Room 6 into Room 7. *Kiev* (988-1056). Beginning of Christianity in Russia. On the walls are mosaics after those in the Cathedral of St. Sophia in Kiev. Small Russian crosses.—Room 8. *Kiev* (from 1056 on). Pictures of saints; marriage crowns; embroideries. On the walls are reproductions of mosaics in St. Sophia's Cathedral at Kiev.—Room 9. *Novgorod*. Watercolours by *Martinov*, representing objects in Russian churches. The walls and ceiling are painted in the style of the Novgorod churches.—Room 10. *Vladimir*. Ornaments in the style of the Uspenski Cathedral.—Room 11 (to the left). *Suzdal*. Ornaments for pictures of saints; pictures of saints. —Room 12. *Rostov*, in the government of Yaroslavl; wedding-crowns (Брáчныe вѣнцы).—Room 13. *Moscow* (down to the beginning of the 15th cent.). The ceiling reproduces the style of ornamentation on the throne of Vladimir Monomákh.—We now return to the staircase and turn to the right into Rooms 18-20, which represent the period of Iván the Terrible.—Room 21. Period of Tzar Feódor Ivánovitch and of Borís Godunóv (end of 16th cent.).—Room 22. The Interregnum (beginning of 17th cent.).

To the S.E. of the Historical Museum, in the middle of the Red Square, stands the *Monument of Minin and Pozhárski* (Пá-мятникъ Мúнину и Пожáрскому; Pl. D 4, *II*), by Martos (1818). The bronze figures of Minin (left) and Pozhárski (right) are borne by a granite pedestal with reliefs representing the self-sacrifice of the Russian people and the flight of the Poles from the Kremlin.

During the Interregnum (1606-13) a butcher of Nizhni-Novgorod, named *Kosmá Minin Sukhorúkov*, called upon the people to free their fatherland from the Poles and to fight for their faith. The summons was answered by levies from Nizhni, and also by recruits from the towns on the Volga and in the Ukraine, and Minin placed these bodies under the command of *Prince Demetrius Mikháilovitch Pozhárski*. On Aug. 20th, 1612, the Russian army appeared before Moscow, defeated the Poles in a battle lasting three days, and compelled King Sigismund to retire.

Near the Cathedral of St. Basil is the **Lóbnoye Myesto** (Pl. D, 4; *II*), *i.e.* Place of a Skull, a kind of rostrum or round platform, surrounded by a stone balustrade.

In 1605 the False Demetrius was formally received at the Lóbnoye Myesto, while the following year the angry people dragged his murdered body hither. Iván Shuiski was proclaimed Tzar here in 1606, and Mikhail Feódorovitch in 1613. This was the place of the execution *en masse* of the Streltzi (p. 289). The solemn processions, in which the Tzar led the ass on which the patriarch sat, passed the Lóbnoye Myesto on their way to the Cathedral of the Assumption. Religious disputations were also held here on Sunday, and the ukases of the Tzar were also proclaimed here.

At the S. end of the square is the ***Cathedral of St. Basil,** or *Vasíli Blazhénni Cathedral,* more properly called the *Cathedral of the Virgin Protectress and Intercessor* (Покро́вскій собо́ръ Васи́лія Блаже́ннаго; Pl. D 4, *II*), a building of very singular appearance, begun by Iván the Terrible in 1554 from plans by the Russian masters *Barma* and *Postnik,* to commemorate the conquest of Kazan. It was consecrated in 1557, but was not really completed until 1679. In 1812 the church was plundered by the French and used by them as a stable, but in 1839-45 it was restored in its original form. It consists of eleven small, dark chapels, arranged in two stories, and combined in a most extraordinary agglomeration. The building is surmounted by a dozen domes and spires, painted in all the colours of the rainbow, and of the most varied forms. Some of them are shaped like bulbs or pine-apples, some are twisted in strange spirals, some are serrated, some covered with facets or scales. All of them bulge out over their supporting drums and are crowned by massive crosses. The decoration, in which numerous Renaissance details may be detected, is of the most exuberant character. The whole effect is quaint and fantastic in the extreme. — The interior contains little of interest.

The E. side of the Krásnaya Square is occupied by the so-called **Trading Rows** (*Torgóvniye Ryadí;* Pl. D 4, *II*). The *Upper Rows* (Ве́рхніе торго́вые ряды́), between the Ilyínka and the Nikólskaya, were built by A. N. Pomerántzev in sandstone in 1888-93, at a total cost of 6,000,000 rb., besides 9,500,000 rb. for the site. They are three stories in height, 275 yds. long, and 95 yds. deep, and are intersected in each direction by three glass-covered corridors, with bridges in the second and third stories. The main building has two towers in the middle. Restaurant in the basement, see p. 271. The Upper Rows (open 8-8; chief entrance in the Red Square) contain about 1000 offices and shops, used for both retail and wholesale trade. Visitors should not omit to walk through them. — The *Middle Rows* between the Ilyínka and Varvárka, were constructed by R. I. Klein, and are chiefly used for wholesale trade.

In the VARVÁRKA (Pl. D, 4; *II*), to the right, is the *Známenski Monastery,* or Convent of the Apparition of the Virgin, founded in

1631 by Tzar Mikhail Feódorovitch, and restored in 1902. Adjacent is the —

*House of the Boyar Románov (Домъ бояръ Романовыхъ; Pl. D 4, *II*), a one-storied building with a frontage of 56 ft., affording an excellent picture of the furnishing of the houses of the wealthier Russians in the 16-17th cent. (adm., see p. 275; entr., Pskovski Pereúlok; fee to the attendant 30 cop.). Owing to the slope of the ground the house presents four stories towards the court. In this house was born Mikhail Feódorovitch, the first Tzar of the Románov family, who afterwards presented it to the Známenski Convent (p. 299). At a later date it was entirely surrounded by other buildings. In 1812 it was plundered by the French, and in 1856 it was, so to speak, rediscovered. Tzar Alexander II. purchased it and caused it to be restored. — The groundfloor is occupied by storerooms, above which are the kitchen and rooms for the servants. In the second floor are the Boyar's rooms. In the Krestóvaya Paláta, or Reception Room of the head of the house, is a glass-case containing the family plate and a silver equestrian statuette of Charles I. of England. The chapel contains some old pictures of saints. In an adjoining room are souvenirs of the Patriarch Philaret, the father of Tzar Mikhail Feódorovitch, and of the Tzar himself. On the uppermost floor is the bedroom of the Patriarch Philaret. The visitor will be struck by the small size of the doors and the narrowness of the staircases.

The central and main street of the Kitái-Gorod, almost exclusively occupied by wholesale houses and banks, is named the ILYÍNKA. On the right side of it stands the **Exchange** (Биржа; Pl. D 4, *II*), erected in 1838 (business-hour, 12-1). Opposite is the handsome *House of the Tróitzko-Sérgiyevskaya Lavra* (p. 325), with shops. The street ends at the *Ilyínskiya Gate*, to the right and left of which are the *Stáraya Square* and the *Nóvaya Square*, extending along the wall of the Kitái-Gorod.

The NIKÓLSKAYA (Pl. D, 4; *II*), the third chief street of the Inner City, also begins at the Red Square. At the corner, to the left, rises the *Kazan Cathedral*, built by Prince Pozhárski in 1625 in gratitude for the deliverance of Russia from the Poles, and restored in 1825. Adjacent is the *Za-Ikóno-Spasski Monastery*, or *Monastery of the Saviour behind the Pictures*, founded in 1660; the first Russian scientific school was established here in 1682, and among its pupils was the celebrated writer Lomonósov (p. 301). The school was suppressed in 1814.

Farther on, to the left, is the *Greek Monastery of St. Nicholas* (Николаевскій греческій мужской монастырь), destined by Iván the Terrible in 1556 for the Greek monks who had come to Moscow from Mt. Athos (services in Greek). — Opposite, at the corner of the street of the same name, is the *Bogoyavlénski Monastery*, founded in 1296, entirely remodelled after 1812, and again restored in 1896. It contains the burial-places of many noble families.

Farther on in the Nikólskaya, to the left, is the **Synodal Printing Office** (Синодáльная типогрáфія; Pl. D 4, *II*), the oldest in Russia, founded by Iván the Terrible in 1563. The present building was erected by Nevyérov in a bastard Gothic style in 1645, and restored in 1814. The library (in the court; adm., see p. 275) contains a copy of the Acts of the Apostles (Апóстолъ) printed in 1564 by Iván Feódorov (ca. 1520-88; p. 310), the first book printed in Russia (No. 24 in the last glass-case to the right of the entrance).

A little beyond the Synodal Printing Office is the busy *Tretyakóvski Proyézd*, leading to the left to the Teatrálni Proyézd (p. 310; Theatre Square, see p. 309). At the N. end of the Nikólskaya is the *Vladímir Gate* (Pl. D, 4; *II*), so called after the church of that name, erected in 1691 to commemorate the deliverance of Russia from the yoke of the Tartars. This brings us to the Lubyánskaya Square (p. 310).

c. South-West Quarter of the City.

University. Rumyántzov Museum. Church of the Redeemer. Convent of the Maidens.

Electric Tramways, see p. 271. Nos. 18, 23, 24, & 34 run from the Theatre Square to the University. Nos. 23, 24, & 34 run from the Theatre Square to the Rumyántzov Museum and to the Church of the Redeemer, and Nos. 17 & 23 to the Convent of the Maidens. The Arbát is traversed by Nos. 4, 15, 17, & 31. — The walk from the Church of the Redeemer to (2¹/₄ M.) the Convent of the Maidens is tedious and uninteresting, so it is advisable to use the tramway.

Along the W. side of the Kremlin, from the Voskresénskaya Square on the N. to the Moskvá on the S., stretches the **Alexander Garden** (Алексáндровскій садъ; Pl. D 4, *II*), laid out by Alexander I. It is divided into two parts by the Tróitzkiya Bridge, connecting the Tróitzkiya Gate of the Kremlin with its outer tower, and is traversed from end to end by an avenue of lindens.

To the W., between the Alexander Garden and the Мохновáя, rises the **Manège** or *Riding School* (Гарнизóнный манéжъ; Pl. D 4, *II*), 200 yds. long, 60 yds. broad, and 45 ft. high, constructed in 1817. It serves as a drill-hall for the Moscow garrison, and is also used for exhibitions, popular fêtes, large concerts, and the like.

To the W., beyond the Riding School, in the Mokhováya, lies the **Imperial University** (Pl. D, 4; *II*), the oldest in Russia, founded by the Empress Elizabeth in 1755, at the suggestion of Lomonósov (see below) and Iván Shuválov. The University, which is attended by 9700 students, consists of two blocks of buildings separated by the Nikítskaya. To the S. is the New University and to the N. is the Old University (Clinics, see p. 306). In front of the New University is a *Bronze Bust of Lomonósov* (Pl. L), by Ivánov, erected in 1876. In the Mokhováya is the *University Library*, a building surmounted by a dome and containing 385,000 vols. (adm., see p. 275; Chief Librarian, Kalishévski). Adjoining the Old University, at the corner of the Bolshaya Nikítskaya and the Dolgorúkovski Pereúlok, is the *Zoological Museum* (adm., see p. 275; catalogue 10 cop.; Director, Prof. G. Kozhévnikov).

In the Bryusóvski Pereúlok, leading to the N.E. from the Bolshaya Nikítskaya, is the *English Church* (Pl. C 4, *II;* p. 274). — The Leóntyevski Pereúlok, another side-street, farther on, contains the **Museum of Domestic Industries** (Кустáрный музéй; Pl. C 4, *II;* adm., see p. 274), which affords a good survey of the home industries of Russia. Most of the exhibits are for sale. ·

The Mokhováya ends on the N. at the Moïséyevskaya Square and the Tverskáya (p. 308), while to the S. it leads, along with its prolongations, to the Convent of the Maidens (p. 307). In the Vozd víznenka, which diverges to the W. from the Mokhováya, are the *Archives of the Foreign Office* (Глáвный архúвъ министéрства инострáнныхъ дѣлъ; Pl. C 4, *II*), containing rich treasures in the shape of documents of the Grand-Princes and Tzars from 1265 to 1801, a library, state seals, and MSS. Among the last are letters written by Queen Elizabeth of England to Ivàn the Terrible. The archives are open to students on week-days, 11-3 (closed on Sat.).

At the corner of the Známenka and the Mokhováya Úlitza is the *Imperial Rumyántzov Museum* (Императóрскій Москóвскій и Румя́нцовскій Музéй; Pl. C 4, *II*), a handsome building in the baroque style erected in 1787 by Kazakóv (?), and occupying a small eminence. The chief façade is adorned with columns and is turned towards the Mokhováya. On the portico is the inscription 'To joy-bringing enlightenment' (На блáгóе просвѣщéніе). The nucleus of the museum is formed by the collections bequeathed to the State by Count Nicholas Rumyántzov (d. 1826), but these have been considerably expanded by gifts and purchases. Director, Prince V. D. Golítzin. Adm., see p. 275; entr. at Vagánkovski Pereúlok 2. Russian and French catalogues.

To the left of the entrance is a portrait of the founder of the museum by *G. Dawe* (1828). — The **Library** (comp. Plan), which contains nearly 1,000,000 vols., is especially rich in historical works and in books printed in ecclesiastical Slavonic and old Russian. Among the MSS. is one of *Giordano Bruno*, from the collection of A. S. Norov. — One of the corridors (Pl. 6) contains archives of Russian masonic lodges and masonic insignia. [Freemasonry was introduced into Russia in 1731, but was suppressed by Alexander I. in 1822.] — The central building contains MSS. (Pl. 9, 18) and an important collection of coins (Pl. 17).

In the N. wing is the **Dashkov Collection of National Costumes** (Pl. 19-32), including a series of 360 figures dressed in the original garments, as well as separate articles of clothing, domestic utensils, and so on. Room 19. Aleutian Islands (Cabinets i-vii); Tlinkits or Koloshes (Cab. vii-ix). — Room 20. Japan (Cab. xiii-xvi); Korea (Cab. xvii & xviii); China (Cab. xix-xxii); Sunda Islands (Cab. xxiii-xxvi). — Room 21. Samoyedes (Cab. 1 & 2); Tunguses (Cab. 3 & 4); Finns from the Volga and

the Urals (Cab. 5-7); West Finns, Esthonians (Cab. 8 & 9); Kalmucks
(Cab. 10-12); Tartars, Kirghizes (Cab. 13-20); Gipsies, Rumanians, Lithuanians, German colonists (Cab. 21-24); Semites (Cab. 25); Caucasian tribes
(Cab. 26-30); in the middle, Turkestan (Cab. 31-40). — Room 22. E. Siberians (Cab. 43-51). — Room 23. Models of houses. — From Room 22 we reach
the upper floor (Slavs). In the middle row: Great Russians (Cab. 54-66);
to the right of the entrance, Little Russians (Cab. 67-72), White Russians

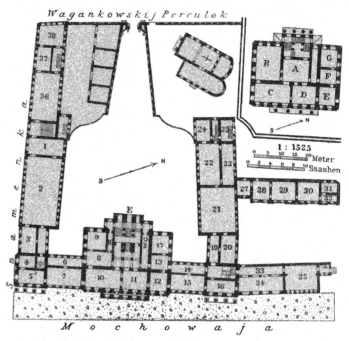

Key to the Numbers on the Plan (not used in the museum itself). 1. Of-
fices; 2. Library of Count Rumyántzov; 3. Catalogue Room; 4 & 5. MSS.
& Reading Rooms; 6. Masonic Insignia; 7 & 8. Library; 9. MSS.; 10-14.
Library; 15. Curator's Offices; 16. Library; 17. Collection of Coins; 18.
MSS.; — 19-26. National Costumes; — 27-32. Kamtchatka and Alaska Col-
lection; — 33-35. Library; 36-38. Reading Rooms.

(Cab. 73-77), Poles (Cab. 77-80), Czechs and Moravians (Cab. 81). We return
along the other side: Slovenians (Cab. 82 & 83), Slovaks (Cab. 84 & 85),
Croats (Cab. 86), Slavs from the Balkans (Cab. 87-93), Ruthenians (Cab. 94
& 95). — Room C. Costumes and other objects. — From Room 21 we enter
the Ethnographical Collection from Kamtchatka and Alaska (Ryabushinski-
Jochelson Expedition; Pl. 27-32); above, Christian and Russian Antiquities.

The **Picture Gallery** is contained in a separate building. (1) Russian Pictures of the 18-19th centuries. Collection Th. I. Pryánishnikov

(d. 1867): *A. A. Ivánov* (d. 1858), 'Behold your King' (Pilate showing Christ
to the people), a large picture upon which the master worked for 20 years;
portraits by *Losénko* (d. 1773; Volkov, the founder of the first Russian
theatre, p. 331), *Levítzki* (d. 1822), *Borovikóvski* (d. 1826), *Lampi* (d. 1830;
Prince Potemkin, unfinished), *Tropinin* (d. 1858), and other masters;
paintings by *K. P. Bryullóv* (d. 1852), *Orlóvski* (d. 1832), etc.; *Fedótov,*
Arrival of the bridegroom, His first decoration; *Peróv,* Burial of a peasant;
Ryepin, I. S. Turgényev; paintings by *Aivazóvski.* — Lvov Collection, with
pictures by *Borovikóvski, Levítzki,* and *Bryullóv.* — Engravings. — Collec
tion of K. T.Soldatyénkov (d. 1901): *Turlúigin,* At work; *Levitan,* Land
scape; *Koróvin,* Detected poacher; *Lébedev,* Peasant-woman; *Myasoyédov,*
Open-air service; *Popóv,* Eating-house; *Trutóvski,* Invalid; *Ratchkóv,*
Dr. Pikulin; *Makóvski,* In the anteroom of the Justice of the Peace;
Zhuravlév, Funeral-feast; *Shishkin,* Landscape; *Siemirádzki,* Sword-
dance; *Shishkin,* Landscape; *Jakobi,* Jester at the court of the Empress
Anna Ivánovna; *Bogátov,* Ploughman; *Kasátkin,* At the door of the
chapel; *Botkin,* Reading the lessons; *Kasátkin,* In the corridor of the
District Court; *Vasílyev,* Thaw; *Vasnetzóv,* Game of cards.

(2) ITALIAN, DUTCH, AND OTHER PICTURES. Italian pictures, many of
them spurious. *Rubens,* Mucius Scævola (sketch); *Snyders,* Butcher's
shop; *Ph. Wouverman,* Hunting-party; *Rembrandt,* Haman at the banquet
with Esther and Ahasuerus (1660); *A. de Gelder,* Lot and his daughters;
A. van der Neer, Conflagration at night; *G. Terburg,* Portrait of a
woman; *J. van der Heyde,* Dutch manor-house; *J. van Ochtervelt,* Lady
at her toilet. The adjoining rooms contain French and German paintings.

Farther on in the Známenka, to the left, at the corner of the
Bolshói Známenski Pereúlok, is the *Alexander Military Academy*
(Pl. C, 4; *II*). — No. 8 Bolshói Známenki Pereúlok is the *House of
Sergius Ivánovitch Shtchukin,* with an admirable collection of
modern French paintings, including examples by Monet, Sisley,
Renoir, Degas, Cézanne, Gauguin, Matisse, and Picasso; adm. on
written application to the owner.

We now return to the Mokhováya, and proceed to the S. along
the Volkhonka. On the right, at the corner of the Antípyevski
Pereúlok, is the **Museum of Fine Arts** or *Museum of Alexander III.* (Музей изящныхъ искусствъ ймени императора
Александра III.; Pl. C 5, *I*), built by R. I. Klein in 1898-1912.
The Museum was founded by I. V. Tzvyetáyev (d. 1913) and belongs
to the University. It contains coloured and bronzed casts and
marble copies of the most important works of art of all countries
and all epochs, Egyptian antiquities, and Italian paintings of the
14th century. Adm., see p. 275. Director, Professor W. K. Malmberg.

To the N.E. of the Church of the Redeemer is a seated figure of
Tzar Alexander III. (in bronze), by Opekúshin (1912).

The *Church of the Redeemer (Храмъ Христа Спасителя;
Pl. C 5, *I*), the most richly decorated church in Moscow, built in 1839-
83 from the plans of *Thon,* in commemoration of the events of 1812-14,
is conspicuously situated in a large square on the left bank of the
Moskvá. It is open for morning service at 8 a.m., and then again
from 11 a.m. until dusk. The total cost of the building, which is
335 ft. high and covers an area of 8020 sq. yds., amounted to upwards

of 15,000,000 rb. The church is in the form of a Greek cross and is surmounted by five gilded domes, the chief of which has a diameter of 100 ft. The outside walls are sheathed in marble. The twelve fine bronze portals, three in each façade, are approached by broad flights of granite steps. The roof is bordered by a bronze-gilt balustrade. The 48 marble alto-reliefs on the façades are by Loganóvski, Ramazánov, and Baron Klodt.

The subjects of the reliefs are as follows: on the W. façade is a figure of Christ; to the right are SS. Alexander Nevski and Nicholas of Novgorod, and to the left SS. Nicholas the Wonder-worker and Elizabeth. At the right angle is a group representing David giving Solomon the plan of the Temple; at the left is the Anointing of Solomon. The saints on the S. side, facing the Moskvá, are those on whose days the Russian battles of 1812 occurred; to the right, Barak and Deborah; to the left, Moses and Miriam; at the corners, Abraham and Melchizedek (r.), and David's reception after the conquest of Goliath (l.). On the E. side, facing the Kremlin, are the saints regarded as the champions and intercessors of Russia; to the left and right, Nativity and Resurrection of Christ. On the N. side are the champions and defenders of the Faith, and saints on whose days the Russians were victorious in 1813-14. At the corner to the right is St. Sergius, consecrating Demetrius of the Don for his struggle with the Tartars; to the left is St. Dionysius blessing Pozhárski and Minin (p. 298).

The INTERIOR, which is abundantly lighted by sixty windows, is elaborately decorated in gold and marble, and makes an impression of great harmony. On festivals and high days, 3700 candles are lighted for divine worship. The vocal music of this church is celebrated.

On the walls of the CORRIDOR running round the interior of the church are 177 marble tablets, bearing imperial manifestoes of the time of the War of Liberation, and also the names of battles and of the officers who fell in them. Four massive piers support the MAIN DOME, which is adorned with a large picture of the Lord of Sabaoth, by *Markov*. Below are representatives of the Old and New Testaments, by *Kóshelev*. In the niches of the piers are the Adoration of the Shepherds, the Adoration of the Magi, the Anointing of David as King, and St. Sergius blessing the Grand-Prince Demetrius of the Don before his contest with the Tartars, four paintings by *V. P. Vereshtchágin* (not to be confounded with V. V. Vereshtchágin, the painter of battle-scenes). In the spandrels are the Transfiguration, the Resurrection, the Ascension, and the Descent of the Holy Ghost, with the Evangelists below, all by *Bruni* and *Sorókin*. The IKONOSTÁS is in the form of a white marble chapel, with a bronze-gilt roof. On the holy door are the Annunciation and the Evangelists, by *Neff*. In the niche behind the high-altar is the throne of the Metropolitan, above which is the Last Supper, a painting by *Siemirádzki*. Still higher is the Nativity, a colossal painting by *V. P. Vereshtchágin*. The paintings to the left (Jesus in Gethsemane, Jesus exposed to the people, Bearing of the Cross) and to the right (Crucifixion, Descent from the Cross, and Entombment) are also by *V. P. Vereshtchágin*. In the upper gallery are the CHAPELS OF SS. NICHOLAS and ALEXANDER NEVSKI, both richly adorned and containing numerous pictures of saints. In the former we should notice the pictures illustrating the history of the church, and in the latter, the four pictures from the life of Alexander Nevski, by *Siemirádtski*. In the W. WING of the church are the following paintings: Baptism of St. Vladimir at Korsun, by *Karnéyev*, with the Baptism of the Grand-Princess Olga, by *Syedov*, above it; Foundation of the Lavra in Kiev, with the Baptism of the Inhabitants of Kiev above it, both by *Bodarévski;* Reception of the Vladimir Virgin, by *Bashilov,* with the Foundation of the Uspenski Cathedral, by *Pryánishnikov,* above it: Virgin appearing to St. Sergius, by *Makóvski,* with the Building of the Tróitzkaya Lavra, by *Pryánishnikov,* above it.

To the S. of the Church of the Redeemer, at Pretchistenskaya Náberezhnaya 29, in a house built by Vaznetzóv, is the *Tzvetkóv Gallery* (Pl. C, 5; *I*), containing upwards of 300 paintings by Russian masters.

The Volkhónka leads to the S.W. of the Church of the Redeemer, and ends at the site of the *Pretchistenka Gate,* whence the boulevard of that name (Pl. C, 4, 5; *I*) leads N. to the *Arbátskaya Square* (p. 307). In this square is a seated bronze figure of *Gogol,* the dramatist (1809-52), by Andréyev (1909). To the N.W. of the square, at Povarskáya 18, is the *Tolstói Museum* (Толстóвскiй музéй; adm., see p. 275), containing souvenirs of Count Leo Nikoláyevitch Tolstói, arranged in seven rooms. The fourth room contains the furniture of the room in which he died at Astapovo (p. 361; Tolstói's house, see below). To the S.W. from the Pretchistenka Gate runs the Pretchístenka (Pl. C, 5; *I*), in which, on the right, at the corner of the Obúkhovski Pereúlok, are the *Headquarters of the Fire Brigade* (Пожáрное депó; Pl. 29, C 5, *I*), while on the left is the *Alexander & Marie Girls' School* (Pl. 2, C 5, *I*). At the end of this street is the Súbovskaya Square, from which the *Smolénski Boulevard* (p. 307) runs to the N., and the *Súbovski Boulevard* (Pl. C, 5; *I*) to the S.E.

From the Pretchistenka Gate the Ostóshenka runs to the S. On its right side, at the corner of the Yerópkinski Pereúlok, is the *Commercial School* (Pl. 24, C 5; *I*), founded by the merchants of Moscow in 1804. Farther on, at the end of the street and at the corner of the Krúimskaya Square, is the *Lyceum of the Tzarévitch Nicholas* (Pl. 41, C 5; *I*), including a high school and a school of law. — Between the Ostóshenka and the Moskvá lies the *Zatchátiyevski Nunnery* (Pl. 54, C 5; *I*), founded in the early 15th century. This was the point from which Prince Pozhárski (p. 298) directed the attack against the Poles in Moscow (1612).

The Pretchistenka is prolonged toward the S.W. by the Bolshaya Tzarítzuinskaya. In the Khamovnítcheski Pereúlok, which diverges to the left, is the *House of Count Leo Tolstói* (No. 21; Pl. C, 5, 6, *I;* see above). In the Bolshaya Tzarítzuinskaya, on the right, is the Field of the Maidens (Дѣвичье пóле; Pl. B 5, *I*), in which, during the time of the Mongolian supremacy, were assembled the maidens who had to be delivered to the Khan along with the yearly tribute in money. No. 15, on the left, is the *Archives of the Ministry of Justice* (Архívъ министéрства юстíцiи; Pl. 11, B 6, *I;* open on week-days, except Sat., 11-3), containing documents of the former municipal government of Moscow. Nearly opposite, to' the right, is a seated bronze figure of *N. I. Pirogóv* (Pl. 43, B 6; *I*), the eminent surgeon (b. at Moscow in 1810, d. 1881), by Sherwood (1897). Adjacent are the *University Clinics* (Pl. B, 6; *I*), completed in 1891.

To the S.W. of the University Clinics is the **Novo-Dyevítchi Convent** or *Convent of the Maidens* (Pl. A, 6; *I*), a building of great historical interest, surrounded by a wall furnished with towers, battlements, and loopholes.

The Novo-Dyevitchi Convent was founded in 1524 by the Tzar Vasíli Ivánovitch to commemorate the reunion of Smolensk with the principality of Moscow. In 1610 bloody combats with the Poles took place here. The convent was then partly destroyed, and was afterwards restored by Tzar Michael. Sophia, the ambitious sister of Peter the Great, was compelled to take the veil here in 1689, under the name of Susanna. The rebellio: of the Streltzi in her favour was suppressed, and 300 of her adherents were hanged before the window of her cell. Napoleon visited the convent in 1812. An attempt to blow up the church on the retreat of the French was frustrated by the courage of the nuns.

The main gate has a tower ending in five pinnacles; through it we enter the court, which contains many graves, including that of A. P. Tchekhov (p. 431). Close behind it is the Cathedral, with its five domes and the tombs of Eudoxia (d. 1731), the first wife of Peter the Great, and of his sisters Catherine, Eudoxia, and Sophia (d. 1704). On the left stands the large bell-tower, with a clock that strikes the quarters. The top of it commands a fine view of the Sparrow Hills and the environs of Moscow.

The *Smolénski Boulevard* (Pl. B, C, 5; *I*), mentioned at p. 306, leads N. to the *Smolénski Ruinok* (Pl. B, C, 5; *I*), whence the busy *Arbát* leads to the Arbátskaya Square (Pl. C 4, *I;* p. 306). — From the Smolénski Ruinok the Smolénskaya leads W. to the *Borodínski Bridge* (Pl. B 5, *I;* steamer, see p. 272). About $^3/_4$ M. to the W. is the *Dorogomílovskaya Zastáva* (Pl. A 5, *I;* tramways Nos. 4 & 31), where the Mozhaisk road reaches Moscow. It was by this road that Napoleon entered Moscow in 1812.

About 1½ M. to the W. of the Zastáva, at **Fili**, is the *Kutúzov Cottage* (Кутузовская изба; open daily, 9-4); this stands on the site of the old cottage (burnt down in 1868) in which, on Sept. 1st (13th), 1812, after the battle of Borodinó, the Russian Council of War determined on the evacuation of Moscow. — It was from the Poklónnaya Gorá, a hill near Fili, and not from the Sparrow Hills, that Napoleon viewed Moscow for the first time (Sept. 14th, 1812). The village of *Pokróvskoye-Fili*, 1½ M. to the N.W. of the Kutúzov Cottage, formerly belonged to Peter the Great's uncle, Leo Kyríllovitch Naríishkin. The Church of the Virgin Protector and Intercessor, a cruciform edifice of 1693, is surrounded by an outside gallery, and contains some old pictures of saints. — *Kúntzevo*, see p. 322.

Going N. from the Smolénski Ruinok along the Novínski Boulevard, we reach the *Kudrínskaya Square* (Pl. B, C, 4; *I*), at the beginning of the Sadóvaya or Garden Street (p. 277). Hence we proceed to the W., passing the *Widows' Home* (Вдовій домъ; Pl. 53, B 4, *I*), built in 1803, and by the Kudrínskaya soon reach the bridge across the *Pryésnenskiye Ponds* (Pl. B, 4; *I*). To the right lie the *Zoological Gardens* (Зоологическій садъ; Pl. B 3, *I;* adm., see p. 275; electric tramways Nos. 16 & 25, from Theatre Square). The *Shtchukin Museum* (Музей П. И. Щукина), bequeathed by P. J. Shtchukin, Málaya Gruzinskaya 21 (Pl. B, 3, 4; *I*), contains Russian antiquities and objects of industrial art. Adm. for students only on application to the director of the Historical Museum (p. 297).

d. North-West Quarter of the City.

The Tverskáya is traversed beyond the Tverskiya Gate by *Electric Tramways* (pp. 271, 272) Nos. 1, 6 (from Lubyánskaya Square), 13, & 25; Trúbnaya Square is served by Nos. 1, 11, 15, 26, 29, & A.

The Tverskáya (Тверскáя ýлица; Pl. C, D, 3, 4, *II*), one of the main streets of Moscow, containing many tempting shops, runs from the Iberian Gate to the N.W. for about 2 M. On the right it passes the *Okhótni Ryad* (p. 277), a square with market-halls; to the left is the Mokhováya (p. 301). Farther on, on the same side, is the *Póstnikov Arcade*. Also to the left is the *Palace of the Governor General* (Домъ генерáлъ-губернáтора; Pl. C, D, 4, *II*). Opposite, in the small Tverskáya Square, is an equestrian statue of *General M. D. Skóbelev* (d. 1882), by Šaimónov (1912).

At the site of the old *Tverskiya Gate* (Pl. C, 3; *II*) the street intersects the boulevards encircling the 'White City' (p. 276).

To the left rises the *Pushkin Monument* (Pl. C, 3; *II*), unveiled in 1880, and consisting of a bronze statue of the poet, from a model by Opekúshin, standing on a granite pedestal. To the right, in the Strastnói Boulevard, is the *Strastnói Monastúir* or *Nunnery of the Passion* (Pl. C, 3; *II*), founded by Tzar Alexis Mikháilovitch in 1654. The bell-tower over the entrance commands a fine view.

Farther on in the Tverskáya, to the right, is the *House of the Civil Governor* (Домъ граждáнскаго губернáтора; Pl. C 3, *II*); to the left is the *Ophthalmic Hospital* (Pl. C, 3; *II*).

Beyond the Sadóvaya the street assumes the name of Bolshaya Tverskáya Yamskáya, and ends at the **Triumphal Gate** (Тріум-фáльныя Ворóта; Pl. B, C, 3, *I*), 2 M. from the Iberian Gate. The Triumphal Gate consists of a single archway in the style of the Arch of Titus at Rome, erected, according to the inscription on the attic, 'in commemoration of the deeds of Alexander I. in 1812'. It is adorned with statues of warriors and with bas-reliefs, and is surmounted by a Victory in a six-horse chariot. Outside the Triumphal Gate, to the left, lies the *Alexander* or *Brest Railway Station* (p. 270), rebuilt in 1912; straight in front is the Peterbúrgskoye Chaussée, running to the Petróvski Park (p. 323). — To the E. of the Triumphal Gate, in the Miyúskaya Square, to the right, is the handsome *Shanyávski People's University* (Pl. 50, C 2; *I*), maintained by the municipality. In the middle of the square the large *Cathedral of St. Alexander Nevski* is being built to commemorate the liberation of the serfs in 1861.

Parallel to the Tverskáya on the E., between the Okhótni Ryad and Strastnói Boulevard (see above), is the Bolshaya Dmítrovka

(Pl. D, 3, 4; *II*). To the left, at the corner of the Okhótni Ryad, is the *Club of the Noblesse* (p. 274). — Beyond the Strastnói Boulevard the street is prolonged under the name of Málaya Dmítrovka, passing on the right the *Church of the Nativity* (Pl. C, 3; *II*), which dates from the 17th century.

On the E. the Okhótni Ryad (p. 308) ends at the spacious Theatre Square (Театра́льная пло́щадь; Pl. D, 4, *II*), one of the largest open spaces in Moscow, measuring 350 yds. in length and 175 yds. in breadth. It is adorned with flower-beds and a fountain, with figures (by Vitali) representing Music and Light and Classical Poetry. On the N. side rises the **Great Imperial Theatre** (Большо́й теа́тръ; Pl. D, 4, *II;* p. 273), rebuilt by *Cavos* after a fire in 1854. The façade is preceded by an Ionic portico. The pediment is adorned with reliefs and surmounted by a colossal group of Phoebus in the Chariot of the Sun. The interior, decorated in white and gold, contains five balconies and accommodates 4000 spectators. — To the E. is the *Little Imperial Theatre* (Ма́лый теа́тръ; Pl. D 4, *II;* p. 273), built in 1841 and having room for 1000 spectators. To the N. of the Little Theatre, between the Petróvka and Neglínni Proyézd, are the Alexander and Solodóvnikov Arcades.

The Theatre Square is adjoined on the S.W. by the Voskresén-skaya Square (Pl. D, 4; *II*), on the E. side of which, in one of the towers of the Kitái-Gorod, is the *Ornithological Museum* (Музе́й птицево́дства; open free on week-days, 10-4).

The Petróvka (Pl. D, 3, 4; *II*), running to the N. from the Theatre Square, is one of the most animated business-streets in the city and contains many fine shops. The shops in the Kuznétzki Most (Smith's Bridge; Pl. D 4, *II*), the first cross-street to the right, running to the Lubyánka, are still better. On the right side of the Petróvka, just short of the Petróvski Boulevard, is the *Vuisóko-Petróvski Monastery* (Pl. D, 3; *II*), founded in the 14th cent., and containing the tombs of the Narúishkin Boyars.

In the N. quarter of the Petróvka, to the left, is the *New Catherine Hospital* (Екатери́нинская больни́ца; Pl. D 3, *II*), and to the right are the *Gendarme* or *Petróvski Barracks* (Pl. D, 3; *II*). From this point to the Sadóvaya the street is known as the Каре́тни Ряд (Pl. C, D, 3; *I*), on account of the numerous carriage-works it contains. Beyond the Sadóvaya, on the Bozhedómski Pereúlok, is the *Ecclesiastical Seminary* (Духо́вная семина́рія; Pl. C, D, 3, *I*). In the Nóvaya Bozhedómskaya are the *Marie Hospital* (Pl. D, 2; *I*), the *Alexander Institute for Girls* (Pl. C, D, 2; *I*), and the German *Frederick William & Victoria Institute*. The garden of the last contains monuments to Emperor William I., Tzar Alexander II. and Prince Bismarck.

From the Vuisóko-Petróvski Monastery we proceed to the E. viâ the *Petróvski Boulevard* to the Trúbnaya Square (Pl. D, 3; *II*), containing the *Hermitage Restaurant* (p. 270; market, see p. 277).

To the N. of the Trúbnaya Square extends the *Tzvyetnói Boulevard* (Pl. D 3, *II;* flower-market, see p. 277), on the left side of which is the building of the German *Gymnastic Society*.

From the Trúbnaya Square we may return to the Theatre Square, either viâ the Neglínni Proyézd (Pl. D, 3, 4; *II*) or through the Rozhdéstvenka. The former contains the *Imperial Bank* (Государственный банкъ; Pl. D, 3, 4, *II*), built by Prof. Buikóvski in 1894, and the *Imperial Dramatic School* (Pl. D, 4; *II*). In the Rozhdéstvenka, immediately to the left, is the *Rozhdéstvenski Nunnery* (Pl. D, 3; *II*), founded in 1386 (?). — Farther on, to the right, is the Stróganov Drawing School, in which the **Industrial Art Museum** (Худóжественно-промы́шленный музéй; Pl. D, 3, 4, *II*) is housed (adm., see p. 275; director, S. V. Noakovski). The museum contains extensive collections of models illustrating Russian architecture, painting, and decorative art, as well as Chinese objects, furniture, works in clay, etc. Some of the contents are for sale.

e. North-East Quarter of the City.

Electric Tramways, see pp. 271, 272. Nos. 10, 17, 19, 32, & 36 (from Lubyánskaya Sq.) run to the Súkharev Tower. Nos. 4, 6, 10, & 29 run from Lubyánskaya Sq. to Sokólniki (in 25 min.; fare 10 cop.), the first two viâ the Myasnítzkaya, No. 10 viâ the Súkharev Tower, and No. 29 viâ the Marosscíka.

From the Theatre Square (p. 309) the Teatrálni Proyézd (p. 301) leads to the E., passing the S. ends of the Neglínni Proyézd and the Rozhdéstvenka (see above). On the S. side is a seated bronze figure by Volnúkhin (1909) of *Iván Feódorov*, the first Russian printer (comp. p. 301). The street ends at the Lubyánskaya Square (Лубянская плóщадь; Pl. D 4, *II*), which lies outside the N. or Vladímir Gate of the Kitái-Gorod. At this square begin two great lines of thoroughfare, the Bolshaya Lubyánka, running to the N., and the Myasnítzkaya (p. 311), running to the N.E. — On the right side of the Bolshaya Lubyánka (Pl. D, 3, 4; *II*) is the *Third High School* (Pl. D, 4; *II*), behind which, to the E., is the lofty *Telephone Office.* At the end of the street, to the left, is the *Sryétenski Monastery* or *Monastery of the Meeting* (Срéтенскій мужскóй монасты́рь; Pl. D 3, *II*), which lies in the *Kutchko Field,* the old place of execution (formerly outside the city), and is said to occupy the spot where the Vladímir Virgin was solemnly received in 1395 (p. 283). — To the E. of the Bolshaya Lubyánka, and parallel with it, runs the Málaya Lubyánka (Pl. D, 3, 4; *II*), on the right side of which lies the Roman Catholic *Church of St. Louis* (Pl. D 4, *II* ; French), founded in 1791. To the right of the end of this street, in the Milyútinski Pereúlok, is the Polish Roman Catholic *Church of SS. Peter & Paul* (Pl. D, 3; *II*).

The N. prolongation of the Bolshaya Lubyánka, beyond the Rozhdéstvenski Boulevard, is known as the Sryétenka (Pl. D, 3; *I*). At the end of this street, and forming a part of the Sadóvaya, is the *Súkharev Square* (market, see p. 274), about 1 M. from the Lub-

yánskaya Square. Here rises the **Súkharev Tower** (Сухарева
башня; Pl. D 3, *I;* no adm.), erected in 1689 by Peter the Great
in honour of the Súkharev Regiment, under the protection of which
the youthful Tzar and his mother were able to find refuge in the
Tróitzkaya Lavra during the rebellion of the Streltzi in 1682. The
building, which was used as a School of Navigation down to 1715,
and then as the seat of the Board of the Admiralty down to 1806,
served from 1834 to 1900 as a reservoir. The lower part consists
of a rectangular building with two stories, 130 ft. in length and
80 ft. in breadth. Over this is an octagonal tower (185 ft. high),
rising in four stages above the gateway connecting the Sryétenka
with the First Myeshtchánskaya.

On the N. side of the Súkharev Square lies the large *Sheremétyev
Hospital & Poor House* (Pl. 51, D, E, 3; *I*), founded by Count
Nicholas Sheremétyev in 1803.

The Pérvaya or First Myeshtchánskaya (Pl. D, 1-3; *I*) runs to the
N. from the Súkharev Tower to the *Krestóvskaya Zastáva* (Pl. D, 1; *I*),
with the *Windau Station* (p. 270) and the two huge *Water Towers* (Кре-
стóвскія башни) of the water system completed in 1893 (open on week-
days 10-4). Each of the towers contains 400,000 gallons of water. The
platform at the top affords a fine view. In the E. tower is the *Museum
of Municipal Administration* (Музéй городскáго хозяйства; adm., see
p. 275; catalogue 10 cop.). — At the Grokhólski Pereúlok are the *Botanical
Gardens* of the University (Pl. D, E, 2, *I*; adm., see p. 275; guide 20 cop.).

Immediately to the left in the Myasnítzkaya, which runs to the
N.E. from the Lubyánskaya Square (p. 310), is the *Ecclesiastical
Consistory* (Духóвная консистóрія; Pl. D 4, *II*). The Consistory
is said to have been built in the time of the Grand-Prince Vasili IV.
Ivánovitch, and to have served at first as the residence of the archbishop (Рязáнское архіерéйское подвóрье). In 1774-1801 it
was the seat of the 'Secret Office', for investigating political offences.
It has served its present purposes since 1833. Farther on, to the left,
is the *School of Art* (Учúлище жúвописи, ваянія и зóдчества;
Pl. D, E, 3, *II*); in the court is a nine-storied building, the tower of
which commands a fine view of the town (elevator 50 cop.). On the
right is the *General Post Office* (Pl. E 3, *II;* p. 272), built by
Novikov in 1910-12; adjacent, at the corner of the Tchistoprúdni
Boulevard, so called after the 'limpid pool' at its S. end, is the *General Telegraph Office* (Pl. E 3, *II;* p. 273). — The Myasnítzkaya ends
at the Sadóvaya ('Garden Street', p. 276), just short of which,
however, the busy Myasnítzki Pereúlok diverges to the right and
leads to the *Red Gate* (Крáсныя Ворóта; Pl. 39, E 3, *I*), a triumphal archway with three passages, erected in the coronation year
of Empress Elizabeth Petróvna (1742) at the expense of the Moscow
merchants.

From the Red Gate the Kalantchévskaya leads N. to the square of
the same name, containing the stations of the *Nicholas, Yaroslavl*,
and *Kazan Railways* (comp. pp. 269, 270).

From the Kalantchévskaya Square the Krasnoprúdnaya and the Sokólniki Chaussée lead N.E. to the **Sokólniki Park** (Соко́ль-ничья Ро́ща; Pl. E-G, 1, *I*), which lies 5 V. (3¹/₄ M.) from the Lubyánskaya Square and forms the most popular promenade in Moscow. From the *New Promenade* (Nóvoye Gulyániye), a rondel containing a band-stand and a café, seven vistas *(Prósyeki)* radiate towards the N. These are connected by transverse alleys. To the W. of the band-stand is the *Old Promenade* (Stároye Gulyániye), a favourite resort of the lower classes on Sun. and holidays, with a summer theatre and various other forms of amusement.

f. East Quarter of the City.

Electric Tramways (pp. 271, 272) Nos. 3, 24, 26, 29, & 31 run along the Pokróvka; Nos. 21, 24, & 30 traverse the Nyemétzkaya. — A visit to the E. quarter of the city offers little interest.

Opposite the *Ilyínskiya Gate* (Pl. D 4, *II;* p. 300), to the N., lies the **Polytechnic Museum** (Политехни́ческій Музе́й; Pl. D 4, *II*), built in 1876 in the Russian style from the plans of *Monighetti* (adm., see p. 275; catalogue 20 cop.). The museum contains extensive collections of technical, architectural, agricultural, and other models, drawings, and the like. — To the right of the Ilyinskiya Gate is a *Chapel* erected in 1887 by the Moscow Regiment of Grenadiers in memory of the comrades who fell at Plevna, Kars, and other places in the Russo-Turkish war of 1877-78.

To the E. of the Ilyínskiya Gate runs the Pokróvka, a thorough-fare 4 M. long, extending (under various names) to the Yáuza. The beginning of the street, as far as the Armyánski Pereúlok, is called the Marosséika, after the Maloróssi or Little Russians who resided here in the 17th century. To the left is the *House of the Philan-thropic Society* (Челове́колюби́вое о́бщество; Pl. D, E, 4, *II*).

In the Armyánski Pereúlok, to the left, is the *Lázarev Institute for Oriental Languages* (Ла́заревскій институ́тъ Восто́чныхъ язы́ковъ; Pl. D 4, *II*), founded in 1814 by the brothers Lázarev. Opposite this is the *Armenian Church* (Pl. E, 4; *II*), built in 1771. — To the S. of the Marosséika, in the Kosmo-Damiánski Pereúlok, is the Lutheran **Church of SS. Peter & Paul** (Петра́ и Па́вла лютера́нская це́рковь; Pl. E 4, *II*), rebuilt from the plans of V. Kosov in 1905. At the end of the street is the *Ivánovski Convent*, or *Nunnery of John the Baptist* (Pl. E, 4; *II*), founded in the 16th cent., burned down by the French in 1812, and rebuilt from the plans of Buikóvski in 1861.

The Pokróvka, properly so called, extends from the Armyánski Pereúlok to the Zemlyanói Val (i.e. Ger. *Wall*) or Boulevard. To the left is the striking **Church of the Assumption** (Pl. E, 4; *II*), built in the time of Borís Godunóv, and also known as the 'Red Church' from the colour of its bricks. Its thirteen domes, arranged in the form of a pyramid, excited the admiration of Napoleon in 1812, and the building was accordingly spared from the flames. — In the

Tchistoprúdni Boulevard, to the left, is the *Borodinó Panorama* (Pl. E 4, *II;* adm., see p. 275), with a battle-picture by Roubaud. — To the S., at Pokrovski Boulevard 5, is the *Commercial Academy* (Pl. E, 4; *II*), founded in 1906, with 105 teachers and 4500 students.

Farther on in the Pokróvka, to the left (No. 31), is the house of *P. Botkin,* containing a collection of paintings by modern French, German, Belgian, and Russian masters (adm., see p. 274).

To the S., in the Mali Kazyónni Pereúlok, is the *Alexander Hospital* (Pl. E, 4; *I*), in the court of which is a bronze bust, by Andréyev (1909), of *Dr. Th. P. Haas*, the philanthropist (d. 1853).

To the E. of the *Zemlyanói Val* lies the *Kursk & Nizhni-Novgorod Railway Station* (Pl. F 4, *I;* p. 270). Beyond the Zemlyanói Val the Pokróvka takes the name of STÁRAYA BASMÁNNAYA. To the right is the *Church of St. Nikíta the Martyr* (Pl. 21, F 3; *I*), founded by Grand-Prince Vasíli in 1517 and restored in 1751.

To the S. of the Church of St. Nikíta, in the Gorókhovski Pereúlok, is the *Constantine School of Surveying* (Константиновскій межевой институтъ; Pl. 52, F 3, *I*). In the Voznesénskaya is the Lutheran *Church of St. Michael* (Pl. 20, F 3; *I*), built in the Gothic style in 1576, and repeatedly restored.

From the *Rasgulyái Square* the *Nóvaya Basmánnaya* leads to the left to the Red Gate (p. 311). The prolongation of the line of streets we have been following is called YELÓKHOVSKAYA from this point to the *Yelókhovskaya Square* (Pl. F, 3; *I*), and thence to the *Pokróvski Bridge* (Pl. G, 2; *I*) it is known as POKRÓVSKAYA ÚLITZA. — Farther to the E., on the left bank of the Yáuza, lies the artisan quarter of *Preobrazhénskoye,* containing several large factories.

The first cross-street, diverging to the S. from the Pokróvskaya, is the NYEMÉTZKAYA (German Street), the focus of the German colony which used to exist here and is still recalled by several of the names. To the E. lies the *Nyemétzki Ruinok* (Pl. F, 3; *I*), the most important market in the E. quarters of the city. To the S.E., on an open space on the Yáuza, rises the *Lefórtovski Palace* (Лефóртовскій дворéцъ; Pl. F, G, 3, *I*), originally built by Peter the Great for General Francis Lefort (born at Geneva in 1656, d. 1699), rebuilt by Paul I. in 1798, and now occupied by military officials. Adjacent is the *Imperial Technical Academy* (Pl. F, 3; *I*), founded in 1832 and attended by 3000 students.

Beyond the Yáuza are the *Red Barracks* (Крáсныя казáрмы) and the *Alexis Military School* (Pl. G, 4; *I*), the former to the left, the latter to the right. — In the large Cadet Square, to the E., are the barracks of the *First & Second Cadet Corps* (Pl. G, 4; *I*). This site was originally occupied by the *Annenhof,* built by the Empress Anna Ivánovna as a summer residence and twice destroyed by fire. In 1784 Catherine II. erected the present imposing palace from plans by Bazhénov at a cost of 4,000,000 rb. — To the N. of the Cadet Square is the *Military Hospital* (Воéнный гóспиталь; Pl. G 3, *I*), a huge building with accommodation for 2000 patients, founded by Peter I. and rebuilt by Alexander I. from plans by Seménov.

g. South-East Quarter of the City.

Electric Tramways, see p. 272. The Andronov Monastery is reached by Nos. 27 & 32, the Novospasski Monastery by No. 16, the Simonov Convent by No. 28. Lines 21, 23, & 30 also serve this quarter.— *Steamboat,* see p. 272.

From the VARVÁRSKAYA SQUARE (Pl. D, 4; *II*), which lies outside the Varvárskaya Gate, the SOLYÁNKA leads to the S.E. to the Yáuzski Bridge (see below). To the right is the main entrance of the imperial **Foundling Hospital** (Воспитáтельный домъ; Pl. E 4, *II*), which is adorned with groups of Charity and Education by Vitali.

The Foundling Hospital (open to visitors on Thurs. and Sun., 1-4) is a colossal white block founded by Catherine II. in 1764. A little later it was occupied by the Court of Wards (see below), and finally by the Nicholas Girls' Orphanage (see below). In 1812 it served as a hospital. The institution receives a yearly subvention from the State amounting to upwards of 1,000,000 rb., chiefly derived from the sale of playing-cards throughout Russia. The Foundling Hospital accommodates 2500 children, besides which 30,000 are boarded out in neighbouring villages.

To the left of the main entrance to the Foundling Hospital in the Solyánka stands the above-mentioned *Court of Wards* (Опекýнскій совѣтъ; Pl. E 4, *II*), which contains valuables, important papers, documents, etc. Adjacent is the *Nicholas School for Girls* (Pl. E, 4; *II*). The Solyánka ends on the S. at the *Yáuzski Bridge* (Pl. E, 4; *II*), leading to the *Rogózhskaya Quarter*, situated on the left bank of the Yáuza.

From the bridge the NIKÓLO-YÁMSKAYA leads to the left to (25 min.) the **Andrónov Monastery** (Спáсо-Андрóніевскій мужскóй монастьíрь; Pl. F 4, *I*), picturesquely situated on the high left bank of the Yáuza. This convent, which includes five churches, was founded in 1365, and was entirely rebuilt after its destruction in 1812. The belfry, 260 ft. high, commands a fine view.

About ³/₄ M. to the S. of the Andrónov Monastery is the *Pokróvski Monastery* (Pl. 45, F 5; *I*), founded in 1655, in the reign of Tzar Alexis Mikháilovitch.

About 1¹/₂ M. to the S. of the above-named Yáuzski Bridge, on the left bank of the Moskvá, lies the **Novospásski Monastery,** or *New Monastery of the Saviour* (Pl. E, 6; *I*), said to be the oldest convent in Moscow. It is surrounded by a white wall and contains five churches. Over the entrance is a belfry 235 ft. in height, rebuilt in 1785. Thé monastery was founded in the time of Iván Kalitá (1328-40) in the Kremlin, and was transferred to its present site in the reign of Iván III. (1462-1505). It was frequently destroyed by fire but always rebuilt. In 1812 it was plundered by the French, while its churches were used as barracks and stables.

The vestibule of the *Church of the Transfiguration* (Спáса Преображéнія), dating from the time of Mikháil Feódorovitch, contains some old mural paintings representing Greek philosophers (below), scenes from Russian ecclesiastical history, and the genealogical tree of Rurik (at the top). On the ikonostás is a miracle-working picture of the Saviour, brought here in 1647 from Vyatka. Behind the altar are portraits of the ten patriarchs. The Treasury *(Riznitza)* contains numerous valuables and gorgeous ecclesiastical vestments. The convent contains the graves of Marfa, the mother of the Tzar Mikháil Feódorovitch, and of various members of the house of Románov as well as of families related to it. Hence we follow the Krutítzki Pereúlok to the S. to the *Krutítzki Barracks* (Pl. E, F, 6; *I*). To the right of the small church at the end of the cul-de-sac is a fine façade (Крутйцкій теремъ; restored), dating from the 17th cent. and richly ornamented with green tiles. We next pass the *Powder Magazine* (Pl. E, F, 6, 7; *I*) and in about $^1/_2$ hr. after leaving the Novospásski Monastery we reach the **Símonov Convent**(Pl. E, 7; *I*), situated on the high bank of the Moskvá (steamer, see p. 272). This convent was founded in 1370 and was captured by the Poles and Lithuanians in 1610 in spite of the wall with which it had been enclosed in 1591. It was partly burned in 1812 and thereafter rebuilt. Field-Marshal Count Bruce (d. 1735) is buried under the refectory. The most interesting of its five churches is the *Cathedral of the Assumption*, the vocal music of which is famous (best on the eves of festivals). The treasury contains valuable crosses, chalices, and censers. The *Bell Tower*, 330 ft. in height, was built in 1839, and commands a view of the city.

Outside the *Simonovskaya Zastáva* lies the *Lizin Pond* (Pl. E, 7; *I*), well known through Karamzin's story of 'Poor Lizzie'.

h. South Quarter of the City.

Tretyakov Gallery. Sparrow Hills.

Electric Tramways (p. 271) Nos. 3, 10, 18 (from the Theatre Square), & 13 traverse the Bolsháya Polyánka, passing near the Tretyakóv Gallery; No. 18 runs to the Kalúzhskaya Zastáva, while No. 7 runs on thence to the Sparrow Hills. — *Izvóshtchik* from the Kremlin to the Tretyakóv Gallery 30-40 cop.; to the Sparrow Hills 2 rb. *Steamer* to the Sparrow Hills, see p. 272.

The quarter of ZAMOSKVARÉTCHYE, situated on the S. bank of the Moskvá, occupied at a very early period on account of the propinquity of the Kremlin, was once the Tartar quarter, but is now becoming a fashionable residential quarter.

To the E. of the Kremlin the iron *Moskvoryétzki Bridge* (Pl. D, 4; *I*) leads across the island separated from the S. part of the town by the *Vodootvódni*, or *Drainage Canal*, while the *Tchugúnni Bridge* (Pl. D, 5; *I*) crosses this canal to the Pyátnitzkaya Úlitza, which ends at the Serpukhovskáya Square.

To the W. of the Kremlin is the *Great Kámenni Bridge* (Pl. D, 5; *I*), built in stone in 1634-82 and replaced by an iron structure in 1859. It leads to the Bersénovskaya Nábereshnaya, in which is the quaint-looking *House of the Archaeological Society* (Pl. 10, D 5; *I*). — To the E. is the *Bolótnaya Square*, with a fruit and vegetable market (p. 277). Steamer to the Sparrow Hills, see p. 272.

The *Tretyakóv Gallery (Pl. D, 5; *I*), Lavrúshinski Pereúlok 12, ranking with the Alexander III. Museum in St. Petersburg as one of the most important collections of modern Russian
paintings (over 2000 in number), was presented to the city by the
brothers P. and S. Tretyakóv in 1892. The gallery is especially rich
in works by *Vasíli Vasílyevitch Vereshtchágin* (1842-1904; landscapes, war scenes), *Vasíli Gregóryevitch Peróv* (1833-82; scenes of
Russian popular life), *Iván Ivánovitch Shishkin* (1831-98; landscapes), *Vasíli Dmítriyevitch Polyénov* (b. 1844; landscapes), *Iván
Nikoláyevitch Kramskói* (1837-87; portraits), *Ilyá Yefímovitch
Ryepin* (b. 1844; genre-scenes, portraits), and *Vladímir Yegórovitch
Makóvski* (b. 1846; genre-scenes).— Admission, see p. 275. French
illustrated catalogue 75, Russian catalogue 15 cop. The pictures are
at present in course of re-
arrangement.—Director,
I. Grabar.

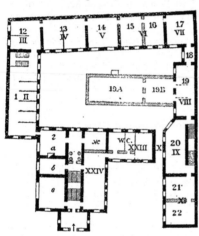

To the left of the main
entrance are the office of
the director, a smoking-
room, and a cloak-room;
to the right are a cloak-
room and lavatory.

Room ж. Modern
French paintings, pre-
sented by M. A. Morózov.
— We then pass through
Room r, which contains
water-colours, into—

Room 1. Drawings
and water-colours. 1 (by
the first window to the
right). *E. P. Tchémesov*

The rooms on the groundfloor are indicated
by Arabic numerals and the letters r and ж,
those on the first floor by Roman numerals,
and the letters a, б, в.

(1737-65), Empress Ca-
therine II.; 66-73. *P. F.
Sokolóv*(1791-1847),Por-
traits; 92-100. *K. P.*

Bryullóv (1799-1852), Sketches and Studies; *F. A. Bruni* (1800-75),
101. Brazen Serpent, 102. Fight between good and evil spirits; 122-124.
A. A. Ivánov (1806-58), Sketches for his chief work, Christ before
Pilate (p. 304); 138. *M. I. Lébedev* (1812-37), Evening in Albano; *P. A.
Fyedótov*(1816-52), 152. Portrait of his father, 166-172. Genre-scenes;
259, 264, 266. *I. I. Shishkin* (1831-98), Landscapes; 267. *N. N. Gay*
(1831-94), Last Supper; 279, 281. *V. G. Peróv* (1833-82), Sketches;
W. G. Schwartz (1838-69), 304. Iván the Terrible going to early
mass, 313. Presentation of his hawking-glove to Iván the Terrible;
342, 343, 345. *I. Y. Ryepin* (b. 1844), Portraits; 369-374. *V. M.*

Vaznetzóv (b. 1848), Sketches for the menu-cards at the coronation banquet of 1883; 387. *F. A. Vasílyev* (1850-73), Boat in the Black Sea.—At the end of the room is a staircase ascending to the

First Floor. — Room II. Older Russian painters. On the left side-wall: 11. *A. P. Lósenko* (1837-73), The artist's studio; 21-29. *V. L. Borovikóvski* (1757-1825), Portraits; 43-61. *V. A. Tropínin* (1776-1857), Portraits; 79-85. *O. A. Kiprénski* (1783-1836), Portraits; 100-112. *S. F. Shtchedrín* (1791-1830), Landscapes; 119-135. *K. P. Bryullóv*, Portraits; 142. *N. G. Tchernetzóv* (1804-79), Pushkin, Kruilóv, Zhukóvski, and Gneditch (1832); 167-174. *M. I. Lébedev*, Landscapes.— On the right side-wall: 197. *P. A. Fyedótov*, Young widow; 252. *K. D. Flavítzki* (1830-66), Death of Princess Tarakánov; 263. *Baron M. K. Klodt* (1832-1902), Sunset; 268. *V. V. Pukirév* (1832-90), An ill-assorted pair; *V. G. Peróv*, 278. Guitar-player, 289. Bird-catcher, 290. Wandering pilgrim, 294. Hunter, 297. Portrait of F. M. Dostoyévski, the author (1872).

Through a door in the far corner we reach three rooms (a, б, & в) containing a portrait of P. Tretyakóv (d. 1898) by *Ryepin*, portraits by older Russian artists, and pictures of saints.

Room III. To the left, 417. *I. M. Pryánishnikov* (1840-94), Jester; 401. *Baron Klodt* (b. 1835), The last spring; 421. *Pryánishnikov*, Retreat of the Grande Armée in 1812; 438. *P. A. Svedómski* (1849-1904), Medusa; 384-390. *A. K. Savrásov* (1830-97), Landscapes; 397. *P. P. Tchistyakóv* (b. 1832), Italian stone-cutter.

Room IV. To the right, 542. *V. M. Maxímov* (b. 1844), Conjurer at a peasant-wedding; *I. K. Aivazóvski* (1817-1900), 454. The Black Sea, above it, 451. Night-view of Gurzuff (p. 420); 553. *I. I. Klever* (b. 1850), Forest-scene; *I. I. Shishkin*, 470. Rye-field, 474. Morning in the forest; 499. *G. G. Myasoyédov* (b. 1835), Fanatics burning themselves; 522, 524-528. *A. I. Kuíndzhi* (1842-1910), Landscapes; 543. *V. M. Maxímov*, Dividing the inheritance. — On a stand in the middle of the room, 473. *I. I. Shishkin*, Forest-scene.

Room V. To the right, Portraits by *I. N. Kramskói*, including one (570) of Count Leo Tolstói (1873). — To the left, Landscapes by *F. A. Vasílyev*; 567. *I. N. Kramskói*, Christ in the wilderness.

Room VI. To the right, *N. N. Gay*, 637. Tzarévitch Alexis cross-examined by Peter the Great at Peterhof, 639. Portrait of Count Leo Tolstói (1884); 680. *A. I. Korzúkhin* (1835-94), In the convent-inn; *N. A. Yaroshénko* (1846-98), 684. Fireman, 686. Student, 701. 'Everywhere is Life' (convicts feeding pigeons from the barred windows of their railway carriage). — On a stand in the middle of the room, Landscapes by *I. P. Pokhitónov* (b. 1850).

Room VII. To the left, 733. *V. G. Peróv*, Disputation between the Orthodox and the Old Believers before the Tzarina Sophia; *V. I. Súrikov* (b. 1848), 739. Mocking the wife of the Boyar Morózov (an Old Believer), 737. Execution of Streltzi, 738. Prince Ménshikov in exile.

ROOM VIII (in three sections). Sec. I: 778. *I. Y. Ryepin,* Petitioners in the government of Kursk. — Sec. II: *I. Y. Ryepin,* 768. Anton Rubinstein (1881), 781. Convict's return, 753. Priest.— Sec. III: *I. Y. Ryepin,* 786. Count Leo Tolstói (1887), 782. Iván the Terrible with the corpse of the son he has just killed, 761. Tzarina Sophia, sister of Peter the Great, compelled to witness the execution of the Streltzi in the Novo-Dyevítchi Convent. — On the side-wall, 776. *I.Y. Ryepin,* Cossacks preparing a letter to the Sultan of Turkey.

ROOM IX. To the left, 858. *I. S. Ostroúkhov* (b. 1858), Landscape, with effect of wind; 846. *V. M. Vaznetzóv,* Joy of the just; 869-877. *I. I. Levitan* (1861-1900), Landscapes; 886. *V. A. Syeróv* (1865-1911), Portrait of the composer N. A. Rimski-Kórsakov (1898); on a stand, *V. M. Vaznetzóv,* Sketches and studies for the mural paintings in the Vladímir Cathedral at Kiev.

ROOM X. To the right, 919-926. *I. I. Levitan,* Landscapes; 932-937. *A. E. Arkhípov* (b. 1862), Genre-scenes; 893. *A. N. Russov* (b. 1844), Slave-girl.

ROOM XXIII. 1826. *K. A. Somov* (b. 1869), Lady in blue; 1774. *M. A. Vrubel* (1856-1910), Pan. — *Room XXIV.* New acquisitions. — We now return to Room IX and enter—

ROOM XI. *V. M. Vaznetzóv,* 950. After the battle of Prince Igor with the Polovtsi, 954. Iván the Terrible, 952. Werwolf, 955. Three heroes, 956-967. Sketches for the mural paintings in the Vladímir Cathedral at Kiev; 972, 973. *N. N. Dubovskói* (b. 1859), Landscapes. — We again return to R. IX and descend to the—

Ground Floor. — ROOM 20. To the left, 1509. *A. D. Kívshenko* (1851-95), Council of War at Fili in 1812, a replica of the picture in the St. Petersburg Academy of Arts.

ROOM 21. To the left, 1536. *S. I. Svyetoslávski* (b. 1857), Beginning of spring; 1540. *N. A. Kasátkin* (b. 1859), Coal-miners.

ROOM 22. *A. A. Borisov* (b. 1866), Studies of scenes in N. Russia. — We now return through RR. 21 & 20 into—

ROOM 19. *V. D. Polyénov* (b. 1844), 1371. Lake of Gennesaret, 1373. Jesus among the Scribes in the Temple; Scenes in Greece, Egypt, and Palestine. — In the middle, 1632. *M. M. Antokólski* (1842-1902), Marble figure of Iván the Terrible. — To the left are—

ROOMS 19 B & 19 *A* (lighted from the roof), containing works by modern foreign artists. Room 19 Б. To the right, 87. *Romney,* Portrait; 88. *Lawrence,* Mrs. Siddons; 89. *Lenbach,* Bismarck; 91. *Kaulbach,* Princess Alix of Hesse, the present Tzarina. — Room 19 A. To the left, 38. *Menzel,* Garden of the Luxembourg; above, 79. *Bastien Lepage,* Declaration of love; 41. *Daubigny,* On the bank of the Oise; 77. *Munkaczy,* Nosegay; 27. *Rousseau,* Barbizon; *Troyon,* 21. Sheep, 19. Bull; 70. *Fortuny,* Snake-charmer; 5. *Corot,* Château of Pierrefonds; 57. *O. Achenbach,* Night festival in Naples; 1. *Corot,* Landscape; 84. *Dagnan-Bouveret,* Newly married couple;

63. *Vollon*, Still-life; 1. *L. David*, Ingres, the artist; 46. *Daubigny*, Landscape; 39. *Menzel*, Wandering gipsies.

Room 18. 1347. *W. G. Schwartz*, Spring pilgrimage of the Tzarina in the reign of Alexis Mikháilovitch.

Room 17. Studies by *A. A. Ivánov* (1806-58). — In the middle 1634. *M. M. Antokólski*, Christian martyr, a marble figure.

Room 16. *V. Y. Makóvski* (b. 1846), 1215. Doctor's waiting-room; 1237. Acquitted; 1247. At the justice's; 1232. Run on the bank.

Room 15. *V. V. Vereshtchágin* (1842-1904), Scenes from the Russo-Turkish war of 1877-78; 1202. Vanquished (mass for the dead); 1203. Skóbelev reviewing troops on the Shipka Pass; 1205. Before the attack; 1206. After the attack.

Room 14. *V. V. Vereshtchágin*, Sketches from his travels in India.

Room 13. *V. V. Vereshtchágin*, 1122. On the ramparts; 1121. Pyramid of skulls, an 'Apotheosis of War'; 1120. Two Turcomans at the door of a mosque; 1040. Spoils of war (human skulls); 1051. Khirgizes on the way to the bazaar; 1052. Gates of Tamerlane; 1068. Khirgiz falconer; 1069. Sale of a young slave; above, 1070. Russian troops attacked by Turcomans; 1071. Subterranean prison in Samarkand; 1077. Dervishes; 1082. Triumph over the vanquished.

Room 12. *V. V. Vereshtchágin*, Pencil drawings and coloured sketches from his journey to Turkestan in 1867-71.

To the S.E. of the Tretyakóv Gallery, Bolshaya Ordúinka 34, is the *Community of Martha and Mary*, a kind of sisterhood founded in 1905 by Grand-Duchess Elizabeth, widow of Grand-Duke Sergius (p. 294) and granddaughter of Queen Victoria.

From the *Mali Kámenni Bridge* the *Yakimánka* leads to (20 min.) the KALÚZHSKAYA SQUARE (Pl. D, 6; *I*). To the right is the *Kruimski Val*, which runs from this square to the Kruimski Bridge. Four long streets, the *Kalúzhskaya, Donskáya, Shábolovka*, and *Múitnaya*, radiate hence towards the S.

The *Múitnaya* leads past the *Kónnaya Square* (horse-market, see p. 277) and the *Serpukhovskáya Zastáva* (Pl. D, 7; *I*), to the E. of which lies the **Danílovski Monastery** (Pl. D, 7; *I*), said to have been founded in 1272 by Grand-Prince Daniel Alexándrovitch. It contains three churches and is surrounded by a wall erected in the time of Iván the Terrible. Gogol (d. 1852), the famous writer, is buried in the graveyard of the monastery.

At the end of the DONSKÁYA rises the **Donskói Monastery** or *Convent of the Virgin of the Don* (Донскóй мужскóй монастьíрь; Pl. C 7, *I*), erected by Tzar Feódor I. Ivánovitch in memory of the victory gained over the Tartars in 1591, and named after the ikon of the Virgin of the Don, to whose protection the Russians had committed themselves. The high red wall of the convent, dating from 1712, encloses seven churches and a cemetery with the graves of many noble families and eminent personages. The principal church, built in 1686-1711 by Catherine, the sister of Peter I., contains a number of mural paintings, chiefly of scenes from Biblical history. Adjoining the holy door are a painting of the Redeemer and the ikon of the Virgin of the Don, richly adorned with gems. In 1812 the convent was plundered by the French, but it afterwards received abundant compensation from the booty of the Don Cossacks.

The Kalúzhskaya contains a series of charitable institutions. To the right, on the high right bank of the Moskvá, is the **Neskútchni Park** (Нескучный садъ; Pl. B, C, 6, 7, *I*), the most beautiful and best kept park in Moscow, containing splendid groups of trees and many flower-beds, small lakes, and pavilions. The imperial *Alexander Palace* (Pl. C, 6; *I*), which lies in the park, is not accessible.

About 1³/₄ M. (tramway No. 18) from the Kalúzhskaya Square, at the S. end of the Kalúzhskaya, is the *Kalúzhskaya Zastáva* (Pl. B, C, 7; *I*). Hence we may proceed by tramway (No. 7; 5 cop.) or on foot (³/₄ hr.), passing *Noyev's Nursery Garden* (Pl. B 7, *I*; café-restaurant), to the

*Sparrow Hills (Воробьевы горы, pron. Varabyóvi Góri; Pl. A 7, *I;* steamer, see p. 272), which afford a panorama of the valley of the Moskvá and of the old city of the Tzars, especially fine at sunset. The view is well seen from the veranda of the *Krwinkin Restaurant* (good, but rather expensive).

View. In the foreground, surrounded by fields of vegetables, is the small white Tikhvinski Church; farther off is the Church of the Redeemer (p. 304); in the background is the many-towered city of Moscow, with the Kremlin; to the left (N.) is the Novo-Dyevítchi Convent (p. 307); to the right (E.), on the high, wooded bank of the Moskvá, is the *Merchants' Poor House* (Pl. 6, B 7; *I*).

39. Environs of Moscow.

As Moscow preserves the memory of the brilliance of the old empire of the Tzars, so do the châteaux and country-seats of the environs recall the existence of a wealthy and ostentatious class of boyars. The neighbourhood of Moscow is at its best in spring. In July the temperature often rises to 100° Fahr. although the evenings are cool.

The most interesting points in the neighborhood of Moscow lie near the railways. It is, however, preferable to hire an izvóshtchik (p. 271) for as long a time as is needed (bargaining advisable).

a. Tcherkizovo. Izmailovo.

About ³/₄ M. to the E. of the *Preobrazhénskaya Zastáva* (Pl. H 1, *I;* tramways Nos. 3, 4, 5, & 10) lies —

Tcherkízovo (Черкизово), formerly the ancestral residence of the family of the Metropolitan Alexis (p. 280). On the E. bank of the lake is an *Almshouse* (Pl. H, 1; *I*), built by Bishop Serapion in 1810. — About 1¹/₄ M. to the E. of the lake lies

Izmáilovo, the old manor of the family of Románov, formerly a model farm and favourite resort of the Tzars. Alexis Mikháilovitch built the Church, which was rebuilt by Feódor III. Alexéyevitch in 1679. On the S. side of the Vinográdni Pond, in the midst of pleasure-gardens, is the Nikolái-Izmáilovski Home for

Old Soldiers (Николаевская Измайловская богадѣльня), erected in 1839-49 from the plans of Thon. The pleasant wood of Izmáilovo, known as *Zvyerínetz* (*i.e.* deer park), lies 1 M. from the pond. About 2 M. to the S.W. of the pond is the Seménovskaya Zastáva (Pl. H 2, *I;* tramway No. 22).

b. Kuskovo. Kosino.

This excursion may be made either by carriage or by railway. In the latter case we may go either by the Moscow & Nizhni Railway (p. 336) to (10 V.) the station of Kuskovo (in 20 min.; fares 30, 15, & 10 cop.), or by the Moscow & Kazan Railway (p. 364) to the station of Veshnyaki (R. 47; in 25 min.; fares 58, 35, & 23 cop.), and return by the Moscow & Kazan Railway from Kosino (in 1/2 hr.: fares 58, 35, & 23 cop.).

Kuskóvo, 1¹/₄ M. to the S.E. of the railway station and 8 M. to the E. of Moscow, has been in possession of the Counts Sheremétyev since the beginning of the 16th century. The sumptuously furnished Manor House (visitors admitted) contains a picture gallery consisting chiefly of family portraits. Adjacent are the Hermitage and a shell grotto. The well-kept garden contains an orangery and numerous marble statues and busts.

From Kuskovo a path leads to the S.E. through the wood to (2 M.) the *White Lake* (Бѣлое óзеро), on the E. bank of which lies the attractively situated village of **Kosinó.** Close to the margin of the lake is the Church of St. Nicholas the Wonder Worker (Цéрковь Святáго Николáя Чудотвóрца), built in 1675 and resembling a fortress with its towers and loopholes. It contains an ikon of St. Nicholas, said by legend to have been found in the Holy Lake (see below). The *Tróitzkaya Church,* the second church of the village, built in 1823, has a diamond-studded shrine containing a picture of the Virgin, painted in Modena and presented in 1717 by Peter the Great, who sometimes visited Kosino. — About 1 M. to the S. of the village is the Kosino station of the Moscow & Kazan Railway (R. 47). — The *Holy Lake* (Святóе óзеро), 1/3 M. to the S.E. of the village, is a deep and clear sheet of water about 1/4 M. across. On the N.W. side, close to the bank, is a quaint little chapel with two domes, marking the position of the wonder-working baths, which draw thousands of pilgrims to Kosino every summer.

c. Lyublino. Kolomenskoye. Tzaritzuino.

Moscow & Kursk Railway (R. 46) to Lyublino in 1/4 hr. (fares 30, 15, & 10 cop.); to Pererva in 20 min. (fares 40, 25, & 15 cop.); to Tzaritzuino in 1/2 hr. (fares 50, 30, & 20 cop.). An electric railway to Podolsk (p. 359), viâ Lyublino and Tzaritzuino, is in contemplation.

Lyublinó-Dátchnoye, 6¹/₂ M. to the S.E. of Moscow, lies amid trees on the hilly banks of a picturesque lake. — About 2 M. to the E. of Lyublino (seat in a linéika 25 cop.) lies **Kuzmínki,** also called

Vlákhernskoye, containing many country-houses. It was formerly the property of Prince Galítzuin, but has belonged since 1912 to the city of Moscow. In the park is a rotunda with 16 columns and a statue (by Vitali) of Empress Marie Feódorovna, wife of Paul I. An obelisk marks the spot where a house of Peter the Great once stood. About 2 M. to the N. of Kuzminki lies Veshnyaki station (p. 364).

12 V. *Perérva,* with a convent. About 2 M. to the W. lies **Kolómenskoye,** founded by inhabitants of the town of Kolomna in 1237 and attractively situated on the right bank of the Moskvá. The lofty Church of the Virgin of Kazan, erected at the beginning of the 17th cent., was restored in 1880. The summer-palace, once a favourite residence of Iván the Terrible, has wholly disappeared. It was frequently visited by Peter the Great, who was brought hither for safety during the first revolution of the Streltzi (Sept. 1st, 1682). — We cross the Moskvá.

18 V. **Tzarítzuino-Dátchnoye,** a village presented by Peter the Great to Prince Kantemir of Moldavia and repurchased by the Empress Catherine II. in 1774. From the railway station we proceed in a straight direction, passing (5 min.) the garden-restaurant of Dippmann (on the right), to the (4 min.) large pond; then, beyond the dam, we turn to the right to (6 min.) the ruins of a château. The château was begun under Catherine. II. from the designs of Bazhénov, but was left unfinished because it reminded the empress of a coffin surrounded by candelabra (the towers). Adjoining the château is the theatre, also left unfinished. The extensive park is laid out in the English style and contains ponds, bridges, grottoes, and pavilions.

d. Kuntzevo.

This excursion may be made by carriage (passing the Dorogomilovskaya Zastáva; Pl. A 5, *I*), or by using the Moscow & Brest or Alexander Railway (R. 32) viâ Fili to (11 V.) the station of Kuntzevo (¹/₄ hr.; fares 35, 20, & 15 cop.).

Kúntzevo, 1 M. to the N. of the railway station and 7 M. to the W. of Moscow, is a pleasant colony of villas (no inn), formerly the property of the Tzar Alexis Mikháilovitch, who presented it to his father-in-law Cyril Narúishkin. The loftily situated Manor House (17th cent.) is surrounded by terraces and a fine park. Opposite is a small church, built in 1744; it contains a few old Bibles printed in Vilna in 1500 and 1575, and a chalice-cover embroidered by Natalia Narúishkin, the mother of Peter the Great. — About 2 M. to the E. lies Pokrovskoye-Fili (p. 307).

About 1¹/₂ M. to the S.E. of Kuntzevo Station lies *Davídkovo,* a pretty village on the *Syetún* and a favourite summer-resort of Moscow. A little to the S. is *Voluínskoye,* with numerous villas and gardens.

e. Petrovski Park. Petrovsko-Razumovskoye. Tushino. Arkhangelskoye. Ilyinskoye.

The Petrovski Park is most conveniently reached by the electric tramway (Nos. 6, 13, & 29, p. 271). For the longer excursion to Arkhangelskoye the traveller should hire a carriage, and follow the highroad from Moscow to Tushino and Ilyinskoye (25 V. or 17 M. from the Triumphal Arch).—Steam tramway from the Butúirskaya Zastáva, see p. 272. Nicholas Railway to the station of (4 V.) Petrovsko-Razumovskoye (fares 25, 15, & 10 cop.), see p. 268. From this point a walk of 20 min. to the W. brings us to the Agricultural Institute. Those who use the Moscow & Windau Railway (R. 33 b) reach Tushino in $1/_2$ hr. (fares 32 & 21 cop.; no first class) and Pavshino, $3^1/_2$ M. to the N.E. of Arkhangelskoye, in 40 minutes.

From the Triumphal Gate (p. 308) the St. Petersburg Road leads to the *Petrovski Park (Pl. A, B, 1, 2; *I*). To the left lies the racecourse. On the same side, farther on, is the *Khodúinskoye Field* (Khoduinskoe Pole; Pl. A 2, *I*), where 1400 men lost their lives on May 18th (30th), 1896, on the occasion of a popular festival held to celebrate the coronation of Tzar Nicholas II. Beyond the Khoduinskoye Field, in the distance, is the summer-camp of the Moscow garrison.

The *Petrovski Palace* (Pl. A, 1), $1^1/_2$ M. from the Triumphal Gate, was built by Kazakóv in 1776, and was occupied by Napoleon in Sept., 1812. On the latter's retreat it was plundered and set on fire by the French; the present handsome two-storied building in the Lombard-Gothic style dates from 1840. The palace is surmounted by a flat dome and surrounded by a colonnade. Its internal equipment is simple. Single visitors are generally admitted by the sentinel at the door, but a party must apply to the superintendent, who occupies an adjoining building to the left. The court is surrounded by a massive wall provided with towers, battlements, and loopholes. This, like the palace itself, is constructed of red bricks with ornamentation in white. The Tzars repair to the Petrovski Palace before their coronation and proceed thence in solemn procession to the Kremlin.— The *Park*, laid out by Tzar Nicholas I. in 1834, contains a summer-theatre, numerous villas, and several restaurants (p. 271). In the E. half of it is a small lake, with bath-houses.

About $3^1/_2$ M. to the N. of the Petrovski Palace, beyond *Súikovo*, lies **Petrovsko-Razumóvskoye.** The château which formerly stood here was built by the Boyar Cyril Narúishkin for his grandson, the future Tzar Peter I. Peter frequently resided here in his youth and took a personal share in the beautification of the park. Several of the old oaks are said to have been planted by his own hand. In 1763 Catherine II. presented the property to Count Razumóvski, and in 1861 it was purchased by the Government. The château was pulled down and an *Agricultural Institute* was built in its place in 1865. This is the most important establishment of the kind in Russia, possessing rich collections, a library, a school of forestry, and a model farm. It is attended by about 1000 students. Beyond the botanical garden is a large and well-kept park containing a lake. Near the entrance is an *Open Air Restaurant*.

About 1¹/₂ M. to the N.W. of the Petrovski Palace is **Vsekh-vsyátskoye,** which lies on the highroad to Tushino. In summer this is frequented as a place of residence by the families of officers on duty in the military camp in the Khoduinskoye Field (p. 323).

About 4 M. to the N.W. of Vsekhsvyatskoye, on the road to Volo-kolamsk, and at the confluence of the *Shodna* and the Moskvá, lies the village of **Túshino,** which was the headquarters of the second *False Demetrius* (the 'Thief of Tushino') in 1608-9.

The large village of **Arkhángelskoye,** containing many datchas, is charmingly situated on the left bank of the Moskvá, 7 M. to the S.W. of Tushino and 13 M. from the Triumphal Arch (izvóshtchik 5, carr. & pair 8, tróika 25 rb.; there & back 6-7 hrs.). The road passes through *Pávshino* (railway station, see p. 323) and *Gályevo.* The manor house (Бáрскiй домъ), belonging to Princess Yusúpov, lies upon a height; it was built at the end of the 18th cent., possibly from the plans of Quarenghi (p. 131), and has a colonnaded façade. The fine park, laid out in the French style and stretching along the slope above the Moskvá, contains numerous marble statues and an orangery. It commands a superb panorama.

About 2¹/₂ M. to the S.W. of Arkhangelskoye, in a high situation overlooking the Moskvá, lies **Пуínskoye** (Ильинское), the pro-perty of Grand-Duchess Elizabeth Feódorovna, with a fine park, orangeries, and two large farms. Visitors are generally admitted to the park on application to the steward (Контóра имѣнія). About 5 M. to the S. of Ilyinskoye is *Odintzóvo* station, on the Moscow & Brest Railway.

f. Ostankino. Alexeyevskoye.

Motor omnibuses run in summer from Máryina Roshtcha (Mariinski; Pl. C, D, 1, *I*) to Ostankino (fare 15 cop.).

About 2¹/₂ M. to the N. of the Krestóvskaya Zastáva lies **Ostán kino,** an ancient possession of the Counts Sheremétyev, with nu-merous summer-villas. The *Château* was built of wood in 1789-96 in the style of a Roman villa by Kazakóv; the wings were added in 1801 by Quarenghi. It contains a series of handsomely furnished rooms and a private theatre (on the upper floor). Visitors are ad-mitted on application to the steward. Adjoining the château is the church, built in 1668. In the park is the so-called Peter or Hero Oak, said to have been planted by Peter the Great.

A little to the E. of Ostankino is **Alexéyevskoye,** once a favourite resort of the Tzar Alexis Mikháilovitch, whose château fell into disrepair and was taken down in 1812. At Alexeyevskoye is the storage basin of the Moscow Waterworks, with a capacity of 800,000 gallons (p. 325; adm. on week-days, 10-4).

40. From Moscow to the Troitzko Sergiyevskaya Lavra.

66 V. (44 M.). Railway in 2 hrs, (fares 2 rb., 1 rb. 20 cop.; reserved seat in the Yaroslavl trains 1½ rb. extra).

Moscow (Yaroslavl Station), see p. 269. The train traverses the Sokolniki forest and then crosses the Yáuza at Alexeyevskoye.— About 1½ M. to the W. of (15 V.) *Tainínskaya* is the village of *Tainínskoye*, with a church dating from the end of the 17th century.

17 V. *Muitíshtchi*, Мытищи (Rail. Restaurant), the station for *Great Muitíshtchi*, a village and colony of datchas, which contains the Moscow Waterworks begun under Catherine II. in 1779, reconstructed in 1853-58, and enlarged in 1890-93. The water is collected from 43 springs and conducted by an aqueduct (Водопроводная труба) to Alexeyevskoye (p. 324), where it is pumped up by steampower into the two water-towers (p. 311).

28 V. *Púshkino* (Railway Restaurant), a large village with numerous datchas and manufactories, situated on a small lake in a pine wood. — 56 V. *Khotkóvo*. To the right, near the railway station, is the Pokrovski Nunnery, founded in 1308 and rebuilt after its pestruction by the Poles in 1610. Its chief church contains the common grave of the parents of St. Sergius (see below). The church festival is celebrated on Sept. 28th (O.S.). At the entrance to the convent are two inns. *

66 V. (44 M.) **Sérgiyevo**, Сергиево. — *Railway Restaurant.* — In the village are three *Inns* maintained by the monastery, R. ½-5 rb. *Izvóshtchik* from the railway station to the monastery 20-25, with two horses 40 cop., to the monastery, and thence to Gethsemane or Bethany and back, 1½ rb. — A hasty visit to the Lavra may be made in 2 hrs., in which case luncheon or dinner may be taken in the railway restaurant.

Sérgiyevo, picturesquely situated on the *Kóshura* and *Glimitza*, contains 27,000 inhabitants. The road from the railway station to (¼ hr.) the Lavra leads to the right. In front of the monastery are some trading rows (Pl. 22).

The *Tróitzko-Sérgiyevskaya Lavra (Троицко-Сергиевская Лавра), or the Trinity Monastery of St. Sergius, situated on gently rising ground, is, after the old and famous Lavra at Kiev (p. 380; comp. p. 130), the richest, the most distinguished, and historically the most important convent in Russia. The lofty and pinnacled outer wall (⅔ M. in circumference and 5 ft. thick) is strengthened with nine towers and encloses 13 churches (the domes and towers of which are resplendent with gilding and painting), a theological academy (Pl. 2), a school for the painting of pictures of saints (Pl. 20), several benevolent institutions, and a number of other large buildings. It is visited annually by upwards of 100,000 pilgrims.

The Troitzkaya monastery was founded in 1340 by *Abbot Sergius* (b. ca. 1319), the son of an impoverished boyar of Rostov. Soon after

his death, which occurred in 1392, the town of Moscow and the Troitzkaya monastery were devastated by a horde of Tartars. On their retreat,
Nikon, the successor of Sergius as abbot, found the body of Sergius
uninjured amid the smoking ruins of the convent. The miraculous preservation of the body of St. Sergius soon became widely known, and crowds
of believers hastened to pray at his grave. The monastery was quickly
rebuilt, and in the middle of the 16th cent. it was surrounded by a lofty
wall. It possessed numerous villages and about 120,000 serfs, and could
place an army of 20,000 men in the field. One of the most glorious pages
in Russian history is the account of the heroic defence of the convent by
the monks in 1608-09 against a Polish army of 30,000 men under Sapieha

Wagner & Debes. Leipzig

1. Abbot's Residence; 2. Academy; 3. Apartments of the Metropolitan of
Moscow; 4. Bakery of the Sacramental Bread; 5. Belfry; 6. Bookshop;
7. Cells; 8. Choristers' Quarters.— CHURCHES: 9. Assumption; 10. Cell of
St. Sergius (now a chapel); 11. Descent of the Holy Ghost; 12. St. Nikon;
13. Trinity.— 14. Holy Gate; 15. Holy Well; 16. Hospice; 17. Obelisk;
18. Office Buildings; 19. Refectory; 20. School of Painting; 21. Tomb of
the Godunovs; 22. Trading Rows; 23. Treasury; 24. Uspenski Gate.

and Lisovski, who were compelled to retire after an unsuccessful siege
of sixteen months. During the general insurrection of the Russians under
Minin and Pozhárski against the Poles (p. 298), the monks of the Troitzkaya convent, of whom the most famous were *Abbot Dionysius* and
Abraham Palitzin, traversed the country and encouraged the peasants
to take up arms. In 1618 another Polish army, under Prince Wladislaus,
besieged the monastery without effect. In 1685 it afforded a refuge to
the young Tzars Iván and Peter the Great from the rebellious Streltzi.
In 1812 the Troitzkaya monastery was not disturbed by the French, and
this immunity is ascribed by the devout to the miraculous powers of the
ikon of St. Sergius.

We pass through the frescoed gateway (Pl. 14), in which pictures
of saints are sold, and follow the main avenue in a straight direction.

Immediately to the left is the bookshop of the monks (Pl. 6), where views of the convent may be obtained.

To the right, behind the railing, stands the *Cathedral of the Assumption* (Успéнскій соббръ; Pl. 9), consecrated in 1585, and surmounted by five domes, the central one of which is gilded. The frescoes in the interior date from the end of the 17th century. To the left, in front of the W. entrance, are the tombs of *Tzar Boris Godunóv* (d. 1605), his wife, and two of his children (Pl. 21).

To the left, lying back a little from the main avenue, is the *Refectory* (Трáпеза; Pl. 19), a gaily-painted building 240 ft. long, completed in 1692. The large dining-hall is adorned with paintings of Biblical scenes. Over the church is the library of the monastery, containing 830 MSS., some of them with miniatures.

To the right of the main avenue, in a chapel, is the *Holy Well* (Pl. 15), from which it is usual for visitors to the monastery to drink. Not far off stands an *Obelisk* (Pl. 17), 36 ft. high, erected by the Metropolitan Plato in 1792 and bearing four gilt panels, on which the chief events in the history of the convent are inscribed. Behind it is the *Belfry* (Pl. 5), a rococo structure built in 1741-67 from designs by Rastrelli (?), and rising in five tiers to a height of 320 ft. (fine view from the top). It contains 40 bells, the heaviest of which is said to weigh 64 tons.

Farther on, to the left, stands the oldest of the convent churches, the small *Cathedral of the Trinity* (Трóицкій соббръ; Pl. 13), erected by St. Nikon in 1422 on the site of the wooden church of St. Sergius. The interior is lavishly adorned with ornaments of gold and silver, pictures of saints, and frescoes by Daniel Tchorni and Andréi Rublév. The last, which date from the beginning of the 15th cent. (comp. p. 338), have frequently been retouched. To the right, near the ikonostás, is the open sarcophagus of St. Sergius, presented by Iván the Terrible. It is made of silver, set with jewels, and above it is a silver canopy given by the Empress Anna Ivánovna. Over the S. door of the ikonostás (to the left of the canopy) is a picture of the saint, painted on a piece of wood from his coffin.

Behind the Cathedral of the Trinity is the *Treasury* (Рíзница; Pl. 23; no admission), the contents of which are valued at 650 million rubles. A series of large glass-cases contain ecclesiastical vessels, mitres, and croziers, most of which are of pure gold and encrusted with precious stones; gospels and missals in golden bindings; richly adorned copes and stoles, altar-cloths, and grave-cloths, literally sown with pearls. Among the articles interesting for their historical or personal associations are a buff hunting-coat of Iván the Terrible; the hair-shirt and wooden bowl of St. Sergius; a cope embroidered by Catherine II.; and a polished agate in the interior of which, by a curious freak of nature, the figure of a monk kneeling before a crucifix may be distinctly discerned.

Adjoining the Cathedral of the Trinity on the S. stands the small *Church of St. Nikon* (Pl. 12), founded in 1548 and renewed in 1840, containing the remains of the saint. — Towards the E. is the *Church of the Descent of the Holy Ghost* (Духовская церковь; Pl. 11), reconstructed in 1554, with the tomb of the Metropolitan Philaret (d. 1867).

The old Palace of the Tzar, a little to the N. of the Uspenski Cathedral, now contains the *Imperial Theological Academy* (Pl. 2), established in 1749 and attended by 250 students.

In a fine wood, about 1½ M. to the E. of the monastery, are the *Hermitage* (Геѳсиманскій Скитъ) and the *Church of Gethsemane*, founded in 1844. Women are not admitted to the former except on Aug. 17th (O.S.). The recluses immured in the cells here, many of which are underground, never quit their voluntary prison, but receive their food through an opening in the door. — About 2¼ M. to the S.E. of the Troitzkaya Monastery is the *Convent of Bethany* (Спа́со-Виѳа́нскій монасты́рь), founded in 1783 by the Metropolitan Plato, including the Church of the Transfiguration (interior worth seeing), as well as Plato's residence and grave. By the pond is an ecclesiastical seminary.

From Sergiyevo to *Yaroslavl* and *Kostroma*, see R. 41.

41. From Moscow to Kostroma viâ Sergiyevo and Yaroslavl.

348 V. (231 M.). Railway in 11½ hrs. (fares 10 rb. 75, 6 rb. 45 cop.; seat-ticket 1½ rb. extra); to Yaroslavl (262 V. or 174 M.) in 7½ hrs.

From Moscow to (66 V.) *Sergiyevo*, see R. 40. — As we leave Sergiyevo we have a view of the Troitzko-Sergiyevskaya Lavra to the left, and enter the government of Vladimir, which, after that of Moscow, is the busiest industrial district in Russia. It is also distinguished by its careful horticulture.

105 V. (70 M.) *Alexándrov* (Rail. Restaurant). The Novgoródsko-Vasílycvski doors in the ikonostás of the Cathedral of the Trinity date from 1336.

From ALEXANDROV TO IVANOVO, 193 V. (128 M.), railway in 6 hrs. 85 V. *Yuryev Polski*, a small town with 8800 inhabitants. The E. and S. walls of the Cathedral of St. George, which was built in 1234, are entirely covered with sculptures in stone. In the interior is the stone cross of Svyatosláv, 5 ft. in height, with the Crucifixion and reliefs of saints (1224). — 193 V. (128 M.) *Ivánovo*, see p. 338.

136 V. *Berendyéyevo.*

About 21 V. (14 M.) to the N.W. of Berendyeyevo (highroad; carr. 2 rb.) lies *Pereyaslávl-Zalyéski*, Переяславль Залѣскій, the chief town of a district, founded in 1152. Pop. 12,700. The Cathedral of the Transfiguration, dating from the 12th cent., has retained its original form. The town lies on *Lake Pleshtchéyevo* (Озеро Плещѣево), on which Peter the Great learned the elements of navigation when a boy.

Beyond (154 V.) *Ryazántzevo* the train enters the government of Yaroslavl, in which both trade and industry flourish.

210 V. (139 M.) **Rostóv-Yaroslávski,** Ростовъ Ярослав-
скій.—*Railway Restaurant,* déj. (12-2) 60 cop., D. (2-7) ³/₄-1 rb.— *Tzar-
kov's Inn,* near the Kremlin, R. 1-2¹/₂, D. ³/₄ rb.— Izvóshtchik from the
railway station to the town 30, per hr. 60 cop.— Illustrated Russian
Guide, by A. Titov, on sale at the museum (50 cop.).

Rostóv, one of the most ancient towns in Russia, founded be-
fore the days of Rurik, came into the possession of Moscow under
Demetrius Donskói (d. 1389), and was until 1788 the seat of a
Greek Catholic archbishop.

The town lies in a semicircle
on the W. side of *Lake Nero*
(Óзеро Нéро), a sheet of water
8 M. in length, 3¹/₄ M. in width,
and abounding in fish. Pop.
18,300. The town is noted for
its pictures of saints on enamel. In the environs are many
market-gardens. — From the
railway station we go straight
on through the Blagovyé-
shtchenskaya to (20 min.) the
Kremlin, which is surrounded by a wall with ten round
towers. This lies on the lake
in the middle of the town, and
eleven streets radiate from it.
Its churches, built in the time
of the Metropolitan Jonas Sui-
soyevitch (1652-91), are good
examples of the Russian architecture of the 17th cent., and
contain contemporary frescoes.

Key to the numbers on the plan.
1. Belfry of the Uspenski Cathedral.
— *Churches:* 2. Redeemer; 3. Redeemer in the Square; 4. Resurrection; 5. Smolensk Mother of God;
6. St. Gregory of Naziantium; 7. St.
John. — 8. Church School (formerly
the Archbishop's Palace); 9. Museum;
10. Red Palace (ruin).

To the N. is the *Church of
the Resurrection* (Цéрковь
Воскресéнія Христóва; Pl.
4), built in 1670; on the S.
side of this is a door with allegorical paintings. The *Church
of the Smolensk Mother of
God* (Цéрковь Смолéнской Бóжіей Мáтери Одигíтріи; Pl. 5),
built in 1691-1701, is surmounted by a dome and painted in
brightly-coloured triangles. In the *Church of St. John* (Цéрковь
Іоáнна Богослóва; Pl. 7), above the choir-gallery, are some interesting canopies. On the S. side of the Kremlin is the Byélaya
Paláta, erected in 1670 for the accommodation of the Tzars. This
building, along with the Terem, now contains the *Museum* (Pl. 9;

entr. at E.), the contents of which include ecclesiastical antiquities, ancient household utensils, and so on (open daily 9-2, at other times on application to the caretaker). A good view of the town and its environs is afforded by its so-called *Garden Tower* (Садовая башня). In the *Church of the Redeemer* (Церковь Спаса на Сѣняхъ; Pl. 2) the ikonostás has been replaced by a screen with five arches. To the N. of the Kremlin is the *Uspenski Cathedral,* consecrated in 1230. On the ikonostás, to the left of the 'holy door', is the picture of the wonder-working Vladímir Virgin, painted by Alimpi (11th cent.). Adjoining is the belfry (Pl. 1), 105 ft. long and 55 ft. high; it dates from the end of the 17th cent., and has four arched openings and four domes (harmonious chime of 13 bells).

About 1 M. to the S.W. of the Kremlin, on Lake Nero, is the *Spaso-Yákovlevski Monastery,* founded in the 14th cent. and containing a rich treasury. About $1^1/_4$ M. farther on is the village of *Bogozlóv,* with a wooden church containing a carved wooden 'holy door' of the 16th century.

262 V. (174 M.) **Yaroslávl**, Ярославль. — The RAILWAY STATION (Pl. B, 6; Restaurant) lies to the S. of the town. — The LANDING PLACE of the steamers is below the Cathedral of the Annunciation (Pl. 4; C, 2). Steam-ferry across the Volga 1 cop., for a carriage 10 cop.

HOTELS. *Kokuyév* (Pl. a ; C, 3), Theatre Square (Театральная площадь); *Bristol* (Pl. d; C, 3), Yekaterininskaya, R. $1^1/_4$-$3^1/_2$ rb., déj. (12-2) 75 cop., D. (2-7) 60 cop. to 1 rb.; *Tzargrád* (Pl. b; C, 3), Yekaterininskaya; *Yevrópa* (Pl. c; C, 3), Vlásyevskaya. — *Restaurant Buttler*, Kazanski Boulevard, to the N. of the theatre (Pl. C, 3), with a concert-garden.

IZVÓSHTCHIK (fixed tariff) per drive 20-25, per hr. 50 cop.; from the landing-place to the town 30-40, to or from the ($2^1/_2$ M.) rail. station 50 cop.

ELECTRIC TRAMWAY from the railway station through the town to the steamboat landing-place and to Vspolye station (beyond Pl. A, 4).

STEAMERS (see above; comp. R. 45) up the river to Ruibinsk in 7 hrs. (fares 1 rb. 95, 1 rb. 25 cop.); down the river to Kostroma in 6 hrs. (1 rb. 65, 1 rb. 10 cop.) and to Nizhni-Novgorod in 32 hrs. (fares 5 rb. 85, 4 rb. 10 cop.). A pleasant trip may be made to Rostov (p. 329).

Yaroslávl, the capital of the prosperous government of the same name and seat of an archbishop, is situated on the right bank of the *Volga,* near its junction with the *Kótorosl.* Pop. 112,000. The Volga is here nearly $1/_2$ M. wide, and the town lies 225 ft. above it. Yaroslavl contains a seminary for priests, a juristic lyceum, and several churches, some of which, dating from the 16-17th cent., are of considerable architectural interest. Its numerous manufactures include cotton (Yaroslávl Cotton Mill, founded in 1722, beyond Pl. A 5), tobacco, and linen. The appearance of the town, especially as seen from the Volga, is very picturesque. — There is a Lutheran Church (Pl. 9; B, 3).

Yaroslavl, first mentioned in 1071, is said to have been founded by *Yarosláv the Wise* (1019-54). In 1238 it was sacked and burned by the Tartars. In 1463 the principality of Yaroslavl was united with Moscow. Catherine II. made the town the capital of a province in 1777. The banished Duke Biron of Courland lived here from 1742 to 1761. The first Russian theatre was founded in Yaroslavl in 1750 by Volkov and Polyúshkin.

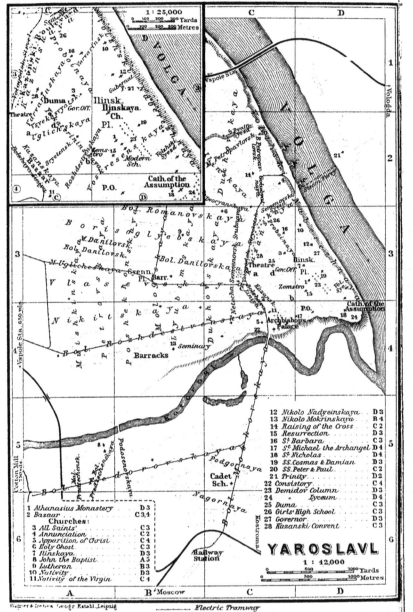

From the Railway Station (Pl. B, C, 6), in the S. part of the town, we follow the broad Bolshaya Moskóvskaya (electric tramway), passing on the left (10 min.) the long building of the *Cadet School* (Pl. C, 5), to the (20 min.) bridge over the Kótorosl.

About 1 M. to the W. of the Cadet School rises the **Church of John the Baptist* (Цéрковь Іоáнна Предтéчи въ Толчкóвѣ, or Предтéчевская цéрковь; Pl. 8, A 5), the chief example of the Yaroslavl style of architecture, built in 1671-87 and possessing no fewer than 15 gilded domes. The walls are covered with coloured tiles. The belfry (110 ft. high) dates from the early 18th century. The church contains interesting mural paintings by Dmitri Grigoryev and others (1694-1701). To the left of the altar is a carved and gilded wooden door leading to a chapel (Придѣлъ Гýрія и Варсонóфія). The key of the church is kept in the cottage to the right of the entrance, in the enclosing wall. The church is most conveniently visited in driving to or from the railway station (30-40 cop. extra).

Beyond the bridge, to the right, lies the *Archiepiscopal Palace* (Архіерéйскій домъ; Pl. C, 4), occupying the buildings of the Spaso-Preobrazhénski Monastery, founded in the early 13th cent. (one of the oldest in Russia) and adapted for its present uses in 1787. A gateway leads to the convent-court, on the E. side of which is the *Church of the Transfiguration* (with a blue cupola), built in 1216-24 and restored in 1516. It contains some mural paintings of 1516, restored in 1563, 1781, and 1814. Adjacent, to the right, is the *Church of SS. Theodore, David, and Constantine* (with a green cupola), erected in 1831 on the site of an old church dating from 1218; to the left of the ikonostás is a silver shrine with the remains of the canonized princes.

To the W. of the archbishop's palace is the *Nikólo-Mokrínskaya Church* (Pl. 13; B, 4), built in 1665-94 and now the regimental church; the 'holy door' of the ikonostás (18th cent.) and the canopies over the 'thrones of the Tzar and the Patriarch' are interesting.

Along the W. side of the inner town runs the KAZÁNSKI BOULEVARD (Pl. C, 3; restaurant, see p. 330), which presents a scene of great animation, especially in the evening.

The Rozhdéstvenskaya, on the N. side of the archbishop's palace, leads to the N.E. to (9 min.) the Ilyinskaya Square (Pl. D, 3), which is adjoined by the *Government Offices* (Присýтственныя мѣстá; Pl. C, 3) and other official buildings. In the middle of the square is the white *Ilyinskaya Church* (Pl. 7; D, 3), built in 1647-50, with two quite dissimilar belfries and surrounded by a railing; it contains frescoes by G. Nikitin and others (1680; comp. p. 334) and a gilt wooden altar-canopy of 1657. — To the S. rises a bronze column (Pl. 23), erected in 1829 in honour of P. G. Demidov (p. 332). — Still farther to the S. is the *Cathedral of the Assumption* (Pl. D, 4), founded in 1215 by the Grand-Prince Constantine Vsévolodovitch, but dating in its present form (with five gilt cupolas) from 1646. In the interior, to the right, are the remains (мо́щи) of the canonized princes of Yaroslavl, Vasili and Constantine Vsévolodovitch. To the left of the 'holy door' of the ikonostás is a picture of the Virgin, said to have been painted in the 12th century. To the E., behind the cathedral, is the *Juristic Lyceum* (Демидовскій юридическій лицей; Pl. 24, D 4), founded by Demidov in 1803 as a college of philosophy and generously endowed.

From the Lyceum the VOLGA BOULEVARD (Волжская набережная; Pl. C, D, 1-3), interrupted by three ravines spanned by viaducts (views), stretches to the N. along the lofty bank of the Volga for a distance of about 2 M. To the left are the *House of the Governor* (Pl. 27), with a garden extending to the Ilyínskaya Square, and the *Nikólo-Nadyéinskaya Church* (Pl. 12), built in 1620, with a carved and gilded ikonostás (1751). The *Church of the Nativity* (Pl. 10) was built in 1644 and restored in 1831. Below the Seménovski Ravine is a steam-ferry (p. 330) plying to the left bank. Not far off are the steamboat landing-places. At the N. end of the boulevard is the *Church of SS. Peter & Paul* (Pl. 20; C, 2).

Yaroslavl is connected with *Ruibinsk* (p. 349) by a branch-railway (79 V. or 52 M.). — From Yaroslavl to *Archangel*, see R. 42.

Beyond Yaroslavl we traverse a monotonous district of field and forest. From (309 V.) *Nérekhta* (Rail. Restaurant), a branch line runs to (63 V.) Yermólino (p. 338). We cross the *Solonítza*.

348 V. (231 M.) **Kostromá,** Кострома. — The *Railway Station* (restaurant) lies on the right bank of the Volga. — HOTELS. *Kostromá,* Voskresénskaya Square, a little to the right of the Susánin Monument, R. ³/₄-2¹/₂, D. (2-6 p.m.) 1¹/₄ rb.; *Moskóvskaya,* Pávlovskaya, a little to the N. of the Susánin Monument. — There is a restaurant in the *Town Park* (Городской садъ), opposite the N. side of the Cathedral of the Assumption, D. (2-6) 1 rb. 20 cop.

Izvóshtchik from the railway station to the town, in summer ³/₄-1 rb. (incl. ferry), in winter 50 cop.; from the steamer landing-place to the town 30-45 cop.; to the Ipátiyev Convent and back, 1-1¹/₄ rb.

STEAMBOATS (landing-place to the S.E., below the Cathedral of the Assumption) upstream to Yaroslavl in 7 hrs. (fare 1 rb. 95 cop.) and to Ruibinsk in 16 hrs. (fare 3 rb. 30 cop.); downstream to Nizhni-Novgorod in 21 hrs. (fare 4 rb. 40 cop.). FERRY over the Volga 2, for a carriage 12 cop.

PEASANTS' WORK on sale at the Kostrómskago Kustárnago Zemstva, Russina 8, to the E. of the Susáninskaya Square.

A hurried visit may be made to the town and to the Ipátiyev Convent by izvóshtchik in 2 hrs. (ca. 2 rb.).

Kostromá (380 ft.), situated on terraces rising from the left bank of the *Volga,* which is here 600 yds. in width, is first mentioned in 1213 and is the capital of the government of the same name and the seat of a Greek Catholic bishop. Pop. 67,000. There are large spinning-mills and a Lutheran church.

A little to the N. of the Volga (in a line with the ferry) lies the great SUSÁNINSKAYA SQUARE, from which all the main streets radiate. In the middle rises the *Monument to Susánin,* by Demut-

Malinóvski (1851). On a granite column is a bronze bust of Tzar Mikhail Feódorovitch (see below); leaning against the column is the peasant Susánin, who, when compelled by the Poles to conduct them to the hiding-place of the newly-elected Tzar, purposely led them astray and was hewn down by them in consequence. This incident furnished the plot for Glinka's opera 'A Life for the Tzar'.

A little to the S.E. of the Susáninskaya Square, close to the river, on the site of the old Kremlin, rises the *Cathedral of the Assumption* (Успéнскій собóръ), built about 1250 by the Grand-Prince Vasili Kostrómski (to whom the Virgin appeared while he was hunting near Kostroma; comp. below). It was rebuilt in 1775-78 after a fire and has six gilded domes. On the ikonostás, to the left of the holy door, is the large wonder-working picture of the Virgin (Чудотвóрная Ѳеóдоровской икóна Бóжіей Мáтери; 13th cent.); also banners of the Opoltchéniye (militia), used in 1812 and 1853-56. The altars stand in the N. part of the church instead of in the E., as the apparition was seen in that quarter of the heavens. — To the eft of the Cathedral of the Assumption stands the lofty belfry, five stories high, of the Cathedral of the Epiphany (Колокóльня Богоявлéнскаго собóра), built after 1773. To the right of the Cathedral of the Assumption is a platform commanding a view of the Volga. In front of the cathedral is a monument (by A. Adamson) to commemorate the 300th anniversary of the rule of the House of Románov, erected in 1913-14. — At the end of the Debrinskaya, which runs to the E. from the Cathedral of the Assumption, stands, to the left, the *Church of the Resurrection*, built about 1650, with frescoes of that date.

On the left side of the Pávlovskaya, which runs N. from the Susáninskaya Square, is the *Románov Museum* (open on Tues., Thurs., Sun., and holidays 12-4, in winter 12-3; adm. 10 cop.), finished in 1913 and containing ecclesiastical antiquities and souvenirs of the reigning dynasty.

On the right bank of the Kostroma, $1^2/_3$ M. to the W. of the Susáninskaya Square, is the **Ipátiyev Monastery** (Ипáтіевскій монастырь).

The Ipátiyev Monastery was founded in 1330 by the Tartar prince *Zacharias Tchet*, the founder of the Godunóv family, who had fled from the Golden Horde to Moscow and had been baptized there. It stands on the site where the Virgin appeared to him in a vision along with St. Ipátiyev. In 1586-90 the monastery was surrounded by a strong stone wall, and at the time of the Interregnum it formed a small fortress which was able to afford shelter to *Mikhail Feódorovitch Románov* in 1613, when persecuted by the Poles. Here, on March 14th (O.S.), he received the representatives of the Muscovite boyars and clergy, who prevailed upon him to accept the crown.

Passing through the gate we find ourselves in the courtyard, with the Cathedral of the Trinity in front of us and the rooms of the Tzar in the background to the right. — Among the numerous

interesting objects in the *Cathedral of the Holy Trinity* (Трби-
цкій соббръ), which was rebuilt in 1586, are mural paintings by
G. Nikitin and others (1685; comp. p. 331); to the right of the
ikonostás is the throne of the Tzar Mikhail Feódorovitch, with a
carved-wood canopy (late 17th cent.). The treasury contains the
picture of the Virgin with which Mikḥaíl's mother, Marfa Ivánovna,
blessed her son at the election; also rare diptychs. To the right of
the cathedral is a belfry (1605).— On the W. side of the convent
is the *House of the Románov Boyárs* (Домъ бояръ Романовыхъ),
preceded by a flight of steps; it was rebuilt in 1863 after the model
of that at Moscow (p. 300). To the left of the entrance-hall are
two rooms which Mikhail Feódorovitch occupied at the time of his
election; to the right are the four rooms occupied by his mother (castellan to the right). The furniture has been copied from old designs.

42. From Yaroslavl to Archangel.

787 V. (522 M.).   RAILWAY in 27 hrs.; beyond Vologda the line is
narrow-gauge.

Yaroslavl, see p. 330. The line crosses the Volga and at first
traverses a well-cultivated region in the government of Yaroslavl.
In the government of Vologda the numerous aspen woods which have
hitherto been predominant are replaced by coniferous forests. The
inhabitants, who are in part of Finnish origin, although they speak
Russian, are in repute as skilled carpenters and stove-fitters.

62 V. *Danílov* (Rail. Restaurant); 91 V. *Pretchístoye;* 149 V.
Gryazóvetz (Rail. Restaurant), a town of 3700 inhab., situated in
a marshy district on both banks of the *Rzhavka.*

192 V. (127 M.) **Vólogda** *(Rail. Restaurant),* see p. 258.

Beyond (223 V.) *Sukhóna* we cross the river of that name. The
line runs through forest, and settlements become less frequent. 322 V.
Vózhega (Rail. Restaurant); 390 V. *Konósha;* 470 V. *Nyandóma*
(Rail. Restaurant). Beyond (544 V.) *Lepsha* the train enters the
government of Archangel and traverses a marshy district.

787 V. (522 M.) **Archangel**, Архáнгельскъ. — The *Railway
Station* (restaurant) is on the left bank of the Dviná ; steam-ferry in sum-
mer to the town (1 hr. in all). — HOTELS. *Hotel Bar,* R. 2½-5 rb.; *Tróitz-
kaya,* Tróitzki Prospékt, R. 1-2½ rb., bed-linen 40, D. (1-7 p.m.) 80 cop.;
Mináyev, Rúinotchnaya Square. — RESTAURANTS in the 'Obshtchestvo
Ofitziantov' and in the 'Kommértcheskoye Sobrániye'. — IZVÓSHTCHIK per
drive 20 cop. to 2 rb.; at night (12-6 a.m.) double fares. — POST & TEL-
EGRAPH OFFICE, Náberézhnaya, corner of the Finlyándskaya. — BRITISH VICE-
CONSUL, *Thomas Woodhouse.* — LLOYD'S AGENT, *Bruno Paetz.* — ENGLISH
CHURCH, Tróitzki Prospékt; service in summer at 10 a.m.

Archangel, the capital of the government of that name, stretches
for a distance of nearly 5 M. along the right bank of the *Northern
Dviná* (Сѣверная Двинá), 28 M. above its mouth in the White

Sea. Pop. 38,000. The city carries on a trade in timber, tar, pitch, fish, flax, and other articles. The harbour is clear of ice from the beginning of May till the beginning of October (O.S.).

On Aug. 24th, 1553, Sir Richard Chancellor, who had been sent out from London to discover a sea-route to India and China round the N. end of Norway, landed at the mouth of the Dviná. He was summoned to Moscow by Iván the Terrible and received important trading privileges for his countrymen. The English settlement, of. which no trace now remains, was at Kholmogori (see below). The town of Archangel was founded in 1584, 46 M. below Kholmogori, and during the 17th cent. formed, as the only seaport of Russia, the emporium of the trade of Moscow with England and Holland. Peter the Great, however, almost entirely suppressed the trade of the town in the interests of St. Petersburg. In 1708 Archangel became the capital of a province.

The chief street of the town is the TRÓITZKI PROSPÉKT, which runs parallel with the Dviná. In this street stands the *Tróitzki Cathedral*, built in 1709-43 with two stories and five domes. In the upper church, under a canopy to the right of the entrance, is a wooden cross, 14 ft. in height, carved by Peter the Great in 1694. — Farther on, to the left, is the old Russian and German Trading Factory, a large building of 1684, now containing the *Custom House* and the *District Court*. In front of the Boys' High School is a tasteless bronze statue of *M. V. Lomonósov* (b. at Kholmogori in 1711; d. 1765), the scholar and poet, erected in 1832 from a design by Martos. À little to the N., in the fashionable 'German Suburb', is the *Duma* or *Town Hall*, with the *Museum*, which contains natural history and ethnographical collections. The museum is open on weekdays 10-2 (in winter 11-2), on Sun. & holidays 12-3 (adm. 10 cop.; Russian catalogue 10 cop.). Farther on, to the left, are the Anglican (p. 334), the Lutheran, and the Roman Catholic churches.

Near the N. end of the Tróitzki Prospékt, and about $2^1/_2$ M. from the cathedral, is a bridge leading across the *Kuznétchikha* to the suburb of SOLOMBÁLA, situated on an island and containing the old Admiralty buildings and a hospice of the Solovétzki Convent (Соловécкое подвóрье). To the left is the island of *Moïséyev.*

At the S. end of the town is the *Convent of the Archangel Michael* (Михáйло-Архáнгельскій монастьíрь), from which Archangel takes its name.

About 46 M. above Archangel lies **Kholmogóri**, a small town with 1350 inhabitants. Anna Leopóldovna, daughter of the Duke Carl Leopold of Mecklenburg-Schwerin, and the former regent of Russia, died here in 1746 as a prisoner. Her husband, Prince Anthony Ulrich of Brunswick-Wolfenbüttl, died here in 1774 and is said to be buried in the Church of the Assumption.

STEAMBOATS ply from Archangel to *Onéga, Kem, Mezen,* and other small towns on the White Sea (Lloyd's agents at these). — Another steamer runs once a week to (5 days) *Vardö* (fare 13 rb. 20 cop.; see *Baedeker's Sweden & Norway*). The steamer calls at *Alexándrovsk*, a small town on the Arctic Ocean, founded in 1899, with a biological station and the ice-free *Catherine Harbour* (Екатерíнинская гáвань).

From Archangel to the Solovetzki Convent, 166 sea-miles, steamboat in 15-17 hrs. The steamboat of the Murman Company plies once weekly (fare 4 rb. 80 cop., meals $2^1/_2$ rb.). The fare on the steamer belonging to the convent, which runs as needed, is $3^1/_2$ rb., but no food can be procured on board. July is the best time for this trip, as in June the steamers are crowded with pilgrims.

The steamer descends the *Maimáxa,* or E. arm of the Dviná, reaches the White Sea in about 2 hrs., and then steers to the N.W.

The **Solovétzki Monastery** (Соловѣцкій монастырь), one of the largest and wealthiest in Russia, lies on the W. side of Solovetzki Island in the White Sea, in 65° N. lat.; the island is 17 M. long and 11 M. broad, and contains numerous lakes and woods. The convent is enclosed by a lofty wall with towers, erected in 1584-94; on the W. side it is bounded by the sea, on the E. side by the *Holy Lake.* — Visitors are put up without charge in the conventual hospices, but a charitable donation is expected. The annual number of pilgrims is 10-15,000.

The Solovetzki Convent was founded in 1429 by *SS. Hermann* and *Sabbatius.* The first church was built by *St. Zosima* in 1436. Most of the present stone buildings were erected in the reign of Iván the Terrible by *Abbot Philip,* who afterwards became Metropolitan of Moscow (p. 268). In the 16-17th cent. the convent was used as a place of exile for both ecclesiastical and secular dignitaries. In 1666 the monks refused to accept the reforms of the Patriarch Nikon (p. lviii). In consequence of this the convent was besieged for years by the troops of the Tzar and taken by storm in 1676.

In the W. side of the wall is the so-called *Holy Gate,* forming the main entrance to the monastery. Above it is the *Armoury* (Оружейная палата), containing weapons from 1578 onwards. Opposite, to the E., is the *Cathedral of the Transfiguration,* built in 1558-66, containing part of the remains of St. Philip (comp. above). Beyond is the *Church of the Trinity,* containing the bones of the founders of the convent. To the N. of the cathedral are the rich *Treasury* (Ризница), the *Church of the Assumption,* and the large *Refectory* (Трапеза), the vaulting of the last being supported by one massive central pillar. — The workshops of the monks supply all the conventual needs in the way of clothing, implements, etc.

43. From Moscow to Nizhni-Novgorod.

412 V. (273 M.). Railway in 10 hrs. (fares 12 rb. 50, 7 rb. 50 cop.; seat-ticket $1^1/_2$ rb.); sleeping-car, during the fair, 3 rb. 30, 2 rb. 45 cop.

The district extending to the E. from Moscow as far as the Volga, and taking in the governments of Vladimir, Kostroma, Nizhni-Novgorod, and part of Ryazan, consists mainly of forest. Various industries are carried on in the towns. The inhabitants are comparatively free from foreign elements and are the best representatives of the Great Russian type (comp. p. xli).

Moscow (Kursk & Nizhni-Novgorod Station; Pl. F 4, *I*), see p. 269. — 10 V. *Kuskóvo,* see p. 321. From (51 V.) *Fryázevo* a branch-railway runs to (14 V.) the manufacturing town of *Bogoródsk.* 64 V. *Pávlovo-Posád* (Rail. Restaurant), with silk and cotton mills.— 84 V. *Oryékhovo* contains the large Morózov cotton mills. A branch-line diverges here to the S. for (28 V.) Kurovskaya (p. 364).—We cross the *Klyazma.* 117 V. *Pyetushkí* (Rail. Restaurant).

The scenery now becomes more cheerful. The railway skirts a range of hills rising from the left bank of the Klyazma and then crosses this river by an iron lattice bridge.

179 V. (119 M.) **Vladímir-on-the-Klyazma,** Владиміръ на Клязьмѣ. — *Railway Restaurant,* D. 1 rb. — HOTELS. *Kommértche-skiye Nomerá,* R. 1-3¹/₂ rb. ; *Centrálnaya,* R. 1-2 rb., both in the Bolshaya Moskóvskaya.— *Tchernetzov Restaurant,* Nizhegorodskáya, D. (1-6) 1 & 1¹/₄ rb.—*Izvóshtchik* from the station to the town 40-50 cop.

Vladímir, the capital of the government of that name and the seat of the Archbishop of Vladimir and Suzdal, is picturesquely situated on the lofty left bank of the *Klyazma.* Pop. 39,000.

The town is said to have been founded by Vladimir Monomákh, Grand-Prince of Kiev, in 1116 and was enlarged and beautified by Andréi Bogolyúbski (1169-75), who made it his place of residence. Within a few decades of his day it extended as far as the village of Bogolyúbovo, which is now several versts distant from the town. In 1238 Vladimir was destroyed by the Tartars under Baty-Khan, and in 1325 the Metro-politan Peter transferred his residence to Moscow. In 1328 the Tartars once more appeared before Vladimir under the leadership of Uzbék, and the Grand-Prince Alexander Mikháilovitch fled to Pskov. Uzbék there-upon presented the principality to Iván, the brother of the Grand-Prince Yuri of Moscow, and from that time onwards Vladimir remained an appanage of the Muscovite house.

We ascend from the railway station straight along the Vokzál-naya, then take the Mironósitzkaya to the left, and the Lukyá-novski Spusk to the right. In 10 min. we reach the Nizhegorod-skáya, which we follow to the left. Immediately to the left is the *Convent of the Nativity of the Virgin* (Рождéственскій монастырь), which is surrounded by a white wall, and has been the residence of the archbishop since 1744. In the court to the left is the Church of the Nativity of the Virgin (Храмъ Рождествá Бóгородицы), founded in 1191 and restored after 1858. It form-erly contained the tomb of St. Alexander Nevski (p. 130). The belfry dates from 1654. We now follow the Nizhegorodskáya for 5 min. more, or keep to the left round the outside of the convent-wall (view of the river and the plain) till we reach (8 min.) an open space, on the S. side of which are the St. Demetrius Cathedral, the *Law Courts,* and the Cathedral of the Assumption. The *Cathedral of St. Demetrius* (Дмитріевскій соборъ), the best-preserved example of the Vladimir-Suzdal style of architecture, is a square building in white limestone, with a central dome and a blue roof. It was erected ca. 1197 under Vsévolod III., and was restored in 1847. The exterior is ornamented with numerous reliefs of saints, fantastic animals, and flowers, which (like the cornice) show Romanesque influence. In the interior are some remains of contemporary mural paintings, which were probably restored in the 15th century. The *Cathedral of the Assumption* (Успéнскій собóръ) built in 1160 by Andréi Bogolyúbski as the burial-church of the Vladimir princes, was enlarged after a fire in 1185, and was restored in 1891. It has five domes, the centre one being gilded. Inside, on the ikonostás, to the left of the holy door, is an old replica of the picture of the Virgin (p. 283) which has been in Moscow since 1395. In the arcade to the left of the ikonostás is a shrine containing the remains of Andréi Bogolyúbski, while to the right is that of his son, Glyeb. The frescoes on the central piers date from the 12th cent., but were restored in the 15th cent. by Andréi Rublév (p. 327). The treasury contains some fragments of princely raiment dating from the 12th century.— The Bolshaya Moskóvskaya, prolonging the Nizhegorodskáya towards the W., is the main street of the town. At its W. end, ¹/₂ M. from the Cathedral of the Assumption, is the so-called *Golden Gate* (Золотыя ворóта), a triumphal arch of 1158 with a gilded dome above the opening. It was restored in 1810. Still farther to the W., in the Dvoryánskaya, is the *Lutheran Church.*

About 35 V. (23 M.) to the N. of Vladimir by highroad, on the *Ká-menka*, lies the little town of **Suzdal** (6000 inhab.), first mentioned in 1024, destroyed by the Tartars in 1238, and under the sway of Moscow from the beginning of the 15th cent. onwards. The *Cathedral of the Nativity* dates in its present form from 1528. Prince D. M. Pozhárski (p. 298) is buried in the *Spáso-Yevfímiyevski Convent*, which was founded in 1352.

From Vladimir a narrow-gauge railway runs to (196 V. or 130 M.; 15 hrs.) *Ryazán* (p. 366).

225 V. (149 M.) *Novki.*

FROM NOVKI TO KINESHMA, 172 V. (114 M.), railway in 7 hrs.— 56 V. *Shuya*, an industrial town with 30,700 inhab., situated on the *Teza*, a tributary of the Klyazma. — 85 V. **Ivánovo**, Ивáново-Вознесéнскъ (*Rail. Restaurant; Natzionálnaya Hotel*; izvóshtchik from the station to the town 40 cop.), on the *Uvod*, is the common name of a group of calico-making towns and villages, containing in all 168,000 inhabitants. It includes the suburb of *Voznesénsk*, lying on the opposite bank of the river. From Ivanovo to (193 V.) *Alexandrov*, see p. 328. — From (104 V.) *Yermólino* a branch-line runs to (63 V.) *Nérekhta* (p. 332). — 172 V. *Kineshma*, see p. 350.

We cross the *Klyazma*.— 239 V. (158 M.) *Kovróv* (Rail. Restaurant), the capital of a district, situated on the lofty bank of the Klyazma and containing 22,200 inhabitants. A branch-line diverges here to the S. for (102 V.) *Murom* (p. 364).— 295 V. *Vyázniki* (Rail. Restaurant).— Beyond (339 V.) *Gorokhovétz* (Rail. Restaurant) the train crosses the Klyazma by a long bridge and enters the government of Nizhni-Novgorod.— On the lofty right bank of the Oká, 8 M. to the S. of (358 V.) *Gorbátovka*, lies the district-town of *Gorbátov* (5100 inhab.). As we approach the Volga the thriving villages become more frequent. — 365 V. *Seíma*, with manufactories.

412 V. (273 M.) *Nizhni-Novgoród* (Rail. Restaurant, good), see p. 339.

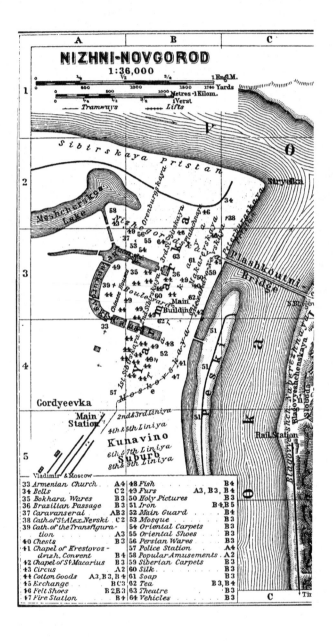

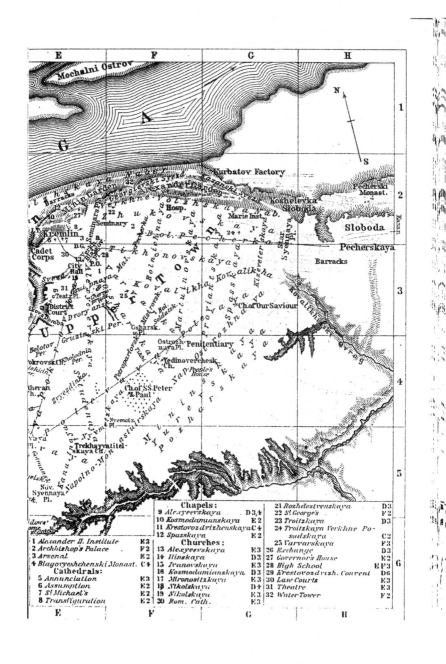

44. Nizhni-Novgorod.

Arrival. The *Main Railway Station* (Pl. A, 5; good restaurant) lies on the Fair Side, in the suburb of Kunavino. Izvóshtchik and electric tramway over the Fair Bridge (p. 345; Pl. C, 3) into the town, see below. — The *Station for Timiryazevo* (Pl. C, 5) lies on the right bank of the Oká. Landing-stages for the *Volga* and *Kama Steamers* at and below Sofrónovskaya Square (Pl. D, 3); the *Oká Steamers* discharge on the right bank of the Oká, above the Fair Bridge (at the Grebnóv Peski during the Fair).

Hotels. In the *Upper Town:* Rossíya (Pl. a; E, 2), Blagovyéshtchenskaya Square, R. with bed-linen 2-12, D. 1¹/₄ rb.; Vostótchni Bazár (Pl. f; D, 3), open in summer only, with a view of the Fair Side, R. 2-10, déj. (11-2) ³/₄ rb., D. (2-6) 85 cop. to 1 rb. 25 cop. — In the *Lower Town:* Birzheváya (Pl. b; D, 3), R. 1-6, déj. (10-2) ³/₄, D. (2-7) 1 rb., St. Petersburg (Pl. c; C, 3), Kommértcheskiye Nomerá (Pl. d; D, 3), these three in the Rozhdéstvenskaya. — On the *Fair Side:* Sóbolev (Pl. e; B, 4), Moskóvskaya 1, open during the Fair only.

Restaurants. Good and inexpensive meals are to be had on the Volga steamers (comp. p. 348). In the upper town: *Vostótchni Bazár* and *Rossíya*, see above; *Minin Gardens* (p. 342), déj. ³/₄, D. (1-7) ³/₄-1¹/₄ rb. On the Fair Side: *Apollo*, cor. of Nizhegorodskáya and Makáryevskaya, D. (2-7) 1¹/₄ rb., variety entertainment in the evening (not cheap); *Birzha*, in the Exchange (Pl. 45; B, 3), D. (12-6) 65 cop. to 1 rb.

Post & Telegraph Office (Pl. E, 3), in Blagovyéshtchenskaya Square; on the Fair Side, during the Fair, in the main building (Pl. B, 3).
Police Station (directory accessible daily, 9-9) in the City Hall (Pl. E, 3).

Izvóshtchik (fixed tariff) from the rail. station to the upper town 50, to the lower town 30, to the Fair 20; per drive in the upper or lower town or in the Fair 20; from the upper to the lower town 25, to the Fair 35; from the Fair to the upper town 45, to the lower town 25; per hr. 60 cop.; for the whole day 4 rb. Carriage with two horses double fare, with rubber tyres 20 cop. extra.

Electric Tramways (uniform fare 3 cop.; from July 1st to Sept. 9th, O.S., 5 cop.; elevators, see below). From the Main Railway Station (Pl. A, 5) viâ the Fair and the Fair Bridge (Pl. C, 3) to the lower end of the Pokhvalínski Elevator (Pl. D, 3), and on to the lower end of the Kremlin Elevator (Pl. E, 2; 2¹/₂ M., in 25 min.). — From the upper end of the Kremlin Elevator viâ the Pokrovka to the Krestovozdvízhenski Convent (Pl. 29, D 6; 1¹/₂ M.). — From the upper end of the Pokhvalínski Elevator viâ the Pol`eváya to the Ostrózhnaya Square (Pl. F, 4; 2 M.).
Horse Tramway from the City Hall (Pl. E, 3) through the Bolshaya Petchérka (Pl. F, G, 2).

Electric Elevators (Элеваторы). *Kremlin Elevator* (Pl. E, 2) from the Rozhdéstvenskaya to the Ivánov Tower (p. 343); *Pokhvalínski Elevator* (Pl. D, 3), from the E. end of the Fair Bridge to the upper town. There is a 5 min. service (fares 5 & 3 cop.).

Theatres. *City Theatre* (Pl. 31; E, 3), in the Theatre Square, open in winter. — *Fair Theatre* (Pl. 63; B, 3), open during the Fair.

Banks. *Imperial Bank* (office-hours 10-3), Osuipnáya (Pl. E, 3; during the Fair in the main building on the Fair Side); *Volga & Kama Bank*, Rozhdéstvenskaya 17 (Pl. D, 3).

Photographs at *A. Karélin's*, at the corner of the Varvárka and Málaya Petchérka (Pl. F, 3); *Dmitriyev*, Osuipnáya (Pl. E, 3), near the theatre.

Baths. *Yermoláyev*, Tchernoprúdski Pereúlok (Чернопрудскій Переулокъ; Pl. E, 3). — *River Baths* in the Volga; the bathing establishments on the Oká are not so good.

Steamers (see p. 348). Landing-places, see p. 339. — Local Steamers from Kunavino to the Kurbátov Manufactory (Pl. G, 2; fares 10 & 5 cop.), and other points. — Volga Steamers (comp. the time-tables; during the height of the travelling season it is advisable to secure tickets in advance). To Kazan, in 20 hrs. (fares 5 rb. 80, 2 rb. 95 cop.); to Simbirsk (10 rb. 60, 6 rb. 60 cop.); to Samara (13 rb. 60, 8 rb. 70 cop.); to Suizran (15 rb. 60, 10 rb. 5 cop.); to Saratov (19 rb. 85, 12 rb. 70 cop.); to Kamuishin (22 rb. 90, 14 rb. 70 cop.); to Tzaritzuin (25 rb. 45, 16 rb. 35 cop.); to Astrakhan, in 5 days (30 rb. 55, 19 rb. 60 cop.). — Kama Steamers to Kazan, in 20 hrs. 5 rb. 15, 2 rb. 60 cop.; to Perm, in 4 days, 15 rb., 10 rb. — Oká Steamers to Murom, Kasimov, and Ryazan.

Principal Attractions (one day). The morning should be devoted to the Fair, beginning at its N. end. In the afternoon it is advisable to ascend viâ the Rozhdéstvenskaya (elevator) to the Kremlin, and visit the Alexander Garden and the Petcherski Convent.

Nizhni-Nóvgorod (*i.e.* Lower Novgorod; Нижній-Новгородъ), also known simply as *Nizhni* (in distinction to Novgorod on Lake Ilmen, p. 262), the capital of the government of the same name and the seat of a Greek Catholic bishop, contains 109,000 inhabitants, among whom, at the time of the Fair, the Tartars are especially conspicuous. It lies at the confluence of the *Oká* (p. 350) and the Volga. The town proper, very picturesquely situated on the right banks of the two rivers, consists of the quiet *Upper Town* (Вéрхній базáръ), and the more lively *Lower Town* (Нижній базáръ). The former is the seat of the authorities, and at the Kremlin reaches a height of 330 ft. above the Volga; the latter is the commercial quarter, and is connected with the Upper Town by winding roads in deep cuttings. On the flat and low-lying tongue of land on the left bank of the Oká lie the *Fair* (the scene of the celebrated annual fair) and the suburb of *Kunávino*. — Nizhni-Novgorod is a busy manufacturing place, but its chief importance lies in its trade in flour, iron, salt, petroleum, and other goods.

Nizhni-Novgorod was founded in 1221 by *Yuri Vsévolodovitch*, Grand-Prince of Vladimir, as a barrier against the inroads of the Mordvins and the Bulgarians. Its prosperity began practically with its foundation. Under *Constantine Vasílyevitch* (1340-55) it became independent, and in 1350 it was made the residence of the Grand-Princes. *Andréi* (1355-63), the son of Constantine, fortified the town with walls and towers; but the completion of these works was hindered by the appearance of the plague. In 1377 Nizhni-Novgorod was burned down by the Tartar hordes, and in 1417 it was united with the principality of Moscow. In 1606 and 1608 the Mordvins besieged the town in vain. The enterprise of Kosmá Minin (p. 298) was initiated in Nizhni-Novgorod. The last warlike event of which the town was witness took place in 1667, when the robber Stenka Razin headed a Cossack and national rising in an unsuccessful attempt to take possession of Nizhni-Novgorod. In 1708 the town was annexed to the government of Kazan, but since 1719 it has been the capital of a separate province bearing its own name.

Crossing the *Fair Bridge* (p. 345) to the Lower Town, we first reach the *Nizhnyaya Blagovyéshtchenskaya Square* (Pl. C, D, 3), in which are the electrical plant and the Pokhválinski Elevator. To the S. of the square rises the *Chapel of St. Alexis* (Часóвня Алексѣ́евская; Pl. 9), named in honour of the Metropolitan Alexis

(14th cent.), and dating in its present form from 1846. From the chapel a road ascends to the right to the *Heights of Dyatlov*. On a spur of these hills, on the side next the Oká, lies the *Convent of the Annunciation* (Благовѣщенскій мужскóй монастѝрь; Pl. 4), founded in 1370 and rebuilt in 1647. The convent contains five churches, the oldest of which is the Cathedral. In the interior, to the left of the Holy Gate, is the Korsun picture of the Virgin, one of the oldest paintings in Russia, painted, according to the inscription, by the Monk Simeon in 993, *i.e.* five years after the introduction of Christianity into Russia (see p. lvii).

To the N.E. of the Nízhnyaya Blagovyéshtchenskaya Square diverges the Rozhdéstvenskaya, the main street of the lower town. Here, to the right, stands the quaint *Rozhdéstvenskaya Church* or *Church of the Nativity* (Pl. 21; D, 3), built in 1719 by Count Gregor Dmítriyevitch Stróganov, and surmounted by five coloured domes. — We now cross the Sofrónovskaya Square (Pl. D, 3), with the *Exchange* (Pl. 26; D, 3), pass (on the left) the *Kosmodamiánskaya Church* (Pl. 16), erected in 1890 from the plans of Dahl, and (on the right) the *Tróitzkaya Church* (Pl. 23), and reach a small square containing the *Gostíni Dvor*. By turning to the left from this point we reach the Nizhnevólzhskaya Náberezhnaya (Pl. D-F, 2), while to the right lies the Zelénski Gorge, containing (on the left) the *Ivánovskaya Church* (Pl. 15) and the *Roman Catholic Church* (Pl. 20).

By ascending through the *Zelénski Gorge* we reach the *Vérkhnyaya Blagovyéshtchenskaya* (Pl. E, 2, 3), the largest square in the Upper Town, from which all the chief streets radiate. To the E. runs the Tikhonovskaya, to the S.E. the Varvárka, and to the S. the Bolshaya Pokróvka, the chief business-street of the town, and the Alexéyevskaya. The entire N. side of the square is occupied by the old walls and towers of the Kremlin.

In the middle of the square rises the *Cathedral of the Annunciation* (Pl. 5), founded at the end of the 14th cent., and rebuilt in 1696. The exterior is notable for a curious cornice of tiles. — Opposite the cathedral, to the S.W., also in an open situation, stands the *Alexéyevskaya Church* (Pl. 13), built in 1719 and remodelled in 1823. Between the two churches is a *Bronze Statue of Tzar Alexander II.*, by Kurpátov (1906). — On the E. side of the square are the *High School* (Pl. 28) and the *Theological Seminary* (Pl. E, F, 2); on the S.W. side is the *City Hall*, by Zeidler (1904).

The *Demetrius Gate* (Дмѝтріевская бáшня; Pl. D. G.), opposite the City Hall, was reconstructed in 1896 and leads to the *Kremlin (Pl. E, 2, 3), which occupies the highest point of the town. It is enclosed by a wall 65-100 ft. in height, which is flanked by 11 (formerly 13) towers.

The building of the Kremlin was first undertaken by the Grand-Prince Demetrius Constantinovitch (1365-84), under whom the Demetrius Gate (p. 343) was completed in 1374. The next was the Ivánov Tower, erected by Iván III. in 1500. In 1508-11 the Kremlin was practically rebuilt under the superintendence of the Italian architect Pietro Francesco (Frasin). Numerous changes have, however, been made in the building since his day. In 1838 a great part of the old moat was filled up, and the shady Kremlin Boulevard was constructed on its site.

On entering the Kremlin we see to our right the long building of the *Arsenal* (Pl. 3). In front of it is the —

Cathedral of the Transfiguration (Спáсопреображéнскій каеедрáльный собóръ; Pl. 8), founded in 1227 in the reign of the Grand-Prince Yuri Vsévolodovitch but afterwards frequently rebuilt. It received its present rectangular form from the architect Yefímov in 1829-34.

INTERIOR. On the pillar to the right of the ikonostás is a large *Picture of the Redeemer*, brought hither from Suzdal in 1352 by the Grand-Prince Constantine Vasílyevitch. On the column to the left, of the ikonostás is the *Ikon of the Virgin*, sent from Constantinople in 1381 through Dionysius, Archbishop of Suzdal and Nizhni. To the left of the holy gate of the ikonostás is the *Ikon of the Iberian Virgin*, painted by Simon Ushakov in 1672. On the N. wall, to the left of the entrance, is the monument of *Kosmá Minin* (d. 1616; p. 298), executed in 1878 by Dahl, in the style of the 16th century. Above the monument are two old *Ecclesiastical Banners*, which accompanied Prince Pozhárski and Minin to Moscow. The grave itself is in the crypt, to which two flights of steps descend. — The *Crypt* also contains the tombs and monuments of ten princes and princesses of Nizhni-Novgorod and of several archbishops. — In the treasury is a *Book of the Gospels*, written on parchment in 1408.

To the N. of the cathedral is the *Governor's House* (Pl. 27), situated on the edge of a slope occupied by the Government Gardens (no admission). — To the W. are the *Minin Gardens* (restaurant, see p. 339; adm. after 7 p.m. 25 cop.) and the *Monument of Minin and Pozhárski*, erected in 1826 and consisting of a granite obelisk 65 ft. high on a base with reliefs and inscriptions. The monument affords an admirable *View of the Volga, the Oká, and the Fair, especially fine towards evening.

To the S.W. of the Cathedral of the Transfiguration is the unassuming *Cathedral of St. Michael* (Собóръ Михайла Архáнгела; Pl. 7), erected in 1227 as the domestic chapel of the Grand Prince Yuri Vsévolodovitch and rebuilt in 1630. The interior contains monuments of several princes of Nizhni-Novgorod. — Between the belfry and the cathedral stands a rectangular *Watch Tower* (entrance through the church). — Close by are the *Cathedral of the Assumption* (Pl. 6), built in 1827, the *Cadet School of Count Araktchéyev* (Кадéтскій грáфа Аракчéева кóрпусъ), transferred hither in 1868 from Novgorod on Lake Ilmen, the *Law Courts* (Присýтственныя мѣстá; Pl. 30), and other buildings. To the N. of the Cadet School is the *Ivánov Tower* (Pl. I. T.; Kremlin Elevator, see p. 339).

To the N.E. of the Kremlin is the **Alexander Garden**
(Александрійскій садъ; Pl. F, 2), an artificial terrace laid out
on the steep slope overhanging the Volga, with extensive and well-
kept pleasure grounds. It affords an admirable *View, seen at its
best in the evening. — Farther to the E., halfway down the slope,
is the —

Petchérski Convent (Печéрскій мужскóй монастЫрь;
Pl. H, 2), the white walls of which gleam picturesquely through the
green foliage of the trees.

The Petcherski Convent was originally erected in the reign of Grand-
Prince Alexander Vasílyevitch, by St. Dionysius, Archbishop of Suzdal
and Nizhni-Novgorod (1329), on the spot where the church of the old
Petchérskaya suburb now lies, $^1/_3$ M. below the convent. Part of the
walls of the old convent, the remains of which are still visible, slid
down the slope of the hill in 1596. The reconstruction on the present site
was begun by Tzar Feódor I. Ivánovitch and completed under Mikhail
Feódorovitch Románov.

The *Church of the Ascension,* in the middle of the convent-court,
was built by Laurénti Vozoyúlin in 1632. It contains some old ecclesiastical vessels and the wonder-working Ikon of the Petchérskaya
Virgin, dating from the 14th cent. (on the pillar to the right, in
front of the ikonostás; comp. p. 345). The *Convent Library* was
formerly very rich, but its treasures have been removed to St. Petersburg. It still contains seven 'synodics', or registers of masses for
the souls of the dead, dating from 1552 to 1654; among the names
in this list are those of the 381 Boyars and other persons executed
by command of Iván the Terrible. The bells of the church are also
notable; one of them was cast in 1492 at Hagenow in Mecklenburg
and was carried off from Dorpat by Iván the Terrible.

Returning from the Petcherski Convent, we turn to the left into
the Bolshaya Petchérka, which is bordered with villas and gardens.
At the W. end of this street, to the right, is the *Kulíbin Industrial
School,* founded in 1872 in commemoration of the inventor I. P.
Kulíbin (d. 1818). In front of us is the *Archbishop's Palace* (Apxie-
рéйскій домъ; Pl. 2), with a large park and remains of the old
earthen wall which formerly surrounded Nizhni.

In the Bolshaya Pokrovka, opposite the District Court (Pl. E, 3),
is the building of the Assembly of the Nobles, containing a small
Museum (entrance from the court), which is open on week-days
10-5 (in winter 10-3) and on Sun. 12-5 (in winter 12-3; adm. 20,
on Sun. 3 cop.; Russian catalogue 15 cop.). Its contents include coins,
antiquities, and paintings by modern Russian masters, among which
may be mentioned the Deposition in the Tomb by Koshelév. Farther
to the S. is the *Lutheran Church* (Pl. E, 4).

From Nizhni-Novgorod to *Moscow,* see R. 43. — From Nizhni-Novgorod
(station, see p. 339) to *Timiryázevo* (Kazan) and *Ruzáyevka* (Penza, Samara), see p. 364.

The Great Fair.

The fair lasts officially from July 15th to Sept. 10th (O.S.), when the offices are closed and the booths must be shut up. All bills of exchange relating to transactions at the fair must be negotiated by Aug. 25th. The liveliest traffic prevails between July 25th and Aug. 12th (O.S.), and the fair is hardly worth visiting before or after these dates. In spring the whole area is generally under water.

HOTELS, etc., see p. 339. — SMOKING is forbidden in the streets of the fair grounds and on the bridge.

The FAIR probably owes its origin to the jealousy felt by the Grand-Prince of Muscovy at the great trade of Kazan, the residence of the Tartar Khans, where an important annual fair was held in July from 1257 onwards, on the field of Arsk. Iván III. (1462-1505) established a similar fair on his territory at *Vasilsúrsk* (p. 351), at the confluence of the Sura with the Volga. After the conquest of Kazan, Mikhaíl Feódorovitch Románov transferred the fair in 1641 to the neighbourhood of the Makáryev Convent (p. 351), which was founded at the beginning of the 15th cent. and dedicated to St. Macarius (b. 1349). The day upon which the saint died (June 25th), a festival frequented by crowds of people, was selected as the opening day of the fair. A fire in 1816 destroyed all the warehouses and booths on this site, and Nizhni-Novgorod was chosen to replace it. In 1822 accordingly, 60 warehouses and more than 2500 stalls were erected here under the superintendence of M. Bétancourt, a general of engineers, at a cost of six million rubles.

Most of the visitors to the fair are Russian merchants and peasants, but it is also attended by representatives of the peoples of the Volga territory and Asiatic Russia, and by Chinese and Persians.

The BUILDINGS OF THE FAIR (Ярмарка, i.e. *Yarmarka,* from the German *Jahrmarkt*) form a regular town of shops and warehouses. The *Ambárs,* or warehouses, generally built of stone and either one or two stories in height, are erected in badly paved streets, which intersect each other at right angles. The so-called tunnels (lavatories) are recognizable by the low towers which rise above them. — The fair grounds are divided into an inner and an outer town. The *Inner Fair,* with 4000 booths, is surrounded by the Bétancourt Canal and intersected by a broad street known as the Boulevard (p. 346). The *Outer Fair,* also with 4000 shops, has gradually grown up round the inner town, and is less regularly laid out. The enormous quantities of goods of all kinds which are exposed to view in the large storage-depots on the side next the Volga, emphasize a peculiar characteristic of this fair, *viz.* that the goods for sale are actually brought to the spot in bulk and are not simply sold by sample as is customary at other fairs. Wares of the same kind are invariably grouped together. The value of the goods brought to the fair in 1910 amounted to 250 million rubles. It is impossible here to give a list of the articles offered for sale at the fair, as it may be truly said that almost everything, from the raw products of the soil to the most costly gold and silver ware, may be procured here. The number of visitors is estimated at 400,000.

The wooden PLASHKOUTNI or FAIR BRIDGE (Pl. C, 3), stretching
: cross the Oká (here ¹/₂ M. broad) from the Nízhnyaya Blagovyéshtchenskaya Square (p. 340), is annually put in place at the beginning
of June, and removed when the frost sets in. This bridge commands a view of the town. On the opposite bank, immediately to
the left, are the *Exchange* (Бирж̀а; Pl. 45) and the *Chapel of the
Petchérski Convent* (p. 343), in which the wonder-working picture
of the Virgin is exhibited during the fair.

NORTH PART OF THE OUTER FAIR. From the Exchange (see
above) the *St. Petersburg Street* and the *Alexander Nevski Street*
(p. 346) lead N. to the Cathedral Square. The former is occupied by
the ironmongers and the sellers of glass and porcelain; the goods
offered for sale in the latter consist of brightly coloured wooden
trunks strengthened with metal mountings (price 2-100 rb. each).
The *Alexander Nevski Cathedral* (Pl. 38; C, 2) was completed in
1881 from the designs of Dahl. The interior is elaborately decorated, and the ikonostás, covered with six rows of pictures of
saints, reaches to the ceiling. To the right of the cathedral lie the
stalls for wooden articles, and behind it is the so-called *Row of
Bells* (Колок̀ольный рядъ; Pl. 34). The bells hang on wooden
frames.

From the *Stryelka* (Pl. C, 2), which affords a good view of the
city, the *Siberian Quay* (Сибир̀ская пристань; Pl. A, B, 2) extends up the Volga. On it lie the offices and warehouses of the
steamboat-companies. From this point we return through the Urál-
skaya and the Orenbúrgskaya (Pl. A, B, 2) to the—

NIZHEGORÓD STREET (Pl. A 2, B 3). At the W. end of this are the
Circus (Pl. 43) and the *Balagani* (Балаг̀аны; Pl. 58), or *Amusement Booths.* Following the Nizhegoród St. to the E., in the direction of the Oká, we reach almost at once a small square with
the *Caravanserai* (Pl. 37), in which rice, raisins (изюмъ), dried
peaches (шептал̀а), pistachio nuts, and other Persian products are
offered for sale. Persian carpets may also be procured here, but
considerable knowledge is requisite for an advantageous purchase.
The *Mosque* (Мечеть; Pl. 53) is surrounded by a lofty brick wall.
On the first floor is a hall with the prayer-niche; the floor is covered with straw mats and carpets, upon which the Mohammedans
perform their devotions (adm. 20 cop.; visitors must take off their
shoes). The goods in the rows of the *Oriental Shoemakers* (Азiят-
ская об̀увь; Pl. 55) include slippers of stamped leather, morocco
cushions with silk embroidery, and shawls. The *Tartar Bridge*
(Pl. A, B, 3) leads S. to the Chinese Rows (p. 346). Farther to the
E., in the Nizhegoród St., Persian goods are on sale, while Simbirsk
shawls may be procured in a side-street. The next cross-street (the
3rd Pozhárski St.) is devoted to tanned hides, which are annually
sold to the value of upwards of 7 million rubles. The *Carriage*

Row (Pl. 64) is interesting, with its droshkies, tarantasses, and other strange-looking vehicles. Farther on to the left are the *Stalls for Felt Shoes* (Вáленая óбувь; Pl. 46), of which 2½ million rubles' worth are sold at the fair. In the middle of the Theatre Square is the *Theatre* (Pl. 63; p. 339), surrounded by inns. The so-called *Brazilian Passage* (Pl. 36) is used by retail dealers in gold and other ornaments. The *Wine Trade* flourishes in the Kizlyár-skaya, which runs parallel with the Nizhegoród St., to the N. of the theatre. The two most important of the other streets crossing the Nizhegoród St. are the Tzárskaya, in which *Soap* is sold, mostly coming from Kazan, and the Macarius St., where *Groceries* and *Spices* are sold. The Nizhegoród St. ends at the Exchange (p. 345).

From the Exchange the *Alexander Nevski Street* leads S. to the INNER FAIR. On the left side of this street are ranged the stalls (Pl. 59) where *Accordions, Ironmongery, Pictures of Saints,* and *Siberian Carpets* (Ковры́; used for horse-blankets; 3-50 rb. each) are sold. The *Chapel of St. Macarius* or *Flag Chapel* (Pl. 42) is a brick structure with five domes. — The so-called *Main Building* (Глáвный домъ; Pl. B, 3), a huge brick structure faced with cement, erected in 1890, is during the fair the seat of the governor, of the committee managing the fair, of the post and telegraph office, of the imperial bank, and of the police. On the groundfloor are an unpretending restaurant and an arcade containing stalls for the sale of trinkets, silk goods, gems from Yekaterinburg, and other articles of luxury (concert in the afternoons). — From the Main Building the *Boulevard*, which is planted with trees, runs to the W. for about 1 M. The shops of the Russian merchants in it are quite in the occidental style, and are devoted to the sale of millinery, ornaments, jewellery, and the like. To the left of the Boulevard, and lying somewhat back from it, is the depot for *Furs* (Пушнóй товáръ; Pl. 49; turnover 32 million rubles), and to the right is that for *Cotton Goods* (Хлопчáто-бумáжныя издѣлія; Pl. 44; turnover 100 million rubles), two of the chief staples of the fair. At the W. end of the Boulevard rises the *Cathedral of the Transfiguration* or *Old Cathedral of the Fair* (Стáрый ярмарóчный собóръ; Pl. 39), built in 1822 from the designs of Monferrand (p. 109). In front of the cathedral is a fountain; to the right and left of it are two *Chinese Rows*, containing the offices of wholesale dealers.

The SOUTH PART OF THE OUTER FAIR offers little of interest to the stranger. Here lie the *Armenian Church* (Pl. 33), warehouses for furs and cotton goods, and the *Fire Station* (Pl. 47), the tower of which commands a good survey of the fair (165 steps; adm. on application to the fire-chief). The Moscow St. leads hence to the *Railway Station* (Pl. A, 5).

On the S. side of the Fair Grounds lies the suburb of **Kunávino** (or *Kunávino*; Pl. A, B, 5), occupied by labourers. The chapel of the *Gorodétz Feódorovski Convent* (Часóвня городéцкаго ѳéдоровскаго

монастырá), built by Dahl, is distinguished by its quaint architectural
style and by its brilliant colouring.

In the Oká, opposite Kunavino, lies the long sandy island of **Peskí**,
to which we cross by a bridge to the N. of the *Chapel of the Convent of
the Raising of the Cross* (Часóвня Крестовоздвѝженскаго монастырá;
Pl. 41, B 4). This island is the depot for two important articles sold at the
fair. The extensive sheds at the *Zhelyéznaya Landing Place* (Желѣзная
прѝстань), which are erected afresh for every fair, contain enormous
quantities of iron, sold annually to the value of 40 million rubles. By
the *Grebnovskáya Landing Place* (Гребновскáя прѝстань) are numerous barges containing enormous piles of dried and salted fish (turnover 16 million rubles).

45. Voyage down the Volga from Tver to Nizhni-Novgorod, Kazan, and Suizran.

The **Volga** (Вóлга, named *Rha* or *Oaros* in antiquity, and *Atel, Itel*,
or *Etel* in the Middle Ages) is the largest river in Europe and the chief
channel of communication in Eastern Russia. It rises in 57° 14′ N. lat.
and 32° 30′ E. long., at a height of 750 ft. above the sea, amid the Valdai
Hills, in the district of Ostashkov, in the W. part of the government of
Tver. It is 2305 M. in length, or about thrice as long as the Rhine, and
flows through nine provinces. The area it drains is nearly three times as
large as France. It enters the Caspian Sea at Astrakhan, in a delta 73 M.
wide. The fall of the Volga is very slight: Tver lies 415 ft. above the
sea, Saratov 7 ft.; Tzaritzuin and Astrakhan lie respectively 50 ft. and
65 ft. below sea-level. At Rzhev the river is 425 ft. wide, at Tver 705 ft.,
at Kostroma 1705-1970 ft., at Nizhni-Novgorod 2460 ft. (increasing in
spring to 13 M.), and at Saratov 6400-15,975 ft. (just over 3 M.). The
main arm at Astrakhan is from 2395 to 6395 ft. wide. The water of the
Volga is of a brown colour, owing to the diluvial deposit and black soil
it carries with it. Traces of the ancient bed of the river are recognizable
in the steppe to the S. of Tzaritzuin in the form of chains of lakes,
while the ancient mouths of the river may be detected on the coast of
the Caspian Sea.

SCENERY. From Tver to the Oká the banks of the Volga consist of
hills of clay, loam, and sand, alternating with low marshes and forest-
land. Beyond the confluence of the Oká with the Volga at Nizhni-Novgorod, the *Right Bank* is bordered all the way to the Caspian Depression
(p. xxxvii) by steep slopes and eminences, attaining at places a height of
1150 ft., while the *Left Bank* consists of plains. The former is thus called
the HILL BANK (Нагóрный бéрегъ), while the left bank is known as
the MEADOW BANK (Луговóй бéрегъ). — The Volga is the highway of
more than 2000 steamers, all using oil-fuel (masút, the refuse of petroleum;
comp. p. 457). The stream is navigable for large steamers up to Tver,
and for smaller vessels up to Rzhev. The chief freights which it bears
are grain, petroleum, and salt, carried in 'tows' of six or more barges,
arranged in double rows. Huge quantities of timber are floated down in
rafts. The navigation is, however, much impeded by the continual silting-
up of the channel, the numerous islands, the low level of the water in
summer, and the six months' frost of winter. — The fishing and the caviare
industry are also important. The finest fish is the sterlet, the best specimens of which are caught in the Surá. The sturgeon is a similar but
very much larger fish. The fishing is said, however, to be deteriorating
owing to the pollution of the river by the oil-fuel used in the steamers.

'Mátushka Volga', or 'Little Mother Volga', is spoken of in Russia
so often and with such affection that it is easy to cherish too high hopes
of the attractions of a voyage upon it. The scenery is nowhere of an
imposing character, and the length of the voyage is very fatiguing; the

trip in the most beautiful part, *i.e.* from Nizhni-Novgorod to Samara, takes 3 days. The simple landscapes of the broad river often recall the peculiar and intense colouring of evening scenes on the Nile, and their variety, as well as the diverse characteristics and customs of the population on the bank, afford considerable interest. The towns and villages arrest our attention through the charm of their colouring. The houses and the church cupolas are painted in gay tints, and form a striking contrast to the green trees and the white sandy banks. Monotonous marshy plains or sombre woods of pine and fir are followed by groves of limes and oaks, green meadows, and smiling fields, while these in turn give place to the endless steppes of the south. At Nizhni-Novgorod we reach the region of mixed population, where the various tribes of the Ural-Altaic family are mingled in inextricable confusion. — Comp. 'The History of the Volga and its Towns', by *W. Barnes Steveni* (1914).

The best Travelling Season is May and the beginning of June (O. S.). The advertised hours of starting of the passenger-steamers represent local time (comp. p. xxxii), not that of St. Petersburg, and are seldom adhered to; in July and August the steamers are often very late. The waiting-rooms on the piers are by no means as comfortable as they might be. At the departure stations (Tver, Ruibinsk, Nizhni-Novgorod, and Astrakhan) cabins may be engaged a day in advance. At the intermediate stations the vacant berths are allotted according to their numbers. They are given out again if those who have secured them are not present when the names are called over. The large passenger paddle-steamers plying from Nizhni-Novgorod are generally well equipped: the cabins are arranged along the upper deck, with the first-class forward and the second-class aft; the gangway surrounds them, and serves as a promenade deck. The cuisine is for the most part excellent: déj. (11-1) 65 cop., D. (2-6) 65 cop. to 1 rb., S. (8-11) 65 cop. Especially popular are caviare (1 rb. per portion), fish dishes, and (in Aug.) crabs. Bed-linen is charged separately: for 1-3 days blankets cost 50, sheets 25, pillows 25, and towels 10 cop. One pud (36 lbs.) of luggage is allowed free. — In consequence of the variable state of the water the vessels are not always able to pass to the right of each other; the steamer descending the river shows a flag (at night a lantern) on the side on which it means to pass, while the other boat repeats the signal in token of comprehension. — The chief steamboat companies are the *Volga Steam Navigation Co.* (Пароходное общество по Волгѣ), founded in 1843; the *Caucasus & Mercury Co.* (Кавказъ и Меркурій, Kavkáz i Merkúri), founded in 1849, and extending its voyages to the ports of the Caspian; the *Samolyót Co.* (Самолётъ), founded in 1853; and the *Russian Co.* (Русь). — For Fares, see under the various towns; tickets may be obtained either from the agents or on board.

In the following description the places at which the steamboats call are indicated by †.

†*Tver*, see p. 267. — 20 V. (l.) †*Orsha*, a village with a Convent of the Ascension. — 87 V. (r.) †*Kórtcheva*, a district-capital, with 2500 inhabitants. — From (125 V.) †*Savélovo* (r.) a railway runs to (121 V.) *Moscow* (comp. p. 270). — 127 V. (l.) †*Kimri*, a village with 10,700 inhab. and important boot-manufactories. — 199 V. (r.) †*Kalyázin*, a district-town with 5700 inhabitants. — 219 V. (l.) †*Priluki*. The banks become higher, but sink again beyond Volga (p. 349).

248 V. (165 M.) †**Uglitch** (r.), the capital of a district in the government of Yaroslavl, contains 9700 inhab. and was founded in the 10th century. On the site where Demetrius (b. 1581), son of Iván the Terrible, was murdered on May 15th, 1591 (probably at the

command of Borís Godunóv), stands the *Church of St. Demetrius* (Це́рковь свята́го царе́вича Дми́трія на кро́ви), erected in the reign of Tzar Mikhail Feódorovitch. To the right, above the landing-place, is the *Château of the Tzarévitch Demetrius*, a small red-brick building with an outside staircase. It was built by Prince Andréi Vasílyevitch in 1481 and was restored in 1892. The interior (open daily; adm. 15 cop.) contains a few souvenirs of the Tzarévitch; visitors are also shown a reproduction (made in the 18th cent.) of the bell which summoned the citizens to punish the murderers, and was accordingly banished by Boris Godunóv to Tobolsk (p. 527). The original bell was melted by a fire in 1677.

281 V. (l.) †*Múishkino,* an unimportant little town.—Just before reaching (302 V.) *Volga* (l.) the steamer passes under the trellis-bridge of the railway from Ruibinsk to Bologoye (p. 267). —337 V. (l.) †*Mológa,* a district-town with 4300 inhabitants.

367 V. (178 M.; r.) †**Ruibinsk.**—HOTELS. *Barkhatov,* R. 1¹/₂ rb.; *Centrálnaya,* R. 1-5, D. (1-6 p.m.) 60 cop. to 1 rb.; *Samokhvalov,* all three in the Krestóvaya.—Izvósitchik from the rail. station to the town 35, to the harbour or vice versâ 45, per drive 25, per hr. 50 cop.—RAILWAY STATION (*Restaurant*) for the Bologoye Railway (p. 267) and for the Yaroslavl Railway (p. 332), 1 M. to the W. of the centre of the town.—STEAMERS on the Volga daily to (5¹/₂ hrs.) *Yaroslavl* (fares 1 rb. 95, 1 rb. 25 cop.); to (15 hrs.) *Kostroma* (fares 3 rb. 30, 2 rb. 20 cop.); to (24 hrs.) *Kineshma* (fares 5 rb. 10, 3 rb. 65 cop.); to (40 hrs.) *Nizhni-Novgorod* (fares 6 rb. 60, 4 rb. 95 cop.).

Ruibinsk (350 ft.), the capital of a district in the government of Yaroslavl, is a brisk river-port situated on rising ground opposite the mouth of the *Tcheksná.* It carries on a trade in grain, and is the centre of the caviare industry. It contains 31,500 inhab., a number raised in summer to 100,000 and even more. The town is known to have existed as far back as the 11th century. On the Volga Quay (На́бережная) rises the conspicuous *Cathedral of the Transfiguration,* built in 1838; adjoining it is a lofty belfry. Close at hand are the Town Park and the Theatre. The town has also a Lutheran Church.

Below Ruibinsk the scenery of the banks becomes monotonous. The stream is broad and dotted with numerous sandbanks.—411 V †*Románov-Borisoglyebsk,* a district-town situated on both banks of the Volga, with 12,300 inhab. and a spinning-mill. In Boriso glyebsk, on the right bank, is the imposing Cathedral of the Resurrection, with five cupolas, erected in 1652-70.— 420 V. (r.) †*Konstantínov,* with chemical works.—435 V. (r.) †*Norskáya Fábrika,* a village with a cotton-mill.—439 V. (l.) †*Tolgski Monastery,* founded in 1314, and rebuilt after its destruction by the Poles in 1609. It has four churches. Beyond the monastery we soon see on the right bank the domes and towers of the picturesquely situated town of —

457 V. (305 M.) †**Yaroslávl** (r.), see p. 330.

469 V. (r.) *Sopelki*, a village where the so-called Byegunes or Stránniki, a sect of the Raskólniks, originated at the end of the 18th century. — 489 V. (r.) †*Babáiki.* About 1 V. from the bank is the *Convent of St. Nicholas the Wonder Worker* (Николо-Бабáевскій монастырь), a frequented place of pilgrimage. — Farther on we pass several sandy islands. — A little short of Kostroma, to the left, is the mouth of the river *Kostromá.*

523 V. (349 M.) †**Kostromá** (l.), see p. 332.

Below Kostroma the scenery improves. —563 V. (l.) †*Krásnoye*, a village where gold and silver ornaments, both genuine and imitation, are manufactured. —580 V. (r.) †*Plyoss* (Плессъ), a prettily situated little town with 2500 inhabitants.

627 V. (418 M.) †**Kíneshma** (r.), a district-town of 25,500 inhab., at the confluence of the *Kineshémka* with the Volga. — A railway (station 1 M. from the pier; izvóshtchik 40 cop.) runs hence to *Novki* (see p. 338).

648 V. (r.) † *Ryeshma*, a village with the *Makáryevski Convent.* — 683 V. (r.) † *Yúryevetz*, a pleasantly situated town with 5500 inhab., opposite which the *Unzha* enters the Volga.

Farther on both banks become flat. 722 V. (r.) † *Pútchezh*, Пучежъ, a market-town with 3200 inhabitants.

The bed of the river continues to increase in breadth, while the contrast between the higher right bank and the lower left bank becomes more strongly marked. — 750 V. (r.) † *Katúnki*, a village in the government of Nizhni-Novgorod, with 2000 inhab. and manufactories of leathern articles. — 758 V. (r.) † *Vasílyev*, a village· with 600 inhabitants.

779 V. (l.) †**Gorodétz**, a straggling village with 6300 inhab., where wooden ware and pryánniki or honey-cakes are made. In the Feódorovski Convent, which was founded at the beginning of the 13th cent., Alexander Nevski (p. 130) spent his last days as a monk, dying here on Nov. 14th, 1263.

792 V. (r.) †*Balakhna*, the capital of a district in the government of Nizhni-Novgorod, with 4700 inhabitants. Soon after leaving Balakhna we obtain a distant view of Nizhni-Novgorod, which, however, quickly vanishes. — 818 V. *Sórmovo*, with a large machine-shop (founded in 1849) and foundries. —A little later appears —

827 V. (551 M.; r.) †**Nizhni-Nóvgorod**, Нижній-Новгородъ (see p. 339), very picturesquely situated at the confluence of the *Oká* (here 700 yds. broad) with the Volga (here 500 yds. broad). The Oká, which is 933 M. in length, forms an ethnographical frontier. The inhabitants of the Volga district above this river are pure Slavs; below it begins the territory of Finnish and Tartar tribes, including Mordvins, Tcheremisses, Tchuvashes, Votyaks, Tartars, and Bashkirs. These races, which rival in number the Russian element of the population, have maintained their own manners and customs,

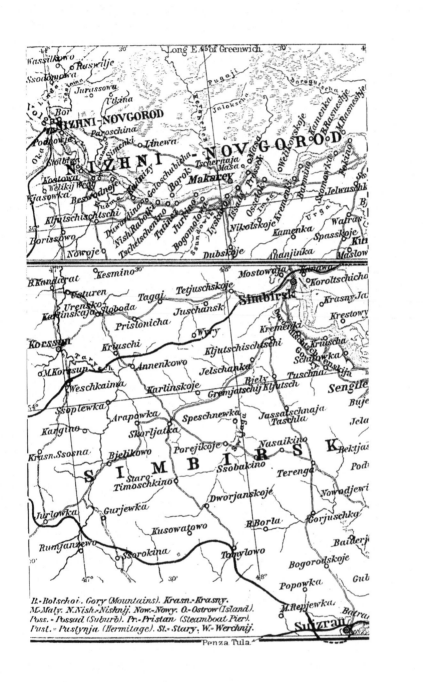

NORTH

Russkaja Ruika
Arda
Semskaja
48°
B.Kok
Sskoje
Kosmodemyansk
Kamarichi
Pojizkoje
Borskaje
Spasso-Geronewskoja Shebega
Seiwalowa
Koshla-Ssa
Tschereshnaja
Sselenikowa
chaishoje
Kushmary
Ujinskaja
Nowo Tronoa
Chaboksari
Nowosartu
Maryinsk
UraPowa
Kuschnikowo
Alexej
Koshwaschi
Nowo Tronoa
Pokrowskoje
Ninssart
Nowaja
Otary
Poi
Junga
Jangildino
Tschekuru
Ruschi
Arina
Tschekutu
Ikowo
Schingassy
Woronowa
Kinel
Isambai
Akramowo
Ziwilsk
Akasino
Koslowko
adrin
Nikolskoje
Ototschewo
Issakowo
Iwanowo
Njurschi
Lipowaja
Tiurlema
Sv
Woldajewo
Schumatowo
B.Schitma
Nowojischino
Beshbatu
na Gora
Russkija Ssorma
Tschuratschikowo
Pigali
Starmary
Nurlaty
K A
Schorkassy
Byssokowka
Nikolskoje
Melekskij
Melekess
Schichrany
Podgornoje
Kud
Nowaja Maina
Moscow
Mosharki
Wladim
Meriklinsk
Lebjashje
Mossejewka
Toburdanowa
W.Ind
Tscheremschan
Fillipowka
54°
Tarninskoje
Bis
Rjasonowo
Annenskaja
Jelchowka
B.Tojaba
Chrjuschtschewka
Kirilowka
Nowaja
Binoradka
Baiterjakowa
Taschelka
Mussorka
Kamenka
Urasgildino
NowyTschitschd
Taschla
Nowy Bujan
Buju
Wysselki
S A M A R A
St.Binoradka
Choroschenkoje
St.Stu
Jagodnoje
Wassiljewka
Krasny Jar
NowyLiptscl
Stawropol
Selenowka
Bogojawlenskoje
Nowo Saraschina
St.Schainu
Sheguli
Selegulewskija Gory
Sarewo Kurganskaja
Kaschin
Samarskaya Luka
Rochestwenskoje
Schawschljajewka
Perewoloka
Binnowka
Sokolija Gor
Alexejew
Natscha
Gjusan
Jermakowa
Wolga
S A M A R A
Wassilje
Obscharowka
Jekaterinowka
Woskressenskoje

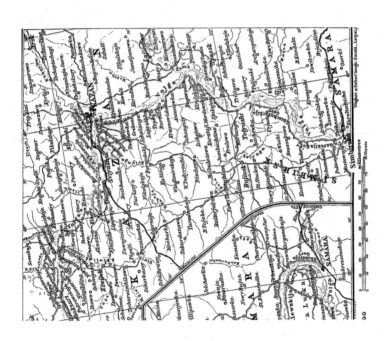

while the Tartars and Bashkirs have preserved to some extent also their national costumes and religion.

RAILWAY from Nizhni-Novgorod to Moscow, see R. 43. — Fares on the STEAMERS, see p. 340.

To the right we see several hamlets. The river increases in width.

49 V. (from Nizhni-Novgorod; r.) *Kádnitzi*, a large village.—
57 V. (r.) † *Rabotki*, a village with 1200 inhabitants. —81 V. (l.) Mouth of the *Kerzhenétz.*

84 V. (r.) *Lúiskovo*, a small town, situated 3 M. from the river, contains 10,200 inhab. and 9 churches. — Opposite, to the left, is the convent of *Makáryev*, marking the site where a yearly fair used to be held (p. 344). The town of Makaryev is now entirely without importance.

87 V. (r.) † *Isádi*, a village on the slope of the *Fadéyevi Hills.* — Near (124 V.: r.) *Bármino* and the village of *Fókino* large quantities of apples and other fruit are grown.

159 V. (r.) † *Vasilsúrsk*, a small town in the province of Nizhui Novgorod, prettily situated on the terraced bank of the river, surrounded by gardens, and lying 1 M. to the S. of the mouth of the *Surá.*

The banks of the Volga become more picturesque. 185 V. (l.) † *Yúrin*, a village with a château belonging to Count Sheremétyev. — To the left is the mouth of the *Vetlúga.*

204 V. (r.) † *Kozmodemyánsk*, the capital of a district in the government of Kazan, opposite the mouth of the *Rutka.* The inhabitants, 5400 in number, carry on a brisk trade in timber; walking-sticks are offered for sale at the pier. — Near Kozmodemyansk begin the settlements of the Tcheremises.

259 V. (r.) † *Tcheboksári*, a district-town with 5500 inhab. and 14 churches. Not far from the bank is the Monastery of the Trinity (Tróitzki), dating from 1566.

289 V. (r.) † *Sunduír*, a market-town situated on the slope. — 349 V. (r.) † *Kozlóvka.* — Farther on we see to the right the towers and domes of the loftily situated Sviyazhsk.

359 V. (r.) † *Vyazóvuiya*, near the railway station of *Sviyazhsk* (P. 364) and the bridge of the Moscow & Kazan Railway (R. 47).

About 8 M. to the S.E. of Vyazovuiya and 2 M. to the S. of the Volga lies the small district-town of **Sviyázhsk,** founded in 1551 by Iván the Terrible. St. Herman (d. 1569), the apostle of this region, is buried in the Bogoródnitzki Convent, which was founded in 1555.

Between *Morkvashí* and *Verkhni Uslón* several attractive points are passed on the right bank.

390 V. (259 M.; l.) † Landing-place for *Kazan* (Kazánskaya Pristan), where the steamer halts for 3-4 hrs. The city lies 4¹/₂ M. inland; izvóshtchiks and tramway, see p. 352. On the way to the town we see, to the left of the embankment, the monument commemorating the conquest of Kazan (p. 352) and the white buildings of the Kremlin with the pointed Syuyumbéka Tower (P. 353).

Kazán, Казань. — Hotels. *Frántziya* (Pl. a; D, 2), R. 1-8 rb., bed-linen 25, D. (2-6) 65 cop. to 1 rb.; *Passage* (Pl. d; D, 2); *Yevropéiskaya* (Pl. b; D, 2); *Centrálnaya* (Pl. c; D, 2), these four in the Voskresénskaya; *Shtchetínkin* (Pl. f; D, 2), Prolómnaya; *Banártzev* (Pl. e; D, 2), Právaya Tchórnoózerskaya, R. from 80 cop.

Restaurants. *Kitái*, Voskresénskaya (Pl. D, 2); *Tchórnoye Ózero* (p. 354), déj. (11-2) 90 cop., D. (2-6) 1¹/₄ rb., military band in the evening.

Pleasure Resorts. *Panáyev Garden* (Pl. E, 2), Bolshaya Lyadskáya, with summer-theatre and variety-show; *Russian Switzerland* (p. 354). Theatre (Pl. E, 2), Theatre Square, in winter only.

Izvóshtchik (tariff) from the steamer-landing to the town or vice versâ 80 cop. to 1 rb.; from the railway station to the town or vice versâ 30 cop.; per drive in the town 20 (at night 30), to Russian Switzerland 30, per hr. within the town 40 cop.

Electric Tramways. From the Steamer Landing (Pl. A, 3) to the Su-kónnaya Suburb (Pl. E, F, 4) viâ the Admiralty Suburb (Pl. B, 2) and the Prolómnaya (Pl. D, 2, 3), 6¹/₄ M., fare 20 cop. — From the Alexander Monu-ment (Pl. 11; D, 2) to Russian Switzerland (Pl. F, 2), fare 5 cop. — From the Gostinodvórskaya (Pl. D, 2) to the S. end of the Yekaterininskaya (Pl. E, 4; Tartar Suburb), fare 5 cop. — From the Railway Station (Pl. D, 3) to the Market viâ the Theatre (Pl. E, 2), fare 5-10 cop.

General Post Office (Pl. E, 2), Theatre Square. — Telegraph Office (Pl. 22; E, 2), Gruzinskaya.

Steamers. On the Volga: to *Nizhni-Novgorod* (fares 5 rb. 80, 2 rb. 95 cop.); to *Simbirsk* (5 rb. 75, 3 rb. 80 cop.); to *Samara* (9 rb. 15, 5 rb. 95 cop.); to *Suizran* (11 rb, 25, 7 rb. 30 cop.); to *Saratov* (15 rb. 85, 10 rb. 20 cop.); to *Kamuishin* (18 rb. 85, 12 rb. 10 cop.); to *Tzaritzuin* (21 rh. 35, 13 rb. 75 cop.); to *Astrakhan* (26 rb. 75, 17 rb. 20 cop.). — On the Kama: to (911 V.; 607 M.) *Perm* (11, 7¹/₂ rb.); to *Ufa*, see p. 370.

The Volga steamers stop at Kazan 3-4 hrs., giving time for a hasty visit to the town. The visitor should take the tramway or an izvóshtchik to the Kremlin and ascend the Syuyumbéka Tower; he should then proceed by cab viâ the Voskresénskaya to the University, and return past the Church of SS. Peter & Paul (view) to the Harbour.

Kazán (260 ft.; Tartar 'kettle'), the capital of the government of that name, the seat of the Archbishop of Kazan and Sviyazhsk, and the headquarters of the 16th Army Corps, lies 4¹/₂ M. from the Volga, on the left bank of the *Kazánka*, on several hills rising in the midst of a plain which is inundated far and wide in spring by the overflow of the two rivers. Pop. 188,000, including 30,000 Tar-tars (comp. p. xlv). Besides numerous Greek Catholic churches, Kazan contains a Lutheran church, a Roman Catholic church, and 13 mosques. Its educational institutions include a university, an imperial theological seminary, and a veterinary institute. — The trade of Kazan is very considerable; it is celebrated for its Russian leather, and also manufactures candles, soap, and other articles.

Kazan was founded on its present site by Khan Ulu-Makhmet in 1437, and became the capital of a Tartar kingdom which was indepen-dent of the Golden Horde. Iván III. captured the town in 1469 and ap-pointed Makhmet-Amin as his vicegerent. This ruler, however, massacred all the Russians in the place in 1504, and invaded the principality of Moscow at the head of his army. Disputes as to the succession after the death of Makhmet-Amin (1519), and continual risings in Kazan led re-peatedly to armed intervention on the part of Iván the Terrible, who finally captured the town on Oct. 2nd, 1552, after a long siege, and incorporated the entire khanate of Kazan with his own dominions. Kazan has been

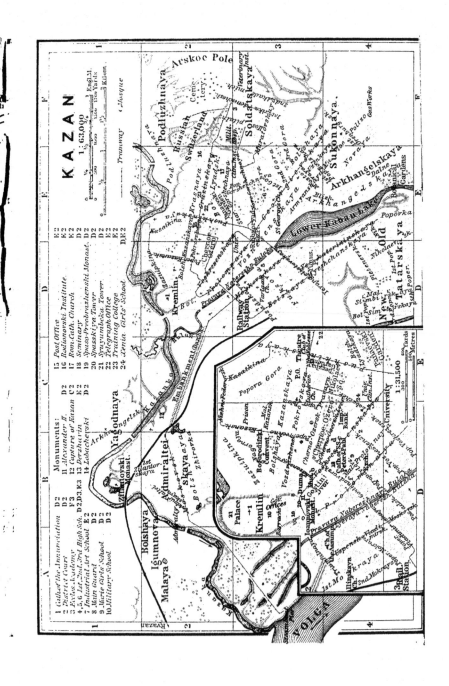

the capital of a province since 1708. In 1774 the town was destroyed by the rebel Pugatchév, but it was rebuilt by Catherine II.

The **Kremlin** (Pl. D, 2), in the N.W. part of the city, was founded and surrounded with palisades by Khan Ulu-Makhmet (p. 352). The stone wall was erected by Iván IV. Three of the old gate-towers still exist: the *Spásskiya* (Спасскія ворота; Pl. 20, D 2), through which the Kremlin is entered from the Voskresén-skaya; the *Táinitzkaya*, which leads to the Kazanka and to the suburb of Kizitcha; and the *Pyátnitzkaya*, on the N.E. side.

Passing through the Spásskiya Gate, or Gate of the Redeemer, we have on our right the extensive *Government Administration Build-ings* (Присутственныя мѣста). To the left stands the *Spaso-Preobrazhénski Convent* (Pl. 19), founded in 1556. Its church con-tains the tombs of several metropolitans and bishops. Farther to the N. is the *Cathedral of the Annunciation* (Pl. 1), built in 1562 and frequently renewed. In the interior, between the two columns on the left, in front of the ikonostás, is a shrine with the relics of Archbp. Guri (d. 1563). The treasury contains rich vestments and ecclesiastical vessels. — Beyond the cathedral is the *Palace,* dating from 1848 and now occupied by the Governor. To the left is the most interesting building in the Kremlin, the brick —

*Syuyumbéka Tower (Башня Сююмбёки; Pl. 21), a relic of Tartar architecture, rising in seven stages to a height of 250 ft. A guide may be obtained at the office of the Governor (in the left wing of the palace). The view from the top is very fine, but the ascent becomes pretty arduous beyond the fourth story. According to legend, the Tartar princess Syuyumbéka threw herself from the top of the tower in 1552, in her despair at the ruin of her native town.

The principal street of Kazan is the VOSKRESÉNSKAYA, begin-ning at the Spásskiya Gate of the Kremlin (see above). The adjoin-ing bronze *Statue of Alexander II.* (Pl. 11) is by Sherwood (1895). At the beginning of the street, to the right, is the **Trading Factory** (Гостиный дворъ; Pl. D, 2); in it is the *Civic Museum,* containing antiquities from Bulgari (p. 355), objects of the Stone Age, Tartar curiosities, paintings, coins, and natural history col-lections. It is open daily, except Mon., 10-5 (adm. 10 or 15 cop., Sun. and holidays 5 cop.; Russian catalogue 5-15 cop.).

To the N. is the *Convent of the Virgin Mother of Kazan* (Казанскій Богородицкій женскій монастырь; Pl. D, 2), dat-ing from 1579. On the spot where the winter-church of the nunnery now stands, tradition relates that a wonder-working picture of the Virgin was found buried in the earth; this is regarded with great veneration, and has been removed to St. Petersburg (comp. p. 104). The Cathedral, built in 1798-1803, is surmounted by a cupola.

A little to the S.E. of the Factory, in a commanding situation, is the two-storied *Cathedral of SS. Peter & Paul* (Pl. D, 2), built by a Florentine architect in 1726. The exterior is decorated with paintings. The terrace affords a fine view. — In the Bolshaya Proló-mnaya (Pl. D, 2, 3) is the interesting *Domestic Industries Museum* (Кустáрный Музéй Казáнскаго губéрнскаго зéмства; open free 10-3, Sun. and holidays 12-3; closed on Sat.). — To the right, at the end of the Voskresénskaya, arc the buildings of the —

University (Pl. D, E, 3), which was founded in 1804 and is attended by 2100 students. To the N.W. is a bust of the mathematician *Lobatchevski* (d. 1846; Pl. 14), by Dillon (1896). With the university are connected a Botanical Garden (Pl. E, 4) and an Ethnographical Museum. The *Library*, the nucleus of which is the collection of Prince Potemkin, contains 304,000 vols. (open in summer 10-2, in winter 9-3; librarian, N. St. Vasilyev).

To the N. of the university are a small and somewhat neglected park named the *Tchórnoye Ózero* (Чёрное Озеро; Pl. D, 2; restaurant, see p. 352), the *Lutheran Church* (Pl. E, 2), and the *Theatre* (Pl. E, 2). In the Derzhávin Garden is a seated bronze figure, by Thon (1846), of the poet *Derzhávin* (1743-1816; Pl. 13), who was a native of Kazan. Farther to the E., and reached by tramway along the Gruzínskaya, is the so-called *Russian Switzerland* (Рýсская Швейцáрія; Pl. E, F, 2), an extensive natural park, at the entrance to which is the pleasure-garden mentioned at p. 352.

The *Tartar Quarter* (Pl. D, E, 4) contains several unpretending mosques (tramway, see p. 352). The steamer trip on *Lake Kabán* (Óзеро Кабáнъ; Pl. E, 3, 4; 2 hrs. in all; fare 20 cop.) is interesting.

About 1 M. to the W. of the city rises the *Memorial of the Capture of Kazan* (Pl. 12; C, 2), erected in 1823 and consisting of a truncated pyramid, 70 ft. in height, with a two-columned portico on each side. The Russian inscription on the W. side is 'Въ пáмять побéды надъ Татáрами 1552'. The interior is fitted up as a chapel, below which is a vault, with a large open coffin containing bones and skulls dug up during the construction of the monument. Fee of 15-20 cop. to the keeper.

The former *Admiralty* (Pl. B, 2), founded by Peter the Great in 1718, has gradually grown to the dimensions of a suburban quarter. A shed here contains the large galley 'Tver', in which the Empress Catherine made her trip down the Volga in 1767 (hardly worth a visit). — A little to the N. of the Admiralty Quarter, on the Zilántov Hill, is the *Zilántov Convent* (Pl. B, 1), founded by Iván IV. in 1559. — The Yágodnaya Slobodá (Pl. B, C, 1), on the right bank of the Kazanka, contains the attractive *Alafúzov People's Palace* and a *Powder Mill* (Пороховóй завóдъ), the latter built in 1776-87.

From Kazan to Perm, 911 V. (607 M.). Steamer up the Kama in 4 days (fares, see p. 352; D. 70 cop. to 1 rb. 10 cop.). — The *Kama*, called by the Tartars *Agh-Idél* or 'White River', is 1764 V. (1150 M.) in length, and flows through the governments of Perm, Ufa, Vyatka, and Kazan. Its banks show as rich a confusion of races as does the Volga between Nizhni-Novgorod and Samara. The races represented on both banks of the Kama include Russians, Bashkirs, Meshtcheryaks, Teptyars, Voguls, Votyaks, and many more. — At (68 V.) *Bogorodsk* (p. 355) the steamer quits the Volga, turns to the left, and enters the Kama. — 185 V. *Tchistopol*, the chief grain-port (rye) on the Kama, lies on the left bank, and is the capital of a district in the province of Kazan. Pop. 25,000. — At (251 V.) *Sokolki* we pass the mouth of the *Vyatka* (left). — 302 V.

Yelábuga, on the right bank, a district-capital in the government of
Vyatka. Pop. 17,400.—Between (394 V.) *Pyáni Bor* and (419 V.) *Kara-
kulino* the *Byélaya* (steamer to Ufa, see p. 370) enters the Kama on the
right.—501 V. *Sarápul,* on the right bank, a district-town in the government of Vyatka. Pop. 19,700 —911 V. (607 M.) *Perm,* see p. 259.

From Kazan to *Timiryázevo* (Penza, Nizhni-Novgorod) and *Moscow,*
see R. 47. The railway station (Pl. C, D, 3; restaurant) lies on the W.
side of the city.

CONTINUATION OF VOLGA VOYAGE. As we leave Kazan we enjoy
a fine retrospect of it to the left. To the right, on the slopes of
the Uslón Hill, is *Verkhni Uslón,* a colony of datchas or villas.—
458 V. (r.) †*Bogorodsk,* a village.

464 V. (l.) *Mouth of the Kama* (comp. p. 354). The clear water
of this stream does not mix very readily with the muddy Volga. The
Kama forms a dividing line in the geognostic profile of the banks of
the Volga. The hitherto predominant marl strata of the Permian
and Triassic formations now give way to Jurassic limestone, which
is soon succeeded by chalk. To the limestone formation belong the
Shtchutchi ('Pike'), *Undáriski,* and *Gorodíshtchenski Hills,* which
begin (with a height of ca. 100 ft.) at Tetyushi. The rest of the
district to the S. of Kazan is covered with forests of oak, pine, fir,
and other trees. Large pastures extend on both banks of the Volga,
and the wool shorn in this district is highly valued.

487 V. (l.) †*Spasski Zatón* is the port for the town of *Spassk*
(3100 inhab.), 8 M. to the E. — The right bank is now again hilly.

507 V. (l.). About 6 V. (4 M.) from the river, near the village of
Uspénskoye or *Bolgár,* are the **Ruins of Bulgári,** which may
be reached from (13 M.) Spasski Zaton (see above) viâ Novo-Mordó-
voye. In the middle of the village stands the Church of the Assumption, about 660 yds. to the S.E. of which is a well-preserved minaret.
The ruins, largely overgrown with vegetation, were rediscovered in
the time of Peter the Great, and were afterwards partly used in the
construction of the village.

The Bulgars or Bulgarians were a Turko-Finnish race, the origins of
which are veiled in darkness. They seem to have reached the Volga
about the beginning of the Christian era. Towards the middle of the
10th cent., when their capital, Bulgari, was a prosperous and important
place, they became converts to Islam. The Mongolian storm, which
swept over E. Europe in the 13th cent., shook the foundations of the
Bulgarian kingdom, though it still retained nominal princes of its own.
It regained a measure of prosperity under the Khans of the Golden
Horde, but Timur put an end to it at the close of the 14th century. A
little later the place of the Bulgarian kingdom was taken by the khanate
of Kazan under Ulu-Makhmet (p. 352).

514 V. (r.) † *Tetyushi,* the capital of a district in the government
of Kazan. Pop. 6000.— We now pass several wooded islands. The
small river *Máina,* to the left, forms the boundary between the
governments of Kazan and Samara. Below it the Volga makes a
wide sweep towards the W.

613 V. (r.) †Simbírsk, Симбирскъ. — Hotels (Номерá). *Staro-Troitzkaya*, Spásskaya, R. 1-3 rb., bed-linen 20 cop., D. (1-6 p.m.) 60 cop. to 1 rb. 20 cop., with fair restaurant; *Kartashóv*, Spásskaya; *Rossíya*, Dvortzóvaya; *Novo-Tróitzkaya*, Moskóvskaya. — Извóзнчик from the steamer-landing to the town 80, from the rail. station to the town 50, to the steamer-landing 60, per drive 25, per hr. 60 cop. — An electric tram-way is to be opened in 1914. — **Promenades.** *Nicholas Garden*, near the Court House; *Vladímir Garden*, in the Venétz, with a summer-theatre (restaurant) and fine view of the Volga.

Simbírsk (Tartar, 'Hill of the Winds'), a provincial capital with 64,000 inhab., lies picturesquely on the steep right bank of the Volga. The elevation (410 ft.) over which the town spreads itself rises between the Volga and the *Sviyaga*, which joins the larger river above Kazan. The town, which is the seat of a Greek Catholic bishop, contains 29 Greek churches, a Roman Catholic church, and a Lutheran church.

Simbirsk was built in 1648 from the designs of the Boyar Khitróvo, who surrounded it with palisades to defend it from the Tartars. He also erected a small fortress with seven towers, 3 M. from the town, and connected the two by the 'Simbirsk Line', consisting of an earthen rampart and a moat. In 1670 Simbirsk was unsuccessfully besieged by Stenka Razin, the robber of the Volga. It became the capital of a province in 1796.

The central and highest part of the town is the *Venétz*, and from it the so-called *Lower Town* descends in steps to the Sviyaga and the Volga. On the slope above the Volga runs the Peter Paul Street (Петропáвловскій спускъ), which is 2 M. in length. From the W. end of the Peter Paul Street we proceed to the N. across the Bol-shaya Sarátovskaya, the shady main street of the town, then turn to the right, and follow the Komissáriatskaya to the Cathedral Square (Собóрная плóщадь), in the middle of which stands the *Tróitzki Cathedral*, erected in 1824-41. Adjacent, to the N., is the Nicholas Garden, on the S.W. side of which is the *Cathedral of St. Nicholas* (1712), while on the S.E. side is the *Court House* (Присýтственныя мѣстá). Opposite the N. side of the Nicholas Garden are the *Club of the Noblesse*, with the Karamzin Public Library and the *Governor's Residence*. To the W. of the last is the Karamzín Square, containing a monument, erected in 1845 from Halberg's designs, to the historian *Karamzín* (1766-1826). On the W. side of the square is the *Convent of the Redeemer* (Спáсскій дѣвичій монасты́рь), founded in 1648.

A branch-railway runs from Simbirsk to (155 V. or 101 M.) *Inza* (p. 367). The station is on the S. side of the town, ¼ hr.'s drive from the centre of it. — Another branch-line runs from *Tchasóvnya* (opposite Simbirsk, on the left bank; railway-bridge in course of construction) to (340 V. or 225 M.) *Bugulma*, whence it is being continued to Ufa (p. 369).

Continuation of the Volga Voyage. Passengers are advised to take the steamer starting from Simbirsk at midnight, in order to traverse the 'Bow of Samara' (p. 357), the most beautiful part of the Volga, by daylight. — Just beyond Simbirsk the contrast between the high right bank and the level steppes of the left bank is particularly marked.

671 V. (r.) †**Sengiléi,** the chief town of a district, with 8800
inhabitants. The chalk hills to the N., W., and S. are known as the
'Ears of Sengilei' (Сенгилéйскіе Ушú). Farther on, to the right,
we pass the *Ilyínski* and the *Novodyevítche Hills.*—719 V. (r.)
†*Novodyevítche,* a village in a ravine, with 4500 inhabitants.—
740 V. (r.) *Usólye,* 2³/₄ M. from the river, contains the manor-house
of Count Orlóv-Davúidov,- the owner of almost the whole of the land
within the 'Bow of Samara' (see below).

To the right are the picturesque *Hills of Zhigulév* (Жигу-
лéвскія гóры), a range of limestone hills, 60 M. long, thickly wooded
with oak and lime, and intersected by numerous ravines. They rise
sharply from the river to a height of 750 ft. Many popular legend
are current about the Volga robbers who once infested the recesses
of these hills.—At this point the left bank is also hilly.

762 V. (l.) †*Stávropol.* The landing-place of the steamers is
3 M. from the town of that name (6500 inhab.).

At Stavropol the Volga is compelled, by the encroachment of the
Zhigulev Hills, to deviate towards the E. About 60 V. (40 M.) farther
on it turns again to the S., while beyond Samara it flows in a W.
direction towards Suizran (100 M.). The neck or chord of this so-
called *Bow of Samara* (Самáрская Лукá), from Zhigúli to *Pere-
válovka,* is only 13 M. in length. The hills on the bank attain a
height of 650-1000 ft.—812 V. (l.) Mouth of the *Sok.* To the S.
rises the huge and conspicuous *Tzarev Kurgán,* a bare hill surrounded by the Sok (two sides) and the Kurúl.— We pass through
the so-called *Samara Gate* (Самáрскія ворóта), between the
Syernuiya Hills on the W. and the Sókolovuiya Hills on the E.

848 V. or 565 M. (l.) †**Samára,** Самара. — The steamer stays here
3-3¹/₂ hrs. Izvóshtchiks (see below) at the landing-stage.—The RAILWAY
STATION (good restaurant) is on the E. side of the town, about 1³/₄ M. from
the Alexéyevskaya Square. [On leaving the square we turn to the left
through the Ulitza Lva Tolstogo, formerly the Mozkatélnaya ; after 25 min.
we turn again to the left through the Dvoryánskaya.]

HOTELS. **National,* cor. of Sarátovskaya and Panskáya, R. 3 rb
Grand-Hôtel, Dvoryánskaya 111, R. 2-5¹/₂ rb., D. (1-6 p.m.) 90 cop. & 1 rb.
20 cop.; *Centrálnaya,* Dvoryánskaya 103, with good restaurant, R. 1-6 rb.,
bed-linen 50 cop., D. (1-6 p.m.) 90 cop. & 1 rb. 20 cop., omn. 50 cop.; *Bristol,*
Dvoryánskaya 86, D. 65 cop. & 1 rb. 10 cop.—*Café Jean,* Dvoryánskaya
76, near the Alexéyevskaya Square (also confectioner).

PLEASURE RESORT. *Strúkovski Garden,* at the N. end of the Dvoryánskaya, with restaurant and fine view of the Volga; music after 7 p.m.

POST & TELEGRAPH OFFICE in the Panskáya, cor. of the Dvoryánskaya.

IZVÓSHTCHIK from the Volga to the rail. station 50, from the station
to the town 40, per drive 25 cop.—TRAMWAY from the station through
the town; also in summer from the Zemstvo Hospital to Dr. Póstnikov's
Establishment (p. 358; fare 10 cop.).

STEAMBOATS *upstream* to Kazan (fares 9 rb. 15, 5 rb. 95 cop.) and to
Nizhni-Novgorod (13 rh. 60, 8 rb. 70 cop.); *downstream* to Suizran (3 rb. 30,
2 rh. 20 cop.), to Saratov (9 rb. 15, 5 rb. 95 cop.), to Kamuishin (12 rb. 25,
7 rb. 90 cop.), to Tzaritzuin (14 rb. 80, 9 rb. 60 cop.), and to Astrakhan
(20 rb. 35, 13 rb. 10 cop.).

Samára (185 ft.), situated at the confluence of the Samara and the Volga, on the high left bank of that river, is the capital of a government, the see of a Greek Catholic bishop, and the headquarters of the 24th Army Corps. Pop. 146,000. It contains 24 Greek churches, a Lutheran church, and two convents, carries on a brisk trade, especially in corn, and is a busy manufacturing place (Zhigu-lévski Brewery). The town is said to have been founded in 1586 to protect the Russian frontier against the inroads of the Kalmucks, Bashkirs, and Nogai Tartars, and to cover the trading-route from Kazan to Astrakhan. It became the capital of a district in 1780 and of a province in 1851.

From the bank of the Volga we ascend to the E. by the Zavód-skaya to the (10 min.) Alexéyevskaya Square, with the *Government Offices* and the *District Court*. In the middle of the square stands a *Monument to Alexander II.*, by Sherwood, unveiled in 1889. The lofty granite pedestal which bears the bronze statue of the Tzar is surrounded by figures of a Peasant, a Circassian, Bulgaria, and Asia, referring respectively to the abolition of serfdom, the conquest of the Caucasus, the delivery of the Balkan Slavs from the Turkish yoke, and the acquisition of Central Asia.— About $3/4$ M. to the S., on the tongue of land between the Volga and Samara, are the *Church of the Kazan Virgin Mother*, built in 1730-35, and the *Spaso Preobrazhénskaya Church*, founded in 1685.

The most important of the streets traversing the town from N. to S. are the *Preobrazhénskaya*, the *Kazánskaya*, the *Voznesén-skaya*, the *Dvoryánskaya*, and the *Sarátovskaya*. The first of these, adjoining the Volga, contains the *Church of the Annunciation*, built in 1785. At the N. end of the Dvoryánskaya, which crosses the Alexéyevskaya Square, and $3/4$ M. from the square, lies the *Strúkovski Garden* (p. 357). To the E. of this are the *Theatre* and the blue-domed *Alexander Nevski Cathedral*, erected in 1894 by Zhiber. The chief business thoroughfares are the Dvoryánskaya and the Panskáya, running at right angles to each other.

About $1^1/_2$ M. to the N. of the cathedral is the *Zemstvo Hospital*. From this point we take the tramway to the N., passing near the *Annáyevo Kumiss Establishment* (on the left), to (2 M.) *Dr. Póstnikov's Kumiss Establishment* (Кумысолечéбное заведéніе дóктора Пóстникова; cab from the Strúkovski Garden in $1/_2$ hr., fare there & back 2 rb., including 1 hr.'s waiting). This establish-ment, the oldest of its kind in Russia (founded in 1858), lies in a park on the high bank of the Volga, $2/_3$ M. from the river, and con-sists of isolated cottages (pens., incl. kumiss, 100 rb. per month).

Kumiss, also known as *Milk Wine*, is prepared by fermentation from mare's milk, and is said to be easily digestible and very nourishing. The process of fermentation produces lactic acid, carbonic acid, and alcohol, the first two of which aid digestion, while the latter imparts lightly stimulating quality. The patient generally begins with one or two bottles daily and gradually raises the number to five. The best time for the cure is spring and early summer.

RAILWAY from Samara to *Moscow*, see R. 48; to *Orenburg*, see R. 49; to *Tchelyabinsk* (Trans-Siberian Railway, R. 77), see R. 50.

Beyond Samara the woods gradually disappear and the hills diminish to a height of 130-165 ft. The geological formation of the banks, consisting of cretaceous and limestone rock honeycombed with caves, continues the same. The left bank consists of undulating prairie, generally covered with luxuriant grass.

883 V. (l.) † *Yekaterinovka;* 922 V. (r.) *Petchérskoye*, with asphalt works. Just short of (937 V.) † *Batraki* (r.), a station on the railway from (Moscow) Suizran to Samara (R. 48), we pass under the large railway-bridge.

963 V. (642 M.; r.) †**Suizran,** Сызрань. — In summer the STEAMER LANDING PLACE is at the island of *Rakov*, 3¹/₃ M. from the town. HOTELS. *Yevropéiskaya*, Bolshaya, R. 1¹/₂-4 rb., bed-linen 40, D. (1-5 p.m.) 65 cop. to 1 rb.; *Centrálnuiye Nomerá.* — IzVÓSHTCHIK from the rail. station to the town 30, from the town to the summer harbour 75 cop.

Suizran, the chief town of a district in the government of Simbirsk, lies on the *Suizran Voloshka* and the little river *Kruimza*, the ravine of which divides the town into two parts. The town, which dates from 1683, was destroyed by fire in 1906, and has since been rebuilt. Pop. 46,000.

RAILWAY STATION (Restaurant, fair) for all lines, about ¹/₂ M. to the N. of the town. Railway to *Samara*, see R. 48a; to *Ryazhsk* (Moscow), see RR. 48a, 48b; to *Ruzáyevka* (Moscow, Nizhni Novgorod), see R. 48c. Voyage down the Volga from Suizran to *Astrakhan*, see R. 61.

46. From Moscow to Tula and Kursk
(Kharkov, Sebastopol).

502 V. (333 M.). Railway in 12 hrs. (ordinary train) or 9¹/₂ hrs. (express; fares 16 rb. 25, 10 rb. 45 cop.; reserved seat 1¹/₂ rb.; sleeping-car 4 rb., 3 rb.).

Moscow, see p. 269. The train starts from the Kursk & Nizhni-Novgorod Station, on leaving which we see the Andrónov Convent (p. 314) on the right. — 10 V. *Lyublinó-Dátchnoye* (p. 321); 18 V. *Tzaritzuino-Dátchnoye* (p. 322); 40 V. *Podólsk*, a small district-town of 9000 inhab. with a large cement factory. Between (60 V.) *Stolbováya* and (70 V.) *Lopásnya* the Russians gained a victory over the Crim-Tartars in 1572.

93 V. **Sérpukhov** *(Railway Restaurant),* an industrial district-town with 36,000 inhab. in the province of Moscow, is situated on the small river *Nara*, which joins the Oká a little farther to the S. The Cathedral of the Trinity was built by Prince Vladímir Andréyevitch in 1380 and remodelled in the 18th century.

About 4 M. beyond Serpukhov the train crosses the *Oká*, which here forms the boundary of the province of Tula and has already

attained a width of 220 yds. — The farther we penetrate to the S.
into the fertile government of Tula, the more do the villages differ
from those in the more northern provinces. The houses are still
usually built of wood, but in a style that unmistakably indicates
that we have passed beyond the luxuriant forests of the N. The
art of wood-carving is lost. The roofs generally consist of thatch.

182 V. (121 M.) **Tula, Тула.** — The *Railway Station* (Restaurant,
very fair; stall for Tula wares, prices high) lies on the W. side of the
town, 2 M. from the Kremlin. — HOTELS. *Tchernuishóvskaya Gostínitza
(Tchaikin's Hotel)*, Kíyevskaya, cor. of Ploshtchadnáya, R. 2, D. 1¹/₄-1³/₄,
omn. ¹/₂ rb., very fair; *Artél*, Kíyevskaya 1, near the Kremlin, R. 1-3¹/₂,
D. (1-7 p.m.) ³/₄-1¹/₄ rb., omn. 40 cop.; *Kommértcheskaya*, Vorónezhskaya.
— RESTAURANT. *Kremlin Garden* (p. 361), D. (1-7 p.m.) ³/₄-1¹/₄ rb. —
IZVÓSHTCHIK from or to the rail. station 50, per hr. 50 cop. — TRAMWAY
(5 cop.) from the station through the town. — *Baths* in the Antónovskiya
Bani, Gryazevskaya.

The so-called *Tula Wares*, consisting of objects in brass (samovars),
nickel-plate, iron, and steel (knives), are widely known, and may be advantageously purchased at the shops of Babáshev (Kíyevskaya 6) and
Shtchelkin (Posólskaya 54). The so-called *Tula Work*, consisting of black
enamel inlaid with silver, is often imitated, most successfully in the
governments of Vologda (Ústyug and Totma) and Moscow. — *Tula Sugar
Biscuits* (Пряники) may be obtained from Byelolípetzki, Pyatnítzkaya 10,
a little to the N. of the Kremlin.

Tula (820 ft.), the industrial capital of the government of the
same name and the seat of the Greek Catholic bishop of Tula and
Byclév, lies on both sides of the *Upá*, an affluent of the Oká. Pop.
137,000 (many artisans). The town contains a Lutheran, a Roman
Catholic, and numerous Greek Catholic churches. Tula is first mentioned in 1146. Like all the towns to the S. of the Oká, it had
much to suffer from the inroads of the Tartars. The iron deposits
in the vicinity of Tula were discovered in the 16th cent., and the
first gun-factory was established in 1632, by a Dutchman named
Vienius. The prosperity of the town dates from 1712, when Peter
the Great established the Imperial Small Arms Factory here.

From the railway station (tramway) we proceed straight along
the Suvórovskaya, and at its end (1¹/₂ M.) we turn to the right
through the Posólskaya. The latter soon turns to the left, and
farther on (7 min.) crosses the Kíyevskaya, the main street of the
town. The N. part of the Kíyevskaya (to the left) passes quite near
the Kremlin (see below); in the S. part are the *Government Offices*
(r.), the *District Court* (l.), the *Assembly House of the Nobles* (r.),
containing a concert-room, and (No. 56, on the right) a *Museum of
Domestic Industries* (porter at the rear of the building). — At the
N. end of the Kíyevskaya, to the left of the entrance to the Kremlin,
is the *City Library*, built in 1912, with a museum. The KREMLIN,
about 985 ft. long and 630 ft. wide, was built in the 16th cent. and
restored in 1784 and 1824. Its N. side abuts on the Upá. Within
its walls lie the guard-house, the *Cathedral of the Assumption*
(1744), and (to the N. of the latter) the *Cathedral of the Epiphany.*

The Kremlin is surrounded by the *Kremlin Garden*, containing a restaurant (p. 360).—A little to the E. of the Kremlin, in the Sadóvi Pereúlok, are the *Archbishop's Palace* and a Collection of Ecclesiastical Antiquities (Пала́та дре́вностей; open free on Sun., 12-2).

On the N. side of the Kremlin is a wooden bridge crossing the Upá, the water of which is dammed up for use in the arms factory. To the left, on the Upá, are the extensive buildings of the IMPERIAL SMALL ARMS FACTORY (Импера́торскій оруже́йный заво́дъ), which was erected under the superintendence of an Englishman named Trewheller. In the grounds, on the S. side, is a bronze statue of Peter the Great by Bach (1912).

FROM TULA TO YELETZ, 229 V. (153 M.), railway in 9 hrs.—Beyond (47 V.) *Uzlováya* (p. 364) the train traverses the *Moscow Coal Basin*. 93 V. *Mályovka* (Малевка), with the coal-pits of Count Bóbrinski; 104 V. *Vólovo* (see below); 155 V. *Yefrémov* (Rail. Restaurant).—229 V. *Yelétz*, see p. 362. From Tula to *Vyazma*, see p. 254; to *Samara*, see R. 48 a.

About $2^1/_4$ M. to the S.W. of (193 V.) *Zásyeka*, a villa-colony (carr. 50 cop.), lies **Yásnaya Polyana** (carr. from Tula and back in 5-6 hrs. 4-5 rb.; the Tolstói Museum at Moscow arranges excursions), the birthplace of Count Leo Nikoláyevitch Tolstói (1828-1910; comp. below). His house may be visited every Sun. (10-1) on the production of tickets obtained gratis in Moscow at the Magasin Pozrédnik, Petróvskiya Line (Pl. D, 3; *II*). In the *Park* (fingerpost, На Моги́лу), on the so-called Stari Zakás Hill, is the tomb of Tolstói, surrounded by nine oaks.—203 V. *Shtchekinó*, about $4^1/_2$ M. from Yasnaya Polyana.—259 V. *Gorbatchóvo.*

FROM GORBATCHOVO TO BOGOYAVLENSK (224 V. or 148 M.), railway in 8 hrs.—59 V. *Vólovo* (Rail. Restaurant), see above.—About 14 M. to the N. of (107 V.) *Kulikóvo Pole*, and not far from the *Don*, is the battlefield of *Kulikóvo*, where Grand-Duke Demetrius Ivánovitch Donskói defeated the Mongols under Khan Mamai on Sept. 8th, 1380; a bronze tablet was erected in 1848 on the Krasni Kholm to commemorate the victory.—169 V. **Astápovo** (Rail. Restaurant). It was here that Count Tolstói (comp. above) died in the house of the station-master on Nov. 7th (20th), 1910. Branch-lines to (105 V.) Yeletz (p. 362) and to (28 V.) Troekurovo (p. 432). — 202 V. *Ranenbúrg*, see p. 432.—224 V. (148 M.) *Bogoyavlénsk* (Rail. Restaurant), see p. 427.

From Gorbatchovo a branch-line runs W. to (132 V.) *Sukhinitchi* (p. 376).

266 V. *Skurátovo* (Rail. Restaurant), a village in the district of Tchern. Just short of (310 V.) *Mtzensk* (Мценскъ), a district-town on the *Zusha*, with 14,500 inhab., we cross the Zusha.

358 V. (239 M.) **Oról**, Орёлъ (pron. Aryól).—The *Railway Station* (Restaurant, fair; D. $^3/_4$-1 rb.), lies on the right bank of the Oká, 2 M. to the E. of the town.—HOTELS. *Berlin*, Gostinaya, R. 1-3, D. (1-7 p.m.) $1^1/_2$ rb., well spoken of; *Yevropéiskaya; Métropole*, R. 1-3, D. (2-6 p.m.) $^1/_2$-1 rb.; *Peterbúrgskaya*, the last three in the Bolkhóvskáya.— *Town Park*, with restaurant; concert and variety entertainment in the evenings.—POST AND TELEGRAPH OFFICE in the Sadóvaya. —IZVÓSHTCHIK from the rail. station to the Oká 40, to the Orlik 50, to the upper town 60, per drive 20, per hr. 50 cop.—ELECTRIC TRAMWAYS run from the station viâ the Moskóvskaya and the Bolkhóvskaya to the Cadet School.

Orél (650 ft.), the capital of the government of that name and
the see of the Bishop of Orel and Syevsk, was founded about the
middle of the 16th century. It is situated at the confluence of the
Orlik with the *Oká* (here 130 yds. in width). Pop. 91,000. — From
the railway station we go to the right, and after 5 min. turn to
the left into the Moskóvskaya, which leads through a poor quarter
of the town to the (2 M.) Oká bridge (view). On the other side of
the bridge we follow the Gostínaya, passing the *City Hall* on the
left. About 6 min. farther on we cross the Orlik and ascend through
the Bolkhovskáya, the main street of the more important part of
the town, which joins the Sadóvaya beside the ($^1/_4$ hr.) *Club of the
Noblesse* (Домъ дворянства; r.). We follow the last-named street
to the right. On the left side of it are the *Government Buildings*
(containing a small local museum), and the *District Court*. On the
right side lies the *Town Park* (Restaurant, see p. 361). Farther
on, to the left, are the *Cathedral of SS. Peter & Paul*, begun in
1794 and completed in 1861, and the *Governor's Residence*, to the
N. of which is the *Cadet School*. By following the Sadóvaya to the
left from the Club of the Noblesse, we reach the *Roman Catholic
Church* and the *Lutheran Church*.

FROM OREL TO GRYAZI, 290 V. (193 M.), railway in 10 hrs. — From (86 V.)
Verkhóvye (Rail. Restaurant) a branch-line runs to (123 V.) Marmuizhi
(p. 428). At (166 V.) *Kazaki* we cross a bridge 130 ft. in height. The
district traversed is attractive. — 184 V. **Yelétz** (Елецъ; *Rail. Restaurant; Peterbúrgskaya; Popóvskaya; Orél;* droshky from the rail. station
to the town 50, per hr. 50 cop.), a district-town in the government of Orel,
is pleasantly situated on the left bank of the *Sosná*, contains numerous
factories, and carries on a trade in cattle. Pop. 58,000. The *Cathedral of
the Virgin* contains some old paintings of saints. The *Nunnery of the
Apparition of the Virgin* resembles a fortress. The chapels of the former
Monastery of the Holy Trinity (12th cent.) are said to have been built
above the graves of those who fell in 1395 while defending the town
against the Tartars. Branch-lines to (105 V.) Astapovo (p. 361) and to
(113 V.) Kastornaya (p. 428); to Tula, see p. 361. — Beyond (209 V.) *Don*
we cross the Don by a lattice-bridge. — 256 V. **Lipetzk** (*Minerálnuiya
Vodi*, a state institution, R. $^3/_4$-4 rb.; droshky from the rail. station to the
town 50 cop.), a district-town in the government of Tambov, situated on
the lofty right bank of the *Vorónezh*, about 2 M. to the S.E. of the station.
Pop. 23,500. The *Alkaline Springs*, containing iron, are said to have been
discovered by Peter I. in 1700. The season lasts from May 20th to Aug.
31st (O.S.); visitors' tax 3 rb. — 290 V. (193 M.) *Gryazi*, see p. 427.

From Orel to *Smolensk*, see p. 253.

Beyond (429 V.) *Malo-Archangel* we enter the province of Kursk.
We have now reached the river-system of the Dnieper, and the hills
gradually disappear and give place to the plain. As we near Kursk
the appearance both of the villages and of the inhabitants changes;
the woodwork of the houses is covered with clay, and wicker-work
frequently takes the place of the wooden beams of the N.

479 V. *Korennáya Pustuin*. About 3 M. from the rail. station,
on the right, is the *Koren Hermitage* (Коренная пýстынь), a

wealthy convent with three churches founded in 1597. On the second Friday after Whitsunday the picture of the Virgin is brought in solemn procession from the Convent of the Apparition of the Virgin, in Kursk, to this spot, where it remains till Sept. 13th (O.S.).

502 V. (333 M.) **Kursk, Курскъ.** — The MAIN RAILWAY STATION (*Restaurant*, fair) lies about 4 M. to the N.E. of the town, with which it is connected by a branch-line (2nd cl. fare 14 cop.). — HOTELS. *Poltorátzki*, Moskóvskaya, near the Krásnaya Square, R. $^3/_4$-5$^1/_2$, D. (2-7 p.m) $^1/_2$-1 rb.; *Bellevue*, R. 1$^1/_2$-5 rb., D. (2-8 p.m.) from 50 cop.; *Hôtel du Nord*, these two in the Moskóvskaya. — IZVÓSHTCHIK from the Main Station to the town 75, per drive 25, per hr. 50 cop.; with rubber tyres 1 rb., 35 cop., or 70 cop. — An ELECTRIC TRAMWAY runs through the town from the Moscow Arch, passing close by the Town Railway Station, to the Kherson Arch.

Kursk (765 ft.), the capital of a government and the see of the Greek Catholic bishop of Kursk and Byelgorod, lies on two ridges at the confluence of the *Kur* and the *Tuskór*, near the point where the latter flows into the *Seim.* Pop. 83,000, including Great and Little Russians, Poles, and about 350 German Russians. Kursk carries on an important trade in grain, linen, leather, and fruit (apples). Kursk, founded in the 9th cent. and first mentioned in a document of 1095, was destroyed by the Mongols in 1240; long belonged to Lithuania, and was eventually annexed to the principality of Moscow.

The more important part of Kursk lies on the left bank of the Kur. We turn to the right on leaving the railway station, and after 2 min. turn again to the right through the Khersónskaya and ascend to (7 min.) the Krásnaya Square, with the Town Park (Restaurant, D. $^1/_2$-1 rb.). On the S. side of the square is the *Convent of the Apparition of the Virgin* (Знаменскій монастырь), erected in 1612 in commemoration of the deliverance from the Poles. Its main church has since 1618 contained the venerated picture of the Apparition of the Virgin, which was found in 1295 in the Koren Hermitage (p. 362). To the left of the convent are the *Government Administration Buildings*, containing a museum (local antiquities, objets d'art, portraits; open daily, except Mon., 11-3; adm. 20 cop.). Opposite is a simple monument to the poet I. F. Bogdanóvitch (d. 1803). On the N. side of Krásnaya Square begins the Moskóvskaya, the main street of town, containing the *Lutheran Church of SS. Peter & Paul* (on the right). A little to the E. is the *Cathedral of the Kazan Virgin Mother* (18th cent.). To the N.W. of the Krásnaya Square, on the high bank of the Kur, is the *Roman Catholic Church.*

FROM KURSK TO KONOTOP (Kiev), 236 V. (155 M.), railway in 7 hrs. 74 V. *Lgov* (Льговъ; Rail. Restaurant; pp. 376, 389); 112 V. *Koréneco* (Rail. Restaurant). — 167 V. *Vorozhbá* (Rail. Restaurant). To Kharkov, see p. 389; light railway to (125 V.) Khutor Mikhailovski (p. 376). — 236 V. (155 M.) *Konotóp* (Rail. Restaurant). To Kiev, see pp. 376, 377.

From Kursk to *Kharkov*, see R. 55 b; to *Voronezh*, see p. 428.

47. From Moscow to Kazan.

903 V. (600 M.). Express train in 24 hrs. (fares 20 rb. 50, 12 rb. 80 cop.; reserved seat 1¹/₂ rb.). Ordinary train in 33 hrs.

Moscow (Kazan Station), see p. 270. — 11 V. *Veshnyakí.* About 1 M. to the N.E. is Kuskovo (p. 321), and about 2 M. to the S. is Kuzminki (p. 321). — 15 V. *Kosinó* (p. 321). — 19 v. *Lyubertzi.* To Ryazan, see R. 48 b. — The train turns towards the E. — 54 V. *Gzhel.* From (82 V.) *Kurovskaya* a branch-railway runs N. to (28 V.) Oryekhovo (p. 337). 147 V. *Tcherusti* (Rail. Restaurant).

270 V. (179 M.) **Murom** (*Rail. Restaurant;* izvóshtchik from the station to the town 25, to the harbour 50 cop.), an old town on the *Oká,* contains 18,600 inhab., and is said to have been founded in the 9th century.

Steamers ply from Murom up the Oká in 2 days to *Ryazán* (p. 366), passing (9 hrs.) *Yelátma,* a small town in the government of Tambov, and *Kasímov,* which in the middle of the 15th cent. was the seat of the Tartar Khan Kasim. Other steamers ply downstream to (15 hrs.) *Nizhni-Nóvgorod* (p. 339), passing (7 hrs.) *Pávlovo,* with its extensive manufactures of knives, locks, and other hardware.

From Murom a branch-railway runs N. to (103 V.) *Kovrov* (p. 338).

Just beyond Murom the train crosses the Oká and farther on the *Tyosha.* — 390 V. *Arzamás* (Rail. Restaurant), a town on the right bank of the Tyosha, with 13,500 inhab. and a school of painting founded by the Academician Stupin in 1800. Many Mordvins live in the environs. From Arzamas a branch-railway runs N. to (120 V.) Nizhni-Novgorod (p. 339).

About 50 V. (33 M.) to the S.W. of Arzamas, in the government of Tambov, lies the *Sarov Convent* (Сáровская пýстынь), founded in the 17th cent., and containing the wonder-working remains of Seraphim (d. 1833), who was canonized in 1903.

The train runs to the S.E. through a corn-district. 449 V. *Lukoyánov* (Rail. Restaurant). From (554 V.) *Timiryázevo* (Rail. Restaurant) a branch-railway runs S. to (52 V.) Ruzayevka (p. 367).

The line turns to the N.E. 674 V. *Alatúir* (Rail. Restaurant), a district-town with 25,600 inhab. on the left bank of the *Surá.* We cross the river. Beyond (860 V.) *Sviyázhsk* (Rail. Restaurant; see p. 351) we cross the Volga by the *Románov Bridge,* built in 1913. — 868 v. *Zelyóni Dol.* — 903 V. (600 M.) *Kazán* (p. 352).

48. From Moscow to Samara *(Siberia, Tashkent).*

a. Viâ Tula and Ryazhsk (Siberia).

1115 V. (738 M.). Railway in 32 hrs. (fares 23 rb. 50, 14 rb. 10 cop.); reserved seat (p. xxiii) 2 rb. 40 cop. extra. *Trans-Siberian Express* twice weekly in 26 hrs. (fares 49 rb., 31 rb. 90 cop.).

From Moscow to (182 V.) *Tula,* see R. 46. — 240 V. *Uzlováya* (Rail. Restaurant; p. 361). 311 V. *Kremlévo,* the junction for the

Moscow-Saratov Railway (R. 60). 336 V. *Skopin* (Rail. Restaurant), a district-town with 16,800 inhab. in the government of Ryazan, lies upon the left bank of the *Verda* (pron. Viórda).— 377 V. **Ryazhsk** (Ряжскъ; *Rail. Restaurant*), a district-town with 15,400 inhab. in the government of Ryazan, situated on the *Khuptá.* To Ryazan, see p. 367; to Kozlov, see p. 427.

Beyond Ryazhsk the railway traverses a prosperous-looking district, where the large villages resemble those in S. Russia. The horses raised here are celebrated. 437 V. *Verda* (pron. Viórda; Rail. Restaurant); 499 V. *Morshánsk* (Rail. Restaurant), a district-town in the government of Tambov, situated on the left bank of the *Tzna,* with 31,800 inhabitants.

The train crosses the Tzna by an iron bridge. Farther on we cross a wide and fruitful plain intersected by low ranges of hills. From (546 V.) *Vernádovka* a branch-railway runs to (121 V.) Kustá-revka (p. 367). 616 V. *Patchélma* (Rail. Restaurant). About 20 M. to the S.W. of (669 V.) *Voyéikovo* is the estate of *Tarkháni,* containing the burial-place of the poet Lérmontov (p. 459).

751 V. (498 M.) **Penza.** — *Rail. Restaurant,* fair.—Hotels. *Pershin,* Moskóvskaya, near the Cathedral Square; *Grand-Hôtel,* in the lower half of the Moskóvskaya, cor. of Rozhdéstvenskaya, R. 1-6 rb., with good restaurant (D. ³/₄ & 1¹/₄ rb.); *Treumann,* cor. of Lékarskaya and Nikólskaya, near the Cathedral Square, hôtel garni, R. 80 cop. to 4 rb., bed-linen 35 cop. — Cab from the railway station to the town 50, per drive 20, per hr. 50 cop.

Penza, the capital of the government of that name and the see of a Greek Catholic bishop, was founded at the beginning of the 17th century. It is situated at the foot of a slope at the confluence of the *Penza* with the *Surá.* Pop. 80,000. From the railway station we bear to the left across the open space and then follow the Lékar-skaya; after 9 min. we turn to the left, and in 2 min. more to the right along the Moskóvskaya, the main street of the town, ascending towards the S. In the shops of this street may be obtained the shawls and other articles of goats' wool (пухóвые), which form a specialty of Penza (5-30 rb., according to size). In the upper part of the town, at the S. end of the Moskóvskaya (a walk of fully 20 min.), is the *Cathedral Square* (Собóрная плóщадь), containing the Greek Catholic *Cathedral,* the *Court House,* and the *Governor's Residence.* On the S. side of the cathedral is a shady square with a bronze bust of Lérmontov (see above). To the S. of this square, at No. 5 Sadóvaya, is the *Selivérstov Drawing Academy* (Рисовáльное учúлище и музéй Н. Д. Селивéрстова), containing a collection of pictures and (first floor) a small archæological museum (open free on week-days 12-3, Sun. & holidays 11-3). The Sadóvaya runs to the W., to-wards the highest part of the town. In the Dvoryánskaya, the second cross-street beyond the Drawing Academy, is the *Lutheran Church.* Hence a road leads W., through a wood 1 M. wide, to the *Horti-cultural School* (Учúлище садовóдства), situated on a hill.

Branch-lines run from Penza to the S. to (148 V.) *Rtishtchevo* (p. 432) and to the N. (separate railway station on the E. side of the town) to (72 V.) *Tanyeyevka* and (132 V.) *Ruzáyevka* (p. 367). About 6 M. to the S.W. of Tanyeyevka is the village of *Suvórovskoye*, once the property of Field Marshal Suvórov, who is commemorated here by a bronze bust, unveiled in 1903, after a design by Rukavíshnikov.

We next traverse a district full of woods, which farther on are largely replaced by tilled land. Beyond (863 V.) *Kuznétzk* (Rail. Restaurant) the train crosses at once the boundary of the government of Simbirsk and the river *Suizran*, the left bank of which it then skirts.

986 V. **Suizran** *(Rail. Restaurant),* see p. 359. — The railway now approaches the Volga, and runs close to its right bank.

About 5 M. beyond (999 V.) *Batraki* (130 ft.; see p. 359) the train crosses the Volga by the imposing *Alexander Bridge,* built in 1875-80. The bridge, which has 13 openings and is 1570 yds. long takes 6 min. to traverse.

Just short of Samara we cross the river of that name.

1115 V. (738 M.) *Samára* (p. 357).

b. Viâ Ryazan (Rostov-on-the-Don) and Ryazhsk (Siberia).

1033 V. (685 M.). Railway in 31 hrs. (fares 22¹/₂ rb., 13¹/₂ rb.; reserved seat 2 rb. 40 cop. extra).

From Moscow to (19 V. or 13 M.) *Lyubertzi,* see R. 47. The train continues to run towards the S.E.

63 V. *Fáustovo* (Rail. Restaurant). From (84 V.) *Voskresénsk* a branch-railway runs to (22 V.) *Yegóryevsk,* with 29,200 inhab. and large cotton-mills.

108 V. **Kolómna** *(Shmelév, Yegórov,* both in the Bolshaya Astrakhanskaya; izvóshtchik from the railway station to the town 40 cop.), a district-town with 29,300 inhab. in the government of Moscow, is situated on the right bank of the *Moskvá.* Kolomna is first mentioned in 1177, and was united with the principality of Moscow in 1305. The *Cathedral of the Assumption,* founded at the end of the 14th cent., was rebuilt in 1672. The *Church of the Resurrection* dates from the middle of the 14th century. The fortified Kremlin was finished in 1533; a relic of it still exists in the *Pyatnítzkiya Gate,* which was restored in 1895.

110 V. *Golutvin* (Rail. Restaurant), with large machine works (Коломенскій машино-стройтельный заводъ; 10,000 hands). The train crosses the Oká near its confluence with the Moskvá. — 128 V. *Lúkhovitzi* (Rail. Restaurant).

From Lukhovitzi a branch-railway (26 V.) runs to *Zaráisk,* a district-town with 8800 inhab., situated on the right bank of the *Osiótr,* an affluent of the Oká. The St. Nicholas Cathedral contains a wonder-working picture of St. Nicholas, brought hither from Korsun in 1224.

186 V. (124 M.) **Ryazán,** Рязáнь. — *Railway Restaurant.* — Hotels. *Steiert,* Astrakhanskaya, R. 1-5, D. (2-6 p.m.) 1¹/₄ rb.; *Lanin,* Sobórnaya; *Morózov,* Sobórnaya, R. ³/₄-2, D. (1-7 p.m.) 1 rb. — Izvóshtchik from the rail. station to the town 40-50, to the pier 60, per hr. 50-75 cop.

Steamers ply daily viâ *Yelatma* (p. 364) and *Murom* (p. 364) to
(650 V.; 433 M.) *Nizhni-Novgorod* (p. 339), taking 2½ days to do the trip
(fares 9 & 7 rb.). This excursion may be recommended.

Ryazán, the capital of the government of that name, is situated
at the confluence of the *Lebedá* with the *Trubésh*, near its junction
with the *Oká*, and is the see of the Greek Catholic archbishop of
Ryazan and Zaraisk. Pop. 41,000. Among its 24 churches are a
Lutheran and a Roman Catholic church. Ryazan possesses important manufactures of metal goods, and, as the centre of a rich
province, carries on a lively trade. The more important part of the
town lies on the hill of the old *Kremlin*, of the fortifications of
which no traces now remain. The *Cathedral of the Assumption* was
built in 1776. Near it are the quaint-looking *Archbishop's Palace*
and the suppressed *Convent of the Holy Ghost*, dating from the
15th century. The *Church of the Raising of the Cross* contains the
tombs of princes and princesses of Ryazan from the 15-16th centuries.

A pleasant excursion may be made to the (48 V.; 32 M.) village of
Old *Ryazan* (Стáрая Рязáнь), situated on the right bank of the Oká,
opposite the steamboat-pier of the district-town of *Spask*. Here are the
remains of the ancient capital and fortress of Ryazan; on the highest
point of the hilly bank is an old earthen rampart.

From Ryazan to *Ruzáyevka*, see R. 48 c; to *Rostov-on-the-Don*, see R. 59.
— A branch-railway runs from Ryazan to (196 V.; 131 M.) *Vladímir* (p. 337).

The train turns to the S. and runs viâ (231 V.) *Starozhílovo* to
(295 V.) *Ryazhsk* (p. 365). Thence viâ Penza to (1033 V. or 685 M.)
Samára, see R. 48 a.

c. Viâ Ryazan and Ruzayevka (Orenburg, Tashkent).

994 V. (659 M.). Express train in 29 hrs. (fares 22 rb., 13 rb. 20 cop.;
seat-ticket 2 rb. 10 cop.; sleeping-car 7 rb. 95, 5 rb. 95 cop.). Ordinary
train in 37 hrs.

From Moscow to (186 V. or 124 M.) *Ryazán*, see R. 48 b. —
The train soon turns to the E. — 289 V. *Shílovo* (Rail. Restaurant).
Beyond (358 V.) *Sásovo* (Rail. Restaurant) we cross the *Tzna*. From
(383 V.) *Kustírevka* a branch-line runs to (121 V.) Vernádovka
(p. 365). Beyond (497 V.) *Arápovo* (Rail. Restaurant) we cross the
Moksha. From (578 V.) *Ruzáyevka* branch-lines run S. to (132 V.)
Penza (p. 365), and N. to Timiryazevo (p. 364). From (683 V.) *Inza*
(Rail. Restaurant) a branch-line runs N.E. to (155 V.) Simbirsk
(p. 356). 865 V. *Suizran* (Rail. Restaurant), see p. 359. — Thence
to (994 V. or 659 M.) *Samára*, see p. 366.

49. From Samara to Orenburg *(Tashkent)*.

393 V. (260 M.). Express train in 11, ordinary train in 15 hrs.

Samára, see p. 357. — At first the railway generally follows
the valley of the *Samara*, on the right bank of which rise various
chains of hills. The edges of the plateau form the watershed be

tween the Samara and the Urál. The government of Samara contains
extensive stretches of the so-called Black Earth (p. xxxvii). The
whole country between the Volga and the Urál is occupied, besides
the Russians, by Bashkirs, Teptiars, Tartars, Meshtcheryaks, Tcheremisses, Tchuvashes, Mordvins, Kalmucks, and Kirghizes.

About 7 M. to the E. of (20 V.) *Smuishlyáyevka* lies *Alexéyevko*,
with a sulphur spring (48° Fahr.). — 39 V. **Kinél** (120 ft.; *Rail.
Restaurant*). To *Tchelyabinsk* (Trans-Siberian Railway; R. 77), see
R. 50. The train turns to the S.E. — 163 V. *Buzulúk* (245 ft.; Rail.
Restaurant), the chief town of a district on the left bank of the
Buzulúk and on the right bank of the *Domashka.* Pop. 18,800.
283 V. *Novo-Sérgiyevskaya* (Rail. Restaurant).

393 V. (260 M.) **Orenbúrg.** — The *Railway Station* (restaurant)
lies to the N.W. of the town. — Hotels. *Centrálnaya,* Nikoláyevskaya,
R. 1-5, D. (1-6 p.m.) 1-1½ rb.; *Amerikánskaya,* R. from 1 rb.; *Birzheváya,* Tróitzkaya, similar prices. — Izvóshtchik from the railway station
to the town 30, per drive 20, per hr. 50 cop.

Orenbúrg (220 ft.), the capital of a government of the same name
and the seat of the Greek Catholic bishop of Orenburg, lies in a wide
plain on the right bank of the *Urál,* which here forms the boundary
between European and Asiatic Russia. Pop. 94,000, including Russians, Tartars, and Kirghizes.

Orenburg was originally laid out in 1735 on the site of the present
Orsk-on-the-Or as the frontier-fortress of the so-called Orenburg Cossack
Line. In 1740 it was removed 118 M. farther towards the Red Hills, to
the spot now occupied by Krasnogórsk, and it was transferred thence to
its present situation in 1743. Orenburg became the capital of a government
at the end of the 18th cent., but was reduced to the status of a district-
town in 1802; since 1865 it has once more enjoyed the privileges of a
provincial capital.

The town contains 35 Greek Catholic churches, a Lutheran
church, a Roman Catholic church, 14 mosques, a theatre, a Kirghiz
school, and a small museum with souvenirs of the period of the
rebel Pugatchév. In summer a band plays daily on the boulevard
(restaurant; view of the Urál). In the middle of the town stands the
rectangular and fortress-like *Trading Factory* (Гостúный дворъ),
provided with four gates and surrounded on three sides by shops.
In this hall are sold rugs and silks from Bokhara and Turkestan;
also the white and grey 'Orenburg shawls', made of pure goats' wool,
so finely knitted that the largest of them will pass through a ring
(the best specimens cost 20-65 rb. per sq. yd.). — The *Hall of Barter*
(Мѣновóй дворъ), on the left bank of the Urál, 3 M. to the S.E. of
the town, is now abandoned.

In the neighbourhood of Orenburg are settlements of Memnonites
and German colonists from S. Russia and the Volga. — About 25 M. to the
N. of Orenburg, in the steppes, is the *Carrick Kumiss Institution* (season
May 20th to Aug. 20th., O.S.; pens. for 3 months 400-550 rb.; comp. p. 358).

Railway to *Tashkent,* see R. 76.

50. From *(Moscow)* Samara to Tchelyabinsk *(Siberia).*

941 V. (625 M.). Ordinary train in 26¹/₂ hrs. Trans-Siberian Express (R. 77) twice weekly in 23¹/₂ hrs. — As far as Ufa the train traverses plains for the most part, then it crosses the S. Urals, after which it passes again through plains. The prettiest part of the S. Urals is the region between Asha-Balashovskaya and Miass.

The **Uráls** or *Urál Mountains* stretch for a distance of about 1600 M. from the Carian Sea on the N. to the steppes of Turkestan on the S. Geologically, they consist of palæozoic slate and limestone, with a central zone of crystalline slate and granite. They are sharply distinguished from the more uniform Russian tableland by the numerous folds of their strata. This folding took place mainly in the carboniferous age. In consequence of the remote antiquity of the range, its forms are, as a rule, gentle and featureless, but in the S. there are several mountains exceeding 5000 ft. in height. The S. Urals, crossed by the railway from Ufa to Tchelyabinsk, are broken up into several ranges by parallel valleys. Their E. slope is short and abrupt. On the other hand, the Central Urals, crossed by the railway from Perm to Biser and Yekaterinburg (p. 259), have such an imperceptible elevation that they can be recognized as a mountain-range from a geological standpoint only. The central and N. parts of the S. Urals form, in virtue of their ores, one of the most important mining and industrial districts of Russia. The first Russian iron foundry was established in 1623, the first auriferous layers of sand were discovered in 1774, and the first platinum was found in 1824. Outside the industrial regions, the Uráls are covered with primitive forest, and are almost uninhabited.

Samára, see p. 357. — 39 V. **Kinél** *(Rail. Restaurant).* To Orenburg, see R. 49. — 74 V. *Krótovka.*

A branch-line runs N. from Krotovka to (81 V.) *Surgút.* — A little to the E. of (78 V.) *Syérnuiya Vodi* is the health-resort of *Sérgiyevskiya Minerálnuiya Vodi*, with cold sulphur springs (R. in the Government Hotels 15-30 rb. per month). Restaurant in the pump-room. Season May 10th to Aug. 25th (O.S.); visitors' tax 3 rb.; sulphur bath 60 cop.

150 V. *Pokhvístnevo* (220 ft.; Rail. Restaurant). About 2 M. to the N. of (169 V.) *Buguruslán* is the town of that name (21,500 inhab.). At (237 V.) *Sarái-Gír* (825 ft.) we cross the watershed between the Volga and the Kama. Beyond (258 V.) *Abdúlino* (530 ft.; Rail. Restaurant), with a huge grain elevator, we enter the government of Ufá. At (328 V.) *Glukhovskáya* (1235 ft.) we cross the watershed between the Kama and the Byélaya. We then follow (all the way to Ufa) the valley of the shallow *Dyoma,* a tributary joining the Byélaya on the left. 383 V. *Ráyevka* (380 ft.; Rail. Restaurant). In entering Ufa we cross the *Byélaya* by a bridge 2100 ft. in length.

491 V. (327 M.) **Ufá.** — The *Railway Station* (restaurant) lies on the Byélaya, 1¹/₂ M. to the N. of the town. — HOTELS. *Bolshaya Sibírskaya,* at the corner of the Uspénskaya and the Alexándrovskaya, R. 1-5 rb., bed-linen 50 cop., D. (1-6 p.m.) 60 cop. to 1 rb.; *Rossíya,* Torgóvaya Square, well spoken of; *Rus.* — Izvóshtchik from the railway station or the steamboat-pier to the town or vice versâ 60 cop. — Ural precious stones at the Urálski Magázin of M. M. Kotz.

Ufá (310 ft.), founded late in the 16th cent. to hold the Bashkirs in check, is the capital of a province, and is prettily situated on the

high right bank of the *Byélaya,* near its confluence with the *Ufá.*
Pop. 103,000. In the middle of the town is a large square with the
Gostini Dvor and the Provincial Museum (on the S. side; open Sun.
& holidays, 12-3). Farther to the S. is the Cathedral, standing in
pleasure-grounds. A little to the E. is the Governor's Residence.

Steamers ply from Ufá down the Byélaya and the Kama (pp. 355, 354)
to *Kazan* (p. 352) in 2¹/₄ days (fares 9 rb. 75, 6 rb. 50 cop.). — Railway in
course of construction from Ufá to *Bugulma* (p. 356).

Just short of (512 V.) *Shakshá* (355 ft.) we cross the Ufá.
Beyond (588 V.) *Ashá-Balashóvskaya* (435 ft.; Rail. Restaurant) the
train enters the Urals (p. 369). — Between (607 V.) *Minyár* (520 ft.)
and Miass (see below) most of the stations have iron-foundries near
them. We cross the *Simá* four times. — 620 V. *Simskáya* (625 ft.),
in a picturesque district. Beyond (642 V.) *Kroptashóvo* (1205 ft.)
we cross the *Yuryuzán.* Farther on the railway is flanked by
lofty cliffs. — 675 V. *Vyazováya* (1060 ft.; Rail. Restaurant). Just
before (743 V.) *Berdyaúsh* (Бердяушъ) we cross the *Satka.*

791V. (527 M.) **Zlatoúst,** Златоустъ. — *Railway Restaurant,* mediocre. — Furnished Rooms from *Mrs. Semyónova* (R. ³/₄-1 rb.) and at the
Nómera Taganai; it is advisable to order in advance. — *Izvóshtchik* from
the rail. station to the town (3 M. to the S.W.) 60 cop. — Photographs may
be more advantageously purchased from *Dunáyev,* in the town, than at
the station. Objects in cast-iron and steel (daggers and sword-blades)
from the factories of the Ural are for sale at the station.

Zlatoúst (1925 ft.; railway station 1495 ft.), a district-town in
the government of Ufá, was founded in 1754 and lies picturesquely
between the lofty hills of *Kosotúr* and *Urengá* (good view of the
town) on the *Ai,* which is dammed up here so as to form a considerable lake. Pop. 34,000. The government works for the manufacture
of sword-blades and side-arms was established in 1811. The arsenal
contains a collection of the weapons manufactured here, shown on
week-days 9-3, by permit obtained on the second floor of the office
adjoining the arsenal on the right. Adjoining the cathedral is a
cast-iron statue of Alexander II. — There is a Lutheran church.

The *Taganai* (3600 ft.) rises on the left. We cross the *Tesmá.*
— Just beyond (809 V.) *Urzhúmka* (1850 ft.), to the right, is a stone
pyramid inscribed Европа and Азiя, indicating the boundary
between Europe and Asia, and also the highest point of the line
between Samara and Tchelyabinsk. — 851 V. *Miáss* (1115 ft.; Rail.
Restaurant), on Lake *Ílmenskoye.* In the vicinity are some gold-
mines. — From (915 V.) *Poletayevo* a branch-line runs S. to (103 V.)
Troitzk (Rail. Restaurant), a town of 37,000 inhabitants.

941 V. (625 M.) **Tchelyábinsk,** Челябинскъ (760 ft.; *Rail.
Restaurant;* Lloyd's Agents, *Kniep & Werner*). Near the station
are large wooden barracks for emigrants to Siberia (267,000 in
1913). The town (Dyadinskiye Nomerá), founded in 1658, lies on
the *Miáss,* 2³/₄ M. from the station. Pop. 70,000.

TRANS-SIBERIAN RAILWAY, see R. 77.

VI. SOUTHERN RUSSIA.

51. From Berlin or Vienna to Odessa viâ Oderberg and Zhmerinka.

FROM BERLIN (Stadtbahn stations) TO ODESSA viâ Oderberg, Cracow, Lemberg, and Podwołoczyska (1084 M.), express train in 37 hrs. (fares 105 *M*, 70 *M*; seatticket 1¹/₂ rb. extra, see p. xxiii). The journey viâ Alexandrovo (or Kalisz), Warsaw, and Brest-Litovsk takes 42 hrs. (fares 102 *M* 45, 68 *M* 15 pf.; seat-ticket 2 rb. 70 cop. extra). — FROM VIENNA (North Railway Station) TO ODESSA viâ Oderberg (932 M.), express train in 36 hrs. (fares 141 *K* 40, 88 *K* 90 *h*; seat-ticket 1¹/₂ rb. extra; sleeping-car rom Vienna to Podwołoczyska 20 *K*, 16 *K*). — St. Petersburg time is 61 min. ahead of that of Central Europe. — *Passports*, see p. xviii.

From *Berlin* to (324 M.) *Oderberg* (Rail. Restaurant; customs examination), see *Baedeker's Northern Germany.* — From *Vienna* to (172 M.) *Oderberg*, see *Baedeker's Austria.*

From Oderberg to (330 M.) *Krasne* (Rail. Restaurant) and (420 M.) *Podwołoczyska*, see *Baedeker's Austria.* Podwołoczyska is the last Austrian station, and the luggage of passengers arriving from Russia is examined here. Krasne is the junction of the railway to (33 M.) Radziwiłłów (p. 375).

From Podwołoczyska the train crosses the *Podhorce* to **Woło-czyska** (Волочйскъ; *Rail. Restaurant,* fair), the Russian frontier station, situated on the left bank of the river. — Passports and luggage are inspected here (see p. xviii).

The railway intersects the fertile government of Podolia. — 59 V. (from Wołoczyska) *Proskurów* (Rail. Restaurant), a district capital, with 41,000 inhab. (many Jews) situated at the confluence of the *Płóskaya* with the Bug. There are large barracks here.

151 V. (100 M.) **Zhmérinka**, Жмеринка, Polish *Żmerynka (Rail. Restaurant),* the junction of the railway to Kazatin (p. 375).

FROM ZHMÉRINKA TO ÓKNITZA, 145 V. (96 M.), railway in 5 hrs. — 29 V. *Bar*, the station for the town of **Bar,** which lies 3 M. to the W. (izvóshtchik 70 cop.) on the *Rov*, a tributary of the Bug. Pop. 22,700. Bar was founded by Sigismund I. of Poland on the site of the town of Rov, which had been destroyed by the Tartars, and received its name in honour of his wife Bona Sforza, who came from Bari in S. Italy. — 52 V. *Kopai Gorod* (Rail. Restaurant). — Beyond (108 V.) *Mohilév-Podólski* (pron. Mohilyóv; Rail. Restaurant), a town with 32,600 inbah., we cross the *Dniester.* — 145 V. *Óknitza* (Rail. Restaurant), see p. 373.

The railway now traverses a wooded and well-tilled region, skirting the height of land which forms the watershed between the *Dniester* and the *Bug.* — From (228 V.) *Vapnyárka* (Rail. Restaurant) a branch-railway runs viâ (112 V.) Christínovka (p. 375) and (241 V.) *Signayevka* (branch-line to *Zlatopol;* 13 V.) to (252 V.) Tzvyetkóvo (p. 387).

From (263 V.) *Rudnitza* a narrow-gauge railway runs viâ (177 V.) Podgoródnaya (p. 393) to (183 V.) *Olviópol,* a town of 9600 inhab., situated at the confluence of the *Sinyukha* with the Bug.

313 V. *Slobodka* (Rail. Restaurant).

FROM SLOBODKA TO NOWOSIELITZA, 375 V. (248 M.), railway in 15 hrs. —
Beyond (47 V.) *Rúibnitza* (Rail. Restaurant) we cross the Dniester by a
girder bridge. — 161 V. *Byeltzi* (Rail. Restaurant), the chief town of a
district in the government of Bessarabia, with 23,600 inbab. and an important cattle-trade. — 247 V. *Óknitza* (Rail. Restaurant), the junction of the
railway to Zhmerinka (p. 372). — About 60 V. · (40 M.; highroad) to the
N. of (312 V.) *Larga*, on a peninsula formed by the small river *Smotritch*,
lies **Kamenétz-Podólski** *(Hotel Bellevue; Grand-Hôtel;* izvóshtchik
per drive 20, per hr. 50 cop.), the picturesque capital of the government of Podolia, formerly a strong Polish fortress, but in the hands of
Russia since 1795. Pop. 49,600. On an elevated situation in the W. part
of the town is the *Château*, surrounded by walls and towers. The *Kazan
Cathedral*, erected in the first half of the 18th cent. as the church of a
Carmelite convent, has been used since 1878 for the Greek form of worship.
The Roman Catholic *Church of SS. Peter & Paul*, founded in the 14th cent.,
has a minaret dating from the time of the Turkish dominion (1672-99). —
375 V. *Nowosielitza* (Rail. Restaurant; customs examination). Hence to
(20 M.) *Czernowitz*, see *Baedeker's Austria*.

We now enter the flat government of Kherson. 337 V. (223 M.)
Bírzula (Бирзула), junction for Kharkov (see pp. 393-387). Near
(389 V.) *Zatishye* are some German settlements.

445 V. (295 M.) **Razdyélnaya** *(Rail. Restaurant).*

FROM RAZDYELNAYA TO UNGENI (Jassy), 212 V. (141 M.), railway in
7 hrs. [The passport must be visé by a Rumanian consul; see p. 394.]
Beyond the (43 V.) former fortress of *Tiraspól* the train crosses the
Dniester, enters the government of Bessarabia, which is partly inhabited
by Rumanians, and traverses an undulating region in which Indian corn
is a frequent crop. — 56 V. **Bendér** (Бендéры; *Rail. Restaurant; Hotel
Peterburgskaya;* izvóshtchik from the rail. station to the town 30, per hr.
50 cop.), a town of 60,000 inhab. on the right bank of the *Dniester*, formerly
a strong fortress but abandoned as such in 1897. It is known in history as
the headquarters of Charles XII. of Sweden in 1709-12; the Swedish camp
was at the village of *Varnitza* on the Dniester, 2 M. to the N. of the town.
Branch-railway to *Reni*, see below. — 112 V. **Kishinév** *(Rail. Restaurant;
London,* Pushkinskaya, R. 1-4, bed-linen ¹/₄, D. ¹/₂-1 rb., *Schweitzárskaya,*
opposite the public garden; *National,* good cuisine), the capital of the
government of Bessarabia, stretches along the right bank of the *Buik.*
Pop. 125,000, nearly half of whom are Jews. A cab from the station
to the town costs 25 cop. (with two horses 50, per hr. 30-50 cop.), and
there is also a tramway running through the Alexándrovskaya and the
Nikoláyevskaya (fare 5 cop.). In the Alexándrovskaya, the principal
street of the town, are the Greek Catholic Cathedral, a bronze statue of
Alexander II., erected in 1886 from a model by Opekúshin, the house of
the Governor, the Lutheran church, and the public garden, containing a
bronze bust of the poet Pushkin, unveiled in 1885. There is a natural
history collection in the Zemstvo Museum. — As we continue, we have a
good view to the left of Kishinev. From (212 V.) *Ungéni* (Rail. Restaurant)
the railway is prolonged across the Pruth to (12¹/₂ M.) *Jassy* (see *Baedeker's
Constantinople,* issued in German only).

FROM BENDER TO RENI, 268 V. (177 M.), railway in 8 hrs. — The train
runs to the S. across the government of Bessarabia. Near the stations
of (35 V.) *Zaim* and (117 V.) *Léipzigskaya* (Rail. Restaurant) lie German
colonies of considerable size. 137 V. *Kilmskaya* (Rail. Restaurant). At
(204 V.) *Trojánov-Val* the line intersects the so-called Wall of Trajan.
— 268 V. **Reni** *(Rail. Restaurant; Hotel Schweitzárskaya,* R. 1-2 rb.,
bed-linen 40 cop.; izvóshtchik from the station to the town 30, from the
steamboat-pier 40 cop.), a town with 10,000 inhab., situated below the con-

fluence of the *Pruth* with the *Danube*. Travellers who wish to visit the Rumanian town of *Galatz* (Bristol, Metropol; see *Baedeker's Constantinople*), which lies 12 M. to the S.W. of Reni, must have their passports visé by a Rumanian consul (see p. 394), and are advised to telegraph from Odessa to the hotel-keeper at Galatz to send a carriage to meet them at the Rumanian frontier on the Pruth.

491 V. *Dátchnaya.*· The train makes a wide circuit round the W. side of the town, passing the suburb of Moldavánka and the goods-station, before reaching the main railway station of (513 V. or 340 M.) *Odessa* (p. 393).

52. From Warsaw to Kiev and to Odessa viâ Zhmerinka.

1124 V. (744 M.). Express train in 27 hrs. (fares 27 rb. 75, 18 rb. 35 cop.; seat-ticket 2 rb. 40 cop. extra); ordinary train in 33 hrs. (fares 23 rb. 50, 14 rb. 10 cop.). The trains start from the Brest Station.—Express trains from Warsaw to *Kiev:* viâ Kazatin (809 V.; 536 M.), in 17¹/₂ hrs. (fares 22 rb. 65, 15 rb. 5 cop.; seat-ticket 1 rb. 80 cop.); viâ Sarni (see below; 710 V. or 491 M.) in 15¹/₂ hrs. (fares 21 rb. 50, 14 rb. 30 cop.; seat-ticket 1 rb. 80 cop.; sleeping-car 5 rb. 90, 4 rb. 45 cop.).

From Warsaw to (199 V. or 132 M.) *Brest-Litóvsk*, see R. 32. The railway traverses the southernmost part of the government of Grodno. Beyond (242 V.) *Maloruíto* the train enters the government of Volhynia and approaches the navigable *Pripet* (Припять, Polish Przypec), a river 506 M. in length, flowing through an extensive district of forest and marsh, the W. part of which we now traverse. Before reaching (275 V.) *Kruimno* we cross the upper Pripet.

316 V. (209 M.) **Kovel** *(Rail. Restaurant)*, a town of 29,000 inhab., is the capital of a district, situated on the *Turiyá*, a tributary of the Pripet, which is crossed by a bridge beyond Kovel.

FROM KOVEL TO KIEV, 423 V. (280 M.), railway in 9-12 hrs.—132 V. *Sarni* (Rail. Restaurant), see p. 39; 277 V. *Korostén* (Rail. Restaurant). —423 V. *Kiev* (p. 377).

From Kovel to *Warsaw*, see R. 6.

Beyond (365 V.) *Rózhitze* (Рожице), we cross the *Stuir*, one of the largest affluents of the Pripet. From (382 V.) *Kivertzi* a branch-line runs S. to (12 V.) *Lutzk*, a town of 32,000 inhab., formerly the capital of Volhynia and now the chief town of a district.

442 V. (293 M.) **Rovno** *(Rail. Restaurant; Frantzúskaya Hotel;* cab from the station to the town 25 cop.), a town and fortress with 39,000 inhab., is the headquarters of the 11th Army Corps. It was founded in the 13th cent., and about the middle of the 18th was the scene of the brilliant court of Prince Lubomirski. To Luninetz and Vilna, see p. 39.

453 V. (300 M.) *Zdolbunóvo* (Rail. Restaurant).

FROM ZDOLBUNOVO TO RADZIWILLOW, 86 V. (57 M.), railway in 2¹/₂ hrs. — From (40 V.) *Dubno*, a fortress with 25,000 inhab., a branch-line runs to (37 V.) *Kremenétz*, a prettily situated district-town with 23,500 inhab. and the scanty remains of a château of Queen Bona Sforza (p. 372). About 25 V. (16¹/₂ M.) to the S. of Kremenetz is the château of *Vishnevétz*, built in

1685, with a beautiful park.— 65 V. *Rudnya-Potcháyevskaya.* About 16 M.
to the S. (izvóshtchik 2 rb.), prettily situated upon a hill (245 ft.), is the
Potcháyevskaya Uspénskaya Lavra (comp. p. 130). In the principal
church, by the first column to the right of the entrance, is shown a foot-
print of the Virgin, of whom there is a wonder-working painting on the
ikonostás.— 86 V. *Radziwillów* (Rail. Restaurant), the Russian frontier-
station. For the continuation of the journey to *Brody* and *Krasne* (p. 372)
in Galicia, see *Baedeker's Austria.*

473 V. *Ozhénin.* The railway now crosses the *Goruin,* a tributary of the Pripet.— 503 V. *Slavuta,* with a Kumiss Institution
(comp. p. 358); 522 V. *Shepetóvka* (Rail. Restaurant), with ferruginous springs; 574 V. *Petchánovka.* Farther on we cross the
Téterev, a tributary of the Dnieper. 599 V. *Tchudnov-Voluinski.*

635 V. (421 M.) **Berdítchev.** — *Railway Restaurant.* — *Continental Hotel,* Byelopólskaya, R. ³/₄-3 rb., bed-linen 40 cop., D. 60 cop. to 1 rb.
20 cop.—*Izvóshtchik* from the station to the town (1 M.) 40, per drive 20,
per hr. 40 cop.—*Tramway* from the rail. station to the town (5 cop.).

Berdítchev, the chief town of a district in the government of
Kiev, stands on a gentle slope rising from the *Gnílopyat,* and contains 77,000 inhab., of whom 80 per cent are Jews. It is the centre
of the Volhynian trade, chiefly in grain and cattle. The Carmelite
Convent, founded in 1627, was suppressed in 1864.

FROM BERDÍTCHEV TO ZHITOMIR, 51 V. (34 M.), light railway in 2¹/₂ hrs.
—**Zhitómir** (Жито́миръ; *Frántziya Hotel,* Kíyevskaya, R. ¹/₂-4 rb., B.
20 cop., D. ¹/₂-1¹/₂ rb., omn. 50 cop.; *Rímskaya Hotel,* Kíyevskaya, similar
prices, very fair; *Venétziya*), the capital of the province of Volhynia, is
situated on the *Téterev,* and is named after one of the comrades of Askold
(p. 378). It has belonged to Russia since 1778, and is the seat of a Greek
Catholic archbishop and a Roman Catholic bishop. Pop. 93,000, half of
whom are Jews. Zhitomir contains a Lutheran Church in the Romanesque
style, built in 1896. It manufactures kid gloves and tobacco, and carries
on a trade in grain and timber. The town is traversed by several electric
tramways, including one from the railway station to the principal square
(fare 8 cop.; cab from the railway station 60, with two horses 90 cop.;
per hr. 65 cop. or 1 rb.).

660 V. (437 M.) **Kazátin** *(Rail. Restaurant),* the junction of
the railway to (149 V.) *Kiev,* see R. 55 b.

FROM KAZATIN TO UMAN, 183 V. (122 M.), railway in 6 hrs. — 163 V.
Christínovka (Rail. Restaurant), see p. 372. — 183 V. *Uman* (Frántziya
Hotel; izvóshtchik from the station to the town 50, from the town to
Sofiyevka 25 cop.), the chief town of a district in the government of Kiev,
with 42,000 inhab., more than half of whom are Jews. The Sadóvaya
or Sofíyevskaya leads from the town to *Sofíyevka,* a country-house built
by Count Felix Potocki for his wife Sophie in 1793, and surrounded by
a beautiful park. It is now the seat of an imperial school of agriculture.

678 V. *Goléndri.* The railway now enters the government of
Podolia. — 718 V. *Vínnitza* (Rail. Restaurant). About 2 M. to the
S.E. of the station (cab 50 cop.) is the town of **Vinnitza** *(Bellevue),*
which is prettily situated on the *Bug,* and is the headquarters of
the 12th Army Corps. Pop. 48,000, half of whom are Jews. Vinnitza contains a Capuchin convent with a large church. — Beyond
(741 V.) *Gnivan* we cross the Bug.

761 V. (504 M.) *Zhmérinka* (p. 372). Hence to (1124 V. or
744 M.) *Odessa,* see R. 51.

53. From Moscow to Kiev.

803 V. (532 M.). Express train in 21 hrs. (fares 19 rb., 11 rb. 40 cop.; seat-ticket 1 rb. 80 cop.; sleeping-car 6 rb. 40, 4 rb. 80 cop.).

Moscow, see p. 269. The trains start from the Bryansk station. —114 V. *Malo-Yaroslávetz*, a small town with 5300 inhab., known for the defeat of Napoleon I. on Oct. 12th (O.S.), 1812, which compelled him to begin his retreat along the devastated route to Smolensk. — From (159 V.) *Tikhonova-Pustuin* (Rail. Restaurant) a branch-line runs to (17 V.) Kaluga (p. 254). From (241 V.) *Sukhínitchi* (Rail. Restaurant) branch-lines run to the W. to (220 V.) Smolensk (p. 253) and to the E. to (132 V.) Gorbatchovo (p. 361).

356 V. (236 M.) **Bryansk**, Брянскъ (525 ft.; *Rail. Restaurant*, fair; *Dudin*, *Rossíya*), an industrial town in the government of Orel, is situated on the high right bank of the *Desná*, about 2 M. from the railway (izvóshtchik 50 cop.). Pop. 30,400. The most noteworthy church is the *Cathedral of the Intercession of the Virgin* (1526). The *Arsenal*, with a gun-foundry, was established in 1783.

An interesting visit may be paid (narrow gauge railway) to the *Máltzov Industrial Works* (Мáльцовскіе завóды), situated to the N. of Bryansk, which employ 20,000 workmen, produce goods (glass, bottles, cement, railway carriages, and machinery) to the annual value of 19 million rubles, and own 900 sq. M. of forest. The head-office is at Dyátkovo, where the permits to visit the works are issued.

A branch-line runs from Bryansk to (197 V.) *Lgov* (p. 363). — To *Smolénsk* and to *Orél*, see p. 253; to *Brest-Litóvsk*, see p. 249.

From (488 V.) *Khutor Mikháilovski* (Rail. Restaurant) a light railway runs to (125 V.) Vorozhba (p. 363). Beyond (585 V.) *Melnya* we cross the *Seim*. — 596 V. *Konotóp* (Rail. Restaurant), a district-town with 28,000 inhab., situated in a marshy district on the *Yezúza*, is the junction for the line from Kursk to Kiev (p. 363). — 623 V. **Bakhmatch**, Бахмачъ *(Rail. Restaurant)*, junction of the line to Odessa (R. 55a) and of that from Vilna to Romni (p. 39).

667 V. (442 M.) *Kruti* (Railway Restaurant).

From Kruti to Tchernigov, 76 V. (50 M.), light railway in 3½ hrs. — Tchernígov *(Rail. Restaurant; Alexándrovskaya Hotel, R. from 1, bed-linen ½, D. ½-1 rb.)*, the capital of the province of the same name in Little Russia, lies on the right bank of the *Desná* and contains 33,000 inhabitants. The railway station lies on the left bank of the Desná, 2 M. from the town (cab with two horses 1 rb.). The *Spasski Cathedral* was founded in the 11th century. In the Smolénskaya (No. 3) is the *Tarnovski Museum of Antiquities of the Ukraine* (Музéй укрáинскихъ дрéвностей В. В. Тарнóвскаго), containing interesting objects from the time of the Cossack dominion. The museum is open free on week-days, Mon. excepted, from 11 to 3, and on Sun. from 12 to 4; it is closed for a month in summer. — Steamers ply from Tchernigov to Kiev (p. 378).

685 V. **Nyezhin** (Нѣжинъ; *Rail. Restaurant*), the chief town of a district, situated on the *Oster* (pron. Ostyór), contains 52,000 inhabitants. The poet Gogol studied at the lyceum here (now the Historical & Philological Institute) from 1821 to 1828, and is com-

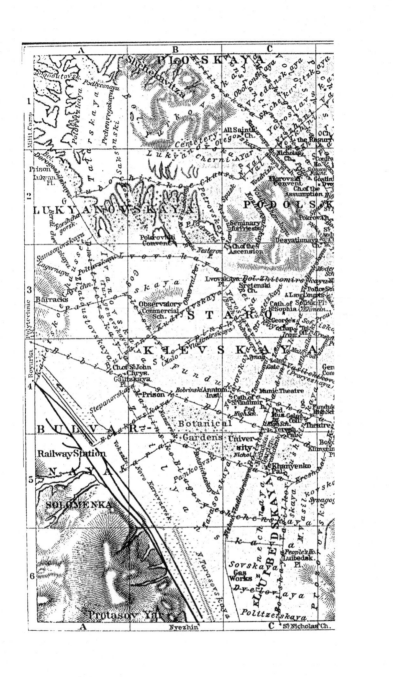

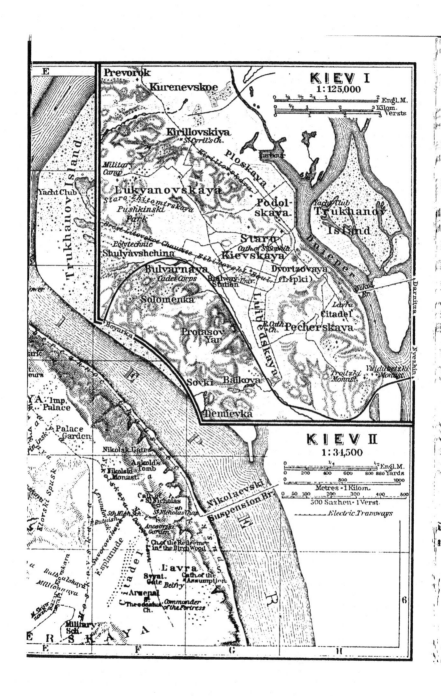

KIEV I
1:125,000

Engl.M.
Kilom.
Versts

Prevorok
Kurenevskoe
Kirillovskiya
St Cyril's Ch.
Ploskaya
Harbour
Military Camp
Yacht Club
Lukyanovskaya
Staro Zhitomirskaya
Pushkinski Park
Podol-skaya
Yacht Club
Trukhanov
Island
Short Levovskoe Chaussée
Polytechnic
Shulyavshchina
Staro Cath. of St Sophia
Kievskaya
Bulvarnaya
Cadet Corps
Railway Junct.
Dvortzovaya (Lipki)
Dnieper
Lukyadskaya
Solomenka
Railway Station
Lavra
Citadel
Boyarka
Protasov Yar
Cath. Ch.
Pecherskaya
Troitzki Monast.
Widdubitzki Monast.
Sovki Baikova
Darnitza
Tvezhin
Temievka

KIEV II
1:34,500

Engl. M.
Yards
Metres -1 Kilom.
Sazhen 1 Verst
Electric Tramways

Imp. Palace
Palace Garden
Nikolski Gate
Askold's Tomb
Nikolski Monast.
Cath. of St Nicholas
5th High Sch.
St Nicholas Ch.
Anatomic Garden
Ch. of the Redeemer in the Birchwood
Electski Spusk
Esplanade
Lavra
Cath. of the Assumption
Svyat. Gate
Belfry
Arsenal
Theodosius Ch.
Commander of the Fortress Ch.
Military Sch.
ERSKAYA

Nikolaevski
Suspension Br

E
F
G
H

6

memorated by a monument with his bust. The railway station lies
$2^1/_2$ M. to the S. of the town (carr. and pair 60 cop.).

Beyond (776 V.) *Brovarí* we traverse wood and cross a long
iron bridge over the *Dnieper*, obtaining a view of the Lavra of
Kiev to the right. Farther on, to the right, we see the two towers
of the Roman Catholic church of St. Nicholas (p. 379).

803 V. (532 M.) *Kiev* (see below).

54. Kiev.

ARRIVAL. The *Railway Station* (Pl. A, 5) lies in the W. part of the
town, $2^1/_2$ V. ($1^1/_2$ M.) from the Kreshtchátik (p. 379). Cab-tariff, see below.
—City Offices of South Western Railway, Pushkinskaya 14 (Pl. C, 4, 5;
open 9-4, Sun. & holidays 9-12); of Moscow & Kiev Railway, Alexándrovskaya 49 (Pl. D, E, 3, 4). Agency of the International Sleeping Car Co.,
Nikoláyevskaya 5 (Pl. D, 4; week-days 9-5, Sun. & holidays 10-12).

Hotels (charges for rooms considerably higher in February, during
the Contract Fair). *HÔTEL CONTINENTAL (Pl. c; D, 4), Nikoláyevskaya 11,
with garden-court, R. from $2^1/_4$, B. $^3/_4$, déj. (12-2) 1, D, (2-6) $1^1/_2$, omn.
$1^1/_2$ rb.; *GRAND-HÔTEL (Pl. a; D, 4), Kreshtchátik 22, R. from $1^1/_2$, B. $^1/_2$,
déj. (1-2) $1^1/_2$, D. (2-8) $2^1/_2$ rb.; HÔTEL DE L'EUROPE (Yevropéiskaya; Pl.
b, D 3), Kreshtchátik 2, R. 1-10, D. 1 rb.—FRANÇOIS (Pl. h; C, 4), Fundukléyevskaya 17, R. $1^1/_4$-6 rb., B. 50, D. (1-6) 60 cop; FRÁNTZIYA (Pl. d;
D, 4), Kreshtchátik 30, R. $1^1/_4$-8, déj. $^3/_4$, D. 1 rb.; GRAND-HÔTEL NATIONAL
(Pl. e; D, 5), Kreshtchátik 47, R. 1-4 rb.; SAVOY HOTEL (Pl. f; D, 4),
Kreshtchátik 38; GLADUINYÚK (Pl. g; C, 4), Fundukléyevskaya 10.

Restaurants at the above-named hotels; also, *Semadéni*, Kreshtchátik
15, opposite the Duma (Pl. D, 4), a frequented luncheon-room and café,
D. (1.30-5 p.m.) 85 cop., foreign newspapers; *Merchants' Club* (see below),
D. (2-6) $^3/_4$-$1^1/_4$, S. (11-1) 1 rb.; *Roots*, Kreshtchátik 1, in the Tzárskaya
Square (Pl. D, 3), déj. (11-2) and D. (2-6) à la carte, S. 1 rb.; *Métropole*,
in the Hôtel François (see above), D. 50-75 cop.

Theatres. *Municipal Theatre* (Pl. C, 4), Fundukléyevskaya, corner of
Vladimirskaya, for operas; *Solovtzóv Theatre* (Pl. D, 4), Nicholas Square,
for dramas; *Bruikin Variety Theatre*, Fundukléyevskaya 5 (Pl. B, C, 4).
—*Apollo*, Meringovskaya 8 (Pl. D, 4), a cabaret.

Pleasure Resorts. *Garden of the Merchants' Club* (Купéческій
клубъ; Pl. D, E, 3; p. 383), with summer-theatre, string-band every evening in summer (adm. 40 cop.); *Château des Fleurs* (Pl. E, 4; burnt down
in 1913), with garden and operetta theatre.—*Circus* (Pl. D, 4; Hippo
Palace), Nikoláyevskaya 7.

Izvóshtchik (see p. xxiv).	15	20	25	30	35	40	45	60	min.
One horse (day)	25	30	35	40	45	50	60	75	cop.
„ (night; 12-7)	35	40	45	50	55	60	70	100	„
Two horses (day)	50	60	70	80	90	100	110	150	„
„ (night)	65	75	85	95	105	115	125	180	„

From the rail. station 10 or 20 cop. more (usual charge 50 cop. for one
horse, 1 rb. for two). Baggage below 3 puds free.

Electric Tramways. The following are the principal lines: 1. *De-
mievka* (beyond Pl. C, 6) to *Tzárskaya Square* (Pl. D, 3) viâ Kreshtchátik,
in $^1/_2$ hr.; fare 8 cop. 2. *Railway Station* (Pl. A, 5) to *Alexander
Square* (Pl. D, 2) viâ Kreshtchátik and Tzárskaya Square; 35 min.; 11 cop.
—3. *Tzárskaya Square* (Pl. D, 3) to the *Lavra* (Pl. F, G, 6); 20 min.;
8 cop.—5. *Bessarábka* (Bogdán-Khmyelnítzki Square; Pl. D, 5) to the

Polytechnic (see Inset Map; 28 min.; 8 cop. — **9.** *Alexander Square* (Pl. D. 2) to *Michael Square* (Pl. D, 3; connecting here with Elevator); 14 min.; 5 cop. — **10.** *Alexander Square* (Pl. D, 2) viâ St. Cyril's Church to *SS. Peter & Paul Square* (see Inset Map); 32 min.; 8 cop.

British Vice-Consul, *J. F. Douglas*, Pushkinskaya 21 (Pl. C, 4, 5).

General Post Office (Pl. D, 4), Kreshtchátik 24. — **Telegraph Office** (Pl. C, 3), Bolshaya Vladimirskaya 23. — **Police Station** (Pl. C, D, 3), Bolshaya Zhitómirskaya 1. *Directory* (with list of addresses), Bolshaya Zhitómirskaya 3, accessible on week-days 10-3 & 6-9, Sun. & holidays 12-2.

Baths. *Centrálnuiya*, Malo-Zhitómirskaya 3 (Pl. D, 3); *Michelsohn*, Karaváyevskaya 6 (Pl. A-C, 5). — RIVER BATHS (Pl. E, 3) on the Naberezhnoye Chaussée, with separate compartments (номерá; 15 cop.).

Steamboats (April-October). On the DNIEPER to (320 V.) *Krementchug* (p. 391) and (476 V.) *Yekaterinoslav* (p. 401); to (629 V.) *Mohilev* (p. 257). — On the PRIPET to (628 V.) *Pinsk* (p. 249). — On the SOZH to (320 V.) *Homel* (p. 39). — On the DESNÁ to (204 V.) *Tchernigov* (p. 376).

DRIED FRUITS (Варéнье), a specialty of Kiev, at *A. Balábukha's*, Nikoláyevskaya 3 (Pl. D, 4).

Principal Attractions (1 day). Kreshtchátik (p. 379), Vladimir Monument (p. 383), Lavra (p. 380), Nikoláyevski Spusk (p. 382), St. Michael's Convent (p. 383), St. Andrew's Church (p. 383), Cathedral of St. Sophia (p. 384), Vladimir Cathedral (p. 385). — It is advisable to take a cab (p. 377) from the Vladimir Monument to the Lavra, and viâ the Nikoláyevski Spusk to St. Michael's Convent.

The churches of the Lavra are open from early morning till 8 p.m. (in winter 6 p.m.), the catacombs till 5 p.m. (in winter 4 p.m.).

  Kiev, Кiевъ, pron. Keeyev (590 ft. above the level of the sea, 295 ft. above the Dnieper), the fortified capital of a government of the same name in Little Russia, is the residence of the Governor-General, the headquarters of the 9th and 21st Army Corps, and the see of a Greek Catholic Metropolitan. It also contains the Vladimir University and a Polytechnic Institution, and carries on an important trade in sugar. Pop. 590,000, including Russians, Poles, and Jews. The city is picturesquely situated on a series of wooded heights, rising abruptly from the right bank of the dirty yellow *Dnieper*, which is here 400-580 yds. in width. At the season of the breaking up of the ice in the second half of April, the river overflows its banks far and wide. Kiev, known as 'the Jerusalem of Russia', is a great resort of pilgrims, and is characterized by the number of its churches, which, however, are inferior in architecture to those of Moscow. The city is divided into three parts. On the S.E. is *Petchérsk* or *Cave Town* (Печéрскъ), including the Lavra; to the N.E. is *Podól*, or trading quarter, which lies in the plain close to the river and is adjoined by suburbs; to the N.W. is the high-lying *Staro Kiev* or *Old Town* (Стáро-Кiевъ). On the heights to the W. of Petchérsk stretches the attractive quarter of *Lipki* or *Linden Town*, the residence of the aristocracy and richer merchants.

  According to legend, Kiev, 'the mother of all the towns of Russia', was founded by the three brothers *Ki*, *Shtchek*, and *Khoriv*, belonging to the stock of the Polyáni, after whose death *Askold* and *Duir*, two Varangian followers of Rurik (p. 262), made themselves masters of the principality in 864. Olég, Rurik's successor, captured Kiev in 882 and made it his capital. Christianity, which was fostered by St. Olga and other members of the princely house, soon gained a foothold here. After the capture of Korsun (p. 410), *St. Vladimir* (p. xlviii) adopted Christianity and married Anna, sister of the Greek Emperors Basil and Constantine, and on his return to his own country in 988 he caused his people to be baptized. Under him and his immediate successors, especially under *Yaroslav I.*, Kiev attained great importance. Its decline began on the death of Yaroslav I. in 1054. Vladimir II. (1113-25) married Gytha, daughter of King Harold of England (p. xlviii). The town became a bone of contention for the princes among whom the territory had been divided, and was destroyed by Andréi Bogolyúbski in 1169, by Svyetosláv Vsévolodovitch in 1171, and by Rurik Rostislávitch in 1204. It was also stormed by the Tartars under Baty-Khan in 1240 and completely sacked. In 1299 the Metropolitan of Kiev, then the foremost ecclesiastical dignitary of the Russian church, removed his seat to Vladimir-on-the-Klyazma. [Political reasons afterwards occasioned the transfer of this dignity to the Patriarch of Moscow; see p. 295.] Gedimin, the Grand-Prince of Lithuania, expelled the Tartars in 1320. His successors encouraged Roman Catholicism to such an extent that in 1455 it was possible for King Casimir IV. of Poland to forbid the erection of new Russian churches. In 1483 Mengli-Girei, the Khan of the Crimea, devastated the town. In 1516 it received, from Sigismund I., the privileges of the 'Magdeburg Code'. The Act of Union was accepted by the Metropolitan Michael Rogoza in 1596, but in 1621 Peter Mogíla re-established the strict orthodox faith. In 1686 Kiev was ceded to Russia by Poland.

The traffic of the city centres in the KRESHTCHÁTIK (Крещатикъ; Pl. D, 4), a thoroughfare about $^3/_4$ M. long and 108 ft. wide, stretching along the ravine between Lipki and Old Kiev. It contains numerous public buildings, such as the *City Hall* (Дума; 1877), the *Exchange* (Биржа; 1883), and the *Post Office* (Почтовая контора), and also the chief hotels, banks, and the like. In front of the City Hall rises a statue, by Ximenes (1913), of *P. A. Stolýpin*, who was assassinated at Kiev in 1911. The Annenkovskaya, or Luteránskaya, diverging to the E. from the Kreshtchátik, contains the *Lutheran Church* (Pl. D, 4), built in 1857. On the S. the Kreshtchátik ends at the *Bogdán Khmyelnítzki Square* (Pl. D, 5), also called *Bessarábka*, which contains the large market hall. [For the Bibikovski Boulevard, see p. 385.]

In the Bolshaya Vasilkóvskaya (Pl. C, 5, 6), which runs to the S. from the Bogdán Khmyelnítzki Square, are the *People's Palace*, built in 1902, and the Roman Catholic *Church of St. Nicholas*, with its two towers, finished from the plans of Gorodétzki in 1909.

On the N. the Kreshtchátik ends at the *Tzárskaya Square* (Царская площадь; Pl. D, 3; tramway, see p. 377), in which there is a *Bronze Statue of the Emperor Alexander II.*, by Ximenes (1911); the groups on the plinth represent the abolition of serfdom. Near by is the new *Public Library*, built by Krivosheyev (open on week-days 10-8, Sun. & holidays 12-4; closed in July); a little to the N.W. is the Roman Catholic *Church of St. Alexander* (Pl. D, 3), built in 1817-49, with a portico of four columns.

From the Tzárskaya Square we may ascend to the left to the Vladimir Monument (p. 383). We follow the ALEXÁNDROVSKAYA

(Pl. D, E, 2-4) to the S.E. On the right is the **Museum of Art and Archaeology** (Музéй дрéвностей и искýсствъ; Pl. E, 4), a building with a hexastyle portico, built by *Gorodétzki* in 1900. It is open daily, 10-3 (adm. 30 cop.; catalogue 15 cop.), but is closed from June 15th to Aug. 15th (O.S.), when, however, strangers may obtain admission by application to the director, N. Byelashévski.

Ground Floor. Opposite the entrance is the vestibule, with autographs and MSS. To the left of the entrance are prehistoric and Slavonic antiquities (period of the Grand-Princes of Kiev).—First Floor. In Room I are coins, paintings, gold and silver vessels. In the corridor are works of art from E. Asia. The Little Russia Room contains textiles, wood-carvings, and tapestry. To the right are ecclesiastical antiquities from Little Russia. To the left of Room I are three rooms for temporary exhibitions.

At the end of the Alexándrovskaya, to the left, is the *Imperial Palace* (Pl. E, 4), a rococo building restored in 1880 (no adm.).

Beyond the *Palace Garden* (Дворцóвый паркъ) we proceed to the left to the *St. Nicholas Gate* (Николáевскія ворóта; Pl. F, 4), outside which begins the Никóльская. To the left stands the *Convent of St. Nicholas* (Николáевскій монастЫрь; Pl. F, 5). Farther on, also to the left, but standing a little back from the street, is the *St. Nicholas Cathedral* (Николáевскій собóръ), built in 1696. Just beyond this the Николáyevski Spusk (p. 382) diverges to the left, while on the right is the Suvórovskaya, leading immediately to the *Esplanade* (Pl. F, 5, 6), used in autumn for horse-races and at other times as a drill-ground. The direct continuation of the Никóльская is called the *Road to the Lavra* (Дорóга въ Лáвру). In this, to the left, is the small *Church of the Redeemer in the Birch-Wood* (Цéрковь Спáса на берестóвѣ; Pl. F, 5), containing remnants of frescoes of the 11th century. Farther on, ca. 2 M. from the Tzárskaya Square, we reach the lofty wall, built in the 17th cent., which encloses the—

*Lavra (Кíево-Печéрская Лáвра; Pl. F, G, 6), the most highly revered convent in Russia (comp. p. 130).

The founder of the *Monastery of the Caves* is supposed to have been the Russian Hilarion, who lived as a hermit in a cave he had himself excavated on the wooded hill rising from the Dnieper, and was afterwards called to be Metropolitan of Kiev. His successor in the hermitage was the monk Anthony, who returned from Mt. Athos in 1051. Among the adherents attracted by the piety of this hermit were SS. Theodosius and the chronicler Nestor (p. 381), and at a later date many of the monks belonged to princely houses. The first abbot was Varlaám, the son of a boyar; the second was the above-mentioned Theodosius (d. 1074). In the 12th cent. the monastery was elevated to the rank of Lavra, and as such it stood under the direct control of the Patriarch, at first of Constantinople, then of Moscow. The Igúmen received the title of Archimandrite, a title now borne by the Metropolitan of Kiev, to whom the monastery has been subordinated since 1786. The yearly revenue of the Lavra amounts to about one million rubles.

Opposite the *Arsenal* (Pl. F, 6) is the *Holy Gate* (СвятЫя вратá), adorned with frescoes from the lives of SS. Anthony and Theodosius and leading into the court of the monastery. Above the gate is the *Church of the Trinity*, containing frescoes of the S.

Russian School, dating from the 18th century. The monastery court
is enclosed on the right and left by the cells of the monks. At the
time of the great festivals (July 15th and Aug. 15th, O. S.), it is the
camping-ground of the pilgrims, of whom 150,000 yearly visit the
Lavra. — To the right stands the *Belfry,* which was built in 1745
and rises to a height of 300 ft. in four diminishing stages (*View;
374 steps; permission of the commandant of the fortress necessary
for the ascent). — In front, farther on, is the —

Uspenski Cathedral, or Cathedral of the Assumption (Pl.
F, G, 7), a building 150 ft. square, with seven gilded domes. It
was consecrated in 1089, destroyed by the Tartars in 1240, rebuilt
in the course of the 15th cent., and restored in the rococo style in
1729, after a fire. The gables are adorned with frescoes.

The mural paintings inside are by V. P. Vereshtchágin (p. 305). The
present *Ikonostás,* made of gilded wood, was a gift of Peter the Great. At
the top, in the middle, is a painting (on cypress-wood) of the Virgin, surrounded by gilded rays and precious stones and said by tradition to have
been brought to Kiev from Byzantium in 1073. To the right as one enters
is a sarcophagus containing the relics of St. Theodosius (p. 380); to the
right of the ikonostás is a silver coffin containing the skull of St. Vladimir.
The church is always so crowded with infirm and other worshippers that
moving about in it is somewhat difficult. — The interesting *Conventual
Treasury* (Ри́зница), also preserved in the cathedral, contains relics and
valuables, permission to see which is obtained from the Metropolitan.

To the right of the cathedral is the *Refectory* (Трапе́за), with
a church built in 1895. Close by is the grave of P. A. Stolýpin, the
Prime Minister (p. 379). Beyond the cathedral we follow the road
immediately in front of us, which is spanned at places by large flying
buttresses, and then descend a flight of covered wooden steps to the
right, leading to the *Church of the Raising of the Cross,* which
contains the entrance to the catacombs of St. Anthony.

The Catacombs of St. Anthony (Бли́жнія пеще́ры преподо́б-
наго Анто́нія) consist of a number of small rectangular chambers
connected by narrow passages, originally excavated in the clay soil
and afterwards supported by masonry. These passages are about
6¹/₂ ft. in height and so narrow that only one person can pass through
them at a time. Some of the small chambers, which were formerly
the cells of the monks, are now used as chapels for the mass.

Visitors are led through the caves in groups by a monk; each is
provided with a wax candle (15-20 cop.). — No fewer than 73 saints are
buried here in niches, the bodies lying like mummies in open coffins and
enveloped in costly garments. Among these are *Anthony* (p. 380), whose
cell with its stone couch is still shown, *Varlaám* (p. 380), and *Nestor*
(d. 1115), the 'father of Russian history'. — The cells in which the more
ascetic hermits immured themselves are also pointed out to visitors, but
the small openings through which they received their food have been
built up. Another curiosity is a head projecting from the ground, and
covered with a mitre said to have been worn by John the Longsuffering
(Іоа́ннъ многострада́льный), who had himself buried in the earth up
to his neck and is said to have lived so for 30 years, while his dead
body was afterwards preserved in the same position (12th cent.).

The more distant CATACOMBS OF ST. THEODOSIUS (Дальнія пещёры преподобнаго Өеодосія) are similar in arrangement to those of St. Anthony, but less extensive and less interesting. They are entered through the *Church of St. Anna.*

The other churches and chapels of the Lavra have no particular interest. The printing-office for religious works was founded in 1606.

Redescending the Lavra Road (p. 380), we proceed to the right to the NIKOLÁYEVSKI SPUSK (fine view), a road about 1 M. in length. [A flight of 225 wooden steps affords a short-cut.] On the left is *Askold's Tomb* (Аскольдова могила; Pl. F, 5), with a chapel (345 ft. above the river; fine view) built in 1810 over the supposed site of Askold's tomb (p. 378). At the end of the road is the *Nicholas Suspension Bridge* (Николаевскій цѣпной мостъ), which spans the Dnieper (carriage-toll 20, with two horses 40 cop., including return; smoking forbidden). This bridge, which is $^1/_2$ M. long and supported by seven piers, five of which are in the water, was constructed by the English engineer Charles de Vigneroles in 1848-53 at a cost of $2^1/_2$ million rubles.

From the Nicholas Bridge the Náberezhnoye Chaussée ascends along the right bank of the Dnieper, leaving Askold's Tomb on the left, and leading in 35 min. to the Pumping Works (Pl. E, 3). Near by, among the bushes, is the *Baptismal Monument* (Памятникъ. крещёнія; Pl. D, E, 3), raised in 1802 to commemorate the introduction of Christianity, and consisting of a pillar-crowned chapel with a spring, the water of which is popularly credited with healing powers. A religious ceremony takes place here on July 15th (O.S.).

Farther to the N. we reach the quarter of **Podól** (Pl. C, D, 1, 2), the seat of the trade of Kiev and the dwelling-place of the poorer part of the population. In the midst of Podól, in the ALEXÁN-DROVSKAYA SQUARE (Александровская площадь; Pl. D, 2), stands the *House of Contracts*, so called from the fact that the bargains made at the 'Contract Fair', the most important sugar-mart of Russia, used to be signed here (new building in view). To the S. are the *Gostini Dvor* and the *Samson Fountain* (Фонтанъ Сампсона), popularly known as the Lion Fountain. Opposite is the BRATSKI CONVENT, containing the large *Cathedral of the Epiphany,* built in 1693 and restored in 1865. Beyond this is the *Imperial Theological Academy* (Императорская духовная академія), founded in 1615 as a church-school. It was converted into an academy in 1701 and is attended by 200 students. Its museum (Музей церковныхъ древностей) contains a rich collection of Old Russian ikons and the like (art-students admitted on application to the director; Russian catalogue, 1897, $1^1/_2$ rb.).

About 2 M. to the N.W. of the Alexándrovskaya Square (tramway, see p. 378) lies the *Church of St. Cyril* (see Inset Map, p. 377), dating from the 12th century. The frescoes in the S. aisle are coeval with the church. The other wall-paintings are by Vrubel (1885).

From the N. end of the Kreshtchátik (p. 379) we may turn to the left and either ascend in 5 min. to the Vladimir Monument (see below) or descend (a short walk) to the attractive *Garden of the Merchants' Club* (Pl. D, 3; p. 377). Near the restaurant, is a pavilion with a beautiful *View, particularly of the Dnieper plain.

The **Vladímir Monument** (Пáмятникъ св. Владимíру; Pl. D, 3), 62 ft. in height, cast in bronze from the design of Baron Klodt, was erected in 1853. The relief on the lofty pedestal represents the baptism of the Russian people (comp. p. 379); above is the figure of the saint holding a cross, which at night is made visible far and near by electric light. — About 400 yds. farther on is a *Pavilion* commanding a view of the Dnieper and Podól.

About the same distance above the Vladimir Monument is another pavilion with a view. Following thence the margin of the steep hill on which Old Kiev (p. 378) lies, we reach the —

Monastery of St. Michael (Михáйловскій монастырь; Pl. D, 3). The church, with its seven gilded domes, situated on the S. side of the enclosing wall, was founded in 1108 and has been frequently restored.

In the interior of the church, on the right side of the ikonostás, is an ancient ikón of the Archangel Michael, richly adorned with precious stones, which Alexander I. carried with him in the war with France. In a side-chapel to the N. is the silver tomb of St. Varvára (Barbara), surmounted by a canopy and dating from the end of the 18th cent.; the remains of the saint are said to have been brought to Kiev in 1070. In the apse are remains of mosaics of the 12th century (Last Supper).

To the W. of the convent are a monument to St. Olga and Sт. Michael's Square. To the N.W. of this we reach the Tryokh-svyatítelskaya, in which, lying back from the street, is the Church of the Three Saints (Цéрковь трёхъ святителей; Pl. D, 3), with a green central dome. This building was erected by St. Vladimir as the *Church of St. Basil,* on the site of the sanctuary of the Slav deity Perun. In 1240 it was destroyed by the Tartars, and about 400 years later it was thoroughly restored by Peter Mogila and consecrated to SS. Basil the Great, Gregory of Nazianzus, & John Chrysostom. Parts of the N. wall, the three apses, and some other fragments of the original building are still extant. — About $^1/_4$ M. farther to the N., in the Tryokhsvyatítelskaya, is the handsome —

Church of St. Andrew (Цéрковь Андрéя Первозвáннаго; Pl. D, 2), built in the baroque style in 1744-67 from the plans of Rastrelli, with white domes and gilt decoration on a white ground. It stands on the highest point in Old Kiev, on the *Andréyevski Hill,* which descends steeply to Podól, and occupies the spot where, according to tradition, the Apostle Andrew, the first preacher of the gospel in Russia, erected a cross. The church stands on a lofty platform, reached by a broad flight of steps. The terrace commands a fine *View of Podól, the river, and the plain to the E.

We now turn to the S. and enter the VLADÍMIRSKAYA, in which, immediately to the right, is the **Desyatínnaya** or *Church of the Tithes* (Десятинная церковь; Pl. C, D, 2, 3), erected by St. Vladimir in 989-996 as the *Church of the Assumption*. It was destroyed by the Tartars in 1240, and was entirely rebuilt in its present square form with five domes in 1828-42. Inside, adjoining the S. wall, is a stair leading down to a vault with the sarcophagus of St. Vladimir.

Proceeding hence in the same direction and crossing the Bolshaya Zhitómirskaya, we reach the SQUARE OF ST. SOPHIA (Софійская площадь; Pl. C, 3), the middle of which is occupied by the fine monument of *Bogdán Khmyelnítzki* (1593-1657; comp. p. 402), the Cossack hetman, erected in 1888 from the design of Mikéshin. This consists of a high block of rock surrounded by vines and bearing the hetman on a rearing steed. — On the S.W. side of the square are the enclosing wall and the belfry (about 1750) of the —

*Cathedral of St. Sophia (Софійскій соборъ; Pl. C, 3), constantly besieged, like the Lavra, by numerous pilgrims and beggars. The church, erected in 1037-49 by the Grand-Prince Yaroslàv, in gratitude for the victory here gained by him over the Petchenegians, is 180 ft. long, 120 ft. wide, and 130 ft. high. It is surmounted by a central dome and 14 subsidiary domes, all gilded. The exterior has suffered from alterations in the 17th cent. and other periods, but the interior is the most interesting architectural picture that Kiev has to show. The five central aisles, all ending in apses, and intersected by a transept, date from the original building.

The INTERIOR (fee to attendant 20-30 cop.) is adorned with mosaics on a gold ground and old frescoes. The richly gilded *Ikonostás*, which formerly reached to the ceiling of the church, is in the rococo style and was erected in the first half of the 18th century. Behind the ikonostás, above the archbishop's throne (Горнее мѣсто), is a figure of the Virgin (the so-called Нерушимая стѣна or 'indestructible wall') and below it is a representation of the Last Supper, two mosaics of the 11th cent. (best viewed from the gallery, see below). The *Chapel of St. Vladimir*, to the left of the ikonostás, contains the monument of Yaroslàv I. (d. 1054), consisting of marble and adorned with reliefs of Christian symbols. In the arcade to the left of the ikonostás is an open and empty stone coffin, supposed to be that of Vladimir Monomäkh. — The approach to the gallery is in a staircase turret, reached from the S. arcade, to the left of the entrance. This turret formerly lay outside the cathedral and connected it with the prince's palace. The walls of the staircase are adorned with *Frescoes of Byzantine court life (11th cent.), including some curious scenes of the circus, the partakers in which are disguised as animals.

To the W. of the cathedral is the *Residence of the Metropolitan*.

From St. Sophia Square the wide BOLSHAYA VLADÍMIRSKAYA, the principal street of Old Kiev, leads towards the S. On the left side of it is the *Irene Monument* (Памятникъ св. Иринѣ; Pl. C, 3, 4), consisting of a block of masonry under a protecting roof, said to be the remains of the Irene Convent founded by the Grand-Prince Yaroslàv. To the right is the *Church of St. George* (Церковь св. Геóргія; 1752). Farther on, also to the right, is the so-called **Golden Gate** (Золотыя ворóта; Pl. C, 4), situated on a small eminence and surrounded by pleasure-grounds; its gates are said to have consisted of gilded bronze. It was erected in 1037 under YaroslÁv I. (p. 379) and was formerly the principal gate of Kiev. It is now a heap of ruins, with traces of the old arches.

From the Golden Gate the Vasiltchikovskaya (Proryeznáya; Pl. C, 5, 4) descends to the E. to the Kreshtchátik (p. 379), passing the *Imperial Conservatoire of Music.* — In the Yaroslávov Rampart, also named the Bolshaya Podválnaya, is the *Synagogue of the Karaïtes* (Pl. C, 4), completed in 1902 from the design of Gorodetzki.

Farther on in the Vladimirskaya, to the right, in the *Municipal Theatre* (Pl. C, 4), built by Schröter in 1900. To the left is the *Museum of Pedagogy* (Pl. C, 4; open free daily, 12-2), completed in 1912. Farther on, to the right, is the **Vladímir University** (Pl. C, 5), a massive dark-red edifice with a portico of eight columns built by Beretti in 1837-42. The University, which was transferred from Vilna to Kiev in 1834, is attended by 3000 students, and possesses valuable natural history, numismatic, and other collections. The library contains about 500,000 volumes. — In front of the E. side of the University lies the *Nicholas Garden,* with a *Bronze Statue of Tzar Nicholas I.* by Tchizhov (1896). Behind the University, to the W., stretch the extensive *Botanical Gardens* (Pl. B, C, 4, 5), which include a *Zoological Garden.*

From the Bogdán Khmyelnítzki Square (p. 379) the poplar-lined Bíbikovski Boulevard runs W. for nearly 2 M. — At No. 9 Tereshtchenkovska is the **Palais Khanyenko** (Pl. C, 5), with an interesting art-collection (visitors admitted in winter and spring on production of their visiting-cards; Russian catalogue 30 cop.).

Among the chief pictures are the following: 17. *Albertinelli,* Deposition in the Tomb; 26. *Perugino,* Madonna; 34. *P. da Cortona,* Monk in a cave; 55. *L. Giordano,* Vision of St. Jerome; 63. *L. Lotto,* Madonna with saints; 66. *Palma the Younger,* Battle of the Amazons; 155. *P. Brueghel the Elder,* Village festival; *Jan Brueghel the Elder,* 158. Flemish village, 159. Flowers; 161. *Hans Jordaens the Elder,* Stranded whale; 171. *K. van Mander,* Adoration of the Shepherds; 259. *Rubens,* River-god and nymphs, a study; 187. *G. Coques,* Family group; 259. *Palamedesz,* Portrait of a woman; 261. *J. Bronchorst,* Concert; 264. *A. van Ostade,* Merry l'leming ('Le grivois flamand'; copy); 270. *Rembrandt (?),* Portrait of a woman; 276. *F. Bol (?),* Joseph accused by Potiphar's wife; 305. *J. van Ruysdael,* Woodland scene; 328. *R. Ruysch,* Flowers; 367. *C. Natoire,* Cupido; 369. *Fr. Boucher,* Village-scene; 394-96. Russian ikons (second half of the 17th cent.).

Farther to the W. in the Bíbikovski Boulevard, on the right, stands the massive **Cathedral of St. Vladímir** (Владúмірскій собóръ; Pl. C, 4), built in the Byzantine style in 1862-96 by *Beretti* and *Bernhardt.* It is 156 ft. long, 90 ft. wide, and 160 ft. high. The seven domes are gilded, and the windows are framed in fine stone ornamentation. Inside are some remarkable *Mural Paintings,* in which the artists have attempted to revive the Byzantine style.

The INTERIOR, which consists of three aisles, was decorated in 1885-96 under the superintendence of Professor Prakhov. The low ikonostás is made of marble. Among the paintings by Vasnetzóv may be mentioned Last Judgment, above the W. entrance-door, with the Baptism of Vladímir and the Baptism of the Russians to the left and right of it; a large head of Christ in the principal dome; Madonna, behind the high-altar, with the Last Supper below; the Prophets, to the right and left of the high-altar; and the figures of SS. Olga, Vladímir, and Alexander Nevski on the ikonostás. By the side-altars are scenes from the Last Days of the Redeemer, by Svedómski, with landscapes painted from nature. In the choir, to the right, behind the altar, is the Nativity, by Nésterov. On the ceiling of the choir are the Transfiguration, by Kotarbinski (to the right), and the Ascension, by Svedómski (to the left).

Continuing to follow the Bibikovski Boulevard from the Vladímir Cathedral, we reach (7 min.) a *Bronze Statue of Count Bóbrinski* (Pl. B, 4), the founder of the Russian sugar-industry, erected in 1872 from the design of Schröder. — To the N.W. of the railway station is the *Polytechnic Institute* (beyond Pl. A, 3), completed in 1901 and attended by 2500 students.

FROM KIEV TO POLTAVA, 329 V. (218 M.), railway in 8¹/₂-10 hrs. — We cross the Dnieper by the bridge mentioned at p. 377. — About 17 M. to the S. of (84 V.) *Pereyaslávskaya* lies *Pereyasláv*, a district-town in the government of Poltava, founded in 993. Pop. 18,600. — 139 V. *Grebenka* (Rail. Restaurant), see below; 178 V. *Lubni* (Rail. Restaurant); 207 V. *Romodán* (Rail. Restaurant), see p. 391. — 329 V. (218 M.) *Poltava*, see p. 389.

From Kiev to *Moscow*, see R. 53; to *Odessa*, see R. 55 b; to *Kovel*, see p. 374.

55. From Moscow to Odessa.

a. Viâ BAKHMATCH AND BOBRINSKAYA.

1229 V. (814 M.). This line, the shortest route between Moscow and Odessa, was at the end of 1913 open for traffic as far as Bobrinskaya. The rest of the line is to be opened in the summer of 1914.

From Moscow to (623 V.) *Bakhmatch*, see p. 376. We diverge to the S. from the Kiev line. — 697 V. *Priluki*, a district-town with 30,500 inhab. and a trade in peasants' tobacco (махóрка); 751 V. *Grebenka* (Railway Restaurant), see above; 808 V. *Zolotonosha*, a district-town with 12,800 inhabitants. We cross the Dnieper. 836 V. *Tcherkássi;* 865 V. *Bóbrinskaya* (Railway Restaurant), see p. 387; 917 V. *Novomirgorod* (Railway Restaurant), a district-town with 11,000 inhab.; 985 V. *Pómoshnaya* (p. 393); 1064 V. *Voznesénsk* (Railway Restaurant), a district-town with 19,300 inhabitants. We cross the *Bug*. — 1229 V. (814 M.) *Odessa* (Bakhmatch Station), see p. 393.

b. Viâ BAKHMATCH AND KIEV.

1415 V. (938 M.). Express train in 37¹/₂ hrs. (fares 28 rb. 95, 18 rb. 15 cop.; seat-ticket 2 rb. 70 cop., see p. xxiii). Slow train in 56 hrs. (fares 27 rb., 16 rb. 20 cop.). — *From Kiev to Odessa*, 612 V. (407 M.), express train in 12¹/₂ hrs. (fares 17 rb. 95, 11 rb. 55 cop.; seat-ticket 1¹/₂ rb.).

From Moscow to (803 V.) *Kiev*, see R. 53. — The train runs to the S.W. through the fruitful and well-tilled government of Kiev.

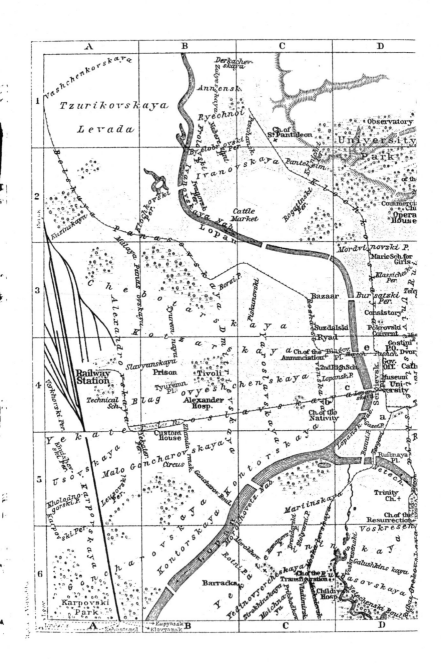

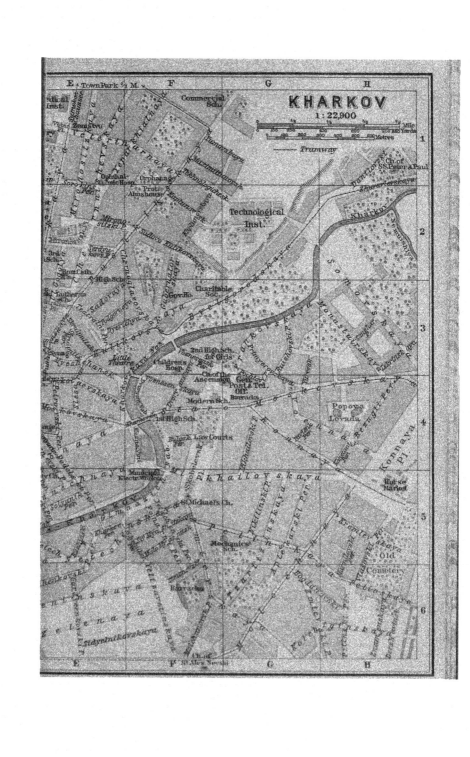

824 V. *Boyárka,* an attractive summer-resort of the citizens of Kiev. About 5 M. to the S. of (837 V.) *Vasilkóv* is the prettily situated town of that name, with 16,800 inhabitants. — 863 V. **Fastov** (Фастовъ; *Railway Restaurant,* fair).

From Fastov to Znamenka, 282 V. (187 M.), railway in 7-10 hrs. 32 V. *Byélaya Tzerkov,* 73 V. *Olshanitza,* 132 V. *Korsún,* 168 V. *Tzvyetkóvo* (p. 372), 199 V. *Bóbrinskaya* (p. 386), all five with rail. restaurants.— 282 V. (187 M.) *Známenka* (p. 391).

952 V. (631 M.) **Kazátin.** Thence to (1415 V.) *Odessa,* see p. 375.

c. Viâ Kursk, Kharkov, and Birzula.

1563 V. (1036 M.). Railway in 43 hrs. (fares 29 rb., 17 rb. 40 cop.; express and seat-tickets extra). — From Moscow to Kharkov, 731 V. (487 M.), express train in 14 hrs. (fares 20 rb. 20 cop., 13 rb.; seat-ticket 1 rb. 80 cop.).

From Moscow to (502 V.) *Kursk,* see R. 46. — About 7 M. beyond Kursk the train crosses the *Seim* and begins to traverse the plain of the 'Black Earth' (p. xxxvii), from the sombre levels of which the miserable gray villages stand out curiously in the glittering sunshine. 575 V. *Kleinmíkhelovo* (Rail. Restaurant). — 652 V. **Byélgorod** (*Rail. Restaurant; Yevropéiskaya Hotel;* cab to the town 30 cop.), a district-town in the government of Kursk, containing 28,000 inhab. and carrying on a brisk trade, is picturesquely situated at the foot of the lofty limestone cliffs on the right bank of the *Donétz.* The Tróitzki Convent, which is reached in 20 min. by turning to the left from the station and then going to the right along the Ulitza Imperátora Nikoláya II, contains the grave of Bishop Ioasaf (d. 1754), who was canonized in 1911. Branch-lines to (139 V.) Basi (p. 389) and to (148 V.) Kupyansk (p. 389).

731 V. (484 M.) **Kharkov,** Харьковъ. — *Rail. Restaurant,* very fair. — Hotels (overcrowded and dear during the large markets, see p. 388). *Grand-Hôtel* (Pl. a; D, 4), Torgóvaya Square, R. from 2, B. ³/₄, déj. (12-2) 1¹/₄, D. (2-7) 1¹/₂-2¹/₂, omn. ¹/₂ or 1 rb.; *Rossiya* (Pl. c; D, 4), Yekaterinoslávskaya 4, R. from 1¹/₄ (with bath from 4), B. ¹/₂, D. (1-7 p.m.) ³/₄-2¹/₄ rb., omn. 60 cop.; *Métropole* (Pl. f; E, 3), Nikoláyevskaya Square 31, R. from 1³/₄, D. (1-6 p.m.) 1¹/₄ & 2¹/₄ rb., good; *Astoria,* Sérgiyevskaya Square (Pl. D, 4) new; *Monnet* (Pl. b; C, 4), Yekaterinoslávskaya 5; *Astrakhánskaya* (Pl. d; D, 3), Nikoláyevskaya Square; *Bolshaya Moskóvskaya* (Pl. e; D, 4), Klotchkóvskaya 1.

Restaurants. *Grand-Hôtel,* see above; *Versailles,* Kontórskaya 1 (Pl. B, C, 5), with garden, D. (2.30 to 5.30) 1¹/₂ & 2¹/₄ rb., very fair; *Astrakhánskaya,* see above; beer at *Zimmermann's,* Sumskaya 11 (Pl. E, 1-3), D. (1-4 p.m.) 60 cop. — Cafés. *Dierberg, Poque,* Moskóvskaya (Pl. E, 4), French and German newspapers at both.

Cab from the railway station to the town 40, with two horses 80; per drive 30 or 60 cop.; second-class one-horse cabs 10 cop. cheaper. A one-horse cab is called a *Vánka.*

Tramways (5 or 8 cop.). From the Railway Station (Pl. A, 4) viâ the Yekaterinoslávskaya to the Torgóvaya Square (Pl. D, E, 4); thence to the N. along the Sumskaya (Pl. E, 1, 2), to the E. along the Staro-Moskóvskaya (Pl. F-H, 4), and to the S. along the Moskályevskaya (Pl. C, 5, 6). Electric cars also run to the Balashóvski Railway Station and to the Town Park.

Post & Telegraph Offices in Voznesénskaya Square (Pl. G, 4) and in the Arcade (Pl. D, 4). - Banks. *Imperial Bank* (Pl. E, 3), Teatrálnaya Square

(open 10-3); *Volga & Kama Bank*, Nikoláyevskaya Square (Pl. D, E, 3, 4), and many others. — Bookseller *A. Dröder*, Moskóvskaya 21 (Pl. E, 4).
BRITISH VICE-CONSUL, *C. Blakey*, Moskóvskaya 27 (Pl. E, 4). —ENGLISH CLUB, *Helfferich-Ladet Sporting Club*.

Kharkov, the capital of the government of that name in Little Russia, lies mainly upon the plateau (755 ft.) which here interrupts the belt of 'Black Earth' (p. xxxvii), about 100 ft. above the *Udi* (an affluent of the Donétz) and the two small streams *Lopan* and *Khárkov*, which unite here. The town, which dates from about 1650, is the see of the Greek Catholic Archbishop of the eparchy of Kharkov and Akhtuirka, and the headquarters of the 10th Army Corps. It is a university town and the administrative centre of the great iron industry and coal-mines of South Russia. The inhabitants, 248,000 in number, carry on a considerable trade in cloth, wool and cattle. The fairs held here on Jan. 6-20th (O.S.), after Easter, after Whitsun, on Aug. 15-30th, and on Oct. 1-20th (the chief one) are of great importance for South Russia.

From the *Railway Station* (Pl. A, 4) the Yekaterinoslávskaya (tramway), leads E. to the Old Town. To the N. of this street, in the Blagovyéshtchenskaya (Pl. A-C, 4), is the *New Opera House*. To the N. of the Blagovyéshtchenskaya Square (Pl. C, D, 4) lies the *Bazaar*

In the Sérgiyevskaya Square is the *University* (Pl. D, 4), which was founded in 1804 and is attended by 3400 students. It contains a library of 240,000 vols., a museum of art (Музéй изящныхъ искýсствъ; paintings, prehistoric antiquities; Tues., Thur., & Sun., 11-2), an ethnographical museum (Wed. & Sun., 12-2), and a zoological collection (Sun. 12-2, from Sept. 1st to May 15th, O.S.). To the N. of the university is the *Municipal Industrial Museum* (Городскóй худóжественно-промышленный музéй), which is open daily, except Mon., 11-4 (adm. 5-10 cop.; closed in June and July, O.S.; Russian catalogue 20 cop.), with a collection of modern Russian paintings and objects illustrating the arts and crafts of Little Russia. To the E. is the *Uspenski Cathedral*, dating from 1781, with a belfry 295 ft. high, completed in 1841. The Moskóvskaya (Pl. E, 4), which runs E. from the cathedral, is the chief business thoroughfare. In the Universitétskaya, to the left, is the *Pokrovski Convent* (Pl. D, 3; 1726). Farther on, to the N., in the Ruimárskaya, are the *Opera House* (Pl. D, 2) and the *Commercial Club*.

The Nikoláyevskaya Square (Pl. D, E, 3, 4) contains several banks, including the handsome building of the *Agrarian Bank* (by Bekétov). Hence the Sumskaya (tramway, see p. 387) leads N., past the *Theatre* (Драматúческiй теáтръ; Pl. D, E, 3), to the *University Park* (Pl. D, 1, 2). Just outside the park, which contains a small zoological collection (adm. 5 cop.), is a bronze statue, by Andrioletti (1907), of *V. N. Karázin* (d. 1842), the founder of Kharkov University. To the N. are the medical buildings of the University and the new *Town Park*. From the *Veterinary*

Institute (Pl. E, 1) we proceed to the E., through the Veterinárnaya and its prolongation, to the high-lying *Technological Institute* (Pl. G, 2; 1400 students). We return to the Old Town by the Púshkin-skaya. In the Úlitza Gógolya are the *Roman Catholic* and *Lutheran Churches* (Pl. E, 2, 3).— On the N. side of the Skóbelevskaya Square are the *Law Courts* (Pl. F, 4).

FROM KHARKOV TO BALASHOV, 630 V. (417 M.), railway in 24 hrs.— From (126 V.) *Kupyánsk* (Rail. Restaurant) branch-lines run S. to (221 V.) Debaltzevo (p. 429) and N. to (148 V.) Byelgorod (p. 387).— 197 V. *Valúiki* (Rail. Restaurant), with a large grain-elevator, is the junction of a branch-line to (207 V.) Kastornaya (p. 428). Beyond (319 V.) *Koponishtche* we traverse an attractive hilly district all the way to Liski. Near (325 V.) *Divnogórskaya Plattfórma* are a monastery and the hills of *Bolshíya Divi* and *Máluiya Divi*, each containing numerous caves. Just before reaching (346 V.) *Liski-on-the-Don* (Лйски на Дону; Rail. Restaurant), the junction of the railway from Voronezh to Rostov (p. 428), we cross the Don. 438 V. *Talovaya* (Rail. Restaurant); 554 V. *Povórino* (Rail. Restaurant), see p. 427.—630 V. (417 M.) *Balashóv* (p. 432).

FROM KHARKOV TO VOROZHBA, 234 V. (155 M.), railway in 6 hrs.— 23 V. *Lyubótin* (Rail. Restaurant) is the junction of the line to Poltava (see below), and of a branch-line to (17 V.) Merefa (p. 400). At (108 V.) *Kirikóvka* a line diverges for (16 V.) *Akhtúirka*, an industrial town with 31,700 inhabitants. Beyond (128 V.) *Smoródino* (Rail. Restaurant) is (174 V.) *Basi*, at the junction of a line to (139 V.) Byelgorod (p. 387).—188 V. Sumi *(Rail. Restaurant; Grand-Hôtel;* izvóshtchik from the rail. station to the town 40 cop.) was founded in 1658, and is the capital of a district in the government of Kharkov. Pop. 51,500. It possesses ancient forti-fications and a large sugar-factory.—234 V. (155 M.) *Vorozhbá* (p. 363)

From Kharkov to *Simferopol (Sebastopol),* see R. 57.— From Kharkov branch-lines also run N.W. to (239 V.) *Lgov* (p. 363) and S.E. to (199 V.) *Slavyansk* (p. 431).

The railway now runs to the S.W. through the government of Kharkov, which, like the neighbouring Poltava, formed a part of the old *Ukraine* or 'borderland' (*i.e.* towards Turkey). Both dis-tricts are very fertile. The great mass of the inhabitants are Little Russians (p. xliii). — 737 V. *Nóvaya Baváriya*, with a large brewery. At (754 V.) *Lyubótin* (Rail. Restaurant; see above). Be-yond (808 V.) *Kólomak* we enter the government of Poltava.

863 V. (572 M.) **Poltáva.**—STATION OF THE KHARKOV & NIKOLAI RAILWAY (*Restaurant,* fair), for all trains, on the E. side of the town, about 2 M. from the Alexándrovskaya Square; STATION OF THE MOSCOW & VORÓNEZH RAILWAY (Полтáва гóродъ; *Restaurant,* fair), for trains to Kiev, to the N.W. of the town, about 1³/₄ M. from the Alexándrovskaya Square. The two stations are connected by a loop-line, which crosses the battlefield mentioned at p. 390.— HOTELS. *Yevropéiskaya,* Petróv-skaya, R. from 1¹/₄ rb., D. (2-7 p.m.) from 60 cop. to 1 rb. 20 cop.; *Vorobyóv,* Preobrazhénskaya; *Grand-Hôtel,* near the Alexándrovskaya Square, R. from 1¹/₂ rb.— ČAB (*Phaeton*) with two horses from the Kharkov Railway Station to the town 75, from the Moscow & Voronezh Railway Station to the town 50, per drive 20-30, per hr. 60 cop.

Poltáva or *Pultóva*, the capital of a government of the same name, is situated on a ridge of ground overlooking the *Vorskla*, contains 84,000 inhab. (many Jews), and carries on an important trade in horses, fat cattle, and grain. — We go straight out of the Kharkov

25*

Station and cross (5 min.) the Vorskla. About 6 min. later we avoid
the turning to the right, and go straight on as far as (25 min.), the
Petrovski Park, where we turn to the right. Passing on our right
the *Zemstvo Building* (1908), which is adorned with majolica and
paintings and contains a museum of natural history and archaeology (Естéственно-историческiй музéй; adm. as at the Gogol
House, see below), we reach (3 min.) the Alexándrovskaya and follow
this street to the right. [The Alexándrovskaya Square lies about
$1/_2$ M. off in the other direction.] Immediately to the right stands
the *Church of the Resurrection* (Воскресéнская цéрковь), built in
1773. Opposite, to the left, is a *Chapel* (Цéрковь Спáса-Неру-
котворéннаго) in which Peter the Great said his prayers after the
battle of Poltava. Behind this is a *Memorial Stone* with military
emblems, set up in 1849, marking the site of the house occupied by
Peter the Great after the battle. At the end of the street is the
Cathedral of the Assumption, built in 1770. Returning through the
Alexándrovskaya, we reach the Gógolevskaya in 10 minutes. In this
street, on the left, is the *Gogol House* (Просвѣти́тельное здáнiе
и́мени Гóголя), containing an ethnographical collection (open free,
Sun. 12-3, week-days, except Mon., in summer 9-2, in winter 10-3).
To the S. is a *Roman Catholic Church*. At the junction of the
Petróvskaya with the Úlitza Kotlyarévskago, the next cross-street,
is a bronze bust by Posen (1903) of the Little Russian poet *I. P.
Kotlyarévski* (d. 1838). Farther on, to the left, is the *Post Office*.
The Alexándrovskaya ends in the circular Alexándrovskaya Square,
in the middle of which rises a *Column of Victory*, 56 ft. in height,
erected in 1809 to commemorate the battle of Poltava. The square
contains the Cadet School, the Governor's Residence, the District
Court, etc., and close by, to the E., is the *Lutheran Church*.
Following the Monastúirskaya from this point we come in 25 min.
to the high-lying *Monastery of the Raising of the Cross* (1650).

The battlefield on which the outcome of the great War of the North was
determined and the position of Russia in Europe established by the victory
of the Russians under Peter the Great over the Swedes under Charles XII.
on June 27th (O. S.), 1709, lies $3^1/_4$ M. to the N.W. of the town (carr. & pair
there & back in $1^1/_2$ hr., fare $1^1/_2$-2 rb.). The Russians had about 42,000 men
and 72 guns, the Swedes 27,000 men and only 4 guns. Under the so-
called Swedish Grave (Швéдская моги́ла), a mound 65 ft. in height surmounted by a large stone cross, are buried the Russian dead, 1345 in
number. Close by are a church and a museum containing relics of the
battle, including a large panel of copper, set up in 1778, on which a representation of the battle of Poltava is engraved; the fallen Swedes lie
under another tumulus less than $1/_2$ M. to the N. (monument erected in
1909). The 16,000 survivors of the Swedish army surrendered to the
Russians at Perevolótchna three days after the battle.

FROM POLTAVA TO LOZOVAYA, 165 V. (109 M.), railway in $5^1/_2$ hrs.—
45 V. *Kárlovka*, with an extensive grand-ducal estate; 76 V. *Konstanti-
nográd* (Rail. Restaurant), a district-town in the government of Poltava,
with 13,700 inhabitants.—165 V. (109 M.) *Lozováya*, see p. 400.

From Poltava to *Kiev*, see p. 386.

Beyond (958 V.) *Potóki* we cross the *Psiól* (Пселъ), a tributary of the Dnieper.

973 V. (645 M.) **Krementchúg**, Кременчугъ. — *Rail. Restaurant.* — HOTELS. *Palmyra*, Khersónskaya, R. 1-5, D. (1-5 p.m.) ¹/₂-1 rb.; *Italiya*, R. ³/₄-2¹/₂, D. (1-5 p.m.) ¹/₂-1 rb.; *Victoria*, cor. of the Khersónskaya and the Birzheváya. — IZVÓSHTCHIK from the rail. station or the steamboat-pier to the town 30, per drive 20, per hr. 40; with two horses 50, 40, 60 cop. — ELECTRIC TRAMWAY from the station through the town to the harbour; also other lines (fare 5 cop.). — STEAMBOATS ply to Yekaterinoslav and Kiev (see p. 378).

Krementchug, the chief town of a district of the government of Poltava, situated on the left bank of the *Dnieper* and frequently exposed to inundations, carries on a lively trade in timber and firewood (numerous saw-mills). Pop. 100,000 (including Kryukov, see below). The noteworthy buildings include the Greek Catholic *Cathedral of the Transfiguration* (founded in 1808), the *Town Hall*, and the large *Arsenal*. Open-air concerts take place in the attractive *Public Park* (restaurant). There is a Lutheran church. — *K. Baer's Nursery* at Pávlovka, 5 M. to the N., is interesting.

FROM KREMENTCHUG TO ROMNI, 201 V. (133 M.), railway in 6 hrs. — 108 V. *Romodán* (Rail. Restaurant), see p. 386; 119 V. *Dubrovski*, with the stud of the Grand-Duke Demetrius Constantinovitch, where the famous Orlov trotters and mares are reared. — 201 V. (133 M.) *Romni* (p. 39).

We cross the Dnieper by a girder-bridge (view of Krementchug to the right) to (983 V.) *Kryukov* (see above). From (1034 V.) *Koristóvka* a branch-line runs to (69 V.) Pyatikhatki (p. 402). — 1069 V. (708 M.) **Známenka**, Знаменка *(Rail. Restaurant)*, junction for Fastov (p. 387).

FROM ZNAMENKA TO KHERSON, 280 V. (185 M.), railway in 8¹/₂ hrs. (express to Nikolayev in 5 hrs.). — 75 V. *Dolínskaya* (Rail. Restaurant). To Yekaterinoslav and (277 V.) Sinelnikovo, see pp. 402, 401.

222 V. (147 M.) **Nikoláyev**, Николаевъ. — *Rail. Restaurant.* — HOTELS. *Lóndonskaya*, R. from 1¹/₂ rb.; *Barbe*, R. from 1¹/₄ rb., B. 50, déj. (12-4) 55-75 cop., D. (4-5) ¹/₂-1¹/₄ rb., both in the Sobórnaya; *Peterburgskaya*, Potémkinskaya. - - CAB from the railway station to the town 50, from the steamer landing-stage 60, per drive 30, per hr. 60 cop. — TRAMWAYS from the station to the town and from the harbour to Spask. — BRITISH VICE-CONSUL, *J. Picton Bagge*, Tavritcheskaya 1. — LLOYD'S AGENT, *Arthur Deacon*.

Nikoláyev or *Nicolaieff*, a town of 120,000 inhab. in the government of Kherson, stands upon a point of land on the left bank of the *Bug*, at its junction with the *Ingúl*. It was founded by Prince Potemkin in 1788 and is the chief grain port of S. Russia. There are both Lutheran and Roman Catholic churches. The Sobórnaya traverses the town from N. to S. In the Sobórnaya Square are a statue of Admiral Greig (p. 76) and the Old Guard House, in which the Vereshtchágin Museum is to be housed. At the S. end of the Sobórnaya, on the Bug, is a large shipbuilding yard; at the N. end, on the Ingúl, are another shipbuilding yard, the Admiralty, and a

well-kept boulevard. At the corner of the Katolitcheskaya and Spásskaya is a branch of the Nicholas Observatory at Pulkovo (p. 189).
To the W. of the town, on the Bug, are the summer villas of *Spask*,
with a promenade (restaurant).

About 25 V. (17 M.) to the S. of Nikolayev, on the right bank of the
Bug, are the ruins of the Milesian colony of *Olbia*. About 25 V. to the
W. of Olbia, on the N. side of the Dnieper Limán, is the fortified town
of *Otchákov*, the ancient Alector.

Steamer from Nikolayev to Odessa daily in 7 hrs. (fare 3 rb.); to
Kherson daily, except Sat., in 6 hrs. (fare 2 rb. 15 cop.).

280 V. **Khersón,** Херсонъ (*Railway Restaurant; Peterbúrgskaya, Odésskaya,* R. in both 1-3 rb.; cab per drive 25, with
two horses 30, per hr. 40 or 60, from the rail. station to the town
50-60 cop.; British vice-consul, *E. Caruana,* Lyuteránskaya 13),
the capital of the government of the same name, lies at an elevation
of 100 ft. on the right bank of the Dnieper, 19 M. above its mouth
in the Dnieper Limán. It contains 93,000 inhab., one-third of whom
are Jews, and carries on a trade in grain and timber. St. Catharine's
Cathedral or Church of the Redeemer, in the Voénni Suburb, contains the tomb of Prince Potemkin (d. 1791; to the right in front
of the ikonostás), who founded the town in 1778. In the centre of
the town is a well-kept boulevard, with a bronze statue of the prince
by Martos (1836). An obelisk near the Greek Catholic Cemetery,
erected in 1828, commemorates the philanthropist John Howard
(1726-90), who died here of camp fever while on a tour of investi-
gation into the causes of the plague. The house in which he lived, in
the Suvórovskaya, is marked by a tablet; he lies buried at Stepá-
novka, 4 M. to the N. of the town ('Vixit propter alios, alios salvos
fecit'). There are a public library, a museum of local antiquities
and a picture gallery. The town also possesses Lutheran and Roman
Catholic churches. Steamers to Alexandrovsk (see p. 402), to Nikolayev (see above), and to Odessa (daily in 10 hrs.; fare 3 rb. 95 cop.).

1117 V. (740 M.) **Yelisavetgrád,** Елисаветградъ.— *Railway
Restaurant.* — Hotels. *Kovalénko,* R. 1-3 rb.; *Rossíya,* R. 1-3 rb., both
with restaurants (D. from 50 cop.); *Syévernaya,* R. 1½-5 rb., D. (1-4 p.m.)
60 cop. to 1¼ rb.; *Grand-Hôtel,* Dvortzóvaya.— *Restaurant Kozlóv,* D.
from 50 cop.— Izvóshtchik from the railway station to the town 40, with
two horses 60, per drive 20 or 30, per hr. 40 or 60 cop.— Electric Tramway
from the station through the town (5 cop.) and to the Town Park (8 cop.).

Yelisavetgrád, a district-town in the government of Kherson,
founded in 1754 in the reign of Empress Elizabeth, contains 76,000
inhab., one-third of whom are Jews, and carries on a brisk trade in
grain, cattle, and wool. It is well built and possesses attractive
boulevards and wide streets, such as the Bolshói Prospékt. Among
its buildings may be mentioned the Cavalry School (in the old imperial palace), the Lutheran Church, and the Roman Catholic Church.
An agricultural show is held annually, April 20-28th (O.S.). — About
1¼ M. from the town is the large Town Park.

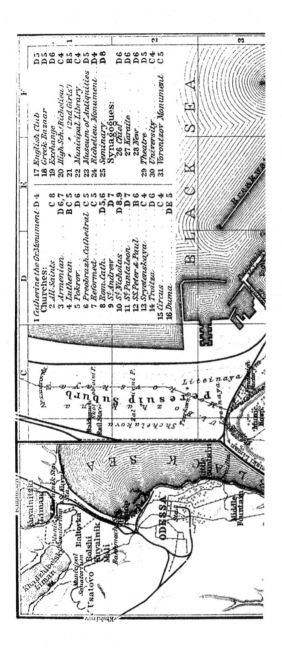

1 Catherine the Gr.Monument.	D.4	
Churches:		
2 All Saints	C 8	
3 Armenian	D 6,7	
4 Lutheran	B C 5	
5 Pokrov	D 6	
6 Preobrazh. Cathedral	C 5	
7 Reformed	C 5	
8 Rom.Cath.	D 5,6	
9 St.Andrew	D 7	
10 St.Nicholas	D 8,9	
11 St.Pantaleon	D 7	
12 SS.Peter & Paul	B 6	
13 Sretenskaya	C 4	
14 Troitza	D 6	
15 Circus	C 4	
16 Duma	D E 5	

17 English Club	D 5
18 Greek Bazaar	D 5
19 Exchange	D 6
20 High Sch.(Richelieu)	C 4
21 " " (2nd Girls')	B 5
22 Municipal Library	C 4
23 Museum of Antiquities	D 5
24 Richelieu Monument	D 4
25 Seminary	D 8
Synagogues:	
26 Chief	D 6
27 Karaite	D 6
28 New	D 6
29 Theatre	D 5
30 University	C 4
31 Vorontzov Monument	C 5

BLACK SEA

ODESSA

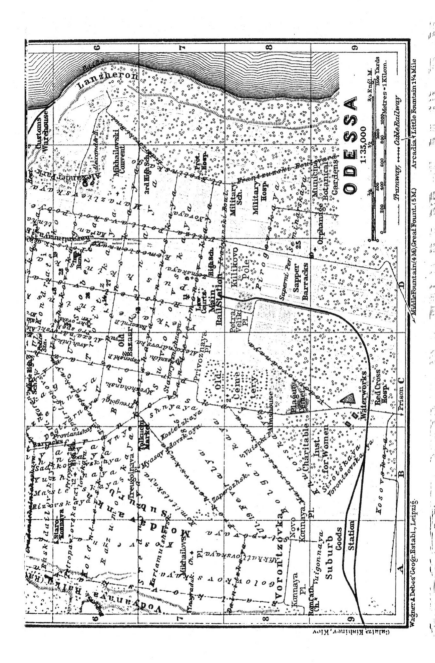

ODESSA

1:35,000

1197 V. (793 M.) *Pómoshnaya* (p. 386); 1242 V. *Podgoród-naya* (p. 372). Beyond (1251 V.) *Goltá* (Rail. Restaurant) we cross the Bug.—1366 V. *Balta.* About 5 M. to the N. lies the district-town of that name (Passage Hotel; izvóshtchik 1 rb.), with 30,000 in-hab. and a considerable trade in grain and cattle.
1387 V. (919 M.) **Bírzula** *(Rail. Restaurant).* From this point to (1563 V.; 1036 M.) *Odessa,* see pp. 373, 374.

56. Odessa and Environs.

RAILWAY STATIONS. *Main Station* (Pl. D, 7), on the Kulikóvo Pole, for the S.W. lines; *Bakhmatch Station* (Pl. B, 1), in the Peresuip Suburb, for R. 55 a; *Odessa Harbour Station* (Pl. D, E, 4) for the Kuyálnitzki Limán (p. 399).—City Office of State Railways, Ulitza Skóbeleva 11 (Pl. C, D, 6), open 10-4 (Sun. & holidays 12-4).

Hotels. *LONDON (Pl. b; D, 5), Nikoláyevski Boulevard 11, quietly situated, with sea-view, R. from 2¹/₂ rb., bed-linen 60 cop., déj. (11-3) 1, D. (3-8) 2 rb.; *ST. PETERSBURG (Pl. c; D, 4), corner of the Yekateríninskaya Square and the Nikoláyevski Boulevard, with sea-view, R. from 2¹/₂, déj. (11-1) 1, D. (1-7) 1¹/₂ rb.; *YEVROPÉISKAYA (Pl. d; D, 5), Púshkinskaya 2, with German waiters, commercial, R. from 2 rb., B. 60 cop., dej. (12-3) 1, D. (2-8) 1¹/₂, omn. 1 rb.; *BRISTOL (Pl. i; D, 5), Púshkinskaya 15, cor. of Ulitza Kondraténko, R. 1¹/₂-15 rb., B. 60 cop., déj. (11-2) 1, D. (1-8) 1-1¹/₂ rb.; HÓTEL PASSAGE (Pl. a; C, 5), corner of the Deribásovskaya and the Preobrazhénskaya, R. from 1³/₄, D. (1-6) ³/₄-1 rb.—BOLSHAYA MOSKÓVSKAYA, Kolodézhni Pereúlok 1, cor. of Deribásovskaya (Pl. D, 5), R. from 1¹/₂ rb.; SAVOY, Khersónskaya 29 (Pl. B, C, 3, 4), R. from 1¹/₂ rb.; HÔT. DE PARIS (Parizhkaya; Pl. f, D 5), Púshkinskaya 6; FRÁNTZIYA (Pl. g; C, D, 5), Deribásovskaya; CENTRÁLNAYA (Pl. h; C, 5), Preobrazhénskaya 34; CONTINENTAL (Pl. e; C, 5), Ulitza Stolýpina 19, R. from 75, bed-linen 50, D. (1-6) 50-80 cop.

Restaurants at the *London, *St. Petersburg, *Yevropéiskaya, and *Bristol Hotels, see above; *Alexander Park* (P. 398), with fine view; *Nicholas Boulevard* (p. 396), open in summer only, déj. 60 cop., D. ³/₄-1 rb.; *Kuznetzóv,* in the Exchange (P. 398), D. 75 cop.; *Palace,* Lanzherónovskaya 13 (Pl. D, 5), D. 75 cop.; *H. Bruhns,* Deribásovskaya 16, in the court, a popular luncheon rendezvous; *Bavaria,* corner of the Deribásovskaya and the Rishelyévskaya (Pl. D, 5), in the basement, D. 50-60 cop.—*Automatic Restaurant,* Preobazhénskaya 36, corner of Grétcheskaya (Pl. C, 5).

Cafés. *Robinat,* Yekaterininskaya, cor. of Lanzherónovskaya (Pl. D, 5); *Fanconi,* Yekaterininskaya, near the Lanzherónovskaya·(Pl. D, 5), both very popular; *Liebmann,* cor. of Preobrazhénskaya and Deribásovskaya (Pl. C, 5).

Cab Tariff (izvóshtchik; comp. p. xxiv). One-horse open cabs somewhat cheaper.	One-horse with cover.	Two-horse phaeton.
From the Main Railway Station, with luggage	70 cop.	1 rb. 20 cop.
To the Main Railway Station, with luggage	45 „	— 70 „
To the Bakhmatch Railway Station, with luggage	10 „	— 75 „
From the Bakhmatch Railway Station, with luggage	80 „	1 rb.
To or from the Quarantine Harbour, with luggage	90 „	1 rb. 40 „
To or from other harbours, with luggage	80 „	1 rb. 20 „
Drive within the town	30 „	— 40 „
Per hour	70 „	1 rb.
Each additional half-hour	35 „	— 50 „
To Lanzherón	60 „	— 90 „
To Little Fountain	90 „	1 rb. 50 „
To Middle Fountain	1 rb. 20	2 rb. 20 „
To Great Fountain	1 rb. 80	3 rb.
To the Limáns	1 rb. 40	2 rb. 40 „

Electric Tramways. The more important lines are: 1. *Khersonski Spusk* (Pl. B, 3) to *Kulikóvo Pole* (Pl. D, 8) viâ Rishelyévskaya.—2. *Naruishkinski Spusk* (Pl. C, 3) to *Old Cemetery* (Pl. C, 7, 8) viâ Preobrazhénskaya. — 3. *Goods Station* (Pl. A, 9) to *Torgóvaya* (Pl. B, C, 4, 5).—4. *Goods Station* (Pl. A, 9) to *Lanzherón* (Pl. F, 6) viâ Uspénskaya.—7. *Moskóvskaya* (Pl. C, 1-3) to *Khadzhibéiski Limán* (see Inset Map).— 14. *Khersónski Spusk* (Pl. B, 3) to *Main Railway Station* (Pl. D, 7).—16. Corner of *Preobrazhénskaya* and *Bolshaya Arnaútskaya* (Pl. C, 6, 7) to *Little Fountain* (beyond Pl. F, 9).—18. *Kulikóvo Pole* (Pl. D, 8) to *Great Fountain* (beyond Pl. D, 9).—19. *Great Fountain* to *Lustdorf* (see Inset Map). --20. *Khersonski Spusk* (Pl. B, 3) to *Khadzhibéiski Limán* (see Inset Map). —22. *Remeslénnaya* (Pl. D, 6, 7) to *Voénni Spusk* (Pl. D, 4) viâ the Harbour. —23. *Kulikóvo Pole* (Pl. D, 8) to *Ólgiyevskaya* (Pl. B, C, 4).—24. Corner of *Preobrazhénskaya* and *Úlitza Zhukóvskago* (Pl. C, 5, 6) to *Lanzherón* (Pl. F, 6).—25. Corner of *Preobrazhénskaya* and *Bolshaya Arnaútskaya* (Pl. C, 6, 7) to *Arcadia* (beyond Pl. F, 9).—27. *Round the Town.*-- 28. *Naruishkinski Spusk* (Pl. C, 3) to *Lanzherón* (Pl. F, 6).—33. *Remeslénnaya* (Pl. D, 6, 7) to *Moskóvskaya Bridge* viâ the Harbour.

Theatres. *City Theatre* (Pl. 29; D, 5), Theatre Square, operas and dramas; *Russian Theatre*, Grétcheskaya 48, cor. of Kolodezni Pereúlok (Pl. C, D, 5), dramas.—VARIETY PERFORMANCES. *Khudózhestvenni Theatre*, Yekaterininskaya 27 (Pl. D, 5-7); *Coliseum*, Khersónskaya 29 (Pl. B, C, 3, 4), with skating rink.

Pleasure Resorts (open in summer only). *Alexander Park* (p. 398); *Arcadia* (p. 399); *Little Fountain* (Мáлый Фонтáнъ; p. 399).—*Circus* (Pl. 15; C, 4), also used for variety performances.

General Post & Telegraph Office (Pl. C, 4, 5; p. 397), Úlitza Stolýpina 8, open for poste restante letters (to the left on entering, on the second floor) from 9 a.m. to 7 p.m., for registered letters from 9 a.m. to 3 p.m. & 5-7 p.m.; on Sun. & holidays from 9 to 11 a.m. The telegraph office is always open (on the groundfloor, to the right of the entrance).

Booksellers. *Becker & Wedde*, *E. Berndt*, Deribásovskaya 18 & 16 (Pl. D, 5); *Rousseau* (French), Rishelyévskaya 6 (Pl. D, 5-7). — GERMAN NEWS-PAPER: *Odessaer Zeitung.* — *Maps of the Crimea*, issued by the General Staff, may be obtained at the Staff Office of the Odessa Military District (Штабъ Одéсскаго воéннаго óкруга), Pirogóvskaya 6 (Pl. D, E, 8).

Banks. *Imperial Bank* (Pl. D, 6), Ulitza Zhukóvskago 11; *Ashkenazi*, Rishelyévskaya 4 (Pl. D, 5-7); *Crédit Lyonnais*, corner of the Rishelyévskaya and the Lanzherónovskaya (Pl. D, 5).

Baths. Warm baths at the hotels (p. 393); also *Rabinóvitch & Fishman*, Ulitza Poltávskoi Pobyédi 27 (Pl. E, 5-7); *Isakóvitch*, Preobrazhénskaya 45 (Pl. C, 4-7).—SEA BATHS. At the Fountains, Lanzherón (stony), Arcadia, Lustdorf (strongest surf), in the Limans (p. 399), etc. Warm sea-baths at *Goikóvitch's*, at the harbour, to the left of the steps; at *Trieger's*, Tchernomórskaya 17; and at *Arcadia* and *Little Fountain* (p. 399).

Physicians. *Dr. Augst*, Ulitza Novosélskago 100, senior physician of the Protestant Hospital; *Dr. Käfer*, Vagneyovski Pereúlok; *Dr. Bernstein*, Púshkinskaya 5; *Dr, Walter* (oculist), Ulitza Novosélskago 59; *Dr. Thomson* (ladies' doctor), Ulitza Stolýpina 16.—DENTISTS. *H. Cornelius* Preobrazhénskaya 5; *Dr. Bondesen*, Púshkinskaya 5; *Dr. Flemmer*, Sobórnaya Square 4.—PROTESTANT HOSPITAL (Pl. E, 7) of the German community, well managed, 3-5 rb. per day.

Consulates. *Great Britain:* J. F. Roberts, C. M. G., consul-general, Tróitzkaya 17 (Pl. C-E, 6); John Lowdon, vice-consul. — *United States:* J. H. Grout, consul, Kazarménni Pereúlok 1 (Pl. D, 4). — *Rumania:* Ulitza Novosélskago 96 (Pl. B, C, 3-6; 11-2); travellers to Rumania must have the visa of the Rumanian consul (5 fr. or 2 rb.; no charge for English, French, German, Austrian, Swiss, Italian, or Belgian travellers).—*Turkey:* Khersónskaya 8 (Pl. B, C, 3, 4; 11-3); travellers to Turkey must have a passport *visé* by the Turkish consul (20 Turkish gold piastres or 1 rb. 80 cop.).

ANGLO-RUSSIAN CHAMBER OF COMMERCE, Púshkinskaya 11.— LLOYD'S AGENT, *E. G. Jacobs*, Quarantine Harbour.

English Church, Remeslénnaya 15 (Pl. D, 6, 7); services in winter at 8.30, 11, & 7 (at 7.30 in the Seamen's Institute), in summer by special arrangement; chaplain, *Rev. R. Courtier-Forster*, Remeslénnaya 15a.

English Clubs. *British & American Club*, Sabancyev Most 4; *Odessa British Athletic Club*, Frantzúzski Boulevard. — HOMES. *Girls' Friendly Society*, Deribásovskaya 4; *Home des Gouvernantes*, Khersónskaya 62; *Foyer Français*, Remeslénnaya 5; *Seamen's Institute*, Lanzherónovskaya 3.

Police Station (Pl. C, 5), Preobrazhénskaya 44; here also is the *Directory* (list of addresses).

Steamers of the *Russian Steam Navigation & Trading Company* (Рýсское óбщество парохóдства и торгóвли; chief office, Lanzherónov- skaya 1) ply to the CRIMEA (see R. 58) and to the CAUCASUS (see R. 62) daily in summer (mail-boats thrice weekly), starting from the Voénni Mole of the Pratique Harbour (Pl. D, 3, 4); ticket-offices in the Deribásov- skaya Arcade (Pl. C, D, 5) and to the left of the entrance to the harbour. — Steamers of the *Russian Transport & Insurance Co.* (Россíйское транспóртное и страховóе óбщество; office, Ulitza Kondraténko 10) to the Crimea and the Caucasus, thrice weekly, starting from the New Mole of the Coaling Harbour (Pl. E, 4). — To CONSTANTINOPLE (comp. *Baedeker's Constantinople* or *Mediterranean*): steamers of the *Russian Steam Navi- gation & Trading Company* once a week in 29 hrs. (on the steamers to Alexandria 23 & 15 rb., incl. meals), starting from the Quarantine Harbour (Pl. E, F, 5). — Also *North German Lloyd* steamers (Mediterranean-Levant service), going on to Genoa and Marseilles, and vessels of the *Austrian Lloyd*, *Società Marittima Italiana*, and *Messageries Maritimes.* — To LONDON, see p. xviii.

Principal Attractions (¹/₂-1 day). Nicholas Boulevard and Catherine Monument (p. 396); drive through the Yekaterininskaya, Preobrazhénskaya, Deribásovskaya, and Púshkinskaya (as far as the Exchange); Alexander Park (p. 398); towards evening, walk or drive to Little Fountain and Arcadia (p. 399).

Odessa, Одесса (pron. Adyéssa), one of the most important commercial towns on the Black Sea, is situated in the govern- ment of Kherson. It is the headquarters of the 8th Army Corps and the seat of a Greek Catholic archbishop and of the New Rus- sian University. Its population is 630,000, one third of whom are Jews and about 30,000 are foreigners. The value of its exports, chiefly consisting of grain and flour, amounted in 1912 to 80 million rubles. In 1912 its harbour was entered by 719 steamers, of 1,450,952 tons (200 British, of 446,339 tons). Odessa lies about 20 M. to the N. of the mouth of the Dniester, in a spacious and deep bay well protected against silting-up. It stretches, at a height of about 150 ft. above the level of the Black Sea, for about 4 M. along the margin of the Pontic Steppe, which here falls more or less abruptly to the sea, and is intersected by numerous deep hollows (so-called Ovrági or Balki). The wide and well-paved streets, cross- ing each other at right angles and generally shaded with trees, make the city one of the most regular and handsome in Russia. Considering the ungrateful nature of the soil, the citizens of Odessa are justified in their pride in the Nicholas Boulevard, the Alexander Park (to the S.E. of the city), and other shady resorts. The slopes descending to the sea are sprinkled with private gardens and villas (datchas). Odessa is built of the soft shell-limestone which is found

at a depth of about 50 ft. below the clay of the steppes, and a part
of the town is entirely undermined by the quarries.

Catherine II. ordered the foundation of the city on May 27th (O. S.),
1794; the first stone was laid by Admiral J. de Ribas on Aug. 22nd of the
same year. The new city occupied the site of the small Turco-Tartar settlement of *Khadzhibéi* and is presumed to have received its name from the
Sarmatian seaport of Ordessus, which lay in this neighbourhood. From
1817 to 1859 Odessa was a free port. The Governors-General Duc de
Richelieu and Prince Vorontzóv were especially prominent in furthering
the growth of the town. On April 13th, 1854, the naval harbour was
bombarded by a Franco-British squadron. On May 12th the British warship
'Tiger' stranded 3 M. to the S. of Odessa during a fog and was set on fire
by the Russian artillery. In 1876-77 Odessa was blockaded by the Turks,
but without success.

The Harbour consists of four parts. To the S.E. is the so-called
Quarantine Harbour (Карантинная гавань; Pl. E, F, 5), for
foreign vessels. On the N. are the *New Harbour* (Новая гавань;
Pl. E, 4), for steamers of the Volunteer Fleet, and the *Coaling
Harbour* (Угольная гавань; Pl. D, E, 4), for steamers of the
Russian Transport and Insurance Co. (comp. p. 395) and other
Russian vessels. To the W. is the *Pratique Harbour* (Практи-
ческая гавань; Pl. D, 3, 4), for steamers of the Russian Steam
Navigation & Trading Co. (comp. p. 395) and sailing-ships.

The most beautiful part of the town is the wide *Nicholas
Boulevard (Николаевский бульваръ; Pl. D, 4, 5), which extends for 500 yds. along the edge of the slope above the harbour,
bounded on one side by handsome buildings and on the other by
pleasure-grounds and four rows of trees. This boulevard commands
a fine view over the sea, and in spring is the favourite resort of the
fashionable world of Odessa, just as the Deribásovskaya (p. 397) is
in winter. At the N. end of the row of houses is the *Vorontzóv
Palace*. Farther to the S. are a café-restaurant (p. 393) and a *Bronze
Statue of the Duc de Richelieu* (Pl. 24), erected in 1826. The duke,
who was Governor-General of Kherson in 1803-14, is represented in
Roman costume. From this point a massive flight of *Granite Steps*
(193), 40 ft. wide and arranged in ten stages, descends to the Nicholas
Church and to the sea and the harbours mentioned above. There
is an elevator to the right (fare 2 or 3 cop.).

A little to the S.W. of the Richelieu Monument is the Catherine
Square, which contains the **Monument of the Empress
Catherine II.** (Pl. 1; D, 4), erected in 1900 from designs by the
architect Dmitrenko and the sculptor Popóv. The bronze figure of
the empress stands upon a granite pedestal resembling a column,
which is surrounded by bronze figures of Prince Potemkin (in front),
Count Zubov (r.), Colonel de Volant, the engineer (l.), and Admiral
J. de Ribas (behind; see above). The monument is 35 ft. in height.

On the W. side of the Nicholas Boulevard is the *Imperial Palace*
(Дворéцъ; Pl. D, 5), at present the residence of the commander-
in-chief of the troops in the Odessa District. At the S. end of the

boulevard rises the *Duma* or *City Hall* (Pl. 16; D, E, 5), with a portico of twelve columns. In front are a fountain (1888), with a bronze bust of the poet *Pushkin* (p. 398), and a cannon (placed here in 1904) from the English warship 'Tiger' (see p. 396).

To the W. of the Duma the boulevard is adjoined by an asphalt square of moderate size at which the Púshkinskaya (p. 398) begins. On the E. side of this square is the **Museum of Antiquities** (Музéй дрéвностей; Pl. 23, D 5), chiefly containing Greek antiquities from the N. coast of the Black Sea. It is open free on week-days, except Wed., 11-4 (in winter 11-3), on Sun. 12-3. Director, E. G. Kagarov. Catalogue 30 cop.

GROUND FLOOR. The entrance-hall leads straight into *Room I*, containing Greek antiquities, chiefly vases from S. Russia (Olbia, Panticapæum). Cab. 4 (third shelf from top), Red-figured Attic vase with Menelaus and Helen, Dish with Bacchic procession; fourth shelf, Hydria with the Rape of Oreithyia by Boreas. Cab. 23. Works in bone. Cab. 27. Greek and Roman glass. — *Room* II (on the right). Fragments of vases of the 6th and 5th cent. B.C. No. 11, to the left of the entrance, limestone slab with Runic inscription (about 10th cent. A.D.; the only document of the kind as yet found in Russia). — *Room* III. Antiquities from Akkerman (Tyras) and Theodosia; bronze vessels, 25, 28, 27. Scythian copper cauldrons; at the second window from the entrance, 32. Scythian bronze vessel, a rare specimen; in the opening into the fourth room, 4. Limestone figure of a Roman legionary. — *Room IV*. Neolithic objects from Preteni. — We retrace our steps through the entrance-hall to *Room V*, with Christian antiquities and weapons. — *Room VI* (Aula). Ancient stelæ with inscriptions; portraits. — *Room VII*. Coins, medals, old books.
BASEMENT (reached from Room V). *Room VIII*. Egyptian antiquities. — *Room* IX. 28 Babi (comp. p. 298); Greek marble fragments. — *Room* X. Marble fragments with Turkish inscriptions.

Following the Lanzherónovskaya towards the W., we pass the *English Club* (Pl. 17; Russian) on the right and reach the THEATRE SQUARE (Театрáльная плóщадь), containing the *City Theatre* (Pl. 29), built in 1887 by Fellner & Helmer.

The next street parallel with the Lanzherónovskaya on the S. is the DERIBÁSOVSKAYA, which contains the most brilliant shops in the city and leads to the W., passing the (right) *Deribásov Garden* (Дерибáсовскiй садъ; Pl. C, D, 5), to the SOBÓRNAYA SQUARE (Pl. C, 5), with its fountains and pleasure-grounds. On the W. side of the square is the **Cathedral of the Transfiguration** (Преображéнскiй собóръ; Pl. 6), founded in 1795. This church, which is 342 ft. long, 138 ft. wide, and 165 ft. high, has a bell-tower 265 ft. in height and a dome above the crossing. To the right of the main entrance is the tomb of Prince Voroutzóv, Governor-General of Odessa in 1823-54; adjacent is a Turkish banner captured in 1828. In the grounds to the N. of the church is a *Bronze Statue of Prince Voroutzóv* (Pl. 31), by F. Brugger (1863). — To the W., at No. 63 Úlitza Novosélskago (Pl. B, C, 3-6) is the *Conservatoire*, founded in 1913.

To the N.W., at No. 8 Úlitza Stolýpina is the *General Post Office* (Пóчта: Pl. C, 4, 5), built by *Kharlámov* in 1899. The lofty delivery-room extends through all three stories. The Ulitza Stolýpina ends at the New Bazaar Square (Новобазáрная плóщадь; Pl. C, 4), in which a daily market is held. Over the spacious market buildings towers the *Sryétenskaya* or *Novobazárnaya Church* (Pl. 13), an imposing building with five domes, completed in 1847.

We return through the Kóblevskaya to the Úlitza Petrá Velíkago, at the right (S.W.) end of which is the *Lutheran Church* (Pl. 4), built in 1897.—Following the Úlitza Petrá Velíkago to the left (N.), we reach the **New Russian University** (Новороссíйскiй университéтъ; 1865; Pl. 30, C 4), situated at the corner of the Khersónskaya. It contains archæological, natural history, and other collections (open on Sun., 12-2), and has 2000 students. At Khersónskaya 13 is the *Municipal Library* (Городскáя публíчная библióтека; Pl. 22, C 4), a building in the Renaissance style, erected by Nestúrkh in 1906. It contains 170,000 vols. and is open on week-days 10-10 (from May till end of Aug., 10-7), on Sun. and festivals 11-5. Farther to the N. are the University Clinics and large hospitals (Pl. B, C, 3). Not far to the E., at Sofíyevskaya 5, on the first floor, to the left, is the *Municipal Museum* (Pl. C, 3, 4), containing Russian and other paintings (open free daily, 11-3; closed in July, Oct., Nov., & Dec.). At the N. end of the Torgóvaya is the *Rusov Picture Gallery.*

On the S. the Khersónskaya leads to the Preobrazhénskaya, near the N. end of which street is the *Commercial School* (Коммéрческое учúлище; Pl. D, 4).—Farther to the E. is Catherine Square (p. 396), at which begins the Yekaterínínskaya, another of the chief streets of Odessa. Following this to the S., we reach the *Roman Catholic Church* (Pl. 8; D, 5, 6), rebuilt in 1853. At the corner of the Tróitzkaya stands the *Tróitzkaya Church* (1808; Pl. 14, D 6); at the E. end of this street is the *Nunnery of St. Michael* (Mikháilovski Convent; Pl. E, 6). The Yekaterininskaya ends at the Privóznaya Square (Pl. C, 7), at the W. end of which is the entrance to the *Old Cemetery* (Pl. C, 8), with the tomb of Captain Giffard, commander of the 'Tiger' (p. 396). To the E. of the Privóznaya Square stand the *Law Courts* and the *Main Railway Station* (Pl. D, 7), two monumental buildings in the style of the Italian Renaissance.— To the S. of the station are a *Cadet School* (1902) and the *Sérgiyev Artillery School* (1913).

From the station we return through the Púshkinskaya to the Duma and the Nicholas Boulevard (p. 396). At the corner of the Púshkinskaya and the Úlitza Kondraténko, to the right, is the *Exchange* (Pl. 19; D, 6), built by Bernadazzi in 1899. The main entrance, with its large archway, is in the N. front. Farther on, to the right, is the Siccard House (No. 17) bearing an inscription to the effect that Pushkin lived here in 1823 (Здѣсь жилъ Пушкинъ 1823 г.).

Immediately to the E. of Odessa lies the **Alexander Park** (Pl. E, 5, 6; restaurant, see p. 393), a popular resort in which open-air concerts are given when the weather permits. The *Monument of Alexander II.*, a lofty column of Labrador stone, erected in 1891, commemorates the visit of the Tzar in 1875. About $^1/_2$ M. farther on lies **Lanzherón** (Restaurant, with open-air concerts), with sea-bathing (tramways, see p. 394). — To the S. of Lanzheron there are numbers of datchas and private gardens skirting the sea. The Frantzúski Boulevard leads (from the Alexander Park, in 1 hr.; cabs, see p. 393; tramway, see p. 394) to **Little Fountain** (Mali Fontán, Малый Фонтанъ; comp. Inset Map, p. 393), with a garden-restaurant (concerts) and good sea-bathing. About $^3/_4$ M. farther on are **Arcadia** (tramway, see p. 394; concerts in the beach-restaurant; warm sea baths) and **Middle Fountain** (Sredni Fontán, Средній Фонтанъ; tramway, see p. 394). About $2^1/_4$ M. to the S. of Middle Fountain is **Great Fountain** (Bolshói Fontán, Большой Фонтанъ; tramways, see p. 394; restaurant near the terminus). This village contains the Convent of the Assumption, to which a yearly pilgrimage is made on Aug. 22nd, O.S. (tramway). Beyond the convent is a lofty lighthouse. The three places derive their names from a spring which formerly furnished Odessa's water-supply. About 4 M. to the S. of Great Fountain (tramway) is the German colony of *Lustdorf* or *Olgino* (Hotel Villa Kitty), a popular sea-bathing resort.

About 50 V. (33 M.) to the S.W. of Odessa (steamer in 5 hrs.; fare 1 rb. 65 cop.), on the *Dniester Limán*, lies *Akkermán* (Centrálnaya, R. from 80 cop.), a district-town in the government of Bessarabia, which occupies the site of the Milesian colony of *Tyras* and possesses the remains of a Genoese fortress built in 1438. Pop. 33,000.

The Limans or Lagoons of Odessa.

Comp. Inset Map, p. 393.

The word *Limán* (from the Greek λιμήν, harbour) is applied to a small inlet at the mouth of a river, separated from the main body of the sea by a narrow strip of land like the Venetian lido, formed by the deposits of the river and named *Péresuip* (Пересыпъ).

The water of the lagoons contains as much salt as a saline spring of average strength; in summer its temperature varies according to the month from 62° to 85° Fahr. — Special importance is attached to the mud-baths made of the slime which covers the bottom of the limáns to a depth of 3-12 ft. These limán baths are efficacious in scrofula, gout, rheumatism, nervous affections, and cutaneous diseases. — Salt is also obtained from the water by evaporation.

The **Kuyálnitzki Limán** (Куяльницкій Лиманъ), 8 V. ($5^1/_2$ M.) to the N. of Odessa, is 20 M. long and $1^1/_4$ M. broad, averages 10 ft. deep, and lies 16 ft. below the surface of the Black Sea, from which it is separated by an isthmus about $1^1/_4$ M. broad. It is reached by a branch-line from Odessa Harbour Station (see p. 393); trains run hourly during the season in 25 min. (fares 25 & 10 cop.; no second class). Near the station is the *Municipal Sanatorium*, built in the Russian style (mud-bath 1-$1^1/_2$ rb., warm limán bath 60, sea-water bath 15 cop.). Rooms may be obtained in the adjacent datchas

for 20-75 rb. a month, and 50-250 rb. for the summer. The season
lasts from May 15th to Sept. 1st (O.S.); the mean temperature in
July is 74° Fahr. There are several other bath-establishments.

The **Kadzhibéiski Limán** (Хаджибéйскій Лимáнъ; tramways, see p. 394), 4½ M. to the N.W. of the town, is 18 M. long
and 2 M. wide, and lies 13 ft. below the level of the Black Sea. Its
péresuip (p. 399) is fully 2½ M. wide. On the W. side are the
bath-houses and datchas for summer-guests (R. 75-275 rb. for the
summer). About 1 M. to the S.W. of the limán lies the *Municipal
Sanatorium*, surrounded by a large park (prices of the baths as in
the Kuyalnitzki Limán, p. 399).

The **Limán** of **Xénievka** (Ксéніевскій Лимáнъ; omn. twice
daily from Odessa in 2 hrs., fare 50 cop.), situated 10 M. to the S.W.
of Odessa, near the German settlement of *Klein-Liebental* or *Xénievka* (Ксéніевка), has preserved its natural condition more fully
than the others. It is 7 M. long; ⅔ M. wide, and 7 ft. deep; it is
separated from the sea by a péresuip (p. 399) only 200 ft. in width.
Beside the Sanatorium there are summer-lodgings in the village.

57. From Kharkov to Simferopol
(Sebastopol).

636 V. (421 M.). Express train in 12½ hrs. (fares 18 rb. 50, 11 rb.
90 cop.; seat-ticket 1½ rb.; sleeping-car 5 rb. 65, 4 rb. 25 cop.). Ordinary
train in 19 hrs. — Through-carriages run from St. Petersburg and Moscow
to Sebastopol, Feodosiya, and Yekaterinoslav.

Kharkov, see p. 387. — The railway traverses the S. part of the
government of Kharkov, which is still within the 'Black Earth' belt
(p. xxxvii). From (23 V.) *Meréfa* a branch-line runs to (17 V.) Lyu-
botin (p. 389). — 41 V. *Borki*. The Church of the Redeemer here,
completed in 1894 from designs by Marfeldt, with a lofty dome,
commemorates the escape of Alexander III. and his family from the
railway accident of Oct. 17th (O.S.), 1888. — Beyond (110 V.) *Krasno-
pávlovka* the train enters the government of Yekaterinosláv. The
cornfields now give place to flat pasture-lands, leading gradually
to the steppes. — 139 V. **Lozováya** *(Rail. Restaurant)* is the
junction of the lines to Rostov (p. 431) and to Poltava (p. 390). 196 V.
Pavlográd, situated on the *Vóltchya*, a tributary of the Dnieper,
is a district-town with 40,500 inhab. and a lively trade in grain
and horses. — 230 V. (152 M.) **Sinélnikovo** *(Rail. Restaurant)*.

From SINELNIKOVO TO KHARTZUISK (Rostov), 234 V. (156 M.), express
train in 5 hrs. — 55 V. *Ulyánovka* (Rail. Restaurant). From (71 V.) *Tchá-
plino* (Rail. Restaurant) a branch-line runs to (83 V.) Pologi (p. 402) and
(193 V.) *Berdyánsk* (Rail. Restaurant; Metropole; Mezhdunaródnaya; izvóshtchik from the station or harbour to the town 30, per drive 20 cop.;
British vice-consul, J. E. Greaves; Lloyd's Agent, François Datodi), a
grain-port of 38,000 inhab., on the N.W. coast of the Sea of Azov. —
148 V. *Gríshino*, 184 V. *Otcheretino*, both with rail. restaurants. 209 V.
Yasinovátaya (Rail. Restaurant); branch-line to (58 V.) Debaltzevo (P. 429);
to Mariupol, see p. 401. — 234 V. (156 M.) *Khartzuísk* (P. 431).

FROM YASINOVATAYA TO MARIUPOL, 137 V. (91 M.), express train in 3³/₄ hrs. — 13 V. *Yúzovo.* About 5¹/₂ M. to the S.E. of Yuzovo lies *Yuzovka* or *Hughesovka* (pop. 49,300), named after John Hughes, who established coal-mines and iron-works here in 1872, thus founding the important mining industry of the Donetz Basin (p. 429). Many of the employees of the New Russian Company are English (English Church of St. David & St. George; services at 8.30, 11, & 7; chaplain, *Rev. J. Leask*). — 37 V. *Yelenovka* (Rail. Restaurant); 68 V. *Volnováкha* (p. 402). — 137 V. (91 M.) *Mariúpol* (Rail. Restaurant; Grand-Hôtel; Continental, R. 1-5, D. ¹/₂-1¹/₂ rb., omn. 40 cop.; izvóshtchik from the station to the town 40, vice versâ 30, per hr. 40 cop.; British vice-consul, W. S. Walton; Lloyd's Agent, F. C. Svorono), a port on the N.W. coast of the Sea of Azov, with 44,600 inhab. and a trade in coal, iron, and grain.

———

FROM SINELNIKOVO TO DOLINSKAYA, 277 V. (183 M.), railway in 8¹/₂ hrs. Just short of Yekaterinoslav we cross the Dnieper by a bridge ³/₄ M. long.

53 V. (35 M.) **Yekaterinosláv,** Екатеринославъ.— *Railway Restaurant.* — HOTELS (all in the Catherine Prospékt). *Lóndonskaya,* R. from 1¹/₂ rb., B. 60 cop., déj. (11-1) ³/₄, D. (1-5) 1¹/₄-2 rb.; *Bristol,* R. from 1³/₄, déj. (11-1) ³/₄, D. (1-7) ³/₄-2 rb.; *Yevropéiskaya; Frántziya* (same proprietor and terms as the Lóndonskaya). — IZVÓSHTCHIK from the railway station to the town 30, per drive within the town 20, per hr. 40 cop.; with two horses 60, 35, & 70 cop. — ELECTRIC TRAMWAY from the station through the Catherine Prospékt to the Cathedral Square (5 cop.).

Yekaterinosláv, situated on the right bank of the Dnieper, was founded by Catherine II. in 1784, and is the capital of the government of the same name. It possesses 218,000 inhab. (including 50,000 Jews), thriving industries, and an active trade in grain, timber, cattle, horses, and wool. The broad Catherine Prospékt (Екатерйнинскій проспéктъ; tramway, see above), the main street of the town, nearly 3 M. long and planted with trees, leads E. from the station to the Cathedral Square. In the Prospékt, on the right, are the *Lutheran Church,* the *Town Park* (with the theatre), the *Roman Catholic Church,* the *Residence of the Governor,* and the *Town Hall;* on the left stand the *Post & Telegraph Office* and the *District Court.* Farther on, in the Cathedral Square, are the *Mining School* and the *Museum of Antiquities* (Областнóй музéй имени А. Н. Нóлн; open daily 9-5, in winter 9-4; adm. 20, catalogue 80 cop.). In the square stands the *Greek Catholic Cathedral,* founded in 1787 and completed in 1835. Adjoining the cathedral on the S. is a bronze statue of the Empress, erected in 1846, which was cast in Berlin in 1782 by order of Potemkin. To the N.E. of the cathedral is the former *Potemkin Palace,* now the club-house of the noblesse of Yekaterinoslav, with its park on the Dnieper.

Between Yekaterinoslav and Alexandrovsk (p. 402) the Dnieper penetrates the S. Russian barrier of gneiss and granite by a series of nine rapids. The *Nenasūitetzki* (the 'Insatiable'; Ненасúтецкій порóгъ), the fifth of these rapids, is fully ¹/₄ M. long and has a fall of 15 ft. It occurs 37 V. (24 M.) to the S. of Yekaterinoslav, below *Nikólskoye,* a village on the right bank (carr. there & back, in one day, 6 rb.; luncheon-basket necessary, as no provisions are obtainable *en route*).

Steamboats (pier near the railway bridge) from Yekaterinoslav to Kiev, see p. 378.

56 V. *Goryainovo*, with large foundries (Александровскій заводъ). From (83 V.) *Zaporózhye* (Rail. Restaurant) a branch-line runs to (10 V.) *Trituznaya*, also with large foundries (Днѣпрóвскій заводъ). From (120 V.) *Verkhóvtzevo* (Rail. Restaurant) a loop-line runs to (112 V.) Dolgintzevo viâ (42 V.) *Pyatikhatki* (p. 391). — 211 V. *Dolgintzevo* (Rail. Restaurant).

FROM DOLGINTZEVO TO VOLNOVAKHA, 399 V. (265 M.), railway in 14 hrs. — From (36 V.) *Apóstolovo* a branch-line diverges to (40 V.) Nikólo-Kozélsk (see below). 92 V. *Nikópol*. Beyond (164 V.) *Kitchkás* we cross the Dnieper by a bridge 355 yds. long. At (185 V.) *Alexándrovsk* we cross the railway from Kharkov to Simferopol (see below). 275 V. *Pologi* (p. 400). — 399 V. (265 M.) *Volnovákha* (p. 401).

We cross the *Ingulétz* just before reaching (223 V.) *Krivói-Rog*, a town of 18,000 inhab., situated in the centre of a productive iron-mining district. From here a branch-line runs to (29 V.) *Nikólo-Kozélsk* (see above). — 277 V. *Dolinskaya*, see p. 391.

Beyond Sinelnikovo (p. 400) the railway proceeds along the rocky plateau on the left bank of the Dnieper, through an almost unbroken grazing country, the monotony of which is varied only by the numerous kurgáns (tumuli).

302 V. (200 M.) **Alexándrovsk** (*Rail. Restaurant; Rossiya;* izvóshtchik from the rail. station to the town 40-50, to the steamboat-pier 70 cop. to 1 rb.), a district-town in the government of Yekaterino-slav, lies 1¹/₃ M. from the Dnieper and contains 51,000 inhabitants. It is the starting-point of the navigation of the Lower Dnieper (trade in grain). The 'Plavni' or old river-bottom, with its luxuriant growth of grass and trees, presents a striking contrast to the steppes. — In the river is the island of *Khórtitza*, formerly the principal stronghold of the Zaporóg Cossacks (see below), but occupied since 1789 by three Mennonite communities.

The *Zaporógs* (meaning 'beyond the rapids'; comp. p. 401), are said to have settled in the 10th cent. on Khortitza and the other islands of the Dnieper between this point and its limán (comp. p. 399). Marauding ex-peditions led to encounters with the Poles, more particularly under the leadership of the Atamán (Hetman) *Tarás Bulba*, whose deeds have been celebrated in verse by Gogol. Under *Hetman Bogdán Khmyelnítzki*, about the middle of the 17th cent., these encounters led to the annexation of the country to Russia, but not without attempts being made later to regain its independence. The last prominent hetman was *Mazeppa (Mazepa)*, who attached himself to Charles XII. of Sweden and died at Bender in 1709. He furnished Byron with the subject of his well-known poem.

From Alexandrovsk to *Kherson*, steamers down the Dnieper twice daily in 18 hrs. (fare 4 rb. 40 cop.; meals extra); the time-table varies with the weather-conditions. — Railway to *Dolgintzevo* or *Volnovakha*, see above.

For some distance farther the railway skirts an arm of the Dnieper and traverses its well-watered plain. — 340 V. *Popóvo*, (366 V.) *Prishib*, and (385 V.) *Fédorovka* are three settlements of the German colonists, chiefly Mennonites from S. Germany, who have settled in the valley of the *Malótchnaya* and raise large quantities of sheep and swine. The most important of these colonies is *Halbstadt* (Гальбштадтъ), 22 V. (14½ M.) to the E. of Prishib.

407 V. **Melitópol** (*Rail. Restaurant; Konidi;* izvóshtchik from the rail. station to the town 50 cop.), a district-capital with 18,500 inhab., stands on the *Malótchnaya*, and is the central point of the trade of the German colonies of this district. — 432 V. *Akimovka* is the first station at which the Tartars are seen in any great number. The scenery now becomes very desolate; the ground is often covered with innumerable fossils, of which the railway embankment is largely constructed. — 492 V. *Novo-Alexéyevka.*

A branch-railway runs from Novo-Alexeyevka in 40 min. to (14 V. or 9 M.) *Genitchésk* (Геническъ), a village of 13,000 inhab., with a trade in salt, on the strait connecting the Sea of Azov with the Putrid Sea. — About 65 V. (43 M.) to the W. of Novo-Alexeyevka is the model estate of *Askania-Nova*, the hereditary property of the Falz-Fein family, which is shown to visitors on previous application. This enormous estate occupies an area of 210 sq.M., and 2000 labourers are regularly employed on it. One of its chief features is the raising of sheep, of which 100,000 are kept in stock. The zoological park, where foreign animals are acclimatized, is also interesting.

The train now runs on a narrow embankment across the *Sivásh*, or *Putrid Sea*, a stagnant lake 93 M. long and 2-14 M. broad, which separates the former island and present peninsula of the *Crimea* from the mainland. — 532 V. *Taganásh* (Rail. Restaurant), the first station on the peninsula. From (550 V.) **Dzhankói**, Джанкой *(Rail. Restaurant)* a branch-line runs to Feodosiya and Kertch (see p. 425). — For some time longer the train runs through a regular steppe, finally approaching the hilly district formed by the N. slopes of the Yaila Mts. (see below). Green meadows and trees resembling those of Central Europe here refresh the eye. We skirt the *Salgír* and reach (636 V.) *Simferópol* (p. 411). Hence to *Sebastopol*, see R. 58b.

58. The Crimea.

From Moscow viâ Kursk and Kharkov to (1440 V.; 955 M.) Sebastopol, see RR. 55c, 57, & 58b; express train in 28½ hrs. (fares 30 rb. 80, 19 rb. 80 cop.; sleeping-car 11 rb. 50, 8 rb. 65 cop.; reserved seat 2 rb. 70 cop.). From this trunk-line branch-lines diverge within the Crimea for the seaports of Feodosiya and Kertch. — Steamers from Odessa to Sebastopol and Kertch (and thence to Batum), see RR. 58a, 58c. — Steamers of the Russian Steam Navigation and Trading Co. ply from Constantinople to Sebastopol once weekly in 30 hrs. (fares 68 fr., 42 fr.; meals extra).

Ordnance maps of the Crimea may be obtained in Odessa (see p. 391). Visitors may consult The Invasion of the Crimea, by *A. W. Kinglake* (1863; students' ed. 1899); The Crimea in 1854 and 1894, by *Sir Evelyn Wood* (1895); The Crimea, by *Thomas Milner* (1855); Through Russia: from St. Petersburg to Astrakhan and the Crimea, by *Mrs. Guthrie* (1874); Around the Black Sea, by *W. E. Curtis* (1911); and Scythians and Greeks, by *Ellis H. Minns* (illus.; 1913).

The *Crimea* (Крымъ) or *Tauric Peninsula*, belonging to the government of Taurida, lies between 44° 23' and 46° 21' N. lat. and has an area of 9750 sq.M. On the N. it is connected with the mainland by the narrow Isthmus of Perekóp, on the E. it is bounded by the Sea of Azov, and on the S. and W. by the Black Sea. — The N. part of the peninsula, almost three-quarters of the whole, consists of a low treeless tableland of Neo-Tertiary 'steppe limestone', which contains salt lakes and kurgáns or tumuli. The vegetation is typical of the steppes, and sheep-raising is carried on here on a large scale. The Tertiary, Cretaceous, and Jurassic strata rise gradually towards the S. to the flat-topped Jurassic *Yáila Mts.* (Tartar Ййла, summer pasture). This range, which occupies the S. part of the peninsula, is a continuation of the Caucasus, and extends from Feodosiya to Balaklava, a distance of 100 M. The highest summits are the *Román-Kosh* and the *Tchatuir-Dágh*, attaining heights of 4955 ft. and 4990 ft. respectively. Grain is cultivated on the foothills; on the higher slopes are beech-woods, and still higher mountain pastures. The abrupt S. face of the Yaila, with its folded slates (Lower Jura) protruding through the limestone, forms a strong contrast to the monotony of the long slope on the N. Thanks to a more abundant rainfall, the upper slopes on the S. are clad with beautiful forests, chiefly of black pine, and the delightful bays of the steep coast are lined with a series of vineyards, gardens, villas, and watering-places, enjoying a mild climate and showing a luxuriant Mediterranean vegetation. The finest point of the coast is the stretch between Baidar Gate and Gurzuff.

The best TRAVELLING SEASON for a visit to the Crimea is early summer or autumn; in the height of summer rain is very rare and the heat often oppressive. The highroads are good. The charge for posting is 4 cop. per horse and verst, with an extra charge for the carriage. For drives of any length the best plan is to hire an izvóshtchik (phaeton 20-25 rb. for 100 V.).

PLAN OF TOUR. For visitors coming from the W. or N., *Sebastopol* is the most suitable starting-point for a visit to the S. coast of the Crimea. The best centre for excursions is Yalta. The following distribution of time may be recommended to hurried travellers:

1st Day. Sebastopol (P. 407).
2nd Day. Motor drive from Sebastopol to Yalta (R. 58 c.).
3rd Day. Carriage drive from Yalta to Livadia, Oreanda (p. 419), and Alupka (pp. 420, 421), returning by the local steamer.
4th Day. Walk viâ Massandra and through the Nikitski Garden (pp. 418, 419) to Gurzuff (p. 421), returning by the local steamer.
5th Day. From Yalta to Bakhtchi-Sarai (p. 423) by carriage; *or* from Yalta to Sebastopol by steamer (p. 424).
6th Day. Bakhtchi-Sarai and environs (pp. 412-414), returning to Sebastopol by railway (pp. 414, 415); *or* excursion from Sebastopol to Bakhtchi-Sarai, going and returning by railway.

The ascent of the Tchatuir-Dágh (p. 422) may also be recommended.

Travellers coming from the Caucasus have time to visit Kertch (p. 426) and Feodosiya (p. 425) while the steamer is waiting, and should then begin as above with Yalta (3rd and 4th Day). 3rd Day. Ascent of the Yaila (p. 423). 4th Day. Motor drive from Yalta to Sebastopol. 5th Day. Sebastopol. 6th Day. Excursion to Bakhtchi-Sarai.

The HOTELS at Sebastopol, Yalta, Suuk-Su, and Gurzuff are fairly good, those in the other places passable. During the height of the season (Aug. 1st to Oct. 15th, O.S.) the hotels are generally overcrowded and the prices raised; it is then advisable to order the rooms in advance. The spring season is in March and April (O.S.).

Among the Tartar national dishes may be mentioned tcheburék (a kind of meat-pie), and shashlúik (mutton roasted on a spit). Buzá is a sourish, viscid drink, made of buckwheat and oatmeal.

SEA BATHING. The bathing-season lasts from the middle of May till the middle of October (O.S.; no bathing-machines). Amongst the bathing-resorts are *Eupatoria* (p. 406); *Yalta* (p. 416), the most fashionable and expensive of all; *Alupka* (p. 421); *Gurzuff* (p. 421); and *Feodosiya* (p. 425). — September is the best month for the GRAPE CURE.

TARTAR WORDS are generally accented on the last syllable.

The earliest inhabitants of the peninsula of whom we have any record were the TAURIANS (Cimmerians), living among the mountains on the coast, and the SCYTHIANS, occupying the corn-growing steppes. A Scythian kingdom was founded in the 2nd cent. B.C., which reached its zenith under Skilurus and Palakus (1st cent. B.C.) and persisted till the third cent. A.D. Its chief towns were *Neapolis* (near Simferopol) and *Palakion* (Balaklava). In the 6th cent. B.C. and following centuries various GREEK COLONIES had settled on the Crimean Coast, such as *Chersonesus* (p. 410), established by the Dorians of Heraclea, and *Theodosia* (p. 425) and *Panticapaeum* (p. 426), sent out by the Ionians of Miletus. Panticapæum became the capital of a kingdom (4th cent. B.C.), which included the E. Crimea (with Theodosia), the peninsula of Taman (with *Phanagoria*), the E. coast of the Sea of Azóv, and the mouth of the Don (with the important city of *Tanais*). This kingdom fell into the hands of Mithridates VI. of Pontus (B.C. 120-63). Under Augustus Pontus became one of the Roman client-states, and about the middle of the 4th cent. A.D. it was wholly incorporated with the Eastern Roman Empire. The so-called Crimean Goths, who began to settle in this region in the 3rd cent. B.C., were completely hellenized. The storms of the Great Migrations destroyed the Greek settlements. In the 13th cent. the GENOESE founded Eupatoria, Balaklava, and other colonies, and under them Kaffa (Feodosiya) became a flourishing commercial town. About the same period, however, the Mohammedan TARTARS took possession of the N. part of the peninsula, while the advance of the Turks and struggles with Venice paved the way for the downfall of the Genoese dominion in 1475. The history of the Tartar khanate is a mixture of palace revolutions, foreign wars, and predatory forays, and in 1478 it became dependent on the Sublime Porte. In 1783 Russia forced the last Khan to abdicate and converted the Crimea into a Russian province. Many of the Tartars then emigrated to Turkey, and those who remained behind are now peaceful tillers of the soil. Their physical type, in consequence of the strong admixture of Greek and other elements, differs considerably from that of their Mongolian relatives. The Crim Tartars are slender in form, and have aquiline noses and eyes which show little obliquity. The process of Russification is going on at an increasing rate, and the number of Tartars is steadily diminishing through emigration. In 1854-55 the Crimea was the scene of the Crimean War (comp. pp. 407 et seq.).

a. Steamer from Odessa to Sebastopol.

176 Sea Miles (1 S.M. = ca. 1³/₄ V.). Steamboats of the *Russian Steam Navigation and Trading Co.* (comp. p. 395) run daily in summer, taking 20 hrs. (fares 11 rb. 50, 8 rb. 75 cop.; food 1 rb. 70, 1 rb. 40 cop.; second cabin fairly comfortable). Steamboats of the *Russian Transport and Insurance Company* also ply thrice weekly (second-class fare 8 rb., meals extra). — Passengers are advised to obtain a stateroom immediately below the upper deck, as the port-holes may be left open here if the sea is not too rough. The tickets are available for 15 days, and allow of breaks in the journey on due notification. — The commissariat of the steamers is good. Breakfast is served from 7 to 9 a.m., déjeuner (2 courses and coffee) at 11.30 a.m., dinner (5 courses and coffee; 4 courses in the second class) about 5.30 p.m., tea between 7 and 9 p.m.

The **Black Sea** (Чёрное море), the *Pontus Euxinus* of antiquity, earns its name in part from the dark-blue colour of its water; this naturally varies with the light, but is never so blue as the Mediterranean Sea. Its area amounts to 163,700 sq.M., not including the *Sea of Azov* (14,500 sq.M.). No tidal movement is perceptible. On the N. side the sea forms two large bays, separated from each other by the Crimea: *viz.* the Bay of Odessa, which at places is 650 ft. deep, and the Sea of Azov, which communicates with the main body of water by a narrow channel only. The Black Sea proper is a huge basin with precipitous sides, being about 4600 ft. deep near the shore and 7365 ft. deep in the middle. The surface-water, owing to the large rivers which flow into it, contains little salt (1.8 per cent), but the lower strata contain more (2.2 to 2.3 per cent). The bottom is covered with black mud, smelling of sulphuretted hydrogen and devoid of animal life. On warm summer nights phosphorescence is visible. Dolphins often follow the steamers.

Odessa, see p. 393. — As we leave the harbour we enjoy a fine retrospect of the town. The steamer soon gains the open sea, steers toward the S.E., and after 14 hrs. reaches —

143 S.M. **Eupatoria,** Евпаторія. — The steamer anchors in the roadstead and passengers are landed in small boats. — HOTELS. *Dyulber*, near the beach, open from May 15th to Sept. 1st, very fair; *Modern*, Lázarevskaya, R. 1¹/₂-8 rb., D. (2-6 p.m.) 80 cop.; *Beiler*, Lázarevskaya, R. from 1¹/₂ rb., with restaurant. — Извóзчик 20 cop. per drive, 1 rb. per hr. — Good sea-bathing (5 cop.) on the sandy beach. — *British Consular Agent*, H. J. B. Martin.

Eupatoria, the chief town of a district on the W. coast of the Crimea, contains 32,000 inhab., who carry on a large trade in salt. During the Crimean War the allied British and French army landed in Sept., 1854, about 20 M. from the town. By the harbour there is a boulevard with a restaurant. Just to the N. of this is the Lázarevskaya, the chief street of the town, with the Greek Catholic Cathedral, completed in 1898, to the E. of it, and the Mosque of Juma-Jami, built in 1552, to the W. About 6 min. from the harbour, to the N., is the theological seminary of the Karaïtes (Караймская кенаса; p. 413). The Thalassa Sanatorium and the Lutheran meeting-house may also be mentioned.

About 2 M. to the S.W. of the harbour (izvóshtchik 50 cop.; electric tramway in view) is the *Moináhskoye Lake*, with mud-baths (R. 1¹/₂-3, bath 1-2¹/₂ rb.). — Highroad to *Simferopol*, see p. 412.

In continuing the voyage the steamer steers to the S. and in 4 hrs. reaches (176 S.M.) *Sebastopol* (p. 407).

Konstantinovskaya
Battery

BAY OF SEBAS

Bay

7th Bastion

People's
Theatre

Comman-
dant

Museum
Custom Ho.

Ch. of St. Nicholas

Techn.
Sch. St. Vladimir

Cath.

Cath.
St. Peter & Paul

Girls' High. Sch.

Luth. Ch.

Modern
Sch.

Munic.
Hospital

Prison

Old
5th Bastion

Novoseltz.

Syernaya
Pl.

Southern Bay

Historical
Panorama

Boulevard

Tatarsk

Rail. Station

SE

Old
4th Bastion

1 Biological Station .... B 2
2 Greek Church .... A 3
3 Lazarev Monument .... C 4
4 Nakhimov Monument .. B 2
5 Naval Officers' Club .. B 2,3
6 Pokrovsk. Church .... B 4
7 St. Nicholas' Chapel .. B 3
8 Todleben Monument .. B 5
----- Electric Tramway

Sebastópol *(Sevastópol).*

LANDING STAGES. Russian Steam Navigation and Trading Co., near
the Gráfskaya Pristan (Pl. C, 2); Russian Transport and Insurance Co., a
little to the S. of the Custom House (Pl. B, C, 3). — The RAILWAY STATION
(Pl. B, C, 6; *Restaurant*) lies to the S. of the town, ¹/₂ hr. from the Gráfskaya Pristan. City office of the Government Railways at Yekateríninskaya 10·(Pl. B, 3).

Hotels. KIST (Pl. a; B, 2), Gráfskaya Pristan, fair, with view, R.
from 3 rb., B. 35 cop., D. (1-6 p.m.) 1¹/₂-2¹/₂ rb.; GRAND-HÔTEL (Pl. b; B, 3),
Yekaterininskaya 1; HÔTEL DU NORD (Cѣверная; Pl. c, B 2), Nakhímovski
Prospékt 7; WETZEL, Yekaterininskaya 6 (Pl. B, 3), with restaurant; BRISTOL
(Pl. e; B, 3), Nakhímovski Prospékt 8, well spoken of, R. 2-4, B. ¹/₂, déj.
(11-1) ¹/₂, D. (1-6 p.m.) ¹/₂-1¹/₄ rb.

Izvóshtchik (regular tariff) from the rail. station to the town by day
or night 40, from the town to the station 50 cop.; per drive or from the
steamer-landing to the town 20 (between 12 & 6 a.m. 30); to the Historic
Boulevard 35; per hr. 50, each additional ¹/₂ hr. 25; hand-luggage free,
trunk 25 cop.; to the Malákhov Kurgán and back, with 1¹/₂ hr.'s stay,
2¹/₂ rb.; to Chersonese, ¹/₂ hr. from the Gráfskaya Pristan, and back, with
1 hr.'s stay, 1 rb. 80 cop.; to St. George's Convent or Balaklava and back,
with 2 hrs.' stay, 3¹/₂ rb.; to the English and French cemeteries (p. 415)
and back, with 1 hr.'s stay, 2 rb.; to Inkerman and back 4 rb. Carriages
with rubber tyres 25 per cent more. — CIRCULAR DRIVE (ca. 5 hrs.; recommended when time is limited): Museum, Vladimir Cathedral, Cathedral
of SS. Peter & Paul, Historic Boulevard, Malakhov, and Chersonese (fare
3¹/₂ rb.; bargaining necessary). The drive by private carriage to Yalta
may be combined with a visit to St. George's Convent and Balaklava.

Electric Tramway (comp. Plan) from the railway station and from
the Gráfskaya Pristan through the town and to the Historic Boulevard
(from the station to the Gráfskaya Pristan ¹/₄ hr.).

Boat (Яликъ; tariff) from the Gráfskaya Pristan across the bay 25-30,
per hr. 30 cop., to Inkerman or to Chersonese and back 1 rb., to the
Inzhenérnaya Harbour (Pl. D, 1, 2; Cemetery of the Brethren) and back
70 cop. — Steam-launches (Катеры) ply between the Gráfskaya Pristan
and Syévernaya Harbour (Pl. C, D, 1) in 9 min. (fare 4 cop.).

Post & Telegraph Office (Pl. B, 3, 4), Yekaterininskaya.

Sea Baths on the Sea Boulevard (10 cop.); stony bottom. — Hot
baths (Pl. B, 2, 3), Kornilovskaya Square.

British Vice-Consul, *K. L. Ringeling* (acting), Yekaterininskaya 22.

Sebastópol or *Sevastópol* (Севастóполь, commonly mispro-
nounced in England), the chief naval harbour of S. Russia, lies on
a bay running into the land from W. to E. for a distance of about
5 M., and was laid out in 1784 on the site of the Tartar village of
Akhtiar. The harbour has an average depth of 65 ft. and is the best
on the Black Sea. The town is specially memorable for the great siege
of 1854-55. Though then almost wholly destroyed, it has quickly
recovered itself and now contains 77,000 inhabitants. Numerous
new buildings (most of them of yellow limestone) and broad streets
provided with rows of trees give the town a pleasant appearance.

After the landing of the Franco-British army at Eupatoria and the
enforced retreat of the Russians from the Alma (comp. p. 412), the siege
of Sebastopol began in Oct., 1854. The attack at first made little progress, as the defensive works, though originally unfinished, were quickly
strengthened by the genius of Todleben, while at the same time various
attempts were made from the outside to raise the siege. These latter led

to the battles of Balaklava (Oct. 13th, O.S.) and Inkerman (Oct. 24th,
O.S.). After the arrival of General Niel, the famous French engineer, the
attack of the French was mainly directed upon the *Malakhov (Malakoff)*
and the *Green Hill (Mamelon Vert)*, while that of the British was directed
to the *Great Redan* (the 3rd bastion). In May, 1855, General Pélissier
assumed the supreme command, but the defenders offered the most obstinate resistance to his vigorous and repeated assaults. It was not until
part of the fortifications had been reduced to a mere heap of earth by
the continuous bombardment that the French succeeded at last, on Aug.
27th (O.S.), in storming and retaining possession of the Malakhov, while
the attack of the British upon the Redan proved futile. The town, however, now became untenable, and the Russians retired to the N. side of
the bay. — The total number of cannon used by the besiegers amounted
to 800, from which, during the 349 days that the siege lasted, 1,350,000
shots were fired. The loss of the Allies amounted to 80,000, that of the
Russians to 120,000 men.

From the *Gráfskaya Pristan* (Pl. B, C, 2), or landing-place, a
broad stone staircase with a twelve-columned portico (1846) ascends
to a square containing the Hotel Kist (p. 407) on the right, and the
Naval Officers' Club (Pl. 5) on the left. A high granite pedestal
in the middle of the square bears a *Bronze Statue of Admiral
Nakhímov* (Pl. 4), by Bilderling and Schröder (1898). — To the N.
lies the **Sea** or **Marine Boulevard** (Примо́рскій бульва́ръ;
Pl. B, 2), the chief promenade of Sebastopol, affording a fine view
of the sea and the city (Restaurant, D. ³/₄-1 rb.; military band on
summer evenings, adm. 10 cop.). Near the shore, on an artificial
rock, is a monument erected in memory of the Russian war-ships
sunk during the Crimean War. A little to the W. is the **Biological
Station** of the Imperial Academy of Sciences at St. Petersburg
(Pl. 1), established in 1897, and containing the *Black Sea Museum*
and an *Aquarium* (open daily, except Mon. and Sat., 10-4; Thurs.
& Sun. free, Tues., Wed., & Frid. 30 cop.; strangers admitted at
other hours also by permission of the director). — The *Nakhímovski
Prospékt* (Pl. B, 3), running to the S., is the chief business thoroughfare of the city. — At the N. end of the Mítchmanski Boulevard
(Pl. B, 3) is a monument to *Captain Kazarski*, who distinguished
himself against the Turks in the naval war of 1828.

To the S. of the Marine Boulevard, in the Yekateríninskaya, is
the **Museum of the Defence of Sebastopol** (Музе́й оборо́ны
Севасто́поля; Pl. B, 3), erected by Kótchetov in 1895, and containing cannon, shot and shells, models of the sunken Russian men-
of-war, maps, plans, and pictures of the siege, and souvenirs of
the defenders. The first floor commands a fine view of the S. bay.
The museum is open on week-days 10-5 (in winter 10-4), on Sun. &
holidays 12-5 (in winter 12-4); adm. 20 cop.; catalogue 40 cop.

From the museum we follow the Yekateríninskaya towards the
S. To the W., reached by a cross-street, is the *Cathedral of SS.
Peter & Paul* (Pl. B, 4), rebuilt after the Crimean War on the model
of the temple of Theseus at Athens. The Yekateríninskaya ends at
the Novoséltzski Square (Pl. B, 5), where, at the site of the 4th bastion,

begins the so-called **Historic Boulevard** (Исторйческій Бул-
вáръ; Pl. B, 5, 6). Memorial stones here mark the positions of the
Russian batteries during the siege. On the N. side is a bronze
Statue of Count Todleben (p. 407; Pl. 8), from a design by Bilderling (1909). Farther to the S. is a *Panorama* (Панорáма обороны
Севастóполя), containing a painting (by Roubaud of Munich) representing the storming of Sebastopol by the British and French on June
6th, 1855 (O.S.; open from 9 a.m. to sunset; adm. 30 cop.). An extensive view is obtained from the roof of the building (adm. 40 cop.).
There is a restaurant opposite. — We may now return by the Sobórnaya (Pl. B, 3, 4), near the N. end of which, to the right, is the
Cathedral of St. Vladímir (Pl. B, 3), surmounted by a central
dome and completed in 1888. The interior of the church is elaborately painted, and on the W. wall is a Last Judgment by Kornéyev.
To the right and left of the ikonostás are steps descending to the
crypt, where, under a cross of black marble, rest Admirals Nakhímov,
Istómin, Kornílov, and Lázarev, all actors in the Crimean War.

Returning to the Gráfskaya Pristan (p. 408), we may now take
a boat to the MARINE QUARTER (Korabélnaya; Pl. D, 3, 4), containing the *Admiralty,* a bronze *Statue of Admiral Lázarev*
(Pl. 3; view; 1866), and dry docks and other naval establishments.
Proceeding hence to the S.E., we reach (1/2 hr.) the **Malákhov** or
Malakoff Hill (Pl. D, 4), an old kurgán or tumulus, now forming
a plateau 1150 ft. long and 490 ft. broad. This is the highest point
in the neighbourhood of Sebastopol, and its storming in 1855 decided
the fate of the town (p. 408). Near the keeper's house is a large
cross of white marble marking the burial-place of the French and
Russian soldiers who fell in the attack. Farther on is the bronze
Monument of Admiral Kornílov, erected in 1895 from the plans
of Bilderling and Schröder. The admiral is depicted at the moment
when he is struck by the fatal bullet; to the right, below, is a figure
of the sailor Koshka. Marble tablets on and adjoining a dilapidated
tower commemorate Admirals Nakhímov and Istómin, who both
fell here.

The large **Russian Cemetery** (Брáтская могйла, *i.e.* Grave of
the Brethren; beyond Pl. D 1), in which more than 100,000 of those who
fell during the siege are buried, is situated in a treeless plain to the
N. of the Bay of Sebastopol. Visitors should take a steamer or rowing-
boat (comp. p. 407) from the Gráfskaya Pristan to the Syévernaya Harbour (Pl. C, D, 1), and then go in a cab (return fare 85 cop.) along the
unshaded road for 10 minutes. The huge collective graves are carefully
tended. At the head of the main avenue, to the left, about 400 yds. from
the entrance, are the tombs of the Russian leaders, Prince Gortchakóv
(d. 1861) and Count Todleben (d. 1884). Near by stands the conspicuous
Church of St. Nicholas, in the form of a pyramid, about 65 ft. in height,
surmounted by a cross; it was consecrated in 1870. On the outside of the
walls is inscribed a list of the regiments which took part in the battle,
with a record of their losses; on the inside are the names of the officers
who fell. The church commands a view of the town and bay.

About 2 M. to the W. of Sebastopol (carr. & boat, see p. 407), on the Karantinnaya Bay, lie the ruins of the city of **Chersonese**, or *Korsún* (the 'Russian Pompeii') and a Greek Catholic convent, with the Cathedral of St. Vladimir.

Chersonesus, afterwards known as *Cherson*, was founded in the 6th cent. B.C. by colonists from Heraclea in Bithynia and carried on (4th cent.) a large trade in wine and other articles. The remains of its massy fortifications (4th cent. B.C.; repeatedly renewed) are visible outside the convent-wall. The Romans made Cherson the military centre of the Crimea. Christianity spread rapidly as early as the 4th century. The excavated remains belong chiefly to the Byzantine period.—The RUINED CITY, the lines of the streets of which are still recognizable, includes the so-called Uvarov Basilica; another church (frequently rebuilt), with mosaics; and several private houses, with baths and fish-ponds. To the E. lies a large Christian necropolis, with a well-preserved martyrs' church (mosaics, relics of frescoes) and a few painted tombs.

The *Cathedral of St. Vladimir* was built in the Byzantine style in 1861-91 and incorporates some remains of the church in which Prince Vladimir of Kiev is said to have been baptized in 988 (see p. 379). In the lower church, to the right and left of the altar, are paintings of the Baptism of Vladimir and the Baptism of the Russians, by Riss. The paintings on the ikonostás of the upper church are by Korzúkhin.—On the Karantinnaya Bay, ca. 300 yds. to the E. of the cathedral, is a *Museum* of Greek, Roman, and Byzantine antiquities (open on week-days 9-12 and from 2 p.m. to sunset; on Sun. and festivals in the afternoon). Opposite the entrance is a *Marble Stele (No. 39)*, 4½ ft. in height but broken across the middle, inscribed with the civic oath of Chersonesus (3rd cent. B.C.). This is the only Greek civic oath which has been preserved to us in the form of an inscription. In the court (Lapidarium) are a model of a basilica and some monuments and tombs from the necropolis.

About 12 V. (8 M.) to the S. of Sebastopol (carr., see p. 407) lies the **Convent of St. George** (Гео́ргіевскій монасты́рь), founded in 988. On entering we turn to the right through a vaulted passage and descend some steps. After the drive across the barren plateau we are agreeably surprised by the vigorous growth of trees on the slopes of the steep bank and by the *View of the open sea. Opposite, rising from the sea, is *St. George's Cliff* (Скала́ свята́го Гео́ргія), with a cross. To the W. (a walk of about 1 hr. along the top of the cliffs) is *Cape Fiolente*, the old promontory of *Parthenium*, supposed to be the site of the sanctuary of Artemis in which Iphigeneia became a priestess. Near the cape is the *Grotto of Diana* (Гро́тъ Діа́ны), accessible by boat.—About 8 V. (5½ M.) to the N. of the convent lies Balaklava (see below).

A carriage-road (cab, see p. 407; motor omnibus 1 rb.) runs to the S.E. from Sebastopol, passing the French cemetery (comp. p. 415) and the country-house of Nikoláyevka, where Lord Raglan, the British commander-in-chief, died on June 28th, 1855, to (14 V.; 9½ M.) **Balaklava** (*Rossiya, Grand-Hôtel*, both on the bay, R. from 1 rb.), the ancient *Palakion*, now an unimportant place with 3200 inhab., picturesquely situated on a small bay enclosed by naked cliffs and entered only by a very narrow opening. During the Crimean War this was the chief base of the English army, the position of which was stormed by the Russians on Oct. 13th, 1854 (O.S.). It is memorable for the famous Charge of the Light Brigade, when, owing to a mistake in giving or receiving orders, the brigade of 607 men rode for 1½ M., exposed all the way to a raking

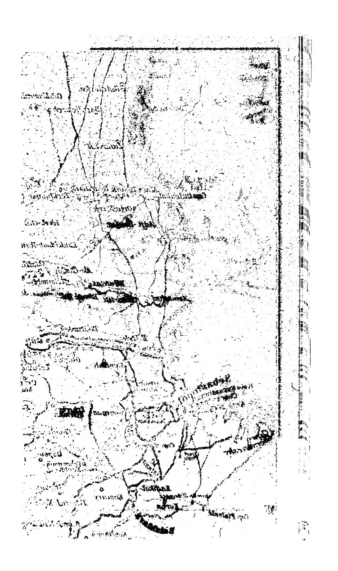

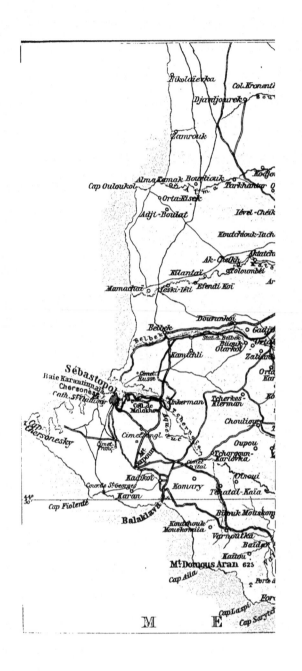

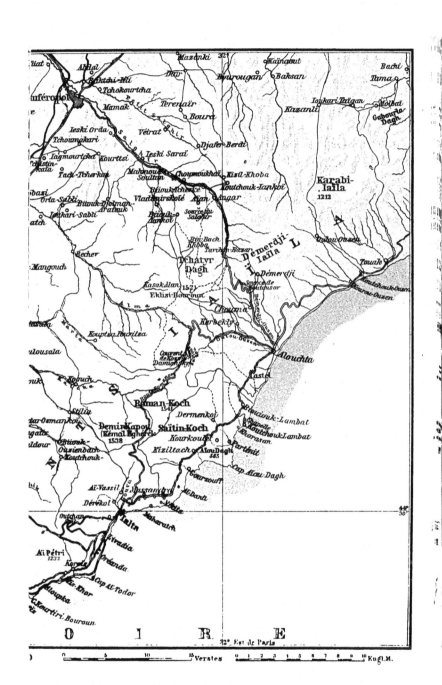

Russian fire, to attack the Russian army in position. The brigade broke into the battery, sabred the gunners, and put the Russian cavalry to flight, but, not being supported, could not hold its ground, and would have been annihilated but for the timely intervention of the French, who stormed the Fedukin heights and put an end to the firing from the N. on the returning remnant (198 men) of the Light Brigade. It is hardly necessary to remind the reader of Tennyson's 'Charge of the Light Brigade', or of the comment of the French general: 'C'est magnifique, mais ce n'est pas la guerre!' There is a monument to the Russian and English combatants.—The Inlet of Balaklava has been wrongly identified with Homer's description of the Bay of the Læstrygonians (Odyssey, X. 86-94). In antiquity it was named *Symbolon Portus*, and as a Genoese colony it received the name of *Cembalo*. Two towers to the S. of the place are relics of the latter (view). The sea-bathing at Balaklava is good.

Balaklava was the chief scene of the activity of *Miss Florence Nightingale* (d. 1910) during the Crimean War. A nook on the hills overlooking the village is still known as 'Miss Nightingale's Seat', and her room at the Convent of St. George (p. 410), where she had her principal hospital, is still shown to visitors.

An attractive excursion may be made from Sebastopol to *Inkerman* (p. 415; frequent steamers on Sun.).

b. Railway from Simferopol to Sebastopol.

73 V. (48 M.). Railway in 2-3 hrs.

Simferópol. — *Railway Restaurant.* — HOTELS. *Yevropéiskaya,* opposite the Public Garden; *Métropole,* Pushkinskaya 8; *Peterbúrgskaya,* a little to the S. of the Cathedral. — CAB (tariff) from or to the station 40, at night 50, per drive 20, per hr. 50 cop. — MOTOR OMNIBUS to Alushta 4 & 3½ rb., to Gurzuff or (90 V. or 60 M.) Yalta 8 & 7 rb.

Simferópol (820 ft.), which has grown out of the Tartar town of *Ak-Metchet* (White Mosque), is the capital of the government of Taurida, and is the seat of the provincial authorities, of a Greek Catholic bishop, of a Mufti, and of the Commandant of the 7th Army Corps. Pop. 70,000, including 7000 Tartars. It lies in a picturesque situation on the *Salgir*. Fruit-preserving is the chief industry. From the railway station a straight walk of 20 min. through the Vokzálnaya and Dolgorúkovskaya brings us to the *Alexander Nevski Cathedral,* in front of which stands a stone obelisk in honour of Prince Dolgorúki, the conqueror of the Crimea in 1771. Opposite the cathedral, to the N.W., is the *Zemstvo Building,* containing natural history collections (Естéственно-историческій музéй; open free on Sun. 12-2, to strangers also on week-days 11-2; director, S. Mokrzhétzki). The Yekaterininskaya, running parallel with the Dolgorúkovskaya on the W., is the chief business street. To the S.W. of the cathedral is the Bazaar Square (bazaar-days Wed., Frid., & Sun.). A little to the S. of the cathedral is the Tartar quarter, with its 12 mosques and its narrow, dirty streets. About 5 min. to the S.E. of the cathedral, on the Salgir, lies the *Public Garden* (restaurant; music; adm. 10-20 cop.), in which stands a bronze statue of Empress Catherine II. by Laverétzki (1890), with figures of Princes Potemkin and Dolgoruki on the front of the pedestal.

From Simferopol to Eupatoria, 63 V. (42 M.), highroad (motor omnibus in 2¹/₂ hrs., 4¹/₂ rb.; carr. 15-20 rb.; provisions should be carried). The road leads through the steppe in a N.W. direction. — 44 V. *Saki*, with a mud-bath establishment on *Lake Sak* (R. 1-5¹/₂ rb., D. 70 cop. to 1 rb. 30 cop.; mud-hath 1³/₄ rb.). — 63 V. (42 M.) *Eupatoria*, see p. 406.

From Simferopol to *Alushta*, see p. 423; to *Kharkov*, see R. 57.

The railway enters the *Yáila Mountains.* — 18 V. **Alma, Альма.** We cross the Alma.

The battlefield of Sept. 8th, 1854 (O.S.), lies about 22 M. to the W., near the village of *Burlyuk;* it is marked by one British and two Russian monuments. — The Russians under Prince Menshikov were drawn up on the heights overlooking the river Alma to bar the Sebastopol road to the Allies (under General Lord Raglan and Marshal St. Arnaud), who were approaching from the N. over an open plain. The French and Turks attacked and severely pressed Menshikov's left, while the British assaulted the front of the Russian position, which they carried in spite of a devastating artillery and musketry fire. The success of this frontal attack dispirited the rest of the defenders, who withdrew to the S. The Russians had 36,800 men and 120 guns, the Allies 59,000 men and 128 guns. The losses of the former were 5700, of the latter 3300.

30 V. (20 M.) **Bakhtchi Sarái, Бахчисарай.** — *Railway Restaurant*, unpretending, with a few bedrooms; those wishing to dine here should notify the landlord in good time. — HOTELS (unpretending). *Grand Hôtel*, R. from ³/₄ rb.; *Centrálnaya*, Bazárnaya, R. from 1 rb. — *Tartar Café* (cup of coffee 5 cop.), opposite the Khan-Sarái. — Specimens of the domestic industries of the Tartars may be obtained in a shop adjoining the café.

CAB from the railway station to the town or vice versâ 40, at night 50, per hr. 50 cop. A pleasant *Circular Drive* of 5-6 hrs. may be taken from the Khan-Sarái viâ Katchikalén, Tchufut-Kaléh, the Uspenski Convent, and back (fare 6-7 rb.; provisions and wine must be taken). — *Guide* (Проводникъ) 1 rb. daily. — *Saddle Horse* 2-3 rb. daily.

Travellers should attend the religious services of the *Howling Dervishes*, which take place on Thurs., 9-12 p.m. (the visitor should time his arrival for 10 p.m.; guide necessary). The dervishes work themselves into a state of ecstasy by violent movements of the upper part of the body and by chanting, sometimes for hours at a time, the Muslim Confession of Faith ('lâ ilâha', etc.) and finally the single word 'hû' (He, *i.e.* God).

Bakhtchi Sarái (ca. 690 ft.), the 'Palace of the Gardens', the residence of the Khans from the end of the 15th cent. till 1783, lies on the *Tchuryúk-Su* (Чурюкъ-су), an affluent of the Katchá, in a narrow rocky valley about 3 M. in length. The town, which contains 17,200 inbab. (two-thirds of them Tartars), has a thoroughly Oriental character. The street-life is seen to greatest advantage in the later morning hours. — From the railway station we follow a road to the left which leads across an unoccupied tract to the Bazárnaya, the main street of the town. This is barely 20 ft. in width and has but few cross-streets. The houses, which are interspersed with vineyards, orchards, Lombardy poplars, and groups of other trees, are converted into workshops and stores simply by letting down the wooden fronts and using them as counters or work-benches. The shops, which sell leather, fruit, and many other articles, are all closed after sunset. In the Bazárnaya, near the middle of the town and about 2 M. from the railway station, lies the —

*Khan Sarái, or Palace of the Khans, surrounded by houses on three sides and enclosed by a lofty wall. The palace was built by Khan Abdul Sahel-Girai in 1518, and was destroyed in 1736, but since then it has been repeatedly restored by the Russian government. The gate-keeper is to be found at the left of the entrance, at which is a column commemorating the visit of Catherine II. Beyond an archway under a pavilion, we enter a rectangular court ca. 425 ft. in length and 125 ft. in breadth. To the right of this stands the palace and to the left the mosque, the latter adjoined by two octagonal domed buildings, forming the mausolea of the Khans.

The MOSQUE, a somewhat dark chamber with grated windows accommodating about 300 persons, was restored in 1894. It is best visited at the hours of prayer (noon or 4 p.m.). The two large octagonal wooden stars on the ceiling are intended for the hanging of lamps. The walls are covered with quotations from the Koran. To the right of the *Mihrab*, or prayer-niche, is a flight of wooden steps ascending to the *Mimbar* or pulpit, in which prayers are read on Fridays. Adjacent is a gallery for the Khan. — The *Minaret* commands a fine view of the town.

The PALACE contains a great number of rooms and halls, all of them bearing special names. Among these are the *Divan;* the *Court Room*, with stained-glass windows and a raised seat for the Khan behind a wooden grating; the *Audience Chamber;* the *Golden Room;* the *Dining Room;* and the *Barber's Room*. The most famous of the springs the palace contains is the so-called '*Spring of Tears*' (Фонтáнъ слезъ), the water of which is caught in 10 shells let into a marble table. The story according to which the Countess Marie Potocka wept away her life as a prisoner here, deaf to the love-making of the Khan Mengli-Girai, has no foundation in fact. The *Garden Room* contains a marble basin and fountain. The only object of interest in the *Harem* is the bathing-room.

The *Mausolea* contain the tombs of the Khans and their wives, the former recognizable by a turban, the latter by a hood. The oldest grave dates from 1592. In a garden behind the mausolea are the tombs of some of the Khans and their court-officials.

In the suburb of SALATCHÍK is a *Medreseh*, or Mohammedan high school. It consists of a square building with 15 rooms disposed round an inner court.

The shadeless ENVIRONS of Bakhtchi-Sarai are best visited by carriage (circular drive, see p. 412). We leave the town towards the W. and first reach the Tartar village of *Azíz*. We next cross a barren plateau and then ascend to the S.E. through the valley of the *Katchá* to the (5¹/₂ M.; drive of 1 hr. from the railway station) *Anastasia Convent* (Скитъ святóй Анастáсіи). A flight of stone steps, continued by a stony footpath, ascends hence to *Katchikalén*, the caves in which are believed to have been hewn in the living rock in prehistoric ages (there & back ³/₄ hr.; a monk officiates as guide). About halfway up is the *Church of St. Sophia*, hollowed out of the rock, and affording room for scarcely a dozen people; divine service is held here once yearly on Sept. 17th (O. S.). About three-fourths of the way up, under a protecting roof, is the *Anastasia Spring*, which, however, has dried up.

Beyond the Convent of Anastasia the road follows the bed of

the Katchá, which is covered with detritus and contains no water in summer. The road then ascends towards the N.

To the left we see the *Tepé-Kermén* (1780 ft.), a mountain containing more than 10,000 caverns, arranged in rows one above the other. These caves, many of which have been partly destroyed by the weather, seem to have been made as dwelling-places or burial-places. The mountain lies about 4 M. to the S.E. of Bakhtchi-Sarai, and it takes 1 hr. to drive to the foot of it from the Anastasia Convent. The ascent, made by the N. side, takes 1 hr. There is no drinking-water at the top.

As we proceed, the Black Sea becomes visible in the distance, to the left. After a drive of 2 hrs. (from the Anastasia Convent) we reach the *Valley of Jehosaphat*. The ancient Karaïte burial-ground here has but few features of interest. A short and good path ascends hence to the ruined town of **Tchufút-Kalé,** or 'Fortress of the Jews' ($2^3/_4$ M. to the E. of Bakhtchi-Sarai). This is perched on a narrow limestone plateau, about $^3/_4$ M. long and $^1/_4$ M. broad, at the top of precipitous cliffs 1640 ft. above the sea, and about 650 ft. above the Valley of Jehosaphat. The inhabitants, belonging to the Jewish sect of the *Karaïtes* or *Qaraites*, i.e. the Disciples of the Letter of the Law (of Moses, as opposed to the traditions of the Elders), have deserted the town since the middle of the 19th century. The only occupant of the place at present is the Rabbi Gakham, who acts as guide ($^3/_4$ hr.). Simple refreshments may be obtained at his house, on the S. side of the ruins. About the middle of the town is the mausoleum of *Nenkedzhan-Khanim*, a daughter of the Khan Tokhtamúish, who is said to have thrown herself from the rocks here in consequence of unrequited love (1437).

From Tchufut-Kale a footpath descends to the S. in a few minutes to the *Uspenski Convent*, founded in the 15th century. One of the five churches, about halfway up the hill and reached by a footpath with steps, is hewn out of the living rock. A great pilgrimage takes place to this resort on Aug. 15th (O. S.). From the convent a walk of $^3/_4$ hr. through a grove of nut-trees brings us to the Khan-Sarai in Bakhtchi-Sarai.

On an eminence about 13 M. to the S. of Bakhtchi-Sarai are the ruins of *Mangup-Kaléh*, now in process of excavation. The basilica, dating from the time of Justinian, and the well-preserved Turkish fort are interesting. To reach the ruins we drive to (2 hrs.) *Kodzha-Sala* (return-fare 6-8 rb.), at first following the Yalta road (p. 423) and then ascending the beautiful valley of the Karalöz. From Kodzha Sala a good path leads to ($1^3/_4$ M.) the ruins.

For the highroad from Bakhtchi-Sarai to (76 V.) *Yalta*, see p. 423 (phaeton 18-25 rb.).

THE RAILWAY TO SEBASTOPOL traverses a hilly district, crosses the *Belbék* by an iron bridge, and enters the narrow rocky valley of the river at the station of (46 V.) *Belbék.* The Black Sea appears for a short time on the right. On leaving the ravine, the train runs to the S. to (55 V.) *Mekénzievi-Gori.* — We pass through

four tunnels and cross the *Tchórnaya* before reaching (63 V.)
Inkermán (boat from Sebastopol, see p. 407), situated in an unhealthy neighbourhood at the E. end of the Bay of Sebastopol, near the
mouth of the Tchornaya. Inkerman is famous for the battle of
Oct. 24th, 1854 (O.S.), when 8000 British soldiers sustained a
hand-to-hand fight for several hours against at least five times that
number of Russian troops, until a reinforcement of 6000 French
enabled them to complete the defeat of the enemy. The field is
marked by Russian and English monuments. Of the old Genoese
fortifications some well-preserved towers and fragments of the ramparts still remain. Below is a convent. In the cliffs are numerous
pagan cave-dwellings. — Farther on the railway describes a wide
sweep, affording fine views of the bay, the Malákhov Hill (p. 408),
and the sea. It then threads two tunnels and skirts the S. bay to—

73 V. (48 M.) *Sebastópol* (p. 406).

c. Drive from Sebastopol to Yalta.

82 V. (61 M.). The excursion is better made in this than in the reverse
direction. MOTOR OMNIBUS EXPRESS in 5 hrs. (fare 10 & 8 rb.); offices at
Yekaterininskaya 18 (Pl. B, 3-5). MOTOR MAIL (fare 8 & 6 rb.); offices at
the Hotel Kist. A motor-car can be hired for 35-45 rb. — CARRIAGES (offices
at the posting station in the Monastúirskaya; Pl. A, B, 5): with two horses
15, three horses 20, four horses 28 rb. It is advisable to start early, in
order to reach Yalta before dusk. A visit to the Convent of St. George
and Balaklava is easily combined with this excursion, but a previous
bargain should be made (1-2 rb. extra). Alupka, Oreanda, and Livadia
are best visited from Yalta.
    The traveller should provide his own food and wine.
    In autumn or winter those who have time enough should pass the
night at the Baidar Gate in order to enjoy the magnificent sunrise. [In
summer the sunrise is not visible.] The inns here, however, are extremely
primitive (comp. p. 416).
    STEAMBOAT VOYAGE, see R. 58 e.

The highroad from Sebastopol (p. 407) to Yalta leads at first
towards the S.E., passing the *English Cemetery* (Áнглійское клáдбище) on the right (obelisk to British soldiers; tomb of Sir George
Cathcart). To the W. of this is the *French Cemetery* (Францýзское
клáдбище), with a chapel in the middle of it. Not far from this point
was the camping-ground of the French and English troops during
the Crimean War. — The road to Balaklava (p. 410) soon diverges
to the right; farther on, on a hill to the left, is a mortuary chapel
(1882), in memory of the Italians who fell in the Crimean War.
—21 V. *Tchatál-Kayá*, a posting-station (simple refreshments).

The road now dips and bends towards the E. into the *Baidár
Valley* (Байдáрская долúна), where at first there is little more
than room for the road and the accompanying brook between the
steep walls of rock on either side. Farther on the valley opens out
into an irregular oval, 11 M. in length and 5-7 M. in breadth. The

road next ascends slowly, passing the houses of (38 V.) *Baidári*, a Tartar village, and through woods of beech and oak. At the top of the ascent we reach the —

44 V. (29 M.) **Baidár Gate** (Байдárскія ворóта; 1635 ft.) which was blasted through the solid limestone in 1848. [Unpretending nightquarters to be had in the posting-station; the inns are very primitive and dear, and it is advisable to fix the price of everything beforehand; R. $1^1/_2$-3 rb.] Here an incomparable *View suddenly opens before us (seen to best advantage from the platform above the gate). In front of the beholder stretches the dark-green sea; at his feet lie a group of ruins; on the left are the cliffs of the Yaila and a far-distant strip of shore, rich with southern vegetation.

Beyond the Baidar Gate the road leads downwards in rapid zigzags, passing first a Greek Catholic church erected in 1892 (fine interior) and then, on the right, the estate of *Forós*. About 3 V. beyond the Baidar Gate we thread a rock tunnel 165 ft. long, and then see on our right the sea and *Cape Sarúitch* (280 ft.), the southernmost point of the Crimea. To our left rise rugged and precipitous cliffs of Jurassic limestone. — We next reach the (55 V.) posting-station of *Kikenëiz*, where the broadening strip of coast affords room for a more luxuriant vegetation. Large walnut-trees grow close to the highroad, and the slopes are covered with hazels. In the woods, oaks and beeches of the sturdiest growth alternate with terebinths and pines, cypresses and laurels with pomegranates, mulberries, and fig-trees. The vineyards of the S. coast also begin here.

64 V. *Simëiz* (Pens. Alexándrov-Dóbnikov; Villa Xenia), a sea-bathing resort, lying below us and 2 M. off the road. A branch of the Nicholas Observatory at Pulkovo (p. 189) is situated here. The road again ascends to a considerable height. 67 V. *Alupka* (p. 421). 70 V. *Mis-Khor* (Мисхоръ; posting-station; comp. p. 420). Farther on we pass *Gaspra*, an estate belonging to the Countess Panin (left), the low-lying promontory of *Ai-Todór* (p. 420; right), and numerous datchas. The abrupt rocky walls on the left now give way to less lofty foothills. — 77 V. *Oreanda* (p. 419). From the highest point of the road here we obtain a magnificent view of the Bay of Yalta. Beyond *Livadia* (p. 419) the road descends to (82 V. or 61 M.) *Yalta.*

d. Yalta and Environs.

The *Harbour* lies to the E. of the town; steamer to Sebastopol and Kertch, see R. 58 e. — Motor Omnibus (notices in Dr. Weber's excursion office, p. 418) to Sebastopol, see R. 58 c, to Simferopol, see p. 411. Town office of the Government Railways (Pl. 1), Tchernómorski Pereúlok.

Hotels (bed-linen usually 50, electric light 25 cop. a day extra). *Rossíya (Pl. a), separated by a terrace (concerts in summer and autumn) from the Náberezhnaya, R. 2-8 rb. (Aug. 15th to Nov. 1st, O.S., 3-10 rb.), B. 75 cop., déj. (11-2) 65 cop. to 1 rb., D. (2-8) $1^1/_2$-$2^1/_2$ rb., pens. (Nov. 1st

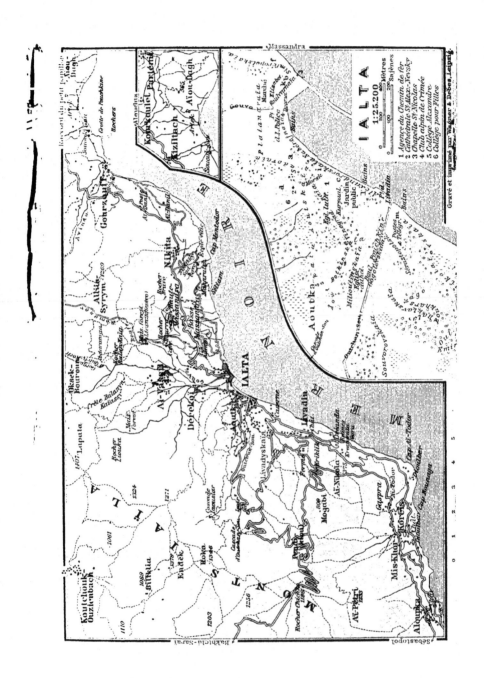

IALTA

1:25.200

0 100 200 300 400 Mètres
0 100 200 Sajènes

1 Agence du Chemin de fer
2 Cathédrale St. Alex.-Nevsky
3 Chapelle St. Nicolas
4 Club alpin de Crimée
5 Collège Alexandre
6 Collège pour Filles

Gravé et imprimé par Wagner & Debes, Leipzig.

to March 15th) 135 rb. per month; VILLA HELENA, Náberezhnaya 51, R. 1¹/₂-6 (Easter and autumn 3-10), B. ¹/₂, déj. ³/₄, D. 1-1¹/₄ rb., new; MARIINO (Pl. i), corner of Náberezhnaya and Morskáya, R. from 1¹/₄ (in autumn from 2), B. ¹/₂, déj. (11-1) ³/₄, D. (1-7 p.m.) 1-1¹/₄ rb.; FRÁNTZIYA (Pl. c), immediately adjoining the Náberezhnaya, R. from 1¹/₂ (in autumn from 2), D. in the sea-pavilion (1-7 p.m.) 1¹/₄ rb.; ST. PETERSBURG (Pl. l), Náberezhnaya, R. from 1¹/₄ (in autumn 2¹/₂-4) rb.; DZHALITA, Náberezhnaya, near the Livadia Bridge, R. 1-5 (in spring and autumn 1¹/₂-8), B. ³/₄, D. ³/₄-1¹/₄ rb.; OREANDA (Pl. m), near the Livadia Bridge, R. from 1 (in autumn from 2) rb., B. 45 cop., déj. ³/₄ rb.; MÉTROPOLE (Pl. e), Vinográdnaya, R. from 1¹/₂ (in autumn from 3), B. ³/₄, déj. ³/₄, D. 1-1¹/₄ rb.; CENTRÁLNAYA (Pl. b), on the harbour, R. from 1 (in autumn 1¹/₂), B. ¹/₂, déj. ³/₄, D. ³/₄-1 rb.; HOTEL-PENSION YALTA (Pl. d), in a high situation, R. from 1 rb., D. 60 cop. to 1 rb. 10 cop.; GRAND-HÔTEL (Pl. f), above the harbour, R. from ³/₄ (in autumn from 1) rb.; BRISTOL (Pl. k), on the harbour, R. from 1 (in autumn from 1¹/₂) rb.

Pensions. *Von Schleier*, Aútskaya, pens. 100-150 rb. per month; *Quisisana* (formerly Weber); *Caputo*, Ulitza Emira Bukharskago 20, pens. 80-100 rb. per month; *Stratéiz*, pens. from 70 rb. per month; *Schultz*; *Wittmer; Tchukurlar*, R. 30-70 rb. (20 per cent more in autumn). — SANATORIA. *Gastria* (proprietor, Dr. Lébedev), pens. 135-175 rb. per month; *Bloch*, pens. 150-300 rb. — Numerous FURNISHED ROOMS, from 50 rb. per month (from 20 rb. out of the season). For invalids the villa district to the S. of the Livadia Bridge is the most suitable.

Restaurants at the above-named hotels. In the Public Garden (Городской садъ): *Sea Pavilion Restaurant*, déj. (11-1) ³/₄-1, D. (1-7) 1¹/₄ rb.; *Vernet* (confectioner's).

Post & Telegraph Office, near the Livadia Bridge, open on weekdays 8-2 & 5-7, on Sun. & holidays 8-10 a.m.

Cabs (good phaetons with two horses; overcharging frequent). *Within the Town:* per drive (incl. that to or from the harbour) 20-70 cop. (luggage 10 cop. extra), per hr. 70, each additional ¹/₂ hr. 30 cop. At night (2-7 a.m.) 50 per cent more. Pleasure-drives within the town are not regulated by the tariff.

Outside the Town (return-fare included in each).	1 or 2 persons	3 or 4 persons
To Lower Massandra or Livadia, with ¹/₂ hr.'s stay	2 rb.	2 rb. 40 cop.
To Isar, with 1 hr.'s stay	3 „	3 „ 60 „
To Upper Massandra or Oreanda (2 hrs.' stay)	4 „	4 „ 80 „
To Ai-Todor or Utchan-Su or Nikitski Park (2¹/₂ hrs.' stay)	5 „	6 „ „
To Alupka or Gurzuff (3 hrs.' stay) . . .	6 rb. 80 cop.	8 „ 20
To Suuk-Su (3 hrs.' stay)	8 „ 20 „	10 „ 20 „

Saddle Horses 3 rb. per day, for ladies 4 rb.; half-day 2 & 3 rb.

Local Steamers (Катеръ; refreshments on board), starting from the Mole, run seven times daily to Alupka (65 cop.), four times daily to Simeïz (80 cop.), four times daily to Gurzuff (55 cop.), and thrice daily to Alushta (1 rb.).

Rowing Boats (bargaining necessary), per hr. 50 cop. (1-3 pers.). To Alupka or Gurzuff and back, with 2 hrs.' stay, 5 rb. (1-7 pers.).

Sea Baths (10-15 cop.) on the Náberezhnaya. The beach is stony, and bathing is not practicable when the sea is rough. Warm salt-water baths at *Pfeifer's*, in the Hotel Frántziya.

Visitors' Tax (for a stay of more than three days), 2¹/₂ rb. per month, 5 rb. per season; families 1¹/₂ or 3 rb. for each member.

The Yalta Section of the **Crimean Mountain Club** (Крымско-Кавказскій горный клубъ; annual subscription 5 rb.) arranges daily drives in the vicinity of Yalta between April and October. The programmes for the week are displayed in the waiting-room (Pl. 4; small museum and observatory) near the Police Bridge. Tickets may also be bought here, between 8 a.m. and 1 p.m. and between 5 and 9 p.m., for 1¹/₂-1³/₄ rb. for a day's excursion (Ai-Petri 25 cop. more), longer excursions at the same rates (members of the club 1 rb.). These entitle the partaker to a seat in a 'lineika' (the two back-seats and the seat beside the driver best for the view), which starts at 9 a.m. (8.30 a.m. for Ai-Petri). Early notification is necessary. Guides for walking excursions 1 rb. daily. The 'Bebesh Excursions' make similar arrangements at similar prices.

TOURIST OFFICE. *Dr. F. Weber's Excursion Office*, in the Dzhalita Hotel (p. 417).

Principal Attractions. For a limited stay (3 days) the itinerary given at p. 401 is recommended.

Yalta (Ялта), a district-town with 30,000 inhab., is picturesquely situated on an amphitheatre rising from a large bay of the Black Sea. It is the most fashionable and most expensive of the Crimean bathing-resorts, and is much frequented from the middle of Aug. till the end of Oct. (O.S.). In the background are the steep slopes of the *Yáila* (ca. 3940 ft.; p. 404), 3-4 M. distant as the crow flies. A fine view of the town and the sea may be had from the lofty harbour-mole. The chief promenades are the Náberezhnaya or Sea Boulevard (Набережная; numerous seats), lighted with electricity at night, and the adjoining small and shady Public Garden (adm. 20 cop.; Kursaal; music; theatre; restaurant, see p. 417). The best shops are in the Náberezhnaya (oriental wares, especially those from the Caucasus, rather dear).

Yalta lies in 44° 30′ N. lat.; and the average annual temperature is 56° Fahr. The hottest months are July and Aug. (mean temperature 75°), the coldest are Jan. and Feb. (with a mean of 39°). The yearly rainfall amounts to 18.5 inches. The bathing-season lasts from the middle of May till the end of Oct. (O.S.), and the grape-cure from Aug. 15th to Oct. 15th. Sudden changes of temperature are common in winter.

Short Excursions. Droshkies, see p. 417. — To the E. of Yalta lies the beautiful park of *Lower Massandra* (Нижняя Массáндра), belonging to the royal domain (adm. in summer from 6 a.m. to 8 p.m. by season-tickets distributed gratis by the management). It is reached by ascending to the right at the Grand-Hôtel (Pl. f.) and then taking the second turn to the left, a few paces farther on. This brings us to (¹/₄ hr.) the lower entrance; but we may also take the upper road to Gurzuff (1 hr.). The trees and shrubs in the park are all provided with labels; among the finest are three beautiful specimens of the Araucaria imbricata and an avenue of roses. — Adjacent, to the N.E., is Upper Massandra (Вéрхняя Массáндра; 1200 ft.) containing a small *Imperial Château,* completed in 1901 in the style of Louis XIV. from plans by Messmacher. To the N. are some natural *Grottoes,* formed of boulders detached from the cliff, and two rocks known as 'Hurrah' and 'Bravo', commanding good views (1320 ft. & 1580 ft. respectively). The large wine-cellar

(Ви́нный подва́лъ; marked 'Cave' on the map) is open to the
public on week-days from 6 a.m. to noon and from 2 to 6 p.m. — To
the N.W. of Upper Massandra and about 5 M. to the W. of Yalta, in
the midst of fine pine-forests, is *Lyesnítchestvo* (1050 ft.), the seat
of the Department of Forestry for Southern Crimea. By ascending
the road from this point for 3 min. and then taking the footpath to
the left, we reach (25 min.) the Abdaraman Square, which affords
a fine view of the *Utch-Kosh Gorge* and of Yalta. — To the E. of
Lower Massandra are the vineyards of *Maharátch* (Магарачъ),
and another wine-cellar ('Cave' on the map). — Still farther to the
E. (ca. 5 M. from Yalta) lies **Nikíta,** with an imperial **Acclima-
tization Garden* (Никитскій садъ), founded in 1812 by C. Steven
(director, M. T. Tcherbakov), a school of horticulture, and a school
of viticulture. The exuberant flora includes cypresses, cedars, palms,
and many other varieties. — To Gurzuff, see p. 421.

About 2¹/₄ M. to the S.W. of Yalta lie the two imperial palaces of
Livadia, which are shown only by special permission of the major
domo (passports may be asked for). — We follow the highroad to
Sebastopol to a point about 1¹/₂ M. beyond the mouth of the brook
Utchán-Su, and then pass through a gate to the left, which admits
to the well-kept vineyards and park of Livadia. In the park is the
New or *Large Palace,* built in 1911 from the plans of Krasnov, and
hard by is the simply-equipped *Small Palace* (Ма́лый дворе́цъ),
on the upper floor of which is the room in which Alexander III. died
on Oct. 20th, 1894. To the W. lie the farm and small château of
Eriklik (1500 ft.). — To the S. is the adjacent park of **Oreanda,**
another piece of imperial property. The château, built in 1843-52
in the Italian style from the designs of Stakenschneider, was burnt
down in 1882 and has been left in ruins. The park, which contains
many rare plants, extends down to the sea. About ¹/₃ M. above the
ruined château is an open *Rotunda.* About ³/₄ M. higher up is the
Hill of the Cross (Krestóvaya Gorá; 615 ft.) surmounted by an iron
cross 13 ft. in height and commanding a view of the Bay of Yalta.
To the right is the cape of Ai-Todor (p. 420), while the hills of
Sudak (p. 424) may be distinguished to the left in clear weather.
— To Alupka, see p. 420.

Longer Excursions (cabs and steamers, see p. 417; guide of the
mountain-club desirable, p. 417).

To the Waterfall of Utchan-Su, 10 V., a walk of 2¹/₄-2¹/₂ hrs.
The first half of the route is shadeless. We start by following the
Aútskaya, and after ¹/₄ hr. we continue in the same direction, avoid-
ing the turn to the left. To the left, in a deep ravine, is the stream
of Utchán-Su, while in front of us tower the steep walls of the Yáila.
At the cross-roads ¹/₂ hr. farther on we turn to the left, and in

2 min. more we cross the brook. The road now ascends slowly and circuitously through wood and after ¹/₂ hr. reaches *Issár.* On an adjacent rocky knoll are the ruins of a Genoese fort. After ¹/₂ hr. we turn to the right, while the road from Livadia joins ours on the left (p. 419). In 20 min. more we reach the simple restaurant adjoining the waterfall, which lies in the midst of a magnificent forest. The road goes on to the left to the top of the Yáila (p. 423). The **Utchán-Su** ('Flying Water'; 1225 ft.) falls over a rocky barrier 330 ft. in height (4 min. from the restaurant), but in summer there is very little water. We have a fine view of Yalta and the sea.

Still more extensive is the view from the *Vtoráya Ploshtchádka* (2-я площáдка, second terrace), a little higher up. In 6 min. we reach a guide-post, showing the way to the Cross Rock (straight on; see below) and to (4 min.) our destination (to the right).—For the Cross Rock we follow the just-mentioned path. In 7 min. we pass a footpath leading to the left to the road up the Yáila. Our path is steep and stony. In ¹/₄ hr. we turn to the right, and in a few paces reach the *Cross Rock* (Крестóвая скалá), a high jutting crag surmounted by a small wooden cross (view no better than that from the Vtoráya Ploshtchádka). The *Shtangéyev Path* (Штангéевская тропá), keeping to the left at the last-mentioned divergence, leads to (4 hrs.) the Shishko Cliff (p. 423).

From the waterfall we return to Yalta by following the path to (20 min.) Issár, and then going straight on. To the left we obtain fine views of Yalta. In 1 hr. we reach the Sebastopol road to the N. of Livadia, which we then follow to the left to (¹/₂ hr.) Yalta.

From Yalta to Alupka, 17 V. or 11 M. (cab and steamer, see p. 417). We quit the town by the Livadia Bridge and turn toward the S.W. — 2 V. *Livadia* (p. 419); 5 V. *Oreanda* (p. 419). — The 'Lower Road' leads near the sea, passing the Moorish château of Grand-Duke Dmitri Constantínovitch just before reaching (12 V.) *Cape Ai-Todór.* Hard by and close to the sea is the Gothic villa known as the 'Swallow's Nest' (Лáсточкино гнѣздó). The manor of Ai-Todór, which belongs to the Grand-Duke Alexander Mikháilovitch, extends hence to the Sebastopol highroad, on which is the entrance. By the sea are considerable remains of a Roman castellum, with two ancient fortified walls, parts of which are in very good repair; the outer wall consists of large blocks of stone, the inner of small partly-hewn stones, built up without mortar. Here, too, are some baths, with a Nymphæum adjoining the second inside wall. Ancient objects found here are placed in the Museum. On the highest point is a lighthouse. — Farther, on are *Kharax,* the English château of Grand-Duke George Mikháilovitch; the *Villa Abrikósov-Kramartch,* in a pseudo-classical style; and the Moorish-looking château of *Dyulber* (i.e. 'Beautiful'), the property of the Grand-Duke Peter Nikoláyevitch. Still farther on are *Koréiz,* the estate of Prince Yusúpov, with a pleasant avenue, and the park of *Mis-Khor* (p. 416), adjoining the sea. — To the left we have a continuous view of the sea.

17 V. (11 M.) **Alúpka.** — HOTELS. *Rossiya* (R. on the map), R. from 1¹/₂ rb., déj. (11-1) 80 cop. to 1 rb., D. (1-7) ³/₄-1¹/₂ rb.; *Frántziya*, R. from 1 rb., déj. 50 - 80 cop., D. ³/₄ - 1¹/₄ rb.; *Dolgov*, déj. ³/₄, D. ³/₄ - 1¹/₄ rb. — Numerous LODGING HOUSES (rather expensive). — The bathing-beach is stony.

The *Château* (interior uninteresting; closed 12-2) was erected for PrinceVorontzóv (d. 1856) in 1837 at a cost of nearly 3,000,000 rb. from the plans of the English architect Blore, who adopted a combination of the Gothic and Moorish styles. In the middle of the S. façade is a large Moorish archway. Opposite this is a wide flight of steps, with six marble lions, descending to the lower part of the park. Close by the sea is the Aivazovski Rock. The larger part of the magnificent *Park (guide desirable; 50 cop.) stretches up the hills at the back of the château. Its attractions comprise a wealth of rare subtropical plants, a beautiful avenue of cedars, flower-beds, some palms, and some magnificent cypresses, including two in the court-yard planted by Potemkin. There are also several pavilions, an orangery, some fountains, and a mosque, the minaret of which commands a pleasant view. — Above the château towers the *Ai-Pétri* (p. 423), which may be ascended in 5 hrs.

FROM YALTA TO GURZUFF, 13 V. (9 M.), highroad (cab and steamer, see p. 417). — The road ascends gradually, commanding a view of the sea to the right. After 4 V. we pass *Lower Massandra* (p. 418) on the right, while the route to *Lyesnítchestvo* (p. 419) diverges to the left. — 5 V. *Upper Massandra* (p. 418); 8 V. *Nikitski Garden* (p. 419); 11 V. *Ai Danil*, a posting-station, beyond which we obtain a fine view. About 1³/₄ V. farther on a branch of the highroad descends to the right in windings to —

13 V. (9 M.) **Gurzúff,** Гурзуфъ (eight large lodging-houses, R. 1-9, déj. ³/₄, D. 1¹/₄ rb.; carriage to Yalta and back 5 rb.), an attractively situated bathing-resort, which may be recommended for a long stay. The beautiful *Park, laid out by the Duc de Richelieu, is illuminated in the evening by electricity. Pushkin lived in the former château of the duke in 1820. By the sea is the Greek Catholic Church of the Assumption. The village contains several Tartar cafés (coffee 5 cop.) and a mosque with a lofty minaret (view from the top; 72 steps). Boat to the Pushkin Grotto 1¹/₂ rb. or more.

About 1 M. to the N.E. of Gurzuff is the bathing-resort of *Suúk-Su*, with four lodging-houses (R. from 1¹/₂ rb., board 45-90 rb. per month). The E. side of the Bay of Gurzuff is bounded by the conspicuous and wooded **Ayu-Dágh** (Аю дагъ; the 'Bear'; 1853 ft.), which rises abruptly from the water and is conspicuous far and near. The ascent is usually begun at *Arték*, 2¹/₄ M. from Gurzuff. We next follow the road to the E., leading to the Tartar village of *Parthenit*, and then take a bridle-path to the right, which leads to the wooded summit in 1 hr. The top, however, commands no view.

From Gurzuff to Alushta, see p. 422.

FROM YALTA TO ALUSHTA. Travellers should go by the Románov Road ('Route Romanov'; fine mountain-scenery) and return by the

27*

Coast Road (phaeton & pair. for 3 days, 30 rb.; motor-car, in one day. 65 rb.). The traveller must bring his own provender.

a. The *Románov Road*, completed in 1913, diverges to the N. from the Coast Road between Upper and Lower Massandra. Beyond Lyesnitchestvo (p. 419) it ascends to the *Red Crag* (Кра́с-ный Ка́мень; two-horse phaeton from Yalta and back 10 rb., motor-car 25 rb.) and reaches its highest point (4760 ft.) on a thinly wooded plateau to the E. of the Demir Kapu (5045 ft.). It then descends slowly round the W. side of the *Román Kosh* (5055 ft.), the highest mountain in the Crimea, and leads through wood, passing the *Babu Dágh*, to the *Nunnery of SS. Cosmas & Damian*, founded in 1856 and situated in the romantic upper valley of the Alma (church festival on July 1st, O.S.; phaeton & pair from Yalta and back. in 2 days, 20 rb.; motor-car 45 rb.). Farther on we traverse woods. About 3¹/₄ M. to the S. of the Eklizi-Burún (see below) the road bends sharply to the S.E. and then leads to the E., down the valley of the *Ulú-Üzén*, to Alushta (see below).

b. *Coast Road*, 42 V. (28 M.; carr. 10-12 rb.; motor mail; steamboat, see p. 417). From Yalta to (11 V.) *Ai-Daníl*, see p. 421. About 1³/₄ V. farther on the route to Gurzuff (p. 421) diverges to the right. 17 V. *Kiziltash*, a village to the left; to the right rises the Ayu-Dágh (p. 421). 25 V. *Karassán* lies below us to the right, with a four-storied château in the Moorish style. Adjacent, to the N is the estate of *Kutchúk-Lambát*. Beyond the posting-station of (28 V.) *Biyúk-Lambát* the road descends gradually through a forest-district, in which we again meet the trees familiar to us in Central Europe. To the left we have a fine view of the Tchatuir-Dágh and the Demerdzhi-Yáila.

42 V. (28 M.) **Alúshta**, Алушта (*Yevropéiskaya*, R. 1¹/₂-6 rb., B. 40 cop., D. ³/₄-1¹/₂ rb.; *Grand-Hôtel; Yushni Béreg;* visitors' tax 3 rb.), a town with 4500 inhab., frequented for sea-bathing. The remains of fortifications date from the Byzantine period. The vineyards, laid out by German settlers in 1826, are now mainly in the possession of Messrs. Tokniakóv & Molotkóv, a visit to whose cellarages is interesting. — Steamboat to Sebastopol or Kertch, see R. 58c.

Alushta is the starting-point for an ascent of the *Tchatuir-Dágh (Чатырда́гъ, 'Tent Mountain'; 4990 ft.), the top of which is 25 V. (17 M.) distant. Horse, with mounted guide, to the caves and back (at least 10 hrs.) 10-12 rb. Pedestrians require 18 hrs. for the complete expedition. Warm clothing is necessary even in the height of summer, and food and wine must also be carried. The start should be made between 4 and 5 a.m. The ascent proper begins after 1³/₄ hr. at the Tartar village of *Kerbekli* (beds to be had at the house of the representative of the Crimean Mountain Club), whence a ride of 3-3¹/₂ hrs. brings us to (18 V.) the plateau, which is about 8 sq. M. in extent. The highest point of the plateau is the *Eklizi-Burún*, which commands an imposing panorama, embracing on the N. the steppe and the foothills of the Yáila, extending on the W. to the Bay of Sebastopol and Eupatoria, and bounded on the S. and E. by the sea. — On the N. side the Tchatuir-Dágh descends in terraces. On the second of these, reached from the Eklizi-Burún (p. 422) in 1 hr. on horse-back or in 1³/₄ hr. on foot, is a simply equipped shelter-hut of the Crimean Mountain Club (nightquarters 20 cop.). Near the hut are the stalactite caves of *Bin-Bash-Khobá* ('Cave of the Thousand Heads') and *Suuk-Khobá* ('Cold Cave'). A charge of 10 cop. is made for admission, and the attendant also expects a gratuity.

To (18 V.) the *Nunnery of SS. Cosmas and Damian* (saddle-horse there & back 4-5 rb., carr. 8 rb.), see p. 422.

FROM ALUSHTA TO SIMFEROPOL, 49 V. (33 M.), motor omnibus, see p. 411 (an attractive drive). The road leads through the deciduous woods of the *Demérdzhi-Uzén* valley, passing (6 V.) the Tartar village of *Shumá* and the *Kutúzov Spring* (Кутузовскій Фонтанъ), so called after Field-Marshal Kutúzov, who was wounded here in 1774 in a battle with the Turks. The road, after ascending along the E. side of the *Tchatúir-Dágh* (p. 422) till it reaches a point nearly halfway up the mountain, descends to (19 V.) *Tavshán-Bazár* (restaurant at the posting-station, with bedrooms), situated in the midst of luxuriant beech-woods. Farther on we skirt the *Salgir* (p. 411), crossed by several bridges. From (29 V.) *Biyúk-Tchevké* a visit may be paid (with guide) to the stalactite cavern of *Kizil-Khobá*, which lies 3 V. to the E. 35 V. *Mahmoud-Sultán* — 49 V. (33 M.) *Simferópol* (p. 411).

From Alushta to (88 V.; 58 M.) *Sudak* (p. 424). Carriage in 2 days; 30-40 rb. There are no regular posting-stations, but the night may be spent in the village of *Kutchúk-Uzén* (28 V.) or *Uskút* (52 V.). Food and wine must be provided. The sea-route is preferable.

FROM YALTA TO BAKHTCHI-SARAI, 76 V. (50 M.), carriage (no diligence) in 12-15 hrs. (fare 25-30 rb.; to the Shishko Cliff and back 10-12 rb.). As far as Fotzsala this is a very attractive drive. — From Yalta to the (10 V.) waterfall of *Utchán-Su*, see pp. 419, 420. — Beyond this point we ascend in windings through woods, which become thinner as we proceed. To the E. we have an unimpeded view of the coast and the sea. The road skirts the *Pendikúl* (2850 ft.), and a finger-post ('Тропа на скалу Пендикюль') to the right directs us to a (3 min.) platform commanding a magnificent view. After numerous windings we reach (25 V.) the top of the *Yáila*, where there is a simple inn with four small bedrooms. Adjacent rises the *Shishkó Cliff* (3885 ft.), a splendid point of view. From this point the top of the *Ai-Petri* (4045 ft.), which rises to the W., may be attained in 1 hr. (guide desirable). — Farther on we traverse a bleak plateau and then a beech-wood, finally descending in windings through an attractive district. To the left is the deep valley of the Kurú-Uzén. — 48 V. *Kokós* (plain inn by the bridge; bargaining advisable), a Tartar village, with a shooting-box of Prince Yusupov's (may be visited in the owner's absence). Farther on the road enters the valley of the *Belbék*. — 54 V. *Fotzsála;* 58 V. *Albát.* At (67 V.) *Biyúk-Syurén* we leave the valley of the Belbék and a little farther on we join the road leading from Sebastopol to Bakhtchi-Sarai. — 76 V. (50 M.) *Bakhtchi-Sarái*, see p. 412.

c. Steamer from Sebastopol to Kertch.

190 Sea Miles. Steamboats of the Russian Steam Navigation & Trading Co. in 24 hrs. (fares 11 rb. 30, 8 rb. 45 cop.; food 3 rb. 20, 2 rb. 60 cop.). For breaks in the journey and other details, see p. 106. From Sebastopol

to Yalta 7 times a week in 5 hrs. (fares 3 rb. 85, 2 rb. 50 cop.); from Yalta to Alushta 4 times a week in 2 hrs. (fares 3 rb. 45, 1 rb. 50 cop.); from Alushta to Sudak 4 times a week (fares 3 rb. 50, 1 rb. 55 cop.); from Sudak to Feodosiya (fares 3 rb. 65, 1 rb. 75 cop.); from Feodosiya to Kertch in 6¹/₂ hrs. (fares 4 rb. 75, 3 rb. 50 cop.). Steamers of the Russian Transport & Insurance Co. also ply from Sebastopol to Kertch via Yalta, Sudak, and Feodosiya thrice weekly (fare 8 rb. 45 cop.). — In Sebastopol, Yalta, and Feodosiya the large steamers lie to at the pier; in the other ports passengers land by small boats. The course of the vessels is generally near the coast; the most beautiful part of it is that between Cape Saruitch and Alushta.

Sebastópol, see p. 407. — The vessel leaves the bay on the W., skirts *Cape Chersonesus*, and then shapes a S.E. course. *Cape Fiolente* (p. 410) and the *Convent of St. George* (p. 410) are both visible. Beyond *Cape Saruitch* (p. 416) begins the 'Russian Riviera', which extends as far as Alushta, and is bounded on the N. by the precipitous Yáila (p. 404). The chief points passed farther on are the manor of *Forós* (p. 416); *Mshatka; Milás*, recognizable by its four towers; the abrupt *Cape Kikenëiz*; the steep and lofty cliff of *Divo*, below Leméni; the handsome château of *Alupka* (p. 421), with the *Ai-Petri* (p. 423) towering above it; the white Moorish château of *Dyulber* (p. 420); and *Cape Ai-Todór* (p. 420), with the villa of Swallow's Nest. Beyond the lighthouse of Ai-Todór we obtain a *View of Yalta, with the Ayu-Dágh (p. 421) rising in the distance to the N.E. After passing *Oreanda* (p. 419) and *Livadia* (p. 419) the steamer halts at the mole of —

54 S.M. **Yalta** (p. 416). Fine view of the town.

As we continue our voyage, *Gurzúff* (p. 421) comes into sight. Beyond the *Ayu-Dágh* (p. 421) are the manor of Kutchuk-Lambat (p. 422) and the wooded hill of *Kastel*. Farther on we pass the mouths of numerous valleys clad with forest or brushwood. Towards the E. the steppe-like character of the scenery becomes gradually more emphasized by the barrenness of the hills.

72 S.M. *Alúshta* (p. 422), to the S. of the *Tchatuir-Dágh* (p. 422).

96 S.M. **Sudák**, Судакъ (*Lórentzov*, R. 1¹/₄-2¹/₂, bed-linen ¹/₂, D. ³/₄-1 rb.), situated in a district producing one of the best wines of the Crimea. In the vicinity are the remains of an old Genoese fortress, adjoining which is a German colony founded in 1805.

About 7 V. (5 M.) to the W. lies *Novi Svyet*, with the vineyards of Prince Golitzuin. — About 18 V. (12 M.) to the N.E. (phaeton 8 rb.), in the midst of a forest, is the convent of *Kiziltásh*, founded in 1853.

FROM SUDAK TO FEODOSIYA there are two roads. The COAST ROAD (52 V. or 34 M.; carr. 12-15 rb.; mail 1¹/₂ rb.) leads viâ *Kozí, Otuzi*, and *Koktebél.* — The SUDAK VALLEY ROAD (63 V. or 42 M.; daily motor service) at first traverses the fertile *Sudák Valley* (Судáкская долúна), rising along the *Taraktásh River* and crossing the E. foothills of the *Yáila Range*. At (20 V.) *Elbúsli* the road bends to the N.E. and touches *Stari-Krim*, at the foot of the *Agarmúish* (2297 ft.). This was the capital of the Crimea from the conquest of the peninsula by the Tartars to the 15th cent.; it is now an unimportant place with 6700 inhabitants. Near *Koshka-Tchokrák* our road joins the highroad from Feodosiya to Simferopol.

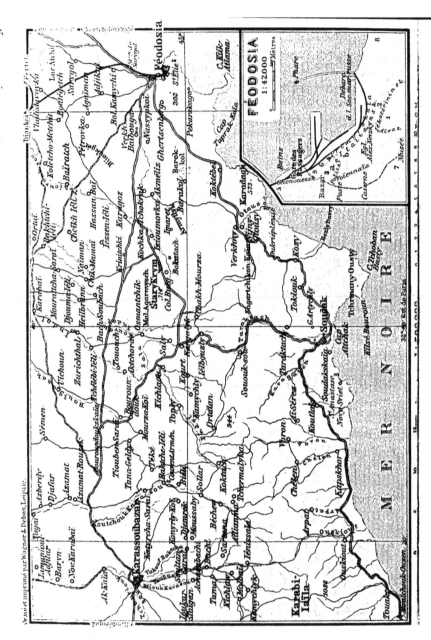

As we proceed, the coast becomes flatter and flatter.

124 S.M. Feodósiya, Θεοдосія. — The wharf of the steamers of the Russian Steam Navigation & Trading Co. is on the S. side of the harbour, near the mole, and about 1 M. from the station of the railway to Dzhankói and Kertch. — HOTELS. *Centrálnaya* (Pl. b), R. 1-5 rb., D. 80 cop.; *Yevropéiskaya* (Pl. a), both in the Italiánskaya; *Rossiya.* — CAB from the harbour to the town, incl. luggage, 40, from or to the rail. station 25-35, per drive 20, per hour 50 (outside the town 75) cop. — BRITISH VICE-CONSUL, *W. E. W. von Stürler.* — LLOYD'S AGENT, *P. S. Bossalini.* — Good sea-bathing at the *Town Baths*, to the N. of the rail. station. — About 2-3 hrs. suffice for a hasty visit to the town.

Key to the Numbers on the adjoining Plan: 1. Roman Catholic Church. — 2. Lutheran Church. — 3. Aivazovski Fountain. — 4. Fountain of the 'Good Genius'. — 5. Aivazovski's House. — 6. Alexander Monument. — 7. Mosque. — 8. Quarantine Station. — 9. Genoese Tower.

՝ *Feodósiya* (Theodosia), situated on the Black Sea on the bay of the same name, is the chief town of a district and contains 38,000 inhabitants. Its excellent sandy beach has made it a popular sea-bathing resort; it also contains several kumiss institutions (comp. p. 358), while its numerous vineyards are utilized for the grape-cure (end of Aug. to Nov.).

Theudosia or *Theodosia* was founded in the 6th cent. B.C. as a colony of Miletus, and soon carried on an extensive trade in the export of grain. In the 13th cent. it was refounded by the Genoese under the name of *Kaffa;* and in the following century it is said to have contained 100,000 inhabitants. In 1475 it was captured by the Tartars.

Along the W. side of the harbour, which was built in 1890-94, runs the Marine Boulevard (Primórskaya). On the right side of this street are the *Fountain of the 'Good Genius'* (Pl. 4) and a *Bronze Statue of Alexander III.* (Pl. 6) by Bach (1896), while to the left, near the Bazaar, is another *Fountain* (Pl. 3), erected in the Turkish style in 1888 from the plans of Aivazovski (restaurant adjacent). A little farther to the N. are an old *Tower* (Pl. 9) of the Genoese period and the *Station* of the railway to Dzhankoi (see below). Beyond the station is the *House of I. K. Aivazovski* (Pl. 5; d. 1900), containing a collection of pictures by this painter of sea-pieces (open daily 11-2 & 5-8; and usually also on the arrival of the larger passenger steamers; adm. 20 cop.). — To the S. of the town is the *Museum of Antiquities,* founded in 1811 and open on week-days 7-7, in winter 9-4 (adm. 15 cop.; Russian catalogue 25 cop.; director, L. Colli). It contains a few Greek inscriptions referring to Pairisades and Sauromates I., Kings of the Bosphorus, and also a number of slabs with Latin inscriptions of the 14-15th century.

FROM FEODOSIYA TO DZHANKOI (Kertch), 112 V. (74 M.), railway in 3¹/₂ hrs. The railway traverses a flat steppe-region affording glimpses to the right of the Sivásh (p. 403). — From (17 V.) *Vladislávovka* (Rail. Restaurant) a branch-line runs through the steppes to (85 V.) *Kertch* (p. 426). — 112 V. (74 M.) *Dzhankói* (p. 403).

From Feodosiya to Sudak, see p. 424.

From Feodosiya the steamer steers to the E. along the flat coast. After about 3¹/₂ hrs. *Opúk* becomes visible, lying at the foot of a table-mountain, covered with huge rocks and the remains of an old castle. Farther on we steer to the N. into the *Straits of Kertch* or *Yenikale*, known in antiquity as the *Cimmerian Bosphorus*.

190 S.M. **Kertch-Yenikale**, Керчь-Еникале.— Hotels. *Primórskaya: Passage; Centrálnaya*, Dvoryánskaya 1, R. from 1¹/₂ rb., B. 40 cop., D. ¹/₂-1 rb. — Cab per drive 25, to the harbour (incl. luggage) 40, to or from the rail. station 50, per hr. 60 cop. — British Vice-Consul & Lloyd's Agent, *M. N. Megalos*. — The Steamers from Batum and Odessa anchor in the roads; the passengers are brought to shore by a tender and are allowed 5 hrs. to visit the town. The antiquities offered for sale in the streets are usually spurious.

Kertch, a commercial port at the entrance to the Sea of Azóv, rises from the beach in the form of an amphitheatre. The population amounts to 56,000, including the old fortress of *Yenikale* (8 M. to the E. of Kertch) and the new fortress of *Paul* (2¹/₄ M. to the S.E.), which together command the strait. The *Church of St. John the Baptist*, in the Predtétchenskaya Square, is said to have been built in the 8th century. The *Archaeological Museum* (open free daily, 9-12 & 2-5; director, V. Shkorpil), Myeshtchánskaya 10, contains 200 ancient glass vessels, remains of wooden sarcophagi, clay vessels, tombstones with Greek inscriptions, slabs of terracotta used for covering graves, fragments of stucco with paintings in the early Pompeian style, and other objects of interest.

The site of Kertch was occupied in antiquity by *Panticapaeum* or *Bosphorus*, a colony established by Miletus in the 6th cent. B.C. Under the dynasty of the Spartocidæ (4th cent.) it became the capital of a large kingdom (comp. p. 405) and carried on a brisk trade in grain with Athens. Mithridates the Great resided here, and here he died in 63 B.C., betrayed by his son Pharnaces. The dynasty of the Sauromates and Rhescuporidæ, established by the Romans, maintained its power down to the 4th cent. A.D. Thereafter the city became dependent on the Goths and Huns, and finally was absorbed by the Byzantine Empire. The valuable objects found in the tombs of Panticapæum are now in the Hermitage at St. Petersburg. — Near the Hotel Centrálnaya is a wide flight of 214 steps ascending in several stages to the *Mithridates Hill* (Горá Митридáтъ). About halfway up (6 min.) are the ruins of a modern temple in the Doric style. Hence we ascend rapidly, passing a small modern Ionic mortuary temple, to the (5 min.) top of the hill crowned by the so-called 'Throne of Mithridates' (Крéсло Митридáта), consisting of a few large stones. The fine view includes the sea and the steppe, with its numerous kurgáns or tumuli. On the slopes of Mithridates Hill numerous graves of the Roman period have been discovered, some of them adorned with paintings. On the N. slope are early Hellenistic and Roman remains, including those of a public building. In the suburb of Glinishtche is the *Melék-Tchésmenski Kurgán* (ca. 3rd cent. B.C.) containing a tomb-chamber, a dromos, and some inscriptions. Adjacent, at Tchetvórtaya Prodólnaya 10, is a painted tomb-chamber of the 1st cent. A.D., with frescoes (to the right and left of the entrance are the deities of the dead, Hermes and Calypso; on the vaulting, Head of Demeter; in the rear lunette, Rape of Persephone). — About $2^1/_2$ M. to the N. of Kertch (carr. & pair there & back in $1^1/_4$ hr., $1^1/_2$ rb.) is the *Tzarski Kurgán*, the best-preserved tumulus in Russia, a wedge-shaped structure consisting of overhanging blocks with a tomb-chamber and a dromos 65 ft. long by $6^1/_2$ ft. broad (4th cent. B.C.). The archæological collection includes tomb-reliefs and the like, a painted head of Persephone (4th cent. B.C.), and the slab-door of a tomb-chamber, with a painted head of Medusa (1st cent. A.D.).

About 14 V. (9 M.) to the N.W. of Kertch is *Lake Tchokráskoye* (Чокрáское солянóе óзеро), with mud-baths. — About $2^1/_2$ M. to the N. of Kertch is the *Bulganákski Mud Volcano*.

RAILWAY to Dzhankoi and Feodosiya, see p. 425. The railway station (restaurant) lies $1^1/_3$ M. from the town

59. From Moscow to Rostov-on-the-Don (Vladikavkaz) viâ Voronezh.

1165 V. (772 M.). Railway in 26-42 hrs. (farés 24 rb., 14 rb. 40 cop.). The trains start from the Kazan Station; the express trains are provided with dining and sleeping cars (berth 9 rb. 30 cop. & 7 rb.).

From Moscow to (295 V.) *Ryazhsk*, see R. 48 b. 344 V. *Bogoyavlénsk* (Rail. Restaurant), junction of the Moscow and Saratov railway (R. 60) and of a branch-line to Gorbatchovo (p. 361).

385 V. **Kozlóv** (*Railway Restaurant; Slavyánskaya*, R. 1-3, B. $^1/_2$, D. $^1/_2$-$1^1/_4$ rb.; *Centrálnaya*, both in the Moskóvskaya; izvóshtchik to the town 20-30 cop.), a district-town in the government of Tambóv, lies on the *Lyesnói-Vorónezh*, and was founded in 1636. Pop. 50,000. — To Moscow or Saratov, see R. 60.

The line traverses the district of the 'Black Earth' (P. xxxvii). — 445 V. (295 M.) *Gryazi* (Грязи; Railway Restaurant, fair), with a huge grain elevator (capacity 27,200 tons).

FROM GRYAZI TO TZARITZUIN, 565 V. (375 M.), railway in 20 hrs. The railway traverses the steppes between the Volga and the Don. Nearly all the stations are unimportant Cossack settlements. — 125 V. *Zhérdevka* (Rail. Restaurant). 197 V. *Borisoglyébsk* (Rail. Restaurant), a town in the government of Tambóv, on the left bank of the *Vórona*, contains 29,000 inhab., and carries on a trade in grain, cattle, and wool. — 222 V. *Povórino* (Rail. Restaurant), see p. 389; 301 V. *Filónovo* (Rail. Restaurant); 420 V. *Artcheda* (Rail. Restaurant). — 565 V. (375 M.) *Tzaritzuin*, see p. 434.

From Gryazi to *Orel*, see p. 362.

515 V. *Gráfskaya*, in the midst of woods. — 545 V. *Otrozhka* is the junction for the branch-line to —

552 V. (366 M.) **Vorónezh**, Воронежъ. — *Railway Restaurant.*

HOTELS. *Bristol*, Bolshaya Dvoryánskaya 23, R. $1^1/_2$-7 rb., omn. 30 cop.; *Centrálnaya*, Bolshaya Dvoryánskaya 22, R. 1-4 rb., bed-linen 30 cop.,

D. (1-6 p.m.) 60 cop. to 1 rb. 20, omn. 30 cop.; *Grand-Hôtel*, Málaya Dvoryánskaya 36, R. 1-5 rb., bed-linen 35 cop., D. (12-6) ¹/₂-1 rb., omn. 30 cop.;
Frántziya, Moskóvskaya, R. 1-5 rb., bed-linen 35, B. 30 cop., D. (12-6)
¹/₂-1 rb.—Izvóshtcuik from or to the rail. station 35, per drive 20, per hr.
40-50 cop.—Tramway from the station viâ the Bolshaya Dvoryánskaya
to the New Cemetery; and through the Bolshaya Moskóvskaya to the
Convent of St. Mitrophanes.

Vorónezh, the capital of the fertile government of Vorónezh
(celebrated for its breeds of horses and cattle), and the headquarters
of the 5th Army Corps, was founded in 1586 as a frontier fortress
against the Tartars and now contains 79,000 inhabitants. It is
pleasantly situated on the high right bank of the *Vorónezh*, here
intersected by numerous ravines, about 5 M. above its confluence
with the Don. An agricultural academy was opened at Voronezh in
1913.— The Bolshaya Dvoryánskaya, the chief street of the town,
is reached by turning to the left on leaving the railway station,
turning to the right after a few yards, and in five minutes turning
to the right again. In following this street from the station we
pass on the left Schwarz's *Bronze Statue of Peter the Great* (1860),
who in 1695 established at Voronezh a shipbuilding-yard for the
fleet of the Don (no longer extant). To the right is the Petróvskaya,
with a *Cadet College*. Farther down the Bolshaya Dvoryánskaya,
to the left, is the *General Post Office*, while to the right, at the
corner of the Bolshaya Sadóvaya, is a statue of the poet *S. Nikítin*
(d. 1861), by Shuklin (1911). At the end of the street, to the right,
1¹/₄ M. from the station, is a bust of the popular poet *Koltzóv*
(d. 1842), by Triscorni (1868). In the Bolshaya Moskóvskaya, diverging to the right at this point, is a *Provincial Museum* (No. 52),
which is open on Sun. & holidays 12-4 (closed June-Aug. O.S.). Another
5 min. brings us to the *Convent of St. Mitrophanes* (d. 1703), with
a conspicuous church (Annunciation). On an island in the river is
the Yacht Club, originally the *Arsenal*, built in 1696. There is a
Lutheran Church in the Bolshaya Sadóvaya and a *Roman Catholic
Church* in the Lyesnaya.

From Voronezh to Kursk, 231 V. (153 M.), railway in 6¹/₂ hrs.— From
(90 V.) *Kastórnaya* (Rail. Restaurant) branch-lines run to the N. to (113 V.)
Yeletz (p. 362) and to the S. to (207 V.) Valuiki (p. 389). 130 V. *Mar-
mvizhí* (p. 362).--231 V. (153 M.) *Kursk*, see p. 363.

The train now returns to Otrozhka (p. 427). — Just beyond (644 V.)
Liski-on-the-Don (Лиски на Дону; Rail. Restaurant), the junction
of the Balashov & Kharkov line (p. 389), we cross the *Don* by a
girder-bridge 350 yds. in length. We then leave the 'Black Earth'
district and enter the steppe. — 752 V. *Yevstrátovka* (Rail. Restaurant); 860 V. *Tchertkóvo* (Rail. Restaurant). — 922 V. *Míllerovo*
(Rail. Restaurant).

From Millerovo to Debaltzevo, 177 V. (117 M.), railway in 8¹/₂ hrs.
— Beyond (80 V.) *Olkhóvaya* the train crosses the N. Donetz. — 105 V.
Lugánsk (*Rail. Restaurant; Grand-Hôtel;* izvóshtchik from the station

to the town 30 cop.) is a district-capital in the Government of Yekaterino-
sláv, with foundries and engine-works, including the Hartmann Locomotive
Works, which employ 7000 hands. Pop. 60,000.—124 V. *Rodakovo;* 145 V.
Altchevskoye, with large iron-works.—177 V. (117 M.) *Debaltzévo* (see below).

967 V. *Glubókaya* (Rail. Restaurant). The railway crosses the
Northern Donétz by a bridge 213 yds. long.—1011 V. *Likhaya.*

FROM LIKHAYA TO TZARITZUIN, 357 V. (237 M.), railway in 13 hrs.—
141 V. *Morózovskaya* (Rail. Restaurant); 300 V. *Krivomúzginskaya* (Rail.
Restaurant), the junction of a branch-line to (18 V.) *Donskaya.*—357 V.
(237 M.) *Tzaritzuin* (Rail. Restaurant), see p. 434.

1034 V. (685 M.) **Zvyérevo** (Звѣрево; *Railway Restaurant*).

FROM ZVYEREVO TO KRAMATORSKAYA, 287 V. (190 M.), railway.—From
(145 V.) *Debaltzévo* branch-lines run to the N.E. to (177 V.) Millerovo (see
above), to the N. to (221 V.) Kupyansk (p. 389), to the W. to (58 V.) Yasinovataya (p. 400), and to the S. to Ilováiskoye (P. 431). At (287 V.) *Kramatórskaya* the railway joins the line from Lozovaya to Rostov (p. 431).—
All these railways traverse the **Coal District of the Donétz,** which is
9600 sq. M. in extent, and contains large deposits of bituminous coal and an-
thracite. Its richest veins are at *Uspénskaya* (p. 431) and in the *Lisítchya
Balka.* The district to the N. of the coal beds is rich in iron-ores.

1052 V. *Sulin* (Rail. Restaurant), with coal-pits and foundries.

1117 V. (740 M.) **Novo-Tcherkássk,** Новочеркасскъ.—*Rail-
way Restaurant.*—HOTELS. *Centrálnaya,* R. 1¹/₄-3³/₄, D. ¹/₂-1 rb.; *Bolshaya
Moskóvskaya,* R. 1-5, D. ¹/₂-1 rb., both at the corner of the Plátovski Prospékt and Moskóvskaya; *Yevropéiskaya,* Atamánskaya, R. 1¹/₂-5, D. ³/₄-1 rb.
—*Berger's Confectionery Shop,* Moskóvskaya.—IZVÓSHTCHIK from the
railway station to the town 40, per drive 20, per hr. 40 cop.—GENERAL
POST OFFICE, Plátovski Prospékt.

Novo-Tcherkássk (340 ft.), the capital of the territory of the
Cossacks of the Don and seat of the Greek Catholic archbishop of
the district of the Don and of a Polytechnic Institute (1907), was
founded by Platov in 1805 and now has 67,000 inhabitants. It is a
straggling town, situated on a plateau intersected by numerous ravines and enclosed on three sides by the *Aksái,* a tributary of the Don,
and the *Tuzlóv.* Large quantities of sparkling wine are made here.
— From the railway station, which lies in the S.E. part of the town,
the Kreshtchénskaya leads direct in ¹/₄ hr. to the Nicholas Square.
Here stand the *Cathedral of the Ascension* (1905), a monument
of the *Hetman Baklanov,* unveiled in 1911, and a *Bronze Statue
of Yermák* (p. 524) after a design by Beklemíshev (1904). From
this square the Plátovski Prospékt runs to the S.W. (left), passing
(on the right, at the corner of the Atamánskaya) the *Don Museum*
(Донской музей), where are preserved Cossack banners, charters,
and trophies, and the sceptre with which the Hetman has been invested since the time of Catherine II.

In the historical section (first floor, to the right) is a glass-case (right
wall) containing souvenirs of the *Hetman Platov* (see p. 430). Among
these is a sword of honour presented to him by the City of London (June 8th,
1814) for the 'consummate skill, brilliant talents, and undaunted bravery
displayed by him during the protracted conflicts in which he has been
engaged for securing the liberties, the repose, and the happiness of Europe.'

Farther on, to the right, diverges the Moskóvskaya, the chief business-street; on the left is a bronze statue (1853), by Baron von Klodt, of the *Hetman M. I. Platov* (d. 1818), a distinguished figure in the wars at the beginning of the 19th century. Behind are the *Hetman's Palace* (Атаманскій дворецъ) and the shady *Alexander Garden*, with a summer-theatre; while at the W. end of the Prospékt, 1¹/₂ M. from the Nikoláyevska Square, is one of the two triumphal arches erected in honour of Alexander I. in 1817 (the other being in the Petersburg Prospékt). There is also a Lutheran Church (1899).

We now approach the *Don*. 1141 V. *Aksái*, with 7600 inhabitants. — 1156 V. *Nakhitcheván* (Нахичевань), an Armenian colony founded in 1780 and containing 71,000 inhabitants. In front of the Greek Catholic Cathedral is a bronze statue of the Empress Catherine II. by Tchizhov; in the Alexander Park is a granite column in honour of Alexander II. An electric tramway runs to Rostov.

1165 V. (772 M.) **Rostóv-on-the-Don,** Ростовъ на Дону́. — *Railway Restaurant.* — Hotels. *Bolshaya Moskóvskaya,* Bolshaya Sadóvaya, well spoken of, R. from 2, D. 1¹/₂-2 rb.; *International,* Moskóvskaya 53, R. from 1¹/₄, D. ¹/₂-1 rb.; *San Remo,* opposite the Bolshaya Moskóvskaya Hotel, R. 1-4, D. (12-6) ³/₄-1 rb.; *Yerrópa,* Bolshaya Sadóvaya, R. from 1¹/₄ rb., B. 35 cop., D. (1-6) ³/₄-2 rb. — Good restaurant in the *Merchants' Club* (Коммерческій клубъ; introduction of guests permitted), at the corner of the Sadóvaya and the Taganrógski Prospékt; concerts in summer in the *Club Garden.* Beer at *Rösner's,* Nikólskaya 111. — Confectioners. *Schweitzárskaya, Filippov, Kharakh-Khiantz,* all in the Bolshaya Sadóvaya.

Izvóshtchik from the rail. station to the town 40, to the station or to the harbour 30, per drive 20, per hr. 50, to Nakhitchevan 50 cop.

Electric Tramways from the station viâ the Bolshaya Sadóvaya to Nakhitchevan, and through all the other main streets.

Post & Telegraph Office, Soborni Pereúlok.

Consulates. British Vice-Consul, *John Lowdon,* Nikoláyevski Pereúlok 44. — U. S. Consular Agent, *G. R. Martin.* Bolshaya Sadóvaya 137.

Rostóv, a brisk commercial town in the territory of the Cossacks of the Don. is prettily situated on the lofty right bank of the *Don,* about 13 M. from its mouth in the Sea of Azóv. Pop. 200,000. After Odessa and Kiev it is the best-built town in S. Russia, but it offers little of interest to the stranger. Its chief exports are wheat, rye, barley, and wool. It contains some important tobacco-factories (Asmólov, Kushnarév). — From the railway station the tramway, running at first on the level and then ascending, leads to the Bolshaya Sadóvaya, the chief thoroughfare of the town, intersecting it from E. & W. To the left are the *Public Garden* (Городской садъ) and the *Duma,* the latter erected in 1897-99 from the plans of Professor Pomerántzev (p. 299); behind is the *Museum.* The Soborni Pereúlok, diverging opposite the Public Garden, leads to the *Greek Catholic Cathedral,* with its lofty belfry. In the square to the N. of the cathedral is a bronze *Statue of Alexander II.,* by

Mikéshin. In an open space to the right, farther on, stands the *Cathedral of St. Alexander Nevski,* completed in 1908 from the plans of Yashtchenko. Rostov also contains Lutheran and Roman Catholic churches. — About 5 M. to the E. (one-horse carr. 1-1½ rb.) is the shady *Armenian Garden* (Армянскій садъ; mediocre restaurant).

FROM ROSTOV TO LOZOVAYA (Kharkov, Moscow), 399 V. (264 M.), express in 8½ hrs. — Just short of (37 V.) *Sinyávskaya* the Sea of Azóv becomes visible on the left, and the train now follows its shore as far as Taganrog. — 68 V. (45 M.) **Taganróg** *(Rail. Restaurant; Yevrópa,* Petróvskaya 57, R. 1¼-5½, D. ¾-1¼ rb.; izvóshtchik from the station to the town 40, to the harbour 60 cop.; British vice-consul & Lloyd's Agent, *E. Clively)* is a pleasant port on the Sea of Azóv, with 72,000 inhabitants. On leaving the station we turn to the left, and then to the right into the Petróvskaya, the principal street. In 12 min. we come to the entrance of the Town Park (l.), in front of which is a bronze statue of Peter the Great (1903) by Antokólski. Farther on, on the same side, is the Tchekhov Museum (Чéховскій музéй), with souvenirs of A. P. Tchekhov (1860-1904), the dramatist, who was a native of Taganrog (comp. p. 307). On the left side of the Varvatziyévski Pereúlok, which joins the Petróvskaya on the right, is the Greek Convent, and opposite it is a bronze statue (by Martos) of Alexander I. (1830). Following the Petróvskaya, we see on the left the District Court. In the next side-street to the left, the Dvortzóvi Pereúlok, on the left, 1 M. from the monument of Peter the Great, is the Imperial Palace, with the room where Alexander I. died in 1825. About ⅓ M. to the S. of the palace is a lighthouse overlooking the harbour. The town contains a Lutheran church. — 131 V. *Uspénskaya* (p. 429); 178 V. *Ilováiskoye* (p. 429); 190 V. *Khartzuisk* (Харцызскъ; Rail. Restaurant), see p. 400; 231 V. *Nikitovka* (Rail. Restaurant); 260 V. *Konstantinorka.* (Rail. Restaurant), with glass-works. At (289 V.) *Kramatórskaya* (Rail. Restaurant; p. 429) are large iron-works. — From (300 V.) *Slavyánsk* (Rail. Restaurant) one branch-line runs to (8 V.) *Rapnáya-Slavyánsk* (565 ft.; Minerálnuiya Vodi, R. from 1¼ rb.), a watering-place with saline and mud baths, and another to (199 V.) Kharkov (p. 387) viâ *Svyatogórskaya,* with the *Svyatogórski Uspénski Convent* (Святогóрскій Успéнскій монастырь), a building on a white cliff on the high right bank of the *Donétz,* surrounded by oaks and lime-trees. It is first mentioned in 1547 and possesses eight churches, some of which are hewn in the living rock. Below is the Uspenski Cathedral, while high above, reached viâ passages in the rock, terraces, and 511 steps, is the Church of St. Nicholas. A pleasant small-boat trip (there & back 20 cop. each) may be made from the convent up the Donétz to the Hermitage (Скить). — 399 V. (264 M.) Lozováya (p. 400).

STEAMERS connect Rostov with *Taganrog* (see above), *Mariupol* (p. 401), *Kertch* (p. 426), and *Feodosiya* (p. 425).

From Rostov to *Vladikavkaz* and *Baku,* see R. 63.

60. From Moscow to Saratov viâ Ranenburg.

796 V. (527 M.). Railway in 21¼ hrs. (fares 21 rb. 90, 13 rb. 10 cop.; seat-ticket 75 cop.; sleeping-car 6 rb. 35, 4 rb. 80 cop.).

Moscow (Saratov Station), see p. 269. The line runs to the S.E. and crosses the *Oká* just short of (102 V.) *Kashira* (Railway Restaurant). 232 V. *Kremlevo* (Rail. Restaurant) is the junction for the railway from Tula to Ryazhsk (R. 48a). 238 V. *Paveletz* (Rail. Restaurant). From (289 V.) *Troekúrovo* a branch-line runs to (28 V.) Astapovo (p. 361). 312 V. *Ranenburg* (p. 361); 334 V. *Bogoyavlénsk*, see p. 427; 374 V. *Kozlóv*, see p. 427.

Turning to the E., the line traverses the fertile but monotonous district of the 'Black Earth' (p. xxxvii).—442 V. **Tambóv** (*Railway Restaurant; Yevropéiskaya;* izvóshtchik from the rail. station to the town 50 cop.), the capital of the government of Tambóv and the seat of a Greek Catholic archbishop, lies on the *Tzna*. Pop. 53,000. The town contains Lutheran and Roman Catholic churches.

FROM TAMBOV TO KAMUISHIN, 445 V. (295 M.), railway in 19 hrs.— Beyond (106 V.) *Oblovka* (Rail. Restaurant) we cross the *Vórona*. From (168 V.) *Tavolzhánka* a branch-line runs to (97 V.) Rtishtchevo (see below). 194 V. *Balashóv* (Rail. Restaurant), see p. 389. Beyond (329 V.) *Ilmen* (Rail. Restaurant) we cross the *Medvyéditza.*—445 V. (295 M.) *Kamúishin* (Rail. Restaurant), see p. 434.

531 V. *Kirsánov* (Rail. Restaurant); 593 V. *Vertunóvskaya* (Rail. Restaurant). From (618 V.) *Rtishtchevo*, Ртищево (Rail. Restaurant) branch-lines run to (97 V.) Tavolzhanka (see above) and to (148 V.) Penza (p. 365).—711 V. *Atkársk* (Rail. Restaurant), a district-town with 12,800 inbah., lies on the *Medvyéditza*, a tributary of the Don· branch-line to (235 V.) Volsk (see below). The ground becomes undulating and then hilly.—796 V. (527 M.) *Saratov*, see p. 433.

61. The Volga from Suizran to Astrakhan.

1208 V. (800 M.). The voyage lasts 3 days.—Fares to *Saratov* 6 rb. 60, 4 rb. 45 cop.; to *Kamuishin* 10 rb. 90, 7 rb. 10 cop.; to *Tzaritzuin* 13 rb. 75, 8 rb. 85 cop.; to *Astrakhan* 19 rb. 40, 12 rb. 50 cop. Fares to Nizhni-Novgorod, etc., see p. 340 & R. 45.—The stations of the steamers are marked with a dagger (†).—Comp. p. 347.

Beyond Suizran (p. 359) the *Volga* skirts the E. margin of a plateau, ca. 650-980 ft. in height, separating it from the Don. All the larger settlements lie on this plateau and none of them upon the flat 'meadow-bank' to the left. — 93 V. (r.) †*Khvalúinsk*, the chief town of a district, with 18,300 inhab., including many Raskolniks and other sectarians, who are numerous in all the towns of the lower Volga. — 115 V. (r.) †*Alexéyevka*, a village with 3000 inhabitants. — 165 V. (l.) †*Balakóvo*, a large village with 20,000 inhab. and a considerable trade in wheat.

185 V. (123 M.) (r.) †**Volsk** (*Volgar;* cab from the steamer to the town 30, from the railway station to the town 60 cop.), a town of 36,000 inbab., lies on the high and treeless chalk bank. A branch-railway runs hence to Atkarsk, see above.

The Volga now enters the region of the steppes. On the left bank begin the German colonies founded by Catherine II., which extend hence all the way to Sarepta (p. 435) and are usually invisible except for their church steeples. The most important of

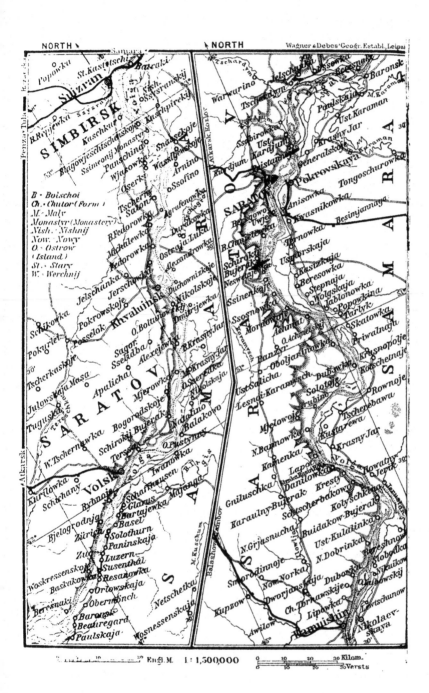

them is (236 V.) *Barónsk-Katharinenstadt *(Bienemann's Hotel)*, named after the Dutch Baron Beauregard (1765), the leader of the colony. The seated bronze figure of the Tzarina Catherine II. is by Baron von Klodt (1840). Pop. 12,000. On the bank of the river are several rows of grain-elevators.

327 V. (217 M.) †**Sarátov,** Саратовъ. — The RAILWAY STATION (restaurant) for *Kozlov* (R. 60) is in the W, part of town, that for *Uralsk* and *Astrakhan* in the Pokróvskaya Slobodá (p. 434), on the left bank of the Volga. — HOTELS. *Rossiya,* Nyemétzkaya, with lift, fair restaurant, and electric light, R. 1-7^1/$_2$, D. (1-6) ^{3}/$_4$-1^1/$_4$ rb.; *Bristol,* Alexándrovskaya, R. 1-3^1/$_2$ rb.; *Yevrópa,* cor. of Alexándrovskaya and Nyemétzkaya; *Bolshaya Moskóvskaya,* cor. of Moskóvskaya and Alexándrovskaya; *Tyurin,* bôtel garni, Nyemétzkaya. — *Jean's Café* (also confectioner's), Nyemétzkaya, cor. of the Nikólskaya. — POST & TELEGRAPH OFFICE, Bolshaya Sérgiyevskaya. — IZVÓSHTOHIK from the wharf to the town 50 (in autumn 80), from the rail. station to the town 40, per drive 20, per hr. 40 cop. — TRAMWAY from the rail. station through the Moskóvskaya to (2^3/$_4$ M.) the Cathedral of the Trinity, on the Volga, and along various other streets.

Sarátov, the capital of the government of that name, founded at the end of the 16th cent., extends from the Volga valley, the floor of which is here at the level of the sea, up the neighbouring hills, which rise round the town like an amphitheatre of garden-clad slopes to a height of 650 ft. A bar of sand separates the town from the main stream. Saratov is the seat of a University founded in 1909, of a Greek Catholic and a Roman Catholic bishop, of a Lutheran provost, and of other officials. Among its 218,000 inhab. are many German Russians. — From the pier we may take the tramway through the Armyánskaya, or we may ascend to the W. along the Bábushkin Vzvoz, passing the pleasure-resort of Vokzál (view of the river) on the right, and reaching the *Public Garden,* also called the 'Lipki', in 7 minutes. To the W. of this is the Cathedral Square, in which are the *Alexander Nevski Cathedral,* built in 1825, the *Government Offices,* and a bronze statue of Alexander II. by Volnúkhin (1911). From the Cathedral Square the Nyemétzkaya, the chief street, containing a *Roman Catholic Church* with two towers (left), runs towards the S.W. The Nikólskaya skirts the S.W. side of the square, its left branch leading S.E. to the *University,* which at present possesses a School of Medicine only, while in the opposite direction it runs past the *Lutheran Church* (left) to the *Radíshtchev Museum* (Радищевскій музей; open daily 10-3, adm. 15 cop.; open free on Sun. & holidays; P. N. Boyev, director; catalogue 10 cop.), which contains modern paintings, objects of industrial art, and relics of the novelist Turgényev (1818-83). To the N.W., behind the Museum, is the *Municipal Theatre.* A little farther on the Nikólskaya is intersected by the Moskóvskaya. By following this to the right, we reach (20 min.) the Offices of the Ryazan-Ural Railway (l.) and the *Cathedral of the Trinity* (Тройцкій соборъ; 1697), situated near the river. To the left the Moskóvskaya leads past the

Moskóvskaya Square, where the new University is' to be built, to the (2 M.) railway station.

On the left bank of the Volga (here about 3 M. wide) lies the *Pokróvskaya Slobodá*, important on account of its grain trade.

From Saratov to Uralsk, 395 V. (262 M.), railway in 20 hrs. (railway station, see p. 133). — 71 V. *Urbach* (Rail. Restaurant; see below). — 158 V. *Yershór* (Rail. Restaurant) is the junction of a branch-line which runs N. to (88 V.) *Nikoláyevsk-Urálski*, the chief town of a district in the government of Samára, situated on the *Irgíz* and containing 15,000 inhabitants.- -395 V. (262 M.) *Urálsk* (Rail. Restaurant; Nomerá Karevoi, Mikháilovskaya; izvóshtchik from the rail. station to the town 40 cop.), a town with 46,000 inhab. on the right bank of the *Urál*. The Modern School contains a small museum.

From Saratov to Astrakhan, 620 V. (411 M.), railway across the steppes in 24 hrs. (station, see p. 433). — 71 V. *Urbach* (Rail. Restaurant), see above. From (102 V.) *Krasni Kut* (Rail. Restaurant) a branch-line runs to the S.E. to (142 V.) *Alexándrov-Gai.* — 199 V. *Pallásovka* (Rail. Restaurant). — To the W. of (295 V.) *Elton* is *Lake Elton*, a saturated salt-pan 65 sq. M. in area and 1-2 ft. deep, possessing no outlet and never frozen over, even in the coldest winter. It takes its name from the Kalmuck 'Altan-nor', *i.e.* Gold Lake. — From (390 V.) *Verkhni Baskuntchák*, situated on the salt-lake of the same name (Баскунчакское оаеро), a branch-line runs W. to (51 V.) Vladimirovka (p. 435). 502 V. *Ashuluk.* — 620 V. (411 M.) *Astrakhan*, see p. 435.

372 V. (r.) *Sosnóvka*, 434 V. (l.) † *Róvnoye*, German colonies with 3-5000 inhabitants. Beyond (462 V.) † *Nizhnyaya Bánnovka* the river-bank is for some distance furrowed by precipitous gorges.

544 V. (361 M.) † *Kamúishin* (Rühl, R. 1-2 rb.; Lichtenwald, R. ³/₄-1¹/₂ rb.; izvóshtchik from the pier or the rail. station to the town 40, from the pier to the station or vice versâ 50 cop.), a district-town with 22,300 inhab., is situated on the high right bank. There is a Lutheran church. By the Volga are the Zemstvo Buildings. A trade is carried on in water melons (арбузъ). Railway to Tambov, see p. 432. — Opposite, on the left bank, is the large *Nikoláyevskaya Slobodá*, with 31,000 inhabitants.

The Volga now reaches the extensive Caspian Depression, the dry bed of a former inland sea, of which the present Caspian Sea (p. 462) is a relic. Vast stretches of the soil are covered with a crust of salt, while at other points it rises in sand-dunes. Vegetation is nowhere visible except for a short time in spring and autumn. — 675 V. (r.) † *Dubovka*, with 18,500 inhab., carries on a trade in melons (дыня).

728 V. (483 M.) † **Tzaritzuin.** — Hotels. *Lux; Stolítchnuiye Nomerá*, Alexándrovskaya Sq., R. ³/₄-5 rb., D. (12-5) 45-90 cop.; *Natzionálnuiye Nomerá.* — Izvóshtchik per drive 20-30, from the pier to the station 50 cop.

Tzaritzuin, a district-capital in the government of Saratov, lies on the right bank of the Volga, and was founded at the end of the 17th cent. as a Cossack outpost. Pop. 100,000. Tzaritzuin has a trade in timber, fish, and grain. At the N. end of the town are the large

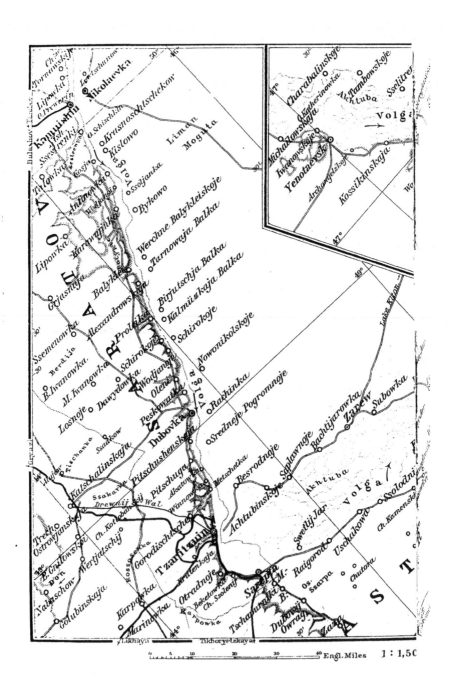

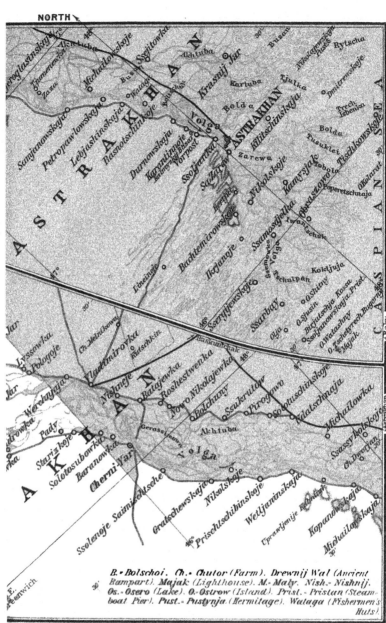

NORTH

A S T R A K H A N

CASPIAN SEA

B. = Bolschoi . Ch. = Chutor (Farm). Drewnij Wal (Ancient Rampart). Majak (Lighthouse). M. = Maly . Nish. = Nishnij. Os. = Osero (Lake). O. = Ostrow (Island). Prist. = Pristan (Steamboat Pier). Pust. = Pustynja (Hermitage). Wataga (Fishermen's Huts).

Wagner & Debes' Geogr. Establ., Leipzig.

Kilometres

Versts

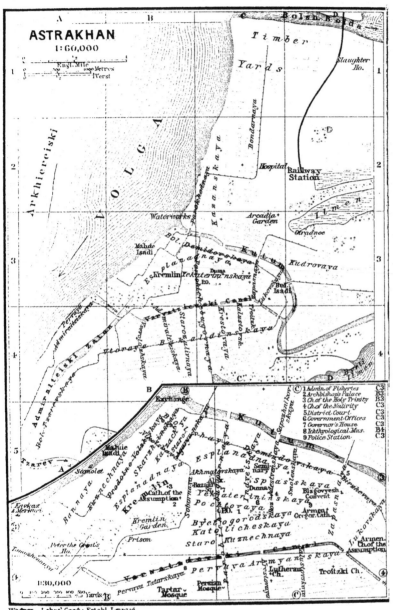

ASTRAKHAN

1:60,000

Engl. Mile
Metres
1 Verst

A   B   c   Bolsh Bolda   D

T i m b e r
Yards

Slaughter
Ho.

Arkhiereiski

V O L G A

Bondarnaya

Hospital   Railway
Station

Waterworks

Kasanskaya

Arcadia
Garden

Gradnoe

L i m e n

Bol. Demidorskaya

Mahie
Isadi

Esplanadnaya

Kutum

Kudrovaya

Kremlin   Yekaterininskaya
Duma
P.O.

Bol. Isadi

Admiralteiski Canal

Krestovaya
Troitski

Starokalidanskaya

Bel.-Tzarevskaya

Pervaya
Admiralteiskaya

Vtoraya   Belakalidinaya

Limen

Exchange

Admin. of Fisheries   C3
1 Archbishop's Palace   B3
2 Ch. of the Holy Trinity   B3
3 Ch. of the Nativity   C3
4 District Court.   C3
5 Government Offices   C3
6 Governor's House.   C2
7 Ichthyological Mus.   B4
8 Police Station   C3
9

Kutum

Saroshanhor-
skaya

Mahie
Isadi

Tzarev

Signolet

Bannaya

Kuznechnaya

Pradoise Mahie

Skarzhinskaya

Kazachava
Staroi

Esplanadnaya

Akhmatovskaya

Al.Sk.

Demidorrvskaya

Deya

Semi-
nary

Spasskaya

Spasskaya

Zaazan

Arkhierevskaya

Knokaz
i Merkur

Esplanadnaya

Kre-

Cath. of the
Assumption

Bazaar

Yekaterininskaya

Pochtoraya

Duma

Blagovyesh
Convent

Armen
Oregr. Cath.

Lukovskaya

Kremlin
Garden.

Sohanova

Byeiogorodskaya

Katoli cheskaya

Prison

Peter the Grent's
Ho.

Staro   Kuznechnaya

Armen.
Ch. of the
Assumption

Tzmeshovanskaya

Vorvats

Pervaya Armyan-
skaya

skaya

Troitzki Ch.

1:30,000

Yards

Pervaya Tatarskaya

Tartar
Mosque

Persian
Mosque

Lutheran
Ch.

A   B   C   D

Wagner Debes' Geog. Establ, Leipzig.

petroleum tanks and the Ural-Volga Foundry. A large Gun Factory was established here by Messrs. Vickers in 1914 (Russian Artillery Works Co.).

About 50 V. (33 M.) to the E. of the town lies *Tzarev*, occupying the site of *Sarái*, the former capital of the Golden Horde, of which a few scanty remains still exist.

FROM TZARITZUIN TO TIKHORYETZKAYA (Caucasus), 502 V. (335 M.), railway in 16 hrs. The railway traverses the steppes. — 24 V. *Sarepta* (see below); 122 V. *Zhútovo* (Rail. Restaurant); 179 V. *Kotélnikovo* (Rail. Restaurant); 253 V. *Zimóvniki* (Rail. Restaurant); 337 V. *Velikoknyázhe- skaya* (Rail. Restaurant); 417 V. *Pestchanokópskaya* (Rail. Restaurant). — 502 V. (335 M.) *Tikhoryétzkaya* (p. 452).

From Tzaritzuin to *Gryazi*, see p. 427; to *Likhaya*, see p. 429.

Below Tzaritzuin the Volga bends to the S.E. and divides into several arms. — 758 V. (r.) †**Sarepta,** the southernmost of the German colonies mentioned at p. 432, is a pleasant-looking place with 6000 inbab., $2^1/_2$ M. from the river. The mustard of Sarepta is known all over Russia. The railway station (see above) is 2 M. from the town (izvóshtchik 40 cop.).

The banks become more and more monotonous; the few settlements are nearly all on the right bank. From (845 V.; l.) †*Vladímirovka* a railway runs to (51 V.) Verkhni Baskuntchak (p. 434).

878 V. (585 M.; r.) †*Tchorni Yar*, a district-town with 8200 inhabitants. — A little beyond (1024 V.; r.) †*Yenotáyevsk*, to the left, is *Tyuményevka*, with a Buddhist temple (Хурулъ) close to the river. — 1200 V. (r.) *Kalmuitzki Bazaar*, the chief settlement of the Kalmucks, with a Buddhist temple, which may be visited with the permission of the Russian director, who resides opposite (guide 40 cop.). From here a local steamer goes to Astrakhan.

1208 V. (800 M.; l.) †**Astrakhan,** Астрахань. — HOTELS. *Bolshaya Moskóvskaya* (Pl. c; B, 3), Kazatchya, R. $1^1/_4$-5, D. (1-5 p.m.) $3/_4$- $1^1/_4$ rb.; *Yevropéiskaya Gostinitza* (Pl. a; B, 3), Skarzhínskaya, R. $1^1/_4$- 5 rb.; *Rossíya* (Pl. b; B, 3), Prodólno-Vólzhskaya, R. $1^1/_2$-5 rb., B. 30 cop., D. (1-5) 60 cop. to 1 rb. [Many travellers pass the night and take their meals (P. 848) on board the steamer during their visit to Astrakhan.] — RESTAURANTS in the Moskóvskaya and Rossíya hotels (see above), in the *Arcadia Garden* (Pl. C, 3; with summer theatre), and in the *Otrádnoye Garden* (Pl. D, 3; electric tramway). — IZVÓSHTCHIK: first-class (with cover), from the harbour to the town 40, second-class 30 cop.; per drive 20 & 15 cop.; per hr. 60 & 40 cop. — Five lines of ELECTRIO TRAMWAY traverse the town (fare 5 cop.). — POST & TELEGRAPH OFFICE (Pl. C, 3), Potchtóvaya.

Astrakhan, the capital of the government of that name, contains 150,000 inhab., and is the seat of Greek Catholic and Armenian archbishops. It lies on an undulating island in the Volga Delta, 90 V. (60 M.) from the mouth of the main branch of the river, and 65 ft. below the level of the Black Sea. As the focus of the commerce of the Great Caspian plain, and as an important transhipment harbour, Astrakhan shows a picturesque mixture of Russians, Tartars, Armenians, Persians, Kalmucks, and other races. Fishing is the chief resource of nearly half the population. The imports consist chiefly of grain and timber, the exports of petroleum, fish, salt caviare, and wool. The town is surrounded by vineyards.

Astrakhan was founded on its present site in the 14th cent. after the destruction by Timur of the older city, which lay about 7 M. to the N., on the right bank of the Volga. Down to its capture by the Russians in 1557, it was the capital of a Tartar khanate. In 1605 it espoused the cause of the False Demetrius; in 1660 it was unsuccessfully besieged by the Tartars, and in 1670 it was taken by Stenka Razin (p. 310). Peter the Great made it the base of his campaign against Persia, constructed shipbuilding-yards, and laid the foundation of its later prosperity.

On the Volga is a market-place (Maluiye Isadi; Pl. B, 3), with large tanks in the river (sadki) for keeping live sturgeon. On the *Sáyatchi Bugór*, the highest point of the town, near the Volga, lies the KREMLIN (Pl. B, 3), which was founded at the end of the 16th century. Only four of its towers are now standing (entrance on the E. side). Within its walls, immediately to the left, rises the *Uspenski Cathedral*, erected in 1700-1710. It has five green cupolas, and consists of an upper and a lower church. The columns and walls of the former are covered with imitation marble, while the ikonostás, 75 ft. high, is made of gilded wood. The treasury contains some objects of interest. — To the E. of the Kremlin is the *Trading Factory* or *Bazaar* (Гостйнный домъ; Pl. B, 3), a busy place for retail-trade and rag-fairs. From this point the Yekaterínin-skaya, the main street, leads to the E., passing numerous Persian shops. To the left is the Alexander Square, with a *Bronze Statue of Alexander II.* (by Opekúshin; 1884); then, also to the left, the *House of the Governor* (Pl. 7) and the new *Duma* (City Hall; Pl. C, 3), containing the *Peter Museum* (natural history and other collections; open daily, 11-2, except Mon.; adm. free). On the right is the *Fiscal Board*. At the end of the street, on the right, is the Armenian *Uspenski Church* or *Church of the Assumption* (Pl. C, 3); farther to the E. is the *Bolshiye Isadi Bazaar* (Pl. C, D, 3), where Persians, Tartars, and others may be seen carrying on their trade in the early morning. To the S. is the *Roman Catholic Church*.

To the S. of the Kremlin, beyond the Varvatziyevski Canal, is an *Ichthyological Museum* (Pl. 8; adm. on application to the director, Th. Kavraiski). Farther to the E. are a Persian *Mosque* (1860; Pl. B, C, 4) and a *Lutheran Church* (1892). — By the old harbour, the wharves of which were removed to Baku (p. 456) in 1868, stands the so-called *House of Peter the Great* (Pl. B, 3), containing his yacht 'Mon Plaisir' (hardly worth visiting).

The fisheries (Батáри) at *Vorpost* (opposite the town on the right bank) and at *Ikryánoye* (20 M. downstream) are interesting. At the latter place the largest are Zapóshnikov's.

From Astrakhan to *Baku*, see R. 64. — Railway along the left bank of the Volga to *Saratov*, see p. 434.

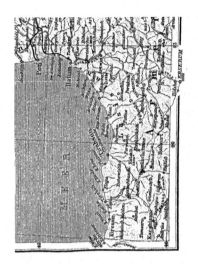

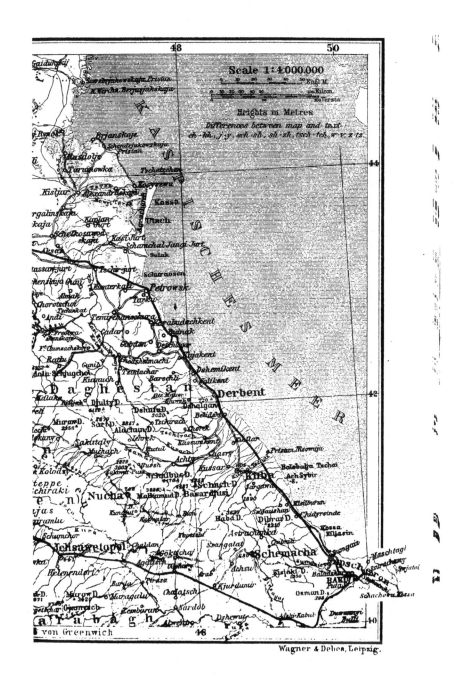

Scale 1:4.000.000

Heights in Metres

Differences between map and text.
ch-kh, j-y, sch-sh, sh-zh, tsch-tch, w-v, z-ts

Wagner & Debes, Leipzig.

VII. THE CAUCASUS.

The Viceroyalty of the **Caucasus** (Кавка́зское наме́стни-чество or Кавка́зъ) consists of seven Governments (Ста́vropol, Tiflis, Kutaïs, the Black Sea, Bakú, Yelisavetpól, and Eriván), five Territories (Terek, Kubán, Kars, Daghestán, and Batúm), and two Districts (Sakatáli and Sukhúm). Its total area is 412,310 sq. V. (181,110 sq. M.), and its population 11,735,000. It lies between 38° 30' and 46° 30' N. lat. and between 37° 20' and 50° 20' E. long., and it is bounded on the N. by the Yeya, the Manúitch, and the Kumá, on the W. by the Black Sea, on the S. by Asia Minor and Persia, and on the E. by the Caspian Sea. The district to the N. of the ·Great Caucasus' (see below) is called *Ciscaucasia* (Сѣверный Кавка́зъ), that to the S. (including the 'Little Caucasus', p. 437) is known as *Transcaucasia* (Закавка́зье).

The **Great Caucasus** (Большо́й Кавка́зъ), a huge range of mountains separating Asia from Europe, begins at the peninsula of *Apsheron* on the Caspian Sea and extends thence in a W. N. W. direction to the point where the *Kubán* pours its waters into the Black Sea. The total length of the range is about 930 M., its width varies from 28 M. to 134 M.

The highest summits, dominated by the huge extinct volcanoes of Elbruz and Kazbek, are found in the central zone, which consists of crystalline slates. On the S. this is adjoined by a girdle of folded slates and limestone, leading by a comparatively short slope to the plains of Transcaucasia. On the N. side the slope is much more gentle, descending by a well-defined series of spurs. The N. foot-hills consist on the E. side, in Daghestán, of folded sedimentary rocks; towards the W., on the other hand, as in the Crimea, we find a stratified plateau inclining gently towards the N., and grad-ually merging in the plain. Many transverse valleys intersect the foothills of the Caucasus, but there are few longitudinal valleys. The middle of the N. slope is deeply indented, near its foot, by the subsidence basin of *Vladikavkaz*. At this point, where the range is at its narrowest, it is crossed by the most important line of communication, viz. the *Gruzinian* or *Georgian Military Road,* which ascends the valley of the Terék, passes Mt. Kazbek, crosses the *Krestóvaya Pass* (7695 ft.), and descends to Tiflis.

To the W. of the *Kazbék* (16,545 ft.) the central ridge extends to the double-peaked *Elbrúz* (18,470 ft. and 18,345 ft.) in the form of a mighty glacier-wall 125 M. long. The average height of its passes is 11,000 ft.; its highest summits are the *Adái-Khokh* (15,245 ft.), the *Duikh-Tau* (17,055 ft.), and the *Shkara* (17,040 ft.). To the E. of the Adai-Khokh is the *Mamison Pass* (9270 ft.), connecting the valleys of the Ardón and the Rión. Glaciers are still to be found over 60 M. away from the Elbruz towards the W., where the lower but still very wild mountains of Abkhasia descend abruptly to the Black Sea. To the E. of the Kazbek isolated snow-clad mountains attaining a height of 13,000 ft. (Tebúlos 14,785 ft.) occur over a distance of 90 M. Beyond that point the mountains of Daghestán decrease in height towards the Caspian Sea, on the shore of which is a small littoral plain.

The snow-line on the S. side of the Caucasus is at a height of 9500 ft.; on the drier N. side it is 1300 ft. higher. The present GLACIERS are quite as important as those of the Alps: the *Duikh-Su Glacier*, the largest, on the Duikh-Tau, is $9^1/_2$ M. long, and is inferior in size to the Aletsch Glacier alone. The effects of the glaciers of the Ice Age are, however, much less marked than in the Alps. For this reason the Caucasus is almost wholly devoid of the charm of lakes and waterfalls. The general character of its scenery is much wilder and more sombre than that of the Alps, owing to the destruction of its forests, while its meadows and pastures lack the Alpine luxuriance. The rivers are rapid, but their volume varies greatly. The *Kubán*, the *Ingúr*, and the *Rión* descend to the Black Sea; the *Terek*, on the N. side of the Caucasus, and the *Kurá*, on the S., flow into the Caspian. Iron and sulphur springs abound.

The S. part of the Caucasus is bounded on the W. by the lowlands of the Rión and on the E. by those of the Kurá. Still farther to the S. extends the **Little Caucasus** or **Anticaucasus,** running nearly parallel to the Great Caucasus and connected with it by the *Surám* or *Mesghian Mts.* The Little Caucasus is not a mountain-range, but merely the margin of the elevated *Armenian Highlands*. It is an extensive high plateau with basaltic overlying strata and lofty volcanic summits, of which the *Great Ararat* and *Mt. Alagöz* alone tower above the snow-line. The N. edge of this plateau, to the W. of the point through which the Kurá has forced a passage, is formed by the *Akhaltzúikh Mountains*, the N. ramifications of which, the *Adshar Mountains,* extend to the Black Sea. At right angles to these mountains is the *Arsiyán* range, running towards the S. and eventually reaching the Pontic hills. The Armenian Highlands contain some large lakes in subsidence basins. The largest of these, in the Russian part of Armenia, is *Lake Goktcha* (6315 ft.; 538 sq. M.). Earthquakes are common in Armenia and in the Transcaucasian plains.

CLIMATE. The N. approach to the Caucasus has a climate similar to that of the steppes, especially in its E. part. The range of temperature is extreme, the mean Jan. temperature at Stavropol being 24°, and that of July 68°. The rainfall is moderate (at Pyatigorsk 21.07 inches annually). It follows that the N. slopes of the mountains are but scantily wooded. The chief rainy season is in early summer. The plains of the Kurá are still drier and are considerably hotter: at Tiflis the mean Jan. temperature is 32°, that of July 76°; at Baku the figures are 38° and 79° respectively. The rainfall at Tiflis is 19.14 inches, at Baku only 9.48 inches. The steppes of the Kurá, especially towards the E., are thus more or less desert. A strong contrast is afforded by the plains of the Rión and by the mountain slopes rising from it and from the Black Sea. The rainfall here at all seasons of the year attains almost tropical dimensions, amounting at Batum to 93.27 inches, and at Poti to 63.55 inches. The winter temperature is also much higher, the Jan. mean temperature at Batum being 43°, that of Aug. 74°. This accounts for the extraordinarily rich afforestation and for the luxuriance of the crops. In the lower parts of this region oak

28*

and beech woods are common, intermingled with yew, box, and tamarisk. Many of the oaks, ashes, and elms are swathed in climbing vines. The forests are often rendered practically impenetrable by creeping plants, such as the thorny sarsaparilla. The rich varieties of underwood include cherry-laurels, ilexes, azaleas, rhododendrons (found 5000 ft. above the sea), and ferns as high as a man. Clearings are carpeted with tiger lilies and other brilliant flowers. The upper valleys are often covered with huge coniferous forests, extending to the very edge of the glaciers, and alpine plants blossom at a height of 13,000 ft. Edelweiss and the European Alpine rose are not known. The extreme temperatures and the small precipitation of the Armenian Highlands cause the vegetation to be of a scanty and steppe-like character (Erivan, 3230 ft.; Jan. temperature 20°, July 77°, rainfall 12.75 inches).

Fever (comp. p. 446) is rampant on the whole coast of the Black Sea, as well as in the valleys of the Rión, the Araxes, and the Kurá; *Leprosy* is scarcely known except among the poorest classes of the Persian population; the so-called *Sartian Sickness* (Годовикъ; comp. p. 506), a kind of eruption, occurs at Yelisavetpol.

Bears are frequently met in the Caucasus, and tigers and panthers occur in the district of Lenkorán. The aurochs or bison (bison bonasus L.; comp. p. 45) is still to be found in the vast forests of the almost unpopulated W. Caucasus, and the chamois and the ibex (ægocerus Pallasii and capra Caucas., two species peculiar to the Caucasus) frequent the higher mountains. Wild boars, hyænas, jackals, wild cats, and antelopes abound on the plains. The valley of the Rión, the ancient *Phasis*, is the original home of the pheasant.

Venomous Serpents are found chiefly in the plains of Transcaucasia and in the steppes near the Kurá. Among them may be noted the vipera euphratica and the deadly vipera ammodytes, which has a horn on its head. The bite of the small yellow *Scorpion* (scorpio avchasicus) is not considered dangerous except in August, but that of the black scorpion (scorpio androctonus bicolor), which occurs at Nakhitchevan and Dzhulfa, is usually fatal. Wounds from the tarantula or phalanges are rare.

Population. In respect of ethnography the Caucasus is one of the strangest and most interesting regions of the globe. Its pathless mountains and isolated valleys have furthered the splitting up of its population into numerous tribes, and have preserved the scattered remnants of various nations which have in the course of ages followed the great routes of migration to the N. and E. The S. part of the district is inhabited by the descendants of the ancient IBERIANS, who all use the common language of *Karthli*, now broken up into numerous dialects. These include the *Georgians*, called by the Russians *Gruzinians*, who occupy the upper and middle valley of the Kurá; the *Mingrelians*, in the district bounded by the Tzkhenis-Tzkali, the Rión, the Ingúr, and the Black Sea; the *Imeretians*, in the valley of the Kviríla and in that of the Rión to its junction with the Tzkhenis-Tzkali; the *Gurians*, to the S. of the Rión; the *Svans* or Svanetians, on the upper courses of the Ingúr and the Tzkhenis-Tzkali; and the *Khevsurs, Pshaves,* and *Tushes,* to the E. of Mt. Kazbek, on the N. and S. slopes of the Caucasus. Even in antiquity the Iberians were regarded as a semi-civilized and peaceful race, as they possessed the art of writing and a literature at a very early stage. Their ancient alphabet (Khutzuri), is allied with the Armenian; their present alphabet is called Mkhedruli. They number about 1,400,000, all members of the Greek church.

To the N. of the mouth of the Ingûr reside about 60,000 *Abkhasians,* the remnant of a race which inhabited this district from antiquity down to 1864, when the bulk of it shared in the Circassian emigration (comp. below). They have been Mohammedans since the 15th century.

On the other hand there has been a considerable immigration of Tartars and Armenians. The ARMENIANS, who number about 1,500,000, and are found mainly in the province of Erivan, have been Christians since the beginning of the 4th century, and have a national church presided over by the Patriarch (Katholikos) of Etchmiadzin (p. 493). They separated from the Roman church after the Council of Chalcedon (451 A. D.), and called themselves Gregorians after Bishop Gregory the Illuminator. Their ritual is almost identical with that of the Russo-Greek church. The service is recited in ancient Armenian, but the sermon is delivered in the modern dialect. — The TARTARS, 2,000,000 in number, are Mohammedans (Sunnites), and are found chiefly in the E. provinces of Transcaucasia. Their speech is closely akin to Turkish. — The greater part of the province of Baku is occupied by the TATS (75,000), an Iranian race, speaking a degraded form of Persian and belonging to the Shiite sect of Mohammedans.

The strip of coast along the Black Sea, in the N.W. part of the Caucasus, has, with the exception of a few Russian colonies, remained almost uninhabited since 1864, when the 400,000 TCHERKESSES or CIRCASSIANS, who formerly occupied it, emigrated *en masse.* The *Kabards,* the chief tribe, however, numbering 145,000 souls, who had long before submitted to Russia, still occupy the N. slope of the mountain, between the Malka and the Terek and between the latter and the Sunzhá. According to their own national tradition, the Circassians, who call themselves *Adighē,* are of Semitic origin; their language is wholly isolated. A number of *Tartars,* the so-called *Mountain Tartars,* have also penetrated the N. valleys of the Central Caucasus and have to a certain extent blended with the Kabards, whose influence is recognizable in their language. The Kabards, who were Christians in the early middle ages, afterwards embraced the doctrines of Islam; but they took no part in the insurrection of Shamyl (p. 444). They are regarded as the most chivalrous of the mountain-races, and their manners and costume have been adopted by many of their neighbours.

The chief garment of the so-called CIRCASSIAN COSTUME (also worn by the Cossacks of the territory) is the *Tcherkéska*, a long, close-fitting coat of coarse woollen stuff, with a small upright collar and long sleeves turned up at the ends; in front this garment is provided with several rows of small pockets or stalls for cartridges. Below this they wear the *Beshmet* or *Arkhalúk*, a somewhat shorter garment of cotton, visible only at the neck and arms. Close-fitting breeches, gaiters, short boots, and a sheepskin cap complete the costume. In cold or wet weather they envelop themselves in the *Burka*, a sleeveless cloak of thick felt, with a hairy exterior. Like all Caucasians, they carry a whole arsenal of weapons, though the bearing of arms is now forbidden. The dress of the Circassian women has little that is characteristic except the bodice, which is adorned with chains and buckles, and the cylindrical hat, richly ornamented with gold and silver, and having chains and loops of the same metals hanging from its upper edge.

The central part of the mountain-range is occupied by the OSSETIANS, who call themselves *Ran* or *Ironi* (Aryan), and are undoubtedly of Aryan origin. Their language is allied to that of the Medo-Persians. They number about 240,000 souls, part Christians and part Mohammedans.

The E. wing of the Caucasus is inhabited by two main groups of tribes, the Tchetchens and the Daghestanians. The TCHETCHENS, who call themselves *Nakh-tchi*, occupy the N. slopes of the range as far as the Terek, but are divided into two separate parts by a large Russian settlement. They number about 305,000, and are divided into several tribes. They are Mohammedans (Sunnites). Their territory was the centre of the great rising, not finally put down until 1859. The *Kists* (6000) and the *Ingushes* (50,000) also belong to the Tchetchen stock.

The DAGHESTANIANS or LESGHIANS (585,000) have also from time immemorial been divided into various tribes, often confined to single villages or valleys and speaking a dialect unintelligible to their nearest neighbours. The most important groups from the linguistic standpoint are the so-called *Avarians* (235,000), occupying the valley of the Avarian Koissu, the native place of Shamyl; the *Darginians* (148,000); and the *Kurinians* (158,000). All are said to be fanatical followers of Mohammed (Sunnites), but they are hard-working and trustworthy. They practise industry, especially the making of carpets and weapons, as well as agriculture; and the Lesghian 'burkas' (see above) are known throughout the Caucasus†.

The RUSSIANS in the Caucasus now amount to nearly 4,000,000. Most of them are settled in the Cossack *Stanitzi* (villages), in the N. part of the government, the districts of the Terek and the Kubán, and the province of Stavropol. Among them, especially in Transcaucasia, are many sectaries (ca. 120,000), such as the *Dukhobórs* (many of whom migrated in 1900 to Canada and E. Siberia)

---

† The villages of Daghestan often bear a striking resemblance to the pueblos of New Mexico. Comp. an admirably illustrated article, by *George Kennan*, in the National Geographic Magazine for Oct., 1913.

and the *Molokáns.* These are found mainly on the plateau of the
Little Caucasus, and their chief occupation is cattle-rearing, while
they also furnish most of the carriers of the territory. — There
are about 60,000 GERMANS, mostly from Wurtemberg (1816-17), in
Tiflis, Helenendorf, and other places.

The different LANGUAGES spoken in the Caucasus cannot here be discussed in detail. [Comp. 'Die Sprachen des kaukasischen Stammes', by
R. von Erckert (Vienna; 1895), and the book by *Abercromby* mentioned
at p. 447.] It should be noted that the names of places, except those formed
on the Russian model, are usually accented on the last syllable. The
transcription of names in the following pages follows the Russian usage.

History. In antiquity the E. coast of the Black Sea appears
as the home of the *Mos-kher* or *Iberians,* occupying the three districts of Colchis, Iberia, and Albania. The Iberians seem to have
early attained a stage of civilization which distinguished them from
the mountain-tribes, while they likewise appear to have no affinity
with their Aryan neighbours. A few Greek colonies, chiefly from
Miletus, were established on the coast of Colchis, in the lowlands
watered by the Phasis. The legends of Prometheus and of Jason and
the Argonauts indicate early relations of this district with Europe.

In the historical period we find IBERIA, the valley of the Kurá,
occupied by the *Georgians,* whose name originated in a Greek
corruption of the Persian *Gurg* or *Gurdj* (Armenian, *Virkh*).
Owing at first a somewhat loose allegiance to Persia, the Georgians
afterwards came under the supremacy of Macedonia. They, however,
threw off this yoke in the 3rd cent. B. C. and maintained their
independence till the middle of the 3rd cent. of the Christian era.
Their kings resided at *Harmotzika* (Georg. *Armas-Tzikhe,* i.e.
castle of Ormuzd), perched on a rock rising over the Kurá, near
Mtzkhet (p. 474). The first dynasty was that of the Pharnavasians
(Pharnabazus), who were followed by an Armenian family. Domestic
struggles, partitions of the kingdom, and ineffectual attempts to
shake off the domination of Persia are the chief features of the
history of Georgia from the 4th to the end of the 6th cent., when
the throne passed into the hands of a Persian dynasty. Christianity
also spread through the country in this period. Tiflis became the
seat of government at the end of the 5th century. The continual
struggles with Persia necessitated an appeal to the Byzantine Empire,
but this involved the recognition of Byzantine suzerainty. The dynasty of the *Guramides* (574-787) was followed by that of the
Bagratides, the first of whom, *Askhót,* fell in a contest with Arab
invaders. Few of this family were able to maintain the independence of Georgia against Byzantium and Persia. The happiest reigns
were those of *David the Restorer* (1089-1125), who made conquests
in Asia Minor, and *Queen Tamára* (1184-1212), to whom all the
great structures of the country are to this day ascribed. At the end

of the 14th cent. Georgia was overrun by Timur the Tartar, whose hordes were not expelled till after the death of their leader.

About the middle of the 15th cent. the kingdom was divided into the three principalities of *Imeretia, Karthlia,* and *Kakhetia.* The effect of this partition was to confirm the dependence of Georgia on the Persian monarchy, which was re-established in the 16th cent., and on the invading Osmanlis. Islam also spread more and more. From the time of Peter the Great the Russians began to threaten Georgia on the N.; in 1774 they obtained possession of the Kabardá and (through alliance with the Ossetians) of the most important pass across the Caucasus range. In the resulting collision with the Persians, the Georgians stood on the side of the Russians. *Prince Heraclius* of Kakhetia and Karthlia, which had been reunited in 1762, became a Russian vassal in 1783; and his successor, *George XIII.,* ceded his territory to Russia in 1801. Imeretia also became a Russian province in 1810. By the Peace of Adrianople (1829) Russia was put in possession of most of the district abutting on the Black Sea; and the independent mountain-tribes were also subdued after a struggle that lasted for more than sixty years. The most obstinate resistance was that offered by the fanatical tribes of the E. Caucasus (1835-59), under the leadership of the *Imaum Shamyl* (d. 1871). His mountain-fastnesses of Veden and Gunib were not captured till after the Crimean War (1856). The struggle lasted still longer on the W., where the Circassians did not surrender till 1865. The risings during the Russo-Turkish War (1877-78) were suppressed without difficulty. By the Peace of San Stefano Russia received the districts of Kars and Batum.

Travelling and Equipment. Those who confine themselves to the railways and to the carriage or motor route between Tiflis and Vladikavkaz do not require any other equipment or knowledge of languages than is desirable for any tour in Russia. For excursions on foot a guide is indispensable, as guide-posts are unknown. It is, however, advisable to make sure that the guide really knows the district; and he should not be paid till the end of the journey. — For tours in the higher mountains it is necessary to have a competent attendant, who knows something of cooking, and can speak not only Russian but also the language of the particular district visited (Georgian, Tartar, or Armenian). Those who travel on foot will require several porters (1-1½ rb. per day) for even the most restricted quantity of baggage (comp. p. 445) or (better) some pack-horses, each of which can carry 5-6 puds. — The best mode of travelling is on horseback (comp. below). It is, however, often difficult to hire a horse at all, and seldom possible without long and tedious bargaining (horse and guide 2-3 rb. per day, acc. to the place and season). For a long tour it is therefore better to buy the horses outright and sell them again at the end of the journey; in Vladikavkaz horses may be purchased for 60 rb. each, in Kutaïs for about 40 rb. Those who hire horses are advised to do so for as much of the journey as possible and even to pay a little more on this account, since this not only saves endless time in bargaining, but also gives both guides and horses time to get used to the traveller. Most of the mountain-paths, including those passes that are not covered with ice, are practicable for horses. The horses must be watched at night to prevent their being stolen. The Caucasian horses, especially those of the Kabard district, are said to be steady, enduring, and docile. The native saddle, with its high horns in front and back, affords a very secure seat; but it takes some time to get used to it. The traveller provides his own bridle, stirrups, and stirrup-leathers. Spurs are not used.

The teléga (p. xxiv) is usually the only wheeled vehicle procurable. The Gruzinian Military Road (R. 68) is, however, equipped with a regular service of motor omnibuses. The rate per horse and verst is 3 cop. in the plains and 4-5 cop. in the mountains, to which have to be added the charge for the carriages, gratuities, and so on.

On mountain-tours it is advisable to start as early as possible and to allow oneself one-third more time than seems absolutely necessary, in order to cope with unforeseen hindrances. The crossing of the mountain-torrents often presents difficulties. Under normal conditions travellers on horseback or by carriage may count on 50-60 versts per day. In cases of doubt a good book or map will be found much more trustworthy than the information of the natives.

Travellers who quit the beaten track should be provided with rugs, a lantern, an air-cushion, rubber overshoes, an alarum-clock, pins and needles, thread, string, straps, preserved meats, condensed milk (all these obtainable in Odessa), bread (seldom obtainable in the mountains and never good) or biscuits, tea, sugar, quinine, opiates, vaseline, carbolic acid, bandages, soap, matches, candles, insect powder, wrapping paper, and writing materials. All these may be obtained in Tiflis, and all except the preserves in Vladivkakaz. — Those who mean to ascend any of the higher mountains should import a tried guide from the Alps; the natives, except at Mt. Kazbek and Mt. Ararat, cannot be depended upon and should not be used except as porters. There are no *Club Huts* or *Refuges* in the Caucasus, with the exception of one on Mt. Kazbek. Besides the ordinary mountaineering requisites, the traveller should have a tent for nightquarters, a sleeping bag, an axe for cutting wood, a hammer, nails for the boot-soles, some spirits of wine and charcoal for making a fire where there is no wood, and torches. Wine should be renounced and tea taken instead. Spirits should not be used except in urgent cases. The baggage is best carried in waterproof-bags, provided with lock and key, and suitable for transport either on horseback or by porters. When wheels are practicable, heavy luggage may be forwarded in an *Arba*, a high-wheeled wooden cart drawn by buffaloes. — Full information is to be found in Merzbacher's book (vol. ii) mentioned at p. 447.

The title of prince (Князь) has been granted by Russia to all the former feudal lords of Georgia, great and small; and it is advisable for the traveller to have as many *Introductions* as possible to influential members of this class as well as a letter of recommendation (Открытый лист) from the Viceroy of the Caucasus, addressed to the Russian provincial officials. Such introductions, however, will not always avail in helping him to surmount the difficulties that arise; many of these can be successfully met only by a resolute bearing on his own part. The Caucasian idea of the value of time is still hazier than that of the Russian: hence patience is the first requisite. The traveller must take care to conceal the fact that he is pressed for time, as otherwise the demands for porters and horses will at once be raised. A bargain should never be concluded until personal inspection has proved everything to be as stated. — *Public Safety* is on a somewhat unstable footing, and it is as well to avoid travelling alone or the exhibition of much money (for permission to carry a revolver, see p. xxviii). It is advisable to keep a sharp look-out on one's belongings, as the natives are not averse from picking up unconsidered trifles. — The *Viceroy's Tourist Committee* was founded in 1914 to develop the touring possibilities of the Caucasus.

Hotels in the European sense are found only in places served by railway or steamer. The *Dukhán*, or inns in the native villages, provide nothing but unfurnished and generally dirty rooms, bread (with cheese 20 cop.), tea, wine, and, at best, eggs and poultry (fowl 60 cop. to 1 rb.). Those who wish for meat must buy a whole sheep (4-5 rb.) or sucking pig (2-3 rb.; comp. p. 405). The so-called *Kantzelyáriyas*, simple rest-houses without furniture, may be used by travellers provided with official introductions. It is, however, often necessary to have recourse to native hospitality, which is seldom refused by the Iberians, but often by the Mohammedan Tartars and Lesghians. A suitable compensation is left on departure; when payment is declined, some small gift (such as a pocket-knife, hand-glass, compass, tobacco, cigarettes, or tea) will be acceptable.

Season. The best season for a visit to the higher mountains is the latter part of summer. September and October are also good months, though the shortness of the days and the coldness of the nights have then to be reckoned with. The rainfall diminishes from W. to E. (comp. p. 439). The lower valleys are best visited in autumn or in spring, when the vegetation is in its glory; in summer they are hot and unhealthy. Fever is very prevalent, even among the mountains, and it is advisable to take small doses of quinine as a preventive. Warm clothing, and especially woollen underwear, should be worn to prevent chills; all drinking-water should be boiled, especially in marshy districts and dirty villages; and a mosquito-net should be used at night.

Travelling Expenses. The necessary expenses in the towns are at least 10-12 rb. per day. On mountain-tours the chief items are the cost of guides (from the Alps), porters, horses, and equipment. A long journey is in general relatively less expensive than a short one. As it is often impossible to change money in the villages, the traveller should have an ample supply of small notes and small coins.

Plan of Tour. At least ten days are required for the most superficial visit to the Caucasus. The best starting-point is Batum, which can be reached by steamer from Odessa or the Crimea in 3-5 days.

Railway from Batum to Tiflis (R. 65), with an excursion from Mikhailovo to Borzhom (p. 490), and on to Bakuryani (pp. 491, 492)	3 Days
Tiflis (R. 66)	1 „
From Tiflis to Baku and back (R. 67; p. 456) .	3 „
Motor omnibus from Tiflis to Vladikavkaz (Gruzinian Military Road; R. 68)	1 „
N. Caucasus Mineral Baths (Kislovodsk, Pyatigorsk, pp. 458 et seq.)	2 „

Among other attractive tours are a visit to Kutaïs and its superb environs (Convent of Gelati, p. 464); the drive along the Mamison Road (R. 69; 5 days); and an excursion over the Latpari Pass to Svanetia (R. 70), which requires 9-10 days from Tiflis. A visit to Ani (pp. 492, 493) takes 3 days from Tiflis, and one to Erivan, Etchmiadzin, and Ararat (R. 73 b) 6-7 days.

Bibliography. Among the numerous works on the Caucasus may be mentioned the following:

Exploration of the Caucasus, by *D. W. Freshfield* (two richly illustrated vols.; 2nd ed., 1902; 3*l.* 3*s.*).

Transcaucasia and Ararat, by *James Bryce* (1877; 4th ed., 1896).

A Vagabond in the Caucasus, by *Stephen Graham* (1911).

My Climbs in the Alps and Caucasus, by *A. F. Mummery* (1895; 1*s.* ed., 1913).

Travels in the Eastern Caucasus, by *Sir A. T. Cunynghame* (1872).

Savage Svanetia (1883) and Sport in the Crimea and Caucasus (1881), by *C. Phillips Woolley.*

The Frosty Caucasus, by *F. C. Grove* (1875).

A Trip through the Eastern Caucasus, with a chapter on the languages of the country, by *Hon. J. Abercromby* (1889).

The Russian Conquest of the Caucasus, by *John F. Baddeley* (1908).

Armenia, by *H. F. B. Lynch* (2 vols., illustrated; 1901).

Contes et Légendes du Caucase, by *J. M. Mourier* (Paris; 1888).

A travers l'Arménie russe, by *Madame B. Chantre* (Paris; 1893).

A travers le Caucase, by *E. Levier* (Paris, 1894; chiefly of botanical interest).

Voyages au Caucase et en Asie centrale, by *Zichy* (Budapest; 1897).

Aus den Hochregionen des Kaukasus, by *G. Merzbacher* (Leipzig, 1901; in two vols., handsomely illustrated; 40 *M*).

Kaukasus, by *M. de Déchy* (Berlin, 1907; 3 vols.; illus.; 80 *M*).

Hundert Kaukasus-Gipfel, by *R. Afanasieff* (Munich, 1913; 4 *M*), with accounts of the ascents of 100 of the principal Caucasian summits.

See also the article 'Caucasus' in the Encyclopædia Britannica (11th ed.; 1910), by *J. T. Bealby* and *Prince Kropotkin*.

The best MAP of the Caucasus is the so-called *Five Verst Map* (i.e. 5 V. to the English inch; 1 : 210,000) published by the Russian General Staff (last ed. 1895-1901; 50 cop. per sheet). About 700 sheets of the new *One Verst Map* (1 : 42,000) have been issued (1870 et seq.); they also cost 50 cop. per sheet, but are not procurable through the ordinary channels. *Merzbacher's* map of the Caucasus range (1 : 140,000; Munich, 1901; three sheets, 9 *M*) and *Freshfield's* map of the central peaks (1 : 210,000; London, 1896) are clear and handy.

The following is a list of terms occurring frequently in names of Turkish, Ossetian, and Georgian origin.

Ag, Ak, white.	*Kau*(pron. ka-oo),village.	*Su*, river, water.
Aúl (pron. a-ool), village.	*Khevi*, gorge, ravine.	*Tau* (ta-oo), mountain.
Aúz(pron. a-ooz), pasture.	*Khokh*, mountain.	*Tchaï*, river.
Bashi, summit of a mountain.	*Kol*, lateral valley.	*Tchala*, river, brook.
	Kom, valley, gorge.	*Tchirán*, glacier.
Don, river and valley.	*Kosh, Kutan*, shepherd's hut.	*Tzkali*, river.
Kará, black.		*Ukiu* (ookioo), small.
Karaúl (pron. kara-ool), guard-house.	*Minghi*, white.	*Ullu* (ooloo), large.
	Mta, mountain.	*Vtzik*, pass.

62. From Kertch *(Odessa)* to Batum by Sea.

369 Nautical Miles. STEAMERS of the *Russian Steam Navigation & Trading Co.* ply from Odessa to Batum 7 times weekly in summer, calling at the Crimean ports of Eupatoria, Sebastopol, Yalta, Feodosiya, and Kertch. The direct steamer (322 S.M.; 3½ days), however, calls only at Sebastopol, Yalta, Feodosiya, Novorossisk, Tuapse, Sotchi, Gagri, and Sukhum-Kale. [The freight-steamers should be avoided.] The fares and charges for meals vary according to steamer and season. Direct mail steamer from Odessa to Novorossisk 20 rb. 55 & 14 rb. 40 cop. (food 6 rb. 40, 5 rb. 20 cop.), to Batum 31 rb. 80 & 21 rb. 90 cop. (food 9 rb. 95, 8 rb. 10 cop.). Mail steamer from Kertch to Novorossisk 5 rb. 40 & 4 rb. 35 cop. (food 1 rb. 85, 1 rb. 50 cop.), to Batum 14 rb. 50 & 11 rb. 35 cop. (food 8 rb. 25, 6 rb. 70 cop.).—A STEAMER of the *Russian Transport & Insurance Co.* also runs thrice weekly from Kertch (Odessa) to Novorossisk (fare 4 rb. 35), Poti (10 rb. 80), and Batum (11 rb. 35 cop.). These rates are for the second cabin (there being no first) and do not include meals.

At Novorossisk, Tuapse, Poti, and Batum the steamers lie-to at the piers, but at other points passengers are landed by small boats, if the sea is calm enough.

Kertch, see p. 426. In continuing the journey we at first see to the left the flat *Peninsula of Taman*, but beyond the mouth of the *Kubán* begin the Caucasian Mountains, which accompany the coast for a distance of 250 M. An extraordinary stillness broods over the forest-clad mountain-slopes; since the emigration of the Circassians (p. 441) no signs of human occupation are seen except a few ruined fortifications or a recent Russian settlement.

48 S.M. *Anápa* (Rossiya), a seaport and bathing-resort with 11,500 inhabitants.

86 S.M. **Novorossísk,** Новороссійскъ. — Hotels. *Yevrópa*, Serebryakóvskaya, in the town, R. 1-3³/₄, D. (12-6) ³/₄-1 rb.; *Frántziya*, at the harbour, R. 1¹/₄-5¹/₂, D. (12-6) ³/₄-1¹/₄ rb. — ·Phaeton from the harbour (steamers land passengers on the quay) to the rail. station or to the town 35, from the old town to the station 50, per hr. 50 cop. — Motor Omnibus from the rail. station to the 'Kurort', as far as the Serebryakóvskaya in ¹/₄ hr. (fare 15 cop.). — British Vice-Consul & Lloyd's Agent, *O. Geelmuyden.*

Novorossísk, a pleasantly situated seaport on a bay 2¹/₂ M. wide and 5 M. long, is the capital of the Government of the Black Sea, and contains 61,000 inhabitants. It has belonged to Russia since 1829. The harbour is one of the best on the whole Pontic coast, though in winter it is exposed to storms raised by a wind resembling the Bora. On the N. side of the bay lies the 'New Town', containing the buildings of the Russian Standard Petroleum Co., the rail. station (³/₄ M. from the harbour and 2¹/₄ M. from the Old Town), the large grain elevator, and a Lutheran church. To the S.E. of the New Town are several cement works; a visit may be made to the quarries of the Black Sea Cement Co. (German officials). On the W. side of the bay is the 'Old Town'. Between this and the New Town lies the *Tzemés Morass*, which is being drained. To the S. of the Old Town is the 'Kurort', with sea-bathing. — In the environs are large vineyards.

From Novorossisk to Sukhum-Kale by the Coast Road, 486 V. (322 M.). This road is provided with posting-stations (indicated below by P.; horse 6 cop. per verst), but lack of horses often causes considerable delay. A private carriage to Sukhum-Kale costs 120 rb.; motor car to Sotchi 300 rb. This is an interesting but somewhat fatiguing trip, best made in August or September. Fair accommodation is found in the larger places. The traveller must be on his guard against fever. — On leaving Novorossisk we proceed towards the S. 24 V. *Kabardinskaya* (P.). Beyond (39 V.) *Gelendzhik* (p. 449; P.) the road gradually ascends to the (60 V.) *Mikháilov Pass* (2625 ft.; P.). Beyond the pass it descends circuitously to the village of *Beregováya.* — 75 V. *Pshádskaya* (P.). — At (94 V.) *Arkhipo-Óssipovka* (P.), a village of 600 inhab., once stood the Mikháilov fort, blown up in 1840 by the private soldier Arkhíp Ossipov at the cost of his own life to prevent its falling into the hands of the Circassians. This deed of heroism is commemorated by a white cross in the middle of the village. — 118 V. *Dzhubga* (p. 449; P.); 129 V. *Tenginski Posád* (P.); 142 V. *Novo-Mikháilovskaya* (P.); 154 V. *Ólginskaya* (P.). Beyond (173 V.) *Nebúgskaya* (P.) we cross the *Agui.* A little farther up the valley, amid an amphitheatre of mountains, is the Circassian 'aul' of *Kárpovka.* 191 V. *Tuapsé* (p. 449; P.). Farther on the scenery is very imposing. 215 V. *Nashé* (P.); 232 V. *Yelisavétinskoye* (P.); 249 V. *Lázarevskoye* (P.); 266 V. *Tchukhúkskaya* (P.); 289 V. *Golovinskaya* (P.); 301 V. *Vardané* (P.), a grand-ducal domain; 315 V. *Dagomúis* (P.), an imperial domain; 332 V. *Sotchi* (p. 449; P.); 352 V. *Hosta* (P.); 364 V. *Adler* (p. 449; P.); 377¹/₂ V. *Sandrípsh* (P.); 404¹/₂ V. *Gagri* (p. 449; P.).

—419$^{1}/_{2}$ V. *Koldokhvára* (P.), in the province of Kutaïs. About 7 M. to the S. lies Pitzunda (see below).—435$^{1}/_{2}$ V. *Svondrípsh* (P.); 445$^{1}/_{2}$ V. *Gudaút* (see below; P.). Beyond this point we traverse wood, passing the (461$^{1}/_{2}$ V.) convent of *Novi Afón* (p. 450; P.).—486 V. *Sukhúm-Kalé* (p. 450)
From Novorossisk to *Tikhoryétzkaya* (Rostov, Baku), see pp. 453, 452.

104 S.M. *Gelendzhík* (Kordes, Peterbúrgskaya, R. $^{3}/_{4}$-2 rb., D. 50-70 cop.), situated on a crescent-shaped bay, with 1800 inhab. and good bathing.—The steamer next halts at (140 S.M.) *Dzhubga*, 2 M. from the village of that name (1000 inhab.; road to Yekaterinodar, p. 452). The mountains now become higher.—163 S.M. **Tuapsé** or *Velyamínovski Posád* (Rossíya), a small town situated on an eminence. Pop. 16,000. The mountains here are about 3000 ft. above the sea. A railway is being built to Maikop (p. 453).

204 S.M. **Sotchi,** Сочи.—HOTELS. *Kavkázskaya Riviera*, three large buildings, overlooking the sea, with café, restaurant, and theatre, closed from Nov. 15th till Easter, R. 1$^{1}/_{2}$-6, déj. (12-2) $^{3}/_{4}$, D. (6-8) 1, board 45-75 rb. per month; *Grand-Hôtel*, R. from 1$^{1}/_{2}$ rb., D. (1-6) from 70 cop., pension from 65 rb. per month.—IZVÓSHTCHIK from the harbour to the Square 50 cop., per day 10-15 rb.—MOTOR SERVICE to Sukhum-Kale.

Sotchi, a town of 11,300 inhab., is noted for its luxuriant southern vegetation, and perhaps occupies the site of the ancient *Nisis*. It consists of an upper part on a plateau and a lower part on the river Sotchi. Pleasant walks may be taken in the Khludovski and Yermólovski parks. In the vicinity are large vineyards and orchards.

About 5 M. to the S.E. of Sotchi are the *Matzestinskiye Sulphur Springs.*—An excursion (taking one day by carriage) may be made to the *Falls of the Matzesta*. We follow the Adler road to the S.E. for 4 V., then turn to the left, and drive 13 V. more to *Siverskiye Khutora*. Here we leave the carriage and proceed on foot to (30-40 min.) the first waterfall, whence it takes 1$^{1}/_{2}$ hr. more to reach the fourth and last.

218 S.M. *Adler* (Yúzhnaya, overlooking the sea, R. $^{3}/_{4}$-2 rb.), at the mouth of the *Mzuimtá*, with 1600 inhabitants.

A road (carr. 12-15; diligence 2$^{1}/_{2}$ rb.) leads N.E. from Adler through the fine valley of the Mzuimtá to (54 V.) the town of *Románovsk* (1970 ft.; Atchishho, R. 1-2 rb.), also called *Krásnaya Polyána*, with 3400 inhabitants. There are several mineral springs in the vicinity. About 5 M. to the N.W. is an imperial hunting lodge.

232 S.M. **Gagri.**—There are four HOTELS (300 rooms), all belonging to the State. R. from 1 rb., B. 40-60, déj. (12-2) 75 cop., D. (6-8) 1$^{1}/_{2}$ rb.— PHAETON per drive 20-30 cop.—Saddle-horse 3 rb. daily.—Sea-bath 30 cop.

Gagri, a bathing-resort established by the Russian Government in 1901 at the instance of Alexander, Duke of Oldenburg, who built a château here, lies by the sea on the S. slope of the coast-mountains, and is sheltered from the N. winds. The mean annual temperature is 60° Fahr. Among the interesting walks in the vicinity are those to the Lower Fall of the Zhoekvara (1 hr.), to the Upper Fall of the Zhoekvara (3 hrs.), and to the source of the Gagripsh (1$^{1}/_{2}$ hr.).

Farther on appears *Pitzínda* (accommodation in the Dukhán, 1 M. from the church), with a conventual church in the Byzantine style (10th cent.). This is supposed to have been the site of the Milesian colony of *Pityusa* ('pine town').—257 S.M. *Gudaút*, a small village.

Luikhni, the ancient capital of Abkhasia, $2^3/_4$ M. to the N., is now an unpretending village with an old Georgian church.

266 S.M. *Novi-Afón* (Новый Аѳонъ, 'New Athos'), a large convent of the monks of Mt. Athos, founded in 1875 (accommodation in the guest-house). An old church found here has been enlarged to serve as the convent-church, and on the highest terrace there is also an imposing cathedral, consecrated in 1900. A good view is obtained from the high-lying Iberian chapel (Иверская часовня). The vineyards and orchards are very well kept. There is a pretty walk to the waterfall and on to a cave (пещера Симона Кананита).

278 S.M. **Sukhúm-Kalé.** — *Hotel Oriental,* R. 1-5 rb. — *Cab* per drive 15, per hr. 40, to Sinope 40 cop., to (16 M.) Novi Afon (see above) and back 5-6 rb. — *Omnibus* to Novi Afon 1 rb. 20 cop.

Sukhúm-Kalé, the chief town of a district in the province of Kutaïs, lies on the flat coast-district, which is here somewhat wider than usual, and contains 25,000 inhabitants. It is surrounded on three sides by mountains, and is noted for its mild climate (mean annual temperature 59°) and rich vegetation. In the middle of the town is the *Alexander Nevski Cathedral.* The other chief objects of interest are the 'Sinope' Garden of the Grand-Duke Alexander Mikháilovitch and the adjoining private gardens, the Botanical Gardens, and the Public Park. A considerable traffic is carried on in tobacco. — *Iskuria,* the name of the promontory to the S., recalls the Milesian colony of *Dioskurias* (the Roman *Sebastopolis*).

Near Sukhum-Kale lie the small German colonies of *Neudorf* and *Gnadenberg* (E.). — Sukhum Military Road, see p. 453.

Another road leads from Sukhum-Kale viâ (58 V.) Otchemtchiri (see below) to (107 V. or 71 M.) *Zugdidi,* capital of Mingrelia, with 4600 inhabitants. Hence a highroad leads to (42 V.; 28 M.) *Novo-Senáki* (see below).

After a short halt at (306 S.M.) *Otchemtchíri* the steamer passes the mouth of the *Ingúr.* The two snow-domes of the Elbruz (p. 485) are visible here in clear weather.

340 S.M. **Poti** (*Colchída; Bellevue;* phaeton from the harbour to the rail. station 50, from the harbour to the town 40, from the station to the town 30 cop., double rates at night; electric tramway through the town; acting British vice-consul and Lloyd's Agent, John Pavoni), a town of 17,500 inhab., lies in a marshy and fever-breeding district at the mouth of the *Rión,* $1^2/_3$ M. from the railway. The river is crossed by a bar of diluvial mud, and in stormy weather the steamer goes on to Batum without calling here. — To the S.E. of the town is the large *Lake Paleostóm,* the ancient mouth of the Rión, beside which lay the Milesian colony of *Phasis.*

FROM POTI TO SAMTREDI, 62 V. (41 M.), railway in 2 hrs. — The line at first traverses a flat marshy country. Beyond (15 V.) *Abasha* we cross the *Tzkhenis-Tzkali,* the *Hippos* of the ancients, forming the boundary between Imeretia and Mingrelia. Soon after we obtain a view to the left of the snow-capped summits of the Laila chain. — Beyond (26 V.) *Novo-Senáki,* the station for the district-capital of that name (4500 inhab.), the train crosses the *Tekhur* at a point 8 M. below the extensive remains of

Nakalakévi. We then reach the exuberantly fertile plain of the Rión, which is surrounded by hills of moderate height. Its endless fields of Indian corn make a somewhat monotonous impression. From Novo-Senaki to Sukhum-Kale, see p. 450. — At (62 V.) *Samtredi* (75 ft.; Rail. Restaurant) our line joins the railway from Batum to Tiflis (see p. 463).

On entering the harbour of Batum, we enjoy a magnificent view of the chain of the Caucasus and of the Adzharian Mts. in Lazistan.

369 S.M. **Batúm.** — HOTELS. *Impérial* (Pl. a), Kutaískaya, R. from 1½ rb., D. 60 & 80 cop.; *Frántziya* (Pl. b), Mikháilovskaya, D. à la carte; *Oriental* (Pl. c), Náberezhnaya, D. 60 & 80 cop. — *Summer Restaurant* in the Boulevard, opposite the Cathedral, D. (12-4) ½-1 rb.. — POST & TELEGRAPH OFFICE (Pl. 3), Mariinski Prospékt. — CAB from the harbour or station to the town or vice versâ 40, per drive 25, per hr. 80 cop. — BOAT per hr. 60 cop. — CONSULS. Great Britain, *P. W. J. Stevens,* Mariinski Prospékt 24; United States, *L. A. Davis,* Sobórnaya Square. — LLOYD'S AGENTS, *F. Burkhardt & Co.,* Náberezhnaya.

STEAMERS to the *Crimea* and *Odessa,* see p. 447. — To *Constantinople* several times a week (comp. *Baedeker's Mediterranean*).

Batúm, the capital of a district and the most important trading town on the E. Pontic coast, lies on a marshy spot at the foot of the W. spurs of the Armenian plateau. Pop. 40,000. The town owes its importance to the railway to Baku, but its trade has dwindled since

1. Alexander Nevski Cathedral; 2. Azizie Mosque; 3. Post and Telegraph Office; 4. Roman Catholic Cathedral; 5. Russian Steam Navigation & Trading Co.; 6. Russian Transport & Insurance Co.

the unrest of 1905-6. The chief exports are petroleum and its by-products, manganese, liquorice, silk-cocoons, and wool. On the W. side of the Petroleum Harbour are bazaar streets, on the E. side petroleum stores. Along the stony beach runs the *Boulevard,* a

palm-fringed street dominated on the S. by the *Alexander Nevski
Cathedral*, built in 1906. Adjoining *Lake Nurie*, in the W. part of
the town, is the *Alexander Park*, with its subtropical vegetation.

About 2 M. from Batum is a group of mediæval ruins known as *Zamok
Tamári*, i.e. Castle of Queen Tamara (comp. p. 443). — *Makhindzhaúri*, 4 M.
to the N., is frequented for its good air; it is a station on the railway
to Tiflis. — The tea-plant and the bamboo are cultivated with some success
in the *Tchakva Valley* (9 M.; p. 463) and in the hilly district adjoining
it. — About 13 M. to the S. of Batum, and reached by an attractive bridle-
path, are the interesting ruins of the old *Church of Makriali.* — To Adzháris-Tzkali (phaeton there & back, in one day, 5-6 rb.; motor-car 10-12 rb.),
see below.

From Batum to Artvin, 92 V. (61 M.), an attractive excursion. A
carriage (phaeton), accomplishing the journey there & back in 3 days, may
be hired for 30-35 rb.; the start has to be made betimes; motor omnibus
6 rb.; cyclists take about 10 hrs. We return to the village of *Kapandidi*,
6 M. to the S. of Batum, by boat (a so-called kayúka) in 6-8 hrs. (fares
5-10 rb.). The kayúkas plying daily to Kapandidi with vegetables take
passengers for 2-3 rb. a head. The road, which runs almost the whole way
along the right bank of the *Tchorókh*, crosses the valley of the *Kakha-
béri*, to the S. of Batum.—16 V. (11 M.) *Adzháris-Tzkali*, a village in
a pretty district, with a bridge over the Adzhára. In the vicinity is the
Goderski Pass, with a petrified forest.—27 V. *Maradidi*, a large village
with a frontier-post; 32 V. *Kheba;* 45 V. *Bortchkha*, on the left bank of
the Tchorókh.—Beyond (69 V.) *Zinkóg* we cross a bridge to (92 V.) *Artvin*
(hotel by the bridge, on the right bank), a straggling town rising in picturesque terraces. The 7300 inhabitants speak Armenian and Turkish.

From Batum to *Tiflis*, see R. 65.

63. From Rostov-on-the-Don to Baku.

Vladikavkaz. North Caucasus Mineral Baths.

1235 V. (818 M.). Express train in 32 hrs. (fares 25 & 15 rb.; reserved
seat 2 rb. 40 cop.; sleeping-car 9 rb. 90 & 7 rb. 40 cop. extra). — From Rostov
to *Vladikavkaz*, 653 V. (433 M.), express train in 16 hrs. (fares 17 rb.,
10 rb. 20 cop.; simple refreshments served on the train); to *Pyatigorsk*,
491 V. (326 M.), express train in 12 hrs. (fares 14 rb., 8 rb. 40 cop.).

Rostóv, see p. 430. The train crosses the *Don* by a girder-
bridge and runs to the S. through the steppe, in which a few Cossack
settlements are seen from time to time. — 118 V. *Kruilóvskaya*
(200 ft.; Rail. Restaurant); 135 V. *Sosuika*, the junction for (133 V.)
Eisk, a port on the Sea of Azóv.

171 V. (114 M.) **Tikhoryetzkaya** (270 ft.; *Rail. Restaurant*).
To Tzaritzuin, see p. 435.

From Tikhoryetzkaya to Novorossisk, 254 V. (168 M.), express train
in 6 hrs. Before the arrival of the train at Novorossisk a representative
of the railway passes through the carriages taking orders for the transport
of luggage, purchase of boat-tickets, and so on. — 68 V. *Stanitchnaya* (130 ft.;
Rail. Restaurant). — 127 V. **Yekaterinodár** (90 ft.; *Rail. Restaurant; Central, Metropole, Yevropa*, R. 1¼-4, D. ½-¾ rb.; cab from the rail. station
to the town 40-50, per drive 20-30, per hr. 50-75 cop.; electric tramway
from the station to the town 5 cop.), the capital of the district of Kubán
(Кубанская область), lies on the right bank of the *Kubán*, and was
founded by Catherine II. as a Cossack settlement in 1794. Pop. 100,000. The
small museum (Статистическій музей), in the Gráfskaya, contains objects
of a late Greek period, found in the Kubán district. A branch-railway runs

to (128 V.) Kavkázskaya (see below). — The train crosses the Kubán and then runs to the W. along the foothills of the Caucasus. 208 V. *Krüimskaya* (105 ft.; Rail. Restaurant), a small Cossack village. Beyond (238 V.) *Tonnélnaya* (720 ft.) we descend first through a tunnel upwards of 1 M. in length and then through a short tunnel. — 254 V. (168 M.) *Novorossísk* (p. 448).

To the left is a low mountain-chain which disappears beyond Nevinnomuisskaya. — 229 V. (153 M.) *Kavkázskaya* (260 ft.; Rail. Restaurant).

A branch-line runs hence to the E. to (145 V.; 96 M.) **Stávropol** (1930 ft.; *Centrálnaya*, R. from 1¹/₄, D. ¹/₂-1¹/₄ rb.; *Rossíya;* cab to the town 50, per drive 25, per hr. 50 cop.), the quiet capital of a government of the same name, with 60,000 inhab. and an attractive public park. — Another branch-line runs to the W. to (128 V.; 85 M.) Yekaterinodar (p. 452).

The railway crosses the *Kubán.* 291 V. *Armavír* (625 ft.; Rail. Restaurant; Bolshaya Moskóvskaya, R. 1-6 rb.; izvóshtchik from the rail. station to the town 20 cop.), with 44,000 inhab., is situated on the left bank of the Kubán.

From Armavir a branch-line runs W. to (124 V. or 82 M.) **Maikóp** (*Rail. Restaurant; Centrálnaya,* Ofitzérskaya Ulitza; izvóshtchik from the rail. station to the town 60 cop.), the capital of the Kubán District, containing 45,000 inhabitants. In the neighbourhood are oil wells (output in 1911, 8 million puds), connected by a conduit 70 M. long with Yekaterinodar (p. 452). The railway is being prolonged to Tuapse (p. 449).

The railway now traverses a plateau lying to the N. of the Caucasus. Just short of (366 V.; 243 M.) **Nevinnomúisskaya** (1080 ft.; *Rail. Restaurant*) we cross the Kubán.

From Nevinnomuisskaya the **Sukhum Military Road** (Военно-Сухýмская дорóга) leads to (316 V. or 209 M.) Sukhum, a horseback journey of 6 days. — A highroad goes S. to (50 V.) *Batalpashínsk* (585 ft.), a Cossack town of 17,800 inhabitants. Beyond this point there is an ordinary carriage-road. 97 V. *Geórgiyevskoye* or *Ossetínskoye.* — We ascend the valley of the *Teberdá.* 130 V. *Teberdínskoye.* About 20 V. farther on the road begins to descend the valley of the *Ganatchkhir* (Ганачхирь). 165 V. *Lake Tumanli-Gel;* 175 V. *Klukhor Barracks* (6280 ft.). Beyond this point a winding bridle-path (12 turns) leads viâ *Lake Teberdínskoye* (188 V.; view) to (189 V.) the *Klukhor Pass* (9235 ft.; not free from snow till Aug.). We descend circuitously into the valleys of the *Kluitch* and the *Kodór.* 232 V. *Adzhari.* — 261 V. *Lati.* Here we again meet a carriage-road, leading to (308 V.) the coast-road, which we follow to the right. — 316 V. (209 M.) *Sukhúm-Kalé* (p. 450).

Beyond (411 V.) *Kúrsavka* (1300 ft.) the peaks of the main chain gradually come into view on the right. They rise like a gigantic wall from the plain, and farther on are dominated by the perennially ice-clad double peaks of the *Elbruz* (18,465 ft.; p. 485). The view of the mountain is generally clearest about sunrise. — 466 V. (309 M.) **Minerálnuiya Vodi** (975 ft.; *Railway Restaurant,* fair), the station for the N. Caucasus mineral baths (see p. 458).

At (554 V.) *Prokhládnaya* (655 ft.; Rail. Restaurant) we cross the *Malka.* The railway now ascends steadily all the way to Nazran (p. 455). — 568 V. *Kotlyarévskaya* (685 ft.; Rail. Restaurant), on the *Terek.*

Railway from Kotlyarevskaya to *Naltchik,* the starting-point for excursions to places in the Central Caucasus, see p. 483.

The Kazbek (p. 475) now becomes visible to the S. Just short of (584 V.) *Murtazovo* (830 ft.) we cross the Terek. Between (600 V.) *Elkhótovo* (1005 ft.) and (611 V.) *Darg-Kokh* (1140 ft.; lineika to Alagir, p. 477, 3-3¹/₂ rb.) the *Ardón* enters the Terek from the right. 632 V. (419 M.) *Beslán* (1605 ft.; Rail. Restaurant).

FROM BESLAN TO VLADIKAVKAZ, 21 V. (14 M.), railway in 1 hr.

Vladikavkáz. — *Railway Restaurant.* — HOTELS. *Yevrópa*, R. from 1¹/₂ rb., D. (12-3) ¹/₂-1¹/₄ rb.; *Grand-Hôtel*, R. 1¹/₂-6, D. (1-7) ³/₄-1¹/₂ rb.; *Parízh; Imperial*, R. 1¹/₂-6 rb., D. (1-5) 60 cop., all in the Alexándrovski Prospékt; *London*, Loris-Mélikovskaya 56, new. — IZVÓSHTCHIK from or to the rail. station 25 cop. by day (with luggage 40 cop.), 50 or 80 cop. by night, per drive 20, per hr. 50 cop. — ELECTRIC TRAMWAY from the rail. station through the town, 5 cop. — MOUNTAIN CLUB (Владикавкáзскiй Гóрный Клубъ), Alexándrovski Prospékt 8.

Vladikavkáz (2345 ft.; railway station 2200 ft.), the clean and formerly fortified capital of the Terek district, was founded in 1784, and lies upon both banks of the *Terek*. Pop. 76,000. The town receives its name ('Mistress of the Caucasus') and its importance from its situation at the entrance of the great Gruzinian (Georgian) military road to Tiflis. It is the headquarters of the 3rd Caucasian Army Corps and is mainly a garrison-town. There is a Lutheran church. — From the railway station, which affords a good view of the mountains, we follow the Moskóvskaya in a straight direction, and at (10 min.) the Grand-Hôtel we turn to the left (S.) and enter the Alexándrovski Prospékt, the main thoroughfare of the town, which is fringed with lime-trees. After following this for 11 min. we reach on the right (W.) the entrance to the *Public Park*, from which we descend to the 'Trek Velocipedistov', with its small lake (adm. 10-20 cop.). The Vorontzóvskaya leads E. from the Public Park to (5 min.) the *Novokavkázski Cathedral*. Opposite the W. front of the cathedral is the *Museum* (Музéй Терскóй Óбласти; open on Sun. and holidays 10-2, adm. 10 cop.; at other times on application to the keeper), containing weapons, plants, minerals, etc. The balcony at the top of the building commands a superb *View of the high mountains. To the N. of the cathedral is the *Roman Catholic Church*. From the Public Park we go on to the S. through the Alexándrovski Prospékt and its continuation, the Kraśnoryádskaya; after 9 min. we turn to the right, and reach the *Terek Bridge* (view of the mountains). On reaching the left bank of the Terek we turn after 4 min. to the left and arrive at the posting-station.

From Vladikavkaz to *Tiflis* by the *Gruzinian Military Road*, see R. 68. Those who do not want to make the whole of this excursion should at least drive in the afternoon to the station of Kazbek, and spend the night there to see the sunrise next day. Or they may drive, starting at 5 a.m., to the guard-house near Gveleti, whence, sending the carriage on to Kazbek, they may ascend to the Dyevdorak Glacier and go on towards evening in a linéika (2 rb.) to Kazbek, where the night is spent. — To *Kutaïs*, on the Ossetian Military Road, see R. 69.

CONTINUATION OF THE RAILWAY TO BAKU. From Beslan to Petrovsk the railway runs towards the E. 654 V. *Nazrán* (1690 ft.), the highest station on the railway. — The train now descends to (734 V.) *Grozni* (420 ft.; Rail. Restaurant; Frántziya, R. 1-5, D. 1 rb.; izvóshtchik from the rail. station to the town 50 cop.), a dirty district-town on the *Sunzhá*, with 30,000 inhabitants. About 8 M. to the N. are important oil-wells (output in 1911, 77 million puds); the crude petroleum is conveyed to the town in pipes.

882 V. (585 M.) **Petróvsk** (75 ft. below the level of the Black Sea; *Railway Restaurant; Centralnáya*, R. 1-5, bed-linen $^1/_2$ rb.), a seaport on the Caspian Sea, with 22,000 inhab. and a roadstead protected by two long moles. The railway station is near the steamboat-pier.

About 3 M. to the S. are the remains of the old town of *Tarkun* (carr. there & back $1^1/_2$-2 rb.), perhaps the Semender of the Khazar kingdom; it is now occupied by Kumuiks and Jews.

A HIGH ROAD (carr. in 5 hrs. 6 rb., omn. 2 rb.) leads from Petrovsk to the S.W. viâ (21 V.) *Alti-Buyun* (posting-station) to (43 V.; 29 M.) *Temir-Khan-Shurá* (1520 ft.; Centrálnuiye Nomerá), the capital of the government of Daghestan, with 13,800 inhab. (to Telav, see p. 489). From this point a visit may be paid to (112 V.; 75 M.) *Gunib* (3935 ft.), a mountain-plateau about 20 sq. M. in extent, which formed the last place of refuge for Shamyl (p. 444). This trip, however, should not be made without influential introductions to the Russian commandants. The plateau is reached by a highroad, but there is often a lack of horses at the stations.

STEAMER from Petrovsk to *Astrakhan* or to *Baku*, see R. 64.

The railway now bends to the S. and skirts the W. coast of the Caspian Sea.

1004 V. (665 M.) **Derbént** (*Rail. Restaurant; Grand-Hôtel*, near the rail. station; izvóshtchik from the station to the town or vice versâ 30, per drive 30, per hr. 50 cop.), a seaport on the Caspian Sea with 33,000 inhabitants. The town, the name of which means 'barrier' or 'iron gate', lies at the most easily defensible point of the only road leading to the N. along the mountains, and was a frequent bone of contention between the various races which overran this district in the Middle Ages. It now stretches picturesquely between the walls of the mediæval fortifications, from the narrow strip of level land on the sea up the slope of the hill, which is crowned by the citadel of *Naruín-Kalé*. In ancient days *Albana*, the capital of Albania, lay here, commanding the pass known as the *Portae Albanae*.

The ridge on which the citadel of Derbent stands attains a height of 1970 ft., and along it stretches, to a point ca. 50 M. inland, a wall erected by the Sassanides.

FROM DERBENT TO NUKHA in Kakhetia, 4-5 days. This rough bridle-path, which is practicable in the height of summer only, skirts the base of the *Shakh-Dágh* (13,960 ft.) and the *Bazardyuzi* (14,700 ft.), the highest summit of the S.E. Caucasus. It then passes *Akhti* (see p. 456) and crosses the central chain by the *Salavat Pass* (9280 ft.). — *Nukhá*, see p. 472.

STEAMER from Derbent to *Astrakhan* and to *Baku*, see R. 64.

Beyond (1025 V.; 679 M.) *Belidzhi* we cross the *Samúr.* From (1081 V.) *Khatchmás* (Rail. Restaurant) a coach runs to (22$^1/_2$ V.) *Kuba,* whence a road leads through the valley of the Samúr to (80 V.) *Akhti* (see p. 455).

1221 V. *Baladzhári,* where our railway joins the Tiflis & Baku line (p. 473). — Shortly before reaching Baku we pass the Tchorni Gorod on the left (see p. 457).

1235 V. (818 M.) **Baku.** — *Railway Restaurant.* — HOTELS. *Europe* (Pl. b; B, 2), Laláyevski Proyézd 4, R. from 1$^1/_2$ rb., with restaurant; *Métropole* (Pl. a; B, 2), Nikoláyevskaya (burnt down in 1914); *Grand-Hôtel* (Pl. c; B, 2), Laláyevski Proyézd, no restaurant; *National,* adjoining the Europe Hotel; *Bolshaya Moskóvskaya* (Pl. e; B, 2), Prátcheshnaya.
Two-HORSE CABS (Phaetons) from the rail. station to the town 60, vice versâ 40; per drive 30, per hr. 70; to the Black Town 60 cop., there & back (including $^1/_2$ hr. waiting) 1 rb. 20 cop.; at night (after 2 a.m.) double fares. — TRAMWAYS from the rail. station to Bailov, Shemakhinka, and the Tchorni Gorod. — POST & TELEGRAPH OFFICE (Pl. 10; B, 2), Merkuryevskaya.
BRITISH VICE-CONSUL, *A. E. Ranald McDonell.* — PHYSICIANS (English-speaking), *Dr. Krimholtz, Dr. Gegershted.* — ENGLISH CHURCH (comp. Pl. A, 4), at Bailov; chaplain, *Rev. T. Linton, M. A.;* service at 11 a.m. *English Club* (comp. Pl. A, 4), at Bailov.

Baku (56 ft. below sea-level) is the capital of the district of the same name, and lies in a treeless district on the S. coast of the peninsula of *Apsheron,* which projects far into the Caspian Sea. The town ascends from the shore in amphitheatre form, and is dominated on the W. by what used to be the citadel. It owes its present importance to the naphtha springs (p. 457), which supply the whole of Russia with petroleum. The population of 225,000 includes Tartars, Armenians, Persians, and Russians. Baku, which takes its name from the Persian *badkubé* (i.e. squall) on account of the N. and N.W. winds which prevail here, is said to have been founded in the 6th century. It belonged during the greater part of its existence to Persia, and passed into the hands of Russia in 1806.

To the N. of the quay (Набережная Александра II.), between the railway station on the E. and the citadel on the W., extends the main part of the modern town, which contains few features of interest. The Greek Catholic *Alexander Nevski Cathedral* (Pl. A, 2) was completed in 1898. The *Armenian Cathedral* (Pl. 1: B, 2) dates from 1871. There are also a *Lutheran Church,* built in 1897 (Pl. 7: C, 1), and a new *Roman Catholic Church* (Pl. 11: C, 2). The chief business thoroughfares are the Ólginskaya (Pl. B, 2) and the Mikháilovskaya (Pl. B, 2). — Along the sea, below the citadel, runs the shadeless *Marine* or *Sea Boulevard* (Pl. B, 3), which is much frequented in the evening. At the S. end of the Ólginskaya is a Cinematograph Theatre (Pl. B, 2), with a roof-restaurant commanding a view of the sea. Kis-Kalé, see p. 457.

The old citadel (Крепость), lying high above the town, and now forming a quarter inhabited chiefly by Tartars, is surrounded

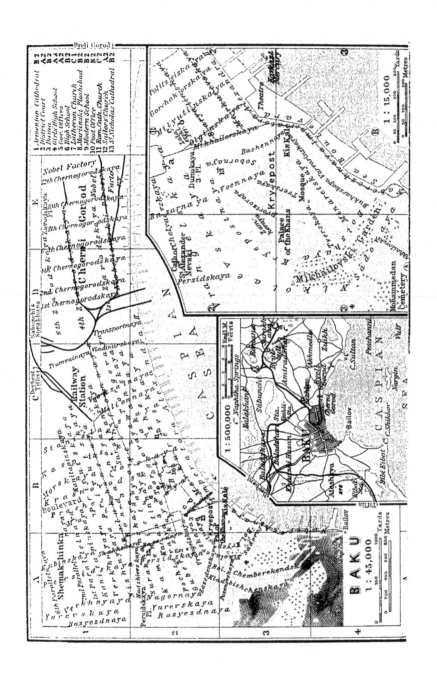

BAKU

1 : 45,000

by a wall nearly $1\frac{1}{2}$ M. in length. Its numerous narrow lanes are gradually giving place to wide modern streets. The dilapidated *Palace of the Khans* (Ха́нскій дворе́цъ; Pl. A, 3; 15th cent.?), now used as a military magazine, contains two mosques (one of them in ruins) and a court of justice (Суди́лище). We reach it most conveniently from the S. end of the Bazárnaya (see below), by passing through the gate of the citadel, and ascending immediately to the right viâ the Málaya Kryepostnáya. At (3 min.) No. 84 we turn to the left into the Zámkovski Pereúlok. No. 74 in this street, on the left, is the entrance to the palace (guide at No. 76; fee 25 cop.). — In the S. part of the citadel (reached from the sea through the Báshennaya) is the most characteristic feature of the town, the *Kis-Kalé* or Virgin Tower (Pl. B, 3), a massive structure, 147 ft. high, dating from the Byzantine period. It is associated with a romantic legend, and served down to 1909 as a lighthouse (no admission).

The S. part of the Bazárnaya (Pl. A, B, 2) and the adjacent streets offer many opportunities for studying the popular life of the place.

In the sea, off the promontory of *Bailov*, to the S. of the town, are the remains of the walls of the ancient town of Baila.

To the E. of the railway station lies *Tchorni Gorod* (i.e. the 'Black Town'; tramway and phaeton, see p. 456), containing the Nobel petroleum works. Farther to the E., is *Byeli Gorod*, or the 'White Town', containing the oil-refineries of Rothschild (Каспі́йское-Черномо́рское Нефтепромы́шленное и Торго́вое О́бщество), Shibáyev (Schibaieff), and other firms.

A railway, flanked on both sides by numerous iron pipes for the conveyance of the oil, runs to the N. from Baku to (8 M.) the *Bala-khani-Sabuntchi-Romaná Oil Field* (area $6\frac{1}{2}$ sq. M.), the most important district of the PETROLEUM WELLS, situated on the peninsula of Ápsheron. Another but smaller field, that of *Bibi-Eybát* (p. 458), lies ca. 3 M. to the S. of Baku. In 1912 no fewer than 2750 wells had been tapped in the two fields, producing ca. 480 million puds of crude petroleum, 12 millions from 'gushers'. The petroleum itself and the natural gas are contained under high pressure in layers of sand and sandstone, separated from each other by beds of clay. The depth of the more productive wells varies from 500 ft. to 2000 ft. The crude oil consists of a fluid and very inflammable substance of a greenish hue, but appearing more of an amber-brown when held against the light; from this the clean and colourless kerosene or petroleum of commerce is obtained by a refining process. In recent years important by-products, including vaseline, have been obtained. The slag or refuse (masút) is brown and tough, and is used as fuel.

An interesting visit may be paid to the *Nobel Refinery* (Това́рищество нефтяно́го произво́дства Бр. Но́бель; Pl. E, 1), the largest in Baku, handling in 1910 no less than 65 million puds of crude oil. Permission may be obtained at the office in the Tchorni Gorod (week-days, 9-12 & 3-5), where most of the upper officials speak German. The traveller should first obtain permission to visit the naphtha works at Sabuntchi, which may be reached by railway in $1/2$ hr. It is, however, better to make this excursion by phaeton, taking half-a-day from Baku and back (fare 5-6 rb.); as the road is very rough, care should be taken that the horses are fresh and strong. After viewing the works in Sabuntchi (which the traveller is recommended to do in his oldest clothes and boots on account of the pools of oil), we drive back to the factory in the Tchorni Gorod in order to witness the processes of distillation and refining. Smoking is, of course, forbidden. — An interesting account of the Russian oil industry is given in 'The Oil Fields of Russia', by *A. B. Thompson* (2nd ed., 1908).

About 19 V. to the N.E. of Baku (railway in 1 hr.) lies *Surakhání* (output in 1912, 36 million puds), containing a *Temple of the Fire Worshippers* (Храмъ огнепоклóнниковъ) built in the 13th cent. in the Indian style and restored in the 17th century. Since 1879 it has been abandoned, but it can be visited on application to the Kokorev works; the lighting of the naphtha gas is no longer allowed. The naphtha gas issuing from the limestone strata outside the temple is used by the adjacent village of Surakhani for lime-burning and other purposes. — There is a gaseous spring rising in the sea at *Bibi-Eybát* (comp. p. 457), but its ignition is forbidden.

Near Baku are several mud-volcanoes occasioned by the subterranean gas bubbling up through liquid mud.

On the left of the railway line runs the oil-conduit from Baku to Batum (540 M. long). It was completed in 1906, and 70 million puds pass through it annually.

Railway to *Tiflis*, see R. 67. — Steamer to *Astrakhan*, see R. 64; to *Krasnovodsk* (Samarkand), see R. 75. — Route to *Teheran*, see R. 74.

North Caucasus Mineral Baths.

From Mineralnuiya Vodi to Kislovodsk, 61 V. (40 M.), railway in $2^1/4$-3 hrs. In summer extra trains run hourly between the different watering places. — In each of the watering-places is an hotel known as Kazyónnaya Gostínitza, belonging to the Russian government, but leased to a private owner. Bath $1/2$-1 rb. — In June and July the watering-places are overcrowded. In point of natural beauty they are far inferior to the South Caucasus resorts (p. 490).

Minerálnuiya Vodi, see p. 453. The train ascends gradually across the high-lying plain. Various isolated ranges and peaks appear in the background to the right and left, but it is not until we pass Essentuki that the line really approaches the mountains. The Elbruz (p. 485) is visible from time to time.

14 V. *Beshtau* (1445 ft.; Rail. Restaurant).

FROM BESHTAU TO ZHELYEZNOVODSK, 5 V. (3 M.), railway in 20 minutes. The line ascends rapidly through woods. — Zhelyeznovódsk (1885-2100 ft.; *Railway Restaurant; Kazyónnaya Gostínitza*, with electric light and lift, R. $1^1/2$-7, D. $1/2$-1, board 2 rb.; cab per drive 25, per hr. 50 cop.), with its ferruginous and alkaline springs (59-120°), lies amid woods on the S. slope of the *Zhelyéznaya Gorá* (2802 ft.; shelter-hut with rfmts.; easy ascent, starting a little to the E. of the covered walk, in $1^1/2$ hr.; the road round the base of the mountain is $3^1/2$ V. in length). The season lasts from May 15th to Sept. 1st. (O.S.); visitors' tax 5 rb. (day ticket 20 cop.).

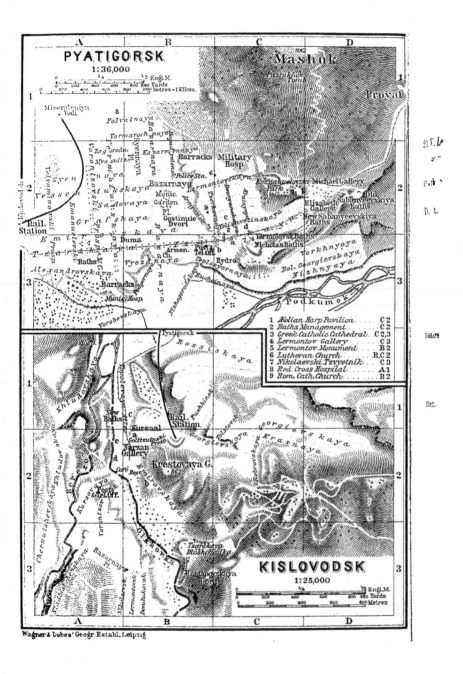

PYATIGORSK

1:36,000

Mashuk

KISLOVODSK

1:25,000

1 Aeolian Harp Pavilion . . . . C 2
2 Baths Management . . . . . C 2
3 Greek Catholic Cathedral . C 2,3
4 Lermontov Gallery . . . . . C 3
5 Lermontov Monument . . . . B 2
6 Lutheran Church . . . . . B,C 2
7 Nikolaevski Tzvyetnik . . . C 3
8 Red Cross Hospital . . . . A 1
9 Rom. Cath. Church . . . . . B 2

Opposite the railway station are the Ostrovskiya Baths, erected in the Moorish style in 1893. There is a covered walk for the use of visitors, adjoined by a theatre. — The ascent of the **Beshtau** (p. 460; easier from Pyatigorsk) takes 2¹/₂ hrs. From the railway station we follow the road to the S., at first through a wood, passing a road-keeper's hut (Но́вая карау́лка), and reach (3 M.) an inn at the *Orlinnaya Gorá*. Hence a footpath leads to the left to (1¹/₂ hr.) the summit.

16 V. *Karras* (1580 ft.), a German colony with a saline spring; 21 V. *Lérmontovski* (p. 460).

25 V. (17 M.) **Pyatigórsk**, Пятигорскъ. — *Railway Restaurant.* — HOTELS. **Bristol* (Pl. d; C, 2), Tzárskaya, R. 3-8, D. (1-5 p.m.) 60 cop. to 1¹/₂ rb., S. (from 9 p.m.) 1 rb. 20 cop.; **Kazyónnaya Gostínitza* (Pl. a; C, 3), with baths, elevator, etc., R. 1¹/₄-6 rb., bed-linen 50, déj. 30-50, D. from 50 cop.; *Yevropéiskaya* (Pl. b; C, 3), Sobórnaya Square, R. 1-9, bed-linen ¹/₂, D. (12-6) ¹/₂-1 rb.; *Centrálnaya* (Pl. c; C, 2), Dvoryánskaya, R. from 1¹/₄, D. (2-8) ¹/₂-1¹/₄ rb. — Numerous *Furnished Lodgings* from 30 rb. per month.

RESTAURANTS at the *Nikoláyevski Tzvyetník*, D. (12-5) 60 cop. to 1 rb. 10 cop., music twice daily (8-9 & 5-7); *Spiridón Tchitáyev* (opposite the Yevropéiskaya Hotel), with garden and both Russian and Caucasian cuisine. — *Café Rabbe*, at the W. entrance to the Nikoláyevski Tzvyetník (Pl. 7). *Season* from May 1st to Sept. 15th (O.S.). Visitors' tax 5 rb.; in addition there is a municipal tax of 2 rb. Day ticket 20 cop.

IZVÓSHTCHIK (tariff) from the rail. station to the town 25 (including hand-luggage), with trunk 50, per drive 20, per hr. 50 cop.; to the Provál 50 cop., there & back, with stay of ¹/₂ hr., 1 rb. — ELECTRIC TRAMWAY from the rail. station to the New Sabaneyevskiya Baths (5 cop.) and from the Nikoláyevski Tzvyetník to the Provál (10 min.; 7 cop.). — POST & TELEGRAPH OFFICE (Pl. B, 3), near the Yevropéiskaya Hotel.

Caucasian Alpine Club (Кавка́зское го́рное о́бщество), in the Kazyónnaya Gostínitza (in summer; 11-1 & 4-6); annual subscription 5 rb. The club arranges excursions for travellers.

Pyatigórsk (1685 ft.), a town with 32,000 inhab., on the left bank of the *Podkúmok*, is much frequented, especially by military men, on account of its warm sulphur springs (75-99°). Its name, meaning 'Five Mountains', is derived from the five peaks by which it is surrounded: *Lúisaya Gorá* (2415 ft.), *Mashúk* (see p. 460), *Zméinaya* (3250 ft.), *Beshtau* (p. 460), and *Zhelyéznaya Gorá* (p. 458). All these summits are of volcanic origin, and each of them, with the exception of the Beshtau, has a deposit of cretaceous limestone overlying the lava. — Near the middle of the town is the Cathedral Square, on the E. side of which stands the *Greek Catholic Cathedral* (Pl. 3; C, 2, 3). On the N. side of the square rises a *Bronze Statue of the Poet Lérmontov* (p. 460; Pl. 5), erected in 1892 by Opekúshin. The terrace in front of it commands a superb **View* of the mountains in general, and in particular of the snow-capped summit of the double-peaked Elbruz (p. 485; 60 M. distant as the crow flies). Farther to the N. are the *Roman Catholic* (Pl. 9) and *Lutheran Churches* (Pl. 6). — To the E. from the Cathedral Square runs the Tzárskaya, which passes on the right the grounds of the Nikoláyevski Tzvyetník (Pl. 7), containing the Lérmontov Gallery (Pl. 4), which is used by visitors as a covered promenade (music and restaurant, see above). Here also are the *Nicholas* and *Yermólov*

Baths (Pl. C, 3). To the S.W. is a well-fitted-up *Hydropathic Establishment*. About 3 min. above the Café Tzvyetník is the *Goryátchaya Gorá*, with a bronze eagle and a view-pavilion. We then follow the Tzárskaya, passing the *New Sabaneyevskiya Baths*, and finally ascend some steps to the *Elizabeth Gallery* (Pl. D, 2), which is reached from the Cathedral Square in ¹/₄ hr., and affords a fine view of the town. It contains a drinking fountain (the Elizabeth Spring). About 150 yds. to the left of the gallery, and visible from it, is the *Lérmontov Grotto*, the entrance to which is protected by a railing. About 250 yds. higher up is the so-called Æolian Harp (Эóлова áрфа; Pl. 1, C 2), a kind of belvedere. — By passing through the arched gateway to the left of the Elizabeth Gallery and ascending the footpath immediately to the left, we reach (2 min.) the *Mikhail Gallery* (Pl. D, 2; no view), with the Mikhail Spring.

The **Prováł** (Pl. D, 1) is reached from the Mikhail Gallery (see above) in ¹/₄ hr. by following the road to the right beyond the Gallery for 2 min. and then bending to the left (tramway, see p. 459). The Prováł is a kind of cavern in the mountain, 88 ft. in depth and open at the top. It contains a warm sulphur spring and is entered by a gallery 148 ft. in length. Opposite the tramway terminus is the Proval Restaurant, with view-terrace (D. 80 cop. to 1 rb. 20 cop.).

The bell-shaped **Mashúk** (3255 ft.; Pl. C, D, 1), which rises to the N.E., is a good point of view. The top may be reached in 1-1¹/₄ hr. (descent in 40 min.) by a somewhat shadeless footpath, 1²/₃ M. in length which ascends in long windings and is provided with benches, or by the somewhat longer carriage-road (phaeton 6 rb.) passing the Prováł. Walkers follow the road to the left from the Mikhail Gallery (see above), and after 1¹/₂ min. take the first footpath to the right, which passes (on the left) the tomb of the Alpinist A. V. Pastukhov (d. 1899). At the top is a shelter-hut (simple rfmts.; nightquarters 1 rb.). The view embraces the central chain of the Caucasus from the Elbruz to the Kazbek. In a straight line beyond the barracks lies *Mt. Yutza* (3186 ft.), connected with Pyatigorsk by an aqueduct; beyond it rise the *Dzhutza* (3933 ft.) and the double peaks of Mt. Elbruz (p. 485), the latter about 55 M. distant. In a depression to the right lies Kislovodsk (p. 461); to the W. are the five peaks of the Beshtau (see below), with the Zhelyeznaya Gora (p. 458) to the right of them. To the N.W. are *Mt. Razváłka* (3032 ft.) and (to the right of it) the Zméinaya (p. 459). To the E. are the Lúisaya Gora (see p. 459) and the town of Georgiyevsk.

Pyatigorsk forms the best starting-point (easier than from Zhelyeznovodsk) for an ascent of the five-peaked **Beshtau** (4593 ft.; shelter-hut with rfmts.; it is advisable to be provided with luncheon). This is an attractive trip, especially between the beginning of June and midsummer. We take a phaeton (2-3 rb., there & back 4-5 rb.) viâ *Lérmontovski Station* (p. 459) to (6 V.) the beginning of the footpath on the edge of the forest (2715 ft.), a walk of ³/₄ hr. from the rail. station. Thence we reach the summit in 1¹/₂ hr., and obtain a fine view of the Elbruz, especially at sunrise. Descent to Zhelyeznovodsk, see p. 459.

From the Prováł a carriage-road skirts the N. base of the Mashúk. After ¹/₄ hr. the road to the top of the Mashúk diverges to the left. In 25 min. more we reach the *Perkalski Springs* (inn not far off); and in a further 25 min. we reach the spot, marked by a monument, where *Lérmontov* fell in a duel in 1841; in ³/₄ hr. more we reach the Nikoláyevski Tzvyetník.

From Pyatigorsk to *Urusbíevo*, see p. 483.

As we proceed, the Beshtau (see above) is visible to the right.

41 V. (27 M.) **Essentukí.** — *Railway Restaurant.* — Hotels. *Nóvaya Kazyónnaya Gostínitza,* R. 1-3¹/₂ rb.; *Stáraya Kazyónnaya Gostínitza,* R. 1-6 rb.; *Métropole.* — Izvóshtchik from the station 20-30, with luggage 40-60, per drive 20, per hr. 60 cop. — The *Season* lasts from May 10th to Sept. 10th (O.S.); visitors' tax 5 rb. (day ticket 20 cop.).

Essentukí (2065 ft.) possesses cold alkaline springs, which are efficacious in affections of the stomach and liver. A little to the S.E. of the railway station begins the park containing the *Nicholas Baths* (1898), the Old Hotel, and the New Hotel. — Among the chief points for excursions in the neighbourhood are the *Otcharovániya Valley* (5¹/₂-6 M.; carr. 4-5 rb.); the *Svistún* mountain (2680 ft.; 4 M. to the S.; carr. 2¹/₂ rb.); and the Beshtau (p. 460; carr. to the guard-house, 11¹/₄ M., 5-6 rb.).

The railway now ascends and crosses the Podkúmok.

61 V. (41 M.) **Kislovódsk** (Plan, see p. 459). — Hotels. *Grand-Hôtel* (Pl. a; B, 2), a temperance hotel with good restaurant (D. 90 cop. to 1 rb. 20 cop.; no gratuities); *Park* (Pl. b; B, 2), a hôtel garni, in the Emírovskaya, R. 3-8 rb.; *Rossiya* (Pl. c; B, 1), in the Tópolevaya Alléya; *Narzán* (Pl. d; A, 2), R. from 1 rb., bed-linen 50 cop.; *Beshtau* (Pl. e; A, 2), R. from 1¹/₂, D. (1-4 p.m.) ¹/₂-1¹/₂ rb., the last two opposite the Narzán Gallery. — Furnished Rooms are to be had in the houses in the Tópolevaya Alléya or Poplar Avenue mentioned below (45 rb. and upwards per month). — Restaurants. *Kursaal* (Pl. B, 1, 2), opposite the rail. station, rather dear, with garden (concerts, adm. 20-50 cop.) and theatre; *Park Restaurant,* under the superintendence of the bath authorities, D. (12-5) 60 cop. to 1 rb. 20 cop. (no gratuities). — Izvóshtchik from the railway station 30, with heavy luggage 50, per drive 25 cop., per hr. 1 rb. — Agency of the *Sleeping Car Co.* in the Grand-Hôtel. — The *Season* lasts from June 1st to Oct. 1st (O.S.); visitors' tax 5 rb. (day ticket 20 cop.).

Kislovódsk (2695 ft.), a town of 14,000 inhab. situated in a narrow valley, is the most fashionable of the North Caucasus baths, and is also visited on account of its elevation. It is surrounded by terrace-like slopes of hard limestone, containing caverns and curious perforations, such as those on the Koltzo Gora (p. 462). — On leaving the railway station (Pl. B, 1), which is opposite the above-mentioned Kursaal, we turn to the left. In 4 min. we see the Narzán Gallery to the left (Pl. A, B, 2), while to the right diverges the *Tópolevaya Alléya* (Тóполевая аллéя; 'Poplar Avenue'; Pl. A, B, 1), containing numerous furnished lodgings. The *Narzán,* named by the Circassians the 'drink of heroes', is a strong carbonic spring (55°; more than 500,000 gallons in a day), the water of which, resembling Apollinaris, is used both for drinking and bathing (bath 75 cop.). The shady park adjoining it on the S. contains a music pavilion. To the right of it is a café, while to the left (higher up) is the above-named restaurant of the bath authorities. A pretty view of Kislovodsk and of its more distant environs may be obtained from the *Románovskaya Gorá* (Pl. B, 3), which we reach by ascending from the music pavilion on the Olkhovka, and turning to the left at (10 min.) the Ladies' Skating Rink. Hence to the summit, partly by steps, 8 min. more. — On the E. side of the town is the *Krestó-*

vaya Gorá (Крестовая ropá; 'Hill of the Cross'; Pl. B, 2; 2920 ft.), reached either from the Kursaal by the bridge across the Golitzuinski Prospékt, and then by an ascent of 7 min., or by turning to the S.E. at the Narzán Gallery up the Emirovskaya and passing the Park Hotel on the right. After 4 min. we skirt the stone fence on the left, keeping to the left at the top of it. In 7 min. more we reach a stone cross affording a view of Kislovodsk, though a perhaps more picturesque view is obtained just before we reach it.

Among the attractive points for excursions are the *Small Waterfall* (Ближній водопадъ; 1¹/₃ M. to the S.); the cliff known as the *Castle of Cunning* (Замокъ Ковáрства; 3¹/₃ M. to the W.; hotel with restaurant; saddle-horse there & back 1-2 rb.); the *Great Waterfall* (10 M. to the S.); the *Koltzo Gora* (Кольцó ropá; 'Ring Hill'; 4 M. to the N.), with a view of the Elbruz (p. 485), especially fine at sunset.

About 32¹/₂ V. (22 M.) to the S.W. of Kislovodsk rises the **Bermamúit** (8500 ft.; comp. Map, p. 485), the ascent of which, easily accomplished from the N. side, is well worth while. This trip is best made in July or at the beginning of Aug. (O.S.) and should be begun not later than 7 p.m. The drive to the mountain takes 7 hrs., and a four-seated spring-cart with four horses may be hired for it (there & back 15-20 rb.). A carriage of the Caucasian Alpine Club (p. 459) also makes the trip once weekly, the charge for which is 8-10 rb. including meals and nightquarters on the mountain. Warm clothing and rugs are necessary. The route ascends steadily from Kislovodsk and leads through wild valleys offering views of the 'Castle of Cunning' and of the 'Great Waterfall' (see above), with the Beshtau (p. 460) and the Mashúk (p. 460) behind us. At a point 26 V. (17 M.) from Kislovodsk, the two summits of the Elbruz come into sight. The top of the Bermamuit commands a magnificent *View of the Elbruz (p. 485), 27 M. to the S., best at sunrise and by early morning light. The small inn here is open from May 15th to Oct. 1st. (O.S.).

64. From Astrakhan to Baku across the Caspian Sea.

476 S.M. STEAMERS of the *Caucasus & Mercury Co.* (p. 348) run daily (the mail steamers, which run thrice weekly, are the best). The journey takes 2-3 days. Fares, including dinner, 24 rb. 45 cop., 19 rb.; luggage 95 cop. per pud.—From Petrovsk there is also a railway (comp. pp. 455, 456).

Astrakhan, see p. 435. A small steamer descends the busy *Volga*, and brings the travellers after a voyage of 9-12 hrs. to (175 V. or 119 M.) *Two Fathom Roads* (Двѣнадцать футовóй рейдъ), in the Caspian, where passengers are transferred to the sea-going steamers.

The **Caspian Sea** (Каспíйское мóре) occupies the deepest part of the depression situated to the W. and S. of the Ural Mts. and is the relic of a larger sea formerly stretching for a long distance towards the N. and E., to which the salt-pools of the Turcoman steppe and the Sea of Aral also belonged. The level of the Caspian Sea is 85 ft. below that of the Black Sea. It is the largest of all inland seas, being 756 M. long, 125-220 M. wide, and 178,857 sq. M. in area. The N. half is nowhere more than 118 ft. deep, but there are two deeply-cut depressions in the S. half, which attain a depth of 3600 ft. The water contains 0.75 to 1.50 per cent of salt. The N. and E. coasts are flat and not easily approached;

the spurs of the Caucasus on the W. bank and Mt. Elburz on the S. approach close to the sea, leaving only a narrow coast-strip free. Storms are frequent and the steamers are not very comfortable, so that navigation is often far from pleasant.

About 15 hrs. after leaving Two Fathom Roads the steamer touches at —

223 S.M. *Petróvsk* (halt of 3 hrs.; see p. 455).

In 7 hrs. more the steamer reaches —

294 S.M. *Derbént* (p. 455; halt of 1 hr.), where it anchors in the open roadstead. — Farther on we round the barren peninsula of *Ápsheron* (p. 456), and 18 hrs. after leaving Derbent we reach

476 S.M. *Baku* (p. 456).

65. From Batum to Tiflis.

327 V. (217 M.). RAILWAY in 11-13 hrs. (fares 10 rb. 75, 6 rb. 45 cop.; reserved seat 1¹/₂ rb.). — This is a very attractive trip.

Batúm (Rail. Restaurant), see p. 451. The line at first follows the coast, with the Black Sea to the left, and the N. slope of the Pontic Mts. to the right. We thread a short tunnel. 13 V. *Tchakva* (p. 452). Beyond (52 V.) *Supsa*, situated on the river of that name, the train turns to the E., and enters the wide and fruitful plain of the *Rión* and its tributaries. This was the ancient *Colchis*, now *Mingrelia* and *Imeretia*. — At (99 V.) *Samtrédi* (75 ft.; Rail. Restaurant) we are joined by the line coming from Poti (pp. 450, 451).

128 V. (85 M.) *Rión* (340 ft.; Rail. Restaurant). To Abbas-Tuman, see p. 492.

FROM RION TO TKVIBULI, 49 V. (33 M.), railway in 4¹/₂ hrs.

8 V. **Kutaïs**, Кутаисъ. — *Railway Restaurant.* — HOTELS. *Frántziya*, R. 1-6 rb., B. 40 cop., D. 1 rb.; *Grand-Hôtel*, similar charges. *Restaurant Yalta*, at the Byeli Bridge, on the Rión, D. ¹/₂-1 rb. — CAB from the rail. station to the town ¹/₂, per drive ¹/₄, per hr. 1 rb. — Preserved fruits at Oganiezov's. — Modern Caucasus arms and shawls can perhaps be purchased more advantageously in Kutaïs than in Tiflis.

Kutaïs (530 ft.), a town of hoar antiquity, originally the capital of Colchis, afterwards that of Imeretia, and now that of the province of Kutaïs, is finely situated on the foaming *Rión*, the banks of which are here connected by three bridges. Pop. 57,000. The beautiful conifers, magnolias, laurels, and myrtles in the Nakashidze Garden and on the so-called Farm (Фéрма), excite the admiration of the traveller. On the Archieréiskaya Gorá, or Bishop's Mountain (carr. & pair there and back in ³/₄ hr., 1 rb. 20 cop.), above the town to the N., on the right bank of the Rión, are the remains of the *Church of Bagrat III.* (Храмъ царя Варрата III.), which was erected at the beginning of the 11th cent. in a mixed Byzantine and Armenian style. Above is a low fortress tower, which commands a good view of the town, the mountains, and the convent of Gelati,

From Kutaïs to *Vladikavkaz*, on the Ossetian Military Road, see R. 69; to *Svanetia* viâ Alpani, see p. 481 and R. 70.

16 V. (11 M.) *Gelàti* (705 ft.), whence a rough path about 2 M. in length ascends to the E. to the convent of that name, which, however, is more conveniently reached from Kutaïs in $1^1/_4$-$1^1/_2$ hr. by phaeton (return-fare 6-7 rb.; provisions should be taken). — The **Convent of Gelati,** founded in 1109 and situated high up on the hillside, is occupied by a few Georgian monks. Its buildings are fast crumbling away. The chief church, the *Cathedral of the Virgin* (Храмъ Рождества́ Богоро́дицы), stands in the middle of the convent court, and dates from the end of the 11th century. It is constructed of huge blocks of sandstone and contains some faded frescoes, with portraits of the Imeretian kings. On the ikonostás are some old pictures of saints. At the corner of the apse is a large mosaic of the 11th cent., representing the Virgin with the archangels Michael (on the left) and Gabriel (on the right). The treasury (Ри́зница; to the right of the ikonostás), contains the Imeretian royal crown, some ancient MSS., and ecclesiastical vestments and vessels. — To the right of the cathedral is a chapel containing the tomb of King David the Restorer (1089-1125), who was the founder of the convent. To the right of the sarcophagus stands one wing of an iron gate dating from 1063, which was brought by the king from the conquered Persian town of Ganzha (Yelisavetpol). About 10 min. walk above the convent (we turn to the right on leaving the court) is the *Elias Chapel,* the *View from which embraces the valley of the *Tzkali-Tzitéli* ('Red River'), an affluent of the *Kvirila.* This valley is bounded by the luxuriantly wooded hills of Imeretia, beyond which rise the spurs of the central chain in the districts of Letchgúm and Radshá.

About 3 M. from Gelati, on a cliff in the valley of the Tzkali-Tzitéli, lies the convent of *Motzaméti,* which, however, contains nothing of interest except an old sarcophagus resting upon lions' feet.

49 V. (33 M.) *Tkvibúli* (2090 ft.), with coal-mines.

Continuation of the Railway to Tiflis. The train now runs to the S.E., skirting the wooded N. slope of the Akhaltzúikh-Imeretian watershed, which here attains a height of 9515 ft. — 156 V. *Kviríli* (520 ft.; Rail. Restaurant), situated on the *Kviríla,* a torrent hurrying down to the Rión. From (160 V.) *Sharopán* (550 ft.; Rail. Restaurant) a narrow-gauge line ascends to the N., through the valley of the Kviríla, to (50 V. or 33 M.) *Satchkheri,* passing (38 V.) *Tchiatúri* (1125 ft.), near which large beds of manganese are quarried. We now leave the hot plain of Colchis and ascend abruptly over viaducts, through a narrow and verdant valley. Beyond (200 V.) *Tzipa* we cross the ridge of the *Surám Mountains,* separating the valleys of Imeretia and Georgia, by a tunnel $2^1/_3$ M. long. At (205 V.)

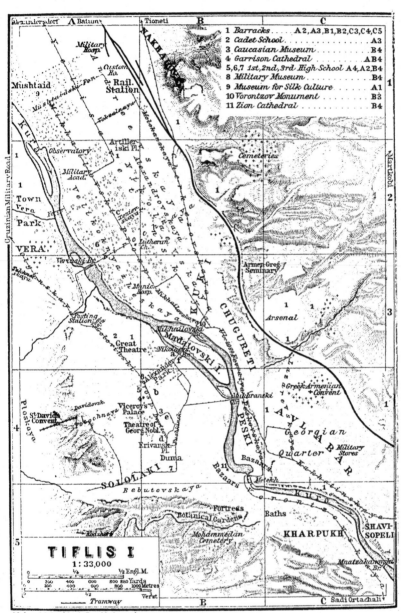

1 Barracks A2, A3, B1, B2, C3, C4, C5
2 Cadet School A3
3 Caucasian Museum B4
4 Garrison Cathedral AB4
5,6,7 1st, 2nd, 3rd High School A4, A2, B4
8 Military Museum B4
9 Museum for Silk Culture A1
10 Vorontzov Monument B3
11 Zion Cathedral B4

TIFLIS I

1 : 33,000

½ Engl. M.

200 400 600 800 880 Yards
0 200 400 600 800 1000 Metres

Tramway

Verst

Wagner & D bes' Geogr Establ, Leipzig

Varvárino (2480 ft.), the highest point on the railway between Batum and Baku, the train reaches the fertile plain of *Suram,* which is surrounded by lofty wooded mountains. We are now in the district of the *Kurá,* through which we descend gradually to —

215 V. (143 M.) **Mikháilovo** (2305 ft.; *Railway Restaurant*). The numerous oil-tanks at the station belong to the Nobel refinery at Baku. Branch-lines run to the N. to (6 V.) Suram and to the S. to (28 V.) Borzhom (p. 490). —The train crosses the *Kurá* and descends along its right bank. Just short of (240 V.) *Kareli* the high mountains begin to appear on the left, and farther on the Kazbek (p. 477) can be seen nearly 60 M. away as the crow flies.

257 V. **Gori** (1915 ft.; *Railway Restaurant; Seméinuiye Nomerá;* izvóshtchik from the rail. station to the town 40 cop.), the chief town of a district, with 20,700 inhab., nearly all of whom are Georgians. It lies on the left bank of the Kurá, at the foot of a conical hill surmounted by the ruins of the castle of *Goris-Tzikhe.*

High up in a cliff about 5 M. to the E. of Gori (phaeton 5-6 rb.), on the left bank of the Kurá, lies the curious cave-town of *Uplis-Tzikhe,* containing a natural tunnel in the sandstone, about 82 yds. in length, which leads down to the level of the Kurá.

From Gori to *Zaramag,* see p. 485.

The character of the scenery now changes, naked and barren cliffs taking the place of the wooded slopes. The parched and monotonous hill-country of Georgia gradually unfolds itself. Below rushes the Kurá in a deep gorge. — Beyond (296 V.) *Xanka* (Ксанка) we cross the Kurá; then we notice on the left, above the *Shio-Mgvinski Convent* (hardly visible from the railway), numerous caves in the vertical cliffs, which are said to have afforded refuge to the Christians at the time of the inroads of the Mongols and Persians.—At (307 V.) *Mtzkhet* (1515 ft.; Railway Restaurant; p. 474) the railway crosses the Gruzinian Military Road. Beyond the rail. station, on the left, is the cathedral.

327 V. (217 M.) *Tiflis* (1490 ft.; Rail. Restaurant).

66. Tiflis.

The bureau of the Government Railways and the agency of the Sleeping Car Co. are in the offices of the Caucasus and Mercury Steam Navigation Co., Eriванskaya Square 3 (Pl. A, B, 4; *II*).

Hotels. *LONDON (Pl. a, B 1; *II*), Madátovskaya 9, R. 2-10 rb., B. 70 cop., déj. & D. à la carte, pens. 8-15 rb.; *ORIENT (Pl. b, A 2, *II;* proprietor, *A. Roth*), Golovinski Prospékt 9, R. 1½-10 rb., B. 50 cop., déj. (12-5) 90 cop. to 2 rb., D. (5-12) 1½-2½, pens. 5-8 rb. (at both these hotels English, French, and German are spoken); WETZEL (Pl. c, A 2; *I*), at the corner of Mikháilovski Prospékt and Xéniyevskaya, R. 1-10 rb., B. 60, D. (1-5) 60 cop. to 1 rb.; KAVKÁZ (Pl. d, A 3; *II*), Erivánskaya Square, frequented by Georgians; PALACE HOTEL, Golovinski Prospékt (Pl. A, 1-3; *II*), new. Hôtels Garnis. SYEVLIRNUIYE NOMERÁ(Pl. e, A 3; *II*), Gräfskaya 1, R. ½-6 rb.; GRAND-HOTEL (Pl. f, B 1; *II*), opposite the London Hotel.

Restaurants at the hotels. Also *Annóna*, under the Arts Club Theatre (Pl. A, 1; *II*), D. (1-5) 60 cop. to 1 rb. 20 cop.; *Restaurant* near the Theatre of the Georgian Noblesse (Pl. A, 3; *II*), D. including wine 1 rb.; *Beau Monde*, Yelisavétinskaya (Pl. A, B, 1-3; *I*) cor. of Nekrásovskaya. — Among the national dishes are the following: shashlúik (p. 405), basturmá (beef roasted on the spit), tchikhirtmá (soup with mutton or fowl, saffron, and other spices), lokó (boiled fish from the Kurá), and plov (the Turkish pilau).

Cabs (two-horse phaetons).

From the rail. station to the town (if the train is more than 1/2 hr.
   late, 30 cop. is charged for each additional 1/2 hr. of waiting) 75 cop.
From the town to the station . . . . 50 „
Per drive . . . . 50 „
Per hour . . . . 1 rb.
To the Mushtaïd Gardens *or* to the Botanical Gardens . . . 80 cop.

Electric Tramways. The chief intersecting points are the Eriván-skaya Square (Pl. B, 4; *I*), and the Samánnaya Square (Pl. D, 4; *II*). 1. From Erivánskaya Square viâ Golovínski Prospékt and the Kirótchnaya to the Railway Station (Pl. A, B, 1; *I*); red disk or lamp.—2. From Tzkhnét-skaya (Pl. A, 3; *I*) viâ Erivánskaya Square and Mikháilovski Prospékt to the Railway Station; white disk.—3. From Erivánskaya Square viâ the Tcherkezovskaya (Pl. B, 2, 3; *I*) to the Railway Station; yellow disk.—4. From the Military Hospital viâ the Kakhetinskaya (Pl. C, 4, 5; *I*), Mukhránski Bridge, and Erivánskaya Square to the Railway Station; blue disk.—6. From Samánnaya Square viâ the Tcherkezovskaya to the Railway Station and back viâ Mikháilovski Prospékt (Pl. A, B 1-3; *I*); green and red disk.—7. From Ortatcháli (beyond Pl. C, 5; *I*) viâ Samánnaya Square and Mikháilovski Prospékt to the Railway Station and back viâ the Tcherkezovskaya; yellow and blue disk. 9. From Sololáki (Pl. A, 4, 5; *I*) viâ Erivánskaya Square to the Olginskaya (Pl. A, 3; *I*); blue disk.

Post Office, Madátovskaya 5 (Pl. B, 1; *II*); new building under construction at the corner of the Golovínski Prospékt and Voyénnaya (Pl. A, 3; *I*). — **Telegraph Office,** Voyénnaya 4, adjoining the Posting Station.— POSTING STATION (Pl. A, 3; *I*), at the N. end of the Golovínski Prospékt.

Theatres. *Great Imperial Theatre* (Казённый Театръ; Pl. A 3, *I*), Golovínski Prospékt; *Artists' Club Theatre* (Театръ артистическаго общества; Pl. A 1, *II*), near the Great Theatre; *Theatre of the Georgian Noblesse* (Театръ грузинскаго дворянства; Pl. A 3, *II*), Dvortzóvaya. — *Georgian Orchestra* ('The Four Sazandári'), in the summer-premises of the Avlabárski Club, Mikháilovskaya (Pl. B, 3; *I*).

Clubs. *German Club,* Mikháilovski Prospékt 129 (Pl. A, 1, 2; *I*). *Kruzhók* (strangers admitted on the introduction of a member; entrance fee 1 rb. 5 cop.), Golovínski Prospékt 10 (Pl. A, 1-3; *II*), summer-premises in the Kirótchnaya, near the Vérinski Bridge (Pl. A, 3; *I*); concerts several times a week in summer, and balls in winter. *Artists' Club* (Pl. A, 1; *II*), summer address, Mikháilovski Prospékt 107 (Pl. A, 1, 2; *I*), with garden and concerts (50 cop.). *Armenian Club* (Тифлисское собрáніе), Golovínski Prospékt 6 (Pl. A, B, 3, 4, *I*; new building at the N. end of this street), summer-premises at Mikháilovski Prospékt 73 (Pl. A, B, 1-3; *I*).

Physicians (German-speaking). *Dr. Von Haffner,* Torgóvaya 10; *Dr. Kirschenblatt* (internal diseases), Xénievskaya 6; *Dr. Maissuryánz,* Loris-Mélikovskaya 9; *Dr. Mykirtchyánz* (ladies' doctor), Bébutov St. 58; *Dr. Rosenbaum* (surgeon), St. Michael's Infirmary. — DENTISTS. *Helmrich,* Golovínski Prospékt 41; *Dr. Mykirtchyánz* (see above). — BATHS at the foot of the fortress, comp. p. 470; fee to the masseur (тёрщикъ) 30-50 cop.

Banks. *Imperial Bank* (Pl. A, B, 2; *II*), Loris-Mélikovskaya; *Bank of Commerce,* Erivánskaya Square (Pl. B, 4; *II*).

Shops (generally shut from 2 to 5 p.m. in the height of summer). Leather and Felt Goods: *Adelkhánov,* Armyánski Bazaar (Pl. B, C, 4; *II*). Preserved Fruits, Groceries, & Foreign Wines; *Nazarbékov,* Dvortzó-

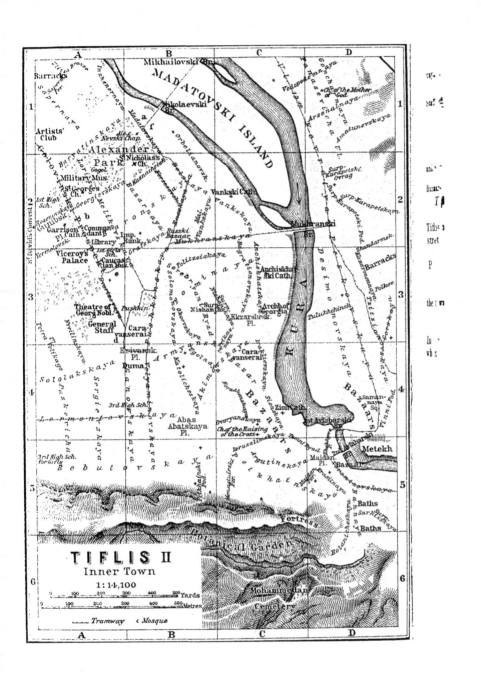

TIFLIS II
Inner Town
1:14,100

Tramway   ‹ Mosque

vaya, under the Theatre of the Georgian Noblesse (Pl. A, 3; *II*). — Underclothing: *Altchvang*, Dvortzóvaya (Pl. A, 3; *II*). — Books: *Hiddekel*, Golovínski Prospékt 11 (Pl. A, 2; *II*). — Maps of the Caucasus at the General Staff Offices (Pl. A, 3; *II*). — Photographs: *D. Yermakóv*, Erivánskaya Square (Pl. B, 4; *II*), next door to the Kavkáz Hotel; photographic materials, *Hagen*, Golovínski Prospékt, adjoining the Military Museum (Pl. A, 2; *II*). — Sporting Guns & Revolvers: *Hägele*, Golovínski Prospékt 19. — Opticians: *Hornig*, Golovínski Prospékt, next door to the Military Museum. — Chemists: Кавказское товарищество торговли аптекарскими товарами, in the Erivánskaya Square, adjoining the Town Hall. — *Bazaars*, see p. 469 (Silk and Silver Ware, etc., *A. N. Akopov*, Armyánski Bazaar, Pl. B, C, 4, *II*).

Principal Attractions (1 day). Morning: Convent of St. David, Bazaars. Afternoon: Sulphur Baths, Botanical Gardens.

Tiflis or Тифлисъ (1495 ft.), Georgian *Tbilis* or *Tbilizi Kalaki*, the capital of the viceroyalty of the Caucasus and of the province of Tiflis, and the headquarters of the 1st and 2nd Caucasian Army Corps, stretches for a distance of about 7 M. along a narrow valley 1-1¹/₂ M. in width and enclosed by barren mountains 2300-2460 ft. in height. Pop. 350,000 (Armenians, Russians, Georgians, etc.). Latitude 41° 13′ N., long. 44° 48′ E. of Greenwich. Through this valley the *Kurá* has hollowed out for itself a deep bed, and in its S.E. course through the town it has a fall of about 60 ft. On the S., where the castle-hill (1580 ft.) on the right bank is faced by a promontory on the left, the channel of the stream contracts to a width of about 100 ft. In consequence of its shut-in position, Tiflis is very hot in summer, when the mean temperature is 74° (in winter 35°, throughout the year 55°). Autumn is the pleasantest season. — Tiflis owes its prosperity to its favourable situation at the intersection of the trading routes from the Caspian to the Black Sea and from the Armenian uplands across the Caucasus to Russia. The most important of its products are carpets, woollen, cotton, and mercerized goods, shoes, wine, and tobacco.

Tiflis derives its name from the warm sulphur springs (Georgian tbili = hot) which the Georgian Tzar Vakhtang Gurgazlan (446-499 A. D.) is said to have discovered while hunting. At the beginning of the 6th cent. it succeeded Mtzkhet (p. 474) as the capital of the Georgian kingdom. In 1395 Timur the Tartar plundered the town. On the division of the kingdom in 1424, Tiflis remained the capital of Kharthlia, generally under the suzerainty of Persia, though at times also menaced by the Turks. In 1795 Tiflis was destroyed by the Persians, and in 1801 it was ceded to Russia.

In the N. part of the town, on the left bank of the Kurá and to the S. of the railway station, stretches the clean GERMAN QUARTER, formerly occupied by German immigrants from Wurtemberg (1818). To the S. is the GRUZINIAN or GEORGIAN QUARTER (Avlabár).

On the right bank of the Kurá is the RUSSIAN QUARTER, the seat of the officials and of the larger business firms. This is adjoined on the S. by the Armenian and Persian BAZAARS.

Perhaps the most interesting feature of Tiflis consists of the STREET SCENES in the native quarters. The streets are generally steep and often so narrow that two carriages cannot pass each other. The houses, mostly adorned with balconies, are perched one above

the other on the mountain-slope, like the steps of a staircase. From
sunrise to sunset, with the exception of the hot midday hours, the
streets are crowded with a motley throng of men and animals, walkers, riders, and carts (arbá; p. 445). The most conspicuous elements
of the population include the Georgian dealers in vegetables, fruit,
and fish, with their large wooden trays on their heads; the Persians,
in their long caftans and their high black fur caps, often with red-
dyed hair and finger-nails; the Tartar seïds and mullahs, in flowing
raiment, with green and white turbans (tchalma); the smooth-shaven
Tartars, in ragged clothing; the representatives of various mountain
tribes, in their picturesque tcherkéskas and shaggy fur caps; and
the porters, bearing heavy burdens on their backs. The Mohammedan
women never appear in the street without their veils. Among other
features are the lively little donkeys bearing heavy loads or ridden
by one or more men, and the horses carrying waterskins, with their
gaily-clad attendants.

The N. part of the town, on the right bank of the Kurá, is occupied by the modern RUSSIAN QUARTER, with its straight streets,
spacious squares, and the more important government-buildings.
In its centre lies the *Alexander Garden* (Александровскій садъ;
Pl. A, B, 1, 2; *II*), with the *Church of St. Nicholas*, the *Alexander
Nevski Chapel*, and a bust of the poet *Gogol*, by Khodoróvitch
(1903). On the W. side of the garden is the *Hall of Fame* or *Military Museum* (Военно-историческій музéй; Pl. A 2, *II;* open
daily, except Sat., 9-2, in winter 10-3; adm. 20 cop.; guide, 1913,
40 cop.; Director, Lieut.-Col. S.S. Esadze), which was built in 1885
and contains numerous portraits, military trophies, and paintings
of the most important events in the conquest of the Caucasus.

The Military Museum faces the *Golovínski Prospékt* or main
street of the town, in the N. part of which is the *Great Theatre*
(Pl. A, 3; *I*), built from designs by Schröter. In this street, on the
right, are the *First High School for Boys* (Pl. A, 2; *II*), the *Garrison Cathedral* (Военный соборъ; Pl. A 2, *II;* 1871-97), with its
massive dome, and the *Palace of the Viceroy* (Pl. A, 2, 3; *II*). —
To the left are the *Office of the Commandant* and the *Public
Library* (Публичная библіотека; Pl. A 2, *II*), the latter containing 50,000 vols. (closed at present). — At the S. end of the Prospékt,
to the left, is the *Caucasian Museum* (Кавказскій музéй; Pl.
A 3, *II*), founded in 1867 by Dr. G. Radde (d. 1903). Director,
Col. A. N. Kaznakóv. It is at present closed on account of rebuilding, but will probably be reopened in 1916.

The S. continuation of the Golovínski Prospékt, the Dvortzóvaya,
passes the *Theatre of the Georgian Noblesse* (Pl. A 3, *II;* on the
right; p. 466), and ends at the Erivánskaya Square (Pl. B, 4; *II*), on
the S. side of which stands the Duma. To the N. of the *Caravanserai* is a bust of the poet Pushkin, by Khodoróvitch,

To the S. of the Russian Quarter lie the *Bazaars (Pl. C, 4, 5; *II*),
a network of narrow lanes and alleys occupied mainly by Armenian
and Persian dealers. A hasty visit, especially if ladies are of the
party, is best made by carriage (1½ hr.) and in the company of a
commissionnaire recommended by the hotel-keeper. Those who have
more time will find it very interesting to stroll through the bazaars
on foot, studying the various popular types at their ease. Among
the most interesting features of the bazaars are the open workshops
of the goldsmiths and armourers; the stalls of the small-ware dealers
and pastrycooks; the bakers' shops, with their flat loaves baked in
huge clay ovens; the cobblers' stalls, displaying their gaudy slippers;
and the wine-merchants' shops, where the wine is kept in sheep or
buffalo skins (burdyúk), with the hair inside.

If extensive purchases are made (comp. the remarks at p. 463) it
is desirable to have the company of an experienced inhabitant, but it
should be remembered that guides recommended by the hotels receive a
percentage on the sales, which naturally comes out of the pocket of the
purchaser. The main rule in buying a number of articles is to offer a
lump sum for the whole collection (about ⅔ of the sum demanded in the
better shops), and not to pay for each object singly. — The most prized
woollen goods come from Daghestan, Kabardá, and Ossetia. Fleecy cloth
costs 5-15 rb. per arshin; the Imeretian cloth is distinguished by its
bright colours and is cheap (25-30 cop. per arshin). — A good burka (p. 440)
costs 12-15 rb., while especially fine and light specimens cost at least
30 rb. — Tiflis is the chief market for Caucasian carpets. As a general rule
the Kubá knotted carpets are twice as dear as those from the Karabágh
and five times as dear as those from Daghestan. The unknotted carpets
are termed zumáks. Genuine old carpets or rugs are steadily becoming
dearer and rarer, and the purchaser should be on his guard against imitations. — The weapons of Daghestan still preserve their old reputation,
but very deceptive imitations are manufactured in Tiflis. Plain daggers
cost 1-3, inlaid with silver 5-12, inlaid with gold 20-50 rb.; sabres cost
5-20, inlaid 50-80 rb.; plain muskets cost 5-10 rb.; old guns inlaid, 50-100
(imitations of the last 10-50) rb.; walking-canes with German silver ornamentation cost 2-5 rb. — Transcaucasian objects include silver belts, often
gilded and adorned with enamel, silver azarpéshi (ladles), silver wine-
vessels with chasings in the Persian style, and the long necked water-jars
of copper. — Tiflis is one of the chief marts in the wine-trade of the Caucasus. Transcaucasia produces yearly 20 million vedros (54,000,000 gallons)
of wine. The best wine is that from Kakhetia (Tzinondáli, Mukuzán,
Napareuli, etc.), the price of which varies from 25 cop. a bottle up to
1 rb. or more. The red wines are rather harsh.

To the S.E. of the Alexander Garden, on the Kurá, rises the Armenian *Vanski Cathedral* (Pl. C, 2; *II*) with its three towers, erected
in the early 18th cent. on the site of an older church. — To the S.
is the Greek Catholic *Antchis-Khatski Cathedral* (Pl. C, 3; *II*),
containing an interesting 8th cent. painting of Christ in a costly
13th cent. frame. — Still farther to the S., on the Kurá, is the *Zion
Cathedral* (Cióнскiй coбóръ; Pl. C 4, *II*), completed in the 7th
cent., frequently destroyed in subsequent times, and restored in 1795
et seq. In the interior, to the left of the ikonostás, is a picture of
St. Nina, behind which is kept the wooden cross of that saint (not
shown to visitors). Near the cathedral is the *Museum of Ecclesias-*

tical Antiquities (Церко́вный музе́й духове́нства Грузи́нской эпа́рхіи), which is open on Tues. & Thurs. 9-11, and on Sun. & holidays 9-1. — To the S. of the Metekhski Bridge are some *Baths* (Pl. D, 5; *II*), where the warm carbonated sulphur-springs (99-114°) which rise here are utilized. The best are the Tzikhis-Abáno, belonging to Prince Orbeliáni (bath 1-1½ rb.).

To the W. of the Baths stretch the shady *Botanical Gardens* (Ботани́ческій садъ; Pl. B, C, 6, *II*), forming a pleasant refuge from the noise of the streets. They are open from 8 a.m. to 7 p.m., in winter till 4 p.m. (director, A. C. Rollov). The *Botanical Museum* contains over 2000 objects, including sections of the different trees of the Caucasus, specimens of plant-fibres, fruits, etc. In the remoter part of the garden is a waterfall, and simple refreshments are to be had a little farther up. Admission to the enclosed part of the gardens may be obtained on payment of 5 cop. — On the S. side of the valley is a Mohammedan cemetery, which, however, is hardly worth visiting. — A steep footpath ascends from the Botanical Gardens to the ruins of the Persian *Fortress* (Pl. C, D, 5; *II*), which rise picturesquely over the bazaars. [The key of the fort-gate must be obtained from the head-gardener.] In clear weather the fort commands a magnificent view of the town and of the range of mountains dominated by the snowy dome of the Kazbek. To the left of the Kazbek (p. 477) are the pyramid of the Gimarai-Khokh and (farther off) the broad ridge of the Tepli group and of the Adái-Khokh.

About ½ M. to the W. of the *Garrison Cathedral* (Pl. A, 2; *II*) is the lower station of the funicular railway (Фуникулёръ) to the top of **Mt. Plóskaya** (3270 ft.), which takes 6 min. for the ascent (fare 15, up & down 20 cop.). About halfway up (station; 5 cop.), on the right, is the Georgian *Convent of St. David* (Pl. A 4, *I;* 1935 ft.; Мтацми́ндскій монасты́рь св. Дави́да Гаре́джійскаго). In a grotto close by is the grave of the Russian poet, A. S. Griboyédov (1795-1829). The upper station (restaurant, D. ³/₄-1 rb.) commands a fine view of the town and mountains, which are seen to best advantage in the morning.

The Metekhski Bridge crosses the Kurá to the GEORGIAN QUARTER on the left bank. Above the bridge rises the *Metékh,* the former palace of the Georgian kings, now a prison. The only part remaining of the old building is the interesting church (Метéхская цéрковь; Pl. D 5, *II;* no admission), which dates from the 5th cent. (dome added in the 13th century).

To the N.E. of the Alexander Garden (p. 468) is the Nicholas Bridge, leading to the Madátovski Island and thence to the left bank of the Kurá. By the bridge stands a bronze statue, by Pímenov (1866), of *Prince Vorontzóv* (d. 1856; Pl. 10, B 3, *I*), who conferred various benefits on the town when governor of the Caucasus. The Mikháilovski Prospékt, with the *Lutheran Church* (Pl. A, B, 2; *I*),

leads hence to the N. through the 'GERMAN QUARTER' (p. 467) to the
Railway Station (Pl. A, 1; I). To the W. of the station lies the
Mushtaïd Park (Pl. A, 1; I), a popular resort with a *Museum of
Silk Culture* (Pl. 9; open free on week-days 10-2, in winter 10-3).
— About 1¹/₄ M. to the N. is the German colony of *Alexandersdorf*.
About 12 M. to the S.W. of Tiflis (motor omnibus 2, return journey
1¹/₂ rb.; phaeton 8 rb.; walking not recommended), high up among the
foothills of the Little Caucasus, rises *Kodzhóri* (4370 ft.), a favourite summer-resort of the residents of Tiflis. *Udzó*, with an old church, and the
ruined fortress of *Ker-Ogli* both afford fine views of the Little Caucasus,
the valley of the Kurá, and of the high mountains. In the environs of
Kodzhori are the ruins of several old Georgian churches, with frescoes and
curiously decorated doors and windows (*Betáni, Kabenski Convent*, etc.).
About 7 M. to the S. of Kodzhori is the German colony of *Elisabethtal*
(ca. 3280 ft.; inn).—From Tiflis a motor omnibus runs to the W. viâ Kodzhori, in 3 hrs. (fare 6 rb.), to (40 M.) the summer-resort of *Manglís*
(3935 ft.), situated amid pine-clad mountains. — A highroad runs to the summer-resort of *Byeli-Klyutch* (4105 ft.), 36 M. to the S.W. of Tiflis. About 3 M.
farther on, high over the river *Khram*, is the ruined castle of *Samshvildo*.
    The interesting convent of *Martkóbi*, 19 M. to the N.E. of Tiflis (an
excursion of two days, phaeton 12-15 rb., saddle-horse 3-5 rb.), was founded
about 415 A. D. — Pleasant day-trip also to *Mtzkhet* (p. 474).
    From Tiflis to *Batum*, see R. 65; to *Vladikavkaz* (Gruzinian Mili-
tary Road), see R. 68; to *Baku*, see R. 67; to *Erivan*, see R. 73 b.—Motor-
cars for excursions may be hired from the company mentioned at p. 473.

67. From Tiflis to Baku.

515 V. (343 M). Express train in 13 hrs. (14 rb. 50, 8 rb. 70 cop.;
reserved seat 1¹/₂ rb.; sleeping-car 4 rb. 10, 3 rb. 10 cop.).

Tiflis (Rail. Restaurant), see p. 465. The line runs to the S.,
along the left bank of the *Kurá*, through a monotonous landscape.
6 V. *Navtlúg* (1515 ft.; p. 492). At (58 V.) *Sogát-Bulákh* (800 ft.)
the foothills of the Armenian highlands on the right approach to
the edge of the Kurá. The train crosses the river before reaching
(75 V.) *Poïli* (915 ft.).

89 V. (59 M.) **Akstafá** (915 ft.; *Railway Restaurant*).

FROM AKSTAFA TO ERIVAN, 175 V. (117 M.), highroad. A motor omnibus runs via Delizhan in 8 hrs. to (149 V.) Karaklis (p. 493; fare 8 rb.),
and another runs from Delizhan viâ Yelenovka in 6 hrs. to Erivan (fare
6 rb.). A four-horse carriage from Akstafa to Delizhan costs 18-20 rb., and
thence to Erivan 25 rb. (post-chaise about 15 rb.). — Railway from Tiflis
to Erivan viâ Alexandropol, see R. 73 b.
    The road ascends to the S.W. through the picturesque Akstafa valley.
9 V. *Kozákh*, a posting-station; 22¹/₄ V. *Uzun-Tálskaya*; 40 V. *Karaván-
Saráï* (accommodation); 58 V. *Kars-Tchai*. Beyond (72 V.) *Delizhán*
(2200 ft.; R. in the posting-station 1-2 rb.), a prettily situated summer
resort, we cross the *Tchubukhli Pass* (6670 ft.), passing the posting
station (91 V.) *Sempónovka*, and reach the *Lake of Goktcha* or *Sevanga*
(6315 ft.; trout-fishing), 557 sq. M. in area. Its E. boundary is formed
by the high volcanic *Karabagh Meridian Mts.* As we proceed along the
W. bank of the lake, we see to the left, on a rock in the lake, the
convent of *Sevanga*, which is well worth a visit (ferry 3¹/₄ M. on this side
of Yelenovka; the night may be spent in the convent). At the village
of (112 V.) *Yelénovka* the road leaves the lake and turn to the W,

Just beyond the posting-station of (129 V.) *Akhti* (5690 ft.) the road
descends, and a magnificent view opens out before us. On the left is
the chain of the *Novo-Bayazét*, with the volcanic cone of *Utchtapalár*
(10,700 ft.); on the right is the Alagöz (p. 494). — The road now enters
the spacious and fertile basin of the *Araxes*, in which once stood the
royal Armenian city of *Artaxata*. — 141 V. *Sukhói-Fontán*, a posting
station; 160 V. *Eilyari*, another posting-station. — As we make a steep
descent to *Erirán* (p. 494), the minarets and cupolas of the town appear
in front of us, with the massive *Mt. Ararat* (p. 495) in the background.

From (133 V.) *Dzegám* (1050 ft.) a road leads to the S. to (25 M.)
Kedabék, with the copper-mines and foundries of Siemens Brothers.

177 V. (118 M.) **Yelisavetpól** (765 ft.; *Railway Restaurant*),
the capital of the district of the same name (1455 ft.; *Centrálnaya*),
lies about $3^1/_3$ M. to the S. of the railway station (tramway 8, izvósh-
tcbik 75 cop.). Pop. 60,000. Before its conquest by the Russians in
1804, the town was called *Ganzha*. The mosque of Shah Abbás (17th
cent.), in the bazaar-square, is surrounded by gigantic plane-trees. —
About 8 M. to the S. is the German colony of *Helenendorf* (1550 ft.).

The line now descends towards the desolate Transcausian Steppe.
Most of the rivers which flow from the mountains dry up in this
desert, so that the Kurá, reinforced by the waters of the *Aráx*
(Araxes) coming from Armenia, is the only one that reaches the
Caspian Sea. — 240 V. *Yevlákh* (30 ft.; Rail. Restaurant), a place
with a bad reputation for fever in summer.

FROM YEVLAKH TO NUKHA, 76 V. (50 M.), highroad; motor omnibus in
4 hrs. (fare 4 rb.). The road leads to the N., passing the posting-stations
of (14 V.) *Khaldán*, (25 V.) *Tchemakhli*, (45 V.) *Sutchminskaya*, and (59 V.)
Ipyaglinskaya. — **Nukhá** (2455 ft.; *Ekonómiya*) is a town of 42,000 inhab.,
with silk-thread factories. In the high-lying citadel is a palace built for
the Khans in 1760. To Derbent, see p. 455; to Telav, see p. 489.

FROM YEVLAKH TO SHUSHA, 104 V. (69 M.), highroad; motor omnibus
in 6 hrs. (fare 6 rb.; narrow-gauge railway projected). The road leads to
the S., passing (23 V.) *Bardá*, formerly the capital of Albania, with a
noteworthy mausoleum. 36 V. *Kotcharlinskaya;* 50 V. *Korvéndskaya;* 65 V.
Agdám; 80 V. *Khodzhalinskaya*. All these are posting-stations. — Shushá
(*Mardi*), in the Armenian highlands, a town of 43,000 inhab., with steep
and narrow streets, manufactures beautiful carpets (20-400 rb. each).

Immediately after leaving Yevlakh we cross the Kurá. 282 V.
Udzhári (40 ft.). The snow-covered mountains of Daghestan now
appear on the left. — 326 V. *Kyurdamír* (20 ft. below sea-level).

FROM KYURDAMIR TO SHEMAKHA, 69 V. (46 M.), highroad. 18 V. *Kara-
sakhkál;* 33 V. *Akh-Su*, where pomegranates and peaches are wonderfully
cheap in autumn; 51 V. *Sheradilskaya*. — Shemakhá (2230 ft.; accommodation at the Shemakhinski Zayészhi Cathedral; food at the Shemakhin-
skoye Artistitcheskoye Obshtchestvo), a finely situated hill-town, with
23,000 inhabitants. The town carries on the manufacture of silk scarves
(1 rb.) and shawls (5-35 rb.).

397 V. *Adzhí-Kabúl* (30 ft.; Rail. Restaurant). The railway now
turns to the N. and from (430 V.) *At-Bulákh* (30 ft. below sea-level)
onwards runs along the shore of the Caspian Sea (on its right),
skirting the S. spurs of the Caucasus. The landscape has the
aspect of a desolate wilderness, in which from time to time rise

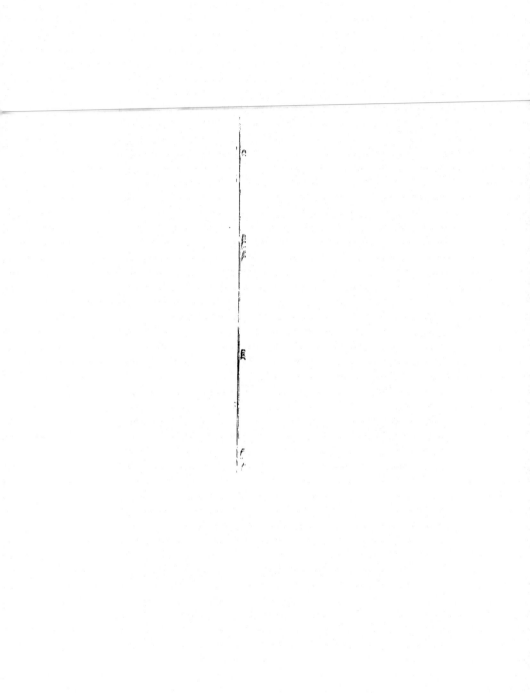

scattered hills or mountain-chains. Beyond (459 V.) *Sangatchál* (60 ft. below sea-level) the line often runs quite close to the sea. 484 V. *Putá,* with mud-volcanoes; 502 V. *Baladzhári* (160 ft.; Rail. Restaurant). Railway to Petrovsk and Rostov, see R. 63.

515 V. (343 M.) *Bakú* (55 ft. below sea-level), see p. 456.

68. From Tiflis to Vladikavkaz.

(Gruzinian or *Georgian Military Road;* Военно-Грузинская Дорога.)

200 V. (132 M.), **High Road.** Motor Omnibuses of the *Société Fran- çaise des Transports Automobiles du Caucase* ply regularly from April 15th to Oct. 15th; they accomplish the journey in 10 hrs., starting at Tiflis from the office at Olginskaya 46 (Pl. A, 3; *I*), and arriving in Vladikavkaz at the Grand-Hôtel (fare 20 rb.; to Kazbek 15^1/$_2$ rb.; one pud of luggage allowed free, excess 2 rb. per pud). The company maintains hotels at Kazbek, Dushet, and Passanaur (dinner-station for passengers from Tiflis); the Mail Posting Stations are only for passengers by the mail. Private motor-car 125 rb. — Horse Posting Arrangements. The posting-rate per horse and verst is 3 cop. In ascending the valley four to six horses are prescribed, in descending three or four. A single traveller should give the driver at each station a fee of 40-50 cop., a party 15-20 cop. each. The best plan is to hire a calèche, which allows the journey to be broken at the traveller's convenience. The charge for a two-seated calèche (Двух- мѣстная коляска) with 4 horses is 52 rb. 13 cop., to which must be added a stamp duty of 4 rb. 80 cop. The traveller will do well to hire a so- called conductor, who blows his horn to clear the way and looks after the luggage at the stations (charge 5 rb. for 3 days, with a fee of 1 rb. per day). The *Station Rest Houses* are built of stone and afford limited accommodation. The best quarters are at Mleti (p. 476) and Kazbek (p. 477; R. with bed-linen and light 1 rb. 40 cop.), but those at Dushet (p. 475), Passanaur (p. 476), Gudaur (p. 476), and Kobi (p. 476) are also tolerable.

The Georgian Military Road, constructed in 1811-1864, is one of the most beautiful mountain roads in the world (height of pass 7800 ft.); the best season of the year is from the beginning of June to the end of Aug. (O. S.). Travellers should pass the night at Kazbek, for the sake of seeing the fine sunrise on the following morning. — Travellers in the reverse direction should leave Vladikavkaz (comp. p. 454) early in the afternoon and also spend the night in Kazbek; hotel-accomodation at Tiflis should be ordered in advance.

The verst-figures in brackets indicate the distances from station to station.

Tiflis, see p. 465. We leave the town on the N. As we descend to the little river *Vera,* we see on the right a cast-iron cross which commemorates the escape of Tzar Nicholas I. from a dangerous accident during his journey in the Caucasus in 1837. — The road first runs along the right bank of the *Kurá,* on the left bank of which *Alexandersdorf* (p. 471) comes in sight. Then, temporarily leaving the river, it crosses the so-called *Plain of Digomi.* — After about 13 V. the valley of the Kurá closes in. To the right, on a hill, stands the picturesquely situated convent of *Dzhváris-Zakdari,* with a church dating from the end of the 7th cent. (?) and said to be built on the spot where St. Nina first erected the cross.

30*

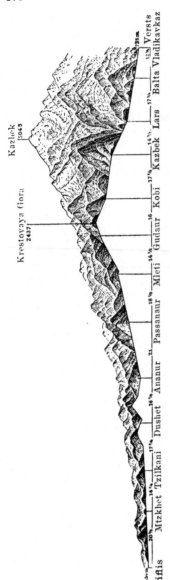

Kazbek 5043

Krestovaya Gora 2437

12½ Versts Balta Vladikavkaz

17¾ Lars Balta

14¾ Kazbek Lars

17¾ Kobi Kazbek

16 Gudaur Kobi

14½ Mleti Gudaur

18¾ Passanaur Mleti

21 Ananur Passanaur

16¾ Dushet Ananur

17¾ Tzilkani Dushet

14½ Mtzkhet Tzilkani

20½ Tiflis Mtzkhet

Tiflis

20½ V. **Mtzkhet** (Мцхетъ; 1600 ft.), a wretched village, lies at the confluence of the Arágva with the *Kurá*, 2 M. from the posting-station. The latter river is crossed here by a stone bridge. Mtzkhet is one of the oldest places in Georgia, and was the capital of the kingdom before Tiflis. The hill opposite the town once bore the castle of *Armás-Tzikhe* (p. 443), the most ancient royal residence in the country. — The most important building is the *Cathedral of Sveti Tzkhoveli*, lying to the left of the highroad and surrounded by a lofty crenelated wall with towers. It is said to have been erected in the 4th cent. on the spot where the alleged vesture of Christ was found, brought hither from Golgotha by a Jew; the present building, with a dome over the crossing, dates from the beginning of the 15th, and was renewed in the 18th century. In this church are buried many of the Georgian kings of the Bagratide dynasty (p. 443), including the last king of all, George XIII. (d. 1801; to the left of the ikonostás). In the apse are some old frescoes that have been restored. — At the end of the village, to the left, is the *Nunnery of Samt-ávro* (Самтáврскій монастырь), with a large church in which Mirian, the first Christian king of Georgia, and his wife lie buried. — In the N.E. part of the cemetery, close by the road, stands an old chapel, on the supposed spot where St. Nina once inhabited her cell. — Every

year, on Oct. 1st (O.S.), the inhabitants of the surrounding districts
assemble in Mtzkhet for a church-festival, forming an exceedingly
interesting ethnographical scene.

Railway to *Tiflis* and to *Batum*, see p. 465; the railway station is
near the posting-station.

Beyond the convent, on both sides of the road, lies the *Necropolis of Samtávro*, consisting of two superimposed layers of the
remains of tombs belonging to the Iron Age. They are made of
slabs of slate in the shape of chests. The skulls found in these
tombs are all dolichocephalous, though the present inhabitants of
the Caucasus are almost all brachycephalous. — Still farther on, to
the right, are the ruins of the fortress of *Natzkhóra*. — We next
pass, by a deeply sunken road, into a fertile district taking its
name from the little river of *Gartishári*, and cross the *Kartha-
linian Plain*, to —

35¹/₄ V. (14³/₄ V.) *Tzilkáni* (2835 ft.).

The road begins to ascend slowly and leads along the wide floor
of the *Arágva* valley. In the distance the Kazbek (p. 477) appears
for a short time. After 49 V. the small *Bazalétskoye Salt Lake*
becomes visible on the left; beyond, in the distance, to the N.W.,
is seen the *Sedlováya Gorá* ('saddle hill'). After this the road
begins to descend; just short of Dushet is the station of the French
motor omnibuses.

53 V. (17³/₄ V.) *Dushét* (2890 ft.; restaurant at the omnibus
station). The village of that name, with 2600 inhab., lies to the E.
of the posting-station. It was the former residence of the Eristave,
i.e. viceroys, of the Arágva domain, and was frequently contended
for in their feuds with the Georgian kings. Relics of these early
times remain in the shape of an old tower (said to have belonged
to the viceregal palace) and the ruins of a fortress; the St. Nicholas
Church is also old.

The road ascends between fields for 4 M. to a mountain ridge,
from which it descends, passing several Georgian and Ossetian
villages, into the valley of the *White Arágva* (Бѣлая Арагва).
A few miles farther down, the river is augmented by the waters
of the *Pshavo-Tchevsurian Arágva*. — Passing some deserted barracks, we come to —

69¹/₄ V. (16¹/₄ V.) *Ananúr* (2695 ft.), picturesquely situated at
the junction of two valleys, and overlooked by the ruins of a fortress (to the left of the road), comprising within its walls two old
churches, the remains of a viceregal residence, and a watch-tower
The posting-station is at the N. end of the place.

From Ananur to *Telav*, see p. 489.

The scenery adjoining the road becomes more and more mountainous. The river rushes more wildly, and the wooded mountains
on either side rise higher and higher.

90¹/₄ V. (21 V.) *Passanaúr* (3335 ft.; hotel-restaurant of the omnibus company, R. from 1¹/₂, déj. from. 1 rb.), in a narrow valley at the confluence of the *Black* (Чёрная) and the *White Arágva*.

The road ascends on the right bank of the White Arágva. Here and there on the steep slopes are hamlets with old churches and half-destroyed towers. The mountains attain a height of 11,500 ft.

108³/₄ V. (18¹/₂ V. **Mleti** (4635 ft.), situated high above the foaming waters of the White Arágva, with a meteorological station.

Just beyond Mleti the road crosses the Arágva and ascends in 18 curves along the almost perpendicular rocky walls of the valley; the rocks are covered with huge streams of lava and often assume the form of columns. A marble tablet at the lowest curve of the road commemorates the construction of this section in 1857-61. Fine views are had to the right and left of the valley and of the Georgian hamlets clinging like swallows' nests to the steep slopes, in the midst of fields and Alpine pastures. We see the *Red Mts.* (Красныя горы) and (as we continue to ascend) the *Seven Brothers* (Семь братьевъ), both groups consisting of volcanic, red-tinted rocks. The road now makes a slight ascent to —

123¹/₄ V. (14¹/₂ V.) *Gudaúr* (7080 ft.), with a meteorological observatory. Even in June the snow often lies quite thickly here.

The road now leads upwards along the edge of giddy precipices (protected in places by walls and galleries against avalanches or landslips), between *Mt. Gud* (Горá Гудъ; on the right) and *Mt. Krestóvaya* (Крестóвая Горá; 8000 ft.; on the left). At last, amid verdant Alpine pastures, we attain the summit of the **Krestóvi Pass** (variously estimated at 7695 ft. and 7815 ft.), which is designated by a small obelisk on the left, and by a cross, said to have been erected by Queen Tamára, on the right. Beyond the top of the pass the road slowly descends; and we pass by an abrupt transition from the imposing, yet lovely, scenery of the S. slope to the bald and severe mountain region of the N. The following section of the road, especially where it bends to the N. and descends into the *Baidára Gorge*, skirting one of the affluents of the *Terek*, is somewhat dangerous in winter and spring on account of frequent avalanches, although protected in places by long snow-sheds. When there has been much snow, it is better to pass over it early in the morning or in the evening. Numerous carbonic and ferruginous springs appear in this region. The massive head of the *Kazbek* (p. 477) now appears.

139¹/₄ V. (16 V.) *Kobi* (6340 ft.) The rest-house lies at the foot of a lava-stream, at the confluence of three small rivers, of which the most important is the Terek proper, issuing from the *Trusso Gorge*.

The valley, which is framed by sheer and barren mountains, now grows broader. Where the cliffs are less precipitous they are occupied by the small hamlets of the Ossetians and the Georgians,

with their occasional square towers. Halfway between Kobi and
Kazbek, the road bends round the old fortress of *Sión*, situated on
a lofty rock, adjoining a large hamlet with a noteworthy ancient
basilica in Georgian style. Farther on, the view into the wide valley
of the *Tzno* opens up on the right.

156½ V. (17¼ V.) *Kazbék* (5625 ft.; Grand-Hôtel, a dépendance
of the hotel of the same name in Vladikavkaz, with a restaurant
and view-terrace, R. 2-5, B. ³/₄, déj. 1-1¹/₂, D. 1¹/₂-2¹/₂, pens.
7-9 rb.). Those who spend the night at the posting-station should
select a room with a view of the Kazbek (charges, see p. 473). The
fountain in front of the station-building commemorates the visit of
the Tzarina Marie Feódorovna in 1888. The village of Kazbek and
the large hamlet of *Gergéti*, lying opposite it on the W., are inhabited by Georgian mountaineers, who maintain themselves by
agriculture and cattle-raising and by hunting the tur or Caúcasian
ibex; the children collect rock-crystals. Near the village church is
the grave of the Georgian poet Prince Alexander Kazbék (d. 1893),
marked by a monument consisting of a marble model of Mt. Kazbek, with a bronze bust of the poet.

To the W., opposite the village, rises the gigantic ice-pyramid
of *Mt. Kazbék,* once an active volcano, the E. peak of which
(16,545 ft.; Mt. Blanc 15,780 ft.) may be seen in clear weather in
all its glory; in the afternoon it is generally veiled in mist. The
W. peak is not visible from the posting-station. It was to Mt. Kazbek, according to the myth, that Prometheus was fastened (other
versions mention the Elbruz). A magnificent *View of the Kazbek,
especially at sunrise, is to be had from the ruined *Church of
Tzminda-Saméba* ('Holy Trinity'; 7120 ft.; reached on horseback
in 1¹/₂ hr., on foot in 2 hrs.; horse 2, guide 1-1¹/₂ rb.). Above the
church grows the Caucasian rhododendron, which blossoms in June.
It is also well worth while to proceed from the church as far as
the foot of the *Or-tzferi Glacier* (9625 ft.; 2 hrs. riding), whence
a superb view is obtained of the Terek valley.

The Kazbek is best ascended from Gveleti (p. 478) viâ the Dyevdorák
Hut (p. 476) and the Yermólov Hut (guide 20-25 rb.; to the Yermólov Hut
3 rb., or, if the night is spent out, 5 rb.). The following guides are recommended: Levan Alibekov, Yegor Kizílkov, Ilya and Levan Kushayev,
and Illico Khutziev. Porters receive 2-3 rb. daily. From the Dyevdorák
Hut (p. 478), we proceed viâ the (1¹/₂ hr.) *Dyevdorák Glacier* (lower end
ca. 7525 ft.) to the (3¹/₂ hrs.) *Yermólov Hut* (Ермоловская хижина) of
the Russian Mountain Club (11,420 ft.; food, wraps, and water must be
provided by the traveller), built in 1903 on the *Bart-Kort Aréte*. From
this point we reach the summit in 6¹/₂-7¹/₂ hrs. viâ the 1st Volgishka,
passing the rock known as Pronessi Gospodi, and being on our guard
against falls of stones. We descend in 3¹/₂ hrs. to the Yermólov Hut, and
in 3 hrs. more to the Dyevdorák Hut.—The first ascent of the Kazbek
was made in 1868 by D. W. Freshfield, A. W. Moore, and C. C. Tucker,
who attacked it from the S. side and found it difficult. 1st Day. Ascent
to the W. from the posting-station; after 6 hrs., camp was pitched for the
night on the S. side of the Or-tzferi Glacier (see above), at a height of
ca 10,820 ft. 2nd Day. To the foot of the ice-wall between the two peaks

in 5¾ hrs.; after a climb of 4 hrs. more the saddle was reached, and in 1¼ hr. more the E. peak. — In 1891, owing to the good condition of the snow, G. Merzbacher ascended the Kazbek on the N. side, from the mineral springs in the *Genaldon Valley*, in 12 hrs., descending in 5 hrs.

Beyond the station of Kazbek the road crosses the *Terek* by an iron bridge, passes two basalt caves 1¼ M. farther on (above, to the left), and then proceeds in windings along the margin of a wide bulge made by the Terek Valley, first ascending slightly and then falling rather rapidly. The road is hewn in the rocks, the vertical and sometimes even overhanging walls of which attain a height of more than 300 ft.; on the right yawns the deep abyss. — Near the old village of (7 V.) *Gveléti* are a bridge over the Terek and a guard-house (4625 ft.).

Saddle-horses (2½ rb., with guide; porter 1-1½ rb.) or an arbá (p. 415; 8 rb.) may be obtained at the guard-house for an excursion to the *Dyevdoruk Hut* (Девдоракская хижина; 7710 ft.; accommodation for travellers, 12 beds), situated 2 hrs. (8 V. or 5¾ M.) to the W.; for the ascent of the Kazbek from this point, see p. 477.

On the farther side of the bridge begins the **Daryál Gorge* (Дарьяльское ущелье) or 'Gate of the Alani', the *Portae Caspiae (Porta Caucasica)* of the ancients, which is about 5 M. long and at its narrowest for ca. ⅔ M. beyond the bridge. Its rocky walls tower perpendicularly above the floor of the valley to a height of 5900 ft., and there is barely room for the road alongside of the river, which here penetrates a secondary chain of the main mountain-range, the average height of which (14,430 ft.) is still 3280 ft. above the snow-line. A little farther on we obtain to the left a **View of the Dyevdorák Glacier and the Kazbek. A small fort guards the end of the gorge, and on a rocky pinnacle opposite to it on the left are the ruins of the *Castle of Tamára*, which has no connection with the famous queen of Georgia (p. 443) beyond a similarity of name.

Between Kazbek and Lars, in the height of summer, the traveller will often meet Khevsûrs (p. 441) in their striking costume, consisting of gaily coloured and ornamented cloaks, with embroidered crosses fastened on the breast and shoulder. They offer for sale embroidered tobacco-pouches, gloves, satzeruli (knuckle-dusters), sabres, and (occasionally) shields.

171 V. (14½ V.) *Lárs* (3610 ft.). Just before reaching this place we cross a bridge leading to the left bank of the Terek. Beyond the posting-station, which is hemmed in by lofty walls of rock, the huge *Yermólov Stone* (Ермоловскій камень), 95 ft. long, 50 ft. wide, and 42 ft. high, rises from the river.

About 2 M. beyond the posting-station of Lars the road touches at the village of the same name, and soon after it enters the *Dzherákhovskoye Gorge*. Numerous watch-towers appear on projecting rocks. The gorge gradually widens. About halfway to Balta the *Dzherákhovski Fort* is seen on the right, and the village of *Tchmi* on the left, the latter containing three prehistoric burial-grounds and vaults (säppäds).

FROM TCHMI TO UNAL, bridle-path (provisions necessary). We proceed to the W. to (10 hrs.) *Dargavsk*, with an old necropolis and a view of the glaciers to the S. [About 6 M. to the N., at the hamlet of *Koban*, is another necropolis.] Continuing towards the W. for 3-4 hrs. more, we reach *Dallakau*, 2 M. to the N. of which is *Dzivgis*, with an old Ossetian sanctuary. From Dallakau we reach *Unal* (see below) in 5-6 hrs., viâ *Khidikus* and the pass of *Dzhimi-Avtzag* (fine view).

188 V. (17 V.) *Balta* (2690 ft.).

The road gradually descends along the left bank of the Terek, between low wooded hills. The mountains recede, especially on the right. At the former fort of (5 V.) *Redánt* we obtain our first view of the plain and town of —

200 V. (12 V.) *Vladikavkáz* (2345 ft.; p. 454).

69. From Vladikavkaz to Kutaïs viâ the Mamison Pass.

(*Ossetian Military Road;* Военно-Оссетйнская Дорóга.)

283 V. (188 M.). The trip takes 5 days by carriage. This road is more attractive than the Georgian Military Road so far as scenery is concerned, but the surface is in a very bad state of repair. The journey from Vladikavkaz to Kutaïs is more interesting than in the reverse direction; trustworthy attendants and horses can also be found at Alagir more easily and cheaply than at Oni or Kutaïs. The best travelling-season is July and August (O. S.). It is desirable to have introductions to the engineers of the road at Vladikavkaz (for the N. part) and Kutaïs (for the S. part).

We may go by railway from Vladikavkaz to (42 V.) Darg-Kokh (p. 454) and thence take a lineika (5-6 rb.) viâ (11 V.) Ardonskaya to (27 V.; 16 V. from Ardonskaya) Alagir. Or we may go from Vladikavkaz to (52 V.) Alagir direct by carriage (10 rb.); but in this case the traveller should stipulate for the route viâ Arkhonskaya and Ardonskaya in order to avoid the somewhat dangerous drive through the Ardón.—From Alagir to Oni (4 days) we proceed either on horseback (3 rb. daily), or in a linéika (20-25 rb. daily) or a 'drogá', an open, springless vehicle of a very primitive character. The traveller must take his own provisions with him, which are best bought in Vladikavkaz; an arbá should be hired to carry the luggage (p. 445; 3 rb. daily; passengers should take 1-2 rb. from the coachman as a security, but should not themselves give any earnest-money).—From Oni a post-chaise (2 horses; ca. 15 rb.) may be taken to (111 V.) Kutaïs; but lack of horses at the posting-stations often causes wearisome delay. There is also an omnibus in 18 hrs. (fare 4¹/₂ rb.).— A phaeton from Kutaïs to Vladikavkaz costs 150-175 rb.

Vladikavkáz, see p. 454. The road leads to the N.W. through the steppe, viâ (17 V.) *Arkhónskaya* and (35 V.) *Ardónskaya* (7¹/₂ M. to the S. of Darg-Kokh, p. 454), whence it runs to the S., through the Ardón valley, to (52 V.) *Alagir* (2050 ft.; Bellevue, R. 1¹/₂ rb.; linéika to Svyatói Nikolai 8-10, there & back in 3 days 15 rb.). — The road begins to ascend the valley of the Ardón, along the left bank of that river. Near the little village of (70 V.) *Biz* (2810 ft.; 265 inhab.) rises the *Káriu-Khokh* (11,160 ft.). 76 V. *Unál,* see above. Beyond the *Gulák-Dukhán* (3165 ft.) the valley

turns to the W. We soon reach the (80 V.) confluence of the *Sadón*
3530 ft.) with the Ardón.

On the right, about 3 M. above the junction of the Sadón, in a side-
valley. lie the copper-works of *Sadón* (4160 ft.). From Sadon to *Stuir-
Digor*, see pp. 484, 485.

The valley of the Ardón becomes more and more beautiful. Soon
after crossing the bridge over the Sadón we reach the ancient hamlet
of (84 V.) *Nuzál*, the 'cradle of the Ossetians', possessing a quaint
old church built of unhewn blocks of stone, and interesting fortifications dug out of the solid rock. The road now runs S. along the
right bank of the Ardón, following the E. slope of the *Adái Khokh*
(p. 488), whence the Karagóm glacier (p. 488) descends to the N.W.
and the Tzeya glacier to the E.

89 V. (59 M.) *Svyatói Nikolái* (3745 ft.), the first halting-place
for the night for passengers coming from Alagir. Accommodation
may be found in the shelter-house of the Vladikavkaz Mountain Club
or in the house of the engineer, who will also give information as to
guides to the Tzeya Glacier (2 rb. there & back, including a saddle-
horse; if the night is spent out, 3 rb.).

The **Tzeya Glacier** (Цейскій ледникъ; 6755 ft. high at its lower
end and 6 M. long) lies 18 V. (12 M.) to the W. of Svyatoi Nikolai (on
foot there & back in 2 days). The expedition is well worth making. The
route leads through the wooded *Tzeya Valley*, passing the hamlets of
Nizhni Tzei (5670 ft.) and (4 hrs.) *Verkhni Tzei* (5740 ft.). About 4 M.
from Verkhni Tzei lies *Rekóm*, the sanctuary of the Ossetians, a log-
cabin the exterior walls of which are hung with the antlers and skulls of
deer, wild-goats, and ibexes (no admission to the interior). About 10 min.
beyond Rekom is the Sanatorium Hotel, open from June 1st to Aug. 15th
(O. S.; R. 1-1½ rb.). The foot of the glacier in reached 2 M. farther on. —
The new footpath to Rekom through the Tzeidon Valley is easier and
shorter, but there is no view (to the glacier 12 V.).

Beyond Svyatoi Nikolai the road enters the imposing *Khassará
Gorge* (2¾ M. long, with remains of old fortifications), and just
after passing the hamlet of (99 V.) *Zaramág* or *Saramág* (accommodation in the Nomerá Kryépost; fine view of the Kaltber; to
Gori, see p. 485) turns to the W. into the *Mamisón Gorge*. The gorge
widens considerably as it reaches (107 V.) the hamlet of *Tib* on the
left; retrospect of the peaks of the Tepli Group, p. 488; in front are
the Khalatza and other mountains. The road reaches the (115 V.) barracks (nightquarters) lying at the foot of the pass, and crosses the—

123 V. **Mamisón Pass** (Мамисóнскій перевáлъ; 9265 ft.;
small shelter), the highest pass practicable for carriages in the
Caucasus (Stelvio, 9055 ft.). From a mountain-ridge to the S.,
several hundred feet higher, a magnificent *View is obtained, especially at sunrise, extending to the Shkara (p. 488) and the Ushbá
(p. 486).

The road descends in windings through the valley of the *Tchan-
tchakha*, traversing beautiful woods of silver fir and beech and
passing near an engineer's house. 137 V. *Gurshévi* (6325 ft.), on

the left; 147 V. *Glola* (4630 ft.), on the right (accommodation in the engineer's house).

About 16 V. to the N.W. of Glola, up the Rión valley, is the village of **Gebi** (3385 ft.; accommodation in the kantzelyáriya). For the Edena Pass and the Tzikhvarga, see p. 488. To the S. of Gebi (1-1½ day) rises the *Shoda* (11,840 ft.).

We traverse the valley of the *Rión*. At (160 V.) *Utzéri* (3475 ft.; hotel) is a carbonic ferruginous spring. — We continue along a shadeless route to (172 V.) *Oni* (2515 ft.; hotel), a posting-station on the left bank of the Rión.

The highroad descends along the beautiful valley of the Rión. 193 V. *Tzossi* (posting-station); 215 V. *Tola* (posting-station); 230 V. *Alpani* (posting-station; accommodation at the posting agent's). To Svanetia, see R. 70.

Beyond Alpani the road leads through several picturesque gorges, by which the Rión has found its way through the limestone rocks of the mountains. 247 V. *Mekvéna* (posting-station); 261 V. *Namokhováni* (posting-station). — Through woods and between luxuriant vineyards and orchards we at length reach (283 V.; 188 M.) *Kutaïs* (p. 463).

70. Svanetia.

Alpani, on the Mamison Road, is the starting-point for a visit to **Svanetia** or **Suanetia**, the name applied to the upper valleys of the Ingúr, bounded on the N. by the Central Caucasus, and on the S. by the *Láila Range* (13,150 ft.) and its spurs. The N.E. part, with the communities of Ushkúl, Kal, Adísh, and Muzhál, is the so-called *Free Svanetia;* the N.W. part, with the communities of Latal, Betcho, etc., takes its name from the princely family of *Dadesh-Keliani*, which has its seat here. — The extensive forests of deciduous trees and the meadows and fields of Svanetia form a pleasing contrast to the rocky and snowy walls of the Central Caucasus towering to the N. The villages still retain their numerous watch-towers (40-80 ft. high), generally whitewashed, and there are many small churches.

August is the best travelling-season. Accommodation may be had at the kantzelyáriyas (p. 446) or in the school-houses. Provisions should be taken for the whole journey. — Map, see p. 485.

FROM ALPANI TO KAL, 85 V. (57 M.), a ride of 3 days, with the nights at Tzagéri and Tcholúr. — *Alpani*, see above. — The road leads to the N. through the picturesque *Ladzhanuri Gorge*, crosses the low watershed between the *Rión* and the *Tzkhenis-Tzkali*, and descends, passing *Orbéli*, a prettily situated place with an old castle, to (19 V.) *Tzagéri* (accommodation at the dukhán), the seat of a district-chief (Уѣздный начáльникъ). This is a good place to hire horses. — We then proceed through magnificent woods, along a bridle-path on the right bank of the Tzkhenis-Tzkali, viâ (27 V. from Tzagéri) *Lentékhi* (2410 ft.) to (19 V. from Lentekhi) *Tcholúr* (3320 ft.).

FROM LENTEKHI TO LATAL. We proceed to the W. to (2¹/₂ hrs.) *Kheldde* and thence to the N. to (8-9 hrs.) *Skimeri.* In 4-5 hrs. more we reach the *Ldila Pass* (ca. 10,800 ft.), with ,its glaciers, whence a view may be had of the Elbruz and the Dongúz-Orun. We next descend in 2¹/₂ hrs. to a saddle some 1640 ft. lower, with a fine view by morning light of Svanetia and the crests of the high mountains. In 2 hrs. more we reach *Tzkhomdri,* and 4-5 hrs. more bring us to *Latál* (see below).

From Tcholur we make a steep zigzagging ascent through beech-woods (6¹/₂ hrs., not including halts) to the **Latpári Pass** (9285 ft. · passable from July till the beginning of Oct.).

The *View (mostly clear at sunrise only) from the top of the pass (or still better from a point situated to the E., some 300 ft. higher) embraces, on the N., the S. side of the central range (with its towering peaks and glaciers), the serrated walls of the Shkara (p. 488) and of the Dzhanga-Tau (p. 488), the bold pyramids of the Gestóla (p. 488) and the Tetnúld (p. 488); on the W., the green mountain-chains of Free Svanetia; on the N.W., the double peaks of the Ushbá (p. 486) and the huge mass of the Dongúz-Orun (p. 486).

From the N. side of the pass we descend in windings to the village of *Kal* (5735 ft.; accommodation in the kantzelyáriya or in the dukhán).

To the N. of Kal is the village of *Iprari,* the watch-towers of which were destroyed by the Russians in 1876. The path from Kal viâ Muzhál, Mestia, and Betcho to *Zugdidi* (p. 450; 4-5 hrs.) is practicable for horses as far as Betcho, but beyond that for walkers only.

To the E. of Kal, up the valley of the Ingúr (2 hrs. riding), lies the community of *Ushkúl* (6760 ft.; accommodation at the school-house), consisting of three villages, with 50 watch-towers, two old castles, and a church containing many interesting antiquities.

From Ushkul the lower end of the *Shkara Glacier* (7835 ft.) can be reached on foot in 3 hrs.—A day's excursion to the *Tzena Valley is well worth making.

FROM KAL TO LATAL, a ride of two days by a bridle-road through the valley of the Ingúr.—*Kal,* see above. The route leads to the N.W. as far as the village of *Ipar* (accommodation in the kantzelyáriya).

From Ipar a bridle-path leads to the E. through the valley of the *Adísh-Tchala* to (3 hrs.' ride) the village of *Adísh* (6690 ft.); about ¹/₄ hr. higher up are an interesting church and the grand *Adísh Glacier* (lower end 7450 ft.). *Tetnúld,* see p. 488.

From Ipar we may also proceed to the N. over the *Uguir Pass* (6300 ft.) to (2 hrs.' ride) the village of *Mulákh* (5500 ft.); a little to the E. of this lies *Muzhál* (accommodation at the priest's house; Tyuber Pass, see p. 487).

Beyond Ipar the landscape grows hilly; to the S. is a fine view of the Láila (p. 483).—*Latál* (4310 ft.), a community consisting of several villages, is the lowest inhabited spot in Free Svanetia. To Lentekhi, see p. 481.

About 3 M. to the N. of Latal lies the village of **Betcho** (accommodation at the kantzelyáriya), the seat of a pristav (police-official), whence a view of the Ushbá (p. 486) is obtained to the N. Horses and porters are not always to be had. To Urusbievo, see p. 486.

Etzéri, to the S.W. of Betcho (a ride of 2½ hrs.), is the seat of Prince Dadesh-Keliani. To the S. is the *Láila;* its N. peak (13,045 ft.) was ascended in 1889 by D. W. Freshfield and C. H. Powell, the middle peak (13,155 ft.) was scaled in the same year by V. Sella, and the S. péak (13,105 ft.), in 1891, by G. Merzbacher and L. Purtscheller. To the N.W. of Etzeri lies *Tchubikhevi* (p. 486).

From Latal a road leads to the N.E. up the valley of the *Mulkhra,* passing *Lenzher,* with frescoes on the exterior of its church, to *Méstiya* (4490 ft.; accommodation in the kantzelyáriya), a village with about 70 watch-towers. This is a walk of 3 hrs. Farther to the E. lies Mulakh (p. 482). From Mestiya to Urusbievo, see p. 486.

71. The Central Caucasus from the Elbruz to the Kazbek.

Mountain-climbers will find a detailed description of the higher peaks in the books by *Freshfeld, Merzbacher, De Déchy,* and *Afanasieff* mentioned at pp. 446, 447. — For equipment, maps, etc., comp. pp. 444, 445, 447.

a. Approaches from the North and from the South.

FROM PYATIGORSK TO URUSBIEVO, 130 V. (86 M.), a trip of 2 days (carr., 3½ rb., to a point 10 V. beyond Atazhukino, and thence on horseback). — *Pyatigórsk,* see p. 459. The road leads to the S.E. viâ *Goryatchevódskaya* and crosses the (32 V.) *Malka,* near *Asháboro,* a village with 3600 inhab. (Kabards). At (52 V.) *Baksánskoye,* where we are joined by a route from Naltchik (see p. 484), our road enters the valley of the *Baksán,* which it ascends towards the S.W. — 78 V. *Atazhúkino* (Atazhutan; accommodation at the chief's house). — About 10 V. higher up (accommodation in the dukhán at the bridge) begins the bridle-path which leads along the Baksán and passes *Ozrokovo* (p. 484). — 130 V. (87 M.) **Urusbíevo** (4940 ft.; accommodation in the dukhán of Prince Urusbíev; saddle-horse for 3 days 5 rb.), a village where good 'burkas' (p. 442) are made. The double-peaked mountain seen at the S. end of the *Aduir-Su Valley* is the Ullu-Tau-Tchana (p. 487).

The *Suiltrán-Kol-Bashi* (12,490 ft.), to the W. of Urusbievo, may be ascended in 6½ hrs. and affords a good view of the Elbruz. Urusbievo is also the best headquarters from which to ascend the *Elbruz* (p. 485). Passes over the Central Caucasus, see p. 486; to Tchegem, p. 484.

FROM KOTLYAREVSKAYA TO NALTCHIK, 47 V. (31 M.), carriage in 5-6 hrs. (fare 6-9 rb.; also railway, opened at the end of 1913). — The highroad leads from *Kotlyarévskaya* (p. 453) to the S.W. through the steppe. — 23½ V. *Dontórskaya,* a posting-station. — 47 V. **Naltchik** (Нальчикъ; 1605 ft.; accommodation at the Club), a small town with 5500 inhab., mostly Russians, and the seat of a district chief (Уѣздный начáльникъ), is situated on the river of the same name. Monday is the market-day here. About 2 M. to the S.W. of Naltchik is the Naltchik Sanatorium for Consumptives; 2 M. to the N.W. is the German colony of *Alexandersdorf.*

FROM NALTCHIK TO URUSBIEVO, 100 V. (66 M.), carriage to a point 10 V. beyond Atazhúkino, thence on horseback, in $1^1/_2$-2 days.— The route leads from *Naltchik* (p. 483) through the partly cultivated steppe of the *Great Kabardá* to (25 V.) *Baksanskoye.* Thence, see p. 483.

FROM NALTCHIK TO TCHEGEM, 60 V. (40 M.), a ride of $1^1/_2$ day. — The route runs N. from *Naltchik* (p. 483), and at (12 V.) *Tchegémski* crosses the Tchegém and ascends to the S.W. along its valley to the village of *Tchegém* (4830 ft.; accommodation at the kantzelyáriya), with 750 Tartar inhabitants.

From Tchegem to the N. viâ *Ozrokovo* (P. 483) to *Urusbievo* (p. 483), a ride of 2 days.—From Tchegem to *Bezingi* (see below), a ride of 4 hrs. —Tyuber Pass, see p. 487.

FROM NALTCHIK TO BEZINGI, 50 V. (33 M.), a ride of 2 days.— The bridle-path from *Naltchik* (p. 483) runs to the S.W. along the left bank of the river of the same name for 8 M., then crosses to the right bank, traverses farther on a thickly wooded country, and descends into the valley of the *Kara-Su-Tchakho.* It finally enters the valley of the *Tcherék (Urvan),* through which it proceeds along the left bank of the river.—50 V. *Bezingi-Túbenel* (4780 ft.; accommodation at the chief's or in the shop at the upper end of the village), a village with 780 Tartar inhabitants.

Bezingi is the headquarters for the ascent of the Gestóla (p. 488), the Shkara (p. 488), the Duikh-Tau (p. 488), the Dzhanga-Tau (p. 488), and other peaks.

On the E. side of the Bezingi Glacier, 8 hrs. above Bezingi, is the so-called **Misses-Kosh** (8365 ft.), a green Alpine plateau, the starting-point for several mountain-ascents (Zaluinán-Bashi, p. 487; Adísh, p. 488; Dzhanga-Tau, p. 488). It is better, however, to select a higher point as the last sleeping-place before the climb.

FROM BEZINGI TO BALKAR, a ride of one day. We either proceed across the *Dumalá Pass* or across the *Bezingi Pass* (10,085 ft.), which is higher and commands more extensive views. The two routes finally unite in the Tchainashki Valley.

FROM NALTCHIK TO BALKAR, 50 V. (33 M.), a ride of $1^1/_2$ day. —The bridle-path proceeds to the S. from *Naltchik* (p. 483) over low hills, descends to the *Tcherék,* and ascends through its valley. Beyond the wild *Tcherék Gorge* the path runs along the left bank. — 50 V. *Kunnyúm* (3800 ft.; accommodation at the chief's), the highest of the Balkar villages, with 750 Tartar inhabitants.

From Kunnyum an ascent of 5 hrs. on horseback brings us to the so-called **Karaúl** (5230 ft.), an Alpine pasture 1 M. long, surrounded by precipitous mountains. In summer the stone huts near the bridge over the *Duikh-Su* are inhabited by shepherds. Passes, see p. 488.

FROM SADON TO STUIR-DIGOR, 45 V. (30 M.), a ride of $1^1/_2$ day. For the copper-works of *Sadón,* see p. 480. — The bridle-path mounts through the *Sadón Valley* to the grassy ridge at the head of the pass, then descends to the W. to the Ossetian village of *Kamuntá* (560 inhab.), in the *Songúta Valley* or the valley of the *Aigamugi-Don.* [To the S. is the *Skatikom Glacier* (lower end

6930 ft.), descending from the Adái-Khokh.] From Kamunta we may
either descend to the N.W. through the valley of the Songúta until
its junction with the *Urukh*, and then ascend through the valley of
the latter river to Stuir-Digor; or we may proceed to the S.W., over
two grass-grown passes, to *Dzinágo*, with its low pyramidal stone
tombs, and thence to (4¹/₂ M.) Stuir-Digor.—**Stuir-Digor** (5015 ft.;
accommodation at the kantzelyáriya), an Ossetian village with 800
inhab., lies in a broad valley, the W. wall of which is formed by the
Labóda group (p. 488). Thence to the foot of the Tana Glacier
(p. 488) in 5 hrs., to the foot of the Karagóm Glacier (p. 488) in
4 hrs. To the Karaúl, see p. 488.

Approaches from the South. FROM GORI TO ZARAMAG, 120 V.
(80 M.), a ride of 3 days. The road leads to the N. from *Gori* (p. 465),
ascending along the *Lyakhva* viâ *Tzkhinvali* to *Patza*. It then proceeds
to the E., ascending through the valley of the Bolshaya Lyakhva, viâ
Dzhomat (*Jomat;* 5575 ft.), to the top of the *Bakh-Fandak Pass* (8815 ft.),
and then descends to the N. through the *Sakki Valley* to *Zaramág*, on the
Mamisón Road (p. 480).

FROM KUTAÏS TO GEBI, 140 V. (93 M.), 2 days (carriage as far as
Glola). Details, see p. 481.

FROM KUTAÏS TO KAL, 135 V. (90 M.), 3 days. The route leads viâ
(52 V.) *Alpani* and the *Latpari Pass*, comp. pp. 481, 482.

b. Main Range of the Caucasus.

The W. buttress of the Central Caucasus is formed by the
*Elbrúz (*Minghi-Tau* or 'White Mountain'), the highest peak
in the Caucasus, a volcanic mass with two snowy and ice-clad
summits (W. peak 18,470 ft., E. peak 18,345 ft.; Mt. Blanc 15,780 ft.),
connected by a saddle (17,285 ft.). The S.E. side of the mountain,
where the *Baksán* takes its rise, and the N. side are covered by
snowfields. The W. side, with the source of the *Kubán*, is the
steepest. On the N. side of the Elbruz is the *Ullu-Tchiran Glacier*
(lower end 9580 ft.), on the W. side is the *Ullu-Kam Glacier* (lower
end 9730 ft.), on the S. side the *Azáu Glacier* (lower end 7650 ft.;
two refuge-huts, no rfmts.) and the *Terskól Glacier* (lower end
8610 ft.), on the E. side the *Irik Glacier* (lower end 8335 ft.;
8¹/₂ sq. M. in area; 6¹/₂ M. long).

The best starting-point for an ascent of the Elbruz is *Urusbievo*
(p. 483), whence it takes 2 days to reach a mountain-ridge to the W. of
the *Terskól River*, where the night is spent at a height of 11,000 ft. In
1868 the E. summit was ascended from this ridge in 8¹/₄ hrs. by Douglas
W. Freshfield, A. W. Moore, and C. C. Tucker, with a Swiss guide and
two hunters from Urusbievo (descent in 4 hrs.); while the W. summit
was conquered in 1874 by F. C. Grove, H. Walker, and F. Gardiner, who
took 7 hrs. to reach a point near the saddle, and 2³/₄ hrs. thence to the
summit (descent in 4 hrs.). In 1889 H. Woolley took 3 days to make the
ascent of the W. summit, going to the N. of Urusbievo through the *Kuir-
tuik-Su Valley* to the N. side of the saddle, and thence in 1³/₄ hr. to the
top.—The magnificent view from the Elbruz comprises on the E. the central range as far as the Kazbek, the characteristic feature of this being the

deep valleys by which the precipitous peaks are separated from each other; farther off are the Pontic and the Abkhasian ridges. On the S. the view takes in the Ushbá (see below), the mountains of Svanetia, and Mt. Ararat. On the W. the Black Sea is seen in the distance. On the N. are the steppes.

Passes from the upper Baksán Valley.

From the W. end of the Baksan Valley the *Tchiper (Jiper) Pass*, a pass with two openings (10,805 and 10,720 ft. respectively), leads to the W. into the *Ulu-Kam (Kubán) Valley;* by following a bridle-path down the valley we reach *Utchkulán* (4660 ft.), from which place there is a track to Batalpashinsk (p. 453).

From Terskol-Kosh to Tchubikhevi (p. 483). The *Tchiper (Jiper)-Azau Pass* (10,720 ft.), which was crossed by M. de Déchy in 1885, is practicable for walkers only. By this route (2-2¹/₂ days), we cross the pass into the *Nenskra Valley* and proceed thence to the E., over the *Bassa Pass* (9955 ft.; not difficult), into the *Nakra Valley.* — Or we may choose the (1¹/₂ day) *Donguz-Órun Pass* (10,495 ft.), the easiest and lowest of the Baksán passes.

From Urusbievo (p. 483) to Betcho (p. 482). One route (17 hrs. on foot) leads across the *Betcho Pass* (11,075 ft.). We ascend the Baksán Valley in 4 hrs., then turn to the S. into the *Ozengi Valley* and reach (in 5 hrs. more) the head of the pass. In descending we cross the outflow of the W. *Ushbá Glacier*, which is a difficult task in the afternoon. An alternative route (1¹/₂-2 days on foot) is the *Akh-Su Pass* (12,465 ft.). A conical snow-clad hill to the W. of the pass commands a fine view of the Elbruz.

From Urusbievo (p. 483) to Mestiya (p. 483) over the *Adwir-Su* or *Mestiya Pass* in 2 days, a route offering no trouble to experts.

To the S. of the Elbruz rises the *Donguz-Órun*. Its middle summit (14,605 ft.) was ascended in 9 hrs. in 1891 by G. Merzbacher and L. Purtscheller, starting from a sleeping-camp (8365 ft.) on the E. slopes of the Donguz-Órun Valley. — To the S.W. of the Donguz-Órun rises the pyramid of the *Shtavler* (13,105 ft.), which was climbed in 6 hrs. in 1903 by Frl. C. von Ficker, H. von Ficker, W. R. Rickmers, F. Scheck, and J. H. Wigner from a camp in a W. side-valley of the Nakra.

In 1903 the following ascents were made from a camp at the end of the *Krish Glacier* (ca. 7220 ft.): to the N., the Donguz-Órun (see above) in 9 hrs. by R. Helbling, F. Reichert, and A. Weber; to the N.W., the *Ledösht-Tau* (12,550 ft.) and the *Hevai* (13,060 ft.), both in 8 hrs., by O. Schuster and J. H. Wigner; to the W., the *Lakra-Tau* (12,190 ft.) in 7 hrs., by L. W. Rolleston and T. G. Longstaff.

Farther to the E. are the two peaks of the **Ushbá**. On the W. side is the *Ushbá Glacier* (lower end 7200 ft.), on the S. side the *Gul Glacier* (lower end 9000 ft.).

The N.E. summit of the Ushbá (15,400 ft.; S.W. peak 13 ft. higher) was ascended by J. G. Cockin in 1888. His route, starting from a camp at the foot of the Gul Glacier (see above), led over steep glaciers and slopes covered with snow and ice to the (10¹/₄ hrs.) saddle between the two summits; thence in 2³/₄ hrs. to the N.E. peak. This is an extremely difficult ascent, and great caution is necessary on account of falling stones. — The ascent of the S.W. summit of the Ushbá, which is also extremely difficult, was accomplished in 1903 in one day by R. Helbling, F. Reichert, A. Schulze, O. Schuster, and A. Weber. — The first successful attempt to combine the two summits in one circular tour was made in Aug., 1903, by L. Distel, G. Leuchs, and H. Pfann. This was an extremely difficult ice and rock tour, and necessitated the spending of 4 nights in the open air, two of these at a height of 14,750 ft. 1st Day: from the camp (ca. 9850 ft.) on the Ushbá Glacier (p. 486) viâ the N. arête to (17 hrs.) a point 14,750 ft. above the sea. 2nd Day: to (2¹/₄ hrs.) the N.E. summit, thence down to (1 hr.) the saddle and across (6 hrs.) its icy knife-edge. 3rd Day: up the N. side to (4¹/₂ hrs.) the S.W. summit and then down to (7¹/₂ hrs.) a camp at a height of ca. 12,800 ft. 4th Day: to (4 hrs.) the Gul Glacier (p. 486).

To the N. of the Ushbá rises the *Shekildi-Tau* (14,175 ft.), ascended in 1903 in one day by R. Helbling, F. Reichert, A. Schulze, and A. Weber, from the tongue of the Ushbá Glacier (p. 486) viâ the S. arête (very difficult). — To the N. is the *Shekildi Glacier* (lower end 7245 ft.; over 10¹/₂ sq. M. in area; 5¹/₂ M. long); to the N.E. is the *Bshedükh* (14,015 ft.), ascended in 1903 by L. Distel, G. Leuchs, and H. Pfann from a camp on the tongue of the Shekildi Glacier (see above) in 14 hrs. (very difficult).

Farther to the E. is the snowy summit of the *Ullukára* (14,115 ft.). To the N. are the *Bashkára* (13,515 ft.) and the *Dzhantugán* (*Jantugán;* 12,790 ft.). — At the S. end of the Aduir-Sü Valley (p. 481) rises the *Latzga* (13,120 ft.), with the *Tcheget-Tau-Tchana* (13,480 ft.) and the *Gumitchi* (12,485 ft.) to the W. of it, and the *Ullu-Tau-Tchana* (13,795 ft.) to the E. The last was ascended in 1903 from the W. side by L. W. Rolleston and T. G. Longstaff, starting from a camp at the foot of the *Margan-Tau* (S.). The lower end of the *Aduir-Sü Glacier* lies at a height of 8165 ft. above the sea. To the S.W. of the Latzga is the *Lekzuir Glacier* (lower end 5690 ft.; 14¹/₂ sq. M. in area; 8 M. long).

Between Urusbievo (p. 483) and Tchegem (p. 484) the following peaks stand in advance of the N. side of the main range: *Aduir-Su-Bashi* (14,280 ft.), ascended in 1896 by H. W. Holder, J. G. Cockin, and H. Woolley in 2 days from the Aduir-Su Valley (caution necessary on account of falling stones); *Dzhailüik (Jailýk) Bashi* (14,870 ft.), the highest of this series of peaks; and the two peaks of the *Sullu-Kol-Bashi*, of which that to the N., 13,970 ft. in height, was ascended by G. Merzbacher and L. Purtscheller in 1891.

The double-peaked *Tikhtengen* (15,265 ft.) was ascended in 1903 by L. W. Rolleston and T. G. Longstaff from the Tzanner Glacier (see below) in 10 hrs. (difficult). To the S.W. is the *Tyuber (Tuiber) Glacier* (lower end 6665 ft.; 21 sq. M.; 6¹/₂ M. long), and to the S. is the *Tzanner (Zanner) Glacier* (lower end 6840 ft.; 15 sq. M.; 7¹/₂ M. long).

From Bezingi and from Tchegem the *Tyuber Pass* (11,730 ft.) leads to *Muzhál* (p. 482).

To the W. of the *Bezingi* or *Ullu Glacier* (lower end 6540 ft.; 17 sq. M.; 8 M. long) lies the snowy summit of the *Zaluinán-Bashí* (14,265 ft.), which was ascended in 1888 by J. G. Cockin and H. W. Holder from the Misses-Kosh (p. 484) in 6¹/₂ hrs. (caution necessary against falling stones).

From the Misses-Kosh to the head of the *Zaluinán (Salynan) Pass* (ca. 13,580 ft.) and back in a trip of 9 hrs.

Farther to the E. is the middle part of the Central Caucasus, consisting of the *Gestóla, Tetnúld, Adish, Dzhanga-Tau, Shkara, Duikh-Tau, Koshtán-Tau,* and other peaks.

The **Gestóla** (15,930 ft.) was ascended in 1886 by C. T. Dent and W. F. Donkin from the S. end of the Bezingi Glacier in 10¹/₄ hrs.—The **Tetnúld** (15,920 ft.) was ascended by D. W. Freshfield in 1887. Starting from his camp (8990 ft.) on the right side of the *Nágeb Glacier* (above *Muzhál*, p. 482), he reached the S. arête in 8¹/₄ hrs., and the summit in 4¹/₄ hrs. more (descent in 5 hrs.).   G. Merzbacher and L. Purtscheller ascended the Tetnúld in 1891 in 6³/₄ hrs., starting from a camp (11,645 ft.) above *Adish* (p. 482; descent in 3¹/₂ hrs.).—The **Adísh** or *Katyún-Tau* (16,295 ft.) was ascended in 1888 by H. W. Holder and H. Woolley from the Misses-Kosh (p. 484) in 12 hrs. (descent in 7¹/₄ hrs.).—The **Dzhánga-Tau** *(Janga-Tau)* has two peaks (W. peak 16,570 ft.; E. peak 16,530 ft.). The E. summit was ascended in 1888 by J. G. Cockin from the Misses-Kosh (p. 484) in 12 hrs., and in the same time in 1891 viâ the N.E. arête by Merzbacher and Purtscheller (descent in 7¹/₄ hrs.). Both summits were ascended in 1903 from the Khalde Valley (7875 ft.) by R. Helbling, F. Reichert, A. Schulze, and A. Weber, who took 3 days for the entire excursion (very difficult).—The **Shkara** (17,040 ft.) was ascended in 1888 by J. G. Cockin from a camp at the foot of the rocky arête descending from the Mishirgi-Tau to the Bezingi Glacier. The mountain-ridge was reached in 5¹/₂ hrs., and after a rest of ³/₄ hr. the summit was attained in 4¹/₂ hrs. more (descent in 6 hrs.).—The **Duikh-Tau** *(Dykh-Tau;* 17,055 ft.), formerly known as the Koshtán-Tau, was ascended in 1888 by Mummery in 8¹/₂ hrs., starting from a camp on the upper Bezingi Glacier on the S. side (descent in 4³/₄ hrs.).—The **Koshtán-Tau** (16,880 ft.), formerly called the Duikh-Tau, was ascended in 1888 from the Karaúl (p. 484) by H. Woolley, who took 3 days for the ascent and descent. W. F. Donkin and H. Fox lost their lives in an unsuccessful attempt earlier in the same year.

PASSES. From the KARAÚL (p. 484) the *Shari-Vtzik Pass* (11,565 ft.; 1¹/₂ day on foot, 2 days with pack-animals) and the *Edena Pass* or *Godi-Vtzik Pass* (11,475 ft.) lead to *Gebi* (p. 481), the *Fuitnargi Pass* (11,100 ft.) into the *Tzena Valley* (p. 482; 2 days), and the *Shtulu-Vtzik Pass* (10,985 ft.; practicable for horses in midsummer only) in 1¹/₂ day to *Stuir-Digor* (p. 485).

To the E. of the Edena Pass (see above) is the *Geze-Tau* (12,755 ft.). — The *Laboda* (14,175 ft.), forming, with three adjoining peaks, the Wetterhörner of the Caucasus, was ascended in 1895 by C. T. Dent and H. Woolley from the Stuir-Digor Valley above the *Tana Glacier* (lower end 7045 ft.).

Farther to the S.E. is the double-peaked *Tzikhvarga* (13,580 ft.). The E. summit was ascended in 1890 from the Karagóm Valley by V. Sella, the W. summit from Gebi (p. 481) by H.'W. Holder and J. G. Cockin. The passage from the W. to the E. summit takes ³/₄ hr.

The *Burdzhula* or *Karagóm-Khokh* (14,295 ft.) was ascended in 1890 in 9 hrs. by H. W. Holder and J. G. Cockin, starting from a camp near the *Natzantzára Brook*, above the Rión.

The massive **Adái-Khokh** (15,245 ft.) was ascended in 1884 by M. de Déchy in 8 hrs., starting from a camp on the Tzéya Glacier (10,825 ft.).

On the N.W. side of the Adái Khokh is the *Karagóm Glacier* (lower end 5790 ft.; 13¹/₂ sq. M.; 9¹/₂ M. long).—*Tzeya Glacier*, see p. 480.—The *Kaltber* (14,465 ft.) was ascended in 5 hrs. by Dr. W. Fischer and O. Schuster, starting from a camp (10,990 ft.) above Rekom (p. 480).

A peak adjoining the *Tepli* (14,510 ft.), between the Adái-Khokh and the Kazbék group, was ascended in 1896 in 7 hrs. by V. Sella from a camp (9840 ft.) above *Kolota*.—The *Zuatizi (Suatisi)-Khokh* (14,695 ft.) was ascended in 1910 in 7¹/₂ hrs. by Dr. W. Fischer, G. Kuhfahl, and O. Schuster, starting from the *Khitzan-Khokh*, a rock in the middle of the Midagravin

Glacier (ca. 11,150 ft.). — The *Gimarai-Khokh* (15,670 ft.), to the W. of the Kazbek, was ascended in 1891 by G. Merzbacher from the huts at the mineral springs (7650 ft.) at the upper end of the *Genaldon Valley.* The ascent took 9½ hrs., and the descent 4¾ hrs. — The *Shau-Khokh (Mitchin-Tzup;* ca. 14,760 ft.) was ascended in 1911 in 5½ hrs. by Dr. W. Fischer, E. Platz, and O. Schuster from a bivouac (11,810 ft.) on the Midagravin Glacier.

Kazbék, see p. 477.

72. Kakhetia. Daghestan.

Several highroads lead from Tiflis to Kakhetia, a district composed of the valleys of the *Yora* and the *Alazán.* Railway from Tiflis to *Signakh* and *Telav* under construction.

From Tiflis to Telav, 95 V. (63 M.), highroad, motor omnibus in 6 hrs. (5 rb.). — *Tiflis,* see p. 465. — The road leads to the E., at first through a monotonous hilly country. 10 V. *Orkhévi.* 24 V. *Vaziáni.*

About 8 V. (5 M.) to the E. of Vaziani is *Marienfeld* (2885 ft.), a German colony. From here a highroad leads to the E. through the valley of the Kakhetian *Yora,* 66 M. long and 5-20 M. wide, viâ (35 V.) *Kakabéti,* a Georgian village on the left bank of the Yora, to (74 V., or 49 M.) Signakh (see below). The valley of the Alazán is the chief wine-growing district of Kakhetia, the whole country producing yearly 6,600,000 gallons of wine, chiefly red.

Beyond Vaziani the road runs to the N., through pretty country, crossing the watershed between the Yora and the Alazán at a height of 5545 ft., and passing the posting-stations of (41 V.) *Udzharma,* (61 V.) *Gambori,* and (77 V.) *Tetris-Tzkale.*

95 V. **Teláv** (2420 ft.; *Seméinuiye Nomerá*), an old town of 17,700 inhab., is beautifully situated on the right bank of the Alazán in the midst of a fertile country, and is the seat of a district chief (Уѣздный начальникъ). It has some remains of fortifications.

About 5 M. to the E. of Telav (phaeton there & back 3-4 rb.) lies the imperial domain of *Tzinondáli,* where the best wine in Kakhetia is produced. — The church of *Alaverdi* (Алавéрдскій соборъ), situated 8 M. to the N.W. of Telav (phaeton there & back 5-6 rb.) and dating from the 10th cent., is visited on Sept. 14th. (O. S.) by hordes of pilgrims. On this occasion the traveller will have an opportunity of studying the types of the mountain-tribes of Khevsurs, Tushes, Kists, etc. — An interesting excursion of 4-5 days may be made from Telav on horseback, viâ *Gremi* and across the *Kodór Pass* (7850 ft.), to *Temir-Khan-Shurá* (p. 455). Gremi, once the residence of the Kakhetian kings, is now an insignificant village. — A highroad leads to the N.W. from Telav, viâ (25 V.) *Akhméti* and (55 V.) *Tionéti,* to (82 V.) Ananur (p. 475). — A rough road, practicable only on foot or on horseback with a trustworthy guide, runs from Telav along the left bank of the Alazán, viâ (51 V.) *Kvareli, Satzkhenisi,* and the *Aldiakho Pass,* to (6-7 days) the Avarian town of *Koi-Su.*

From Telav to Nukha, 211 V. (140 M.), highroad (motor omnibus from Tiflis to Lagodekhi viâ Bakurtzikhe, 165 V. in 8 hrs., fare 9 rb.). — *Telav,* see above; 16 V. *Akuri;* 30 V. *Mukuzán* (1720 ft.); 47 V. *Bakurtzikhe.*

62 V. **Signákh** (2590 ft.; *Kakhétiya*), a district-town with 16,000 inhab., picturesquely situated on a lofty projecting rock,

possesses the ruins of a fortress. In a nunnery is the Sepulchral
Church of St. Nina, said to date from the 4th, but as a matter of
fact probably from the 6th century. St. George's Chapel commands
a fine view. Signakh is reached by carriage from Telav in 6-7 hrs.,
but may also be reached from Tiflis direct (103 V. or 68 M.) by
motor omnibus in 6 hrs. (6 rb.). Highroad to Marienfeld, see p. 489.

Beyond Signakh the highroad runs first to the E. At (70 V.)
Tznoris-Tzkali it turns to the N., crosses the *Alazán*, and leads
through fine forest viâ (90 V.) *Tchiaúri* to (104 V.) *Lagodékhi*
(Restaurant in the Military Club). — 121 V. *Byelokáni*, a village
inhabited by Lesghians; 143 V. *Zakatáli* (1785 ft.; accommodation
at the club); 162 V. *Gyillyúk.* — 177 V. *Kakhi* (2600 ft.), whence
we take the highroad viâ (198 V.) *Nizhni Geinyúk* to (211 V.)
Nukhá (p. 472). Or we may go on horseback in 3-4 days viâ *Yelisú*,
Saruíbásh, and the *Salavat Pass* to the district in which the
Samúr takes its rise, and on to *Akhtí* (p. 456).

73. Georgia. Armenia. Karabagh.

a. South Caucasus Mineral Baths.

From *Mikháilovo* (p. 465) a branch-railway runs through the
Borzhóm Ravine to (28 V.) *Borzhóm* (Rail. Restaurant). Thence a
narrow-gauge line (carriages changed) runs to (6 V.) *Borzhóm Park.*

Borzhóm. — HOTELS. *Stárokavalérskaya* (Pl. a), on the left bank
of the Borzhómka, R. 1¹/₂-4 rb., bed-linen 50, B. 60 cop., D. (from
1 o'clock) 1-2 rb.; board 75 rb. per month; *Minerálnuiya Vodi* (Pl. b), opposite, on the right bank of the Borzhómka, R. from 1¹/₂ rb.; *Firuze* (Pl. c),
on the right bank of the Borzhómka, R. 1-10 rb.; *Borzhóm* (Pl. d), on the
right bank of the Kurá, a little to the E. of the Park station, R. 1¹/₄-3 rb.;
Centrálnaya (Pl. e), on the right bank of the Kurá, near the Olginski Bridge,
open throughout the year. — PHAETON from Borzhom station to the town
75, from Borzhom Park station to the town 40, per drive 30, to Likani 40
(there & back, with stay of ¹/₂ hr., 80) cop., per hr. 1 rb. 20 cop. — SADDLE
HORSE 4-5 rb. per day. — *Season.* June 10th to Sept. 10th (O. S.). Visitors'
Tax 3 rb. (two days free).

Borzhóm (2620 ft.), with 5800 inhab., lies on both banks of
the *Kurá*, at its confluence with the *Borzhómka*. It is one of the
most beautiful places in the Little Caucasus, is surrounded by richly
wooded hills, and recalls many scenes in the S. part of the Black
Forest. Much rain falls during May and June. On the right bank of
the Kurá are Borzhom Park station and the mineral baths (alkaline
hot springs, the Catherine Spring of 82° and the Eugene Spring of
71° Fahr.; bath 50 cop.). On the left bank is the newer part of
the town, with the Moorish-looking château of the Grand-Duke
Mikhail Nikoláyevitch. Interesting walks may be taken in the
Remertovski Park, with a seismological observatory (Pl. 11) and a
bronze bust (1913) of Grand-Duke Mikhail Nikoláyevitch; in the
Vorontzóv Park (3095 ft.; 20 min. above the Minerálnuiya Vodi

Hotel); and in the Borzhómka ravine.—About 2 M. to the S.W. of
Borzhom, on the left bank of the Kurá, lies *Likani*, a château of
the Grand-Duke Nikolái Mikháilovitch, built in 1895 in the Renaissance style. Opposite Likani, towards the E., are the ruins of the
castle of *Petres-Tzikhe*, on a hill.

The *Lomis-Mta*, or Lion Mountain (7165 ft.), situated 23 M. to the W.,
commands in clear weather a splendid view of the Elbruz, Ushbá, Tetnúld,
Duikh-Tau, and Kazbek.

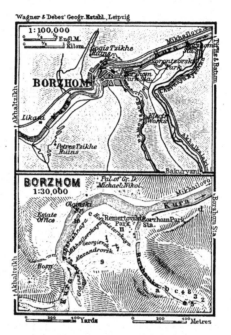

Explanation of the Numbers on the Map: 1. Armenian Church; 2. Catherine
Spring; 3. Catherine Spring Baths; 4. Chemical Laboratory; 5. Eugene
Spring; 6. Eugene Spring Baths; 7. Greek Church; 8. Mineral Waters
Export Office; 9. Palace of Grand-Duke Sergius Nikoláyevitch; 10. Post
and Telegraph Office; 11. Seismological Observatory.

FROM BORZHOM TO BAKURYANI, 41 V. (27 M.), narrow- gauge railway in
3¹/₂ hrs. (2nd class fare 94 cop.). The train (at the end of which is an
open observation car) ascends circuitously through the attractive valley
of the *Tchórnaya Retchka*. We start at *Borzhóm Park Station.*—6 V.
Borzhóm (p. 490).—19 V. *Tzagveri*, with an alkaline spring. About
3 M. to the E. is the village of *Timotis-Ubani*, with a ruined church,
near which, in the abrupt cliffs, are many cell-like hollows.—As we

continue, we notice on the right the section of the line just traversed, and a little later it appears on the left. Beyond (23 V.) *Tzemi* (4395 ft.), with a sanatorium for children (pens. 50-60 rb. per month), we pass through fine woods. Opposite the railway station of (29 V.) *Nikoláyevo* is a pavilion commanding a view of the valley. At (33 V.) *Sakotchavi* we reach the top of the plateau. — 41 V. **Bakuryani** (5415 ft.; *Rail. Restaurant*, with good trout). We now pass on to the S., either on foot or on horseback, to the (10 M.) *Tzkhra-Tzkharo* ('Nine Springs'; 8895 ft.), affording a fine view of the mountains, the forests of Borzhom, and the great Armenian plateau. About 6½ M. farther to the S. is *Lake Tabistzkhúri* (6195 ft.), which abounds in trout.

From Borzhom to Abbas-Tuman, 75 V. (50 M.), a fine posting-road; motor omnibus in 4 hrs. (fare 5 rb.); post-chaise in 7-8 hrs. (fare 16 rb.); phaeton 20-30 rb. (without changing horses; 1 day). — The road ascends the left bank of the Kurá. 18 V. *Strashni-Okóp*, a posting-station; 30 V. *Atzkhúr* (3180 ft.), a posting-station, with the remains of a church of the 7th cent; 50 V. *Akhaltzikh* (3375 ft.; good meals at the club-house), a town and posting-station, with an old fortress and 21,500 inhab., famed for their work in silver filigree; 62 V. *Benara*, a posting-station.

75 V. (50 M.) **Abbás-Tumán.**—Hotels. *Minerálnuiya Vodi*, R. 1-10 rb., D. (12-5) 60 cop. to 1 rb. 20 cop., pens. from 60 rb. per month; *Mirakov*, R. from .2, D. (12-6) 1-1³/₄, pens. 6-8 rb. — Furnished Lodgings. *Röschel*, R. from 1 rb.; *Weisse*, R. 1-2 rb. — Izvóshtchik per drive 20-30, per hr. 60 cop.; to the (2½ M.) Vorota Otcharovániya & back, with stay of ½ hr., 2 rb. — *Season*, June 1st to Oct. 1st (O. S.). Visitors' Tax 3 rb.

Abbás-Tumán (4255 ft.) is a much frequented watering-place in a valley-basin, with warm sulphur springs (93-119°; good bathing arrangements) and two grand-ducal villas (burned down in 1913). The ravine of the *Abbastumánka*, about 7 M. long, ascends to the Zekarski Pass (see below); a chapel stands on the spot where the heir-apparent, George Alexandrovitch, died in 1899. Farther on is the *Vorota Otcharovániya*, or Gate of Delight (izvóshtchik, see above).

From Abbas-Tuman to Rion, 73 V. (48 M.), carriage-road (no posting; phaeton 30-35 rb.). This road, which is one of the most beautiful in the Caucasus, leads to the N. to the (16 V.) *Zekarski Pass* (7080 ft.), affording a magnificent view of the Great and Little Caucasus. It then sinks rapidly to the valleys of the *Khani-Tzkali* and the *Rión*, the Alpine meadows being succeeded by luxuriant woods with subtropical vegetation. About 40 V. (27 M.) from Abbas-Tuman is the village of *Kersheveti* (accommodation at the road-surveyor's). The road continues through woods passing several villages, to (65 V.) *Baydad* and (73 V.; 48 M.) *Rión* (p. 463).

b. From Tiflis to Erivan *(Etchmiadzin, Ararat, Tabriz).*

353 V. (233 M.). Railway in 18 hrs. There are few railway restaurants.

Tiflis, see p. 465. — Beyond (6 V.) *Navtlúg* (1510 ft.; p. 471) we cross the *Kurá* and enter a small plain. To the right are the saline lake of *Kodi* and the Armenian pilgrim-resort of *Shav-Nabát*, on a conical hill. — 35 V. *Sandar*. About 13 M. to the W. (omn. 80 cop.) is the large German colony of *Katharinenfeld* (ca. 2625 ft.).— 62 V. *Sadákhlo* (1370 ft.). The line, which ascends steadily as far as Dzhadzhur (see below), enters the wild and romantic *Bambák Defile,* through which flows the *Debedá-Tchai* (Bortchalínka).

86 V. *Akhtalá* (1865 ft.), with copper works (French). To the left of the station is the beautiful *Akhtalá Ravine.* A little way up this defile is a large cathedral, standing on the verge of a precipice; adjoining it are two smaller churches and the remains of a palace.

104 V. *Sanaïn* (Rail. Restaurant). The line threads several short tunnels.— 142 V. *Karaklís* (4290 ft.; Rail. Restaurant). Motor omnibus to Akstafa viâ Delizhan (Erivan), see p. 471.—The railway turns to the W., crosses the watershed between the Araxes and the Kura at (188 V.) *Dzhadzhur* (6035 ft.), and reaches the barren upland plateau of *Shirák.* The Alagöz (p. 494) comes into sight.

207 V. (137 M.) **Alexandrópol** (5055 ft.; *Rail. Restaurant; Ángliya;* izvóshtchik from the station to the town 40, at night 80 cop.), with 49,000 Armenian inhab., was once fortified and an important frontier-post between Georgia, Persia, and Turkey.

FROM ALEXANDROPOL TO KARS, 72 V. (48 M.), railway in 3¼ hrs. The line leads to the W. over a barren upland plateau.— 72 V. (48 M.) **Kars** (5750 ft.; *Railway Restaurant; Impérial;* izvóshtchik from the station to the town 40, per hr. 60 cop.), a fortified place with 35,000 inhab., at the entrance to the deep and rocky gorge of the *Kars-Tchai,* is known to have existed as a strong fortress in the 9th century. Later it came into the possession of the Turks, who defended it brilliantly, under the English General Williams, against the Russians for six months in 1855. On Nov. 6th, 1877 (O. S.), however, it was finally stormed by the Russians, and since then it has belonged to Russia.. To the N. W., beyond the Old Town, is the Citadel, which is situated on a high conical lava mound. Near the Turkish quarter is a church dating from 930, transformed by the Turks into a mosque, and now a Greek Catholic Garrison Church. There is a Russian memorial of the campaigns of 1828, 1855, and 1877, by Mikéshin (1910). Outside the town is the German colony of *Petrovka.*—In 1913 a railway was opened from Kars to *Sarakamuish,* the Russian frontier-station on the road to Erzerum.

FROM ALEXANDROPOL TO ANI, 45 V. (30 M.), carriage there & back in 1 day 20-25 rb.; it is advisable to start as early as possible (railway, see p. 494), and provisions must be carried. — We drive first to the W. for 1½ hr. along a good carriage-road, passing the ruins of a loftily-situated ancient Armenian castle. We then cross the *Kars-Tchai,* to the S. of which we touch at several Armenian villages. To the right tower the volcanic cones of the *Aladzhá Mts.,* to the left is the Alagöz (p. 494). It is not until we are quite close to Ani that this ruined town becomes visible.

*Ani (4955 ft.), the 'town with a thousand and one churches', already mentioned in the 4th cent. A. D., was until 1046 the residence of the kings of the Bagratide dynasty. It was ravaged by the Seljuk Turks in 1064, and by the Mongols in 1239, while in 1319 it was overthrown by a violent earthquake. It lies upon a tongue of rock, surrounded, except on the N. side, by gorges 100-200 ft. deep, between the *Arpá-Tchai* (on the E.) and the *Aladzhá-Tchai* (on the W.); its circumference amounted to over 3 M. An Armenian monk, who acts as guide, and a single family of peasants are now the only inhabitants.—The town is entered from the N. side through a double wall about 1100 yds. long. The outer wall, which is in a good state of preservation and strengthened by about 30 square towers, consists of regularly hewn blocks of reddish-brown stone, ornamented with bands, crosses, and inlaid-work of dark stone. On a hill at the N.W. corner of the town are the remains of a palace (12-13th cent.), wrongly called the Palace of the Bagratides

(Дворе́цъ Багратуніевъ). About 300 yds. to the S.E. is the Cathedral
(Собо́ръ), built in 989-1001, the central tower of which has fallen in.
About 200 yds. to the E. of the cathedral is the Church of Gregory the
Illuminator (Це́рковь Григо́рія Просвѣти́теля), which contains some
well-preserved frescoes. A little to the S.W. of the Cathedral is the
Manutchc Mosque (10th & 12th cent.), with the Museum. Still farther
to the S. are the remains of the Viceroy's Palace (Ца́рскій дворе́цъ).

The ascent of the highest (13,445 ft.) of the four peaks of the **Alagöz**
takes 1-2 days from Alexandropol and is not difficult for experts. The
trip, like that to Mt. Ararat (p. 495), is not without danger on account of the
nomadic Kurds: the traveller should therefore carry a revolver and obtain
a mounted police escort at Alexandropol. We first ride to the E. viâ (9 M.)
Bolshói Kapanák, and then to the S. viâ the villages of *Golgát*, *Norashén*,
and *Bolshiye Arikhvéli*, finally crossing some high-lying fields and pastures
of the Kurds and Tartars and reaching (8 hrs.) a stony lateral arête of
the Alagöz. We then dismount and proceed to (4¹/₄ hrs.) the top. Among
the four summits of the mountain lies a crater 1¹/₄ M. in diameter and
1540 ft. deep, filled with névé. On the S.E. the rim of the crater is
broken by a deep gorge, from which the *Dadalyú-Tchai* issues. On the
slopes of the Alagöz are numerous lakes of various sizes.

From Alexandropol a road leads to the N. viâ *Khertvis* to (103 M.)
Akhaltzíkh (p. 492).

The railway to Erivan leads to the S. from Alexandropol along an
upland plateau and across the lavas of the Alagöz (see above), which
long remains visible on the left. — 231 V. *Agin*. On the right the
ruins of Ani are plainly discernible. — 250 V. *Ani*. About 5¹/₂ M. to
the N.W. of the station is the ruined town of that name (p. 493), which
is more conveniently reached by carriage from Alexandropol (no
carriages, guides, or provisions at the station). — 267 V. *Alagöz*
(Rail. Restaurant). The railway now turns to the S.E.; on the right
(S.) appears Mt. Ararat (p. 495). Beyond (297 V.) *Aráx* the
line gradually sinks to the salt steppe of the Araxes. — 327 V.
Etchmiadzín. About 8 M. to the N. is the town of that name
(p. 495; omnibus 50 cop., phaeton 2 rb.). — 339 V. *Ulukhanlu*
(2545 ft.; Rail. Restaurant). To Dzhulfa (Tabriz), see p. 496. — The
railway now makes a sudden turn to the N.

353 V. (233 M.) **Eriván.** — The *Railway Station* (restaurant) is
1³/₄ M. to the W. of the town. — HOTELS. *Orient*, Kryepostnáya, R. 1-3,
D. (1-5 p.m.) from ¹/₂ rb.; *Lyon*, Astáfyevskaya, R. 1-3 rb.; *Grand-Hôtel*.
Izvóshtchik from the station to the town 60, per drive 20, per hr. 60 cop.
to 1 rb.; double fares at night.

Eriván (3230 ft.), often a bone of contention between the
Turks and the Persians, but belonging to Russia since 1827, is the
capital of the government of the same name and has 33,000 inhab.
(Armenians and Tartars). It lies on the *Zanga River*, and has a
fine view to the W. of the Alagöz (see above), and to the S. of Mt.
Ararat (p. 495), 40 M. away. On the W. side of the town stands the
Gök-Jami, a mosque built in the time of Nadir Shah (d. 1747), now
in ruins; to the right of the pishták (p. 517) is a minaret, the exterior of which is overlaid with glazed and coloured tiles. On the
S. side of the town are the remains of the former fortress. The
town also possesses a large Oriental bazaar.

About 12 M. to the W. of Erivan (phaeton there & back in one day, 5 rb.; railway, see p. 494), near the village of *Vagarshapát*, lies the convent of **Etchmiadzín** (Эчміадзинъ; 2840 ft.), the seat of the Armenian Katholikos.

The Armenian Church is a national church (comp. p. 441). The Katholikos is chosen by the whole nation, including Russian, Turkish, Persian, and Indian Armenians, and the choice must be confirmed by the Tzar of Russia. The Armenian Church is administered from Etchmiadzin through the synod, under the presidency of the Katholikos, and with the co-operation of a procurator nominated by the Tzar. — The first Armenian Katholiki resided in Artaxata (p. 472), but at the end of the 4th or the beginning of the 5th cent. they transferred their seat to Etchmiadzin, the convent of which down to the 10th cent. was known as Vagarshapát. For a time also they settled at Dvin and Ani (p. 493), and at Siss in Cilicia; but since 1441 Etchmiadzin has been their permanent residence and the centre of the spiritual life of Armenia.

The convent, with its extensive buildings and the theological academy, lies on the plateau, and is surrounded by a wall with towers. In the middle of the large convent-court (116 by 112 yds.) stands the *Cathedral of the Virgin*, built, according to the Armenian legend, in 303 by Gregory the Illuminator on the spot where God's only Son appeared to him; hence the name Etchmiadzín, which means 'the only-begotten Son is descended'. The porch of the W. portal is richly adorned with decorative reliefs in stone. Behind the E. apse is the treasury, where the spear and the hand of St. Gregory are preserved. Outside the cathedral, to the right of the main portal, is the grave of *Sir John Macdonald*, a British envoy who died at Tabriz in 1830. The library possesses a fine Evangelium of the 10th cent., engrossed on parchment and bound in ivory (4th cent. ?). — In a small museum have been preserved some capitals of columns and other objects of archæological interest. The convent has about 40 inmates, some of whom speak German.

About 1¼ M. to the E. of the convent is the *Church of St. Ripsimé*, a square building with a central dome, which is well worth seeing. It was rebuilt in the 7th century. The porch was added in 1653 or 1790. — To the S. of the road to Erivan is the ruined church of *Tzuartnots*. — A visit should also be paid to the ruins of the Round Church of Gregory the Illuminator, which was built about the middle of the 7th century.

About 40 V. (26 M.) to the S. of Erivan (carriage in 6 hrs., 7 rb.), and 12 V. (8 M.) to the S. of Kamarlyu (p. 496; phaeton 4-5 rb.), lies the village of *Araláikh* (2760 ft.), the best starting-point for the ascent of **Mt. Ararat** (Armenian *Massis*, Turkish *Aghri-Dágh*). This volcanic mountain stands completely isolated, at the spot where the boundaries of Russia, Persia, and Turkey meet. In front, on the right, rises the icy dome of the *Great Ararat* (17,055 ft.; Mt. Blanc 15,780), which falls off steeply toward the W.; on the left is the pointed peak of the *Little Ararat* (12,845 ft.); between them is the saddle of *Sardár-Bulág* (8335 ft.). Old Testament tradition identifies Ararat with the mountain where Noah's ark rested after the flood.

The best season for the ascent is Aug. and September. Rugs, cooking utensils, tea, red wine, rice, and two bags of coal must be carried. Information may be had from the frontier-officer or from the village-chief at Araluikh. Each porter receives 5 rb. for the whole excursion. — As the traveller may possibly be molested by the nomadic Kurds, he is advised to take a revolver and procure an escort of Cossacks from the frontier-officer.

On the 1st day we ride from Araluikh to (22 M.; 7 hrs.; saddle-horse 1¹/₂-2 rb.) *Sardár-Bulág* (p. 495), with a spring and a fortified Cossack station, and ascend thence to the snow-line, where the night is spent. On the 2nd day we have a toilsome climb over blocks of lava and fields of débris to the summit of the *Great Ararat* (11 hrs. from Sardar-Bulag), returning to our camp at the snow-line.

The summit of the *Great Ararat*, first ascended by Dr. Parrot in 1829, is about 100 ft. in diameter. A vast panorama stretches out on all sides, embracing a radius of about 170 M. Viscount Bryce, who ascended the mountain in Sept., 1876, describes the view as 'not beautiful or splendid but rather stern, grim, and monotonous'. To the N. is the brown and parched plateau of the Araxes, behind it, the Alagöz (p. 494), the mountains of the Armenian plateau, and the chain of the Central Caucasus, with the Kazbek and the Elbruz. To the S.W. is the region where the Euphrates, the Kurá, and the Araxes take their rise. To the S. and S.E. are the Plain of Bayazét, Lake Van in Turkey, and Lake Urmia in Persia. To the E. is the snowy summit of the Zavalán (15,790 ft.), rising over the Caspian Sea. — On the N. side of the Great Ararat is the deep *Jacob Valley*, in which is the main glacier of the mountain. In its lower part is the Tartar village of *Akhúri* (5700 ft.), with a military outpost.

On the 3rd day we return viâ Sardar-Bulag to Araluikh.

The ascent of the *Little Ararat* from Sardar-Bulag takes 5-6 hrs.

About 20 M. to the N.W. of Erivan lies *Garni* or *Karni*, with the remains of a building in the Ionic style, and the convent of *Kegart* or *Airivánk*, hewn out of the rock.

From ERIVAN TO KARS, 232 V. (154 M.), highroad (diligence in 2 days 20 rb.; railway, see pp. 491, 493), affording a fine view of the Armenian plateau. — 18 V. *Etchmiadzin* (p. 495); 37 V. *Markára;* 54 V. *Igdúir*, where the night is spent. Beyond (74 V.) *Karakanli* the *Araxes* emerges from a ravine into the plain; here also lie the ruins of an old and extensive fortress, *Kará-Kalá* ('Black Fortress'), possibly the *Tigranocerta* which was founded in the 6th cent. B.C. — 92 V. *Kulp*, with rock-salt mines; 113 V. *Agabék;* 136 V. *Akh-Tchái;* 154 V. *Kaguizmán* (nightquarters), with rock-salt mines; 172 V. *Ketak;* 190 V. *Pasli;* 209 V. *Kaostchai.* — 232 V. (154 M.) *Kars* (p. 493).

From ERIVAN TO DZHULFA, 192 V. (127 M.), railway in 7 hrs. Photographing is forbidden. — 14 V. *Ulukhanlu.* To Tiflis, see pp. 494-492. The train turns to the S.E., and crosses a barren plateau; to the right are the Araxes and Mt. Ararat (p. 495). — 30 V. *Kamarlyu* (2560 ft.). About 8 M. to the S. is Araluikh (p. 495). — 149 V. *Nakhitchevan-Erivanski* (2495 ft.; Railway Restaurant; Dvortzóvuiye Nomerá; izvóshtchik from the rail. station to the town 80, vice versâ 50 cop.), a district capital with 8300 Tartar inhabitants. Outside the town is an Armenian churchyard, with the alleged grave of Noah. — 192 V. (127 M.) *Dzhulfa, Julfa,* or Джульфа (2210 ft.; Rail. Restaurant; Frántziya), on the frontier between Russia and Persia.

From Dzhulfa a highroad (carriages to be had; railway under construction) leads S. to (140 V., or 93 M.) **Tabriz** (4430 ft.; Brit. consul, *H. S. Shipley, C. M. G.;* U. S. consul, *G. Paddock*), the capital of the Persian province of Azerbaijan, with 200,000 inbah. (mostly Tartars) and an important trade (carpets, cotton, tropical fruit, tragacanth, etc.). Its chief features of interest are the half-destroyed Blue Mosque (middle of the 15th cent.), the bazaars, and the citadel, which towers above the city.

From Erivan to Akstafa, see pp. 472, 471.

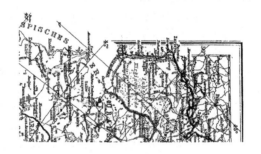

VIII. TEHERAN.
RAILWAYS IN ASIATIC RUSSIA. PORT
ARTHUR. PEKING.

74. From Baku to Teheran.

FROM BAKU TO ENZELI, 343 V. (227 M.), mail steamer of the *Caucasus & Mercury Co.* (p. 462) twice weekly direct in 18 hrs. (fares 20 & 12 rb., including dinner). — FROM ENZELI TO RESHT, 28 V., carriage in $3\frac{1}{2}$ hrs. (fare 50 kran, including a toll). — FROM RESHT TO TEHERAN, 333 V. or 221 M. (54 farsákhs or parasangs; 1 farsákh = ca. 4 M. = ca. $6\frac{1}{4}$ kilo-mètres), carriages of the *Bakhman-Bahram Co.* (p. 499) in 2 or 3 days (motor omnibus service projected; ordinary mail-coaches used by natives only). A four-seated landau or coupé costs 674 kran 13 shahi, a two-seated droshky 619 kran 13 shahi; in addition there are tips amounting to 72 kran and a toll of 59 kran 10 shahi; 1 pud (36 lbs.) of luggage is allowed for each carriage (each additional man, *i.e.* $6\frac{1}{2}$ lbs., 2 kran 15 shahi extra).

PASSPORT. For entrance into Persia a passport provided with the visa of a Persian consul is necessary. This may be obtained at Baku or Tiflis (fee 2 rb. 40 cop.); in case of necessity, however, the visa may be procured on application in Enzeli for a fee of 13 kran 12 shahi. — PERSIAN MONEY The currency consists of silver coins of 1, 2, and

5 kran in value, nickel coins worth $^1/_{10}$ and $^1/_{20}$ of a kran, and banknotes of the Imperial Bank of Persia from 1 tomán upwards (1 tomán = 10 kran; 1 kran = 20 shahi = $4^1/_2 d.$). Persian money may be obtained in Enzeli or in Resht. The rate of exchange varies greatly, the average being $5^1/_2$-6 krans for 1 ruble and $54^1/_2$ krans for 1$l.$ Russian gold pieces are not universally accepted in Persia.

EQUIPMENT. The traveller should provide himself with woollen underclothing (even in spring or late summer, for the changes of temperature are sudden), smoked spectacles, a pith helmet (in summer), rugs, a cushion, insect-powder, a medicine-chest, and a saddle for horseback-excursions in the vicinity of Teheran. Weapons are not necessary. For a stay of some duration in Teheran, a frock-coat and evening dress are desirable, as well as an introduction to one of the legations. — A native servant (not indispensable) can best be obtained at Resht (20-50 rb. per month, besides food). — Precautions should be taken against theft, and the luggage should be carefully looked after. — Excellent SHOOTING is to be had in the vicinity of Enzeli, Resht, and Teheran.

The best TRAVELLING SEASON in North Persia is from the middle of March till the middle of May and from the middle of Sept. till the middle of December. The summer is very hot. The climate, if due regard be paid to diet and clothing, is not unhealthy. Travellers should *on no account* drink *unboiled water.* There is a good deal of fever in Resht and in the marshy province of Gilán; anyone who is subject to it should take quinine daily after leaving Enzeli.

A visit to Resht and Teheran may be made in 16 days, reckoned from Baku. The total travelling expenses, including those of the native servant, will amount to about 600 rb. — The tour is best divided up as follows: steamer from Baku to Enzeli and drive to Resht, 1 day; drive from Resht to Teheran (one day's rest at Kazvin), 4 days; stay at Teheran, 6 days; return from Teheran to Baku (one day's rest at Resht), 5 days.

The Russian General Staff has issued a map of Persia on a scale of 1 : 840,000. The India Office Map of Persia (1 : 2,534,400) is convenient (Stanford; 1$s.$ 6$d.$). The following German maps by A. F. Stahl are recommended: North Persia on a scale of 1 : 840,000 (supplement No. 122 of Petermann's Mitteilungen, 1897), North-West Persia (Petermann's Mitt., 1909), and the Environs of Teheran (1 : 210,000; Petermann's Mitt., 1900).

The following are some common Persian words (the accent generally falls on the last syllable, even in the case of compound words): resthouse, *tchaparkhaneh;* room, *utagh;* horse, *asp;* carriage, *kaliskeh;* driver, *kalisketchi;* mail-driver, *suhtchi;* servant, *nouker;* doorkeeper, *dalundar;* drive faster, *tund bero;* stop, *va ist;* slow, *yavash;* quick, *zud;* how far?, *tche kadr ra;* go away, *bero;* come here, *bia inja;* wait, *sabr kun;* how much does it cost?, *tche kadr or tchand;* too much, *ziad;* dear, *giran;* money, *pul;* give me, *bedih;* tea, *tchai;* bread, *nun;* milk, *shir;* water, *ab;* clean water, *ab-i-pak;* drinking-water, *ab-khurden;* hot water, *ab-i-garm;* boiling water, *ab-i-jush;* sugar, *shekar, kand;* fowl, *murgh;* egg, *tokhm-i-murgh;* boiled rice, *tchilau;* rice with meat and seasoning, *pilau.* Cardinal numbers: 1, *yek;* 2, *du;* 3, *sĕ;* 4, *tchehar;* 5, *penj;* 6, *shish;* 7, *heft;* 8, *hesht;* 9, *nuh;* 10, *dah;* 15, *punsdah;* 20, *bist;* 25, *bist u penj;* 30, *sĩ;* 40, *tchihil;* 50, *penjah;* 75, *heftad u penj;* 100, *sad.* — The following books may be found useful: *Rosen's* Modern Persian Colloquial Grammar (London, 1898); *St. Clair Tisdall's* Modern Persian Conversation Grammar (London & Heidelberg; 1902); Persian Self-Taught, in *Marlborough's Series* (London; 1909).

BIBLIOGRAPHY. *S. G. Benjamin,* Persia and the Persians (3rd ed.; 1887). — *E. G. Browne,* The Revolution in Persia (1910). — *Lord Curzon,* Persia and the Persian Question (2 vols.; 1892). — *Sven Hedin,* Overland to India (2 vols.; 1910). — *A. V. Williams Jackson,* Persia, Past and Present (New York, 1906). — *Ella C. Sykes,* Persia and its People (1910). — *P. M. Sykes,* Ten Thousand Miles in Persia (1902). — *C. J. Wills,* The Land of the Lion and the Sun (1883). — *J. G. Wishard,* Twenty Years in Persia (New York, 1904). — Comp. the article 'Persia' in the *Encyclopaedia Britannica* (11th ed.; 1911).

a. From Baku to Resht.

Steamboat from Baku to Enzeli, see p. 497.—*Carriages* for Resht (comp. p. 497) await the arrival of the steamer at Enzeli-Kazian; there is also a motor omnibus service (fares 20 & 15 kran).

Bakú, see p. 456 — On leaving the town the steamer steers to the S. through the Caspian Sea (p. 462), and after 18 hrs. sail reaches the wharf of the Persian seaport of —

Enzelí-Kazián (75 ft. below sea-level; luggage examined and passports scrutinized in the custom-house), situated on the E. side of the mouth of the Lagoon (Murdáb) of Enzeli. In *Kazián* (accommodation in the rest-house, comp. below; post office), not far from the landing-place, is the large establishment of Lianózov Brothers for the production of caviare and salted fish. To the W., beyond the mouth of the lagoon, lies *Enzeli* (inn), with 1500 inhabitants. — The lagoon abounds with cormorants, geese, swans, ducks, pelicans, cranes, and snipe, and affords good sport.

From Enzeli-Kazian we drive along the highroad (comp. below), which skirts the lagoon in an easterly direction, to (15 V.) the station of *Hassanrud* and (28 V.) —

Resht (*Hôtel d'Europe*, R. 15-25, D. 5-7 kran; *Bellevue;* British vice-consul, *E. Bristow;* agencies of the banks mentioned at p. 501), lying 3 ft. below the level of the sea, the capital of the province of Gilán. Pop. 40,000. Resht is the centre of the Persian silk trade, and has an important silk industry, importing the eggs of the silkworm and exporting cocoons and raw silk. An interesting visit may be paid to the silkworm-breeding establishment of M. Bonnet, from Marseilles. The town also possesses a post office, several good chemists, and an American mission.

b. By Carriage from Resht to Teheran.

Fares, see p. 497. — Immediately on arrival at Resht, passengers should secure their carriages at the agent's, and satisfy themselves as to their condition. Tinned foods, biscuits, wine, tea, and mineral waters must be taken; heavy luggage may be entrusted to the mail, but should be very carefully covered with gunny.

The road from Enzeli and Resht to Teheran belongs to the Общество Энзели-Тегеранской шоссейной дороги, the head office of which is in Москов, while it has representatives in Resht, Kazvin, and Teheran. The maintenance of the stages and rest-houses is leased to the Persian *Bakhman-Bahram Co.* (headquarters in Teheran), which also manages the postal arrangements. The distances given below in versts are reckoned from Enzeli, while those in farsakhs (p. 497) are reckoned from station to station.

At each station horses and driver are changed, a process sometimes entailing many hours' delay. The retiring driver should not receive his tip (3-4 kran) until everything is ready for continuing the journey. — The *Station Rest Houses*, connected with one another by telephone, are very primitive (the tariff hangs on the wall). They supply only bread (poor), rice, milk, hot water, sugar, tea, poultry, and eggs. Beds in private rooms cost 1 kran per hr. The night should not be spent at the intermediate rest-houses except in case of necessity.

32*

Many travellers continue the journey without a break, and reach Teheran in about 50 hrs. Those who are not prepared for such unremitting exertion, and wish to avoid travelling at night (not without its dangers on account of precipices), are advised to divide the journey into three parts. 1st Day, a drive of 12 hrs. in dry weather. We start from Resht at 7 a.m., spend the noonday-halt at Rustemabad, and stop for the night at Mendjil. — 2nd Day. From Mendjil to Kazvin, a drive of 18 hrs. — 3rd Day. From Kazvin to Teheran, a drive of 17 hrs. It is necessary in this case to start early, as the gates of Teheran are closed 3 hrs. after sunset.

From Resht (p. 499) the road leads at first to the S. through a marshy district to (63 V. from Enzeli; 4 farsákh from Resht) *Gudúm* (195 ft.; rest-house). Farther on it ascends slowly through a picturesque mountainous and wooded district, following at places the left bank of the *Sefid-rud* ('White River'), viâ (72 V.; 1½ farsákh) the intermediate station of *Sefid-Ketileh*, to (91 V.; 3 farsákh) *Rustemabád* (595 ft.; rest-house, tolerable). Farther on we go S.W. viâ (106 V.; 2¼ farsákh) the intermediate station of *Rudbár* (600 ft.), with its numerous olive-trees, and after crossing the Scfid-rud by the Mendjil Bridge enter (118 V.; 2 farsákh) *Mendjil* (1090 ft.; rest-house, tolerable; post office). The route runs to the S.E. along the right bank of the *Shah-rud* ('King's River') viâ (128 V.; 1½ farsákh) the intermediate station of *Bala-Balá*, and then to the S. along the left bank of the *Mulla-Ali* to (143 V.; 2¼ farsákh) *Paitchinár* ('Foot of the Plane-tree'; 1275 ft.; rest-house). Thence we ascend steadily, viâ (155 V.; 2 farsákh) *Mulla-Ali* (rest-house), to (172 V.; 3 farsákh) *Yuz-Bashi-Tchai* (3200 ft.; rest-house, tolerable), where a bridge crosses to the right bank of the Mulla-Alí. We now proceed to the E., viâ (183 V.; 1¾ farsákh) the intermediate station of *Bekendi* (4360 ft.), to (189 V.) the watershed of the plateau (5080 ft.). We next descend, viâ (198 V.; 2¼ farsákh) *Buinák* (4820 ft.; rest-house), a large village in a fertile district, with 5000 inbah., to (225 V.; 4 farsákh) —

Kazvín (4215 ft.; rest-house, tolerable; post office; branch of the Imperial Bank of Persia), a town of 30,000 inbab., founded in the 3rd or 4th cent. A.D. In the 16th century it was the residence of Shah Tahmasp I., and it is said to have had at that time 200,000 inhabitants. On the E. side of the town lies the burial mosque of Hussein, son of the eighth Imam, Ali III. er-Riza (p. 511).

About 30 M. to the N.E. of Kazvin, among the mountains round the source of the Shah-rud, lies *Alamút* ('Vultures' Nest'), the old fort of the Assassins, which from 1090 to 1256 was the seat of the 'Old Man of the Mountain'.

From Kazvin a highroad leads S.W. to (278 V.) *Hamadán.*

The road from Kazvin to Teheran leads S.E. over an elevated plateau and is somewhat uninteresting. The stations are: 247 V. (3½ farsákh) *Kevendeh*, 270 V. (4 farsákh) *Kishlák*, 295 V. (4 farsákh) *Yeng-i-Imám* (4080 ft.), 315 V. (3½ farsákh) *Hisarék* (4125 ft.), 339 V. (4 farsákh) *Shahabád* (3275 ft.). Finally we come to (361 V.; 3¾ farsákh) *Teheran.* Our first view is of a sea of flat roofs and

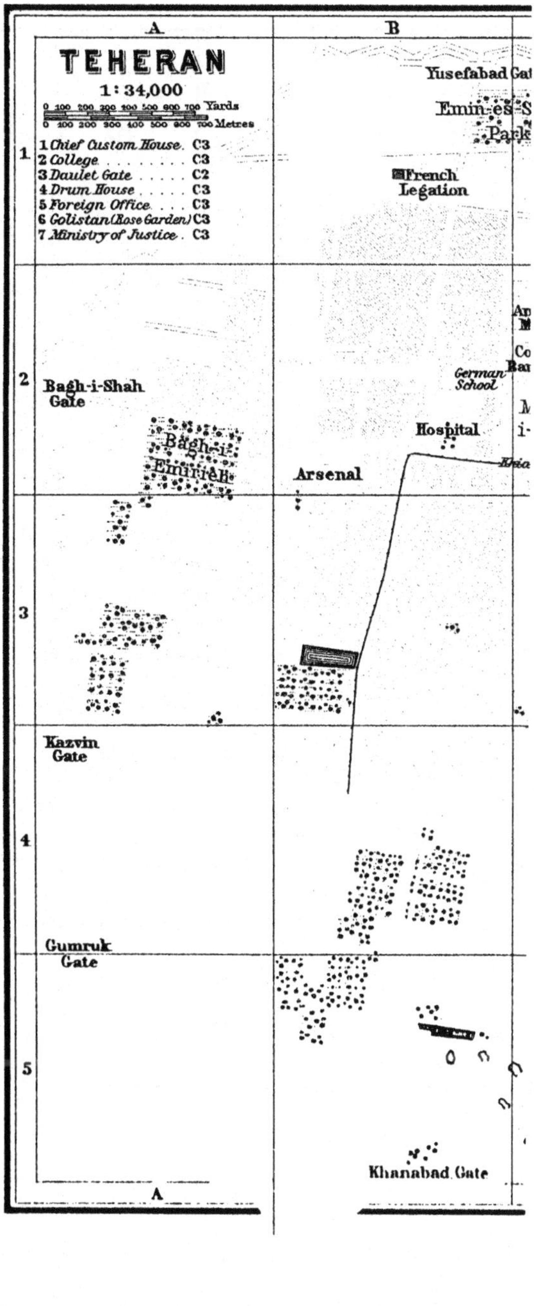

TEHERAN

1 : 34,000

0 100 200 300 400 500 600 700 Yards
0 100 200 300 400 500 600 700 Metres

1 *Chief Custom House* . C3
2 *College* C3
3 *Daulet Gate* C2
4 *Drum House* C3
5 *Foreign Office* C3
6 *Golistan (Rose Garden)* C3
7 *Ministry of Justice* . C3

Yusefabad Gat

Emin-es-S
Park

French
Legation

An
M
Co
Ban

German
School

M
i-

Hospital

Bagh-i-Shah
Gate

Bagh-i-
Eminveh

Arsenal

Kazvin
Gate

Gumruk
Gate

Khanabad Gate

A   **B**

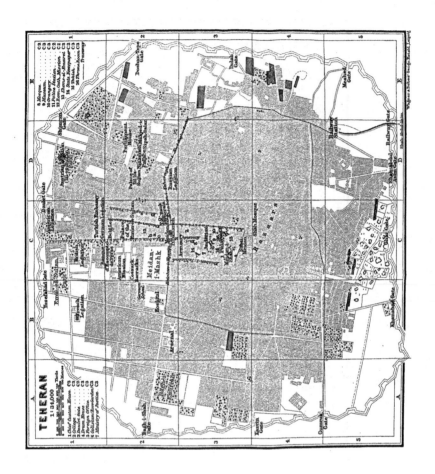

TEHERAN
1:34,000

1. Chief Custom House C3
2. College C3
3. Dutch Gate C3
4. Drum House C3
5. Foreign Office ... C3
6. Golestan Enclosure . C3
7. Ministry of Justice .. C3

8. Mosque C3
9. Museum C3
10. Menagery C3
11. Police Station . C3
12. Rom. Cath. Mission C2
13. Russ. Cath. Mission C3
14. State Newspaper C3
15. Tekieh C3
16. Throne-room ... C3
Tramway

cupolas interspersed with green sycamores, and enclosed on the N. and E. by the mountains of the Elbúrz, with the snow-covered Demavénd (p. 505).

c. Teheran.

Hotels (unpretending). HÔTEL DE PARIS (Pl. a, C 2; formerly English Hotel), English cuisine; HÔTEL DE FRANCE (Pl. b; C, 2), R. 10-15, déj. (12-2 p.m.) 5, D. (7.30-9 p.m.) 5 kran; HÔTEL DE L'EUROPE (Pl. c; C, 2), plain, patronized especially by Russians and Austrians, these three in the Khiaban-i-Ala-ed-Dauleh. — R. and table d'hôte (déj. 6, D. 8 kran) also in the *Club de Téhéran* (Pl. d, C 1; entrance-fee 200, monthly subscription 50 kran; introduction through a member necessary), Khiaban-i-Ala-ed-Dauleh.

Carriages (phaetons) in the Meidán-i-Tupkhaneh (Pl. C, 2; p. 501) 4 kran per hr. within the town, 5 kran outside the town; per drive 2 kran.

Tramways (special compartment for Mohammedan women), fare 5 shahi. The general starting-point is the Meidán-i-Tupkhaneh (Pl. C, 2) mentioned at p. 503, from which lines run through the Khiaban-i-Lalezár; through the Khiaban-i-Tcheragh-gas to the station of the railway to Shah-Abdul-Azim; through the Khiaban-i-Nasirieh to the Sabzi-Meidán and past the Meidán-i-Mashk to the neighbourhood of the Kazvín Gate.

Post Office (Pl. C, 2), at the S. end of the Khiaban-i-Lalezár. Mails are despatched to Europe twice a week. Persia belongs to the Postal Union. The ordinary letter rate of postage within Persia is 6 shahi per $^1/_3$ oz., registered letter 21 shahi; to Europe ($^1/_2$ oz.) 13, registered 26 shahi. Inland post-card 2, foreign 6 shahi. — **Telegraph Office**, Khiaban-i-Nasirieh (Pl. C, 3). Rate per word to England 4 kran 10 shahi; United States 7 kr. 11 sh. to 9 kr. 11 sh.; France 4 kr. 2 sh.; Germany 3 kr. 12 sh.; Austria-Hungary 3 kr. 12 sh.; Russia 2 kr. 6 sh.

Legations. Great Britain, *Sir Walter B. Townley, K.C.M.G.* — United States of America, *Mr. Charles W. Russell.* — France, Germany, Austria-Hungary, Italy, Belgium, the Netherlands, Spain, and Russia also have legations, Sweden and Norway consulates, and Turkey an embassy.

English Religious Services are held on Sun. at 11 a.m. in the American Presbyterian Mission (Pl. C, 2). There is a *Roman Catholic Mission* (Pl. 12; C, 2) carried on by the Lazarists and the St. Vincent Sisters of Charity.

Banks. *Imperial Bank of Persia* (English; Pl. C, 2), Meidán-i-Tupkhaneh; *Banque d'Escompte de Perse* (Учётно-ссу́дный банкъ Персіи, headquarters at St. Petersburg; Pl. C, 1, 2), Khiaban-i-Ala-ed-Dauleh. — **Shops.** *Magasin Hollandais, Comptoir Français*, both in the Khiaban-i-Lalezár (Pl. C, 2); *Magasin Russe*, Khiaban-i-Ala-ed-Dauleh (Pl. C, 2).

HOSPITALS. *Persian Hospital* (Pl. B, 2), under Surgeon-Major Ilberg, physician to the German Legation (house physician, Dr. Becker); *American Mission Hospital*, under Dr. Wishard. — PHYSICIAN, *Dr. Anthony Neligan*, at the British Legation. — CHEMISTS (German). *E. Bonali, W. Bergande*, both in Khiaban-i-Nasirieh (Pl. C, 3). — The so-called *Turkish Baths* are open to Mohammedans only, and the Armenian baths are best avoided.

DISTRIBUTION OF TIME. Permission to view the Palace of the Shah and other places of interest may be obtained from one of the legations. A guide (best engaged through the hotel) receives about 15 kran a week, besides meals.

1st Day. Drive through the European Quarter and the Persian parts of the town (Ark, City Rampart). The bazaars are best visited on foot.

2nd Day. The morning may be devoted to the bazaars. Excursion to Shah-Abdul-Azim (much frequented by Persians on Fridays). Rhages, and the Tower of Silence. Those who travel by railway should order a saddle horse to meet them at Shah-Abdul-Azim.

3rd Day. Excursion to the Mint (permission necessary); on the way back, the Gardens of the Château of Kasr-i-Kajár.

4th Day. Palace of the Shah (permission to view should be applied for immediately after the traveller's arrival). Visits should be paid to the house of a Persian grandee and of a rich Persian merchant.

5th Day. Excursion to Doshan-Teppeh; Royal College (permission necessary).

6th Day. Visit to a caravanserai.

Teherán (3810 ft.), formerly called *Tiran*, the capital of Persia and residence of the Shah, lies upon an extensive upland plateau to the S. of the Elbúrz Mts. The exact situation of the city (long. 51° 25′ 2″ E. of Greenwich, lat. 35° 41′ 43″ N.) is marked on a column at the N.W. corner of the grounds of the British Legation. Pop. 280,000, including 600 Europeans, 5000 Jews, and 4000 Armenians. In 1870-74 the Shah Nasr ed-Din surrounded the town with a new rampart and moat about 11 M. in length. The interior is reached by twelve gates adorned with glazed tiles, which are closed 3 hrs. after sunset and opened at sunrise. [The Kazvín Gate lies on the W. side.] About the middle of Teheran rises the Ark, with the palace of the Shah (p. 504); the European Quarter, containing the legations, lies to the N., while the native city, with its large covered bazaars and narrow crooked streets, lies to the S. of the Ark. In summer the natives of the upper classes retire to resorts among the mountains.— None but Mohammedans may visit the mosques, and the Persians are very apt to resent any scrutinizing of the veiled women. — Lord Curzon describes Teheran as a city which was born and nurtured in the East, but is beginning to clothe itself at a West-End tailor's.

Teheran is first mentioned by the Arabian author Yakut (b. ca. 1179) as an unimportant place near the town of Re (the old Rhagæ, p. 505). The population steadily grew under the Sufi or Sufawid dynasty, which was founded by Shah Ismail and lasted from 1501 to 1721. Sir Thomas Herbert, who visited Teheran in 1627, calls it *Tyroan*. *Shah Suleiman* (1666-94) built a palace here. *Shah Agha Mohammed*, the founder of the present reigning house of the Kajárs, chose Teheran for his residence, and at his death (1797) the badly-built town contained 15,000 residents. *Shah Feth-Ali* (1797-1834) beautified the town to some extent, and the population increased in his time to 60,000. Under *Shah Nasr ed-Din* (1848-96) Teheran attained its present importance. *Shah Musaffer ed-Din* (1896-1907) gave Persia a constitution on Aug. 5th, 1906, and on Oct. 8th he opened the first Parliament (Majliss or Mejliss). His successor *Shah Mohammed Ali* abdicated in 1909 in favour of his son *Shah Sultan Ahmed* (b. 1898).

The STREET SCENES, especially in the vicinity of the Ark (p. 504), are full of interest. Among the prominent features are the Persian grandees in their carriages, attended by numerous servants; the white-turbaned mullahs; the Seïds, or descendants of the Prophet, in dark-blue turbans; long-haired dervishes; merchants on mules or asses; officials in long coats and with high brimless caps of lambskin (kuláh); the running footmen (shatér) of the Shah in their costume dating from the time of Shah Abbas (1586-1628); soldiers on horseback in a uniform resembling that of the Russian Cossacks; Kurdish and Bactrian cavalry; strolling folk (luti) with apes, bears, and lions; women enveloped in large mantles of indigo-blue (tchadér), with yellow shoes, their faces covered with a white veil (rubénd). When the harem of the Shah drives out, we must either avoid the streets through which the procession passes or look the other way.

We should not miss the busy scenes in the BAZAARS (p. 504), in which the cry of the drivers (kharbardár; look out!) is forever ringing in our ears. The genuineness of the colours of silk and woollen *Rugs* (25-200 kran per sq. yd.) may be tested in most cases by pressing them firmly with a damp white cloth; if the colours are not fast they come off. Old rugs are becoming scarcer every day; a good rug should have 85-95 stitches to the square inch. The old *Porcelain Industry* has decayed in consequence of the importation of European and Chinese ware. The traveller should beware of machine-made imitations.

In the N. part of Teheran lies the MEIDÁN-I-TUPKHANEH, or SQUARE OF CANNONS (Pl. C, 2), generally known under the short form Tup-Meidán. The square, which is 268 yds. in length and 120 yds. in breadth, is enclosed on three sides by the artillery barracks, the Imperial Bank of Persia (E. side), and the Police Station (Pl. 11; W. side). In the middle is a pond, surrounded by trees. Handsome gates, adorned with glazed tiles, open on to the principal streets of the town.

Towards the N. run the *Khiaban-i-Ala-ed-Dauleh,* or *Rue des Légations* (Pl. C, 2), and the *Khiaban-i-Lalezár,* the main streets of the **European Quarter.** To the N. of this is the *Emin-es-Sultan Park* (Pl. B, C, 1), the attractive buildings in which, formerly the Grand-Vizier's Residence, are now used by the Swedish gendarmerie.

Leaving the Tup-Meidán on the W. by the Khiaban-i-Kazvín, we reach the *Meidán-i-Mashk* (Pl. C, 2), a large square where reviews are held. On the N. side of the square are the *Cossack Barracks;* opposite, to the W., is the *German School* (Pl. B, 2; built in 1907), with six German masters and 250 pupils.

To the E. of the Tup-Meidán is the Khiaban-i-Tcheragh-gas (Rue du Gaz; Pl. C, D, 2), with the former gas-works, leading to the Russian Legation. To the N. of this is the *Masjed-i-Sipah-Salár* (Pl. D, 2), a fine modern mosque. Behind is the *Parliament House* (Pl. D, 2), the former Baharistán Palace, probably the finest building in the city. It has a stately portico and variegated tile-ornamentation. Built in 1879-81, it was used later for lodging distinguished European visitors. In 1907 the first parliament (Majliss; comp. p. 502) was held here. After the bombardment and sack of 1909 the interior was altered to suit the European idea of a deliberative assembly, and it now contains the chamber proper (with galleries), committee and party rooms, and the other usual adjuncts of a house of parliament.

From the S.W. corner of the Tup-Meidán the Khiaban-i-Almasich (Diamond Street) leads to the main entrance to the Ark (p. 504). — From the S.E. corner of the square the *Khiaban-i-Nasirich* (Pl. C, 3) leads to the S. On the right is the *College of Science and Art* (Dar-ul-Fonún; Pl. 2; founded in 1850), with four European teachers. Farther on, to the right, is the *Shems-el-Emarét* (Pl. 13), a lofty pavilion erected by Shah Nasr ed-Din, with two quadrangular towers at the sides, and a small clock-tower in the middle. The street then leads along the E. side of the Palace, turns to the right, and reaches the *Sabzi-Meidán* (Pl. C, 3), with the entrance to the *Bazaar* (p. 503). Close by is the *Meidán-i-Shah* (p. 505).

The *Ark*, or former citadel, contains the —

Palace of the Shah (Pl. C, 3). Its principal entrance is the *Almasieh Gate* on the N. side, with a loggia constructed in 1875 and richly decorated with pieces of looking-glass; but there are other entrances in the Meidán-i-Shah (S.), adjoining the Foreign Office (W.), and adjoining the Anderún or Harem (N.). — From the gate in the Meidán-i-Shah we first enter the Salaam Court, on the N. side of which is the large Takht-i-Khaneh or *Throne Room* (Pl. 16), containing a throne of white marble used by the Shah at his New Year's reception (March 21st of our calendar). To the right and left of the throne-room are rooms for the reception of the Diplomatic Corps, while on the upper floor are the *Tribunal of the Foreign Office* and the *Ministry of the Interior*. Farther on, to the E., is a narrow court, adjoined by the *Office of the Commandant of the Imperial Guards*, the *Apartments of the Grand Vizier*, and the *Imperial Archives*. Beyond this again is the shady *Golistán* or Rose Garden (Pl. 6), on the N. side of which stands the main palace, containing among other rooms the *Library* (many valuable MSS.) and the *Museum* (Pl. 9), founded in 1873 by Shah Nasr ed-Din after his first European tour, and comprising European and Asiatic objects.

The PERSIAN CROWN JEWELS, the value of which is usually stated as 9,600,000l., though probably not more than a tenth of that sum, are now kept in the *Treasure Vault*. Among the contents are large vases with gems and pearls; the swords of Timur the Tartar and other early rulers; a large terrestrial globe thickly encrusted with jewels, there being no fewer than 51,366 gems with a total weight of 118 oz. troy, besides gold to the weight of 80 lbs.; and a throne incorporating parts of the famous Takht-i-Taús or Peacock Throne, carried off by Nadir Shah on his conquest of Delhi in 1739. The diamond known as the Darya-i-Nur, or 'Sea of Light', another piece of booty obtained by Nadir Shah at Delhi, weighs 186 carats and is said to have been once in the possession of Timur.

To the E. of the museum is the so-called *Orangery* (Narendsh-Khaneh; Pl. 10), containing the entrance to the Harem (Anderún). The W. side of the orangery is adjoined by the so-called *Crystal Room* (Utagh-i-Bulúr) and other apartments. On the E. side of the Golistán is the Shems-el-Emarét, mentioned above. To the S. is the *Takieh* (Pl. 15), a hall resembling a circus, where the Taziych, the dramatic representation of the deaths of Hassan and Hussein, the grandsons of the Prophet, is given in the month of Moharrem. — To

the S. of the Ark is the *Meidán-i-Shah* (Pl. C, 3), with the so-called
Pearl Cannon (Tup-i-Morvaríd), taken from the Portuguese at Ormuz
in 1622; this cannon is considered as 'bast', *i.e.* a free place or
sanctuary, and a fugitive taking refuge under it is secure from
molestation. On the N. side of the square lies the *Chief Custom
House* (Pl. 1), and on the S. is the so-called *Drum House* (Nak-
kareh-Khaneh; Pl. 4), where the sunset is greeted by a burst of
curious music made by trumpets and kettledrums.

The ministers and high court-officials occupy houses surrounded
by gardens, all near the city-wall and most of them on the N. and
N.E. side, where a fine view is obtained of the Elbúrz Mts. with
the Demavénd.

Environs. In the vicinity of the town are four châteaux belonging
to the Shah: the *Kasr-i-Kajár*, about 2 M. to the N. of Teheran, on
the way to Gulahek; the *Sultanetabád*, about 590 ft. above Gulahek; the
Eshretabád, ²/₃ M. to the N. of Teheran; and the *Doshan-Teppeh*, 3 M. to
the E. of Teheran, reached by a good road and possessing a large garden
(pretty view) and a small menagerie. Near it is a racecourse. — About
4¹/₂ M. to the N. is the *Mint*. About 6 M. to the N., on the slope of the Elbúrz
range, is *Shimrán*, with the summer-residences of the foreign representatives
at *Gulahék*, *Zergendeh*, and *Tajrísh*. — About 5¹/₂ M. to the S. (light railway
in 20 min., comp. Pl. D 5; fares 2 & 1 kr.), among the ruins of Rhagæ,
lies *Shah-Abdul-Azím*, a Shiite place of pilgrimage, with a mosque to which
Mohammedans only are admitted. Shah Nasr ed-Din was assassinated
here on May 1st, 1896. The very ancient town of *Rhagae* was destroyed
by Jenghiz Khan and Timur; among its remains are a ruined tower and
rock-reliefs of the Sassanide dynasty (226-651 A.D.). In the neighbourhood
of the Borj-i-Yezid Tower, which was completely rebuilt in 1892, are the
Tcheshme-Ali Springs, with rock-reliefs representing Shah Feth-Ali on the
throne (comp. p. 502). About 2 M. to the E. of this point are the ruins of
the *Tower of Silence* (Dakhmeh), a burial-place of the Fire Worshippers,
where the dead bodies are exposed without coffins and devoured by birds of
prey. A view of the interior may be obtained from the top. — About 15 M.
to the E. is the hunting-château of *Jajerúd*, belonging to the Shah. — The
village of *Veramin*, 35 M. to the S.E., contains the remains of a temple
of the Fire Worshippers. — The snow-clad volcanic **Demavénd** (18,600 ft.),
the 'Dwelling-place of the Spirits', rises 56 M. to the N.E. of Teheran. The
ascent, which is best made between the middle of July and the middle of
Aug., is fatiguing, but offers no danger to experts. Mules, tents, provisions, and guides are necessary. The starting-point is *Reneh*, on the S.E.
side of the mountain. Hence we ascend to a point about 11,800 ft. above
the sea-level and to the S. of the summit, where the night is spent. By
starting next morning at 3 o'clock, the summit may be reached about midday. From Reneh a caravan-road (25 farsákh; 4-6 days from Teheran by
caravan in a good season) leads viâ Amol and Barfcrush through splendid
mountain scenery to *Meshed-i-Sar*, on the Caspian Sea, whence steamboats
of the Caucasus & Mercury Co. ply to Krasnovodsk (p. 510) and Baku
(p. 456).

The environs of Teheran afford excellent *Sport*, abounding in hares,
ducks, geese, snipe, quails, partridges, grouse, and other birds; there are
also ibexes in the mountains and gazelles on the plains. Permission to
shoot must first be obtained from the Shah.

75. From Baku to Tashkent *(Turkestan)*.

STEAMERS of the Caucasus & Mercury Co. ply from (Astrakhan) Baku to Krasnovodsk once a day in 16 hrs. (fares 15, 10 rb.). — RAILWAY from Krasnovodsk to Tashkent, 1748 V. (1159 M.); two trains daily in 58 hrs. (fares 31 rb., 18 rb. 60 cop.; seat-ticket for the 'passenger train' 3 rb. 60 cop.); to Samarkand, 1416 V. (939 M.), in 46 hrs. (fares 27 rb., 16 rb. 20 cop.; seat-ticket 2 rb. 70 cop.). Break of journey, see p. xxiii. A dining-car, simple in its appointments but affording good meals, is attached to the 'passenger train'. The railway restaurants (few and far between) are only tolerable.

Foreigners are not allowed to visit Turkestan except by special permission of the Russian Government. The traveller must send in his request through his country's embassy at St. Petersburg at the latest 6 months before the beginning of his journey. He must detail his proposed route, give an account of the places he desires to visit in their proper order, and state the length of time he intends to stay. The Pamirs, the route from Merv to Kushka, and some others are closed to foreigners. Shooting expeditions in Russian Turkestan are forbidden. Immediately on arrival at Askhabad, Bokhara, or Tashkent, the traveller should call upon the Russian diplomatic officials (dress clothes *de rigueur*).

The Russian General Government of **Turkestán** (Туркестанъ), including the khanate of *Khiva* and the emirate of *Bokhará*, is 790,000 sq. M. in area (nearly 16 times as large as England), and contains 10,110,000 inbah., of whom 7 per cent are Russians. It is bounded on the W. by the Caspian Sea, on the S. by Persia and Afghanistan, on the E. by the Chinese Empire, and on the N. by Siberia. The W. and the E. part of Turkestan are sharply distinguished from each other in physical features. From the Caspian Sea to the point where the Suir-Darya and the Amú-Darya emerge from the E. mountain-district, the whole country consists of an ancient sea-bed now covered by sand. This huge expanse of sand is intersected by six large rivers: the *Tedzhén (Tején)*, the *Murgháb*, the *Amú-Darya* (the *Oxus* of the ancients), the *Zeravshán*, the *Suir-Darya* (*Syr* or *Sir Daria; Jaxartes* in antiquity), and the *Tchu*. The Amú-Darya and the Suir-Darya empty their waters into the salt *Sea of Arál*, which is 26,200 sq. M. in extent and lies 155 ft. above the level of the Mediterranean; the other rivers end either in lakes or in marshes amid the sandy desert. — The crops include wheat, rice, and cotton (principally in Ferghana and Bokhara; produce over 14½ million puds in 1909, or more than half the needs of the entire Russian people). Large quantities of sheep, horses, and camels are also raised.

The CLIMATE of Turkestan is not, on the whole, unhealthy, but its high summer-temperature, its low winter-temperature, and its exiguous rainfall make it of an extreme continental nature. Tashkent has a mean yearly temperature of 56° Fahr. and an annual rainfall of 15 in., while its lowest temperature is 13-14° below zero, its highest 106°. — In April and October the daily range is so large that the lightest possible clothing is needed while the sun shines, though warm rugs and blankets are indispensable at night.

The water should never be drunk until it has been boiled. For washing, the traveller should be provided with an indiarubber bath or basin, and he should disinfect the water with lysoform. — The so-called Sartian sickness or pendinka (identical with the Aleppo or Bagdad boil; comp. p. 440), especially prevalent in Aug. and Sept., and the rishta (thread-worm, filaria medinensis), which burrows under the skin, seem both to be propagated by the water.

The **Population** of Turkestan is divided into the *Settled Tribes* (Sarts, Tajiks, Uzbeks, immigrant Russians, etc.) and *Nomads* (Turcomans, Kirghizes, and allied tribes).

The SARTS, who form 24 per cent of the population, and belong to the Sunnite sect of Islâm, are a hybrid race, partly of Turkish (Uzbek) and partly of Iranian elements, speaking Turkish with Iranian modifications. They are chiefly occupied as tillers of the soil, artisans, and merchants. The houses of the well-to-do classes are built in the Persian style, while the rooms are gaily painted and provided with numerous niches. The Sart considers loud laughing and speaking and hurried movements as marks of bad breeding. — The costume of the men consists of undergarments of white cotton, surmounted by a greater or lesser number (according to the season) of long coloured outer garments (khalât). The outermost of these is kept in place by a shawl 10-20 ft. in length, wound several times round the body and fastened by knots. The feet are shod with heelless top-boots of soft leather, over which are drawn leathern overshoes. The head is covered by a coloured and embroidered cap, often surmounted by a large turban. The general effect of the costume is distinctly gaudy. — The Sarts are very partial to sitting about and gossipping in the bazaars and the numerous tea-houses, drinking meanwhile green tea out of flat bowls. — The woman is practically the slave of her husband, and Bokhara is said to have been the centre of the theological doctrine that women have no souls and should not be allowed to pray.

The Iranian TAJIKS, forming 10 per cent of the population, still speak the original Persian dialect, and are diligent cultivators of the soil. The entire system of irrigation in the country originated in the time when the Tajiks formed the bulk of the inhabitants of the Turanian civilization.

Among the Turkish tribes, which have occupied the district since the beginning of the Middle Ages, the most important are the Turcomans (see below) and the UZBEKS. Pure-blooded Uzbeks are to be found only in a few districts in Central and Eastern Bokhara. The reigning houses and other leading families of the khanates of Central Asia have also for centuries been of Uzbek race.

The TURCOMANS, numbering about 400,000, are to be found chiefly in Merv, in the oasis of Akhal, and on the lower Atrek. They are largely pure nomads, only the poorer among them, who do not possess enough cattle, condescending to do a little farming and fruit-growing. Their language is a Turkish idiom, differing materially from that of the Sarts. The Turcoman is easily recognizable by his huge hemispherical sheepskin cap, which he wears both in summer and winter. His 'khalât' usually consists of home-made cotton, with reddish-brown stripes, lined with cotton-wool. The yurteh, or dwelling of the Turcoman, resembles a beehive, and consists of a circular wooden framework covered with dark brown felt. Before the Russian occupation of the country the Turcomans were the most dreaded robbers in the whole of Central Asia, and their predatory forays ('alaman') often extended far into the Persian Khorasan. — The women enjoy an almost unrestricted freedom, and their face is never veiled. — The Turcoman is nominally a Mohammedan, but as a matter of fact he pays very little attention to any of the commands of the Koran.

The KIRGHIZES of Turkestan, forming about 36 per cent of the population, occupy mainly the steppes of the Suir-Darya district and the most mountainous parts of Ferghana. They call themselves 'Kazaks', and belong to the Turco-Tartar branch of the Mongolian race. Nominally they are Sunnite Mohammedans. The Kirghizes are nomads, and their chief wealth consists of flocks of sheep (the Siberian Kirghizes are horse-breeders). Physically they are of middle height, with broad shoulders, and little hair upon their face. The most characteristic article of their attire is the pointed gray felt hat, with a curved brim, which they wear in summer; but their dress differs also in other respects from that of the Sarts and Turcomans. Their coat is shorter, while their trousers, made of cotton in summer and of leather in winter, are so capacious that the whole of the upper garments can be stowed away inside them. Their outer coat is the most valuable, and generally consists of silk; below that is one of cloth adorned with embroidery, while below that again is one of cotton. They wear long leathern boots, while round their waist is a metal-mounted belt, from which hang a knife and a pocket containing comb, toothpicks, and flints. The dress of the women resembles that of the men, except that its colours are as gaudy as possible, while the head is covered by a huge basket-like cap of stiff white cloth. — The 'kibitka' or Kirghiz house is a round, almost hemispherical tent, consisting of a crinoline-like wooden framework covered with strips of felt. The floor is covered with pieces of felt, only the wealthier classes having carpets. The food consists entirely of sheep's milk, kumiss (p. 358), and cheese, with flesh at rare intervals. The place of bread is taken by pieces of dough soaked in sheep's fat. — The ties of kinship are peculiarly strong among the Kirghizes, and one of their proverbs says 'better to be a shepherd in one's own family than a king among strangers'. They buy their wives, but the position of women is notwithstanding comparatively free.

History. Herodotus has much to relate about the *Massageti*, who lived beyond the Jaxartes (Suir-Darya), and about the peoples who occupied *Bactria* and *Sogdiana*, in the extreme N.E. of the Persian Empire. If Schack's interpretation of Firdusi's *Book of the Kings* be accepted, and we recognize in the old Persian heroic legend the poetic reflection of the primæval history of E. Irania and the lands on the N. boundary, we must reckon not only Bactria (Balkh) but also the regions on the Murghab, on the Zeravshán, and on the Middle Oxus (Amú-Darya) among the earliest seats of human culture. A number of passages in the *Avesta (Zend-Avesta)*, the Books of Wisdom of Zoroaster, seem to point in the same direction. — From the time of *Cyrus* onwards the whole district as far as the Suir-Darya belonged to the Persian Empire. *Alexander the Great* (comp. p. 516) had a long and weary struggle with the Aryan population of the regions of the Oxus. On his death the entire Orient fell into the hands of the Seleucidæ, and *Seleucus I. Nicator* (d. 281 B.C.) constructed extensive circular walls round the oasis of Merv to protect it against the nomads of the N. *Diodotus*, viceroy of Bactria under *Antiochus II. Theos*, made himself (about 255 B.C.) the independent ruler of the territory between the Oxus and the Hindu-Kush. This Hellenistic state succeeded in maintaining itself for a century and a half, when it was conquered by the Parthians. These were succeeded as lords of the soil by the Persian *Sassanides* (226-642 A.D.), and they in turn by the *Arabs*. During the Arabian epoch began the forward movement of the Turkish tribes into Turania. Merv (comp. p. 512), the capital of the Perso-Arabian empire of Khorasan, attained great prosperity as one of the largest towns in the East, and became the cradle of the dynasty of the Abbasides. The inroad of the Mongols under *Jenghiz* or *Genghis Khan* overthrew the civilization of the entire region; in 1216 Bokhara, Samarkand, and Khiva were all stormed and burned down. After the death of Jenghiz Khan his successors divided the empire among them. But *Timur*, named *Tamerlane* from his lameness, succeeded in once more combining Central and Hither Asia in one kingdom. At that time Turkestan belonged to the kingdom of the Jenghisides of Jagatai; but Timur overthrew this power, took possession of Samarkand in 1370, and held a brilliant court here from that time till his death (1405; comp. p. 517). The successors of Timur ruled over Central Asia till the end of the 15th cent., when they gave way to the *Uzbeks*. The domination of the Uzbeks lasted until the conquest of Turkestan by the Russians, and Bokhara and Khiva are to this day governed by vassal princes of Uzbek race.

Peter the Great and Nicholas I. in vain attempted the conquest of Khiva, the one in 1717, the other in 1839. In 1863 Vambéry (d. 1913), disguised as a dervish, succeeded in visiting Bokhara and Khiva. In 1865 Tashkent fell into the hand of the Russians. In 1866-68 the combined power of Bokhara and Kokand was overthrown, and Samarkand and Khodzhent passed into Russian possession. Under *General K. P. von Kauffmann*, who was governor and organizer of the district in 1867-82, the power of Khiva was humbled in 1873. In 1876 the remnant of the khanate of Kokand was incorporated with the Russian Empire under the name of Ferghana. In 1881 the courage and ruthlessness of *General Skóbelev* succeeded in overcoming the resistance of the Tekke Turcomans (Tekintzi; comp. p. 511). In 1884 the Turcomans of Merv submitted without a struggle. In 1895 the greater part of the Pamir plateau was annexed, so that Russia is now separated from British India only by a strip of nominally Afghan territory a few leagues in width.

In Aug., 1880, during the Turcoman campaign of Skóbelev, General Annenkov began the building of the *Central Asiatic* or *Transcaspian Railway*, which reached Merv in 1886, Samarkand in 1888, and Tashkent and Andizhan in 1898. The shifting sands of the deserts and arid steppes made the construction of this railway a task of peculiar difficulty. The railway from Orenburg to Tashkent was opened in 1905.

The best TRAVELLING SEASON in Turkestan is from the middle of March till the end of April (O. S.) and from the middle of Aug. till the beginning of October. In summer the heat is almost unbearable, while the dust irritates the respiratory organs in a highly unpleasant manner. Winter is very cold, and all nature seems dead. — It is desirable to be provided with *Introductions* to the higher Russian officials.

The best CLOTHING for this journey consists of a suit of khaki, with undergarments of raw silk or wool (of which an abundant supply should be taken, as they have to be very frequently changed). Starched linen should be avoided. Among the other necessities are a dress-suit, sheets, pillows, dust-spectacles, and a saddle (for excursions into the country). It is also well to be provided with biscuits, as the native bread is not always very palatable. Weapons are unnecessary.

PLAN AND EXPENSE OF TOUR. A flying visit to Turkestan may be made from Krasnovodsk in a fortnight, including days of rest.

Railway journey from Krasnovodsk to Kokand and back . . 6 days
Bokhara . . . . 2 „
Samarkand . . . . 2 „
Kokand (pleasanter than Tashkent) . . . . 1 day
Ruins of Old Merv (town itself best visited on Thurs. or Sun.) 1 „

Those who do not wish to travel twice on the Transcaspian Railway should return from Tashkent viâ Orenburg (R. 76).

The daily expenses for hotels, carriages, and the like, amount in the towns to 7-10 rb. The hotels, with a few exceptions, are never more than tolerable. A dragoman acquainted with the Sartian dialect receives from 10 to 20 rb. per week. If the traveller brings his dragoman with him from Caucasia, he should take care that he understands Sartian, as this dialect is very different from the form of East Turkish (so-called Tartar) spoken in the Caucasus. — The total expenses of a fortnight's tour may be reckoned at about 300 rb. The *Russo-Asiatic Bank* (comp. p. 525) has branches at the larger towns. ·

BIBLIOGRAPHY. *A. Vambéry*, Travels in Central Asia (1864), Sketches of Central Asia (1867), and History of Bokhara (1873). — *F. Burnaby*, A Ride to Khiva (1877; new ed., 1905). — *G. N. Curzon* (Lord Curzon), Russia in Central Asia (1889). — Дмитріевъ-Мамоновъ, Путеводитель по Туркестану (5th ed.; С.-Петербургъ, 1912). — *R. Karutz*, Von Lübeck nach Kokand (Lübeck, 1904). — *H. Krafft*, A travers le Turkestan russe (Paris, 1902). — *Rev. H. Lansdell*, Russian Central Asia (1885; abridged edition, 1887). — *Annette Meakin*, In Russian Turkestan (1903). — *A. F. O. H. Olufsen*, The Emir of Bokhara and his Country (1911). — *Capt. J. N. Price Wood*, Travel and Sport in Turkestan (1910). — *R. Pumpelly*, Explorations in Turkestan (Washington, 1905). — *W. Rickmer Rickmers*, The Duab of Turkestan (1913). — *Graf von Schweinitz*, Orientalische Wanderungen (Berlin, 1910). — *F. H. Skrine & E. D. Ross*, The Heart of Asia (1899). — *G. F. Wright*, Asiatic Russia (New York, 1903).

a. From Baku to Samarkand. Bokhara.

Steamboats and *Railway*, see p. 506.

The steamer takes about 16 hrs. to cross the Caspian Sea (p. 462) from *Baku* (p. 456) to Krasnovodsk.

Krasnovódsk (70 ft. below the level of the sea; *Railway Restaurant; London*), the chief town of a district, with 7800 inhab. and a fort, was founded in 1869 at the foot of rocky bills (800 ft.) on the Bay of Krasnovodsk in the Caspian Sea, and is the starting-point of the Central Asiatic or Transcaspian Railway. Sailors or porters ('ambal') transport the luggage from the harbour to the adjacent railway station (trunks 10, smaller articles 5 cop.).

The railway skirts the light-green Bay of Krasnovodsk, which cuts deeply into the land, while to the left rises a barren rocky chain. 47 V. *Kará-Tengír* (15 ft.); 77 V. *Belék* (70 ft. below sea-level). Excellent crabs, caught in the Bay of Krasnovodsk, are offered for sale at the stations. Farther on the rocky wilderness on the left comes close up to the railway. — 126 V. *Dzhebél* (25 ft. below sea-level; Rail. Restaurant). — 156 V. *Ballá-Ishem* (35 ft. below sea-level). About 21 M. to the S.W. is the so-called Naphtha Mountain (Нефтяная ropá). To the left lies the *Uzbói*, a waterless valley extending from the lower course of the Amú-Darya through the desert to a point near the Bay of Krasnovodsk. — 200 V. *Perevál* (140 ft.), the highest point the railway reaches in its course through the depression between the chain of the *Great Balkhán* on the left and the *Little Balkhán* on the right. — At (246 V.) *Kazandzhík* (110 ft.; Rail. Restaurant), a Russian village of 650 inhab., in a malarial district, begin, to the right, the marginal chains of the high Irán, the *Kyuren-Dágh* and *Kopet-Dágh*, which the railway now follows for a distance of more than 400 V. (267 M.) — Just short of (315 V.) *Kizúil-Arvát* (325 ft.; Rail. Restaurant), a small town of 5400 inhab. with railway-workshops, the train reaches the home of the Tekke Turcomans, the *Akhál Oasis*. This is the largest oasis in the Transcaspian Territory, being 160 M. long and 6-13 M. wide. In spring it resembles a flowery prairie, interrupted by isolated patches of tilled and garden land, watered by small brooks. The desert is continually visible in the distance to the left, and its mirages and sand-spouts are often seen at a distance of a few miles. — 366 V. *Bamí* (245 ft.), with groves of poplar and acacia; 396 V. *Artchmán* (290 ft.); 426 V. *Bakhardén* (525 ft.).

478 V. (317 M.) **Geók-Tepé** (665 ft.). Opposite the railway station is a small *Museum*, containing relics of the campaign of 1881, portraits (including an equestrian portrait of General Skóbelev, by Svertchkóv), and a painting by Roubaud of Munich, representing the storming of the fortress. Behind the museum rise the clay walls of the former Turcoman fortress of *Dengíl-Tepé*, now rapidly falling into

decay. This fortress was stormed by the Russians under Skóbelev, on Jan. 12th, 1881, after a siege of 23 days. The trains stop here 10-15 minutes, which gives time for a rapid glance at the museum and for the ascent of the fortress-walls. The fort contains a stone monument erected in 1901 in memory of the Russians who fell at the siege, but is otherwise empty.

In plan the fortress is an irregular parallelogram about $1^1/_2$ M. in circumference. The perpendicular ramparts were 26-33 ft. high from the bottom of the moat and 20-40 ft. thick, and were provided with a breast-work at the top. The garrison consisted of 25,000 armed men, while the attacking force consisted of 6000 men with 79 guns. At the S.E. angle is a large breach, made by the explosion of a powder-mine in preparing for the storm-party.

500 V. *Bezmein* (770 ft.). The Kopet-Dágh reaches a height of 9770 ft.

520 V. (345 M.) **Askhabád,** Асхабадъ (730 ft.; *Railway Restaurant; Frantzúskiye Nomerá,* kept by Mme. Révillon, R. 1-$2^1/_2$ rb., D. 60 cop.; *Germania; London;* restaurant at the Civil Casino; good bath in the so-called 'Marble Bath', 60 cop.; phaeton from the rail. station to the town 25, per drive 20 cop.), the capital of the Transcaspian district and the headquarters of the 2nd Turkestan Army Corps, contains over 50,000 inhab., who carry on a brisk trade with Persia. In summer the heat and dust make the place almost unendurable; we must be on our guard against Sartian sickness (p. 506). From the rail. station the Ánnenkovskaya ($1^1/_2$ M. long) leads to the Persian and Armenian trading quarter. The Museum contains collections of ethnography (groundfloor) and natural history (first floor; open in summer week-days 9-1, Sun. & holidays 11-1, in winter 10-2 & 11-2; adm. 10 cop.; closed in July; director, St. Y. Bilkevitch). Many of the inhabitants belong to the Persian sect of the *Babists,* founded between 1830 and 1840 by Ali Mohammed of Shiraz. A large mosque was built here in 1910.

From Askhabad a highroad, crossing the Kopet-Dágh 5 times, leads to (143 M.; a drive of 4 days) *Meshhéd* (3180 ft.), a Persian commercial town with 60,000 inhabitants. The interior of the town (inaccessible to Europeans) contains a mosque built in 1602, in which is the tomb of the eighth Imam, Ali III. er-Riza (d. 818), visited annually by upwards of 50,000 Shiite pilgrims. From Meshhed a bridle-route (2 or 3 days) leads to Kaakhka (see below).

About 3 M. from the railway station of (528 V.) *Anau* (740 ft.) is the ruined town of that name, with the remains of a very fine old mosque. About 2 M. to the S. of (609 V.) *Artúik* (740 ft.) is the Persian town of *Lyutfabád.* — 641 V. *Kaakhká* (950 ft.). Route to Meshhéd, see above. — The train now follows the frontier between Russia and Persia, indicated by conical mounds of earth, and sometimes approaching within a few yards of the railway. — At (680 V.; 450 M.) *Dushák* (810 ft.; Rail. Restaurant) the train quits the S.E. direction which it has hitherto been following, turns to the N.E., and enters the region of the river *Tedzhén (Tején),* the second-largest in the Transcaspian district. Here begins the huge sandy

desert which extends almost all the way to the Amú-Darya, interrupted only by the Oasis of Merv. — About $^3/_4$ M. beyond (724 V.)
Tedzhén (605 ft.) we cross the river of that name.

From Tedzhen a road runs along the right bank of the river to (81 M.)
the frontier-town of *Serákhs* and the *Zulfkár Pass*, situated at the angle
where Russia, Persia, and Afghanistan meet.

Farther on we cross the *Murgháb* (see below).

842 V. (558 M.) **Merv.** — *Railway Restaurant.* — HOTELS. *Yevro-
péiskiye Nomerá; Frántziya*, near the rail. station. — *Elias Yakubóv* has
a large selection of native Afghanistan and Beluchistan carpets, but bargaining is necessary in dealing with him. — *Phaeton* per drive 20, from
the rail. station with luggage 40 cop. Three-horse carriage to Old Merv
& back 10-12 rb. (the excursion takes one day; we must start early and
take provisions).

New Merv (735 ft.), a district-town with 20,000 inhab., on both
sides of the Murgháb, was founded in the oasis of the same name
in 1884. Since 1896 it has been greatly devastated by malaria.
Outside the town, on the left bank of the Murgháb, is the spacious
Market Place, well worth a visit on Mon. & Thurs., when all kinds
of fruit are displayed.

The *Oasis of Merv*, about 1430 sq. M. in area, is formed by the
breaking up of the copious *Murgháb*, which takes its rise in Afghanistan,
and here splits up into a great multitude of small arms and canals, forming a kind of delta district. About 30 M. below the town the last trace
of the river disappears in a morass surrounded by sand-dunes. Cotton
is extensively cultivated in this district. — The Turcomans round Merv
make the best woollen carpets in the whole of W. Asia, but their quality
has of late materially deteriorated in consequence of the immense demand
for them. Comp. 'Merv, Queen of the World', by *C. Marvin* (1881), and
'The Merv Oasis', by *E. O'Donovan* (1882).

From Merv a branch-railway (thrice weekly; comp. p. 504) leads S. to
(294 V. or 195 M.) *Kushka* (2060 ft.), a Russian fortress on the Afghanistan
frontier, which may not be crossed without the special permission of the
Emir of Afghanistan. This railway leads viâ (77 V. or 51 M.) *Sultan Bent*
(885 ft.), with the remains of the huge dam across the Murgháb (comp.
below); an attempt to restore this dam in 1887-89 was unsuccessful.

868 V. *Bairám-Alí* (770 ft.; Railway Restaurant), with the headquarters of the imperial *Demesne of Murgháb* (Мурра́бское Госу-
да́рево име́ніе), which is 435 sq. M. in area, and extends down
both sides of the Murgháb from Sultan-Bent (see above). Intending
visitors should provide themselves with an introduction to the director. The irrigation system of the manor was completed in 1895.
There are large cotton-presses and cotton-cleansing factories.

Opposite the railway station begin the **Ruins of Old Merv*,
covering an area of 16 sq. M., through which the railway now runs.
Those who have not come by carriage from New Merv (2$^1/_2$ hrs.)
should apply to the manager of the Murgháb Manor and request
his assistance in procuring carriages or horses. The traveller is
also dependent for his nightquarters on the courtesy of the officials.

Merv, mentioned in the Avesta (p. 508) as *Muru*, is one of the oldest
cities in the world. It is the *Antiochia Margiana* of classic writers, and

was named by the Turcomans *Kunia-Merv* (Old Merv). Seleucus Nicator founded a Hellenistic colony here. During the 6th cent. A.D. most of its inhabitants were Christians (Nestorians). The city attained the culmination of its prosperity in the 7th cent. under Arab rule. Along with its well-irrigated oasis and the huge dams of the Murgháb, it then ranked among the wonders of the world, and it rivalled Bagdad for the position of the greatest city of the Orient. Jenghiz Khan, enraged by the death of his grandson before its walls, utterly destroyed the city in 1219. According to Arabic writers, upwards of one million human beings were slain by the Mongols on this occasion. In the 15th cent. Merv was rebuilt, and it continued to exist, alternately as an Uzbek and as a Persian town, down to 1795, when the Emir of Bokhara captured it and converted it into a desert by the destruction of Sultan Bent (p. 512). The inhabitants were removed to Bokhara.

In visiting the ruins the traveller should confine himself to the part situated to the N. of the railway and should take with him a supply of food and drink. The Turcomans pasturing their sheep among the ruins are quite inoffensive; they often offer for sale coins and other small objects found among the ruins. — From the railway station we follow the railway embankment a short way towards the E., then bend to the left, and proceed in a straight direction over heaps of rubbish to the entrance gate of *Bairám Alí Khan-Kaláh*, which breaks the long wall stretching from N. to S., and is flanked by two towers. This fortress, which was founded by a son of Timur, and was destroyed by the hordes of Bokhara, consists

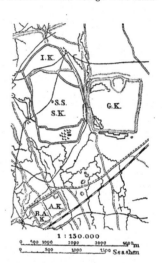

1 : 150.000

N. Part of Old Merv
(after V. A. Zhukovski).

A. K. = Abdulláh Khan-Kaláb;
B. A. K. = Bairám Ali Khan-Kaláh; G. K. = Giaur-Kaláh;
I. K. = Iskender-Kaláh; S. K. = Sultan-Kaláh; S. S. = Tomb Mosque of Sultan Zandshar.

of a rectangle of walls enclosing an area about 1 M. in circumference, the ground of which is strewn with numerous fragments of buildings of baked or crude brick. Immediately to the E. of it is a similar and larger enclosure called *Abdulláh Khan-Kaláh*. The road leads to the E., traversing both of these enclosures. Before leaving by the E. gate the traveller should climb the wall, in order to obtain a view of the extensive ruins. The area, however, was never completely built up and occupied at the same time; the various enceintes show the fortified nucleus of the town at different periods. Farther on the route turns to the N. and passes the ruins of two

small tomb-mosques (Могилы проповѣдниковъ), where, according
to legend, are buried two brothers, the banner-bearers of Mohammed. The road then proceeds towards a large and conspicuous building. forming what remains of the tomb-mosque of Sultan Zandshar,
and said to date from the 12th century. This part of the ruins is
named *Sultan-Kaláh*, and formed the capital of the Seljuks, which
was destroyed by the Mongols in 1219. To the E., surrounded by
long earthen ramparts and covering an area of 1¹/₂ sq. M., lies
Giaur-Kaláh, the Merv of the Nestorian and Arab eras, which has
been in ruins since the 12th century. To the N. lies *Iskender
Kaláh*, probably the site of the town of the Seleucidæ. From the
rampart separating Sultan-Kaláh from Iskender-Kaláh, which we
may ascend, we now drive back to the (4 M.) railway station.

Just beyond Bairam-Ali the railway enters the desert of *Kara-
Kum* ('black sand'), formerly enjoying an evil reputation as the
'Grave of the Caravans'. The shifting sand-dunes near the railway
have, however, been to some extent fixed by the planting of saxaul
(Haloxylon ammodendron). — 944 V. *Utch-Ádzhi* (Rail. Restaurant);
1003 V. *Repeték* (605 ft.), situated in the midst of the desert and surrounded by interminable sand-dunes. A short way beyond (1048 V.)
Barkhani (650 ft.), a dark strip becomes visible on the E. horizon,
indicating the vegetation along the course of the Amú-Darya. — Just
beyond (1070 V.) *Tchardzhui* (625 ft.; Rail. Restaurant; good
melons), in the emirate of Bokhara, we cross the *Amú-Darya* by
an iron bridge.1 M. in length, completed in 1901. The part of the
emirate of Bokhara traversed by the railway consists of alternate
stretches of sand and alkaline desert and well-irrigated arable lands.

1077 V. *Faráb* (605 ft.); 1117 V. *Karákul* (645 ft.).

1182 V. (784 M.) **Kagán.** — *Railway Restaurant.* — Hotels. *Bolshaya Moskóvskaya*, new, with restaurant; *Kommértcheskaya.* — Phaeton
from the station to the town 30-40, per drive 30, per hr. 60 cop.; to Bokhara,
in 1 hr., 1¹/₂-2 rb.

Kagán or *New Bokhará* (730 ft.), with 2000 inhab., is the seat
of a Russian political agent, to whom the traveller should pay a
visit as soon after his arrival as possible.

___

For the visit to (8 M.) *Bokhará* the highroad (carriage, see
above) is, except in hot and dusty weather, preferable to the railway (40 & 20 cop.).

Bokhará (*Turan Hotel*, at the railway station, with restaurant), the purely Asiatic capital of the emirate of the same name
and the most important commercial city in Central Asia, contains
over 80,000 inhabitants. It is surrounded by an earthen wall,
25 ft. high and 7¹/₂ M. in circumference, the numerous gates of
which are closed between sunset and sunrise. [A pleasant ride of

1¹/₂-2 hrs. may be taken round this wall.] The low, flat-roofed houses, built of sun-dried bricks, are almost windowless towards the street. The drinking-water, which is conducted from the *Zeravshán* through the Shakh-rud Canal into a number of ponds, is extremely unwholesome.

In the reign of *Ismail*, a member of the dynasty of the *Samanides*, the rulers of Bokhara from 873 to 1004, the town laid the foundation of its fame, which it still retains, as the intellectual and religious focus of the Sunnite sect of E. Islam. In 1220 Bokhara was razed to the ground by *Jenghiz Khan*. *Timur*, who ascended the throne in 1370, removed the seat of the government to Samarkand; yet Bokhara enjoyed a new era of prosperity under him and his successors, especially in the time of *Ulu-Beg*. From 1499 to 1597 the ruling dynasty was that of the *Sheibanides*, who transferred their residence back to Bokhara. The most capable member of this dynasty was *Abdullah-Khan* (d. 1597). Next came the *Ashtarkhanides*, who ruled until 1784, and under whom the gradual decay of the place began. Since 1784 the ruling family has been the *Mangites*. The present Emir, *Seid-Mir-Alim-Khan*, who is dependent upon Russia, ascended the throne in 1911.

Sir Anthony Jenkinson (p. lii), one of the pioneers of Anglo-Russian commerce and the first Englishman who ever saw the Caspian Sea, extended his journey to Bokhara and Khiva (1557-58).

Bokhara contains 364 mosques and 109 medresehs or theological colleges, which, however, lack the architectural interest possessed by similar buildings in Samarkand.

The chief sight of the town is the very extensive and richly stocked **Bazaar**. The narrow covered passages in the various sections (tíms) of the bazaar are thronged by Persians, Kirghizes, Hindoos, Armenians, Tartars, Afghans, Turcomans, Uzbeks, and Tajiks, most of them wearing light-coloured garments. As in all Oriental towns the various industries are separately grouped in the bazaar, while manufacturing and sale are (when possible) carried on at the same spot. To give some protection against the burning rays of the sun, the streets are either arched over or covered in with mats, linen, or canvas. Among the most attractive goods in the bazaar are the carpets, the fine silks, the copper and other metal wares, and the black lambskins known as 'karákul', good specimens of which cost at least 6 rb. The spacious points of intersection of the bazaar streets are covered with domes and are called 'tchar-su'. The frequent shout of 'posht, posht' means 'look out!' Tea-booths are numerous; and a large platform has been built out over the canal in front of the gate to provide a place for the tea-drinkers. — Purchases of any extent should not be made without the assistance of an intelligent resident. The shopkeepers, with the exception of the Jews seldom understand Russian. The Bokhara 'tenga' is a silver coin worth about 15 cop., while the brass 'puhl' is worth only ¹/₄ copeck.

The *Ark*, or Castle of the Emir, stands on an artificial earthen mound 50 ft. in height. In front of it stretches the *Registán*, an open space covered with fruit-stalls; behind it is an interesting prison (gratuity).

Near the castle lies the large *Kalyan Mosque*, in which the Emir, when in Bokhara, attends service every Friday between 12 and 2 p.m. The light-blue tiles of the dome are still in good preservation. The minaret of the mosque, which is 200 ft. in height, is known as *Manari-Kalyan* or 'Criminals' Tower', because criminals used to be thrown headlong from it (ascent not allowed). — The *Labi-Khaus Mosque* dates from 1611. The square in front of it offers interesting types of popular life. — The most important medreseh is the *Mir-Arab*, situated opposite the Kalyan Mosque and dating from the end of the 16th century. In the middle of the main façade is the large keel-arch of the entrance-door (pishtak), the magnificent tile casing of which has, to a great extent, disappeared. The pishtaks of the *Sargeryan Medreseh* and of the *Timur Medreseh* are well preserved.

About 2 M. to the W. of the town lies *Shirbudun*, a country-house of the Emir, built about 1870 and standing in a large garden.

1223 V. *Kizuil-Tepé* (Rail. Restaurant). — 1269 V. (841 M.) *Kermineh* (1305 ft.). About 8 M. to the N. is the town of this name, containing 12,000 inhab. and a château which forms the usual residence of the Emir of Bokhara. — A little short of (1343 V.) *Katti-Kurgan* we reach the Russian territory of Samarkand. Distant mountains are seen both to the right and left. — 1416 V. (939 M.) *Samarkánd* (Rail. Restaurant; station, Pl. A 1).

Samarkánd.

HOTELS (in Sept. and Oct. rooms should telegraphed for in advance). *Centrálnaya*, *Grand-Hôtel*, *Kommértcheskaya*, *Peterbúrgskiye Nomerá*, all in the Russian Quarter. — Good cuisine at the *Civil Casino* (Обще́ст-венное собра́ние), to which travellers must be introduced by a member.

PHAETON from the railway station to the (3 M.) Russian Town 60 (in winter 75), from the Russian to the Native Town 30, per drive 20, per hr. 50 cop. — BANKS. *Imperial Bank* (Pl. 3; B, 3); *Russo-Asiatic Bank* (Pl. 13; C, 3).

Photographs may be obtained at *Litvíntzev's* and *Polyakov's*.

Principal Attractions (two days). On the first day the traveller should visit the buildings of the town, while he may devote the second to Shakh-Zinda, Afro-Siab, and an excursion in the environs.

The abstraction of coloured tiles and other relics is promptly and severely punished by the officials.

Samarkánd (2255 ft.), the capital of a district of the same name, contains 90,000 inhab., and lies in the valley of the *Zeravshán*, in the midst of a fertile and well-watered plain. It carries on a trade in raisins and other dried fruit. The mean temperature is 56° Fahr. but in summer the shade temperature sometimes reaches 100° Fahr.

The date of the foundation of the town is lost in the mists of antiquity. Its early name was *Maracanda*. In 329 B. C. the town was captured by *Alexander the Great*, who signalized his stay here by stabbing, in the midst of a banquet (328 B. C.), his favourite general Clitus, who had saved his life on the Granicus. In the 7th century of our era Samar-

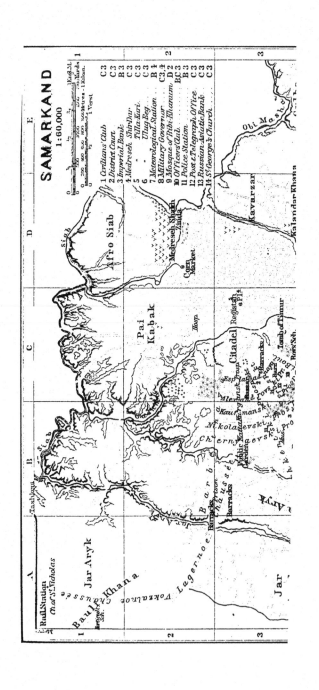

SAMARKAND

1:60,000

1 Civilians' Club	C 3
2 District Court	C 3
3 Imperial Bank	B 3
4 Medreseh Shir-Dar	C 3
5 — Tilla-Kari	C 3
6 — Ulug-Beg	C 3
7 Meteorological Station	B 4
8 Military Governor	C 3,4
9 Mosque of Bibi-Khanum	D 2
10 Officers' Club	B C 3
11 Police Station	B 3
12 Post & Telegraph Office	C 3
13 Russian Asiatic Bank	C 3
14 St George's Church	C 3

kand was taken by the Arabs, and in 1221, in spite of a vigorous resistance, it had to yield to Jenghiz Khan. In 1369 *Timur* (comp. p. 508) made it his capital and residence, and the magnificent buildings he erected still form, though in a somewhat dilapidated condition, the chief sights of the city. At a later date the city was in the hands of the Sheibanides and Mangites (p. 515), but in 1868 it was taken possession of by Russia.

The city consists of two quarters, the mediæval native town, and the Russian town, dating only from 1871. To the N. lies the site of the ancient Maracanda.

The RUSSIAN TOWN, the seat of the officials, is traversed by wide streets adorned with double rows of shady acacias and elms. A military band plays frequently in the public gardens (Pl. B, 3).

A little to the E. of the Russian town is the *Mausoleum of Timur (Gur-Emir;* Pl. C, 3), 110 ft. high and now in a very ruinous condition. It is surmounted by a massive blue dome, the tiles on the drum of which form the best preserved part of the decorations.

We enter the mausoleum by a small door on the left side of the forecourt, leading to a corridor covered with a series of small domes. Here stand the mullahs in charge of the building, one of whom takes visitors round for a fee of 20-25 cop. each. From the corridor a door leads to the right to a square inner chamber 70 ft. high, 1075 sq. ft. in area and covered by the main dome. There are nine tombstones here, eight of which are surrounded by marble railings, while the ninth is in a niche opposite the entrance; the graves are in a crypt below. In the middle is the *Tombstone of Timur,* who died in 1405 at the age of 70. This consists of two greenish-black blocks of nephrite fitted into each other; they are the largest pieces known of this rare stone, measuring $6\frac{1}{2}$ ft. in length, $1\frac{1}{3}$ ft. in width, and 1 ft. in height. The other tombstones, all of relatives or friends of Timur, are of grey marble or alabaster. Behind the lamp ('lanterne des morts') are two masts, one bearing a horse's tail, the other a white banner. The wainscoting consists of octagonal blocks of alabaster, while higher up is a band of jasper, on which the genealogy and deeds of Timur are recorded in Arabic characters. The lateral recesses have beautiful stalactite-vaulting.

Between the Russian quarter and the native town lies the CITA DEL (Pl. C, 3), completed in 1882 (accessible only by permission of the commandant). In an old castle, now used as an artillery depôt, is the so-called *Coronation Stone of Timur* (Тронъ Тимýра; Kok-Tash), a rectangular block of greyish-black marble $11\frac{1}{2}$ ft. long, with arabesques on the sides and half-columns at the angles.

The NATIVE TOWN is rich in monuments of the best period of Mohammedan architecture.

Most of the buildings are made of either kiln-dried or crude bricks. The vault is the prevailing architectural feature, and the outer form of the domes is that of a melon. The decoration consists of dark-blue, light-blue, green, or white glazed bricks, or of coloured tiles with ornamental patterns in low relief. The colours are still beautifully fresh. The large main portals (*Pishtak*) of the mosques (*Metchét*) are surmounted by keel-arches. The minarets are not quite perpendicular, but lean a little to one side.

The rectangular *Registán* or *Market Place* (Pl. C, 3), which is 77 yds. long and 66 yds. wide, affords a good opportunity for

studying the manners and customs of the people. On its E. side is
the mosque of Shir-Dar, on the N. side the mosque of Tillah-Kari,
on the W. side the mosque of Ulug-Beg, and on the S. a row of
traders' stalls. Attached to all three mosques are medresehs, in
each of which the cells of the students surround a plastered, rectangular, paved court with a water-basin in the middle of it. — The
Mosque of Shir-Dar (Pl. 4; C, 3), built in 1616, has a façade elaborately adorned with mosaics. The pishtak is about 75 ft. high.
Visitors may ascend the round minaret on the left or to the platform
above the pishtak; but the steps are very high, and the ascent is
rather uncomfortable for ladies. The view from the top includes
the native town, with its gaily-coloured tiled buildings, but nothing is seen of the Russian quarter except the trees in its avenues.
In front of the mosque is the tomb monument of a saint. — The
decorations of the mosque of *Tillah-Kari* (Pl. 5; C, 3), which dates
from 1618, are in a bad state of preservation. — The *Mosque of
Ulug-Beg* (Pl. 6; C, 3), part of which is in ruins, was built in 1434 by
Timur's grandson, Mirza Ulug-Beg, 'the prince of the astronomers'.

Near the Registan is the cemetery of *Tchil-Dukhtar*, containing upwards of 40 marble monuments of rulers of the period before Timur.

To the E. of the Registan stretches the *Bazaar* (Pl. B, 3), which
unlike that of Bokhara, has broad, well-lighted streets, and is distinctly inferior in interest.

At the E. end of the bazaar-street, about $^1/_3$ M. from the Registan,
rise the massive remains of the *Mosque of Bibi-Khanum* (Pl.
9; D, 2), erected by Timur in 1399, in honour of his favourite wife
and brilliantly decorated. The main portal, opening on the court,
is flanked by two minarets, one of which has preserved its beautiful
mosaic ornamentations. In the court stands a huge koran-desk,
consisting of two colossal wedge-shaped stones lying upon a pedestal $7^1/_2$ ft. long and $6^1/_2$ ft. wide. Mohammedans believe that child-
less women who creep below the desk will infallibly be blest with
offspring. The pishtak of the mosque has a keel-shaped arch 185 ft.
in height, and its mosaics are also well preserved. Opposite the
mosque is the dilapidated mausoleum of Bibi-Khanum. — Between
the mosque of Bibi-Khanum and the Registan lies the *Monument of
Sheibani-Khan*, consisting of a block of marble 20 ft. long, $17^1/_2$ ft.
wide, and 7 ft. high, covered with thirty tombstones.

To the N. of the native town, up the slope to the plateau of the
ancient Maracanda, stretches **Shakh-Zinda** (Pl. D, 2), a group of
mausolea. The decorations here consist of glazed and coloured tiles of
fayence, and their brilliancy of colouring and delicacy of execution
can hardly be exaggerated. — The portal, which was erected in 1434
by Ulug-Beg (see above), gives on a passage, to the right and left
of which lie eighteen buildings of some size. To the left, above the
flight of steps, is the *Mausoleum of Oldsha Aïm*, the nurse of

Timur. Farther on, to the right, is the *Mausoleum of Shirin-Bika-Aka* (1385), while opposite, to the left, is the *Mausoleum of Dshushuk-Bika* (1371), with a fine entrance-door; these contain the remains of two sisters of Timur. To the right, towards the end of the passage, is the *Mausoleum of Shakh-Zinda* (Kazim-ibn-Abbas) with a beautifully carved walnut door. Besides the tomb of the saint, it contains a copy of the Koran about 6 ft. in width.

Above Shakh-Zinda lies the extensive plateau on which *Maracanda* (p. 514) lay; the natives call it *Afro-Siab* (Pl. D, 1), after a legendary Shah of Turan. The nearer part of Afro-Siab is occupied by Mohammedan cemeteries. The plateau, which rises abruptly from the Zeravshán valley, is 3 M. in circumference. The ancient ramparts and the approaches from below are still recognizable, and also numerous round reservoirs, resembling those still in use at Bokhara. We also see the mound of the former citadel, where the castle of the princes of Sogdiana stood, and probably the spot on which Alexander the Great held his court. — About 3 M. to the N.E. of Samarkand is the interesting *Observatory of Ulug-Beg*, excavated in 1910, and commanding a superb view of the Zeravshán valley and the Hissar Mts.

A road leads from the town through the middle of Afro-Siab, and, at the farther end of the latter, descends into the river valley. Here lies (7 M.) the *Tomb of Daniel*, regarded by Mohammedan tradition as a companion of Kazim-ibn-Abbas (comp. above). — About 6 M. from the town, in the steppe, stands the so-called 'Camp of Timur', the remains of a summer-residence of that ruler. — Below Afro-Siab, on the left bank of the Zeravshán, rises a colossal brick archway, known as the *Bridge of Timur*, and probably a relic of a large dam and sluice for the regulation of the Zeravshán. A second arch, at right angles to that just mentioned, has fallen in.

b. From Samarkand to Tashkent.

332 V. (220 M.). Railway in 12 hrs.

Samarkánd, see p. 516. The train runs to the N.E. to (30 V.) *Rostóvtzevo* (2480 ft.), the highest-lying station on the Central Asiatic Railway. It then crosses a range of mountains, at first running through a shallow depression, and then, as it nears Dzhizak, in a narrow winding pass known as the 'Gate of Timur' (Тамерланова ворóта). Here are two Arabic inscriptions, referring to the armies that have penetrated this pass (1425 and 1571), and a bronze tablet with a Russian inscription commemorating the construction of the railway. — 107 V. (71 M.) *Dzhizak* (1280 ft.; Rail. Restaurant), a district-town of 12,000 inhab., is one of the most unhealthy spots in Turkestan. — We now enter the 'Starvation Steppe' (Голóдная степь), a triangle between the Suir-Darya on the N.E., the foothills of the Turkestan mountains on the S., and the Kuizuil-Kum ('Red Sand') on the W. — 190 V. (126 M.) *Tchernyáyevo* (1180 ft.; Rail. Restaurant).

FROM TCHERNYAYEVO TO ANDIZHAN, 306 V. (203 M.), *Ferghána Railway* in 12 hrs. [It is desirable to be provided with introductions to the representatives of the large Russian cotton-dealers.] This journey is full of interest as far as Gortchakovo. Rich fields of cotton, sorghum (durra), and rice, the thriving villages, and the elaborate network of irrigation canals afford a graphic picture of the peculiar system of cultivation depending mainly on the presence of flowing water. None of the copious mountain-streams descending from the Alai Mountains reaches the Suir-Darya, as their water is exhausted in irrigating the fields. In clear weather we have a fine view to the N. of the *Alatau Mts.*, and to the S. of the *Alai Mts,* both of which are covered with snow till well on in the summer.

75 V. *Khodzhént* (1330 ft.; Rail. Restaurant). The town of this name, the ancient Kyropolis, lies 6¹/₂ M. to the N.W., on the Suir-Darya (izvóshtchik 1¹/₂ rb.), and contains 40,000 inhabitants. — The railway now enters the Ferghana District.

179 V. (119 M.) **Kokánd** (1375 ft.; *Rail. Restaurant; Centrálnaya,* opp. the Town Park, R. 2-4 rb., D. 60 cop. to 1 rb.; new hotel to be opened by the Brothers Vadyaev; phaeton from the rail. station to the Russian town 35, to the old town 45, per drive 20 cop.), the capital of an independent khanate down to 1875, but since then in the hands of Russia, is a city of 114,000 inhab. (6000 Russians), situated on a canal of the *Sokh* and surrounded by a ruinous wall. It is the most important trading town in Turkestan, although in respect to population, and the size and business of its bazaar, it is inferior to Bokhara. In recent years malaria has been much less prevalent. The former palace of the Khan, completed in 1870, now a barrack, has a façade of glazed and coloured tiles (adm. on appli cation to the commandant). The throne-room has been fitted up as a Greek Catholic Chapel. The traffic in cotton begins yearly in the middle of Aug. (O. S.) and is taken part in by representatives of the great Russian cotton-dealers.

A railway leads to the N. to (84 V., or 56 M.) *Namangán* (Nomerá Agaluikov, Kuropátkinskaya; Nomerá Yug, Barónskaya), a town with 74,000 inbah., whence Tashkent may be reached on horseback in 4-5 days.

244 V. *Gortchakóvo* (1675 ft.; Rail. Restaurant, well spoken of). The station adjoins the S. wall of *Old Margelán* (Старый Маргелáнъ), a very ancient town with 47,000 inhabitants. About 3 M. to the N. of the rail. station (phaeton, 50 cop.) is the Great Bazaar, near which is the alleged grave of Alexander the Great (Могила Искáндери пашú).

A branch-line runs to (8 V.) **Skóbelevo,** known as *New Margelán* up to 1907 (*Rail. Restaurant; Grand-Hôtel,* clean; phaeton from the rail. station to the town 40, at night 60-80 cop., to Old Margelan & back 3¹/₂, after rain 4-6 rb.), the capital of the Ferghana District, founded by the Russians in 1877. Pop. 15,500. Its museum is worth inspection (open on Sun., 11-12). Magnificent view of the mountains from the fields to the S. of the town.

306 V. (203 M.) *Andizhán* (1635 ft.; Rail. Restaurant; Rossíya), a town of 76,000 inbah., destroyed by an earthquake in 1902 but almost wholly rebuilt since. Cotton is extensively grown in the vicinity. A highroad leads from Andizhan to the S.E. to (46 V., or 31 M.) *Osh* (ca. 4265 ft.; 47,000 inhab.), the starting-point for travelling ̃on the Pamir Plateau and in Chinese East Turkestan. The *Pamirs* are reached by a military road, practicable for artillery, which traverses a series of very elevated passes and several wild valleys. Permission to make this journey is seldom granted, and the crossing of the Indian frontier is possible only by an express arrangement between Russia and the British government. — From Osh (see above) a route leads to the S.E. to (280 M.) Kashgar. The first part of the route consists of a road leading viâ (50 V. or 33 M.) *Gultcha* and *Sufi-Kurgan* (6825 ft.) to (80 V., or 53 M. from Gultcha) the *Tallduik Pass* (11,865 ft.). [At Sufi-Kurgan diverges the route over the *Terekdavan Pass* (13,515 ft.).] From the Tallduik Pass a bridle-path leads to the Russian frontier-fortress of *Irkeshtam*, and thence viâ the Chinese fortified station of *Ullugtchat* to *Kashgar* (ca. 4265 ft.), a Chinese town of 65,000 inbah., with a British consul-general *(Sir G. Macartney, K.C.I.E.)*. It also contains a branch of the Russo-Asiatic Bank.

Beyond (257 V.) *Suir-Dáryinskaya* (860 ft.), the railway to Tashkent crosses the *Suir-Darya* by an iron bridge 370 yds. in length, and enters the province of Suir-Darya.

332 V. (220 M.) **Tashként.** — *Railway Restaurant.* — HOTELS. *Tzakho (Regina)*, with restaurant, fair; *Rossíya; Stáraya Frántziya; Grand-Hôtel*, R. from 2 rb., D. (12-7) 80 cop. — *Anona Restaurant.* — IzvÓsHTCHIK from the rail. station to the Russian Town 50, per drive in the Russian Town 20, to the Native Town 50, per hr. 60 cop. — TRAMWAY from the station to the Native Town.

Tashként (Ташкентъ; 1570 ft.), captured on June 15th, 1865, by the Russians under General Tchernyayev, is the seat of the Governor General of Turkestan and of the 1st Turkestan Army Corps, and contains 272,000 inbab., including 118,000 Russians. A remarkable phenomenon is the absolutely windless calm which prevails during nearly the whole year in the city and its environs. The town contains a Lutheran Church, built in 1896. — The broad streets of the Russian Town are flanked with rows of trees and canals. In the Konstantinov Square is the monument of *K. P. von Kauffmann* (p. 506), by Schleifer (1913). The *Kauffmann Library*, containing over 80,000 vols., is rich in works on Turkestan, and also possesses a small ethnographical collection (open on Sun., 12-2). A monument, by Mikéshin, in the Town Park, erected in 1904, commemorates the taking of the town. It represents a Russian soldier planting the colours on the city-wall. — The Native Town is extensive, but it is inferior to Bokhara in the picturesqueness of its street-scenes, and cannot vie with Samarkand in architecture. — In summer (from June on) the higher officials and the upper classes of the citizens retire to their datchas in the *Tchimgán Ravine* (Чимгáнское ущéлье; 4690 ft.), which lies 86 V. (57 M.) from the town (carriage 25 rb.).

From Tashkent to *Orenburg*, see R. 76.

76· From Orenburg to Tashkent.

1736 V. (1150 M.). Express train, with through-carriages from St. Petersburg and Moscow, once daily in 44 hrs. (fares 31 rb., 18 rb. 60 cop.; reserved seat 3 rb. 30 cop.). Sleeping Car of the International Sleeping Car Co. twice weekly (13 rb. 90, 10 rb. 40 cop.). The daily mail-train takes 60 hrs. — Permission to visit Turkestan, hints on the preservation of health, etc., see pp. 506 et seq.

The railway traverses the Kirghiz Steppe, touches the N.E. corner of the Sea of Arál (p. 506) at (802 V., or 532 M.) Arálskoye More, and farther on follows the valley of the Suir-Darya (pp. 506 et seq.).

Orenburg, see p. 368. — The railway turns towards the S. and crosses the *Úrál River*. — 72 V. *Ilétzk*, a district-town with 15,800 inhab., and extensive deposits of rock-salt, which are being exploited. — We now proceed towards the E., first on the right, then on the left bank of the *Ilék*· 119 V. *Ak-Bulák* (Rail. Restaurant); 254 V. *Aktyubinsk* (Rail. Restaurant), a district-town with 14,000 inhab., in the province of Turgái. Beyond (434 V.) *Emba* we cross the *Mugodzharskiya Mts.* 492 V. *Ber-Tchogúr;* 598 V. *Tchelkár;* 753 V. *Saxaulskaya* (Саксаульская), all three with railway restaurants.

802 V. (532 M.) *Arálskoye More* (Rail. Restaurant), at the N.E. corner of the Sea of Arál. — 922 V. *Kazalinsk* (255 ft.; Rail. Restaurant), the station for the district-town of that name, which lies in the Suir-Darya district, 7 M. to the W., and contains 12,300 inhabitants.

The train now follows the course of the Suir-Darya, keeping to its right bank.· Beyond (1084 V.) *Dzhusali*, and again just before reaching (1199 V.) *Kara-Uzyák* (Кара-Узякъ), we cross the *Kara-Uzyák*, a right-bank tributary of the Suir-Darya.— 1222 V. *Perovsk* (460 ft.; Rail. Restaurant), about 1 M. from the district-town of that name (8300 inhab.); 1342 V. *Tchiili* (Rail. Restaurant). — 1488 V. (986 M.) *Turkestán* (720 ft.). About 3 M. to the N.E. (izvóshtchik 75 cop.) lies the town of that name, the capital of a district and containing 16,300 inhabitants. It was captured by the Russians in 1864, and contains the Khazrat-Sultan tomb-mosque (erected by Timur in honour of a Mohammedan saint), which attracts many pilgrims in·the spring. — 1540 V. *Timúr*. On the right is a large kurgán or tumulus, which is said to date from the period of Timur. Just short of (1640 V.) *Aruis* (815 ft.; Rail. Restaurant) we cross the river of that name. — From (1661 V.) *Kabul-Sai* (Rail. Restaurant) a highroad leads to (740 V. or 490 M.) *Vyerni*, a town with 36,000 inhabitants. The train crosses the crest of the *Sari-Agatch* at a height of 1865 ft. above the level of the sea, then descends into the valley of the *Dzhilga (Jilga)*, and runs on, crossing several small bridges, to (1736 V. or 1150 M.) *Tashként* (p. 521).

From Tashkent to *Samarkand* and *Krasnovodsk* (Baku), see R. 75.

77. From Moscow to Vladivostok
viâ Tchelyabinsk *(Trans-Siberian Railway)*.

8134 V. (5391 M.). Railway from Moscow to Tchelyabinsk, 2056 V.; Trans-Siberian Railway from Tchelyabinsk to Irkutsk, 3049 V.; Trans-Baikal Railway from Irkutsk to Mandshuriya, 1424 V.; Chinese Eastern Railway from Mandshuriya to Pogranitchnaya, 1388 V.; Ussuri Railway from Pogranitchnaya to Vladivostok, 217 V. — *Customs Examination.* On the outward journey Chinese officials examine passengers' luggage at Mandshuriya, and Russian officials at Pogranitchnaya (registered luggage at Vladivostok). On the return-journey there is a Chinese examination at Pogranitchnaya, and Russian examinations at Mandshuriya, Tankhoi, and Irkutsk. — Two Express Trains weekly in 8²/₃ days, one being operated by the International Sleeping Car Co. (Междунаро́дный по́ѣздъ), and the other by the State Railways (Казённый по́ѣздъ). Carriages are changed at Irkutsk. Fares 327 rb. 44, 212 rb. 77 cop. (first-class compartment reserved for a single traveller 523 rb. 70 cop.); from Berlin to Vladivostok 673 ℳ, 424³/₄ ℳ: from London to Vladivostok 37-38*l.*, 23-25*l.* The first-class compartments or sections are for two persons, the second-class for four. The railway tickets (apply early) are available for 22 days if bought in Russia, or 3 months if bought elsewhere. If the journey is broken, it is necessary to obtain a new seat-ticket for the rest of the journey. Thus, *e.g.*, a new seat-ticket from Omsk to Irkutsk costs 18 rb. 40 or 13 rb. 80 cop. The amount of luggage allowed free is 60 Russian lbs. (54 lbs.), but through passengers from foreign countries are entitled to twice as much. Each additional 10 lbs. (9 lbs.) costs 2 rb. 69 cop. The charges in the Dining Car are B. 55 cop., déj. 1¹/₄, D. 1¹/₂ rb. — Mail Train daily in 13 days (fares 158 rb. 93, 96 rb. 76 cop.; carriages changed at Tchelyabinsk, Irkutsk, and Mandshuriya). Also 'Passenger Train' daily as far as Mandshuriya (seat ticket, see p. xxiii). — The journey from Moscow to *Tsuruga* (Yokohama) viâ Vladivostok takes 12 days (fares 365 rb. 19, 250 rb. 51 cop.); to *Nagasaki* 12 days (fares 380 rb. 48, 265 rb. 81 cop.); to *Shanghai* 14 days (fares 410 rb. 7, 295 rb. 39 cop.).

From St. Petersburg to Vladivostok, viâ Perm and Tchelyabinsk, 8269 V. (5481 M.), express train twice weekly in 9 days (fares 329 rb. 35, 214 rb. 25 cop.). Carriages are changed at Irkutsk. Comp. R. 35.

Through-passengers from W. Europe to the Far East must have their passports *visé* by a Russian consul (comp. pp. xviii, xix); registered luggage is not examined before it reaches the frontier of the country of destination. — Tickets (available for 2 years) are obtainable for the journey to the Far East by railway and back by steamer, or vice versâ. The steamer-journey may be begun or ended at Shanghai, Yokohama, Kobe, or Nagasaki.

Siberia (Сибѝрь) has an area (4,784,034 sq. M.) 1¹/₂ times greater than Europe, 2¹/₃ times larger than Russia in Europe, and more than 10 times larger than the United Kingdom of Great Britain and Ireland. In 1910 its population was estimated at 8,220,000. It extends from the Ural Mts. (59° E. long.) on the W. to the Sea of Japan and the Okhotsk and Behring Seas on the E. (Cape Deshnev or East Cape, 174° 24' E. long.), and from the Arctic Ocean on the N. to China on the S. It is divided into the two *Governments of Tomsk* and *Tobolsk* (which together formerly constituted the General-Government of West Siberia); the *General-Government of Irkutsk*, which includes the Governments of Yeniseisk and Irkutsk and the Territories of Yakutsk and Transbaikal; and the *General-Government of the Amur Territory*, comprising the Amur and Maritime Provinces, Kamtchatka, and the N. half of the island of Sakhalin. The N.W. part of the *General-Government of the Steppes* (the Akmolinsk and Semipalatinsk Territories) belongs officially to Russian Central Asia.

Western Siberia, from the Urals to the Yeniséi, is for the most part a flat plain, with good arable land and pastures in its central and S. portions. Eastern Siberia, which is three times as large, is mountainous and less fertile, labouring under the disadvantages of a severe climate in its W. part and of periodical inundations in the E. In N. Siberia most of the ground is covered with forest *(Taigá)*, gradually passing over into a waste of barren lands *(Tundras)*, which are frozen for the greater part of the year and marshy in the summer. To the S. and S.E. are the *Altái Mts.* (p. 526), the chief peak of which is the Byelúkha (14,900 ft.); the *Sayán Mts.* (Саянскія горы; highest peak *Munku-Sarduik*, 11,275 ft.); the *Yáblonovi Hills;* and the *Stanovói Hills*, all of crystalline formation. —Into the Arctic Ocean flow the *Ob* (2240 M. long), with its greatest tributary the *Irtúish* or *Irtýsh* (about 2200 M. in Siberia and 330 M. in China, where it is known as the Black Irtúish); the *Yeniséi* (about 2490 M. long); and the *Lena* (2860 M. long). The *Amúr* (p. 537), which with the *Argún* is over 2720 M. long, flows into the Sea of Okhótsk. The largest lake is *Lake Baikál* (p. 533).

The CLIMATE of Siberia runs to extremes both of heat and of cold; the winter is severe and the air dry except on the E. coast. The coldest month is January, the hottest July. At Tomsk the range is from — 3.3° Fahr. to + 65.6°, while the mean annual temperature is + 30.7°. The corresponding figures at Irkutsk are — 5.4°, + 65.1°, and + 31.3°; at Siberia and 330 M. in Blagovyeshtchensk, on the Amúr — 13.9°, + 70.5°, and + 33.3°; at Vladivostok — 14.1°, + 87.1°, and + 40.3° F.

Siberia is rich in coniferous trees. The deciduous trees of W. Siberia lack variety, consisting mainly of birches, aspens, alders, and poplars; to the E. of the Yáblonovi range the list receives many additions, such as the oak, walnut, and elm. The Territory of the Amúr, on the other hand, abounds in deciduous trees.—Siberia is especially rich in minerals. These include gold (output in 1909, 2895 pud or 1,524,762 oz.), silver, lead, copper, iron, coal, and graphite. Exports to the W. include wheat, rye, oats, and butter (in 1911 more than 4,300,000 pud or 69,320 tons, most of it viâ Windau).

The great majority of the INHABITANTS of Siberia, especially those in the towns and along the railway, are Russians, including free immigrants (peasants and Cossacks) and the exiles and their descendants (comp. p. 261). [Between 1896 and 1910 there were 3,970,000 immigrants.] The Turkish (Kirghizes, Tartars, Yakuts), Finnish (Voguls, Ostyaks), and Mongolian (Teleuts, Buriats, Samoyedes, Tunguses) races are also represented.—The exiles, most of whom are to be found in E. Siberia, consist of criminals condemned to penal servitude, those compelled to settle in prescribed communities, and those banished by administrative process. As a result of an Imperial Ukase of June 10th, 1900, the banishment to Siberia has been considerably limited.

HISTORY. The Russian conquest of Siberia began in the reign of *Iván the Terrible,* who in 1574 invested the merchants *Jacob* and *Gregory Stróganov* with the right to build forts upon the banks of the rivers Toból, Irtúish, etc. In 1575, for the protection of their extensive domains, the Stróganovs took into their service 800 Cossacks under *Yermák,* the former Volga pirate, who penetrated far into the interior of Siberia. and (on Oct. 26th, 1581) captured *Iskér* or *Sibír* (p. 528), the capital of the Siberian Tartar Empire. Yermák was drowned after a fight in 1584 while attempting to escape by swimming across the Irtúish.—Thenceforward the Russians pressed steadily eastward and northward, and easily vanquished the inhabitants who opposed them. Tobolsk was founded in 1587, Tomsk in 1604, Yakutsk in 1632, Irkutsk in 1652. In 1649 the Cossack Hetman *Khabaróv* fitted out an expedition to take possession of the Amúr district, but the peace of Nertchinsk (1689) gave this territory back to China. The scientific exploration of the land was undertaken during the reign of Peter the Great, when Behring discovered the strait which bears his name.—In 1854 *Count Muravyév* (Amúrski), Governor-General of Eastern Siberia, descended the Amúr with a military force, and in 1857 the left bank of that river was ceded to Russia by China. In 1860, by the treaty of Peking, Russia acquired the Ussuri province; and in the same year Vladivostok was founded. During the construction of the Trans-Siberian Railway (1891-1903) the Russians leased the peninsula of Kuan-tung (with Port Arthur) from the Chinese (1898). The Russians occupied Manchuria in 1900, and their refusal to evacuate it at the request of Japan brought on the Russo-Japanese war of 1904, which ended in the defeat of the Russians. By the Peace of Portsmouth (1905) Russia lost Kuan-tung, Manchuria, and the S. half of Sakhalin.

The best TRAVELLING SEASON for Siberia extends from the middle of May (O. S.) to the middle of June. July is a very hot month, but August is pleasant, while September is a favourable season for Manchuria (voyage on the Amúr, see p. 539). Those who make the trip in summer should take light clothing and a warm overcoat, while woollen underwear is the best safeguard against the sudden changes of temperature. Travellers should *on no account* drink *unboiled water*. High goloshes or 'rubber boots' are desirable, as the unpaved streets of the towns are almost impassable in spring and autumn; in winter felt overshoes or 'arctics' (пимы́) are also necessary. A mosquito-veil is desirable in E. Siberia and Manchuria during the summer. It is desirable to carry a revolver in Manchuria and in trips away from the railway.—The HOTELS are almost invariably dear and indifferent. Bed-linen, soap, etc., should always be taken. A disturbing feature is the inevitable concert or 'sing-song' in the dining room, which usually lasts far into the night. Travel in Siberia is about one-third more expensive than in Russia in Europe.

The traveller must be on his guard against *Thieves*. Thus, when he quits his compartment at a railway station he should have the door locked by the provodník (p. xxi).

Travellers in Siberia should avoid carrying large sums of money on them. Instead they should have orders on the *Russo-Asiatic Bank* (Русско-Азіатскій банкъ; comp. p. 96), on the *Commercial Bank of Siberia* (Сибирскій торговый банкъ), or (for the East) on the firm of *Kunst & Albers* at Vladivostok (branch at Hamburg).

BIBLIOGRAPHY. More or less extensive accounts of Siberia will be found in the following works: *A. Bordeaux*, Sibérie et Californie (Paris, 1903). — *A. J. Dmitriev-Mamonov* and *A. F. Zdziarski*, Guide to the Great Siberian Railway (1900). — *J. F. Fraser*, The Real Siberia (1902). — *W. Gerrare*, Greater Russia (1903). — *Sir A. Hosie*, Manchuria (1901). — *G. Kennan*, Siberia and the Exile System (4th ed., 1897) and Tent Life in Siberia (New York, 1893). — *J. Legras*, En Sibérie (Paris, 1913). — *M. P. Price*, Siberia of To-day (1912). — *P. A. Stolypin & A. V. Krivoshein*, Kolonisation Sibiriens (Berlin, 1912). — *M. L. Taft*, Strange Siberia (New York, 1911). — *S. Turner*, Siberia (2nd ed., 1911). — *Chas. Wenyon*, Four Thousand Miles across Siberia (5th ed., 1909). — *R. L. Wright* and *Bassett Digby*, Through Siberia (1913).

a. From Moscow to Irkutsk. Tomsk.

5105 V. (3384 M.). EXPRESS TRAIN twice weekly (from Tchelyabinsk on also twice weekly by the train coming from St. Petersburg) in 5¹/₂ days (fares 167 rb. 65, 110 rb. 5 cop.). The ticket is valid for 14 days; break of journey, see p. 523. Luggage to the amount of 40 Russian lbs. (36 lbs.) allowed free; each additional 10 lbs. (9 lbs.) 1 rh. 64 cop. 'PASSENGER TRAIN' in 6¹/₂ days (73 rb. 50, 44 rh. 10 cop.; reserved seat 6 rb. 10 cop.). — St. Petersburg time (comp. p. xxxii) is kept at all railway stations.

From Tchelyabinsk to the Ob the train passes through grassy steppes inhabited by the horse-breeding Kirghizes (p. 507) and producing immense quantities of Siberian butter. From Novo-Nikolayevsk (p. 528) to Krasnoyarsk (p. 530) we traverse the *Taigá* (virgin forest), which has been thinned out in the vicinity of the railway-line and near Atchinsk (p. 530) alternates with meadow-land. From Krasnoyarsk to Irkutsk (p. 531) the country is comparatively animated and well cultivated.

From Moscow to (2056 V. or 1363 M.) *Tchelyábinsk* viâ *Tula, Ryazhsk, Samára,* and *Kinél,* see RR. 48 a and 50.

The Trans-Siberian Railway runs to the E. from Tchelyabinsk (p. 370) through the province of Orenburg, which is part of European Russia.—83 V. (from Tchelyabinsk) *Tchumlyák* (560 ft.); 117 V. *Shumíkha* (580 ft.), 156 V. *Mishkino* (510 ft.), both with railway restaurants; 188 V. *Yurgamúish.* About 200 V. from Tchelyabinsk the line passes from the province of Orenburg into that of Tobolsk (Siberia).

241 V. *Kurgán* (260 ft.; Rail. Restaurant). The town of that name (Bogdánov; izvóshtchik from the railway station to the town, 50 cop.) lies 1 M. distant, on the right bank of the *Toból,* a tributary of the Irtúish. Pop. 24,600. The dramatist A. von Kotzebue (d. 1819) spent the year 1800 in exile here. Kurgan exports large quantities of butter, and contains representatives of several English firms. The huge butter-making industry of Siberia is said to have been originated by the English wife of a Russian landowner near Tyumen (p. 261).—About 6 V. beyond Kurgan we cross the Toból by a bridge 512 yds. long. 363 V. *Makúshino* (465 ft.; Rail. Restaurant), in a marshy district. Beyond (449 V.) *Mamlyútka* (450 ft.) we enter the territory of Akmolinsk and cross the (482 V.) *Ishim,* a tributary of the Irtúish, by a bridge 256 yds. long.

490 V. *Petropávlovsk* (455 ft.; Rail. Restaurant). The district town (Nomerá Nazárova, R. from $1^{1}/_{2}$ rb.; Centrálnuiye Nomerá; izvóshtchik from the station to the town 50 cop.), founded in 1752, lies on the right bank of the Ishim, 2 M. to the N.E. of the station, and contains 43,000 inhab. (15,000 Mohammedans). The old court of barter (Мѣновóй дворъ) is a sort of caravanserai with the shops opening upon the inner quadrangle only. Petropavlovsk has a large trade in cattle and hides.

The train now skirts the N. margin of the *Kamuishlovsko-Irtúish Valley,* which is dotted with salt lakes. 617 V. *Isil-Kul* (420 ft.; Rail. Restaurant). About 2 M. short of Omsk the *Irtúish* (p. 524) is crossed by a bridge 750 yds. in length.

746 V. (495 M.) **Omsk,** Омскъ.—Branch-line from the rail. station (restaurant) to the ($3^{1}/_{2}$ V.) town; it is, however, better to take an izvóshtchik (see below).—HOTELS. *Rossíya,* Lyúbinski Prospékt, R. $1^{1}/_{2}$-6, D. (1-6) $^{3}/_{4}$-$1^{1}/_{4}$ rb.; *Yevropéiskaya,* Dvortzóvaya, R. 2-4 rb., D. (2-6) 60 cop. to 1 rb.; *Kommértcheskiye Nomerá,* Kostyólnaya.—IZVÓSHTCHIK from the Main Railway Station to the town 1 rb., from the Town Station 40, per drive 30, per hr. 75 cop.—GENERAL POST OFFICE, Potchtóvaya.—BRITISH VICE-CONSUL, *S. R. Randrup.* There is also a U. S. CONSULAR AGENT.

Omsk (285 ft.), founded in 1717, is the headquarters of the 4th Siberian Army Corps and the capital of the General-Government of the Steppes (comp. p. 523). It is situated on the right bank of the *Irtúish,* just above its confluence with the *Om.* Pop. 128,000. —From the main railway station, adjoining which is a settlement with about 20,000 inhab. and large railway-workshops, we proceed to the N. to the Nikólskaya Square, passing a park with the *Officers' Summer Casino.* In the square is the *Church of St. Nicholas,* containing an alleged banner of Yermák (p. 524), brought hither from Berezov on the lower Ob. Adjacent are the large *Cadet School,* a three-story building, and a *Roman Catholic Church.* We continue to the N. along the Dvortzóvaya and then cross an iron bridge over the Om, with the steamboat-wharf to the left. At the other end of the bridge we reach the Lyúbinski Prospékt. Adjacent, on the bank of the Om, is the *Dyetski* or *Children's Playground,* with a summer theatre. The Lyúbinski Prospékt ascends to the Bazaar Square, with the *Museum* of the Imperial Russian Geographical Society, which is open in summer (except from June 10th to Aug. 10th) on Thurs. & Sun., in winter Frid. & Sun., 12-3 (adm. 15 cop.; conservator, A. N. Sedelnikov). The contents of the Museum include ethnographic collections from the steppes, specimens of the domestic industries of the district, a collection of birds, and prehistoric relics. Close by are a *Lutheran Church* and a *Municipal Theatre.* Behind the Museum lay the old fortress, the four gates of which are still standing. The building in which the author F. M. Dostoyévski (d. 1881) was imprisoned from 1849 to 1853, and in which he wrote his 'Recollections of a Dead House' (Engl. translation entitled 'Buried Alive in Siberia'), stood in the N.E. corner of the fortress, but has been removed. — About $^2/_3$ M. to the N. of the town is a Birch Grove (Загородная роща), much frequented by the inhabitants of Omsk (izvóshtchik 50 cop.).

Railway from Omsk to *Yekaterinburg,* see p. 261.

FROM OMSK TO TOBOLSK, 1127 V. (747 M.), steamer down the Irtúish in 4-5 days (fare 8 rb.). The *Irtúish,* the largest tributary of the Ob, rises on the S.W. slopes of the Altái Mts. and is 2500 M. long. The right bank is higher than the left. — 380 V. *Tara,* on the left bank, a district-town with 12,500 inhabitants. Near (770 V.) *Ust-Ishim* the Ishim joins the Irtúish on the left.

1127 V. (747 M.) **Tobólsk,** Тобольскъ (*Loskútnaya; Kommértcheskaya,* kept by Ackermann, R. 1-1³/₄ rb., bed-linen 30 cop.; izvóshtchik from the landing-stage to the lower town 40, to the upper town 50, per drive 25 cop.; steamer to Tomsk, see p. 530, to Tyumen, see p. 261), the capital of the Government of Tobolsk and seat of the Greek Catholic Bishop of Tobolsk and Siberia, has 21,400 inhabitants. It was founded in 1587 on the steep right bank of the *Irtúish,* opposite the mouth of the *Toból,* and consists of an upper and a lower town, the latter being unhealthy. In the upper town is a *Kremlin* enclosed within walls and containing a 'Swedish Tower', built with the labour of captured Swedes after the battle of Poltava (see p. 390). At the entrance to the *Yermák Garden* is a *Museum* (open daily except Mon., in summer 12-7, in winter 12-3; adm. 20 cop.; director, V. N. Pignatti), with works on Siberia, bronzes, and an ethnographical collection (Ostyak and Samoyede curiosities). The Yermák Garden also contains a marble *Obelisk* erected in 1839 to the memory of Yermák. Adjoining the *Bishop's Palace* is a chapel, in which the Bell of Uglitch (see p. 348) hung down to 1892. In the Tulyatzkáya, which leads from the upper to the lower town, is the *Lutheran Church.* Not far off is a *Roman Catholic Church.* On the bank of the Irtúish stands the *Známenski Monastery,* the oldest in Siberia. - About 13 M.

from Tobolsk, on the right bank of the Irtúish, lies *Kutchúmovo Goro-dishtche*, with the ruins of the old town of *Iskér* (p. 524).

FROM OMSK TO SEMIPALATINSK, 992 V. (658 M.), steamer up the Irtúish in 4-5 days (fare 14 rb.).—548 V. *Pavlodár*, on the right bank, with 9000 inbab., chiefly Cossacks and Kirghizes.—992 V. *Semipalatinsk* (Irtúish; Rossíya), capital of the territory of the same name, with 35,000 inbab. (half of whom are Mohammedans), lies on the right bank. It contains a Museum of the Imperial Geographical Society.

790 V. *Kormílovka* (370 ft.). Beyond (859 V.) *Kolóniya* (360 ft.) we enter the Government of Tomsk. 904 V. *Tartárskaya* (Rail. Restaurant); 953 V. *Tchani* (365 ft.), 30 M. to the S.W. of which is *Lake Tchani*, well stocked with fish (area 1266 sq. M.).—1049 V. *Kaïnsk Tomski* (400 ft.; Rail. Restáurant). The district-town of this name with 6500 inbab., chiefly exiled Jews and their descendants, lies 8 M. to the N. (izvóshtchik 1½ rb.).—Beyond (1090 V.) *Kozhurlá* (455 ft.) the line crosses the river of that name, and then the *Karapúz*. 1209 V. *Tchulúimskaya* (460 ft.; Rail. Restaurant).—About 3 V. before reaching (1285 V.) *Kotchenóvo* (545 ft.) the train crosses the *Kargát;* and 32 V. farther on it crosses the *Krivodónka*. About 4 V. beyond (1324 V.) *Krivoshtchékovo* we cross the *Ob* by a bridge 865 yds. long.

1332 V. **Novo-Nikoláyevsk** (*Rail. Restaurant; Yefremov,* Gudimovskaya; *Novo-Nikoláyevskoye Podvórye,* Nikoláyevski Prospékt, R. 1-3½ rb.), founded in 1896 at the time of the construction of the Trans-Siberian Railway, has already 70,600 inhabitants. It is prettily situated on the high right bank of the Ob. In the middle of. the town is the Alexander Nevski Church. Novo-Nikolayevsk is a favourite starting-point for sportsmen in pursuit of the wapiti, mountain-sheep, ibex, and other big game on the N. slope of the Altái. Steamer to Tomsk or Biisk, see p. 530.

About 224 V. (150 M.) to the S. (post-road; steamer, see p. 530) lies **Barnaúl** (*Centrálnaya*) a town of 61,000 inhab., on the left bank of the Ob, the headquarters of the Altai Administration and the centre of the fertile 'Cabinet' estates (*i.e.* belonging to the Tzar). It carries on an important butter-trade. It was founded in 1738 by A. N. Demidóv, in whose honour a monument has been erected. He also opened the first mines in the Altái district. The town possesses a good mineralogical museum (Горный музей) and a Lutheran church.

From Barnaul a post-road (160 V. or 106 M.) and a steamer (280 V. or 186 M.; comp. p. 530) go to *Biisk* (Moskóvskoye Podvórye), a district-town of 29,000 inbah. on the *Biya*, in the province of Tomsk. It carries on a trade in wool.

Biisk is the starting-point for an excursion to the RUSSIAN ALTÁI, a range of mountains culminating in the *Byelúkha* (14,900 ft.) and the *Iiktu* (13,780 ft.), in the central Katun-Tchuya Chain. Glaciers are found as low as the forest-level (6560-8200 ft.). The inhabitants of this bleak mountain district are Russian peasants and nomads, such as the Altaians and Khirgizes. There are no regular posting-stations; but the peasants furnish carriages and horses (10-12 cop. per verst). The traveller should bring tinned provisions with him, as he can count upon nothing in the villages but bread, milk, and eggs. Comp. 'Пути по Русскому Алтаю' (Tomsk, 1912), by Prof. V. V. Sapózhnikov (p. 529), the chief authoity on these monntains.—From Biisk the Uimonski Road leads S., viâ the villages of *Altaiskoye, Kulgan, Tchorno-Anuiskoye, Ust-Kanskoye, Abaiskoye,*

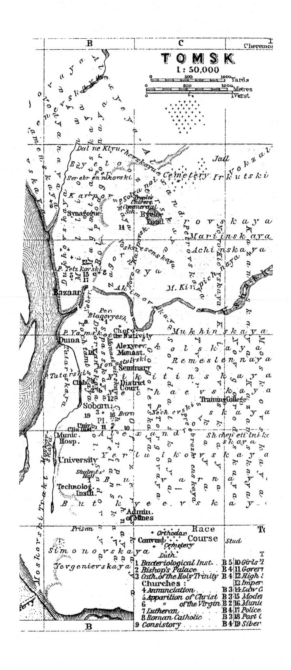

TOMSK
1 : 50,000

1	Bacteriological Inst.	B 5
2	Bishop's Palace	B 4
3	Cath. of the Holy Trinity	B 4
	Churches :	
4	Annunciation	B 3
5	Apparition of Christ	B 3
6	" of the Virgin	B 2
7	Lutheran	B 4
8	Roman Catholic	B 3
9	Consistory	B 4
10	Girls'	
11	Gover	
12	High	
	Imper	
14	Law C	
15	Mode	
16	Muni	
17	Police	
18	Post	
19	Siber	

and *Uimonskoye,* to (360 V.) *Kotanda.* From this point we may reach the *Akkem Glacier,* on the N. slope of the Byelukha, in 2 days, or the *Ieduigem Glacier,* on the E. slope, in 4 days.

The railway runs on towards the N.E. to Mariinsk, then to the E. to Kansk, and thence to the S.E. to Irkutsk.— 1366 V. *Sokúr* (760 ft.); 1450 V. *Bolotnaya* (Rail. Restaurant). About 3 M. short of (1489 V.) *Tutalskaya* (435 ft.) the *Tom* is crossed.— 1546 V. *Taigá* (845 ft.; Rail. Restaurant), with 10,300 inhabitants.

FROM TAIGA TO TOMSK, 82 V. (54 M.), branch-railway in 3 hrs.

Tomsk, Томскъ. — *Railway Restaurant.* — HOTELS. *Yevrópa* (Pl. a; B, 3), cor. of Potchtámskaya and Blagovyéshtchenski Pereúlok, R. 1½-8 rb. *Rossiya* (Pl. b; B, 4), Spásskaya; *Métropol,* Magistrátskaya 11 (Pl. B, 1-3) all three with cafés chantants; *Dresden* (Pl. c; B, 3), Magistrátskaya, quiet, without café chantant. — RESTAURANTS. At the two first named hotels; at the *Club* (Общественное собрáніе; Pl. B, 4; introduction by a member necessary), Potchtámskaya; beer at *Krüger's,* Potchtámskaya.

IZVÓSHTCHIK from or to the railway stations 75 cop. (luggage included); to the steamboat wharf, see p. 530; per drive 20-25, at night (12-6) 30 or 35, per hr. 40, at night 60, each additional hr. 30 or 45 cop.

POST & TELEGRAPH OFFICE (Pl. 18; B, 4), Potchtámskaya. — Bookseller, *I. I. Makúshin,* Blagovyéshtchenski Pereúlok (Pl. B, 3).

The city-office of the railway is in the Magistrátskaya (Pl. B, 1-3).

Tomsk (485 ft.), situated on the high right bank of the *Tom* (free from ice May 1st to Nov. 1st) and at the mouth of the *Ushdika,* in lat. 56°29′ N., is the capital of the government of the same name and the seat of a Greek Catholic bishop. Pop. 112,000. It was founded in 1604. — In the S.W. quarter stands the UNIVERSITY, founded in 1888 (Pl. B, 5; 1000 students), the only one in Siberia. It consists of a medical and a legal faculty. Its collections include an *Archaeological and Ethnological Museum* (open free daily 12-3; director, P. Bogayevski); a *Zoological Museum* (closed at present; director, N. F. Káshtchenko); a *Botanical Cabinet* (open on week-days in winter 10-1; director, V. V. Sapózhnikov); a *Mineralogical Museum* (open Sun. and holidays in winter 12-1; closed in June, July, and Aug.; director, P. Pilipenko); and the *Library,* with 250,000 volumes. Near the University is a *Students' Dining Hall* (Pl. B, 5). A *Technological Institute* (Pl. B, 5) was opened in 1900; it is attended by 1200 students. — The Greek Catholic *Cathedral of the Trinity* (Трóицкій собóръ; Pl. 3, B 4) was finished in 1900. The recluse Theodore Kuzmitch (d. 1861), widely known on account of his resemblance to the Tzar Alexander I., is buried in the *Alexéyevski Monastery* (Богорóдице-Алексѣевскій мужскóй монастырь; Pl. B, 4), which was founded in 1605; the cell actually occupied by him is still shown in the Tchistakov House, in the Monastúirskaya. The *Nikólskaya Church* (Church of the Nativity; Pl. B, 3) occupies the site of an old nunnery, where, in 1740, Princess Catherine Dolgoruki, the bride of Peter II., was forced to take the veil. She was, however, freed from her vows in

1742 by the Empress Elizabeth. Tomsk contains a *Lutheran Church*
(Pl. 7; B, 4) and a *Roman Catholic Church* (Pl. 8; B, 3). — The
town is the headquarters of a mining district (comp. Pl. B, 5), and
possesses gold-smelting works.

STEAMBOAT from Tomsk (wharf to the N. of the town near the Tche-
remóshniki railway station; izvóshtchik 1 rb.) to *Biisk* (p. 528; 1174 V.
in 5 days, 19½ rb.) viâ *Novo-Nikolayevsk* (p. 528; 361 V. in 1-1½ days,
6 rb.) and *Barnaul* (p. 528; 894 V. in 3 days, 12 rb.). Also to *Tyumen*
(p. 261; 2220 V., 15 rb.) viâ *Tobolsk* (p. 527; 1814 V. in 3-5 days, 10 rb.).
These services are often interrupted in summer by low water.

CONTINUATION OF THE RAILWAY JOURNEY TO IRKUTSK. The train
runs at first on through the 'Taigá' (p. 524). — 1583 V. *Súdzhenka*
(810 ft.), with coal-pits. Just before reaching (1617 V.) *Izhmor-
skáya* (790 ft.) we cross the auriferous *Yaya.* — 1685 V. *Mariinsk*
(450 ft.; Rail. Restaurant), a district-town with 18,700 inhab., on
the left bank of the *Kiya.* About 2 V. farther on the train crosses
the Kiya by a bridge 232 yds. long, and then ascends to the watershed
between this stream and the *Tyazhín.* — 1810 V. *Bogotól* (975 ft.;
Rail. Restaurant). Beyond (1841 V.) *Kritovo* the line passes from
the Tomsk Government into that of Yeniseisk, and crosses the
Tchulúim by a bridge 302 yds. long. — 1875 V. *Átchinsk* (700 ft.;
Rail. Restaurant). About 2 V. from the railway station is the district
town of that name, situated on the high right bank of the Tchulúim,
with a population of 11,000. It is the northernmost town (lat. 56°
16′ N.) on the Trans-Siberian Railway. A highroad runs hence to
the S. to (333 V. or 221 M.) Minusinsk (p. 531).

The country now becomes hilly. 1910 V. *Tchernoryétchenskaya*
(885 ft.; Rail. Restaurant). The train now ascends the watershed
of the *Great Kemtchug* and the *Katcha*, crosses the Katcha just
short of (1995 V.) *Katcha* (1545 ft.), and then descends to —

2040 V. (1352 M.) **Krasnoyársk**, Красноярскъ (520 ft. ·
Railway Restaurant; Métropole, Voskresénskaya, without café
chantant; R. from 1¼ rb., D. from 50 cop.; *Stáraya Rossíya*,
Blagovyéshtchenskaya; izvóshtchik to the town 50 cop.; British
vice-consul), the finely situated capital of the Government of
Yeniséi, with 80,000 inhabitants. It was founded in 1628, and
lies on the left bank of the *Yeniséi*, here ⅔ M. broad, at the mouth
of the Katcha. Near the railway station, on the W. side of the
town, are the *Railway Technical School* and the *Town Park*
(restaurant at the club). A fine view is obtained from the promenade above the steamboat-wharfs. The Municipal Museum is open
free in winter on Sun. and holidays 11-3 (closed from May 15th to
Aug. 15th). Besides 18 Greek Catholic churches, there are a Lutheran
and a Roman Catholic church.

We may proceed by the pretty highroad (330 V. or 219 M.), or by steamboat down the Yeniséi, to *Yeniséisk*, a district-town of 12,000 inhab., pleasantly situated on the left bank of the Yeniséi. It has a Municipal Museum.

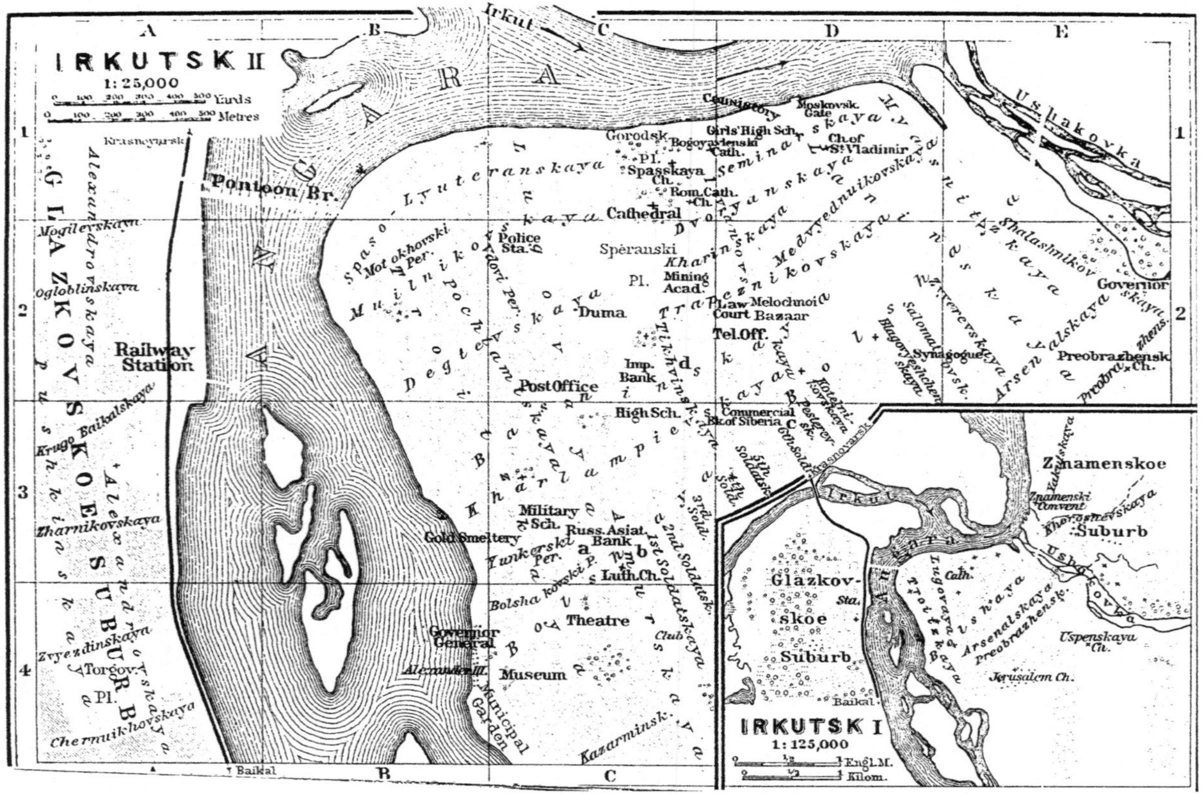

IRKUTSK II

1:25,000

IRKUTSK I

1:125,000

RIVER ANGARA

Pontoon Br.

Railway Station

Alexandrovskaya

GLAZKOVSKOE SUBURB
pushkinskaia

Cathedral

Cadet Corps

Spasskaya Ch.

Court Bazaar

Post Office

Police Sta.

Telof.

Theatre

Museum

Municipal Garden

Governor General

Gold cemetery

Military Sch.

Russ. Asiat. Bank

Commercial Bank of Siberia

Imp. Bank

High Sch.

Mining Acad.

Girls' High Sch.

Preobrashensk Ch.

Znamenskoe

Glazkovskoe Suburb

Baikal

A very enjoyable steamboat trip (4-5 days; magnificent scenery at first) may be taken up the Yeniséi, which is here generally flanked by lofty rocky banks, to *Minusinsk* (Rossiya), a district-capital in the government of Yeniséi, with 15,600 inhabitants. The Municipal Museum, founded by N. M. Martyanov in 1877, and containing 70,000 objects, is worth visiting (open free, Sat. 11-3, Sun. 11-2). Highroad to Atchinsk, see p. 530.

Just beyond Krasnoyarsk the train crosses the *Yeniséi* by a bridge of six spans, having a total length of 1010 yds. 2044 V. *Yeniséi*. About 4 M. beyond (2163 V.) *Klyúkvennaya* (1205 ft.; Rail. Restaurant) we cross the *Rúibnaya*. Beyond (2211 V.) *Kamala* (1085 ft.) the train crosses the watershed of the *Tuirbúil* and the *Little Uryá* and traverses the *Kan* valley. 2267 V. *Kansk Yeniséiski* (680 ft.; Rail. Restaurant), a district-town on the left bank of the Kan, with 17,500 inhabitants. About 2 M. farther on we cross the Kan by a bridge 278 yds. long. 2293 V. *Ilánskaya* (885 ft.; Rail. Restaurant); 2374 V. *Klyutchi* (1280 ft.). After crossing the auriferous *Biryusá*, the line enters the Government of Irkutsk. Beyond (2425 V.) *Taishét* (1040 ft.; Rail. Restaurant) we traverse hilly country viâ (2531 V.) *Kamuishét* (1175 ft.), with cement-works, and (2547 V.) *Uk* (1635 ft.) as far as (2573 V.) *Nizhne-Udinsk* (1360 ft.; Rail. Restaurant), a mountain-girt district-town on the *Udá*, with 6500 inhabitants.

We now proceed through a cultivated district, crossing the Udá, to (2618 V.) *Khudoelánskaya* (1915 ft.), the highest-lying station between Tchelyabinsk and Irkutsk. 2683 V. *Tulún* (1635 ft.; Rail. Restaurant). About 2 M. beyond (2813 V.) *Zimá* (1510 ft.; Rail. Restaurant) we cross the *Oká* by a bridge 510 yds. long. — 2952 V. *Polovína* (1790 ft.; Rail. Restaurant). We cross the *Byélaya* 11 M. farther on. About 10 M. to the N.E. of (2994 V.) *Telma* (1425 ft.) is the village of *Alexándrovskoye* (p. 532). We cross the *Kitói* 5 M. beyond Telma. — 3042 V. *Innokéntyevskaya* (1455 ft.; Rail. Restaurant), 2 M. from which is the *Voznesenski Monastery,* founded in 1672, and containing the bones of St. Innocent (d. 1713) in its principal church (to the right). — Just before reaching Irkutsk we cross the *Irkút*.

3049 V. (2021 M.) **Irkútsk,** Иркутскъ. — The RAILWAY STATION *(Restaurant)* is on the left bank of the Angará, in the suburb of Glázkovskoye, which is connected with the town in summer by a pontoon bridge. *Offices of the State Railways* in the Náberezhnaya Angari, cor. of the Kharlampiyevskaya (Pl. B, C, 3), open on week-days 8-12 & 1-6 (winter 1-4), Sun. & holidays 8-12; the sale of tickets ceases 2 days before the departure of the train; English, French, and German spoken.

HOTELS. *Central* (Pl. b; C, 3), Bolshaya, R. 1¹/₂-8¹/₂ rb.; *Grand-Hôtel* (Pl. c; D, 3), Bolshaya; *Kommértcheskoye Podvorye* (Pl. d; C, 2), cor. of the Tíkhvinskaya and Básninskaya, R. 1¹/₂-4 rb., bed-linen 40, D. (1-5 p.m.) 60-75 cop.; *Centrálnoye Deko*, Bolshaya; *Métropole* (Pl. a; C, 3), Lugováya, R. 1¹/₂-6¹/₂, D. (2-6 p.m.) ¹/₂-1¹/₄ rb. - *Restaurant Modern*, in the Central Hotel (see above).

Izvóshtchik from the rail. station to the town 90 cop., at night (10-7) 1 rb. 20 cop., incl. bridge-toll; per drive 25 (at night 50) cop.

34*

POST OFFICE (Pl. C, 2), Potchtámskaya. —BATHS at *Kurbatov's*, cor. of the Náberezhnaya Angari and Savinski Pereúlok; bath from 1 rb. BANKS. *Commercial Bank of Siberia* (Pl. D, 3), Bolshaya; *Russo-Asiatic Bank* (Pl. C, 3), Bolshaya. —*Makushin Library*, Bolshaya.

Irkútsk (1455 ft.) is situated in 52° 17′ N. lat. and 104° 16′ E. long., on the right bank of the clear and swift-flowing *Angará* (here 660 yds. wide), 44 M. from Lake Baikál, and opposite the mouth of the *Irkút*. It was founded in 1652, and is the see of a Greek Catholic bishopric, the capital of the General Government and of the Government of Irkutsk, and the headquarters of the 3rd Siberian Army Corps. Pop. 113,000. — On the N. side of the town, in the centre of a large open space, is the *Cathedral of the Virgin of Kazan* (Pl. C, 1), a modern building, with five domes and a detached belfry. Opposite the Cathedral is a *Roman Catholic Church*. In the Bolshaya, the main street of the town, which it traverses from S.W. to N.E., are the *Lutheran Church* (Pl. C, 3), the *Theatre* (Pl. C, 4), completed in 1897 from the plans of Schröter, and the *Residence of the Governor-General* (Pl. B, 4), facing the Angará. Opposite the last is the interesting *Museum* of the Imperial Russian Geographical Society (Pl. C, 4), which is open on week-days (except Sat.) 1-3, on Sun. 11-3; adm. 10 cop. (at other times adm. 50 cop.; conservator, N. N. Bogorodski). It contains archæological collections from E. Siberia, Buddhistic objects of worship, mammoth remains, and Chinese birds. The Observatory is open from dusk to 10 or 11 p.m.; adm. 30-50 cop. On the Angará is a bronze *Statue of Alexander III.* (Pl. B, 4), by Bach (1908).

About 70 V. (46 M.) to the N.W. of Irkutsk (post-horse 3 cop. per verst) is the village of *Alexándrovskoye* (comp. p. 531), containing a large and well-equipped prison on the radiating system (Александровская центра́льная ка́торжная тюрьма́). Visitors are generally admitted on application to the director, but it is as well to have an introduction from the Governor of Irkutsk.

b. **From Irkutsk to Vladivostok viâ Karuimskaya** *(Sryetensk)* and **Kharbin** *(Dairen, Peking).*

3029 V. (2008 M.). EXPRESS TRAIN (1st & 2nd class; sleeping and dining cars) four times weekly in 3¹/₃ days (fares 167 rb. 45, 108 rb. 10 cop.; to Kharbin 119 rb. 5, 77 rb. 15 cop.; comp. p. 523). The railway-ticket is good for 11 days (comp. p. 523). The allowance of free luggage is 60 Russian lbs. (54 lbs.) for through-passengers, and 40 lbs. for others; each 10 lbs. (9 lbs.) additional costs 1 rb. 39 cop. —MAIL TRAIN once daily in 5¹/₄ days (fares 142 rb. 20, 55 rb. 95 cop.; to Kharbin 99 rb. 65, 38 rb. 95 cop.); half-a-day is saved by taking the 'Passenger Train' as far as Mandshuriya. Carriages are changed at Mandshuriya (Manchuri).

The so-called zonal tariff of the (Russian) Chinese Eastern Railway is much higher than that of the Russian State Railways, as the following selected fares show: 176 V., 8 rb. 40 cop. & 5 rb.; 625 V., 25 rb. & 15 rb. 65 cop.; 876 V., 36 & 22¹/₂ rb.; 1100 V., 44 & 27¹/₂ rb.; 1400 V., 56 & 35 rb. --Custom-house examination, see p. 523. —The railway-clocks show Irkutsk time (4 hrs. 56 min. ahead of St. Petersburg time) between Lake Baikál and Mandshuriya, and Kharbin time (6 hrs. 25 min. ahead of St. Petersburg time) between Mandshuriya and Vladivostok.

From Irkutsk to Muisovaya the train passes through superb scenery. At first we skirt the Angará to Lake Baikál (see below), girt with huge grey cliffs stretching away to the horizon; then, from Baikal to Muiso- vaya (see below), the line runs on a ledge cut in the rocky bank of the lake, whence, as we emerge from each tunnel, we obtain fresh views of the lake and its girdle of mountains. From Muisovaya to Tchita (p. 534) the country is wooded and hilly, and at times picturesque. [From Tchita (Karuimskaya) to Sryetensk (p. 535) we follow the wild and precipitous bank of the Ingodá.] From Tchita to the Manchurian frontier and thence to Yakeshi (p. 536) the train passes through steppes; from Yakeshi to Barim (p. 536) we traverse a succession of picturesque valleys; between Barim and Pogranitchnaya (p. 537) the steppes begin again, becoming more hilly as we near Pogranitchnaya; thence to Vladivostok (p. 538) we traverse mountains, descending to the sea through a wild and wooded country. Manchuria is an endless steppe, well cultivated in places, bounded on the S. by bare hills, and intersected by four great rivers.

Irkútsk, see p. 531. The railway follows the right bank of the *Angará* (splendid views). 23 V. *Mikhalévo* (1450 ft.). — 61 V. *Bai- kál* (1520 ft.; Rail. Restaurant), where the Angará issues from the lake.

Lake Baikál (1560 ft.), called by the Mongolians the *Bai-Kul* ('Rich Lake'), is surrounded with rocky mountains about 4600 ft. high, many of them covered with forest. It is 13,185 sq. M. in area, 400 M. in length, and from 18 to 56 M. in width. Lake Baikál is the deepest lake in the world (over 6500 ft. in places); moreover, next to the Great Lakes of America and the Victoria Nyanza and Lake Tanganyika in Africa it is the largest fresh-water lake in the world. Its water is extraordinarily clear and very cold. It freezes over about the end of December (O. S.). Storms are very frequent and violent, but least so in June and July. The mountains on the É. side are already snow-covered by October. Lake Baikal is rich in fish. The coregonus omul Lepech. (a kind of whitefish) and the Baikal seal (phoca baicalensis) are peculiar to its waters.

From Baikal the train rounds the S. end of Lake Baikal, thread- ing forty tunnels and passing through numerous cuttings and over numerous bridges. 105 V. *Maritui* (Rail. Restaurant). From (140 V.) *Kultúk* a highroad leads to Kyakhta (p. 534). The train now turns to the E. 150 V. *Slyudyánka* (Rail. Restaurant); 201 V. *Múrino* (Rail. Restaurant); 251 V. *Tankhói* (Rail. Restaurant; customs examination for passengers from the Trans-Baikál district).

305 V. *Muisováya* (1540 ft.; Rail. Restaurant), on the S.E. shore of Lake Baikál. The line now runs near the lake as far as (349 V.) *Posólskaya* (1570 ft.), but it then enters the broad valley of the *Selengá* and follows the left bank of that stream. 384 V. *Selengá* (1580 ft.; Rail. Restaurant), near the village of *Ilyínskoye*, with the Svyáto-Tróitzki Monastery founded in the 16th century. About 7 M. beyond (423 V.) *Tataúrovo* (1620 ft.), where the valley con- tracts, the train crosses the Selengá by a bridge 595 yds. long.

459 V. *Verkhne-Udínsk* (1785 ft.; Rail. Restaurant; Sibir, R. 1-3 rb., bed-linen 35 cop., D. ³/₄-1¹/₄ rb.; izvóshtchik from the rail. station to the town ¹/₂, at night 1 rb.), a prettily situated district town at the junction of the *Udá* and Selengá, is the headquarters of the Western Trans-Baikál Mining Administration. Pop. 15,000.

A highroad, shorter but less interesting than that from Kultuk (see above), runs from Verkhne-Udinsk to the S. to *Selenginsk* (the scene, in

1818-41, of the missionary labours of Wm. Stallybrass and Edw. Swan, who translated the Bible into the Mongolian tongue), *Troitzkosavsk*, and (219 V.) *Kyakhta-Maimátchin*, two towns (the former Russian, the latter Chinese) on the frontier between Russia and Mongolia, formerly the centre of the overland tea trade from China to Russia (now unimportant). At Kyakhta is an agency of the Russo-Asiatic Bank.

About 5 M. beyond Verkhne-Udinsk the train crosses the *Udá.* 492 V. *Onokhói* (1770 ft.), a village occupied by Buryats and Mongols. — 512 V. *Zaïgráyevo* (1880 ft.), with cement-works. We cross the *Bryan.* — The train next ascends viâ (561 V.) *Gorkhón* (2325 ft.) to (593 V.) *Petrovski Zavód* (2635 ft.; Rail. Restaurant), near which is the Petrovski Foundry established in 1790. Farther on we follow the right bank of the *Khilók.* 642 V. *Tolbaga* (2420 ft.). Beyond (685 V.) *Badá* (2535 ft.; Rail. Restaurant) is a short tunnel. 733 V. *Khilók* (2640 ft.; Rail. Restaurant); 846 V. *Mogzón* (2975 ft.; Rail. Restaurant). — About 10 V. beyond (885 V.) *Sokhondó* (3095 ft.) the train leaves the valley of the Khilók crosses the *Yáblonovi Range,* and penetrates a tunnel 93 yds. long, inscribed at its W. entrance 'To the Great Ocean' (къ Великому океану) and at its E. entrance 'To the Atlantic Ocean' (къ Атлантическому океану). We then descend rapidly to (907 V.) *Yáblonovaya* (2775 ft.; Rail. Restaurant), beyond which we follow the winding and picturesque valley of the *Ingodá.* 941 V. *Ingodá* (2265 ft.; Rail. Restaurant).

978 V. (648 M.) **Tchitá** (Чита; 2150 ft.; *Railway Restaurant*); 980 V. *Tchitá Town Station.* The prettily situated town (Daúrskoye Podvórye; izvóshtchik to the town 50, at night 80 cop.), situated on the left bank of the Tchitá, near its confluence with the Ingodá, is the capital of the Trans-Baikál Territory and the headquarters of the 2nd Siberian Army Corps. Pop. 73,000. The *Museum* of the Imperial Russian Geographical Society has an interesting collection of objects relating to the mining and smuggling of gold (open free in winter on Sun., 10-1; at other times on application to the conservator, P. M. Tolmatchev; closed from June to Aug.). Many of the Decabrists (the St. Petersburg revolutionaries of Dec. 14th, 1825) were banished to Tchita.

We cross the Tchitá and then traverse hilly country as far as Kitaiski Razyezd. 1033 V. *Makkavyéyevo* (2035 ft.). — 1071 V *Karúimskaya* (1985 ft.; Rail. Restaurant).

From KARUIMSKAYA to SRYETENSK, 266 V. (176 M.), railway in 9 hrs. — 13 V. *Kitáiski Razyézd* (p. 535). About $^2/_3$ M. beyond (39 V.) *Urulgá* (1865 ft.; Rail. Restaurant) we cross the river of that name, and farther on we cross the *Tolbagá.* — 116 V. *Onón* (1690 ft.), at the confluence of the Onón and the Ingodá, which here form the *Shilka.* The train now runs along a ledge hewn out of the steep left bank of this river. — 139 V. *Shilka* (1655 ft.; Rail. Restaurant).

From (183 V.) *Nértchinsk* (1585 ft.; Rail. Restaurant) a branch-line runs to the (10 V.) district-town of that name (Métropole; izvóshtchik from the rail. station to the town 1 rb.), with 11,300 inhabitants. It is the headquarters of the E. Trans-Baikál Mining District, and contains a small municipal museum (open free on Sun. and holidays, 12-2; at other times on application to the director).

About 296 V. (196 M.) to the E. lies *Nértchinski Zavód*, the capital of the district of that name, in the mines of which those prisoners who are condemned to hard labour (като́рга) undergo their punishment.

We cross the *Nertcha* by a bridge 350 yds. long. Beyond (207 V.) *Byánkino* (1550 ft.; Rail. Restaurant) we cross the *Kuyengá*. 220 V. *Kuyengá*, the junction for the Amur Railway (p. 539); 234 V. *Bayán*, with cement-works.

266 V. (176 M.) **Sryétensk,** Срѣте́нскъ (1490 ft.; *Railway Restaurant; Dalni Vostók*, in the town, ¹/₂ M. from the steamer landing, R. 1³/₄-4 rb.; izvóshtchik from the rail. station to the town 60 cop. in winter, 1 rb. 60 cop. in summer), a Cossack stanitza with 6800 inhab., lies on the right bank of the *Shilka*, which is here about ¹/₃ M. in width. The rail. station is close to the left bank, not far from the wharf of the mail-steamers.

Steamboat to *Kharbárovsk* (Vladivostok), see p. 539.

CONTINUATION OF RAILWAY JOURNEY TO KHARBIN. The railway runs for the most part through a steppe-like district inhabited by Cossacks and Buddhistic Buryats. The winter here is very cold. — At (1084 V.) *Kitáiski Razyézd* (Кита́йскій Разъѣ́здъ; 1930 ft.) the line to Sryetensk diverges to the E. (p. 534), while our line runs towards the S. About 1 V. beyond the station we cross the *Ingodá*. Beyond (1091 V.) *Adriánovka* (2075 ft.; Rail. Restaurant) we ascend to the watershed (2885 ft.) between the Ingodá and the Agá, and then descend to (1120 V.) *Buryátskaya* (2580 ft.). 1144 V. *Mogotni* (Rail. Restaurant). A little short of (1165 V.) *Agá* (2060 ft.) we cross the river of that name. Hard by is the Aginski Datzán, a Buryat convent. Beyond (1211 V.) *Olovyánnaya* (Rail. Restaurant) we cross the *Onón*, and near (1245 V.) *Buirka* we cross the *Turgá*. 1273 V. *Khadabulak* (Rail. Restaurant). About 7 M. to the W. of (1304 V.) *Borzyá* (Rail. Restaurant) is the *Tchindátskaya Cossack Stanitza*. 1342 V. *Kharanór* (Rail. Restaurant). About 2 V. beyond (1404 V.) *Matziyévskaya* the railway enters Manchuria.

1424 V. (944 M.) **Mandshúriya** (*Manchuria*, Маньчжу́рія; 2135 ft.; *Rail. Restaurant*), with 10,000 inhab., founded since 1900, is the frontier-station between Russia and Manchuria, and the starting-point of the Chinese Eastern Railway (Кита́йская-Восто́чная желѣ́зная доро́га). Passengers' luggage is examined here.

As far as the Great Khingán Mountains the train runs through a flat steppe-district. Among the prominent features of interest are the fortified station-buildings (sometimes adorned with apes, dragons, and other Chinese ornaments), the lofty loopholed water-towers, the rude Chinese carts with their two high wheels, and the camels at pasture. — At (28 V. from Mandshuriya) *Tchalainor* (Чжалай-норъ†; 1825 ft.) we cross the outlets of *Lake Kulun* (Dalai-nor), flowing in the direction of the *Argún*. In this vicinity are several coal-pits. Farther on, we traverse the valley of the *Khailár*.

176 V. *Khailár*, Хайларъ (2030 ft.; Rail. Restaurant). Near the station (izvóshtchik, 25 cop.) is the modern town (Popóv Hotel), with 4000 inhab. and a branch of the Russo-Asiatic Bank. The interesting old town, surrounded by a mud wall, lies 2 M. off. An important trade is carried on in the pelts of the bobak or marmot (Russ., Тарбаганъ). — We cross the *Emin*. 228 V. *Tcharomte*, Чжаромтэ (2095 ft.), in a good arable district.

253 V. *Yakeshi*, Якэши (2200 ft.), at the foot of the *Great Khingán Mts.*, the E. slopes of which are richly wooded. Farther on we ascend, viâ (283 V.) *Myandukhe* (Rail. Restaurant) and (340 V.) *Irekte* (2870 ft.; Rail. Restaurant), to (349 V.) *Khingán* (Хинганъ) and to the top of the pass, threading a tunnel (3155 ft.) 2 M. long just beyond the station. We then descend in windings, including the so-called 'Hingan Loop', to (372 V.) *Bukhedu* (2210 ft.; Rail. Restaurant), in the *Valley of the Yal*.

At (429 V.) *Barim* (1460 ft.) we obtain a fine view of the mountains. Farther on the steppes begin again, but on this side of the Khingán they are more fertile than to the W. of it. 487 V. *Tchalantun*, Чжаланьтунь (1055 ft.; Rail. Restaurant), a straggling village; 517 V. *Tchingis-Khan*, Чингисъ-Ханъ (865 ft.), named after Jenghiz Khan, the Mongolian conqueror (d. 1227), whose home is said to have been a little to the N.

Beyond (603 V.) *Khurkhura* (Хурхура; 525 ft.) we cross the *Nonni* and reach (623 V.) *Tzitzikar*, Цицикаръ (Rail. Restaurant).

A light railway, with a station of its own, runs hence (fares 80 & 60 cop.) to (25 V.) Tzitzikar or *Tsitsikar* (Chinese inns only; Russo-Asiatic Bank), the capital of the Manchurian province of Heilungchiang, founded in 1692 and situated near the left bank of the *Nonni*. It is surrounded by a wall and carries on a trade in grain. Pop. 70,000.

From this point to Kharbin the train traverses a treeless and almost uninhabited plateau. 758 V. *Anda* (495 ft.; Rail. Restaurant). At (847 V.) *Duitzinshan*, Дуйциньшань (405 ft.), the train leaves the plateau and approaches the Súngari, which it crosses by an eight-arched bridge 1035 yds. in length (view).

876 V. (581 M.) **Kharbín**, Харбинъ. — *Railway Restaurant.*
Hotels (all in the New Town). *Grand-Hôtel*, near the station, R. 2¹/₂-7 rb., B. 55 cop., déj. (12 to 3.30 p.m.) 90 cop. to 1¹/₂ rb., D. (7-9 p.m.) 1-1¹/₂ rb.; *Métropole*, *Oriant*, R. from 2 rb. — Izvóshtchik from the New Town to the Harbour Suburb 40, to the Old Town 80 cop.; from the Harbour Suburb

† The station-names are taken from the official Russian time-tables.

to the Old Town 1 rb. 20; per drive within any one quarter of the town 25, per hr. 80 cop. Double fares at night. — BANKS. Branches of the *Russo-Asiatic, Hongkong & Shanghai,* and *Yokohama Specie Banks.* Branch Office of Kunst & Albers (comp. p. 538). — International Sleeping Car Co. at the Grand-Hôtel (p. 536). — CONSULS. British, *H. E. Sly;* American, *S. P. Warner.* — LLOYD'S AGENTS, *Kunst & Albers.* — ENGLISH CHURCH SERVICES are held about once a month.

Kharbin or *Harbin* (500 ft.), in a marshy district on the navigable *Súngari,* is a town of 80,000 inhab., including 30,000 Russians but not counting the strong garrison. Except for the old town it was founded about 1900, and it owes its importance to the Russo-Japanese war. It consists of four parts: the *New Town* (Новый Харбинъ), with the Railway Station, the Headquarters of the Chinese Maritime Customs for Manchuria, the Russian Post Office, the Head Office of the Chinese Eastern Railway, and the residences of the railway and other officials; the *Harbour Suburb* (Пристань), on the Súngari, 2¹/₂ M. to the N., with the larger business houses, most of which are in the Kitáiskaya; the Chinese Town of *Fudzyadyan,* to the E. of the Harbour Suburb; and the *Old Town* (Старый Харбинъ), to the S. of the New Town, and now without any importance. The former Chinese Citadel, 5 M. to the E. of the Súngari, was razed by the Russians in 1900.

To *Mukden* and *Port Arthur,* see R. 78; to *Mukden* and *Peking,* see RR. 78, 79.

The railway to Vladivostok runs to the E. through a mountainous region. 915 V. *Ashikhe,* Ашихэ (445 ft.), with 40,000 inbab. and a Mission Station of the United Free Church of Scotland. At (934 V.) *Ertzendyantzi,* or Эрцендяньцзы, is a hill consisting of white marble (quarries).' Beyond (1028 V.) *Imyanpo* (700 ft.; Rail. Restaurant), a Manchurian town with a Russian colony, we ascend through verdant valleys to (1109 V.) *Gaolintzi,* Гаолиньцзы (2075 ft.). 1131 V. *Khandaokhetzi,* Ханьдаохэцзы (1410 ft.; Rail. Restaurant), with 3000 inhabitants. — Just short of (1230 V.) *Modaoshi,* Модаоши (1045 ft.), a prettily situated settlement, we cross the *Mudan-kiang.* About 13 M. to the S., in a fertile plain on the left bank of the Mudan-kiang, is the fur-trading town of *Ninguta.* — We ascend through three tunnels to (1254 V.) *Daimagou,* Даймагоу (2065 ft.), and then descend to (1278 V.) *Mulin* (1080 ft.; Rail. Restaurant). 1309 V. *Matzyaokhe,* Мацяохэ (1065 ft.), in a fertile plain; 1345 V. *Silinkhe,* Силинхэ (1265 ft.).

1388 V. *Pogranitchnaya* (1505 ft.; Rail. Restaurant; Russian custom-house, comp. p. 535), the frontier-station between Manchuria and the Russian coast-district. It is also the N.E. terminus of the Chinese Eastern Railway. — The Ussuri Railway, which begins here, descends through six tunnels to (1413 V.) *Grodekovo* (585 ft.). 1471 V. *Golenki* (395 ft.), in a grassy plain.

1504 V. *Nikólsk Ussuríski* (75 ft.; Rail. Restaurant; Grand-Hôtel, Nikoláyevskaya 7, with good cuisine; izvóshtchik from the

station to the town 50 cop., at night 1 rb.), a district-town in a
fertile neighbourhood, was founded in 1866 and contains 52,000
inhabitants. It is the headquarters of the 1st Siberian Army Corps.
The sportsman will find good shooting in the neighbourhood (musk-
deer, roe-deer, and wild-boar). — About 20 V. beyond Nikolsk Ussu-
riski the railway traverses a romantic rocky district (Суйфунскія
щёкп) on the steep bank of the *Zuifun.* 1539 V. *Razdólnoye* (25 ft.).
Beyond (1563 V.) *Nadézhdinskaya* (70 ft.; Rail. Restaurant) are
some coal-pits. The train now skirts the *Gulf of Amúr,* passing
the villa-colonies of *Okeanskaya* and *Sedanka,* and finally reaching the station of *Vladivostók,* on the W. side of the Golden Horn.

1605 V. (1064 M.) **Vladivostók,** Владивостокъ. — *Railway
Restaurant.* — HOTELS. *Hotel-Restaurant d'Allemagne* (Нѣмѣцкая гости́-
ница; Pl. a, B 2), cor. of Kitáiskaya and Pekinskaya, R. 2-6, bed-linen ¹/₂,
B. ³/₄ rb., déj. (12.30 to 2) 80 cop. to 1¹/₄ rb., D. (7.30 to 9 p.m.) 1¹/₂ rb.; *Ver-
sailles* (Pl. b; A, 2), Svyetlánskaya 10, cor. of Koréiskaya, these two well
spoken of; *Grand-Hôtel* (Pl. c; A, 3), Aleútskaya, opposite the rail. station;
Centrálnaya (Pl. d; A, 2), cor of Svyetlánskaya and Aleútskaya, R. 1¹/₂-4,
D. (12-4 p.m.) ³/₄-1 rb.

RESTAURANTS. *Zolotói Rog* or *Golden Horn,* Svyetlánskaya 15, with
view over the bay, déj. (11-1) ³/₄-1, D. (12-5) ¹/₂-1¹/₄ rb.; *Shuin,* Svyetlánskaya 36; *Unterberger,* Svyetlánskaya 35.

IZVÓSHTCHIK from the station to the town 25 cop. (luggage 20 cop.),
per hr. 1 rb.; at night (12-7 a.m.) double fares. — ELECTRIC TRAMWAY
(8-20 cop.) from the railway station (Pl. A, B, 3) along the Svyetlánskaya.

POST & TELEGRAPH OFFICE (Pl. 5; B, 2), Svyetlánskaya. — CONSULS.
British, *R. Macleod Hodgson;* American, *J. F. Jewell.* — Head Office of the
great commercial and banking house of *Kunst & Albers* (Pl. K & A; B, 2),
Svyetlánskaya; agents for the Hongkong & Shanghai Banking Corporation,
the Hamburg-American Line, the North German Lloyd, the Pacific Mail
Steamship Company, and the Occidental & Oriental Steamship Company.

Imperial Bank (Pl. 1; B, 2), Svyetlánskaya; *Russo-Asiatic Bank* (Pl. 7;
A, 2), Aleútskaya (open 9.30 to 2). — *International Sleeping Car Co.,* Aleútskaya 4 (Pl. A, 2, 3).

Local time is 6³/₄ hrs. ahead of St. Petersburg time.

Vladivostók ('Mistress of the East'; 10 ft.) is the prettily situated capital of the Maritime Province, the headquarters of the
4th Siberian Army Corps, and a fortified naval and commercial
harbour. It lies in 43°7′ N. lat. and 131°54′ E. long., on the slopes
of the Coast Range, at the S.W. extremity of a peninsula between
the *Amúr Gulf* on the W. and the *Ussuri Gulf* on the E. The
harbour is formed by the bay of the *Golden Horn* (Золотóй рогъ),
4 M. long and ²/₃ M. wide, on the W. and N. sides of which the town
lies. The town, founded in 1860, was a free port from 1865 to
1909. It has about 120,000 inhab., including many soldiers and
some Chinese, Koreans, and Japanese. Living is extremely dear.
The mean annual temperature is about 40° F. (comp. p. 522), and the
climate is unattractive, Sept. being the most agreeable month. The
bay is ice-bound from the middle of Dec. to the beginning of March,
but sea-communication is rendered possible by ice-breakers.

The main street of the town, the **Svyetlánskaya** (Pl. A-D, 2, 3),

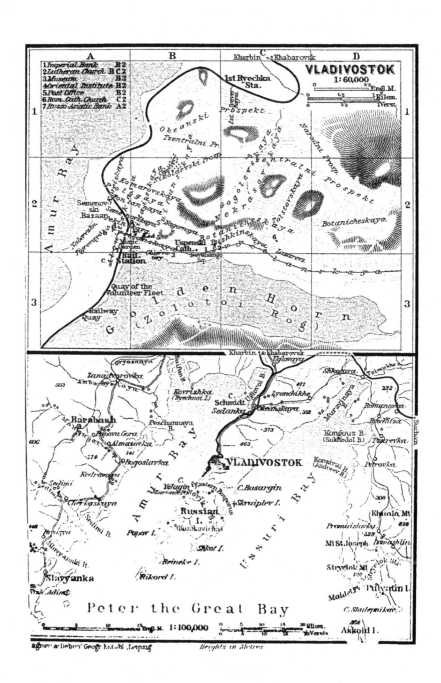

runs from E. to W. not far from the Golden Horn and is crossed by the railway. On the S. side of it lie the *Municipal Garden* (Pl. A, B, 2) and the *Museum* of the Amúr Exploration Society (Pl. 3, B 3; open free on Tues., Frid., & Sun. 10-4; at other times, on application to the Director; entr. at Úlitza Petrá Velíkago 7), containing costumes and weapons of the Russian Far East; on the N. side is a monument to *Admiral Zavoiko*, erected in 1908. Farther to the E. are the Greek Catholic *Uspenski Cathedral* (Pl. B, 2) and a memorial (1897) to *Admiral G. I. Nevélski* (d. 1876), who in 1848 discovered the Amúr estuary. On it are inscribed the words of Nicholas I.:— Гдѣ разъ поднятъ русскій флагъ, онъ уже спускаться не долженъ ('Where once the Russian flag has been unfurled, it must never be lowered'). Here also are a *Lutheran Church* (Pl. 2; B, 2) and the docks and barracks. A fine view is obtained from the heights above the *Observatory*. Also worthy of mention are the *Roman Catholic Church* (Pl. 6; C, 2) and (in the Púshkinskaya) the *Oriental Institute* (Восточный институтъ; Pl. 4, B 2), for the study of E. Asiatic languages, opened in 1899.

About 30 M. to the S.E. of Vladivostok is the island of *Askold*, on which the Manchurian sika deer ('spot deer') is preserved.

Steamers of the Russian Volunteer Fleet (Добровольный Флотъ) run viâ *Nagasaki* to *Odessa* in 40-45 days (fare 500 rb., including food); to *Tsuruga* (branch-line to Yokohama & Tokio), twice weekly in 40 hrs. (fare 37 rb., including food); to *Shanghai*, once weekly (fare 81 rb., including food).—Japanese steamers (Nippon Yusen Kaisha) ply to *Kobe*, *Nagasaki*, *Shanghai*, *Hong Kong*, and other ports.

From Vladivostok to *Khabarovsk* on the Amúr, see p. 542.

c. From Sryetensk to Khabarovsk by Steamer down the Amur and thence to Vladivostok by Railway.

Steamer from *Sryetensk* to *Khabarovsk*, 2141 V. (1419 M.). Mail-steamer of the Amúr Steamship Co. (Амурское общество пароходства и торговли) every five days from the beginning of May to the end of Sept. (O.S.), with change of boats at Blagovyeshtchensk (fares 53 rb. 53, 32 rb. 13 cop.; meals 2¹/₄ rb. per day; luggage 2 rb. 14 cop. per pud); the voyage to Blagovyeshtchensk takes 5 days (upstream, 8), from that point to Khabarovsk we take 3¹/₂ days (upstream, 5¹/₂). When the water is unusually low, passengers are sometimes carried as far as Pokrovskaya or Blagovyeshtchensk on barges towed by a tug. The best travelling seasons are May (O. S.), the first half of June, and August. Occasional spots of considerable beauty are passed, especially on the Shilka, but the voyage, on the whole, is very tiresome owing to its length and the absence of places of any size.—The Amúr Railway, which was begun in 1908 and is eventually to connect *Kuyenga* (p. 535) with Khabarovsk (p. 541), was opened at the end of 1913 as far as (777 V. or 515 M., in 36 hrs.) *Kerak;* the section from Kerak to *Alexándrovskaya*, with a branch-line to Blagovyeshtchensk (p. 540), is to be opened shortly.

Railway from *Khabarovsk* to *Vladivostok*, 717 V. (475 M.) in 30 hrs.

The Amúr, Амуръ, 2750 V. (1825 M.) in length, is formed by the confluence of the *Shilka* and the *Argún*, and at Nikolayevsk, opposite the island of Sakhalin, flows into the Gulf of Tartary, which connects the Sea of Okhótsk with the Sea of Japan. There are no fewer than 120 shoals (перекатъ) in the course of the stream. Its sturgeon, salmon, and other fisheries are important. In the forests on the right or Chinese bank the

Siberian tiger (Felis tigris mongolica; the largest in the world) is found. On the left bank, between Pokrovskaya and Khabarovsk, are many stanitzas or Cossack settlements, planted here in 1858 and later to protect the frontier against the Manchurians of the right bank.

Sryétensk, see p. 535. — The steamer descends the *Shilka* towards the N.E. — 24 V. *Lomovskáya,* a Cossack stanitza, situated (like all the rest) on the left bank of the river. The steep bank consists of limestone and contains many caves.— 109 V. *Ust-Kara,* at the mouth of the *Kara,* on which, about $6^1/_2$ M. off, are several gold-mines.— 162 V. *Gorbitza* (1220 ft.).

373 V. *Pokróvskaya,* the first village in the Territory of the Amúr, is situated 4 V. below the union of the Shilka and the *Argún,* which together form the *Amúr.*

As far as Albazin the river is flanked by high rocky banks covered with pine-woods. 437 V. *Ignáshino;* on the right bank is the *Hill of Bears* (Медвѣжья сóпка). Beyond *Svérbeyevski* the *Oldói* joins the Amúr on the left. The Amúr now enters a defile 15 M. in length. Beyond *Orlovski* the valley again expands, and the river contains many attractive islands.

580 V. *Albazín,* on the site of a fort founded by the Cossack Hetman, *Khabaróv* (p. 524), in 1651. This fort was heroically defended by *Tólbuzin* against the Chinese in 1686-87, but was destroyed by the Chinese after the departure of the Russians in 1689.

The banks of the river are continuously hilly, but deciduous trees become more numerous. Between Albazin and *Permíkinski* the Amúr flows through several channels, and in places attains a width of two miles. At *Ólginski* it contracts to a width of 220 yds.— 788 V. *Tchernyáyeva.* The Amúr turns to the S.E. On the right bank, 6 M. short of *Kuznetzóvski,* is a natural colonnade formed by four columnar rocks (Кáменные столбы). The valley expands.

About 1 M. below *Yermákovski,* the *Onón* flows into the Amúr on the left. At *Tzagayán* are the so-called Burning Mountain and the Lama Rock (Скалá лáмы), a spot considered holy by the Mongolians. Beyond (920 V.) *Novo-Voskresénskoye* the stream widens to $2^1/_4$ M.; the left bank, consisting of red sandstone, is over 300 ft. high. About 2 M. short of (998 V.) *Kumárskaya,* on the left bank, opposite the mouth of the *Kumára,* is a promontory (Мысъ Корсакóва) crowned by a conspicuous iron cross.

The mountains gradually recede. Beyond *Samadón* the stream follows a very circuitous course. Between *Bibikovski* and *Yekateríninskaya* it is sometimes $6^1/_2$ M. wide.

1212 V. (803 M.) **Blagovyéshtchensk,** Благовѣщенскъ. —
Hotels. *Grand-Hôtel, Rossíya,* R. 3-7 rb. — Извóзитсик, per hr. 60 cop., at night (after 11 p.m.) 1 rb. 20 cop. — Branches of the *Russo-Asiatic Bank,* the *Commercial Bank of Siberia,* and *Kunst & Albers* (p. 525).

Blagovyéshtchensk, on the left bank of the Amúr, at its confluence with the *Zeya* (50° 15′ N. lat.), was founded in 1856, and is the capital of the Amúr Territory. Pop. 76,500. The town was bombarded in 1900 by the Boxers, an action which resulted in the sending of the Orlóv punitive expedition to Manchuria. On the bank of the Amúr are a boulevard and a triumphal arch erected in 1891 in commemoration of the visit of the Tzarevitch Nicholas Alexándrovitch, the present Tzar. The Municipal Museum is open free on Sun., 1-4. — Amúr Railway, see p. 539.

The Amúr now runs towards the E. The left bank is bordered by a steppe-like plain, but the right is hilly. — 1243 V. *Aigún,* on the right or Manchurian bank, was totally destroyed by the Russians in 1900 (comp. above). 1371 V. *Poyárkovo.* Above (1493 V.) *Innokéntyevskaya,* on the left, is the mouth of the river *Buréya.* The country becomes hilly. Beyond *Páshkovski* the abrupt mountains of the *Little Khingán* trench closely on the Amúr, which here follows a very circuitous course, and contracts to a width of 660 yds. 1633 V. *Radde,* prettily situated.

Beyond (1752 V.) *Yekaterino-Nikólskaya* the stream again becomes wider, and flows towards the N.E., as far as Khabarovsk between low-lying banks. *Blagoslovénnoye,* a village occupied by Koreans. — 1888 V. To the right is the mouth of the *Súngari.* — 1916 V. *Mikháilo-Seménovski.* Farther on, we pass a few insignificant settlements. At *Nízhne-Spásski,* on the right, is the mouth of the *Ussurí,* which is here $^2/_3$ M. in breadth. A column marks the frontier between Russia and Manchuria.

2141 V. (1419 M.) **Khabaróvsk,** Хабаровскъ. — The *Railway Station* (restaurant) lies 2 M. to the N.E. of the town. — HOTELS. *Esplanade; Centrálnuiye Nomerá; Bristol.* — Izvóshtchik from the rail. station to the town $^3/_4$-1 rb., per hr. 1 rb. — Branches of the *Russo-Asiatic Bank* and of *Messrs. Kunst & Albers* (p. 538).

Khabaróvsk (315 ft.) is situated on three terraced hills on the rocky right bank of the Amúr (here 2 M. in width) in 48°28′ N. latitude. It was founded by Count Muravyév (p. 524) in 1858, and named after *Khabaróv* (p. 524), the Hetman of the Cossacks. It is now the capital of the General Government of the Amúr and the headquarters of the 5th Siberian Army Corps. Pop. 55,000, including 4000 Chinese. The mean annual temperature is 33° F. In the Alexéyevskaya, to the left of the house of the Commandant, is the interesting *Museum* of the Imperial Russian Geographical Society, open on Thurs. & Sun., in summer 10-6, in winter 12-4 (free on Sun., adm. on Thurs. 15 cop.). Adjoining is the *Town Park,* containing a bronze statue of *Count Muravyév-Amúrski* (d. 1881), standing upon a pedestal 33 ft. high, and erected in 1891 from the designs of Opekúshin. On the Artillery Hill is the new palace of the Governor-General. The Cadet School was completed in 1904. About $^3/_4$ M. from the station is a School of Railway Engineering. A new bridge is being constructed for the Amúr Railway (p. 539).

From Khabarovsk a steamer plies in 3 days (fares 22 rb. 15, 13 rb. 20 cop.) to (940 V. or 623 M.) *Nikoláyevsk* (Obshtchéstvennoye Sobrániye;

branches of the Russo-Asiatic Bank and Kunst & Albers, comp. p. 538), a district-town with 16,500 inhab. on the left bank of the Amúr, situated 86 M. from its mouth in the Gulf of Tartary.

FROM KHABAROVSK TO VLADIVOSTOK, 717 V. (475 M.), Ussuri Railway in 32 hrs.—The railway runs to the S. along the right bank of the *Ussuri*, the total length of which is 850 V. (565 M.). As far as Yevgenyevka (see below) it traverses a very thinly-peopled district. The left bank belongs to Manchuria.—Beyond (64 V.) *Vyérino* (270 ft.) we cross the *Kiya*, and farther on the *Khor*. Both these streams join the Ussuri on the right.—121 V. *Vyázemskaya* (235 ft.; Rail. Restaurant). Beyond (142 V.) *Kóti-kovo* (195 ft.) the banks become hilly and are covered with wood. We pass many bridges.—Beyond *Gedike Razyézd* the railway reaches its highest point (445 ft.). Beyond (219 V.) *Bikin* (195 ft.; Rail. Restaurant) we cross the river of that name. The scenery is hilly and attractive.—330 V. *Iman* (195 ft.; Rail. Restaurant), a flourishing place with 30,000 inhab., beyond which we cross the Iman.

340 V. *Muravyév-Amúrski* (215 ft.). Shortly before reaching (389 V.) *Ussuri* (225 ft.) we cross the Ussuri and enter the steppe-like *Prikhankóiskaya Basin* on *Lake Khanka*, a favourite resort of duck-hunters in autumn. 424 V. *Shmakovka* (245 ft.), with the Svyato-Tróitzki Convent, founded in 1895.

493 V. *Yevgényevka* (315 ft.; Rail. Restaurant), a prettily situated village with 1000 inhabitants. Villages and cultivated fields now become more numerous.—532 V. *Mútchnáya* (260 ft.), a village with 1300 inhabitants. We cross the *Lefú* and then descend into the valley of the *Zuifun*.

616 V. *Nikólsk Ússuriski* (75 ft.; Rail. Restaurant). From this point to (717 V. or 475 M.) *Vladivostók*, see pp. 537, 538.

78. From Kharbin to Dairen (Dalny) and Port Arthur (Ryōjun) viâ Mukden.

FROM KHARBIN TO KUANTCHENTZI (Ch'ang-ch'un), 222 V. (147 M.), *Chinese Eastern Railway*. Express train (through-carriages, with dining and sleeping cars, from Irkutsk) thrice weekly in 6 hrs. (fares 13 rb. 73, 8 rb. 48 cop.); mail train once daily in 8½ hrs. (9 rb. 15, 5 rb. 65 cop.). The time-tables give St. Petersburg time, which is 6 hrs. 26 min. behind Kharbin time.— FROM KUANTCHENTZI TO DAIREN (Dalny), 436 M., *South Manchuria Railway* (headquarters in Dairen); express train with sleeping-car and dining-car (B. 1, déj. 1¼, D. 1½ yen) thrice weekly in 15 hrs. (fare 34 yen 45 sen), to Mukden in 6¾ hrs. (fare 18½ yen); 100 kin or 132 lbs. of luggage free. There is also an ordinary train twice daily. The time-tables show Chinese coast-time, which is 22 min. behind Kharbin time, and 6 hrs. 4 min. ahead of St. Petersburg time.

For the transliteration and pronunciation of Chinese names, see p. 549. 1 yen (= 100 sen) = 2*s*. Money may be changed at Kuantchentzi.

Kharbin, see p. 536. The Chinese Eastern Railway diverges to the S. from the line to Vladivostok (p. 537) and traverses the fertile S.E. part of Manchuria. Beyond (115V.) *Tao-lai-chao*, Таолайчжао

(225 ft.) we cross the *Súngari* by a bridge $^1/_2$ M. long. 152 V. *Yao-mén*, Ямынь (615 ft.; Rail. Restaurant). — 222 V. (147 M.) **Kuan-tchentzi** (Куаньченцзы) or **Ch'ang-ch'un** (760 ft.; *Rail. Restaurant; Yamato Hotel*), a town with 130,000 inhab. and an important trade in soy or soya beans. There are branch-offices of the Russo-Asiatic Bank and the Yokohama Specie Bank, as well as a mission-school and infirmary of the Presbyterian Church in Ireland.

A branch-railway (80 M., in $5^1/_2$ hrs.; fare 6 yen) runs hence to the E. to *Kirin* (690 ft.), situated on the left bank of the Sungari and surrounded by a wall 13 ft. high. It has a population of 100,000 and carries on a trade in tobacco, timber, and soya beans. Here too are a mission-school and infirmary of the Presbyterian Church in Ireland.

From the Ch'ang-ch'un station the South Manchuria Railway ascends to the S., with a range of mountains on the left. — 38 M. *Kung-chuling* (685 ft.); 145 M. *T'ieh-ling* (215 ft.; Rail. Restaurant), a commercial town with 30,000 inhab. and a mission-school of the United Free Church of Scotland.

189 M. **Mukden** or **Fêng-t'ien.** — *Railway Restaurant.* — HOTELS. *Astor House* (O. Diedering), in the inner town, R. $ 3-4, B. $ 1, déj. (12.30 to 2 p.m.) $ $1^1/_2$, D. (7.30 to 9 p.m.) $ 2, pens. $ 7 (for the dollar, comp. p. 549); *Yamato Hotel*, near the station, R. $3^1/_2$-5, B. 1, déj. $1^1/_2$, D. $1^3/_4$ yen. — CARRIAGE from the rail. station to the town 1 yen. — TRAMWAY from the station to the W. city-gate. — Rickshaws (comp. p. 553) and saddle-horses (not easily procured) can best be ordered at the hotel. — CONSULATES. British Consul-General, *P. O'Brien-Butler.* American Consul-General, *F. D. Fisher.* — *Yokohama Specie Bank*, in the inner town.

Mukden (160 ft.), the old capital of Manchuria, on the right bank of the *Hún-ho* (a tributary of the Liáo-ho), and 3 M. to the E. of the station, is surrounded by an earthen wall 11 M. long, and contains ca. 175,000 inhabitants. It has an important trade in wheat, soya beans, and furs, a mission-school and hospital of the United Free Church of Scotland, and a Mission of the Presbyterian Church in Ireland. In the S. suburb is a Roman Catholic Cathedral. A strong wall surrounds the inner town, in which is an *Imperial Palace*, built in 1631 and restored in 1909 (adm. obtainable through the Consulate, also for the tombs of the emperors mentioned below). It consists of a group of gaily-coloured, one-storied buildings, mostly of wood, and separated from each other by courtyards. To the right of the Great Court is the Throne Room, with the ancient carved-wood throne. The Treasury contains official robes, embroideries, paintings, weapons of the Emperor Ch'ien-lúng (1736-96), jewels, porcelain, and other curiosities. Another building (inaccessible) contains the archives of the former Manchurian dynasty.

About $3^1/_2$ M. to the N. of the town, amid pine and oak woods, is the **Péi-ling** ('North Tomb'), the burial-place of T'ái-tsung (d. 1643), father of the first Emperor of the Manchurian dynasty (adm., see above). We follow the dilapidated outer avenue, flanked by figures of animals, to the brightly painted S. Gate (usually closed), whence we proceed to the left, round the wall, to the W. entrance. Thence we follow the inner avenue, beginning at the above-mentioned S. Gate, to a building containing a large tortoise in calcareous marble that bears a stone tablet on which are engraved the events of Tʻái-tsung's life. We next pass through a tower-gateway into the inner court, on a terrace in the middle of which is the Hall of Ancestors. Beyond this are the so-called Spirit Walls (with sacrificial utensils) and the inaccessible tumulus or grave-hill, on which grows a stunted tree (view of the hill from the wall). — About 11 M. to the E. of Mukden, in a picturesque situation near the Hún-ho, is the *Túng-ling* ('East Tomb'), the burial-place of Tʻai-tsu (d. 1626), father of the above-mentioned Tʻái-tsung. It resembles the Péi-ling in its arrangement but is much less easily reached.

About 12 M. to the S. of Mukden begins the **Battlefield of Mukden,** the scene of the deciding contest of the Russo-Japanese War (Feb. 25th to March 10th, 1905). The Russian forces, under the supreme command of *General Kuropátkin*, consisted of the 2nd army under *Baron Kaulbars* on the right wing, the 3rd army under *Baron Bilderling* in the centre, and the 1st army under *General Linévitch* on the left wing, and numbered in all 310,000 men, with 1100 guns. Its strongly fortified position was 90 M. in length and 12-15 M. in depth. The Japanese army, under the supreme command of *Marshal Oyama*, had entrenched itself in a position immediately opposite the Russians. It included five different armies: the 5th under *General Kawamura*, on the right wing; the 1st under *General Kuroki*, the 4th under *General Nozu*, the 2nd under *General Oku*, and the reserve, in the centre; and finally the 3rd army, under *General Nogi*, on the left wing. At the very outside it numbered 300,000 men, with 892 guns. Its front was 50-60 M. long; its depth 20-30 M. The Japanese attacked the left wing of the Russians, while at the same time their 3rd army began to outflank the Russian right wing. Up to March 1st they obtained no decided advantage, but afterwards the Russians were gradually forced back. On March 8th the Russians retreated across the Hún-ho and took up a position on the opposite bank. On the night of March 8-9th Nozu crossed the frozen river, and by penetrating the centre of the Russian position threatened to invest Mukden. On the following night the Russians evacuated the town, and their retreat partly degenerated into a disorderly flight. The loss on the Russian side amounted to upwards of 87,000 men (including 29,000 prisoners), while the Japanese lost 67,000 men.

From Mukden a branch-railway runs to the S.E. to *An-tung* (Seoul, Fusan). To *Peking*, see R. 79.

We cross the Hún-ho. From (199 M.) *Su-chia-túng* a branch-line runs to (34 M.) *Fu-shun* (Hotel), with the coal-mines of the South Manchuria Railway Company (output in 1911, 1,200,000 tons). — The train intersects the W. part of the battlefield of Mukden (see above), which was occupied by the 3rd Russian and 4th Japanese armies. To the left is the Putilov Hill, with a granite column commemorating the Japanese who fell in the battle. A little before reaching Liao-yáng we cross the *Tai-tzŭ-ho*.

229 M. **Liao-yáng** (85 ft.; *Rail. Restaurant*), on the left bank of the Tai-tzŭ-ho, is one of the oldest towns in Manchuria and possesses many orchards. Pop. 100,000. The conspicuous pagoda is a massive stone building in the form of a cone. So-called Samshu

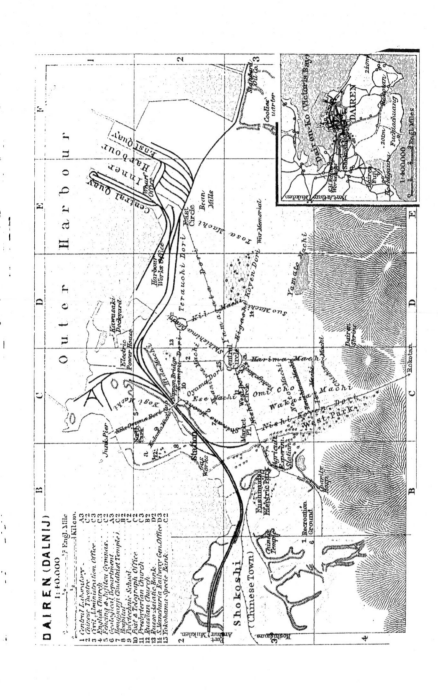

DAIREN (DALNIJ)
1:40,000

1 Central Laboratory A3
2 Chinese Theatre C2
3 Civil Administration Office . . . C3
4 English Church C3
5 Fencing & Children Grounds . . . A3
6 Geological Department A3
7 Honganji (Buddhist Temple) . . . B2
8 Hospital B2
9 Polytechnic School C3
10 Post & Telegraph Office C2
11 Presbyterian Church B2
12 Russian Church D2
13 Russo-Asiatic Bank D2
14 S.Manchuria Railway Gen.Office . D3
15 Yokohama Specie Bank C2

brandy is distilled here. The United Free Church of Scotland has a Mission and a hospital at Liao-yáng. — A branch-line runs to (10 M.) *Yen-t'ai*, with a coal-mine.

The *Battle of Liáo-yáng* lasted from Aug. 30th to Sept. 3rd, 1904. The Russians, 135,000 men in all, had established themselves to the S. of Liao-yáng in two fortified lines, the outer 16 M. in length, the inner 10 M. The right wing of the Japanese, whose total numbers were about the same, forced a passage across the Tai-tzŭ-ho, whereupon the Russians evacuated the outer line (Aug. 31st) and, after making an unsuccessful attack on Sept. 3rd, retired in good order to Mukden. On Sept. 5th the Japanese occupied Liao-yáng. The Russians lost 16,000 men, the Japanese 23,000.

254 M. *Tang-kang-tzŭ*, with warm sulphur springs. About 10 M. to the E. is the Buddhist convent of *Chien-shan*, in a picturesque rocky district. — 267 M. *Hái-ch'êng* (100 ft.).

287 M. *Ta-shih-ch'iáo* (60 ft.; Rail. Restaurant).

From Ta-shih-ch'iáo a branch-line runs to the W. to (14 M.) **Ying-k'óu**, also known as *Niú-chuang* or *Newchwang* (25 ft.; *Astor House*, 2 M. from the Japanese railway station, carr. 60-80 sen), a town with 60,000 inhab., on the left bank of the Liáo-ho, which is here 490 yds. wide and enters the Gulf of Liao-túng a little lower down. The chief exports are bean-cakes and bean-oil. The town contains British (W. J. Clennell), American (W. P. Kent), and other consuls, branch-offices of the Russo-Asiatic and Yokohama Specie Banks, and a mission-station and hospital of the Presbyterian Church in Ireland. — Chinese Railway (station on the right bank of the Liáo-ho, 2 M. from the Astor House; ferry from the Astor House, 10 sen) to Kao-pêng-tzŭ (Peking), see p. 550.

The train now enters the S. part of the peninsula of *Liao-túng*, a mountainous and barren district, the summit of which attains a height of 2985 feet. — 305 M. *Kai-p'ing*, with a silk trade; 325 M. *Hsiung-yüeh-ch'êng*, with hot springs. At (371 M.) *Wa-fang-tien* (Rail. Restaurant) the Japanese, on June 15th, 1904, defeated a Russian attempt to relieve Port Arthur. Just short of (401 M.) *San-shih-li-pu* begins the *Kuan-tung Territory*, leased in 1898 by China to Russia, which parted with its rights in favour of Japan in 1905. — 415 M. *Chín-chou.* On May 26th, 1904, the Russians under General Stössel were thrown back from this point on Port Arthur. — 430 M. *Chou-shui-tzŭ*, with cement-works. The railway to Port Arthur diverges here (see p. 546). Our line turns towards the S.

436 M. **Dairen** or **Dalny.** — HOTELS. *Yamato Hotel* (Pl. a; B, 2), to the N.W. of the station, R. 2³/₄-12, B. 1, déj. (12.30 to 2) 1¹/₂, D. (6.30 to 8.30) 1³/₄ yen, a new building in the Central Circle (Pl. a; C, 3); *Ryoto Hotel* (Pl. b; C, 2), to the S.E. of the station, Japanese. — *Dairen Club* (Pl. C, 2), to the N., near the Nippon Bridge.

CABS, per drive 25-40 sen; per hr. 1¹/₂, with two horses 2, per day 6 & 10 yen. — RICKSHAW, per drive 10-30 sen. — ELECTRIC TRAMWAYS (1st cl. 5 sen) from the rail. station or the harbour through the town to the White City and the Chinese Quarter.

GENERAL POST OFFICE (Pl. 10; C, 2), Kambu-döri. — Agency of the *Hongkong & Shanghai Banking Corporation*, Yamagata-döri (Pl. D, 2, 3); *Yokohama Specie Bank* (Pl. 15; C, 2), Central Circle; *Russo-Asiatic Bank* (Pl. 13; D, 2). Agents for the Hamburg-American Line, *Arnhold, Karberg, & Co.*

CONSULS. British. *H. G. Parlett;* American, *A. W. Pontius.* — Passports for the journey through Siberia (comp. pp. xviii, xix) are obtained from the Russian consul.

CHURCH SERVICES. *English Church* (Pl. 4; C, 3), at 11 a.m. & 6 p.m.; Rev. H. Hibberd. *Presbyterian Church* (Pl. 11; C, 3), West Circle.

Dairen, a Japanese town of 50,000 inhab., is the chief port of Manchuria and the S.E. terminus of the express line of the South Manchuria Railway. It lies on the E. coast of the peninsula of Liao-túng, in 38° 56′ N. lat. and 121° 36′ E. longitude. The mean annual temperature is 52° F., rising in July to 92° F. and falling in January to zero. The town, laid out by the Russian government at a cost of 20 million rubles, was still unfinished when it was occupied (May 30th, 1904) by the Japanese, who have since completed it in a thoroughly modern style. The harbour is shallow and exposed to E. winds, but is never frozen over; it is protected by a massive breakwater. The exports include soya beans and bean-oil. From the Railway Station (Pl. B, C, 2) the Nippon Bridge leads S.E. to the town proper, the main streets of which radiate from five circles. In the Central Circle (Pl. C, 3) is the Civil Administration Office, and in the Higashi-koyen-dōri, which runs hence to the E., are the large Head Offices of the South Manchuria Railway (Pl. 14; D, 3). In the West Circle (Pl. C, 3) is the Presbyterian Church (Pl. 11). On the W. side of the town are the Western Park (Pl. C, 3, 4) and the so-called White City or Electric Park (Pl. B, 3), a pleasure-resort. Still farther to the W. is the Chinese Quarter (Pl. A, 3). To the N. of the station is the old Russian official quarter.

About 4¹/₂ M. to the S.E. is the sea-bathing place of *Lao-hu-tan* or *Rōkotan* (cab there & back 2¹/₂ yen). — *Hoshiga-ura* (Yamato Hotel; cab there & back 2¹/₂ yen), 6 M. to the S.W. of Dairen, is another sea-bathing place.

From Dairen steamers ply once weekly to *Tsingtau* (p. 552), and twice weekly to *Shanghai* (2 days; fares, 40 & 25 yen). — Mail steamers of the Osaka Shosen Kaisha also run to *Kobe* (42, 24 yen) and *Osaka*, to *Chemulpo*, and to other ports.

FROM DALNY TO PORT ARTHUR, 37 M., railway viâ *Chou-shui-tzŭ* (P. 545) in 1¹/₂ hr. (fare 2¹/₄ yen). Just before reaching Port Arthur we see the so-called 203-Mètre Hill to the right (p. 548).

Port Arthur or **Ryōjun** (*Yamato Hotel*, Pl. a, ¹/₄ hr's drive from the station, R. 2¹/₂-10, B. 1, tiffin 1¹/₂, D. 1³/₄ yen; cab per hr. 50 sen, per day 5 yen; Yokohama Specie Bank), a Japanese naval and commercial port with 19,000 inhab., lies at the S.E. extremity of the Liao-túng peninsula, on the N. and E. sides of a bay of the Yellow Sea 2¹/₂ M. in length, and surrounded by rocky hills 655 ft. high. The harbour, which is never frozen over, is entered by a channel 1000 vds. long and 385 vds. broad. The town consists of two parts; to the W. of the railway station is the *New Town*, containing the residence of the Governor-General of the Kuantung territory, the College of Engineering, and the Yamato Hotel. To the E. of the station are the *Old Town* and the *Chinese Quarter*.

The fortress of Port Arthur, constructed by the Chinese viceroy Li Hung-cháng (d. 1901), was captured by the Japanese in 1894 by an attack from the land side. In 1898 it was ceded by China

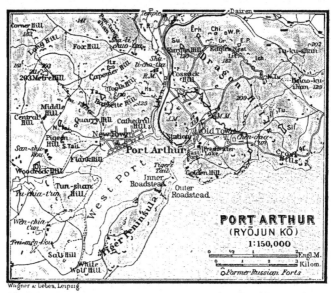

J. M. Japanese Monument, M. M. Military Museum, R. M. Russian Monument.—*Old Russian Fortifications:* Chi., Chi-kuan-shan; E. P., East Panlung-shan; Érh., Érh-lung-shan; Hs., Hsiao-an-shu-shan; Ich., Ichino-he; Itz., Itzŭ-shan; L., Lao-lu-tsui; N. Tai., North Tai-yan-k'ou; N. Tu., North Tung-shih-kuan-shan; Sil., Silver Hill; Su., Sung-shu-shan; S. Tai., South Tai-yan-k'ou; T. R., Temple Redoubt; Ta., Ta-an-tzŭ-shan; Tu., Tung-shih-kuan-shan; W. P., West Pan-lung-shan.

to Russia on a 25 years' lease, and in 1904 it was recaptured by the Japanese after an obstinately contested siege, which lasted five months. The fortifications are left much as they were on the surrender of the town, and are open to visitors. Those on the sea-side and on the S.E. front are inaccessible. Guides at the hotels.

On Feb. 8th, 1904, the Russo-Japanese War began with a successful attack of *Admiral Togo* on the Russian fleet in the outer roads of Port Arthur. On April 13th an attempt of the Russian fleet to reach the open sea was repulsed, and the Russian flagship 'Petropavlovsk', with *Admiral Makárov* on board, was blown up by a submarine mine. After the battle of Chin-chou (p. 545) the unfinished fortress, defended by *General Stössel*, was invested by the Japanese under *General Nogi*. After several preliminary engagements the attack on the fortress proper was begun on Aug. 8th. On Aug. 9th the *Ta-ku-shan Hill* (665 ft.; E.) was seized, and from this point a heavy fire was directed on the Russian fleet, which was thus forced to leave the shelter of the harbour, and fell a victim to the Japanese fleet. By Nov. 2nd the besieged Russians had been driven back to their main line of defence, but the struggle had cost their assailants dear; thus they lost 15,000 men on Aug. 19th in the attempt to carry *Fort Pan-lung-shan* (N.E.) by storm. The Japanese then had recourse to mining operations, but on Nov. 26th they attempted a second attack on Fort Pan-lung-shan, which was repulsed and cost them 8-9000 men. After an attack lasting several days, the *203-Mètre Hill* (N.W.), the key of the Russian position, was captured on Dec. 5th. The losses of the Japanese between Nov. 27th and Dec. 5th amounted to 12,000 men. The brave Russian *General Kondraténko* fell on Dec. 15th in the defence of the North Chi-kuan-shan Fort. On the capture of the N.E. forts, *Érh-lung-shan* and *Sung-shu-shan*, the Russians evacuated the N. front. General Stössel offered to surrender on Jan. 1st, 1905, and a capitulation was signed the following day. The Russians lost about 50,000 men (including 25,000 prisoners), but the capture is said to have cost the Japanese 60-70,000 men.

To the N., between the New and the Old Town, is the *Monument Hill* (Hakugyoku-zan; Pl. J. M.), with a monument covering the remains of 22,000 Japanese soldiers, and a memorial tower (220 ft. high) erected in 1909. The hill commands a good view of the town and forts. To the E. of the Old Town, on an entrenched hill, is the *Military Museum* (Chinretsu-jyō; Pl. M. M.; open free daily 8-5, except Mon.), with many reminiscences of the last siege. Among the most noteworthy are the models of the forts before and after the capture. — To the N. of the New Town is a temple erected in 1908 by the Japanese Government to the memory of the fallen Russians (Pl. R. M.). Farther to the W. (4 M. to the N.W. of the New Town) is the steep *203-Mètre Hill* (Nihyaku-sanko-chi), the scene of the bloodiest and bravest attack and the most obstinate resistance of the whole siege; its furrowed sides show the effects of the heavy fire. The top, commanding a good view of the forts, town, and harbour, is reached by a zigzag path in 20 minutes. — On the N.E. front are the fairly well preserved ruins of *Forts Sung-shu-shan* and *Érh-lung-shan*, which, after a long series of mining operations, were taken by assault.

79. From Mukden to Peking.

522 M. (787 V.), *North Chinese Railway*. Through Express Train once weekly in 23¹/₂ hrs. (fares $ 33.65, $ 20.85 c.), with dining-car (B. $ ¹/₂-1, déj. or D. $ 1¹/₂) and sleeping-car (extra fare $ 5 & $ 2¹/₂). From Moscow to Peking once weekly in 10 days (fares 341 rb. 2, 218 rb. 58 cop.); carriages changed at Kuantchentzi and Mukden. There are also a Through Mail Train once a week, in 23¹/₂ hrs., and an ordinary train daily, taking

2 days and stopping for the night at Shan-hai-kuán (fares $ 31.65, $ 19.85 c.). Passengers must take their own provisions to Shan-hai-kuán, beyond which there is a dining-car to Peking. The carriages are all corridor-cars and resemble those of the Russian railways. Those of the second and third class are not used by Europeans. — The free allowance of luggage is 150 lbs. for first-class passengers. — The names of the stations are exhibited on posts in both English and Chinese. For Chinese coast-time, comp. R. 78.

Chinese Language. — The TRANSLITERATION employed in our text is that of Sir Thomas Wade (with the addition of pronunciation accents), which has also been adopted by the South Manchuria and North Chinese Railways. According to this system the Peking pronunciation is approximately as follows: *a* = a in father; *ai* = ai in aisle; *ei* = ey in grey; *ê* = u in fun; *i* = ee (but sometimes short, like i in chivalry); *o* = o in ore; *ou* = ow in cow (nearly); *u* = oo in too; *ü* = French u in tu. Of the consonants, *ch, k, p,* and *t* are pronounced almost like the English j, g, b, and d; *ch', k', p',* and *t'* are aspirated; *j* = French j in jour. — The traveller may consult 'Chinese without a Teacher', by *Prof. H. A. Giles* (6th ed., 1908), and 'The Chinese Language and How to Learn it' and 'The Pocket Dictionary of Peking Colloquial', two elementary works by *Sir Walter Hillier.*

NUMERALS. 1, *yi-ko* (*i.e.* one piece); 2, *liáng-ko;* 3, *sán-ko;* 4, *ssŭ-ko;* 5, *wú-ko;* 6, *líu-ko;* 7, *ch'i-ko;* 8, *pá-ko;* 9, *chiú-ko;* 10, *shih-ko;* 11, *shih-yi-ko;* 12, *shih-êrh-ko;* 20, *êrh-shih;* 21, *êrh-shih-yi;* 30, *sán-shih;* 31, *san-shih-yí;* 100, *yi-pai;* 300, *sán-pai;* 1000, *yi-ch'ien.*

MONEY (comp. p. 553). One dollar, *yi-k'uai-ch'ien;* $ 2, *liang-k'uai ch'ien;* $ 15, *shih-wú-k'uai-ch'ien;* $ 53, *wu-shih-sán-k'uai-ch'ien;* $ 1½, *yi-k'uai-pán;* $ 2½, *liang-k'uai-pán;* 10 cents, *yi-mao-ch'ien;* 20 c., *êrh mao-ch'ien;* 30 c., *sán-mao-ch'ien:* $ 1.30 c., *yi-k'uai-san-máo.* — Change, *huán-i-huan;* I want 110 c. (11 ten-cent pieces), *yao shih-yi-mao-ch'ien;* I want 10 c. more (comp. p. 554), *hái yao yi-mao-ch'ien.*

TIME. To-day, *chin-t'ien;* to-morrow, *ming-t'ien;* the day after to-morrow, *hóu-t'ien;* in the morning, *tsáo-ch'i;* at noon (midday), *shang wu;* in the evening, *wán-shang;* one o'clock, *yi-tien-chung;* two o'clock, *liáng-tien-chung;* 1.30 p.m., *yi-tien-pán (-chung);* 2.30 p.m., *liáng-tien-pán;* come again to-morrow at 2.30, *ming-t'ien sán-tien-pán-chung huí-lai;* this evening at 7 o'clock, *chin-t'ien wán-shang ch'i-tien-chung.*

RICKSHAWS (p. 553). Rickshaw coolie, *la-ch'é-ti;* (drive to the) British Legation, *(la) Ying-kuo-fú* or *wang Ying-kuo-fú-ch'ü;* (drive) to the hotel, *(la) fán-tien* or *wang fán-tien-ch'ü;* drive to the N., *wang péi ch'ü;* drive to the S., *wang nán ch'ü;* to the E., *wang túng ch'ü;* to the W., *wang hsi ch'ü;* N.E., *túng-pei;* N.W., *hsi-pei;* S.E., *túng-nan:* S.W., *hsi-nan;* stop, *chán-cho;* wait a little, *têng-i-têng* or *tái-i-ta'rh;* turn round, *huí-ch'ü;* back to the hotel, *huí fántien;* home, *huí-chiá.*

IN A SHOP. How much? *tó shao-ch'ien;* what is the price of this article? *chê-ko túng-hsi mai tó shao-ch'ien;* too dear, *t'ai kuei;* not good, not pretty, *pu háo;* thank you, *lao-chiá, lao-chiá* (I have troubled you; used especially if one has bought nothing); good-bye, farewell, *tsai-chién.*

IN A HOTEL *(fán-tien).* Cold water, *liáng-shui* (pron. shwey); warm water, *jó-shui;* hot water, *k'ái-shui;* soda-water, *ch'i-shui;* hock, *pái-chiu;* claret, *húng-chiu;* champagne, *shán-pin-chiu;* beer, *p'i-chiu;* bottle of beer, *yi p'ing-tzŭ p'i-chiu;* knife, *yi-pa táo-tzŭ:* fork, *yi-pa ch'á-tzŭ;* glass, tumbler, *pó-li-pei;* wine-glass, *chiu-péi.*

RAILWAY. Railway station, *huo-ch'ê-chán;* ticket, *ch'ê-p'iao;* first-class, *ti-yi-têng tsó-wei.*

MISCELLANEOUS. Slowly, later, gradually, *man-mán-ti;* quick, *k'uai-k'uái-ti;* come, *lai;* bring here, *ná-lai;* take away, *ná-ch'ü;* yes, *shih;* no, *pú-shih* or *mei-yó;* I do not wish, *pu yáo;* I do not understand, *pu túng;* good day, have you already dined (popular greeting)? *ch'ih-fán-la' mei-yó;* make way, *chieh k'uáng;* go away, *ch'ü pa.*

35*

Mukden, see p. 543. The train runs first to the N.W., then to the S.W. through the district of the Liáo-ho and its tributaries, passing extensive cornfields. — Before reaching (30 M.) *Chu-liu-ho* we cross the *Liáo-ho* by a bridge 730 yds. long. At (37 M.) *Hsin-min-fu (Hsin-min-tʻing)* there is an Irish Presbyterian Mission and Hospital. We go on in a S.W. direction.

From (107 M.) *Kou-pang-tzu (Kao-pêng-tzŭ)* a branch-line runs to (58 M.; 3-3³/₄ hrs.) Ying-kʻóu (p. 545).

Between this point and Tʻáng-shan (p. 551) we have a hilly region to the right. On this side of (132 M.) *Tʻai-liny-hó* we cross the river of that name. — 147 M. *Chín-chou,* 191 M. *Níng-yüan-chou,* two walled towns. To the left, in the *Gulf of Liao-túng,* is seen the island of *Tao-hao-táo.* — Just short of (221 M.) *Sui-chung-hsien (Chung-ho-só)* we cross the *Chung-ho.* Beyond (249 M.) *Chʻien-só (Tsʻien-só)* the railway passes through the *Great Wall* (p. 567), which goes on for 3¹/₂ M. more to the S.E. as far as the Gulf of Liao-túng.

261 M. **Shan-hai-kuán** (*i.e.* 'mountain and sea barrier'; *Railway Hotel,* a little to the W. of the station, pens. \$7; *Tako-kuan,* Japanese), the night-station for the ordinary trains to and from Peking, is frequented as a summer-resort.

The line crosses the *Shih-ho* by a long bridge and traverses a mountainous district to (272 M.) *Tʻáng-ho.*

A short branch-line runs to **Chin-wang-táo** (Rest House Hotel; pop. 5000), a sea-bathing town and seaport on the Gulf of Liao-túng, with an ice-free roadstead (landing-stage 610 yds. long), which is used by the steamers in winter instead of Tientsin.

The railway diverges more and more from the coast. — 283 M. *Pei-tai-hó.* The sea-bathing town of the same name (³/₄ hr. by litter from the station), with a good hotel and beach, as well as a considerable extent of forest, is much frequented by Europeans. It is the summer-seat of the British and German Legations and a health-station for the German troops. — 300 M. *Chʻang-lí,* a town so named since the Chin (Kin) dynasty (1189), has a station of the American Board of Missions and rich orchards. — We cross the Luán-ho and have (on the right) a pretty view upstream. 322 M. *Lán-chou,* an old town on the right bank of the *Luán-ho,* also possesses orchards.

The Luán-ho rises in the S. part of the Great Khingán Mts. (p. 536), near the imperial hunting-preserves (Wéi-chʻang). In its middle course it receives, on the left, the *Jó-ho* or *Jé-ho* ('Warm Water'), on which, amid beautiful scenery, lies **Jehól** or *Chʻêng-tê-fú,* the ancient summer-residence of the Manchu dynasty, with its palaces, Lama temples, gardens, and deer-parks. Jehól lies to the N.E. of Peking, from which it may be reached on horseback in 5 days; the return-journey is generally made by boat down the Luán-ho to Lán-chou, taking 2-4 days according to the condition of the water.

Farther on we pass through a pleasant district and reach (331 M *Lei-chuang.* — 340 M. *Ku-yéh,* a small place with coal-mines.

355 M. *T'áng-shan,* a town with 40,000 inhabitants. The railway station lies at the foot of a hill, the slopes of which are dotted
with European villas. It commands a fine view of the barren hills
and pinnacled mountain-ranges, which gradually disappear farther
on. Excellent coal is yielded by the important coal-pits, and there
are also large railway-workshops.

The train now enters the great North Chinese plain, here a well-
watered lowland, the farmhouses and villages of which are situated
on artificial eminences. Many of these were destroyed during the
Boxer Rebellion in 1900. 383 M. *Lu-t'ái,* on the *Cháo-ho* or *Lu-
t'ai-hó,* which is navigable for junks up to this point. Beyond
(388 M.) *Hán-ku* we cross the Cháo-ho. — 402 M. *Pei-t'áng,* a seaport on the Cháo-ho, protected by several forts. It was captured
by the united British and French forces in 1860. Beyond this
point we traverse a swampy region.

408 M. **Tángku,** *T'áng-ku* (*Rail. Restaurant; Station Hotel,*
pens. $ 6; agency of Carlowitz & Co. of Tientsin), situated in a
desolate district on the left bank of the muddy yellow *Pái-ho.* Its
grayish-yellow clay huts make a very dreary impression, especially
on those arriving by sea. Whenever the water is so low that the
Tientsin steamers have to wait too long outside the bar of the Pái-ho,
the passengers are landed in a steam-pinnace and go on by railway
(porter to the railway station 10 c. for each piece of luggage). Works
are now going on for the improvement of the navigation of the river;
its course has already been considerably shortened by four cuttings
between Tientsin and Ta-kú.

A little way down the river lies *Ta-kú,* the forts of which protected
the mouth of the Pái-ho and were stormed by the Allies on June 17th, 1900.
They have since been razed.

The train now runs to the W. through an almost untilled plain,
sprinkled with funeral mounds. 410 M. *Hsin-ho;* 420 M. *Chün-
liang-ch'éng,* with two forts.

435 M. **Tientsin.** — Two RAILWAY STATIONS, both on the left bank
of the Pái-ho: *Tientsin East,* for the Foreign Colony, and *Tientsin Central,*
for the Chinese Town and for the railway to Tsinanfu (Tsingtau; p. 552).

HOTELS (carriages in waiting at Tientsin East). *Astor House,* German,
pens. $6-10, tiffin (1-3 p.m.) $1½, S. (8-10 p.m.) $1½, very fair; *Hôtel de
la Paix,* R. $ 3-6, B. $ 1, tiffin (12-2 p.m.) $1½, S. (7.30 to 9 p.m.) $1½, pens.
$ 6-10; *Hôt. Impérial; Queen's Hotel.* — CONFECTIONER, *Kiessling.*

RICKSHAWS: 5-10 c. for short drive in the Concessions; 20 c. per hour.
— CARRIAGES ('Tattersall's Horse Repository'): first hour $ 2, second hour
$ 1, each additional hour 50 c. — ELECTRIC TRAMWAY through the Foreign
Colony and the Chinese Town.

BANKS. *Hongkong & Shanghai Banking Corporation; Chartered Bank
of India, Australia, & China; Banque de l'Indo-Chine; German-Asiatic
Bank; Russo-Asiatic Bank; Yokohama Specie Bank.* — BUSINESS FIRMS.
*H. Blow & Co., Hall & Holtz, Hirsbrunner & Co., A. H. Jaques & Co.,
E. Lee,* all in Victoria Road. — BRITISH POST OFFICE (also German, French,
Russian, Japanese, and Chinese). — CHINESE TELEGRAPH ADMINISTRATION,
14 Rue du Chemin de Fer. — STEAMSHIP AGENTS. *Carlowitz* (Hamburg-

American Line), *Melchers* (North German Lloyd), *Jardine, Matheson, &
Co.* (P. & O. Line), *Butterfield & Swire* (China Navigation Co.).
PHYSICIANS. *Drs. Irwin, Brown, & Shaw,* 54 Meadows Road; *Dr. Gordon
O'Neill.* 18 Victoria Road; *Dr. Peck*, Victoria Buildings. --DENTISTS. *Dr.
P. Atwood,* 20 Victoria Terrace; *Dr. A. W. Davis,* 19 Rue de France; *Dr.
D. B. Nye.* 29 Recreation Road.--HOSPITALS. *Queen Victoria Memorial
Hospital; Isolation Hospital.*--DISPENSARIES. *Watson & Co.,* 1 Victoria
Road; *Woollen, Vosy, & Co.,* 34 Rue de France; *Betines & Co.,* 11 Vic-
toria Road.
CONSULS. British, *H. E. Fulford, C.M.G.,* consul-general; United
States, *S. E. Knabenshue.*--CHURCHES. *All Saints* (Episcopal), Racecourse
Road; *Union Church,* Taku Road; *Church of St. Louis* (Rom. Cath.), in
the French Concession.--ENGLISH NEWSPAPERS. *Peking & Tientsin Times;
China Times; China Critic.* — CLUBS. *Tientsin Club,* Victoria Road;
Race Club.

Tientsin (pron. T'ién-ching), the seat of the Provincial Governor of Chih-li, is an important seaport, open to foreign nations
since 1860. In 1912 the value of its trade amounted to 15,611,926 *l.*
In 1900 the city was besieged by the Boxers and Chinese troops
from June 15th to July 13th, since when it has been occupied by
foreign troops (4500 men), including three British regiments and
one American. Pop. 800,000 (4000 foreigners). The city lies in the
barren and marshy lowland of the *Pái-ho,* 47 M. above its mouth
in the Gulf of Pe-chi-li (Pei-chih-li), and at the point where it is
joined by the *Imperial Canal* (Yú-ho) and the *Lut'ái Canal.* The
river is crossed by several bridges. Tientsin consists of two separate towns: *Tientsin Settlement,* entirely occupied by Europeans,
on both banks of the river; and *Tientsin City,* the Chinese town,
situated to the N.W., on the right bank of the Pái-ho. In the Foreign
Colony are the Concessions of the various European powers. In the
British Quarter are the Anglo-Chinese College, with a small museum,
and Gordon Hall, containing memorial brasses to troops of all
nationalities who fell in 1900. There are also memorials in the
Russian Park and in the German Concession. The river is frozen
from Nov. till the end of Feb., during which season the shipping
is diverted to Chin-wang-táo (p. 550).

From Tientsin a RAILWAY runs in 11 hrs. to (255 M.) *Tsinanfú* or
Chi-nan-fú (Trendel; Stein; British Consul, J. L. Smith; U. S. Consular
Agent; German-Asiatic Bank), the capital of the province of Shan-tung.
From Tsinanfú the Shan-tung Railway runs in 11 hrs. more to (256 M.)
Tsingtau (see below).

From Tientsin or Tángku (in winter from Chin-wang-táo) a STEAMER
of the Hamburg-American Line runs in 22 hrs. to *Chefoo* or *Chih-fú* (Beach
Hotel; Astor House Hotel; British Consul, C. C. Kirke; U. S. Consul,
J. H. Arnold), a seaport with 54,000 inhabitants on the N. coast of the
Shan-tung peninsula, which has been open to European trade since 1860.
--From Chefoo the steamer goes on in 22 hrs. to **Tsingtau** or *Ch'ing-tao*
(Green Island; *Prinz Heinrich; Strand Hotel;* German-Asiatic Bank),
situated on the S.E. coast of the *Bay of Kiáutschou* (pron. Chiáo-chou),
and the capital (since 1898) of the territory leased to Germany. Detailed
information will be found in the little guidebook by Behme & Krieger
(Engl. ed., 1910).

From Tientsin East the train runs through a large cemetery to
Tientsin Central, crossing the Lu-t'ái Canal and the city wall.

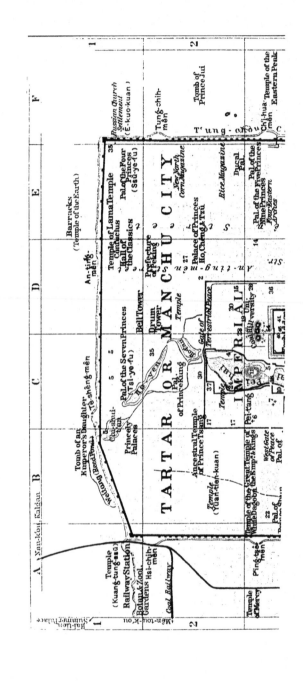

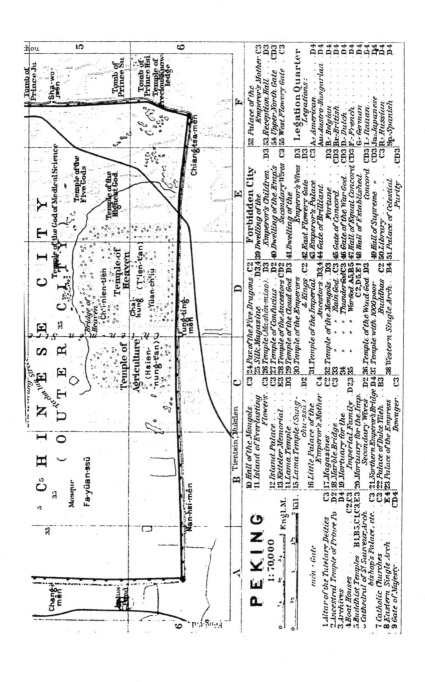

PEKING

1:70,000

Engl.M.

Kil.

mén · Gate

1. Altar of the Tutelary Deities	C3
2. Ancestral Temple of Prince Po	D2
3. Archives	D4
4. Boat Houses	C2,C3
5. Buddhist Temples	B1,B5,C1,C3,E3
– Cathedral of St.Sauveur.Arch.	
– bishop's Palace, etc.	C3
7. Catholic Churches	E4
8. Eastern Single Arch	CD4
9. Gate of Majesty	

B Tientsin, Mukden	
10. Hall of the Mongols	C3
11. Island of Everlasting Flowers	C3
12. Island Palace	C3
13. Ketteler Memorial	C3
14. Lama Temple	D3
15. Lama Temple (Sung-chu-ssu)	D2
16. Little Palace of the Emperor's Mother	C4
17. Magazines	C2
18. Marble Bridge	C3
19. Mortuary for the Imperial Family	D2,C3
20. Mortuary for the Imp. Secondary Wives	C3
21. Northern Emperor's Bridge	D4
22. Palace of Duke Yieh	B3
23. Palace of the Empress Dowager	CD4

C	
24. Pax of the Five Dragons	C2
25. Silk Magazine	D3,4
26. Temple M(a-shén-miao)	D3
27. Temple of Confucius	C3
28. Temple of the Ancestors	E3
29. Temple of the Cloud God	D3
30. Temple of the Emperors & Kings	D2
31. Temple of the Imperial Ancestors	D3,4
32. Temple of the Mongols	C2
33. " Rain God	C3
34. " " Thunder God	C3
35. " " War God	D2,3
36. Temple of the Wind God	C2,D5,E1
37. Temple with 1000 poor	D4
38. Western Single Arch	B3

Forbidden City

39. Dwelling of the Emperor's Children	D3
40. Dwelling of the Emp's Secondary Wives	C3
41. Dwelling of the Emperor's Wives	D3
42. East Flowery Gate	D3
43. Emperor's Palace	C3
44. Gate of Brilliant Fortune	D4
45. Gate of Concord	D3
46. Gate of the War God	C3
47. Hall of Equal Concord	CD3
48. Hall of Established Concord	D3
49. Hall of Supreme "	D3
50. Library	C3
51. Palace of Celestial Purity	CD3
52. Palace of the Emperor's Mother	C3
53. Reception Hall	D3
54. Upper North Gate	CD3
55. West Flowery Gate	C3

Legation Quarter

Legations:

A. American	D4
Au.Austro-Hungarian	D4
B. Belgian	D4
Br.British	D4
D.Dutch	D4
F.French	D4
G.German	D4
I.Itaian	D4
Ja.Japanese	D4
R.Russian	D4
Sp.Spanish	CD3

CHINESE CITY (OUTER CITY)

Mosque
Fa-yüan-ssü

Tomb of Prince Ju
Sha-wo-mén
Tomb of Prince Su
Tomb of Prince Hsi
Temple of Medical Knowledge

Temple of the God of Medical Science
Temple of the Five Gods
Temple of the Highest God

Temple of Heaven
Ch'i-nien-tien
Chai-kung (T'ien-tan)
Yüan-chiu

Bridge of Heaven

Temple of Agriculture
(Hsien-nung-tan)

Nan-hsi-mén
Chiang-tsa-mén
Yung-ting-mén
Chang-mén
Lotus Pond

A little farther on, to the left, we see the West Arsenal (Hsi-kú). The train then runs to the N.W. through a barren and featureless plain to (453 M.) *Yang-ts´ün.* — We then cross the Pái-ho and reach a somewhat less dreary district. 466 M. *Lao-fa* or *Lo-fá; 475 M. Láng-fang,* the extreme point reached by the Seymour Expedition for the relief of Peking in 1900. — 499 M. *Huang-ts´ún,* at the S.W. corner of *Hái-tzŭ,* an imperial deer-park surrounded by an earthen wall 50 M. in length (now disused and in a state of decay). To the left rise the *Hsi-shan* or West Mts. — 510 M. *Féng-t´ai,* the starting-point of the railway to Kalgan (p. 567).

The wall of Peking now becomes visible on the horizon. We pass Ma-chia-p´ú, the old station for Peking, and reach (517 M.) *Peking Yung-ting-mén.* The train then turns to the E. and passes through a breach in the S. wall into the 'Chinese City' (p. 564), the huge and vast unoccupied spaces of which produce the impression of an unwalled nomádic settlement. We then run to the W., skirting the wall of the 'Tartar City', and enter the terminus.

522 M. *Peking-Ch´ién-mén,* adjoining the Legation Quarter (p. 559), which we enter through the 'Water Gate' (Pl. D, 4; p. 560).

80. Peking and Environs.

ARRIVAL. Hotel-porters and rickshaws meet the train at the *Peking Ch´ién-mén Station* (Pl. D, 4; see above; *mén* = gate). — Agency of the International Sleeping Car Co. in the Grand-Hôtel des Wagons-Lits (see below).

Hotels (comp. p. 549), all with restaurants. GRAND-HÔTEL DES WAGONS-LITS (Pl. a; D, 4), Legation Street, on the Canal, with central heating and baths, pens. $8-12, B. (8-10 a.m.) $1, tiffin (12.30 to 2 p.m.) $1¹/₂, S. (8-10 p.m.) $2 (rooms better ordered in advance by telegraph); HÔT. DE PÉKIN (Pl. c; D, 4), opposite the Italian Legation, with baths, pens. $5-6, B. $1, tiffin (12.30 to 2 p.m.) $1¹/₂, S. (7.30 to 9 p.m.) $1¹/₂; HÔT. DU NORD (Pl. b; E, 4), to the N. of the Ha-ta-mén, pens. $4-6. — *Peking Club* (introduction necessary), R. $2¹/₂.

CHINESE RESTAURANTS. Among the best of these, in the N.W. part of the Chinese or Outer City, are *Tsui-ch´iung Lin* and *Hui-féng T´ang.* European knives and forks are often obtainable.

Conveyances. — The ordinary conveyance is the *Rickshaw* (lá-ch´è, yáng-ch´è), a small two-wheeled vehicle with springs and movable top, drawn by one or more coolies (two desirable in bad weather). The fare is 10-20 c. per drive, 20-30 c. per hr. (40-60 c. if the trip is continuous). In longer trips it is customary to advance about 20 c. to the coolies at the resting places. In the case of any difficulty in indicating the exact destination, it is customary just to tell the coolie the point of the compass he is to make for (comp. p. 549). — The *Peking Tattersall Ltd.* supplies motor-cars (first hour $7, each succeeding hr. $5, per day $25), carriages ($1 per hr., with two horses $1.20 c., per day $5 & $6¹/₂), and saddle-ponies ($3 per day, 8 a.m. to 7 p.m.).

Currency (comp. p. 549). The usual basis of reckoning is the Mexican *Silver Dollar* ($), which is worth about half as much as the United States dollar (*i.e.* ca. 2s.). There are also silver coins of 10 and 20 *Cents* (c.). All these coins are often counterfeited. The *Cash* is a small copper coin with a hole in the middle, worth about ¹/₄₀ of a penny (1000 cash

= $ 1). Sums above $ 10 are paid by cheque, in the case of the Chinese in bullion. — In changing money with the Chinese the traveller should insist on receiving 110 c. for the dollar (comp. p. 549).

Banks. *Hongkong & Shanghai Banking Corporation* (Hui-fêng), *International Banking Corporation* (Hua-ch'i), *German-Asiatic Bank*, *Banque de l'Indo-Chine*, *Russo-Asiatic Bank*, *Yokohama Specie Bank*, all in Legation Street (Pl. D, 4).

Shops. — GENERAL STORES. *Gillard & Co.*, *Kicrulff & Co.*, *Culty & Co.*, all in Legation Street; *Viccajee & Co.*, *Wauiee*, both in Ha-ta-mên Street. — CHEMISTS. *Betines & Co.*, Ha-ta-mên Street. — PHOTOGRAPHERS (Châo-hsiang-p'ú). *Camera Craft Co.*, *Hartung*, both in Legation Street, near the Hôtel des Wagons-Lits; *Yamamoto*, to the N. of the Hôtel de Pékin (p. 553). — JEWELLERS. *Sennet Frères*, opposite the American Legation. — SADDLE MAKER. *Reitzig*, Legation Street. — CURIO SHOPS (Ku-wan-p'u), in Liu-li-ch'áng, Ha-ta-mên, and Wáng-fu-ching Streets. — BOOKSELLERS, see p. 564; *Market* beside the Lúng-fu-ssŭ Temple, see p. 562; *Cloisonné Enamel Factory*, see p. 564. In the Chinese shops bargaining is absolutely necessary (comp. p. 549). — NEWSPAPERS. *Peking Daily News; Peking Gazette; Journal de Pékin.*

Post Offices. Chinese, German, French, Russian, and Japanese, all in the Legation Quarter (p. 559).

Telegraph Offices (Pl. D, 4). *Chinese Telegraph Administration, Great Northern Telegraph Co. of Copenhagen, Eastern Extension of the Australasian & China Telegraph Co. of London*, all in the same building, which faces the glacis to the N. of the Austro-Hungarian Legation; per word to Russia 2 fr.; Great Britain $ 2.25 c.; U.S.A. ca. $ 2.50 c.; Australia $ 1.50 c.

Legations, comp. p. 559 and the Plan. British Minister, *Sir John N. Jordan, G.C.I.E.;* United States Chargé d'Affaires, *Hon. Edward T. Williams.* — For the journey through Siberia passports must be *visé* at the Russian consulate (comp. pp. XVIII, XIX).

Religious Services. *Church of England*, in the British Legation Chapel; *Union Church* (Pl. D, E, 3), in the Têng-shih-k'ou. — *Roman Catholic*, St. Michel, Legation St.; St. Sauveur (Lazarists), see p. 562. — *Greek Catholic*, at the Russian Church Settlement (È-kuo-kuan; Pl. E, F, 1).

Hospitals. *Union Medical College Hospital*, facing the Ketteler Memorial (Pl. 13; E, 3), *St. Michel* (French), Legation Street, both of which receive foreign patients; *German Military Hospital* (p. 559), with dispensary. — DOCTORS are attached to most of the Legations.

Peking (120 ft.), Chinese *Péi-ching*, also called *Shun-t'ien-fú* as the capital of a district, and popularly known as *Ching-tu* or *Ching-ch'êng (i.e.* capital), the capital of the Chinese Empire, lies in the great plain of N. China, in lat. 39°54′ N. and long. 116°28′ E. Its total circumference is 21 M., and it contains 700,000 inhab., including the Legation guards of the Great Powers and many other foreigners. The city is divided into five distinct parts, separated by walls. On the N. are the *Manchu* or *Tartar City* (Néi-ch'êng, *i.e.* Inner City), the *Legation Quarter*, and the *Imperial City* (Huáng-ch'êng), the last including the *Purple* or *Forbidden City* (Tzŭ-chin-ch'êng); to the S. lies the *Chinese City* (Nán-ch'êng, *i.e.* S. City, or Wái-ch'êng, *i.e.* Outer City). The Manchu City, the W. part of which is the fashionable quarter, was originally reserved for the so-called Bannermen (Ch'i-jên), *i.e.* the warriors who came to China along with the Manchu dynasty, while the native population lived outside the wall. This distinction has, however, vanished (comp. p. 558). The wall of the Tartar City is 50 ft. high and 40 ft. wide at the top; that of the Chinese City is 30 ft. high and 15-25 ft. thick (comp. p. 559).

In spite of the monotony of its grey brick houses, the city has many picturesque points; the sunset view of the Western Hills from the city wall is singularly beautiful. The more important streets are now well-kept; the other streets, however, are extremely dirty, malodorous (especially in summer), and often practically impassable after rain. The main business-streets of the Inner or Tartar City are the *Wáng-fu-ching* and *An-ting-mên Tá-chieh* (Tá-chieh, main street; Pl. D, 1-4), leading N. from the Legation Quarter to the Án-ting-mén, and the *Há-ta-mên Tá-chieh* (Pl. E, 1-4), running N. from the Ha-ta-mén. The chief streets in the Outer or Chinese City are the *Ch'ién-mên Tá-chieh;* Pl. C, D, 4-6), running S. from the Ch'ién-mên to the Yung-ting-mén, and the *Liu-li-ch'áng* (see p. 564). The well-cultivated environs with their numerous water-courses and canals, their scattered groves and clumps of trees, are often very attractive. — The CLIMATE is continental but quite healthy owing to the dryness of the air. In summer the temperature rises to a maximum of 104° F. in the shade, while in winter it falls to − 4° F. The storms of sand and dust are specially frequent in spring; the rainy season comes in July and August. The pleasantest part of the year is autumn (Oct.). Winter has always plenty of sunshine, and the cold is never unbearable except in a high wind. The visitor should not drink unboiled water, and in summer he should be on his guard against diarrhœa.

History. — The Chinese carry the history of Peking back to 1121 B.C., when *Wú-wang* invested his relative *Shih* with the principality of *Yen*, of which *Chi* was the capital. Chi is said to have stood pretty much on the site of the present Peking; many authorities believe, though perhaps wrongly, that the old Mongolian wall to the N. of the town (p. 566) is the last remnant of this city. In 222 B.C. Yen was conquered by *Shih-huáng-ti* and made a province of the unified Empire of China. For many centuries thereafter Chi remained simply the chief town of the district. Under the *Han Dynasty* (ca. 200 B.C. to 200 A.D.) it received the name of *Yen*, and in the time of the *T'ang Dynasty* (618-907) it was known as *Yú-chou*. At this time it was the seat of a military governor and lay to the S.W. of the present city. The temple of Fá-yüan-ssŭ (p. 565) lay near its S.E. corner, and the W. part of its enclosing wall passed between the Temple of the White Cloud and the Temple of Celestial Peace (p. 565).

In 936 Yú-chou was captured by the *Kítan* (Chitan) or *Liao Tartars*, who dominated a part of N. China down to 1122. [They destroyed the old city and built a new and larger one in its place; this was first known as *Nán-ching* ('Southern Capital') or *Yú-tu-fú* and after 1013 as *Yén-ching*. A fragment of its N. wall is still extant near the Temple of the White Cloud (p. 565), and its S.W. angle is visible at the hamlet of O-fang-ying, $1^1/_4$ M. to the S.W. of Peking. In 1122-25 Peking, under the name of *Yen-shan-fú*, was in the hands of the *Sung Dynasty*, which ruled over Central and Southern China. The Sung were driven out by the *Chin* (Kin) or *Júchên*, the ancestors, or at least the kinsmen, of the present Manchus. These doubled the size of the town by extending it to the E., and in 1151 made it their residence under the name of *Chúng-tu* ('Middle Capital') or *Ta-hsing-fú*.

In 1215 the city fell into the hands of *Jenghiz Khan* (p. 536), whose great-grandson *Kublaï Khan* (d. 1294; see below), the first emperor of the *Mongol* or *Yüan Dynasty*, selected it as his residence in 1264, and in 1267 built a town to the N.E. of it called *Ta-tú* ('Great Capital'; Mongol, *Khan-balik* or 'Town of the Princes'). On the E., W., and S., its limits corresponded to the present Tartar city; the N. wall, however, was formed by the old rampart (T'ú-ch'êng, p. 566), so that the Bell and Drum towers (p. 563) lay in the middle of the town.

Hung-wú, the founder of the *Ming Dynasty*, who expelled the Mongols in 1368, reduced the town to the dimensions of the present 'Tartar City' and called it *Pei-p'ing-fú*. Under his son *Yung-ló*, who took up his residence here in 1409 and built a brick wall in place of the earthen ramparts of the Mongols, it received the name of *Péi-ching* (Peking, 'North Capital') and the administrative designation of *Shun-t'ien-fú*, which have clung to it since that time. The 'Chinese City' was not incorporated till 1524, and its wall was built in 1544. — The *Manchu Dynasty (Ta-ch'ing)*, which conquered the empire in 1644, did not enlarge the city. The 'golden age' of the Chinese porcelain industry falls in the reign of the Emperor K'áng-hsi (p. 557).

The beginning of European intercourse with Peking took place under the Yüan Dynasty. In addition to a number of European artisans and artists as well as Arabian astronomers, the first Roman Catholic missionaries (Ruysbroek, De Montecorvino, Arnold von Köln, and others) came in the 13th cent. to Peking, where an archbishopric was soon founded. *Marco Polo* (d. 1323), the most celebrated traveller of the Middle Ages, to whom we owe the first description of Peking, was for many years the private secretary of Kublaï Khan. Under the Ming Dynasty intercourse with Europe was practically suspended. It was not till 1601 that Matteo Ricci, the Jesuit, obtained permission from the emperor to establish a community in Peking. Since that date a *Jesuit Mission* has flourished here continuously, with a few short interruptions; its members obtained an advantageous position at the imperial court through the skilful use of their ample knowledge, and endeavoured

(not without success) to promote the mutual understanding of China
and Europe. Their best opportunity for this came under the two
most celebrated emperors of the Manchu Dynasty, viz. *K῾áng-hsi*
(1662-1723) and *Ch῾ien-lúng* (1736-95), who, like Kublaï Khan,
showed a friendly disposition towards European culture, and entrusted the Jesuits with the solution of a number of scientific,
artistic, and technical problems. Remainders of this period exist
in the buildings of the Yüan-ming-yüán (p. 566) and in the shell-
ornamentation of the façades of some Peking houses. Specimens
of cloisonné enamel with rococo figures of the time of Ch῾ien-lúng
are still occasionally met with in the shops.

During the war of 1860 the allied British and French troops
occupied Peking on Oct. 13th and destroyed the imperial summer
palace of Yüan-ming-yüán (p. 566). A series of bad harvests and
the economic stress occasioned by the construction of railways
and other foreign enterprises led (in June, 1900) to the outbreak
of the so-called *Boxers* (I-ho-ch῾üán), which was directed against
all foreigners. The name 'Boxer' comes from the confusion of the
word 'ch῾üán', *i.e.* 'fist', with the name 'I-ho-t῾uán', *i.e.* 'League
of Friends', one of the secret societies which are so common in
China. This rebellion resulted in the assassination of the German
ambassador, Baron von Ketteler (June 20th, 1900) and in the siege
of the Europeans in the Legation Quarter and in the Pei-t῾áng.
On Aug. 14th Peking was occupied by the allied forces of the
Great European Powers, the United States, and Japan. — On Feb.
12th, 1912, the Imperial House of the Manchu Dynasty ceased to
rule over China, which thereupon became a Republic with Yüan
Shih-k῾ái as temporary President. On April 8th, 1913, the first
Parliament was inaugurated, consisting of a Senate (Ts῾án-i-yüan;
274 members) and a House of Representatives (Chúng-i-yüan; 596
members). Yüan Shih-k῾ái was formally elected first President of
the Republic on Oct. 6th, 1913.

Religion. — China has three main religions: Confucianism,
Taoism, and Buddhism, the last in two forms, Foism and Lamaism.

CONFUCIANISM, founded in the 5th cent. B.C. by *Confucius*
(K῾úng-tzŭ), in close touch with the primitive forms of Chinese
faith, is less a religion than a code of morals regarding the duties
of mankind towards the family, the neighbourhood, and (above all)
the state. The cult, though doubtless somewhat altered by Buddhistic and Taoistic influences, is in the main of primitive simplicity.
It allows no idols, but represents the Deity and ancestors by inscribed tablets before which worship is performed with the aid of
prayer, incense, and the sacrifice of animals. — TAOISM, reaching
back to the mystic philosopher *Láo-tzŭ* (6th cent. B.C.?), was originally a form of pantheism, probably influenced by India, but it
afterwards degenerated through the adoption of Buddhistic and

other Indian ideas into a chaotic polytheism and thaumaturgism. Its forms of worship, including the adoration of idols, are all exactly the same as those of Buddhism. — BUDDHISM, which reached China in a very corrupt and polytheistic form, has on its side borrowed much from its two predecessors; in particular it has had to reconcile itself to the national worship of ancestors. In its purer form of *Foism*, it was recognized as the religion of the State in 67 A.D. *Lamaism*, a degenerate and strictly hierarchical form, was introduced from Tibet in the 13th cent. and is practically confined to N. and N.W. China. The Buddhistic worship consists mainly in meditation, the repetition of formal prayers (in Lamaism with the aid of praying-wheels), and in bloodless sacrifices to numerous idols.

Population. Street Life. Dwelling Houses. — The native population consists of *Chinese* and *Manchus* (comp. p. 554). The two races are distinguished mainly by their physiognomy and by certain peculiarities in their language. There is also a considerable difference in the dress of the women. The Chinese women wear a short upper garment, showing wide trousers below; their hair is bound up in a sort of chignon at the back of the head, and their feet are compressed in childhood by the use of bandages, which latter custom, however, is now dying out. The Manchu women wear long robes, leave the feet of their natural size, and dress their hair in a sort of wing-like arrangement on the top of the head.

The main thoroughfares traversing the town from S. to N. are generally very animated, especially in summer. The shops are usually open towards the street, but of the dwelling-places little is seen except the walls of house and courtyard. Along the roadways, many of which are now metalled, moves a constant stream of carts, horsemen, mule-trains, camel-caravans, funerals, and wedding-processions. Along the sidewalk, both to the right and to the left, are the booths and tents of cook-shop keepers, wine-dealers, and traders of all kinds, between which the stream of pedestrians and rickshaws winds its way. Story-tellers, jugglers, and pertinacious beggars are all in full force; hawkers spread their goods (mainly of European manufacture) on the ground; and the sellers of various kinds of edibles call out their wares. The noise lasts till late in the night, and indeed is often added to after dark by the letting-off of fireworks at all kinds of entertainments.

The Chinese dwelling is usually in the form of a small enclosure, consisting of three one-storied houses arranged round a court in such a way that the main building, opposite the gate of the court, faces towards the S. The court is often shaded by trees. Behind the gateway (and sometimes also in front of it) is a wall or wooden screen as a protection against evil spirits; hence the passers-by cannot see into the court. Each house stands on a massive terrace of masonry, filled in with a core of compressed earth, and generally about $1^1/_2$-2 ft. high. The back-wall and the side-walls are usually windowless, while the four columns of the front wall are built of masonry only to a height of 3 ft., the upper part consisting of lattice-work covered inside with silk paper. The door, which has a very high threshold, is also made mainly of lattice-work and is always in the middle of the front wall. The interior is divided by carved wooden partitions into three chambers; these as a rule have no ceilings of their own, so that the common tent-like roof constructed of concrete and hollow tiles, is visible from within.

a. The City.

Before beginning a detailed inspection of the sights, it is desirable to take a *Drive round the Forbidden City (2-2^1/$_2$ hrs.), which gives a good general idea of Peking and its street-life. From the *Legation Quarter* we proceed to the N. through Thomann Street (Pl. D, 4) and its continuation, the Wáng-fu-ching Tá-chieh (Pl. D, 3, 4), then turn to the left through the *East Gate of Flowers* (Túng-hua-mên; official name, *East Gate of Peace*, Túng-an-mên; Pl. D, 3), and enter the *Imperial City*, which we traverse up to the inaccessible *Purple* or *Forbidden City* (p. 560). We then skirt its E. side to the picturesque N.E. angle, where we turn to the W. and go past the *Coal Hill* (r.; p. 561) and over the *Marble Bridge* (p. 561) to the *West Gate of Peace* (Pl. B, C, 3). We then return along the W. and S. sides of the Imperial City back to the Legation Quarter.

A *Walk on the Wall of the Tartar City (also practicable by rickshaw), either in the evening or the morning, is also well worth while. From the Ha-ta-mên (Pl. E, 4), where we ascend the wall, we may go either W. to the Ch'ién-mên (Pl. C, D, 4; comp. p. 564), which was re-erected after its destruction in 1900, or E. to the architecturally interesting corner-tower, and then N. to the Imperial Observatory (p. 562), each trip taking ^{1}/$_2$-^{3}/$_4$ hr. The walk to the W. affords a commanding view over the Legation Quarter and the Chinese Town as well as a magnificent prospect of the West Mts. (especially beautiful in the glowing light of sunset). In keeping to the E. we enjoy a beautiful view of the T'úng-chou Canal and the country to the E. of Peking.

The Legation Quarter (Pl. D, 4), in and near which are the hotels mentioned at p. 553, has since 1900 assumed a more and more European character. Its cleanliness and quietness offer a pleasing contrast to the other parts of the city. On the N., E., and W. it is protected by a glacis, partly provided with a moat in front. On the S. side runs the S. wall of the Tartar City, which is strengthened by blockhouses towards the Ha-ta-mên (Hata Gate) and the Ch'ién-mên. The quarter is divided by the *Imperial Canal* (Yü-ho) into an E. and a W. part (walk on the wall, see above). The main thoroughfare is the —

Legation Street, which runs from E. to W. Proceeding from the Ha-ta-mên, we have on the right the *German Officers' Casino*, and on the left the *Waldersee Barracks* (good canteen).

In the Schwartzhoff Street, which diverges to the right, is the *German Military Hospital* (p. 554).

Farther on, to the left, is the *Belgian Legation* (Pl. B.), while

to the right are the German-Asiatic Bank and the Roman Catholic
Cathedral of St. Michel.

Soden Street, which here diverges to the left, leads to an approach to
the wall of the Tartar City. — To the right is Thomann Street, running
N., at first between the E. wall of the French Legation and the French
Barracks. Farther on, to the left, are the *House of Mr. Aglen*, Director
of the Maritime Customs, and the *Italian Legation* (Pl. I.). On the right
are the *International Club* and the *Austro-Hungarian Legation* (Pl. Au.),
with a statue (1909) of Emp. Francis Joseph (by J. Benk).

Farther on in the Legation Street, to the right, is the *French
Legation* (Pl. F.). Opposite, to the left, is the *German Legation*
(Pl. G.), in the garden of which is a marble cross erected to the
memory of the ambassador, Baron von Ketteler (comp. pp. 557,
562). Next come, on the right, the French and Japanese post offices,
the *Spanish Legation* (Pl. Sp.), and the Yokohama Specie Bank; on
the left are the Hongkong & Shanghai Bank and the Grand-Hôtel
des Wagons-Lits (Pl. a).

[Legation St. is here intersected by Canal Street. The left
branch of this leads S. past the German post office to the *Water
Gate* and the *Tientsin Railway Station* (Pl. D, 4; comp. p. 553).
In that part of Canal Street which lies to the N. of Legation Street
are (on the right) the *Japanese Legation* (Pl. Ja.) and the Japanese
and Italian Barracks. To the W. of the Canal lies the large *British
Legation* (Ying-kuo-fú; Pl. Br.), with its church and beautiful
garden. On a part of the N. wall are marks made by bullets during
the siege of 1900 and the inscription 'Lest we forget'.]

Returning along the Canal to Legation Street, we continue to
follow it to the W. On the right is the *Russian Legation* (Pl. R.),
with its chapel; on the left are the Indo-Chinese Bank, the International Banking Corporation, the Russo-Asiatic Bank, the *Dutch
Legation* (Pl. D.), the *American Legation* (Pl. A.), and the American Barracks. Opposite the American Legation are several shops
and the French *Hospital of St Michel* (Pl. D, 4); to the S.W. is
the Ch'ién-mên (p. 564).

The PURPLE or FORBIDDEN CITY (Pl. C, D, 3), so named on account
of the purplish colour of its enclosing wall, contains the Imperial
Palace and is open to only a few privileged persons. All that the
ordinary traveller will see are the yellow roofs (yellow being the
imperial colour) of the palaces and temples overtopping the wall.

The present entrance is by the *Gate of Celestial Peace* (T'ién-
an-mên; Pl. C, D, 4), on the S., which leads into a park planted with
fir-trees and containing the *Temple of the Imperial Ancestors*
(T'ái-miao; Pl. 31) and the *Altar of the Tutelary Deities* (Shê-chi-
t'án; Pl. 1). Visitors proceed straight on and by passing through
the Gate of Majesty (Pl. 9; C, D, 4) reach the *Noonday Gate* (Wú-
mên; Pl. C, D, 3), the entrance proper to the Forbidden City. Here
begins a series of halls stretching towards the N., which are chiefly

used for audiences and similar occasions, and are separated by courts and monumental gateways. First comes the *Hall of Supreme Concord* (T'ái-ho-tién; Pl. 49), followed by the *Hall of Equal Concord* (Chúng-ho-tién; Pl. 47), and the *Hall of Established Concord* (Páo-ho-tién; Pl. 48), the last being the seat of the examinations formerly held under the presidency of the Emperor, for the highest degree of scholarship, that of the Hán-lin or Academicians. The *Palace of Celestial Purity* (Ch'ién-ch'ing-kúng; Pl. 51) was used for the audiences held at 5 a.m., which, however, sometimes took place in the adjacent Chün-chi-ch'ú. In the *Chiáo-t'ai-kúng* were kept the imperial seals, the oldest of which is said to date from 240 B.C. To the N. and on both sides of the above-mentioned buildings are the palaces of the Emperor, the Empress, the imperial children, and so on. — Outside the wall, to the N., is the so-called *Coal Hill* (Méi-shan, officially Ching-shan or Prospect Hill; Pl. C, D, 3), a tree-clad mound 215 ft. high, probably thrown up under the Ming Dynasty. Its five symmetrical terraces are each crowned with a temple, intended to protect the imperial palace from evil influences. The hill, which is at present (1914) inaccessible, is to be converted into a public park. The tree is still preserved on which the last Ming emperor hanged himself in 1644, in order not to outlive his power.

To the W. of the above-mentioned buildings is the former *Winter Palace*, with gardens and lakes, some of which date back as far as the Júchên Dynasty. The Marble Bridge, or Bridge of the Imperial River (Yü-ho-ch'iáo; Pl. 18), which is now open to traffic and connects the E. and W. quarters of the Inner City, divides the whole into two parts. To the N. is the *Péi-hai* or 'North Lake' (Pl. C, 2, 3), with the artificial island of Ch'iúng-hua-táo ('Island of Everlasting Flowers'; Pl. 11), containing a prominent dagoba (Pai-t'á) or memorial tomb. The portion to the S. of the bridge now forms the residence of Yüan Shih-k'ái and is entered on the S. by the *New Flowery Gate* (Hsin-hua-mên; Pl. C, 4). The *Nán-hai* or 'South Lake' (Pl. C, 3, 4) contains the island-palace (Pl. 12) of the Emperor Kuang-hsü (d. 1908). On the W. side of the *Chúng-hai* or 'Middle Lake' (Pl. C, 3) is the Palace of the late Empress-Dowager Tzü-hsi.

In the IMPERIAL CITY, to the N.E. of the Coal Hill (see above), lies the **University** (Pl. D, 3), formerly the palace of an imperial princess. From the second court we have a fine view of the Coal Hill. The *Government University* (Ta-hsüeh-hsiao), founded in 1902 as the Imperial University (Ta-hsüeh-t'áng), and remodelled in 1910, is attended by 300 students. It is to be transferred to a new building near the Yellow Temple (p. 565), while the old building will be retained for preparatory training. The University is managed by a Director-General and consists of six faculties: the Philosophical and Philological Faculty (with Chinese professors), the Faculty of Political Economy (with English professors), the Faculty of Physical Science (German), the Juristic Faculty (French and English), the Technical Faculty (American), and the Agricultural Faculty (Japanese); it is planned to add a Medical Faculty to these. The University also possesses a Library of European and Chinese books (with a reading-room), and a Natural Science and Technical Laboratory and Collection.

Not far from the W. gate of the Imperial City is the **Pei-t'áng**, the property of the Roman Catholic Lazarist Mission of Chih-li, with the *Cathedral of St. Sauveur* (Pl. 6, C 3; consecrated in 1888), the residence of the Archbishop (Mgr. Jarlin), seminaries, a monastery, and a nunnery. The Pei-t'áng is celebrated for its heroic defence from Aug. 14th to Aug. 16th, 1900. The tumulus erected over the graves of the fallen commands a wide panorama.

S.E. PART OF THE INNER OR TARTAR CITY. The *Imperial Observatory* (Kuán-hsiang-t'ái; Pl. E, 4), easily reached from the Ha-ta-mén (Pl. E, 4) by the city wall (comp. p. 559), was built in 1279. Some of the instruments, which were made under supervision of the Jesuits in 1673, were taken to Germany (Potsdam) in 1900.— Adjoining the S. wall of the city is the *German Cemetery* (Pl. E, 4). To the N. of the Observatory, on the site of the Examination Hall, is the new *Parliament Building* (Pl. E, 4), founded in 1911.

Not far off is the *Lúng-fu-ssŭ* (Pl. 14; D, E, 3), a Lama temple built in 1451 and partly destroyed by fire a short time ago. The vicinity of this temple offers a lively scene on the 9th, 19th, and 29th day of each Chinese month, when a market is held here for all sorts of utensils, toys, books, flowers, and other miscellaneous articles.

The N. PART OF THE INNER OR TARTAR CITY contains a few of the chief sights of Peking. We drive up the Ha-ta-mén Street (p. 555), pass through the Eastern Single Arch (Túng-tan P'ái-lou · Pl. 8, E 4), the *Ketteler Memorial* (Pl. 13, E 3; p. 560), erected in 1903 in expiation of the murder of the German ambassador of that name, and the *Four Eastern Arches* (Túng-ssŭ p'ái-lou; Pl. E, 3), and enter (3 M.) the N. end of the Tartar City.—A little to the N.E. of the Ketteler Arch is the *Wái-chiao-pú* (Pl. E, 3) or Ministry of Foreign Affairs.

The *****Lama Temple** (Yung-ho-kúng or Láma-miao; Pl. E, 1), built before 1722 as the palace of the later Emperor Yung-chéng, is the largest Lama temple in the city and the dwelling-place of a 'living Buddha' (huo Fó; not accessible to visitors). The gates and other fine architectural features are well worthy of notice; so, too, are the Temple of the Great Buddha, with a wooden statue 75 ft. high, and the Hall of Prayer, where the traveller may have an opportunity of seeing the Lamas at their devotions.

Opposite, to the W., is the *Temple of Confucius (Wén-miao,
Ta-ch'êng-tién or K'úng-miao; Pl. D, E, 1), renewed by the Emperor
Ch'ien-lúng (p. 557). In the first court are several rows of stone
tablets (some dating from the Ming period), with the names of successful graduates. It will be noticed that the name of the reformer
Kang Yu-wéi has been chiselled out by imperial order. Under the
entrance-portico of the second court, with its ancient cypresses, are
the celebrated 'stone drums' (shíh-ku), the inscriptions on which
date from the early Chou Dynasty (11-8th cent. B. C.; rubbings
sold at $ 5). Opposite is the Temple of Confucius proper, where
the Emperor, either in person or by deputy, offered incense twice a
year to the manes of the great sage. Opposite the entrance is the
ancestral tablet of Confucius, bearing the inscription: 'Spirit tablet
of the soul of the supremely holy teacher K'ung (Confucius)'. To the
right and left, in double rows, are those of his chief pupils (Mêng-
tzŭ, etc.). The solemn restfulness of the court and the unadorned
architecture of the Temple Hall are in keeping with the simple dignity
of the primitive Chinese cult. — Adjoining, to the W., is the *Old
University* (Kuó-tzŭ-chién), with the **Hall of the Classics** (Pi-
yung-kúng; Pl. D, 1), built by Ch'ien-lúng. A marvellous gate
(p'ai-lou) of glazed tiles leads into the marble-paved square court,
in the middle of which, surrounded according to ancient prescrip-
tion by a circular pond, rises the main hall, where the Emperor
used to preside over the examination. Around the court are the
halls containing the sacred writings of Confucianism carved in
stone, and also a marble sun-dial. The beauty and restfulness of
this spot, combined with its incipient decay, make a profound impression on the beholder.

In the middle of the N. quarter of the city rises the so-called
*Drum Tower (Kú-lou; Pl. C, D, 2), 100 ft. in height, built in
1272. A steep flight of stone steps ascends to the first floor, containing a colossal drum, which is sounded at 8 p.m. and every
hour thereafter during the night. The bell in the Bell Tower is
pealed at the same time. The gallery commands a splendid panorama. To the S. is Peking, resembling a forest extending to the
horizon, with the roofs of the main buildings rising above the trees.
To the N. and W. are cultivated fields, with hills in the background.
In clear weather the Yellow Temple (p. 565) may be descried to
the N., and the Summer Palace (Wan-shou-shán; p. 566) and Yü-
ch'üan-shán (p. 567) to the N.W. — About 110 yds. to the N. rises
the **Bell Tower** (Chúng-lou; Pl. C, D, 1, 2), of nearly equal height
This was erected by Yung-ló a little to the N.W. of the Bell
Tower of the Yüan Dynasty, which marked the centre of the old
Mongolian capital, and was renewed by Ch'ien-lúng in 1745 after
a fire. The staircase is darker and steeper than that of the Drum
Tower. At the top is a gigantic bronze bell weighing over 40 tons,

which is one of the largest bells actually hung (comp. p. 281; fine view).

A visit should also be paid to the CHINESE or OUTER CITY (comp. p. 554), the S. quarter of Peking. The chief entrance from the N. is the *Ch'ién-mên* ('Front Gate'; Pl. C, D, 4), from which the *Ch'ién-mên Tá-chieh* (Pl. C, D, 4-6), the main thoroughfare, runs towards the S. between the Temple of Heaven and the Temple of Agriculture, both of which are surrounded by walled parks.

The **Temple of Heaven* (T'ien-t'án, *i.e.* Altar of Heaven; Pl. D, 5, 6) was built by Yung-ló in 1420, and restored by Ch'ien-lúng in 1753. It belongs to the Confucian cult and is dedicated to the worship of Heaven. The only worshipper was the Emperor, in his capacity as 'Son of Heaven', and his duty was performed thrice yearly by the offering of sacrifice. The temples and the marble altars and terraces are all circular in shape on account of the supposed form of the heavens; the buildings are roofed with blue glazed tiles. Visitors are admitted to the Great Hall of *Ch'i-nien-tién*, with its throne and balustrades; to the altar of *Yüan-ch'iú* ('Round Hill'), to the S. of the temple, where the Emperor performed his devotions; and to the *Chái-kung* or Hall of Abstinence, to the W., where the Emperor passed the night before the sacrifice in fasting. The view looking N. from the altar of Yüan-ch'iú is highly picturesque owing to the variety of colours, while the massive simplicity of the whole produces an impression of great solemnity. — A fee of 10-20 c. is given to the guide and to each of the doorkeepers.

Less imposing, though also full of interest, is the **Temple of Agriculture** (Hsien-nung-t'án, *i.e.* Altar of the First Husbandman; Pl. C, 5, 6), which stands to the W. of the Temple of Heaven. It was built by Chia-ch'ing in the 16th cent. and restored by Ch'ien-lúng, and also belongs to the Confucian cult. Every spring the Emperor made an annual offering here to the 'Nine Hills', the 'Four Rivers', the 'Four Seas', and the God of Husbandry. The altars and temples are rectangular in form and lower than those of the Temple of Heaven; the tiles are dark brown, *i.e.* the colour of the soil. Noteworthy is the terrace of *Chin-hêng-t'ái*, with the field in which the Emperor ploughed eight furrows every year, the princes ten, and the chief officials eighteen. The field, the produce of which was formerly devoted to sacrificial purposes, is now used for experimental horticulture. The sacrificial vessels and other ceremonial objects used in this temple and in the Temple of Heaven are now kept in one of the large halls of the Temple of Agriculture. On festivals they are occasionally exhibited to the public. — Fees as above.

To the S.W. of the Ch'ién-mên (see above) is the interesting **Liu-li-ch'áng* ('Glazed-tile Yard'; Pl. C, 4, 5), a street containing the best shops for books and curios (high prices).

From the Liu-li-ch'áng a side-street leads N.W. to a manufacturing quarter (formerly the imperial brick-yard), where visitors may inspect the making of cloisonné enamel, Chinese and European furniture, carpets, and the like. — Hard by are the remains of an ancient wall, and near it a *School of Occidental Learning*, excellently managed by Chinese teachers.

In the S.W. part of the town is the Buddhistic temple of *Fá-yüan-ssŭ* (Pl. B, 5), dating from the time of the Tʻang Dynasty and dedicated to the Goddess of Mercy (Kuán-yin), whose relics are said to have been dug up at this spot. The park, with a small dagoba and a pond (generally dry), is interesting.

b. Environs of Peking.

In a picturesque district, $^2/_3$ M. to the W. of the *Hsi-pien-mên* (Pl. A, 4), is the Taoistic *Temple of the White Cloud* (Po-yün-kuán; Pl. A, 4), to the S. of which stands the *Temple of Celestial Peace* (Tʻién-ning-ssŭ; Pl. A, 4), with a beautiful thirteen-storied pagoda, the oldest in Peking, begun in the 7th cent. and finished under the Tʻang Dynasty.

To the N.W. of the Temple of the White Cloud are traces of the old wall of *Yén-ching* (p. 556).

About $^2/_3$ M. to the E. of the *Chʻi-hua-mên* (Pl. F, 3) lies the **Temple of the Eastern Peak** (Túng-yüeh-miáo; Pl. F, 3), another Taoistic building. Along the sides of the second court are a number of small chapels, containing plastic representations of the good and evil deities of Taoism, and many votive tablets. Especially interesting is the chapel of the Son-giving Deity, to the left of the entrance, which is much frequented by women. In the third court is the Temple of the Wonder-Working Mule; patients seek relief here by rubbing the bronze figure of the sacred animal on that part of its body in which they themselves are suffering. Thus, owing to the prevalence of affections of the eyes among the Chinese, the eyes of the mule have had several times to be renewed, and have now again nearly vanished.

A visit may also be paid to the Yellow Temple outside the *Án-ting-mén* (Pl. D, 1), reached from Peking by a drive of $^1/_2$ hr. towards the N. The route passes near the former *Temple of the Earth* (Ti-tʻán; Pl. E, 1; now barracks), erected by the Yüan emperors and restored in the 16th cent. under Chia-chʻing. Farther on is the *Russian Cemetery*, desecrated by the Boxers in 1900.

The *Yellow Temple (Huáng-ssŭ), belonging to the Lamaistic cult, was built in 1651-94 on the site of an earlier temple. It consists of two parts, the Túng-Huang-ssŭ to the E. and the Hsi-Huang-ssŭ to the W. The most interesting part of the *Túng-Huang-ssŭ* is the main temple, on account of the beauty of its inside architecture, which is unique among the buildings of Peking. The arcades and columns, with capital and egg-moulding base, clearly indicate Indian influences. [Similar columns are found in the upper gallery of the two-storied palace in the Hsi-Huang-ssŭ, shut

up because of its dangerous condition; below are Chinese columns.]
In front of the temple is a square with fine old trees. The *Hsi-Huang-ssŭ*, renewed by Ch'ien-lúng in 1771, served as lodgings
for the subject Mongol princes, who brought their tribute to the
Emperor at the Chinese New Year (Feb. of our calendar). This
ceremony was accompanied by a kind of fair, in which Mongolian
furs and various industrial products could be obtained cheap. Visitors should notice the dagoba erected by Ch'ien-lúng over the clothes
of a Téshi-Lama who died at Peking of small-pox, probably the
most beautiful Buddhist monument in Peking. It consists of white
marble and is decorated in alto-relief with scenes from the life of
the last incarnation of the Lama; many of the figures were mutil-
ated by the Japanese in 1900.

A walk of 25 min. from this point brings us to the *T'ú-ch'êng,
the ancient N. rampart of Mongolian Peking (comp. p. 555), from the top
of which we have a fine prospect of the well-cultivated district, with
its clusters of trees and tombs, and of the distant city-wall of Peking.

About 1½ M. to the N.W. of the Yellow Temple lies the *Temple of
the Great Bell* (Tá-chung-ssŭ), built in 1735. The bell was cast under
the Ming Emperor Yung-ló (1403-25) and is covered, both outside and in,
with Chinese and Sanskrit characters.

To the Summer Palace and the Yü-ch'üan-shán, 6 M. to the
N.W. Carriages and ponies, see p. 553; motor-car to the Summer
Palace, $15 (for 4 hrs.), carr. $6½; the traveller must bring his
own provisions. The Summer Palace, the summer residence of the
Chinese Court, is at present open to visitors on the 5th, 15th, and
25th of each Chinese month. Cards of admission are obtained
(through the traveller's legation) from the Wái-chiao-pú (p. 562.)

From the Hsi-chih-mén (Pl. A, 2) a well-paved street leads
N.W. through a pleasant region, with many cemeteries and ham-
lets; the hills are constantly in sight. We first cross the Kalgau
Railway (p. 567), and at the end of the suburb we pass the imperial boat-houses. On the left we have a good view of the Indian
Temple of the Five Towers (Wu-t'a-ssŭ). Beyond the village of
Hái-tien are the barracks and drill-ground of the Manchu Guards.
Behind lies the *Summer Palace* (I-ho-yüán, Park of the Peaceful Age, commonly known as Wan-shou-shán), above the walls of
which tower the yellow roofs of the great temple. The Palace (adm.,
see above; fee to official guide, $1 for each person, besides 10 c.
for the opening of each door), constructed by the Emperor K'áng-
hsi (p. 557), consists of a number of pavilions and courts picturesquely grouped round an artificial lake. In the lake is the famous
marble houseboat, with its wooden superstructure. On the artificial
hill called the Hill of Endless Longevity (Wan-shou-shán) are some
pavilions and a temple, reached from the front by a fine flight of
steps; at the sides are grotto-like pathways (good panorama). —
A little to the N.E. is the so-called *Old Summer Palace* (Yüán-
ming-yüán; always open), with the interesting ruins of the baroque

buildings (comp. p. 557) erected by the Jesuit missionaries about the middle of the 18th cent., and destroyed in 1860.

To the W. of the Summer Palace is the **Yŭ-ch'üan-shán** or Hill of the Jade Spring, the steep outlier of the *Hsi-shan* or 'Western Hills'. It is covered with beautiful pleasure-grounds, begun under Liao and completed in the 17th cent. by K'áng-hsi. We ascend by a winding, mosaic-paved path, passing several temples and kiosques, to a *Grotto* containing Buddhist scenes hewn in the rock in alto-relief. On the top is the seven-storied *Pagoda* (T'ai-chŭn-lóu), which affords a panorama of the picturesque barren mountains, the Wan-shou-shán (p. 566), the ruinous Summer Palace of Yŭán-ming-yŭán, and the richly cultivated and well-watered plain extending, with its monuments and villages, to Peking. The descent may be made to the *Yŭ-ch'üan* or 'Jade Spring', with its excellent water, and to the charming park with the imperial boat-house. We return by the same route.

To the Great Wall and the Ming Tombs, an excursion of two days. 1st Day. From the railway station at the Hsi-chih-mén (Pl. A, 2; rickshaw in 1¼ hr.) we take the early train of the Kalgan Railway (first-class fare $ 1.80 c.) to (25 M. ; 1³/₄ hr.) **Nan-k'óu** (655 ft. ; *Ching-Érh Hotel; Railway Hotel*, Chinese landlord but European equipment and cuisine, well spoken of, pens. $ 7; donkey $ 1 per day, chair $ 5), with large railway work shops. We then follow the highroad, ascending the valley along the railway, to the (4¹/₂ M.) small fort of *Chü-yung-kuán*, with its beautiful sculptures and inscriptions. Farther on we ascend the narrow defile to *Pa-ta-ling* (2065 ft.), at the head of the pass, where (6 M. from Chü-yung-kuán) we reach the **Great Wall** (Wan-li-ch'ang-ch'éng or 'Wall of Ten Thousand Miles'). The wall was completed towards the end of the 3rd cent. B.C. as a protection against the inroads of the Hsiúng-nu or Huns, but in its present form it probably does not go farther back than the time of the Ming Dynasty. It is constructed mainly of bricks and is in a ruinous condition. We ascend to the top of the wall at the gateway. [A perhaps more usual way of making this excursion is to take the 'Construction Train' of the Kalgan Railway to the station of *Ching-lung-ch'iao*. We return to Nan-k'óu for the night.]—2nd Day. In the morning we proceed to the N.E. to the (7¹/₂ M.) **Ming Tombs** (Ming-ling), passing through an ornamental gate (p'ai-lou) with five openings, built of white marble in 1541. In 10 min. we reach a large red gate, affording a fine view of the valley, which is surrounded by pinnacled mountain walls and is open towards the S. only. Farther on is a red pavilion covered with yellow tiles, containing a stone 'Pei' or tomb-monument 12 ft. in length (inscribed stone tablet resting on a tortoise, the symbol of eternity). Passing two elaborately-worked stone pillars 15 ft. high, we enter the *Sacred Way* or *Avenue of Animals*, consisting of 32 gigantic figures of animals and men, each carved from a single block of marble (early 15th cent.). We first see four lions, then four rams, four camels, four elephants, four fabulous monsters, and four horses. Beyond these comes a series of military and civil mandarins. From this point a walk of 1 hr. brings us to the *Tomb of the Emperor Yung-ló* (p. 554), known as the Ch'áng-ling, the finest and largest of the 13 Ming tombs (fee to the caretaker $ ¹/₂-³/₄). It is hardly worth while going on to the other tombs. The tumulus is covered with cypresses, oaks, and firs, and is about 1 M. in circumference. To the S. of it lies the Temple area, in which, on a terrace of white marble, stands the main hall, borne by 32 columns of teak, 36 ft. in height. To the left and right of the blocked-up entrance of the tomb are vaulted passages, ascending to the terrace, which commands a splendid panorama. We then return to Nan-k'óu and take the midday train back to Peking.

To THE HSÍ-LING, an excursion of two days; the traveller must bring his own provisions (or cook) and bedding. 1st Day. By the early train of the Peking-Hankow Railway (station, see Pl. C, 4; through-carriage; first-class $ 4¹/₂) we reach *Liáng-ku-chuáng* in 4¹/₂ hrs. We then proceed on foot along a beautiful road shaded by trees, and after ¹/₄ hr. we pass (in a side-valley on the right) the tomb of the Emperor Kuang-hsü (d. 1908), which is now in course of building (visit permitted). In 1 hr. we reach the **Hsí-ling** ('West Tombs'), the mausoleum of several members of the Manchu dynasty. The tombs (adm., 20 c. each) lie amid extensive and magnificent pleasure-grounds, framed by the serrated ridges of the neighbouring mountains. In T'ái-ling-chên ('Market Town by the T'ái-ling') the traveller can obtain accommodation ($ 1 per day) by sending his card to the commandant. In the afternoon a visit should be paid to the *T'ái-ling* (Tomb of the Emperor Yung-chêng; 1723-36) and the *Ch'áng-ling* (Tomb of the Emperor Chia-ch'íng; 1796-1821). — 2nd Day. In the morning we make a short excursion to (1-1¹/₄ hr.) the *Mú-ling* (Tomb of the Emperor Tao-kuáng; 1821-51), returning to Peking by the midday train (through-carriage).

From Hsí-ling a visit may be paid to the Pass of Tzŭ-ching-kuán. In the afternoon we go on foot, or by donkey or mule, to the village of *Hó-lung-huá* (tolerable inn), whence we walk (there & back in one day), viâ the village of *P'o-ti-hsiá*, to the picturesque *Pass of Tzŭ-ching-kuán*, with an hotel and a beautiful little temple. This was the scene of the German engagement of 28-29th Oct., 1900. The ascent of the pass-wall is rather fatiguing but well repays the trouble on account of the wide view, extending W. to the Great Wall.

To *Jehól*, see p. 550.

INDEX.

Printed by Grimme & Trömel, Leipzig.

28378

Baedeker, Karl   Russia.

Lightning Source UK Ltd.
Milton Keynes UK
UKOW05f1922060217
293762UK00015B/889/P